Tahiti
& French Polynesia
Guide

Jan Prince

D0017552

Le Meridien Bora Bora

Fakarava

Cruising Around French Polynesia!

Moorea

Kia Ora, Rangiroa

Bora Bora

InterContinental,
Tahiti

Lotus

Traditional Dancers

Outrigger Canoe race,
Bora Bora

Taha'a

Tikehau

Waterfall on Tahiti

Lunch in the
Water, Bora Bora

Paradise in
Moorea

Cruising with
Haumana

Snorkeling with a
great backdrop!

Hotel Bora Bora

Papenoo Valley, Tahiti

Rangiroa

Dive
Tahiti!

Relais Mahana,
Huahine

Tahiti
& French Polynesia
Guide

Jan Prince

*Get the book written by Tahiti's foremost travel expert
– the guidebook insiders call "the bible of Tahitian travel."*

OPEN ROAD PUBLISHING

We offer travel guides to American and foreign locales. Our books tell it like it is, often with an opinionated edge, and our experienced authors always give you all the information you need to have the trip of a lifetime. Check out our website to see all our titles.

Open Road Publishing
P.O. Box 284, Cold Spring Harbor, NY 11724
www.openroadguides.com

6th Edition

Front cover photo courtesy of Manihi Pearl Beach Resort. Back cover photo copyright©InterContinental Beachcomber Resort Tahiti. Photo insert credits: p. 1, p. 4 middle, p. 7 top, p. 8 middle: Le Meriden; p. 2 top: Frederic Jacquot (wikimedia.com); p. 2 middle: A.www.viajar24h.com (flickr.com); p. 2 bottom, p. 3 bottom: InterContinental Beachcomber Resorts; p. 3 top: Kia Ora; p. 3 middle: tiarescott (flickr.com); p. 4 top, p. 5 top: kckellner (flickr.com); p. 4 bottom, p. 6 top: thelastminute (flickr.com); p. 5 middle: lander2006 (flickr.com); p. 5 bottom, p. 7 bottom: Jean-Sebastien Roy (flickr.com); p. 6 middle: Mr. Dotcom; p. 6 bottom: Haunama; p. 7 middle: veroyama; p. 8 top: Fouka Riddim (flickr.com); p. 8 bottom: Relais Mahana.
Maps by DesignMaps.
All information, including prices, is subject to change. The author has made every effort to be as accurate as possible, but neither she nor the publisher assumes responsibility for the services provided by any business listed in this guide; for any errors or omissions; or any loss, damage, or disruptions in your travel for any reason.

TABLE OF CONTENTS

1. Introduction   11

2. Overview   12

3. The Best of French Polynesia   22

4. Land & People   33

5. A Short History   46

6. Planning Your Trip   54
When to Go   54
What to Pack   56
Entrance Requirements   57
Making Reservations   60
Useful Websites in Tahiti   65
Where to Find More Information   65
Getting to French Polynesia   66
    Baggage Allowances   66
    By Air   67
    By Passenger Ship   69
    By Private Boat   70
    Customs Allowances   71
    Traveling on Your Own   72
Getting Around Tahiti and Her Islands   72
    By Air   72
    By Inter-Island Passenger Boats & Freighters   76
    By Cruise Ships Based in Tahiti   81
    By Charter Boat   83
    By Live-Aboard Dive Boats, Cruise & Dive Charters   84
    By Car   87
Accommodations   88

7. Basic Information   92
Business Hours   92
Cost of Living & Travel   92
Electricity   93
Festivals & Holidays   93
Getting Married   93

Health Concerns   95
Internet Service   99
Maps & Maritime Charts   100
Money & Banking   101
Movies & DVD/Videos About Tahiti   103
Post Office & Courier Services   105
Publications About Tahiti   106
Radio   110
Retiring in Tahiti/Buying Land or Houses in French Polynesia   111
Shopping   111
    Tahiti Cultured Pearls   111
Staying Out of Trouble   115
    Women Traveling Alone   116
Tax Refunds on Value Added Tax   117
Telephones & Telecommunications   117
Television   120
Time   120
Tipping   121
Weights & Measures   121

8. Calendar of Events   123

9. Taking the Kids   130

10. Food & Drink   135

11. Tahiti   140
Arrivals & Departures   140
Orientation   144
Papeete & Environs   144
    Getting Around Town   146
    Where to Stay   149
    Where to Eat   167
    Seeing the Sights   183
    Nightlife & Entertainment   198
    Sports & Recreation   201
    Shopping   210
        Where to Buy Tahitian Cultured Pearls   212
    Massages & Spas   213
    Tattoos   214
    Day Tour to Moorea   215
    Day Tours to Bora Bora   217
    Practical Information   217

12. Moorea   222
Arrivals & Departures   223
Orientation   225
Getting Around   227
Where to Stay   229
Where to Eat   258
Seeing the Sights   273
Nightlife & Entertainment   277
Sports & Recreation   279
Shopping   290
   Tahitian Cultured Pearls   291
Massages & Spas   293
Tattoos   296
Practical Information   297

13. Huahine   301
Arrivals & Departures   303
Orientation   304
Getting Around   305
Where to Stay   306
Where to Eat   320
Seeing the Sights   323
Sports & Recreation   324
Shopping   327
Special Services, Massage, Natural Therapy, Relaxation   328
Practical Information   328

14. Raiatea   330
Arrivals & Departures   334
Orientation   336
Getting Around   337
Where to Stay   338
Where to Eat   347
Seeing the Sights   350
Sports & Recreation   351
Shopping   357
Special Services, Massage, Natural Therapy, Relaxation   358
Tattoos   358
Practical Information   359

15. Tahaa   362
Arrivals & Departures   363
Orientation   365

Getting Around   366
Where to Stay   366
Where to Eat   375
Seeing the Sights   378
Sports & Recreation   380
Shopping   382
Massages & Spas   382
Tattoos   383
Practical Information   383

16. Bora Bora   385
Arrivals & Departures   387
Orientation   390
Getting Around   390
Where to Stay   391
Where to Eat   412
Seeing the Sights   422
Nightlife & Entertainment   428
Sports & Recreation   429
Shopping   438
    Tahitian Cultured Pearls   439
Massages & Spas   441
Tattoos   444
Practical Information   444

17. Maupiti   448
Arrivals & Departures   449
Orientation   450
Getting Around   450
Where to Stay & Eat   451
Seeing the Sights/Sports & Recreation   457
Practical Information   458

18. Tuamotu Islands   459
Rangiroa   460
    Where to Stay   463
    Where to Eat   473
Manihi   479
    Where to Stay & Eat   481
Tikehau   487
    Where to Stay   489
    Where to Eat   495

Fakarava   497
    Where to Stay   500
    Where to Eat   509

19. Marquesas Islands   514
Nuku Hiva   518
    Where to Stay   521
    Where to Eat   526
Ua Pou   534
    Where to Stay   536
    Where to Eat   538
Ua Huka   540
    Where to Stay   543
    Where to Eat   545
Hiva Oa   548
    Where to Stay   552
    Where to Eat   557
Tahuata   561
    Where to Stay & Eat   563
Fatu Hiva   564
    Where to Stay   567
    Where to Eat   567

20. Austral Islands   570
Rurutu   572
    Where to Stay   576
    Where to Eat   579
Tubuai   582
    Where to Stay   584
    Where to Eat   587
Rimatara   589
    Where to Stay & Eat   590
Raivavae   590
    Where to Stay & Eat   592
Rapa   596
    Where to Stay & Eat   597

21. Glossary of Tahitian Terms   598

General Index   605

Lodging Index   619

Sidebars

New to this Edition! 11

Tahiti, Where Love Lives 15

How To Wear Your Flowers 34

The Mystical-Magical Intoxicating Ti Plant 35

Polynesian Aristocracy 42

The Very Friendly People of Tahiti 44

U.S. Consulate in Tahiti 59

Scuba Diving Terms 85

Addressing a Letter to French Polynesia 105

Ordering From a French Menu 136

Drinking Laws 138

A Tahitian Prophecy 141

Land of the Double Rainbow 191

The Monoi Road (La Route Du Monoi) 194

Let the Music Play 200

What to Do on Tahiti Iti 209

Dolphin & Whale Watching Expeditions 284

Moorea's Best Dive Sites 287

Huahine's Archaeological Sites 303

The "Lapita Village" Museum 311

Tiare Apetahi – Raiatea's Endangered Flower 333

Hibiscus Foundation Saves the Sea Turtles 381

Paul-Emile Victor – The Colors of Bora Bora 385

Legend of Hiro 386

Bora Bora Today 388

Tupapau 428

Bora Bora's Sharkfeeding Show 432

"Many Lagoons" by Ralph Varady 460

Maps

French Polynesia   13

Tahiti   150

Papeete City   184

Moorea   231

Huahine   307

Raiatea   339

Tahaa   367

Bora Bora   392

Maupiti   452

Rangiroa   464

Manihi   482

Tikehau   490

Fakarava   501

Marquesas Islands   515

Nuku Hiva   523

Hiva Oa   553

Austral Islands   571

Rurutu   577

Tubuai   585

Raivavae   593

1. Introduction

Unlike many armchair travelers and other romantics I harbored no childhood dreams to escape to Tahiti—the Isle of Illusion and Love under the swaying palms. Surely I had heard the magical name "Tahiti" when I saw the old movies about the South Seas, but they made no lasting impression on me.

But when I saw a picture of Bora Bora in a *Sports Illustrated* magazine in January 1968, I was swept away by the beauty of the island. For the next six months I read every book on Tahiti and the South Pacific that I could find in the Public Library in Houston, where I was living at the time.

When I arrived in Tahiti later that year I was prepared to accept Tahiti as she is, not as a starry-eyed tourist. I could even appreciate the wonder and beauty of a volcanic black sand beach. I knew that I would like the smell of a coconut fire and the musty odor of copra. I longed to hear the rumble of the surf crashing on the coral reef and the squawking cries of the sea birds as they fished in the lagoon. I also knew that I would enjoy the fun loving Tahitian people, their dignity, humor and sensuous dances. I understood that it was more important to absorb the colorful sights, sounds and fragrant smells of the people and scenery around me than to see Tahiti through the lens of a camera.

My husband and I spent three weeks on Tahiti, Moorea and Bora Bora, and returned again in 1970 to do it all again. When we moved to Tahiti in 1971, I chose to discover my own Tahiti. That's what I've been doing for more than 40 years. I've experienced Tahiti as an American tourist and as an expatriate full-time resident, as a journalist, travel writer and tour guide. I've explored most of the inhabited islands in five archipelagoes, traveling by airplanes, luxury liners, inter-island cargo ships, small fishing boats and by private sail boats. I've stayed in all the best hotels, at several of the pensions and hostels, and I've lived for weeks at a time with Polynesian families in the outer islands. I learned to speak French with an American accent and enough of the Tahitian language to be understood. However, you can get by with English, gestures and smiles almost everywhere you go in these islands.

French Polynesia is not just another destination for vacations. It is a completely different world; a different lifestyle made up of the special light in the sky, the special color of the water, the special smile of the people.

Along with the travel information you'll find in this book are tidbits of my own experiences in Tahiti and Her Islands, which are officially known as French Polynesia. I'm confident that the travel advice in this book will help you discover your own Tahiti!

NEW TO THIS EDITION!
In addition to the **color photos** and **new maps** added last edition, we have a new list of *Bests* (see Chapter 3), such as Best Atolls, Best Resort Beaches, Best Luxury Accommodations, Best Seafood Buffet, Best Sunrise, Best Surfing – and much more!

2. Overview

Visitors to **Tahiti** often ask me which is my favorite island in French Polynesia, which is the prettiest and which I think they would most enjoy visiting.

Although I do have my favorites, each island has its own beauty, charm and specific personality. Almost everywhere you go in French Polynesia you will meet hospitable, friendly people, which helps to give meaning to the natural assets of the island. The latter question is dependent on the amount of time and interest you have to explore the islands, the people and the culture.

From the first moment I laid eyes on the lagoon of **Bora Bora** I was entranced. Each time I have returned to Bora Bora over the years I still gasp in awe at the beautiful colors of the lagoon. I find myself gazing at Otemanu and Pahia mountains from all angles around the island, and especially when I'm taking a boat trip around the lagoon.

The mountains and bays of **Moorea** are simply breathtaking, and this is the cleanest island of the Society group, with neatly trimmed lawns and flower gardens. Moorea has been my home since I moved here from Tahiti in 1992. You will find some of the flavor, and certainly the rhythm of the islands by sitting beside the lagoon at a resort hotel and listening to Tahitian musicians playing their guitars and ukuleles and singing their favorite Polynesian songs at sunset time. My favorite activities include a Safari Tour by 4WD that takes you into the Opunohu Valley and a Dolphin and Whale Watching Excursion with Dr. Michael Poole. The humpbacks are here from July-Oct. The spinner dolphins are here all year.

Tetiaroa is a sanctuary for thousands of sea birds that lay their eggs on the white powdery sands of the beaches. Here you can easily observe crested terns, brown noddy birds, red- and blue-footed booby birds, white-bellied gannets, petrels, the beautiful white fairy terns with black eyes, and the occasional red-breasted frigate birds, whose fledglings of fluffy white feathers are larger than their mothers are. At 42 km. (26 mi.) from Tahiti, Tetiaroa is just the right distance for a day-tour by sailboat that will take you over in the morning and bring you back to Papeete at night. You can walk from the reef across a shallow part of the lagoon to Bird Island, have a picnic on the beach and swim in the enclosed lagoon that is bordered by 12 flat islets called *motu*.

The Hotel Tetiaroa Village and the private airstrip were closed several years ago, prior to the death of owner Marlon Brando on July 1, 2004. In 2009 Pacific Beachcomber SC (PBSC) began construction on **The Brando**. PBSC is a company in Tahiti that owns 4 Intercontinental hotels in Tahiti, Moorea and Bora Bora, 2 Maitai hotels in Bora Bora and Rangiroa, plus the *Paul Gauguin* cruise ship. The Brando is located on Motu Onetahi, where the extended airport runway has been rebuilt. This will be a 100% energy-independent hotel that will open in late 2012

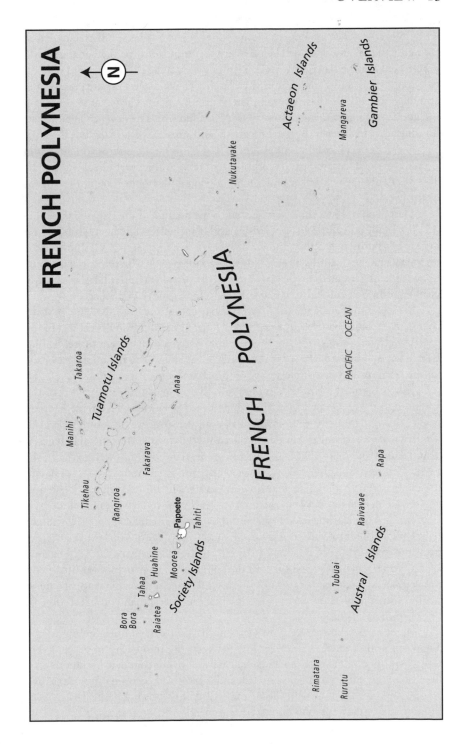

with 35 private villas totaling 40 rooms. These deluxe villas are discreetly placed facing the beach and there will be no overwater bungalows on Tetiaroa, which is a protected marine sanctuary. The 35 units will include 30 single room villas, 4 two-room villas, and 1 three-room villa. Each villa will have a private plunge pool and the resort will also have a communal swimming pool. The 6-star facilities will include 2 restaurants, 2 bars, a Bird's Nest Spa built over a fresh water lagoon, staff housing and a maintenance area. This eco-friendly resort will also include the same SWAC (sea water air conditioning) system that is used at the Intercontinental Bora Bora Resort & Thalasso Spa. In addition to The Brando resort, there will also be The Residences, which will be built on private lots with architecture similar to that of the hotel.

The island of **Huahine** is very special to me because of the Polynesian people who live in the quiet little villages, fishing and planting vegetables and fruit in their little *fa'apu* farms in the valley. In 1977 I was aboard a sailboat that was shipwrecked on the reef facing the little village of Parea, and the people who came to our rescue became lifelong friends. As you drive around the island you can still feel the history of Huahine when you visit the stone *marae* temples in Maeva Village.

Raiatea and **Taha'a** are ideal for sailboat chartering, and there are 4 yacht charter companies based in Raiatea. There are numerous *motu* islets inside the protected lagoon where you can drop anchor, watch a magnificent sunset behind Bora Bora, and listen to the roar of the surf on the reef as you fire up the barbecue on the stern of the boat, while a huge tropical moon rises above the sea.

Tahiti is still the land of double rainbows for me, the regal Queen of the Pacific, and the Diadème Mountain, which can best be viewed from the Fautaua bridge east of Papeete, is even shaped like a crown. A drive around the island of Tahiti will reveal seascapes that are reminiscent of all the island groups of Polynesia. Tahiti is an island that's alive with color, from the flamboyant flowers to the bright *pareo* clothing to the pink, yellow, orange, blue and green houses you'll see beside the circle island road. There are numerous waterfalls in the verdant valleys and you'll find challenging hikes in the mountains if you want to get off-track.

Tahiti is perhaps the most magical and beautiful island of all, but she will not reveal her treasures to you as readily as the smaller islands do. You have to get away from the mainstream of hotels and Papeete to feel the essence of this seductive island, which remains constant amidst the apparent changes of modern life. If you can appreciate the special beauty of a black sand beach of volcanic sand, or a quiet stroll through a forest of *mape* (Tahitian chestnut) trees, then you'll feel some of the spirit of old Tahiti.

Many of us who live on Polynesia's high islands dream of escaping to the **Tuamotu atolls**, where we can get lost between the immensity of sea and sky. Rangiroa, Manihi, Fakarava and Tikehau are the islands that may beckon to you, like a siren call. Here you can live on fish and lobster and coconuts, and scuba dive among an abundance of wild life in the wonderfully clear lagoons that attract professional underwater photographers from the world's top magazines.

TAHITI, WHERE LOVE LIVES

"Tahiti, where love lives" is one of the most popular slogans adopted by the Tahiti Tourist office to promote Tahiti and Her Islands to the American market. This campaign is aimed at busy executives from homes where both husband and wife work and have very little time to spend together.

When you choose the Islands of Tahiti for your vacation, you will find a complete change of scenery and a rhythm of life that is slow and relaxed, very conducive to romance. Tahiti is still the Island of Love. Here we take the time to enjoy one another. Time to simply be. One of Tahiti's favorite expressions is Haere Maru, which means "take it easy." That's what you'll learn to do when you get here.

The mysterious **Marquesas Islands** hold a fascination for an increasing number of voyagers, who seek the authenticity of lifestyle that is still lived in the isolated valleys of these distant islands of brooding beauty. The wood carvers on each island create magnificent sculptures for their churches, and to sell in the artisan centers. The young people dance the traditional *haka* and bird dance, and the herds of horses, goats and cattle watch the scenery from their pastures on the precipitous cliffs overlooking the bays.

Whenever I hear a *himene* group singing the old Polynesian hymns and chants, I am carried away in spirit to the **Austral Islands**, where the villagers gather in their Protestant meeting houses almost nightly to practice their songs for the Sunday church services. I can almost smell the *couronnes sauvages*, the necklaces of flowers and herbs that are placed around your shoulders when you arrive on the joyful island of Rurutu. And I can see the handsome, muscled young men who spend their days in the taro fields, while the women sit on *peue* mats on their terraces or in their living rooms, weaving hats, bags and mats from pandanus fronds.

The **Gambier Islands** represent another page from Polynesia's colorful and often tragic past. Under the severe staff of Father Honoré Laval, the docile, gentle people of Mangareva were converted to Catholicism and lost their lives while submitting to the forced labor of building churches. A neo-gothic city of 116 buildings of coral and stone and a cathedral for 2,000 people is a reminder of the priest who had a driving need to build.

Here's a quick preview of what Open Road's *Tahiti & French Polynesia Guide* offers you:

Society Islands

The **Society Islands** are the main tourist destinations in French Polynesia. They are the islands the furthest west in French Polynesia, and the home of more than 3/4 of the population. They are divided into the **Windward Islands** or *Iles du*

Vent and the **Leeward Islands** or *Iles sous le Vent*, so named because of their position in relation to the prevailing wind.

The Windward Islands include the high islands of **Tahiti** and **Moorea**, and the uninhabited volcanic crater of **Mehetia**; plus the coral atoll of **Tetiaroa**, the late Marlon Brando's former retreat. The mostly flat island of **Maiao** still has its doors closed to the outside world, and visitors are not encouraged to spend the night ashore.

In the Leeward Islands the high islands of **Huahine, Raiatea, Taha'a, Bora Bora** and **Maupiti** lie 180 to 260 km. (112 to 161 mi.) northwest of Tahiti. The atolls of **Tupai, Mopelia, Scilly** and **Bellinghausen** are the westernmost islands of the Society group. These 4 atolls are either uninhabited or have no tourist facilities, but you can visit by sailboat from Bora Bora.

The high islands of the Leeward and Windward Society group are some of the most beautiful islands in the world, offering countless photogenic scenes of saw-tooth mountain ranges, deep blue bays, green valleys and sparkling turquoise lagoons inside the fringing or barrier reefs. These are the names you've heard so much about: Tahiti, Moorea, Huahine, Raiatea, Taha'a, Bora Bora and Maupiti. On most of these islands you can explore the valleys, waterfalls and *marae* stone temples on a safari tour, or while hiking with a guide or on your own. In the opalescent lagoons you can swim, snorkel, scuba dive, water-ski, jet-ski, surf, kitesurf and windsurf, paddle an outrigger canoe, feed the rays, go sailing and picnic on the *motu*. And you can photograph the island, lagoon and reef while parasailing or taking a flight-seeing helicopter tour.

The airport and hotel on **Tetiaroa** were both closed in early 2004, but you can still explore this privately owned atoll during a day's sailing excursion from Tahiti. And you can make plans to stay at The Brando when this new hotel opens in late 2012.

Tuamotu Islands

The **Tuamotu Archipelago** consists of two parallel island chains of 77 coral atolls and one upraised island, located between the Society and Marquesas Islands. These specks of land form one of the world's largest collections of atolls in the vastness of the blue Pacific. They are strewn across 10 latitudes and stretch more than 1,500 km. (930 mi.) from northwest to southeast and more than 500 km. (310 mi.) from east to west. Forming the shapes of a doughnut, a bean or cigar, an egg or a slice of pie, several of these half-drowned atolls enclose lagoons that are inhabited by the black-lip *Pinctada Margaritifera* oyster, which produces the world's finest quality pearls, now called Tahiti cultured pearls rather than black pearls.

One of these atolls is **Rangiroa**, which is one of the largest atolls in the world, with a lagoon that is so spacious it could accommodate the entire island of Tahiti within its perimeter. You'll find international class accommodations on Rangiroa, **Manihi, Tikehau** and **Fakarava**, as well as thatched roof bungalows or rooms in small family hotels and pensions. There are also guest facilities with families on the atolls of **Ahe, Anaa, Apataki, Hao, Kauehi, Kaukura, Makemo, Mataiva, Reao, Takapoto** and **Takaroa.** Several of the Tuamotu atolls are uninhabited due to a lack of water.

Lagoon excursions on Rangiroa include snorkeling through the pass, along with hundreds of fish and sharks. You can watch the dolphins, look at the fish through a glass bottom boat, visit the *motu* islets around the vast lagoon, picnic on a *motu,* fish inside the lagoon or open ocean, and parasail above the immense watery playground. Scuba diving in the Tuamotus is rated world class by the experts, especially in Rangiroa, Manihi, Fakarava, Tikehau, Toau and Mataiva. Manihi's lovely lagoon is a haven for the black lipped oyster, and you can visit a pearl farm, picnic on a *motu*, snorkel, go line or drag fishing, join a sunset cruise and learn to scuba dive. Tikehau has an unspoiled lagoon with pink sand beaches just waiting for a footprint, and Fakarava is becoming so popular with scuba divers that an international class hotel, small family hotels and several guest houses have been built. Wherever you go in the Tuamotus you will find a warm reception, laughter, music, lots of fresh air and sunshine, and an abundance of fresh lagoon fish.

Marquesas Islands

The **Marquesas Islands** lie northwest by southeast along a 360-km. (223-mi.) submarine chain 7º-10º south of the Equator. Two geographical groups are separated by 96 km. (60 mi.) of open ocean, with a combined land area of 1,279 sq. km. (492 sq. mi.). The southern group consists of the 4 high islands of **Fatu Hiva, Tahuata** and **Hiva Oa**, which are inhabited, plus **Mohotani** and the small uninhabited islet of **Fatu Huku.**

The northern group comprises the 3 high islands of **Ua Pou, Nuku Hiva** and **Ua Huka**, all inhabited, plus the small islets of **Motu Iti, Eiao** and **Hatutu**, which are uninhabited. The most important island, Nuku Hiva, is about 1,500 km. (932 mi.) northeast of Tahiti, and Hiva Oa, in the southern group, lies 1,400 km. (868 mi.) northeast of Tahiti. The Marquesas Islands are younger than the Society Islands and do not have protective coral reefs. The wild ocean beats endlessly against the craggy, sculpted coasts, unbroken by any barriers for almost 6,400 km. (4,000 mi.).

Accommodations are available on all the inhabited islands, either in small international class hotels or in family pensions. Most of the rooms and meals are reasonably priced in the Marquesas, but the cost of land and sea transport is very expensive. Read the information on the *Aranui* in the chapter on *Planning Your Trip.* This is the best way to visit the Marquesas Islands, unless you want to stay a few days on one or more of the islands. You can also take an Air Tahiti flight to the Marquesas and board the *Aranui* there and fly back to Tahiti if you prefer.

In the Marquesas you can visit restored archaeological sites with giant stone tikis, hike to waterfalls and high plateaus and ride horses to remote villages. You can scuba dive among a wealth of wild sealift, charter a sailboat for a dive and sail outing through the islands, go deep sea fishing, and watch the wood carvers at work.

Austral Islands

The **Austral Islands** are the southernmost island chain in French Polynesia, lying on both sides of the Tropic of Capricorn and extending in a northwest-southeasterly direction across 1,280 km. (794 mi.) of ocean. They are part of a vast mountain range, an extension of the same submerged chain that comprises the Cook Islands.

The Austral Islands include the high islands of **Rurutu, Tubuai, Rimatara, Raivavae** and **Rapa**, plus the low, uninhabited islands of **Maria** (or Hull) and the **Marotiri** (or Bass) **Rocks**. These islands lie between 538-1,280 km. (334-794 mi.) south of Tahiti, and are separated from one another by a great distance of open ocean. These are French Polynesia's more temperate islands, where taro and potatoes, cabbages and carrots are grown for the market in Papeete.

You can fly to Rurutu, Rimatara, Raivavae and Tubuai, but you can get to Rapa only by boat, as the Rapan inhabitants have voted against this intrusion on their solitude. Raivavae and Rapa are the most beautiful of the Austral Islands and Rurutu is the most lively of all the group. You'll enjoy the communal spirit that exists here, in the taro fields, the artisan shops and in the churches of Rurutu. The people are enthusiastic in both work and play, and they keep their culture alive with annual tours to visit the religious and historic sites of the island.

You can explore Rurutu by horseback or 4WD vehicle, picnic on a white sand beach and hike to waterfalls and limestone grottoes with stalactites and stalagmites. Tubuai is noted for its sandy beaches of various shades, its *motu* islets and fish-filled lagoon. Raivavae has the most beautiful *motu* I have ever seen, but certain parts of its lovely lagoon are now contaminated with *ciguatera*, which prohibits the consumption of fish and *pahua (tridacna* reef clam).

HOTEL CATEGORIES AND RATES

Most of the public (rack) rates for the international class resorts change according to the times of year when the rooms are most in demand. The seasons may vary a little for the different hotels, but generally, the High Season is June 1-Nov. 15, and Dec. 22-31. Low Season is Jan. 1-May 31 and Nov. 16-Dec. 21. Some of the hotels also add a mandatory charge for Christmas Eve dinner and/or New Year's Eve dinner for any room booked on Dec. 31. Check with the hotels of your choice to get the details.

You won't find many real bargains for a hotel room in Tahiti and Her Islands, unless you get way off the tourist track or stay at a hotel with a construction project underway. However, some of the top resorts are now offering an American breakfast or breakfast and dinner, as well as free nights, even during the high seasons. Check out the promotions on their individual websites, or see a list of hotel specials on *www.truetahitivacation.com.*

The hotels in this guide are classified according to their rack rates, facilities and amenities. The rates are for two people per night for a room, bungalow or villa. Some of the hotels have accommodations in two categories. Prestige = US $1,000 and more; Deluxe = $600-$1,000; Superior = $300-$600; Moderate = $200-$300; Economy = $200 or less.

FAMILY HOTELS (PENSIONS) AND RATES

Small family hotels are found on all the islands listed in this guide book. You have several choices of accommodations and prices ranging from $40-$250 per night for a double room. Most of the more remote islands (Maupiti, Tuamotus, Marquesas and Austral Islands) include breakfast and dinner or all meals for two in their rates. Therefore, the cost of a room or bungalow with MAP (half-board or demi-pension) will be around $114-$319, depending on the lodging.

These are the categories of lodgings in the small family hotels:

Bed & Breakfast Guest Rooms

For one night or more, you will be greeted as friends in the home of residents who have converted part of their house or its surroundings to welcome you. In a pleasant and quiet environment, with a maximum of 4 rooms and/or bungalows that can lodge up to 12 people, you will enjoy a convivial stay while discovering the island. Whether the household is modest or affluent, breakfast is always included, which will be the occasion to appreciate local specialties using fresh products, based on availability and the inspiration of the lady of the house. Breakfast is served in a common space that can be the family's dining room, covered terrace or *fare pote'e* shelter.

Pensions - Holiday Family Home

A maximum of 9 furnished bungalows for 27 people, located on or near the family property, with private bathrooms, or shared guest-only bathrooms. Besides breakfast, which is included in the rate, the hostess proposes a half-board formula for meals in the dining room that are sometimes taken with the host family. Please note that this is not a restaurant, but family-style dining providing guests with a maximum of friendly surroundings.

Guest Houses or Family Residences

A maximum of 9 furnished bungalows for 27 people located on or near the family property, with private bathrooms. Guests can cook their own meals as this type of lodging features an equipped kitchen or kitchenette. There is an office and the owners are present full time, always providing guests with the warmest welcome, recommending nearby restaurants and/or snack bars for a taste of the island's traditional food. A communal area is reserved for guests. Upon request, a bungalow cleaning service is provided every three days.

Family Hotels
Small family hotels have a maximum limit of 12 units that can host up to 36 people, with furnished rooms or bungalows arranged as collective or individual structures, all with individual bathrooms. There is a reception desk, offices, a laundry room (with or without charge), a laundry service (with or without charge), a bar and a dining room. Breakfast is included in the rate, and there is a full meal plan or à la carte plan available, offering menus. There's also a daily cleaning service provided for all accommodations. Never forget that you will be staying in people's homes, which cannot be expected to provide the same services as a hotel.

Meal plans are: EP (European Plan, room only with no meals included); MAP (Modified American Plan, with breakfast and dinner, also called *demi-pension* or *half-board*); AP (American Plan, with breakfast, lunch and dinner, also called *pension complete* or full-board).

See additional information on hotels and family hotels in Chapter 6 *Planning Your Trip*. There are still a few backpackers' lodgings and campgrounds available on some islands. Check the accommodation information in each Island chapter.

TAXES – WHAT YOU WILL PAY

This information will come in handy when you are calculating what your visit to Tahiti & French Polynesia will cost.

Add **5% government hotel tax** (also called tourist development tax) to room rates in the international classified hotels and cabins of cruise ships based in French Polynesia. The small family hotels, pensions and guesthouses are not subject to this tax.

Add **5% value added tax** (VAT in English, TVA in French) to all room rates in international classified hotels, as well as non-classified hotels, family pensions, campgrounds and ships. This 5% VAT is also added to prepaid meal plans and all transfers the hotel or pension provides between the airport or boat dock and the hotel or pension or ship.

Add **4% service charge** on accommodations, food and beverage costs in the international classified hotels and cabins of cruise ships based in French Polynesia.

Add **150 CFP municipal tax** (also called sojourn tax, visitors tax, city tax or tourist tax) per person per day to your bill at the international classified hotels, international cruises or any other establishment of equal characteristics. Children under the age of 12 staying with their parents are exempt from the municipal tax.

Add **50 CFP sojourn tax** per person per day on non-classified hotels, family pensions or campgrounds on the following islands: Tahiti, Moorea, Huahine, Taha'a, Raiatea, Bora Bora, Rangiroa, Manihi, Tikehau, Ahe, Mataiva and Nuku Hiva. The tax on Fakarava is **40 CFP**. A 10% VAT is added to tourist services such as transfers made by a taxi or transfer service, all restaurants and snacks, all tours and excursions. A 6% VAT is added to all inter-island transportation by air and boat, including charter flights and chartered boat trips. The 6% VAT also applies to non-alcoholic beverages, medicines, books, newspapers and magazines. Alcoholic beverages are taxed 16%.

Passengers on international cruises are charged 200 CFP per day for Tourist Development Tax while the ship is visiting French Polynesia. They are also charged 500 CFP per person per day on cruising activity (T.A.C.) for any tours or excursions they take.

Unless specified, most of the rates quoted in this guide do not include taxes, which are subject to change at any time.

3. The Best of French Polynesia

ITINERARIES
The Best One-Island Choice

If your ideal vacation is to fly to one island, check into a hotel, unpack and settle in, then I suggest that you choose a hotel on Tahiti, Moorea or Bora Bora if this is your first visit to French Polynesia. You will have more choices of restaurants and entertainment on the main islands and there is enough activity to keep you busy on land and in the lagoon for at least a week.

If you add Moorea to your itinerary, then I suggest that you fly direct from Tahiti to Moorea, providing you don't have to wait too long at the airport in Tahiti. Better yet, schedule an international flight that will allow you to connect from Tahiti to Moorea immediately after arrival at the Tahiti-Faa'a International Airport. The first Air Tahiti flight from Tahiti to Moorea begins at 7am. on Mon., Wed., Thurs., and Fri.; at 7:45am on Sun., at 8am on Sat., and at 10:30am on Tues. If your overseas flight arrives in Tahiti in the middle of the night, as some of them do, you may want to pre-register in a hotel or family pension in Tahiti and continue your trip the next day.

The most important idea is for you to get settled into your hotel as quickly as possible, take a refreshing shower and nap, and go swimming in the lagoon when you awaken. As soon as you get out of your traveling clothes and into your swimsuit, shorts or *pareo*, you'll feel yourself starting to relax.

If you are staying on the island of Tahiti you owe it to yourself to visit Moorea at least for a day. You can hop aboard an inter-island fast catamaran for a 30-min. trip or you can take a 10-min. air shuttle flight to get to Moorea. And if you are staying on Moorea and want to go shopping and sightseeing in Tahiti, you can commute to Tahiti in the morning and return in the afternoon. Details for this inter-island connection are given in the *Moorea* chapter and the *Tahiti* chapter contains information on Day Tours to Moorea.

If you only want to stay on **Moorea** and **Tahiti**, I suggest you spend the first few nights on Moorea and the final part of your visit in Tahiti. One of the statements I hear the most often from visitors when they arrive in Moorea is: "Oh, how I wish I had come here first."

In Tahiti you "must" take a trip around the island, whether by guided tour or renting a car. The 4WD Safari Tour across the interior of the island is also very different and interesting. Be sure to visit the public market, the Marché Municipale, during the day, and in late afternoon find a good spot to watch the sunset behind Moorea. See *Best Sunset* in this chapter.

The best things to do on Moorea are to take a 4WD Safari Tour to visit the Belvedere Lookout and the restored stone *marae* in Opunohu Valley. If you are young enough in body and spirit to enjoy riding an ATV, this is a noisy but popular choice of exploring the interior of the island. Go on a **dolphin watch** boat excursion to see the spinner dolphins that live in the open ocean. You can also enjoy some whale watching on this trip from July-Oct. If you want to swim with dolphins, then visit the Dolphin Park at ICH Moorea Resort.

The Best of the Leeward Society Islands

Almost everyone yearns to see **Bora Bora**, yet there are some visitors who deny themselves this privilege, claiming that it is too expensive or that they don't have time. If you think you'll never pass this way again, then I urge you to indulge yourself and just go ahead and do it. I do not recommend a day tour to Bora Bora, because so much of your time is spent at airports and just getting there and back to Tahiti in one day. Do spend at least 1-2 nights, and be sure to take an outrigger tour to discover the incredibly beautiful lagoon and motu islets. Stops are made to feed the stingrays and sharks and to let you swim and snorkel in the clear warm lagoon. If your budget will stretch that far, then book yourself and your significant other into an overwater bungalow for the complete Bora Bora experience. **Huahine** and **Taha'a** are now counted among the main tourist islands, especially since the opening of luxurious international hotels. **Raiatea** still retains its flavor of old Polynesia, with accommodations in several guesthouses, as well as two 3-star international class hotels and a deluxe boutique hotel. **Maupiti** makes a good day trip by boat from Bora Bora, or you can fly there and stay in a family hotel. There are no international hotels on this island.

The Leeward Islands provide the **best sailing area** for those who want to do some **bareboat cruising** or join a programmed **yacht charter** with captain and crew. These waters also provide some of **the best fishing grounds** for sportfishing, with prize-winning catches of blue marlin and swordfish. If you have dreams of taking a **helicopter flight** somewhere in the islands, then I suggest you do it in Bora Bora. Better yet, fly by helicopter from Bora Bora to Le Taha'a Island Resort & Spa and treat yourself to a real hedonistic experience by staying a few days in one of their magnificent villas. A word of advice: visit Moorea before you stay in one of the super luxurious hotel resorts in the Leeward Islands. The hotel facilities, beaches and views on Moorea may disappoint you by comparison to those in Bora Bora or Taha'a.

The Best Atolls

Rangiroa, Tikehau, Manihi and **Fakarava** are now being added to the itineraries of travelers who wish to discover the quiet beauty of the unspoiled Tuamotu atolls. **Scuba divers** are especially thrilled to drift dive through the passes, surrounded by thousands of fish and sharks. There are international class hotels and small family hotels on each of these 4 atolls and they are easy to get to by airplane. There are plenty of activities organized to visit the lagoon by boat, with a picnic on an uninhabited motu islet and visits to a pearl farm. The Paul Gauguin Cruises calendar for 2012 includes visits to Rangiroa and Fakarava. Archipels Croisières (Dream Yacht Charter) offers sailing programs in Rangiroa and Tahiti Yacht Charter has a sailboat based in Fakarava. *Aquatiki* offers cruise and dive charters in the Tuamotu Archipelago, starting from Fakarava. See chapters on *Rangiroa* and *Fakarava*.

The Best Islands Off Track

All 6 of the **Marquesas Islands** can best be visited by taking a 14-day cruise from Tahiti on board the *Aranui 3* passenger/cargo ship. The *Paul Gauguin* stops at 4 of the Marquesas Islands during its 14-day cruises through the Marquesas, Tuamotus and Society Islands. In Sept. 2012 the *Paul Gauguin* will visit the Austral Island of Rurutu, the Island of Whales, during an 11-day cruise that also includes the Society Islands.

The Best Way to Visit the Islands

The wholesale tour operators who specialize in package programs to Tahiti and Her Islands offer vacation choices that will allow you to visit several islands. Some of these programs will schedule you to fly direct from the airport in Tahiti to one of the outer islands, and they sometimes include an overnight stay in Tahiti on the way back home.

Air Tahiti offers an interesting choice of "air passes" that will allow you to island hop among the Societies, the Tuamotu, the Marquesas and the Austral Islands. Their "Island Adventures" packages include airfare, lodging and some meals in all 5 archipelagoes. See details on these programs in chapter on *Planning Your Trip*.

The Best Way to Spend Your Last Evening in Tahiti

One of the questions visitors most frequently ask me is where should they go on their last evening in Tahiti. They are usually flying into Tahiti from one of the outer islands sometime during the afternoon and they have to fly home that night. What to do with the hours in between flights if they have no hotel or family pension room to go to? Many times this happens on a Sunday, when the shops are closed.

I tell them to check their luggage at the airport storage room and take *le truck* into Papeete. There they can walk around and have dinner on the roulottes. They can also have a good draft beer at Les Trois Brasseurs micro brewery, with dinner if desired. Then they take *le truck* or a taxi back to the airport in time for check-in. Another suggestion I give them is to check their luggage and take *le truck* or a taxi to the nearby Intercontinental Tahiti Resort. They can hang around the hotel grounds and swimming pools and have a drink at Le Lotus swim-up bar while watching the sunset over Moorea. A third recommendation is to go to Le Belvedere restaurant for the sunset and an early dinner. They will pick you up at the airport or ferry dock and take you and your luggage up the mountain to the restaurant. Afterward, they will take you to the airport in plenty of time for your flight. See details in *Tahiti* chapter.

The Best of the Best Resorts: My Favorites

Hilton Moorea Lagoon, Hilton Bora Bora Nui, Bora Bora Pearl Beach, Tikehau Pearl Beach Resort, Manihi Pearl Beach Resort, Le Taha'a Island Resort & Spa.

Best Overwater Bungalows/Suites/Villas

Moorea: Hilton Moorea Lagoon Resort.

Huahine: Te Tiare Resort.

Taha'a: Le Taha'a Island Resort & Spa.

Bora Bora: Hilton Bora Bora Nui Resort, Four Seasons Resort, St. Regis Resort, Sofitel Private Island Resort (formerly Sofitel Le Motu), ICH Bora Bora Le Moana Resort.

Tikehau: Tikehau Pearl Beach Resort. Their overwater suites are my favorite accommodations in all the islands.

Manihi: Manihi Pearl Beach Resort. The furnishings are a bit dated, but comfortable, and I love to watch the multi-hued parrot fish nibbling on the coral just below the bungalows.

Best Beach Bungalows/Suites/Villas

Moorea: Sofitel Ia Ora Moorea Resort; ICH Moorea Resort.

Taha'a: Le Taha'a Island Resort & Spa. The beach villas here get my top rating.

Bora Bora: Bora Bora Pearl Beach Resort, Le Meridien Bora Bora.

Rangiroa: Hotel Kia Ora has deluxe beach bungalows with a Jacuzzi or pool.

Tikehau: Tikehau Pearl Beach Resort. The a/c bungalows are very popular.

Best Garden Bungalows

Moorea: Moorea Pearl Beach Resort has garden bungalows with or without pools. The Sofitel Ia Ora, Hilton Moorea Lagoon and ICH Moorea have also added plunge pools adjacent to their garden bungalows.

Bora Bora: The garden suites at Bora Bora Pearl Beach have plunge pools, a sundeck and covered gazebo, plus a privacy fence.

Best Luxury Accommodations

Taha'a: Le Taha'a Island Resort & Spa's Royal Beach Villa.

Bora Bora: St. Regis Resort's 3-bedroom Royal Estate, Royal Beach Pool Villa, Royal Overwater Pool Villa; Four Seasons' Presidential Suite; ICH Thalasso's Poevai Overwater Suite; Bora Bora Nui's Royal Horizon Overwater Villa and Royal Hillside Villa.

Best Honeymoon Resorts

Tahiti and Her Islands provide the ideal setting for a romantic honeymoon, and the deluxe hotels with overwater bungalows are a favorite destination for newlyweds and other lovers. All the tour operators have honeymoon programs, or they can create a personalized package according to your wishes. I suggest that you also contact the hotels of your choice for information on their honeymoon programs.

Stepping down into the lagoon from the steps of your overwater bungalow is an unforgettable sensual delight, and there are many other pleasures to be enjoyed in these units. Unfortunately, privacy is not one of them. Most of the overwater bungalows are built too close together to provide total discretion, and your neighbors may be sharing your passion, albeit unwittingly.

Tahiti: ICH Tahiti Resort, Le Méridien Tahiti

Moorea: Hilton Moorea Lagoon Resort, ICH Moorea Resort, Sofitel Ia Ora Moorea Resort, Moorea Pearl Resort.

Huahine: Te Tiare Beach Resort.

Taha'a: Le Taha'a Island Resort & Spa, Vahine Island.

Bora Bora: St. Regis Resort, Four Seasons Resort, ICH Thalasso, Bora Bora Nui, Bora Bora Pearl Beach, Sofitel Private Island.

Rangiroa: Hotel Kia Ora, Kia Ora Sauvage.

Manihi: Manihi Pearl Beach Resort.

Tikehau: Tikehau Pearl Beach Resort.

Fakarava: White Sand Beach Resort Fakarava.

Nuku Hiva: Nuku Hiva Keikahanui Pearl Lodge

Hiva Oa: Hanakee Hiva Oa Pearl Lodge.

Best Resort for Privacy

Tahiti: ICH Tahiti Resort, Radisson Plaza Resort, Hotel Tahiti Nui.

Moorea: Villa Corallina, Dream Island

Huahine: Te Tiare Resort

Rangiroa: Kia Ora Sauvage

Tikehau: Tikehau Pearl Beach Resort

Best Family Lodgings

Tahiti: Radisson Plaza, ICH Tahiti Resort, Sofitel Maeva Beach Tahiti Resort, Manava Suite Resort Tahiti, Royal Tahitien.

Moorea: ICH Moorea Resort, Moorea Pearl Resort, Les Tipaniers, Hotel Hibiscus, Fare Hamara, Te Nunoa Bungalow, Mark's Place Moorea Bungalows.

Huahine: Relais Mahana, Maitai La Pita Village, Villas Bougainville.

Bora Bora: Le Méridien, Four Seasons, St. Regis, Bora Bora Pearl Beach Resort, Le Maitai Polynesia, Hotel Matira.

Best Beds

Bora Bora: Hilton Bora Bora Nui, Sofitel Marara Bora Bora Beach and Private Island all have wonderfully comfortable mattresses. The beds at St. Regis are also great except for the hard-to-see black base that juts out around the mattress, which can bruise your legs when you stumble against it. Four Seasons Resort Bora Bora was given a 5-star sleep rating by TripAdvisor.

Best Bathrooms

Moorea: Hilton Moorea Lagoon has claw footed bathtubs and a separate shower with oversize rain nozzle.

Huahine: Te Tiare Resort has a Jacuzzi bathtub and separate shower with powerful water pressure.

Bora Bora: St. Regis Resort has a deep bathtub, a separate shower with an oversize rain nozzle plus a hand held nozzle, and Acqua de Parma bath products. Hilton Bora Bora Nui has a huge well lit bathroom of pink marble with an oversize bathtub, a separate shower with rain nozzle and hand held jet nozzle, separate toilet and bidet. Four Seasons has glass floor panels in the marble bathrooms of the overwater bungalows, as well as bathtubs with a view of the lagoon.

Best Resort Spas

Tahiti: Le Spa at the Radisson Resort.

Moorea: Hélène'Spa at ICH Moorea Resort; Moorea Lagoon Spa at Hotel Hilton Moorea Lagoon, and Manea Spa at Moorea Pearl Resort.

Taha'a: Manea Spa at Le Taha'a Island Resort & Spa.

Bora Bora: Thalasso Deep Ocean Spa at ICH Bora Bora Resort; Manea Spa at Bora Bora Pearl Beach Resort, Hina Spa at Hilton Bora Bora Nui, Kahaia Spa at Four Seasons, and Miri Miri Spa at St. Regis.

Manihi: Try the sensuous Monoi Poe massage at Manihi Pearl Beach Resort that involves a string of pearls.

Best Resort Wedding Chapels

Bora Bora: ICH Thalasso, Le Méridien, Four Seasons.

Best Tahitian Wedding Ceremonies

Moorea: Tiki Village.

Bora Bora: Patrick Taurua of Patrick's Activities/Maohi Nui.

Best Resort Beaches

Moorea: Sofitel Ia Ora Moorea Resort

Huahine: Relais Mahana

Bora Bora: Hilton Bora Bora Nui, Le Méridien, St. Regis.

Best Resorts for Snorkeling
Moorea: Hilton Moorea Lagoon
Huahine: Relais Mahana.
Taha'a: Le Taha'a Island Resort & Spa.
Bora Bora: Sofitel Private Island, Bora Bora Pearl Resort.
Manihi: Manihi Pearl Beach Resort.

Best Resorts for Safe Swimming in Lagoon without much coral
Moorea: Sofitel Ia Ora Moorea Resort, ICH Moorea Resort, in inner lagoon.
Huahine: Relais Mahana (great swimming); Te Tiare.
Bora Bora: Le Méridien's inner lagoon, lagoonarium at St. Regis Resort.
Tikehau: Tikehau Pearl Beach Resort, in front of beach bungalows.

Best Views
Tahiti: any hotel with a view of Moorea.
Moorea: Hilton Moorea Lagoon Resort; Sofitel Ia Ora Moorea Resort, Legends Resort.
Raiatea: Taha'a, Bora Bora and Huahine viewed from Mt. Tapioi.
Taha'a: Le Taha'a has an excellent view of Bora Bora.
Bora Bora: Otemanu Mountain viewed from Bora Bora Pearl Beach, ICH Le Moana Resort, Sofitel Marara Private Motu, ICH Thalasso, Le Méridien, St. Regis and Four Seasons.

Best Landscaping & Gardens
Tahiti: Le Royal Tahitien
Moorea: Hilton Moorea Lagoon, ICH Moorea Resort.
Bora Bora: Hilton Bora Bora Nui.

Best Small Resorts
Moorea: Club Bali Hai, Les Tipaniers.
Huahine: Relais Mahana, Maitai La Pita Village.
Raiatea: Opoa Beach Hotel; Raiatea Lodge Hotel.
Taha'a: Hotel Vahine Island; Hotel La Pirogue.
Bora Bora: Hotel Matira.
Rangiroa: Maitai Rangiroa Lagoon Resort.

Best Small Upscale Accommodations
Moorea: Dream Island, Villa Corallina, Fenua Mata'i'oa, Green Lodge, Te Nunoa Bungalow, Robinson's Cove Villa, Taoahere Beach House.
Huahine: Villas Bougainville, Huahine Vacances
Taha'a: Fare Pea Iti, Tiare Breeze.
Bora Bora: Rohotu Fare Lodge, Blue Heaven Island; Bora Bora Condos.
Rangiroa: Motu Teta

Tikehau: Ninamu Resort, Relais Royal Tikehau.
Fakarava: Raimiti

Best Restaurants
Tahiti: Restaurant Jimmy's for Thai, Vietnamese & Chinese food, Coco's for French gourmet cuisine; Pink Coconut for La Nouvelle Cuisine Française; Lotus Restaurant at ICH Tahiti for best fusion cuisine; Hotel Royal Tahitien for poisson cru and great local style meals; Western Grill for BBQ ribs; Chez Loula et Remy in Taravao for fresh seafood and local dishes. Vaitohi Restaurant at Manava Suite Hotel is open until midnight and serves good local and international food.
Moorea: Aito Restaurant for poisson cru, fresh lagoon fish and coconut crab (in season); Rudy's for parrotfish stuffed with crab, Restaurant Tiahura (Chez Irene) for fish and seafood, Le Mayflower for French gastronomic cuisine; Te Honu Iti for steaks and sauces; Painapo Beach for Tahitian food (ma'a Tahiti).
Huahine: Restaurant Mauarii for Polynesian food, fish and seafood; Te Tiare Resort for mahi mahi burger; Chez Tara for ma'a Tahiti.
Raiatea: Opoa Beach Hotel and Raiatea Lodge Hotel for gastronomic French cuisine; Jade Garden for Chinese dishes.
Taha'a: Chez Louise for Polynesian meals and seafood; La Pirogue for Japanese Teppanyaki and other international cuisines; Restaurant Taha'a for local style meals prepared by a Frenchman.
Bora Bora: Villa Mahana for the best French gastronomic cuisine; Fare Manuia for French dishes; Bloody Mary's for fish, excellent burgers, draft beer and cocktails; Mai Kai Marina & Yacht Club for fresh seafood and a variety of good food.
Rangiroa: Rangiroa Lagoon Grill for good sandwiches, Kobe beef, fresh fish and lobster; Vaimario for French cuisine; Chez August & Antoinette (Puhipuhi) for fresh fish and local style Chinese dishes.
Manihi: Manihi Pearl Beach Resort for best fresh lagoon fish.
Fakarava: Pension Raimiti for all their excellent and beautifully presented meals.
Nuku Hiva: Chez Yvonne Katupa in Hatiheu for best restaurant in the Marquesas Islands.

Best Snacks & Patisseries
Tahiti: L'Oasis du Vaima, Patachoux, Les Roulottes
Moorea: Caraméline at Post Office in Maharepa, Le Rotui in Pao Pao, Le Motu in Haapiti, A l'Heure du Sud Roulotte, near Le Petit Village.
Huahine: Snack New Marara
Bora Bora: Snack Matira, Roulotte Matira.

Best Pizza
Tahiti: Lou Pescadou
Moorea: Daniel's Pizza, Pizzeria Luciano in Maharepa.

Huahine: Haamene Pizza
Bora Bora: La Bounty
Rangiroa: Vaimario

Best Seafood Buffet
Tahiti: La Soirée Merveilleuse at Intercontinental Tahiti Resort

Best Bars
Tahiti: Tiki Bar at ICH Tahiti Resort has Happy Hour 4:30-5:30pm daily and live music Wed.-Sun. Best night to meet locals is on Thurs. Manava Suite Resort has jazz or dance shows at the Taapuna Pool Bar on Thurs., Fri., and Sat. evenings, and their Punavai Lounge Bar is open nightly until 1am, serving excellent cocktails.
Moorea: Eimeo Lounge Bar at Hilton Moorea Lagoon has live music on special evenings. Motu Iti Bar at ICH Moorea Resort, and Autera'a Bar at Moorea Pearl Resort have a good selection of cocktails, with local musicians performing during Happy Hour. Hotel Kaveka has live music (Ron Falconer) each Tues. and a local band on Fri. & Sat.
Taha'a: Manuia Bar at Le Taha'a. Bartender Maurice makes great cocktails.
Bora Bora: All the resort hotels have music during Happy Hour. Bloody Mary's and the Mai Kai Lounge Bar are the best bars for drinks and fun.

Best Polynesian Show
Tahiti: ICH Tahiti Resort has live dance shows at least 3 times a week, including a Marquesan group on Wed., and Les Grands Ballets de Tahiti on Fri. and Sat. nights. Tumata Robinson's Tahiti Ora dancers perform each Fri. evening at Le Méridien Resort.
Moorea: Tiki Village Theatre has a big dance show with 60 performers 4 nights a week. Club Bali Hai has a dance show on Wed. evening. Dance shows are also presented at Sofitel Ia Ora Moorea and Tahiti Pearl Resort, and on Tues. and Sat. evenings there is a fire dancing show at the Hilton Moorea Lagoon.
Bora Bora: Maohi Nui dancers, led by Patrick Taurua, perform several nights a week in various hotels, including fire dancing. Kevin's group also has fire dancing.

Best Land Excursions and Best Guides
Tahiti: Circle Island Tour with William Leeteg of Adventure Eagle Tours. A Full Day Cross the Island Tour by Patrick Cordier of Patrick Adventure.
Moorea: 4WD Safari Tour by Albert Tours (Blanc-Blanc or Tom). ATV tour with Karl Haring of ATV Fun Tours.
Huahine: 4WD Island Echo Tour by Paul Atallah.
Raiatea: Circle Island Tours and Visits to Marae Taputapuatea. Christian & Nella work with American tourists and have a good reputation for their minibus tours.

Taha'a: 4WD Safari Tours by Dave's Tours, Vai Poe Excursions or Vanilla Tours.

Bora Bora: Circle Island Tour with Simplet Taxi. 4WD Safari Tours with Patrick Taurua of Maohi Nui Private Excursions.

Best Lagoon Excursions and Best Guides

Moorea: Dolphin & Whale Watching Expedition by Dr. Michael Poole; Dolphin & Lagoonarium Tours by Harold Wright; Picnic on the Motu with Albert Tours.

Huahine: Lagoon Excursions, Shark Feeding Excursions, and Picnics on the Motu with Marc Garnier of Huahine Nautique.

Raiatea: Lagoon & Motu Excursion by Faaroa Tours or West Coast Charters.

Taha'a: Lagoon Excursions and Visits to Pearl Farms with Vai Po'e Excursions.

Bora Bora: A Boat Trip Around the Island with Shark Observation and Ray Feeding, with Shark Boy of Bora Bora or Raanui Tours. Patrick Taurua of Maohi Nui Private Excursions is the best guide for private tours and picnics on the motu. If he is not available, try Etienne or Keishi Tours. Reef Discovery, led by Christophe Poch, a French Navy veteran who speaks perfect English, is one of the most popular activities in Bora Bora.

Best Diving

There is world class diving in the passes of **Rangiroa, Manihi, Tikehau, Fakarava, Ahe, Toau,** and most other atolls in the Tuamotu Archipelago that open to the ocean. The Society Islands also offer exciting dives. There are dive centers on 13 islands and atolls in French Polynesia. The best known are TOPDIVE-Bathys, Bora Bora Blue Nui, Manihi Blue Nui, Tikehau Blue Nui and Raie Manta Club.

Best Surfing

Tahiti: Taapuna Pass near Fisherman's Point, Taharu'u in Papara, Hava'e Pass in Teahupoo on Tahiti-Iti, and Papenoo on the east coast.

Moorea: Haapiti, Temae

Huahine: Pass at Fare and Ara Ara Pass in Parea.

Rangiroa: Avatoru Pass

Tikehau: Tuheiava Pass

Best Sunrise

Tahiti: Between Tautira and Teahupoo on Tahiti Iti peninsula (watching the sun rise out of the ocean).

Moorea: Sofitel Ia Ora Moorea (watching the sun rise over Tahiti).

Huahine: Relais Mahana and Pension Mauarii (watching the sky turn pink over Parea).

Maupiti: Le Kuriri (watching the sun rise over Bora Bora).
Rangiroa: Kia Ora Sauvage (watching the sun rise out of the ocean).

Best Sunset

Tahiti: Sunset beside Moorea as seen from Point Venus, and sunset behind Moorea as seen from Tahiti's west coast, especially from ICH Tahiti Resort.

Moorea: Hotel Hilton Moorea (Apr.-Sept.) Anywhere in the beach area of Haapiti most of the year. You can see the sun drop behind the ocean, often with a green flash.

Raiatea: From Sunset Beach Motel or anywhere nearby.

Bora Bora: From Matira Beach you can watch the sun go to bed behind Maupiti. The Mai Kai Marina & Yacht Club faces the pass and the sunset, so this is a good place to go for a Sundowner.

Fakarava: From the beach or pier at Pension Havaiki Nui. Anywhere on the lagoon.

At Sea as viewed from the *Aranui* between Tahiti and the Marquesas Islands.

Best Moonrise

Tahiti: Between Tautira and Teahupoo on Tahiti Iti peninsula.
Rangiroa: This is a beautiful sight from Kia Ora Sauvage.
Tikehau: Tikehau Pearl Beach Resort.
Manihi: Manihi Pearl Beach Resort.

Best Stargazing

Manihi Pearl Beach Resort on the airport runway, Kia Ora Sauvage on the beach, Tikehau Pearl Beach Resort on the beach, Pension Raimiti in Fakarava. Anywhere away from lights.

Best Budget Friendly Islands

Huahine, Raiatea, Maupiti, Marquesas and Austral Islands.

4. Land & People

LAND

Tahiti and Her Islands, officially known as French Polynesia, are sprinkled over 5,030 million sq. km. (almost 2 million sq. mi.) of ocean in the eastern South Pacific. French Polynesia is east of the International Date Line. Tahiti is 6,200 km. (3,844 mi.) from Los Angeles; 3,900 km. (2,418 mi.) from Auckland, New Zealand; and 8,800 km. (5,456 mi.) from Tokyo. The most northerly island in the Marquesas archipelago, Eiao, also known as Hatutu, is more than 2,000 km. (1,240 mi.) from the Austral Island of Rapa, the most southerly island.

The word Polynesia means "many islands." The total land area of these 118 Polynesian islands and atolls adds up to only 3,500 sq. km. (1,365 sq. mi.). The territory is geographically and politically divided into five archipelagoes: the Society Islands, Austral Islands, Marquesas Islands, Tuamotu Islands and the Gambier Islands. These island groups differ in terrain, climate and, to a lesser degree, the people.

High Volcanic Islands & Low Coral Atolls

All the Polynesian islands are basically of volcanic origin that were formed millions of years ago when volcanoes erupted from a rising column of magma in the asthenosphere called a "hot spot." Five strips of islands correspond to a succession of hot spots along the Pacific seabed. The MacDonald hot spot, southeast of Rapa, is believed to have come to life 15 or 20 millions of years ago, and is still intermittently active. A 2006 geological study of the Society Islands stated that Mehetia is estimated at 1.16-2.03 milion years in age; Tahiti Iti at 0.45-0.78 million; Tahiti Nui at 0.19-1.37 million; Moorea at 1.36-1.72 million, Huahine at 2.91-3.08 million, Taha'a at 1.10-1.41/2.62-3.39 million; Raiatea at 2.44-2.75 million; Bora Bora at 3.21-3.48 million, and Maupiti seems to have come into existence 4.21-4.51 million years ago.

During Charles Darwin's visit to Tahiti in 1842 he climbed a mountain and discovered that the flat coral atoll is actually a high island that has sunk deeper into the ocean when the original volcano disappeared completely under the water. The old volcanic core still remains underneath the atoll, but all you see is the coral ring, which encircles the lagoon. The coral rim of the atoll indicates how big the island once was. A series of small coral islets, strung together by often-submerged coral reefs, are seldom more than a quarter of a mile wide and only a few feet above the sea. Inside this narrow strip of coral the lagoon can be the size of a salt-water pond or as big as an inland sea.

White beaches of coarse and fine coral sand create a border between the sea and the green oasis of coconut forests, flowering trees and scented bushes. The live coral gardens of the reefs and inner lagoons are filled with a fantastic variety of tropical fish, sharks, rays, turtles, crustaceans, and other marine fauna.

Flora

From the moment you step off your plane in Tahiti you become aware that you are surrounded by flowers. The first scent is the sweet perfume of the beautiful white **Tiare Tahiti** (*Gardenia taitensis*) that a smiling *vahine* offers to welcome you to this luxuriant land of flowers.

This traditional custom of the islands existed long before there were passenger ships and airplanes. Until recently, when the Tahitians were traveling between the islands, they were adorned with crowns and leis of flowers. This sign of the traveler is still a custom in some of the remote islands, but the health department now prohibits transporting food and plants from Tahiti to the outer islands because of the fruit fly and other destructive insects.

Walk through the public market in the heart of downtown Papeete and just watch for a few minutes as the vendors sell their brilliantly colored anthuriums, birds of paradise, asters, carnations, red and pink ginger flowers, delicate orchids, vivid roses, and myriads of varied bouquets. You won't be complaining about the prices here. A drive around the island will give you an opportunity to see the many varieties of flowers flourishing in the rich soil of Tahiti.

HOW TO WEAR YOUR FLOWERS

"They are very fond of flowers," wrote Captain Cook, when he first visited Tahiti in 1769. "Especially of the Cape Jasmine (Gardenia taitensis, known as the Tiare Tahiti), of which they have great plenty planted near their houses; these they stick into the holes of their ears and into their hair..."

Many of the visitors to Tahiti have noticed that there is a custom of conversing through the wearing of flowers, and this language of the flowers still exists. Learn to read what they are saying when you see a big, husky man digging a ditch and wearing his Tiare Tahiti bud behind his ear; or when you see a young lady with her long hair coifed so nicely for that special evening and laced with orchids; when you see the proud Tahitian grandmothers with their woven hats and a hibiscus behind an ear.

When you wear your flower behind your right ear—it means you are single, available and looking. When you wear your flower behind your left ear—it means you are married, engaged or otherwise taken. When you wear flowers behind both ears—it means you are married but are still available. When you wear your flower backward behind your ear—it means "follow me and you'll find out how available I am." When you wear a flower backward behind both ears—it means anything goes. And when you see the young vahine with flowers in her hair—it means she's desperate, you'd better hurry up!

Here in the Polynesian islands, we incorporate flowers into our daily lives. Both men and women can be seen wearing a fragrant blossom behind their ears, even while performing the most humdrum tasks. Often you can hear them softly singing to themselves. Wearing flowers does make you want to sing.

Traditional Tahitian Food Plants

On all the islands and atolls of French Polynesia you will find the graceful coconut palm, the "tree of life" to the Polynesians, which can be used in dozens of ways. Other trees and plants that provide traditional Tahitian foods are breadfruit, bananas, *fei* plantains, taro, tarua, manioc, arrowroot, sweet potato and yams. Complimentary food plants include: sugarcane, pandanus, *mape* (Tahitian chestnut), ti or *auti* (*cordyline fruticosa*), *vi* Tahiti or Tahitian apple (*Spondias dulcis*), kava (*Pometia pinnata Forster*), *nono* (*Morinda citrifolia*), small ginger roots called *rea*, bamboo, the candlenut tree (*Aleurites molucanna*), the wild hibiscus called *purau (Hibiscus tiliaceus)*, the *hotu* fruit of the *Barringtonia asiatica*, and varieties of purslane and cress, as well as several types of ferns.

Imported Food Plants

The European explorers, botanists, sailors, missionaries, traders and civil servants brought many species of economic flora to Tahiti, which flourish on most of the islands today. Among these food plants you will find varieties of: avocado, bay rum tree, Brazilian plum, cantaloupe, cashew nut, cayenne pepper, citron,

---

THE MYSTICAL-MAGICAL INTOXICATING TI PLANT

The ancient Tahitians had 13 varieties of the **ti plant** (Cordyline terminalis or fructicosa) that they called **auti**. The most sacred of all ti plants in old Tahiti was the Ti-'uti, which was a fine variety planted chiefly in the marae enclosures for the gods and religious uses. Beautiful varieties of ti have been introduced in recent years, but it is still the glossy green leaves that were worn by orators, warriors and enchanters that are worn today by dancers, high priests and firewalkers. This small tree of the Liliaceae family is believed to possess mystical-magical qualities that will protect the house from fire, and hedges of auti surround many of the homes in the islands. The broad leaves are used as food wrappers and to line the pits where breadfruit is preserved by fermentation.

The ti is also used in traditional healing for diarrhea, vomiting, abscesses or ear infections. The root can be cooked in the underground stone oven to replace the breadfruit and the taro, and the large fibrous tuber was formerly made into candy. This root is very rich in sugar, and during the reign of King Pomare II, natives from the Sandwich Islands (now Hawaii) taught the Tahitians how to build a still and produce a potent liqueur from the auti root.

coffee, custard apple, grapefruit, guava, gooseberry tree, jackfruit, Java almond, lime, lychee, mamee apple, mandarin, mango, orange, pakai, Panama cherry, papaya, passion fruit, pineapple, pistachio, pomegranate, quenette, rambutan, sea grape, soursop, Spanish plum, Surinam cherry, star apple, sugar apple, tamarind, vanilla and watermelon.

Chinese Gardens

Chinese immigrants brought their garden vegetables with them, which they plant in the high valleys of Tahiti. These colorful vegetables can best be seen at the Papeete market, where you will recognize varieties of bok choy, cabbages, carrots, cilantro, cucumbers, eggplant, ginger root, green peppers, jicama, lettuce, long beans and snap beans, parsley, pumpkins, soy bean sprouts, spinach, squashes, tomatoes, watercress, white radishes and zucchini.

Sacred Trees of Old Polynesia

The sacred trees of old Polynesia were chosen for their medicinal value, and the quality of their wood, bark, leaves or roots. Some of these trees are still used for carving into furniture, *umete* bowls, platters, small canoes, tikis and ceremonial clubs. These precious trees are the *tamanu* or *ati* (*Calophyllum inophyllum*), the *tou* (*Cordia subcordata*), rosewood or *miro* (*Thespesia populnea*), banyan or *ora* (*Ficus prolixa*), *aito* or ironwood (*Casuarina equisetifolia*), *reva* or *hotureva* (*Cerbera odollam*) and the *pua* (*Fagraea berteriana*).

Land-Based Fauna

There are no snakes in Tahiti and Her Islands and there are no poisonous spiders or fearsome land animals, except for the centipede (*Scolopendra subspinipes*), which lives in dark, humid areas, under rocks and in palm frond structures. Its bite is venomous and very painful to humans. It is nocturnal by nature and its diet is made up exclusively of cockroaches, while the centipede itself is a delicacy for chickens. So don't strangle the roosters that crow outside your hotel window all night long!

Almost every home in the Polynesian islands has a few house pets in the form of the *mo'o*, a yellow lizard that lives on the ceilings, where they feed on mosquitoes and other flying insects and bananas if they're available. Sometimes these critters find their way into hotel rooms, which has been known to disrupt the tranquility of the human occupants. Some tourists are so upset by the presence of a lizard in their room that they want to change hotels in the middle of the night—not wanting to accept the fact that there is no such thing as a lizard-proof room in the tropics. These geckos are harmless, but they do seem to occasionally take delight in dropping "whitewash" on inappropriate places, such as your bed or head. The reptile population includes four gecko species and three lizard species, none of which are to be feared.

Here you will find the yellowish-red Tahitian dog, some of whom are descendants of the barkless vegetarian dogs that crossed the ocean aboard the double-hulled voyaging canoes of the pioneer Polynesians. They eat meat these days and sometimes they bark all night, in tandem with the cocks.

Along with the dog, the pig was the only domestic animal known to the Polynesian before the arrival of the Europeans. Both animals were raised for food. The pig is still baked in the underground ovens for special feasts, and dogs are still served in a "special Chinese sauce" during big celebrations. Some of the pigs have taken to the bush and men on the high islands organize wild boar hunts.

Captain Wallis gave a cat to the high chiefess Purea in 1767, and it found a mate somewhere during its trip to Tahiti, because today cats abound in all the inhabited islands and atolls. The little Polynesian rat and its cousins, who arrived aboard ships and boats, are threats to coconut trees without the metal bands. The *Rattus norvegicus*, a large brown rat, carries *leptospirosis* (Tahitian meningitis) and other contagious diseases. They also steal birds' eggs and fruit, and love to make their nests in thatched roofs.

In the Marquesas Islands you will see wild goats, sheep and cattle grazing on the precipitous cliffs overlooking the sea. Wild and tamed horses roam the plains of Ua Huka. The ancestors of these small horses were brought from Chile by Dupetit-Thouars in 1842.

A land crab called *tupa* lives in holes in the ground close to the lagoon and as far as a mile inland. They're edible if you pen them up and feed them coconut for ten days. Some people feed the *tupa* crabs to their pigs, but few families eat them now.

The mosquito and *nono* (sandfly) are two obnoxious pests that can truly ruin your vacation if you don't protect yourself from their stings. They particularly favor visitors, so be sure to bring a good insect repellent with you.

For many years herbicides and pesticides were used in massive quantities, which is a concern for the public because of the risks of pollution and toxic effects in rivers and lagoons. In recent years more attention is being paid to the dangers of these chemicals and "bio" gardening is becoming fashionable. However, most people do not really understand the concept of organic gardening and the advantages of using compost. Training programs are now being held on this subject, but there are no controls yet on commercial gardens. Fresh water shrimp and blue-eyed eels with long ears still live in some of the rivers and streams, although many of the rivers are choked with litter. Regular clean-up campaigns of the waterways and the lagoons are organized by conscientious groups.

Birds

The early Polynesians and European explorers brought birds (*manu*) into these islands and other species have been introduced from Asia, Africa, Australasia and the Americas. Habitat changes and introduced species of birds are believed to be accountable for the extinction of certain species that formerly inhabited the Windward Society Islands.

Polynesia's terrestrial avifauna consists of some 33 species: two species of heron, one duck, one sandpiper, one rail, nine pigeons, three loris, two swiftlets, four kingfishers, one swallow, five reed-warblers and four flycatchers. Because of the diversity of habitats the terrestrial avifauna of the volcanic islands is more varied than that of the coral atolls.

In contrast French Polynesia has 28 species of breeding seabird, making it one of the richest tropical areas for marine species. Murphy's petrel (*Pterodroma ultima*) is the only species that lives in Polynesia all the time. The birds you may see include terns, boobies, noddies, frigatebirds, petrels and the graceful white tropicbirds (phaetons), identified by two long white plumes that form the tip of the tail as they soar high over the valleys from the rocky cavities where they nest. The white sand beaches and the bushes on the *motus* inside the reef on Tetiaroa atoll are nesting grounds for several species of sea birds, and the Tuamotu atolls have numerous bird islands. Except for some small volcanic islets, the atolls generally shelter more marine birds, who find an abundance of food in their vast lagoons and around the islands. Almost a million sooty terns (*kaveka*) live on a small island offshore Ua Huka in the Marquesas Islands.

French Polynesia is also an important wintering area for several migratory bird species such as bristle-thighed curlew and long-tailed koel. At least 13 species of land-birds coming from North America and Siberia reach these islands on a regular basis.

The main land bird you will see is the Indian mynah (*Acridotheres Tristis*), which was imported to Tahiti around 1903 to eradicate a beetle that was destroying the young coconuts. The cheeky mynah also wiped out several species of birds by robbing their nests. The turtledove (*geopelia striata*) was introduced in 1950, and the red-tailed bulbul (*Pyconotus cafer*), a native of Asia, was introduced more recently, brought in from Rarotonga in the Cook Islands. The Tahitians gave the name vini to several small finch-like birds, which include the chestnut-breasted mannikin (*Lonchura Castaneothorax*), common waxbill (*Estrilda Astrild*), red-browed waxbill (*Estrilda Temporalis*), crimson-backed tanager (*Ramphocelus dimidiatus*) and the gray-backed white-eye (*Zosterops Lateralis*).

The Tahiti lorikeet (*Vini peruviana*) disappeared from Tahiti around the end of the last century, when the swamp harrier was introduced. This pretty little blue and white bird, also known as lori-nonette, is still found on some of the Tuamotu atolls, but is on the endangered species list, along with the pihiti (*Vini ultramarine-Kuhl*) of the Marquesas Islands and all the other lorikeets.

The mo'a oviri or wild cock is a jungle fowl of the Gallus Gallus family, which was introduced by the early Polynesians. The roosters are brightly colored with red, green and black feathers, and the hens are beige, brown or black. These birds can fly for several yards and they live in a free state, not really belonging to any family, but roost in trees and bushes close to a good source of food, such as my house. The roosters crow at all hours of the night, especially during the full moon, and of course, when you're trying to take a nap in the afternoon. I buy rice and bread for them and imported frozen chickens for myself. Their biggest enemies, apart from the swamp harrier, are little Tahitian boys, who catch the roosters and use them as fighting cocks.

Ocean, Reef & Lagoon Fauna

Scientists specializing in coral reefs have inventoried more than 800 species of shore fishes in Tahiti and Her Islands, with 633 species reported in the Society Islands. The oceanic slope is the richest part of a coral reef, and this is where you will have a better chance of finding crayfish or rock lobsters (*Panulirus penicillatus* called *oura miti*) and slipper lobsters (*Parribacus antarticus* called *tianee* in Tahitian). The near surface zones of the reef abound with surgeonfish, parrotfish, wrasses and red mullets. The external reef is also inhabited by various species of triggerfish, soldier-fish, squirrelfish, bass, perch, rock cod, angelfish, demoiselle-fish, mullet, and gray sharks and moray eels. You may also come across a green turtle (*Chelonia mydas*) or see a rare jellyfish or an occasional sea snake in this underwater zone.

Most of the mollusks and crustacea are found on the reef flats, which are also favored by pencil sea urchins and holothurians (sea cucumbers, called *rori* in Tahitian). The trigger-fish, puffer-fish, rock cods, box-fish, rascass and butterfly cod make their permanent homes here, and parrot-fish, surgeon-fish, angel-fish and small sharks, usually the harmless black-tipped and white-tipped variety, will visit the reef flats at high tide. Submerged coral plateaus act as passages between the oceanic slopes and the lagoons, and are the homes for echinoderms, particularly sea urchins, clam shells, octopus, small sponges and anemones, annelid worms and a variety of crabs. Lizardfish, puffer-fish and trumpet-fish are also common in this area. At high tide small schools of red mullet, jacks and parrotfish cross the zone on their way from the ocean to the lagoons.

On the lagoon slopes, as well as in the passes and the cracks in the reef (*hoa*), which have a sandy bottom sloping gradually to the center of the lagoon, is the favorite area of sponges, sand crabs, seashells (littorinids, nerites, ceriths), oysters, pearl oysters, cowries, strombs, spider shells, cones, all types of holothuria, *Ophiuridae*, starfish, *taramea*, some species of sea urchins (*vana*), soles, sand goby (*avaava*), leopard rays and some red mullets.

The coral outcrops and pinnacles are habitats of bivalve mollusks, including the colorful velvet-mantled reef clam (*Tridacna maxima*), called *pahua* locally. Numerous small species of fishes also gather here: surgeonfish, angelfish, butterfly fish, soldier-fish, harp-fish, butterfly cod, trumpet-fish, box-fish, porcupine-fish and trigger-fish.

There is almost no living coral or algae on the bottom of the lagoons, which are colonized by clamshells, pearl oysters, stony oysters and ark shells. Spider shells, a rare helmet shell or conch shell live on the softer sand bottom, but the majority of shells, including the pencil shells, miters, harp shells, olives, ceriths and several cones, remain hidden in the sand during the daytime.

The open lagoon waters are the habitat of roving fishes, including unicorn-fish (*ume*), *rotea, kukina,* coral trout (*tonu*), chameleon sea bass (*hoa*), lagoon sharks and stingrays. The (*lutjanus*) snappers, sweetlip, flying fish, garfish, great barracuda (*ono*), sea-pike barracuda (*tiatio*), jacks and mullets come and go between the lagoon and the ocean, and the silver scad (*ature*) also visit the lagoon for brief periods during certain seasons.

The flora of the fringing reefs is rich, and trochus are abundant in many parts of the fringing reef, but the fishes found here are usually in the juvenile stage. These may include moray eels, rock eels, rascasse, surgeonfish, wrasses, gobies, blennies and angelfish.

Three types of rays are found in Polynesian waters, and they are not aggressive unless threatened. The biggest danger is when a bather treads on a ray that is buried in the sand in shallow water. The most spectacular and famous member of the family is the giant manta ray (*Manta alfredi (Macleay), fafa piti),* that has a wingspan up to 25 feet across and may weigh almost two tons. The spotted eagle ray (*Aetobatis nari nari Euphrasen*) is the "bird ray" (*fai manu*) to the Tahitians because of its protruding head and narrow snout. They feed on mollusks and are one of the most important predators of the valuable pearl oysters in the lagoons of the Tuamotu and Gambier Islands. Several species of rays equipped with venomous spines on their tails are found in Polynesia. The stingray (*Himantura sp., fai iu)* lives near coral reefs or in the brackish water of some large bays around the high islands. The pectoral fins or wings of these species, as well as those of most other rays, are tasty and considered a delicacy, sometimes appearing on the menu in seafood restaurants in Tahiti and Moorea.

Sea turtles (*honu*) were once reserved for the high chiefs and priests of Tahiti, as this marine reptile was held *tapu* (sacred and forbidden). The three species living in Polynesian waters are the leathery turtle, the green turtle and the hawksbill turtle, which are on the list of endangered species and, therefore, *tapu.* However, these turtles are still massacred for their flesh and carapaces.

The most important commercial fishes found in the ocean depths surrounding French Polynesia include several species of the tuna family, principally, the yellow fin tuna (*Neothunnus albacora macropterus, aahi),* which are fished year round. Along with the tuna, the mahi mahi dolphinfish (*Coryphaena hippurus*) is the favorite fish served in restaurants. The great barracuda (*Sphyraena barracuda, ono*), the wahoo (*Acanthocybium solandri, paere*), the deep-water swordfish (*Xyphias gladius, haura or meka*), and the salmon of the gods (*Lampris Luna),* are also served in seafood restaurants. The bonito (*Katsuwonus pelamis, auhopu*) is the most commonly caught fish, and is preferred by most Tahitians to any other fish, but the taste is a bit too "fishy" for most visitors. Many other species of edible fish abound in this oceanic wonderland, which are taken home by the local fishermen for their own dinner.

Roughly one-third (or 25) of the species of dolphins and whales in the world are found in the waters of Tahiti and Her Islands. The spinner dolphins (*Stenella longirostris)* are the easiest to find around Tahiti and Moorea because they live the closest to shore. The humpback whales *(Megaptera novaeangliae)* can be seen and heard offshore Moorea between Jul.-Oct., when they come up from Antarctica to mate and give birth. They also escape the austral winters by visiting the Australs, Gambier and Tuamotu Islands, as well as the Leeward Society group and the Marquesas Islands. Black and white killer whales *(Orcinus Orca)* have been sighted numerous times in the Marquesas Islands, especially around Nuku Hiva, where there is a scuba diving center.

According to Richard H. Johnson, an American marine biologist and local shark specialist living in Tahiti, there are an estimated 35 species of sharks in French Polynesian waters. The sharks visitors normally see during a shark feeding or shark observation excursion inside the lagoon are the blackfin reef shark or *Carcharhinus Melanopterus.*

Natural Dangers

The ocean, coral reef, lagoons and coral gardens do have a few inhabitants that are not man's best friend. Sea snakes are rare in Polynesia and only one species *(Pelamis platurus)* is occasionally seen and caught along the coasts of some of the islands. This bi-colored snake has a brownish back and yellow belly and its venom is dangerous to humans. The theory is that these serpents hitchhiked on the bottoms of ships arriving in Tahiti from islands to our west, where the snakes are prevalent.

The natural dangers you want to avoid in the lagoon are: the "crown of thorns" starfish, called *taramea* in Tahitian; the sting of the jellyfish; burns from the Holuthurian or sea cucumber, also called sea leech, *rori* in Tahitian, and its cousin with spaghetti-like sticky tubules; burns from the sea anemone; the sting of the stone fish, called *nohu* in Tahitian; the sting of the scorpion fish and fire coral; the sting of sea urchin spines, called *vana* in Tahitian; and the highly poisonous varieties of cone shells, members of the *Conidae* family. There are 60 species of cones in Polynesia, but the most dangerous are the geographic, textile, marbled, aulicus and tulip cones. The best way to protect yourself from any of these unpleasant encounters is to wear plastic reef sandals or other appropriate shoes when walking in the lagoon or on the reef, and to watch where you put your hands and body when snorkeling or scuba diving.

The moray eel rarely attacks humans, but it will bite when it is provoked and feels threatened. Keep your hands safely out of the crevices or cavities in the coral, where the moray eel may be lurking.

Shark attacks occur most frequently in the atolls, along the exterior of the barrier reefs and in the shallow fissures between the exterior reef and the interior lagoons. Some of these attacks happen when a spear fisherman is trailing a string of fish behind him. Several scuba diving and snorkeling excursions include feeding the sharks and moray eels, who have been "tamed" by repetitive feedings.

You can avoid any potential problems by swimming only in the areas where you see the locals swimming; do not swim in the ocean at night; leave your bright jewelry at your hotel when you go swimming, snorkeling or scuba diving, as it can reflect the sun and refracted light in the water, and attract the attention of moray eels and sharks; and wear protective footgear when you're swimming in the lagoons and walking on the reef.

PEOPLE

The census of September 2007 counted 259,596 residents of French Polynesia, an increase of 14,750 people (6%) since the last census of November 2002, and the estimated population in July 2011 was 294,935. Three-quarters of the population live in the Windward Society Islands; 13% in the Leeward Society Islands; and the rest in the Marquesas, Austral and Gambier Islands.

On the island of Tahiti, the commune of Faa'a remains the most populated, with 29,851 inhabitants, followed by Papeete with 26,017 residents. The Moorea-Maiao commune had an increase of 13% (now with 16,500 residents), while the commune of Bora Bora has 4% more people than in 2002 for a total population of 8,992.

Life expectancy in the islands is 74.6 years for men and 79.7 years for women. The median age is 29.1 years and the number of male and female residents is about equal. There were 15.53% births per 1,000 people and 4.87% deaths per 1,000 inhabitants. Deaths on the road and suicide by hanging or drinking herbicides takes the lives of several young people each year.

The Polynesians

The majority (78%) of the people who live in the 5 island groups of French Polynesia are the **Maohi** people or Eastern Polynesians. Whether they live in the

---

POLYNESIAN ARISTOCRACY

The first Europeans to discover Tahiti found a highly evolved aristocratic society divided into three distinct groups. The first was the **Arii** or princely caste, whose king or Arii Rahi, was considered a sacred being. The **Raatira** were minor chiefs and landowners, and the **Manahune** were the common people. The **Arioi** were a kind of sect or religious fraternity that originated in Bora Bora. Their rank in the society was identified by their tattoos. They excelled in dancing and good manners and lived totally promiscuous lives, killing their children at birth. They traveled like troubadours from island to island, performing erotic ballets and political skits. The Manahune or *kaina* of today's Tahiti still forms the majority of the population. These Polynesians are the blue-collar workers, at the bottom end of the economic structure, with the least political power today.

Society Islands, the Marquesas, Tuamotu-Gambier or Austral Islands, they are commonly referred to as **Tahitians**. The Polynesians refer to one another according to their island or archipelago, such as a Marquesan, a Paumotu (native of the Tuamotu Islands), a Rurutu or Rapa Iti, a Mangareva, and so forth.

Two distinct racial types settled the Marquesas Islands and some of the Marquesans have longer, narrow heads. Red hair was added by European sailors from exploration ships and whalers. There are striking differences in the Paumotu physical types, as well as their language and culture. Some of the men on the Tuamotu atolls are big strapping fellows, with wide flat noses, while others are more squat, with big heads, small button noses and dark brown skin. Still others have thin lips, aquiline features, slim bodies and light tan skin. The Austral Islanders resemble their neighbors in the Cook Islands, with almost blue-black hair, Spanish eyes and heavy beards. In Mangareva and the other Gambier Islands the earliest settlers appear to have been castaways from the Tuamotu archipelago, the Marquesas and Rarotonga.

The first European visitors to Tahiti were impressed by the personal cleanliness of the people. They may take 3-4 cold water showers a day. A group of dancers or workers or spectators on a hot day smell only of soap, *monoi* or flowers. Being dirty or wearing dirty clothes was traditionally a matter of shame. There are, of course, many exceptions to this custom today.

The Chinese

The first Chinese were brought to Tahiti during the American Civil War to work for the Tahiti Cotton and Coffee Plantation Company in Atimaono, on Tahiti's south coast districts of Papara and Mataiea. A contingent of 329 Chinese laborers arrived in Tahiti from Hong Kong on February 28, 1865, coming from a district around Canton and the Kwangtung Province, who spoke the Hakka dialect. Eleven months later Atimaono had a total of 1,010 Chinese workers who planted cotton, coconut trees, coffee, sugar cane, fruit trees and vegetable gardens at Atimaono.

At the end of the war there was no money to send the Chinese home, so most of them took jobs to earn their return fare. About a hundred of these Chinese workers remained in Tahiti and began growing vegetables on rented land, opening small stores in Tahiti and several of the outer islands. A second wave of Chinese immigrants arrived in Tahiti in 1890, who had a higher social standing, and the first Chinese women arrived in 1907. Gradually these Chinese businessmen acquired wealth and today they are integrated in all the professions, but are primarily the merchants of French Polynesia. Many of the Chinese intermarried with the Tahitians and were eventually allowed to become French citizens, when several families changed their names to sound more "Frenchified." Today Mr. Wong has Chinese cousins who use the name of Vongue. The Chinese comprise 12% of the population today.

The French

French people from all walks of life began arriving in Tahiti as early as 1843, when the Protectorate was created in Tahiti, with Papeete as the government capital. French civil servants, lawyers, *notaires*, small businessmen, schoolteachers, medical professionals, missionaries and military men settled here, often intermarrying with the most important families of Tahiti.

Most of the French live on the island of Tahiti and her sister island of Moorea. There are small settlements of French *fonctionnaires* or retired civil servants living on Raiatea, Taha'a and Bora Bora, and in the Marquesas Islands of Hiva Oa and Nuku Hiva, with just a scattering of French on the more isolated islands. Today 6% of the population is comprised of "local French" and 4% are Metropolitan French.

The Expatriates

There are some 300 Americans living in French Polynesia, primarily in the Society Islands, where they are employed in tourism and the cultured pearl industry, or they have retired from business.

Even though the French and other Europeans have never settled in large numbers in French Polynesia, there has been a recent influx of French moving to these islands, as well as some other citizens of the European Union. The population also includes a few expatriates from Australia, New Zealand and other South Pacific Islands.

The Demi

A *demi* is a Polynesian with mixed blood. The first half-caste or *demi* was born about nine months after the Spanish caravel *San Lesmes* was wrecked on the reef of Amaru in the Tuamotu atolls in 1526. After that came more Spaniards, followed by the Dutch and then the British sailors, who arrived in Tahiti in 1767. The French followed and then Tahiti became a favored destination for sea rovers, merchants, lotus-eaters, writers, painters and wastrels.

Throughout the years the pure Polynesian stock has been diminished by contact with the French, English, Americans, Germans, Russian, Swedish, Norwegians, Spanish, South Americans, Japanese, Africans—you name it. The *demi* is often very attractive and reasonably intelligent, and usually has a pretty good

---

THE VERY FRIENDLY PEOPLE OF TAHITI

During a 1981 interview on the *East-West Connection* television program in Los Angeles, the hostess asked Tahiti's Minister of Tourism: "What is the racial breakdown of the majority of the people?" He replied: "We used to say in Tahiti that the whole world slept with Tahiti."

education, and a good job with the local government, quite frequently obtained through family connections. The *demi* can also be one of the most confused people you'll ever meet, because they live between two cultures.

On one hand they want to be sophisticated and snobbish French, and on the other hand, they are happiest when they're slurping up the *ma'a* Tahiti with their fingers and singing *kaina* songs in Tahitian during a boozy *bringue*. Some of them are adept at combining the two contrasting cultures. There's a saying in Tahiti that describes the dilemma of the average Tahitian-European person: "When he wakes up the morning, the *demi* doesn't know which side of the bed to get out of."

5. A Short History

GENERAL HISTORY OF FRENCH POLYNESIA
The Polynesian Migrations

Archaeologists, ethnologists, anthropologists, linguists and other scholars have long debated the questions of when, why, and how the pioneer Polynesians crossed thousands of miles of open ocean to settle on these islands in the Eastern Pacific that are now called **French Polynesia**. New archaeological evidence and improved techniques of radiocarbon dating may refine the theories, but at present most of the experts who study this subject agree that the Australoid ancestors of the Melanesian, Micronesian and Polynesian people came from Southeast Asia. They walked across the landmass that existed in the final Ice Age to reach what are now the Indonesian islands of Sumatra, Java and Borneo, and on to Australia and New Guinea, which were then joined, settling in the Southwest Pacific around 30,000 BC. A group of dark-skinned people called the Papuans also came from Southeast Asia, arriving in the southwestern Pacific area between 7,000 and 3,500 BC.

Several thousands of years later, between 3,000 and 1,000 BC, a group of lighter-skinned Austronesians from Asia forced the Papuans to moved further inland in what is now Irian Jaya and Papua New Guinea. Some of these wanderers then set out to explore the more eastern South Pacific islands, eventually settling on every speck of land that could support life. They sailed eastward in their huge double ocean going canoes, using the sun, stars, wind, ocean currents, and the flight patterns of birds as their guides, referring to their crude stick charts to navigate to new islands. Carrying 100-500 people on board these canoes made of lashed planks with sails of pandanus matting, they brought with them their women and children, pigs and dogs, coconuts and taro, breadfruit tree seedlings and roots, shrubs and trees, as well as flowering plants, which were to be used for food, clothing, medicines, and other household needs. Historians believe this eastward progress occurred over 5,000 years, and departures from a settled island were necessitated due to overpopulation, food and water shortage or because of internal fighting.

The Polynesian culture is believed to have evolved in the central Pacific, in Tonga or Samoa, which they called Havaiki, their ancestral religious center. After a pause of 1,000 years, a migratory wave from this "cradle" of Polynesia brought the new explorers even farther eastward, and some archaeologists believe that as far back as 500 BC the first of these double-hulled canoes reached the Marquesas Islands. A tall and stately race of proud and cultured people settled on some of the 20 islands, which they called *Te Fenua Te Enata*, or *Te Henua Te Enana*, "The Land of the Men."

During the next migratory movement of the Polynesians, some 500 years after arriving in the Marquesas, the voyaging canoes sailed south and west to the

Tuamotu Archipelago and Mangareva, north to the Hawaiian Islands, and even farther eastward to discover and populate Easter Island, all around 850 AD. The great Polynesian migrations then proceeded southwest, with canoes departing from the new religious and cultural center of Havaiki, Raiatea in the Leeward Society Islands, around 1,000 AD. These voyagers settled in Rarotonga in the Cook Islands and in New Zealand, completing a triangle of Polynesian colonization. The Polynesian people of French Polynesia, the Cook Islanders, Easter Islanders, native Hawaiians and the Maoris of New Zealand all speak variations of the Maohi language, the native tongue of their Marquesan ancestors.

European Exploration

In 1513 the Spanish explorer **Vasco Nuñez de Balboa** crossed the Isthmus of Panama and sighted the mighty Pacific Ocean. Seven years later, in 1520, **Ferdinand Magellan**, a Portuguese in the service of the Spanish, sailed to the Philippines, but the only island he sighted in Polynesia was the atoll of Puka Puka in the northeastern Tuamotu archipelago. The Spanish caravel *San Lesmes* was wrecked on the reef in Amaru in the Tuamotus around 1526 and the shipwrecked sailors supposedly married Polynesian women. In 1595 **Alvaro de Mendaña de Neira** was searching for the Solomon Islands, which he had discovered in 1567, and during this second voyage into the South Seas he discovered the southern group of the Marquesas Islands. In 1606, 80 years after the disappearance of the *San Lesmes*, **Pedro Fernández de Quiros**, who had been Mendaña's chief pilot, discovered a number of the Tuamotu Islands before continuing on to other island groups further west. This was the last of the Spanish explorations in the Pacific during that era.

In 1615-16 the Dutch explorers **Le Maire** and **Schouten** discovered several atolls in the Tuamotus, and in 1722 **Jacob Roggeveen**, another Dutch captain, sailed through the Tuamotus and passed the island of Makatea on his way to the Society Islands, where he sighted Maupiti in the Leeward Society Islands. But he failed to see Bora Bora, Raiatea or Taha'a, all high islands that are visible from Maupiti.

The Dutch were then followed by the British, with **Commodore John Byron**, grandfather of the famous poet, discovering more of the Tuamotu atolls aboard the *H.M.S. Dolphin* in 1765. If any of the European explorers found Tahiti, they left no record of their discovery.

The *Dolphin* returned to the South Seas in 1767 under the command of **Captain Samuel Wallis**, who discovered the island of Tahiti, and anchored in Matavai Bay on June 23, 1767. He was followed just 10 months later by French **Admiral Louis Antoine de Bougainville**, who also discovered Tahiti, and claimed the island for France during his visit in April 1768. In April 1769, Lieutenant **James Cook**, aboard the *H.M.S. Endeavour*, made his first trip to Tahiti. He returned again in 1773, 1774 and 1777. Cook visited Moorea and discovered the Leeward Islands of Raiatea, Taha'a, Huahine, Bora Bora, Tupai and Maupiti, which he named the Society Islands, as they lay contiguous to each other.

In 1772 Spanish captain **Don Domingo de Boenechea** anchored his ship, the *Aguilla*, in the lagoon of Tautira on the Tahiti Iti peninsula. After claiming the island for his country and king, Boenechea sailed for Peru, but returned in 1774 to establish the first long-term European settlement on the island, with two missionaries and two military men. The Spanish rule ended in Tahiti following the death of Boenechea, when the missionaries returned to Peru.

"Breadfruit Bligh" & The Bounty

The story of **Captain William Bligh** and the mutinous crew aboard the *H.M.S. Bounty* provided a colorful chapter in Tahiti's history following their arrival at Point Venus in Matavai Bay on October 26, 1788. Once ashore, Bligh and his men had to wait five months before the breadfruit they sought would be at the right stage for transplanting. The sailors happily accepted this respite from Bligh's tight discipline, and willingly adapted to the Tahitian *aita pea pea* (no problem) philosophy of life, complete with all the pleasures any sailor could ever imagine.

When the *Bounty* weighed anchor on April 4, 1789, and headed toward the Leeward Islands of the Society group, Bligh was faced with a moody, belligerent crew. The punishments Bligh meted out for his men, and his insults to his officers were too harsh to endure after the idyllic life the men had enjoyed in Tahiti. Acting Lieutenant Fletcher Christian was especially disturbed, and his fury finally exploded into a dramatic mutiny, which is remembered as the most famous mutiny in history.

Bligh was hauled out of bed early on the morning of April 28, tied up and dragged on deck. He and 18 of his officers and men were put into an open launch with food and water, some wine and rum, a compass, a quadrant, some canvas, and lines and sails. Then the boat was set adrift in the open ocean, a few miles from Tofua in the Tongan Islands, whose inhabitants were extremely unfriendly in those days. Bligh's success in sailing the small open boat across 5,800 km. (3,600 mi.) of ocean to Timor and Batavia in the Dutch Indies, is one of the most remarkable voyages in history.

Twice Fletcher Christian sailed the *Bounty* to Tubuai, 568 km. (355 mi.) due south of Tahiti in the Austral Islands, but they were unable to stay there because the natives were so hostile. They returned to Tahiti for supplies, and when the *Bounty* left Matavai Bay for the last time, some of the British sailors remained ashore at Point Venus. Aboard the ship with Christian were 8 of his fellow mutineers, 6 Tahitian men, 12 Tahitian women and a little girl. This small group reached the uninhabited island of Pitcairn, where they burned the *Bounty* and began a new life ashore. There was no news of Christian and his party for 18 years.

The 16 men from the *Bounty* who chose to remain in Tahiti settled down with their wives and families. Two of them had died by the time the H.M.S. *Pandora* anchored in Matavai Bay in 1791, but **Captain Edward Edwards**, who had been sent from England in search of the mutineers, arrested the remaining 14 men. The

Pandora was shipwrecked and 4 of the men were drowned before they could reach England for their trial. During a court martial inquiry in England, 3 of the men were condemned to death and hanged, and the remaining 7 were set free. **Peter Heywood** wrote the first Tahitian dictionary in prison while awaiting his trial.

Captain Bligh had also undergone a trial by the English court, which cleared his name for any guilt in the *Bounty* mutiny, and he sailed back to Tahiti, arriving in Matavai Bay on April 10, 1792, as commander of the *H.M.S. Providence* and her armed tender, the *Assistance*.

Bligh remained in Tahiti for three months, collecting 2,126 breadfruit trees and 500 other plants to take back to the West Indies. The breadfruit seedlings were planted in St. Vincent and in Port Royal, Jamaica. When the trees grew and began to bear fruit, the Negro slaves refused to eat the starchy breadfruit because they didn't like the taste.

The English Lose to the French

The English Protestant missionaries from the London Missionary Society (LMS) arrived aboard the *Duff* and landed at Point Venus on March 5, 1797, to convert the Tahitians to the Gospel. **George Pritchard** of the LMS gained the confidence of **Queen Pomare IV** and convinced her that Tahiti should be under the protection of England. Although **Queen Victoria** was unwilling to declare Tahiti a protectorate of England, a power struggle between the English Protestants and the French Catholic missionaries in Tahiti almost brought England and France to the brink of war.

The end result was that Queen Pomare IV and the LMS missionaries lost their battle with the French, under the guns of *La Reine Blanche*, a French warship commanded by **Admiral Dupetit-Thouars**. Tahiti became a French protectorate in 1842 and guerrilla rebellions on Tahiti and some of the other islands resisted the French invasion until 1846, when France gained control over Tahiti and Moorea.

French Colonialism

Tahiti and her dependencies became a full-fledged French colony on December 29, 1880, when the century-old reign of the Pomare family formally came to an end and French nationality and rights were bestowed on all Tahitians.

The Pomare's dominions included Tahiti, Moorea, Maiao, Mehetia, the Tuamotu islands and Tubuai and Raivavae in the Austral Islands. The French had already annexed the Marquesas Islands in 1842 and all the other islands were annexed by 1901.

In 1903 the *Etablissements Français de l'Océanie* (EFO), or French Territories of Oceania, were established, incorporating all of the French holdings in the Eastern Pacific into one colony. Copra, cotton, mother-of-pearl shell, phosphate, vanilla and fruits were exported in exchange for manufactured goods. By 1911 there were about 3,500 colonists, mostly French, living in Polynesia, plus the

Chinese immigrants who had been brought to Tahiti in the 1860s to work in the cotton fields of Atimaono.

Although Tahiti was geographically far from the main theaters of the two world wars, the colony was politically involved because of its French connection. During World War I almost 1,000 Tahitian soldiers fought against the Germans in Europe, and the town of Papeete was bombarded by 2 German cruisers on Sept. 22, 1914, when they sank a French navy ship in the harbor.

During World War II young men from Tahiti joined the Pacific Battalion, were shipped to Europe, and fought side by side with the forces of the Free French. Bora Bora was used as a military supply base for the American forces, with 5,000 soldiers, sailors and Seabees arriving on the small island in 1942. Besides a few cannon in the hills and some old Quonset huts, the only reminders of the American presence in Bora Bora today are some blue-eyed Tahitians with light hair and skin.

French Polynesia

A 1957 statute changed the *Etablissements Français de l'Océanie* colony into a French Overseas Territory, with the official name of French Polynesia. In the early 1960s a large harbor was built in Papeete, an international airport was opened in Faaa, the French established the *Centre d'expérimentations du Pacifique* (CEP), the Pacific Experimentation Center in Tahiti, and MGM brought a big film crew to make another movie of *Mutiny on the Bounty*. All of these rapid changes brought French Polynesia into the modern age, accompanied by problems of inflation, unemployment, housing problems, pollution, emotional instability, juvenile delinquency and political discontent among an increasing number of the population.

French Nuclear Testing

French Polynesia entered the nuclear age in 1963 when the French chose the Tuamotu atolls of Moruroa, 1,200 km. (720 mi.) southeast of Tahiti, and Fangataufa, 40 km. (24 mi.) south of Moruroa, as sites for the *Centre d'expérimentations du Pacifique* (CEP), Pacific Experimentation Center. Although the local political parties protested the invasion, President Charles de Gaulle responded by outlawing political parties.

On Sept. 11, 1966, De Gaulle watched from an offshore French warship as the first nuclear test was carried out, exploding in the atmosphere almost 600 m. (2,000 ft.) above the turquoise lagoon of Moruroa. Between 1966-1974, the French made 41 atmospheric tests in Moruroa and Fangataufa, and between 1975-1991, some 134 underground tests were completed, by drilling a shaft deep into the coral foundation under the lagoons. President François Mitterand suspended the nuclear testing in April 1992 and most of the 7,750 employees of the CEP returned to France or to their islands in French Polynesia. In June 1995, France's newly elected president, Jacques Chirac, announced a new series of eight nuclear tests, to be completed by the end of May 1996.

The shock of this announcement reverberated around the world, and on Sept. 5, 1995, when a 20-kiloton explosion was carried out in Moruroa, the result was disastrous for France, and especially for French Polynesia's tourism and economy. Severe rioting broke out in Papeete, with several buildings burned, the Tahiti-Faaa International Airport terminal was partially burned, and the vehicles in the parking lot were damaged and burned. On Jan. 27, 1996, France made its 6th and final nuclear test at Fangataufa, and 2 days later President Chirac announced that the tests were finished forever.

Some of the 1,500 workers, technicians and scientists, brought from France and Tahiti for these tests, finished their work and studies and went home, while the French Army and Legionnaires dismantled the 2 nuclear bases.

Internal Autonomy Government

In 1977 the French government granted **administrative autonomy** to French Polynesia, and domestic or internal autonomy was given in 1984, consolidated in 1990 and extended in 1996. On February 12, 2004, the French government gave French Polynesia the status of a **French Overseas Community**, rather than a Territory, which means that the Assembly of French Polynesia can adopt "laws" in the most important areas, and not just "resolutions", or acts of an administrative nature. This revision of the Constitution also enlarges the field of responsibilities of French Polynesia, which can negotiate international agreements with foreign states, in matters relevant to its responsibility. It also may become a member of international organizations and have representation in foreign states.

The French Polynesian Government consists of a president, who is elected for a 5-year term by the Assembly and Council of Ministers whom he appoints before submitting the list to the Assembly's vote. The 57 members of the Assembly are elected by vote every 5 years and represent the 5 archipelagoes. The French Polynesian Government is represented in the French Parliament by 2 deputies and 2 senators, plus an advisor in the French Social and Economic Council.

A French High Commissioner represents the State in French Polynesia, and the Republic of France controls defense, law and order, justice, worldwide international responsibility and the currency. The French *gendarmes* have brigades on all the larger islands and each *commune* has one or more Tahitian *mutoi*, municipal policemen, whose duties may include directing school traffic and tracking down scooters or cars that were "borrowed" on a Saturday night. His job also includes keeping peace in his own neighborhood. There are also other branches of law enforcement in Tahiti, including the secret service police and the municipal police who patrol the "hot spots" of downtown Papeete on weekends, searching for drinking minors, drugs, fights and vehicles with boom boxes blaring at top volume, which are all illegal.

Today the Tahitian flag, white with red borders at top and bottom, with an emblem representing a double outrigger sailing canoe, flies side by side with the tricolor of the French flag. The archipelagoes also have their own emblems. The

Territorial anthem "Ia Ora 'O Tahiti Nui" is sung or played wherever French Polynesia participates in international meetings or sports events throughout the Pacific. You can listen to this anthem and learn all about the French Polynesian Government at *www.presidence.pf.*

Post-Nuclear Progress Pact for Self-Sufficiency

A **Progress Pact** between the French Polynesia and the Republic of France was signed in January 1993, to compensate for the loss of financial resources due to the ending of the CEP French nuclear tests in the Tuamotu Islands. A 10-year adjustment law and development contracts for 5-year periods were adopted in 1994, with the State providing assistance in the fields of education, training, research, health and transport infrastructures, agriculture, tourism and housing.

When French President Jacques Chirac decided in 1996 to halt all nuclear testing, France committed itself to maintaining the same amount of spending in CFP in French Polynesia. The spending level agreed to was 18 billion French Pacific francs (about US $1.8 million dollars) per year for 10 years, which was made possible by a reconversion fund. This agreement for strengthening the economic autonomy was signed between the French State and French Polynesia on July 26, 1996, and was valid until 2005. President Chirac then removed all boundaries on the reconversion fund payments so that French Polynesia is supposed to receive 18 billion CFP per year in perpetuity.

French Polynesia's main economic resources are **tourism** and **pearl farming**. In recent years, **deep-sea commercial fishing** has also shown promise, particularly with an increase in exports. **Agricultural products**, such as fruit, flowers and nono or noni (*Morinda citrifolia*), have also had some export success.

2011 Political Instability and Economic Crisis

As I write this in mid-2011 Tahiti is struggling to recover from the effects of the world economic recession that began in 2008. Standard and Poors came to Tahiti in 2010 to study the situation and reported that French Polynesia has to turn to a new economic base, especially on tourism, to replace the model based on French state transfers. The number of tourists began declining in 2008 and several restaurants, hotels, boutiques and other tourist-related businesses have had to close. The market for Tahitian cultured pearls has also suffered. The number of overseas visitors took an upswing in 2011 as more Americans began to book their dream vacations in these enchanting islands, and tourism professionals are now feeling more optimistic for the future.

French Polynesia has had 13 changes of government since 2004, and the current president, Oscar Temaru, is in office for the fifth time. He heads the pro-independence party. Instead of using the palatial Presidency for his offices, Temaru chose to occupy the Vice-President's smaller headquarters. He suggested that this grandiose colonial style building be used as a casino. (He will have to persuade the churches that this is a good idea). His suggestion for improving the economy is to legalize the sale of marijuana (pakalolo). We are not sure if he was serious, but some of the Assembly members agree with him, pointing out that Tahiti's "Hotel Nuutania" (prison) wouldn't be so overcrowded if the "paka" growers were liberated. And if they pay their taxes, then the salaries of the government representatives won't have to be reduced. In addition to the taxes that have already been increased for those of us who work for ourselves, the Temaru government also intends to begin a personal income tax system to help boost the economic growth.

Other measures to cut expenses will be to consolidate or close several of the government agencies. These include stopping the publication of *Tahiti Presse*, the government's on-line press agency, and transforming TNTV, the government-owned television station, into an on-line Web TV. Temaru, who is also the Minister of Tourism, wants to close all the overseas offices for Tahiti Tourism and hire outside companies to promote Tahiti and Her Islands.

6. Planning Your Trip

WHEN TO GO

"When is the best time to go to Tahiti?" is a question I'll answer by asking you: "What do you want to do once you get here?" If you want to scuba dive, you'll have the best underwater visibility during the dry season. If you want to snorkel and swim in the limpid lagoons, then come between Oct.-June, when the water temperature is at least 80° Fahrenheit. If your goal is to photograph the most marvelous sunsets, complete with a "green flash", then come in Jul.-Aug., when the evening skies are more likely to be free of clouds. If you want to see Tahiti dressed in her most beautiful finery of flowering trees and ripening fruits, then come in the "springtime" months of Oct.-Dec. If you want to surf the huge rollers, make your reservations for Jan.-Mar. The waves are usually high in Aug. also, when the Billabong Surfing championships are held in Teahupoo.

If you intend to catch a record-setting marlin, then your guess is as good as the experts, who tell me they're now reeling in the big ones all year long, rather than just during the summer months. If you want to see the humpback whales, they come up from Antarctica between Jul.-Oct., and play around just offshore, in the passes and sometimes in the bays of the Society Islands. Whale-watching expeditions will take you just offshore Moorea or Tahiti to sight the gigantic visitors, and on the Austral Island of Rurutu a scuba diving company may let you swim with the whales.

If you want to charter a yacht and sail from island to island, the balmy trade winds blow most of the year, and are most pleasant from May-Sept. If your interest is outrigger canoe racing, the biggest competitions are in Jul.-Oct. And if you want to party with the Polynesians during the biggest celebration of the year, then reserve now for a room during the Heiva Festivals that begin in late June, reach a peak in July and continue throughout most of Aug. with mini-Heiva programs in some of the larger hotels.

You may want to consult the *Calendar of Events* chapter before making your decision, as well as checking out the legal holidays in French Polynesia, which are listed in Chapter 7, *Basic Information*.

Another thing to keep in mind may be the school holidays, which can influence the availability of international and domestic flights, as well as accommodations in the small hotels and family operated hotels or pensions. The students have a week's vacation the last week in Sept., the second week of Nov., a month's holiday from mid-Dec. to mid-Jan., another week off during the third week of Feb., 2 weeks during the first half of April, the third week in May and 6 weeks off during the month of July and the first half of Aug. Add to that the 14 legal holidays that fall during the school week, plus time off when the teachers have a pedagogic meeting. When, you might ask, do these kids get an education? If you have any questions about the exact dates, the Tahiti Tourisme office can answer them.

Climate & Weather

The climate of these islands is usually benign, sunny and pleasant, and the cool, gentle breezes of the South Pacific Ocean and the northeasterly trade winds provide a natural a/c system. Meteorologists consider the months of Nov.-Mar. as the "rainy" season, when the climate is warmer and more humid, and Apr.-Oct. as the "dry" season, with a cooler drier climate. The yearly average ambient temperature is 27°C (80.6°F). Most of the rain falls during the warmer season (1,800 mm or 70.9 in.), but there are also many days of sunshine during these months (average of 2,500-2,900 hours) with refreshing trade winds. Mean relative humidity in Tahiti for an average year is 77.4%.

The central and northern Tuamotus have warmer temperatures and less rainfall than in the Society Islands. There are no mountains to create cooling night breezes, as the elevation of these atolls ranges from 6-20 ft. above sea level. They can experience desert-like hot periods between Nov.-Apr., with devastating storms and cyclones.

The Marquesas Islands are closer to the equator, and temperatures and humidity tend to be slightly higher than in Tahiti, with more rainfall in verdant Fatu Hiva and more arid conditions in Ua Huka. The Marquesas archipelago lies in the midst of a trade wind belt from the northern latitudes, bringing northeasterly winds most of the year, with seasons that are reversed to those in the Society Islands. Although there is no real rainy season, trekking through the steep valleys to visit tikis and archaeological sites in the Marquesas can be a very steamy and often muddy hike at any time of the year.

The climate in the Australs is more temperate and less rainy than in Tahiti, and the seasons are more clearly defined. These islands lie at the southern boundary of the southeast trade winds, which blow from Nov.-Mar. In the cold season, from May- Sept., the winds are more variable and generally westerly, with temperatures of 50°-70° F.

French Polynesia is on the far eastern edge of the South Pacific cyclone (hurricane) belt, and has suffered serious damage from cyclones, tropical depressions, and other effects of El Niño.

Dry Season

From Jul.-Sept. the *mara'amu* trade winds can bring blustery, howling weather and rain from the south. But the rains don't always accompany these chilling winds. I lost the roof of my house one year in July during the *mara'amu* and I looked up to see a beautiful, bright sky filled with a moon and stars.

The dry seasons are sometimes too dry in many of the islands, when we suffer droughts and water rationing. This is especially true during June-Sept. We have also had a shortage of water in Jan., but our visitors enjoyed the bright, sunny days when they could work on their tans in the midst of Tahiti's so-called rainy season. Winter storms in the southern latitudes, down around the "Roaring 40s" south of the Austral Islands, can stir up some powerful waves, with 16-ft. swells damaging homes and hotels throughout the Society Islands.

These inclement weather conditions should not affect your vacation plans, as the months of July-Sept. or Oct. are especially beautiful in the islands, with day after day of glorious sunshine, and cool nights good for snuggling and gazing at the Southern Cross and other tropical stars. If your hotel is located on the southern coast of any of the Society Islands, just bring along a windbreaker or sweater, and throw an extra blanket on the bed.

Wet Season

"Is it going to rain during my vacation/honeymoon?" I get several e-mail inquiries on that subject every year. The answer is, "it's highly possible". But don't let it stop you from coming. During the height of the rainy season, it can rain very heavily for days and days. During this time the trade winds stop and the temperature and humidity levels rise. When this happens the mugginess may make you feel hot, sticky and irritable if you stay indoors. The best thing to do is to take a walk in the refreshing rain or swim in the lagoon to cool off. It's true that you cannot work on your tan during this weather, but you can tour around the island and watch the double rainbows over the emerald green valley when the sun breaks through the clouds for a few minutes. This is also a great time to go shopping for your own special Tahiti cultured pearls!

Weather Report

You can get a 10-day weather report for Tahiti on the Internet at *www.weather.com, www.intellicast.com;* and at *www.tahitiplanet.com/webcam.htm* you can get the weather plus the sunrise, sunset, moon and star movements. Another site is *www.weatherunderground.com.*

WHAT TO PACK

Casual and cool are the keywords to packing for this tropical climate. Light, loose, wash and wear garments of cotton and other natural fabrics are best. Unless you are taking a cruise ship to Tahiti you can leave your formal dining clothes and coats and ties at home. Women should pack a few pairs of shorts and slacks, along with a couple of skirts and tops or comfortable dresses, plus 1-2 swimsuits. Men will be properly dressed in shorts and tee shirts almost everywhere, except for dinner in a few hotels, fancy restaurants and nightclubs, where you'll have to put on long pants, an open-neck shirt and real shoes. You can both buy some colorful *pareos* once you are here to complement your wardrobes. Yes, men wear them too! But only around the hotel grounds or on the beach. Most Polynesians do not wear their *pareos* to town.

Both men and women will be in style on most occasions in sandals or flip-flop rubber thongs, except for some restaurants or nightclubs, as mentioned above. Be sure to include aqua socks or protective footgear, such as old tennis shoes, for walking on the coral reef and in the lagoons. Plastic sandals can be purchased in the islands for about $15, which can be worn in the lagoon and while walking in the valleys.

A lightweight sweater or windbreaker will feel good on cool evenings, especially during the months of Jul.-Sept., and anytime you are on the sea at night. Along with a hat or visor, don't forget to pack a good pair of sunglasses and your sun block or screen. A folding umbrella or a lightweight plastic rain coat or poncho that fits into a pocket or purse may also come in handy during tropical rain showers, which are refreshing rather than cold.

Some of the budget hotels and hostels or family pensions do not supply face cloths, and in some of the backpacker's lodgings you will have to bring your own soap and towel. A universal sink plug is handy for most lavabos and bathtubs. Other useful items include an alarm clock, portable clothes line and pegs, small bags of soap powder, clothes hangers, beach towel, pocket flashlight, corkscrew, tin opener or Swiss Army knife, plastic fork and spoon, folding plastic insulated cup and zip-lock plastic bags to contain anything spillable. Bring a small first-aid kit containing your personal medicines, aspirin, indigestion tablets, vitamins, insect repellent, antiseptic cream, aloe gel, Band-Aids or other sticking plasters. Pack your toiletries and just a few cosmetics, and you may want to bring along your binoculars. Remember to put your sharp items in your luggage to be checked, rather than in your carry-on bag.

Don't forget to bring your camera, and make sure you know how to operate it before you get here, to prevent losing that perfect shot. Be sure to include lots of film and a battery plus charger, as well as a waterproof bag to protect your camera from salt and spray during boat excursions. Also pack a small travel bag in which to carry your things when you're on tours and excursions.

Hair-dryers are provided in the luxury hotels, and if you bring a hair-dryer, make sure it can convert to 220 voltage, or bring a small adapter (transformer). Always ask at your hotel reception before plugging in your electrical appliances. You may want to bring your own supply of reading material. You can exchange books at most hotels. If you bring a Kindle, be sure to bring the charger too. Some folks bring their own booze, which is expensive here. Last but not least—bring your passport, airline tickets, driver's license, cash and international credit cards.

ENTRANCE REQUIREMENTS: PASSPORTS/VISAS

All U.S. citizens and nationals can apply for a passport by completing the application form DS-11, which is available in U.S. post offices. You can download this form from the **U.S. State Department** website (*www.travel.state.gov/passport*) or call the National **Passport Information Center**, (Tel. 877/487-2778), which has offices in several cities. Complete the form and return it to the Passport Agency or to your nearest post office or federal courthouse.

All non-French citizens must have a valid passport to enter French Polynesia, as well as an airline ticket back to their resident country or to at least 2 more continuing destinations. Your passport or travel document must be valid for at least 6, months beyond your return date. Your first and last name on your passport must match your international air tickets.

Nationals from the following countries are entitled to a 3-month stay without a visa:

European Union: Austria, Belgium, Denmark, Estonia, Finland, Germany, Greece, Hungary, Ireland, Italy, Latvia, Lithuania, Luxembourg, Malta, The Netherlands, Norway, Poland, Portugal, Czech Republic, United Kingdom, Slovakia, Slovenia, Sweden and Spain.

Other countries: Andorra, Australia, Cyprus, Iceland, Liechtenstein, Monaco, St. Martin, Switzerland and the Vatican.

Maximum stay of 3 months per semester: Brazil, China, and Chinese citizens holding a valid passport from Hong Kong, Macao and Bulgaria.

Refugees and stateless persons: If holding a travel authorization delivered by France.

Nationals from the following countries are entitled to a 1-month stay without visa:

North, Central and South America: Argentina, Bolivia, Canada, Costa Rica, Chile, El Salvador, Ecuador, Guatemala, Honduras, Mexico, Nicaragua, Panama, Paraguay, Uruguay, and the USA.

Asia-Pacific: Brunei, New Zealand, Japan, Malaysia, Singapore and South Korea.

Europe: Croatia.

Nationals from all other countries require visas, which may be obtained from the French Embassy or French Consulate in the country of residence. The visa must be endorsed "valid for French Polynesia", which applies also to aliens holding temporary visitor's permits (one year in metropolitan France). Aliens holding residence cards for metropolitan France are exempt from visa requirements. Except for nationals of the European Union and aliens holding a 10-year residence for metropolitan France, all foreigners entering French Polynesia must have a return ticket. For further information please visit the website: *www.polynesie-francaise.pref.gouv.fr.*

A foreigner with a residence card for the US is not exempt from having a visa for visiting French Polynesia. This visa exemption is subject to change at short notice. It is advisable to contact the nearest French Consulate or an airline serving Tahiti for specific information.

If you think you will want to extend your stay in French Polynesia beyond the 1-month visa exemption for US citizens, you should apply for a 3-month visa at a French Consulate office prior to coming to Tahiti.

If there is some unforeseen reason why you will need to extend your visa once you are here, you can ask for another month or two at the Immigration office at the Tahiti-Faa'a airport, *Tel. 80.06.00.* This must be done at least one week before the exemption expires. The Police Aux Frontière (PAF) who control this office have sometimes refused requests for visa extensions because they want you to get the visa before you arrive in Tahiti. All visitors must have a sufficient amount of resources to cover their planned stay in French Polynesia. Temporary residency visas for up to one year are more difficult to obtain, and have to be applied for at a French Consulate or Embassy before you arrive in French Polynesia.

Transit Visa to Get Through the US to Tahiti
French nationals require only a National Identity Card to stay in French Polynesia. However, the Delphine passport is necessary when traveling to or from French Polynesia via the US. They will also need to register online at *https:// esta.cbp.dhs.gov* more than 72 hours before leaving home. This is the Electronic System for Travel Authorization (ESTA) program administered by the U.S. Department of Homeland Security (*www.dhs.gov*), and applies to citizens of 27 countries, including most European nations, the U.K., Australia and New Zealand. In order to travel to Tahiti through the U.S., even if they don't leave the airport in Los Angeles, citizens from all other countries must have either a visitor visa to the U.S. or a C-1 transit visa from the U.S. State Department (*www.unitedstatesvisas.gov*).

In the US
• **Embassy of France:** 4101 Reservoir Rd., NW, Washington, DC 20007-2185, *Tel. 202/944-6200, Fax 202/944-6166; www.info-france-usa.org.*
• **French Consulates.** New York: 10 East 74th St., New York, NY 10021, *Tel. 212/ 606-3601; Fax 212/606-3670; www.consulfrance-newyork.org.* Visa Service New York: Tel. 202/944-6195; Fax 202/944-6148; visa@consulfrance-newyork.org. San Francisco: 540 Bush St., San Francisco, CA 94108, *Tel. 415/397-4330, Fax 415/433-8357; www.consulfrance-sanfrancisco.org.* Los Angeles: 10390 Santa Monica Blvd., Suite 410, Los Angeles, CA 90025; *Fax 310/235-3200; Fax 310/479-4813; www.consulfrance-los angeles.org.*

U.S. CONSULATE IN TAHITI

A Consular Agency of the United States opened in Tahiti in 2004, after an absence of 38 years. This office is located in Punaauia on the upper level of the Tamanu Iti Center. Christopher Kozely, the vice consul, cannot issue or renew passports, but his services include helping Americans who have problems due to sickness or death or who have lost their passports. You can contact this office at B.P. 10765, Paea, Tahiti 98711, French Polynesia; *Tel. 689/42.65.35; Fax 689/50.80.96; E-mail: usconsul@mail.pf; or ckozely@mail.pf.* In US *917/464-7457.* For emergencies only *Tel. 21.93.19.*

Other French consulate offices are in Atlanta, Boston, Chicago, Houston, Los Angeles, Miami, New Orleans and Washington, DC. Residents of those cities are required to apply there. If there is no French consulate in your town, please contact the French Embassy in Washington, DC, listed above.

In Canada

• **Embassy of France:** 42 Sussex Drive, Ottawa, Ontario, KIM 2C9, *Tel. 613/789-1795, Fax 613/562-3735: www.ambafrance-ca.org.* The French Consulate in Ottawa is now closed.

• **French Consulates:** Montreal: 1501, McGill College, Bureau 1000, Montreal (QC) H3A 3M8; *Tel. 514/878/4385; Fax 514/878-6272; www.consulfrance-montreal.org.* Toronto: 2 Bloor Street East, Suite 2200, Toronto (ON) M4W 1AB; *Tel. 416/847-1900; Fax 416/847-1901; www.consulfrance-toronto.org.* Vancouver: 1130 West Pender St., Suite 1100, Vancouver (BC), V6E 4A4 Canada; *Tel. 604/637-5301; Fax 604/637-5300; www.consulfrance-vancouver.org.*

MAKING RESERVATIONS

It is so much simpler to talk with your favorite travel agent to take care of all the reservations and details in planning your trip to Tahiti and Her Islands. Or you can arrange your entire trip by yourself, by contacting the airlines and hotels directly, going through one of the travel agencies in Tahiti, and checking the individual websites of the lodgings that interest you. The airlines have special fares and passes, which will cost you less if you reserve 2 weeks to a month in advance. The airfares vary according to whether you go in the high or peak season, the shoulder season or the basic season. Check with the airline companies online, by telephone or in person to learn which season will be in effect when you want to fly. If you are traveling on a tight budget, ask for their lowest fares, and be sure to learn what restrictions apply.

The Internet websites offer some of the best deals you'll find on airfare, as well as hotels and car rentals. Two of the most popular travel sites are **Microsoft Expedia**, *www.expedia.com*, and **Travelocity**, *www.travelocity.com*. **Johnny Jet** is on Facebook and Twitter and you can get travel deals, stories, tips, destinations and contact information for airlines, hotels, car rentals, etc. from his site: *www.johnnyjet.com.*

Package Tours

The travel agencies listed in this chapter can suggest package tours that include international air travel to French Polynesia, accommodations, some meals, ground transfers, inter-island travel by airplane or boat, and some tours and excursions. Be sure to read the fine print in all tour packages so that you understand what you are paying for. You don't want to limit yourself to eating all your meals in the same hotel when there are enticing restaurants to explore on the island.

Using Travel Specialists/Agents in USA and Canada
Contact the Tahiti Tourisme office for brochures, schedules and information: **Tahiti Tourisme North America**, 300 Continental Boulevard, Suite 160, El Segundo, CA 90245; *Tel 310/414-8484; Fax 310/414-8490; info@tahiti-tourisme.com; www.tahiti-tourisme.com.*

The list below includes some of the wholesale travel companies, tour operators and travel agencies that have been approved by the Tahiti Tourisme office in Los Angeles. Should your local travel agency need additional brochures and information, they can contact one of these companies, who are financially sound and have a well-trained staff with a good knowledge of Tahiti and Her Islands. Some of the wholesalers also work directly with the public. The list also includes some agents I can personally recommend for their vast knowledge of and love for these islands.

U.S.
• **Brendan Vacations**, *Tel. 800/421-8446; 818/428-6000; www.brendanvacations.com.* This family owned business offers escorted, locally guided and independent vacation packages to Tahiti and French Polynesia.

• **Crossroads Travel, Inc.** *Tel. 800/322-0224; 804/794-7700; uschi@crttravel.com; www.crttravel.com.* Uschi and David Helfrich own this full service travel company, with two offices in Midlothian, VA. They are a member of Virtuoso and make frequent trips to Tahiti and Her Islands to gather information that helps in organizing the best programs for their clients. Uschi can definitely be called a Tahiti Expert because of her detailed knowledge of what's happening in the tourist business. Her special interest is family travel, but you will see from their website that they cover every aspect of discovering these fabulous islands.

• **Custom Tahiti Travel**, *Tel./Fax: 404/348-4407; 800-678-9964; www.CustomTahiti.com.* Richard Bondurant owned and managed Tahiti Travel Planners (New Millennium and GoTahiti.com) for many years, then he spent an extended period of time in Tahiti and wrote the book, "Cocktails in Tahiti". He then took over operations of Custom Tahiti Travel, a division of Tahiti Enterprises, LLC in Decatur, GA. This company is solely focused on travel to Tahiti, whose knowledgeable and well-trained agents provide high-end and celebration travel services to the islands with an emphasis on honeymoons, milestone anniversaries, significant birthday events, retirement celebrations etc. Visit their website to read the letters of praise written by their satisfied clients.

• **Islands in the Sun**, *Tel. 800/828-6877, 310/536-0051; www.islandsinthesun.com.* The late Ted Cook founded this company in 1965 and since then thousands of travelers have booked their South Pacific vacations through this well-informed and very helpful team.

• **Jetabout Island Vacations**, *Tel. 800/548-7509; www.jetabouttahitivacations.com.* This company is based in El Segundo, CA and was formerly Qantas Vacations. They have some good packages for Tahiti.

- **Pleasant Holidays**, *Tel. 800/742-9244; www.pleasantholidays.com.* This big company is known for their packages to Hawaii and Mexico, but they also have interesting programs for Tahiti. They are a subsidiary of the Automobile Club of CA.
- **Sunspots International**, *Tel. 800/266-6115, Fax 503/661-7771; www.sunspotsintl.com.* This is a travel company based in Portland, OR, selling family travel and Island Romance packages to French Polynesia and other South Pacific destinations.
- **Swain Tahiti Tours**, *Tel. 800/227-9246; 610/896-9595; www.swaintours.com.* They are based in Ardmore, PA, selling cruises, wedding packages and independent travel packages that also include Manihi and Tikehau. They have some good programs for families.
- **Tahiti Discount Travel**, *Tel. 877/426-7262; www.tahiti-discounttravel.com.* The owners formerly worked for Discover Wholesale Travel before they closed. See their website for low-priced packages to Tahiti and Her Islands.
- **Tahiti Legends**, *Tel. 800/200-1213, 714/374-5656; www.tahiti-legends.com.* This tour operator is based in Huntington Beach, CA. I highly recommended them for their well-trained staff, who are not only very familiar with Tahiti and Her Islands, but are truly in love with the islands, the people, the hotels, cruise ships and tourist activities.
- **Tahiti Travel**, *Tel. 800/747-9997, 323/655-2181, www.tahiti-explorer.com.* This is an online travel agency owned by Frenchman Yves Courbet in Los Angeles that has been in business since 1995, promoting discounted rates for customized vacations or honeymoons to all the Islands of Tahiti. His travel specialists can also help you to choose from the special packages listed on his website. See also *Website Forums and Bulletin Boards* in this chapter.
- **Tahiti Travel Planners**, (a Division of New Millennium Tours, Inc.), *Tel. 800/ 772-9231, 773/935-4707; www.gotahiti.com.* This Chicago based travel agency specializes solely in vacations to Tahiti and Her Islands and claim they are the world's leading experts for travel, vacation and honeymoon planning for the islands of French Polynesia. Their *www.gotahiti.com* website describes dozens of travel packages. Their *www.tahitimoons.com* website includes romantic honeymoon programs.
- **Tahiti Vacations**, *Tel. 800/553-3477; Fax 818/772-6492; www.tahitivacation.com; www.tahitivacations.net.* This company is owned by Brendan Vacations in Chatsworth, CA., specializing in packages to Tahiti and Moorea, as well as choices for all the other islands served by Air Tahiti.
- **The Adventure Travel Company**, *Tel. 212/397-9792; Fax 212/397-9504; theadventuretravelcompany@gmail.com.* Owner Camilla Mork is an adventure travel specialist agent in Manhattan, NY, who plans soft adventure tours for small groups. She and her husband Steve are escorts for an 18-day tour that includes Tahiti, Moorea, Bora Bora, Easter Island and Fakarava. She also organizes other customized tours.

Canada
- **Island Escapes by Goway**, *Tel. 800/387-8850, 604/264-8088; www.goway.com*. This company was founded in Toronto in 1970 and has an excellent reputation.
- **Fun Sun Vacations**. *Tel. 800/938-6786, 780/421-1272; www.funsun.ca*. This Canadian owned family business is one of Canada's top three tour wholesalers and sells through retail travel agencies.

Diving
- **Dive Tahiti Blue**, *Tel. 689/56.25.33; Tel./Fax (USA) 310/507-0211; www.divetahitiblue.com*. This company is owned by Laurel and James Samuela, who live on the island of Moorea. Laurel grew up in California and is a PADI certified dive master. James, who is Tahitian, grew up on Moorea and was once the youngest guide on the island, leading horse rides along the beach when he was 13. Now he is a diver and tattoo master. They know which scuba diving center is best suited to dealing with American clientele, and they provide full travel service, coordinating everything from airline tickets to transfers, lodging and scuba diving. They can even plan a live aboard scuba diving trip for you on board the *Aquatiki*. See also their website for *truetahitivacation.com*.
- **Diving in Tahiti and Her Islands**, *Tel. 689/53.34.96; www.diving-tahiti.com*. This is the Tahiti-based office representing all scuba diving centers in French Polynesia.
- **PADI Travel Network**, *Tel. 800/729-7234, 949/858-7234; www.padi.com*. They have packages for scuba divers.
- **World of Diving & Adventure Vacations**, *Tel. 800/Go-Diving (800/900-7657) or 310/322-8100; www.worldofdiving.com*.

Using Inbound Travel Agents in Tahiti
You may want to contact one or more of these inbound agents when planning your trip. These are tourism professionals who live in Tahiti or Moorea and they can give you detailed information about every aspect of traveling in French Polynesia. The travel agencies can also arrange for you to be transferred from the international airport to your lodging, and handle any other land, sea or air transportation you may need.
- **Marama Tours**, B.P. 6266, Faa'a, Tahiti, 98702. *Tel. 689/50.74.74; Fax 689/82.16.75; www.maramatours.com*. This company was founded in 1973 by Mata and Emile Cowan, a Polynesian family whose children and grandchildren also grew up in the tourist business and now take active roles in managing this popular agency. They are a full service travel agency with one of the largest transportation fleets. They also have travel desks in the big hotels.
- **Paradise Tours**, B.P. 2430, Papeete, Tahiti, 98713. *Tel. 689/42.49.36/77.07.63; Fax 689/42.48.62; www.paradisetourstahiti.com*. This is one of the oldest agencies in Tahiti handling inbound tours, founded in 1965.

- **South Pacific Tours**, B.P. 1588, Papeete, Tahiti 98713. *Tel. 689/80.35.00; Fax 689/80.35.12; www.south-pacific-tours.com.* In addition to being the biggest inbound agency in Tahiti for the Japanese market, they also handle clients from the U.S.A. and Europe.
- **Tahiti Nui Travel**, B.P. 718, Papeete, Tahiti 98713. *Tel. 689/46.41.41; Fax 689/ 46.41.30; www.tahitinuitravel.biz.* This is Tahiti's largest travel agency, and handles inbound tours for individuals and groups from all countries. They have a well-earned reputation for their professionalism. They have travel desks in the big hotels.
- **Tahiti Tours**, B.P. 627, Papeete, Tahiti 98713. *Tel. 689/46.40.46; Fax 689/ 42.50.50; www.tahiti-tours.com.* This agency has been in business for more almost 50 years and is owned by Tahiti Nui Travel. They handle a lot of inbound tours and local excursions and day tours and they are the American Express representatives in Tahiti.
- **Tekura Tahiti Travel**, B.P. 2971, Papeete, Tahiti 98713. *Tel. 689/43.12.00, Fax 689/42.84.60, www.tahiti-tekuratravel.com.* The knowledgeable English-speaking staff can book your hotel rooms, guest houses, villas, transfers, excursions, diving, cruises, yacht charters, sailboats, domestic flights, boat transportation to outer islands and car rentals.
- **True Tahiti Vacation**, *Tel. 689/56.25.33; (USA) 310/464-1490; www.truetahitivacation.com.* This is a full service travel company based in Moorea, providing expert guidance in the general, honeymoon and spa markets. American owner Laurel Samuela and her Tahitian husband, James Samuela, know every island first hand and have personally visited every hotel and pension. Their goal is to use their insider knowledge of the islands to make your vacation as extraordinary as possible. True Tahiti Vacation is owned and operated by SARL Dive Tahiti Blue, a partner of Tahiti Nui Travel, who books all their air, hotels and transfers. See their website listed under *Diving, www.divetahitiblue.com,* as well the websites for Moorea Tattoo, *www.mooreatattoo.com,* and Te Nunoa Bungalow, *www.mooreabungalow.*

Other Destination Management Companies in Tahiti
- **Haere Mai Federation**, B.P. 4517, Papeete, Tahiti 98713. *haere-mai@mail.pf; www.haere-mai.pf; www.haere-mai.com.* This association was created in 1997 and represents 172 family pensions and guesthouses on 21 islands in all 5 archipelagoes of French Polynesia. Contact them for online booking and information.
- **Islands Adventures Air Tahiti**, B.P. 314, Papeete, Tahiti 98713; *Tel. 689/ 86.43.68; Fax 689/86.42.67; islands.adventures@airtahiti.pf; www.air-tahiti-islands-adventures.com.* See information under Air Tahiti Island Stays in this chapter.
- **Website Forums** and **Bulletin Boards.** These are also a good source of information on deciding which islands to visit and where to stay. Not only do they have

trip reports and photos of various hotels, pensions, activities and tourist sites in French Polynesia, but also you have access to an endless number of opinions on each subject. A very popular Tahiti Forum in English is *www.tahiti-explorer.com*, which is sponsored by Tahiti Travel in Los Angeles, with over 5,000 members. *www.tripadvisor.com* lists comments on hotels, restaurants and activities in French Polynesia, and even gives ratings on each establishment covered. The Tahiti experts on this forum are also part-time residents of Moorea or come here often enough to consider themselves residents. *www.tahititalk.com* has a rather limited selection of posters, but most of them are very familiar with these islands and enjoy helping others to discover various aspects of Tahiti and Her Islands. If you're planning to visit the islands by cruise ship, then tune into the Cruise Critic forum, *www.cruisecritic.com*, and find out what former passengers have to say about the ship and shore excursions you'll be taking.

USEFUL WEBSITES IN TAHITI

Tahiti Guide, *www.tahitiguide.com*, has tourist information on all the islands, hotels, pensions, and activities. Owner Gilles Loubeyre also has a reservation website, *www.tahitiresa.com*. **Tahiti Traveler,** *www.thetahititraveler.com,* has information on hotel resorts, small hotels and guesthouses, and it's partner, E-Tahiti Travel, *www.etahititravel,* can make the bookings for you. Another on-line travel agency is *www.easytahiti.com*.

TahitiWeb is the search engine to Tahiti's Websites: *www.tahitiweb.com*. If you want to find information about the **French Polynesia Government**, go to *www.presidence.pf,* and for information on the assembly, go to *http:// histoire.assemblee.pf.* Tahiti Presse is the government-owned press service with the news reported daily in French and a small blurb in English, *www.tahitipresse.pf.*

An encyclopedia of Polynesian patrimony is presented in various languages on *www.tahitiheritage.pf.* See *www.tahiti-realestate.com* if you want to rent or buy a house, bungalow or apartment in Tahiti and Her Islands. For information on the specific islands, most have their own website which you can reach by typing the name of the island preceded by *www. (moorea.com, raiatea.com, borabora.com, rangiroa.com, marquises.com, tahiti.com and papeete.com)*, or you can type the name of the island plus the word «island» and you'll get another site, such as *mooreaisland.com, huahineisland.com* and so on. Some of these sites are owned by the Tahiti Travel Net and others belong to other travel agencies, who can help you plan your trip.

WHERE TO FIND MORE INFORMATION

• **Tahiti Tourisme,** B.P. 65 Papeete, Tahiti 98713, French Polynesia. *Tel. 689/ 50.57.00; Fax 689/43.66.19; tahiti-tourisme@mail.pf; www.tahiti-tourisme.pf.* This office is on the harbor side of the Papeete waterfront in Fare Manihini. English-speaking Polynesian hosts and hostesses are on duty to answer your questions in the visitors' center. Here you will find brochures and informational sheets on lodgings, activities, tours and excursions, le truck, taxis, rental cars, ferries, boats and air services to the outer islands, as well as maps and anything else related to tourism. The visitor's bureau is open Mon.-Fri. from 7:30am-5:30pm, on Sat. from 8am-4pm, and on Sun. from 8am-12pm. The offices for overseas promotion are located in the connecting buildings. Video and DVD films, posters, T-shirts, caps and sun visors can be purchased in the promotional materials department.

* **Department of Tourism**, B.P. 4527, Papeete, Tahiti 98713, French Polynesia. *Tel. 689/47.62.00; Fax 689/47.62.02; sto@tourisme.gov.pf.* This office is in charge of the development and quality control of tourist accommodations, cruises and charter boats, land-based leisure activities and travel agencies.
* **Ministry of Tourism**, French Polynesia Government, The Presidency, *B.P. 2551, Papeete, Tahiti 98713. Tel. 689/48.40.00; Fax 689/48.40.14; www.tourisme.gov.pf* (site under construction).
* **Chamber of Commerce, Industry, Services and Trade**, B.P. 118, Papeete, Tahiti 98713. *Tel. 689/47.27.00; Fax 689/54.07.01; cci.tahiti@mail.pf; www.ccism.pf.* Use this contact for questions regarding any business or trade in Tahiti.
* **Te Fare Tauhiti Nui Cultural Center (House of Culture)**, B.P. 1709, Papeete, Tahiti 98713, French Polynesia. *Tel. 689/54.45.44, www.maisondelaculture.pf.* The House of Culture is in charge of selected cultural events throughout the year. There is a library on the premises.
* **Oceanian Studies Society**, c/o Territorial Records, Tipaerui, B.P. 110, Papeete, Tahiti 98713, French Polynesia. *Tel./Fax 689/41.96.03; seo@archives.gov.pf.* Researchers may obtain permission to use the library and archives of the Société des Etudes Océaniennes.
* **Friends of Tahiti**, P.O. Box 2224, Newport Beach, CA 92659; *friendsoftahiti@yahoo.com.* Te Mau Hoa No Tahiti is the Tahitian name for this cultural and charitable association, whose objectives include promoting friendship and cultural understanding between the people of French Polynesia and the United States through education, cultural arts exposure and travel. If you live in Southern California perhaps you can join them for their Tahitian galas and fundraiser programs, which include traditional Tahitian buffets and dance shows. They also organize a Heiva Festival each July; *www.heivausa.com.*

GETTING TO FRENCH POLYNESIA

Baggage Allowances

Airline regulations for most international flights serving Tahiti entitle each first-class, business-class or premium economy-class passenger to a "free" baggage limit of 2 bags totaling 32 kg. (70 lbs.). Economy-class passengers are allowed 1 bag weighing no more than 23 kg. (50 lbs.). Check the website of the airlines for their extra bag charges.

All passengers are allowed a carry-on bag that will fit in the overhead compartment or under the seat, which means that it cannot exceed total measurements of 115 cm. (45 in.), and the weight limit varies from 7-12 kg. (15-26 lbs.). This 1-bag carry-on limit applies to all classes of service. All passengers may carry a small handbag on board, and most airlines will also allow you to board with one other accessory, such as a portable computer or camera bag, providing it does not weigh more than 7 kg. (15 lbs.).

Air Tahiti, the domestic inter-island company in Tahiti, has a baggage limit of 10 kg. (22 lbs.) for each passenger who is flying to another island within French Polynesia. If you have a ticket connecting with an international flight within seven days, or if you are flying to/from the Cook Islands on Air Tahiti's international flight, your baggage limit is 20 kg. (44 lbs.). Passengers with a diving card and confirmed reservations with a scuba diving company are allowed an extra 5 kg. (11 lbs.) of baggage weight. You are allowed 50 kg. (110 lbs.) when you purchase a "Z" class ticket on Air Tahiti, but you should have two bags weighing 25 kg. each, rather than one heavy bag. Air Tahiti's carry-on limit is 3 kg. (6.6 lbs.).

Baggage Storage

A baggage storage room at the Tahiti-Faa'a airport terminal, *Tel. 86.42.21*, is open daily from 6am-10pm on Mon.-Tues. On Wed., Thurs, Fri and Sat. they are open from 7am-10pm and on Sun. from 5:30-11am and 1-10pm. Their rates for 24-hr. storage are 410 CFP for a small bag, 670 CFP for a medium size bag, and 765 CFP for a large bag. The hotels and some family pensions offer free baggage storage for their guests. For details on baggage, excess charges, security and packing tips, go to *www.airtahitinui-usa.com/traveldesk/baggage.asp#checked*.

Dangerous Goods

It is advisable to contact your airline representative for the latest information on what is allowed as carry-on baggage and what you'll have to pack in your checked luggage. The following items are prohibited in both hold and carry-on baggage: compressed gas or other explosives, inflammable liquids, corrosives, poisons, irritants, and substances or materials that are oxidizing, toxic, radioactive or magnetized. Safety regulations prohibit certain articles from being carried into the aircraft cabins. These include firearms, munitions, knives, scissors and other sharp or pointed instruments.

By Air From North America

All international flights arrive at the **Tahiti-Faa'a International Airport** on the island of Tahiti. The airline companies serving Tahiti from North America usually depart from the Los Angeles International Airport, for a 7 1/2-hour direct flight to Tahiti. If you are flying to Los Angeles from another city or state, be sure to allow sufficient time between flights to make the connection. When your flight lands in Los Angeles it takes a while to transfer your bags from a domestic airline terminal to the international terminal. Due to increased safety measures, airport check-in time is three hours before each international flight departure.

The following airline companies have one or more flights weekly between Los Angeles and Tahiti. Extra flights are added during the high seasons, which vary. The busiest seasons are generally the months of Jul.-Aug. and the Christmas-New Year's season. Once you arrive in Tahiti and want to check on arriving or departing flights you can contact the Tahiti-Faa'a International Airport at *Tel. 86.60.60/ 86.60.92; www.tahiti-aeroport.pf.*

Airlines Serving Tahiti from Los Angeles

AIR FRANCE, in US *Tel. 800/321-4538 / 800/237-2747; in Canada 800/ 667-2747; in Tahiti Tel. 689/47.47.47; Fax 689/47.47.90. www.airfrance.com/pf.* France's international carrier has 4 Paris-Los Angeles-Papeete flights a week, flying 272-seat Airbus A340 aircraft. The Air France Tahiti office is on rue LaGarde in downtown Papeete.

AIR NEW ZEALAND, in US *Tel. 800/262-1234 / 310/615-1111, Fax 648- 7017; in Canada Tel. 800/799-5494 (English) or 800/663-5494 (French); Fax 604/ 606-0155; in Tahiti Tel. 689/54.07.47, Fax 689/42.45.44; www.airnewzealand.com or www.airnz.co.nz.* In April 2007 Air New Zealand stopped flying from Los Angeles to Tahiti, but they have code sharing with Air Tahiti Nui for flights from Los Angeles-Papeete. The Tahiti office is on the ground floor of the Vaima Center, on the corner of rue Jeanne d'Arc and rue du General du Gaulle.

AIR TAHITI NUI, in US, *Tel. 877/824-4846; Fax 310/640-3683; res@airtahitinui-usa.com; in Tahiti Tel. 689/46.03.03; Tel. 689/46.02.20; Fax 689/46.02.90; res@airtahitinui.pf; www.airtahitinui.com.* This is Tahiti's international airline company, and shouldn't be confused with Air Tahiti, which is the national carrier. Air Tahiti Nui has 5-7 flights a week from Paris to LAX and Papeete, depending on the season, and 5 flights a week to Papeete that originate in Los Angeles. Air France, Qantas and Air New Zealand have code-sharing agreements for some of the US-Tahiti flights. Air Tahiti Nui has 5 Airbus 340-300 airplanes with 6 first class, 24 business class and 264 economy class seats. Passengers are welcomed in traditional Tahitian style by smiling Polynesians who offer them a Tiare Tahiti flower when they board Air Tahiti Nui in Los Angeles and Paris. The airplanes provide individual movie screens in front of the seats, with a choice of 6 films, as well as telephones and music. The Air Tahiti Nui office in Papeete is located in Immeuble Dexter on rue Paul Gauguin at the Pont de l'Est.

QANTAS AIRWAYS, in US *Tel. 800/227-4500; in Tahiti Tel. 689/50.70.64; Fax 689/43.10.52; qantas@southpacificrepresentation.pf.* Their aircraft no longer flies to Tahiti, but Qantas maintains a code share agreement with Air Tahiti Nui for the Los Angeles to Tahiti service. The GSA Tahiti office is located upstairs at the Vaima Center in Papeete.

By Other Air Routes

AIR CALEDONIE INTERNATIONAL, in US *Tel. 800/254-7251;* in Noumea *Tel. 687/26.5500;* in Tahiti *Tel. 689/85.09.04; Fax 689/85.09.05;*

www.aircalin.com. Aircalin has a direct flight from Noumea, New Caledonia, to Tahiti each Thurs., with an Airbus A320 airplane. The Tahiti office is on the first floor upstairs at the Tahiti-Faa'a International Airport.

AIR NEW ZEALAND, in US *Tel. 800/262-1234 or 310/615-1111;* in Tahiti *Tel. 689/54.07.40; Fax 689/42.45.44; www.airnewzealand.com* has 2 direct flights a week from Auckland to Papeete, code-sharing with Air Tahiti Nui. The Tahiti office is on the ground floor of the Vaima Center, on the corner of rue Jeanne d'Arc and rue du General du Gaulle.

AIR TAHITI, *Tel. 689/86.42.42; Fax 689/86.40.99; reservation@airtahiti.pf; www.airtahiti.com*. Air Tahiti is French Polynesia's domestic airline that goes international once a week when it flies an ATR 42 airplane to Rarotonga in the Cook Islands. This service began in Apr. 2007 when Air New Zealand dropped Rarotonga from its Auckland-Papeete route. The twice-weekly flights operate on Thurs. and Sat. during July and the first 2 weeks of Aug., and only on Thurs. the rest of the year. There are 3 airfare classes and free baggage is limited to 20 kg. per passenger, with a 3 kg. allowance for 1 carry-on bag. Check in 2 hours before scheduled flight time at the Air Tahiti desks in the domestic terminal.

AIR TAHITI NUI, *Tel. 689/46.03.03* in Tahiti; *www.airtahitinui.co.jp or www.airtahitinui.com* has 2 direct flights from Tokyo to Papeete each week. You can also fly Air Tahiti Nui from Auckland to Papeete 2 times a week. They have code share programs with Qantas and Air New Zealand that provide connections from Australia to New Zealand and on to Tahiti and Los Angeles.

HAWAIIAN AIRLINES, in the continental US, Alaska and Canada *Tel. 800/ 367-5320; in Honolulu 808/838-1555;* in Tahiti *Tel. 689/86.60.00; Fax 689/ 45.14.51; ppt.admin@hawaiianair.pf; www.hawaiianair.com*. There is only one regular flight a week between Honolulu and Tahiti, departing Honolulu each Sat. The Tahiti office is located on the ground floor of the International Airport of Tahiti-Faa'a.

LAN AIRLINES, in US *Tel. 800/735-5526; in Tahiti Tel. 689/42.64.55; www.lan.com*. LAN (formerly LAN Chile) has 1 flight per week from Santiago, Chile and Easter Island, arriving in Tahiti on Wed. night. The Tahiti office is located upstairs at the Vaima Center in Papeete.

QANTAS AIRWAYS, in US *Tel. 800/227-4500;* in Tahiti *Tel. 689/50.70.64; Fax 689/43.10.52; E-mail: qantas@southpacificrepresentation.pf*. Qantas code shares with Air New Zealand for the 2 flights a week from Auckland to Papeete.

By Passenger Ship

Tahiti's cruise ship season usually begins in Nov. and ends in Apr., with most of the passenger liners calling during the months of Jan.-Mar. The 2010-2011 season began in Aug. 2010 with the arrival of the *Dawn Princess*, followed by *M/ S Clipper Odyssey, Sapphire Princess, Rhapsody of the Seas, Royal Princess, M/S Rotterdam, M/V Hanseatic, Seabourn Sojourn, Regent Seven Seas Cruises Voyager,*

Crystal Serenity, M/V Deutschland, Silver Spirit, Balmoral, Pacific Princess, M/S Columbus, Aurora, M/S Bremen, M/V Pacific Pearl.
Ship day in Tahiti usually is limited to an early morning arrival in the harbor and a late afternoon departure, allowing enough time to make a tour of the island, perhaps to explore the coral gardens or tropical valleys and shop for post cards and souvenirs. South Pacific cruises also include Tahiti, Moorea, Huahine, Raiatea and Bora Bora in their itineraries, and some of the ships are now calling at the Marquesas Islands, as well as Rangiroa and Fakarava and other atolls in the Tuamotu Archipelago, and the Austral Islands of Raivavae and Tubuai in their shore programs.
The 2012 and 2013 programs include 10-night Tahiti & Polynesia cruises on board the *Ocean Princess* in Jan. and Feb. of each year. In Jan. 2012 Oceania Cruises has an 18-night Papeete-Auckland cruise, and in May they have a 21-night Papeete-San Francisco cruise. P & O's *Oriana* will include Tahiti in the Auckland-San Francisco sailing in March 2012, which is sold by Disabled Holidays. Celebrity Cruises will include Tahiti in the 30-day Sydney to Honolulu cruise in March, and *M/S Hanseatic* of Hapag-Lloyd Cruises will sail from Tahiti to Fiji during a 14-day cruise in March. There are many more scheduled cruises to Tahiti as part of a South Pacific program or World Cruise. Details are available on-line and from your travel agent. See *Paul Gauguin Cruises* under *Getting Around by Cruise Ships Based in Tahiti* in this chapter.

By Private Boat
The best way to visit Tahiti and Her Islands is, of course, the leisurely way. Hundreds of cruising yachts from all over the world pass through the islands each year, with some boats stopping only long enough to get provisions for the next leg of the journey, while others linger until the authorities ask them to move on.
Their contact with the villagers in remote islands is often rewarding for all concerned, with the "yachties" often getting involved in the daily lives of the friendly Polynesians. Outgoing visitors are frequently invited to join in volleyball and soccer games and fishing expeditions. The young people will take you to hunt for tiny shells that are strung into pretty necklaces, and the women will teach you how to weave hats, mats, and baskets from palm fronds. You can also eat delicious seafood direct from the shell while standing on a Technicolor reef. In the evenings, you can sit on the pier under a starlit sky and watch the Southern Cross as you listen to the young men from the village playing melodic island tunes on their guitars and ukuleles.
There's a sailing adage that goes: "A month at sea can cure all the ills of the land." However, a month at sea with an incompatible crew can make you ill or want to kill. Sailing to Tahiti sounds so very romantic, and many people do realize their life-long dreams of anchoring inside an opalescent lagoon and tying a line around a coconut tree. It takes a month and sometimes much longer to sail from the US West Coast or Panama to the Marquesas Islands, the first landfall in French

Polynesia. This long crossing is also disastrous for many relationships, so it is very important to know the dispositions of the other people on the yacht, and to be as easy-going and tolerant as you can be.

Valid passports and tourist visas are required for the captain and each crew member. The Immigration Service in French Polynesia can issue a 3-month visa that is good for all of French Polynesia. In addition to the required visa, each crew member must also deposit money into a special account at a local bank or at the Trésorerie Générale that is equal to the airfare from Tahiti back to their country of origin. Crew changes can only be made in harbors where there is a *gendarmerie*, and the Chief of Immigration must be advised of any crew changes. For information on visa for yachtsmen, contact CMA-CGM; *Tel. 54.52.46/54.52.50/77.08.90/71.42.71; email: ppt.yachts@cma-cgm.com.*

CUSTOMS ALLOWANCES

In addition to your personal effects, when you come to French Polynesia you may legally bring in duty free: 200 cigarettes or 100 cigarillos or 50 cigars or 250 grams of smoking tobacco, 50 grams of perfume, 1/4 liter of *eau de toilette*, 500 grams of coffee, 100 grams of tea and 2 liters of spirits. Visitors under 17 years of age are not allowed to import tobacco or spirits. Each traveler over the age of 15 years can bring in other goods worth 30.000 CFP and under 15 years the limit is 15.000 CFP.

Prohibited items include narcotics, copyright infringements (pirated video and audiotapes), guns and weapons of all kinds, ammunition, dangerous drugs, counterfeit items or imitation brand names. Cultured pearls of non-French Polynesian origin are prohibited.

No domestic pets can be imported without authorization from the Food and Veterinary Department, *Tel. 689/42.81.47, Fax 689/42.08.31.* The importation of live animals, animal products and products of animal origin is subject to prior authorization. Plants and plant products are subject to phytosanitary control. In Dec. 2007 Tahiti's Service of Rural Development announced plans to open a quarantine station for animals and plants in the Tipaerui section of Papeete, but that hasn't happened yet. For further information you can contact the Department of Agriculture, B.P. 100, Papeete, Tahiti, or at Tahiti-Faa'a Airport, *Tel. 689/82.49.99,* or at the Port of Papeete, *Tel. 689/54.45.85.* The Department of Customs and Indirect Duties also publishes information on the web site of the Ministry of Economics, Finance and Industry at: *www.finances.gouv.fr/douanes.*

Returning Home

US customs allows an exemption of $800 in goods for each US resident, including one liter of liquor, 200 cigarettes and 100 cigars. A *Know Before You Go* brochure is published by US customs, which you can read at *www.cbp.gov/travel.*

US law allows the importation, duty-free, of original works of art. Because of concessions made to developing countries, jewelry made in Tahiti may qualify as original art, and thus be duty-free. The US customs has waived the import duty on Tahiti cultured pearls or pearl jewelry made in French Polynesia, so you will not be charged duty by the customs for these purchases. California residents will be charged a State tax on pearls if you declare them. If you purchase pearls or pearl jewelry, make sure to get a certificate from the place of purchase stating that the jewelry was made in the islands. See information on VAT Tax Refunds in *Basic Information* chapter.

Canadian residents have a personal exemption of Can$750 if they are absent from Canada for at least 7 days. You can learn all about their regulations at *www.cbsa-gc.ca.*

TRAVELING ON YOUR OWN

Having the time to be flexible in your travels and being open to adventure and new experiences can bring you infinite rewards in discovering wonderful places and people. If you like to travel "by the seat of your pants" you can come to Tahiti without a hotel reservation and let serendipity be your guide. You can usually get a hotel room or a bed in a guesthouse or small family hotel on the most popular tourist islands without any advance notice if you are willing to settle for whatever accommodation is available. I have found spur-of-the-moment lodgings for friends who wanted to spend a couple of days in Bora Bora during the July Festival, which is normally overbooked at that time of year. Although Polynesians are now more discerning about inviting strangers into their homes, there are still numerous visitors who get "adopted" by a local Tahitian, French or Chinese family. One woman I know went to Huahine where she intended camping out, but she was invited to stay in the home of a Tahitian woman she met, who has a *roulotte* on the boat dock in Fare. The *Tahiti Beach Press* receives several letters each year, written by tourists who want to nominate a local resident for the "Mauruuru Award" because that local has been exceptionally kind to them. The hospitality extended to our visitors includes everything from giving a free ride and a tour around the island to inviting the tourist to their homes for a shower, a meal and quite often, free room and board for several days.

Tourism is very far from reaching the level of saturation in these islands, and the only long lines you'll normally find are at the Tahiti-Faa'a International Airport while you are waiting to pass through Immigration. You can usually get a last-minute seat on an airplane, a cabin on an inter-island ship, a berth on a sailboat, or a place on any of the tours and excursions that are available on each island. However, it is certainly recommended to reserve in advance if you want to avoid delays, especially for airline flights.

GETTING AROUND TAHITI & HER ISLANDS BY AIR

AIR TAHITI, Tahiti-Faa'a International Airport, B.P. 314, Papeete, Tahiti; reservations *Tel. 689/86.42.42;* information on flight arrivals *689/86.60.61/ 86.41.84; Fax 689/86.40.99; www.airtahiti.pf.* The main ticket office, *Tel. 47.44.00,* is located on the corner of rue du Genéral de Gaulle and rue Edouard Ahnne, across the street from Fare Loto in downtown Papeete. Office hours are Mon.-Fri. 8am-5pm and on Sat. from 8-11am. The airport office, *Tel. 86.41.84,* is open daily from 6am-4:30pm.

Air Tahiti Network

Air Tahiti operates domestic scheduled flights between the islands of French Polynesia, with a network of 47 islands, covering all 5 archipelagoes. A modern fleet of twin-turboprop aircraft comprises 3 ATR 42-500 planes with 48 seats, 7 ATR 72-500 planes with 66 seats, 1 Twin-Otter plane with 19 seats that is based in the Marquesas Islands, and 1 Beechcraft with 8 seats. All the aircraft have high wings, offering you great views of the beautiful islands if you are seated by the window. Air Tahiti also flies to Rarotonga in the Cook Islands each Thurs., and on Sat. during July and the first half of Aug. See information for international flights *By Other Air Routes* in this chapter.

Air Passes

Air Tahiti offers 5 different **air passes** with 2 extension possibilities, which all begin in Papeete and are subject to special conditions. Your travel agent can arrange an air pass for you to visit several islands, which is the most popular and least expensive means of island hopping. Rates quoted here are for adults who buy their tickets in French Polynesia. You can also buy the Air Passes before you get here, except for the Blue Pass and Discovery Blue Pass, which can be purchased only in French Polynesia. The Air Pass rates will increase, along with the additional fees that Air Tahiti will charge for airport security, according to an announcement made at the beginning of Sept. 2011. Contact an Air Tahiti sales office for more information or go to: *www.airtahiti.com.*

Air Passes to the Society Islands

Pass MD230 is called the **Discovery Pass**, which will take you from Tahiti to Moorea and on to Huahine and Raiatea for 31.000 CFP. Pass MD 215 is called the **Bora Bora Pass**, which lets you visit all 6 of the major islands in the Society group: Tahiti, Moorea, Huahine, Raiatea, Bora Bora and Maupiti. You are not allowed to transit in Papeete within the pass nor to fly back to Papeete before the end of the pass, which is sold for 36.900 CFP.

Air Passes to the Society Islands & Tuamotu Archipelago

Pass MD220 is the **Lagoon Pass**, which costs 43.000 CFP and combines a visit to Moorea with Rangiroa, Tikehau, Manihi, Fakarava and Ahe. One transit is allowed through Papeete between Moorea and the Tuamotu Archipelago. Pass MD213 (**Bora Bora-Tuamotu Pass**) is one of the most popular choices, especially for honeymooners and scuba divers. This pass costs 58.600 CFP and takes you from Tahiti to Moorea, Huahine, Raiatea, Bora Bora and Maupiti in the Society group, and on to Rangiroa, Tikehau, Manihi, Fakarava and Ahe in the Tuamotu atolls.

A **Moana Pass** (Code BD216) takes you from Tahiti direct to Huahine, Raiatea, Bora Bora, and then to Moorea. This pass is sold in French Polynesia only and costs 32.300 CFP. It is subject to specific conditions and cannot be combined with the Austral or Marquesas Islands extensions. A **Ninamu Pass** (Code BD236) for 26.100 CFP is good for Huahine, Raiatea and Moorea.

Air Pass to the Marquesas Islands

You can also visit the islands of Nuku Hiva, Hiva Oa, Ua Pou and Ua Huka with an Air Tahiti **Marquesas Pass** (Code MD240), which is priced at 73.500 CFP.

Air Pass Extensions

Should you wish to discover some of the more remote archipelagoes you can take advantage of 2 Air Pass Extensions, which must be purchased with one of the basic Air Passes available. The extensions to the Marquesas or Austral Islands can be used either before or after the pass, and you can buy both extensions if you so choose. A stopover in Tahiti is permitted before or after the extensions.

Code A is the **Austral Islands Extension,** which includes the islands of Rurutu, Tubuai, Raivavae and Rimatara for an additional 35.200 CFP. Code M is a **Marquesas Extension** that will takes you to the islands of Nuku Hiva and Hiva Oa for an additional 63.500 CFP.

Island Stays

Air Tahiti's **Island Adventures** specializes in off the beaten track stays in all 5 island groups, with ready made packages at preferential prices that include round-trip air fares between Tahiti and the outer island chosen, plus accommodations in a hotel, guest house or small family hotel; meeting and greeting with flower leis and travel documents; ground transfers, and most of the government taxes. Depending on your package, you may also have 1-3 daily meals included, and an excursion thrown in. All the packages are detailed on *www.islandsadventures.com*, which is supposed to be in English. However, this website address automatically reverts to the French language site of *www.sejoursdanslesiles.pf.* Fax them at *689/86.40.99.*

Baggage

The normal baggage allowance of 10 kg. (22 lbs.) is raised to 20 kg. (44 lbs.) on most domestic destinations if you are connecting to/from an international flight. If you purchase your domestic flights locally then your limit is 10 kg. Divers are allowed an extra 5 kg. if proof is provided when checking in. Excess baggage fares vary according to destination. Rather than having to pay for excess baggage at each inter-island flight, you may choose the special "round-trip formula" available upon check-in at the Tahiti or Moorea airports. This will save you 30%

off the normal round-trip rate. Carry-on bags should not exceed 3 kg. (6.6 lbs). See information on Baggage Allowances under *Getting to French Polynesia* in this chapter.

Reconfirmations

You are not required to reconfirm your reservations with Air Tahiti, except in the following conditions. If Air Tahiti has no contact number for you then you should reconfirm 24 hrs. before your scheduled flight. If you take a flight for which you have no reservation or if you should choose to travel by other means, then you should reconfirm any subsequent reservations you've already made with Air Tahiti. If you are flying on board a Beechcraft or Twin Otter to the Eastern Tuamotu, the Gambier Islands or to Marquesas Islands you should reconfirm a week in advance. Air Tahiti advises that you verify the departure time of your flight in the event of a delay or flight cancellation, at *Tel. 86.42.42.*

Other Information

Check-in time for Air Tahiti flights is 1 hour in advance of your flight. If you haven't checked in by 20 min. before flight departure your reservation will be canceled. All Air Tahiti flights are non-smoking. Air Tahiti issues new timetables on Apr. 1 and Nov. 1, one for local distribution and the other for overseas markets. The rates quoted here were taken from the local distribution timetable that expired Oct. 31, 2011. All Air Tahiti airfares quoted in this book will increase with the addition of new fees to cover the cost of fuel to operate the ground security vehicles at each airport. Please check Air Tahiti's website for updated airfares and information at *www.airtahiti.aero.*

Charter Flights

AIR TAHITI, Tahiti-Faa'a Airport, B.P. 314, Papeete, Tahiti 98713. *Tel. 689/86.40.12/86.42.42; Fax 689/86.40.69; reservation@airtahiti.pf; www.airtahiti.aero.* Various aircraft available for charter within French Polynesia.

POL'AIR, Tahiti-Faa'a Airport, *Tel. 689/74.23.11; www.compagniepolair.com.* This privately owned company has a Beechcraft 1900D for charter to any of the islands in French Polynesia that has an airstrip. It will hold 2 pilots and 19 passengers. They also have a BN2A 1-2 pilot, 9 passenger plane that can be chartered to fly yourself if you have a pilot's license.

By Helicopter

TAHITI HELICOPTER SERVICE. *Tel. 689/50.40.75; Fax 689/50.40.76; contact@tahiti-heicopters.com; www.tahiti-helicopters.com.* This service is the only private helicopter service in French Polynesia. It began in 2011 and was still developing at press time. When complete, their fleet will consist of three Ecureuil (Squirrel) helicopters with 1 pilot and 5 passenger seats. These include: an Ecureuil AS-355 F1, twin-turbo helicopter designed for carrying heavy loads at longer distances; an AS-350 single-engine helicopter for fast and short connections; and an AS-355 N motorized version of the Squirrel that is designed to carry heavy loads at a significant speed in a hot environment. In Dec. 2011 they will receive a smaller, lighter aircraft, the Robinson R-44, that can carry 1 pilot and 3 passengers on short-haul routes between Tahiti and Moorea.

Tahiti Helicopter Service is based at the Tahiti-Faa'a airport in Tahiti, providing sightseeing flights and charters on request to visit Tahiti and Moorea. There is also a 5-passenger helicopter based in Bora Bora (*Tel. 67.54.90*), and one 5-passenger Ecureuil will be based permanently in the Marquesas Islands starting in 2012, where they will provide transfers from the Nuku Hiva airport to Taiohae village and other nearby islands, as well as photographic flights. Contact the company directly for private charters See further information in the destination chapters on *Tahiti, Moorea, Bora Bora* and *Nuku Hiva* in the Marquesas.

GETTING AROUND BY INTER-ISLAND PASSENGER BOATS & FREIGHTERS

Windward Society Islands

Tahiti and Moorea are connected by a fast catamaran that provides 30-min. crossings several times daily between Papeete and the Vaiare ferry dock in Moorea. **Aremiti V**, *Tel. 689/50.57.57/50.57.92* in Tahiti and *Tel. 689/56.43.24* in Moorea; *www.aremiti.pf* transports 697 passengers, 30 lightweight cars and 2-wheel vehicles.

Passengers, cars and larger vehicles are transported on this route by the **Aremiti Ferry**, *Tel. 689/50.57.57/56.31.10*, and the **Moorea Ferry**, *Tel. 689/50.11.11/56.34.34*, for the 1-hr. trips across the Sea of Moons, as the channel is called. For rates and schedules see *Arriving by Boat* and *Departing by Boat* in the **Moorea** chapter.

Leeward Society Islands

HAWAIKI NUI, *B.P. 635, Papeete, Tahiti, Tel. 689/54.99.54, Fax 689/45.24.44; contact@stim.pf.*

The Hawaiki Nui is a cargo/passenger ship that provides twice-weekly inter-island service between Papeete and the Leeward Society Islands of Huahine, Raiatea, Taha'a and Bora Bora. Departures from Papeete are each Tues. and Thurs. See schedules and fares in each Island chapter. This ship carries only 12 passengers, who sleep on the deck or share cabins. Meals are available on board the ship. Cars can also be transported. See *Arriving by Boat* and *Departing by Boat* in the Huahine, Raiatea, Taha'a and Bora Bora chapters.

MAUPITI EXPRESS II, *Tel. 66.37.81/78.27.22; www.maupitiexpress.com.* This 140-passenger launch transports passengers between Raiatea, Taha'a, Bora Bora and Maupiti. See each Island chapter for the schedules and rates. If you want to take a day-trip from Bora Bora to Maupiti, you should contact owner/captain Gérald Sachet by cell phone. He also has a small boat in Maupiti that is used for

Maupiti Poe Iti Lagoon Tours and his wife runs Pension Poe Iti in Maupiti. See *Arriving by Boat* and *Departing by Boat* in the Raiatea, Bora Bora and Maupiti chapters.

Marquesas Islands

ARANUI 3, operated by Compagnie Polynésienne de Transport Maritime, 2028 El Camino Real South, Suite B, San Mateo, California 94403; in US *Tel. 800/972-7268 or 650/574-2575; Fax 650/574-6221; cptm@aranui.com; www.aranui.com.* The Tahiti office is located at Motu Uta, across the harbor and bridge from Papeete, *Tel. 689/42.62.40; Fax 689/43.48.89.*

In my opinion the *Aranui* is the best way to visit French Polynesia if you have the time and interest to enjoy an authentic experience of ship-day in a small secluded valley in the Marquesas Islands. The *Aranui 3* was custom-built in Rumania and began service in March 2003, replacing the *Aranui 2*, offering the same friendly atmosphere that has made the worldwide reputation of the Aranui ships and Polynesian crew. The *Aranui 3* is a working cargo/copra ship—not a cruise ship in the usual sense, where you put on your best finery to dine at the captain's table. You'll be more practically dressed in a cool shirt or blouse and shorts or pants that you don't mind getting wet and dirty when you get into the whaleboat for shore excursions. And don't forget your plastic sandals, protective hat, sunglasses, sunscreen and a good repellent against mosquitoes and *nono*s (sand fleas). The 200-passenger *Aranui 3* was specially designed with added space and the passengers' comfort in mind. The ship is 117.65 m. (386 ft.) long, 17.68 m. (58 ft.) wide and cruises at a speed of 15 knots. The ship has a/c in all passenger areas and indoor public spaces. There are accommodations for 208 passengers in 63 standard "A" cabins, 9 deluxe cabins, 14 suites, and a dormitory with 30 bunk style beds. All the cabins and suites have a telephone and personal safe.

The spacious suites all have picture windows and 12 suites even have a balcony. In addition to a queen-size bed with reading lights, there is a desk, chest of drawers, hanging closet, comfortable chairs and coffee table in the sitting space, a refrigerator, TV with video channel, private bathroom with bathtub/shower, and a selection of amenities. The 2012 rates for a suite start at US $4,982 per person, depending on location or whether it has a balcony.

The 9 deluxe cabins are large outside cabins with picture windows, a queen-size bed or 2 twin beds, refrigerator and private facilities with bathtub/shower, for US $4,560 per person. The 63 standard "A" class cabins are all outside, with 2 lower berths and private facilities with showers, for US $3,827 per person. The class "C" dormitory style accommodations for 30 passengers are located on the restaurant deck. They have a/c and share the toilet facilities. These upper and lower berths are US $2,234 per person and are not accessible to children younger than 15 years.

The public facilities of the *Aranui 3* include a reception, colorful dining room with your choice of seating, a non-smoking lounge-library, boutique, video room, meeting rooms, elevator, gym, and infirmary with a doctor. There are 2 bars and lounges, a sun deck and salt-water swimming pool. Special marine facilities make it easy for you to fish, swim, snorkel and go scuba diving. There is daily maid service, twice-weekly laundry service and trained hostesses and guides. Organized shore excursions include picnics, Marquesan feasts, guided hikes to waterfalls, stone tikis and archaeological sites, visits to wood carvers and artisan workshops, plus inland and upland tours by 4WD vehicles.

Between Feb. 4-Dec. 15, 2012 the *Aranui 3* will have 16 departures from Tahiti to the Marquesas Islands, with a brief stop at the Tuamotu atoll of Fakarava on the outbound trip, and in Rangiroa atoll on the return voyage. brief stops in the Tuamotus. The complete round-trip takes 14 days, but you can also choose an Inter-Marquesas cruise on board the *Aranui*, which is only 7 days, starting and ending in Nuku Hiva.

The *Aranui* means "The Great Highway" in the Tahitian language and it serves as a lifeline to the Marquesas Islanders, as the ship calls at each principal village and several remote valleys on the 6 inhabited islands. The big cargo holds contain food, fuel, cement and other building materials, trucks, fishing boats, beer, bedding and other necessities to offload in the distant Marquesas Islands. Copra, citrus fruit, fish and barrels of *noni* (*Morinda citrifolia*) are embarked to take back to Papeete.

Watching the *Aranui*'s muscular crew perform their tasks is part of the attraction and charm of this voyage. Even if hydraulics are not your favorite thing, you'll enjoy watching a pickup truck being loaded from the ship's hold onto a barge or double platform balanced on top of two whale boats lashed together. What's even more interesting is to see how the crew gets the truck safely ashore while the waves are bouncing the whaleboats up and down.

On-board guest lecturers are experts in their fields of Marquesan art, archaeology, history or customs, and they accompany the passengers ashore to enrich their visit by explaining the meaning of the designs in wood carvings, the stone tikis, the *paepae* platforms and *tohua* meeting grounds in the valleys. While you're watching the young people dance for you in the villages, tasting special Marquesan food and visiting the archaeological sites, the Marquesan men and boys are helping the *Aranui* crew to load burlap bags of copra in the whaleboats to be shipped to the copra processing plant in Papeete. A trip aboard the *Aranui* will give you many opportunities to meet the friendly and natural Polynesians, far removed from the normal tourist scene.

The 2012 rates quoted here are based on per person double occupancy and include 3 meals a day with wine at lunch and dinner, plus picnics and programmed meals on shore, as well as guided excursions. Add 50% for single occupancy. Children pay the adult fare. Adults sharing a cabin with 3 Pullman beds will have a 25% reduction from the full fare for the 3rd person. Port taxes, cruise tax, tourism tax and fuel surcharges are added to the above rates.

Activities such as horseback riding, scuba diving and helicopter tours are optional. The *Aranui* now includes Sports Fishing for its passengers, with a choice of 3 fishing packages allowing 3-8 hours of angling for wahoo, tuna, marlin, mahi mahi, and a large variety of delicious lagoon fish. For a sample itinerary of your voyage and other details, go to: *www.aranui.com/download/aranui-english.pdf.*

Tuamotu Islands

Before planning a trip to the Tuamotu Archipelago aboard any of the ships listed below, you should verify if the vessel is still in service. The treacherous reefs of the atolls are a graveyard for ships that have been wrecked on these coral shores. These distant atolls were named the Dangerous Archipelago for a good reason. During the past few years some of the older ships were destroyed by fire and/or sank at sea. Because these freighters are allowed to carry only 12 passengers, the owners have asked me not to list their ships anymore because they cannot even meet the needs of the inhabitants of the atolls. Other ships have been removed from this list because new rulings will not allow any passengers on board. The offices of these *goëlettes* (tramp boats) are located in the port area of Motu Uta, reached by bridge across the Papeete harbor.

ST. XAVIER MARIS STELLA III, operated by Société Navigation Tuamotu, B.P. 14160, Arue, Tahiti 98701; *Tel. 689/42.23.58; Fax 689/43.03.73; cell 77.22.88; E-mail: maris-stella@mail.pf.* The office is in a warehouse on the inter-island goëlette pier at Motu Uta.

This 207-ft. long red-hulled steel ship began its service to the Tuamotu atolls in June 2001. This ship carries only 12 passengers and priority is given to the people who live in the islands. They bring their woven mats and bedding and sleep on the deck or pay extra for a berth in a shared cabin. Meals are served. The ship reaches Rangiroa after 20 hours at sea, then continues on to all the western Tuamotu atolls: Ahe, Manihi, Takaroa, Takapoto, Arutua, Apataki, Kaukura, Toau, Fakarava, Kauehi, Raraka, Niau and Papeete. Only one day is spent in each port and the itinerary changes according to the freight on board. The ship leaves Papeete every 15 days and it takes 10 days to make the round-trip circuit. The one-way deck fares, with 3 meals per day included, are 7.070 CFP for Mataiva, Rangiroa and Tikehau, 8.484 CFP for Ahe and Manihi, and 11.830 CFP for Fakarava. The one-way fare for a berth in a cabin is 10.000 CFP for Mataiva, Rangiroa and Tikehau, 15.000 CFP for Ahe and Manihi, and 30.000 CFP for Fakarava.

MAREVA NUI is operated by Siméon Richmond, B.P. 1816, Papeete, Tahiti 98713. *Tel. 689/42.25.53, Fax 689/42.25.57.* The office is at the Motu Uta inter-island cargo ship pier.

This is a 181-ft. steel ship that transports passengers and cargo between Tahiti and the western Tuamotu atolls, with departures from Papeete every 15 days for the 8-day round trip voyage. There are 12 passenger berths and no cabins. The ship calls at Makatea, Mataiva, Tikehau, Rangiroa, Ahe, Manihi, Takaroa, Takapoto, Raraka, Kauehi, Apataki, Arutua, Kaukura, Niau, Fakarava, and then returns to Papeete. The one-way fares for a berth and 3 meals daily are 7.350 CFP to Tikehau, 10.100 CFP to Rangiroa, 17.000 CFP to Manihi and 19.800 CFP to Fakarava.

COBIA III, *Tel./Fax 43.36.43*, leaves Tahiti at 3pm each Mon., arriving in Fakarava Wed. night or Thurs morning. There are accommodations for 12 passengers in 3 cabins. The one-way fare is 6.300 CFP, and no meals are available on board.

NUKU HAU, managed by Roland Paquier of S.T.I.M., B.P. 635, Papeete, Tahiti 98713, *Tel. 689/54.99.54/45.24.44*, is based at the Motu Uta quay.

This is a 210-ft. cargo ship that can take 12 passengers from Tahiti to the eastern Tuamotu and Gambier Islands during the 18-day round-trip voyages it makes once every 25 days. There is no cabin space but you will be served three meals a day on board. The itinerary includes Hao, Nengo Nengo, Tureia, Vanavana, Marutea Sud, Rikitea, Tematangi, Anuanuraro, Nukutepipi and Hereheretue, before returning to Papeete.

Other ships serving the Tuamotus are **Dory III**, *Tel./Fax 42.30.55*; and **Kura Ora IV**, *Tel/Fax 45.55.44; Cell 78.82.92*.

Austral Islands

TUHAA PAE II, operated by Société Anonyme d'Economie Mixte de Navigation des Australes, B.P. 1890, Papeete, Tahiti, *Tel. 689/50.96.09; Fax 689/ 42.06.08; E-mail: snathp@mail.pf.*

This is a steel hull ship, 59 m. (196 ft.) long that carries passengers and supplies to the Austral Islands. It makes 3 voyages a month from Tahiti to the Austral Islands, calling at Tubuai, Rimatara, Raivavae and Rurutu, then returning to Papeete. The itinerary may vary. The ship visits Rapa once every 2 months. The cabins are very basic, usually with 4 bunk beds, no portholes and no air. The showers and toilets are on a separate level from the cabins. The local passengers sleep in berths in a big open room up top, which is cooler but not private.

TUHAA PAE IV was expected to arrive in Tahiti in Sept. 2011 to replace the *Tuhaa Pae II*. This brand new ship was built in the Philippines by an Australian shipyard and is 80 m. (262 ft.) long and 13 m. (43 ft.) wide. There are 7 decks and a/c accommodations for 100 passengers in 12 cabins and 4 suites. The Amiral and Vice-Amiral suites have private balconies, a king size bed, 2 sofas, mini-bar, bathtub and room service. Guest services include a panoramic restaurant, an open-air snack bar, boutique, swimming pool and self-service laundry. On the public Rapa deck there are 50 individual berths with reclining back rests, separate toilet and shower facilities for men and women, and machines for sandwiches and hot and cold drinks.

The 7-day programs will leave Papeete on Monday and return the following Monday. The passengers will visit Rurutu, Tubuai, Raivavae and Rimatara, going ashore at 8am and returning to the ship at 4pm. They will discover the island by bus during the morning, have lunch in a restaurant, and spend the afternoon in cultural pursuits. Individual activities will be available at the passenger's charge, such as visiting grottos, horseback riding or hiking. The *Tuhaa Pae IV* will include Rapa in their 10-day itinerary every two months. During the voyages when the ship is transporting fuel to the Austral Islands, the number of passengers will be limited to 25. The company will open a website and decide on the passenger fares by the time the new ship goes into service.

GETTING AROUND BY CRUISE SHIPS BASED IN TAHITI

M/S PAUL GAUGUIN was bought in 2009 by Pacific Beachcomber S.C. (PBSC), the leader in French Polynesia luxury destination resorts. Dick Bailey is President and CEO of PBSC, and he also heads Paul Gauguin Cruises. (Please see information under *Locally Owned Hotel Chains* in this chapter). *Tel. 800/848-6172 (inside U.S. or Canada); +1 425/440-6171 (international); www.pgcruises.com.*

The 332-passenger *Paul Gauguin* was built in France to be based year-round in Tahiti. In January 1998 it began regular 8 day/7 night cruises in the Society Islands.

The 2012 itineraries include 6-night and 7-night Holiday Cruises in Tahiti & Society Islands, 10-night cruises to the Society Islands & Tuamotus, 11-night Cook Islands & Society Islands cruises, an 11-night cruise to the Australs & Society Islands, a 12-night cruise on the Fiji Eastbound Itinerary, a 13-night cruise on the Fiji Westbound Itinerary, 14-night cruises to the Marquesas, Tuamotus & Society Islands, and a 17-night South Pacific Discovery cruise plus 3 nights in Sydney. Cruise fares start at US $3,997 for the 7-night sailing that takes you from Papeete to the Leeward Society Islands of Raiatea, Taha'a, Bora Bora and then to Moorea and back to Tahiti. The sailing programs and fares are listed on *www.pgcruises.com.*

The Paul Gauguin's Culinary Sailings will feature Michelin-starred Chef Jean-Pierre Vigato on the June 23, 2012 sailing to Tahiti & the Society Islands. Jean-Michel Cousteau will join the Paul Gauguin on the July 11, 2012 sailing to the Society Islands & Tuamotus; the Nov. 20, 2012 sailing to Fiji, Tonga, Cook & Society Islands; and the Dec. 1, 2012 sailing to the Marquesas, Tuamotus & Society Islands. Mr. Cousteau will offer a series of lectures with videos of his work in the world's oceans, as well as accompany several dives from the ship. Other guest hosts will also be on board during some sailings, including the Paul Gauguin Cruises President Dick Bailey.

The Paul Gauguin is 156.5 m. (513 ft.) long, 21.6 m. (71 ft. wide), with a draft of 5.15 m. (16.9 ft.), and a gross tonnage of 19,200. All of the 160 staterooms and suites are outside, with sweeping ocean and lagoon views. Nearly 70% of the staterooms have private balconies or verandas. One of the Owner's Suites has 457 sq. ft. of living space plus a 77 sq. ft. veranda. The Grand Suites have 529 sq. ft., including a private balcony and veranda. There are Veranda Suites, Veranda Staterooms, C & D Balcony Staterooms with a 360° view, E Window Staterooms, and F Porthole Staterooms. The smallest cabin is 200 sq. ft. and has two portholes.

The staterooms and suites have individual temperature control and are decorated in a contemporary motif, with exotic woods and warm colors. They each contain a queen-size bed or twin beds, white marble appointed bathroom with a full-size bathtub and shower, hair dryer and terry cloth robes, TV, CD and DVD player, direct dial telephone, personal safe, numerous shelves and spacious closets.

There is also a refrigerator stocked with soft drinks and mineral waters. Butler service and in-suite/stateroom bar setup are provided in higher categories. There is one wheelchair-access stateroom, and select staterooms can accommodate three guests. There is an international crew of 217, including a sufficient number of cabin stewards to provide individual service round-the-clock.

The 9-deck ship has 2 elegant restaurants and a poolside grill, plus a 24-hr. room service menu. Passengers can choose single, open seating dining at their leisure to enjoy 6-star gastronomic meals featuring the menus created by Le Cordon Bleu Chefs of France. Well-being and vegetarian selections and special dietetic meals are prepared on request. Fare Tahiti is an on-board museum, gallery and special information center with books, videos, and other materials on the ethnic art, history, geography and culture of Tahiti and Her Islands.

There is an Internet Café with computers and WiFi Hotspots are accessible throughout the ship. In addition to 2 bars and lounges, there is a duty free boutique and **Tahia Pearls** shop, a panoramic nightclub and piano bar, a disco, casino, medical center and beauty salon. A full spa and fitness center is operated by **Deep Nature Spa by Algotherm**, and includes a steam room and full beauty services. A recent addition is the gold massage, inspired by traditional Russian massage methods, and Algo silhouette contouring, toning and firming techniques. A new Algotherm machine for facial treatments has been introduced. You can click on the Spa Menu on the website to see the choices of massages, body wraps and facials available. In addition to the fully equipped Fitness Center and swimming pool, there is a nautical sports center with a retractable water sports platform. Water-skiing, windsurfing, sailing, kayaking and snorkeling are offered, as well as optional scuba dive programs for novices and experts. The staff of PADI dive masters also lead certification programs. Nightly entertainment is presented in the main lounge. The "Gauguines" or "Gauguin's Girls" are pretty Tahitian *vahines* who sing and dance and act as gracious hostesses aboard the ship.

In addition to your suite or stateroom the all inclusive fares cover meals, preselected wines with meals, non-alcoholic beverages and mineral waters, and all nautical sports from the Marina nautical sports center except scuba diving. You will have complimentary use of the Paul Gauguin's exclusive, private white sand beach in Bora Bora with bar service, volleyball and great snorkeling. There is also a complimentary day on the Paul Gauguin's private islet, Motu Mahana, off the coast of Taha'a, featuring snorkeling, watersports, barbecue with full bar service, and Polynesian hospitality. Also included are on-board gratuities, welcome at the Tahiti-Faa'a International airport and transfer to a first-class hotel, use of hotel rooms for the morning on departure day, brunch at the hotel, transfers from the hotel to the *Paul Gauguin* in the afternoon, and transfers from the ship to the airport at the end of the cruise for international departure. Check their website or see your travel agent to learn how you can save 50% and enjoy Free Air when you book your cruise aboard the Paul Gauguin, which in 2011 was named the Gold Magellan Award Winner in the Small Cruise Ship category by Travel Weekly.

GETTING AROUND BY CHARTER BOAT

If your romantic spirit is stirred at the sight of a white-sailed ship beating out to the wide sea, you can put yourself aboard your dream by chartering a sailboat in Tahiti. Comfortable modern yachts of every description are available for chartering by the day or week, with bases in Tahiti, Raiatea, Taha'a, Rangiroa and Fakarava. Please check each island section for details on chartering a sailboat.

Billowing sails, white against the horizon, beckon you to "come aboard" one of the sleek yachts you see gliding gracefully across the lagoon, within the protective embrace of the barrier reef that encloses Raiatea and Taha'a. Sailing conditions are ideal in the Leeward Islands and a large variety of yachts can be chartered in Raiatea for bare-boating, day sailing or for longer excursions with skipper and crew.

ARCHIPELS CROISIÈRES (DREAM YACHT CHARTER), *Tel. 689/ 66.18.80; Fax. 689/66.18.76; polynesie@dreamyachtcharter.com; www.dreamyachtcharter.com. Jérome Touze, base manager, cell 30.55.02; François Guais, customer service, cell 28.42.64.*

Archipels Cruises operated a nautical base in Moorea for several years, and have now transferred their base to the Apooiti Marina in Raiatea since they were purchased by Dream Yacht Charter in 2009. The Archipels fleet consists of 3 Harmony monohulls 47-52 ft. long and 5 Marquises and Eleuthera catamarans 56-60 ft. in length, which can be chartered only with a skipper. Dream Yacht Charter also has 8 Catana catamarans from 41-50 ft. long that can be chartered to sail yourself (if qualified). All of these yachts are based permanently in Raiatea, except during the high season, when 1-2 yachts are kept in Rangiroa. Please see information in the *Raiatea* and *Rangiroa* chapters.

THE MOORINGS, *B.P. 165, Uturoa, Raiatea 98735. Tel. 689/66.35.93/ 78.35.93; Fax 689/66.20.94. www.moorings.com. North American reservations: Tel. 800/669-6529, outside US and Canada Tel. 727/535-1446.* The Moorings has been operating in Raiatea since 1985. The nautical base was taken over by First Choice Holidays in 2007, along with Sunsail. It is located at Apooiti Marina in Raiatea and has an average fleet of 20 yachts that can be chartered bareboat, ready to sail away or with skipper and hostess/cook. Please see further information in *Raiatea* chapter.

SUNSAIL, *B.P. 331, Uturoa, Raiatea 98735. Tel. 689/60.04.85; Fax 689/ 66.23.19; www.sunsail.com.* This nautical base has been moved to Apooiti Marina in Raiatea and is now owned by First Choice Holidays. They have a fleet of 14 sailing yachts. Please see further information in *Raiatea* chapter.

TAHITI YACHT CHARTER, *Tahiti office: Monette Aline, B.P. 364, Papeete, Tahiti 98713; Tel. 689/45.04.00; Fax 689/42.76.00; tyc@mail.pf; www.tahitiyachtcharter.com. Raiatea base: Tel. 689/66.28.86; Fax 689/66.28.85.*

Tahiti Yacht Charter is a 100% locally owned company that is very service oriented. They have a fleet of 28 catamarans, most of them less than 2 years old, all based at the Apooiti Marina in Raiatea, with Papeete as a possible departure point. Their sailing range is mainly the Leeward Islands, including Maupiti when weather conditions allow it. You can also sail to the Tuamotu and Marquesas Islands with a Tahiti Yacht Charter skipper on board.

Their original cruises are targeted to couples as well as families or groups of friends. These programs include a 2 day/1 night "Ia Orana" cruise inside the lagoon of Raiatea and Taha'a, a 7 day/6 night "Tahiti Twosome" private cruise in the Leeward Society Islands, and a 7 day/6 night Tuamotu Atoll cruise that takes you from Fakarava to Toau and back to Fakarava. Please see further information in *Raiatea* chapter.

TAHITI HAUMANA CHARTERS, *Tahiti Cruise, B.P. 9240, Motu Uta, Papeete, Tahiti 98713; Tel. 689/50.06.74; Fax 689/50.06.72; www.tahiti-haumana-charter.com.*

Following a full refurbishment in 2010 this 110 ft.-long charter yacht now has 9 guest cabins (160 sq. ft.) and one master suite (480 sq. ft.). All cabins are outside and have individually controlled a/c, queen-size beds, safe, minibar, flat screen TV with DVD-CD player, and private bathrooms. The master suite also has a living area. There is an a/c restaurant, a panoramic lounge, sundeck with Jacuzzi, a Taurumi massage room and a marina platform. In addition to 2 tender boats, there are kayaks, snorkeling gear, fishing equipment. Guests can also rent a deluxe wave runner. The *Haumana* is available for charters.

Other Charter Yachts described in the Island chapters include: **Atara Royal**, based in Raiatea; **Catamaran Tane**, based in Raiatea; **Bisou Futé** and **Fai Manu**, based in Taha'a; and **Eden Martin**, based in Huahine.

GETTING AROUND BY LIVE ABOARD DIVE BOATS, CRUISE & DIVE CHARTERS

AQUA TIKI II. *Contact Patrice Poiry in Fakarava at Tel. 689/73.47.31; www.aquapolynesie.com.*

This brand new 60-ft. (18 m.) Fountain Pajot Eleuthera type catamaran can accommodate 9 passengers (8 divers) in 5 cabins. Each cabin has its own bathroom. You can rent a cabin or charter the whole boat for cruises that begin in Fakarava, take you to the neighboring atolls of Kauehi, Toau, Tahanea, Aratika and to the north and south passes of Fakarava, depending on the cruise program chosen. In addition to scuba diving, activities include snorkeling, water-skiing, wake-board-ing, kayaking and big-game fishing. Please see information under *Sports & Recreation* in the *Fakarava* chapter.

Scuba Diving Conditions & Requirements

The clear, tropical waters of Tahiti and Her Islands are ideal for year-round diving, providing a diversity of magnificent dive sites in the lagoons, passes and outer coral reefs. Because French Polynesia covers such a vast area, with varying degrees of latitude and longitude, the underwater scenery is different from archipelago to archipelago, from island to island. The average water temperature

---

SCUBA DIVING TERMS

For the uninitiated in the vernacular of scuba diving, **PADI** is the **Professional Association of Diving Instructors**. An OWDI is an overwater diving instructor. The PADI system of training divers is used in North America. The techniques differ from those of the French system of **CMAS** (**Confédération Mondiale des Activités Subaquatiques**), which is the World Underwater Federation. Most of the diving monitors and instructors in Tahiti and Her Islands are qualified to teach both PADI and CMAS.

The **FFESSM** is the **Fèderation Française des Activités Subaquatiques**, or French Underwater Federation. A level of B.E. training in the FFESSM equals a CMAS one star rating; the first echelon or level equals a two-star rating in CMAS; and autonomous diver equals a three-star rating in CMAS. In France a monitor (moniteur) is more qualified than an instructor. A moniteur d'Etat is the equivalent of a State instructor, with levels of BEES 1, 2 or 3. BEES 3 is the highest level you can reach, except for a moniteur federal, who is not supposed to accept money for giving lessons. All the instructors and monitors in Tahiti are paid for their services.

---

is 29 °C/85°F during the summer months of Nov.-Mar., and 25°C/79°F during the Austral winter months of Apr.-Oct. Underwater visibility is normally good up to distances of 30 m. (100 ft.).

All non-certified scuba divers must have a certificate from a doctor indicating that you are in good health. A medical exam can be taken in Tahiti for the necessary papers, and examinations are available to obtain diving diplomas.

Around the island of Tahiti you will find some of the best scuba diving conditions for the beginner or the veteran diver who needs a reorientation. Due to the location of dive centers on the west coast of the island, in the lee of the prevailing easterly winds, you will find minimal currents and calm surface conditions. There are colorful small reef fish, friendly moray eels, eagle rays, small white-tip sharks and nurse sharks. Dive attractions also include a sunken inter-island schooner and a seaplane, and a vertical cliff on the outer reef that descends to infinity from a plateau 4.5 m. (15 ft.) deep. Moorea's special diving features are the feeding of moray eels, barracuda and large lemon sharks, plus a friendly encounter with leopard rays and large Napoleon fish. A sunken ship is clearly seen in the translucent waters of Papetoai.

Bora Bora is famous for its multihued lagoon, but also for the abundance of large-species marine life that inhabit this environment, especially the graceful manta rays that are sometimes found in groups of 10 or more, swimming inside the lagoon and in the pass. In the lagoon surrounding Huahine Nui and Huahine Iti you can feed sharks and see large schools of barracudas, big red snappers, tuna, turtles, rays and Napoleons. The lagoon that is shared by Raiatea and Taha'a attracts large schools of pelagic fish, leopard rays and a few manta rays. Divers can watch or join in the feeding of the large blue-green Napoleon fish, pet moray eels, and observe white-tip, black-tip and gray sharks.

In the Tuamotu atolls you will find world-class diving in luminescent waters with very good visibility inside the lagoons and passes. Rangiroa is one of the top diving destinations in the world. This is the largest atoll in the Southern Hemisphere and one of the largest in the world. Rangiroa's two most famous diving spots are the Avatoru and Tiputa passes through the coral reef. Schools of sharks, squadrons of eagle rays, jacks, tuna, barracuda, manta rays, turtles and dolphins swim through these passes when the very strong currents from the ocean flow into the lagoon or rush back out to sea.

Manihi is famous for the **pearl farms** inside its crystal clear lagoon. Excellent diving conditions are favorable for beginners and experienced divers. The sites include a beautiful variety of coral gardens, big Napoleon fish, black-tip reef sharks, gray sharks, eagle and manta rays, schools of snappers and big tuna fish. One favorite site is a breathtaking wall that drops 3 to 1,350 m. (10-4,500 ft.). When the famous French diver Jacques Cousteau explored the lagoon in Tikehau he said that it contained more fish than any of the other lagoons in this part of the Pacific. The inhabitants ship parrotfish and other lagoon fish from the Tikehau lagoon to Tahiti by airplane and fishing ships. Fakarava is the second largest atoll in the Tuamotu archipelago, where scuba diving is the most spectacular in the Garuae Pass, which is one km. (.62 mi.) wide and 16 m. (52 ft.) deep.

Experienced divers will be treated to a panorama of underwater life that includes manta rays, dolphins, barracudas, tiger sharks, hammerhead sharks and whale sharks. A dive center is now open on the atoll of Makemo, where a virtually unexplored scuba diver's paradise awaits discovery. Some of the dive boats include Toau, Kauehi, Tahanea and Aratika on their itinerary.

The northern group of the Marquesas Islands offers underwater caves with large fauna, recommended for adventurous, experienced divers only. Some of the world's most famous underwater photographers come here to dive and photograph the dozens of manta rays, leopard rays, stingrays, friendly hammerhead sharks and pigmy killer whales that inhabit the open waters surrounding the islands.

In the southern latitudes of the Austral Islands the humpback whales are a big attraction for scuba divers just offshore the island of Rurutu. These mammals, which are 14-18 m. (46-59 ft.) in length, are seen during the months of July-Oct., when they come up from Antarctica to mate and give birth, while escaping the austral winters. Several humpbacks also visit Moorea, Tahiti and the Tuamotu atolls.

There are more than 30 scuba diving clubs in French Polynesia, located on the islands of Tahiti, Moorea, Huahine, Raiatea, Taha'a, Bora Bora and Maupiti in the Society Islands; the atolls of Rangiroa, Tikehau, Manihi, Fakarava, Makemo and Hao in the Tuamotu archipelago; on Nuku Hiva in the Marquesas Islands; and on

Rurutu and Tubuai in the Austral Islands. Please check each destination chapter for information on the most popular diving clubs used by tourists.

GETTING AROUND BY CAR

In the Society Islands most of the roads that circle the islands are paved. There are a few places in Raiatea and Taha'a where the road is not sealed but they are pretty well graded. Following heavy rains there are frequently holes in the road that can be very dangerous, especially if you are riding a scooter or bicycle. In most of the Marquesas Islands the 4-wheel drive vehicles (called 4x4, pronounced "cat-cat") are usually rented with driver, because the roads are abominable. However, you can rent a self-drive 4WD on most of the islands. Rangiroa has a paved road between the two passes and there's nowhere else to go by car. The Austral Islands have mostly concrete or unpaved roads, which you can drive in a normal car, except for some places in Rurutu, where a 4WD is required.

You will drive on the right side of the road in French Polynesia, just as you do in North America and continental Europe. A valid diver's license from your State or home country will be honored here. Should you buy an international driver's license, which is not at all necessary, you will still need to show your normal driver's license in order to rent a car or scooter. The minimum age is 21 years to rent a 4WD vehicle and to rent 2-wheel vehicles the driver must be 18 or 19 years old, depending on the island. If you are 70 years old or more, then you must have a doctor's certificate proving that you are still capable of driving.

Speed limits are 40 km. per hour (24 mi. per hour) in the towns and villages, 60 km. (37 mi. per hour) on the winding roads of most of the islands and 80-110 km. (50-68 mi. per hour) on a short stretch of freeway leading from Tahiti's west coast to downtown Papeete. Seat belts are mandatory for the driver and all passengers in the front and back seats of vehicles on all islands, and very stiff fines will be charged if you don't fasten-up and the gendarmes stop you. Helmets are required for anyone riding a motorcycle or scooter.

Anyone driving a 2-wheel vehicle should remember to go single file if you are on the main road. Some of the local drivers are in a mighty big hurry to get somewhere, even with nowhere to go. After all, they take their driver's lessons from the French! There are now some bicycle paths, but not usually all around the island. You should also be alert for drunk drivers, especially late at night, and young boys doing "wheelies" on bicycles or scooters, often with no lights at night. You also have to look out for children and dogs when you pass through the villages around the island.

Liability Insurance

Vehicle insurance includes third party liability insurance. It is possible, depending on the conditions of the driving license and age, to take a comprehensive insurance that covers collision, damage and waiver.

Automobile Rental
Europcar and Avis-Pacificar are the biggest names for rental cars in French Polynesia, although Hertz also has offices in the more popular tourist islands. There are also a few individuals who rent cars, scooters and bicycles. See information for each island in the *Getting Around Town* section.

HOTELS AND VILLAS – INTERNATIONAL CLASS ACCOMMODATIONS
In mid-2011 Tahiti and Her Islands had 27 international class hotels on 8 islands, offering 2,500 rooms (including 915 overwater bungalows or villas) in the 4- and 5-star categories. These up-market hotel accommodations include deluxe rooms, suites and villas with a/c, direct dial international telephones, WiFi Internet access, individual safes, refrigerators or mini-bars, coffee/tea making facilities, hair dryers, satellite TV and room service. Some of these accommodations are similar to American hotel or motel rooms, usually in concrete buildings of 2 or more levels. Most of the outer island hotels also offer these conveniences in their deluxe- or superior-class Polynesian style bungalows.

Mid-range accommodations are also available on 10 islands, offering 566 rooms (including 19 overwater bungalows) in 21 small hotels with 2- and 3-star ratings. These may be an air-conditioned room in downtown Papeete or an in-transit motel at the airport. an older small hotel on Moorea or in the more distant islands. Some of the newer 3-star hotels are actually adorable boutique hotels with 4-32 rooms and 5-star furnishings.

On several of the islands you will now find superior-class accommodations for couples or families in a self-contained, totally equipped bungalow, villa or house with all the modern conveniences and many extras. Some of the rentals also include a car or boat, and sometimes both.

The typical Polynesian style bungalows can be very elegant, especially when they are built overwater, with a glass panel or table in the floor, allowing you to have a peek at what the fish are doing in the coral gardens below. These bungalows often have thatched roofs of woven pandanus leaves and woven bamboo walls. The interior walls are sometimes covered with pandanus matting from Indonesia, and a chic Polynesian decor incorporates all the flamboyant colors you'll find in the tropical gardens, or it reflects the softer colors of the lagoon. The most deluxe hotels have replaced the Polynesian furnishings with a neutral decor of off-white, cream and beige, adding accent colors with cushions. Most of the bungalows have air-conditioning, large bathrooms with a bathtub/shower, bathtub and separate rain or power-shower, or Jacuzzi and separate shower. They also have lighted dressing tables and living areas, plus a terrace or veranda, and the overwater bungalows have steps leading into the lagoon, with a shower on the landing. Some of the overwater villas in Bora Bora now have swimming pools, and the deluxe hotels in Moorea, Huahine, Taha'a, Bora Bora and Rangiroa have also added plunge pools to their garden or beach units. To answer the demands of their American guests, the hotel rooms most frequently chosen by honeymooners are also equipped with a satellite

TV, plus a DVD and CD player. Some even have 2 TV's and an espresso machine. Most of these hotels have added a spa whose services include a relaxing massage for two, sometimes at the edge of the lagoon at sunset time or under the starry sky. The cost of a standard room in a deluxe hotel on the island of Tahiti varies from $197-$361 double. The rates for a standard double room in a medium-priced classified hotel start at $151 in Tahiti, $130 in Moorea, $153 in Raiatea, $231 in Bora Bora, and $90 in Rurutu. Bungalows in deluxe hotels start at $428 on Moorea, $615 on Huahine, $295 on Raiatea, $651 on Taha'a, $908 on Bora Bora, $766 (MAP for 2) on Rangiroa, $315 on Fakarava, and $293 on Nuku Hiva.

Overwater bungalows are the most popular accommodations with honeymooners. At the Intercontinental Tahiti Resort an overwater bungalow on the motu costs $529 and the newer units over the lagoon are $767 during low season. Le Méridien Tahiti sells their overwater bungalows for $656. The lowest priced overwater units in Moorea are $971, except for Club Bali Hai, where you will pay $183.

On Raiatea an overwater bungalow starts at $339, and on Huahine the lowest rack rates are $869 for an overwater bungalow; on Rangiroa they are priced at $1,285 (MAP for 2), on Tikehau the lowest price is $843, and on Manihi the rates start at $855. On Taha'a an overwater unit at Vahine Island is $814, and at Le Taha'a Island Resort & Spa the lowest priced overwater unit is $1,169. Bora Bora's 9 hotels with overwater bungalows start at $530 at Le Maitai Polynesia, and escalate to $1,293 per night for the least expensive overwater villa at the St. Regis.

International Hotel Chains

The **Intercontinental** chain represents a hotel in Tahiti, Moorea and 2 in Bora Bora. The **Hilton** brand replaced **Sheraton Hotels** in Jan. 2009, representing a hotel in Moorea and another in Bora Bora. **Starwood Hotels** and **Resorts** represents St Regis in Bora Bora and has a minor interest in Le Meridien Tahiti and Le Meridien Bora Bora. The French group **Accor** has a **Sofitel** hotel on Tahiti, Moorea and Bora Bora. **Radisson** has a hotel in Tahiti. **Four Seasons Resort** is located in Bora Bora.

Locally-Owned and Managed Hotel Chains

Pacific Beachcomber SC, is headed by President and CEO, Dick Bailey, an American resident of Tahiti. This company owns and manages the Intercontinental Tahiti Resort & Spa, Intercontinental Moorea Resort & Spa, Intercontinental Bora Bora Le Moana Resort, and Intercontinental Bora Bora Resort & Thalasso Spa. In 2009 the PBSC assumed operation of the *M/S Paul Gauguin*, and Dick Bailey is President and CEO of the Paul Gauguin Cruises. Also in 2009 PBSC began construction on The Brando, a 100% energy-independent 6-star hotel that will open in late 2012 on Tetiaroa with 35 private villas (40 rooms). See information in Chapter 2 *Overview*.

Hotel Management & Services (HMS), a partner of Pacific Beachcomber SC, is also headed by Dick Bailey. They own Le Maitai Polynesia in Bora Bora and the Maitai Rangiroa Lagoon Resort. They also handle the management and marketing of the Maitai Lapita Village in Huahine, which opened on Sept. 1, 2011.

Financière Hôtelière Polynésienne (FHP) is a Tahiti company comprised primarily of Air Tahiti and Banque Socredo, along with private investors. They own and manage the 5-star Le Taha'a Island Resort & Spa, which is a member of the prestigious **Le Relais et Chateaux** association. They also own all the Pearl Resorts and manage the Nuku Hiva Keikahanui Pearl Lodge and the Hiva Oa Hanakee Pearl Lodge.

South Pacific Management (SPM) is a locally owned company that manages the Manava Suite Resort Tahiti, Moorea Pearl Resort, Bora Bora Pearl Beach Resort, Tikehau Pearl Beach Resort, Manihi Bearl Beach Resort and Te Tiare Resort in Huahine. Since Jan. 2009 SPM has operated the Bora Bora Nui Resort and the Moorea Lagoon Resort under the Hilton franchise.

FAMILY HOTELS, BED & BREAKFAST GUEST ROOMS & GUEST HOUSES

On all the islands listed in this guide book you will find accommodations with Tahitian, Chinese or French hosts who welcome visitors for home stays in their bed and breakfast houses, guest rooms, guest houses and small family hotels. These lodgings are generally referred to as *family pensions*; however, the "Haere Mai" Federation that represents the associations of family lodgings on 21 islands is now calling them *family hotels.*

The small *fare* (FAH-rey) in the family operated lodgings often has a thatched roof, overhead fan and colorful linens and curtains. Some are screened, and most have a porch or terrace. In the family hotels or guesthouses you usually have a private room or bungalow. In some of these lodgings you have cooking facilities and in others you eat what your hosts prepare. You may have a bathroom to yourself with a hot water shower, or share the outdoor facilities, which may have a cold water shower. On some of the more arid islands your water supply may be limited.

These small family hotels and guest rooms are the heart and soul of tourism in Tahiti and Her Islands. According to the chosen type of lodging, this experience can offer a total immersion in the daily life of a local family. It provides an opportunity to share, see, hear, feel and taste life in the islands as if you were a distant relative finally coming back to the source. Some of you will go fishing on the lagoon with your hosts. Others will follow the children in their mountain explorations, looking for waterfalls and rock pools to bathe in. Still others will take their hosts' advice and discover the local produce and cuisine. You will live in a *fare* made of traditional or modern materials, on often unknown but grandiose sites. In the friendly and spontaneous warmth of Tahitian families, this is a unique experience that fulfills the demands and needs of visitors for authenticity, conviviality, nature, quiet and intimacy. It is also a way of participating in the improvement and preservation of the environment and cultural heritage of the islands.

A classification system offered in this type of lodging allows visitors to plan their stay under the best possible conditions. The very rigorous rating is established by the French Polynesia Government's Tourism Department, which monitors the application of some 100 rating criteria. The classification commission has the power to downgrade, or even exclude establishments that no longer meet required hygiene and safety standards.

Small family hotels and guest rooms are rated from one to three Tiare Tahiti flowers. The quality and attractiveness of the site, the level of comfort and amenities and the services offered are paid particular attention. These ratings are still a work-in-progress, but you will see from the family hotels listed in each chapter which lodgings have been awarded one or more Tiares:

One Tiare : Simple comfort, excellent quality-to-price relationship.
Two tiares : Good comfort at the best possible rate.
Three tiares : Excellent comfort, attentive service at reasonable rates.

Please see Chapter 2 *Overview* for a description of the categories of these lodgings. For more information on the classification criteria, please contact the French Polynesia Tourism Ministry at *www.tourisme.gov.pf.* For further information on the guesthouses and family accommodations, contact *www.haere-mai.com.*

Activities

Family hotels, guesthouses and other moderate or economy accommodations can offer fascinating activities, sometimes directly, or through the most competent excursion operators. The pension owners know the hiking trails, the secret beaches, the surfing spots, the ancient ruins hidden in the valleys, the lagoon or ocean locations where fish are plentiful. They can help you organize excursions and picnics on motu (islets inside the lagoon) or on remote beaches. In some places, you will discover sea kayaking, in others you'll visit a Tahitian cultured pearl farm, or be initiated into the mysteries of weaving by a Tahitian "mama." Given their experience and local contacts, your hosts can advise you on other activities, such as scuba diving or horseback riding.

For those who like giving their holiday a theme, be it sports, nature or exploration, family hotels in Tahiti and Her Islands are the ideal accommodations, providing the closest to what you are seeking.

7. Basic Information

Listed here, in alphabetical order by topic, are recommendations and practical information for your trip to Tahiti and Her Islands.

BUSINESS HOURS

Several of the small restaurant/snacks and the Papeete Municipal Market, **le Marché**, open around 5am, and between 7:30-8am the post office, government offices, banks, airline offices, travel agencies and boutiques open. Many of the shops and offices still close for lunch between 12pm and 1:30 or 2pm, while others are now remaining open through the lunch period. Except for the restaurants and sidewalk cafés and bars, most of Papeete is closed down by 6pm.

The suburban shopping centers remain open until 7-8pm. Most businesses close at noon on Sat. and all day Sun. and holidays. The food stores are open on Sat. afternoon and usually open on Sun. and holidays from 6-8am, with a few *magasins* remaining open until noon and then reopening between 5-7pm.

COST OF LIVING & TRAVEL

French Polynesia can be very expensive and it can also be affordable, depending on how you choose to go. I've been living in Tahiti and Moorea since 1971 and I have never ceased to be amazed at the costs. We pay the same prices as you will when we go to the restaurants and grocery stores, take a taxi or buy gas for our automobiles. Only recently have the residents begun to benefit from reductions on inter-island airfares, hotel rates and some of the excursions. Many Americans spend their entire vacation complaining about the cost of Coca-Cola, beer, water and food. Some of these tourists are so concerned with how much money they're spending that they cannot even enjoy their vacations.

Even though some of the prices here are still astronomical compared to what you'll pay in the United States, Canada or wherever you are, they are actually lower for many items than we paid a few years ago. I remember when a package of celery, or a head of cauliflower or broccoli cost 1.300 CFP! Today, in Moorea I pay 560 CFP a kilo for broccoli imported from Australia or the USA. I pay 404 CFP for a head of cauliflower imported from the USA. Imported celery is 396 CFP for 16 oz. Locally grown frisée lettuce is 709 CFP a kilo, green peppers are 707 CFP per kilo, cucumbers are 284-425 CFP a kilo and locally grown tomatoes are 520-620 CFP a kilo, depending on the season. Watermelons from Maupiti or Huahine sell for 1.000-1.500 CFP each in Tahiti and up to double the price in Moorea.

With the opening of the "mega" markets (Carrefour, Hyper-U Tropic Import, Cash and Carry, Price Club, Hyper Champion and Casino) in Tahiti, competition brought the prices down a little. Larger supermarkets have also opened in the outer islands, providing a wider choice of goodies at slightly lower prices. But then, the value added tax brings them up again.

Transportation Costs

See each Island chapter for details and costs on how to get around. You can rent a car on all the Society Islands, in Rangiroa, on most of the Marquesas Islands and on some of the Austral Islands. Gasoline is sold by the liter (4 liters = 1.06 gallons), and in Moorea you'll pay 167 CFP per liter for unleaded gas, or 668 CFP per gallon, which is used by most of the rental cars. Diesel fuel is 155 CFP a liter or 620 CFP per gallon. Most service stations sell Total and Mobil products, and Shell has a few stations on the island of Tahiti and Moorea.

ELECTRICITY

The current is 220 volts, 50 cycles in most hotels and family homes. Some of the newer upscale hotels have outlets for both 220 and 110 volts. Most hotels provide 110-volt outlets for shavers, and hair dryers are usually provided. It's best to ask the management before you plug in hair dryers, battery chargers and computers. Adapters are usually necessary for American appliances, as the French plugs have two round prongs. You can bring your adapters with you or buy them at a general store in Tahiti. The hotels sometimes, but not always, have a transformer or converter for your electrical appliance.

FESTIVALS & HOLIDAYS

All of French Polynesia celebrate New Year's Day, Missionaries Day (March 5), Good Friday, Easter Sunday, Easter Monday, May Day (May 1, which is Labor Day), May 8, which was also Victory Day 1945, Pentecost (7th Sunday after Easter), Pentecost Monday, Ascension Day (June 1), Internal Autonomy Day (June 29), Bastille Day (July 14), Assumption (August 15), All Saints Day (November 1), Armistice Day 1918 (November 11), and Christmas Day.

All government offices, banks, airline offices, travel agencies and most private offices are closed on official holidays, and if it falls on a Thurs. or Tues., quite often the businesses will make a bridge, giving their employees an extra day off to enjoy a long weekend. See *Calendar of Events* chapter.

GETTING MARRIED

Tahiti, the Island of Love, has long been a favorite honeymoon destination for lovers of all ages. Having a symbolic wedding or renewal of vows in Paradise has also become a popular activity for some of our visitors. In all the favorite tourist islands of French Polynesia couples from around the world are now saying "Oui" at the Mairie (Town Hall), "Hai" in the wedding chapels at the hotels, and "Eh" while standing in front of a Tahitian high priest.

Now you can legally tie the knot in French Polynesia. In May 2009 the French National Assembly passed a new law that allows foreign visitors to get married legally here without having to reside in Tahiti 30 continuous days prior to a civil ceremony. The reduced waiting time allows the couple to expedite the proceedings once they reserve their flight and hotel. At the same time they can request a civil marriage ceremony at the (Mairie) City Hall where their hotel is located. They can then go ahead with their wedding celebrations and honeymoon as soon as they arrive.

The waiting time may be shorter now, but there is still quite a bit of paperwork involved in getting married in a French country. All legal weddings must take place at the City Hall. This may be followed by the symbolic ceremony of your choice. Overseas visitors who wish to be married in French Polynesia should choose several possible dates for the ceremony, keeping in mind that civil weddings cannot be performed on Sundays and holidays. This is to make sure that the City Hall will be available when and where you would like to have the marriage performed.

The couple must submit an application form to the chosen municipality or commune at least one month and 10 days prior to the date of the civil ceremony, for the publication of the banns (official marriage notice made by the commune). This "Marriage of foreign citizens in French Polynesia" form, as well as other pertinent information, can be obtained from *www.tahiti-tourisme.com*.

Locally based multi-lingual Wedding Planner services can help you with all the administrative paperwork, planning and on-site coordination. These include: Tahiti Nui Travel, *Tel. 689/46.41.41*, wedding@tahitinuitravel.com; Laurel Samuela, *Tel. 689/56.25.33, www.truetahitivacation.com*; and Legal Tahitian Wedding Ceremony Company, *Tel. 689/72.49.75, legaltahitianwedding@ymail.com*. The international class hotels in all the tourist islands of French Polynesia can also advise and assist you in preparing for this romantic event.

Polynesian Wedding Ceremonies

The historical change in French Polynesia's law that allows foreigners to get legally married without the formerly required 30-day residence period has created a fantastic opportunity for visitors to combine their civil wedding with a traditional Polynesian ceremony and a memorable honeymoon experience.

For some 20 years Tiki Village in Moorea has specialized in Polynesian weddings. Couples of all ages and nationalities have chosen to splurge for a fun-filled colorful Maohi wedding ceremony in the authentic tradition of old Polynesia. These productions are a pure Tahitian experience and are not legally recognized or binding marriages. And it's not just newlyweds who get married in the Tahitian style, but also loving couples who are celebrating their anniversaries, who wish to renew their vows to one another.

Olivier Briac, owner of Tiki Village, said that the romantic Tahitian wedding is something absolutely unique. "There have been a lot of visitors who wanted to be married, but they wanted a legal wedding. With this new law in effect, now you can get both in the same place. It's done, it's finished, it's fabulous," he said. (Please see information on *Wedding Ceremonies* in Moorea chapter).

Romantic Weddings on the Hotel Beaches and in Wedding Chapels
Symbolic weddings can also be performed at all of the international class hotels in Tahiti and Her Islands. You may choose a simple and private ceremony on a white sand beach at sunset, or a royal event in the authentic tradition of old Polynesia. The higher priced options include a Tahitian priest, singers, dancers and musicians, traditional costumes and pareos, flower leis, a wedding bouquet, a gastronomic dinner, a bottle of champagne and wedding cake, and your king size bed will be covered with beautiful tropical flowers.

Some of the most extravagant weddings are performed in the wedding chapels of Bora Bora. These are located at Bora Bora Pearl Beach Resort & Spa, Hilton Bora Bora Nui Resort & Spa, Four Seasons Resort & Spa, Intercontinental Bora Bora Resort & Thalasso Spa and Le Méridien Bora Bora.

The international class hotels all have a special package for couples who wish to celebrate an engagement, have a wedding ceremony performed, renew their vows, or toast their wedding anniversary.

The Hilton Moorea Lagoon Resort & Spa, voted by TripAdvisor Readers as the No. 1 Hotel for Romance in the World and No. 1 Hotel for Romance in the South Pacific for 2010, can arrange civil weddings as well as Polynesian wedding ceremonies. Religious and Continental weddings may also be organized.

Maohi Nui Polynesian Weddings in Bora Bora
Patrick Tairua is a charismatic Polynesian man of Bora Bora who performs wedding ceremonies in the most touching, romantic manner that a couple in love could experience anywhere. (Please see information under *Wedding Ceremonies* in the Bora Bora chapter).

HEALTH CONCERNS
On the island of Tahiti you will have access to a large government hospital, 2 private clinics, and numerous specialists who provide good medical and dental services. In addition to the allopathic doctors, you have alternative health care in the form of homeopathic medicine, acupuncturists, Chinese herbalists, traditional Tahitian healers, massage therapy, magnetizers and thalassotherapy. Many of these specialists speak English. Moorea, Raiatea, Nuku Hiva and Tubuai have small hospitals, and all the other islands have medical centers, infirmaries or dispensaries. The more populous islands also have pharmacies and dentists. In Tahiti and Moorea there are optical services, where you can have minor repairs made to your eyeglasses or new glasses made, and should you need emergency attention for your hearing aid, that is also available in Papeete.

All the islands maintain hygienic controls to combat potential epidemics of tropical diseases, such as the dengue fever, which is also known as "breakbone" fever, because of the intense pain in the head and muscles. This viral disease is carried by the *Aëdes aegypti* mosquito, which also lives indoors and bites during the daytime. In addition to a high fever, excruciating headache, pain in the joints and back, and a general feeling of weakness, the victims also develop an itchy body rash. Unfortunately, there is no vaccine, and you cannot take aspirin for the pains, as it may cause the stomach to bleed. The doctors can treat this disease with a *dengue cocktail*, which is an injection of Vitamin C and other vitamins, but the symptoms can last from 7-10 days. There are several forms of *dengue*, and the most severe type can cause death in children, although this is very rare in French Polynesia.

Leptospirosis or Weil's disease has some of the same symptoms as the dengue: high fever, severe headaches, chills, muscle aches, vomiting, jaundice, red eyes, abdominal pain, diarrhea or a rash. This is caused by bacteria of the genus *Leptospira* and affects humans and animals. Most of the cases reported in French Polynesia are caused by dried rat urine that is mixed with the food, water or soil. You can also get this disease from swimming downriver from pigpens. In addition to causing kidney damage, meningitis, liver failure and respiratory distress, the disease is usually fatal. Be sure to wipe off the tops of all bottles and cans before drinking, because rats live in all the storerooms in the tropics. Better yet, drink from a clean glass.

Malaria is not present in the islands of French Polynesia, and the inhabitants generally have a high standard of health. There is an occasional outbreak of conjunctivitis, and some of the long time residents have suffered from filariasis or elephantiasis, an insect-borne disease that attacks the lymphatic system. Preventive medicine is distributed free every 6 months in all the islands, which keeps this disease well under control, and it is not a threat to the short-term visitor.

Pests & Pets

Mosquitoes are tropical pests, and in addition to the high cost of living and the noise of the roosters, the biggest complaints in French Polynesia are about the hungry mosquitoes that just love fresh blood from our visitors. There's not much you can do about the inflated prices and the crowing rooster you'd love to throttle at 2-3-4-5am, but you can avoid being bitten. In the high-end hotels, you will find an electric diffuser or mosquito destroyer that uses a bottle of liquid or blue pastilles, treated with Allethrin, to ward off mosquitoes. Other lodgings usually provide mosquito coils that you can burn, or you can buy them at any food store.

Bring a good mosquito repellent with you or go to the pharmacy once you're here and buy your defense products. I have found Dolmix Pic cream to be effective, which is sold in pharmacies. Aerogard spray or lotion is a good Australian product and can be purchased in the supermarkets. Tourists have also reported satisfactory results with *monoi* oil mixed with citronella, and this is available in most supermarkets, small *magasins* and hotel gift shops. My favorite anti-mosquito cream is Rid, which is made in Australia, but it is not sold in Tahiti. It is available in other Pacific Island groups, however. American friends who spend several months in Moorea each year tell me that Buggspray (2GS) with 25% DEET and a vanilla scent works well for them. You can order it at *www.buggspray.com*. Be aware that mosquitoes will bite you day and night, and are most active when the weather is hot and sticky, which means during our rainy seasons. You have to remember to reapply your mosquito protection throughout the day or evening, especially if you are perspiring or swimming, as the water and sweat wash the product away.

On some of the islands you may encounter the *nono*, which is a minuscule "no-see-um" sand fly with a nasty sting. They are most prevalent at daybreak and late in the afternoon, when they come to chew on your ankles. You might not even know you've been bitten until hours later, when the itching starts. Do not scratch it, however, as that will only aggravate the pain and cause an infected sore. Slathering yourself in oil is the best way to keep these little buggers at bay, as they just slide off your skin. Any kind of oil will do, although Avon's Skin So Soft from the States, or *monoi* oil, which is sold all over French Polynesia, will certainly smell better than cooking oil. Daily doses of 500 milligrams of vitamin B1 will help to ward off the pesky nonos.

If you do get stung by a mosquito, nono, wasp or bee, or cut yourself on coral, a good first aid treatment is to squeeze fresh lime juice on the wound to avoid infection. Cuts and scratches infect easily and take a long time to heal, so it is important to prevent any problems. Creams are also sold to take away pain from stings. Just remember to include an antibacterial cream in your traveling first aid kit, which you should definitely pack for your trip. The ingredients of such a kit will vary according to your own needs. The most important items to include would be any prescription drugs you take. Bring an extra pair of eyeglasses if you use them.

Ciguatera

More than 400 species of lagoon and reef fish are potential carriers of **ciguatera**, a poisoning from eating infected fish. This phenomenon existed in some of the coral islands before the arrival of the first Europeans, and is caused by a microscopic marine organism that lives on or near the coral reef, especially reefs that have been disturbed by cyclones, shipwrecks, port construction and other developments.

The larger carnivorous fish, such as the parrot fish, surgeon fish, coral bass, sea perch, snappers and jack fish are all potential carriers of ciguatera, as well as the big barracuda, as they tend to store the toxins found in the smaller coral fish on which they feed. The open ocean fish, such as mahi mahi, tuna, swordfish, salmon of the gods and marlin and other pelagics do not carry the ciguatera toxin.

If you catch your own fish, it is best to get the advice of the local people before you cook it. They know which spots are more likely to be affected by ciguatera. The seafood served in the restaurants of French Polynesia is as safe as you'll find anywhere. Just avoid eating the head, gonads, liver and viscera of the fish.

Drinking Water

The Department of Health in French Polynesia reports that the tap water in Papeete has been treated with chlorine and is potable, and the water on the islands of Bora Bora, Taha'a and Tubuai is drinkable. For the rest of the island of Tahiti and on all the other islands, it is advisable to drink bottled water. Eau Royale and Vaimato are two of the companies in Tahiti that sell bottled water, and the lab tests have given a higher rating to Vaimato for purity and cleanliness. There are also several brands of bottled water imported from France. Some of the hotels have water filter systems.

Too Much Sunshine!

More vacations have been ruined from an overdose of sun than from any other factor. So many of the elderly tourists, who come ashore from their air-conditioned cruise ships, walk along the road in the heat and humidity of the noonday sun. Back home they drive round and round the parking lot, hoping to find a parking place close to the entrance to the shopping center or super market. When they come here they decide to walk the equivalent of several blocks or even kilometers, with the sun blazing on their heads.

I have escorted groups of American doctors to Marlon Brando's atoll of Tetiaroa for a day tour. No matter how much they were warned about the dangers of the sun, when it was time to fly back to Tahiti in the afternoon, all the doctors in the group, including the dermatologists, were as red as a boiled lobster. The Tahitian name for white people is *popa'a*, which is derived from the Tahitian word for "red lobster."

Fair-skinned people have to be especially careful in the tropics. Do your jogging, take your walk and work on your tan at the beginning of the morning or in the late afternoon, when distant clouds low on the horizon filter the ultra violet rays. During your picnic on the *motu* or while riding in any open boat, make sure you apply a sufficiently strong sunscreen or sunblock (containing 25 to 50 sunburn protection factor) on all the exposed parts of your body. Wrap up like a mummy if there is no sun protector on the boat. Don't forget to rub the lotion on your feet and reapply the sunblock throughout the day, as you sweat and swim. Always wear a hat when exposed to the sun, and protect your nose and lips with zinc or a similar barrier cream.

Should you forget this advice and get yourself "cooked" while vacationing in Tahiti and Her Islands, there are several remedies to ease the pain and help the healing process. These include applying tomato juice or vinegar to the sunburned parts, as well as Calamine lotion, aloe vera gel, tamanu oil, and a range of other products, which are available at the pharmacies in your country and in Tahiti.

Diarrhea

The abundance of tropical fruits you'll find so tempting in Tahiti are also very good for you if you exercise moderation. If you go overboard on the tropical fruit, you may regret it. Your system is not accustomed to so much Vitamin C, which can have a cataclysmic effect on your bowels.

The change of water, food and climate are the primary reasons for an upset digestive system. Drink bottled mineral water, eat in balanced proportions and get plenty of rest, and you will most likely avoid any disruptive problems. When you're packing for your trip to Tahiti be sure to include a remedy for treating diarrhea. There are many products on the market from which to choose, such as Imodium and Lomotil.

Should symptoms of diarrhea manifest, it would be best to avoid the consumption of raw vegetables and chilled beverages. Eat steamed white rice and boiled eggs and yogurt, and drink lots of bottled water to restore body fluids lost through dehydration.

Sex in the South Seas

Exercise the same precautions you would apply back home. Since the arrival of the first European ships in 1767, Tahiti has earned a worldwide reputation as a sexually permissive port-of-call. Even with the strong influence of all the missionaries and church groups that have worked for over 200 years to change the sexual mores of the Polynesians, the promiscuous practices have not been completely eliminated.

Papeete is a hot spot of very young female prostitutes and *raerae* (male transvestites), who frequent the nightclubs and bars and hang out on the corner of Boulevard Pomare and Avenue Prince Hinoi, looking for a pick-up. Safe sex in Tahiti often means that when boy meets girl for a clandestine rendezvous, they are both reasonably sure that his wives and girlfriends and her husband and/or boyfriends are not going to catch them in the act—this time. Even though there is an on-going educational program on the dangers of unprotected sexual encounters, there is still a reticence to put the knowledge into action. Thankfully, French Polynesia today has one of the world's lowest rates of the Acquired Immune Deficiency Syndrome (AIDS) virus, known as SIDA in French. This terrible disease has already claimed several lives in Tahiti, however, and all the other sexually transmitted diseases are prevalent here as well.

Vaccinations

No immunizations are required for entry into French Polynesia unless you are arriving from an infected area. The U.S. State Department has a 24-hour **Travel Advisory**, *Toll Free 888/407-4747; www.travel.state.gov/travel/warnings.html.* Check their website for up-to-date overseas health information, as well as crime and politics in foreign countries, and information on medical insurance overseas. The US Center for Disease Control in Atlanta, Georgia, gives travel advisories on an **International Traveler's Hotline**, *Toll Free 877/FYI-TRIP (877/394-8747); www.cdc.gov/travel/default.aspx.*

INTERNET SERVICE

Many of our visitors choose to bring their own laptop when they visit Tahiti and Her Islands. They can keep in touch with friends and family and learn what's happening in the "real world" while they are gazing at the translucent lagoon below their overwater bungalow. They can listen to music, have a slideshow of the humpback whales they saw during that morning's boat excursion, watch DVD movies and play electronic games.

Most hotels and several of the small family hotels or pensions provide wireless Internet connections (WiFi) or high-speed dataports in the guest rooms, and also have "hotspots" in some of the hotel's public areas. Through your own computer or with those provided by your hotel, you can connect to Mana, the local Internet service provider, which is a subsidiary of the OPT (Post and Telecommunications Office), either by modem or by ADSL. You type in 36-88-88, and log-in as anonymous, using the Password anonymous. This type of modem connection is available in all the archipelagos of French Polynesia.

Mana has installed WiFi "surfing spots" (*www.manaspot.pf*) around Tahiti, on Moorea, Huahine, Raiatea, Bora Bora, Rangiroa and several of the outer islands. This service provides high-speed wireless Internet access for portable computers and cell phones in all 5 archipelagoes. They have issued "ManaSpot" WiFi cards that sell for 660 CFP for 1 hr., or 3.960 CFP for a 10-hr. card. Monthly rates with unlimited volume are available for professionals. You can buy these cards at any post office.

Hotspot-WDG, *Tel. 71.96.57*; **Iaoranet**, *Tel. 77.24.86*; and **Wifi Tiki**, Tel. *56.35.67*, also provide cyber-spaces. Read the *Internet* section of each Island chapter to learn more about this service and where to find the public computers and WiFi cards that will enable you to get connected on-line.

MAPS AND MARITIME CHARTS

Free maps are available at the Tahiti Tourisme office, including a map of downtown Papeete. The *Tahiti Beach Press* includes folkloric maps of Papeete and the islands of Tahiti, Moorea and Bora Bora. You'll also find maps in the bookstores and newsstands. Pacific Promotion's *39 Tourist Maps of Tahiti and Her Islands* includes outdated locations of all hotels and pensions. **Librairie Klima**, *Tel. 42.00.63*, at Place Notre Dame in Papeete, sells oceanographic charts of the islands. **Nauti-Sport**, *Tel. 50.59.59*, in Fare Ute, also sells French nautical charts of Polynesia. **Bluewater Books & Charts** in Fort Lauderdale, FL, *www.bluewaterweb.com* is a good source of navigational charts of the Pacific.

The Topographic Section of the **Service de l'Urbanisme**, *Tel. 46.82.18*, is located on the 4th floor of the Administrative Building at 11 Rue du Commandant Destremeau, where you can find topographical maps of the islands. **Pacific Image**, *Tel. 50.34.34/77.17.75; infos@pacific-image.pf; www.pacific-image.com; www.tahitiphotos.com* has CD-Rom maps, photos and posters of French Polynesia. You can see on-line maps at *www.tahitiguide.com*.

MONEY & BANKING

The **French Pacific franc**, written as **CFP**, or **XPF** in banking circles, is the official currency of French Polynesia. One of the banks in Tahiti told me that CFP stands for *cour de franc Pacifique*, and in the currency exchanges on the Internet XPF means *comptoirs français du Pacifique franc*. The colorful CFP notes, which may look like play money to you, are issued in denominations of 500, 1.000, 5.000 and 10.000 francs (CFP); and coins are 1, 2, 5, 10, 20, 50 and 100 francs (CFP).

The CFP franc has been anchored to the euro since January 1, 1999, on a fixed parity basis. With 1.000 CFP you have 8.38 Euros (**1 euro = 119.33 CFP**). Even though the French franc was replaced by the Euro starting January 1, 2002, the French Pacific franc (CFP) will continue, for the time being, to exist as a separate monetary entity. This currency is valid only in the French Overseas Communities and Territories of the Pacific: French Polynesia, New Caledonia and Wallis and Fetuna.

The 7 Euro bills are in denominations of 500, 200, 100, 50, 20, 10 and 5. The 8 coins are the 2 Euro coin, the 1 Euro coin, and cents—50, 20, 10, 5, 2 and 1 Euro cents. The local banks will accept Euro bills, just as they accept American dollars, but they will not accept Euro coins or American coins. Some of the stores, shops, boutiques and other small vendors will not accept even the Euro bills. Most shops will accept American dollars, but you probably won't get good exchange rates in the process.

The exchange rate for the US dollar fluctuates daily in the banks and by the second on the Internet. The average yearly US dollar exchange rate has steadily dropped from 105.7 CFP in 2003 to 96.1 CFP for 2004 and 2005, to 95.1 CFP for 2006, to 87.1 CFP for 2007. At my deadline time for the No. 5 edition of this guide in 2008 the CFP received for a dollar was down to 81.5 and it continued to decline into the 70's. **As I write this on October 13, 2001, the bank-to-bank exchange rate on the Internet was 86.9032 CFP for one US dollar.** This means that a consumer would get about 79-80 CFP in French Polynesia, or 6-7 points less in exchange.

If you have access to the Internet you can get currency conversions on *www.xe.com/ucc/full.shtml.*

Ready Cash

In the main terminal of the International Airport of Tahiti-Faa'a there are two automatic teller machines (**ATM's**), which are called a *distributeur*. One is at the Banque de Polynésie facing the door you will exit after clearing Immigration/ Customs; and the Socredo Banque ATM is to the right of the door, near the restaurant/bar and Air Tahiti domestic terminal. There is no longer an exchange counter open at the airport for international arrivals and departures, and the two ATM's often run out of money. If you fly to Tahiti between Thursday and Tuesday it is advisable to arrive with enough French Pacific francs (CFP) in your pocket to get you started.

Where to buy your CFP before leaving home is a subject that is well-discussed in the Forum section of *www.tahiti-explorer.com*. The people who advise inquirers on the Forum live in French Polynesia full- or part-time or they visit the islands several times a year for long stays. They suggest you buy francs from Wells Fargo, which you can do in person, by phone or online at *https://www.wellsfargo.com/ foreignexchange*. American Express, *www.amextravelresources.com* is also another source you might try.

Banque de Polynésie, Banque de Tahiti and Banque Socredo have offices on most of the main tourist islands and they all have ATM windows. Some of the post offices also have ATM windows. Most, but not all, of these machines will accept your Visa and MasterCard transactions, as well as Eurocard, but you may have trouble using your American Express card for ready cash. Although you may see the Cirrus logo on the ATM, these machines will process only Cirrus from France.

You can get cash advances with your Visa and MasterCard at the Banque de Tahiti, and at some of the Banque de Polynesie branches, but the amount may be limited according to the type of credit card you have. American Express cash advances can be transacted at Tahiti Tours in Papeete and some of the banks are able to handle American Express transactions as well. Socredo will not handle any transactions unless you have an account with them.

Currency Exchanges

The Banque de Tahiti and the Banque de Polynésie will exchange currency, and you will pay around 1.000 CFP for this service. You can also exchange your dollars for CFP at your hotel, which is sometimes necessary, but you will not receive as good a rate as you'll get at the bank. Banque de Tahiti is the only bank that still exchanges Travelers Checks, which the other banks consider too easy to counterfeit.

Credit Cards & Personal Checks

Visa is the most widely accepted credit card in the tourist islands of French Polynesia. The international class hotels, airlines, car rental agencies and some of the pearl shops will accept all major credit cards. Some restaurants and shops accept American Express, MasterCard and Diner's Club.

All the banks in Tahiti can help you with any questions regarding Visa and MasterCard. **Tahiti Tours**, *Tel. 54.02.55*, is the local representative for American Express services; **Socredo Bank**, *Tel. 41.51.23*, handles JCB; and **Banque de Polynésie**, *Tel. 46.66.66*, is the representative for Diner's Club. Many of the small hostels and pensions do not accept credit cards.

To secure a reservation in a hotel or hostel, you may send a personal check for the required deposit, but once you arrive, most businesses will not accept personal checks unless they are written on a local bank account. Some of the owners of art galleries and pearl shops will occasionally accept a personal account on a foreign bank if you are making a big purchase.

To get the best exchange rate for your dollar I recommend charging your hotel bill, restaurants, activities, pearls, gifts and all other purchases on your credit cards. You will need some local cash in your pocket for incidentals, and if you have CFP left over at the end of your stay, then apply it to your hotel bill.

MOVIES AND DVD/VIDEOS

The impact of movies showing the South Sea Islands has been so motivating that several people moved down here to live forever after seeing films such as *Tabu, Sadie Thompson* (also known as *Rain*), *Return to Paradise*, one or more versions of *Mutiny on the Bounty*, and the 1958 release of *South Pacific*, starring Mitzi Gaynor, John Kerr and Rosanno Brazzi.

I was once the tour guide for a group of Japanese tourists, who sang "Bali Hai," "Bloody Mary," "Happy Talk" and other songs from *South Pacific* all day, as we drove around the island of Tahiti. This movie was not made in Tahiti, nor did the book or film ever indicate that Tahiti, Moorea or Bora Bora was the setting, yet many people still assume otherwise. The former Bali Hai hotels on Moorea, Huahine and Raiatea, as well as the Club Bali Hai on Moorea, were named for the movie, not the other way round. The "Bali Hai" mountain on Moorea (Mou'a Roa or 'long mountain' in Tahitian) does not even resemble the "Bali-ha'i" of the original movie. Still, escapist dreams are very good for tourism and for the well being of the dreamer.

ABC Productions made a remake of *South Pacific* in 2000, which was shown on American TV and is now available in VHS and DVD. Although most of the movie was filmed at Port Douglas in Queensland, Australia, ABC Productions chose Opunohu Bay in Moorea for the scenes that include the spectacular beauty of the island of Bali-ha'i and the Mou'a Roa mountain. Thus, the legend became reality and the mountain named Bali Hai by the Hotel Bali Hai "boys" is now immortalized on film as the famous Bali-ha'i peak that beckons to the sailors across the sea. I can see the "Bali Hai" mountain from my home office in Urufara beside Opunohu Bay.

Movies to Set the Mood

Here is an abbreviated list of movies that were either filmed in Tahiti, or supposedly used stories or settings from Tahiti. Perhaps you can locate a few of these in your local video rental stores. And you, too, can dream of Tahiti and Her Islands.

White Shadows in the South Seas (1927), *The Pagan* (1928), *Tabu* (1931), *Never the Twain Shall Meet* (1931), *Bird of Paradise* (1932), *Mutiny on the Bounty* (1935) with Charles Laughton and Clark Gable, *Hurricane* (1937), *Aloma of the South Seas* (1941), *Son of Fury* (1942), *The Moon and Sixpence* (1941), *South of Tahiti* (1941), *The Tuttles of Tahiti* (1942), *Bird of Paradise* (1951), *Drums of Tahiti* (1953), *Cinerama South Sea Adventure* (1958), *Enchanted Island* (1958),

Mutiny on the Bounty (1962), Trevor Howard, Marlon Brando and Tarita Teriipaia, *Tiko and the Shark* (1963), *Donavan's Reef* (1963), *Hurricane* (1978). *Beyond the Reef*, also known as *The Boy and The Shark*, was filmed on Bora Bora by Dino de Laurentiis, immediately following the *Hurricane*, using some of the same decor. *The Bounty* (1984) was filmed in Moorea with Mel Gibson as Fletcher Christian and Anthony Hopkins as a more sympathetic Captain Bligh. *A Love Affair* (1994) was a Warner Brothers movie filmed in Moorea, starring Warren Beatty and Annette Bening.

The Stone Cutter is a 35-mm. film written, narrated and produced in 2001 by Moorea resident Aad van der Heyde. The 72-min. movie, based on a fairy tale, has an all-Tahitian cast and no dialogue and was filmed on Moorea. The DVD is now available at Tower Records, Blockbuster, Walmart and other video stores in the USA and Canada.

Tahiti's government-owned audiovisual company, Institut de la Communication Audiovisuelle (ICA), has a good selection of video films and TNTV programs. These include performances by Tahiti's best professional dance troupes, Heiva festivals, old movies made in Tahiti, and video films featuring various islands of French Polynesia. Contact them at *dca@mail.pf* or *www.ica.pf.*

Tahiti has several private companies that produce video films on all the islands, from the land, sea and sky. The most notable is Teva Sylvain's Pacific Promotion. The quality of the color is excellent and most, but not all, of these films are compatible with the American DVD/video systems. The Tahiti Tourisme office has a selection of promotional films for sale, and you'll find some commercial films at Odyssey, a big bookstore-music shop behind the Cathedral in downtown Papeete. Tahiti Music has closed its shop.

Media Shot in Tahiti

The beautiful island of Bora Bora and some of our other islands benefit from the promotion of American television programs that have been filmed in French Polynesia. In Aug. and Sept. 2011 Bora Bora was featured in 3 episodes of E!'s hit show, "Keeping Up With the Kardashians." During the filming Kris & Bruce Jenner and Kim Kardashian & Kris Humphries were lodged in $5,000 a night overwater Presidential Villas at the Hilton Bora Bora Nui Resort & Spa. These are the only 2-story overwater villas in French Polynesia. Two episodes of "Rudy Maxa's in French Polynesia" was due to air on PBS in the Fall of 2011. The trip took Rudy Maxa from Papeete to Bora Bora, Moorea, Fakarava and Hiva Oa on board the *Paul Gauguin*. Macy's 2011 Summer Fashion Book and "Journey" promotional campaign was filmed at the Bora Bora Pearl Beach Resort.

The 2010 Season Finals for "The Bachelorette" generated an enormous amount of publicity for Le Taha'a Island Resort & Spa, as well as the Hilton Bora Bora Nui Resort & Spa. "Couple's Retreat", starring Vince Vaughn, was a 2009 American comedy filmed at the glamorous St. Regis Resort & Spa in Bora Bora. For more productions, see *www.tahiti-tourisme.com/multimedia.*

POST OFFICE & COURIER SERVICES

You can leave your American stamps at home because they won't be acceptable for mailing your postcards overseas from any of the islands in French Polynesia. I say this because I've met some Americans who do bring their stamps to Tahiti, thinking they'll be saving money on postage. Each country has its own postal system, and in Tahiti this is an important source of revenue for the country.

The cost of mailing letters weighing less than 20 grams is 140 CFP to all international destinations except France and French Overseas Departments and Territories.

The main post office is on Boulevard Pomare in downtown Papeete. Services include stamps for letters and parcels, express delivery service, international telephone calls, telegrams, telex, fax, phone cards, and a philatelic center. Post offices also have Internet service for the public. There are post offices on all the inhabited islands of French Polynesia.

General Delivery mail service is available at all the post offices. On the envelope you should write the person's name, c/o Poste Restante, and the name of the island, and make sure that this is followed by French Polynesia.

B.P. = *bôite postale* **or post office box**

You will note that most of the addresses listed in this book show the initials B.P., which stand for *bôite postale*, the equivalent of post office box in the US. You can write P.O. Box or B.P. and your letter to French Polynesia will be processed

---

ADDRESSING A LETTER TO FRENCH POLYNESIA

When addressing a letter or package to anyone living in French Polynesia, it is necessary to include the name of the person, hotel or business, the B.P. (boite postale) number, the town or village where the post office is located, the island, the zip code if known, and the country. Example: **Jan Prince, B.P. 298, Maharepa, Moorea, 98728 French Polynesia.** On some of the islands the PK number is used instead of a B.P., which should always be followed by the name of the village and any other specifics you may have, then the name of the island and country. Example: **Jan Prince, Chez Monnier, PK 20,1, côté montagne, Papetoai, Moorea, French Polynesia 98729.**

Zip codes are a relatively recent addition to our postal services and many people still don't know what their zip code is. I haven't included the name of the country in the addresses given in this book, but each address should always include the name of the island, followed by French Polynesia.

with no problem.

PK = *poste kilometre*, the number of kilometers from the *mairie* or post office
Should you be given an address with a PK number instead of B.P., on the island of Tahiti, this indicates how many kilometers that person lives from the *mairie* (town hall) in Papeete. On other islands, such as Moorea, the 0-kilometer can be at the post office. PK stands for *poste kilometre*, and when you're driving around the Society Islands you will see the kilometer markers on the mountainside of the road. Look for the red-capped white painted stone or concrete markers with the kilometer number painted in black on two sides.

For Stamp Collectors

The **Philatelic Center** of the Offices Des Postes et Télécommunications (OPT) in Tahiti is located in the main post office, where you can buy sets of collector stamps, along with a stamped "first day" envelope. The themes for these beautiful stamps include the fruits, flowers, fishes and fauna of Polynesia, along with pictures of pretty *vahines*, fancy hats, outrigger sailing canoes, old *goelette* schooners and lovely seascapes. All the major post offices in the islands also carry selections of these collectors' items. You can also order stamps from home: Centre Philatélique de Polynésie Française, Office des Postes et Télécommunications, Mahina 98709 Tahiti, French Polynesia, *Tel. 689/41.43.35; Fax 689/45.25.86;* or through the Internet, *E-mail: phila@mail.opt.pf, www.tahiti-postoffice.com.*

Courier Services

DHL Worldwide Express, B.P. 62255, Faa'a, Tahiti, *Tel. 83.73.73, Fax 83.73.74,* is located in the Immeuble Tavararo, at PK 4.8 in Faa'a, a building on the right just before you reach the entrance leading to the Tahiti-Faa'a International Airport. Open Mon.-Thurs. 7:30am-4pm and on Fri. until 3pm. They do not close at lunch. They provide 4-day delivery service from Tahiti to the USA. They charge 6.156 CFP to ship documents weighing less than 500 grams from Tahiti to NY, and 8.775 CFP up to a kilo. A 1-kilo package is 10.113 CFP. No vanilla, liquids, flowers, pearls or jewelry can be shipped.

Federal Express (Fedex), *Tel. 45.36.45,* has an office in the Immeuble Polyfix building in Faaa. Open Mon.-Fri. from 7:30am-4:30pm. They charge 5.945 CFP for shipping documents and 6.709 CFP for a package weighing less than 1 kg. to the United States.

PUBLICATIONS ABOUT TAHITI
Newspapers & Magazines

Tahiti Beach Press is an English language magazine that is published monthly and distributed weekly for visitors. You will find it in hotels in Tahiti, Moorea, Huahine, Raiatea, Bora Bora and Rangiroa. You can also pick up a copy at Tahiti Tourist Bureau, the airports, ferry docks, car-rental agencies, and in the restaurants and businesses that advertise in the *Tahiti Beach Press*. A one-year subscription to this publication is $39.95 for airmail postage to the U.S. Address your subscription request to *Tahiti Beach Press*, B.P. 887, Papeete, Tahiti 98713, French Polynesia. *Tel. 689/42.68.50; tahitibeachpres@mail.pf; www.tahitibeachpress.com.*

La Dépêche de Tahiti and Les Nouvelles are Tahiti's daily French-language newspapers. The *International Herald Tribune, USA Today, Time* and *Newsweek* are sold at Le Kiosk in front of the Vaima Center on Boulevard Pomare and at La Maison de la Presse on Boulevard Pomare in Papeete. The copies you can find in Tahiti will not be the most current editions. You can also find newspapers and magazines on Moorea at Kina Booksellers, adjacent to the post office in Maharepa, at La Pirogue in Le Petit Village, and in the gift shops of the larger hotels. La Maison de la Presse in Bora Bora also carries magazines and newspapers.

Books

You may still find some of the reference books and novels in public libraries, specialized bookstores and secondhand shops. Free catalogs of publications may be requested from: **Bishop Museum Press**, Honolulu, HI, *www.bishopmuseum.org/ press*; **University of Hawaii Press**, *www.uhpress.hawaii.edu*. The **Book Bin**, in Corvallis and Salem OR, *www.bookbin.com;* **Mutual Publishing**, Honolulu, HI, *www.mutualpublishing.com.* **Pacific Island Books**; *www.pacificislandbooks.com.* **Serendipity Books**, *www.serendipitybooks.com.au.* **Jean-Louis Boglio** in Queensland, *www.maritimebooks.com.au* is a good source for books on the French territories of the Pacific. **Colin Hinchcliffe**, 12 Queens Staith Mews, York, YO1 1HH, England; *www.empirebooks.org.uk.* **Société des Océanistes Catalogue**, Musée de l'Homme, 75116, Paris, France; *www.oceanistes.org.*

You can also buy books about Tahiti and Her Islands, including this travel guide, online at *www.amazon.com* and *www.bn.com.*

Reference Books

Ancient Tahiti (Bulletin 48 Bernice P. Bishop Museum, Honolulu) by Teuira Henry, is based on material recorded by her grandfather, the Reverend J. M. Orsmond, who came to Moorea as a Protestant missionary in 1817. This is my primary reference book for the plants, flowers, trees, religion, culture and legends of the Society Islands. *Ancient Tahitian Society* (The University Press of Hawaii, Honolulu, 1974) is a 3-dome collection by Douglas L. Oliver. These scholarly studies are an excellent reference for the history and culture of the Tahitians.

Bengt Danielsson, a Swedish anthropologist and historian, who crossed the Pacific from Peru to the Tuamotus with Thor Heyerdahl aboard the *Kon-Tiki* raft in 1947, settled in Tahiti until his death in 1997, and published a wide variety of books. They include: *The Happy Island* (London, 1952), *Work and Life on Raroia* (Stockholm, 1955), *From Raft to Raft* (London, 1960), *Forgotten Islands of the South Seas, Love in the South Seas* (Mutual, 1986), *Tahiti-Circle Island Tour Guide* (Les Editions du Pacifique, 1976), and *Moruroa Mon Amour—the French Nuclear*

Tests in the Pacific (1977), by Bengt & Marie-Thérèse Danielsson.

Fatu-Hiva—Back to Nature (Penguin Books, 1976) is Thor Heyerdahl's account of the sojourn he and his wife undertook for more than a year on this lonely island in the Marquesas Archipelago, just before the outbreak of World War II. *History and Culture in the Society Islands* (Honolulu, 1930), *Marquesan Legends* (Honolulu, 1930), *Polynesian Religion* (Honolulu, 1927), and *The Native Culture in the Marquesas*, Honolulu, 1923), all by Craighill Handy.

Polynesian Researches (1829) by William Ellis, is a 2-volume work by a missionary who spent nearly 6 years in the South Sea Islands. *Polynesia's Sacred Isle* (Dodd, Mead & Company, New York, 1976), by Edward Dodd, is part of a 3-volume *Ring of Fire* set about the island of Raiatea.

Ra'ivavae—An expedition to the most fascinating and mysterious island in Polynesia (Doubleday & Company, Inc., New York, 1961). Author-anthropologist Donald Marshall describes life on Ra'ivavae, one of the Austral islands south of Tahiti.

Return to the Sea (John deGraff, Inc., New York, 1972), by William Albert Robinson, is the story of Robinson's 70-ft. brigantine *Varua*, in which he sailed to Tahiti in 1945, to settle in Paea, where his house still stands. Robinson used *Varua* as a floating laboratory to travel throughout the Pacific Islands, helping to eradicate the filariasis parasite transmitted by mosquitoes that causes elephantiasis.

Robert Suggs, an American archaeologist who did seminal work for the American Museum of Natural History of New York in the Marquesas Islands during the 1950s and 1960s, has written *The Island Civilizations of Polynesia* (New American Library, Mentor Books, New York, 1960), *Hidden Worlds of Polynesia* (Harcourt, Brace and World, New York, 1963) and *Marquesan Sexual Behavior* (Harcourt, Brace and World, New York, 1966), which are interesting reading and good reference books for anyone interested in the Marquesas Islands. His latest book is *Manuiota'a, Journal of a Voyage to the Marquesas Islands*, which was written with Burgl Lichtenstein and published by Pa'eke Press in 2001.

Many archaeologists and historians who specialize in the South Seas consider Patrick V. Kirch the expert authority on Polynesian pre-history. His works include *On the Road of the Winds: An Archaeological History of the Pacific Islands Before European Contact,* (University of California Press, May 2000), *The Lapita Peoples: Ancestors of the Oceanic World (The Peoples of South-East Asia and the Pacific),* (Blackwell Publishers, December 1996), *The Evolution of the Polynesian Chiefdoms* (Cambridge University Press, reprint edition August 1989), and *Historical Ecology in the Pacific Islands: Prehistoric Environment and Landscape Change* (co-authored with Terry L Hunt, Yale University Press, March 1997).

Tahiti, Island of Love by Robert Langdon is a popular account of Tahiti's history, and it's easy reading. *Tahitian Journal* (University of Minnesota Press, 1968) is a diary written by George Biddle between 1917 and 1922, along with paintings and drawings by the author. The setting is Tautira on the Tahiti-Iti peninsula, where Biddle lived among the Tahitians. *Tahitians—Mind & Experi-*

ence in the Society Islands (University of Chicago Press, 1973) by Robert I. Levy is an anthropologist's reference book for anthropologists, containing a wealth of cultural information. *The Journals of Captain James Cook* (Cambridge University, 1955, 1961, 1967), edited by J. C. Beaglehole, were published in 3 volumes.

Mystic Isles of the South Seas (Garden City Publishing Company, Inc., New York, 1921) by Frederick O'Brien, is based on his visit to Tahiti during one of three journeys he made to the South Seas. His story of Lovina Gooding, the colorful character who owned the Tiare Hotel in Papeete, is classic. O'Brien's *White Shadows in the South Seas* are about the Marquesas Islands, and *Atolls of the Sun* feature the Tuamotu Archipelago.

South Sea Idylls (James R. Osgood & Co., Boston – 1873), was written by Charles Warren Stoddard, about life in the Marquesas Islands during his visit in the 1800s. This is one you may have to search for in specialized shops. *Tahiti* (Grant Richards Ltd., London) by Tihoti, the Tahitianized name of George Calderon, who visited Tahiti in 1906. He was killed in the war in Gallipoli in 1915, and the book was completed from his notes. This is truly a collector's item and is illustrated with Calderon's drawings of the people he met while wandering around the island of Tahiti.

Tales of the South Pacific (1947) and *Return to Paradise* by James A. Michener are all-time classics by a very descriptive writer. *The Bounty Trilogy* (1932) by Charles Nordhoff and James Norman Hall comprises the three volumes of *Mutiny on the Bounty, Men Against the Sea* and *Pitcairn's Island*. *The Dark River* (1946) by Charles Nordhoff and James Norman Hall, is set in the wild and natural *fenua 'aihere*—the Land of Forests—of the Taiarapu peninsula on Tahiti-Iti. The descriptions of this savage beauty transport us right onto the scene of this lonely land. *The Hurricane* (1935) by Charles Nordhoff and James Norman Hall is an exciting story set in the Dangerous Archipelago of the Tuamotus. *Typee: a Real Romance of the South Seas; Omoo; a Narrative of Adventures in the South Seas, a Sequel to Typee and Marquesas Islands* by Herman Melville are all based on Melville's experiences in the islands.

A Tahitian and English Dictionary (Haere Po No Tahiti, 1985) with introductory remarks on the Polynesian language and a short grammar of the Tahitian dialect. This was first printed in 1851 at the London Missionary Society's Press. *Fa'atoro Parau* is a 684-page illustrated Tahitian/English-English/Tahitian dictionary written by Sven Wahlroos, Ph.D., also known as Taote Tivini.

Recent Novels, Island Tales & Modern Accounts

All of the following books can be ordered from *www.amazon.com*.

To Live in Paradise is an autobiography by Renée Roosevelt Denis, a long-time resident of Tahiti and Moorea. It takes us from Bali to Haiti to Tahiti and is filled with tales of adventure with her grandfather, André Roosevelt, her famous parents, her Tahitian husband and children, her years with Club Med in Moorea and her meetings with Marlon Brando on his private atoll in Tetiaroa.

Together Alone is a 2004 publication written by Ron Falconer, my former Scottish neighbor in Moorea. Ron tells the true story of his experiences sailing around the world and settling on Caroline Island, an uninhabited atoll in Kiribati, now known as Millennium Island. He spent almost 4 years on this desert island, along with his French wife and their 2 children who were under the age of 5 years. In this book you will meet some of the characters that still live on Moorea, Tahiti and Ahe, in the Tuamotu Islands.

Tahiti Blue by Alex W. duPrel, who lives in Moorea and publishes *Tahiti Pacifique Magazine*. *Breadfruit, Frangipani, and Tiare in Bloom*, 3 books by Célestine Hitiura Vaite, a young Tahitian woman who lives in Australia. *Varua Tupu*, a collection of stories and poems written by residents of French Polynesia that are translated into English. *The Old Broom Road Tahiti* edited by Fran Dieudonne and Ann Kuhns. *Omai, The Prince Who Never Was*, by Richard Connaughton. *Cocktails in Tahiti* by Richard Bondurant. *Teahupoo: Tahiti's Mythic Wave*, by Tim McKenna. *Tahiti: Polynesian Peasants and Proletarians*, by Ben R. Finney. *Tahiti of Yesteryear*, black and white photos by Stafford-Ames Morse. *Polynesian Interconnections: Samoa to Tahiti to Hawaii*, a scientific education book for young adults, by Peter Leiataua AhChing. *Ra'ivavae*, by Edmundo Edwards; and *Runaway to Tahiti*, a sailing story by Harry F. McIntyre.

Ila France Porcher, a Canadian artist who lived with her French husband in Tahiti and Moorea for several years, wrote *My Sunset Rendez-vous: Crisis in Tahiti*, published in 2010 by Strategic Book Group. First I bought the Kindle edition from *www.amazon.com*; then I ordered the 632-page paperback edition. This very sensitive and well-written book is one the most interesting and compelling books I have read in many years. It is the story of the author's years of nose-to-nose study of the blackfin sharks who lived in the lagoon near her house. Ila has dedicated her book to Martha, her favorite friend among the hundreds of sharks she sketched, photographed, fed and swam with during her years of interaction with the blackfins. When a company from Singapore began finning the sharks in 2003, Ila sought to protect them from this cruel and wasteful practice. Through her hard work, determination and with the help of many wildlife advocates, the sharks of Polynesia finally found protection in 2006.

Books Available in English in Tahiti
    Odyssey, behind the Cathedral, and **Archipels**, on rue des Remparts, stock some Polynesian books in English. The **Museum of Tahiti and Her Islands** and **Paul Gauguin Museum** in Papeari sell a few books and booklets in English.
    Paperback editions of books by James Norman Hall can be purchased at the **James Norman Hall House and Library** on the mountainside at PK 5.5 in Arue, *Tel. 50.01.61/50.01.60; www.jamesnormanhallhome.pf.*

RADIO

Radio Polynésie 1ère, also known as Radio Tahiti (FM 89, 89.6, 89.9, 91.8), is the official station, which operates with French and Tahitian broadcasts. There are also several other stations that broadcast in French and Tahitian. The most popular station for the young listeners is Radio NRJ, (FM 88.6), which plays the Top 40 hits. Just turn the dial from 88.6 to 106, until you find music to your liking. Don't rely on your radio for soft music for dreaming while you contemplate the clouds or classical music for a superb sunset. You'll have a hard time finding it.

RETIRING IN TAHITI, BUYING LAND OR HOUSES IN FRENCH POLYNESIA

If you have a dream of living in Tahiti and Her Islands, then I suggest that you come here on a visit first and get a feel of the place before you take the next step. Spending a relaxing vacation on a small island in the middle of the South Pacific is quite different from living so far removed from the choices and conveniences of life in a big modern country. The complexities are even more magnified if you do not speak or read and write French, which is the official language of French Polynesia.

In the past it was possible, although not easy, for foreigners to buy land or houses here, and some American couples have retired quite happily in these islands. Others divide their time between their homes in the States and their "fares" on Tahiti, Moorea, Huahine or wherever in the islands. They can have the best of both worlds. During the past few years, however, it has become increasingly difficult for non-Polynesians to buy property here. The government's approvals or denials are made on an individual basis.

Another option to actually buying the land is to take a long-term rental or a lease for 30 years or more. There are about 3 dozen real estate agencies in Tahiti that can answer your questions regarding the purchase of land, houses, villas, condos and apartments. Please do not contact me with questions about real estate. I have no experience with realtors and cannot tell you the correct price of land or houses.

SHOPPING

All the main tourist islands have souvenir shops and arts and crafts centers, where you can find hand-painted *pareos*, locally made T-shirts, carved Marquesan bowls, ceremonial spears, drums, ukuleles, tables and tikis, plus tapa bark paintings, Tahitian dancing costumes, basketry and woven hats, shell jewelry, mother-of-pearl creations, *tifaifai* bed covers, vanilla beans, Tahitian music and video films, *monoi* oil, soaps and perfumes, and beautiful Tahiti cultured pearls. See information in each Island chapter.

Tahiti Cultured Pearls

The emerald and turquoise lagoons of the Tuamotu and Gambier Islands of French Polynesia are a natural haven for the black-lipped oyster, the *Pinctada*

Margaritifera (*Cumingi variety*), which produces the world's finest black pearls. At the beginning of the 19th century the lagoons of Polynesia were filled with pearl oysters, also called *nacres*. From 1802-1940 the smoky gray mother-of-pearl shell was sought after as material for buttons. With the introduction of watertight diving glasses the divers could go deeper and deeper to find oysters of an acceptable size, as they exhausted the ready supply. With the advent of synthetic buttons and the depletion of accessible oysters in the lagoons, the adventurous days of the famous South Seas pearl divers ended after World War II, with controlled diving seasons continuing into the 1960s.

During the highlight of the pearl diving days there was an average of one pearl found among 15,000 oysters killed. The *Pinctada margaritifera* came very close to extinction, until researchers experimented with techniques to harvest the spawn of the *nacre* to collect the baby spats that would grow into oysters.

The first trials were made at culturing black pearls in the lagoon of Hikueru in 1962 and in Bora Bora in 1964, using the grafting technique that was invented in Japan in 1893, and refined by Mikimoto in the early 1900s. The first undersea pearl farm was established in the lagoon of Manihi in the 1970s, and the culturing of black pearls slowly grew from an isolated experiment into an industry. In 1976 the Gemological Institute of America (G.I.A.) gave formal recognition to the authentic character of the cultured pearls of Tahiti, and in 1989 the official designation of this gem became "Perle de Culture de Tahiti," the label decided upon by the *Confederation Internationale de la Bijouterie Joaillerie et Orfèverie* (CINJO). Just a few years ago there were about 900 more or less functioning pearl farms, essentially in the Tuamotu and Gambier atolls, with a few small pearl farms in the Society Islands of Huahine, Taha'a, Raiatea and Maupiti. That number has been greatly reduced today as the government has imposed more restrictions to improve the quality of the pearls.

The Tahiti cultured pearl is French Polynesia's biggest export item and the most sought after souvenir purchase made by visitors to Tahiti and Her Islands. Just a few years ago this pearl was virtually unknown in the United States, and today you can buy Tahitian pearl jewelry through the Home Shopper's Channel on TV, as well as on E-bay and several other websites on the Internet. Some of the pearl merchants in French Polynesia also have their own shopping websites.

When you shop for your pearls you can make a better choice if you know what to look for in choosing a quality pearl. The main criteria are size, shape, surface quality, luster and color.

Size: Although you can find a few Tahiti cultured pearls with a diameter of 7 or 7.5 millimeters, they usually start at 8 millimeters. The average size is 9.5-11.5 millimeters, and anything over 16.5 millimeters is very rare and often valuable. The bigger the pearl, the more it costs. The largest round Tahiti pearl on record is the Robert Wan, which measures 20.92 millimeters (over 13/16 of an inch) and weighs 12.5 grams. This beauty is on display at Robert Wan Pearl Museum in Papeete.

Shape: The shape or form of the pearl is judged by roundness and symmetry.

They are graded as round, semi-round, semi-baroque, baroque and circle. The round pearls are rare, therefore more expensive, but a drop or pear-shaped pearl that is perfectly symmetrical can be as expensive as a round pearl.

Surface quality: In 2001 the French Polynesia Assembly adopted measures that revised the classification of Tahiti's cultured pearls. The pearls are graded Gem, A, B, C, and D quality according to the number of flaws, pits, scratches and rays that blemish the surface.

A "Gem" quality pearl is extremely rare, as it is perfect, with no blemishes. "A" category pearls have no more than one imperfection or a group of localized imperfections concentrated over less than 10% of a pearl's surface. These pearls also have a very beautiful luster. "B" category pearls are defined as those with some imperfections "concentrated" over less than a third of their surface and with a beautiful or average luster. Instead of just having imperfections over less than a third of their surface, the imperfections must now be concentrated. The majority of pearls are "C" quality, those with "light concentrations" of imperfections over less than two-thirds of their surface and an average luster. Before the new ruling in 2001, the imperfections did not have to be lightly concentrated over less than two-thirds of a pearl's surface. "D" category pearls are pearls with "light" imperfections over more than two-thirds of their surface and "no deep imperfections;" or "D Category" pearls are those with deep concentrations "over less than half of their surface" and with "a soft luster." When I sold pearls I used to tell people that a "D" quality pearl looks like your dog has been chewing on it, leaving lots of tooth marks. Some pearl shops have started grading their pearls as AAA, AA, B+, B-, C+, C-, and so on.

Luster or orient: The most important criteria in judging the quality of a Tahiti cultured pearl are its luster or orient. Luster is the reflective quality or mirror-like shine on the pearl's surface. Orient is the iridescence or radiance from the inner-layer quality of the pearl. The thicker the mother-of-pearl (nacre) covering the nucleus inside the pearl, the more light it reflects. From the grafting to the harvesting of a pearl, a period of 18 to 24 months is necessary to achieve the desirable thickness that produces a fine quality pearl with a good luster and orient. The minimum nacre thickness required was formerly set at 0.6 millimeters, but the Tahitian government increased the minimum thickness to 0.8 millimeters, effective July 1, 2002. Reputable pearl dealers sell only those pearls with a nacre thickness of 1.5 to 2 millimeters, which can be determined by knowing the size of the nucleus that was grafted into the oyster and measuring the diameter of the finished pearl. No x-rays are needed for this information, but some of the more aggressive pearl dealers use gimmick advertising, claiming that you will receive an x-ray of the pearl you buy.

Color: After years of publicity campaigns to promote black pearls in overseas markets, including Elizabeth Taylor's "Black Pearl Perfume", the marketing experts decided to change the name from Tahitian black pearl to Tahiti cultured pearl. They feel this better describes the product and helps to eliminate confusion when people see that the pearls come in many colors. Black pearls are rarely black, which may come as a surprise to you, but they are called black pearls because they come from the black-lipped oyster.

The color of a Tahiti cultured pearl may range from white to lunar gray, with gradations of cream, peacock green, rainbow tints, aubergine (eggplant), blue, pink and golden. The color of the pearl depends on the color of the mantle or lip of the donor oyster used to graft into the producing oysters during the cultivating process. The grafter trims the outer mantle, the epithelium, of a donor oyster and cuts it into about 50 small pieces. Then he takes one tiny sliver of this living cell and transplants it into the gonad gland of a three-year old oyster, along with a nucleus, a small white round ball that is made from the shell of the Mississippi River mussel. The grafted oysters are then placed in wire nets and suspended from platforms under the lagoon, where they live for 18 to 24 months while the oyster is covering the nucleus with up to 16,000 micron-thin layers of mother-of-pearl, which is comprised of aragonite. The pearls that are produced from the slivers of mantle from one oyster will all be different, as there are no two pearls exactly alike.

Color is also affected by the mineral salts present in the water, the degree of salinity, the plankton that the oysters feed on, and the water temperature. Although some pearl sales people will tell you that the nuances of color do not affect the price of a pearl, they actually do. Pearls with a prevalence of white or gray are priced lower and pearls with rare hues, such as rainbow, aubergine, fly-wing green and shiny black, are more expensive.

Where to Buy Your Pearls

I have covered this subject in the individual Island chapters. My recommendation for choosing your pearl is to find a sales person you like and a pearl that "winks" at you. I sold pearls on a part-time basis in Moorea for five years, and I learned that certain pearls naturally attract the attention of the person who should be wearing them. They have their own magic, you know. In Moorea and the outer islands of the Societies and Tuamotus, some of the pearl shops are owned by people who have their own pearl farms and jewelers, or they own the shop, so there's no middle man to pay. Therefore, they can sell the pearls at a lower price than in Papeete. Plus you have the advantage of being able to walk outside the boutique and look at the pearls in the natural light, which truly brings out the beauty of this living jewel, especially in the early morning, at sunset time and on cloudy days. The same tactic won't work on a bright sunny day at noon.

People often ask if a pearl costs less when you buy it from a pearl farm, such as on Manihi, Rangiroa and Fakarava. The answer is yes, but the best pearls are usually shipped to Tahiti to be set into jewelry, or sold at auction to the big name buyers from overseas. Most of the smaller pearl farms belong to a co-operative that sells their pearls at an international auction held twice a year.

Get a receipt and a certificate of origin and authenticity for each pearl you buy. You can claim a tax refund (Value added Tax or VAT) for pearl jewelry you purchase in French Polynesia, but this exemption does not cover unset pearls or precious stones. See information under *Taxes* in this chapter. Keep in mind there is no import duty on Tahiti cultured pearls when you pass through US Customs on your way home.

You will probably be warned against buying pearls from street vendors. This notice is to protect you against the possibility of receiving stolen goods and buying inferior merchandise. Customs officials at the international airport in Tahiti now have powerful x-ray machines that can see everything in your suitcases, carry-on bags and containers. Some people have been caught trying to leave Tahiti with quantities of inferior quality black pearls that haven't been claimed as export items. Normally, these reject pearls are dumped into the ocean under controlled conditions.

Smuggling Tahiti cultured pearls out of the country will get you into a lot of expensive trouble. An American tourist heading for Honolulu was caught by the x-ray machine with 220 reject pearls. Another person with a ticket to Easter Island had a cooler filled with pork ribs and two raw ducks. The x-ray machine revealed two sacks of mediocre quality pearls stuffed inside the ducks. If you buy pearls in quantity you will have to present your pearls to the Service de la Perliculture to receive an export certificate, once they have determined the quality of the pearls you have purchased.

STAYING OUT OF TROUBLE

When you're packing your bags for a trip to Tahiti please do not include any drugs that are illegal in your country. They are also illegal here and the French Immigration and Customs authorities do not consider the importation of any stupifiants as a light matter. "Dope dogs" are trained to sniff out anything suspicious in your luggage when it's unloaded from the plane, and x-ray machines make it possible for the officials to see everything inside your suitcases. Heavy fines and jail sentences are a sure way to ruin a good vacation. Should you decide to risk it anyway, then please use discretion and do not give or sell any illegal drugs to a local person. This is a very small place and news travels amazingly fast via the "Coconut Radio."

When I first came from Houston, Texas, to Tahiti as a tourist in 1968 I remember that I was so afraid of theft that I took my handbag with me when I took a ride across the beautiful Bora Bora lagoon aboard an outrigger sailing canoe. Inside the bag were my passport, return plane tickets, traveler's checks, money, driver's license and other important papers. After I moved to Tahiti I learned to relax more and to leave the watch and handbag in my hotel room when I went out in a boat. Many times there were no doors to lock and no windows to close.

Due to the increasing hotel room thefts, most of the rooms are now more protected. Experience has taught me to lock the valuable papers inside the personal safe provided in the hotels. Many of the small family hotels or pensions now provide safes in their rooms. Be sure to lock the door to your room or bungalow and close the windows when you leave the room.

For police, dial 17.

The shops, boutiques and especially the *roulottes* (mobile diners) in Papeete have their share of thefts, and you should watch out for purse-snatchers in the city, which also includes pre-teenage girls. The delinquency problems are not so pronounced that you have to be afraid to take your eyes off your suitcase at the airport. Please don't let fear ruin your vacation, when you should be relaxed and carefree, but just be cautious and use the same common sense that you would use when traveling anywhere.

If you want to discover Papeete-by-night, stay in the main stream of lighted streets, sidewalk cafés and bars, where lots of people are on the streets. Avoid drunk Tahitians and you'll enjoy yourself more. A municipal police station is close to Papeete's municipal market, adjacent to the Loto (lottery) building on rue Edouard Ahnne. You can also dial 17 at any telephone booth without having to use a phone card and you will be connected to the *gendarmerie*, the French national police station.

Women Traveling Alone

If you're a woman traveling alone or with a girlfriend, then you should be aware that the crime rate in Tahiti is low compared to most cities anywhere in the world, but you should still use caution. Back in the 1970s and 1980s, in my pub-crawling days, I used to feel totally at ease running around in Papeete at any time of the night, popping into a nightclub here and there to see what was going on and to dance the night away. Experience has since taught me to heed my own advice and avoid drunk men and dark streets.

Another word to the wise for women alone: do not sunbathe in the nude or even topless on secluded beaches. Some of the Tahitian males see this as an open invitation, and they will pursue you, even if it takes all day. This warning needs to be heeded in the remote islands as well as in the more popular tourist islands.

A form of rape called *mafera* existed in these islands long before the Europeans arrived, not to be confused with *motoro*, the traditional courtship practice of a fellow slipping into his girlfriend's bed or onto her *peue* mat for consensual sex. The difference between the two customs depends on whether or not the girl agrees. If she does, then they are simply making love. If she objects and he does it anyway, then it is *mafera* or rape. Older Tahitian men on various islands claim that neither custom is practiced on their island today because the young people are better educated now. Others say that the *tane haere po* (guy who creeps around in the dark) is more interested in smoking his *pakalolo* (marijuana) than peeking or crawling through windows.

Tahitian men can be very charming and are always ready for sexual encounters. Many of them have told me that they do not notice whether a woman is young or old, fat or skinny, pretty or not. What they see is a woman. One of their favorite expressions is: "Age makes no difference. It's love that counts." What woman would want to argue with that philosophy? Should you succumb to the erotic mist that covers these tropical isles, then be sure that you provide your own protection against sexually transmitted diseases, which exist in Tahiti and Her Islands just as they do back home. Do not rely on your partner for anything except a brief moment of pleasure, which is not even guaranteed.

A woman visiting the islands by herself is often open to all kinds of experiences, which may include being invited to stay in the home of a Tahitian family. Should this happen to you, then chances are you'll create a lifelong friendship and wonderful memories. Just use your female intuition in making your decision.

TAX REFUNDS ON VALUE ADDED TAX (VAT)

If you are visiting French Polynesia for less than 6 months you can claim a tax refund (Value Added Tax or VAT) for eligible goods you take home. The value of purchases from any single store, tax included, must total at least 5.000 CFP. All the goods must be taken back with you, in your carry-on or checked luggage, when you leave French Polynesia. All tax refunds must be claimed within 6 months of purchasing the goods. Not all stores are participating in the tax-free program; therefore, prior to your purchase, verify this with the store concerned. If they do participate, you will have to prove that you are not a resident of French Polynesia and that you are 15 years old or over. Most people who apply for this tax refund have bought Tahiti cultured pearl jewelry of some value.

At the Tahiti-Faa'a International Airport you should present the 3 copies of the Retail Export Form, as well as the goods purchased under the tax-free program. Customs will retain the pink copy #3 and will stamp the other two copies. You need to return the stamped pink copy #2 to the store for your refund. The green copy #4 is for your records.

Do not forget to keep the goods with you at all times when you apply for Customs endorsement of the Retail Export Form at Tahiti-Faa'a International Airport. Customs officers may want to check them. Within a reasonable period of time, once you are back home, you should receive the amount of refunded tax from the store, credited directly to you credit card. Once you are back home, you may still claim the tax refund if the Retail Export Form has not been endorsed by Customs upon leaving French Polynesia. However, the process is time consuming and may be more expensive than the amount of tax refund that you are claiming.

There is no refund for tax you pay on food products and beverages, tobacco products, medicine, firearms, unset precious stones and pearls, cultural property, automobiles, motorcycles, boats, planes, as well as their parts and accessories. Nor is there a refund on taxes for purchases of a commercial nature (in such quantities that it is reasonable to believe they are not intended for your personal use).

TELEPHONES & TELECOMMUNICATIONS

Dial 4490 to reach a long-distance operator in Tahiti from any of the islands of French Polynesia. Dial 4499 for information on telephone numbers within

French Polynesia and for international information. The telephone numbers for government offices, hotels and other private businesses, as well as all home phone numbers, contain only 6 digits.

Public pay phones are easily identifiable booths of metal and glass, with black letters on a yellow background. There are several phone booths in the most populous islands, and you will probably even find a public phone in the most remote village of the Marquesas Islands, the Gambier Islands, or Rapa in the Austral Islands. Many small family hotels have a "point phone" for the convenience of their guests.

The pay phones and point phones require an OPTcard, (formerly called télécarte), a prepaid phone card that you can buy at any post office and in many shops and newsstands. These plastic cards are often decorated with some of the same scenes as the postage stamps, and are collectors' items as well. After dialing 44.10.00, you will reach the prepaid service, and a vocal machine will guide you in French, English and Tahitian. The OPTcards sell for 1.000 CFP, 2.000 CFP and 5.000 CFP. A digital readout on the phone states how many units remain on your card as you talk with your party.

You can also go to an Internet café and call home via Yahoo Messenger or Skype.

Calling Tahiti

When dialing direct to Tahiti and Her Islands, dial the proper International Access Code + 689 (Country Code) + the local number. The International Access Code if calling from the US is 011. Therefore, if you were calling me at the *Tahiti Beach Press*, you would dial 011+689+42.68.50. Some businesses and individuals are now listing their phone numbers as 426-850, rather than 42.68.50. The same codes apply when sending faxes. You can look up telephone or fax numbers in French Polynesia online at *www.annuaireopt.pf.*

Calling Home from Tahiti

To call overseas from anywhere in Tahiti and Her Islands, dial 00, then the country code (1 for the US and Canada), followed by the area code and phone number. You can dial direct from your hotel room or by going to the nearest post office, point phone or phone booth. In the post offices you give the postal clerk the number you are calling and she will direct you to one of the booths when your call is placed.

Automatic direct dial calls to Hawaii, the US mainland or Canada from Tahiti at any time during the day or night, Sun. and holidays included, cost 68 CFP per min. to a fixed phone and 85 CFP per min. to a mobile phone. This rate also applies to metropolitan France, New Zealand, New Caledonia, Australia, Japan and the Cook Islands. The cost of calling most European countries is 102/119 CFP per min. To call Mexico, South America, Asia or Eastern Europe, you will pay 137/153 CFP per min.

At the post office you can pay directly for the call, place a collect call or charge the call to your long-distance calling card if you live in the US or Canada. You can dial 1-800 numbers direct from French Polynesia, but these calls are billed at the rate of a normal overseas phone call.

Calling Within Tahiti and Her Islands

When calling from a fixed phone to a fixed phone, intra-island calls (on the same island) cost 34 CFP for every 4 min. Inter-island calls (such as from Tahiti to Huahine or Rangiroa to Nuku Hiva) cost 34 CFP for every 2 min. and 30 seconds between 6am-10pm, and 34 CFP for 5 min. between 10pm-6am. Just dial the 6-digit telephone number, as there are no area codes within French Polynesia.

Most individuals and business people now carry their cell phones wherever they go. These numbers have a prefix of 7, 2 or 3. If you are calling from a fixed telephone to a mobile vini (cell) phone, the local cost is 60 CFP per min. from 6am-6pm during the week, from Mon.-Fri. The price is reduced to 34 CFP per min. between 6pm-6am Mon.-Fri., and the 34 CFP per min. rate applies day and night on weekends and holidays. These rates include taxes.

Calling from Hotels

Whether you dial direct from your hotel room or go through the hotel switchboard, the surcharge can often double the cost of your international call.

Cellular or Mobile Phones

If you want to bring your own cell phone with you when you visit French Polynesia, make sure that it is an unblocked phone that can operate on a 900-megahertz system. If you have a Global System for Mobiles (GSM) phone you should buy a prepaid SIM card for French Polynesia. (Cellular Abroad in Santa Monica, CA., *Tel. 800/287-3020; www.cellularabroad.com* has these).

Or you can wait until you get to Tahiti and have a new Vini chip inserted in your cell phone at a post office or at one of the many shops that sell Vini phones. (Vini is the name of a small finch that lives in these islands and it is also the name used by the Tikiphone department of the telephone company). Save your original chip to put back in once you are on your way home. You will also be given a local phone number. This number can be reached from overseas by dialing 011+689 + your 6-digit mobile phone number. This phone number is valid for 180 days unless you replace it with your original chip.

The cost of this prepaid Vinicard is 1.000 CFP, which gives you a calling credit of 15 min. of local calls. The amount of credit for international calls depends on the destination and duration of the call. If you want to continue the service, make sure you buy a replacement card before the credit is used up. The recharge cards cost 500, 1.000, and 2.000 CFP.

You will also have voice mail service when you buy the Vini card. Be sure you specify that you want an English-speaking version; so that you will understand when she tells you how much credit you have left. Because your credit can be used up very quickly, it is best to buy a phone card (OPTcard) for long conversations. If you're on a yacht or somewhere else where a phone isn't available, then quickly call your family and friends on your cell phone and ask them to call you back.

For further information, contact the Tikiphone Vini Network at *www.opt.pf,* or *www.vini.pf.* Details of how to use the Vinicard and prices for international visitors are listed in English, and you can also check their map of network coverage. Once you arrive you can also get information at the Tikiphone Customer Service in Papeete in the OPT (*Office Postes Télécommunications*) building at the Pont de l'Est, *Tel. 689/48.13.13; Fax 689/48.72.48; www.vini.pf.* The Travel Insider, *www.thetravelinsider.info,* is also a good source for understanding the intricacies of preparing your cell phone for a trip to Tahiti.

Other options are to rent a cell phone in the US from RoadPost, *Tel. 888/290-1606 or 905/272-5665; www.roadpost.com.* In Tahiti you can buy a cell phone starting at 4.900 CFP plus the prepaid Vinicard. Call customer service *3950* for more information.

TELEVISION
In 2010 the French state's RFO Télé Polynésie changed its name to **Polynésie Première**. At the same time Tahiti switched from analog to digital television broadcasting, giving viewers free access to France Télévision's five public channels: France 2, France 3, France 4, France 5 and France Ô. Besides Polynésie 1ère, **Tahiti Nui Satellite (TNS)** provides 27 channels of cable service, including CNN and TCM in English. More programs will be available in early 2012, including one in HD. Most hotels in the Society Islands have access to the TNS programs, especially CNN, which is the version made for the Asia-Pacific region rather than the United States programs you are used to seeing. **Canal+** is another cable service.

Tahiti Nui Television **(TNTV)**, is a free channel owned by the French Polynesia government, with local news and other programs in French and Tahitian. Due to financial strain, the government has announced that TNTV will become a Web-TV and the government's on-line news agency **Tahiti Presse** will also be eliminated by the end of 2011. Supporters are currently signing a petition to keep Tahiti Presse online.

TIME
The island of Tahiti, as well as all the rest of the Society Islands, the Tuamotu Archipelago and the Austral Islands, is **10 hours behind Greenwich Mean Time.** These islands are in the same time zone as Hawaii, and are 2 hours behind US Pacific Standard Time and 5 hours behind US Eastern Standard Time. You'll add one-hour difference in time between Tahiti and the US when daylight saving time is in effect in the US. This means that between the first Sunday in April and the last Sunday in October, when it is noon in Tahiti, it is 6pm in New York and 3pm in Los Angeles; and between the last Sunday in October and the first Sunday in April, when it is noon in Tahiti, it is 5pm in New York and 2pm in Los Angeles.

The Gambier Islands, which form the most eastern archipelago in the territory, are an hour ahead of the rest of French Polynesia, and a half-hour ahead of the Marquesas Islands, which are a half-hour ahead of the Tuamotus, Societies and Australs. Therefore, when it is noon in Tahiti, it is 12:30pm in the Marquesas and 1pm in the Gambier Islands.

French Polynesia is east of the International Date Line, with the same date as the US. These islands are one day behind Tonga, Fiji, New Zealand and Australia. Tahiti is 20 hours behind Australian Eastern Standard Time.

TIPPING

The brochures published by the Tahiti Tourisme office state: "Tipping is not customary in Polynesian culture and is not expected. However, tipping is welcomed for exemplary service."

In 2008 when Tahiti's economic, social and cultural council (CESC) proposed adding 4% to all customer bills in restaurants, snacks, bars, cafés, hotels, family pensions, etc., the Ministry of Tourism agreed that it was time to get away from the no-tipping "taboo" that was invented. This obligatory 4% service charge was approved by the Assembly of French Polynesia as a means of increasing the salaries of hotel and restaurant employees, including those who have no direct contact with the public.

Most of the international class hotels and some restaurants in the tourist islands have a printed form that includes a place to add tips when you sign to your room or pay your bill. At the bottom of the menu in some restaurants you'll occasionally see a notice that tips are appreciated, or simply "Tips?". There may also be a "Tips Accepted" sign posted in some obvious place inside the restaurant.

In some tourist guides and brochures you will read that a Tahitian will be offended if you try to tip them. I have been tipping wait staff, bellmen and even polite and helpful taxi drivers for many years. If you want to tip someone, you will make him or her happy and you'll feel good about it yourself, because you are probably accustomed to tipping back home.

WEIGHTS & MEASURES

French Polynesia is on the metric system, but for your convenience, I have converted kilometers to miles, meters to feet, kilos to pounds, liters to gallons, and Celsius to Fahrenheit, where appropriate. To facilitate your own conversions, here are the equations:

1 meter = 3.28 feet	1 foot = 0.30 meters
1 meter = 1.09 yards	1 yard = 0.91 meters
1 square meter = 10.7639 square feet	1 square foot = 0.09 square meter
1 square meter = 1,1960 square yards	1 square yard = .08 square meter
1 hectare = 2.4710 acres	1 acre = .04 hectares

1 kilometer = .62 miles	1 mile = 1.61 kilometers
1 liter = 1.06 quarts	1 quart = 0.95 liters
4 liters = 1.06 gallons	1 gallon = 3.79 liters
1 kilogram = 2.20 pounds	1 pound = 0.45 kilograms

Temperature Guide

0° Celsius = 32° Fahrenheit	=	Freezing point of water
10° Celsius = 50° Fahrenheit	=	Winter in the Austral Islands
20° Celsius = 68° Fahrenheit	=	Comfortable for you, chilly for some of Tahiti's residents
30° Celsius = 86° Fahrenheit	=	Quite warm-almost hot
37° Celsius = 98.6 Fahrenheit	=	Normal body temperature
40° Celsius = 104° Fahrenheit	=	Heat wave conditions
100° Celsius = 212° Fahrenheit	=	Boiling point of water

8. Calendar of Events

There's something happening throughout the year in these Festive Islands of Tahiti. The calendar listed here only touches the highlights. For a more complete list of sports competitions, arts and crafts exhibits, dance shows, music festivals, golf challenges and raids on various islands, as well as Mahana Pae (Friday) celebrations in Papeete, contact: Tahiti Tourisme in Tahiti, *Tel. 689/50.57.00*; or in Los Angeles, *Tel. 310/414-8484; www.tahiti-tourisme.com/discover/events.asp.*

January
Tahiti "Tere Fa'ati". This celebration is held every other year on the first Sunday of the New Year. Following a tradition in Tahiti you will ride around the island in a flower decorated *le truck*, complete with a band of musicians playing the guitar, ukulele and "gut-bucket" bass, and singing "kaina" style Tahitian songs, while you rattle 2 spoons in a beer bottle and sing along until you're hoarse. There are normally about 10 *le trucks* and 300 people on this tour and you stop at several of the most beautiful natural sites to visit waterfalls, public gardens, parks and beaches, with a traditional Tahitian feast served on the beach in Tautira. This 12-hr. tour ends on the beach at Point Venus, with the election of a King and Queen and a fire dance is performed against the golden rays of the setting sun.
Chinese New Year. The Year of the Dragon begins on Jan. 23, 2012. Tahiti's Chinese community welcomes in the New Year of the Chinese horoscope, which takes place the end of Jan. or the first part of Feb. Celebrations include parades, the Dance of the Lion and Dragon, and open house on Cultural Day at the Chinese temple in the Mamao suburb of Papeete. There are traditional dances, martial arts demonstrations, food tasting, calligraphy, paintings and fortune telling. A Grand Ball with dinner and entertainment is also a highlight of this celebration. The colorful events end two weeks later with a Parade of Lanterns and a fireworks show over Papeete harbor. Contact: *sinitong@mail.pf; Tel. 689/42.74.18.*

February
FIFO Tahiti 9th edition
The International Oceanian Documentary Film Festival of Tahiti will take place on Feb. 6-12, 2012. The screenings, workshops, symposiums, meetings and digital encounters will be held at the Maison de la Culture. Contact: "Te Fare Tauhiti Nui" Cultural Center, *Tel. 689/54.45.44; www.fifotahiti.org.*
Moorea Marathon, 24th edition. A 42.195 km. scenic marathon is held each Feb. on the island of Moorea, with some 700 runners participating. A 21 km. Half-Marathon and a 6 km. Fun Run are also held in conjunction with the international event. First aid, refreshment and sponge stations are located every 2.5 km. and

Tahitian music along the route helps to keep the pace lively. A Pasta Party and Tahitian Feast with a dance show are organized each year as part of the activities. The 24th edition will be held on Sat., Feb. 18, 2012. Contact: Te Moorea Club Assoc., *Tel. 689/56.25.79; info@mooreaevents.org; www.mooreaevents.org.*

Moorea "Tere Fa'ati". This island tour around Moorea by "le truck" is similar to the circle island tour organized in Tahiti at the beginning of Jan., complete with Tahitian musicians, singers and dancers. The Moorea outing takes place in mid-Feb. on the Sun. following the Moorea Marathon. The tour stops at all the best sights and sites on the island.

Valentine's Day. Tahiti has long been known as the "Island of Love", so what better place to spend Feb. 14th, Valentine's Day! This world-famous holiday is celebrated by all romantics throughout Tahiti and Her Islands. Visitors will find entertainment in the streets of Papeete, and can admire the Valentine window decorations in the boutiques and shops. These usually include sexy French lingerie and lovely pearl jewelry, as well as boxes of chocolates and red roses. Be sure to reserve a table in advance at your favorite restaurant.

March

Missionaries Day. March 5 is a public holiday each year to commemorate the arrival of the first English Protestant Missionaries on Mar. 5, 1797. Reenactment ceremonies are held in the Evangelical churches and at some of the stadiums in the Society Islands and special activities are sometimes held in the Austral Islands. Contact: *Maohi Protestant Church, Tel. 689/46.06.00.*

National Women's Day. The women's associations from throughout French Polynesia meet in Papeete on Mar. 8 to discuss the Women's Condition. Songs, dances and skits punctuate these well-attended colorful and meaningful gatherings.

April

Tahiti Traditional Sports Championship. Polynesia's traditional sports include javelin throwing, stone lifting, coconut tree climbing, a fruit carrier's race, outrigger canoe paddling and other trials. Contact: Traditional Sports and Games Federation, *Tel. 689/50.31.11; enoch@mail.pf.*

Tifaifai Exhibition. Traditional Tahitian quilts and wall hangings are on display at the City Hall of Papeete in late April to early May. Contact: Dept. of Traditional Arts and Crafts, *Tel. 689/54.54.00;* lydia.laugeon-duchek@artisanat.gov.pf.

May

Raiatea International Billfish Tournament (RIBT) was held in May in 2011 and sometimes takes place in Feb. or Mar. in the Leeward Islands. Blue marlins weighing more than 500 kg. (1,010 lbs.) have been caught by Polynesian fishermen ever since Zane Grey discovered the Tahitian waters in the 1930s. The best-recorded catch so far was the 707 kg. (1,560-lb.) blue marlin caught by the Bonnet/

Tavanae team in 1986. Contact Dominique Goche, *Tel. 689/60.05.45; raiateabillfish@mail.pf; www.fishwbs.com.*

Tahiti Pearl Regatta. This international yachting regatta is held in the Leeward Islands, starting from Raiatea and sailing to Taha'a and Bora Bora. Trophies for each leg are awarded to the winners of various categories and each day ends with a Polynesian dinner and a dance show. Activities include diving, snorkeling, Polynesian games, outrigger canoes and Hobie cats. Participants usually fly to Tahiti and charter yachts in Raiatea. The next Tahiti Pearl Regatta will be held May 16-21, 2012. Contact: Pierre Dinard, *Tel. 689/79.54.44; tpr@mail.pf; www.tahitipearlregatta.org.pf.*

"Me" is celebrated during the month of May in each Maohi Protestant (Evangelical) parish throughout the islands. This religious festival is also a fundraising event and the money collected not only finances the churches' projects but is also given as aid to the underprivileged. At the end of the ceremony a huge feast is prepared by the church members to thank everyone for their generosity.

Miss Dragon is elected in Tahiti each year in May or June. The winner then represents Tahiti's Chinese community in the Miss Asia Pacific beauty pageant.

Festivities of the Pleiades "Matari'i i Raro. This is a cultural commemoration for the end of the cycle of abundance, and the beginning of the dry period when the land stops producing. This usually takes place in mid-May when the star group Pleiades disappears from sight for six months.

Taps Junior Surfing Competition. The 2-day competition for amateur surfers (16-18) takes place at the Taapuna Pass in Punaauia.

Taapuna Master Surfing. A 4-day surf competition in the Taapuna Pass with the best amateur and professional surfers and body-boarders. This competition is sometimes held in late Sept. Contact: Taapuna Surf Club, *Tel. 689/78.60.87; taapunamastertahiti@mail.pf; www.taapunasurf.pf.*

June
Dance Schools Heiva. Performances by the traditional dance schools are presented during the month of June at Place To'ata in Papeete at the beginning of the Heiva i Tahiti Festival.

Tahiti-Moorea Sailing Rendez-Vous. This is an annual sailing rally from the island of Tahiti (Papeete Yacht Harbor) to the island of Moorea (Vaiare Bay Marina), organized by Tahiti Tourisme. This voyage is meant to welcome and create a gathering of charter boat passengers, crews of cruising yachts stopping over in French Polynesia, sailing fans from the islands, the local population, as well as marine sport and tourism professionals. The 3-day festivities on Moorea include Polynesian traditional sports. Contact: Stephanie Betz, *Tel. 689/28.08.44; archipelagoes@mail.pf; www.portdepapeete.pf.*

Tahiti Toa Va'a. A 62-km. open ocean 6-paddler outrigger canoe race between Tautira and Papeete. Contact: Charles Maitere, *Tel. 689/73.16.99; cmaitere@cps.pf; www.tahiti-toavaa.com.*

Miss Tahiti Contest. Lovely and talented young *vahines* compete for the coveted title of Miss Tahiti during the first part of the month. The winner then goes to Paris to vie for the title of Miss France in December.

Anniversary of Internal Autonomy Day. June 29 commemorates the anniversary of a French parliamentary statue that was adopted in 1984, giving French Polynesia increased self-governing powers. The autonomists gather at the stele at the Pont de l'Est in Papeete, and the members of the independence party meet at the stele of Tavararo in Faaa to recall that Tahiti's Pomare V ceded his kingdom to the French protectorate on June 29, 1880.

July

Heiva i Tahiti. The Heiva Festival is the biggest event of the year. It begins in late June and continues for almost a month. There are daily activities, but the main events are scheduled at Place To'ata for Thurs.-Sun. each week, as well as in some of the other communes around the island. In addition to traditional Polynesian sports such as stone lifting, fruit carrier races, copra preparation and javelin throwing, Tahiti's competitions also include outrigger sailing canoe races, bicycle races and a beer race of restaurant and bar waiters. Outrigger paddle canoe races are held inside the lagoon and in the open ocean. The program includes a fire walking ceremony, song and dance competitions and all-night balls. Carnival type rides and fairground booths called *baraques* are set up in two locations, where the kids of all ages can munch popcorn and cotton candy and jump on the Ferris wheel, merry-go-round and other thrilling rides. Contact: Heiva Nui, *Tel. 689/50.31.00; com@heivanui.pf; www.heivanui.com.*

Heiva of the Artisans. The Rima'i Crafts Festival is a star attraction during the Heiva activities in Tahiti, with dozens of exhibits of handcrafts from all the island groups. Live concerts, song and dance competitions, Polynesian meals and various games accompany daily demonstrations of traditional arts and crafts. The Crafts Festival at the Salle Aorai Tini Hau in Pirae is a 3-week event and includes 100 or more arts and crafts stands. Contact: *Tel. 689/54.54.00; lydia.laugeon-duchek@artisanat.gov.pf.*

Tiurai i Papeete. As part of the Heiva i Tahiti festivities, the City Hall of Papeete presents a program of cultural activities such as arts and crafts exhibits, dance shows, traditional sports and games, and musical entertainment. Contact: Dept. of Traditional Arts and Crafts; *Tel. 689/54.54.00.*

Heiva Festivals on all the Islands. These festivals usually begin at the end of June and continue through July featuring traditional sports competitions, including fruit carriers' races, javelin throwing, copra chopping contests and outrigger canoe races, arts and crafts stands and games for children. The singing and dancing contests are the highlight of each festival. The communes of Faa'a and Papara on the island of Tahiti have active programs and some of the smaller communes also have dance shows and singing competitions. The most popular outer island festivals take place on Bora Bora, Raiatea, Taha'a and Huahine.

French Bastille Day Parade. France's National Holiday of July 14th is celebrated throughout French Polynesia with parades, parties and all night balls. Large hotels also organize special evenings for this event. A small military parade is staged on Blvd. Pomare along the Papeete waterfront, followed by a champagne party at the residence of the French High Commissioner. Medals and merit badges are presented to some of the outstanding citizens during this occasion. Horse races and bicycle races are usually scheduled for that afternoon.

Te Aito Va'a. Almost 300 individual outrigger canoe racers compete in this 10-km. course in Tahiti's Matavai Bay, which is held in mid-July. The 100 top Aito (Polynesian warrior) winners of this race qualify to paddle in the Super Aito competitions. Contact: Charles Maitere, *Tel. 689/73.16.99; cmaitere@cps.pf; www.superaito-tahiti.com.*

August

   Mini Heiva Festivals. The Intercontinental Tahiti Resort and Le Méridien invite the winners of the Heiva i Tahiti song and dance competitions to perform during a Mini Heiva Festival that is held over a period of 3 or more evenings. Gastronomic feasts are accompanied by first class entertainment.

   Te Vai Ari'i Marathon - Super Aito Individual Outrigger Canoe Channel Race. Along with the local paddlers who qualify for this most important individual va'a competition, foreign paddlers are invited to join the 4-leg race that is held over a 3-day period in mid-Aug. The first 3 legs take place in Tahiti and the 4th leg is a distance of 21.5 km. (13.3 mi.) starting at Moorea's Temae Beach and ending at Place To'ata in Tahiti. Women's competitions are also held. The winners receive cash prizes. Contact: Charles Maitere, *Tel. 689/73.16.99; cmaitere@cps.pf; www.superaito-tahiti.com.*

   Air Tahiti Nui/Von Zipper Trials. Qualifying surf competition in Teahupoo, Tahiti, prior to the famous Billabong Pro, which brings together foreign and local surf pros. Contact: Tahitian Surf Federation, *Tel. 689/43.86.93; fedesurf@live.fr; www.surf.pf.*

   Billabong Tahiti Pro Surfing Tournament. Each year during the month of Aug. the top 44 professional surfers in the world face the impressive rollers offshore Teahupoo on Tahiti-Iti. This event is part of the World Cup Tournament (WCT) of international surfing. Surfers and spectators enjoy the friendliness, warmth and local color provided by the residents of Teahupoo, the little village at the end of the road on the Tahiti-Iti peninsula, closest to the surfing action. Contact: Tahitian Surf Federation, *Tel. 689/43.86.93; fedesurf@live.fr; www.surf.pf.*

   Tahiti Agricultural Fair. Farmers from all 5 archipelagoes of the territory gather in Tahiti for this big event, which is held in late Aug. or early Sept. Along with stands of fruits, vegetables and flowers, there are displays of arts and crafts, Tahiti cultured pearls and other local products, as well as *ahima'a* (earth ovens) with Polynesian food.

September
World Tourism Day. All the tourist islands participate in this annual celebration in honor of our visitors. World Tourism Day is Sept. 27, and that entire week is filled with traditional singing and dancing shows, arts and crafts exhibits, and Polynesian bands playing music in the streets while hostesses distribute flowers to tourists. The airports, hotels, tourist offices, banks and other offices are decorated with flowers for the occasion. Contact: GIE Tahiti Tourisme; *Tel. 689/50.57.12; info@tahiti-tourisme.pf; www.tahiti-tourisme.pf.*

Raid Painapo. This annual event is held on the island of Moorea, with teams of 3 making a trail run of 20 km. across the Opunohu Valley, where pineapple (painapo) plantations slope down the mountainside. Amateurs run 8 km. Contact: Te Moorea Club Assoc., *Tel. 689/56.25.79; info@mooreaevents.org.*

October
Hawaiki Nui Va'a. This is a 4-day outrigger canoe race between the Leeward Islands of Huahine, Raiatea, Taha'a and Bora Bora, with more than 100 canoes and hundreds of paddlers. The finish line is at Matira Beach in Bora Bora. This is the ultimate va'a competition, which is held each year in Oct. Contact: *fivaa@ifrance.com; www.hawaikinuivaa.pf.*

Tahiti International Pro/Am Golf Open. This popular event is sponsored by the Australasia Pro Golf Association Tour (PGAT). It attracts golfers from many parts of the world, who compete for the cash prizes at the Olivier Breaud International Golf Course in Atimaono, on Tahiti's south coast of Papara. It is sometimes held in July, Aug. or Sept. Contact: Temauri Foster; *Tel. 689/77.72.33; tamauri.foster@mail.pf; www.pgatour.com.*

November
All Saints Day. Nov. 1 is a public holiday. The graves in the cemeteries and in the yards of private homes are weeded and cleaned in preparation for this annual event. Flower stands are set up all around the island and families decorate the graves with dozens of fresh and plastic flowers. That night the cemeteries are lighted with candles as the families sing hymns and recite prayers for their departed loved ones.

Tattoonesia. This is a 4-day gathering of tattoo artists from all the archipelagoes of Tahiti and Her Islands, as well as overseas participants. Contests are held in Tahiti for the best tribal tattoos and the best modern designs. This event is usually held in the early part of Nov. Contact: Jerome Levy, *Tel. 689/29.27.25; info@tahitievent.com; www.tattoonesia.com.*

Festivities of the Pleiades "Matari'i i Nia". This cultural celebration has become an annual event that lasts for a month in Tahiti, from mid-Nov. to mid-Dec. The highlight of the festivities takes place when the star group Pleiades reappears in the sky, marking the return of the season of abundance, when the produce of the earth and sea abound. Cultural re-enactments, songs and dances are performed during this month of welcoming.

Matari'i Toa Nui. Traditional sports and games in the Paofai Gardens and in the Museum of Tahiti and Her Islands – Te Fare Manaha in Punaauia. Contact: Traditional Sports and Games Federation, *Tel. 689/50.31.11; enoch@mail.pf.*
Trail Rotui. Individual running competition for amateurs (14 km. and 7 km.) in Opunohu Valley on Moorea. Contact: Te Moorea Club Assoc., *Tel. 689/56.25.79; info@mooreaevents.org; www.mooreaevents.org.*
Monoi Here. This annual sales exhibit and showing of documentary films promoting Monoi products is held at the Maison de la Culture. Contact: Institut du Monoi, *Tel. 689/43.18.49; monoi.de.tahiti@mail.pf.*

December
Tiare Tahiti Festival. Tahiti's national flower, the fragrant white Tiare Tahiti (*gardenia taitensis*), is honored during this 3-day annual event that usually takes place during the first week of Dec. On the major tourist islands the airports, hotels, some restaurants, tourist offices, post offices and banks are decorated with garlands of Tiare Tahiti blossoms, and Tiare Tahiti flowers are presented to tourists on the streets. A public ball is also held to pay tribute to this lovely flower. Contact: Tahitian Women Grouping Solidarity, *Tel. 689/78.87.42; gsft@mail.pf.*
Hura Tapairu. Annual dance competition held in early Dec. at the Maison de la Culture (cultural center). The 4-day event presents small groups of dancers and also includes individual dancers competing for prizes. Contact: Te Fare Tauhiti Nui, *Tel. 689/54.45.44; communication@maisondelaculture.pf; www.maisondelaculture.pf.*
Christmas Fair. This annual event features the arts and crafts of more than 100 artisan groups who display their creations at the Salle Aorai Tini Hau in Pirae. Exhibits range from bone, wood or stone sculptures to basket-weaving, jewelry, tifaifai quilts, pareos and clothing. Contact: Dept. of Traditional Arts and Crafts; *Tel. 689/54.54.00; lydia.laugeon-duchek@artisanat.gov.pf.*
Christmas in Tahiti. Santa Claus or "Papa Noel" arrives in Tahiti by outrigger canoe, jet ski, helicopter or horse, accompanied by Polynesian musicians as he distributes candies to the children in Papeete. The streets and city halls of each commune are decorated and Christmas villages in Papeete and Faa'a have rides and games for the children. The major hotels in the tourist islands and several restaurants offer special menus and entertainment on Christmas Eve and Christmas Day, which also include roast turkey with chestnut dressing. And the perfect French wine to accompany the meal, of course!
New Year's Eve. St. Sylvestre is celebrated with more feasting, either at private parties or in restaurants featuring special menus and entertainment. This banquet usually includes fresh oysters, smoked salmon, shrimp, crab, lobster and other seafood, raw and cooked fish, foie gras, various cold cuts and salads, roast beef, lamb or duck, smoked turkey, pheasant or wild game, depending on which restaurant you choose. Plus there are rich desserts, cheese platters and lots of French champagne to toast in the New Year. If you are dancing the night away, some of the hotel restaurants serve French onion soup as a finale at the end of the soirée.

9. Taking the Kids

Tahiti and Her Islands are a haven for the young! So bring your kids and let them enjoy the attention they'll receive from the friendly Polynesians, who adore babies and little children. If they're still young enough to be picked up easily, that will be even more fun for the child and the Tahitians, who love to kiss and hug little people, little puppies and anything that is still a baby. When they get older and bigger, that's another story for the animals and local kids, but the Tahitians will still treat visiting children with genuine warmth and patience.

International airline companies and Air Tahiti give preferential seating to families traveling with children. Kids generally pay only half the adult fare on international airline routings. Air Tahiti gives at least a 50% discount to children between 2-11 years and the fare for babies less than 2 years is 10% of the adult fare. Most of the hotels, hostels, guest houses and pensions will let kids younger than 11-12 years stay for free if sharing a room with their parents, or they only charge for an extra bed. Some of the international class hotels have extended the free accommodations to the age of 15.

Your travel agent can make all the reservations for you, securing spacious bulkhead seats on airlines and determining which flights are least crowded. They can also seek out the best deals on lodging and meals.

When traveling with children of any age, make sure their vaccinations are up to date and bring their health records and any special medications they made need. In the event of an emergency, there are medical facilities on all the islands. **The new government- operated Taaone Hospital in Tahiti has a modern pediatric department.** Make sure that your repatriation insurance also covers your child.

Don't show up hungry at the airport. Feed yourself and all the family before you go so that you are not waiting in line at the limited number of airport eateries. Also, bring food for you and your family to eat on the plane should you be stuck on the tarmac.

Traveling with Babies

Hopefully, you'll be at least two people to bring a baby on a long airplane flight to Tahiti. Bring a suitcase filled with baby supplies, including a sufficient supply of disposable diapers, food, light clothes that cover the whole body, a sun hat, favorite toys, Q-Tips, baby wipes, a first aid kit with sun block, mosquito repellent, baby aspirin, thermometer and a treatment for diarrhea. The supermarkets and small magasin stores carry fresh or powdered whole milk, bottled mineral water, dry cereals that must be cooked, canned fruits and jars of baby food, but you'll pay much more for these items in Tahiti than you will back home. Bring a stroller with sunshade or cloth carrier for your baby, or a car seat-sleeper combination. Only a few of the hotels can provide cribs and high chairs for babies.

Toddlers & Little Tykes

Along with the shorts, T-shirts, sweater, waterproof shoes and sun hat you pack for your small children, you should also include some of their favorite snacks, books and toys. If they're big enough to snorkel, pack their own snorkel gear, plus a bucket and shovel and inflatable beach ball. In their first-aid kit be sure to include some preventive drops for swimmer's ear. Cleanse and treat any minor cuts or abrasions immediately to prevent staph infection. Make sure they're protected from the hot tropical sun and mosquitoes and that they drink a sufficient amount of water throughout the day.

Juniors & Adolescents

The warm climate, natural setting, aquatic games and lack of poisonous creatures make Tahiti and Her Islands a paradise for children of all ages. Many of the hotels have swimming pools and beach activities, such as outrigger paddle canoes, pedal boats and windsurf boards. Swimming or playing in the reef-protected lagoon waters is also relatively safe, as long as you keep an eye on the little ones, because there are no lifeguards. Children enjoy lagoon excursions, picnics on the motu, feeding the fish, rays and sharks, sailing and other water activities. Some of the scuba diving centers will accept divers as young as four years. Some of the hotels and guesthouses provide bicycles for their guests, or you can rent them on most of the islands.

McDonald's is located in downtown Papeete and there is another outlet next to the Marina Taina in Punaauia, which has a pool and playground equipment for children. A new McDonald's outlet has opened in the Arue commune of Tahiti, and yet another one opened in 2011 in Taravao on the isthmus of Tahiti Nui and Tahiti Iti. On several of the islands you'll find hamburgers, sandwiches, pizzas, tacos, pancakes and crêpes. All the food stores carry some American snacks and good ice cream. Most of the hotels have children's menus and give special discount rates for buffets and Tahitian feasts for children. The more luxurious hotels have room service, which can be convenient for families, and several of the moderate range hotels and family pensions provide kitchen facilities.

Babysitters

Hotels that welcome children generally have no problem arranging babysitters. If you're staying in a pension or guesthouse, ask your hostess to find a babysitter for you. Make sure they speak some English.

Travel Agents Specializing in Family Travel

RASCALS IN PARADISE, *500 Sansome St., Suite 601, San Francisco, CA 94111, Tel. 415/273.2224; Fax 415/433-3354; www.rascalsinparadise.com.* They specialize in customized vacations for parents and/or grandparents who want to travel with their children or grandchildren. Their South Pacific tours for families with kids can include accommodations at a carefully selected resort, so that you can relax and enjoy some "down time" with the little ones. After your trip you can post your photos and comments online at: kids@rascalsinparadise.com. **CROSSROADS TRAVEL, INC.** *11400 W. Huguenot Rd., Suite 114, Midlothian, VA 23113; Tel. 804/794-7700; 800/322-0224; uschi@crttravel.com; www.crttravel.com.* Owner Uschi Helfrich has a special interest in family travel. She visits Tahiti and Her Islands several times a year to gather information that helps in organizing the best programs for her clients, and she knows which resort hotels are the most "kid friendly." Crossroads Travel is a member of Virtuoso.

Check the website for Tahiti Tourism North America: *www.tahiti-tourisme.com.* They list the travel agents and tour operators who promote Family Vacation Deals. These include programs that offer free air, hotel and meals for children.

Special Family Activities at Hotels
FOUR SEASONS RESORT BORA BORA. *B.P. 547, Vaitape, Bora Bora 98730. Tel. 689/60.31.30; www.fourseasons.com/borabora. Reservations: USA and Canada 1 800/819-5053.* This family friendly resort is spacious and well planned so that kids of any age will not have an impact on the honeymooners or non-family travelers. They have a Kids Club (Tamarii Club) for children 5-12 years old that includes an indoor area with a playroom, video games and a room for resting. The outdoor area features a playground and a shallow children's splash pad close to the beach and restaurants. Their complimentary Kids For All Seasons supervised program for children 5-12 years old includes exercise, arts and crafts, water-based games and creative play. The majority of the activities take place outdoors, with children returning to the Tamarii Club for snacks at the end of an action-packed day.

Children's amenities provided by Four Seasons include welcome treats, child-size bathrobes and slippers, children's menus, items to childproof guest rooms, complimentary cribs, use of stroller, high chair, playpen, bottles and toys. For the pool and beach there are toys and a toy cart, "little swimmers" diapers, sunblock sticks, woven sun hats, fishing-net activities, and water-balloon activities. Baby-sitting can be arranged for children 2-years or older.

Older children will enjoy the Young Adults Center located on Chill Island. Guests from 13-17 years of age receive a welcome kit upon check-in that includes a weekly activity schedule. Chill Island has a private beach and is equipped with water games and snorkeling equipment, offering an opportunity for safe fun in the Resort's lagoon. The Center is located near the tennis court, and also features foosball, table tennis, a badminton net and a beach volleyball court. The indoor game room and lounge are furnished with a pool table, library, television, video equipment and Internet café.

Organized and operated by the Resort's recreation team, Chill Island takes advantage of the resources available on the island and highlights a variety of youth-oriented activities, including: personal fitness programs; swimming, kayaking, stand-up paddle board and windsurfing races, WaveRunner rides, snorkeling, introductory dive lesson (only available during high season), kite-surfing lessons, table tennis tournaments, beach volleyball matches, movies, BBQs, and foam parties in the evenings, underwater treasure hunts, arts and crafts, triathlons including swimming, boating and volleyball, interactive cooking lessons with the Resort's chef (only available during high season), coral nursery grafting with a marine research officer, and marine biology presentations.

INTERCONTINENTAL MOOREA RESORT & SPA. *B.P. 1019, Tiahura, Moorea 98729. Tel. 689/55.19.19, Fax 689/55.19.55; reservationspf@interconti.com; www.moorea.interconti.com.* The Moorea Dolphin Center is located at the Intercontinental Moorea Resort & Spa. This is a big attraction for children, who delight in their interactive sessions with the trained bottlenose dolphins that live inside a lagoon park. There are programs designed for children in different age groups. The whole family will also enjoy a visit to the Sea Turtle Care Center and Nursery on the IC Moorea Resort property.

LE MÉRIDIEN BORA BORA. *B.P. 190, Bora Bora 98730. Tel. 689/ 60.51.51; Fax 689/60.51.52. Reservations 689/47.07.29; Fax 689/47.07.28; rez@lemeridien-tahiti.pf; www.lemeridien.com/borabora.* This family friendly resort has added a fully equipped children's playground. They provide small snorkeling gear for kids from 2 years old, small cha-cha sailboats and a small windsurf board that an 8-year old can handle. An exclusive treat for guests of all ages at Le Méridien is to visit the Turtle Observatory on the hotel property and watch dozens of baby sea turtles being fed at 10:30 each morning. A new Ecological Center has been built near the Turtle Sanctuary, and a French biologist explains that the hawksbill and green sea turtle eggs are hatched on the hotel's beach and the turtles are released from the nursery into the ocean a year later, then tracked by satellite as part of an environmental program. You can even swim with the turtles inside the clear waters of a *hoa* channel that flows from the ocean into the protected lagoon. You can also become a godparent to one of the turtles and receive news of its progress.

PEARL RESORTS. *Reservations: Tel. 689/50.84.45; Fax 689/43.17.86; res@spmhotels.pf; www.spmhotels.pf.* The Pearl Resorts are especially attentive to the needs of children, providing cribs, rollaway beds and baby-sitting services in all their hotels. The Pearl Resorts in Moorea, Bora Bora, Manihi and Tikehau also provide a welcome basket of candies, plus beach toys (rake, spade, bucket) for the 3-8 year olds, and board games for the 8-12 year olds. They have life jackets and snorkeling gear for children, DVD with cartoons for kids, special children's menus or child's portions of food. In Manihi and Tikehau children are also given drawing kits at the dining table. At the Bora Bora Pearl Beach Resort there are bathroom amenities for kids, including slippers and bathrobe. Some of the Pearl Resorts also offer ukulele, palm frond weaving and Tahitian dance classes for their young guests. The Bora Bora Pearl Beach Resort and Manihi Pearl Resort have a mini-golf course, and there is even a movie theatre at the Pearl Resort in Bora Bora. The Pearl Beach Resort in Bora Bora also has the To'a Nui Coral nursery and Coral Fare that is educational and interesting for all family members.

In all the Pearl Resorts the accommodations are free for children less than 16 years old if they are sharing a room with parents, and according to the existing bedding configuration. They pay 50% on transfers and meals (not including beverages) ordered from the kids' menu.

ST REGIS RESORT BORA BORA CREATIVITY CLUB. *B.P. 506, Bora Bora, 98730. Tel. 689/60.78.88; Fax 689/60.78.60; www.stregis.com/borabora; www.starwoodhotels.com/stregis.* St. Regis Resort, Bora Bora has a Kids Creativity Club with facilities built especially for their littlest guests. These include a secluded beach and an indoor play area for children between 5-12 years of age. From discovering the surrounding nature to learning about Polynesian craftsmanship, kids will be overjoyed by the diverse indoor and outdoor activities.

They can participate in the complimentary St. Regis Resort activities, such as beach games, building sand castles, swimming with the marine life in the protected lagoonarium, snorkeling (free equipment), paddling a kayak or outrigger canoe, Hobie cat sailing, windsurfing and paddle boating. They can also play tennis (complimentary equipment). With a responsible adult, children can participate in paid activities such as Aqua Safari, a Bora Bora lagoon cruise, deep sea fishing, jeep safari, jet ski lagoon circle, Lagoonarium, motu picnic, motu private barbecue, submarine, water-skiing and wakeboarding. For guests with children the St. Regis Resort provides cribs and child-sized bathrobes in the rooms, and in the restaurants there are high chairs and special dishes for children. A selection of children-friendly movies and in-room toys are at your disposal by simply calling your St. Regis Butler. With a 24-hour notice, they can arrange reliable babysitting services for your little ones. A fee applies to babysitting, and this service is available only for children one year old and over.

House, Boat & Car Packages

Another good idea for family travel in Tahiti and Her Islands is to rent a self-contained house or villa where you can do your own cooking. I have listed several lodgings on most of the islands that include kitchen facilities. Have a look at the Huahine chapter and see the choices for renting a villa with a boat and car included in the package price. Some of the facilities even include a washing machine on the premises.

10. Food & Drink

I've listened to big beefy American men comparing prices while standing in a hotel swimming pool beside Moorea's Cook's Bay, totally ignoring the incredible beauty of the mountains and lagoon, as they talked about how they managed to cut costs on their trip to Moorea. One of them bragged that he had collected free packages of coffee, tea, sugar, cream, mustard, ketchup, mayonnaise, crackers and other condiments from the fast food outlets in his town, and had brought them along.

Others described all the snacks, soft drinks and alcohol they had packed into a cooler for the trip. These people were not eating in the hotel or nearby restaurants. They spent their week surviving on processed snack foods they brought with them, plus the crusty French *baguette* bread, luncheon meats, cheese and crackers bought at the nearest food store. Although the hotel had (it is now closed) a no-food-in-the-room policy, it was usually ignored, and some of the guests were unwilling to spend 200 CFP for a cup of coffee in the hotel restaurant.

If you decide to travel on a very tight budget, try not to let the high prices occupy so much of your attention that you cannot even enjoy these magnificent islands. You may want to have a look in the larger supermarkets in Tahiti, where there are deli counters with a varied selection of prepared foods. The smaller *magasins* in Tahiti and the outer islands sell tasty take-away meals of rice with chicken, meat or fish, and containers of *poisson cru* for about 1.000 CFP. The mobile diners, *les roulottes*, are found in most of the islands, where you can have a good meal for about 1.200 CFP. There are also small, inexpensive restaurant/ snacks, which are listed under *Where to Eat* for each island.

You can buy a soft drink for 135 CFP in the supermarket and you'll pay around 220 CFP at a few of the *roulottes* and snack bars, but this same canned drink will cost you up to 700 CFP in a hotel bar. Tahiti's favorite locally brewed beer is Hinano, which sells for 211 CFP for a 33 cl. can in grocery stores, and from 450-700 CFP in restaurants and bars. Some restaurants serve *vin ordinaire* (table wine) by the carafe, and an acceptable quality of Bordeaux can be purchased at the grocery stores for around 1.300-1.500 CFP a bottle.

For most of us, one of the greatest pleasures of traveling to a foreign country is to sample the local cuisine. If your budget allows a few meals in a restaurant while you're visiting Tahiti, Moorea, Bora Bora or any of the other islands in French Polynesia, then chances are you will have a superb meal.

La Nouvelle Cuisine Tahitienne

The hotels and restaurants in Tahiti have earned a reputation among gourmet visitors for serving choice cuisine. The chefs have united the flavors of Europe and

---

ORDERING FROM A FRENCH MENU

Helpful hints in ordering from a French menu should include a translation of how you want your steak cooked.

- **Bleu** = rare
- **Saignant** = medium-rare
- **à Point** = medium
- **Bien Cuit** = well done.

If you have the audacity to order a steak *bien cuit*, however, most French chefs will send it out to you when it is about half-cooked.

---

the Orient, spiked with a fresh tropical island accent. Whether he came from France, Switzerland, Italy, South America or Asia, each newcomer brought his little sprig of thyme, his chili pepper, soybean or ginger, perhaps to ward off the effects of home sickness in a foreign land.

Culinary choices feature French *haute cuisine*, 7-course Imperial dinners from the provinces of China, Vietnamese *nems*, Italian pasta, Algerian *couscous*, Spanish *paella*, spicy West Indian specialties and Alsatian *choucroute*. These imaginative and creative chefs have also introduced a *nouvelle cuisine Tahitienne* that is a combination of the traditional recipes of their own home countries and the fresh bounty of the Polynesian waters and fruit orchards. Dishes may include fresh local snapper infused with vanilla sauce, a lagoon *bouillabaisse*, reef clams in garlic butter, sautéed crab with ginger, *varo* with champagne and cream, roast duck with papaya or chicken drumsticks with *fafa* and taro.

To accompany these memorable meals are fine French wines and champagnes, locally brewed beer, or a selection of imported beers and wines. Most of the bars bill themselves as a "Bar Americaine" and serve mixed cocktails. Freshly squeezed orange, grapefruit or pineapple juices are sometimes available, or you will be served fruit juices from the cartons of the Moorea Fruit Juice Factory and Distillery. Perrier and a wide variety of boutique carbonated waters are stocked, as well as the most popular soda pops, sometimes including carbonated diet drinks. Bottled waters from Tahiti and France are also served, and can cost as much as 850 CFP for a bottle of sparkling water such as San Benedetto, while in the supermarkets it is only 180 CFP.

Snack Bars, Fast Food, Salons de Thè & Patisseries

You'll find an abundance of small restaurants in Tahiti and Her Islands that are advertised as Snacks or Restaurant/Snacks. Most of these places are clean and serve daily specials of local style home cooking. The food is usually delicious and inexpensive. The choices often include *poisson cru* with coconut milk, beef or lamb stew, an assortment of curry dishes, fresh lagoon fish, chicken and vegetables, prawns in garlic sauce, pork and taro, chow mein, or *ma'a tinito haricots rouge*, which is a Chinese dish of red beans, macaroni, pork or chicken, Chinese vermicelli noodles and a few more good things.

Fast foods have definitely arrived on the scene in Tahiti, with international and local style hamburger stands popping up all over the island. McDonald's has a prime site in downtown Papeete. There is also a McDonald's adjacent to Marina Taina in Punaauia on Tahiti's west coast, which replaced a Kentucky Fried Chicken site that closed soon after opening. There is now a McDonald's in Arue and another outlet in Taravao. The McDonald's counter at the Tahiti-Faa'a Airport sells only muffins, soft drinks and ice cream. These days you hardly have to pause at all in your shopping to have a bite to eat. You can walk up to a sidewalk food stand and order a *casse-croûte*, a ham and cheese *croissant*, a small pizza or a *panini* sandwich. Or you can beat the heat of the Papeete streets while enjoying some of the world's best ice cream.

Salons de thè serve a variety of teas and *infusions*, as well as *espressos* and vanilla flavored coffee from Pacific plantations. *Patisseries* provide people watching in air-conditioned comfort while nibbling on your choice of flaky pastries.

Les Roulottes

Les roulottes (not roulettes) are mobile diners (roach coaches) that set up shop each evening near the cruise ship dock at Place Vaiete on the Papeete waterfront. They serve hot meals until the wee hours of the morning. These colorful food vans provide good, fast food at reasonable prices, as well as a barstool or a table with chairs, where you can sit and watch the waterfront scene of Papeete-by-night.

You can order barbecue steaks, chicken and *brochettes* (shish kabob), served with French fries, *poisson cru*, or *salade russe*, which is potato salad with beets. Specialty diners serve pizza cooked in a wood-burning stove, *couscous*, grilled fish and chips, Tahitian food, barbecue veal and freshly wokked hot delicacies from the provinces of China. Your dinner can be a veritable moveable feast, with a tempting choice of *crêpes* for dessert. No alcohol is served here, but the bars and nightclubs are just across the street.

Place Vaiete has been modernized and is now an attractive, well-lit and popular gathering place at night because of the 30 roulottes that rent space here and also because of the free music concerts frequently presented in the music gazebo. In addition to public restrooms there is also a special place where the *roulotte* owners can wash dishes and pots and pans. These facilities and all of Place Vaiete are kept clean at all times by a special group of women who are government employees.

Tahitian Feasts

Several hotels and individually owned restaurants in Tahiti and the other tourist islands feature regular Tahitian feasts. The *tamaara'a* (tah-mah-AH-rah-ah) is Tahiti's equivalent to the luau served in Hawaii, only much more authentic.

This feast features *ma'a Tahiti* (MAH-ah), foods that are cooked for several hours in an underground *ahima'a* (ah-HEE-mah-ah*)* oven. These usually include roast pig, *taro* root, *tarua* root, breadfruit, yams, bananas, *fei* (fey-ee) plantains, *fafa* (taro leaves cooked with chicken and coconut milk that tastes like spinach), and accompanied by coconut sauces. Dessert is a gooey pudding called *po'e*, (PO-eh), which is made with bananas, papaya, pumpkin or other fruits and flavored with coconut milk.

The national dish of Tahiti is *ei'a ota* (ee-ah OH-ta), which the French call *poisson cru*. It is made with small cubes of fresh tuna or bonito fish that have been marinated in lime juice and mixed with chopped tomatoes, grated carrots, thinly sliced onions and cucumbers and coconut milk. It's delicious and even better with a French *baguette*. If you have an adventurous palate then you'll want to try *fafaru*, slices of fish marinated in a stinky sauce that most Tahitians just adore. The traditional manner of eating *ma'a Tahiti* is with your fingers, although forks are normally supplied. Most hotel restaurants also serve a buffet of Continental foods along with the Tahitian dishes. In hotels the *tamaara'a* is normally accompanied by Tahitian music and an hour-long folkloric dance show. The colorfully costumed entertainers perform the traditional dances of Tahiti and the musicians play exciting music on their drums, guitars and ukuleles. The dancers may even invite you to dance the *tamure*.

Meals for the Health-Conscious, Vegetarians, & Vegans

Tahiti is not a paradise for dieters or vegetarians, and even less so for vegans. Most of the restaurants serve rich dishes made with real butter, knowing that few people go out to diet. It is difficult to get a piece of grilled fish or steak without having a generous serving of parsley butter on the top. French chefs are also very partial to crème fraiche, a thickened fresh cream that is served on most meals you order in a French restaurant. Vegetarians probably won't mind this unless they are pure vegans. Lagoon fish and prawns are sometimes served with the heads intact, so if you're squeamish about having your dinner looking at you, order a fish filet

---

DRINKING LAWS

Beer, wine and all other alcoholic beverages are sold in the larger supermarkets and *magasins* in Tahiti and most of the outer islands. The legal age for buying alcohol is 18 years. You can buy beer and booze on Sun. mornings and public holidays before 10am in some of the shops and in others not at all. A new law went into effect in Jan. 2008 stating that no drinking is allowed in public places. This means no drinking in front of the *magasin* stores (a favorite place for groups of Tahitian men), in public parks, on the quays and beaches or beside the road. Offenders will be charged the price of a case of the big bottles of Hinano beer.

or something else. Vegetarians usually have a choice of rice, potatoes, carrots, green beans and salads, plus fresh fruits, French cheeses and tempting desserts. A few restaurants do have vegetarian plates and sandwiches. These are indicated in the *Where to Eat* section of each island.

Health conscious visitors will find whole grains, breads, cereals, crackers, dried legumes, nuts and fruits at La Vie Pacifique, a health food store located on rue Emile Martin in the Quartier du Commerce in downtown Papeete. They also carry vitamins, soya milk and vegetable juices. Another source for these items is at La Vie et Sante, *Tel. 50.82.56*, a health food shop operated by the Seventh Day Adventist Church, located on Cours de l'Union Sacrée in Fautaua. Take Avenue Prince Hinoi from downtown Papeete towards Pirae and turn right at the Seventh Day Adventist Church. Most of their products come from France and New Zealand. The large supermarkets in Tahiti, such as Carrefour in Punaauia and Arue, Champion in Papeete and Hyper U in Pirae, carry a line of health food products, including soya milk and tofu. You can buy fresh tofu, as well as fresh fruits, vegetables and herbs, at Le Marché, the public market in the center of Papeete.

On Moorea you can usually find soya milk and tofu at Champion Fare Toa in Afareaitu and at Supermarché Are in Pao Pao. Champion Fare Toa has a special organic (bio) section that contains a small selection of Swedish (Björg) products of whole grain pastas, breads, cereals, galettes, lentils, soup, bouillon, herbal salt and a few bottled or packaged sauces with low sodium and sugar. I even found polenta there, but never have I found corn meal in these islands, except at Supermarché Cecile (years ago) and at the Adventist store. Most of the supermarkets on Moorea carry a very small selection of fresh and dried fruits and nuts, fresh vegetables and supplies for spring rolls. I also checked the supermarkets in Bora Bora and Raiatea and found that they had long life soya milk and tofu on the shelves. Most of the supermarkets have yogurt, including the low sugar and added bifidus Nature yogurt.

If you have lodgings with access to a kitchen, you should have no problems finding enough nutritious food to eat while visiting Tahiti and Her Islands. Otherwise, you'll have to pick and choose carefully from the hotel menu, or have a heart to heart talk with the chef de cuisine.

11. Tahiti

Queen of the Pacific

Polynesian mythology tells of a lovely *vahine* named Terehe, who defied the gods of great Havai'i on the island of Raiatea by swimming in the river during a period of sacred restriction. The angry gods caused the young maiden to be overcome by a feeling of numbness and she sank to the bottom of the river and was swallowed by a giant eel. Terehe's spirit then possessed the eel, who thrashed about, tearing away the earth between Raiatea and Taha'a. The eel's body was magically transformed into a fish, which swam away from Havai'i toward the East. Tu-rahu-nui, artisan of Ta'aroa, the supreme god, guided the fish in its course, and the warrior Tafai used a powerful ax to cut the sinews of the fish, to stabilize the new land. Thus were formed lofty mountain ranges, winding gulfs, an isthmus, bluffs and caves. The insouciant soul of Terehe lives today in this transplanted land called **Tahiti**.

Tahiti Nui Mare'are'a, Great Tahiti of the Golden Haze, the Polynesians sang. This is Tahiti of many shaded waters; various are the songs of the birds. Great Tahiti, the mounting place of the sun. The Tahitian people of old had to boast, because the people of Raiatea, the sacred island of Havai'i, regarded Tahiti as a plebeian island with no gods.

When the Europeans discovered Tahiti, beginning with the arrival of English Captain Samuel Wallis in 1767, followed by Frenchman de Bougainville, Captain James Cook, Captain Bligh and the famous *Bounty* crew, they too shouted the praises of this seductive island, where dreams are lived. Explorers, artists, writers and poets, sea-weary sailors and beachcombers of all makes spread the word. The myth of Tahiti as an earthly paradise was born.

Throughout the years Tahiti has become known as the Land of the Double Rainbows, the Romantic Isle, Beloved Island, Isle of Illusion, Island of Love, the Amorous Isle and the World's Most Glamorous Tropic Isle. Tahiti, the living Spirit of Terehe, is hailed as the most famous island in the South Seas—Queen of the Pacific.

ARRIVALS & DEPARTURES
Arriving By Air

If you are flying from a cold country to Tahiti, then make sure you can take off heavy garments once you arrive here, especially if you are continuing on to Moorea, Bora Bora or any of the other outer islands. You'll probably arrive in the cooler hours of the night, but once the sun rises you'll be sweltering in sweaters, woolens and polyesters. So layer your traveling clothes.

A TAHITIAN PROPHECY

The ancient Tahitian seer named Pau'e prophesied: "There are coming children of the glorious princess, by a canoe without an outrigger, who are covered from head to foot." **King Pomare I**, hearing him say so, inquired how a canoe without an outrigger could hold its balance and not upset; so to illustrate his subject, Pau'e took an 'umete (wooden trough) and set it afloat with a few stones placed in it in a pool of water close by; then turning to the King he said: "What will upset that 'umete without an outrigger. It is balanced by its breadth, and so also is the canoe without an outrigger that is coming."

Pau'e also said: "There will come a new king to whom this government will be given, and new manners will be adopted in this land; the tapa and the cloth-beating mallet will go out of use in Tahiti, and the people will wear different, foreign clothes."

Three days afterwards Pau'e died, and a little later the Dolphin arrived with Captain Wallis, when the people exclaimed: "There is the canoe without the outrigger of Pau'e, and there are the children of the glorious princess!" When the Dolphin coasted the Taiarapu peninsula of Tahiti Iti, the natives approached the ship, headed by a man who held up a banana shoot, which to them was an effigy of their own persons, and after a welcome speech, he dropped it into the sea, signifying that their intentions were friendly and that the sea was sacred to all, for the Tahitians regarded it as a great moving marae or temple.

— Extract from *Ancient Tahiti* by Teuira Henry

If you are on a package tour you will be met inside the baggage room or immediately outside the Customs area of the **International Airport of Tahiti-Faaa**. The tour operators hold signs listing the names of their arriving guests. The Banque de Polynésie at the airport is no longer open for incoming international flights. There are ATM windows in the main terminal at the Banque de Polynésie and Banque Socredo, but they often run out of money, especially on weekends. Therefore, I advise you to arrive with a few French Pacific francs (CFP) to get you started. See details on *Money & Banking* in *Chapter 7 Basic Information*. If you need to make a phone call, book a room or continuing flight, rent a car, pick up a map, post a letter, go to the restroom, eat or drink, shop for a gift or check your e-mail, you can do it all inside the airport terminal.

The airport is located at PK 5.5 (3.4 mi.), west of downtown Papeete. If you arrive between 8pm and 6am be prepared to pay the night rates for a taxi. See details under *Taxi & Limousine Service* in this chapter. If you arrive in the daytime and want to save money, you can walk out to the main road and catch *le truck*. When you leave the airport you'll turn right on the main road (Route 1) to go to the west coast hotels and turn left to go downtown and to the east coast. You have a choice of the old coastal route or the freeway, (Route 5), which is called the RDO. You'll see the freeway entry almost in front of the airport.

If you are flying to Moorea or to any of the outer islands you can push your baggage cart to the Air Tahiti counter, which is at the extreme right of the main terminal when you come out of the Customs area. There is a baggage storage room next to the flower/shell stands in front of the terminal building. See information on *Baggage Allowances & Storage* in chapter 6 on *Planning Your Trip*. The hotels and some of the family pensions have a baggage storage room, which is free for their guests.

Arriving By Boat

If you arrive in Tahiti on board a passenger cruise ship you will disembark at the **Quai d'Honneur** or at one of the concrete piers in downtown Papeete. Tour buses, taxis, guides and tourism representatives meet each ship's arrival, and a Tahitian dance show is often performed for the visitors. A covered reception area with public restrooms, telephones and artisan stands has been built adjacent to the Tahiti Tourist office beside the ship dock.

Before arriving in the port of Papeete by yacht you must notify the port authorities via channel 12 or HF 2683 KHz. You can anchor at the quay or close to the Protestant church, and you are supposed to check in with Immigration as soon as possible. If you arrive on a Fri. afternoon then you'll have to wait until Mon. morning before checking in, as offices for Immigration, Customs and the Harbormaster are all closed on weekends and holidays. Their offices are in the Bureau des Yachts, Quai des Paqueboats, close to the tourist office on the waterfront in Papeete.

The Harbormaster's office, *Tel. 689/50.54.51/50.54.82*; Fax 689/43.36.12 is open Mon.-Thurs. from 7:15-11:30am and from 12:15-4pm, and on Fri. from 7:15-11:30am and 12:15-3pm. The office hours for Immigration, *Tel./Fax 689/42.20.74*; are Mon.-Fri. from 8am-12pm and from 1:30-4pm. The Customs office, *Tel. 42.01.22*, is open Mon.-Thurs. from 7am-2:45pm, and on Fri. from 7am-1:30pm.

You will have to complete a Port Documentation form at the Port Captain's office, *Tel. 50.54.62*. This paper contains information for boats that are entering, moving or leaving the port. It also includes port fees for docking, electricity, water and garbage pick-up if you want to tie up at the yacht quay along the waterfront.

There is no marina as such in Papeete harbor, but the waterfront has been upgraded with new, large pontoons providing stern-to docking, water and electricity for at least 25 boats. These three new pontoons are security controlled 24-7 with lockable gates. Visiting yachts can also dock stern-to at the quay (with water and electricity) along Boulevard Pomare, a busy avenue in the heart of Papeete. Hurricane chains have been laid in the harbor and occasionally yachts foul their anchor on them. Theft has been a problem in the past for boats moored along the quay but the situation has improved with guards patrolling the quay 24/7. Although both options in Papeete harbor can be noisy, most people prefer to stay here at least a few days as it is only a few steps from the market, post office, banks, restaurants, repair facilities and the various offices.

Other anchorages for yachts staying longer may be found in front of the Intercontinental Tahiti Resort & Spa, at the Yacht Club in Arue, and at the Tahiti Nautic Center at Port Phaeton in Taravao.

Marina Taina on Tahiti's west coast is administered by the Papeete Port Authority. All dock spaces are occupied by local yachts, although there is a visitor's quay for large yachts. In 2009 mooring buoys were added that are half the cost of a slip. Water, fuel, laundry, garbage disposal services and use of the dinghy dock are all included.

Yachts sailing or motoring to and from Taapuna, west channel, or Marina Taina must request permission to cross the airfield axis east or west 10 minutes before doing so by calling VIGIE on VHF Channel 12.

Each crewmember is required to have a return air ticket or pay a repatriation bond to your home country. See more information in Chapter 6, *Planning Your Trip*.

Departing By Air

You should reconfirm your international flight no later than 72 hours before your departure date. Check-in time for departing international flights is 3 hours prior to departure. You can exchange your francs for dollars at the Banque de Polynésie office inside the terminal, if they are still open when you leave. Once you pass Immigration and go into the international departure lounge, you will find a couple of duty free shops that sell cigarettes, liquors, French perfumes, Tahitian music, Tahitian cultured pearls and various gift items.

Departing By Boat

The cruise ship company or travel agency arranging your cruise will give you details of what you will do when you arrive in Tahiti to board a passenger ship. Groups are met at the airport and transferred to a hotel until time to board the ship, when they will be transferred by boat to the Quai d'Honneur in Papeete, where the ship is moored.

Permission should be obtained for any cruise that takes a yacht more than 50 miles from Tahiti. If you are departing by private yacht you must advise the Immigration office in Papeete of your final departure, and the Police Air Frontière (PAF) who run this office will issue a release from the bond that you were required to post upon arrival. This document must be presented to the *gendarmes* on the last island you visit before leaving French Polynesia, and your bond will be refunded.

ORIENTATION

Tahiti is located in the Windward Islands of the Society archipelago of French Polynesia. This is the largest of the 118 islands and atolls, with a population of around 180,000 people living in 12 *communes* on Tahiti Nui (big Tahiti) and Tahiti Iti (little Tahiti), also known as the Taiarapu peninsula.

Tahiti Nui and **Tahiti Iti** are shaped as a turtle, a lady's hand mirror or a reclining figure 8. Geologists say that these two majestic green islands emerged from the sea in separate volcanic births millions of years apart. Comprising a total of 1,042 sq. km. (402 sq. mi.) of land, Tahiti Nui and Tahiti Iti are joined by the narrow isthmus of **Taravao**, 60 km. (37 mi.) from the noise of **Papeete** by the west coast and 54 km. (34 mi.) by the east coast.

The circle island tour around the coastal road of Tahiti Nui is 114 km. (71 mi.). Away from the metropolitan area close to Papeete the paved roads are 2 lanes, with very few straight stretches, and there are usually no streetlights and very few guardrails at the edge of the seaside cliffs. The east coast is less developed, with numerous waterfalls and deep verdant valleys, modest homes and beautiful flower gardens beside the road. Here you will find the golden-brown sands of the volcanic beaches and cool streams ferrying tiny boats of flower blossoms to the sea. A fringing reef borders the shoreline in a few places, but most of the coast is battered by the waves of the frequently turbulent open ocean.

The west coast is much more congested, with houses and traffic, and high fences around the luxurious homes that often conceal ocean views to the motorists. A few strips of white sand beaches border the shoreline and the shimmering turquoise lagoon is protected by a coral reef. Beyond the reef, across the Sea of Moons, is the island of Moorea.

Tahiti Iti has 18 km. (11 mi.) of paved road on the eastern and western coasts and a 7 km. (4 mi.) interior road that leads past dairy farms and citrus groves to a panoramic view of the Plateau of Taravao. Beyond the road's end of the peninsula's southern tip lies the *fenua 'aihere*, the magnificent bush land, and the steep sea cliffs known as Te Pari. You can explore this coast by boat or hike across the rivers and volcanic bluffs.

PAPEETE & ENVIRONS

The busy, bustling town of **Papeete**, on Tahiti's north coast, is the capital of French Polynesia. This is the administrative center for the estimated 270,000 people (census of Sept. 2007 counted 259,596 inhabitants) who live in the 5 archipelagoes that comprise this French Overseas Country (*Pays d'Outre Mer* or POM).

Papeete (Pah-pay-eh-tay) is a Tahitian word meaning «a basket of water». The town is spread along the waterfront on Tahiti's north coast, 5 km. (3 mi.) east of the airport, facing the island of Moorea across the channel. Papeete harbor is an international port, as well as home base for the *Paul Gauguin* cruise ship, the *Aranui 3* passenger/cargo ship, and other inter-island ships, copra freighters, fishing boats, ferries, plus a small fleet of French naval ships.

In the suburbs just east of the downtown area you will find a new government operated general hospital with 520 beds in the Taaone section of Pirae. In the winding streets of Papeete there are 2 private clinics, pharmacies, French and Tahitian government offices, tribunal courts, *gendarmerie*, municipal police, port authorities and post office with international communications. Services also include the tourist bureau, banks, airline offices, shipping and travel agencies, TV and radio stations, newspapers in French, English and Tahitian, hotel and technical schools, lycée and university, cathedrals and temples, sports centers and stadiums, health clubs and gyms, a cultural center, museums, art galleries, movie theaters, shopping centers, boutiques, crafts centers and a public market.

Dreams for a Better Tomorrow

Papeete's waterfront has been improved during the past few years, with the addition of 2 concrete piers for cruise ships and the extension of the boardwalk along the waterfront, which will eventually go all the way to the Olympic swimming pool adjacent to the cultural center (Te Fare Tauhiti Nui). The cultural center was updated in 2011 with a high wall to help keep the street noises from disturbing performances inside the Grand Theatre, which now has a state-of-the-art acoustics system.

A big landfill project between the yacht quay and Place To'ata has added the Jardins de Paofai with 12.4 acres of parks and playgrounds, the Hokule'a Beach, and a space that is used for beach sports and games, as well as the carnival rides and *baraques* (stands) for the Heiva Festival each July.

At the other end of the Papeete waterfront is the 3-level maritime building that will serve as the ferry terminal for Papeete-Moorea. Construction began in Oct. 2009 and should be finished by the end of 2011, with the overall completion date for this project planned for 2012.

A long-term plan for Papeete includes tearing down some of the old buildings along Blvd. Pomare and creating a vast esplanade so that the public Marché will open onto the quay. The buildings on rue Colette and Leboucher will be destroyed, thereby providing a direct view of Papeete harbor and the cruise ship docks. New office and apartment buildings of 10-stories or more will be built on the mountainside in Paofai, Vaiami and the Bambridge stadium, and a second phase will add buildings in the To'ata and Aroa Nui Ave. Pouvanaa a Oopa (formerly Ave. Bruat) areas. It was announced in mid-2010 that a 5-story building will open in 2012 on the site of the old Le Pitate nightclub and will house the Maison de la Perle. This possibility was still being debated in the Assembly in mid-2011.

Today's Reality

These are just a few of the changes envisioned by Tahiti's leaders for years to come. In the meantime, several of the businesses in Papeete are for sale or have simply closed shop due to the effects of the economic depression.

Tahiti's security forces have their hands full with more unpleasant changes that are taking place in the capital. A municipal police station is located near the public marché, which is the center of town. Even though there are more security personnel patrolling the streets of Papeete, the crime rate for purse snatching and other petty thefts comprises 50% of infractions reported, and thefts with violence increased by 21% in 2010. Break-ins increased by 15.6% in private homes and 60% for businesses.

Authorities report that the increase of juvenile delinquency is due to alcohol and drugs. The consumption of cocaine and ice and other hard drugs has increased during the past few years and the gendarmes have made some amazing discoveries of abundant "paka" plantations of marijuana on several islands.

Young male and female prostitutes are rampant. You'll find them in the bars, sidewalk cafés and nightclubs on Rue des Ecoles and near Avenue Prince Hinoi, and some of the transvestites are glamorously attired in satins, sequins, feathers, makeup and wigs when they cruise the sidewalks at night. The street surveillance teams also keep an eye on their behavior and even their well-being, as sexual attacks have increased by 7.5%. An anti-noise law was passed in 2004 to eliminate the loud music booming from cars and 4WD vehicles in downtown Papeete or anywhere on the island. Few revelers, however, pay any attention to this law.

GETTING AROUND TOWN
Car & Motorcycle Rentals

Note: The minimum age for renting a 4-wheel vehicle is 21 years and for 2-wheel vehicles it is 18 or 19 years, depending on the island. The driver must have a valid driver's license of one-year minimum from his country of residence or an international driver's license corresponding to the class of vehicle rented. Anyone 70-years old or older who wishes to rent a vehicle must present a medical certificate in addition to their driver's license. You will have to pay a guarantee deposit when renting cars, scooters and bicycles. When you rent a car, do not leave anything at all inside the car when you're not in it. All major credit cards are accepted.

• **Avis**, *in US Tel. 800/230-4898; in Tahiti, Tel. 689/54.10.10; avis.tahiti@mail.pf; www.avis-tahiti.com.* The main office for **Avis-Pacificar** is at 56 Rue des Remparts at the Pont de l'Est in Papeete, and there are also sales offices at the Tahiti-Faaa International Airport, *Tel. 85.02.84* and in Taravao, *Tel. 57.70.70.* Several choices of vehicles are available for rent by the day, week or month. You can also rent an audio Tikiguide for the islands of Tahiti and Moorea.

• **Europcar**, *in US Tel. 800/227-7368; in Tahiti, Tel. 689/86.61.96/81.07.00; tahiti@europcar.pf; www.europcar.com.* The main sales office is in the Vaima Center in Papeete, and there is a sales counter at the Tahiti-Faaa International Airport. Europcar offers a variety of choices in all price ranges.

• **Hertz**, *in US Tel. 800/654.3001; in Tahiti, Tel. 689/42.04.71 (Office), Tel. 689/ 82.55.86 (Airport); Fax 689/43.49.03; hertz@mail.pf; www.hertztahiti.com.* They have a sales counter at the Tahiti-Faaa International Airport and sales desks at the major hotels. A 3-door a/c Peugeot 107 is 9.520 CFP for one day and an a/c Peugeot 206 with automatic transmission is 14.760 CFP. A 9-passenger Hyundai minivan with a/c is 23.100 CFP. All rates include unlimited mileage and insurance, and 3-day packages are available.

* **Tahiti Rent A Car**, *Tel. 689/81.94.00*, has an office at the airport. A 3-door Hyundai-Getz is 8.976 CFP for a one-day package, and a 5-passenger a/c Peugeot 206 is 12.113 CFP, including insurance and unlimited mileage.
* **Tahiti Auto Center**, *Tel. 689/82.33.33; Fax 689/83.33.34; www.tahitiautocenter.pf.* This car rental agency claims to offer the lowest rates. They are located at PK 20.200 in Paea on Tahiti's west coast. Open Mon.-Fri. 7am-5pm and on Sat. 8-11:30am. A 3-door a/c Renault Twingo is 5.500 CFP a day, a 5-door a/c Peugeot 206 is 7.500 CFP, and a 9-seat Hyundai minibus is 15.000 CFP. Weekly and monthly rates available. Rates include insurance and unlimited mileage. They also rent scooters and motorcycles.

Other rental agencies include: **Daniel Rent-A-Car**, *Tel. 689/81.96.32/ 82.30.04; Fax 689/85.62.64; daniel.location@mail.pf.* They have a sales counter at the airport. **Renault Rent**, *Tel. 46.39.86; renaultrent@sodiva.pf; www.renault.pf.* Sodiva Renault is located at Fare Ute in Papeete and reservations should be made at least 48 hours in advance. A Twingo is 6.900 CFP for one day, a Clio II is 8.900 CFP and an automatic Clio III is 10.900 CFP. Minivans and larger vehicles are also available. **Pacific Rent**, *Tel. 689/73.66.76; pacific.rent@mail.pf,* has luxury cars for rent, including a Hummer H3, Porsche Cayenne, Chevrolet Camaro and a Mercedes Class C.

Tahitian Rider, *Tel. 78.75.61; tahitianrider@mail.pf,* rents Harley-Davidson motorcycles. A one-day rental (9am-5pm) is 20.000 CFP, including insurance. A deposit of 100.000 CFP is required.

Taxi & Limousine Service

A taxi stand is located at the Tahiti-Faaa International Airport, *Tel. 86.60.66,* at the Vaima Center, *Tel. 43.72.47,* and on Blvd. Pomare in front of the former Mana Rock Café (now closed), *Tel. 41.23.42.* Your hotel reception can also call a taxi for you.

A taxi ride between the airport and downtown Papeete is 1.500 CFP during the day and 2.500 CFP between 8pm and 6am. The taxi fare between the airport and the west coast hotels, as far as Sofitel Maeva Beach, is 1.000 CFP during the day and 1.500 CFP at night. The daytime fare from the airport to Le Méridien is 2.000 CFP and 4.500 CFP at night. Between the Intercontinental Tahiti Resort and downtown Papeete you will pay 1.700 CFP in the daytime and 2.900 CFP at night, and from Le Méridien Tahiti to Papeete the fare is 2.500 CFP during the day and 5.000 CFP at night. From the airport to the Royal Tahitien the taxi fare is 2.500 CFP during the day and 3.500 CFP at night, and to the Radisson Plaza Resort the daytime fare is 3.500 CFP and 5.000 CFP at night. The official cost of

a circle island tour by taxi is 16.000 CFP, and the hourly rate for a taxi is 4.000 CFP. Drivers charge 100 CFP for each big bag transported.
Carl's Taxi, *Tel. 77.13.69/82.22.72*, is operated by Carl Emery, who grew up in Australia and speaks excellent 'Aussie' English. He has an 8-passenger a/c Toyota High Ace mini-van that he uses for private taxi service and tours. **Mami Elisa Taxi**, *Tel. 72.46.31*, is available 24-hrs. a day to drive you wherever you want to go. I have used her on several occasions and she is very reliable as well as friendly. **Taxi Mike**, *Tel. 24.29.20; Fax 83.77.89*, is owned by Michael from the Cook Islands, who speaks excellent English. He drives a luxurious Logan Break.

Tour & Transport Companies
When you book your visit to Tahiti through a travel agent, your ground transportation is normally part of the package. If you are traveling on your own, you can contact a local tour and transport company to drive you between your hotel and the airport or ferry dock. Be sure to reserve at least one day in advance. The taxi fares are sometimes more reasonable than the transport companies' rates. See the list of Tahiti's inbound travel agencies in Chapter 6, *Planning Your Trip*.

Le Truck & "Busscar" Transportation System
Tahiti's public transport system was traditionally provided by *le truck*, which is a brightly painted wooden cabin mounted on the rear of a flatbed truck. Some of these colorful vehicles still operate during the daylight hours, with night transportation provided from downtown Papeete only to the airport and hotels on the west coast, as far as Sofitel Maeva Beach Resort. The last run depends on what is happening in Papeete. Each *le truck* has a specific route, with the destination usually painted on the top or sides of the vehicle.

Except for some urban routes, Tahiti's famous *le truck* has been replaced with modern buses, which are locally called "**Busscar**." The buses are painted according to the zone they serve. The red buses are for the urban zone from Pirae to Punaauia; orange is for the West coast, from Punaauia to Taravao and Teahupoo, and green is for the East coast, between Tautira and Papeete. The name and number of the zone served is also shown on the front of the bus, just like buses in the United States.

The minimum fare is 130 CFP, which is valid between the Sofitel Maeva Beach Resort and downtown, and you'll have to pay 200 CFP at night. The one-way fare to the end of the road in Teahupoo or Tautira on the Tahiti Iti peninsula is 400-520 CFP. The Tahiti Tourist office can give you specific details on where to catch the bus to your destination.

So, with all this modernization program, what will happen to the beloved *le truck*? Some of them have been kept in Tahiti to transport groups of tourists who arrive aboard the passenger liners or for "Kaina Island" tours around Tahiti. Other *le trucks* have been shipped to the outer islands.

WHERE TO STAY

Downtown Papeete – Superior to Moderate

HOTEL TAHITI NUI, *B.P. 302, Papeete, Tahiti 98713. Tel. 689/46.38.99; Fax 689/85.12.99; www.hoteltahitinui.pf. On Ave. Prince Hinoi 4 blocks from Papeete waterfront. 91 rooms. All major credit cards.*

This 3-star 7-story cosmopolitan boutique hotel opened in early 2009 with standard rooms, junior suites and executive/family suites with kitchens. Some of the standard rooms also have small kitchenettes. The décor in the clean, large rooms is very modern and minimalist, all in black, white, grey or brown, with dark wood furniture and tiled floors. The platform beds are reported to be very comfortable and guests are impressed with the crisp white sheets and the toilet room that is separate from the bath/shower. They have complained, however, about the poor lighting in the bathrooms and the hallways, as well as the lack of baggage services. Each room has a/c, direct telephone, TV with international channels (no CNN), free Internet connection, mini-bar, coffee/tea facilities, hair dryer, iron, and a private balcony. There is a safe available for guest use at the reception desk. Because it is located on a busy street with traffic noises, the rooms overlooking the road all have double-glassed windows for soundproofing. However, it is advisable to request a room on the mountainside and to make sure the balcony doors are well closed.

The hotel is built around an interior atrium and facilities include an open-air swimming pool and Jacuzzi, plus a well-equipped fitness center, and a 2-level dimly lit garage. Wireless Internet is available in the spacious lobby, the bar and in the computer center, where there are two computers and a printer. The Brown Velvet restaurant on the street level serves gastronomic cuisine and the Chocco Latte lounge bar overhangs the restaurant. The Dhana Spa has a Turkish bath as well as complete spa services.

This is the newest hotel in Papeete and is owned by the same local Chinese family who owned the former Le Mandarin hotel and the restaurant Le Mandarin. It is a good choice for anyone who wants to be in the heart of the city, whether for business, in-transit between airplanes, cruises or yacht charters, or just to discover Papeete at a leisurely pace.

Moderate

HOTEL TIARE TAHITI, *B.P. 2359, Papeete, Tahiti 98713. Tel. 689/ 50.01.00; Fax 689/43.68.47; hotltiaretahiti@mail.pf; www.hoteltiaretahiti.info. Blvd. Pomare, on waterfront adjacent to Papeete Post Office. All major credit cards.*

This hotel is near the Papeete Post Office, overlooking Boulevard Pomare and the yacht quay on the waterfront. It is the best choice for a moderate hotel in the downtown area and reservations have to be made well in advance. You can have an early check-in at 3am by paying 50% of the regular room rate. The 38 rooms are located in a five-story building with an elevator. They have a/c, private bathrooms with showers, telephone, cable television and a hair dryer on request. 33 of the

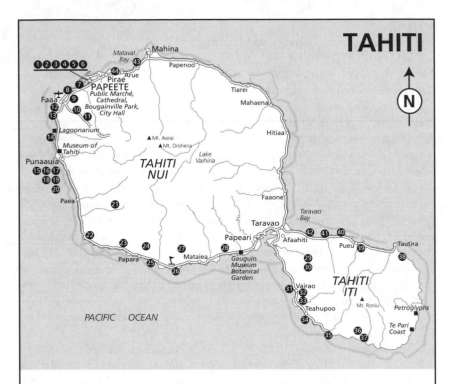

1. Hotel Tahiti Nui	18. Taaroa Lodge	35. Teahupoo Surfing Site
2. Ahitea Lodge	19. Relais Fenua	36. Pension Te Pari Village
3. Pension Puea	20. Te Miti	37. Bonjouir Lodge Paradise
4. Hotel Tiare Tahiti	21. Marae Arahurahu	38. Pension Te Hihi o Te Ra
5. Fare Suisse	22. Marae Grottos	39. Pueu Village
6. Chez Myrna	23. Hiti Moana Villa	40. Punatea Village
7. Heitiare Inn	24. Papara Village	41. Chez Flotahia
8. Tahiti-Faa'a Airport	25. Fare Ratere	42. Fare Maithe
9. Tahiti Airport Motel	26. Papara Surfing Beach	43. Radisson Plaza Resort
10. Chez Lola	27. Atimaono Golf Course	44. Hotel Royal Tahitien
11. Pension Damyr	28. Vaipahi Garden & Waterfall	
12. Intercontinental Tahiti Resort & Spa	29. Taravao Plateau	
13. Sofitel Maeva Beach Tahiti Resort	30. Chez Jeannine	
	31. Meherio Iti	
14. Manava Suite Resort Tahiti	32. Pension Chayan	
15. Hotel Le Meridien Tahiti	33. Vanira Lodge	
16. Pension de la Plage	34. La Vague Bleue (Tauhanihani)	
17. Pension Otaha		

rooms have private balconies with a view of the harbor. Breakfast is served in the cafeteria above the reception. Several restaurants, bars and boutiques are less than a block away.

Economy

AHITEA LODGE, *B.P. 5597, Pirae, Tahiti 98716. Tel. 689/53.13.53/ 76.63.88; Fax 689/42.09.35; pension.ahitea@mail.pf; www.ahitea-lodge.com. In Fariipiti, 15 min. from airport and 900 m. (3,000 ft.) from ferry dock. AE, MC, V.*

This renovated 2-story bed and breakfast is in an alley between Ave. Chef Vairaatoa and Ave. Prince Hinoi, facing the Plomberie and Suzanna Shop in the Fariipiti neighborhood of Papeete. This is a working class neighborhood of Tahitian families, complete with children and dogs. The 10 comfortable standard guest rooms give you a choice of a room for 2 people or 2 adults and 2 children, with private or shared bathrooms and hot water showers. Each room has a ceiling fan, and 2 rooms have a/c, TV and a mini-refrigerator. The best bedrooms are in the main house, and the upstairs rooms open onto a balcony. The least expensive rooms are in an adjacent building. A tropical breakfast is included and is served in the dining room or on the terrace, and guests share a kitchen with refrigerator and microwave oven. There is a charge for laundry, ironing and locker storage room. There is also a pond with tropical fish and a swimming pool in the garden, which is surrounded by a high fence. You can walk or take Le Truck or a taxi about 5 blocks to the downtown restaurants, snacks and the roulotte food wagons. Owners Ado and Michel Moevai also own Puea Pension.

FARE SUISSE, *B.P. 20255, Papeete, Tahiti 98713. Tel./Fax 689/42.00.30; info@fare-suisse.com; www.fare-suisse.com. Rue des Poilus Tahitiens in Quartier Buillard in Paofai, 10 min. from airport and 3 blocks inland from Papeete waterfront. Free airport transfers. MC, V.*

This is a one-story white concrete house operating as a bed and breakfast. Since its opening in 2006 the Fare Suisse has become very popular with European visitors as well as guests from many other countries. Owner Beni and his wife Therese are highly praised by former clients for their friendly, helpful and reliable service, as well as the immaculately clean, comfortable and spacious rooms they provide. Some say that this is the best place they have ever stayed anywhere in the world! This 4-bedroom house is located in a quiet, safe, secluded gated community up the hill from Champion Supermarket on rue du Commandant Destremeau, a 10-min. walk from the center of downtown Papeete. The Maupiti Room has a double bed with a private shower, the Tahiti Room has a double bed, and the Moorea Room has 2 single beds. Guests in these rooms share the well equipped kitchen, the terrace and BBQ grill. The Bora Bora Room has a double bed and a single bed, with a private living area and kitchen, terrace and BBQ grill. The well-appointed rooms are airy, bright, clean and cozy. The bathrooms have been described by some guests as luxurious, with a basket of towels and little soaps for guests to use. Breakfast is served on the terrace. A washing machine is available for guest use and Beni will also store your luggage while you visit the outer islands. He will drive you to the ferry or to the airport and pick you up when you return, at no extra charge.

CHEZ MYRNA, *B.P. 790, Papeete, Tahiti 98713. Tel./Fax 689/42.64.11; cell 689/77.09.75; dammeyer.family@mail.pf. In Tipaerui valley, a five minute walk inland from Rue du Commandant Destremeau. No credit cards.*

Myrna and her husband Walter Dahmmeyer have a concrete 5-bedroom house with a double bed in each room, with a private or shared bathroom. There is also a dormitory and kitchen. Only breakfast is served. You can walk to nearby restaurants, snack bars and *magasins*. Luggage storage available.

Northeast Coast: Arue/Pirae – Deluxe

RADISSON PLAZA RESORT TAHITI, *B.P. 14170, Arue, Tahiti 98701. Tel. 689/48.88.88; Fax 689/48.88.89; www.radisson.com/tahiti. On Lafayette Beach in Arue Commune, 7 km (4.3 mi) northeast of Papeete. All major credit cards.*

The Radisson Plaza Resort was originally planned as a residence hotel with kitchens and large balconies overlooking 2,600 ft. (792 m) of black sand beside the lagoon at Lafayette Beach on Tahiti's northern coast of Arue. The 7 concrete buildings that are spread out around an 8,611 sq. ft. (800 sq. m) swimming pool were already under construction when the owner decided to upgrade his project to that of a 5-star hotel with 165 rooms. He has since sold one of the buildings and the units with kitchens are no longer rented to hotel guests.

All the 135 remaining guest rooms and suites are located on 4 levels and there are elevators and underground parking. Each unit overlooks the ocean and they all have a 140 sq. ft. (13 sq. m) balcony or lanai, thus creating an external living room. There are 45 deluxe rooms, 30 rooms with a Jacuzzi on the covered balcony, and 60 suites and duplexes. All the suites are furnished with a king size bed or 2 double beds and a sofa bed and can accommodate 3 adults and a baby bed. Each of the rooms has a king size bed. All units have individually controlled a/c, satellite TV, IDD telephones, voice mail, free broadband Internet access, bathroom with shower and bathtub, in-room safe, minibar, coffee and tea facilities, hair dryer and daily housekeeping service. There are no CD or DVD players. Room service is available.

The guest rooms and suites, as well as the restaurant, bar, lounge, reception and all other public areas are decorated in a mixture of trendy modern and exotic Polynesian, with furnishings from all over the world. Hiti Mahana, the resort's signature restaurant, overlooks Lafayette Beach and historic Matavai Bay. See further information under *Where to Eat* in this chapter.

The resort's Lafayette Bar is named for the (in-)famous Lafayette after hours nightclub that was located here from the 1940s through the early 1970s. This upmarket bar is a weekend gathering place for Tahiti's young international set of beautiful people who come to listen to music played by local bands. The James Norman Hall Lounge, located to the right of the reception, is the perfect place to relax with a cup of coffee or tea while waiting to meet a friend or business associate.

Le Spa is a full-service spa on the resort's 3rd floor and is reached by elevator. A trained staff welcomes hotel and non-hotel guests for treatments on appointment. Hotel guests can use their room key for access to the a/c Fitness Center, which is adjacent to Le Spa. In addition to the Star Trac Pro equipment, there are locker rooms, 2 showers, a sauna and a steam room. There is extensive cardio fitness and free-weight equipment, and professional yoga and aquagym classes are available. See more information under *Massages and Spas* in this chapter.

At the entrance to the Radisson you will find an interesting arts and crafts shop with colorful displays of *tifaifai* quilts, pareos, woven hats and bags, mother-of-pearl jewelry and drums. There is also a beauty parlor and a boutique selling Tahitian cultured pearls. You can rent a car or a 4-wheel bicycle and plan your island excursions at the activities desk.

Hotel guests have access to the business center at any hour. In addition to computers with free Internet access, there are facilities for faxing, printing and photocopying. General secretarial services, typing and translating can be arranged on request. The hotel's meeting rooms and events spaces are named after some of the famous European explorers and ships that visited Tahiti and especially Matavai Bay in the latter half of the 1700s. These include the Endeavour Room, Captain Samuel Wallis Room, Captain James Cook Room, Captain Louis A. Bougainville Room, the Dolphin Meeting Room, the Restaurant Hiti Mahana, the Lafayette Bar, the Endeavour patio and Endeavour garden.

Like all the favorite Honeymoon Hotels in Polynesia, Radisson Plaza Resort Tahiti also has special packages for newlywed guests and other loving couples. Please contact the hotel directly for all details on the Romantic Packages and Polynesian Weddings.

Moderate

HOTEL ROYAL TAHITIEN, *B.P. 5001, Pirae, Tahiti 98716. Tel. 689/ 50.40.40; Fax 689/50.40.41; royalres@mail.pf; www.hotelroyaltahitien.com. On the beach in Pirae, on Tahiti's north shore, 3 km (1.9 mi) east of Papeete. All major credit cards.*

Although this is an old hotel that was built in the 1960s, it is still very popular with travelers who want to be close to Papeete but away from the noise and dirt of the city. They also appreciate the moderate rates and beautiful grounds. The 40 a/c rooms are located in 2-story motel-type structures that are now rather sad and in need of a good facelift. The spacious garden is decorated with flowering trees and a small river meandering toward the sea. The rooms have one or two beds, a direct dial telephone, Wireless Internet connections, refrigerator and tea/coffee facilities, bathtub/shower and a private balcony or terrace overlooking the tropical gardens. Tahiti's royal family once owned this land. You can swim in the lagoon beside a black sand beach, relax in a Jacuzzi spa and sunbathe on the adjacent wooden deck, or you can cool off under the waterfall in the tropical swimming pool in the garden. Very good meals are served in the thatched roof Tahitian style dining room or under the shade of huge almond trees on the terrace. There is also a snack *fare* adjacent to the swimming pool. This hotel is a favorite destination for local diners and the Happy Hour crowd who come to the spacious bar on Fri. evenings to dance to tunes played by Tahiti's favorite musicians. For more information see *Where to Eat* in this chapter.

Airport Area: Faaa/Punaauia – Deluxe
  INTERCONTINENTAL TAHITI RESORT & SPA *(formerly Tahiti Beachcomber Inter-Continental), B.P. 6014, Faaa, Tahiti. 98702. Tel. 689/86.51.10; Fax 689/86.51.30; www.tahiti.intercontinental.com. 260 rooms. All major credit cards.*

  The Intercontinental Tahiti Resort opened as the Travelodge in 1974 and was later known as the Beachcomber, Beachcomber Parkroyal and Beachcomber Inter-Continental. Although the Beachcomber name was dropped at the beginning of 2005, local residents, as well as many tour operators and tourists, continue to call it the Tahiti Beachcomber. It is located on 30 acres (12 ha.) of lush tropical gardens on the western shore of Tahiti, facing the island of Moorea, built among palm trees and grassy lawns, and has its own white sand beaches and inner lagoon.

  The 260 accommodation units include fully renovated garden and lagoon view rooms, each with 307 sq. ft. (28.5 sq. m.) of floor space plus a balcony. These rooms give you a choice of a king size bed or two twin beds. The 1,237 sq. ft. (115 sq, m.) Antares Suite is located in the main building, with a bedroom, bathroom, lounge, private bar, plus a living room/dining room area.

  An extension of 60 panoramic view rooms is located in 2 additional 3-story buildings. These units offer 414 sq. ft. (38.5 sq. m.) of living space, plus a wide terrace overlooking the sandy bottom swimming pool adjacent to the Lotus Restaurant, and the island of Moorea across the Sea of Moons. The decor is tropical colonial, with bamboo, wood and wicker furniture, wooden floors, and a canopy and padded headboard for the 2 queen size beds or 1 king size bed. A shuttered window between the bedroom and bathroom can be opened if you want to gaze at the lagoon while soaking in the big oval bathtub. There is also a separate shower with 2 adjustable showerheads, and there are 2 lavabos of black marble. The panoramic suite is also in this section.

  On a private motu across a bridge from the main hotel property are 16 overwater bungalows with 30.5 sq. m. (328 sq. ft.) of living space. The overwater bungalows are built in the Polynesian style, with thatched roofs and natural woods. In addition to a/c they also have a ceiling fan, screened windows and sliding glass doors, as well as private balconies and sun decks with steps leading into the lagoon. They are equipped with a king size bed and a double sofa bed. There are 15 beautifully appointed overwater junior suites at the Restaurant Lotus end of the property. These units have 38.5 sq. m. (414 sq. ft.) of living space, excluding the terrace and deck. You can reach these bungalows by taking the hotel's *le truck* or electric cart, or by a leisurely stroll through the hotel gardens. The water is deeper here and the current is sometimes too choppy for good swimming, but these units provide the most intimacy. On request, guests staying in the overwater bungalows can be served breakfast by outrigger canoe.

All rooms and bungalows have adjustable a/c, separate bathrooms with bathtubs and courtesy soaps, *monoi*, bath gel, shampoo, conditioner, body lotion, and lots of other amenities. Each room has blackout curtains, a stocked mini-bar, coffee and tea facilities, personal safe, hair-dryer, make-up mirror, satellite cable TV, video access on demand, IDD telephone and Internet connections. There is twice-a-day maid service, 3 guest laundry rooms, and same-day laundry and dry-cleaning service. Room service is available round-the-clock.

A 1,000 sq. ft. (93 sq. m.) villa with modern amenities is also built over the water on the private motu. This unit is a model of the overwater villas that were built for the Intercontinental Bora Bora Resort & Thalasso Spa. There is a king size bed and 2 sofa beds, providing sleeping accommodations for 4 adults or 3 adults and 2 children.

In the reception area of the main building is a lobby with comfortable sofas and easy chairs. In addition to 24-hour reception, there is a concierge service and public relations counter. There are desks for guest activities, rental cars, excursions, and day trips to outer islands. Also on this level you will find a duty free gift shop and newsstand, a Tahiti Pearls boutique, and function rooms that are used for conferences, seminars and art shows. One of the hotel's 3 bars is in the corner of the lobby, and is open from 10pm-5am, serving drinks and snacks for late arrivals. You can take the elevators or the stairways to the ground level, where you will find the spacious Tiki Bar and open-air Tiare Restaurant, which has all-day dining. The a/c Hibiscus Restaurant is on the second floor and is used for special occasions. Le Lotus Restaurant is built over the lagoon and offers the most romantic setting of any restaurant on the island, with a lovely view of Moorea. See information under *Where to Eat* in this chapter.

The landscaped tropical gardens surrounding the hotel include a 1-mile jogging track and exercise area. Guests can use the snorkel equipment, kayaks, tennis rackets, balls and 2 floodlit tennis courts free for 1 hour. They have free access to 2 large fresh water swimming pools, an outdoor Jacuzzi and 2 white sand beaches. Aquagym classes are held daily except Sun. and you can help feed the fish in the interior lagoon every day at 9 am and 3pm. The Deep Nature Spa has a large selection of massages and beauty treatments, and hotel clients can sign up for TAO lessons in the Fitness Room, which are given several times a week at no charge. Watersports activities, including scuba diving, are organized at TOPDIVE/Bathys Diving Center. See information on *Nautical Activities Centers* and *Scuba Diving* in this chapter. The hotel has an a/c shuttle van that makes 4 trips to Papeete a day for 400 CFP per passenger. There is also a helipad on the hotel grounds.

A daily program of cultural activities takes place at the Tiare swimming pool or Tiki Bar, which includes an arts and crafts exhibit, pareo dying and tying demonstrations, dance lessons, and lessons on how to create floral crowns, tifaifai patchwork bed covers, or how to make the famous Tahitian fish salad called *poisson cru.* Happy Hour is held in the Tiki Bar from 4:30-5:30pm every afternoon. The bar is very active on Thurs.-Fri.-Sat. evenings when popular local musicians entertain the crowds of young people who come to meet their friends and enjoy the ambience. Hotel guests and other tourists can also safely mix with the friendly locals in this secure environment.

When newlyweds mention "Honeymoon" on their reservations at the Intercontinental Tahiti Resort & Spa they will receive special gifts and treats on their arrival at the hotel. A catalog of 'Romantic Ideas' has been prepared for honeymooners and other lovers, which tells you all about the Romantic Touches that can be added. These even include a choice of Traditional Tahitian Wedding Ceremonies. Contact the hotel directly for details.

Superior

HOTEL LE MERIDIEN TAHITI, *B.P. 380595, Tamanu, Punaauia, Tahiti 98718. Tel. 689/47.07.07; Fax 689/47.07.08; Reservations Tel. 689/47.07.26, Fax 689/47.07.28; in North America 800/543-4300; rez@lemeridien-tahiti.pf; www.lemeridien-tahiti.com. Beside the lagoon in Punaauia, 15 km (9.3 mi.) from downtown Papeete and 10 km (6.2 mi.) west of the international airport. 150 units. All major credit cards.*

Le Méridien Tahiti opened in June 1998, on 11.12 acres (4.5 ha.) of land close to the Museum of Tahiti and Her Islands and just 20 min. from the Atimaono International Golf Course. It is now a member of the prestigious Starwood family.

An important renovation project was completed in 2011, resulting in a re-landscaped entrance, lobby and reception area. The lobby features modern red, black and white furnishings including large sofas and comfortable chairs, inspired by the Tahitian tiare flower. Polynesian artwork is everywhere, including a 39-foot painting, a 60-foot sepia cultural print, and a unique wall covering featuring local tapa (Tahitian papyrus) and paint. The lobby now has three personal check-in stations, three computers for guest use, a new concierge desk, and a corner espresso bar with lounge seating.

Lodging facilities include 12 a/c overwater bungalows with thatched roofs, and 130 a/c guestrooms and 8 suites in 4-story concrete buildings. The Polynesian style thatched roof overwater bungalows are 60 sq. m. (646 sq. ft.) in size and have a spacious living area opening onto a deck with an open view of Moorea. The suites include 5 junior suites, 2 deluxe suites and 1 presidential suite. All the rooms can accommodate 3 adults or 2 adults and 1 child. New interiors for all deluxe lagoon-view and deluxe panoramic-view rooms and suites feature contemporary neutral-toned furniture and linens, soothing lighting and authentic Polynesian textures, including bamboo, for an ambience that is energizing by day and relaxing at night. Additional Polynesian touches include authentic "tapa" cloth lights and tables shaped like surfboards. All deluxe accommodations also have new hardwood floors. Standard amenities include IDD telephones, wireless high speed Internet connections, satellite TV, DVD players, refrigerators, in-room safes, coffee and tea facilities, hair dryers, toiletries, separate bathtubs, walk-in showers, bathrobe and slippers, handy makeup mirrors, a full length mirror, plus an iron and board. Room service is provided round-the-clock and same day laundry service and ironing are also available. Some of the amenities may not be available in all the rooms, or fees may apply. You can request a non-smoking room, a room for disabled guests or interconnecting rooms. From each room you can see the lagoon and the island of Moorea across the Sea of Moons.

There is a transit room for guests who need somewhere to stay or put their luggage after they have checked out of their room. In addition to a business center, a gift shop and pearl jewelry boutique, travel agency and car rental desk in the main building, there are 5 conference and banquet rooms accommodating from 20-500 people.

La Plantation, the hotel's main restaurant, and the Astrolabe bar have been renewed and updated in a contemporary style, complete with natural colored wood and woven furniture mixed with brightly colored accents of orange and green to enhance the Polynesian theme. The spaces have been designed to allow for both indoor and outdoor seating, with dividable "green walls" for added privacy. Le Carré, the beachside restaurant, has also had a face-lifting. They serve gastronomic cuisine for lunch and dinner and it is best to reserve. You can get panini sandwiches and burgers at the Pool Bar during the day. Please see further information under *Where to Eat* in this chapter.

The hotel's 2,500 sq. m. (26,910 sq. ft.) sand bottom swimming pool is prolonged by a stream, providing a vast watery playground in the hotel gardens close to the beach. Free activities also include snorkeling equipment, kayaks, aquagym classes, yoga classes, ping-pong, beach volley, bocce ball, and tennis on the hotel's court. Activities for children include beach games (bucket and shovel), video games and board games. Optional activities are scuba diving with Eleuthera Plongée, joining a snorkeling safari, sailing cruise, or a dolphin/whale watch expedition. You can go deep sea fishing, charter a private boat for a half-day's outing, play golf or discover Tahiti's charms on a circle island tour. You can also opt for a relaxing massage in your room. The travel desk in the lobby can book your tours and excursions or rent you a car for your own personal explorations. Le Méridien operates a shuttle service aboard a 'le truck' that will take you to Papeete and back for 1.000 CFP per person. This shuttle operates twice-daily except on Sun. Or you can walk out to the circle island road and catch a local bus and pay the one-way fare of 130 CFP.

An interesting activity at Le Méridien is an atelier (artist's workshop) located on the 6th floor for painters, sculptors and photographers. Visiting artists can exhibit their works here and some of them even give lessons to hotel guests or other students who are interested in learning their craft. Le Méridien has also added L'Atelier du Chef for guests who want to learn how to prepare French cuisine as well as some local specialties.

SOFITEL MAEVA BEACH TAHITI RESORT, *B.P. 60008, Faaa, Tahiti 98702. Tel. 689/86.66.00; Fax 689/41.05.05; HO547@accor.com; www.sofitel.com. Beside the lagoon in Punaauia, 7.5 km (4.6 mi) west of Papeete and 2.5 km (1.5 mi) west of the airport. All major credit cards.*

The Sofitel Maeva Beach opened in 1969, offering a fabulous view of the island of Moorea across the Sea of Moons. Accommodations include 216 a/c rooms and suites in a 7-story pyramid shaped building. The Classic rooms face the mountains and the Superior rooms overlook the lagoon and Moorea. Each room is tiled and has a terrace or balcony, bathtub and rain shower, a separate toilet, IDD telephone, voice mail, wireless Internet connections, plasma TV with satellite/cable, radio, personal safe, minibar, tea and coffee facilities, hair-dryers and makeup mirror. The rooms also include a king-size bed or two twin beds, plus a daybed. These are Sofitel's patented My Bed, which are covered with bougainvillea-inspired bedspreads. The interior design of the Sofitel Tahiti's rooms uses vibrant colors and striking contrasts reminiscent of Paul Gauguin's paintings.

The guest rooms and bathrooms were renovated in 2005, along with the hotel's reception and lobby. There are desks for car rentals, tours and activities, plus a Heipoe Tahiti jewelry, gift and sundries shop. Seminars and banquets can be held in the 3 meeting rooms, which can seat up to 200 people. A business center and secretarial service are provided, as well as fax, copy/print facilities, Internet connections, translators and interpreters.

Breakfast, lunch and dinner are served in the open-air Bougainville restaurant on the ground level and the Sakura is a Japanese teppanyaki restaurant adjacent to the hotel lobby that is open for dinner. See *Where to Eat* in this chapter. Room service is available from 6am-10pm. The Moorea Bar is open from 9am-11pm, serving light snacks and your favorite cocktails beside the renovated swimming pool. Happy Hour is held here daily from 5-6pm, with live music starting at 6pm on Fri. and Sat. evenings.

Aquagym classes are held in the big swimming pool and are very popular with resident French and Tahitian women. There are also yoga classes, as well as 2 lighted tennis courts and a golf driving range on the hotel premises. During holiday weekends and school vacations this hotel receives a lot of local business and the pool and beach area become very lively. It is quieter during the week.

MANAVA SUITE RESORT TAHITI, *Tel. 689/47.31.00; Fax 689/47.31.01; info@manavatahitiresort.pf; www.spmhotels.com. Beside the lagoon at PK 10.5 in Punaauia, between the airport and Le Méridien. All major credit cards.*

This is the newest hotel on Tahiti's sunset coast of Punaauia, which opened in March 2009 on the lagoon site of the former Iaorana Villa, offering a spectacular view of Moorea. The 121 guest accommodations in 5 buildings include 4 floors with modern comfortable rooms, suites, studio suites, and duplex suites with 1-3 bedrooms.

The size of the units range from 30 sq. m. (323 sq. ft.) for a room up to 139 sq. m. (1,496 sq. ft.) for the 2-bedroom duplex suites, plus a terrace. The 12 rooms are above the lobby-reception area, and the 109 studios have terraces providing either Garden or Lagoon views. All the rooms and suites have a/c and a ceiling fan and most of the units have kitchens. I have stayed in a 2-bedroom duplex suite (living room and full kitchen downstairs and 2 bedrooms and 2 bathrooms upstairs, plus a terrace facing the garden and distant mountains. I have also stayed in one of the ground-level studio suites with a terrace facing the lagoon, the white sand beach and the swimming pool, which is the largest infinity pool on Tahiti. Free Aquagym classes are held twice a day Mon.-Fri. and once on Sat. There is even a swim-up bar, and you can also swim in the lagoon beside the motu islet facing Moorea. These apartment style suites for 1-3 people have a well-equipped kitchen, a bathroom with bathtub and a walk-in shower with a power nozzle plus a rainshower, a lighted make-up mirror and a full-length wall mirror. There is a separate European style water closet with a high toilet and tiny lavabo, and 2 hanging closets in the hallway contain an iron and board and a safe. In the bedroom area there is a very comfortable king-size bed and a sofa bed with a contemporary beige bedspread, a flat screen TV and a DVD player (the films can be rented in the gift shop), a convenient counter-desk in front of a big wall mirror and good overhead lighting for reading or working. There is also an Internet LAN cable connection on the desk that is free. The minibar has automatic billing if you move anything in it. Touches of Polynesia are provided with inlaid mother-of-pearl in the furniture, carved wooden posts beside the desk-counter and a wooden tiki in the bathroom.

The Manava Suite Resort has an underground parking garage, a spacious lobby-reception area, elevators, the Vaitohi Restaurant and Punavai Bar, the Taapuna Pool Bar, 2 conference rooms, the Manea Spa, a fitness room, and a business center with 2 computers. There is free WiFi access here and in the lobby and restaurant. At the Marama Tours activities desk in the gift shop you can rent a car or book your island tours. The Manava Digest is the hotel's program of weekly activities, which include a paid shuttle service to Papeete at 8am and 2pm daily except Sun., and a paid shuttle service to the Carrefour shopping center on Tues., Thurs., Sat. at 2:30pm. The Taapuna Pool Bar is the center of attraction on Thurs., Fri., and Sat. evenings, with live entertainment of jazz, or Tahitian or Marquesan dance groups that may include fire dancing. The torches around the bar and pool area are lighted each evening, providing a romantic tropical touch.

This 4-star resort is locally owned and is managed by South Pacific Management (SPM), the same Tahiti-based company that represents the Pearl Resorts in Moorea, Huahine, Bora Bora, Tikehau and Manihi. Whether you are staying overnight before heading to the outer islands or home again, looking for a honeymoon hotel or have business meetings in Tahiti, this hotel is a very good choice. Families are especially welcomed; children under 15 are given free accommodations when sharing the room with their parents, and there is no charge for their meals. In addition to a children's menu and drawing kit at the table, there are kids' life jackets for the water activities. The swimming pool is very popular with

Tahiti's residents and weekends are usually very active with young people having a good time on their skateboards, in the pool and on the man-made beach. Manava Suite Resort Tahiti was chosen as the Best Relaxation/Spa Hotel by TripAdvisor® in its 2010 Travelers' Choice Awards. Several of the trip reports for 2011 stated that the food here is excellent and one writer said that the cuisine served in the Vaitohi Restaurant was better than that he had eaten at the Four Seasons in Bora Bora. Room service is also available from 6am-11pm. For more information see *Where to Eat* and *Massages & Spas* in this chapter.

Moderate

TAHITI AIRPORT MOTEL, *B.P. 60113, Faaa, Tahiti 98702. Tel. 689/ 50.40.00; Fax 689/50.40.01; www.tahitiairportmotel.com. On mountainside facing Tahiti Faaa airport. All major credit cards.*

This 2-star lodging has a/c 46 rooms, including 1 room for guests with reduced mobility, just across the road from the airport. You'll have to take a taxi from the airport or pull your suitcases up the airport access road or stairs to get to the main road, then up an incline to get to the entrance of the motel. The 3-story motel has no elevators, but luggage service is normally available. The rooms are equipped with a double bed or 2 twin beds, refrigerator, TV, free WiFi access, coffee/tea machines, safe, a closet and bathroom with hot water shower. An iron and board are available on request. There is parking for 14 vehicles and they have a baggage storage service. There is no restaurant here, but there are drink and snack machines, plus a coffee machine in the lobby. A Continental breakfast is available to all guests free of charge. No smoking allowed in the motel. Warning: On four occasions in early 2011 tourists were attacked and robbed at night or in the early morning while pulling their luggage from the airport to the motel. Get a taxi or transfer.

Economy

CHEZ LOLA, *B.P. 6102, Faaa, Tahiti 98702. Tel./Fax 689/81.91.75; cell 78.08.52; holozet.lola@mail.pf. PK 4.5 mountainside in the Sainte-Hilaire neighborhood in Faaa Commune, 1 km inland from airport. No credit cards.*

Lola rents out 2 bedrooms in her family home, which is a modern concrete house above the airport. Each room has a double bed and a fan. There's hot water in the bathroom, which you'll share with the other guests. House linens are provided. You'll also have use of the living room, dining room, TV and terrace. Not only does Lola meet you at the airport upon arrival, but she will also drive you to the main road to catch *le truck* to Papeete, and come to fetch you at the airport after you've finished your sightseeing and shopping. Free breakfast. Dinner on request.

PENSION DAMYR, *B.P. 6492, Faa'a, Tahiti 98702. Tel./Fax 689/83.69.13; cell 70.81.31. On the mountainside at PK 5 in the Aubry quartier of Faa'a, overlooking the airport and the island of Moorea. Free round-trip transfers provided. No credit cards.*

Daniel and Myrtille Duquenne have a large property with 2 rooms for guests in the house, who share a bathroom with hot water, as well as the dining room and terrace. Each room has a double bed, large closet and electric fan. There is also a completely equipped studio with a private bathroom and hot water, kitchen, dining room and terrace, plus cable television, a ceiling fan in the bedroom and an electric fan in the living room. A *magasin* store is about 650 ft. away. I have booked several American and Australian friends here and they were all very impressed with the cleanliness of the house, as well as the friendliness and efficiency of the hosts. Tahiti Tourisme has given this pension a 2-Tiare rating.

Southwest Coast: Punaauia to Mataiea – Economy to Moderate
    PENSION DE LA PLAGE, *B. P. 381593, Tamanu, Punaauia, Tahiti 98718. Tel. 689/45.56.12; Fax 689/82.85.48; laplage@mail.pf; www.pensiondelaplage.com. PK 15.4 on mountainside in Punaauia Commune, 9.5 mi from downtown. Look for the sign beside the road. MC, V.*

This pension is close to the Tamanu shopping center, the Museum of Tahiti and Her Islands and several restaurants, including those at Le Méridien hotel. Even though the name indicates that it is a guesthouse on the beach, it is actually on the mountainside, with access to the beach, which is only 100 m. away. There are 12 rooms located in 2 one-story concrete buildings, each with a dbl. bed or sgl. beds, and private bathroom with hot water. The bright, cheerful rooms have bamboo furniture, a refrigerator, ceiling fan and TV, and they open onto a terrace facing the swimming pool and flower gardens. Some of the units have a kitchenette. You can also have owner Anne-Marie Moreels cook your meals for you. She is a French woman who uses fresh local products.

    PENSION OTAHA, *B.P. 380231, Tamanu 98718 Punaauia, Tahiti; Tel. 689/58.24.52/71.55.54; otahalodge@hotmail.com; www.otaha-lodge.com. PK 17.3 on seaside in Punaauia Commune, 17.3 km (10.7 mi) from downtown and 14 km (8.7 mi) from the airport. No credit cards. 2-night stay required.*

Titaua Schenck runs this popular pension beside the white sand beach in Punaauia, and she speaks English. There's a big sign beside the road and you get off Le Truck right at the driveway to the pension. Choices include garden and beach studios or bungalows with kitchenette. All guests have access to a washing machine, kayaks and snorkeling gear. There are restaurants, snack bars and roulottes, as well as various Chinese *magasin* stores selling food in this area.

    TAAROA LODGE, *B.P. 498, Papeete, Tahiti 98713. Tel/Fax 689/58.39.21; Cell 689/78.84.86; taaroalodge@mail.pf; www.taaroalodge.com. PK 18.2, beside the beach in Punaauia behind Snack PK 18. MC, V.*

Ralph Sanford welcomes surfers, backpackers and anyone else who wants to stay beside one of Tahiti's nicest beaches. He has a large chalet style wooden bungalow with a bedroom and double bed on the ground floor, complete with a private bathroom and hot water. On the mezzanine is a 7-mattress dormitory, whose occupants share a bathroom with hot water. All guests have use of the kitchen, dining room and big terrace. Two wooden bungalows overlooking the lagoon have a double bed and a single bed in each, as well as a refrigerator, microwave oven and facilities for coffee and tea. They also have a small covered terrace, where you can sit and watch Moorea and the sunset. No meals are served, but the Sanfords will bring you fresh bread and fruit in the mornings, and there is a restaurant/snack in front of the house. You can catch *le truck* to the airport or town in front of the house and airport transfers are also available.

RELAIS FENUA, *B.P. 381585, Tamanu, Punaauia, Tahiti 98718. Tel. 689/ 45.01.98/77.25.45; Fax 689/45.30.03; relais.fenua@mail.pf; www.relais-fenua.com. PK 18.25 on mountainside in Punaauia, right across the road from Taaroa Lodge and 150 m from the public beach of Mahana Park. MC, V.*

This pension has been awarded a 3-Tiare rating by Tahiti Tourisme. The modern white concrete house contains 7 neo-colonial style rooms for singles, doubles and families, and one room can accommodate handicapped guests. Some of the rooms have a/c and all of them have ceiling fans, TV, personal safes and a private bathroom with hot water. There is a boutique of local arts and crafts on the premises, and a small swimming pool and whirlpool are located in the tropical garden. The public bus passes along the coastal road just 150 m. in front of the property. This guesthouse is convenient to scuba diving centers, marinas, the Museum of Tahiti and Her Islands, the Lagoonarium and the big hotels on Tahiti's west coast. A restaurant-bar and food store are also close by.

TE MITI, *B.P. 130088, Moana Nui, Punaauia, Tahiti 98717. Tel./Fax 689/ 58.48.61; Cell 689/78.60.80; pensiontemiti@mail.pf; www.pensiontemiti.com PK 18.6, mountainside, 11.5 mi from Papeete in Lotissement Papehue, in Paea Commune, 100 m (328 ft.) after the Paea sign, across road from Mahana Park public beach. MC, V.*

A "Bed and Breakfast" sign on the mountainside of the circle island road points the way to this hostel, which is located on 1/4-acre of land with lots of fruit trees. This pension is a good choice for surfers and backpackers, as it is just 200 m (218 yds.) from Tahiti's prettiest white sand beach at Mahana Park. Three clean, modern houses provide 5 bedrooms with ceiling fans, mosquito nets and plenty of storage space. Two dorms have 4 beds each. Guests share 2 fully equipped kitchens, 3 bathrooms with hot water, a TV corner, a washing machine and several spacious patios. Breakfast included. Other services include telephone, fax and Internet access. Snorkeling gear is provided and all arrangements can be made for 4WD excursions, scuba diving and surf schools. Nearby are car and scooter rentals, restaurants, snacks and *magasin* food stores. This is a highly rated hostel according to the tourist feedback at the Tahiti Tourisme Bureau. Frédéric and Christelle are a young, dynamic couple who treat their guests very well.

HITI MOANA VILLA, *B.P. 10865, Paea, Tahiti 98711. Tel. 689/57.93.93; Fax 57.94.44; cell 74.16.67; hitimoanavilla@mail.pf; www.hitimoanavilla.com. At PK 32, 19.8 mi from Papeete beside the lagoon in Papara Commune, 10 min. from golf course and surfing beach. AE, MC, V.*

This is a clean, modern pension built in a lovely flower garden between the road and the lagoon in Papara, just 10 min. by car from the international golf course and the international surfing beach of Taharuu. There are 4 concrete studios with tiled floors, each with a double bed in the separate bedroom and 2 single beds in the living room, plus a private kitchen, private bathroom with hot water, TV, ceiling fans and a covered narrow terrace facing the lagoon. Paved walkways also lead to the 4 newer bungalows that are built in the local government subsidized style with wood shake roofs, a double bed in the sleeping/living room, a private bathroom with hot water, ceiling fan, TV and a terrace overlooking the flower garden and lagoon.

All the rooms are very attractively decorated in bright Polynesian motifs. In addition to a swimming pool, you'll also have the advantage of a private pontoon. Owner Steeve Brotherson can arrange a circle island tour by minivan, fishing, and outings on a barge for you, and help you organize other activities. Four double kayaks available for guest use. A washing machine is available for guest use at a charge, and there is a public telephone booth beside the road in front of the pension. The Restaurant Nuutere is across the street and supermarkets and snack bars are close by. Tahiti Tourisme has awarded a 3-Tiare rating to this family pension.

Other Family Pensions, Guest Houses, Surf Lodges, & Dormitories on Tahiti Nui (Big Tahiti)

PENSION PUEA, *Tel. 85.43.43/77.84.84; pension.puea@mail.pf; www.pensionpuea.com is at 87 Rue Octave Moreau in Fariipiti.* 8 double rooms and 2 communal bathrooms. A/C extra. Rates include breakfast. AE, MC, V.

HEITIARE INN, *Tel. 83.33.52; sylvie.faafatua@mail.pf; PK 4.3, Faa'a, near airport,* has 20 rooms (some with a/c) and private bathrooms. Snack open at night. Airport transfers. A lady friend who stayed here for two weeks said that there is some "hot pillow" business going on here, but the hosts were nice to her.

PAPARA VILLAGE, *Tel. 57.41.41; pacificresort@paparavillage.com*; at PK 38 on the mountainside in Papara. 1 family house with kitchen and 2 bungalows with kitchenette. Swimming pool and *Fare Pote'e* shelter. No restaurant services.

FARE RATERE, *Tel. 57.54.04; sanford.e@mail.pf; www.frenchpolynesia lodging.com.* Beside the Taharuu surfing beach at PK 39.2 in Papara. 2 Beach Bungalows and 3 duplex Garden Studios, with kitchens, TV, and hot water showers, plus a dormitory for surfers.

Tahiti Iti Peninsula (Little Tahiti)

Transfer service by mini-bus is available from Papeete or the airport to Tahiti Iti. Contact: You can rent a car at the airport, your hotel or in Taravao to drive yourself to the Tahiti Iti peninsula. You can also take a public bus for 400-520 CFP each way depending on how far you want to go.

Te Reva Nei, *Tel. 56.20.01/71.81.24; terevanei@hotmail.com.* This small company has a special tour to visit Tahiti Iti for the day. They take you to visit the

Taravao Plateau, the famous surf spot of Teahupoo, and swimming from a black sand beach. Lunch is served at Beach Kaikai, the restaurant terrace at Pension La Vague Bleue, also known as Tauhanihani Village Lodge. This 9am-4pm excursion costs US $135 per person for 4-6 passengers.

Tahiti Iti – Economy to Moderate

PENSION CHAYAN, *B.P. 8836, Taravao, Tahiti 98719. Tel./Fax 689/ 57.46.00; cell 72.28.40; pensionchayan@mail.pf; www.pensionchayantahiti.pf. On mountainside at PK 14 in Vairao, on west coast of Tahiti Iti. MC, V.*

This pension has been awarded a 3-Tiare rating by Tahiti Tourisme. Chayan is a contraction of Chantal and Yannick Salmon, the owners of this 4-bungalow pension they opened in Dec. 2002, between the mountain and the lagoon of Vairao. Although they are on the mountain side of the road, their guests have access to a small beach and a pier built over the lagoon. Their own verdant property has a waterfall and basin in the back yard, and in the middle flows a stream where fresh water eels swim and feed. The 4 concrete bungalows are far enough apart to insure privacy. Each unit has an attractively decorated bedroom with a queen size bed, louvered windows, a fully equipped kitchen, a tiled bathroom with hot water shower, and a terrace. Kayaks are available for guest use, and your hosts can help you arrange all boating excursions and other activities.

VANIRA LODGE, *B.P. 8458, Teahupoo, Tahiti 98719. Tel./689/72.69.62; Fax 689/57.70.18; vaniralodge@mail.pf; www.vaniralodge.com; Skype: vaniralodge. On the mountainside at PK 15.6 in Teahupoo, 75.6 km. (46.9 mi.) from the airport. MC, V.*

Tahiti Tourisme has awarded this pension with the top rating of 3 Tiares. The 6 artistically designed bungalows are built in a 5 acre (2 ha.) park on a plateau 164 ft. (50 m.) above sea level, offering a magnificent 180° view of the lagoon, the surfing waves of Teahupoo, and the tropical sunset. The grounds include fruit trees, a swimming pool, a small waterfall and a pond for goldfish and ducks.

Anyone who ever saw the bungalows at the now defunct Fare Nana'o in Taravao and the former Hana Iti in Huahine (destroyed by a cyclone in the 1990's) will recognize the creative touch of French builder Jean-Claude Michel in the bungalows at Vanira Lodge. Three of the naturalistic style units are made of wood, stone, bamboo and a thatched roof shaped like a turtle shell, with accommodations for up to 5 people. These *fares* have a private bathroom and kitchen. 2 other bungalows have a private garden, bathroom and kitchen and can sleep 4 or 6 people, A 6th unit can sleep 2 people, and has a fridge, kettle and coffee machine, but no kitchen. There are fans and mosquito nets in all the rooms, and they are cleaned every other day. Continental or American breakfasts are served in the gazebo, local dishes are available for lunch, and dinner is catered on request. Free WiFi connections are also available in the gazebo.

French owner Karine Lavalle can help you arrange your activities to go surfing, discovering the Tahiti Iti peninsula by boat or car, tramping to Te Pari, riding horses at the Rauvau Ranch on the Taravao plateau, or finding good restaurants and snacks nearby. The steep track from the road to the lodge can be slippery when wet. The kayaks are free of charge and are located at the marina some 984 ft. (300 m.) from the lodge. They also have rental bikes. Karine also knows the person who can give you a good massage in your room.

LA VAGUE BLEUE (Tauhanihani Village Lodge), *B.P. 66, Taravao, Tahiti 98719. Tel./Fax 689/57.23.23; cell 74.81.82; kotyvaguebleue@mail.pf. Beside the lagoon at PK 16 in Teahupoo village, 76 km. (47 mi) from the airport.. AE, MC, V.*

Koty and Réné Manuireva have 5 local style FEI (government subsidized) bungalows on their property at the edge of the lagoon in the middle of Teahupoo village facing the famous Hava'e Pass. They have two sons who surf and take care of the family pension. Everyone here speaks English. Each bungalow has a king size bed and two single beds (or 5 single beds for surfers), a ceiling fan or electric fan, color TV, a private bathroom with hot water shower, and a covered terrace. The beach units also have a refrigerator and coffee maker. There is a small beach here and kayaks for the guests. They also have a 12-passenger boat they use for excursions to explore the wild coast of Te Pari at the south end of Tahiti Iti for picnics, visits to Vaipoiri grotto and to shuttle the surfers out to the big waves. Beach Kaikai is the name of the on-site restaurant, where Koty serves family style meals.

TE PARI VILLAGE, *B.P. 697, Papeete, Tahiti 98713. Tel. 689/42.59.12/ 42.01.49/78.91.12; Fax 689/42.59.12; teparivillage@yahoo.fr. 2 km (1.2 mi) beyond the end of the road in the Fenua Aihere (wild land), a 30-min. walk or a 10-min. boat ride from the Teahupoo dock on the south coast of Tahiti Iti. No credit cards.*

Vanina Teamotuaitau and Désirée Liant have 4 simple wooden bungalows in a big grassy area beside the lagoon in a tropical garden of coconut groves, fruit trees, coffee and vanilla plantations and flowers. Units contain 1 or 2 double beds, private bathroom with hot water, and a terrace. The bungalows are spacious and clean, decorated with Tahitian fabrics and a mosquito net. All guests share the living room and dining area. American plan is obligatory and the minimum stay is 2 nights. A 5-min. boat ride takes you to the most fabulous surfing spot in Polynesia and you can hike to the waterfalls and tropical jungle of Te Pari cliffs. Canoes and kayaks are provided and you can swim, dive and visit the grotto of Vaipoiri. Most of the clientele are French people who live in Tahiti and want to get away for the weekend or a few days in a quiet, peaceful environment.

BONJOUIR LODGE PARADISE, *B.P. 8255, Taravao, Tahiti 98719. Tel. 689/77.89.69/57.02.15; bonjouir@mail.pf; www.bonjouir.com. Beside the lagoon on the south coast of Tahiti Iti in an area called Te Pari, a 12-min. boat ride beyond the end of the road and the Teahupoo boat dock. No credit cards.*

Owner Annick Paofai calls her pension the 'Eden of Tahiti', as the lush green property is located between the mountains and the lagoon and a river flows through it. The 6 simply furnished bungalows, 5 *fares*, 2 studios, 3 rooms and suite offer a variety of accommodations, including private bathrooms with hot water showers, and mosquito nets over the beds. 4 bungalows are equipped with private kitchens. You can take a 4 km. (2.5-mi.) hike along the seashore to buy food at the *magasin* store in Teahupoo. The pension also operates a shuttle boat service daily at 12pm and 5pm that will take you to Teahupoo and back for a fee. Meals are served in the pension's main restaurant. Breakfast costs 1.500 CFP and dinner is 3.500 CFP. Beer, wine and cocktails are also available.

A one-way car transfer between the airport and Teahupoo boat dock is 7.000 CFP per person. One-way boat transfers between Teahupoo dock and the pension are 2.200 CFP per person. Private parking is 500 CFP per day.

A shuttle boat is available to transfer surfers to the famous spots of Hava'e, Te Ava Iti and to the Vairao pass. The mornings here are especially magnificent, as you can see the sun rising from behind the horizon of the sea. A special sunset cruise or moonlight cruise can be arranged, as well as picnics on the motu.

Kayaks are free for guest use, but you should bring your own snorkeling gear. There is a TV in the restaurant/bar area, and there are facilities for soccer, volleyball and bocce ball. You can also swim, hike, walk to the waterfall, go fishing in the river or lagoon or chill out in a hammock under the big Fare Pote'e gazebo.

PUNATEA VILLAGE, *B.P. 8840, Taravao, Tahiti 98719. Tel. 689/57.71.10/ 77.20.31; punatea-village@mail.pf; www.punatea.com. On seaside at PK 4.7 in Afaahiti on the east coast of the Tahiti Iti peninsula, 64.7 km (40 mi) from Papeete. MC, V.*

This pension has a 3-Tiare rating and is built on 18.5 acres of land beside the lagoon in Afaahiti between Taravao and Pueu. There are 4 separate bungalows and a block of 5 rooms, all built of wood and cedar shake roofs in the style that has become the "norm" for pensions that receive special financial support from the local government. Each of the bungalows contains a double bed and a convertible sofa, a private bathroom with hot water, plus a kitchen and covered porch. There are ceiling fans and electric mosquito repellants. People staying in the rooms share the bath facilities. Owner/manager Titaua Bordes speaks English and is very helpful with her guests. They have access to a kitchen with a micro-wave and meals are also served à la carte in 2 dining *fares* by the sea. Free activities for guests include a fresh water swimming pool, swings for kids, volleyball net, kayaks and bicycles. Paid activities include WiFi access, horseback riding, trips to visit a private waterfall, picnics on Motu Nono and boat excursions to Te Pari on the end of the peninsula.

Other Family Pensions, Guest Houses, Surf Lodges & Dormitories on Tahiti Iti (Little Tahiti)

CHEZ FLOTAHIA, *Tel./Fax 57.97.38; cell 79.92.77; www.flotahia.com.* 3 rooms in modern house on seaside at PK 5,6 in Afaahiti on Tahiti Iti peninsula. Florentine Heitaa provides a Marquesan welcome and colorful décor. EP, MAP, AP, share kitchen, bathroom with hot water, TV, WiFi access, swimming pool. No credit cards.

CHEZ JEANNINE, *Tel./Fax 57.07.49/77.27.37, PK 4, Taravao Plateau on Tahiti Iti.* This lodging has a 1-Tiare rating. There are 5 rooms and 4 bungalows, plus a Vietnamese Restaurant on the premises.

FARE MAITHE, *Tel./Fax. 57.18.24; www.chez-maithe.com.* A 2-room guesthouse with communal kitchen and private bathrooms beside the sea at PK 4.5 in Afaahiti, on the east coast of the Tahiti Iti peninsula. Private transfer in minibus available.

PENSION TE HIHI O TE RA, *Tel./Fax 57.92.78. cell 72.85.24;* Haapii Haro has 3 rooms with a communal kitchen and bathroom with hot water in Tautira, at the start of the hiking trail to the Fenua Aihere on the Tahiti Iti Peninsula. MAP and AP meals available. Mosquito nets and TV. Boat transfer from the marina in Tautira. No credit cards.

MEHERIO ITI, *Tel. 72.45.50, Fax 57.68.49,* on the seaside at PK 11.9 in Vairao, has 6 simple bungalows.

PUEU VILLAGE, *Tel./Fax 57.57.87/74.71.99; www.pueuvillage.com. On the seaside at PK 9.8 in Pueu on the east coast of the Tahiti Iti peninsula.* Owner Victor Van Cam has 4 bungalows with king size beds, private bathrooms with hot water, fans, minibar and terrace. Swimming pool on premises. This used to be the Hotel Te Anuanua.

WHERE TO EAT

Tahiti Nui (Big Tahiti) – Hotel Restaurants

INTERCONTINENTAL TAHITI RESORT, *Tel. 86.51.10. PK 7, Faaa. Open daily for B.,L.,D. All credit cards.*

Tiare Restaurant is the main restaurant, offering all day dining from 6am-9:30pm. The American breakfast buffet for 3.247 CFP also includes Japanese foods such as miso soup, rice and pickled vegetables. Burgers, salads and other light meals are served for lunch as well as a 3-course *table d'hôte* menu. Dinner features local dishes and international cuisine.

A buffet of Tahitian and Marquesan specialties is featured on Wed. night, followed by the Toa Huhina Marquesan dance show, for 6.900 CFP per person. The *Soiree Merveilleuse* (Marvelous Evening) is held on Fri. night, with a lavish seafood buffet for 9.870 CFP and entertainment provided by Les Grands Ballet de Tahiti, the premiere professional dance group of Tahiti. A Bounty Dinner and Show is held on Sat. nights, with a special buffet of imaginative dishes prepared with local products and a musical re-enactment of the "Mutiny on the Bounty" story of Captain Bligh and Fletcher Christian performed by Les Grands Ballet de Tahiti. Cost is 8.950 CFP. A Tahitian brunch for 4.700 CFP is served in the Tiare restaurant every Sun. morning from 7-10am, which gives you the opportunity of tasting some very unusual treats such as *taioro, firi firi* and vanilla coffee laced with coconut milk.

Le Lotus is an overwater restaurant adjacent to a sandy bottom swimming pool with an outdoor Jacuzzi and swim-up bar. From 10am to 6pm you can sip a tropical cocktail while sitting on your underwater barstool and gazing at the beautiful island of Moorea across the Sea of Moons, and watching the outrigger canoe paddlers glide past in the opalescent lagoon. This is one of Tahiti's most beautiful and romantic restaurants and you'll think you're in a movie setting of the South Seas.

Le Lotus is open daily 12-2pm and 6:30-9:30pm, serving a trendy alliance inspired by world foods and European culinary traditions. The hotel management signed a partnership agreement in 2001 with Paul Haeberlin of Alsace and his restaurant, l'Auberge de l'Ill, one of the grand names of French gastronomy, who has a 3-star Michelin rating. A Haeberlin chef now collaborates with the Lotus' own chef to combine Tahiti's fresh products with the recipes from l'Auberge de l'Ill. You should reserve.

Luncheon choices range from a Lotus Express one-plate meal to a 3-course gourmand selection. The main courses include a fusion of Mexican, Oriental, Asian and Mediterranean cuisine.

Dinner can be a 2-course Fine Bouche meal for 7.600 CFP, a 3-course Gourmet meal for 8.900 CFP, or a 4-course Degustation (Tasting) selection for 10.800 CFP. Appetizers on the à la carte menu are 2.900-3.900 CFP; fish and seafood dishes are 3.400-4.900 CFP, and meats are 4.200-4.900 CFP. The menu changes frequently, and includes such tempting dishes as boned pigeon with foie gras, pan-fried scallops, caramelized quail, guinea fowl supreme, filet of Angus beef, or filet mignon of veal with an emulsion of truffles and porto. Hard to resist desserts are 1.350 CFP. You can choose your wines and champagnes from an extensive menu, and toast one another to the musical accompaniment of your old favorites that are played softly on the piano as you dine.

Tiki Bar is the name of the main bar, which is open daily from 10am-midnight. This is one of the most popular gathering places in Tahiti for young professionals looking for entertainment. Happy Hour starts at 4:30pm daily and lasts for 2 hours on Thurs., with live music from 5-9pm. Musical groups also perform each Wed., Sat. and Sun., starting at 5pm. The **Lobby Bar** is open daily from 10pm-5:30am, with light meals served on request.

LE MERIDIEN, *Tel. 47.07.07. PK 15, Punaauia. Open daily for B.,L.,D. All credit cards.*

La Plantation, *Tel. 47.07.34,* is the hotel's main restaurant, where you can serve yourself from the new Signature Breakfast Buffet. Dinner is à la carte except on Fri. evening when a seafood buffet is served, accompanied by Tumata Robinson's Tahiti Ora Polynesian dance show. Cost is 8.500 CFP. An Asiatic Wok buffet is served on some Sat. nights, for 6.060 CFP, which includes live entertainment. Once a month on Sat. they have a Tahitian Buffet and a Heiva du Feu show of Polynesians dancing with knives and fire.

Le Carré is a gastronomic restaurant beside the beach, where you can sit on the sundeck under a big umbrella at lunchtime or under the stars at night while dining by candlelight. Inside the square restaurant are square tables and chairs, square place settings, napkins and dishes, all designed to carry out the theme of Le

Carré—the square. Luncheon choices offer an appetizer for 2.100 CFP, a one-course meal with dessert or a 3-course meal. A lunch express menu is 3.990 CFP, which includes one course, a gourmet coffee and 1/2 bottle of water. Some of the suggestions include eggplant fritters with fresh goat cheese on a green salad, carpaccio of venison, tender poultry stuffed with shrimp and ginger, and crème brûlée with pineapple and crystallized ginger.

Dinner at Le Carré gives you choices of Formula dining. You can opt for the Cold Discoveries appetizers, which give you either salmon, lobster, crab, rabbit or pork starter courses. The Tasting Menu is 9.990 CFP, and they also suggest Le Carré Salé, Le Carré Sucré or Le Grand Carré, which includes the starter, main course and dessert. There are also à la carte selections, including vegetarian dishes, sea bass or the chef's cassoulet. The wine cabinet is filled with select choices of wine from Spain, Chile, Argentina, Australia, California, South Africa, France, New Zealand and Tahiti.

The **Pool Bar** serves light snacks, drinks and ice cream. **L'Astrolabe** is the main bar just above La Plantation Restaurant. Here you can order your favorite exotic cocktails and other libations from a prize-winning barman. A local band entertains here on Thurs. and Sat. evenings. Cocktails are half-price during Happy Hour from 6-7pm each Sun.-Thurs.

MANAVA SUITE RESORT TAHITI, *Tel. 47.31.00. Open daily for B.,L.,D. All credit cards.*

Restaurant Vaitohi serves a Continental breakfast buffet for 2.090 CFP and an American breakfast for 2.900 CFP, which you can enjoy on a covered terrace facing the hotel's lush gardens or inside the dining room. Light luncheon meals include sushi and a smoked fish plate or delicious dishes such as mahi mahi and a lentil salad, served until 3:30pm. Word should be passed around that this restaurant doesn't close until midnight, which is good news for late diners. Another fact that should be broadcast is that the food here is not only varied, with fine cuisines from France, the Mediterranean, the Pacific Rim and Polynesia, but it is also excellent and highly praised by diners from all parts of the world. There is an extensive wine list and the service is friendly and polite.

Punavai Lounge Bar is adjacent to the restaurant and lobby and is open daily from 10am-1am. Tapas are served from 5:30-10pm. The bartenders are noted for their excellent cocktails.

Taapuna Pool Bar is open daily from 10am-7pm, and a light lunch is served between 11:30am-3:30pm. Happy Hour includes live music on Thurs.-Sat.

RADISSON PLAZA RESORT TAHITI, *Tel. 48.88.88. Open daily for B.,L.,D. All credit cards.*

Restaurant Hiti Mahana is the resort's signature restaurant, overlooking Lafayette Beach and Matavai Bay. A Sun. morning Tahitian brunch is 3.950 CFP and a Sun. luncheon brunch is 4.950 CFP.

Lunch can be a burger, a choice of fresh salads or fresh fish, and set menus are available for dinner. A round-the-world buffet or Tahitian specialties are served on certain nights, accompanied by a Tahitian or Marquesan dance show for 6.000 CFP.

Le 5 Sens is open for dinner Thurs.-Sun., serving fusion cuisine from different countries.

Lafayette Bar is on the hotel's upper level, serving Happy Hour cocktails with live music from 5:30-6:30pm.

SOFITEL TAHITI MAEVA BEACH RESORT, *Tel. 86.66.00. PK 7.5 Punaauia. Open daily for B.,L.,D. All credit cards.*

Restaurant Bougainville, on the ground level, is an open-air restaurant for 200 people. Open daily for B.,L.,D serving international cuisine. Lunch includes a salad bar and burgers, as well as a tasting menu of new South Pacific flavors, presenting several small dishes on one plate. The a la carte dinner menu lists salads and appetizers from 1.200-2.200 CFP, and main courses from 2.600-5.000 CFP. A barbecue is served on Sat. nights and a Tahitian buffet is held on Sun. noon once a month and on special occasions. This is accompanied by a Polynesian dance show and costs 6.200 CFP per person. Sandwiches, hamburgers and salads are available during the daytime at the **Moorea Bar** beside the swimming pool, and you can also enjoy your favorite cocktails at this outdoor bar, which is open daily from 9am-11pm.

Sakura is a Japanese restaurant located adjacent to the lobby of the Sofitel Tahiti Maeva Beach Resort. Open Tues.-Sat. 6:30pm-9:30pm. Teppanyaki show cooking is featured, with main dishes of fish, chicken, steak, shrimp and scallops. The vegetables do not include mushrooms and bean sprouts, as you normally find in this type of cooking. A combination meal with dessert costs around 7.500 CFP. Nonetheless, all the chefs (who are mostly Tahitian) are kept busy and reservations are a must.

ROYAL TAHITIEN, *Tel. 50.40.40. On waterfront in Pirae at the Hotel Royal Tahitien. All credit cards. Open daily for B.,L.,D.*

This is one of Tahiti's most popular restaurants with local residents. You can dine on an open deck overlooking the black sand beach and lagoon, or inside the Polynesian style restaurant, which has an intricately woven pandanus ceiling that is reminiscent of Tahiti's "la belle epoch" of the good old days. Breakfast includes choices of French, Continental, American or Tahitian foods.

The lunch or dinner menu offers so many of my favorite foods that it is difficult to choose, and most of the prices have not changed in several years. I usually get the excellent poisson cru or the nems and sashimi combo for lunch, and the breaded veal cutlet Cordon Bleu for dinner, or you can order the mahi mahi Cordon Bleu. Soups include gazpacho or onion soup. Special Island dishes include chicken and fafa (taro leaves) or breaded mahi mahi in grated coconut. They also have American style BBQ ribs. Cheeseburgers, mahi mahi burgers or steak burgers are served with fries for around 1.500 CFP. Desserts include coconut pie or a banana split.

The bar and terrace become a hot spot for cool jazz played by a local band each Wed. evening, and on Fri. nights there is live music for dancing, accompanied by a special BBQ dinner. This is a good place to meet the friendly people of Tahiti.

HOTEL TAHITI NUI, *Tel. 46.38.99, Ave. Prince Hinoi, Papeete. Open daily for B.,L.,D. All major credit cards.*

Velvet Restaurant is on the street level, offering a cool, quiet atmosphere and French gastronomic cuisine. The luncheon chef's suggestions are priced at 2.200-3.400 CFP, and the dinner menu lists creative dishes of local fish and seafood for 2.900-3.400 CFP, meats for 2.700-3.700 CFP and sweets for 500-1.500 CFP. A Continental breakfast is 2.126 CFP and an American breakfast is 3.107 CFP.

Downtown Papeete – Deluxe

CORBEILLE D'EAU, *Tel. 43.77.14. Blvd. Pomare, Paofai. AE, MC, V. Open for L.,D. except for Sat. noon, all day Sun. and holidays. Reserve.*

The name of this small elegant restaurant is the French version of Papeete, which means, "water basket" and it's located in the block just west of the Protestant Church in Paofai across from the waterfront. If you're walking from downtown it is worth the few extra steps to experience the gastronomic French cuisine that is served in a very intimate a/c setting. The menu changes very frequently, featuring 4-6 modern and inventive selections according to the market. You may not understand what you're reading on the menu, but the *maître d'hotel* will graciously explain it all to you, as well as suggesting the appropriate wines for your meal.

Superior

L'O A LA BOUCHE, *Tel. 45.29.76; obouche@mail.pf. Passage Cardella. AE, MC, V. Open for L.,D. Closed Sat. noon and all day Sun. Must Reserve.*

This is one of the best-rated restaurants in Tahiti, right in the heart of Papeete. The name indicates that you'll be salivating when you order the original specialties of fusion cuisine. The menu changes every 6 months, offering luncheon appetizers from 1.600-3.400 CFP, fish and seafood dishes at 3.400-3.650 CFP and meats from 3.390-3.950. Vegetarian platters are also served. This a/c restaurant has a modern French décor and a faithful clientele.

LA PETITE AUBERGE, *Tel. 42.86.13. Rue des Remparts at the Pont de l'Est. All major credit cards. Open Mon.-Sun. 11:30am-1:30pm, and Mon.-Sat. 7-9:30pm. Closed Sun.*

This small, intimate a/c restaurant is a favorite gathering place for cognizant gourmets of traditional French cuisine. There is also outdoor dining beside a busy street. The menu includes St Jacques scallops grilled with crusty echalottes, Queue de Boeuf, and Tournedos Rossini.

ROYAL KIKIRIRI, *Tel. 43.58.64. Rue Colette, between Rue Paul Gauguin and Rue des Ecoles. AE, MC, V. Open Mon.-Sat. 11:30am-2pm, and Wed.-Sat. 7-9:30pm. Closed all day Sun. and at night on Mon. and Tues.*

This small, simply decorated restaurant is a/c and is located above the Kikiriri nightclub, serving very good Chinese and local style food as well as French cuisine. Fresh lagoon fish is frequently imported from the Tuamotu atolls.

Moderate to Superior

LA ROMANA, *Tel. 41.33.64. 3 Rue du Commandant Destremeau. AE, MC, V. Open for lunch Mon.-Fri. 11am-2pm and for dinner Mon.-Sat. 6-10pm. Closed for lunch on Sat. and all day Sun.*

This a/c restaurant has an active lunchtime business as it is located near the complex of government offices. The décor is supposed to be reminiscent of Tuscany, with a restful, old world decor and soft lighting, along with plastic trees and flowers. On Thurs., Fri. and Sat. nights fish and meats are grilled on a wood fire.

LA SAIGONNAISE, *Tel. 42.05.35. Ave. Prince Hinoi. V. Open for lunch and dinner. Closed Sun. MC, V.*

To reach this Vietnamese restaurant if you're walking from downtown Papeete, follow Avenue Prince Hinoi from the waterfront to the first traffic light, and continue straight ahead, walking on the left side of the street until you see the restaurant in the next block. It across the street from Hotel Tahiti Nui. You can relax in the small, a/c dining room while choosing your meal from a varied menu, which hasn't changed in 30 years. In addition to the soups and salads, which are light and pleasing to the palate, you'll want to try some of the house specialties, such as the *nems*, a Vietnamese omelet or the very light and tender fried balls of pork.

LE CAFE DES NEGOCIANTS, *Tel. 48.08.48; www.lecafédesnégociants.pf; 10 Rue Jean-Gilbert, Quartier du Commerce. MC, V. Meals served 8am-1am Mon.-Fri. and Sat. night. Closed Sat. noon and all day Sun.*

You will find this small French bistro from the waterfront street of Boulevard Pomare by following the side street behind *La Maison de la Presse*. There are also tables outside, beside the pedestrian street. The menu includes a creative selection of salads, carpaccios, poisson cru and tartares, as well as French specialties such as Couscous Royale. Live music nightly.

LE MANDARIN, *Tel. 50.33.50. 26, Rue des Ecoles; www.restaurantlemandarin.pf. All major credit cards. Open daily 11am-1:30pm and 6-9:30pm.*

If you're in downtown Papeete and are in the mood for good Chinese food, this a/c restaurant is one of the better choices. The upstairs dining room is decorated in an elaborate Chinese Mandarin motif and serves authentic Cantonese specialties, using local seafood and fresh produce. The menu changes weekly, featuring unusual dishes such as soup made from chicken and *bêche de mer* (sea cucumber), *cigale de mer* (slipper lobster), steamed *limande* (flounder) and Peking duck. The talented chef will also prepare you an unforgettable dinner of *ta pen lou* (Chinese seafood fondue) if you give him a day's advance notice. The wine cellar contains a varied selection of the best of Bordeaux. Live music is performed during lunch on Fri. and in the evenings on weekends.

MORRISON'S CAFE, *Tel. 42.78.61. On fourth level of the Vaima Center. MC, V. Open 11:30am-2pm Mon.-Fri., and 7-10pm Tues.-Sat. Restaurant open to midnight on Fri.-Sat. Happy Hour 5-7pm Thurs.-Fri. Closed Sat. noon and Sun. Nightclub open to 5am on weekends.*

Take the private outside elevator between L'Oasis and Air New Zealand to reach this rooftop restaurant with a/c dining or a table on the garden terrace. Workers from the travel agencies and airline offices in Papeete meet here for lunch to gossip while feasting on low calorie salads or specialties from the garden menu. A wine cellar carries a large selection of wines from the vineyards of France. As a very young man, owner "Pasha" Allouch used to wash dishes in a restaurant in Houston, Texas, where Jim Morrison and The Doors rock band were playing. He became such a Jim Morrison fan that he named his restaurant after the famous singer.

RESTAURANT JIMMY, *Tel. 43.63.32; restaurant-jimmy@mail.pf; 31, Rue des Ecoles (behind the Papeete Mairie). MC, V. Open 11am-2pm and 6-9pm during week and 6-9:30pm on weekends and holidays. Closed Sun. Reserve.*

This popular a/c restaurant has seating for 100 people on two levels and there is a pretty aquarium on the ground floor. The menu includes Thai, Vietnamese and Chinese favorites and they also serve vegetarian dishes including tofu with spicy sauce or cooked with black mushrooms, sautéed vegetables and eggplant sautéed with garlic. Beignets of bananas, pineapple, taro or apples are served for dessert. Wine is sold by the half bottle or full bottle. Some people believe that the food is not as tasty as it was under the management of the former Cambodian owner and his Canadian wife, but the new Chinese owner says that the cooks did not change.

Moderate

MANGO CAFÉ, *Tel. 43.25.55. Ground floor of Vaima Center on Rue Jeanne d'Arc. AE, MC, V. Open Mon.-Sat. L., D. Closed Sun.*

This is a popular restaurant for lunch with a salad bar and an a la carte menu. At night it is transformed into a party atmosphere.

L'APIZZERIA, *Tel. 42.98.30. Blvd. Pomare. AE, MC, V. Open 11:30am-10pm with nonstop service. Closed Sun.*

This garden restaurant has been serving Italian specialties and French food on the waterfront since 1968. In addition to a choice of pizzas cooked in a wood-burning oven, you may also want to try the lasagna, fresh mahi mahi, a barbecued steak or veal Marsala. Parking is available on the mountain side of the restaurant.

LA TERRASSE API, *Tel. 43.01.98. Rue du General de Gaulle. MC, V. Open 6am to 7pm. Closed Sun.*

This indoor-outdoor restaurant is located on the corner of Fare Tony, across the street from the Vaima Center. The tendency here is to linger over a meal or a draft beer (*pression*), while sitting on the covered terrace and people watching. The menu includes a choice of burgers, fresh salads, and daily luncheon specials such as filet of mahi mahi, veal, chicken, duck or beef dishes.

LES TROIS BRASSEURS, *Tel. 50.60.25. Blvd. Pomare, across street from Moorea ferryboats. MC, V. Open daily 7am-1am with continuous food service. Live music on weekends.*

This sidewalk restaurant and microbrewery continues to be one of the most frequented spots in Tahiti. The name means the three brewers, and it is Tahiti's first and only boutique brewery, serving beer fresh from the copper holding tank into your glass. Choices include blond, amber, white and brown beer, which you can order by the glass, mug or pitcher.

They also offer all the services of a classic restaurant and bar, with a snack menu, daily luncheon specials, and French brasserie choices such as grilled pork and lentils, or *choucroute* (sauerkraut, heaping portions of pork, and boiled potatoes). Their homemade 'Flammekeuches', or flambé tarts, are made with cheese, onions, mushrooms, bacon, white cheese, fresh cream and other ingredients, which you slice like a quiche and eat with your fingers to accompany your brew.

LOU PESCADOU, *Tel. 43.74.26. Rue Anne-Marie Javouhey. MC, V. Open Tues-Sat. 11am-2:30pm and 6:30-11pm. Closed Sun.-Mon.*

This lively Italian restaurant is Tahiti's most popular pizza parlor, offering 12 choices of pizza, plus Italian or French Provençal specialties. Mario, the colorful owner-chef who always kept the place lively, died in 2009, and now it's his son Marino who tries to uphold the family tradition in an ambiance of good cheer, good smells and good food. Even the decor is boisterous and happy, with murals of waterfront scenes from the Mediterranean coast, Chianti wine bottles tied to the support posts, with checkered tablecloths and bottles of spicy olive oil on the tables. The friendly waitresses are mostly big Tahitian "mamas" who have been part of the staff for up to three decades, and they all wear ample sized tee-shirts sporting Mario's face with a grizzled beard. Behind the Cathedral of Notre Dame, on the same street as the Clinique Cardella. Closed every year from Dec. 15-Jan. 15, and May 1-10.

SHABU ZEN, *Tel. 58.48.00/29.99.95. Passage Cardella. All major credit cards. Open for L, D, except Sat. noon, all day Sun. and Mon. night.*

This is a very friendly restaurant serving Japanese and Taiwanese specialties. Luncheon choices include Sushi royal, Japanese beef curry, Mustard chicken, or Mapo tofu for 1.900 CFP. Dinner suggestions feature a Zen menu for 2.980 CFP, and the house special fondues that you cook at your table can be a meat platter for 2.750 CFP, a seafood platter or a royal mix platter for 3.600 CFP.

SUSHI BAR, *Tel. 45.35.25. On second level of Vaima Center. All major credit cards. Open Mon.-Sat. for lunch and on Wed., Thurs., Fri. and Sat. for dinner. Closed Sun.*

In addition to plates of tempting sushi they also serve miso soup, poisson cru, tuna sashimi, tartare or carpaccio, California rolls and vegetarian sushi. You can eat in the small restaurant or order take away.

Economy to Moderate
LE MARCHE, *(Papeete Public Market), Tel. 42.25.37. Rue Edouard Ahnne, one block inland from Blvd. Pomare. V. Open 5am-4pm. Closed Sun.*

On the ground floor of the public market are take-out counters where you can get a selection of very good Chinese pastry, sandwiches, *casse-croûtes* and fries.

Coffee and soft drinks are also available here, but you have to eat and drink standing up.

Go up the escalator to the second floor of the public market and you will find a cafeteria-style restaurant where you can eat breakfast, lunch or a snack, and you can order a freshly squeezed pineapple juice or orange juice. Fri. is *ma'a Tahiti* day with traditional Tahitian food and a live band to keep you entertained while you eat. (You are not allowed to take food from the first floor to eat upstairs).

LE RETRO, *Tel. 42.86.83. Street level of Vaima Center, Blvd. Pomare. All major credit cards. Open daily with non-stop service until 11pm.*

This is an all-purpose restaurant for breakfast, lunch and dinner, a snack, *salon de thé* and bar. It is a great place to people watch as it is on the waterfront street across from the boat docks. The menu changes daily, and includes salads, *poisson cru*, burgers, pizza, pasta and daily specials, which are priced around 2.000 CFP.

MARKET COFFEE, *Tel. 45.60.70. 4 Rue Edouard Ahnne. Open Mon.-Sat. from 5:30am-3pm. Open for D. Tues.-Fri. Closed Sun. AE, M, V.*

Their breakfast formula includes a choice of a fresh fruit plate, croissant or pain au chocolat, grilled fish, poisson cru and omelets, bacon and eggs, fried chicken, or sautéed beef with vegetables. Each item is served with coffee, tea, chocolate, bread, butter and jam, and costs 1.200 CFP. On Sat. they also have roast pork, poisson cru and firi firi for 1.700 CFP. Lunch and dinner choices include fish and seafood dishes for 1.500-2.400 CFP, and meat dishes for 1.500-2.000 CFP. Desserts are 500 CFP. You can also order beer, cocktails, or bottled wines.

PATACHOUX, *Tel. 83.72.82/78.95.90. In Fare Tony Center between Snack Hollywood and La Terrasse Api on Rue LaGarde. Open Mon.-Sat. 6am-5pm. Closed Sun. No credit cards.*

This is a very popular pastry and chocolate shop, as well as a bakery, take-away service and snack restaurant with tables on a covered terrace beside a pedestrian street in the heart of Papeete. Choices include a slice of pizza, guacamole, vegetable tacos, sandwiches, salads, poisson cru, and luncheon daily specials of fresh fish and vegetables. You can also get chocolates, pastries, cakes and breads to take with you. If you have a car you may want to stop at their **Pastryland** shop *on the seaside at PK 12.5 in Punaauia, Tel. 45.03.33.*

Economy

LA MARQUISIENNE, *Tel. 42.83.52. Rue Colette. No credit cards. Open Tues.-Fri. 5am-5pm, on Sat. 5am until 12pm and on Sun. until 10am. Closed Mon.*

The smell of the coffee will lure you into this a/c pastry shop, but you won't regret following your nose, because you'll discover a wonderful selection of French pastries, cakes, pies, quiches, slices of pizza and sandwiches that will make you glad you came.

LE MOTU, *street level of Vaima Center, on the corner of Rue General de Gaulle and rue Georges LaGarde. No credit cards.*

This kiosk on the back side of the Vaima block serves a good selection of takeout sandwiches, cheese *croissants* and crusty *casse-croûtes*, as well as soft drinks and ice cream. They even have hotdogs.

L'OASIS DU VAIMA, *Tel. 45.45.01. Street level of Vaima Center, on corner of rue Jeanne d'Arc and Ave. General de Gaulle. No credit cards. Open 6am-6pm. Closed Sun.*

You can buy a sandwich or choose from 10 panini selections at the kiosk counter and eat as you go, or you can sit on the covered dining terrace and watch the daily drama of people passing, while sipping a cold *pression*. You can serve yourself from the salad bar and dine on the daily specials of French food in the a/ c restaurant a few steps up.

McDONALD'S TAHITI, *Tel. 53.37.37. Rue General de Gaulle. No credit cards. Open daily 6am-10:30 or 11pm.*

McDonald's has been firmly established in Tahiti since 1996 and this was the first location to open. School kids, government officials and visiting South Pacific dignitaries all stand in line to order their Big Macs, fries and soft drink. You won't find the bargains here that you are used to back home, but that doesn't keep the people of Tahiti from flocking here on a regular basis. There is also a big McDonald's in Punaauia and a new one in Pirae, plus a small kiosk at the Tahiti-Faa'a airport that doesn't sell burgers. Another outlet will open in Taravao in late 2011.

East of Papeete to Mahina – Deluxe
LE BELVEDERE, *Tel. 42.73.44. Fare Rau Ape Valley, Pirae. AE, MC, V. Open daily for lunch and dinner.*

You will feel on top of the world in this rustic setting, 600 m (1,800 ft.) above the sea, overlooking Point Venus and Moorea. Tetiaroa atoll is visible some 42 km. (26 mi.) to the north. The mountains of Huahine, an island 150 km. (93.2 mi.) from Tahiti, can be seen on a clear evening at sunset, with the help of the telescope on the terrace.

Le Belvedere's bright yellow *le truck* provides unforgettable transportation from your hotel, and you will feel and smell the change of air as *le truck* winds up the one lane road with some 70 hairpin curves, climbing through the Fare Rau Ape Valley.

The restaurant is a combination of a wooden Swiss chalet and Polynesian decor. There are 4 dining areas, but you will probably want to sit on the terrace for the best view, if the air isn't too chilly. During the "winter" months of June, July and Aug., the manager sometimes has to close the windows of the restaurant and light a fire in the fireplace, just like in a real Swiss chalet!

The *fondue bourguignonne* (beef fondue) is the house specialty, with tender slices of New Zealand beef that you cook to your own taste. This is accompanied by a salad bar, hot French fries, tasty sauces and carafes of white or red wine, with ice cream and coffee served afterward. The cheese fondue and seafood fondue are also great favorites, as well as French onion soup, mahi-mahi, *couscous* and pepper steak.

The tourist menu, which includes transportation, a choice of beef or cheese fondue, fish or steak, is 6.000 CFP per person. They also have seafood fondue. Reserve for your transportation. Pick-up at the hotels on the west coast begins at 11:30am for lunch, 4:30pm for sunset and dinner, and 7pm for the last service. If you have a plane to catch during the night and are looking for a place to spend your last evening in Tahiti, why not take advantage of the Belvedere's free *le truck*. The driver will pick you up at 4:30pm somewhere near the airport, ferry dock, tourist office or at your hotel, and after dinner he will drop you off at the airport around 8pm. You can also bring your luggage with you to the restaurant.

Superior

LE LION D'OR, *Tel. 42.66.50. Rue Afareii, Pirae. All major credit cards. Open for L, D. Mon.-Fri. and Sat. for D. Closed Sat. noon and all day Sun. Reserve.*

This is a gastronomic restaurant specializing in seafood and French cuisine, a 5-10 minute drive from Papeete via Ave. Prince Hinoi to Pirae. The a/c restaurant is upstairs behind the Banque de Tahiti and a pharmacy on the right side of the road in a small shopping center. Seafood choices include a dozen fresh oysters, escargots, shrimp flambé, grilled fish, lobster, and their special seafood platter.

Moderate to Superior

DAHLIA, *Tel. 42.59.87. PK 4.2, Arue. MC, V. Open 10:45am-1pm and 6-9pm. Closed Sun.*

This a/c Chinese restaurant is located on the seaside, across the road from the former French military base in Arue. Soups are 1.190-1.300 CFP and the prices range from 1.470 CFP for chicken dishes to 6.900 CFP for a whole Peking duck. You can even order a whole turbot fish for 12.500 CFP and abalones with oyster sauce for 8.600 CFP. The sizzling platters are very popular and seasonal additions are algae, crab, lobster, cuttlefish and river shrimp.

LE CHEVAL D'OR, *Tel. 42.98.89. Fariipiti, Taunoa. V. Open Mon.-Sat. for L, D. Closed Sun.*

Whenever I eat here I always order the *riz Cantonnais Cheval D'or*, which is fried rice with bits of shrimp and fish, the house specialty of the "Golden Horse". Some of my other choices are the eggplant stuffed with fish paste, and shrimp cooked in a spicy sauce and served on a sizzling platter. The roast suckling pig in coconut sauce is served only on weekends. This a/c restaurant is almost always packed with Chinese, French, Tahitian and American residents, which gives me the impression that it's a popular restaurant with everyone who knows how to find it. You'll need transportation and a map to get here from downtown. The simplest way is to turn right from Boulevard Pomare onto Avenue du Chef Vairaatoa and continue about 12 blocks until you come to Cours de l'Union Sacrée. Turn left and head toward the sea, where you'll find the restaurant in front of you where the inland road ends.

West of Papeete to Paea – Deluxe

COCO'S, *Tel. 58.21.08. PK 13.5, (seaside) Punaauia. Open Tues.-Sun. for L., D. Closed Sun. night and Mon. AE, MC, V. Reserve.*

The magnificent tropical setting of casual elegance, orchids and ferns, a gentle or booming surf on the shore and romance in the air presents old Tahiti at its best. There is a thatched roof over the restaurant and woven bamboo covers the walls, with the soft glow of gas lamps, colorful paintings by resident artists, pink tablecloths and gentle music wafting through the air to complete the venue. You begin your evening with a glass of champagne on the lawn beside the lagoon, watching the last rays of the sunset fade into mauve and purple behind the peaks of Moorea. Then you adjourn to your table inside the open sided dining room, to enjoy your gastronomic meal of French cuisine.

The menu changes every four months and set menus are suggested for 9.950-14.950 CFP to allow you to sample 4-7 courses. The pastry desserts are 2.200 CFP and the wine cellar includes prestige *grands crus* as well as dessert wines.

Coco's was taken over in 2008 by Benedicte and Thierry Sauvage, who formerly ran Café Koke in Papeete. She is the pastry chef.

Superior

CAPTAIN BLIGH, *Tel. 43.62.90. PK 11.4 (seaside), Punaauia. AE, MC, V. Open for L, D. Closed Sun. night and all day Mon.*

Just 7 miles from Papeete, on Tahiti's "Gold Coast" overlooking Moorea, this overwater restaurant can seat more than 300 diners. A deluxe seafood buffet is served each Fri. and Sat. night for 5.250 CFP, which includes a Tahitian dance show. Live music is played each Sun. during the noon buffet of *ma'a Tahiti* (a Tahitian feast) for 4.350 CFP. The à la carte menu lists salads for 600-900 CFP, *poisson cru* for 1.350 CFP, shrimp cocktail for 1.600 CFP, a seafood plate for 1.800 CFP, filet mignon for 2.500 CFP and steak and lobster for 3.800 CFP. A pier beside the restaurant leads to the Lagoonarium, and admission is free when you dine in the restaurant.

PINK COCONUT, *Tel. 41.22.23, www.pinkcoconuttahiti.com. Marina Taina, PK 9 (seaside) Punaauia. Open Mon.-Sat. 10am-midnight. Closed Sun. AE, MC, V.*

Painted palm branches and coconuts create the decor in this open sided restaurant at the water's edge. Beyond the luxury yachts berthed at the marina, the island of Moorea beckons across the Sea of Moons. The menu here features French *nouvelle cuisine* that is very pleasing to the eye as well as the palate. Starter courses and a selection of carpaccios are 1.950-2.400 CFP. Fish and seafood are 2.350-3.450 CFP and meat dishes are 1.950-2.400 CFP. Desserts are 990-1.100 CFP. This is definitely a place to come back to. Co-owner Teiva LC and his Vintage musicians entertain at the Pink Coconut and the neighboring restaurant, Quai des Îles. A daily Happy Hour from 5:30-6:30pm features special drinks from the cocktail menu.

QUAI DES ÎLES, *Tel. 81.02.38, Marina Taina, PK 9 (seaside), Punaauia. Open 11:30am-2:30pm Tues.-Sun., 7-9:30pm Tues.-Thurs., and on Fri.-Sat. from 7-10:30pm. Closed Sun. night and all day Mon. AE, MC, V.*

This popular restaurant at Marina Taina is adjacent to the Pink Coconut, and you can gaze at the yachts while enjoying a meal in open-air splendor. Exotic cuisine from the Caribbean or Madras dishes from the Indian Ocean are featured, such as Colombo d'Agneau, beef curry, or a Creole plate, between 2.350 CFP-2.750 CFP. They have an interesting choice of tapas from 990-2.450 CFP, including a basket of ribs, boudin or spicy crab farci. I especially like the way they prepare fish dishes from the Polynesian lagoons, such as parrotfish and ature, which are available in season. Desserts are 990 CFP. Happy Hour is held from 5-7pm each Thurs.-Fri.-Sat. Live music Thurs.-Sat. nights.

BLUE BANANA, *Tel. 41.22.24/81.02.89; www.bluebanana-tahiti.com. PK 11,3 beside the lagoon in Punaauia. Open for L. D. Tues. noon to Sun. noon. Closed Sun. night and all day Mon. AE, MC, V.*

This restaurant was formerly the Auberge du Pacifique and is now owned by Capucine and Steve Baker. Her father is Dr. Christian Jonville (now retired) and Steve is the son of American expat Bill Baker. Their mothers are lovely Chinese ladies from Tahiti. The menu includes gastronomic French cuisine as well as fresh fish daily, a large choice of pizzas, and big burgers with fries. The main courses are 2.200-3.800 CFP and a 3-course tourist menu is 4.500 CFP. They serve "ma'a Tahiti" (traditional Tahitian food cooked in an underground oven) on some Sundays. There is a play area for children and a shaded dining terrace with a wonderful view of Moorea.

CHEZ REMY, *Tel. 58.21.61, PK 15, (seaside) Tamanu Iti Center, Punaauia.. Open daily for L., D. except Sat. night, all day Sun. and holidays. AE, MC, V.*

The manager of this small restaurant and bar describes the cuisine as semi-gastronomic, meaning that it has quantity as well as quality. The menu features French specialties such as stewed rabbit, kidneys and sweetbreads. Starters are 1.550-2.750 CFP, salads are 1.650-2.600 CFP, fish dishes are 2.350-2.900 CFP, and meats are 1.900-3.900 CFP. Chateaubriand steak for two is 7.000 CFP, and desserts are 700-1.100 CFP.

Moderate to Superior

LE CIGALON, *Tel. 42.40.84; pacificburger@mail.pf; PK 14.9, (seaside) Punaauia between Tamanu Iti Center and Hotel Le Méridien. Open Mon.-Sat. for L., D. Closed Sun. AE, MC, V.*

You can eat in the a/c restaurant or on the outdoor terrace beside a small pool. The French cuisine includes appetizers for 1.880-2.780 CFP, fish and seafood for 2.380-3.580 CFP, and meats and poultry for 2.180-3.850 CFP. Desserts are 750-1.080 CFP and you can order draft beer, imported beers and a variety of wines. The daily specials feature traditional French cuisine. The Pacific Burger snack-bar on the terrace serves hot dogs for 420 CFP, burgers from 450-850 CFP, 6 chicken nuggets for 370 CFP, and 3 dozen choices of pizzas and calzones for 970-1.900 CFP.

WESTERN GRILL, *Tel. 41.30.56; ww.westerngrill-tahiti.com. On seaside at PK 12.6 in Punaauia, near school 2+2=4. Open daily for L, D. 2 services on Thurs.-Fri.-Sat. (6:45 and 9pm) with live entertainment. V. Reservations advised.*

If the name doesn't prepare you for this experience, then you'll certainly get the idea when you walk through the swinging saloon doors into this frontier scene right out of the old Wild West. Cowhide rugs, longhorn chairs, wagon wheels, gunny sacks, horseshoes, guitars, serapes, sombreros, leather saddles, Native American pictures, dream catchers and woven art, gold mining pans, lassos, miniature covered wagons, and a ceiling covered with old flags all provide the rustic décor for this most unusual restaurant. Of course there's a long wooden bar and country music, and it's only natural that the waiters are dressed in western gear, complete with big cowboy hats.

The place mat menus list a mouth-watering choice of good grub described as Tex-Mex, but the dishes are named after several States and there's also a touch of New Orleans, complete with Cajun spices. They specialize in giant sized shish kabobs (brochettes) and meats flambéed in whisky. The excellent draft beer is brewed at Les Trois Brasseurs in Papeete (my favorite watering hole). There are also cocktails and wines, so you can wet your whistle while you gnaw away on your smoked ribs, which are served with a tasty BBQ sauce.

Moderate

CASA BIANCA, *Tel. 43.91.35; www.casabianca-tahiti.com. Marina Taina, PK 9 (seaside), Punaauia. All credit cards. Open daily for L., D.*

This Italian restaurant replaced the Casablanca, and features 18 choices of pizzas and calzones for 1.200-1.800 CFP. The house specialty is pizza by the meter for 3.300 CFP for 1/2m and 6.000 CFP for 1m (for 6 people). They also have pasta for 1.600-2.200 CFP, meats for 1.950-2.700 CFP, and each Fri.-Sat. night they grill veal on a spit for 1.700 CFP. Happy Hour is from 5-6pm each Thurs. evening with live entertainment in the **Dinghy Lounge/Bar** on weekends (listed on their website). In addition to Italian wines and grappa you can also order a draft beer brewed by Les Trois Brasseurs in Papeete, who have added this bar and restaurant to their growing list of restaurants and bars in Tahiti. This is a fun place with good food.

CÔTÉ JARDIN, *Tel. 43.26.19, Moana Nui Shopping Center, PK 8.3, Punaauia. MC, V. Open Mon.-Sat. 8am-8pm. Closed Sun.*

This is a handy place to rest and people watch while you're shopping at Carrefour or waiting for someone who is browsing around the mall. You can sit at a table on the mall level or go upstairs to the a/c dining room, where you can order from an interesting menu that includes 10 kinds of pizza, salads, pasta dishes, *poisson cru* and Japanese sashimi. The main courses include fish, poultry and grilled meats and you can order wine by the glass, carafe or bottle. They also have fresh fruit juices, Hinano on draft, and a list of Belgian beers.

Economy
CHOCOLATINE, *Tel. 43.26.31. Moana Nui Shopping Center, PK 8.3, Punaauia. No credit cards. Open daily 7am-7pm.*
This busy snack stand is located at the exit doors of Carrefour super market and they also have a counter inside the store. They sell casse-croûte sandwiches for 230-320 CFP, hamburgers for 590 CFP, salads for 690-990 CFP, and the daily lunch specials start at 1.390 CFP. Service is cafeteria style. They have Italian ice cream as well as a good selection of soft drinks and fresh juices.
McDONALD'S TAHITI, *Tel. 48.07.07. Taina Beach, PK 9, Punaauia. No credit cards. Open daily 9:30am-10pm.*
This is the second McDonald's outlet in Tahiti. You'll find all the familiar burgers and fries and fast service here and there is also a drive-through window and games for the kids in the parking lot. There is a white sand beach behind the restaurant with an entry into the lagoon. In addition to this branch and the main McDonald's in downtown Papeete, there is also an outlet in Pirae and another one will open in Taravao in late 2011.

Elsewhere Around Tahiti Nui (Big Tahiti) – Moderate to Superior
GAUGUIN MUSEUM RESTAURANT, *Tel. 57.13.80. PK 50.5, Papeari. AE, MC, V. Open daily for lunch.*
This popular restaurant is built over the lagoon in Papeari, 50.5 km (31 mi.) west of Papeete and just 364 m. (400 yds.) west of the Paul Gauguin Museum and Harrison Smith Botanical gardens. Chances are you'll be able to admire a double rainbow over Tahiti-Iti while dining on stuffed crab, grilled mahi mahi, shrimp dishes and Continental cuisine, complete with yummy homemade coconut, papaya or lime pie. On Sundays there is a buffet of salads and Tahitian food for 4.000 CFP, with fresh fruits and coconut for dessert. Englishman Roger Gowan and his Chinese wife, Juliette, opened the restaurant in 1968, and the staff includes people from the neighborhood in Papeari, some of whom have worked in the kitchen right from the beginning. Be sure to look at the fish and sharks in the enclosures beside the restaurant.

Moderate
CLUB HOUSE, *Tel. 57.40.32/71.95.11; www.clubhousetahiti.com. PK 40,2 in Papara, at the Atimaono Golf Course. Open daily for L., D. AE, MC, V.*
This is the Golf Course restaurant and is open to the public. The menu includes salads, poisson cru and other fresh fish and shellfish dishes, plus char-broiled steaks and other meats. Roast pig in bamboo and coconut crab are Sunday specials, with a local band.
RESTAURANT JARDIN BOTANIQUE, *Tel. 57.17.59. PK 51.5, Papeari. Open daily 11:30am-3:30pm. MC, V.*
After you have visited the Paul Gauguin Museum and strolled through the Harrison Smith Botanical gardens, you'll be able to quench your thirst or enjoy a

really good meal in the restaurant beside the parking lot. You can dine in the open sided restaurant where there is usually a good breeze beside the lagoon. The menu includes poisson cru, burgers and fries, daily specials of fish, shrimp and meat dishes, desserts and fresh juice, beer and wine. Fresh river shrimp from Papeari is a delicious treat for 2.850 CFP. Ma'a Tahiti (Tahitian food) is served each Sun. for 3.600 CFP.

Economy to Moderate
BEACH BURGER, *Tel. 57.41.03. PK39, Papara. Open Sun.-Thurs. 8:30am-9pm and Fri-Sat. 8:30am-9:30pm. MC, V.*

This restaurant-snack is located near the surfing beach in Papara and is a convenient roadside stop when you're driving around the island. They serve hot dogs, burger combinations, pizzas, and steaks. There are also daily specials, milk shakes, chocolate sundaes, wine and beer. American owner Skip Anderson has added an a/c room for more comfortable dining.

Tahiti Iti (Little Tahiti)
AUBERGE DU PARI, *Tel. 57.13.44. PK 17.8, Teahupoo, Tahiti-Iti. Open 12-3pm on Sat., Sun. and holidays, and at night by reserving a day in advance. MC, V.*

This simple open-air restaurant is located beside the lagoon in Teahupoo village, almost at the end of the road on the west coast of the Tahiti-Iti peninsula, with a good view of the famous international surfer's spot of Hava'e Pass. This is a nice place to linger over a long lunch of shrimp, crab, or lobster while sharing a bottle of wine. The menu depends on seasons and what the fishermen catch. Spicy prawns are 2.700 CFP, and a seafood platter for two is 10.000 CFP.

CHEZ LOULA ET REMY, *Tel. 57.74.99. Turn off from circle island road onto Tautira road and drive to Taravao center. Take first road to right after post office. Open daily for L, D. except Sun. night. All major credit cards.*

It is worth a drive from Papeete to Taravao just to eat at this excellent restaurant. Remy, a rotund Frenchman, wears a baseball cap as he circulates among the various sections of his restaurant, which include an a/c room for 20 people, and he creates a noisy, lively atmosphere with his *joie de vivre*. This is not a fancy place, but the customers don't seem to mind the plastic flowers on the tables. They come here again and again for the superb choices and quality of the food.

I highly recommend the shrimp and ginger. It is heavenly—what more need I say? A Neptune Royal plate consists of sashimi, carpaccio, tuna tartare, seared tuna and raw shrimp. A Reef plate contains grilled shrimp, gambas, *cigales* (slipper lobster) and rock lobster. Grilled lobster Maori is flambéed with Armagnac, and other specials may include frog legs, fresh local rabbit, cassoulet of stuffed crab Antillais style, filet of sole meunieres and seafood paella. A truly rare treat you can sometimes find here is varo (sea centipede). Desserts include apple pie and profiteroles. Wines start at 2.500 CFP.

CHEZ MYRIAM, *Tel. 57.12.56, PK 60, Taravao. Open Mon.-Sat. 7am-11pm and Sun. 9am-3pm. MC, V.*

This friendly restaurant and open terrace snack bar is on the mountainside at the crossroads of Tahiti-Nui and Tahiti-Iti. Myriam is a Chinese-Tahitian lady who speaks English and likes to meet people, and she serves traditional French cuisine and quality Chinese food. She serves *ma'a Tahiti* (Tahitian food) on weekends, which is complete with all the traditional foods, including roast pig.

Other Restaurants & Snacks on Tahiti Iti

Restaurant Taumatai, *Tel. 57.13.59,* is on the left side of the road leading from Taravao to Tautira, catty-cornered to Chez Loula et Remy. I have heard several reports that this is the best restaurant on Tahiti Iti, but unfortunately, it was closed on the two occasions when I went to check it out. A young couple from Taravao are said to serve food that is even better than Chez Loula et Remy, which will take some doing to beat. **Chez L'Eurasienne,** *Tel. 57.07.49,* is a Vietnamese Restaurant at Pension Jeannine on the Taravao Plateau. **La Plage de Maui** (Maui Beach), *Tel. 74.71.74,* in Toahotu has a small strip of white sand beach, a good snack bar and a good reputation. Fresh river shrimp and wild Marquesan goat are menu specialties. Open daily for L. and on Fri.-Sat. for D. **Snack Hinerava,** *Tel. 81.93.61/79.06.11,* at the end of the road in Teahupoo (PK 18) facing the surfers' famous Havae Pass, is open from 8am-10pm Tues-Sun. Dine in a/c restaurant or on terrace.

SEEING THE SIGHTS

Papeete Highlights

The best way to visit Papeete is to take a walking tour, which you can do on your own or with a guide. You will enjoy the walk more if you do it in the cool of the morning. Everyone gets going early around here, so you shouldn't have any problems with closed shops if you begin your stroll around 7:30am

Start your tour at the **Tahiti Tourisme Bureau** on the waterfront side of Boulevard Pomare, at the corner of Rue Paul Gauguin. This building is called **Fare Manihini,** which is the Tahitian word for "Visitor's House." The helpful hosts speak good English and will give you brochures and a map of the city and they will answer any questions you may have. You can also follow the map printed on pages 8-9 of the *Tahiti Beach Press* Guide Section, which is available at the Tourist Bureau.

On the right, just outside Fare Manihini, is the **Captain Tamarii a Teai Square,** named in honor of a former Tahitian merchant marine officer. This is an attractive place with benches and shade trees, where you can relax and enjoy watching the activity on the waterfront after your stroll. Some of the phone numbers on the informational panels may be out of date, but they also show maps, and give information on the birds and fish that are found around Tahiti.

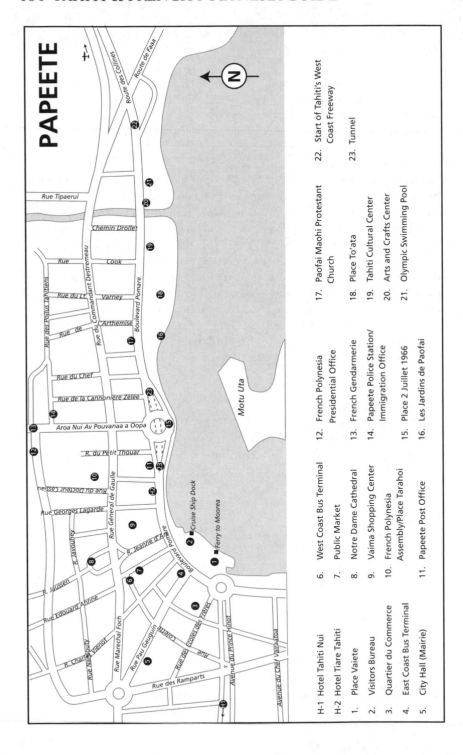

PAPEETE

H-1 Hotel Tahiti Nui
H-2 Hotel Tiare Tahiti

1. Place Vaiete
2. Visitors Bureau
3. Quartier du Commerce
4. East Coast Bus Terminal
5. City Hall (Mairie)
6. West Coast Bus Terminal
7. Public Market
8. Notre Dame Cathedral
9. Vaima Shopping Center
10. French Polynesia Assembly/Place Tarahoi
11. Papeete Post Office
12. French Polynesia Presidential Office
13. French Gendarmerie
14. Papeete Police Station/Immigration Office
15. Place 2 Juillet 1966
16. Les Jardins de Paofai
17. Paofai Maohi Protestant Church
18. Place To'ata
19. Tahiti Cultural Center
20. Arts and Crafts Center
21. Olympic Swimming Pool
22. Start of Tahiti's West Coast Freeway
23. Tunnel

Across the road is the **Vaima Center**, a 4-story mall of boutiques, pearl shops, restaurants, a bookstore, travel and airline agencies, and business offices. It was named for the Snack Vaima, a very popular restaurant and sidewalk café that has been replaced by Le Retro.

All set to go? Walk westward along the renovated **yacht quay** and you will see the catamarans and dive boats that are loading passengers for a day sail to Moorea or Tetiaroa. Cruising yachts tie up here during the peak sailing months of Apr. to Sept., while the owners make necessary repairs and provision their boats for the next leg of their journey.

Across the Papeete harbor the international container ships dock to unload cars, lumber, household furnishings, food, fuel, and numerous other supplies. Several inter-island cargo vessels are based at **Motu Uta**, Tahiti's shipping port of wharves and warehouses, which is connected by a bridge to the industrial area of Fare Ute and downtown Papeete.

This little motu used to be a quiet islet that was reached only by boat or strong swimmers. It was formerly owned by the Pomare family, whom the first Europeans considered the royalty of Tahiti. Chances are you will also see the fast catamarans and ferries that connect Papeete with Moorea. This is one of the busiest French-owned harbors in the world, due to the passenger traffic between Tahiti and Moorea.

Walking along the quay past the **Bounty Tunnel** you will come to a traffic roundabout where **Aroa Nui Avenue Pouvanaa a Oopa** (formerly **Avenue Bruat**) joins **Boulevard Pomare**, the waterfront road. This grassy area is decorated with flags from several countries and a pedestrian walkway leads to **Place 2 Juillet 1966** (formerly **Jacques Chirac Square**), a pleasant semicircular-shaped landfill in a garden setting of trees and flowers. The French Polynesia government renamed this waterfront park to mark the first of France's 181 nuclear weapons tests in the South Pacific, which began on July 2, 1966. A stele of 5 stones represents the 5 archipelagoes of Tahiti and Her Islands, where most of the workers came from who were stationed on the Tuamotu atolls of Moruroa and Fangataufa during the 30 years that France carried out nuclear tests in that area. These stones form a "paepae", a gathering place where people can come and go freely, and the history of their origin is printed on a tableau stand in French, Tahitian and English.

Several stairways lead down to the underground parking garage below the garden, and an extended boardwalk allows you to continue your leisurely stroll beside the harbor. Docking facilities, complete with water and electrical hookups, have been added for the sailboats from many countries around the world, whose owners are living their dreams of cruising the South Pacific.

The **Jardins de Paofai** (Gardens of Paofai) cover an area of 12.4 acres beside the lagoon on the west end of Papeete, with flower-bordered walkways meandering around 25 small islands, waterfalls and basins, five pergolas and two *fare pote'e* open-air shelters. Benches are placed throughout the gardens and there are two enclosed playgrounds for children as well as two public toilets and changing rooms.

In the waterfront area of the gardens is **Hokule'a Beach**, where you will see several outrigger canoes on supports. You may even be able to watch some of Tahiti's canoe teams practicing for the next big race, which is a national passion. You will also see the marae and monument in honor of the *Hokule'a*, a replica of an ancient Polynesian voyaging canoe that was built in Hawaii. It is sponsored by the Hawaiian Voyaging Society to retrace the sailing routes of the Polynesian pioneers who settled the tiny specks of land that make up the Polynesian triangle. The *Hokule'a* made its first voyage to Tahiti in 1976, navigating by the winds, stars and sea currents, and arrived in Tahiti to an overwhelming welcome by thousands of Tahitians.

Your destination on this side of the street is **Place To'ata**, also called **Tahua To'ata**, which is an immense outdoor theater, concert arena and meeting place, complete with public restrooms and showers and exhibit space. Visitors enjoy coming here to sit on a bench among the flower gardens and watch the activity in the harbor, as well as the families who bring their children to skate or ride their scooters in the fresh air. All the restaurants here were rebuilt in 2007.

The **Maison de la Culture** at Fare Tauhiti Nui, adjacent to Place To'ata, is Tahiti's cultural center, library and theater/concert hall, which was renovated in 2011, with a high stone wall on the street side. The **Olympic swimming pool** is just beyond the cultural center, and beyond that is the **Artisan Center**, where you can buy arts and crafts made in Tahiti and Her Islands.

When you get ready to head back toward the center of town, perhaps you will prefer to go up the stairs to the crossover bridge in front of the Artisan Center to get to the other side of the road. Or you can use the designated crossing in front of Place To'ata. Trying to get across the five lanes of traffic can be quite tricky and even dangerous in Papeete, even though there are pedestrian zones.

Once you have negotiated getting across Boulevard Pomare, you will soon come to the **Clinique Paofai**, then the **Protestant Temple**, which used to be part of the Evangelical Society of French Polynesia. In mid-2004 all the former Evangelical churches changed their name to Maohi Protestant Church and all the preachers are Tahitian. The missionaries from the London Missionary Society brought the Gospel to Tahiti in 1797 and the Protestant religion was predominant in the Windward Society Islands until the year 2000, when a poll revealed that 45 percent of the population is Catholic and 34 percent is Protestant.

The **Robert Wan Pearl Museum** is also located in this area of Paofai, on the same side of the street as the Maohi Protestant Church. This is the only pearl museum in the world and is definitely worth a visit. It is open Mon.-Sat. from 9 a.m-5pm, but it is best to get there at least by 4:30pm.

Continue down Boulevard Pomare and turn right on Aroa Nui Avenue Pouvanaa a Oopa (still called Avenue Bruat by most residents). Walk a block and cross the street on Rue du Commandant Destremeau, which changes to Rue du General de Gaulle at this corner. Walk under the shady trees up Avenue Pouvanaa A Oopa and see the government buildings and war memorials.

Here you will find the French court or *tribunal*, the Police station, the *gendarmerie*, and the **Presidential Palace**, the impressive building that formerly housed the offices of the President of French Polynesia, as well as 500 employees. Oscar Temaru, the independence party President who was in office at press-time (for the 5th time in 9 years), refused to use this expensive showcase, choosing the Vice-President's office instead. Across the street is the **Ministry of Culture** and its lovely flower gardens. In front of these colonial buildings are the memorials for the Polynesian soldiers who were killed during the First World War of 1914-1918, as well as plaques for the men killed in Korea, Indochina, Madagascar, North Africa and in other war battles.

Go back to Rue du General de Gaulle and continue toward the center of town, passing more government buildings. On your right is **Place Tarahoi**, where Queen Pomare IV lived in an elaborate mansion before the French took control in 1842, and used Tarahoi as their headquarters. The offices and home of the **French High Commissioner** are located in the building on the right. The roof has 5 points, representing the 5 archipelagoes of French Polynesia. Against the fence in the parking lot is the **Pacific Battalion Monument**, a tribute to the French Polynesians who fought with General Charles de Gaulle's Free French forces during World War II.

To the left of the French High Commissioner's office is the French Polynesia **Assembly** building, where the local politicians have a good go at one another during their hot debates. In front of the building is a monument to **Pouvanaa a Oopa** (1895-1977), a man from the island of Huahine who was a decorated hero fighting for France during World War I. He became an even bigger hero to the Tahitian people when he was sentenced to prison in France while seeking independence for his own country. After spending 15 years behind bars during the 1960s and 1970s, Pouvanaa returned to Tahiti, but was sent back to France again, this time as Tahiti's representative in the French Senate.

Cross Rue du General de Gaulle again in the crosswalk between Place Tarahoi and the rear of the **Papeete Post Office**, just before you get to McDonald's, Tahiti's favorite fast-food joint. (One of Tahiti's local newspapers recently reported that a McDonald's cheeseburger in Tahiti costs more than 10 full meals in China).

Double back toward the west for a few yards until you see the green oasis of **Bougainville Park** on your right, adjacent to the post office. A gurgling stream meanders through the tree-shaded gardens. This was Queen Pomare's favorite bathing pool when she lived at Place Tarahoi, and it was from this little river that Papeete received its name: *Pape* (pah-pey) means water in the Tahitian language; and *ete* (eh-tey) means basket; therefore, Papeete means water basket. Before the houses were equipped with water pipes, the people used to come to this spring with their gourds wrapped in woven leaves and take the *pape* home in their *ete*.

Although this park was named for the French explorer, Louis Antoine de Bougainville, he never laid eyes on this site, because he spent his entire brief visit to Tahiti on the east coast of Hitiaa. However, he was the first French discoverer, and his statue stands between the **two cannons** that are adjacent to the sidewalk on the Boulevard Pomare side of the park.

The cannon nearest the post office was taken from the *Seeadler*, a World War I German raider that belonged to the luckless Count Felix von Luckner. His ship ran aground on Mopelia atoll, in the Leeward Society Islands in 1917, after having captured 14 British, French and American ships in the South Pacific. The other gun comes from the *Zélée*, a small French navy vessel that was sunk in Papeete harbor in 1914 when the German raiders *Scharnhorst* and *Gneisenau* bombarded Papeete.

After you have walked around the cannons, continue toward the center of Papeete on Boulevard Pomare. Turn right on Rue Jeanne d'Arc beside the Vaima Center and you'll see the **Cathédrale de l'Immaculée Conception**, which is usually called the **Cathedral of Notre Dame**. This cathedral was built in 1875 and has been restored a few times. If the door is unlocked go inside, where it is quiet and cool, and look at the paintings of the Crucifixion.

Cross over to the left side of the street at the Pharmacie de la Cathedrale, which is on the corner opposite Place Notre Dame. Walk past Tahiti Music and turn left at the end of the block. The sidewalk here is usually quite crowded with Tahitians who are shopping or hanging out, talking with friends. Walk past the police station and you will see the public market, the **Marché Municipale**, which is the heart and breadbasket of Papeete. The Tahitian "mamas" and even young men sell orchids, anthuriums, ginger flowers, roses, and other flowers of every imaginable hue.

Past the flower vendors inside *le Marché* you will see traditional Tahitian fruits and tubers on the left of the aisle and vegetables sold by the Chinese are on the right. The fish and meat markets are off to the right and upstairs you'll find all kinds of locally made products, including some nice *tifaifai* bed covers or wall hangings and lots of seashells. Outside *le Marché* are hundreds of colorful *pareos*. The cotton ones were made in Tahiti and the rayon *pareos* with fringe are imported from Indonesia.

Leave *le Marché* and go out the door closest to the counters selling woven hats, bags and grass skirts. Walk straight ahead on Rue Colette for one block until you come to Rue Paul Gauguin. Turn right at the corner and you will see the **Mairie of Papeete on** the left. This impressive building is the town hall, called *Hôtel de Ville* in French and *Fare Oire* in Tahitian; it is a replica of Queen Pomare's royal palace that once stood at Place Tarahoi. The elaborate building, with crystal chandeliers and pink marble imported from Italy, was inaugurated in 1990. Former French President **François Mitterand** was the guest of honor for the dedication ceremonies. Walk up the steps into the building and take the elevator to the third floor. There are frequent art exhibits on display in the room to the left as you get off the elevator. Walk around the building and admire the decor, and be sure to see the stone carvings in the gardens all around the outside of the building. They were made by sculptors living in Tahiti, the Marquesas and Easter Island.

Following your tour of the town hall, walk back toward the waterfront and the Tahiti Tourist Bureau. Cross Boulevard Pomare to the harbor side, and as you approach Fare Manihini, take a little detour to the right to have a look at **Place**

Vaiete, also called Tahua Vaiete. This square was the site of the first territorial parliament in 1945. It was also the place where the 4th Festival of Pacific Arts was held in 1985. For many years the traditional song and dance competitions took place here during the July *fête* celebrations, and the carnival type stalls, carousel, Ferris wheel and *papio* rides for children were built next to the amphitheater.

In 2001 this square was enlarged to a tiled area of 1,200 sq. m (129 sq. ft.). A low stone wall encloses Place Vaiete and there are benches and a waterfall, public toilets, and round-the-clock security guards. The roulottes (mobile diners) still set up shop here in the evenings, but they are now limited to 30, and there is even a washroom where they can clean their dishes and pots and pans. Many of the roulottes bring their own linoleum to spread under their vans to protect the tile from grease spots, and some of them place tables and chairs beside the roulotte for more comfortable dining. Local musicians give free concerts in the bandstand and the audience sits on the low wall, the benches and the tiled floor of the square.

If this 2-hour walk is too long for you, it can be shortened by crossing Boulevard Pomare at Avenue Pouvanaa Oopa, after you have visited the waterfront and had a look at the yachts. You can head inland to see the government buildings and continue the above itinerary from there. You will eliminate the extra walk to the Gardens of Paofai, I Iokule'a Beach, Place To'ata, the Cultural Center, Artisan Center, Protestant Temple, and Robert Wan's Tahitian Pearl Museum, which you will certainly want to visit another time.

Around the Island

Most tour drivers follow the northeast coast through Papeete's neighboring *communes* of Pirae, Arue and Mahina. Ask your driver to stop at the James Norman Hall House and Library, at PK 5.5 in Arue. It is well worth a visit. See information under *Museums & Special Sightseeing Stops* in this chapter. From the Tahara'a Lookout Point at PK (poste kilometre) 8.1 in Arue you can see historic Matavai Bay. When Captain James Cook sailed the *Endeavour* into this bay in 1769, he sighted a single tree (*Erythrina indica*) with bright red-orange flowers growing on the promontory above the bay. He used the tree as a navigational landmark and named this reference point "One Tree Hill." Although the gnarled old tree has disappeared, this lookout provides a spectacular panoramic view of the island of Moorea, the Sea of Moons, the coral reef and lagoon, and Tahiti's majestic fern-softened mountains.

The next stop will be at Point Venus at PK 10 in Mahina. This historic site beside Matavai Bay is where English Captain Samuel Wallis of the *H.M.S. Dolphin* came ashore in 1767, to become the first European to discover Tahiti. When Captain Cook led an expedition of scientists to Tahiti to observe the transit of the planet Venus across the sun on June 3, 1769, he named the site Point Venus. Captain William Bligh and the *Bounty* crew came here in 1788 to collect breadfruit plants, and representatives of the London Missionary Society waded ashore in 1797, in search of souls to save.

In addition to the monuments in honor of Captain Cook and the missionaries, you'll see a lighthouse, picnic tables, an arts and crafts center, toilet facilities, tropical gardens and a black sand beach, usually decorated with topless sunbathers, mostly French women. Raise your gaze from the bare twin peaks on the beach and look up at the double summit of Tahiti's highest mountain, Mt. Orohena, reaching 2,241 m (7,353 ft.) high into a crown of clouds. Point Venus is a lovely spot to photograph the bathing beauties as well as the tropical sunset, with a magnificent view of the nearby island of Moorea.

Continuing along the east coast you'll see the surfers riding the waves offshore Papenoo, before coming to the tunnel beside the **Blow Hole of Arahoho**. This 449 ft. (137m.) long tunnel should be open by the end of 2011, although the road work along this section of the east coast will continue until 2014.

At PK 22 in Tiarei, turn off the main road and head into the valley to visit the **Three Cascades of Fa'arumai**. The Vaimahuta waterfall is easily reached by a 5-min. walk across the bridge over the Vaipuu river, following a well defined path under a cool canopy of wild chestnut (*mape*) trees and *Barringtonia asiatica (hutu)* trees. Countless waterfalls cascade in misty plumes and broken curtains down the mountainside to tumble into a crisp, refreshing pool. This is a good swimming hole, but don't forget your mosquito repellent.

Back on the circle island road you will pass country villages, modern concrete homes and modest little *fare* huts brightly painted in yellow, pink and blue. Flowers and hedges of every shape and hue border the road and breadfruit, mangoes, papaya and banana trees fill the luxuriant gardens. Birdhouse-shaped boxes stand by the road in front of each home, ready to receive the daily delivery of fresh French *baguettes* that are baked by the Chinese and eaten by the Tahitians as their staple food.

At PK 37.6 in Hitiaa your guide may point out a plaque beside the bridge. The French explorer, **Louis Antoine de Bougainville**, made a deed of annexation in Apr. 1768, when his ships *Boudeuse* and *Etoile* dropped anchor just inside 2 islets offshore the village. Bougainville proclaimed French sovereignty over the island, which he named New Cytherea. He placed the deed in a bottle and buried it in the ground between the river and the beach. Bougainville's ships lost 6 anchors during his 10-day visit.

At PK 60 you'll be in the village of Taravao, the isthmus that connects Tahiti Nui with Tahiti Iti, the Taiarapu peninsula. If you're saving your discovery of Tahiti Iti for another delightful day, then continue on to **Papeari**, where you'll find the **Paul Gauguin Museum** and the **Harrison Smith Botanical Gardens** (see information under *Museums* and also under *Gardens* in this chapter).

Most tour buses stop for lunch in the vicinity of Taravao or Papeari, where you have a good selection of restaurants and snack bars. The most popular luncheon choice is the **Gauguin Museum Restaurant**, *Tel. 57.13.80*, at PK 50.5 in Papeari. This very spacious restaurant and bar is built over the lagoon, just 400 yds. west of the Paul Gauguin Museum and Harrison Smith Botanical gardens. (See description in the *Where to Eat* section).

> ## LAND OF THE DOUBLE RAINBOW
> When you stop at the **Vaipahi Gardens and Cascade** in Mataiea, look out over the lagoon and perhaps you'll catch sight of a double rainbow arching over the peninsula of Tahiti Iti. This is where I fell in love with Tahiti during my first visit to the island in 1968. There's magic in the air here, a haunting beauty that touches the soul.

The latter half of your tour will take you to the **Vaipahi Gardens and Cascade**, at PK 49 in Mataiea. If you are making the island tour on your own, then stop at the **Vaima River**, PK 48.5 in Mataiea, very close to the public gardens. This is one of Tahiti's favorite watering holes, complete with underground springs that bubble up like a cold Jacuzzi. Leave your car in the parking lot and wade waist-deep through the clear, refreshing river. Wild hibiscus (*purau*) trees lend their shade and purple water hyacinths add their color to the scene. This is a welcome treat on a hot sunny day.

On the southwest coast you'll pass the **Atimaono Golf Course**, *Tel. 57.40.52*, at PK 40.2, where international championship tournaments are played each July. A little further on you'll see the black sand beach and the impressive waves of **Papara**, where world-class surfers compete.

The side road leading into the valley to the **Marae of Arahurahu** is at PK 22.5 in Paea. Follow the road to the parking area and walk a few steps to the 2 restored open-air stone temples, which were used in pre-Christian days for religious ceremonies, meetings, cultural rites, sacrifices and burials. There is no entry fee to visit the *marae* except during special performances that sometimes take place during the **Heiva Festival** in July and Aug. These colorful reenactment ceremonies choose various themes, such as the crowning of a king and royal weddings, with a cast of dozens of beautifully costumed Tahitian dancers, musicians, warriors and *tahua* priests.

The **Grottos of Mara'a** at PK 28.5 in Paea are joined by a flower-bordered walkway. The **Paroa cave** is the largest of 3 natural grottos, where overhead springs drip through wild ferns and moss, forming a pool where children play. **Queen Pomare** used to bathe here and **Paul Gauguin** wrote of swimming inside this cave. Drops of water from the overhead ferns reflect rainbow hues in the rays of the afternoon sun. There is no entry fee, but the grotto may be closed because of loose rocks falling from above the spring.

On the west coast of the island you'll see a sign on the seaside at PK 15.7 in Punaauia, directing you to the **Museum of Tahiti and Her Islands** (**Musée des Iles**). Some of the tour guides stop here. See information under *Museums*.

In the communes of Paea and Punaauia, you will catch only glimpses of Tahiti's lovely beachfront properties behind the walls and thick hedge fences that protect them from the road. You may even see some old Polynesian style homes that are built of pandanus and woven bamboo, but these are now rare. The millionaires' modern villas are up in the mountains, overlooking the island of Moorea. Here suburbia Tahiti blends the past with today. The thatched roof *fare*, colonial mansions and concrete homes are neighbors with schools, shopping malls, used car lots and DVD shops. Supermarkets sell foods for all tastes and boutiques sell surfboards and beachwear from California and Hawaii.

From 1897 to 1901, the artist **Paul Gauguin** lived in a comfortable villa at PK 12.6 in Punaauia, before he left for the Marquesas Islands in search of a wild and savage beauty. Your guide may point out the **2+2=4 school** that was built adjacent to Gauguin's former property.

Museums & Special Sightseeing Stops

Robert Wan Pearl Museum (Musée de la Perle). On Blvd. Pomare in the Paofai section west of downtown Papeete near Protestant Church. Open Mon.-Sat. 9:30am-5pm. Last entry at 4:45pm. This is the only museum in the world dedicated to pearls. Several promenades and themes teach you many lessons about the history and culture of the pearl, a gem that has been regarded as a wonder and a mystery to man and woman since time immemorial. No entry fee. For information or private visits: *Tel. 46.15.54; www.robertwan.com.*

James Norman Hall House and Library, *Tel. 50.01.61/50.01.60; www.jamesnormanhallhome.pf.* On mountainside at PK 5.5 in Arue. Open Tues.-Sat. 9am-4pm. Entry 600 CFP. This colonial style green house is a replica of the famous author's original home, and his library of more than 3,000 books is displayed in numerous bookshelves. James Norman Hall and Charles Nordhoff, both American heroes of World War I, moved to Tahiti in 1920. Hall wrote 17 books by himself and co-authored 12 books with Nordhoff. Their most famous works included *Mutiny on the Bounty, Men Against the Sea, Pitcairn's Island, The Hurricane,* and *The High Barbaree.* Hall's office library contains his original writing desk and typewriter and is arranged exactly as it was on the day he died in 1951. The house is filled with antique wooden furniture, family pictures, Hall's poems written to his family, his favorite paintings, gramophone and other personal effects. One of the 3 Oscars awarded to his son, the late Conrad L. Hall, for his achievements as a cinematographer in Hollywood films, is also on display. Be sure to visit Mama Lala's Tea Room, named in memory of Hall's wife, Sarah Winchester Hall.

Paul Gauguin Museum, *Tel. 57.10.58.* Beside the lagoon at PK 51.2 in Papeari, adjacent to the Harrison Smith Botanical Gardens. Open daily 9am-5pm. Entry 300 CFP. This is a memorial to the late French artist, with only a few original carvings and wood blocks located in the Salle Henri Bing. Reproductions of Gauguin's paintings and carvings are exhibited in 3 buildings beside the sea. In the 2nd building you can see where the originals of Gauguin's works of art are located today. 3 ancient stone *tikis* from Raivavae in the Austral Islands stand in the gardens surrounding the museum, and now the people of Raivavae want them returned to their original sites.

Museum of Tahiti and Her Islands (Te Fare Iamanaha), *Tel. 54.84.35,* on the sea side at PK 15.7 in Punaauia, at Fisherman's Point (Pointe des Pêcheurs). Open Tues.-Sat. 9:30am-5:30pm. Entry 600 CFP. Closed Sun.-Mon. This museum presents the natural environment, Polynesian migrations, history, culture and ethnology in 4 exhibit halls. On display are stone and wooden tikis, hand-hewn canoes, intricate sculptures, tapa bark, seashells and other traditional Polynesian objects and tools. Walk out to the beach and watch the surfers before you continue your tour. Breathe deeply and smell the fresh salty air. If you plan to visit the museum by public transportation, you should know that the last bus for Papeete passes in front of the Tamanu shopping center at 4pm, except during the Heiva Festival in July, when they run a little later.

Lagoonarium, *Tel. 43.62.90,* at PK 11.4 in Punaauia at the Captain Bligh Restaurant. Open daily 9am-5:30pm. Entry 500 CFP for adults and 300 CFP for children 3-12 years old. No entry charge if you eat in the restaurant. 4 big fish parks are built into the lagoon, filled with thousands of fish, sharks, rays, turtles and moray eels. If you arrive at noon you can watch the daily shark feeding show.

Parks & Gardens

Mahana Park is beside the lagoon at PK 18.2 in Paea. Open daily. No entry fee. This public park covers a 1-acre grassy lawn and parking area and borders a beach facing the island of Moorea. The tranquil lagoon is good for swimming. There are public toilets and showers and you can picnic at one of the tables under the trees.

Harrison W. Smith Botanical Gardens at PK 51.2 in Papeari, adjacent to the Paul Gauguin Museum. Open daily 9am-5pm. Entry is 600 CFP. Protect yourself from mosquitoes and stroll through the 137 ha. (340 acres) of tropical gardens, streams and water lily ponds. You will see hundreds of trees, shrubs, plants and flowers gathered from tropical regions throughout the world by Smith, who was an American physics teacher who escaped to the South Seas in 1919 and created his own Garden of Eden in Tahiti. The most impressive part of this park is a natural forest of Tahitian *mape* trees, with their convoluted roots above the ground. This grove provides a cool and pleasant walk, with a small stream meandering through the shaded garden. Main attractions in the gardens are two huge land turtles, which were brought to Tahiti in the 1930's from the Galapagos Islands. These pets placidly pose for photographs and will stop eating to raise their long wrinkled necks and stare at the cameras.

Vaipahi Gardens and Cascade, on the mountainside at PK 49 in Mataiea. Open daily. Free entry. Take a pleasant stroll through these public gardens and discover a sparkling waterfall at the end of a short path. Huge tree ferns and giant leaves of elephant ear plants provide a natural setting for the cascade, which is a popular photographic choice for travel brochures on Tahiti. The gardens are filled

THE MONOI ROAD (*LA ROUTE DU MONOI*)

From traditions that stretch back thousands of years the sacred **monoi oil** of the Polynesians is much more than a natural personal care product. Obtained by macerating fresh Tiare Tahiti (Tahitian gardenia) flowers in refined coconut oil, it is a precious concentrate of sensuality, naturality, and authenticity.

Follow the **Monoi Road** for an extraordinary fragrant journey through the land where Tahiti's famous monoi was born. You can drive yourself or take a guided tour around the island of Tahiti to visit as many of the 22 stops as you wish.

Along the route you will learn all about the botany, manufacture and use of monoi. You will visit fields of Tiare Tahiti flowers, a coconut grove with copra dryer, ethnobotanical gardens, a cosmetology lab, soap factory, traditional monoi makers and monoi perfume manufacturers. Five of the stops will give you an introduction to Polynesian beauty rituals. The Monoi Road includes visits to masseurs and spas, the Monoi Institute, the Papeete Market, and to a large crafts center at Aorai Tini Hau in Pirae, where the Tahitian "mamas" exhibit and sell their traditionally prepared monoi. Be sure to make an appointment for a Taurumi massage.

Most of the 22 stops are admission-free. There is a charge at the Botanical Gardens of Motu Oviri in Papeari, and charges are made for any treatments such as massages. The Huilerie de Tahiti invites the public to visit the coconut oil refinery each year during the Monoi Here Festival, which takes place during the month of November. You will have a grandstand view of the schooners unloading bags of copra from all over the French Polynesian islands. You can follow the production stages whereby coconut is turned into copra oil for the food industry or fuel and refined copra oil for Monoi de Tahiti 'Appellation of Origin.'

Monoi de Tahiti is the first cosmetic product to have obtained an Appellation of Origin. This stamp guarantees the quality of its manufacturing process and of the selection and authenticity of its Polynesian ingredients. Monoi de Tahiti can be used pure or as an ingredient in the composition of personal care products. For complete details and a map of the Monoi Road, go to *www.monoiaddict.com*.

with luxuriant vegetation, including *rambutan* fruit, fragrant *pua* flowers, ground orchids and the exotic jade vine. Crotons and hibiscus add to the flamboyance in these gardens of dancing color. You can enjoy a picnic at a table on the seaside if you are touring the island by private car.

Guided Island Tours

You can book your sightseeing tours through the travel desk at your hotel in Tahiti and see the island with a knowledgeable guide aboard an a/c bus, minivan or Mercedes luxury car.

A **Half Day Circle Island Tour** starts at 4.500 CFP plus entrance fees to the museums and gardens visited. These tours operate daily between 8:30am and 12:30pm, or between 1:30 and 5:30pm. A **Full Day Circle Island Tour** starts at 4.900 CFP plus entrance fees and lunch, with a pickup at your hotel at 9:30am, returning around 3:30 to 4pm.

A knowledgeable guide who speaks good English is essential for your introduction to the sights and stories of Tahiti. For 17 years I worked as a tour guide in Tahiti, in addition to my journalistic endeavors, and I will recommend the best guides so that you'll be able to make an agreeable choice when you book a tour.

Adventure Eagle Tours, *Tel. 77.20.03; eagletourguide@gmail.com; www.adveagletour.com.* William Leeteg is the son of Edgar Leeteg, the famous black velvet painter who lived in Moorea until he died in a motorcycle accident in 1953. William has a great sense of humor and knowledge of Tahiti's history as well as current events, and his English is very good. He may even sing for you as he drives you around the island in his a/c 9-seat minibus. He has a half-day West Coast Tour, and Grand Circle Island Tour of Tahiti, with morning or afternoon departures. Private tours and night tour on request.

Dave's VIP Tours, *Tel. 79.75.65; tahiti1viptours@yahoo.com.* Dave Ellard is an English-speaking guide who will take you on a half-day tour of Tahiti in his 10-seat a/c minibus.

Marama Tours Tahiti, *Tel. 50.74.74; www.maramatours.com* has a number of guides who do a good job of telling Tahiti's tales. Mata and Emile Cowan, both Polynesians, are owners of the company. Emile taught me to be a guide way back in the early 1970s. They have travel desks at the Intercontinental Tahiti, Sofitel Maeva Beach, Manava Suite Resort and at the airport. They offer full-day circle island tours every day, plus many other choices of excursions.

Tahiti Nui Travel, *Tel. 46.42.01,* has a travel desk in some of the hotels and at the airport, plus a variety of interesting tours and multi-lingual guides. Their full-day circle-island tour is available only on Sunday.

If you have the time and the inclination, I suggest that you take a guided tour around Tahiti Nui (big Tahiti) and on another day rent a car and drive around the island, stopping where you choose and exploring both coasts of Tahiti Iti (little Tahiti), as well as driving up the Plateau of Taravao, where you will see horses and cattle grazing in rolling green pastures bordered by eucalyptus trees and orange groves. Or better yet, spend a few days in a bed and breakfast or family pension on Tahiti Iti and get a totally different perspective of life on this island.

Mountain & Waterfall Safari Tours

Excursions by four-wheel drive vehicle (4x4) are designed for you to get off the beaten track and up into the mountains and valleys of Tahiti. The "Queen of the Pacific" will disclose a few of her mysteries and magic as you are driven in a/c or open-air Land Rovers or other 4WDs through the tropical forests of giant ferns, centuries old Tahitian *mape* chestnut trees, wild mango and guava trees, and more waterfalls than you can count.

A **Half-Day Mountain Tour** can be made in the morning or afternoon. This excursion takes you to a height of 4,800 ft. up **Mount Marau** via the **Tamanu Canyon**. Or you can choose a **Half Day East Coast Tour**, which also takes you to Mount Marau and the Tamanu Canyon, plus you will see the **Blowhole of Arahoho** and the **Fa'arumai Cascades of Tiarei**. This tour is noted for the numerous waterfalls you will see.

A **Full Day Across the Island Tour** takes you from Mataiea in the south to the **Papenoo Valley** in the north, crossing the main crater of Tahiti. You leave the circle island road at PK 47.5 in Mataiea and follow the winding track that leads 11.2 km (7.4 mi.) up to **Lake Vaihiria**. At an altitude of 465 m (1,550 ft.) above the sea, this is Tahiti's only fresh water lake. The scenery along the way seems almost vertical, with a saw-tooth mountain range, deep ravines and tumbling cascades above and below you. As you snake to dizzying heights around the curves you will pass small catchment lakes, dams and hydroelectric substations.

After you traverse the **Urufau Tunnel**, which is 110 m. (361 ft.) long, your guide will probably stop to let you look out over the Papenoo Valley. It is believed that from 10,000 to 20,000 Maohi people once inhabited this area, and the valley was totally deserted by 1850. At this height of (780 m.) 2,558 ft. you will have an impressive view of Tahiti Nui's great extinct volcano. The Relais de la Maroto hotel in Papenoo Valley has reopened and now serves lunch. If you have brought your own lunch, then your driver will usually continue on to a site in the Papenoo Valley that is known as **Fare Hape**. This is an area rich in archaeological sites, and some 190 *marae* and sanctuaries have been found in the high valley since the road was built. After a refreshing swim under a sparkling waterfall and a satisfying picnic lunch eaten at a table under a big covered shelter, you can walk with your guide to visit the Fare Hape site. Several of the *marae* temples have been restored and there are archery sites, house foundations and a huge boulder carved with petroglyphs.

Note: due to frequent landslides portions of the road may be closed for months at a time, making it impossible to reach Lake Vaihiria and the Papenoo Valley from the Mataiea side. Most drivers are now avoiding this entry to the valley because the residents have blocked the road and want to charge admission to drive across their land. 4WD excursions are still possible from Papenoo.

Tahiti Safari Expedition, *Tel. 42.14.15/77.80.76; tahiti.safari@mail.pf; www.tahiti-safari.com.* Land Rovers with English-speaking guides are available to take you on half-or full-day mountain tours of Papenoo Valley. Bring your own picnic lunch, swimsuit, towels, cameras and film. Owner Patrice Bordes was the pioneer of the inner island tours in 1990, and he's still the leader. These excursions are not for pregnant women or anyone who is frail, as the unpaved roads can be quite bumpy, and most uncomfortable if you are sitting on the bench in the back. These lush green valleys get a lot of rain and you will also get wet unless the side flaps are closed, creating a hothouse effect for the passengers, who can no longer see the misty beauty of the rainforest. Patrice advises his passengers not to wear the color blue as it attracts mosquitoes.

Patrick Adventure, *Tel. 83.29.29/79.08.09; patrickaventure@mail.pf; www.papeete.com.* Patrick Cordier has a 9-passenger Mazda 4WD and he is a very knowledgeable guide who covers the entire range of subjects concerning Tahiti: the history, culture, legends, geology, archaeology, agriculture, botany, religion, foods, modern life and everything else any visitor would want to know about an island and its people. His full day tour is 6.500 CFP and also takes you around the island of Tahiti Nui. Bring your own lunch to eat at a picnic table in the covered shelter at **Fare Hape** in the Papenoo Valley, and then swim in the pool under the waterfall just behind the picnic area. Patrick takes you to visit the restored *marae* temples on the premises. He also has a half-day mountain tour to visit Tahiti's east coast for 4.500 CFP. Children pay half-price on all his tours.

Natura Excursions, *Tel. 43.03.83/79.31.21; natura.explo@mail.pf; www.natura-exploration.com.* Owner Arnaud Luccioni leads half-day Landrover tours for 8 passengers to Mount Marau or to the Papenoo Valley. He takes you across the central crater of Tahiti Nui to follow the tracks of the *Bounty* mutineers who hid out in this valley when their ship was leaving Tahiti. Private group rates available.

Marama Safari, *Tel. 78.40.11/50.74.74,* is a 4x4 Safari operated by Teva Cowan of Marama Tours. A half-day tour is 5.500 CFP and a full-day excursion is 8.700 CFP. Teva's guides take you into the Papenoo Valley where you can enjoy your picnic lunch on the shores of Lake Vaihiria, Tahiti's only fresh water lake.

Tahiti Nui Travel, *Tel. 46.42.01,* offers half-day morning or afternoon tours to visit Mount Marau, for 4.950 CFP. 4WD Safari Tours are also provided by **Maima Tours Safari,** *Tel. 48.35.85/78.68.69;* **Mato-Nui Excursions,** *Tel. 78.95.47;* **Natura Exploration,** *Tel. 43.03.83/79.31.21,* and **Tahitian Safari Expeditions,** *Tel. 82.69.96/72.24.18,* and **Tahitian Excursion,** *Tel. 82.69.96/72.24.18; www.tahitian-excursions.com* also lead 4WD safari tours.

SSV Rhino Excursions is a unique way to visit Tahiti's mountains and inland valleys. These open-sided 4WD vehicles have a sunroof and are operated by **Tahiti Adventures,** *Tel. 29.01.60; www.tahiti-adventures.net,* based at the Intercontinental Tahiti Resort. A 2-hr. guided tour to Mont Marau is 15.000 CFP for 1-2 people and a 4-hr outing to the Papenoo Valley is 22.000 CFP.

Helicopter Tours

A helicopter tour offers the best of Tahiti's scenic sights, giving you a close-up look at the tallest mountains, dipping into the lush green valleys to hover like a hummingbird in front of a sparkling waterfall, and soaring over the lagoon, reef and sea. Go early in the morning before the clouds veil the view.

Tahiti Helicopter Service. *Tel. 50.40.75; contact@tahiti-helicopters.com; www.tahiti-helicopters.com.* This new company is the only commercial helicopter service operating in French Polynesia in mid-2011. (See information on **Helicopters** under *Planning Your Trip* in Chapter 6). A 5-seat "Squirrel" AS 355 F1 twin-turbine helicopter can accommodate 1 pilot and 5 passengers. It is based at the Tahiti-Faa'a airport and is available for tourist flights around Tahiti, transfers to Moorea, and specific charters on request. A 40-min. complete circuit flight around Tahiti Nui is 52.800 CFP per person for 4/5 passengers on board, 62.000 CFP per person for 3 passengers, and 73.000 CFP per person for 2 passengers. A 60-min. complete circuit flight-seeing tour of Tahiti Nui and Tahiti Iti starts at 68.000 CFP per person for 4/5. Shorter flights of 15-20-30 mins. are also available. A 35-min. flight from the airport in Tahiti to circuit the island of Moorea is 46.200 CFP per person for 4/5 passengers and 64.600 CFP per person for only 2 people.

NIGHTLIFE & ENTERTAINMENT

Reputed as the South Seas heart of hedonism, Papeete by night is prowl-about time. The shops are closed and nightclubs swing. Sounds of techno, disco, zouk, beguine, salsa, reggae, calypso, rock, rap, waltz and jazz compete with the pulsating rhythm of the *tamure*, Tahiti's tantalizing national dance.

Some of Tahiti's larger hotels feature folkloric dance shows and Tahitian orchestras for dancing, and there are frequent all-night balls presented by the various sports clubs and friendship organizations on the island. These events always include live music and entertainment and the Tahitians never tire of seeing their professional or amateur dance groups performing the *ori Tahiti*. After the show the beautifully dressed Tahitians, Chinese and French diners fill the dance floor, where they glide so gracefully to the upbeat tunes of the fox trot and Tahitian waltz. When the tempo suddenly erupts into the sensual *toere* drumbeat of the hip-swiveling, rubber-legging *tamure*, the floor is suddenly packed with Tahitians, who involve their whole being—body, mind and soul—into vigorously performing their favorite dance.

Most of the bars, nightclubs and cafés are located in the heart of Papeete, along the waterfront street of Blvd. Pomare and rarely no more than a block inland. The nightclubs and casinos require proper attire. This means that the women cannot wear shorts and the men should wear a shirt, rather than a tank top, plus shoes, rather than rubber thongs or going barefoot. The nightclubs usually charge an entry fee for men, which includes a drink, and unescorted ladies get in free most of the time, sometimes with the bonus of a complimentary first drink. Some of these nightclubs change ownership and names frequently, so don't be surprised if you don't find the place you're looking for. Just ask a few people at your hotel to give you the new name, and you'll probably get mixed answers.

Local Style

LE ROYAL KIKIRIRI, *Tel. 43.58.64, on Rue Colette between Avenue Prince*

Hinoi and the Mairie of Papeete (town hall). This place started out as a true Tahitian bar, where the musicians tuned up for an evening of *kaina* music, playing the songs of the islands on their guitars and ukuleles, strumming the chords of a gut bucket bass or rattling 2 spoons together in a beer bottle. The revelers enthusiastically sang and danced as they got happy on Hinano beer or Johnny Walker whisky, and the chairs had a hard time staying upright in the general melee. This bar has now been transformed into a chic a/c nightclub that attracts a completely different type of clientele. For several years it has been one of the choice nightspots in Papeete, where good-looking, well-dressed young people gather to dance to live and recorded Tahitian and disco type music.

LE ROYAL TAHITIEN, *Tel. 50.40.40*, in Pirae, is the Happy Hour gathering place for many of Tahiti's office workers each Fri. afternoon, when local residents come to dance at the bar and on the terrace to the tunes of Polynesian music played by a live band. A special barbecue dinner is also served for those who feel like diluting their booze with some veal cooked on a spit. The security is good here and no fights take place, according to manager Lionel Kennedy, an expatriate Aussie, who is also a musician. He plays jazz with other musicians each Wed. evening at the bar.

Discos & Jazz

LE PIANO BAR, *Tel. 42.88.24*, on Rue des Ecoles, 1/2 block inland from Blvd. Pomare. If you want to see a female impersonator strip show Tahitian style, this is the place to go. The transvestite *mahu* dancers, Polynesia's "third sex," are friendly. This can be a fun place and is quite harmless, unless you try to make out with someone else's boyfriend.

LE PARADISE, *Tel. 42.73.05*, on Blvd. Pomare, across from the French naval station. Le Paradise normally has a European ambiance, but it can also resonate to an Afro-Caribbean rhythm. This is the second choice of "best" nightclubs chosen by some of my swinging friends in Tahiti, while others tell me it's awful.

MORRISON'S CAFÉ, *Tel. 42.78.61*, in the Vaima Center, with a private elevator located on Rue General de Gaulle, adjacent to the Air New Zealand office. This is an indoor/outdoor restaurant and café, where the sounds of sweet jazz sing out over the rooftops of Papeete, played by American or French musicians who are frequently imported to liven up the scene. This café is named after Jim Morrison (of The Doors), and the musical ambiance is a combination of American rock music, jazz and modern Tahitian rock bands.

CLUB 106, *Tel. 42.72.92*, on Boulevard Pomare adjacent to the Moana Iti restaurant. This is one of the oldest private dance clubs in Papeete. There's no entry charge, but you must take care of your "look" to be permitted. Simply ring the bell at the front door downstairs and then join Papeete's "in crowd" and dance to taped music for all tastes.

Here are some of the other night spots: **Le Manhattan** is a nightclub on the lower end of Blvd. Pomare across from the ferry terminal. **Metropolis** (ex-Shark, ex-Zizou), also across from the ferry dock, combines a local ambience with recorded disco tunes. **Café des Négociants**, in the Quartier du Commerce, and **Les Trois Brasseurs** on Blvd. Pomare, have live rock bands on Fri. and Sat. nights. **Bar Taina** is in the same block as Les Trois Brasseurs, and is a bar preferred by Tahitians and French military men. Couples or women without escorts may find the atmosphere a little too rough, but men in search of meeting a friendly Tahitian *vahine* or *mahu* may find it to their liking. You can drink on the covered terrace outside and dance to recorded music inside the bar. There's a live Tahitian band every Fri. night. Keep your wallet safely hidden.

New "cool" night spots include the **Ute Ute Restaurant**, **Le Gaia** and Mango Tahiti. **Place Vaiete** on the waterfront near the ferry dock has free concerts and dance performances on some weekends. Outside of town on the West Coast the

---

LET THE MUSIC PLAY

The Tahitian custom of inviting someone to dance is rather subtle. You are sitting at the bar or a table, alone or with friends. A young man begins to stare at you, trying to get your attention, or perhaps returning your own flirtatious glance. When he catches your eye, he just lifts his eyebrows and nods his head toward the dance floor. You can ignore him, shake your head negatively, or raise your own eyebrows in a positive reply and meet him on the dance floor. Tahitian men assume that if a woman isn't dancing with anyone, she is available to dance with him, even if she is sitting with a man.

Dancing with a Tahitian **tane** involves little or no conversation. Normally there is no desire for introductions before or during the first few dances. People are there to dance, and grab a feel, perhaps, but not to talk. Each trip to the floor lasts for the duration of two songs, played to similar tempos. This gives you a good opportunity to get to know one another, with little or no conversation transpiring between you. But there is definitely a communication going on.

If you continue to dance with the same man, for the first hour or so of the evening he is very polite and dances beautifully, as he holds you at a respectful distance. He smells divine, wearing the best perfume of his sister, wife or live-in vahine, the mother of some of his children. After he has drunk a few bottles of Hinano beer he becomes more relaxed and informal. Also much more intimate. He squeezes you close and his hands become freer in their wanderings around your body. He might ask you to leave with him after the dance, as he nuzzles your neck and presses his body close to yours. The next hour after that is when you have to start holding him up, if you are still on the scene by that time.

Western Grill at PK 12.6 in Punaauia presents a Western Show, Drag Show or Elvis impersonator during dinner on Thurs., Fri. and Sat. nights. Reservations are required. The **Pink Coconut, Quai des Iles** and **Casa Bianca** are 3 restaurants at the Marina Taina that have live entertainment on weekends.

SPORTS & RECREATION
ATV-Quad, SSV-Rhino and Jet-Ski Excursions

Tahiti Aventures, *Tel. 29.01.60*; *www.tahiti-aventures.net* is based at the Intercontinental Tahiti Resort, offering you another way to discover the island. You will have an unforgettable experience when you join a guided SSV-Rhino outing into the Papenoo Valley, up to the heights of Mount Marau or around the island. Protective goggles and head gear provided. The hotel travel desks charge 15.000 CFP for 1-2 people for 2-hr. excursions, 22.000 CFP for a 4-hr. trip to the Papenoo Valley, and 32.000 CFP for a full day for 2 people with picnic included.

Tahiti Aventures also has guided Jet-Ski excursions starting at 10.000 CFP for 30 min., and 33.000 CFP for a 2-hr. ride for two people. A Discovery Pack with 2 hrs. on the SSV Rhino and 1 hr. on a Jet-Ski is 28.000 CFP.

Golf

If golf is your game you can tee off at the **Olivier Breaud International Golf Course of Atimaono**, at PK 40.2 in Papara, *Tel. 57.40.32*. Located between the mountains and the sea 25 miles from Papeete on Tahiti's southwest coast, you'll find an 18-hole course 6,900 yd. long, par 72, mostly flat, and well known for some of the world's toughest par 3's. The greens are planted with hybrid Bermuda grass from Hawaii. Two artificial lakes and wide, hilly fairways surrounded by fruit trees add to the beauty and pleasure of this course, which attracts professional and amateur golfers from overseas, who compete in the annual Tahiti International Pro/Am Open, held each July or Aug. This event is now part of the Australian PGA circuit.

The Club House has locker rooms and showers for men and women, a full bar and a restaurant serving French and local foods daily for lunch and dinner. There is a swimming pool, spa pool and a driving range, plus a pro shop and boutique for sales and rentals. The course is open daily from 8am to 4pm.

Marama Tours, Tahiti Nui Travel and **Tekura Tahiti Travel** have travel desks located in the hotel lobbies that sell a golf package for 27.180 CFP for one person and 36.900 CFP per couple. This includes round-trip transportation between your hotel or ship and the golf course, the greens fee, a set of clubs, practice balls, a motorized golf car, golfer's lunch and the souvenir and play package.

Hiking

Feel like taking a hike? Tahiti's mountains and valleys and rugged Te Pari coast offer an interesting choice of treks. Even though you may be tempted to set out on your own to discover the lava tubes, burial caves and hidden grottos, my advice is to go with a guide and the proper equipment. The weather can be variable in the heights, and sudden downpours can suddenly swell the rivers, making them impassable for several days.

The **Hiking Guides Association** (Syndicat des Guides de Randonnées), *Tel. 79.31.21/43.03.83; natura.explo@mail.pf* can give you a list of qualified mountain guides and answer any other questions concerning hiking and canyoning in Tahiti and Her Islands.

Polynesian Adventure, *Tel./Fax 43.25.95, cell 77.24.37; polynesianadv@mail.pf; http://www.polynesianadv.com*. Vincent Dubousquet is a professional guide who specializes in 20 different hikes on Tahiti and Moorea, including exploring the lava tubes. Following are some of his most popular hikes.

The **Fautaua Valley** is one of the easiest walks, which most people accomplish in four to seven hours. The waterfall here was the romantic setting described in *The Marriage of Loti*, a novel written by a French sailor named Louis Marie Julien Viaud, who came to Tahiti in the 1880s. A minimum of two people is required for this half-day outing, or to visit other valleys on Tahiti's east coast, including **Le Belvedere, Tuauru** or **Faananu**. The cost for a half-day hike is 5.600 CFP per person, plus there is an access fee of 700 CFP per person to visit the Fautaua Valley and another 700 CFP to get to the Diadème Pass.

Half-day hikes to the west coast valleys of **Vaipohe** or **Mateoro** are rated easy to sportive and also cost 5.600 CFP per person for a minimum of two people. All-day easy to medium level hikes can be made to the **Fautaua Valley**, the **Hamuta Pass** 900 m (2,952 ft.) high on the **Aorai** trail, to the basaltic organs of **Tuauru Valley** in Mahina, to **Te Faaiti Valley** in Papenoo, which is a park with natural Jacuzzis, or to **Faananu Valley** in Tiare, all on the east coast. The west coast hikes can take you to the canyon of **Vaipohe Valley** in Paea, or to **Mateoro Valley** in Papara, where there is a small canyon and lots of flowers. All these hikes require a minimum of four people and cost 7.500 CFP per person, plus an access fee of 700 CFP per person to enter the Fautaua Valley.

You should be in good physical condition and not subject to vertigo to climb to **Fare Ata**, the second refuge, at a height of 1,810 m (5,937 ft.) on **Mount Aorai**, which at 2,066 m (6,776 ft.), is the second highest peak on Tahiti. Vincent includes this one-day hike in his "sportive" level, which requires a minimum of four people. Other rugged hikes are to the **Teovere** Pass in Papeete, which gives you a good view of the Fautaua Valley and **Le Diadème**, the crown mountain; to the high waterfalls of **Te Faaiti Valley** in Papenoo; and to **Vaihi Valley** in Hitia'a with lovely waterfalls and a view of the east coast. You'll need at least four hikers to go to the **Lava Tubes**, river and tunnels in Hitia'a; up to the refuge of Faaroa and the rugged cliffs of **Te Pari** in Teahupoo; or to **Vaipoiri Grotto** on Tahiti Iti. Each of these tougher treks costs 9.700 CFP per person and you will have to pay an access fee of 700 CFP to get to Teovere Pass.

Two or three hikers can divide the total cost and still make the treks that normally require a minimum of four. All material is provided for the hikes in Tahiti

Iti and Hitiaa. Boat transfers are also provided on the Tahiti Iti treks. Ground transfers are free up to 35 km from pick-up point to the trail entrance. Minimum age for these hikes is 12 years. Polynesian Adventure also has two-day camping hikes into the valleys of Tahiti Nui and Tahiti Iti, for 18.300 CFP a person, including meals. Vincent Dubousquet also leads all-day treks in Moorea.

Rando Pacific, *Tel. 70.56.18; rando.pacific@mail.pf; www.randopacific.com.* Michel Veuillet specializes in canyoning trips that take you to the lava tubes of Hitia'a, and he leads hikes for confirmed mountain climbers, using ropes and rappel techniques. Also see information for Tahiti Evasion in *Moorea* chapter.

Tahiti Evasion, *Tel. 74.67.13/56.48.77; tahitievasion@mail.pf; www.tahitievasion.com.* Eric LeNoble leads day hikes into the Fautaua Valley and Orofero Valley, which are rated as family outings without difficulty. He will take confirmed hikers up to a height of 1,400 m (4,522 ft.) on Mount Aorai. He also leads 3-day hikes to the Pari and Fenua Aihere wild lands of Tahiti Iti, including a 2-night bivouac on the beach. You need to be in good physical condition and able to walk on varied terrain for this trek. His rates start at 4.000 CFP per person, including transfers.

Tahiti Reva Trek, *Tel. 74.77.20; pirimato@mail.pf; www.tahitirevatrek.com.* Angelina Bordas is a fully qualified local guide who offers a wide range of trekking options, half-day trips, full-day or two-day hikes with overnight camping. She also organizes gentle strolls for families, challenging athletic raids, photo safari adventures and mountaineering.

Other well-known guides include: Noella Tutavae, *Tel. 78.36.31; hinatrekking@hotmail.fr;* Luccioni Arnaud, *Tel. 79.31.21; naturaexplo@mail.pf;* Guillaume Dor of Tiare Mato Excursions, *Tel. 43.92.76/77.48.11; tiaremat@mail.pf;* Mataa'e Rangimakea of Presqu'ile Loisirs, *Tel. 57.00.57;* and Hervé Maraetaata of Mato-Nui Excursions, *Tel. 78.95.47.*

Horseback Riding

Most of the horses in Tahiti are from the Marquesas Islands, descendants of Chilean stock. The equestrian clubs now have thoroughbreds from New Zealand as well. You can ride by the sea or in the mountains with a guide, who will take along a picnic lunch upon request. The **Club Equestre de Tahiti**, at the Pirae Hippodrome race track, *Tel. 42.70.41,* and **L'Eperon de Pirae**, *Tel. 42.79.87,* in a nearby stable, have both races of steeds.

Ranch Rauvau, *Tel 73.84.43/43.50.79; www.ranch-du-plateau.kazio.com,* is located at PK 2.5 on the Taravao Plateau of Tahiti Iti. You'll need to reserve in advance if you wish to explore "little Tahiti" by horseback, but the magnificent views are worth the effort. There are 16 horses available for renting for an hour, a half-day or an all-day ride with picnic. This ranch is also called L'Amour de la Nature A Cheval (Love of Nature by Horseback).

Tennis

Tahiti's climate is ideal for playing tennis year-round, by scheduling a match in the early morning or at sunset time, to avoid the hottest hours of a tropical day. Tennis courts are located at the following hotels: **Le Méridien, Intercontinental Tahiti Resort** and **Sofitel Maeva Beach Tahiti Resort**. Sports clubs and private tennis clubs also have their own courts, where you can play for a nominal fee and meet some of the local resident players. These include the **Tennis Club of Fautaua**, just to the west of downtown Papeete, *Tel. 42.00.59*; **Fei Pi Tennis Club** at PK 3.2 in Arue, *Tel. 42.53.87*; and the **Excelsior Tennis Club** in the Mission Quarter of Papeete, *Tel. 43.91.46.*

Deep Sea Fishing

Zane Grey put Tahiti on the world map of outstanding deep-sea fishing spots in the 1930s, when the American novelist had his own fishing camp in Vairao on the Tahiti Iti peninsula. Game fishing has become a year-round sport in Tahiti, and your chances are very good of reeling in a big blue marlin, sailfish, swordfish, yellow fin tuna, mahi mahi, wahoo, ocean bonito or tiger shark. You may also catch jack crevally, blue crevally, rainbow runner, dogtooth tuna and barracuda just outside the reef.

You have a choice of several professional fishing boats throughout the islands, whose crews compete in local tournaments in preparation for the **Tahiti International Billfish Tournament**, which is held every two years. Eric Malmezac is the president of this association, *Tel. 58.36.26; tibt@mail.pf; tiba@mail.pf.* The **Raiatea International Billfish Tournament** is held in the Leeward Islands soon after the TIBT takes place in Tahiti.

Haura Club of Tahiti, *Tel. 42.37.14/77.09.29; pat.four@mail.pf,* presided by Georges Poroi, is based at Marina Taina in Punaauia. This is the game fishing club or marlin club of Tahiti. They can also give you the names of sports fishing boats for charter.

Nautical Centers & Clubs

Intercontinental Tahiti Resort & Spa. Guests of the hotel can use the snorkeling equipment free for one hour. Otherwise, the cost is 1.000 CFP for the mask & snorkel, with a deposit. The same rules apply for tennis rackets and balls and use of tennis courts. Guests have an hour's free use of a kayak, then they pay 1.500 CFP for each additional hour. You can get a boat transfer to the floating sun deck for 1.500 CFP, join a 2-hr. Dolphin Cruise for 9.000 CFP, a snorkeling tour for 5.500 CFP, have a water-skiing or wakeboard initiation for 11.000 CFP, or sign up for a Sunset Cruise with Sea Angels for 6.900 CFP. You can hire a Jet-Ski for 15.000 CFP an hour, or a SSV Rhino for a 2-hour guided excursion, for 15.000 CFP. Even if you are not staying at the hotel, you can take part in the activities by making reservations. See more information under *Scuba Diving* in this chapter.

Le Méridien Tahiti Watersports Activities Center, *Tel. 47.07.07*, is open daily from 8am to 6pm. Snorkeling equipment and kayaks are free for Le Méridien hotel guests, as well as the Aquagym classes that are held in the sandy bottom swimming pool. They can organize snorkeling excursions, a Dolphin Watch, a Lagoon Safari, a 3-hour Whale Watch (Aug.-Oct.), and a 4-hour excursion by private boat. The Eleuthera scuba dive center is based here, offering all levels of diving and lessons.

Marinas

Marina Taina, *B.P. 13003-98717, Punaauia, Tahiti; Tel. 689/41.02.25/ 78.92.46; Fax 689/45.27.58; VHF channel 9; marinataina@mail.pf; www.marina-taina.com*. This modern marina is located at PK 9 in Punaauia, 6 nautical miles south of Papeete on Tahiti's west coast, facing the island of Moorea. This marina is administered by the Papeete Port Authority and is mainly aimed at the resident motor cruiser market, with berths and moorings for about 550 local boats. There is also a visitor's quay for 50 large yachts plus mooring buoys. Services include water, electricity, fuel, garbage disposal, mail handling, office communication, on-board telephones, cable TV, car rental, laundry service and much more. The Eleuthera Dive Center, Haura Fishing Club and 3 restaurants and a computer center are on the premises, as well as a ship chandler, repair shop and a marine gas station. Whether you want information on chartering a sports fishing boat, a luxury motor yacht or a safe mooring for your own sailboat, you can contact manager Eric Malmezac and his efficient staff.

Tahiti Nautic Center Marina, *B.P. 7305-98719, Taravao, Tahiti; Tel. 689/ 54.76.16; Fax 689/57.05.07; tnc@mail.pf; www.tahitinauticcenter.pf*. Located at PK 56 in Taravao, beside Phaeton Bay, with berths for 40 boats up to 50 ft. long catamarans and a maximum draft of 2 m. On the premises are a restaurant, clubhouse, laundry service, naval shipyard, superstructure store and mechanical workshop.

Tahiti Yacht Club, *Tel 689/42.78.03; Fax 689/42.37.07; VHF Channel 6; yctahiti@mail.pf*. Located in Arue, 5 km east of Papeete, the Tahiti Yacht Club is a welcoming and friendly yacht club with an active racing fleet. The Club docks are full with local boats and often do not have anchoring spaces for visitors. Contact the club first and ask for advice. The manager, Michel Alcon, is very helpful.

For information on anchoring in the **Port of Papeete** see information in this chapter under *Arrivals & Departures, By Boat*.

Sailing Charters

Tahiti Yacht Charter, *Tahiti office: Monette Aline, B.P. 364, Papeete, Tahiti 98713; Tel. 689/45.04.00; tyc@mail.pf; www.tahitiyachtcharter.com. Raiatea base: Tel. 689/66.28.86; Fax 689/66.28.85*.

Tahiti Yacht Charter is a 100% locally owned company. They have been established in French Polynesia for 20 years, chartering bareboats or crewed boats.

They have a fleet of 28 catamarans, most of them less than 2 years old, based at the Apooiti Marina in Raiatea, with Papeete as a possible departure point. Details are listed in the chapter on *Planning Your Trip* and in the *Raiatea* chapter under *Sailing Charter Yachts*.

Day Sailing & Boat Excursions

You'll find day sailing and other boat excursions easy to arrange once you're here, simply by booking with your hotel activities desk or walking along the quay at the Papeete waterfront, across from the post office, and talking with the captain of the boat you choose to fulfill your dream.

A Blue Island, *Tel./Fax 83.29.29; cell 77.94.10; ablueisland@mail.pf; www.ablueisland.com.* The fleet consists of a 46-ft. Bahia catamaran, a 50-ft. Beneteau monohull and a 52-ft. Gib Sea sloop, based at the Marina Taina in Punaauia.. They can be chartered with skipper and hostess for a day cruise to Tahiti, Moorea or Tetiaroa, for a sunset sail or a full moon outing. Diving cruises are also available.

Easy Boat, *Tel. 29.83.90; easyboat@mail.pf; www.easyboat-tahiti.com.* Captain Michel provides lagoon discovery tours of the east or west coast of Tahiti, day excursions to Moorea, snorkeling, and dolphin watching. He is also government-certified to take you whale watching between Aug.-Oct. His 28-ft. long motor boat "Remi Nui" has a sun roof and can also be hired as a taxi boat.

Jet France, *Tel./Fax 56.15.62,* is the name of a company that provides day sailing charters to Tetiaroa. Jean-Jacques Besson keeps his 15-m. (49-ft.) yacht *Vehia* tied up at the yacht quay on the Papeete waterfront.

L'Escapade, *Tel. 72.85.31, Satellite Tel. 00.872.76.25.24.382; escapade@mail.pf; www.escapade-croisieres.com.* This 48-ft. catamaran is owned by Anne-Marie and Paul Gasparini, who have 20 years' experience in sailing, spent cruising around the world with their family, and chartering in the Caribbean. You can join them for a relaxing day in Tetiaroa, with departures from the Papeete waterfront quay at 6am on request. You will arrive in Tetiaroa at 10am and visit the motu islets, the seabird sanctuary and swim in the clear warm lagoon. Lunch is served on board and the boat leaves Tetiaroa at 3:15pm, arriving in Tahiti at 6:30pm. Breakfast, lunch and drinks included for the price of 13.000 CFP per person. They also do long cruises to the outer islands on request.

Sea Angels, *Tel. 32.55.35, sea-angels@mail.pf; www.sea-angels-tahiti.com.* This activity is based at the Intercontinental Tahiti Resort & Spa, offering helmet dives and sunset cruises in the lagoon. Free pick-up provided.

Tahiti Cruise/Margouillat, *Tel. 72.23.45; mahi@mail.pf; www.tahiticruise.pf.* Margouillat is a 43-ft. catamaran based at Marina Taina in Punaauia that can accommodate 8 passengers in 4 double cabins for a long cruise and 14 people for a day sail. Daily cruises with or without meals will take you around Tahiti, Moorea or Tetiaroa, on outings to discover the dolphins and whales, or for sunset cruises for groups. Other choices include a half-day sailing & snorkeling lagoon cruise, a full day cruise with lunch on board, and a sunset cruise with cocktail. A weekend in Moorea cruise of two days and one night departs from Papeete on Sat. morning and returns on Sun. evening, or you can arrange cruises of 3 days to 3 weeks or more. A skipper and hostess will accompany you. Contact Jean-Marie Libeau. **Tahiti Voile & Lagon,** *Tel. 74.16.97/28.31.41; tahitivoileetlagon@mail.pf; www.tahitivoileetlagon.com.* You have a choice of a 46-ft. Bahia catamaran or a 50-ft. Beneteau monohull with skipper to take you on a discovery sail of the Tahiti Iti peninsula, Moorea or Tetiaroa. You can see these boats at the quay on the Papeete waterfront across from Le Retro in the Vaima Center. A day sail to Tetiaroa is 13.000 CFP per person, lunch included, for a min. of 8 passengers. A 1 1/2 hr. sunset cruise is 4.500 CFP for 6-12 people, including a cocktail.

Scuba Diving

The protected lagoons, passes and outer coral reefs offer ideal conditions for scuba diving year-round and you'll discover an abundance of dive clubs on the island of Tahiti. The diving instructors are highly qualified and speak English to varying degrees. Safe, dependable boats are used to take you to discover several beautiful locations, which may include "**The Aquarium,**" a calm, clear, fish feeding site; "**The Wrecks,**" a ship and aircraft on the same dive; and "**The Tahiti Wall & Shark Cave,**" an outer reef drop-off with canyons, crevices and shark cave. The small reef sharks and moray eels are fed by hand.

TOPDIVE-Bathys Tahiti, *Tel. 689/53.34.96; tahiti@topdive.com; www.topdive.com.* This is the largest scuba diving center with 8 locations on 5 islands. The 5-star Tahiti center is based at the Intercontinental Resort Tahiti, offering fun dives, PADI certifications, night dives and introductory dives. Special programs include Blue honeymoon dives, whale and dolphin watching, shark experiences and private dives on 12 sites on the west and north coasts of Tahiti. Dives start at 7.900 CFP and Nitrox is available at no extra charge. Free pick-up service.

Eleuthera, *Tel. 689/42.49.29/77.65.68; info@dive-tahiti.com; www.eleuthera.pf.* This 5-star PADI center is located at Marina Taina in Punaauia. Managers Nicolas Castel and Joshua Rouger are International CMAS ** and *** instructors, BEES 1 federal instructors, Sea-Guides and PADI, OWSI and ANMP certified instructors. They provide 4 outings per day, including ocean dives at 9am and 2pm. They offer programs from beginners to certified divers, specifically adapted to each level. Free pick-up at hotels and family pensions.

Fluid Dive Center, *Tel./Fax 689/85.41.46; Cell 70.83.75; fluid@mail.pf; www.fluidtahiti.com.* Yannis Saint-Pé is a scuba dive instructor who provides personalized service aboard his boat **Fluid** for up to 6 divers or snorkelers, including the diving equipment. He has 2-tank dives and half-day dolphin and whale (in season) watching excursions. All levels of PADI and CMAS/ANMP courses available. Refreshments served on board. Underwater video and camera rental.

Tahiti Iti Diving, *Tel. 42.25.33/71.80.77; tahiti-iti-diving@mail.pf; www.tahiti-iti-diving.com.* This Aqualung center opened in April 2009 and is operated by Lionel Heatrich at PK 58,100 in Taravao beside Phaeton Bay. The new equipment includes diving gear for 12 and a dive boat for 14 passengers. There is a boutique with diving equipment and T-shirts for sale, plus a locker room, hot showers and refreshments. Certification for PADI, CMAS and FFESSM. Nitrox and Trimix available. Dive sites include the west coast of Tahiti-iti and Tahiti-Nui, as well as departures from the marinas of Teahupoo and Tautira.

Surfing

The Tahitians claim that their Maohi ancestors invented surfing, and the chiefs of Tahiti used to compete with one another on long wooden boards. Surfers come to Tahiti from all around the world to surf the edges of the passes, and international surfing champions have found challenging waves offshore Teahupoo at the end of the Tahiti Iti peninsula. Between Oct. and March strong swells from the north bring sizable waves, and from Apr. to Sept. the Antarctic winds from the south produce powerful waves that are great for riding the tube.

Prime surf spots include the break at the mouth of the **Papenoo River** at PK 17 on Tahiti's northeast coast. Southwest of Papeete the **Taapuna pass** at PK 15, close to Fisherman's Point in Punaauia, is a favorite reef break spot for local surfers. Further along the coast you'll find the **Taharuu black sand beach** at PK 36 in Papara, where the waves are good enough for the popular **Horue open**, an international competition held each July. The **Billabong Pro Tahiti** is part of the World Championship Tour (W.C.T.). This competition formerly took place in May and is now held in August, and is reserved exclusively for the 44 best surfers in the world. Accompanying the big name surfers are the international press and crowds of spectators who flock to the beautiful untamed coastline of **Te Pari**, at the southern tip of Tahiti Iti. The passes of **Hava'e**, **Te Ava Ino** and **Tapueraha** are good for riding the waves to the left, and **Te Ava Piti** pass sends you to the right.

Tura'i Mata'are Surf School, *Tel./Fax 41.91.37; cell 77.27.69; surfschool@mail.pf; www.tahitisurfschool.info* is operated by Olivier Napias (contact him through the Kelly Surf Shop in the Fare Tony Center in Papeete). Half-day classes in surfing or bodyboarding are given by certified surf instructors, and all material, transportation and insurance is included for 4.800 CFP. Surfboard rentals cost 1.500 CFP per hour, 3.000 CFP for a half-day and 4.000 CFP for a full-day.

Spectator Sports

Soccer is Tahiti's favorite sport, and during the *futbol* season enthusiastic crowds gather at the **Fautaua Stadium** near Papeete on weeknights and during weekends to cheer their team to victory.

Outrigger canoe racing is the top traditional sport. At almost any time of the year you will see the muscled young men practicing for the next big *pirogue* race. The

WHAT TO DO ON TAHITI ITI

Tahiti Iti Tour and Surf, *Tel. 57.97.39/78.27.99/75.55.66; riou@mail.pf; www.tahitiititourandsurf.pf* is owned by Georges Riou, whose nautical sports base is at PK 10.100 in Vairao. His taxi boat service is official, with insurance for his passengers. He can take you to the surf spots, to visit the Vaipoiri Cave, Te Pari cliffs, the coral garden, and to look for dolphins and whales during the season of July-Oct. He offers a day tour on the motu for a min. of 4 passengers, for 8.000 CFP each, or a half-day tour for 5.000 CFP per person. He can also take you waterskiing, wakeboarding and fishing.

Teahupoo Excursions, *Tel. 75.11.98; teahupooexcursions@mail.pf* belongs to a young Frenchman named Michaël, whose boat can take up to 6 passengers to visit Motu Fenua Aino, to swim in the Vaipoiri River and to photograph the rugged Te Pari coastline. He will also take surfers out to the best waves in Teahupoo or to surf the waves of Vairao.

Moana Paofai's Eden Day Adventure Boat Trip, *Tel. 57.02.15/ 77.89.69,* to explore the Fenua Aihere and Te Pari is an outrigger excursion for 2 or more passengers that takes you to visit the southern coast of Tahiti Iti, exploring a hidden tributary, hiking through a rain forest to enter a cave and swimming in the refreshing clear waters of the underground grotto of Vaipoiri. Guests staying at his wife's Bonjouir Lodge Paradise pay 6.000 CFP per person. All others pay 10.500 CFP per person, which includes lunch for a minimum of 2 adults. If you come to Teahupoo for an Eden Day Tour Moana will meet you at the Eden boat beside the lagoon just before the end of the road in Teahupoo. If you rent a car to get here then you can leave it in his private parking area. You can also get a round-trip mini-bus or car transfer.

Iti Nui Surf School, *Tel. 73.14.21, surfitinui@mail.pf.* You can find Doumé at the Mitirapa Pizzeria in Taravao on the road to Teahupoo. He is a qualified surfing instructor who also has the surfboards and boogieboards to teach his students the skills and techniques required to master the impressive waves on the Tahiti Iti peninsula. He charges 4.000 CFP a lesson and 19.000 CFP for 5 lessons. He also teaches courses in stand-up paddle boarding.

Valentin Maino, *Tel. 70.49.82,* is a trained mountain guide who knows all the secrets of Te Pari. He charges 7.000 CFP for a half-day outing, which includes the boat transfers and a picnic, as well as a hike adapted to the level of the walkers. He also organizes 2-day hikes for 15.000 CFP per person. (More guides and treks are listed under *Hiking* in this chapter).

racing season begins around May, and the best teams of male and female paddlers compete in the Heiva Festival races in July, which are held inside the lagoon and in the open ocean. More races are held in Aug. and Sept. to select the teams who will compete in the **Hawaiki Nui Va'a Race** that is held each Nov. During this 3-day event, the paddlers race from Huahine to Raiatea, then to Taha'a and on to Bora Bora. Tahitian-style **horse racing** is held on special occasions at the **Pirae Hippodrome**, where jockeys used to ride bareback, wearing only a brightly colored *pareo* and a crown of flowers. Safety regulations now require saddles and helmets. You can place your bets, but the payoffs are very small. **Cockfighting** is another Sun. afternoon event. Although it is officially illegal, everyone seems to know where the fights will take place on a certain day. Ask at your hotel for specific details.

Almost every weekend in Tahiti or Moorea you will find a marathon or triathlon or bicycle-racing event going on. Other competitions are held for Hobie Cats, kite surfers and jet-skiers, as well as tennis, golf, *petanque* or bocce-ball, volleyball, basketball, boxing, archery, rugby and track. Futsal is a relatively new sport that is soccer (futbol) played inside a salle d'omnisports (covered stadium).

Astronomy Club

The **Astronomers Club of Tahiti** (SAT) has frequent open house visits at their observatory in the Cité de l'Air overlooking the International Airport of Tahiti-Faa'a. You can come alone or with a group to gaze at the celestial lights above the island through their powerful telescopes. To find out exact dates of observation, call Claude LaMotte at *Tel. 82.17.83/75.09.77*; *sat@mail.pf; www.astrosurf.com/sat*. Also check out the English language website of Roland Santallo, who has a privately owned observatory in Faa'a, *www.southernstars-observatory.org*.

SHOPPING

Tahiti is not a shopper's paradise, but some of the merchandise is different from what you're used to seeing back home. Made-in-Tahiti items can be good souvenir purchases, but be aware that some of the wooden masks, clothing and pearly shells that are sold in boutiques and curio shops were imported from Indonesia or the Philippines. The *pareu* or *pareo*, which is called a sarong or lava lava in other countries, is Tahiti's national garment. It is made from a piece of cotton fabric approximately 2 yards long and 1 yard wide and tie-dyed, airbrushed or hand painted. You will find these in shops along the Papeete waterfront, at sidewalk stands, in arts and crafts centers all around the island, in hotel boutiques, and displayed at the colorful kiosks set up permanently outside and upstairs at **le Marché**, the municipal market in the heart of Papeete.

One of the nicest selections of hand painted pareos, shirts, caftans (boubou) and beach cover-ups is at **Le Tiare de Tahiti** boutique on the second level of the Vaima Center. Fabrics to make your own *pareos* or brightly patterned shirts and dresses are sold by the meter at **Tahiti Art**, **Tahiti Beach**, the **Venus** fabric stores and other Chinese-owned shops in the vicinity of the public market.

Polynesian style bikinis, beachwear and ball gowns are fabricated by local factories and couturiers in attractive hand-blocked materials. You'll find the choicest selections in the hotel boutiques, and in dozens of shops in Papeete, including **Tahiti Art, Marie Ah You, Celina** and **Tiare Shop** on Boulevard Pomare, **Anémone** on Rue Marital Foch, **Shop Gauguin Curios** on Rue Gauguin, **Tamara Curios** in Fare Tony Center, **Vaima Shirts, Bikini Boutique** and several other shops in the Vaima Center. **Tahiti Shirts**, on Boulevard Pomare, carries several lines of quality shirts that are designed by young artists in Tahiti. **Tahiti Art** also sells wall hangings, tapestries, lampshades, candles, jewelry boxes, paintings and engravings, all with Polynesian designs. Sports and Surf clothes are sold all over town, as well as in the Moana Nui (Carrefour) center in Punaauia, where you will find **Kelly Surf, Tahiti Sport** and **Graffity**. **Hinano Boutique**, beside the Cathedral, sells tee shirts, dresses, swimsuits, caps, cups, glasses, ashtrays and all sorts of gift items bearing the famous Hinano beer label.

Look upstairs at **le Marché** for carved Marquesan bowls, ceremonial spears, drums, ukuleles, tables and tikis, plus many other gift items. You can also shop upstairs and downstairs at the market for Tahitian dancing costumes, basketry and woven hats, plus shell jewelry, mother-of-pearl creations, *tifaifai* bed covers or wall hangings, embroidered cushion covers and wood carvings. The **Artisan Village** adjacent to Tahiti's Maison de la Culture (cultural center) on the Papeete waterfront in Tipaerui should have some interesting carvings. Handcrafts stand or artisan centers are located in almost every village around the island, and the major hotels have arts and crafts demonstrations several times a week. You can buy very pleasing souvenir gifts directly from the person who created them.

Monoi oil is an especially nice and inexpensive purchase, made from coconut oil and the essence of flowers. The most popular fragrance is the Tiare Tahiti, the white gardenia. Other floral choices of *monoi* are made with Pitate, Ylang Ylang, Tipanie (Frangipani or Plumeria), and you can also buy vanilla, coconut and sandalwood scented *monoi* products. *Monoi* oil can be used as a moisturizing lotion, a perfume, suntan lotion, mosquito repellent, hairdressing and a massage lotion. This can be purchased, along with *monoi* soaps, shampoos, bath gels and balms, in pharmacies, super markets, hotel boutiques and in many shops in Papeete and all around the island. Tamanu oil and creams are also popular, as well as beauty and health products made from the Tahitian noni fruit and tamanu fruit.

Tahitian vanilla beans make an unusual souvenir item, and are found in **le Marché** and in souvenir shops and grocery stores. Candies, cookies, *confitures* and coconut toddy, all Tahiti products, are good for gifts. And don't forget the Tahitian musical choices, in cassettes, CDs, video and DVD films of the islands. There are French perfumes, French fashions, crystal ware and French *patés* and cheeses. Duty Free Shops are found in Papeete and at the International Airport of Tahiti-Faaa. Very French-y style lingerie is on display in several of the shop windows. **Vahine's Secret**, beside the Cathedral, carries name brands of lace bras and thongs or strings, such as Calvin Klein, Aubade, Morgan, Simone Pérèle, Diesel and the Rien Collection.

Gastronomic gift items can be found at **Boutique Comtess du Barry** on Rue Edouard Ahnne in Papeete. In addition to a large selection of French wines, champagnes, aperitifs and digestifs, you'll find bamboo platters and wicker baskets filled with foie gras, confit de canard, jars of baba au rhum, fruit confitures, gourmet nuts and French chocolates. The shops at Tahiti-Faa'a International Airport carry a wide selection of gift items, including Tahitian calendars, mouse pads, music, glasses and cups, T-shirts, pareos, and locally made soaps and lotions. Once you pass Immigration you can buy Duty Free items, including Tahitian pearl jewelry, at the shops inside the waiting area.

Art Galleries
   Galerie Winkler, *Tel. 42.81.77*, is located on Rue Jeanne d'Arc in Papeete, where you will find a variety of paintings, pottery, sculptures and other art works. **Galerie Les Tropiques**, *Tel. 41.05.00*, is on the corner of Boulevard Pomare and Rue Cook, a few blocks west of the Vaima Center. Frequent exhibits feature the works of resident artists. **Galerie Olivier Creations**, *Tel. 50.71.71*. Rue Paul Gauguin, facing Air Tahiti Nui office, between the Papeete Mairie and the Pont de l'Est. The paintings of Joannis and Thierry Fiérin are among the exhibits of paintings by contemporary resident artists you'll find in this interesting gallery. **Au Chevalet**, *Tel. 42.12.55*, is at 158 Boulevard Pomare in Fariipiti. **Ganesha**, *Tel. 43.04.18*, is on the second level of the Vaima Center, with paintings, tapa bark cloth, wood and stone carvings, traditional culture and contemporary art. **Océanie Art Gallery**, is in the Passage Cardella, showcasing original art from local painters as well as the sculptures, carvers, engravers, tapa makers, and works from throughout the Pacific Islands. **Galerie Antipodes**, *Tel. 54.05.05*, is in the Fare Tony Building in Papeete. **No Name Gallery**, *Tel. 41.90.54/78.71.38*, is upstairs in the Matisse Bldg. on the Papeete waterfront. The **SaraHina** atelier of Sabrina Birk Levy is located in her home at *PK 57.5 in Taravao, Tel. 70.10.79; www.sarahina.over-blog.com*. Her paintings illustrate the legends of Polynesia.

Where to Buy Tahitian Cultured Pearls
   Tahiti's biggest export item is the Tahitian cultured pearl, which is also the most sought-after souvenir item. Exquisite jewelry, fashioned of pearls, 18-karat gold and diamonds, can be purchased in Tahiti, as well as pearls set in crystallized Pyrex and pure crystal, or braided coconut fibers, plus unset pearls of all sizes, shapes, quality and prices. Shops selling these jewels of the sea are found on practically every block in downtown Papeete, in addition to all the hotel boutiques.
   I like the creative settings, quality and colors of the pearls sold at **Tahia Pearls**, *Tel. 54.06.00*, on the corner of Avenue Prince Hinoi and Boulevard Pomare, as well as the friendliness and knowledge of the sales staff. Their main showroom is in Moorea, and they also have 2 pearl shops in Bora Bora and a boutique on board the *Paul Gauguin* ship.

The biggest name in the pearl business here is **Robert Wan Tahiti Perles**, who specializes in long rope necklaces of big pearls from his own pearl farms. He also owns Tahiti Pearl Museum. **Vaima Perles**, *Tel. 42.55.57*, upstairs in the Vaima Center, is another good shop for creative designs, and **Dany's Black Pearl**, *Tel. 54.58.89*, on Blvd. Pomare, has nice selections of pearl jewelry. **Tahiti Pearl Market**, *Tel. 54.30.60*, at 25 Rue Colette, between the Papeete Marché and Mairie, has 150,000 pearls direct from the producer's pearl farm, from which you can make your selections. They will even help you to drill your pearls and create you own jewelry. **Orau Pearls**, *Tel. 58.21.25*, is a wholesaler-retailer upstairs in a building on the corner of Rue Paul Gauguin and Rue Colette, between the Papeete City Hall and Le Marche. **Mihiarii Pearls**, *Tel. 41.28.15/41.92.14*, has a boutique adjacent to Le Marché and another one in the Quartier du Commerce, offering a large choice of loose pearls at producer prices.

Tua at **Ariihau Nui Pearls & Handicrafts**, *Tel. 42.66.12*, is my contact for inexpensive pearls. Her shop is upstairs at Le Marché (the Papeete Market). Take the escalator and walk through the restaurant and you will find Tua at the 4th or 5th shop on the left. You'll see the pearls in a showcase, as well as jillions of tie-dyed pareos, mother-of-pearl jewelry, carved artifacts and many more items. Tua and her children keep busy making all these items, which they also sell to boutiques and shops throughout the islands. She takes credit cards, including American Express and she speaks English. The photographs on the wall are of her great-great-grandmother, Teha'apapa, known as the warrior queen, who was the last queen of Huahine. See more information on pearls under Shopping section of *Basic Information* chapter.

MASSAGES & SPAS

Deep Nature Spa, *Tel. 86.51.51/86.51.10*, is a Spa and Fitness Center behind the main swimming pool at the Intercontinental Tahiti Resort & Spa. In addition to the Spa reception, changing room, lockers and showers, there is a steam room, rainshower, cold plunge, tea salon and five treatment areas, including an anti-gravity bed. The 3,230 square foot oasis features Algotherm treatments and products containing marine vitamins extracted from the ocean's depths, the same as used in the Deep Ocean Spa at the ICH Thalasso Spa in Bora Bora. The spa menu also includes treatments with traditional Polynesian Hei Poa, the exotic and highly calming Polynesian massage products, to provide spa-goers with the ultimate experience of tranquility and well-being. The signature "Tahitian Wave" massage is 16.500 CFP for 75 min., and a 4-hr. "Chill Out in Tahiti" massage and body care treatment is 53.200 CFP.

Dhana Spa, *Tel. 46.38.99*, is located at the Hotel Tahiti Nui on Ave. Prince Hinoi. Their services include facial and body care for men and women, plus various massage choices: Dhana, Taurumi, Shirodara, Oriental, reflexology, Ayurvedic and Thai, starting at 10.000 CFP for 55 min. A sports massage for men is 16.000 CFP for 80 min. There is also a Jacuzzi, Turkish bath and gym here.

Just Relax Tahiti, *Tel. 26.32.42/86.66.00* is a Beauty Institute located at the Sofitel Maeva Beach. Open daily except all day Sun. and on Mon. morning. Facials, manicures and waxing are available as well as a California massage, a combo massage or couples massage.

Le Spa, *Tel. 48.88.21; lespa@radisson-tahiti.pf* is on the upper level of the Radisson Plaza Resort in Arue. Open daily 9:30am-8pm. They carry their own clothing line and products created exclusively for Le Spa. There are two single and two double treatment rooms with jet baths, saunas, steam rooms, a rainfall shower and a full-service salon for facial care, makeup, manicure and pedicure. Signature treatments feature black sand and volcanic stones as well as indigenous fruits such as mango, guava, papaya, coconut and vanilla. Be sure to try a Sakura sauna and a Yumeji gentle massage. A 24-hour fitness center with cardio and strength training equipment as well as a yoga center is located next to Le Spa.

Manea Spa, *Tel. 50.84.45*, is located at the Manava Suite Resort Tahiti. Open daily 9am-6pm, providing massages, exfoliating, energizing and tonifying beauty care treatments. Manicures, pedicures, waxing and facials are also available. Massages start at 4.000 CFP for 30-min. and you can have a couples massage in your suite or on the motu in front of the resort. Manea Spa carries its own line of products derived from natural extracts such as pineapple, ginger, bamboo, Tiare Tahiti flowers, tamanu, noni, and white sand from the beaches of Bora Bora. There is also a fitness center.

Rikardo "The Relaxer," *Tel. 73.18.18*, is a one-man massage service operated by Richard Hammill, an American expatriate resident of Tahiti. He is located in the Tiniouru Medical Building, behind the Cathedral, across the road from Odyssey bookstore. He's on the first level, which Americans know as the second floor.

Philippe Girodeau, *Tel./Fax 689/56.40.42, cell phone 77.54.79*, will bring his massage table to your room and make you feel like a new person after he works on your body, mind and soul. He opens your chakra energy centers and heals your aches and pains with magnetism and a pair of very strong hands. He charges 10.000 CFP, but the massage usually lasts more than an hour. He lives in Moorea and goes to Papeete a couple of times a week on request. This is my preferred massage therapist.

Frederic Precloux, *Tel. 42.23.30*, is a chiropractor who studied at the Los Angeles College of Chiropractic. He speaks very good English and his office is located behind the Cathedral in Papeete, in the Tiniouru Medical Building, facing the Odyssey bookstore. He's on the second floor, just above the street level.

TATTOOS

Aroma Tattoo Art, *Tel. 78.06.73; demonaroma@yahoo.com*. Aroma Salmon is located upstairs at the Papeete public market, along with his brother, Manu Salmon of **Manu Tattoo Art**. They are both professional tattoo artists. Their parents, Manihi and Tila Salmon, own Pension Motu Aito Paradise in Fakarava.

Both brothers speak English and work in hygienic conditions. You'll also find some good tattoo artists from the Marquesas Islands on this level of the Papeete market. Tattoo rates start at 5.000 CFP and average 10.000 CFP.

DAY TOUR TO MOOREA

Moorea is only 17 km. (11 mi.) across the channel from Tahiti, and the rugged profile of her mountains beckon you to cross the Sea of Moons, so named by the ancient Polynesians. This is where the residents of Tahiti go when they need to "escape" for a day or weekend. If your plans do not include a stay on Moorea, then a day tour is certainly on the "must do" list.

You can book your excursion at the Tahiti Nui Travel or Marama Tours travel desk in your hotel lobby. They will make all the arrangements so that you can be totally carefree. Following are some of the standard tours, which require a minimum of 2 people Some tours are not available on Sun. and public holidays. The bus drivers on Moorea are not always willing to work on Sun. and holidays, so it would be wise to rent a car at the ferry dock to visit the island.

Marama Tours sells **A Day Tour of Moorea with a Beach Picnic on a Motu & Ray Feeding** for 14.100 CFP per person, including round-trip transfers by land and sea. At the Club Bali Hai on Moorea you board a Moana Tours excursion boat that takes you to visit Cook's Bay and Opunohu Bay, with a stop to feed the friendly stingrays on your way to the motu islet. You can swim and snorkel while your beach barbecue is being prepared.

The hotel travel desks also sell a Moorea Day Tour for 12.800 CFP, which includes all transfers in Tahiti and Moorea, the round-trip fast catamaran, a 4-hr. circle island tour of Moorea by 4WD, or a 2-hr. tour by mini-van. You will be driven up the mountain to the **Belvedere** lookout point with a stop at the *marae* stone temples in Opunohu Valley. This tour can also include lunch at the Hilton Moorea Lagoon for a total of 13.600 CFP.

A **Dolphin Experience** can be combined with a Moorea Day Tour at the Intercontinental Moorea. The cost of round-trip boat fare, land transfers and the Dolphin Center starts at 32.000 CFP without lunch.

A **Moorea Tiki Village Day Tour**, available from Tues.-Sat., includes a visit to the Tiki Village. The cost of 16.700 CFP covers all transfers, round-trip fare on the fast catamaran, lunch and a bus tour from the boat dock in Moorea through **Cook's Bay** to the **Moorea Distillery and Fruit Juice Factory** and the **Belvedere** lookout point, and on around the island. The beach at Tiki Village is not as pretty as some others on the island, and the lagoon is very shallow and warm close to the shore. But you will certainly find all the entertainment you want. Here in this typical **Polynesian village**, you'll see Tahitians weaving palm fronds, dying *pareos*, making floral crowns, sculpting wood or stone, tattooing and creating jewelry from Tahitian cultured pearls. You can paddle a canoe and go snorkeling in the coral gardens. You can eat lunch in the **Papayer Restaurant** and watch a mini-show of **Polynesian dances** performed in the white sand.

You can also visit Moorea quite easily on your own. The least expensive way will cost you a minimum of 3.590 CFP for land and sea transportation. You can catch le *truck* from your hotel to downtown Papeete for 130 CFP, get off on Boulevard Pomare by the Banque de Polynésie, cross the street to Fare Manihini, the Tahiti Tourist Bureau, and walk along the wharf a couple of blocks until you come to the dock for the Moorea ferries. You'll see the ticket office for *Aremiti V* catamaran *(Tel. 50.57.57)* in a small building on the waterfront (or in the new terminal building when it opens). The round-trip fare for non-resident adults is 2.730 CFP and 1.680 for children. The *Aremiti V* is a/c and comfortable. The service from Papeete to Moorea starts at 6:05am Mon.-Fri., and at 7:35am on Sat.-Sun. Visitors usually like to take the boat that leaves Papeete at 9:15am daily. You will arrive in Moorea just 30 min. later, which gives you time for a full day of discovering this lovely island.

You can reserve a guided tour of Moorea through your travel desk in Tahiti, or you can rent a car across the road from the **Vaiare** boat dock in Moorea. Should you decide on the least expensive way to visit Moorea for the day, just walk to the parking lot in front of the ferry terminal, where you will see at least 2 buses loading passengers. One of the buses serves the **North Coast** of Moorea, passing by the hotels Sofitel Moorea Ia Ora Resort & Spa, Moorea Pearl Resort & Spa, Hotel Kaveka, Club Bali Hai, Hilton Moorea Lagoon, Intercontinental Moorea Resort & Spa, Hotel Les Tipaniers, and Hotel Hibiscus. The other bus goes around the **South Coast** of Moorea, passing by Hotel Linareva, the Tiki Village, and Hotel Hibiscus, stopping at Le Petit Village, which is within easy walking distance of the hotels in that vicinity. Be sure to ask the bus driver which direction he's headed, and you pay him 300 CFP before boarding the bus. There's just one standard fare.

The **best public beach** on the island is at Temae Motu, just past the Sofitel Moorea Ia Ora Resort, a short walk from the circle island road. Ask the driver to let you off at the turn-off for the *plage publique de Temae* and follow the dirt road for a couple of blocks. There are changing rooms, toilets and showers here, as well as *roulotte* food vans that sell snacks, soft drinks and bottled water.

If you want to see the coastal sights of Moorea, then take one of the buses to **Haapiti**, and get off at the end of the line, which is at Le Petit Village. From there you can walk across the street to the island's **second best white sand beach**. You can also choose one of the hotels in the vicinity as your home for the day. They have public showers and toilets and you'll find several restaurants, snack bars, boutiques and pearl shops within easy walking distance of Le Petit Village.

Tahia'manu Beach (also called **Mareto**) in Opunohu Bay is another good beach open to the public, within easy walking distance of the Hilton. Picnic tables are shaded by beautiful old tamanu trees and a white sand beach slopes into the normally clear and calm lagoon. There is a fresh water shower here.

If you visit Moorea on a Sun., you may want to go to the **Painapo Beach**, where you can swim, snorkel, and have lunch under the shade of an almond tree beside the lagoon. They have a Tahitian feast on the first Sunday of each month.

The buses depart from **Le Petit Village** one hour before each arrival and departure of the ferries. Therefore, if you are taking the last *Aremiti V* from Moorea to Tahiti, which leaves at 4:45pm Mon.-Thurs., at 5pm on Fri.-Sat., and at 5:45pm on Sun., just stand beside the road an hour before departure time and wave for the driver to stop. (Don't expect bus service on Sun).

When you get back to Papeete you'll have to walk back to the bus stop. Then you will need to find a *le truck* or bus that will take you to the hotels on the west coast, but there will be fewer of them running on weekends.

DAY TOURS TO BORA BORA

The travel desks in your hotel lobby can sell you a Day Tour to Bora Bora, starting at 52.450 CFP per person, which includes a barbecue picnic on the motu at Lagoonarium. I personally do not recommend anyone going to Bora Bora just for the day, because so much time is spent just getting there and back that you have very little time left to see the island. If it is at all possible to do so, I suggest you try to spend at least one night on Bora Bora, so that you can enjoy the overwhelming beauty of the lagoon. Some of the family pensions have good rates for budget travelers.

PRACTICAL INFORMATION

Books, Newspapers and Magazines

La Maison de la Presse, *Tel. 50.93.93*, is on Blvd. Pomare across the street from Place Vaiete. **The Tahiti BOOK Store**, *Tel. 82.40.11/76.47.58*, is on the top level of the Vaima Center in Papeete. **Librairie Archipels**, *Tel. 42.47.30*, is on Rue des Remparts, across from the Mairie of Papeete (town hall). **Odyssey**, *Tel. 54.25.25*, is behind the Cathedral, adjacent to the Aorai building. They have books, CD's, DVD's and office supplies.

Churches & Religious Services

Many religions and denominations are represented in French Polynesia. Following are the main numbers for the religious offices on the island of Tahiti:
• **Protestant Evangelical Church, (Maohi Protestant Church)** *Tel. 46.06.00*
• **Catholic Church**, *Tel. 50.30.00* (Cathedrale parish), *Tel. 50.23.51* (Archdiocese)
•**Mormon Church**, *Tel. 50.55.05*
• **Seventh Day Adventists**, *Tel. 50/82.50/50.55.05* (regional office)
• **Sanito**, *Tel. 42.22.58*
• **Jehovah's Witnesses**, *Tel. 54.70.00*
• **Alleluia Church**, *Tel. 42.95.88*
• **Assembly of God Pentecostal Church**, *Tel. 45.36.61*
• **Neo-Apostolic**, *Tel. 57.93.02*
• **Israelite Synagogue**, *Tel. 41.03.92, cell 72.66.17*

Church services on Sun. morning will offer you an insight into the Tahitian culture away from the hotel scene. You'll enjoy the singing, which is best in the Protestant churches or temples, formerly called **Eglise Evangelique**. This name was changed in 2004 to **Eglise Maohi Protestant**. The missionaries taught the Tahitians to sing the old time hymns in the early 1800s, and over the years the people have transformed the old religious songs into their own versions called *himene*. The singing is a capella, with the men sitting behind the women and the kids running around everywhere. Be prepared to sit on the side up front, where you can look at the parishioners and they can smile back at you. They are used to visitors and will warmly welcome you.

Consulates
• **Consular Agency of the United States**, *B.P. 10765, Paea, Tahiti 98711, Tamanu Iti Center, (1st floor), Punaauia. Tel. 689/42.65.35, Fax 689/50.80.96; usconsul@mail.pf/ ckozely@mail.pf. Fax in USA 917/464-7457.* Consular sessions are held each Tues. between 10am-12pm. You can contact Christopher Kozely 24 hours a day for emergencies only at *cell 21.93.19*.
• **Australia and Canada**, *Tel. 689/46.88.53; Fax 689/46.39.26*.
• **Great Britain**, *Tel. 689/70.63.82*.

Currency Exchange
Banque de Polynésie, Boulevard Pomare, *Tel. 46.66.66*; **Banque de Tahiti**, Rue Cardella, *Tel. 41.70.00*; **Banque Socredo**, Rue Dumont d'Urville, *Tel. 41.51.23;* client relations *Tel. 47.00.00*. There are several branch offices of these banks in downtown Papeete and around the island of Tahiti, with various business hours, and all the major locations have an ATM. See sections on *Ready Cash and Currency Exchanges* in Chapter on *Basic Information*.

Hospitals & Doctors
You can find English-speaking doctors, dentists, nurses and other medical personnel in Tahiti, but they are not common. The Hospital of Pirae and the two private clinics are open 24 hrs. There is also a hospital in Taravao. See Health Concerns in *Basic Information* chapter for further details.

Pirae Hospital, *Tel. 46.62.62* (switchboard), *Tel. 42.01.01* or *15* (emergency), is the new government operated medical center in Taaone, a suburb just east of Papeete. Taravao Hospital, *Tel. 54.77.68* (switchboard), *Tel. 57.76.76* (emergency). **Clinique Cardella**, *Tel. 46.04.00* (switchboard), *Tel. 46.04.25* (emergency), and **Clinique Paofai**, *Tel. 46.18.18* (switchboard), *Tel. 46.18.90* (emergency) are privately owned clinics in Papeete. **S.O.S. Medecins**, *Tel. 42.34.56*, is an emergency unit of doctors and other medical personnel, who will come to the hotel to attend to your needs.

Optika Vaima, also called **Krys Vaima**, is in the Vaima Center, Tel. *50.11.85*, and **Pacific Optic Nguyen**, Rue Yves Martin in the Quartier du Commerce, 1 block inland from Boulevard Pomare, *Tel. 42.70.78,* will repair your glasses while you wait. **Surdité de Polynésie,** *Tel. 43.33.04,* in the Quartier du Commerce close to the Tracqui store will solve your hearing aid problems while you're in Tahiti.

Internet Service – Cyber Cafés

Tahiti's Internet service provider is **Mana,** which has installed WiFi "surfing spots" *(www.manaspot.pf)* around Tahiti, such as the post offices, Tahiti Tourisme, Place To'ata, Bougainville Park, Fare Tony pedestrian area, the Cathedral, Vaima Center, the quay for visiting passenger ships, and at the airport. There are also Manaspots on Moorea and several of the outer islands. This service provides high-speed wireless Internet access for portable computers and cell phones in all 5 archipelagoes. They have issued "ManaSpot" WiFi cards that sell for 660 CFP for 1 hr., or 3.960 CFP for a 10-hr. card. Monthly rates with unlimited volume are available for professionals. You can buy these cards at any post office.

Cybernesia, *Tel. 85.43.67; cybernesia@mail.pf; www.cybernesia.pf.* This cyber-space is on the third level of the Vaima Center above the Concorde Cinema in the heart of Papeete. There are computers with Internet access or you can plug your laptop into the network. Other services include color printing, copies and CD engraving. Open Mon.-Fri. 8:30am-5:30pm and on Sat. 9am-1pm.

@Business Center, *Tel. 83.63.88.* This business center and cyber café is located at the Tahiti-Faa'a Airport at the entrance to the domestic terminal. Services include Internet access, e-mail, color copying, scanning, documents copied to digital files, digital photo cards transferred and CD-Rom engraving.

Tahiti Tourisme Cyber Center, *Tel. 50.57.12* is located in the welcome center of the Visitors Bureau on the Papeete waterfront. There are 2 computers and a printer.

Maison de La Culture, "Te Fare Tauhiti Nui", *Tel. 54.45.44,* at 646 Blvd. Pomare adjacent to Place To'ata, provides Internet access and is a WiFi Manaspot. All of the big hotels, many of the small family owned family hotels and pensions have Internet access, and several restaurants also provide this service for a fee.

Laundry Service

All the larger hotels provide laundry service, and can arrange to have your dry cleaning done. **Laverie,** *Tel. 43.71.59,* is located at 64 Rue Gauguin, facing the Papeete Mairie (town hall) near the Pont de l'Est. They will wash, dry and fold 7 kg. (15 lbs.) of clothes for 1.900 CFP. A quilt is 2.500 CFP. Ironing is also available.

Pharmacies / Drugstores

There are half a dozen pharmacies in the Papeete area, and several around the island. One of the easiest to find in Papeete is the **Pharmacie du Vaima,** *Tel. 42.97.73,* on Rue de Général de Gaulle at Rue Georges La Garde, behind the Vaima Center close to McDonald's Hamburgers. The pharmacist is Nguyen Ngoc-Tran, who speaks English.

Pharmacie Moana Nui, *Tel. 43.16.98*, is in the Carrefour shopping mall in Punaauia, convenient to the Intercontinental Tahiti Resort and Sofitel Tahiti Resort. **Pharmacie Tamanu**, *Tel. 58.20.34*, is located in the Tamanu shopping center in Punaauia, next door to Le Méridien. The pharmacies rotate night and weekend/holiday duty, so it is best to check with your hotel to find out which one is available should you need medical supplies after hours. The medicines sold in French Polynesia are French brands.

Police

The main headquarters of the French gendarmerie, *Tel. 46.73.67* or *17*, is located on Avenue Bruat in Papeete. There are also brigades in Faaa, Punaauia, Paea, Papara, Taravao, Tiarei and Arue. The municipal police can be reached at *Tel. 48.48.48*.

Post Office

The main post office is on Blvd. Pomare in downtown Papeete, *Tel. 41.42.42*. There are also several branches all around the island.

Restrooms

There are public toilets on the Papeete waterfront at the passenger ship dock, just outside the **Tahiti Tourisme Bureau**. The public facilities at **Tahua Vaiete** (Place Vaiete) and **Tahua To'ata** (Place To'ata), on opposite ends of the waterfront, are kept clean 24-hours a day by a team of Tahitian government employees. You'll also find public toilets in the new terminal building for the Moorea ferries on the Papeete waterfront. Bring your own paper just in case. You can also use the restrooms in the restaurants downtown.

Around the island, you'll find public restrooms at the main tourist stops, such as Point Venus, the Blowhole of Arahoho and the Three Cascades of Tiarei, the Paul Gauguin Museum, the Vaipahi Gardens and Waterfall, and at the Grottoes of Mara'a.

Yacht Services

Polynesia Yacht Services, *Tel. 77.12.30; Fax 689/56.18.79; pys@mail.pf.* Laurent Bernaert is a young Frenchmen whose efficient and friendly "no hassle attitude" will make your visit to French Polynesia smooth and pleasant.

His services include: all official formalities with Customs, Immigration and Port; visa extension, bond exemption for non EEC crew members, duty free fuel formalities; advanced port and marina berth reservation, security arrangements, agency discounts for parts and ship's chandlery, Customs brokerage service for import/export orders; express courier shipments; coordination of all kinds of repairs and maintenance; shipyard and refit consultancy; dry docking storage in Tahiti or Raiatea; absentee yacht management; domestic services (laundry, dry cleaning, etc.); dive guides, PADI certifications, underwater yacht services; cruise programs, books and charts for all of Pacific Ocean; gas bottle refills, waste oil removal; international and local travel arrangements; hotel accommodations; rental cars, taxis, VIP services (private plane, helicopter); food and beverage provisioning; medical and dental assistance; mail drop, phone, fax WiFi connection; mobile phone and local SIM cards rental; monthly payment; banking services.

Association de Voiliers en Polynesie, *BP 43442 Papeete, Tahiti, Tel. 689/ 74.10.02; VHF Channel 69 "Teva 3"; http://avp.over-blog.org, avp.tahiti@gmail.com.* Call Michel, the president, on the VHF in the Maeva Beach anchorage. This association was created in 1981 to help visiting cruising sailors and to protect the rights of sailors in French Polynesia. Since 1997, the association tries to keep the Maeva Beach anchorage open to passing boats. It can also inform you about the "etiquette" in the anchorage and the latest security and theft problems. The association organizes and promotes events like nautical flea markets, beach cleanups, potlucks, boat parades, etc. It maintains close contact with the written press and local television to inform the local population about cruising, living aboard, rallies and other cruising related info. AVP maintains a trash disposal container at the disposition of cruisers who are welcome to join the association or give a donation.

12. Moorea

Scientists say that **Moorea** (Mo-oh-RAY-ah) is shaped like an isosceles triangle, and romantics believe the island is in the form of a heart. I think it looks like a swimming turtle. Geologists say that Moorea is twice as old as Tahiti and once contained a volcano that reached 3,300 m (11,000 ft.) into the sky. Polynesian legend tells us that Moorea was created when a magical fish swam from the lagoon of Raiatea and Taha'a to become the island of Tahiti; and the second dorsal fin of this enormous fish grew into land that was called "Aimeo i te rara varu" for the eight mountain ridges that separate the island. The traditional shortened name of this island was Aimeho, Aimeo or Eimeo. Following a vision by one of the Polynesian high priests, the name was later changed to Moorea, which means, "yellow lizard."

Moorea offers you the tropical South Seas island that you expect to find when you fly to Tahiti, just 17 km (11 mi.) across the Sea of Moons. Some people say it's worth the airfare to Tahiti just to see Moorea. Others say that Moorea was created so that people on Tahiti would have something to stare at across the sea.

Moorea's magnificent beauty covers an area of 136 sq. km (53 sq. mi.), which is the south rim of a crater that was formed following cataclysmic explosions eons ago. The lofty cathedral-shaped peaks and jade velvet spires that you will see reflected in the lapis lazuli waters of **Cook's Bay** and **Opunohu** (belly-of-the-stone-fish) **Bay** are the basaltic remains of the crater's interior wall.

The volcanic peaks of the mountain range resemble a fairy castle or a serrated shark's jaw, dominated by **Tohive'a** (hot spade) at 1,207 m (3,983 ft.). **Mou'a Roa** (long mountain), with an altitude of 880 m (2,904 ft.), resembles a shark's tooth. This is the most photographed of the spectacular wonders, and it is often pointed out to visitors as "Bali Ha'i." **Mou'a Puta** (split rock), the 830 m- (2,739 ft.-) high mountain with a hole in its top, is a tempting challenge for hikers. The hole is said to have been made by the spear of Pai, a favorite son of the gods of old Polynesia, who was warned that Hiro, god of thieves, wanted to steal the sacred **Rotui** Mountain and take it home to Raiatea. The warrior Pai threw a spear from Tahiti that pierced the top of Mou'a Puta and the noise woke up all the roosters on Moorea, who crowed so loudly that the thieves were forced to flee. But Hiro did manage to take a piece of Rotui's crest and this stolen land can be seen on top of a mountain in Raiatea, covered with the *toa* (ironwood) trees similar to those that grow on **Mou'a Rotui**.

Moorea's crystalline lagoons, filled with gardens of fanciful coral and exotic sea creatures, are said to have been a gift from Ruahatu, king of the ocean. This benevolent god specially created the azure waters of the fjord-like bays. Tane, the Polynesian god of beauty, bordered the lagoons with white sand beaches and planted an abundance of fragrant white Tiare Tahiti blossoms among the majestic coconut palms.

ARRIVALS & DEPARTURES

Arriving By Air

Air Tahiti, *Tel. 86.42.42, www.airtahiti.pf,* provides direct ATR flight service between Tahiti and Moorea, replacing Air Moorea, which stopped all flights on Oct. 31, 2010. Check in at the Air Tahiti counter in the domestic terminal in the same building used for international flights. There are 3-5 flights a day, with the first flight leaving Tahiti at 7am on Mon., Wed., Thurs., and Fri.; at 7:45am on Sun., at 8am on Sat., and at 10:30am on Tues. The last flight leaves Tahiti at 5pm daily, arriving in Moorea 10-15 min. later. The one-way fare is 4.130 CFP per adult, 2.930 CFP for a child 2-11 years, and 300 CFP for a baby.

There is an ATR flight daily from Bora Bora to Huahine to Moorea. The one-way adult fare is 20.430 CFP from Bora Bora and 14.830 CFP from Huahine. Reduced fares for children and babies.

You can also charter an airplane to Moorea with **Air Tahiti**, *Tel. 86.42.42,* and **Pol'Air**, *Tel. 74.23.11.* Helicopter flights can be organized with **Tahiti Helicopters**, *Tel. 50.40.75; Fax 50.40.76.*

The **Temae Airport** terminal in Moorea has restrooms and information counters for tour and excursion companies. Taxi service is usually available for all arriving flights, and there is a taxi phone at the main entrance. There is no bus service provided directly to the airport. If you are not carrying heavy bags and wish to walk about 4 blocks to the main road to catch the bus, you want to be sure that you schedule your arrival with that of the ferries from Tahiti, when the public transportation service will be operating. You can stand beside the Total Station and wave down the first bus that passes, which will be going from the Vaiare ferry dock toward Cook's Bay. **Torea Nui Transport** provides land transfer service for 700 CFP per person. See details under *Tour & Transport Companies* in this chapter.

Arriving By Boat

The **Moorea Boat Dock** (Gallieni Wharf) in Papeete, a couple of blocks east of the Tahiti Tourist Bureau on the waterfront, is where you will find the fast catamaran and two ferries that transport passengers between Tahiti and Moorea. You can buy tickets in the new terminal building adjacent to the ferry dock, which will hopefully be finished by the time you arrive. Original plans included a parking garage, but the terminal is so grandiose and costly that the government ran out of money and no provisions have been made for parking in Papeete. The ferry dock in Moorea also has an improvement project under way, which will provide more parking at a fee. The **Moorea Express** fast catamaran is out of service indefinitely, and the company is looking for a replacement boat.

Aremiti V, *Tel. 50.57.57/50.57.92* in Tahiti and *Tel. 56.43.24* in Moorea; *www.aremiti.pf.* The air-conditioned fast catamaran *Aremiti V* is 56 m. (184 ft.) long and 14.4 m. (47 ft.) wide, with 2 bridges and 3 passenger salons, a snack bar with tables in the rear, clean toilets, TV screens, comfortable seating for 697 passengers, including 70 places on the upper sundeck, and space for 30 passenger cars and scooters. The crossings from quay to quay take 30 minutes. Non-resident one-way fares in mid-2011 were 1.365 CFP for adults and 840 CFP for a child under 12 years. These rates will increase when they start using the new ferry terminal.

The *Aremiti V* leaves Papeete each Mon.-Thurs. at 6:05am, 7:35am and 9:15am, 12pm, 4pm and 5:30pm, with the exception of Wed., when the 12pm departure actually leaves at 12:20pm. The Wed. schedule of 12:20pm also applies for Fri., with the addition of an extra crossing leaving Papeete at 2:40pm on Fri., and the departures are at 4:15pm and 5:45pm. The Sat. departures from Papeete to Moorea are at 7:35am and 9:15am, 12:20pm, 2:40pm, 4:15pm and 5:45pm. On Sun. the boat leaves Papeete at 7:35am and 9:15am, and at 3:25pm, 5pm and 6:30pm. Be sure to verify the schedules before or when you get to the ticket window, because they are subject to change at any time without much advance notice. See further information on the **Aremiti** boats under *Inter-Island Cruise Ships, Passenger Boats & Freighters* in the chapter on *Planning Your Trip*.

Aremiti Ferry, *Tel. 50.57.57* in Tahiti and *Tel. 56.31.10* in Moorea. This is a 272-ft. long steel hull catamaran that transports cars, big trucks and construction equipment, and up to 502 passengers between the two islands. A one-way crossing takes 50 minutes. There are toilets, an a/c lounge and a snack bar on board. This boat is not recommended for people who have difficulty climbing steep stairs. The *Aremiti Ferry* leaves Papeete for Moorea on Mon.-Fri. at 6am and 9:30am. On Mon.-Thurs. afternoons the ship leaves Tahiti at 3:10pm, and on Fri. the ship leaves Tahiti at 12:30pm and 4:30pm. On Sat. the *Aremiti Ferry* leaves Papeete at 6:45am and 9:30am, and 12:30pm. The hours on Sun. are 7:45am, and 5:30pm. **Note:** These hours are subject to change whenever the *Aremiti V* is unable to transport passengers, so it is best to verify the schedule once you are in Tahiti.

The one-way passenger fares for non-residents are 1.365 CFP per adult and 840 CFP for a child under 12 years. The round-trip cost to transport a passenger car starts at 5.800 CFP.

Moorea Ferry, *Tel. 50.11.11* in Tahiti, *Tel. 56.34.34/56.43.43* in Moorea; www.mooreaferry.pf. This is a 190-ft. long steel hull ship that can transport 300 passengers, cars, heavy trucks and freight during the 1-hour crossings between Tahiti and Moorea. On board are a lounge, snack bar and toilets. The one-way adult fare is 1.050 CFP and half-price for children 4 to 12 years. Lightweight cars are 2.920 CFP one-way, and bicycles are 240 CFP. The Papeete-Moorea schedule for Mon.-Fri. has departures at 6am, 10:15am, 2pm and 4:45pm. The *Moorea Ferry* leaves Papeete each Sat. at 6:30am, 9:30am, 12pm and 5:15pm. On Sun. it leaves Papeete at 7:30am, 4:15pm and 6:45pm.

You will find public telephones, scooter rental agencies, taxi service, toilets, fruit stands and snack bars at the two terminal buildings on the **Vaiare Ferry dock or quay**. The car rental agencies are across the road.

Public ground transportation in Moorea is provided by buses, with vehicles waiting in front of the terminal upon the arrival of the catamaran and ferries from

Tahiti. Give the driver the name of your destination and verify that you're getting onto the right bus, as one goes on the north coast to **Cook's Bay** and onward to the **former Club Med** area, and the other bus heads in the opposite direction, towards **Afareaitu** and on to **Haapiti** and the **Club Med** area, by way of the south coast. You pay the driver 300 CFP before boarding, and pull the cord, ring the bell or holler "stop" when you want to get off.

Departing By Air

Air Tahiti, *Tel. 86.42.42/86.41.84* on weekends in Tahiti or *Tel. 55.06.00* in Moorea, provides ATR service from Moorea to the Leeward Islands. You can fly direct from Moorea to Huahine once a day. There are 3 flights a day between Moorea and Bora Bora, including direct service or with a stop in Huahine or Raiatea. There are direct flights from Moorea to Raiatea on Mon., Tues., Wed. and Sun., and the Fri. flight and one Sun. flight stops first in Bora Bora. One-way fares to Huahine or Raiatea are 13.000 CFP and 18.400 CFP to Bora Bora.

Departing By Boat

Aremiti V Catamaran, *Tel. 56.31.10/50.57.57,* leaves Moorea for Papeete Mon.-Fri. at 5:20, 6:50, and 8:20am. A 10:45am departure is made on Mon., Tues. and Thurs., and on Wed. and Fri. at 11:35am, to coincide with the school program. The afternoon boats leave Moorea at 2:45pm and 4:45pm Mon.-Thurs., and at 1:45pm, 3:25pm and 5pm on Fri. On Sat. the boat leaves Moorea at 6am, 8:20am and 10:45am, and at 1:45pm, 3:25pm, and 5pm. The Sun. schedule is at 6:30am, 8:20am, 2:40pm, 4:15pm and 5:45pm. Ticket counters for the *Aremiti* catamaran and ferry are located at the new terminal of the Vaiare Ferry dock in Moorea. One-way fare is 1.365 CFP for adults and 840 CFP for a child under 12 years.

Aremiti Ferry, *Tel. 56.31.10/50.57.57,* leaves Moorea for Papeete Mon.-Thurs. at 7:30am, 1:30pm and 4:20pm, and on Fri. at 7:30am, 10:45am, 2:30pm, and 5:45pm. The Sat. departures from Vaiare are at 8am, 10:45am and at 4:45pm. The Sun. ferry leaves Vaiare at 4:15pm and 7pm. One-way fare is 1.365 CFP for adults and 840 CFP for a child under 12 years.

Moorea Ferry, *Tel. 56.34.34/56.43.43/50.11.11*, provides passenger and car service between Moorea and Papeete Mon.-Thurs. at 4:45am, 8:15am, 12:30pm (12pm on Wed.) and 3:30pm. The Fri. departures from Moorea are at 4:45am, 8:15am, 12:30pm, and at 3:15pm. The *Moorea Ferry* leaves Vaiare on Sat. at 5am, 8am, 10:45am and 4pm. The Sun. departures from Vaiare are at 6am, 3pm and 5:30pm. The ticket window is in the old terminal and the one-way fare is 1.050 CFP per adult and 525 CFP for children. One-way fares to transport cars starts at 2.920 CFP, and a bicycle is 400 CFP.

ORIENTATION

A paved road hugs the coast for 60 km (37 mi.) around Moorea, where you'll see thatched roof *fares* with bamboo walls, little shacks with tin roofs and lovely villas with stone walls. The census of Sept. 2007 counted 16,329 inhabitants and most of them live on the mountainside of the road, with a sprinkling of homes along the white sand beaches. Gardens of fruit and flowers border the road and during the summer months (Nov.-Mar.) you will see the flamboyant red or yellow Royal Poinciana trees in bloom.

You can happily take pictures on this beautiful island without having electric lines mar the photograph. All the cables are underground. However, you now have to shoot the scenery while trying to avoid the streetlights that have been placed beside the road in the tourist sections of the island. Although there has been a lot of grumbling about these lights, they are helpful for visitors who wish to walk beside the road at night when searching for a place to eat, and they also help drivers to better negotiate the twists and curves along the coastal road at night, while trying to avoid the kids on bikes, people walking in the road and dogs lying or just standing on the pavement.

Moorea doesn't have a town and until recently there was no central shopping area on the island. The administrative center is in the village of **Afareaitu**, which most visitors never see except from a tour bus. Located on the eastern coast facing Tahiti, this sleepy little settlement contains the principal *mairie* (town hall), local government offices and hospital. Most of the churches, schools, supermarkets, small *magasin* stores, banks, boutiques and restaurants are located in the villages of **Maharepa**, **Pao Pao**, **Papetoai** and **Haapiti**. Most of the hotels, hostels and family pensions are found beside **Cook's Bay** or bordering a white sand beach in **Haapiti** or **Temae**, although you can now find accommodations all around the island. The **Raihau Center** in Maharepa is adjacent to the **Socredo Center** that includes a bank, post office, newsstand, snack stand and a few other shops. The **Centre Noha** is across the road. This area is slowly building up with new boutiques and pearl shops opening here and there. At PK 2.7 in Tiaia, **Centre Tumai** is a shopping area located on both sides of the road between Maharepa and the airport in Temae. You will find clothing, pearls and souvenir shops here, as well as a restaurant and snack. The **Cook's Bay Center** and the **Maeva Center** in Pao Pao have a few small shops operated by resident artisans.

There are many enjoyable ways to spend your vacation on this special island. You can tee off at the 18-hole Moorea Green Pearl Golf Course near the airport. The beautiful clear lagoon invites you to come on in for a swim, or you can snorkel, scuba dive, water-ski and jet-ski. You can view the fish and coral through a glass bottom boat, wear a Jules Verne type helmet to walk on the sandy bottom of the lagoon gardens with Aqua Blue, or grab onto a motorized Sea Trailer and snorkel to the reef. You can zoom across the lagoon in a motorboat, kayak, pirogue or lagoon jet, and you can let the trade winds propel you on a flysurf or windsurf board. There are sailing excursions, beach barbecues and fishing trips. You can take a Dolphin & Whale Watching Expedition, or feed the friendly stingrays inside the lagoon. Lessons are available for all water sports, as well as for tennis at various hotel courts, and for horseback riding in Opunohu Valley. You can take your aerial photos during a helicopter or airplane tour of Moorea, and you can soar above the lagoon on a parasail. You can also discover the island by rental car, scooter, bicycle or on foot. Guided tours will show you Moorea's most breathtaking scenery, around the coastal road, in the interior valleys, up the mountains and to the Atiraa waterfalls of Afareaitu. You can visit a fruit juice factory and distillery, and sample a tall cool drink at a lively Happy Hour. At the hotels and at Tiki Theatre Village you can photograph traditional dance shows, learn to tie a *pareo*, grate a coconut and dance Tahitian style. You can even "get married" in a traditional non-binding Polynesian ritual or truly tie the knot in a legal ceremony.

Moorea's restaurants and snack bars have menu selections for all tastes and prices for all budgets. The highlight of your culinary explorations in Moorea should include a *tamaara'a*, an authentic Tahitian feast.

GETTING AROUND MOOREA
Car, Scooter & Bicycle Rentals
• **Albert Rent-a-Car**, at the Moorea Airport, *Tel. 55.21.10*; facing Club Bali Hai, *Tel. 56.19.28*, facing Moorea Pearl Resort, *Tel. 56.30.58*, facing Interconti-nental Moorea, *Tel. 56.33.75*. You can rent a 5-door Chery with a/c and radio for 6.000 CFP for 4 hrs., 7.500 CFP for 8 hrs., and 8.500 CFP for 24 hrs. A 5-door a/c Hyundai Getz with automatic drive and radio starts at 8.000 CFP for 4 hrs. Longer rentals available. 50cc scooters rent for 5.000 CFP for 4 hrs. and 5.500 CFP for 8 hrs. Insurance and free mileage are included in all rentals.
• **Avis-Pacificar** has a sales office across the road from the Vaiare Ferry Dock, *Tel. 56.32.68*, at Club Bali Hai, *Tel. 56.52.04* and at the Intercontinental Resort Moorea, *Tel. 55.19.50*; *vaiare.avismoorea@mail.pf*; *www.avis-tahiti.com*. A 5-door a/c Ford Fiesta, Renault Clio or Hyundai Getz costs 7.260 CFP for 4 hrs., 9.922 CFP for 8 hrs., and 12.500 CFP for 24 hrs. Rates include taxes, unlimited mileage and insurance. Rentals are available for several days and by the week or month.
• **Europcar** is located across the road from the Vaiare Ferry Dock, *Tel. 56.28.64*, and near Le Petit Village in Haapiti, *Tel. 56.34.00/73.82.03*; *moorea@europcar.pf; www.europcarpolynesie.com*. A 4-place a/c Renault Twingo rents for 6.950 CFP for 4 hrs., 7.980 CFP for 8 hrs., and 9.450 CFP for 24 hrs. You can also rent an a/c 5-door Hyundai Getz starting at 8.250 CFP for 4 hrs. A Logan mini-bus with 8/9 places starts at 15.640 CFP for 4 hrs. Bugsters rent for 7.650 or 13.200 CFP for 4 hrs. Europcar also has a special overnight rate if you rent a car at 5pm and return it the next morning by 8am. These rates include taxes, unlimited mileage and insurance. Fuel and flat tires are not included.
• **Moorea Fun Bike**, *Tel. 70.96.95; moorea-fun-bike@hotmail.fr*. Single, 21 speed, tandem and trail bikes, plus Les Rosalies covered bikes for up to six people. Delivered to your holiday place anywhere on Moorea.

- **Rent A Bike/Rent a Scoot,** *Tel. 71.11.09*; *rentabike-rentascooter@hotmail.fr* is beside the road adjacent to Le Petit Village in Haapiti. Free pick-up service is available. They rent 18-speed mountain bicycles for 1.000 CFP for 4 hrs., 1.200 CFP for 8 hrs. and 1.500 CFP for 24 hrs. They also rent motorbikes or scooters for 3.500 CFP for 2 hrs. up to 5.500 CFP for 24 hrs. Gas is not included.
- **Tehotu Location Scooter,** *Tel. 56.52.96/78.42.48*, has an office at the Vaiare ferry dock, where you can rent a scooter for 5.000 CFP for 4 hours, 5.500 CFP for 8 hours, 6.000 CFP for 24 hours. The scooter is insured and you will be required to wear a helmet, which is included.
  Some of the hotels and pensions rent bicycles to their guests. Check with your hotel activities desk for details.

Taxis

You'll find a taxi stand at the airport, *Tel. 56.10.18*, but the drivers are there only when a plane arrives. You can also call: Albert Transport, *Tel. 77.47.21*; D'esli Grand, *Tel. 73.37.19*; Edgard Ienfa, *Tel. 78.52.69*; Ghislaine Mahotu, *Tel. 78.70.88/72.84.87*; John Teamo, *Tel. 77.57.56*; Justin, *Tel. 77.48.26*; Nadette, *Tel. 70.37.45*; Pero and Elizabeth Teraiharoa, *Tel. 56.14.93*; and Sandy, *Tel. 78.80.89*. All the taxis have the rates displayed in their cabs. The fare between the airport and ferry dock is 1.500 CFP for a distance of 2.4 mi. (3.9 km). It will cost you 1.500 CFP from the airport to the Sofitel Ia Ora Moorea, 1.900 CFP from the airport to the Moorea Pearl Resort, 2.200 CFP to the Hotel Kaveka in Cook's Bay, 2.700 CFP to the Club Bali Hai in Pao Pao, 3.200 CFP to the Hilton, 4.200 CFP to the Intercontinental Moorea, and 4.500 CFP to the area of Le Petit Village in Haapiti.

Tour & Transport Companies

Some of the Tour and Transport Companies handle round-trip transfers between the airport or ferry dock and your hotel. They will also provide taxi service if you want to dine out in the evening or arrange a special shopping tour. The best deal you can get is with Loulou and Mate at Torea Nui Transport, *Tel. 56.12.48/ 76.81.31*; *enttoreanui@mail.pf; www.toreanui.com*. They have an office at the Moorea Airport and they provide a transfer service from the airport to any hotel on the island for 700 CFP per person (min. 2 people). Once you arrive at the airport in Moorea go to the Torea Nui Transport counter and buy your ticket there and they will drive you to your destination as long as it is beside the circle island road.

While you are on Moorea you can also use their transfer services in the day time hours to get from one hotel to another, to one side of the island to the other, to go shopping, or whatever, as long as it is on the main road, for just 700 CFP one way. Solo passengers pay 1.400 CFP. You have to reserve a week in advance for any of their transfers. Their last transfer is at 5pm when the last Air Tahiti flight arrives from Tahiti.

Buses & Le Truck

Public transportation is provided by several privately owned companies that rotate the service, using various kinds of buses and a couple of the traditional wooden bodied *les trucks*. In 2010 newer buses were brought over from Tahiti to replace some of the ancient vehicles. The buses operate schedules that coincide with the arrivals and departures of the fast catamarans and ferries from Tahiti, and with the school programs. Note: Do not count on having bus service on Sundays because many of the drivers will not work that day.

The **bus terminals** are located at Le Petit Village in Haapiti, and at the Vaiare Ferry dock. The buses leave Le Petit Village at least an hour before the fast catamarans are scheduled to leave Moorea for Papeete. The ferry schedules are subject to change, so it would be advisable to ask about the bus service at your hotel or pension. From Le Petit Village terminal the buses and *le truck* head in both directions around the island to get to the Vaiare Ferry dock. You just stand beside the road and wave to the driver to stop, and you pay 300 CFP when you get off.

You can use this service for other purposes in addition to your arrival and departure transfers, and you can even go around the island for 600 CFP, as long as you coordinate your plans with the bus schedules, which the drivers normally adhere to.

WHERE TO STAY
Airport & Motu Temae
Deluxe

SOFITEL MOOREA IA ORA BEACH RESORT, *B.P. 28, Maharepa, Moorea, 98728. Tel. 689/55.12.12, Fax 689/55.12.00; HO566@accor.com; Reservations 689/86.66.66, Fax 689/41.05.05; reservation.tahiti@accor.com; www.sofitel.com. Beside the lagoon at PK 2 in Temae, on northeast coast facing Tahiti, 2 km (1.2 mi.) from the airport and 2 km from the ferry dock. 114 bungalows. All major credit cards.*

Following a US$40 million overhaul in 2006, the 35-acre Sofitel Ia Ora Moorea Beach Resort now has 114 beach, garden and overwater bungalows, ranging in size from 31-75 sq. m. (330-807 sq. ft.). The exterior of each bungalow is traditional Polynesian, with a thatched pandanus roof and walls of Kohu wood. The interior decoration is modern, featuring wooden floors, Sofitel's famous "My Bed" with white bed covers and mosquito netting, and orange tables that are supposed to resemble the color of the Tahitian fe'i (plantain) when it is cooked. All rooms have a/c, ceiling fans, a bathroom with a rain shower, separate toilet, hair dryer and make-up mirrors, a mini-bar, individual safe, direct dial phone, coffee and tea making facilities, and a plasma TV with satellite cable. Bathrobes and toiletries are furnished. The overwater bungalows have a window floor for fish watching and there is also a covered terrace, plus steps leading into the lagoon and a shower to rinse off when you come out of the water. The 19 new deluxe overwater units also have an outside shower that is an extension of the tiled shower in the bathroom. They have a walk-in closet, as well as a larger terrace furnished with two lounge chairs. The 20 older overwater units are classified superior and have 2 sitting chairs on a smaller terrace. Some of the overwater bungalows face the beach, some face the horizon, and some units face other bungalows. The deluxe beach bungalows also have a walk-in closet and a private garden where you can shower. Three bungalows are equipped to accommodate disabled guests. There is a sofa bed in some of the bungalows, and no rollaway beds are allowed in any unit. The 2011 published rates for the bungalows were US $469-$1,099 per day. The American breakfast was included in most packages. Early bird deals, free meals and free nights for long stays during certain times of the year were also available.

In addition to two restaurants and a bar, room service is available from 6:30am-10pm. Dance shows are performed each evening during dinner. See information under *Where to Eat* in this chapter. The business center has Internet service and WiFi access is available at the Spa, the pool, the bar and in the restaurants. There are modern meeting rooms, a conference room, gift shop and Pearl Romance shop on the property. An activities desk and car rental desk are located in the lobby.

The new luxurious Le Spa offers 7 treatment rooms. See information under *Massages & Spas* in this chapter. Among the spacious grounds are a dive shop and nautical activities center, and an enlarged infinity swimming pool is located beside the white sandy beach. This resort has the best beach on the island and the most beautiful clear aquamarine lagoon. There are lounge chairs for guests that can be shaded by the tamanu trees along the beach, but there are no beach umbrellas. This beach is off limits to the public.

Superior
  GREEN LODGE, *B.P. 3005, Temae Teavaro, Moorea 98728. Tel./Fax 689/ 56.31.00; cell 77.62.26 (Isabelle), 77.07.86 (Jean-Luc); www.greenlodge.pf. Beside the ocean on Motu Temae, 1/2 mile behind the golf course. AE, MC, V.*

Isabelle and Jean-Luc Geronimo, the young French couple who own Green Lodge, went to Indonesia to buy all the teak furniture and decorations for their beautifully furnished family hotel. They even had their dining room table specially made in Bali, and after dinner it is transformed into a pool table. There are guest accommodations in 6 units, which include 2 beach bungalows, 2 adjoining units with connecting doors in the garden and a separate garden bungalow. There is also a room in the main house that faces the ocean and has its own bathroom and terrace. The room and the garden bungalows all have a queen-size bed, and the beach units have a king-size bed and a sofa bed. The amenities in the bungalows include a/c, ceiling fan, mosquito net, satellite TV, CD and DVD players, closet, iron, safe, mini-fridge, an electric kettle for coffee or tea, a 110/220V hair dryer, a covered patio and lounge chair. Each unit has its own bathroom with an attractive shower wall made from Moorea rocks.

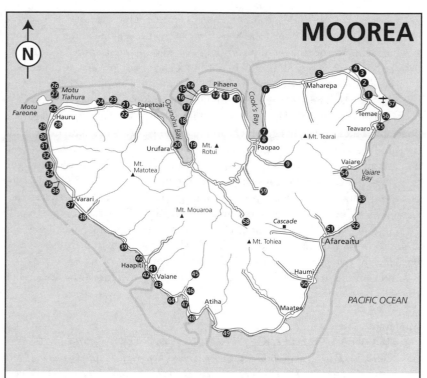

MOOREA

1. Temae Airport
2. Moorea Golf Lodge
3. Green Lodge
4. Moorea Golf Course
5. Moorea Pearl Resort
6. Hotel Kaveka
7. Club Bali Hai
8. Motel Albert
9. Village Temanoha
10. Fruit Juice Factory
11. Pension/Restaurant Aito
12. Pension Motu Iti
13. Hilton Moorea Lagoon Resort & Spa
14. Fare Nani
15. Faimano Village
16. Pension Maheata
17. Fare Vaihere
18. Fare Hamara
19. Robinson's Cove Villa
20. Les Tipaniers Iti

21. Intercontinental Moorea Resort & Spa
22. Legends Resort Moorea
23. Fenua Mata'I'Oa
24. Taoahere Beach House
25. Hotel Les Tipaniers
26. Dream Island
27. Villa Corallina
28. Le Petit Village
29. Hotel Hibiscus
30. Fare Vaimoana
31. Camping Nelson
32. Moorea Beach Lodge
33. Moorea Fare Miti
33. Tapu Lodge
35. Te Fare Mihi
36. Fare Manuia
37. Fare Pole
38. Te Nunoa
39. Fare Edith
40. Residence Linareva

41. Mark's Place Moorea
42. Haapiti Surf Lodge
43. Fare d'Hôte Tehuarupe
44. Tarariki Village
45. La Maison de la Nature
46. Fare Vainui
47. Pension Tifai
48. Fare Arana
49. Fare Aute
50. Vaihau Village
51. Pension Te Ora Hau
52. Motu Ahi
53. Atuana Lodge
54. Vaiare Ferry Dock
55. Sofitel Ia Ora Moorea Beach Resort
56. Temae Public Beach
57. Fare Maeva
58. Belvedere Lookout
59. Opunohu Valley Ranch

Guest services include a complimentary Continental breakfast that is served from 7:30-10am on the pool deck. Sunset cocktails are available in the 2 *fare potée* gazebos facing the ocean, and dinner can be served on request, for 3.780 CFP per person. No lunch is served, but there is a snack and small grocery store nearby.

In addition to the rectangular-shaped swimming pool, deck chairs and hammock, Green Lodge offers a comfortable living room with large flat screen TV, home cinema and Hi-Fi. There is also a reading area, DVD library, board games, pool table, bikes, aquagym equipment and snorkeling gear. Extra charges are made for laundry service and transfers to the ferry or airport. There is a WiFi Hot Spot here and all bungalows have Internet access for a charge. Jean-Luc is a certified golf instructor and can arrange for golf lessons on request. The beach in front of the pension is coral sand with the reef coming right to the edge. It is therefore not suitable for swimming; however, the large white sand public beach of Temae is only 10 min away. This is an excellent choice on Moorea for those seeking a Zen atmosphere of comfort and peace. Low/high season rates for the room and breakfast for two are 15.750/18.585 CFP; a garden bungalow is 18.375/21.683 CFP dbl, and a beach bungalow is 26.250/30.975 CFP dbl, including taxes. High season is June 1-Nov. 16.

Moderate

MOOREA GOLF LODGE, *B.P. 60222, Faa'a Centre, Tahiti 98702. Tel. 689/55.08.55; Fax 689/56.27.27; www.mooreagolflodge.pf. Beside lagoon on Motu Temae, on the same road as the public beach. Drive to the end of the airport, 5 min. from golf course, 10 min. from airport and 15 min. from Vaiare Ferry dock. AE, MC, V.*

This family pension has won Tahiti Tourisme's highest rating of 3 Tiares for the 4 sturdy wooden bungalows that offer two types of lodging. The 2 beachside bungalows each have 2 a/c bedrooms, a living room, bathroom, fully equipped kitchen and a large sundeck. Each unit can accommodate 2-6 people. One of the garden bungalows can also sleep 2-6 people and has 2 a/c bedrooms, and the smaller bungalow with a garden view has one a/c bedroom and can sleep 3 people. Both garden units have a living room, kitchen, bathroom and a large sundeck. All the bungalows have a flat screen TV and a telephone, ceiling fan, safe and hairdryer. The garden bungalows are 14.320 CFP dbl. for one night and 12.530 CFP per night for two nights. The beach bungalows are 16.350 CFP dbl. for one night and 14.320 CFP per night for two nights. WiFi is available at extra cost and there is a pay phone on the premises.

Free activities include snorkeling gear, billiards and petanque bowls. The pension has direct access to the beach. Owner Francis Chung-Tan also operates the Motu Lodge, a restaurant-snack-bar that is located adjacent to Moorea Golf Lodge. It is open daily from 10am to 2pm and 6-9pm, serving Chinese food and BBQ to eat there or take-away.

FARE MAEVA, *B.P. 3170 Temae, Moorea 98728. Tel. 689/56.18.10; faremaevamoorea@mail.pf; www.faremaevamoorea.com. On the ocean side on Motu Temae, 4.5 km (2.8 mi.) from the ferry dock and 2 km (1.2 mi.) from the airport. No credit cards.*

This modern and clean family pension is located just after Kerebel Jeweler on Temae motu, which is really a peninsula connected to the main island. Follow the dusty road beside the airport landing strip and look for the sign. There are 3 garden bungalows, each with a double bed, well-equipped kitchen and private bathroom with hot water. The sheets and towels are changed every 3 days. There is also a small terrace plus a *fare pote'e* shelter for each unit, complete with a table and chairs. A bungalow for 1 night is 12.290 CFP sgl/dbl., and 10.600 CFP per night for 2 days. Continental breakfast on request 1.000 CFP per person (min. 2).

The trees and plants here are similar to those found on an atoll and the beachy scene is accented by a yard filled with white sand. You also have access to a nice white sand beach, but there is no lagoon here, just the reef and open ocean. The public beach, which does have a nice lagoon, is very close by and one of Moorea's most popular surfing spots is also in this vicinity. Your hostess, Maeva Jacquemin, is a young Polynesian-French woman who specializes in arts and crafts. She teaches her guests how to make *poisson cru*, dye and tie a *pareo*, and how to open and grate a coconut. Guests have free use of bicycles. Free pick-up by some restaurants for dinner. Internet and laundry service are extra.

Cook's Bay Area: Maharepa to Paopao
Deluxe

MOOREA PEARL RESORT & SPA, *B.P. 3410, Temae, Moorea 98728. Tel. 689/55.17.50; Fax 689/55.17.51; res@spmhotels.pf; www.spmhotels.com. Beside lagoon at PK 5, between Moorea airport and Cook's Bay, 5 km (3 mi.) from the airport and 9 km (5.5 mi.) from the Vaiare ferry dock. 94 units. All major credit cards.*

The 4-star Moorea Pearl Resort is situated on 7.5 acres of land beside the lagoon just 2 miles from Cook's Bay. This traditional Polynesian style hotel offers 28 overwater bungalows, 8 beach bungalows, 28 garden bungalows with private pool, and 30 garden rooms, single or duplex. All units are a/c and the bungalows also have a ceiling fan. The garden view rooms and duplexes have a king size bed or two twin beds, and all the other units have a king-size bed or 2 twin beds plus a sofa. All units feature a balcony or terrace, coffee/tea making facilities, iron and ironing board, mini bar on request, hair dryer, safety box, satellite television with 26" flat screen plus DVD/CD player, I-pod player, and IDD telephone. WiFi Internet service is available for your laptop in your room and throughout the hotel property for 500 CFP per hour. The overwater bungalows have bathtubs and separate showers, glass tables to view the aquatic life of the lagoon, a large sundeck and sitting area with direct access by steps to the water. Two garden pool bungalows are specially equipped for guests in wheelchairs, and public areas and the pool are easily accessible. There are wide cement paths, ramps and an elevator.

The hotel has 2 restaurants, a bar, boutique/pearl shop, and an activities desk. A 108-person conference room can be used as 3 separate rooms, complete with all the audio-visual equipment for meetings. The Manea Spa offers a full range of relaxing and esthetic treatments. See more information under *Massages & Spas* in this chapter. Room service, laundry service, secretarial services, currency exchange, public Internet service, and a daily newsletter are all available.

There is a 7,500 sq. ft. infinity edge swimming pool, which you can see by Webcam on the hotel's website. Beside the hotel's overwater bungalows is a coral nursery called To'a Nui, where 700 fish have settled and developed in this unique environment. Although the water here is not ideally clear, snorkelers can observe the colony of coral that is regenerating in ecological conditions.

There is an in-house photographer, Polynesian tattooer and the Moorea Blue Diving scuba center. Guests have free use of snorkeling gear, outrigger paddle canoes and kayaks, and they can also play beach volleyball, badminton, ping-pong and petanque (French bowls). Beach toys and child size life jackets and snorkeling gear are also available, as well as a child's menu in the restaurant and babysitting service.

The Autera'a Bar and Terrace becomes a lively place around sunset, when there is often a trio of Tahitian musicians playing island songs. A Polynesian buffet dinner and dance show takes place each Wed. night at the Mahanai Restaurant, and an International buffet with Polynesian dances is held on Sat. nights.

The rack rates until Mar. 2012 are 29.000/35.000 CFP (low/high season) for a Garden View Room; 38.000/45.000 CFP for a Garden View Duplex; 44.000/51.000 CFP for a Beach Bungalow; 49.000/56.000 CFP for a Garden Pool Bungalow; 52.000/62.000 CFP for a Premium Beach Bungalow; 65.000/77.000 CFP for an Overwater Bungalow; 69.000/82.000 CFP for a Premium Overwater Bungalow; and 7.000 CFP for a third person. High season is June 1-Oct. 31. Meal plan rates are listed under *Where to Eat* in this chapter.

Honeymooners and all other lovers have a choice of Romantic Rendez-Vous programs. These include Romantic Welcomes, Romantic Interludes, Romantic Escapades, and Polynesian Wedding Ceremonies, complete with champagne and photos. Contact the hotel directly for details.

Moderate

KAVEKA, *B.P. 373, Maharepa, Moorea 98728. Tel. 689/56.50.50; Fax 689/56.52.63; kaveka@mail.pf; www.hotelkaveka.com. Beside lagoon at PK 7 on east side of Cook's Bay, 7 km (4.3 mi.) from the airport and 11 km (7 mi.) from the ferry dock. AE, MC, V.*

There are 25 wooden bungalows in the gardens, at the edge of the lagoon and beside a small white sand beach that slopes into the warm water of Cook's Bay. This 2-star hotel offers a multi-millionaire's view of the postcard scenery of mountains, coral reef, sea and sky. Some of the bungalows have a/c and all units have a ceiling fan. Most of the rooms have a TV, mini-refrigerator, bathroom with hot water shower, a tiled floor and a covered terrace with two lounge chairs. Beds are either king size or double, with 1-2 single beds in room. The lanai rooms are sold as a bare bones, no frills package deal, but you can rent refrigerators, TV's, and cell phones on request. There are no coffee/tea makers in any of the bungalows, but they all have a private safe in the closet and they are also furnished with blackout curtains. A high rock wall helps to eliminate noises from the road while giving the hotel more privacy. A lanai bungalow without a/c is 13.500 sgl./dbl., and the a/c bungalows in the garden, lagoon view and on the beach are 16.500-26.500 CFP sgl./dbl.

Restaurant Kaveka is built overwater, providing indoor or outdoor dining and a truly breathtaking view of Cook's Bay, especially from the long pier. Live musical entertainment on Tues., Fri. and Sat. Other services and amenities include a small beach, reception/activities/tour desk, free transportation to the shopping center, church and public beach, staff with expert local knowledge, security and on-site owners. You can rent snorkeling gear, bicycles and canoes. There are 2 computers in the lobby and WiFi is available in the bungalows for 500 CFP for 1 hour. Please see more information under *Where to Eat* in this chapter.

CLUB BALI HAI, *B.P. 8, Maharepa, Moorea 98728. Tel. 689/56.13.68, Fax 689/56.42.44; reservations@clubbalihai.pf; www.clubbalihai.com. Beside the lagoon at PK 8 in Cook's Bay, near Pao Pao village, 8 km (5 mi.) from the airport and 12 km (7.5 mi.) from the ferry dock. All major credit cards.*

Club Bali Hai overlooks the panoramic beauty of Cook's Bay and the surrounding mountains of cathedral peaks and spires. The 44 A/C units include 13 overwater bungalows, 6 beachfront bungalows, 5 garden rooms with no kitchen, and 20 rooms in a two-story colonial style building that was built in the 1960s. Most of the rooms in the building have kitchenettes and they all have coffee machines. A bayview room will be quieter as the road traffic can be quite noisy, but the advantage of the mountain view rooms is the lower price plus a kitchenette. The overwater and beach bungalows are Polynesian in decor, with a bedroom, separate kitchen/dining area and terrace facing the spectacular scenery. Some of these units have been renovated in the past few years. The floors and bathrooms are tiled and there are plenty of mirrors in the bedroom and bathroom. These units are furnished with a ceiling fan, a queen size bed in the bedroom and a twin bed in the living room, with a door in between for a little privacy, although the wall does not extend all the way to the ceiling. The kitchen contains a stove and oven, as well as a microwave and coffee/tea making facilities. The windows are screened, but not the sliding door leading to the sundeck. All the bathrooms have hot water showers. Club Bali Hai is a hotel with a Vacation Time-Share program, which is affiliated with Resort & Condominium International (RCI).

The Blue Pineapple (l'Ananas Bleu) is a snack bar located on the hotel premises beside the bay. Matahi Hunter and his wife Virginia and their crew serve breakfast and lunch daily from 7am to 3pm, which you can enjoy while gazing at the magnificent view of the mountains overlooking Cook's Bay. They also serve wine and beer, but there are no other alcoholic beverages available unless you bring them. The hotel staff includes Tahitians who have worked for the Hotel Bali Hai and/or Club Bali Hai for many years. There is a boutique at the hotel entrance next to the reception area and you can watch CNN on a TV in the lounge beside the reception desk. A public phone is on the wall near the reception and you can buy a phone card in the boutique. Free WiFi Internet service is available in all the rooms. There are a few restaurants near the hotel and most restaurants in the Cook's Bay area provide free transportation for dinner.

Club Bali Hai offers their guests a fresh water swimming pool and a small white sand beach with good swimming in Cook's Bay. Avis has a desk in the lobby and other rental cars, scooters and bikes can be rented across the street. Moana Lagoon Tours has picnic and snorkeling excursions and ATV Quad tours also has an office across the street.

The hotel rack rates for a bayview room are 11.550/11.700 CFP sgl/dbl.; a beach bungalow is 13.830/13.980 CFP sgl/dbl; and an overwater bungalow is 16.110/16.260 CFP sgl/dbl, including taxes. Check the Internet on the Club Bali Hai website, as they often have specials that can mean big savings for your next vacation on Moorea. They offer the lowest prices in French Polynesia on overwater bungalows.

VILLAGE TEMANOHA, *B.P. 94, Maharepa, Moorea 98728. Tel./Fax 689/ 55.25.00, cell 77.17.00; Fax 689/55.25.01; temanoha@mail.pf; www.temanoha.com. In Pao Pao Valley behind school, 10 km (6 mi.) from the airport, 14 km (9 mi.) from the ferry dock, and 1.2 km (.07 mi.) from the circle island road. MC, V. Paypal.*

There are 6 high quality wooden bungalows with 40 or 50 sq. m (431 or 538 sq. ft.) of living space built around a swimming pool in a tropical garden of 5,000 sq. m (53,820 sq. ft.) at the foot of Mount Rotui and Mou'a Puta. You'll have cooler temperatures and a wonderful view of the cathedral shaped mountains from this elevation, and the quiet setting is ideal for those who enjoy meditating, taking long walks, lying beside the pool with a book and simply being. Each bungalow contains a double bed and a single bed with mosquito nets, a small living room, equipped kitchen, 1 free bottle of water, private bathroom of wood and river stone paving and a solar hot water shower, plus a covered terrace. There is a ceiling fan in the living room, split bamboo wall coverings, natural tapa on the doors, teak furniture, TV and electric mosquito repellent in each bungalow. Housekeeping service is provided and a Continental breakfast is served to your bungalow on request for 1.551 CFP per person. Free Internet access for messages. Bicycles are available for 1.500 CFP per day. The Tiare *fare* for 2 people is 13.485 CFP and the Rotui *fare* is 15.036 CFP, including TVA. The rocky road from Pao Pao to the pension is recommended for 4WD vehicles only, but once you arrive you will want to stay. Moorea Explorer is the only tour company that will take you directly to Temanoha Village. Hosts Christa and Mathieu Castellani will help you arrange your island tours.

Economy
MOTEL ALBERT, *B.P. 27, Pao Pao, Moorea 98728. Tel. 689/56.12.76; Fax 689/56.58.58; motel.albert@laposte.net. Mountainside at PK 8 in Pao Pao, across from Club Bali Hai, 8 km (5 mi.) from the airport and 12 km (8 mi.) from the ferry dock. No credit cards.*

This is a good choice if you are traveling on a tight budget and want to be in the Cook's Bay area, where you can see the famous mountains surrounding the bay. You'll also be within easy walking distance of supermarkets, restaurants and snacks. There are 4 rooms, plus 4 big bungalows available to rent by the night. All the others have been rented on a long term basis. The wooden bungalows are on stilts, each with two bedrooms, living room, a spacious kitchen with regular stove and big refrigerator, large screened in terrace, screened windows and sliding glass doors, and private bathroom with hot water shower. This family pension was built some 40 years ago and the decor is old Polynesia with pareo cloth bedspreads and curtains. There are one or two double beds in the rooms, as well as a kitchen and private bathroom with hot water shower. The gardens are filled with flowers and fruit trees. Heidi, the manager, speaks some English, and is very friendly. A room is 6.500 CFP sgl./dbl. and a bungalow is 9.740 CFP for 1-4 people and 10.850 CFP for 5 people.

Opunohu-Papetoai Area
Deluxe
HILTON MOOREA LAGOON RESORT & SPA, *B.P. 1005, Papetoai, Moorea 98729. Tel. 689/55.11.11; Fax 689/55.11.55; info@hilton-moorea.pf; www.hilton.com. Beside the lagoon at PK 14 between Cook's Bay and Opunohu Bay, 14 km (8.7 mi.) from the airport and 18 km (11 mi.) from the ferry dock. 104 bungalows. All major credit cards.*

In 2010 the French Polynesian Ministry of Tourism awarded the Hilton Moorea Lagoon Resort & Spa a 5-star rating, the only resort on Moorea or Tahiti to receive such an honor. Also in 2010 the TripAdvisor Traveler's choice awards voted the Hilton Moorea Lagoon the Top Resort for Romance in the World, the Top Romance Resort in the South Pacific, and #4 of the Resorts for Relaxation & Spa in the South Pacific. During the 2011 TripAdvisor Traveler's Choice Awards, the Hilton Moorea Lagoon was #4 of the Top 10 Hotels for Romance in the South Pacific and #7 in the category of Resorts for Relaxation & Spa in the South Pacific.

Most guests obviously love this thatched roof Polynesian style hotel, which is located in 12 acres of tropical gardens, coconut palms and gnarled old tamanu trees, along a white sandy beach. Upon arrival at the Hilton Moorea Lagoon you will be greeted with a Tiare Tahiti flower, a cold face cloth and a fresh coconut. After completing your registration one of the friendly Tahitian valets will drive you and your luggage to your room in an electric golf cart.

This is the only all-bungalow resort on the island, with 104 spacious units located among the lovely flower gardens, along the white sand beach and suspended on stilts over the transparent lagoon and colorful coral gardens. An extensive renovation and refurbishing project of 15 million dollars began soon after this resort became part of the Hilton brand in January 2009, replacing Sheraton Hotels as managers.

Now there are 45 garden bungalows with new plunge pools, 3 lagoon bungalows, 2 garden pool suites, and 54 overwater bungalows. Units for handicapped guests in wheelchairs are also provided. All the bungalows are air-conditioned and also have a ceiling fan. The rooms are decorated in a contemporary Polynesian motif. They contain a king-size bed or two twin beds, a sofa bed and writing table. The furniture is made of local semi-precious woods, and includes outdoor dining facilities and sun lounges on the partially shaded terraces. Each bungalow is equipped with electronic door locks, smoke detector, fire sprinkler system, blackout draperies, 110/220-volt electrical outlets, personal safe, mini bar and coffee/tea making facilities. A flat screen TV broadcasts CNN in English and other satellite programs in French or English. There is a DVD player, CD player, alarm clock/radio, international direct-dial telephone, voicemail, I-pod station and wireless Internet connection in each bungalow. An iron & ironing board are in the closet. Twice daily maid service is provided and next day laundry service is also possible. All of the hotel's units have an extendible lighted makeup mirror and full-length mirror and hair dryer. A nice selection of bathroom toiletries is replenished daily.

The two garden pool suites have 1,712 sq. ft. of living space. They each have a bedroom with a king-size bed and a pop-up TV, and there are two sofas in the lounge, as well as a bar with a wine cellar. They have a 142-sq. ft. pool, a privacy fence, wooden deck, gazebo and Japanese garden. Another feature is the use of Led lights, giving you a choice of changing the color of the water in the pool to pink, blue, green or yellow.

If you have booked an overwater bungalow be prepared for a wonderful surprise when you enter your room. Your eyes are immediately drawn to the picture postcard scenery of the shimmering turquoise lagoon and velvet green mountains visible beyond your terrace. You have a feeling of being suspended in space above the water, which indeed you are. It's simply stunning! Following the extensive modernization project all 54 overwater bungalows now have new furniture, curtains and bathrooms. In addition to a claw-footed bathtub, there is a separate shower stall with a marvelous overhead rain shower as well as a powerful massage nozzle. An electronic curtain between the bathroom and bedroom allows you to gaze at the lagoon while brushing your teeth or to close the curtain for privacy when desired. The overwater bungalows have steps that let you shimmy down into the warm lagoon, which is about 4 feet deep, and there is an outdoor shower on a landing above the water. Guests staying in the overwater bungalows have use of two sets of snorkeling gear, two robes and slippers. The overwater units also have a small glass floor for fish watching, and you are guaranteed an interesting performance of jewel-colored fish in these coral-rich waters. Thousands of new fish and more coral were added to this area in 2004 and you'll find some of the best snorkeling on Moorea in the vicinity of the Hilton's overwater bungalows.

The Hilton Moorea Lagoon's public buildings carry out the theme of Polynesian architecture with enormous thatched roofs, local woods, and shell lamps hanging from the ceiling. The gardens are carefully landscaped with basaltic boulders and huge hibiscus flowers of every hue. Walkways take you from the spacious reception area and activities desk past gardens of white ginger, ixora and other lush tropical plants. Waterfalls cascade into fern-rimmed pools where golden carp frolic and swim. Robert Wan's Tahiti Perles jewelry shop displays chokers and earrings of Tahitian cultured pearls. Kaimana Boutique is a shopper's dream of tropical clothing, *tifaifai* wall hangings and unusual gift items.

In addition to the Arii Vahine Steackhouse Restaurant, Rotui Grill & Bar, Toatea Bar on the pier, and the Eimeo Bar and Lounge, there is also room service available from 6:30am-10:30pm. There are special theme evenings with Tahitian dance shows and live entertainment in the main bar. See more information under *Where to Eat* in this chapter. Hotel services include 24-hour front desk service, 24-hour security, laundry and dry cleaning service, valet service, guest ice machines, multilingual concierge service, pre-registration service, currency exchange, banquet and meeting facilities, daily newsletters and a business center. Guests can buy an Internet card to use the two computers and printer in the lounge section of the Eimeo Bar, where there is a wide-screen TV and a billiards table. There is also an activities desk in the lounge where you can rent a bicycle and arrange for tours. In the main lobby you will find a guest relations desk and a car rental agency.

The hotel's infinity free form swimming pool is a popular place to relax and to get the kinks out of your body after your long flight across the Pacific. There is also a Jacuzzi next to the pool. You can get towels from the beach *fare*. Be sure to visit the Moorea Lagoon Spa, also on the beach level, where you will find well-trained massage therapists who will work wonders on your aches and pains. Indulge in your sensual well being with a Taurumi Maohi massage from old Polynesia, a volcanic stone massage from Hawaii, a lymphatic massage from Bali or a Heaven & Earth massage from China. They can provide a couples' massage, exfoliations, wraps and exotic facials. There is also a Jacuzzi and steam room. See more information under *Massages & Spas* in this chapter. At the Water Sports Center and PADI Scuba Diving Center on the beach in-house guests can check out free snorkeling gear and a free kayak. You can sign up for snorkeling lessons, scuba diving, deep-sea fishing, Aquablue underwater walks, Jet-ski excursions, water-skiing, circle island tours by boat with ray-feeding and a picnic on the motu, sailing cruises, speedboat rental with pilot, and parasailing. See more information under *Nautical Activities Centers* and *Scuba Diving* in this chapter. Across the road from the hotel is a Fitness Center with brand new Precor equipment, two changing rooms, lockers and showers. There are also two lighted tennis courts that are open 24/24 and are free to in-house guests.

The terrace of the Eimeo Bar overlooks the Hilton's white sand beach and turquoise lagoon of diamonds dancing in the sun. This is a great place to watch a gorgeous sunset while sipping a colorful cocktail ordered from the special drink menu. Some of the honeymooners and other guests like to gather on the end of the hotel pier just beyond bungalow 109. There are benches placed here for gazing at the sea and sky, and young lovers meet other couples, also with their champagne and cameras. They compare the positive and negative aspects of their bungalows and the hotel's amenities and services, and make plans to dine together or to explore the island with their newfound friends. Many of the hotel guests prefer to watch the romantic sunset from the terraces of their bungalows. Others are still snorkeling among the purple coral gardens and brightly painted fishes during this magical moment.

In keeping with the Romantic theme, the Hilton Moorea Lagoon Resort & Spa has created Romantic Dining destinations for their loving guests. These champagne dinners and sundowners are all served on the white sand beach under the tropical sky or on the deck of your bungalow. They also have a list of Celebration Gift & Romantic Experience items that can be delivered to your bungalow. These can be as simple as a plate of chocolate cookies, as exotic as a flower bath, as unusual as an original polished shell, or as extravagant as a Royal Spa gift voucher. Or you could order the Exclusive Romantic turn down service, complete with a flower bath, music and candles. The Wedding Planner for the Hilton Moorea Lagoon Resort & Spa can arrange modern weddings, civil weddings, and Polynesian wedding ceremonies. Religious weddings may also be organized. You can visit their website for details and special packages.

Superior

ROBINSON'S COVE VILLA, *B.P. 4118, Vaiare, Moorea 98728. Tel. 689/ 79.95/38; www/robinsoncove.com. Beside lagoon at PK 16,3 in Opunohu Bay, 16.3 km (10.1 mi.) from the airport and 20.3 km (12.6 mi.) from the ferry dock. All credit cards.*

Every afternoon when the setting sun reflects on Rotui, Moorea's sacred mountain, I stand in my front yard and look across Opunohu Bay at the 3 green-roofed bungalows that comprise Robinson's Cove Villa. Often I can see someone lying in a hammock beside the white sand beach, where they are probably enjoying a lovely view of Mou'a Roa (the Bali Hai Mountain), as well as the magnificent splendor of a tropical sunset. I am sure that lucky person knows he or she is in Paradise.

Denis Laxenaire, owner of Robinson's Cove Villa, chose the names of three famous explorers for his lodgings. Villa Cook has 1,600 sq. ft. of living space and includes 2 a/c bedrooms, 2 bathrooms and a mezzanine with beds, providing sleeping accommodations for 6-8 people. There is also a large living room, kitchen, office, a wrap-around partially covered deck with a dining area, and an outside living room facing the beach and that marvelous view. There are also outside showers.

Villa Wallis is the newest unit and can sleep 2-6 people, and Villa Bougainville can sleep 2 people. Each villa contains a well equipped kitchen with a large refrigerator; a washing machine, clothes dryer and iron; solar hot water; a telephone, WiFi, TV, DVD player and a library. Snorkeling equipment, kayak, a picnic basket and ice box are also provided. The villas are cleaned once a week or more frequently as an optional choice. On request, Alix, the on-site caretaker, will prepare your breakfast for 1.500 CFP per person, and she will also cook your dinner for 3.000 CFP should you wish.

The website lists the Villa rates in Euros according to low, medium and high seasons and there is a 5-night minimum, with discounts for longer stays. A villa for 2 people starts at 265 Euros or 31.623 CFP (about US $381) a night during the low season, and a villa for 3-4 people starts at 350 Euros or 41.766 CFP (about US $504) per night during the low season of Jan-Mar. Check the website for other information and rates.

FARE HAMARA, *Tel. 689/56.25.65. On mountainside at PK 16.4 overlooking Opunohu Bay. Reservations: Bob Hammar, Tel. 253/564-0180; hamara@harbornet.com; www.farehamara.com. Moorea contact: Jacques, Tel. 689/83.77.10.*

Fare Hamara was built as a private home of Lindal cedar with 2 bedrooms: 1 king, 1 queen. A twin trundle in the great room and 2 sleeping mats afford sleep space for 8. The large bathroom has a double shower and twin sinks. The American style kitchen is fully equipped. The house is a well-planned octagon shape with a wrap-around deck. Features: personal safe, screened windows & doors, linens, washer & dryer, BBQ on deck. Fantastic views of Opunohu Bay.

Moderate

PENSION MOTU ITI, *B.P. 189, Paopao, Moorea 98728. Tel. 689/55.05.20/74.43.38; Fax 689/55.05.21; pensionmotuiti@mail.pf; www.pensionmotuiti.com Beside lagoon at PK 13.2 between Cook's Bay and Opunohu Bay, 13 km (8 mi.) from the airport and 17 km (11 mi.) from the Vaiare ferry dock. AE, MC, V. Reserve.*

Each of the 5 modern Polynesian style bungalows has a wood shingle roof and the interior walls are covered with pandanus matting. The big bamboo furniture includes a king-size bed and desk. Each unit has a ceiling fan, TV and a bathroom with tiled shower and hot water. The windows and sliding glass door are unscreened, but each room is equipped with an electric machine for mosquito repellent. There are chairs on the terrace and a faucet is placed beside the steps at the front entrance to rinse off sandy feet. You can have room service on your terrace for breakfast, lunch or your favorite drinks. A 20-bed dormitory over the reception area is cooled by a large opening on the lagoon side, as well as a series of fans. There are two clean bathrooms with hot water downstairs. The garden bungalows are 10.500 CFP sgl./dbl., and the beach bungalows are 12.000 CFP. A bed in the dormitory is 1.650 CFP. Taxes are included.

A high stone wall on the roadside helps to keep traffic noises to a minimum. An overwater *fare* provides shelter as well as a sundeck for guests who want to spend a few quiet hours reading, napping in a lounge chair or gazing at the sea and sky.

Kayaks are provided free of charge and owner Auguste Ienfa will drive you to the Hilton to join a tour or excursion. There are computers in the reception with Internet service. The Motu Iti restaurant is on a covered terrace facing the lagoon, and the Aito Restaurant is just next door.

MAHEATA, *B.P. 152, Maharepa, Moorea 98728. Tel./Fax 689/56.25.45; Cell 78.34.74; www.maheata.com. Beside the lagoon at PK 14,3 in Pihaena, 300 m. from the Hilton Moorea Lagoon Resort; www.maheata.com. No credit cards.*

Maheata is a Tahitian word meaning "where the clouds disappear". O'ea Calinaud has 3 Polynesian style bungalows and 2 studios in the garden of her nice property, which has direct beach access to the white sand beach facing the sparkling lagoon at the beginning of Opunohu Bay. These units have a/c at an extra cost, and other amenities include a ceiling fan, mosquito nets over the beds, satellite TV, DVD, a kitchen with microwave oven and refrigerator, and a bathroom with hot water shower. A bungalow for 2/3 adults is 12.500 CFP for 1 night and 9.000 CFP for more than 2 nights. A studio for 4/5 adults is 15.000 CFP for 1 night and 11.600 CFP for 2 or more nights. WiFi and a point phone are also available.

A common area with a sun deck faces the beach and ocean. Guests can enjoy free use of the snorkel gear, kayak, hammocks, petanque (French bowls), ping-pong and drinking water fountain. Paid services include a/c, laundry, telephone, transportation to the supermarket in Pao Pao, baby sitting, local cooking classes, pareo painting, chakras balancing and psycho bio-acupressure.

FARE VAIHERE, *B.P. 55, Maharepa, Moorea 98728. Tel./Fax 689/56.19.19; Cell 29.07.19; farevaihere@mail.pf; www.farevaihere.com. Beside the lagoon at PK 15.5 in Opunohu Bay, 15.5 km (9.6 mi.) from the airport and 19.5 km (12 mi.) from the ferry dock. MC, V.*

This quiet family pension offers a taste of old Moorea, with local style architecture, thatched roofs and woven bamboo walls, on the verdant east coast of Opunohu Bay. Look for a sign with the design of a breadfruit leaf at the entrance, and ring the bell at the gate. There are 4 bungalows for a maximum of 3 people, and each unit has a different color scheme with a queen size bed and a single bed, a tiled bathroom with hot water shower, and a covered porch. They are furnished with a desk, small refrigerator, and a kettle with supplies of coffee and tea. A fan is available on request. The communal *fare* serves as a dining room and there is a mezzanine lounge with a small library, TV and DVD player. Guests have free Internet access.

A bungalow with breakfast is 18.000 CFP sgl./18.900 CFP dbl., and dinner is served on request for 3.900 CFP per person. Corinne is noted for the delicious meals she cooks Parisian style using local products, and according to the comments of former guests, Philippe Guery is also a great cook. The meals can be served in the dining room or at a big table beside the lagoon.

Both of the hosts at Fare Vaihere are appreciated by guests for their attention to detail. Guests have free use of the bicycles, snorkeling gear and kayaks. Philippe is an OWSI PADI instructor who gives personal diving tours and leads snorkeling excursions in Opunohu Bay. Smaller kids can play in the shallow water beside a narrow beach. There will soon be lagoon excursions by motor boat. Eventually, the pension's long pier will be rebuilt. It was blown away during Cyclone Oli in Feb. 2010.

West Coast: Papetoai to Haapiti
Deluxe
INTERCONTINENTAL MOOREA RESORT & SPA, *B.P. 1019, Tiahura, Moorea 98729. Tel. 689/55.19.19, Fax 689/55.19.55; reservationspf@interconti.com; www.moorea.interconti.com. Beside the lagoon at PK 24 between Papetoai and Haapiti, 24 km (14.8 mi.) from the airport and 28 km (17.3 mi.) from the ferry dock. 144 rooms and bungalows. All major credit cards.*

This property has the largest grounds of any hotel on Moorea and encompasses 27 acres (11 hectares) of beautiful gardens with more than 165 species of trees, plants, and flowers. The beach wraps around the hotel giving one the sense that there is always a private area available. The resort provides a magnificent setting for a memorable South Seas vacation, and you will not be disturbed by road noises from any of the bungalows.

In 2010 a multi-million dollar improvement project was completed, adding private plunge pools to the garden bungalows, extending terraces and adding thatched roof gazebo shelters (fare potée) to the garden, beach and overwater bungalows. Another new addition is a 2-level infinity swimming pool with a combined surface of 4,521 sq. ft. (420 sq. m.), just steps away from the beach. This large pool also has swim-up barstools beside the new Motu Oné bar, where you can order drinks and light snacks.

The Intercontinental Moorea features a variety of luxury accommodations with traditional Polynesian décor and furnishings set among the gardens, beaches, and lagoons of the resort. There are 48 a/c lanai rooms, including 2 wheelchair accessible rooms, plus 1 suite, all located in colonial style 2-story concrete buildings. Each room has a king-size bed or two twin beds and a balcony or lanai overlooking the lagoon. The suite also has a living room and 2 convertible sofas. The 17 garden pool bungalows, 28 beach bungalows and 50 overwater bungalows are all suites that are built in the traditional Polynesian design with thatched roofs. These units have a king-size bed, separate sitting area with a writing desk, a convertible sofa bed and a pull-out bed. With their extended terraces and thatched gazebos, these bungalows provide a shaded dining area, complete with table and chairs. Each air-conditioned bungalow has a ceiling fan, bathroom with bathtub and separate shower and a private toilet section. Standard amenities in all rooms and bungalows include international direct dial telephones with 2 sets, satellite/cable color TV, in-house video movies, radio, CD player, and WiFi internet access. There is a fully stocked self-service mini-bar/refrigerator in each room and bungalow, as well as complimentary tea and coffee making facilities, a personal electronic safety box, a hair dryer, 240/110-volt electrical outlets and complimentary grooming items. The overwater bungalows are just at the edge of the lagoon and have steps leading into the water. The beach bungalows open right onto the beach and the garden bungalows now have their own private plunge pool.

An enormous thatched roof building houses the reception, Fare Nui restaurant for 250 diners, Fare Hana poolside restaurant for 80 people, Motu Iti bar with seating for 70 people, a conference room for 80-100 diners or 150 theater-style seats, a concierge service and public relations activities desk, taxi, car and bike rental desk, gift shop and pearl shop. Guest services include twice a day maid service, next day laundry and dry cleaning service (Mon.-Fri.), iron and ironing board on request, currency exchange, and mail and postal service. In-room dining is available from 6:30am-9:30pm. A special romantic touch for guests staying in most of the overwater bungalows is to order breakfast served to their balcony by flower decorated outrigger canoe.

Guests have free use of the hotel's 2 fresh water swimming pools, two tennis courts and white sand beaches, and snorkeling equipment and outrigger paddle canoes are also provided. They can also use the kayaks for 2 hrs. at no charge. There is an on-site nautical sports center and TOPDIVE-Bathy's has a scuba dive center here. See more information under *Nautical Activities Centers* and *Scuba Diving* in this chapter. The Moorea Dolphin Center is a big attraction for people who want to play with the dolphins in an enclosed environment and there is also a turtle sanctuary. Helicopter rides are available with a landing pad on the hotel grounds. In addition to a daily program of activities presented at the hotel, you will also have an interesting choice of excursions to discover the romantic beauty of Moorea's seashore and interior valleys. Should you feel in the mood to just relax and be pampered, you can treat yourself to a fresh floral bath and massage at Hélène' Spa, located on the hotel grounds. See more information under *Massages & Spas* in this chapter.

Musicians play songs from the islands around the bar at sunset, and various activities are organized in the lobby or at the Motu Iti bar. These include pareo-tying demonstrations, tamure lessons, learning how to prepare Tahitian marinated fish and watching video films on the Tahitian cultured pearl. The weekly entertainment program begins on Mon. evening with Polynesian Night, when a buffet of Tahitian and seafood specialties is served, followed by a dance show. Barbecue Night is held each Wed. beside the swimming pool, accompanied by a Polynesian show, and the *Soirée Merveilleuse* held each Sat. evening is a gastronomic buffet featuring a variety of fresh seafood, usually served on the beach under the stars and tropical moon. A Tahitian dance group performs on a stage set between two graceful coconut trees. A Sun. Buffet lunch is served in the Fare Hana beside the pool, to the tune of a musical trio. See more information under *Where to Eat* in this chapter.

The ICH Moorea has a catalog of "Romantic Ideas," "Celebrations of Romance" and "Romantic Touches" for honeymooners and other lovers. You can exchange vows in a non-binding Polynesian wedding ceremony or use the services of the ICH Moorea Wedding Planner to get married at the town hall in Moorea and even exchange vows in a church wedding.

The 2012 room rates had not been released in July 2011 when I did my update on the Intercontinental Moorea Resort & Spa. Their 2011 low/high season rates were 30.393/ 37.691 CFP for a lanai room; 45.295/53.166 CFP for a beach bungalow; 55.234/65.978 CFP for a garden pool bungalow; 58.417/69.224 CFP for a beach premium bungalow; 72.047/84.662 CFP for an overwater bungalow; and 76.227/ 90.373 CFP for an overwater premium bungalow or for a lanai suite. Add taxes.

LEGENDS RESORT MOOREA, *B.P. 1951, Papetoai, Moorea 98729. Tel. 689/55.15.15; Fax 689/55.15.01; www.legendsresortvillas.com. On the mountainside at PK 25 between Papetoai and Haapiti, 25 km (15.5 mi.) from the airport and 29 km (18 mi.) from the ferry dock. All major credit cards.*

Legends Resort is located on a 17.3-acre (7 ha.) hillside on Moorea's northeast coast, overlooking the Intercontinental Moorea Resort & Spa, the lagoon and 3 motu islets inside the lagoon. This 4-star resort opened in July 2008 and has 46 private 2- and 3-bedroom contemporary style villas, plus the main villa that serves as the reception and lounge areas. Here you will also find a gift shop/newsstand, small grocery store, delicatessen, and the Legends Gourmet breakfast and lunch café. La Villa des Sens is the gastronomic dinner restaurant and bar located at the entrance to the resort, and Legends Resort offers in-villa catering. There is an infinity swimming pool and a tennis court (non-lit), as well as a fitness room and spa. A free shuttle boat transfers guests to the resort's private beach on a motu, and snorkels and masks are provided. On the mountain side near the resort there are trails for interesting walks.

The villas are built of wood and stone and stand on tall stilts on a sloping hillside. They are classified as "Nui" (big) or "Iti" (little). The big villas for 2-6 people are 1,883 sq. ft. (175 sq. m), and the little villas for 2-4 people have 1,292 sq. ft. (120 sq. m). Each villa has spacious a/c bedrooms with queen size or twin beds, en suite bathrooms, desk, in-room safe, a separate sitting area with a flat panel LCD TV and satellite service, a DVD player, direct dial telephone, voice mail, and CD player. WiFi is available at 500 CFP per hour, and guests can borrow DVD films free of charge from the reception. The fully equipped kitchen has a stove, microwave, refrigerator, coffee/tea-maker and complimentary bottled water. A washer and dryer are located in the second bathroom. There is a separate dining area, and you can also eat under the small *fare potée* shelter on the panoramic deck. There is a Jacuzzi on the large terrace and a shower in the garden.

The units at Legends Resort are managed collectively as a residence resort, which is different from the time-sharing or condominium concepts. It is a fractional ownership, which is similar to time-sharing. Daily maid service is not automatically available as in hotel resorts. Here you have a choice between maximum privacy and intimacy or the use of such hotel services as the changing of household linen, daily villa cleaning and daily breakfast. The staff will bring you fresh towels on request.

Almost everyone who has stayed at Legends Resort agrees that the views of the lagoon, motu islets, ocean and sunsets are simply stunning. Star-gazing from your terrace is an experience you will treasure. The less enjoyable aspects of staying on the hillside is that there are mosquitoes, ants, geckos and centipedes in the rooms, and birds fly into the villa through the open space between the walls and the roof. There are no screens and some of the windows have only wooden slats instead of glass. The biggest complaint is about the noisy roosters that crow under the bedroom windows in the very early hours of the morning. Only 2 of the 3-bedroom units have a/c and there are no ceiling fans to alleviate the heat. During the periods of strong winds the rooms cannot be closed off. Villa #14 is the closest to the reception and is preferred by guests who do not want to hike up the steep hill to get from their unit to go to breakfast or to the pool. The very helpful staff will happily come to get you in a modified golf cart if you call reception for a ride. They will also drive you to the magasin store beside the main road just at the entrance to Legends Resort. If you haven't brought bug spray with you, you can get it here.

Public rates for the 2-bedroom villas are 44.153 CFP-57.279 CFP per day; the 3-bedroom villas are 73.986 CFP-85.919 CFP; and the Rapa Nui Premium Suite is 105.012 CFP. Add taxes. See more information under *Where to Eat* and *Massages & Spas* in this chapter.

FENUA MATA'I'OA, *B. P. 1192, Papetoai, Moorea, 98729. Tel. 689/55/ 00.25; Fax 689/55.00.26; eileenb@mail.pf; www.fenua-mataioa.com. Beside the lagoon in Tiahura Village, between the Intercontinental Moorea Resort and Hotel Les Tipaniers. MC, V.*

This unique lodging is an exclusive, elegant *residence* located in a gated community. Eileen Bossuot, the hostess, is a former designer for the Relais et Chateaux properties in France, and she and her husband Serge have filled their lagoon-side home with all the treasures of their many voyages throughout the world, including Eileen's collection of 2,500 owls. The décor is a blend of Tahitian, French Provincial, European and Asian, and each item has its own story. Along with the mirrors, lamps, sconces, and objets d'art, there are many colorful tableaux that were painted by Moorea's resident artists. Fenua Mata'i'oa offers a choice of 6 suites for 2-3 guests or a 2-level duplex suite with beds for 4 guests. These include the Princess Lokelani Prestige Suite, the Princess Maimiti Presidential Suite, the Mahealani Suite, the Royal Suite, and the Hereiti and Reva Junior Suites. All the rooms are a/c and furnished with a king-size bed, large sleeping sofa, color satellite TV, music system, 2 telephones, a computer with WiFi, a mini-bar and coffee and tea making facilities. Each of the rooms also has a private bathroom with a large shower, 2 lavabos, toilet, hair-dryer and tasteful decor. In the suite the upstairs bedroom has a private safety box, and the bathroom contains a Jacuzzi bathtub and shower. Daily rates are 30.000-60.000 CFP for 2 people.

Guests can enjoy their refined meals in the privacy of their rooms, on the pier or in the small interior or exterior dining rooms. There is also room service provided until 9pm. There is no beach here, but lounge chairs and palapa type thatched roof umbrellas line the wooden deck beside the lagoon and there is a Jacuzzi pool in the garden. Snorkeling equipment is provided at no extra charge, as well as kayaks and bicycles. This private hotel even has its own dance group, the Pupu Mata'i'oa, and Eileen Bossuot will arrange Polynesian style wedding ceremonies for you.

DREAM ISLAND, *B. P. 1175, Papetoai, Moorea 98729. Tel. 689/77.84.70; Fax 689/56.38.81; www.dream-island.com. 3 deluxe houses on a private motu facing former Club Med property in Haapiti. Taxes included. No credit cards.*

Kolka and Josy Muller say that this is the private island everybody dreams about without believing it could really exist...yet it does. Their 3 deluxe houses are surrounded by unspoiled beauty on a white sand beach just a 5-minute boat ride from the main island. Fare Polynésie is a 3 bedroom, 2 bath house with a private apartment, large lounge, kitchen, dining room and 2 terraces; Fare Pacifique has 2 bedrooms, 2 bathrooms, a lounge, kitchen and 2 terraces; and Fare Gauguin has 2 bedrooms, a master bathroom and another bathroom, a lounge, kitchen and dining room. Each house is equipped with a TV, telephone, lovely furnishings and homey touches. Check out the photos on their website and contact them for the rates.

VILLA CORALLINA, *B.P. 19, Maharepa, Moorea 98728. Tel. 689/77.05.90; Fax 689/56.36.65; manager@villacorallina.com; www.villacorallina.com. A 2-bedroom villa on the west side of Motu Fareone, across the channel from the former Club Med in Haapiti, 27 km (16.7 mi.) from the airport and 5 minutes by boat from main island. No credit cards.*

Marco Ciucci's Villa Corallina offers 6,000 sq. m (64,583 sq. feet) of private grounds on a quiet motu islet, providing panoramic views of the lagoon, coral reef, deep ocean and open skies. There are accommodations for up to 8 people when renting all the lodgings. The main house offers 3,000 sq. ft. of living space, including an upstairs bedroom with screened windows and bathroom. On the ground level is an open living-entertainment area, dining room, breakfast area, fully equipped kitchen, office, beach terrace with barbecue, and a private white sand beach with lounge chairs. The furniture is rattan and bamboo. Amenities include ceiling fans, TV, a DVD player, CD player, books, refrigerator, freezer and house linens. The master bedroom is located in a separate oceanfront bungalow of 750 sq. ft. It contains a king-size tester bed with mosquito net in the bedroom, a ceiling fan, TV, CD player, bathroom and covered veranda with outdoor sofa.

Rental rates start at US $300 per night for 2 people in the main villa and US $390 for 2 people in the main villa with the separate master bedroom suite. A minimum of 4 nights is required. There is also a cute one-bedroom self-contained garden cottage on the interior of the property that can be rented for US $250 a night. This is rented only when the main villa is not in use by another party. See the website for details.

Guests have free use of snorkeling equipment, 2 kayaks and outrigger paddle canoe. They can also use 2 aluminum boats with a 30 h.p. motor, but they must be accompanied by a staff member. A courtesy shuttle is available from 6am-6pm to transfer you to the main island. A catering service is available for meals prepared by the Sunset Restaurant on the main island. Valet service for shopping and cooking is possible except on Sundays.

Superior

TAOAHERE BEACH HOUSE, *B.P. 1937, Papetoai, Moorea 98729. Tel./ Fax 689/56.13.30; Cell 70.77.04; www.taoahere.com. Beside the lagoon in Tiahura Village, Hauru, between the Intercontinental Moorea Resort and Hotel Les Tipaniers. D, MC, V.*

This new bed and breakfast guest house is owned by Alain and Tehei Malmezac, who warmly welcome their guests and lend a helping hand in various ways to insure their comfort and pleasure. There are 3 modern wooden bungalows with thatched roofs overlooking the lagoon in a high-end gated community. They are all decorated with furniture and colorful furnishings from Indonesia.

The Tipanier and Tiare bungalows are each 60 sq. m. (646 sq. ft.) and can sleep 4 people for 40.000 CFP per night including breakfast. They have a private terrace and a Jacuzzi. The Pineapple bungalow is built on high stilts with a terrace that offers an incredible panoramic view of the lagoon, coral reef and ocean. It has 25 sq. m. (269 sq. ft.) of living space and can sleep 2 people for 25.000 CFP per night, with breakfast included. All other meals are available on request. All the bungalows have a/c, a big-screen LCD satellite TV, a safe, an equipped kitchen with microwave, refrigerator and coffee maker, and a bathroom with hot water shower, bathtub, soap, shampoo and hair dryer. Extra charges include a point telephone, Internet connection and airport transfers.

There are several places to sit in the garden facing the lagoon, with thatched roof palapa type shelters and various types of lawn chairs and tree trunk stools. Guest services include a BBQ grill, pool table, petanque bowls, adult bicycles, 2-person outrigger canoes, and snorkeling gear. Alain will tell you where to go to visit the sting rays in the lagoon or find a white sandy beach on a nearby motu islet.

Moderate

HOTEL LES TIPANIERS, *B.P. 1002, Papetoai, Moorea 98729. Tel. 689/ 56.12.67, Fax 689/56.29.25; tipaniersresa@mail.pf; www.lestipaniers.com. Beside the lagoon at PK 25 in Haapiti, 25 km (15.5 mi.) from the airport and 29 km (18 mi.) from the ferry dock. 22 bungalows. All major credit cards.*

"Les Tipaniers" means frangipani or plumeria, the trees of white, pink, orange and yellow flowers you will see and smell throughout the gardens of this very Polynesian style hotel. The local style bungalows have a thatched roof and can sleep 3 or 4 people, with or without a kitchen. The vanilla style units are built in the French colonial architecture with gingerbread trim and have kitchens, accommodating up to 7 people. Each bungalow has a porch or terrace, as well as screens on the windows but not on the sliding glass doors. All the bungalows were renovated in 2003, and this popular hotel enjoys 85 percent occupancy year-round. Rates start at 14.250 CFP for a standard bungalow sgl./dbl., or a local style garden bungalow with kitchen. A beach bungalow with kitchen is 16.250 CFP sgl./dbl. A simple room with a fridge and fan is 7.600 CFP plus taxes.

The beachside restaurant-bar is open for breakfast, lunch and sunset cocktails, and the main restaurant is open for dinner. See information under *Where to Eat* in this chapter. You can easily walk from this hotel to several restaurants, shops, boutiques and pearl shops.

Free activities include outrigger paddle canoes, volleyball, ping-pong, and petanque (French bowls). You can rent mountain bikes. Facing the hotel's white sand beach are three *motu* islets, which you can reach by canoe or boat. Tip'Nautic activities center is on the premises and will arrange your outings on the lagoon. See more information under *Nautical Activities* in this chapter. Scubapiti is a dive center based at the hotel, with a qualified instructor. See more information under *Scuba Diving* in this chapter. The reception staff will help you to arrange your vehicle rentals and paid activities, which can include hiking with Tahiti Evasion. See more information under *Hiking* in this chapter.

LES TIPANIERS ITI, *an annex to the main hotel, is located beside the lagoon at PK 20 in Papetoai, 4 km (2.5 mi.) from Hotel Les Tipaniers, 20 km (12.4 mi.) from the airport and 24 km (14.8 mi.) from the ferry dock. 5 local style bungalows with kitchens can accommodate up to 4 people. All major credit cards.*

"Little Tipaniers" has 5 thatched-roof bungalows with kitchenettes and beds for 3-4 people. A sun deck type wharf overlooks the entrance to magnificent Opunohu Bay. You have access to all the activities available at Les Tipaniers. A complimentary shuttle van will transfer you to the main hotel for dinner on request. The bungalows are 8.300 CFP sgl/dbl and 9.050 CFP for 3-4 people per night, plus taxes. Special rates starting 7th night. Add 4.980 CFP per person for MAP and 8.620 CFP for AP meals at the main hotel.

HOTEL HIBISCUS, *B.P. 1009, Papetoai, Moorea 98729. Tel. 689/56.12.20, Fax 689/56.20.69; hibiscus@mail.pf; www.hotel-hibiscus.pf. Beside the lagoon at PK 27 in Haapiti, next door to the former Club Med, 27 km (16.7 mi.) from the airport and 31 km (19.2 mi.) from the ferry dock. All major credit cards.*

The Hotel Hibiscus is built on one of the nicest properties on Moorea's sunset coast. It is now under new management and they are slowly renovating the bungalows and making other much needed improvements.

The 29 thatched roof bungalows are compact but comfortable, with beds for 3-4 people, tiled bathrooms with hot water showers, a separate toilet compartment, double sinks, a kitchen corner with a mini-refrigerator and 3-burner hot plate, plus cooking and eating utensils, wardrobe closet, ceiling fan, mosquito nets, hair dryer, and a covered terrace with table and chairs. There are also 10 a/c rooms for 3 people and 2 a/c studios in a 2-story building beside the swimming pool that can sleep 3-5 people. These units also have a kitchenette and a balcony or private garden. A safety box is available at reception. A garden bungalow with fan is 15.000 CFP dbl;

a lagoon view bungalow with fan is 18.000 CFP dbl; an A/C room is 15.000 CFP dbl; an A/C studio for 4 is 20.000 CFP and for 5 people the A/C studio is 22.000 CFP. Add taxes.

Le Sunset Restaurant is beside the white sand beach in front of Hotel Hibiscus, serving pizza and French, Italian and local cuisine. They host Full Moon parties every month, Happy Hour with local singers on Fri. night, special Jazz evenings, and other entertainment. See more information in *Where to Eat* in this chapter. In addition to a fresh water hibiscus-shaped swimming pool in the hotel's spacious gardens, there is a white sand beach. You can rent a bicycle or kayak at the reception desk, sign up for island tours or check your e-mail with the Internet service provided.

MOOREA BEACH LODGE, *Haapiti, Moorea 98729. Tel. 689/77.04.59; www.mooreabeachlodge.com. Beside lagoon at PK 27.5 in Haapiti, 27.5 km. (16.7 mi.) from the airport and 31.5 km. (19.2 mi.) from the ferry dock.*

When Frenchman John Labaysse was a child he fell in love with the beautiful white sand beach and good swimming in the coral-free lagoon at this location, which was formerly known as Moorea Camping. He is now the owner of this beautiful property and has a building project underway, with plans to be open by April 2010.

Moorea Beach Lodge will have at least 12 bungalows, with 5 units on the beach and 7 in the garden. Each bungalow will be different and will all have a pandanus roof and white walls, white floors and nice furniture. John's wife, Maya Lo, who is a well-known interior architect/designer, will lend her creative touch. She decorated the villas at the Relais & Chateau Hotel (Le Taha'a Island Resort & Spa) and several of the luxury hotels in Bora Bora. John said that each bungalow will have a double bed and a single bed will be provided on request. They will also have a private bathroom with hot water shower, plus a terrace. Amenities will include a personal safe, mini-fridge, hair-dryer, and free WiFi access.

The big buildings on the property will be old plantation colonial style with tin roofs. These will include the reception, boutique, and the Azur Tahiti pearl shop, featuring the jewelry designed by Stéphane Labaysse, John's brother, who will also be the hotel manager. The communal facilities will include a lounge with TV and pay telephone, laundry facilities and a recreation area with a ping pong table. Guests will have free use of bicycles, snorkeling equipment, kayaks and paddle boards. Moorea Fun Dive is just next door.

A free courtesy van will provide round-trip transfers from/to the ferry quay, and a free Continental, American or local style breakfast will be served to all bungalows. A Chinese take-away restaurant, chicken roulotte and food store are all very close by, and there are several other restaurants and snacks in the neighborhood. Guests are welcome to bring their own ice-chests and drinks and sit in a lawn chair on the beachside terrace. This is one of the best places on the island to watch Moorea's famous sunsets.

Rates for a beach bungalow will be 15.000 CFP and the garden bungalows will be 10.000-12.000 CFP dbl. or with a child.

MOOREA FARE MITI, *B.P. 1569, Papetoai, Moorea 98729. Tel. 689/Fax 689/56.57.42; Cell 21.65.59; mooreafaremiti@mail.pf; www.mooreafaremiti.com. Beside the lagoon at PK 27.5 in Haapiti, 27 km. (16.7 mi.) from the airport and 32 km. (19.2 mi.) from the ferry dock by the north coast. No credit cards.*

There are 7 garden bungalows and 1 beach bungalow for rent on the property that was formerly part of the Hotel Moorea Village before it closed in Oct. 2005. These Polynesian style bungalows have a thatched roof, woven bamboo walls, screened windows and sliding glass doors with screens. Each unit has a bedroom with a queen size bed, living room with 2 day beds, floor fan, equipped kitchen with 2-burner electric stove, small refrigerator, pots and pans and dishes and utensils, bathroom with hot water shower, covered veranda with a big table and 4 chairs. A mattress can be added for a 5th person. A Garden bungalow for 1-4 people is 13.000 CFP and a Beach bungalow is 15.000 CFP, plus taxes. A long white sand beach extends to the former Club Med and you can swim to the little man-made motu in front of the pension. Sunset watching is magnificent from the beach. There are rental bikes and kayaks on the premises, as well as an activities bureau and a small stock of food supplies in the reception area. Bread and meals can be delivered on request, and it is only a 10-minute walk to a food store, restaurants, snacks and shopping. WiFi connection.

FARE TAPU LODGE, *B.P. 2025, Papetoai, Moorea 98729. Tel. 689/ 55.20.55; Fax 689/56.32.79; Cell 79.39.89; www.tapulodge.com. On mountainside at PK 28.2 in Haapiti, 1 km. (0.62) miles from Le Petit Village. MC, V.*

This guest house has been awarded 2 Tiares by Tahiti Tourisme. Six modern concrete units are built on stilts on the mountain slope overlooking Moorea's sunset coast of Haapiti. The smaller units are 70 sq. m. (753 sq. ft.) and have a king size bed plus a mezzanine with a single bed. The large *fares* are 120 sq. m (1,292 sq. ft.), with 2 bedrooms, each furnished with a king size bed with a foam mattress. There are also 2 single beds in the living room. All units have TV, free WiFi, a fully equipped kitchen, bathroom with hot water, and a balcony. The small *fares* are 12.900 CFP sgl./dbl., and the large *fares* are 21.500 CFP; add 1.500 CFP for extra bed. Add taxes. Minimum 2 nights. A white sand beach is just 50 m. (164 ft.) away. All excursions are provided by Moorea Mahana Tours, and guest staying here will get a free lagoon activity.

TE FARE MIHI, *B.P. 111 H, Haapiti, Moorea 98729. Tel. 689/56.34.85; Fax 689/56.38.66; www.tefaremihi.com. Beside lagoon at PK 28,5 in Haapiti. AE, MC, V.*

This 2-Tiare family pension is owned by Moise and Félicie Ruta, who also operate Moorea Mahana Tours. There are 3 modern concrete houses on a fenced property next to a white sand beach. Each unit has a bedroom with a double bed, a sofa bed in the living room, a tiled bathroom with solar hot water, and a complete kitchen with a big refrigerator, a microwave oven and 4-burner stove with oven. There is a dining table on the covered terrace, a BBQ grill, and an outside sink and wash area. Each bungalow has a mosquito net, ceiling fan, safe and TV. Rates start at 16.500 CFP for a lanai bungalow. Guests have free use of kayaks, pedal boats and outrigger canoes, plus they will have one free boat transfer to the motu.

Economy
CAMPING NELSON, *B.P. 1309, Papetoai, Moorea 98729. Tel./Fax 689/ 56.15.18; campingnelson@mail.pf; www.camping-nelson.pf. Beside the lagoon at PK 27.1 in Haapiti, 27.1 km (17 mi.) from the airport and 31.1 km (19.5 mi.) from the ferry dock. AE, MC, V.*

In addition to a spacious campground by the sea, this backpacker's hostel offers 10 dormitory rooms for 2 people, plus a variety of rooms and *fares*. Everyone shares the 7 toilets, 7 showers with cold water and the lavabos and there is also a toilet and shower for handicapped guests. The communal kitchen and dining room are adjacent to the reception area. Information on activities and rental vehicles and kayaks is available at reception. Camping is 1.500-1.800 CFP per person for 1 day, depending on whether you choose the garden or beach. Bring your own tent. A dormitory bed is 2.200 CFP; a very small A-frame Tahitian *fare* is 5.400 CFP sgl./ dbl; the Maire room is 5.000 CFP dbl.; and the Aito room close to the beach is 6.600 CFP sgl./dbl. Discounts on all accommodations starting second night. Taxes included. There are restaurants, snacks, food stores, pearl shops and souvenir shops in the immediate neighborhood.

Haapiti to Afareaitu
Superior
TE NUNOA BUNGALOW, *PK 32, Haapiti-Varari, Moorea 98729. Tel. 689/56.25.33; US 310/464-1490; www.mooreabungalow.com. On the mountainside of the road, 32 km. (19.8 mi.) from the airport and 37 km. (22.9 mi.) from the ferry dock by the north coast. AE, MC, V, JCB.*

This beautifully appointed guesthouse is a Polynesian style bungalow owned by Laurel and James Samuela. She is American and he is Tahitian and they live next door with their 2 children. Laurel owns 2 online travel companies: *wwwtruetahitivacation.com*, and *www.divetahitiblue.com*. James has a tattoo studio on the premises.

Te Nunoa, which means red sky or "that particular sunset when everything is red" is a true gem and an ideal choice for those who long to experience the Tahiti that exists outside of the hotels, without sacrificing luxury and comfort. The bungalow and its lush tropical garden are surrounded by a protective wall of bamboo and stone. Complete with a thatched roof and bamboo walls, the bungalow is lovingly furnished with a very comfy king size bed with a Memory Foam mattress, covered by a mosquito net. There is also a twin day bed with a twin trundle bed underneath that can slide out to accommodate a child. The furniture is teak, including 2 steamer lounge chairs. There are 2 ceiling fans, lamps, an electronic wall safe, satellite TV, CD player, telephone and high speed Internet access. The stainless steel kitchenette is on one wall of the big room, with nice wood cabinets, a 2-burner stove, toaster oven, and a big refrigerator with a freezer. The bathroom has tile from Spain, a hot water shower with a rain nozzle, a hair dryer and specially made fluffy bath and beach towels. Guest toiletries are from Moana Beauty, including Monoi grooming products. There is original art on the walls, including black and white photos by Laurel and tattoo designs by James. Maid service is provided daily and laundry service is available for 2.000 CFP per load. A high chair and port-a-crib are available on request. Sliding doors lead to the private garden, where there is a *fare pote'e* shelter, a hammock and BBQ grill. Bicycles, snorkeling equipment and kayaks are available for guest use, and you will also have access to a pretty white sand beach across the road. The nearest food store is just a 5-min. walk and Le Petit Village is a 15-min. bike ride. Free transportation is provided to take you to a nearby dive center. The bungalow rents for 22.000 CFP (about US $240) per night for 1-2 adults during the low season and 25.000 CFP (about US $270) per night during the high season. Children under 12 are free of charge with adults.

Moderate

FARE EDITH, *B.P. 1400, Papetoai, Moorea 98729. Tel. 689/56.35.34/ 75.01.05; www.fareedith.com. Beside lagoon at PK 32.52 in Varari-Haapiti. No credit cards.*

Tahiti Tourisme rates this pension as 3-Tiares. Pierre & Edith Teissier give their guests a check-out time of 3pm, which is most unusual in family pensions, who normally want the rooms cleared by 10am. They have 4 bungalows in colorful gardens or on the beach, with accommodations for a couple or a family of 3-6 people in one or two bedrooms and living room. All the units have a well-equipped kitchen, a private bathroom with hot water, ceiling fans, TV, mosquito nets, a washing machine and a covered terrace. Rates start at 8.000 CFP sgl., 11.500 CFP dbl. Fare Fara is a family unit for 6 people, with a/c in one of the 2 bedrooms, a sofa bed in the living room, a terrace with a lagoon view, and a garage. This unit is 13.000 CFP-17.000 CFP.

RESIDENCE LINAREVA, *B.P. 1 H, Haapiti, Moorea 98729. Tel. 689/ 55.05.65/31.12.19; Fax 689/55.05.67; linareva@mail.pf; www.linareva.com. Beside the lagoon at PK 34,5 in Haapiti, 21 km (13 mi.) from the ferry dock and 25 km (15.5 mi.) from the airport around the south coast. MC, V.*

This small family hotel overlooks a small beach and Moorea's sunset sea and has a 3-tiare rating from the Tahiti Tourist office. The new owners since 2009 are Roland and Edmée Emfeld, who have refurbished the 8 units, adding new kitchens and bathrooms, as well as other updated comforts and decorations. You have a choice of king size, double or single beds, according to the unit chosen. Some of the units have a/c and they all have a ceiling fan, TV, free WiFi, safety box, library of books, private tiled bathroom with hot water shower, and a covered terrace. All the kitchens are well equipped with stove and refrigerator, toaster and coffee maker, and cleaning products are provided daily. Rates start at 14.500 CFP for 1-2 people staying in a garden studio. A beach studio is 18.000 CFP, and a 4-person suite for 1-2 people is 20.000 CFP. There are also accommodations for families or groups of up to 7 people. You can even have breakfast delivered to your room. A Continental breakfast is 1.550 CFP and an American breakfast is 1.950 CFP. For 3.500 CFP per person you can have a 3-course dinner served on your private veranda or join the other guests on the party deck.

Free activities include bicycles, snorkeling gear, outrigger canoes, kayaks and bocce ball. Barbecue grills are free for guest use, and there's a sunbathing deck on the long pier.

Roland, who is a scuba diving instructor, has a shark-feeding show at the end of the pier each afternoon at sunset. This is a big success with the guests.

FARE D'HÔTE TEHUARUPE, *B.P. 80151, Papetoai, Moorea 98729. Tel./ Fax 689/56.57.33; Cell 77.32.95; tehaurupe@mail.pf; www.moorea-paradise.com. On mountainside at PK 22,500 in Haapiti. All credit cards.*

When Elda Whittaker was building her 4-bungalow guest house, she was mindful of protecting the natural resources of Moorea. Using all natural materials, almost exclusively in exotic woods, the units have high ceilings and insulation, providing air circulation and an insect-free environment. The water is recycled, a waste sorting system insures maximum recycling, and she uses only biodegradable cleaning products. Tahiti Tourisme has awarded this guest house the highest rating of 3 Tiares.

The rooms are beautifully and tastefully furnished, and each unit has an orthopedic king-size mattress, mosquito net, ceiling fan, safe, TV, free WiFi, equipped kitchen with microwave oven and refrigerator, and private bathroom with hot water shower. From each private terrace you will have a panoramic view of the lagoon, coral reef and ocean. The breathtaking scenery is even more impressive from the infinity pool. Bikes and a kayak are also available for guest use. Elda and her team can help you arrange your other activities. From Mon.-Thurs. a bungalow is 13.000 CFP for 2 people and 14.000 CFP per couple on weekends.

FARE ARANA, *B.P. 610, Papetoai, Moorea 98729. Tel./Fax 689/56.44.03; Cell 76.94.77; www.farearana.com. On mountainside at PK 19.5 in Atiha, 15 min. from the ferry dock and 20 min. from the airport. No credit cards.*

Rated by Tahiti Tourisme as a 2-Tiare family pension, Fare Arana sits high on a hillside overlooking Avarapa Bay, offering panoramic views of the ever-changing colors of the lagoon and ocean. The verdant gardens are filled with fruit trees and flowers, providing the perfect setting for 4 thatched roof bungalows of high quality and craftsmanship. Three of the concrete bungalows have a/c and 70 sq. m. (753 sq. ft.) of living space. On the mezzanine there are 2 double beds and 1 single bed, all with mosquito nets. The ground floor has a living/dining area with TV and ceiling fan, a well-equipped kitchen, and a bathroom with hot water shower. The furniture is teak and bamboo and the windows and doors are screened. Steps from the covered terrace and open sundeck lead down to the gardens and swimming pool area, where you can relax in an elegant hammock. There is also a smaller bungalow with a double bed and a folding settee, a ceiling fan, kitchen, bathroom with hot water, and an iron. A BBQ grill is available on request and guests can use the washing machine. The small bungalow rents for 9.900 CFP sgl./dbl., and a large bungalow is 11.900 CFP. Add 2.500 for 3rd person. Taxes included.

Free activities include the swimming pool, *petanque* (French bowls) and kayaks. Owner Fabienne Gautier and her team can help you arrange hikes, 4WD excursions, boat tours, deep-sea fishing, quad excursions, and a visit to Tiki Village.

FARE AUTE, *BP 528, Maharepa, Moorea 98728. Tel./Fax 689/56.45.19; Cell 78.23.34; www.pensionaute.com. Beside a white sand beach at PK 16.4 in Atiha. MC, V.*

This pension has a 2-Tiare rating for this Polynesian style village with 5 garden bungalows, 2 beach bungalows and 1 seaside house spread across the spacious grounds. The garden units are priced from 11.000 CFP for 2 people, and the beach bungalows are 13.000 CFP double, with accommodations for 4 people. All the well-equipped bungalows have kitchens, ceiling fans, mosquito nets, private bathrooms, hot water, TV, washing machine and a covered terrace. The seaside house has 4 bedrooms with a/c in one room, 3 bathrooms with hot water, a living room with TV, and a kitchen. This is priced at 24.000 CFP for 5 people. You can also rent a car or scooter on the premises.

Economy

MARK'S PLACE MOOREA BUNGALOWS, *B.P. 41, Maharepa, Moorea 98728. Tel./Fax 689/56.43.02; cell 78.93.65; www.marksplacemoorea.com; On mountainside at PK 23.5 in Haapiti, in front of the surfing pass, 25 min. from Vaiare ferry dock and 35 min. from Temae airport. Minimum 2 day stay. MC, V.*

Look for the Mark's Place Moorea Bungalows sign beside the circle island road just past the Eglise de la Sainte Famille, the Catholic Church with twin towers. Follow the dirt road into the valley until you see the bungalow complex on the right. Owner Mark Walker, an American expatriate builder and wood worker who has lived in French Polynesia for many years, has built 7 quality bungalows on his grassy property. He is constantly improving his accommodations, which include wooden studios and bungalows that are perfect for couples, families or groups, with sleeping accommodations for 2, 6 or 8 people. Prices start at 8.000 CFP sgl./dbl. during low seasons and 10.000 CFP during high seasons. All units are equipped with a kitchen, bathroom, satellite TV and WiFi (cards sold at reception). Some of the studios and bungalows also have a living room, deck and barbecue grill. There are no mosquito nets and no meals. Check Mark's website to choose the accommodation you prefer.

Bicycle and kayak rentals are available for 1.000 CFP per day, and a snorkeling mask and fins are 500 CFP per day. A load of washing is 1.000 CFP and there is a public phone on the premises. In addition to surfing the pass in Haapiti, Mark's guests enjoy hiking over the mountains and participating in the other activities that are available on Moorea.

HAAPITI SURF LODGE, *Haapiti, Moorea 98729. Tel./Fax 689/56.40.36; cell 72.64.84; haapitisurf@mail.pf. On the mountainside at PK 22.5 in Haapiti. Round-trip transfers included. No credit cards.*

Tahiti Tourisme has awarded a rating of 2 Tiares to this very popular family pension. There are 4 modern white concrete bungalows on the mountainside overlooking the surfing pass of Haapiti, where the spinner dolphins play inside the lagoon year round and the humpback whales swim just beyond the reef between July and early November. Petero Tehuritaua, the young Tahitian owner, built his surfing lodge in 2001 and has everything well organized for his guests. Each clean and attractively furnished bungalow has a double bed, TV, ceiling fan, (a/c on request), equipped kitchen and a bathroom with hot water and a bathtub/shower, as well as a terrace with a dining table and individual barbecue grills. One of the units is a Honeymoon bungalow, built a little higher than the other three, offering a better view of the lagoon, the pass and the romantic tropical sunsets. Guests with children can put up a tent in the yard beside their bungalow. There is also an outdoor shower. A room is 8.500 CFP sgl/dbl for the first night, with digressive rates for longer stays. Add 1.500 CFP per day for a/c and 1.500 CFP per day for extra bed. No charge for child under 12 years. Add taxes.

Petero provides his guests with kayaks and bicycles at no charge, and he will also take you on a tour of the island in his 4WD. There is a long pier on the beach side of his property, where you can fish and swim You can buy fish from vendors on the road or bike to the nearest magasin store for food supplies, which is only a kilometer away. Meals can be provided on request for charter groups of 8-10 people. They will even provide laundry service for long-stay guests.

Afareaitu to Temae
Moderate

TE ORA HAU, *B.P. 4005, Maharepa, Moorea 98728. Tel./Fax 689/56.35.35; cell 77.48.22; vahineheipua@gmail.com; www.teorahau.com. Beside lagoon at PK 8.2 in Afareaitu, facing Motu Ahi, 4.2 km (2.6 mi.) from the Vaiare ferry dock and 8.2 km (5 mi.) from the airport. No credit cards.*

You'll sleep to the sounds of the ocean in this environment that resembles that of the Tuamotu Islands, complete with a white sand beach, sea breezes blowing through the pandanus trees, and a motu islet right in front of you. In the distance, however, you can clearly see the island of Tahiti with its mountains and houses. Your Polynesian hostess, Heipua Bordes, has 3 large wooden bungalows or *fares* that are completely equipped with a kitchen, washing machine and bathroom with hot water shower. The bungalows are clean, modern and very tastefully decorated and the bed linens are changed every 3 days. BBQ grills and kayaks are provided. EP rates start at 13.500 CFP dbl; and the 6-person *fare* is 22.000 CFP, plus visitor tax. She gives 10% discounts for a minimum of 2 nights.

Heipua is well versed in the culture and legends of Polynesia and she has taught her cleaning staff to speak a little English. You can shop for groceries at Champion

Fare Toa, which is 1.7 mi. from the pension. Cars, scooters and bicycles can be rented at the nearby ferry dock in Vaiare. Heipua also owns Te Ora Hau-Tahiti in Afaahiti on the Tahiti-Iti peninsula.

ATUANA LODGE, *B.P. 4118, Vaiare, Moorea 98728. Tel. 689/56.36.03/ 77.60.26; Fax 689/55.06.30; www.atuanalodge.com. Beside lagoon at PK 6,3 in Afareaitu, 2 min. from Vaiare ferry dock. Free transfers. No credit cards.*

Bertille and Atuona Temauri have 2 bedrooms for rent in their 2-story neo-colonial style white house and a thatched roof bungalow in their garden. A high wall in front of the property helps to muffle most of the road noise, and is closed with an automatic gate. On the beach side you can swim and snorkel, watch the fishermen, sailboats and ferries, and look for the spinner dolphins, as well as the humpback whales that come into the ship channel between July and early Nov. The lights of Tahiti are visible at night across the Sea of Moons.

The local style bungalow has a bedroom with a king-size bed and 2 bunk beds, mosquito nets, a ceiling fan, safe, TV, free WiFi, and hairdryer. The kitchen is equipped with a gas stove, microwave oven, refrigerator and freezer. The bathroom has a hot water shower and there is also an outdoor shower to use after swimming or fishing. There are 3 eating locations around the bungalow, and you can even grill your meat or fish on the barbecue and watch the full moon rise above the mountains of Tahiti. The big supermarket Champion Fare Toa is just a 5-min. drive from Atuona Lodge. This individual bungalow is 14.500 CFP a night for 2 people and 1.650 CFP extra for each additional guest over 12 years, up to 4 people. If you don't feel like cooking, Tuana serves half-board meals with breakfast and dinner for 4.200 CFP per person.

Each of the bedrooms in the main house is a/c, has a king-size bed, TV, free WiFi, safe, private bathroom, and access to the Spa on the terrace. A guest room with a Continental breakfast and dinner is 19.800 CFP per day for 2 people. Beach towels are provided for all guests, as well as snorkel gear and kayak.

Other Family Pensions, Guest Houses, Surf Lodges, Dormitories & Camp Sites

Faimano Village, *Tel. 689/56.10.20, Fax 689/56.36.47; faimanodenis@mail.pf; www.faimanovillage.com.* 7 very seasoned Polynesian style bungalows, each with private bathroom (solar hot water), kitchen, TV, and BBQ grill in the gardens and facing the white sand beach at PK 14.1 in Pihaena, near the Hilton Moorea Lagoon Resort. MC, V.

Fare Nani, *Tel./Fax 689/56.19.99; Cell 79.89.73.* Beside the lagoon in Pihaena at PK 14.1, between the Hilton Moorea Lagoon Resort and Faimano Village. 3 little thatched roof *fares* with a double bed, mosquito net and small electric fan, a lounge with sofa and mattresses, a kitchen and outside bathroom with cold water. Owner Maeva Bougues speaks English. 10.000 CFP for couple and 2 children under 12 years. No credit cards.

Fare Vaimoana, *Tel. 689/56.17.14; Fax 689/56.28.78; www.fare-vaimoana.com.* 14 white concrete bungalows with thatched roofs beside the lagoon at PK 27 in Haapiti. The windows are not screened and some of the units have no fans or hot water. The restaurant has closed. All major credit cards.

Fare Manuia, *Tel. 689/56.26.17; Fax 689/56.10.30; faremanuia@gmail.com; www.tahitiguide.com.* 6 bungalows on lagoon side at PK 30 in Haapiti. Standard, garden and beach bungalows for 1-6 people. All units have kitchens, terrace and hot water showers. Owner Janine Salmon speaks English. No credit cards.

Fare Pole, *Tel. 689/56.59.17/27.70.27; www.farepolemoorea.com.* Beside lagoon at PK 30,6 in Varari, 2 km. (1.2 mi.) from Le Petit Village. 2 bungalows on beachfront and 1 garden bungalow, all with kitchens, starting at 13.200 CFP per night. No credit cards

Tarariki Village, *Tel. 689/55.21.05; pensiontarariki@mail.pf.* 6 rustic bungalows, tree houses and 2 dormitories beside beach at PK 21,3 in Vaianae, near surfing pass. Dorm 1.600-2.300 CFP, bungalow 5.500 CFP sgl/dbl. No meals. Min. 2 nights. No credit cards.

Nature House of Mou'a Roa, *Tel. 689/56.58.62/72.62.58; Fax 689/56.40.47; mouaroa@mail.pf; www.lamaisondelanature.com.* 8 rooms in a big colonial style house on an agricultural farm in Vaianae valley at PK 21 between Haapiti and Atiha. Experience a "green" vacation and biologic meals. MAP room 9.900 CFP; AP room 10.900 CFP. Guided hikes. No credit cards.

Pension Tifai, *Tel./Fax 689/56.29.56; www.pensiontifai.pf.* 4 modern white concrete bungalows on mountainside at PK 20,300 in Vaianae. The 2 smaller units can sleep 2 people and the larger *fare* has 1 dbl. bed in bedroom and 2 single beds in living room. All units have kitchen, bathroom with hot water, small terrace, fan, optional a/c, TV, and disabled facilities. Activities include a swimming pool and boat excursions provided by owners. Special weekend rates for 2 people are 20.250 CFP, including breakfast and boat transfer to motu at Club Med. Normal rate is 27.000 CFP for small bungalow and 52.400 CFP for 4-person bungalow. No credit cards.

Atiha Lodge Moorea, *Tel. 33.97.41; atihalodge@moorea@gmail.com; www.atihalodge.blogspot.com.* 2 simple plywood houses on mountainside at PK 16,1 in Atiha. B&B for 3.500 CFP sgl./5.000 CFP dbl. Dorm & breakfast for 2.500 CFP per person. House and breakfast for 8 people for 28.000 CFP. Private beach access with kayaks and snorkel gear. Hiking, massages, relaxation center and acupuncture. No credit cards.

Vaihau Village, *Tel. 689/77.37.38.* Alain Mai-Manate has 3 *fares* on stilts on mountainside in Haumi, Afareaitu. Kitchen with microwave and fridge, bathroom with hot water. No credit cards.

WHERE TO EAT
Airport & Motu Temae
Deluxe
SOFITEL IA ORA MOOREA BEACH RESORT, *Tel. 55.12.12/55.12.26. Restaurant Pure is open daily for B, L, D and snacks. Restaurant K serves D only. Bar Vue on the beach is open daily 10am-10:30pm. All credit cards.*

Restaurant **Pure** is the main dining room featuring international cuisine in a contemporary setting. There is an *a la carte* lunch and dinner menu, and several theme nights that include a Polynesian buffet on Thurs. for 7.100 CFP, serving traditional Tahitian food cooked in the underground oven. There is a dance show each night during dinner in Restaurant Pure.

Restaurant **K** (for Kahaia tree) is the resort's world class gourmet restaurant, where you are required to dress elegantly for dining with your feet in the sand floor. The beachy atmosphere becomes a romantic setting with candlelight and you can see the lights of Tahiti twinkling across the Sea of Moons. The menu lists choices from 1.900-6.500 CFP, which include parrotfish, gambas, roast pig, veal chops, beef filet and lobster. Diners are entertained by the Te Vahine show on Tues. and Sat. evenings. Closed on Thurs. and Sun.

Vue Bar faces the lagoon and the swimming pool. Set in a Polynesian atmosphere this bar serves all your favorite drinks plus some exotic cocktails. You can also order snacks and ice cream. You do not see the sun dipping behind the horizon on this side of the island, but you can sit on the terrace and watch the clouds over Tahiti reflecting the colors of the sunset. Vue Bar has weekly entertainment during cocktail hours.

Superior

MIKI MIKI RESTAURANT & BAR, *Tel. 56.26.70. Call for free shuttle. AE, V.*

Le Miki Miki is located at the Moorea Green Pearl Golf Course Clubhouse, and is open for lunch from 12-3pm on Tues.-Sun. and from 6:30pm in the evening on Wed., Thurs., Fri., and Sat. Closed Sun. night, all day Mon. and Tues. night, except on holidays. The bar is open daily from 10am. Musical parties are held each Fri. evening, with a DJ, live band, or dinner-dance shows. Entrance fees charged for non-diners on Fri., which usually include a drink.

The menu lists burgers for 1.100-1.350 CFP, salads for 950-1.550 CFP, pasta and risotto for 1.450-2.300 CFP, and starter courses for 1.500-2.250 CFP, which include beef or tuna tartare and fried foie gras. The fish choices are 2.500-2.600 CFP, and meats are 2.450 CFP for lamb shoulder and 2.950 CFP for beef filet or a double entrecôte (rib steak) with fries. Desserts are 1.000 CFP. The French chef worked in gastronomic restaurants in France, London and Geneva before coming to French Polynesia in 2006. He cooked at the former Sheraton on Moorea and also aboard the *Aranui III*.

Cook's Bay Area: Maharepa to Paopao – Deluxe

MOOREA PEARL RESORT & SPA, *Tel. 55.17.50. Mahanai Restaurant is open daily for B.,L.,D. Matiehani Restaurant is open for D. Autera'a Bar & Terrasse serves L and cocktails. All credit cards.*

The **Mahanai Restaurant** opens onto the view of the swimming pool, lagoon and overwater bungalows. An American breakfast is 3.200 CFP, and the Canoe breakfast delivered by outrigger canoe to the terrace of the overwater bungalows is

11.300 CFP for two people. A 2-course set luncheon menu is 3.700 CFP and the 3-course set dinner menu is 6.500 CFP. The MAP rate for half-board is 9.200 CFP per person, and the AP full-board rate is 12.500 CFP. A new luncheon menu features Polynesian and Asiatic cold starters, followed by fish & chips or Mediterranean dishes. The dinner menu presents the Chef's specialties, including wahoo tournedos with confit of sesame seaweed. The Polynesian buffet is held each Wed. night for 7.500 CFP, followed by a Polynesian dance show, and a Round-the-World buffet and dance show takes place each Sat. night, for 6.000 CFP per person. At publication time this consisted of Hirinaki's troupe of female dancers who perform to recorded music. A local trio plays music on Mon, evenings and on Fri. nights the rhythm will have you swaying to a salsa beat.

You can also eat your lunch while sitting at the spacious **Autera'a Bar & Terrasse** facing the pool. A choice of luncheon menus allows you to eat between 12 and 2pm and snacks are served between 2-9:30pm (except Wed. & Fri., when snacks are served until 4:30pm). Interesting selections include paninis, Caesar salad with grilled chicken or shrimp, a club sandwich, a Moorea salad with shrimp and pineapple, burgers and fries, and a Polynesian plate, which includes sashimi, tuna tartare and poisson cru.

Matiehani is the name of the a/c gourmet restaurant that serves gastronomic French cuisine nightly except on Wed. and Sun. Seating for a maximum of 12 people. Candlelight dining is also available on the terrace overlooking the lagoon.

Superior
HONU ITI, *Tel. 56.19.84, PK 8, beside Cook's Bay, Pao Pao. Open for L, D. except all day Sun. and at noon on Mon. Courtesy shuttles as far as Sofitel Ia Ora and Intercontinental Moorea Resort. MC, V. Reserve.*

In 1974 Roger Igual won France's most prestigious diploma for chefs—the Concours National de la Poêle d'Or. That same year he brought his cooking skills to Tahiti, and since 1991 Roger has been serving his gourmet specialties to Moorea diners. The overwater terrace of his Honu Iti restaurant provides a privileged setting, where you can gaze at the romantic scenery of Cook's Bay, bordered by pineapple fields and fairy castle mountains, while enjoying some of the island's finest French cuisine. In the evening you can feed the rays and fish that swim close to the terrace, hoping for handouts.

Appetizers are 1.600-2.200 CFP, which include a tasty French onion soup. Fish and seafood specialties are 2.800-3.200 CFP, featuring mahi mahi with vanilla sauce and scallops served with leeks. The meat and poultry dishes are priced from 3.200-3.500 CFP. My favorite meat choice is the very tender beef Bourguignon, marinated in red wine for 2.600 CFP, and there is also osso bucco Milanese. The chef's suggestions are 2.600-2.800 CFP. Desserts are 1.200-1.500 CFP and include Roger's special apple pie with ice cream, as well as homemade chocolate cake. Crêpes Suzette are 1.800 CFP. A 3-course tourist menu is 5.000 CFP. Wines feature some tempting *grands crus* from France's best vineyards.

LE MAHOGANY, *Tel. 56.39.73, PK 5, mountainside, Maharepa. MC, V. Open 11am-2:30pm and 6-9:30pm. Closed Wed. Reserve for dinner. Pick-up service available.*

This popular indoor-outdoor restaurant is the first restaurant on the mountainside you will see when coming from the airport or ferry dock toward Cook's Bay. A street-side chalkboard lists the daily specials, which may be veal Marengo, cassoulet, or gambas. In addition to a varied menu of French cuisine, they also serve a few Chinese dishes, including good chow mein from 1.750-2.150 CFP. The shrimp curry with coconut sauce is highly recommended. A 3-course tourist menu is 4.650 CFP. Burgers and fries are served at lunchtime, along with a selection of salads and grilled rib eye steak.

LE COCOTIER, *Tel. 56.12.10, PK 4.7, mountainside, Maharepa. Diners, V. Open Mon.-Fri. L, D. Closed Sat. noon, and all day Sun. Free pick-up service between Sofitel and Hilton resorts.*

Pascal Mathieu, the manager and chef, presents a varied menu of well-prepared classic French cuisine that is served in the open-air restaurant, on the terrace or inside the a/c dining room. A chalkboard on the wall lists the chef's suggestions of the day, which may include beef tartare, bouillabaisse, stuffed crab, or *St. Jacques au calvados.* You can order wine by the glass or bottle, and choices include some of the *grands crus* from the best vineyards of France. The main courses are priced between 2.400-3.600 CFP. The French *gendarmes* stationed in Moorea eat here.

LE SUD, *Tel. 56.42.95, Pizzeria, Tel. 76.42.40. PK 5.5, seaside on Cook's Bay, Maharepa. MC, V. Open L, D. Tues.-Sat., and D. on Sun. Closed Sun. noon and all day Mon. Free pick-up service from Sofitel to Hilton Resort.*

The décor of this open air unpretentious restaurant is plantation style and the ambience is casual, with occasional evenings of karaoke or live entertainers. Owner Leon is from the South "Le Sud" of France and his cuisine reflects his origins, featuring Provençal style dishes and the flavors of Spain and Italy, with an additional touch of Polynesia. You can order pastas, seafood couscous, paella and tournedos Rossini. He also serves shrimp and chicken curry with coconut, and moule-frites (mussels and fries). Main courses are 1.900-3.500 CFP. You can also order thin-crust pizzas to eat here or take away. Free transfer service does not apply if you order only pizza.

RUDY'S, *Tel. 56.58.00/70.47.47. On mountainside at PK 6 in Maharepa. MC, V. Open daily for dinner only. Free pick-up service. Reserve.*

This Spanish hacienda style restaurant opened in early 2007 featuring fine steaks and seafood, with seating for 50-60 people. Owner Syd Pollock has successfully owned or managed several hotels and restaurants in Moorea and Tahiti since 1968, and is known for his hospitality in receiving and pleasing his guests. Although he is training his son Rodolphe (Rudy) to take over the reigns of the business, Syd is usually on hand to lend a hand and say hello. Rudy's has been voted the #1 restaurant in Moorea by TripAdvisor, and they deserve their great reputation.

Starter courses are priced at 450-1.950 CFP and include garlic bread, French onion soup, goat cheese salad, seafood pasta, snails in puff pastry and lobster ravioli. Fish and seafood dishes are 2.700-4.950 CFP, featuring their signature dish of parrot fish stuffed with crabmeat, for 2.900 CFP. Meats are a specialty at Rudy's, priced at 2.400-3.200 CFP. Choices include beef *bourguignon*, T-bone steak, filet mignon with morilles mushrooms, brandy braised beef ribs, and rack of lamb. The yummy desserts are 850-1.100 CFP and Rudy's has just the right wine to accompany your meal, sold by the glass or bottle. The recorded soft jazz adds to the relaxed ambience, the portions are generous, the food is fantastic and the service is usually fast, with Syd running everywhere at once when the restaurant is full.

Moderate

HOTEL KAVEKA RESTAURANT, *Tel. 56.50.50, PK 7, Maharepa. All credit cards. Open daily for breakfast, lunch and dinner. Courtesy shuttle available. AE, MC, V.*

This spacious overwater restaurant has a fantastic view of Cook's Bay and the peaked mountains that fringe the mirror-like waters of the bay and lagoon. This is an especially agreeable place to cool off during the hot tropical summers, while enjoying a glass of cold beer or a good meal.

To start the day you have a choice of a Parisian breakfast, the Continental buffet or an American breakfast. The luncheon and dinner menu includes an appealing list of appetizers, salads, burgers, sandwiches and pizzas. As well as the fish, seafood and meat dishes, there is a menu of Chinese specialties, such as a combination of nems and sashimi. Burgers and sandwiches are priced at 850-1.950 CFP and the main courses are 1.100-2.850 CFP. They also have a kid's menu. The big wide pier built over the lagoon is an ideal spot for sunset cocktails, which are served from the portable bar. Scottish singer Ron Falconer plays his body harp and harmonica at the Kaveka Restaurant/Bar every Tuesday evening. There is a live traditional band on Fri. and Sat. nights.

ALLO-PIZZA, *Tel. 56.18.22, is on the mountainside at PK 7.8 in Pao Pao, across the road from the French gendarmerie (police station). Open 11am-2pm and 5-9pm Tues.-Sat. Closed all day Sun. and Mon. noon. No credit cards.*

You have a choice of 43 thin crust pizzas cooked in a wood burning pizza oven, which includes salmon pizza and banana pizza, priced from 1.200-1.900 CFP. Be sure to try the homemade chocolate mousse and freshly baked garlic bread. You can eat at the counter or take it to your room. They will deliver a minimum of 2 pizzas to your hotel within the limits of Sofitel Ia Ora Moorea and Hilton Moorea.

BLUE PINEAPPLE (l'ananas bleu), *Tel. 56.12.06. Club Bali Hai Bar, Pao Pao. MC, V. Open daily 7am-3pm and for dinner on Wed. nights. MC, V.*

This waterside restaurant offers an incomparable view of Cook's Bay, yachts in the harbor and pineapple fields on the jagged mountain slopes across the bay. You can start the day with a Continental breakfast, a Spanish omelet, pancakes, or eggs with ham or bacon, accompanied by a glass of fresh pineapple juice. On

Sunday mornings or holidays owner Matahai Hunter prepares a typical Tahitian breakfast of marinated fish with coconut milk, grilled fish, *taioro* (sour coconut sauce with onions), *firi firi* (a figure 8 donut), and coffee flavored with vanilla and sweetened with coconut milk and sugar. Breakfast is 600 CFP-1.900 CFP. For lunch you have a choice of burgers with fries, *poisson cru*, grilled fish, or beef curry, priced from 750-1.750 CFP. They serve soft drinks, juice, a milkshake and even a banana split, as well as beer and wine. The Wed. night BBQ follows the free Tahitian dance show presented by Club Bali Hai. You can order chicken, steak, or seafood kabobs for 1.500-2.400 CFP. Matahai frequently organizes special entertainment featuring popular musicians and dance groups from Tahiti.

RESTAURANT LE MARTINEZ, *Tel. 56.17.71, PK 8.5, mountainside, Cook's Bay, Pao Pao. Open daily except Tues. for L., D. Free pick-up service. AE, MC, V.*

Didier Martinez cooked at Le Sud Restaurant in Maharepa for many years before buying the restaurant in Pao Pao that was formerly called Alfredo's. He has a long menu and specializes in seafood, but the only complimentary reports I have received from local residents were that he makes good Maitai's and his beer is cold. Someone posted on TripAdvisor (in French) that he is a non-pretentious chef who serves very good food. I haven't been there myself.

CHEZ JEAN-PIERRE, *Tel. 56.18.51, PK 9, beside the quay in Cook's Bay, Pao Pao. Open 11:15am-2:30pm and 6:15-9:30pm. Closed Mon. night, all day Wed. and Sun. noon. MC, V.*

The specialty in this non-pretentious waterside restaurant is family style Chinese food, but they also have some French dishes, which are quickly prepared and served in their two dining rooms adjacent to the fishing boat dock at Cook's Bay. The main courses are 1.650-2.450 CFP, and include lemon chicken, mahi mahi with lemon sauce, eggplant stuffed with fish paste, nems, chow mein and chop soy, Chinese *poisson cru*, tofu, braised beef, Mandarin duck and various pork dishes.

Economy to Moderate

CARAMÉLINE, *Tel. 56.15.88, PK 5, Maharepa, in shopping center on mountain side, along with Socredo Banque and the post office. MC, V. Open daily 7am-5pm.*

Here is the ideal place to sit and write your post cards while enjoying something good to eat and drink. You can exchange your dollars at the bank, buy post cards at Kina newsstand, write them at Carameline and mail them at the post office, all in the same small center.

Breakfast is available all day at this popular snack and pastry shop. A Continental breakfast is 1.100 CFP, an American breakfast is 1.750 CFP, and a Tahitian breakfast that includes fish and coconut milk is 2.300 CFP. They serve ham and cheese croissants, quiches and pizzas, hot dogs, burgers, crêpes, and good salads at affordable prices. Poisson cru with coconut milk is 1.500 CFP and the daily luncheon specials start at 1.100 CFP, which may be steak and fries, veal in a white sauce, garlic shrimp or mahi mahi with rice or fries. Along with fresh fruit juices, fresh limeade and Hinano beer, you will also have a good choice of ice creams for 200-400 CFP, 25 flavors of milkshakes for 500 CFP, and a banana split or pineapple split for 990 CFP. Don't forget to check out the pastry counter inside. Service may be slow when the place gets crowded.

Economy

SNACK ROTUI, *Tel. 56.18.16, PK 9.5, beside Cook's Bay, just after Are's Supermarket in Pao Pao. No credit cards. Closed Mon.*

This is the best snack bar on the island, with very fresh food at budget prices. You can sit on a stool at the counter, eat at one of the tables in back or take away a sandwich and soft drink, a *poisson cru*, lemon chicken, or other prepared Chinese dishes served with rice for 700 CFP. Don't resist having a piece of yummy chocolate cake. For 220 CFP you can get a *casse-croûte* (omelet, chow mein, ham and cheese, tuna or ground beef), and the big nems or spring rolls and fried chicken are also good here.

Paopao to Haapiti – Deluxe

HILTON MOOREA LAGOON RESORT & SPA, *Tel. 55.11.11. Arii Vahine Restaurant serves B. & D. daily and L. & D. are also served at Rotui Bar & Grill. Toatea Bar on the pier serves crêpes in the evening. Snacks and cocktails are available in the Eimeo Lounge Bar. All major credit cards.*

In the **Arii Vahine Steackhouse Restaurant** the American breakfast buffet is served from 6:30-10:30am and costs 3.580 CFP. The Sunday morning buffet is 4.200 CFP and includes Tahitian specials as well as the American breakfast. The dinner menu reflects the Executive Chef's passion for preparing cuisine with pronounced Mediterranean influences and a touch of Asia. Some of his favorite culinary creations include steamed parrot fish with green tea sencha, 9-hr. braised lamb shoulder and duck foie gras with passion fruit jelly and cornbread. The à la carte appetizers are 1.700-2.700 CFP, the main course dishes are 2.400-3.900 CFP, vegetarian choices are 1.900-2.400 CFP, and desserts are 1.200-1.500 CFP. A barbecue buffet is presented each Tues. evening for 6.900 CFP, which includes a Polynesian dance show with fire dancing. A special Polynesian buffet on Sat. night is also 6.900 CFP per person, with a traditional dance show and fire dancing from 8-9pm.

Rotui Bar & Grill, beside the Hilton's white sand beach, is open from 11:30am-9:30pm daily except Tues. and Sat. when they close at 6pm because there are special buffets and a dance show in the Arii Vahine Restaurant.

The lunch menu includes really good poisson cru with coconut milk for 1.890 CFP. Other starter courses are 1.290-1.790 CFP, and salads are 990-1.590 CFP. Sandwiches and burgers are 1.390-1.690 CFP, including a Moorea shrimp sandwich. A McLangouste or Mc Spiny Lobster burger contains a whole lobster for

3.190 CFP. The menu of grilled fish, shrimp, chicken and meat is 1.390-1.990 CFP. Desserts for 790-1.150 CFP include crème brûlée with Tahitian vanilla, smooth dark chocolate mousse in coconut crust, a mango sundae, and tasty fruit sorbets. This is one of my favorite restaurants on Moorea. Wine is sold by the glass or bottle and they have Hinano beer on draft.

Toatea Bar is built on the overwater pier nearest the main buildings of the Hilton. While enjoying your meal you can watch the black tip reef sharks, sting rays and colorful fish swimming in the natural aquarium lagoon below. This is the place to be when the romantic full moon rises above the mountains of Moorea. The friendly chef serves Brittany crêpes for 1.500-2.100 CFP, Chef's Special crêpes for 1.900-2.300 CFP, and sweet crêpes for 1.000-1.800 CFP. Open daily 5:30-10pm.

Eimeo Lounge Bar is open daily 5:30-10pm serving your favorite libation. Short drinks include Margaritas, Cosmopolitan, and whisky sour, and the menu of long drinks features Mojito, Pasco sour and Long Island Ice Tea. They also have exotic Polynesian cocktails, which you can sip while watching a glorious sunset from the panoramic terrace. You can also order dry snacks (mini quiches, spicy buffalo wings, Asiatic plate or shrimp cocktail) to accompany your drinks.

INTERCONTINENTAL MOOREA RESORT & SPA, *Tel. 55.19.19. Fare Nui Restaurant is open daily for B., D., and Fare Hana Restaurant is open daily for L. All credit cards.*

Fare Nui Restaurant presents a Continental breakfast from the cold buffet for 3.036 CFP, and the full buffet or American breakfast is 3.702 CFP. Breakfast delivered by outrigger canoe to guests in overwater bungalows is 7.362 CFP per person. The dinner menu features gourmet *à la carte* dining, with starter courses from 1.560-2.690 CFP, barbecue at 2.000-3.100 CFP, and fish and seafood dishes from 2.390-4.880 CFP. Meats are 2.860-3.590 CFP and desserts are 1.200-1.350 CFP. A 2-course lunch is 3.990 CFP and a fixed 3-course dinner menu is 7.706 CFP. Polynesian Night is held each Mon. with a buffet for 7.706 CFP and a dance show. Barbecue Night is held each Wed. beside the swimming pool, accompanied by a Tahitian dance show, for 7.706 CFP. The *Soirée Merveilleuse* on Sat. evening is a gastronomic buffet featuring a variety of fresh seafood, usually served on the beach under the stars, accompanied by A Tahitian dance group. This costs 8.500 CFP. Prices include tax.

Fare Hana Restaurant beside the pool is open daily from 11:30am-9:30pm, serving a luncheon of salads, grilled meats, and Polynesian dishes such as shrimp, tuna, sashimi, and smoked fish. The hamburgers are really good and cost 1.950 CFP-2.590 CFP. Fries are extra. They also serve a Club Sandwich, steak sandwich, and Mahi Mahi sandwich, priced at 1.850-2.290 CFP. A Sunday Buffet lunch is served to the tune of a musical trio.

Motu Oné Bar is a new swim-up bar beside the large infinity pool on the beach. Light meals are served from 11am-8pm and drinks from 8am-10:30pm. Their menu includes salads from 800-1.525 CFP, crêpes, hot dogs, paninis, and sandwiches for 1.450 CFP each. Ice cream, sorbets or a fresh fruit platter are 1.300 CFP.

Non-hotel guests can buy a day-pass for 9.200 CFP that includes a 3-course lunch, a bottle of water or a glass of wine, plus access to the pool, use of a beach towel and deck chair, from 11:30am-5pm.

Motu Iti Bar is an attractive, spacious lounge and sit-down bar in the main building, overlooking the pool and beach. The drink menu lists non-alcoholic cocktails, classic cocktails, and their own cocktails. Here you can order a Sea Breeze, Cucumber Martini, Balsamic Martini, Frozen Mango Margarita or a Strawberry Daiquiri. They also have Hinano beer on tap. Open daily 10am-11pm. **LEGENDS RESORT MOOREA**, Tel. 55.15.15. All major credit cards.

Legends Gourmet is adjacent to reception lounge and is open daily from 7am-8pm, serving a Continental breakfast for 2.200 CFP and a bountiful American breakfast for 2.900 CFP. You can sit on a shaded terrace beside the infinity swimming pool for breakfast, lunch or for sunset cocktails and tapas. Lunch choices are 800-2.300 CFP and include fresh salads, sashimi, tuna tartare or carpaccio, spring rolls, shrimp curry, baked lasagna, and moonfish with pepper berry sauce.

La Villa Des Sens, is near the entrance to Legends Resort and is open for dinner only on Wed.-Sun, from 5-10pm. This gastronomic restaurant features fusion cuisine in an impressive setting that is dominated by a glass wine cellar with more than 120 references to choose from. You can request to be seated at the VIP table or Chef's Table, where you can dine in privacy while enjoying a view of the Chef preparing your meal in the kitchen. The first course choices are priced at 2.200-2.900 CFP and include homemade foie gras cooked torchon-style, served with toasted brioche and balsamic strawberry chutney. The fish and shellfish are 2.850-3.300 CFP and suggest wok-style monkfish with Chinese noodles and shiitake mushrooms sautéed with parsley, or bass cooked on one side and served with lobster bisque and crunchy vegetables. The meat and poultry selections are 2.950-3.600 CFP and give you a choice of rack of lamb, pigeon glazed with Marquesan honey, veal fricassee, or seared beef tenderloin. The gourmet desserts start at 1.200 CFP, and highlight the famous La Villa des Sens warm soufflé with fresh raspberries for 1.400 CFP. It will be difficult to choose just one dessert once you read the menu, which is available on-line at *www.legendsresortvillas.com*. You can also check out the extensive wine list that even includes a Château Lafitte Rothschild 2001, Premier Cru Classé, for 125.000 CFP. Free transfers are provided from/to all hotels on Moorea on reservation.

Superior

AITO RESTAURANT, *Tel. 56.45.52/23.27.63. Beside lagoon at PK 13.1 between Cook's Bay and Opunohu Bay. Closed all day Tues. and at noon on Wed. MC, V. Free pick-up service to some hotels.*

In a previous edition of this book I wrote that every island needs a funky beach-shack restaurant where you can eat deliciously prepared fish served by a "boozy" Corsican, and that Jean-Baptiste Cipriani and his Aito Restaurant play this role in Moorea. I have to scratch the "boozy" part, because he now follows doctor's orders and drinks only non-alcoholic beverages. This restaurant is not for everyone, and I have read some very negative reports about it on TripAdvisor, but everyone I have ever taken here just loved the setting, the food and Jean-Baptiste, who is a real character. Only a few complained about the high prices.

Aito Restaurant is a thatch-covered terrace at the edge of the lagoon. Tall Australian pines (*aito* in Tahitian) shade the small beach and three big *aito* trees grow right through the floor and sagging palm-frond ceiling of the restaurant. A series of Plexiglas windows can be propped open with a stick so you can enjoy the fresh ocean breezes. This is a most delightful place to be on a hot summer's day, when you can feel the trade winds blowing, gaze across the sparkling lagoon to the white line of spume on the reef and watch the gray herons and white fairy terns as they fish nearby.

Vanina, Jean-Baptiste's Tahitian wife, is in charge of the kitchen and makes superb poisson cru, tuna carpaccio and local style fish dishes. The daily specials are listed on a chalk board, which may be Antillaise style stuffed crab, stuffed lobster, carpaccio of korori, poisson cru with fresh coconut milk, shrimp flambéed with pastis, filet of parrot fish, fried or steamed lagoon fish, meka with ginger and soy sauce, tuna cooked with fruit Polynesian style, flambéed slipper lobster (cigale de mer), lobster Rossini with foie gras from Perigourd, or kaveu (coconut crab from Makatea in the Tuamotu Islands). Starter courses are 1.950-2.850 CFP, and the main dishes range from 2.600-4.950 CFP, with the exception of the lobster Rossini and coconut crab, which are available only during certain seasons and are priced accordingly, i.e., 7.650 CFP for the lobster and 8.500 CFP for the kaveu coconut crab.

There is also a printed menu that includes other tempting choices, such as bouillabaisse, and mahi mahi with grated coconut and coconut cream. It takes Jean-Baptiste 10 hours to make the special sauce for his Corsican dishes. He puts small bowls of hot pepper sauce on each table, which he says goes well with the food he serves, accompanied by crunchy baguette bread and butter. It's even better when you wash it down with a spicy Bloody Mary or a bottle of Chardonnay white wine or Corsican Rosé, which is a dry, fruity wine. If you are feeling especially affluent, you may want to order a bottle of champagne for 48.000 CFP!

Desserts may include coconut or banana pie, tarte tatin or a pineapple surprise. The house specialty is the Crêpe Aito. Jean-Baptiste has some interesting after dinner liqueurs you might want to sample, along with a cup of Blue Mountain coffee from Jamaica, for 950 CFP. He also has coffees from Kona, Kenya, Costa Rica, Guatemala, Brazil, Ethiopia, that are 380-420 CFP.

There is musical entertainment on occasion and Jean-Baptiste provides free transfers for lunch or dinner guests staying at the Intercontinental Moorea Resort, Hilton Moorea Lagoon, Club Bali Hai, Kaveka, Moorea Pearl Resort or in family pensions in those areas. Transfers to the Sofitel Ia Ora Moorea Beach Resort are free for a minimum of 4 people.

Economy
   SNACK MAHANA, *Tel. 56.41.70. Beside lagoon at PK 23,200 in Papetoai. Open Mon.-Sat. for lunch only. No credit cards.*
   Heifara is noted for her very good and reasonably priced fish dishes. These include carpaccio, sashimi, tuna tartare, and mahi mahi breaded in coconut with coconut sauce. She also prepares Chinese food and other local style dishes, which are served to guests sitting in her back yard.

West Coast: Haapiti
Superior
   LA PLANTATION, *Tel. 56.45.10, www.laplantationmoorea.com, PK 27, on mountain side just past Le Petit Village in Haapiti. Open 11am-9pm, non-stop service. Closed all day Tues. Free pick-up service to certain hotels. AE, MC, V.*
   This large open-air restaurant has seating for 70 inside and on the covered terrace near the street, which can be quite noisy in the daytime. Refined French cuisine features pan-fried foie gras, as well as crab, lobster, shrimp and other local products prepared with lots of spices. You will also find the Cajun flavor of Louisiana in the Creole gazpacho, crabcake, jambalaya, and roasted crawfish dishes. A Discovery Menu is 4.500 CFP and a Cajun Menu is 5.100 CFP. Desserts include chocolate brownies with vanilla ice cream and maple syrup caramel, or a Plantation Cup with praline vanilla, chocolate, whipped cream and Donatella sauce. Cocktails include drinks with such names as Cajun Bloody Mary, Blue Suede Shoes, Hit the Road Jack, and Soul Man, and there is a varied selection of wines for 2.420-69.270 CFP.
   A simple light menu of salads, poisson cru and sashimi is served in between lunch and dinner for afternoon diners. You can also come to La Plantation for drinks without having to order food. They have a stage and a piano and every other week they feature live entertainment. The music for dancing includes jazz, rock and roll, rhythm and blues and soul music. There is no reggae, techno or local music played here. Free pick-up service is provided for a minimum of 2 people staying at the Intercontinental Moorea and for 4 people staying at the Hilton Moorea Lagoon.
   LE MAYFLOWER, *Tel. 56.53.59, PK 27, Haapiti, seaside; www.restaurant mayflower.com. Open Tues.-Sun. 11:30am-2:30pm and 6:30-10:30pm. Closed all day Mon. and Sat. noon. AE, MC and V.*
   This is the best restaurant in the Haapiti section of Moorea, and for many residents and visitors it is perhaps the choice place to dine out on the island. It is located beside the road next door to Hotel Hibiscus. Laurence and Bertrand Papin are the French owners who chose the name Le Mayflower because Americans identify with that name. The nautical décor includes an old oak barrel, photos of ships, wooden ceiling, walls and floor, brass lights, oil lamps and thick cords of rope. An intimate ambience is added by soft lighting and soft music, live plants, pink tablecloths and fresh flowers on the table.

Bertrand is a young chef from the Loire region of France, whose impressive *haute-cuisine française* has pleased Moorea diners for years, first at Le Cocotier, then at Le Pitcairn restaurant, before he opened his own restaurant. Salads are priced at 950-2.150 CFP; hot appetizers are 1.650-2.300 CFP; fish and seafood dishes are 1.850-2.950 CFP; and meat and poultry choices are 1.950-3.250 CFP. His specialties change nightly, and may include beef Bourguignon for 2.300 CFP, osso bucco Milanaise for 2.300 CFP, or scallops sautéed with Calvados sauce for 2.900 CFP. The *piece de resistance* is lobster ravioli, which is usually available as an appetizer or main dish for 1.900-2.850 CFP. There are also vegetarian dishes for 1.500-1.950 CFP. A child's menu of chicken nuggets and ice cream is 1.200 CFP, and a 3-course tourist menu is 4.200 CFP. Desserts may include crème brûlée for 950 CFP, and profiteroles with hot melted chocolate sauce and whipped cream for 1.050 CFP. Wines are priced from 1.970-17.950 CFP. You can see the entire menu on their website. This is definitely a restaurant worth trying and returning to again and again.

PAINAPO BEACH, *Tel. 28.3370; painapo@mail.pf; is on the seaside at Painapo Beach, PK 33 in Haapiti. Open for lunch Sat.-Sun. 9am-3pm. Closed Mon.-Fri. No credit cards. Must reserve.*

Look for the giant sized tattooed warrior beside the road, and park across the road on the mountainside. This is a good place to spend the day, swimming in the lagoon, petting the stingrays, sunbathing on the white sand beach and enjoying a delicious lunch under the shade of almond trees overlooking the lagoon. Or you can eat inside the big thatched roof dining room with a white sand floor. A platter of *poisson cru*, red tuna sashimi, carpaccio of tuna and tuna tartare makes a nice lunch for two and costs 4.800 CFP. It is served with taro and breadfruit chips and rice. Add a few slices of fresh French baguette and a nice bottle of wine, and you might not even have room for dessert. Other specials include a selection of cooked fish, shrimp, fresh *pahua* (tridacna clams) from the reef or crab with garlic or ginger sauce. You can also order sandwiches, salads and other light meals, as well as drinks, at the thatched roof snack bar beside the road. Ma'a Tahiti (Tahitian food) is served on the last Sunday of each month, accompanied by singer Hauata and her band, whose repertoire includes all the old favorite Polynesian songs of the islands. See more information under *Tahitian Feasts* in this chapter.

Moderate

LES TIPANIERS, *Tel. 56.12.67, PK 25, seaside, Haapiti. Beach Bar Restaurant open daily 7-9:30am and 12-2pm. Main restaurant open daily for dinner 6:30-9:15pm. All credit cards. Best to reserve.*

Although the beach space is limited here, you will usually find groups of French people sunbathing, swimming in the lagoon, participating in a variety of water sports, or reading in the shade. Breakfast and lunch are served in the beachside restaurant. You can order burgers and sandwiches for 980-1.380 CFP, salads from 650 CFP, and pasta from 980 CFP. Fish and grilled meats are 1.800

CFP. Take-away sandwiches are less than 500 CFP. Live Tahitian music at the beach bar each Fri. from 5:45-6:45pm.

Dinner is served in the **GARDEN RESTAURANT**, the main restaurant beside the road. Their friendly staff serves pasta and fine Italian specialties from 980-1.580 CFP, and French dishes such as fish soup for 1.050 CFP and lamb sirloin with goat cheese for 1.980 CFP. The main courses are 1.850-3.250 CFP. Ron Falconer plays the body harp and harmonica and sings Scottish and folk songs, blues and old favorites from the 1970s every other Sat. night, starting at 7pm in the main restaurant.

COCO BEACH SNACK-RESTAURANT, *Tel. 72.57.26*, is located on Motu Tiahura. See information under *Special Activities & Sightseeing Stops Around the Island* in this chapter.

RESTAURANT TIAHURA, *Tel. 56.52.33/26.34.89, PK 25.5 on mountainside, between Les Tipaniers and Le Petit Village in Haapiti. Open for L., D. daily except Wed. Open for Sun. Tahitian breakfast on request. MC, V. Pick-up service to some hotels.*

This is a very popular and friendly local style restaurant that was formerly called Restaurant Irene, named after the Tahitian owner. Irene claims this is the best seafood restaurant on Moorea, and she may have a point. Meals are served on the open-air terrace and inside the restaurant, which may be rather hot during the daytime as this restaurant does not benefit from ocean breezes. Starter courses are 1.300-2.200 CFP, fresh shrimp is 1.750-2.300 CFP, fish dishes are 1.850-2.200 CFP and octopus dishes are 1.800-2.450 CFP. The delicious poisson cru with fresh coconut milk is only 1.300 CFP. A really good choice is the steamed seafood, which is a bamboo basket of mahi mahi, shrimp, scallops, and octopus, served with breadfruit, taro and steamed bananas for 2.500 CFP. She also has chicken and meat choices. Desserts include such delights as fried bananas and ice cream or baked papaya with ice cream.

IGUANE ROCK CAFÉ, *Tel. 56.17.16, PK 26 in Le Petit Village in Haapiti. Open daily with non-stop service from 7am to midnight. Closed Sun. night. MC, V.*

This is an ice cream parlor, bar, snack, pizza parlor and a full service restaurant, with a menu offering French, Tahitian and Chinese foods. The dining rooms can seat 150 people and a special area is provided for children, where they play in security while the parents dine in tranquility. Burgers start at 1.350 CFP and pizzas are 1.300-1.600 CFP. There is a cybercafé with Internet connections in the back corner.

LE SUNSET, *Tel. 56.26.00, PK 27, on the beach at Hotel Hibiscus, Haapiti. MC, V. Open daily for B.,L.,D.*

You can eat pizzas, grilled meats and homemade pastas or sip a cold beer while sitting at a picnic table on the open deck overlooking the white sand beach, the lagoon and the nearby *motu* islets. Or you can sit inside the restaurant and look at the enormous rubber trees that grow at the edge of the hotel's spacious lawn. The food has improved here since the new management took over in 2011, and there are new activities such as live musical entertainment on Thurs. or Fri. evening and a full moon barbecue each month, with a Tahitian singer performing. The menu is quite extensive and includes sandwiches, burgers, thin-crust pizza and salads for lunch or dinner, as well as lasagna, fettuccini and scallops in a vanilla sauce, shrimp and scallops in puff pastry with a saffron sauce, and other fish and meat choices.. The main course dishes are 1.850-3.200 CFP and a 3-course tourist menu is 3.300 CFP. **RESTAURANT PK 0**, *Tel. 22.84.01; www.pkomoorea.com. On lagoon side of road at PK 27,3 in Haapiti. Open for L.,D., daily except Mon. Reserve.*

Julien and Charlotte prepare and serve Japanese and local dishes in this small open-air restaurant. He was trained by a master chef in the fine arts of Japanese cuisine and has a menu that features poisson cru for 1.350 CFP, smoked fish for 1.200 CFP, vegetable and shrimp tempura for 1.850 CFP. Sashimi is 1.100-2.200 CFP. The sushi specialties start at 400 CFP for 2 pieces, or you can order an assortment of 32 pieces for 4.100 CFP. There are donburis made with red tuna, chicken, duck, beef or local shrimp with pineapple, priced at 1.600-2.100 CFP. Desserts are 850-950 CFP and include panna cotta with coconut milk and hibiscus syrup. Entertainment often includes local singers or karaoke.

LE PAPAYER, *Tel. 55.02.50, PK 30, at Tiki Village in Haapiti. AE, MC, V. Open Tues.-Sat. 12-3pm. and 6-10pm. Closed Sun. and Mon.*

This is a good luncheon choice while you are visiting the traditional Tahitian style Tiki Village. The thatched roof open-air restaurant overlooks the lagoon and coral reef, providing a beautiful view as well as good food, served *a la carte*. A mini-show is provided at 1pm by the young dancers and musicians from the Tiki Theatre Village.

A big buffet of Tahitian food and international dishes is served in Le Papayer restaurant each Tues., Wed., Fri. and Sat. evening, when the Tiki Theatre Village dancers and musicians present a spectacular Polynesian show. Please see further information under *Tahitian Feasts* and the *Nightlife & Entertainment* sections of this chapter.

Economy to Moderate

LE MOTU, *Tel. 56.16.70, PK 26, Haapiti, in St. Jacques Center, right across street from ex-Club Med. MC, V. Open Tues.-Sat. 11am-2:30pm and 5-8pm. Closed Sun. and Mon.*

This is a good choice for salads from 1.400-1.900 CFP, crêpes for 300-1.200 CFP, 11 choices of pizzas from 1.000-1.200 CFP. Sashimi, carpaccio of tuna and poisson cru are 1.700 CFP. You can choose from 6 kinds of burgers for 500-540 CFP, and a plate of fries is 450 CFP. Steaks are 1.600-2.100 CFP and daily specials are 1.400 to 1.700 CFP.

Economy

DANIEL'S PIZZA, *Tel. 56.39.95. PK 34.1 seaside, close to Linareva in Haapiti. No credit cards. Open 11am-9pm. Closed Thurs.*

This is where you'll find the best pizza on the island. Daniel gave up his life in Paris, where he was a patissier. Instead of making croissants and brioches, he now cooks excellent pizzas in a wood-fired pizza oven in his garage. He offers 13 choices of pizza priced from 1.300-1.500 CFP. You can sit on a stool and eat at the wooden counter or take your pizza with you. No alcohol is served. Look for his sign beside the road on the seaside just before you get to Residence Linareva.

Other Restaurants, Snacks & Roulottes

Jules et Claudine, a stationary roulotte beside the quay and fish market in Cook's Bay, Pao Pao. Quality of food varies but is usually good. **Motu Iti**, *Tel. 55.05.20*, Restaurant for Pension Motu Iti at PK 13.2 in Pihaena. B., L., D. Salads, pizzas and local style meals. **Le Miri Miri**, *Tel. 56.51.99*. A restaurant and café in Le Petit Village in Haapiti. Open Tues.-Thurs. 8am-5pm and on Fri.-Sat. until 10pm. **A l'Heure du Sud Roulotte**, a stationary roulotte on mountainside between Le Petit Village and La Plantation restaurant. Very good choice of burgers, casse-croûtes and paninis with fries at 450-700 CFP. **Snack Coco d'Isle**, *Tel. 56.59.07*. On lagoon side at PK 27.5, Haapiti. Good food, good prices. Closed Sun. Pizza, chow mein, special Backpacker, Globetrotter or Surfer plates. **La Paillotte**, a stationary roulotte on mountain side, opposite Restaurant PK 0 in Haapiti. Provençal style rotisserie chicken and rosemary herbed potatoes to go. **Chez Teina**, *Tel. 56.29.29*. Restaurant/snack at PK 13,200 on seaside in Maatea. Open L.,D. Closed Mon. Chinese food for 1.100-1.300 CFP a plate. Eat here or takeout.

Tahitian Feasts

TIKI THEATRE VILLAGE, *Tel. 55.02.50, PK 30, Haapiti, AE, MC, V.*

A big buffet of Tahitian food, as well as grilled meats and fish, is served in Le Papayer Restaurant each Tues., Wed., Fri. and Sat. evening, when the Tiki Theatre Village dancers and musicians present a spectacular Polynesian show, complete with fire dancing. The *ahima'a* underground oven is opened as part of the cultural visit through the village. Even if you don't like the looks or tastes of Tahitian food, there are other, more familiar choices of foods served. The total price for unlimited welcome punch, the dinner buffet with all the house wine you want, a guided visit through the Tiki Village and a dance show with 60 performers is 9.950 CFP. A round trip bus transfer from the airport, the boat dock or any hotel on the island is 1.250 CFP.

PAINAPO BEACH, *Tel. 28.33.70, on the seaside at Painapo Beach Village, PK 33 in Haapiti. No credit cards. Reserve.*

A Tahitian feast is served buffet style at noon on the last Sunday of each month, and it is best to telephone and reserve in advance. All the traditional favorites are included: *poisson cru* with coconut milk, *pua'a chou* (a pork stew with cabbage and carrots), *poulet fafa* (chicken and taro leaves with coconut milk), roast breadfruit, *fei*, (mountain plantains), cooked bananas, sweet potatoes, taro and tarua (root vegetables), baked fish, roast pig, *po'e* (a sweet dish with coconut milk and bananas, papaya or pumpkin), and both fresh and fermented coconut milk sauces to dip your food into. *Fafaru* (a stinky but good marinated fish once you've acquired the taste for it) is also on the buffet table, covered with a plate to hold the smell inside. This excellent food costs 3.500 CFP per person and you can go back for seconds if you wish to. You can eat outdoors under the shade of almond trees or inside the thatched roof dining area with a sand floor. A Tahitian band and singer perform while you enjoy your ma'a Tahiti.

INTERCONTINENTAL MOOREA RESORT & SPA, *Tel. 55.19.19. All major credit cards.* Polynesian Night is held each Mon. evening in the Fare Nui Restaurant, with a buffet for 7.706 CFP and a dance show of Tahitian songs and dances.

MOOREA PEARL RESORT & SPA, *Tel. 55.17.50. All credit cards.* A Polynesian buffet is held in the Mahanai Restaurant each Wed. night for 7.500 CFP, followed by a Polynesian dance show of Hirinaki's all-female troupe performing to recorded music.

SOFITEL MOOREA BEACH RESORT, *Tel. 55.12.12, PK 2, Temae. All major credit cards.* The Tahitian underground oven is opened at 6:30pm each Thurs. evening and a Polynesian buffet of Tahitian food is served in Restaurant Pure, followed by a Polynesian dance show at 7:30pm, which sometimes includes fire dancing. The cost of 7.100 CFP per person is for the food and show only.

HILTON MOOREA LAGOON RESORT & SPA, *Tel. 55.11.11. All major credit cards.* A special Polynesian buffet is served at 7pm each Sat. night in the Arii Vahine Restaurant, followed by a traditional dance show of Polynesian songs, dances and fire dancing from 8-9pm. Cost is 6.900 CFP per person.

SEEING THE SIGHTS

Look for the **PK** (*poste kilometre*) markers on the mountainside of the road, which are placed one km (.62 mi.) apart. The signs are in concrete in the shape of Moorea, which resembles a heart. PK 0 is located at the old post office in **Temae**, close to the airport road. If you're coming from the airport and turn right onto the circle island road, you'll soon see the PK 1 marker opposite Lake Temae, which was actually a swamp filled with nonos (stinging flies) before the golf course was built. You can see the Moorea Green Pearl Golf Course on both sides of the road.

The distance markers continue on around the northwest coast to the village of **Haapiti** to PK 35, and then there's a gap in the numbering system. Here you'll want to photograph the **Mou'a Roa** and **Tohive'a mountains** that rise in the distance behind the soccer field. On the seaside is a Protestant Church. The next marker you'll see will be PK 24, where another lovely landscape of the mountains is visible from the courtyard of the Catholic Church, **Eglise de la Saint Famille**. The PK numbers then descend from PK 24 to PK 4, where you'll find the Ferry dock at **Vaiare Bay**, and then on down to PK 0, where you'll see the old Temae post office again. The newer post office is in the commercial center of **Maharepa** at PK 5.

At the end of Opunohu Bay at PK 18 you can leave the circle island road and turn left onto a partially paved inland road that passes through the **Opunohu Valley**. Here you will see horses, cows, sheep and goats grazing in verdant green pastures under the shadow of Moorea's sacred **Rotui Mountain**. There is an agricultural school in this valley and the students look after the livestock. Beside this road, in a forest of *mape* Tahitian chestnut trees, are restored *marae* temples of stone and ancient archery platforms, where the Maohi chiefs and priests used to worship and play. **Le Belvedere** is a popular destination at the top of a steep and winding road, and from the **Lookout Point**, at the end of a torturous road, you have the visual pleasure of **Cook's Bay** and **Opunohu Bay** far below, which are separated by Mt. Rotui. You continue on along the *route des ananas* (the pineapple road), where you'll see the mountain slopes of Pao Pao valley covered with pineapple plantations. Forests of mahogany, teak, acacia and mangoes border the rutted red dirt road, which leads you back to the circle island road at PK 9 in the village of **Pao Pao**.

Land Tours

The **Circle Island Tour** takes you by minivan or large bus on a 3.5 to 4-hr. voyage along the coastal road, winding around Cook's Bay and Opunohu Bay and inland to the Opunohu Valley, with stops at the *marae* of Titiroa and the other Polynesian stone temples and archery platforms in this area, the Belvedere Lookout, pineapple fields, vanilla plantation, and to the Moorea Fruit Juice Factory & Distillery, where you can taste different liqueurs made with the fruits of Moorea. This tour sells for 3.500 CFP up.

The **Mountain Safari Tours** and **Photo Safari Excursions** are also usually half-day tours, varying according to the guides, which sell for 4.000-6.000 CFP. In addition to the sights and sites mentioned above, these 4WD excursions also take you off the main road to discover groves of oranges and pamplemousse (grapefruit), gardens of lush tropical fruits, medicinal plants, rosewood, tamanu, coffee plantations, soft green meadows and a jungle undergrowth of ferns and bamboo. The highlight of this excursion is a visit to the waterfalls of Afareaitu, which includes a 15-min. hike uphill and a refreshing splash under the cascade of water. You will discover Moorea from the mountain to the sea and learn all about the history, culture and daily lives of the people of Moorea.

Here are some of the companies and guides who will be happy to show you Moorea:

Albert Transport & Activities, *Tel. 55.21.10/55.21.11; www.albert-transport.net.* This family business was established in 1962 and is the oldest operating tour company on Moorea. Albert Haring's guides include his sons, who grew up in the tour business. They provide a combined circle island tour and interior island tour by a/c bus with shopping at their family-owned Heivai pearl boutique. 4WD safari tours, private VIP tours, transfers and taxi service are also available, as well as rental cars and scooters.

Hiro's Tours/What To Do On Moorea, *Tel. 78.70.10/22.56.18; wtdmoorea@mail.pf; www.hirotour.com.* Hiro Kelley provides 4-hour photo safari tours by 4WD, lagoon excursions with a shark show, ray feeding and dolphin stop, or a barbecue picnic with open bar on a motu, which also includes a cruise of two bays and a snorkeling stop. Special Land & Sea combinations are also available. Hiro's guides speak English and know the history and legends of Moorea. Free pick-up included.

Inner Island Safari Tours, *Tel. 56.20.09/78.70.88/72.84.87; Fax 56.34.43;inner-saf@mail.pf.* Alex and Ghislaine Mahotu operate half-day inner island photo tours in a/c and open jeeps. They also take you to "Magic Mountain," where you will climb the side of a crater for a 360-degree view. Be sure to bring your camera. These are very well informed guides, who speak good English. Ghislaine also provides taxi service between hotels.

Julienne's Safari Tours Moorea, *Tel. 78.65.40; juliennesafari@hotmail.fr.* A 3 1/2-hr. Opunohu Tour is 4.000 CFP and takes you to the Belvedere lookout, to the marae sites, the agricultural school, pineapple fields and to the Moorea Tropical Garden for free jam and vanilla tasting. A 5-hr. circle island tour is 6.000 CFP and includes the Opunohu sites plus a visit to the Moorea Dolphin Center, Moorea Fruit Juice factory, Le Petit Village, and a stop at the Toatea Viewpoint looking toward the island of Tahiti.

Moorea Explorer, *Tel. 56.12.86; Fax 56.25.52; www.mooreatransport.com* (under renovation). Moorea Transport has a big fleet of Explorer yellow buses, vans and 4WD vehicles, all decorated with fish. You'll see them everywhere on the island. They'll take you on a half-day circle island tour (Belvedere) by a/c bus, or you can sign up for the off-road half-day safari tour by 4WD. They also offer private safari and sunset safari tours, as well as a special shopping tour at Le Petit Village.

Torea Nui Transport & Safari, *Tel. 56.12.48/76.81.31; enttoreanui@mail.pf; www.toreanui.com.* They offer a half-day 4WD safari tour for 4.000 CFP, bus tours around the island, lagoon tours with a picnic and a dinner show at Tiki Village. They also operate a transfer service for only 700 CFP per person (min. 2 people), providing daily transportation service from the airport or ferry dock to your hotel, or from your hotel to other locations on the island. You must reserve one week in advance for this service. See additional information under *Tour & Transport Companies* in this chapter.

Special Activities & Sightseeing Stops Around the Island

Agricultural Lycée of Opunohu has a Fare Boutique, *Tel. 56.11.34, www.etablissement-opunohu.com.* On the right as you drive up the mountain to visit Le Belvedere. In addition to tasting the delicious fresh fruit juices, you can buy their vanilla and coffee beans, dried bananas, crystallized fruits, homemade jams and hand-painted *pareos.* You can also visit the high school farm and see the vanilla plantations, greenhouse, tropical orchards and vegetable gardens. The Fare Boutique has maps of three discovery walkways that will take you along marked paths for hikes of 1-2 hrs. for each choice. Open Mon.-Thurs. 8am-4:30pm, on Fri. 8am-3:30pm, and on Sat. 8am-2:30pm. If you want to hike a trail be sure to arrive at least 2 hours before closing time.

Moorea Fruit Juice Factory and Manutea Tahiti, *Tel. 55.20.00*, on the mountainside at PK 12 in Cook's Bay. Boutique open Mon.-Fri. 8:30am-4:30pm and Sat. 9am-4pm. Visit distillery Mon.-Thurs. You can taste the various liqueurs, including the prize-winning ginger brandy, and you can take home Rotui fruit juices, Paina Colada (*paina* means «drunk» in Tahitian), chocolate and coconut liqueur, Tahiti Drink rum punch, bottles of Tahitian rum and a whole range of Tahiti-Manutea confections and candies made with local fruits.

Moorea Tropical Garden, *Tel. 70.53.63; www.tgardenmoorea.centerblog.net.* Look for the sign on the mountainside at PK 16 in the Vaihere area of Opunohu Bay, and you will find Moorea Tropical Garden at the top of a steep concrete road. This is a family operated business that opened in Sept. 2010. You can visit the vanilla greenhouse and learn all about the vanilla plant and how to cross-pollinate or "marry" the vanilla flower. After walking through the gardens of tropical fruits and colorful flowers, you should visit the sales *fare* and sample some of the homegrown products. There are fruit juices, jams, dried fruits and sorbets, as well as local crafts and postcards. From this height you will have a marvelous view of Opunohu Bay and the Ta'areu Pass.

Nature House of Mou'a Roa, *Tel. 56.58.62; www.lamaisondelanature.com*, is located in the Vaianae Valley between Haapiti and Atiha. You turn off the circle island road at PK 21 (there is a sign) and walk up the valley until you come to the big colonial house that was built in 1900. It is surrounded by lush green foliage and tropical flowers and twin rivers flow through the property. Be sure to sample the farm's homemade organic jams, honey and fruit pies. Phone ahead if you want to stay for lunch or spend the night. You may even want to participate in one of the sports activities organized by Bernard Genton. These include archery, rope rappelling down to the river, mountain skating, riding mountain bikes and hiking. A 4WD Photo Safari takes you into the heart of Vaianae valley. Morning and afternoon departures daily.

Coco Beach Snack-Restaurant, *Tel. 72.57.26*, was formerly called **Restaurant La Plage** or **Motu Moea**. This rustic style restaurant is located on Motu Tiahura, across the channel from Les Tipaniers and the ex-Club Med beach. You can spend a few hours snorkeling in the coral gardens, enjoying the private white sand beach or lounging in a hammock under the shady trees in this privileged setting. It is open Wed.-Sun., from 11am to sunset. There are 10 or more outside tables with umbrellas, a thatched hut for shade and a small outbuilding for toilets. Many of the delicious dishes are prepared on the outside barbecue. These include mahi mahi, shrimp, grilled chicken, and entrecôte steak, all served with salad and fries, priced at 1.950-2.200 CFP. They have a child's menu. There are also 2 daily specials, as well as sandwiches and burgers, poisson cru and tuna tartare. You can even order a fancy cocktail or an expensive bottle of wine from "the cave". A boat shuttle from the Coco Beach pontoon to the motu is 700 CFP per adult and 500 CFP per child. Or they will pick you up at one of the nearby boat docks on request. **Maiau Beach**, *Tel. 70.78.58*, is on Motu Moea (Motu Tiahura). A private section of the white sand beach has been transformed into a protected environment where individuals, organized groups, clubs or associations can spend the day on the beach, take a private snorkeling tour, sunset cruise or enjoy a feast of *ma'a Tahiti* cooked in an underground *ahima'a* oven. Bill Gates celebrated his 40th birthday here in Nov. 2005, along with Paul Allen and 22 other guests from Allen's super yacht. Maire and Jean-Pierre transfer their clients from the beach at Hotel Les Tipaniers to their private paradise, where you will find lounge chairs, an ice chest, refrigerator, barbecue grill, and picnic tables. This is not a snack or restaurant, but they do have bottled water and ingredients for a barbecue.

Tahiti Arome, *Tel. 56.14.51*, is at PK 26 in Haapiti, behind the Royal Tahiti Noni factory. Open Mon.-Thurs. 8:30am-3:30pm. The botanical gardens here contain the largest plantation of Tiare Tahiti in French Polynesia, as well as 50 species of plants used throughout the world in the manufacture of cosmetics and perfumes. Here you will see how the vanilla orchids are "married" and learn about the healing powers of tamanu oil.

Temae Beach is where the locals go to swim, play games on the beach and in the water and have picnics on the white sand. A good surfing spot is located nearby. This is also the starting or ending point for outrigger canoe races, international marathons and other big events. There are public toilets and showers, as well as trashcans, but unfortunately, the whole area gets littered during busy holidays or long weekends. Turn off the circle island road across from the old post office at PK 0, and follow the dirt road for about one km, bearing left where you see a fork, and you can park in the shade across from the public park. This beach connects with the private beach fronting the Sofitel Ia Ora Moorea Beach Resort, which is off-limits to the public.

Ta'ahiamanu Beach is better known as **Maretto Beach**, and is located in Opunohu Bay. This public beach provides a beautiful spot for sunbathing and swimming. There are several picnic tables with benches shaded by graceful old tamanu trees. A sailing school and cruising yachts anchored in the turquoise lagoon add to the charm of this popular site.

NIGHTLIFE & ENTERTAINMENT

Tiki Village Theatre, *Tel. 55.02.50*, at PK 30 in Haapiti, is a unique cultural and folkloric center that you can visit by day or four evenings a week. From 11am-3pm on Tues. through Sat. you can spend the day for 5.000 CFP. Multilingual guides will lead you through the village of thatched roof traditional style Tahitian huts, and explain how the ancient Tahitians built their homes and meeting houses. You will see demonstrations of tattooing, how to carve tikis from stone, how to sculpt wooden bowls, weave a hat, and make a floral crown. You will learn how to tie-dye a pareo that you get to keep. You will see an exhibition of Tahitian dance costumes, visit a replica of Paul Gauguin's house of pleasure to admire the reproductions of his paintings, and visit the Sylvain *fare* that contains black and white photos of Tahiti of Yesteryear.

You can taste Tahitian culinary specialties while enjoying lunch in Le Papayer restaurant. You will be offered a fresh tropical fruit cocktail, a main course, or dessert. The Tiki Village dancers will then perform a mini-dance show at 1pm.

In the afternoon you can swim and snorkel in the lagoon, sunbathe on the beach, or take an outrigger canoe ride to visit a black pearl farm in the lagoon. You can also browse around in the Tiki Village boutique and Virgin's black pearl shop. For an extra charge you can have a half-hour Tahitian dancing class. Another option at extra cost is an exotic massage with perfumed monoi oil in the floating *fare*.

Each Tues., Wed., Fri. and Sat. evening the 60 dancers and musicians at the Tiki Theatre Village present a Polynesian extravaganza. The program begins at 6pm with a welcome fruit drink or rum punch. You will be immersed in the culture and tradition of Polynesia, with demonstrations of arts and crafts and dancing techniques. After the opening of the *ahima'a* underground oven a bountiful buffet is set out, featuring Tahitian specialties, Continental cuisine, barbecued fish, chicken and meats, along with a salad bar and dessert table. Be sure to sample the delicious fried coconut beignets.

While you are enjoying your meal you'll be treated to a very lively demonstration of how to wear the pareo. After dinner the big show gets underway at 9pm in the open-air theater with a white sand floor. This spectacular dance show includes several fire dancers, all muscular men with beautiful tattoos. Everyone here works very hard and puts all their energy and enthusiasm into entertaining you. I highly recommend this Great Polynesian Revue. The cost of the buffet dinner, all the punch you want, as much wine as you wish to drink during dinner, plus the extravaganza show, is 9.950 CFP. The cost of seeing the show without dinner is 4.950 CFP, plus a round-trip transfer charge of 1.250 CFP.

Hotel Hibiscus, Tel. 56.12.20/56.26.00. Each month they have a Full-Moon Party with a buffet on the beach and music provided by Tahitian singer Hauata, and her Kaina Trio. They also have Happy Hour with live music on Fridays, and Jazz evenings on some Sundays.

La Plantation, *Tel. 56.45.10*, in Haapiti has musical evenings several times a month.

Legends Resort, Tel. 55.15.15, organizes special musical evenings on a regular basis, with performers from various countries.

Le Kaveka, *Tel. 56.50.50*, has a traditional Tahitian musical group every Fri. and Sat. evening. On Tues. evenings **Ron** plays the auto harp and harmonica and sings songs from the 1960s and 1970s, plus a little country and Celtic folk songs. You can also catch Ron's act at **Les Tipaniers**, *Tel. 56.12.67*, every other Sat. night, and he performs occasionally at various other restaurants on Moorea.

Le Miki Miki at the **Moorea Green Pearl Golf Course Club House**, *Tel. 56.26.70*, has live entertainment and music for dancing every Fri. evening. **PK 0**, *Tel. 22.84.01*, has live bands performing frequently. **Restaurant Aito**, *Tel. 56.45.52*, has live musical performers and karaoke evenings according to number of reservations.

Several of the larger hotels have barbecues, special theme evenings and Tahitian feasts, followed by Tahitian dance shows. The regular events are listed for each hotel in the *Where to Stay* section of this chapter. More entertainment is added during the high seasons of July-August and for the Christmas-New Year holidays.

SPORTS & RECREATION
All Terrain Vehicle/Quad
ATV Fun Tours, *Tel. 74.62.05/55.21.11; www.albert-atv.com*. This is one of the many activities provided by the enterprising family of Albert Haring, who also have 4x4 Safaris, Wave Runner Tours, Jet Ski Tours, Moana Lagoon Tours, Picnics on the Motu, Private Boat Tours, Taxi and Transfer Service, and combinations of land and lagoon tours. Karl is the youngest son of Albert Haring, and he operates the ATV Fun Tours. He leads a maximum of 7 couples on his shiny red Quads, which are just like the ones used by ATV Moorea Tour. His excursions are for 3 hours and cost 17.000 CFP for rider and passenger, and he takes you to the same places described below. He also provides free pick-up service. Which company to choose? Karl gets good comments on TripAdvisor, but I know that ATV Moorea Tour is also busy year-round, because I watch them go past my house twice a day. Or maybe that's Karl's tours. I cannot tell the difference because the Quads are the same.

ATV Moorea Tour, *Tel. 56.16.60/70.73.45; www.atvmoorea.com*. Located at PK 24.6 in Tiahura, across road from Intercontinental Moorea Resort. Free pick-up. The 6 Bombardier Can Am Outlander ATV Max 400 Quads are especially built for 2 people. A 2 1/2 hr. Discovery Tour with guide is 12.000 CFP for the driver, plus 2.000 CFP for a passenger. A 3 1/2 hr. Adventure Raid takes you on the Discovery Tour plus the pineapple plantations and up to the Bounty Plateau for a clear view of Moorea's mountain chain. Then you will visit Magic Mountain in the center of the volcano for a 360° view. This tour is 19.000 CFP for driver plus 2.000 CFP for passenger. Private VIP tours can be organized.

Golf
Moorea Green Pearl Golf Course Polynesia, *Tel. 56.27.32; www.mooreagolf-resort.com*. Open daily 7:30am-5pm. This Jack Nicklaus Design golf course lies on both sides of the circle island road between Moorea's airport and the village of Temae. There are 18-holes, par 70, and it is 6,676 yards long. A tunnel under the road allows golf carts to circulate from the lagoon to the mountain side of the course. There is a clubhouse with a restaurant and bar, a pro shop, driving range on the lake, putting green and chipping green.

The overall golf course project is spread out over nearly 165 hectares (408 acres) of land with 650m. (2,132 ft.) of white sand beach. The original plans included adding a 150-room 5-star hotel to be managed by the Warwick chain, plus a 3-star 130-room hotel and a complex of 115 residential villas. These projects are still on the back burner due to the economic depression that began in 2008, the year the construction was supposed to begin.

The pro shop is open daily from 7:30am to 5:30pm. You can rent clubs, golf balls, shoes, caddies and golf carts. Green fees are 6.000 CFP for 9 holes and 10.000 CFP with a golf cart. An 18 hole green fee with golf cart is 18.000 CFP, and a practice bucket of balls is 700 CFP. Professional golf lessons are also available. Private lessons are 2.500 CFP for 30 min. and 4.000 CFP for 1 hr. Free shuttle service is provided from all hotels, boat docks and the airport.

The Miki Miki Restaurant is open for lunch Tues.-Sun. and for dinner on Wed., Thurs., Fri., and Sat. Closed Sun. night, all day Mon. and Tues. night. The bar is open daily from 10am. Musical parties are held each Fri. evening, with a DJ, or live band, or dinner-dance shows. See more information under *Where to Eat* in this chapter.

Hiking

Opunohu Agricultural College has opened three circular trails that you can walk alone or with a guide, where you can see the work of the school students and explore one section of the Opunohu domain. A small brochure with the detailed notes on the plant life on the trails is available in four languages (French, English, German and Spanish). Ask for information on guided tours at the Fare Boutique on the right side of the road leading to Le Belvedere lookout.

Moorea Hiking - Hiro Hiking Moorea, *Tel. 79.41.54; hirohiking@gmail.com.* Hiro Damide and his guides operate half-day hikes through the agricultural trails in Opunohu Valley, including the Marae Titiroa, the Belvedere lookout, the Three Pines, and Three Coconut Trees. The hikers are served fresh pineapple, *pamplemousse* (grapefruit) and other fruits, and the cost is 5.250 CFP, including taxes. Hiro also leads all-day hikes into the Opunohu Valley, 18-23 km. (11-14 mi.) hikes across the island from Vaiare to Haapiti, following the trail of the ancient Polynesians. The full-day hike costs 7.350 CFP and includes a picnic lunch. Mountain climbing expeditions up Rotui Mountain and Mou'a Puta, the mountain with the hole in the top can also be arranged.

Polynesian Adventure, *Tel./Fax 43.25.95, cell 77.24.37; polynesianadv@mail.pf.* Vincent Dubousquet is a specialized professional guide who will accompany you on a day's hike to walk across the mountains of Moorea from Vaiare to Pao Pao or to visit the Three Coconut Trees pass. These are easy to medium level walks for a minimum of four people and each hike costs 7.200 CFP per person. He will take you for a day's hike to Mou'a Puta or Rotui Mountain, or to cross Moorea from Haapiti to Vaiare, walking over two passes. You should be in good physical condition and fit for these hikes, which also require a minimum of four people. Each hike costs 9.300 CFP per person. The above rates do not include taxes, food and drinks and boat transfers from Tahiti. Bring a casse-croûte sandwich and water.

Tahiti Evasion, *Tel./Fax 689/56.48.77, cell 70.56.18; www.tahitievasion.com.* Michel Veuillet is the guide who will take you into the green sanctuary of Moorea's valleys and mountains for half- or full-day treks. He will introduce you to the archaeological sites in the Opunohu Valley, the pineapple fields and the Three Coconut Trees pass. This is an easy 2.5- to 3-hour hike for 4.500 CFP. A medium level hike takes you to the *marae* temples and the *mape* (chestnut tree) forests of Opunohu Valley and then to the Three Coconut Trees pass. This 3- to 3.5-hour trek is 4.500 CFP.

An all-day hike takes you to the waterfalls in Afareaitu and on to Mou'a Puta, the mountain with a hole in the top. From this height you will have a magnificent 360-degree view of the island of Moorea and you can also see Tahiti from here. You must be in good physical condition and not subject to vertigo to attempt this climb. A minimum of 2 people is required and transfers are included for the cost of 8.000 CFP per person.

Hiking Discovery, *Tel. 70.73.31; tamislands.discovery@mail.pf.* Heinrich Tamatoa Salmon leads private hiking tours on Moorea. A half-day tour will take you to the archaeological sites in Opunohu Valley and to the Three Pines Pass, to the Three Coconuts Pass, or to the waterfalls in Afareaitu, for 4.500 CFP per person. A full-day hike is 8.000 CFP and takes you to the big loop of Three Pines in Opunohu Valley, across the Vaiare caldera and archaeological path, and to the pierced mountain, Mou'a Puta.

Horseback Riding

Opunohu Valley Ranch, *Tel. 56.28.55/78.42.47; ranch_opunohu_valley@yahoo.fr* is located on the *route des ananas* (pineapple road) in Opunohu Valley, on the right side of the road past the turn-off for Le Belvedere, 2 km (1.2 mi.) from the circle island road at Opunohu Bay. Terai Maihi leads guided excursions for a maximum of 8 riders through mountain trails and into the valley, passing the river, forests of Tahitian chestnut trees (*mape*) and pineapple plantations. The morning ride is from 8:30-10:30am and the afternoon ride is from 2:30 to 4:30pm. Closed on Sun. afternoon and all day Mon. Free hotel pick-up.

Helicopter Tours

Tahiti Helicopter Service, *Tel. 50.40.75; www.tahiti-helicopters.com.* A 5-seat "Squirrel" Ecureuil helicopter has a 35-min. circuit of Moorea starting from the Tahiti-Faa'a Airport, priced at 46.200 CFP per person for 4/5 passengers, and 64.500 CFP per person for 2 passengers. A 15-min. flight-seeing tour of Moorea starting and ending at the Moorea Airport is 39.900 CFP per person for 4/5 passengers.

Nautical Activities Centers

    Intercontinental Moorea Resort, *Tel. 55.19.19.* You'll find a variety of interesting activities here, which are available to hotel guests and anyone else who wants to explore the lagoon. In addition to snorkeling, windsurfing, scuba diving, day sailing, parasailing, fishing, lagoon tours, and pedal boat rentals, you can also get a round-trip boat transfer to a *motu* for 1.060 CFP, or rent a 5-passenger Spyder boat with captain for 18.060 CFP for 1 hr. A self-piloted boat with a 4 HP engine is 7.350 CFP for 2 hrs., and 9.450 CFP for 4 hrs. You can rent a jet-ski or wave-runner with a guide for 9.820 CFP for 1/2 hr. or 15.400 CFP for 1 hr., water-ski for 3.500 CFP for a 10-minute tour, join a snorkeling and ray-feeding expedition in the lagoon for 4.500 CFP, take a sunset cruise for 4.500-6.500 CFP, view the coral gardens through the windows of a self-piloted glass bottom boat for 8.250 CFP, or through an Aquablue diving helmet as you Aqua-Walk on the bottom of the lagoon for 7.500 CFP. You can also rent a talking snorkel for a 40-min. excursion in the lagoon.

    Moorea Pearl Resort, *Tel. 55.17.50.* Hotel guests can use the snorkeling equipment, kayaks and outrigger canoes free of charge. You can rent jet skis and small motorboats to self-pilot without a license. A boat excursion to visit the two bays with ray-feeding includes a picnic on the motu for 6.400 CFP. Water-skiing is 5.000 CFP for beginners, and 4.300 CFP for certified; a sunset cruise is 5.910 CFP and a sunset sailing cruise for 4-6 people is 6.500 CFP each. Other nautical activities include Jet-ski tours, Aquablue helmet dives, picnics on the motu, deep-sea fishing trips, dolphin and whale watching excursions, and scuba diving with Moorea Blue Diving, which is located on the premises.

    Hilton Moorea Lagoon Resort, *Tel. 55.11.11.* Guests staying in the hotel have free use of the snorkeling equipment, kayaks and outrigger paddle canoes. A Jet Ski with guide is 10.300 CFP for 30 min. or 16.200 CFP for 1 hr. Water-skiing for a certified skier is 3.000 CFP for 10 min. A speedboat with pilot is 18.900 CFP per hour, a circle island boat tour with ray feeding and a stop on the motu is 8.200 CFP, a circle island tour with ray feeding and a picnic on the motu is 11.900 CFP, or you can go directly to the motu at 9:45am for the picnic and return to the hotel at 2:30pm for 8.100 CFP. A half-day deep-sea fishing charter for 1-6 people is 18.700 CFP each, and a private fishing charter is 74.800 CFP for a half-day outing. A romantic sailing sunset cruise with cocktail is 7.280 CFP, and a private sunset cruise with cocktail is 75.600 CFP. TOPDIVE-Bathys has a scuba dive center on the premises.

    Sofitel Ia Ora Moorea Beach Resort, *Tel. 55.12.12.* The Fare Nautique is open daily from 7:30am-5pm. They rent bicycles, pedal boats, sea trailers, small boats with or without a license, Jet-skis, windsurf boards, Hobie cats, sea kayaks, water skiing and wake-boards. Snorkeling gear is free for hotel guests. They can also arrange boat tours to a motu for a picnic, day-sailing, deep-sea fishing, scuba diving, and dolphin watch tours.

Tip'Nautic, *Tel. 78.76.73*; *tipnautic@mail.pf,* is a nautical base located at Hotel Les Tipaniers. You can rent snorkeling gear, kayaks, stand up paddle boards, underwater sea trailers for 4.000 CFP for 2 hours, and underwater cameras for 4.000 CFP. You can also catch a boat transfer to the motu for 700 CFP; join a lagoon excursion to discover the sharks, rays and underwater tikis for 4.000 CFP; or pay 7.500 CFP for a discovery of the two bays; go on a dolphin watch (and see humpback whales during their annual visit) for 8.000 CFP; or take a sunset cruise for 6.000 CFP per person.

Boat Rentals, Glass Bottom Boat, Kayaks, Cata-Jet, Jet-Ski and Wave Runners
Albert Wave Runners, *Tel. 78.46.60/30.52.22.* This popular jet-ski tour is operated by the Albert Haring family who also provide several other land and lagoon excursions as well as taxi service, transfers and rental cars and scooters. A 2-hr. Jet Ski tour is 22.000 CFP for 1-2 people, and a unique 3-hr. tour takes you around the island by Jet Ski for 26.000 CFP for 1-2 people.
Glass Bottom Boat, *Tel. 74.32.50; glassbottomboatmoorea@hotmail.com.* Tuatini Activities Moorea excursions depart from the beach at Hotel Hibiscus. The glass bottom boat tour operates daily at 9:30am and costs 4.500 CFP for 2 1/2-3 hrs, which includes ray feeding. A sunset cruise with Maitai punch is 5.500 CFP. They can organize picnics or a Tahitian feast for groups on Maiau Beach, and private tours for snorkeling and ray feeding. Transfers to the motu are 700 CFP per person.
Moorea Jet Ski Tours, *Tel. 77.02.19; halfon@mail.pf; www.tahiti-jetski.com.* Jean-Pierre Halfon has 2-hour Bombardier Seadoo jet ski tours to visit Cook's Bay and Opunohu Bay, the dolphins, rays and sharks. Excursions start at 9.500 CFP for 30 minutes.
Moorea Locaboat, *Tel. 78.13.39/30.05.04; moorealocaboat@mail.pf* is located on the beach at Moe Moea (Fare Condominium). Open daily 8am-5pm. Isabelle and Vanessa have small boats with a 6 HP engine that you can rent without a license. Rates start at 5.500 CFP for one hour, gas included. Transfer service provided.
You can rent a glass bottom boat with no license at Intercontinental Moorea for 8.250 CFP for 2 hrs. or 10.450 CFP for 4 hrs.

Deep Sea Fishing
Tea Nui Services, *Tel./Fax 56.35.95; teanuiservices@mail.pf.* Captain Chris Lilley has a 31-ft. Bertram Flybridge Sportfisher named *Tea Nui* that is professionally equipped with Penn International reels and all that you need to realize your dream of catching marlin, tuna, wahoo or mahi mahi offshore Moorea. Chris, who is an American resident of Moorea, has 30 years' experience fishing in local waters. The *Tea Nui* is based at Intercontinental Moorea. Chris charges US $175 per person for a minimum of 4 on a half-day charter and US $650 for a maximum of 6 people on a private half-day fishing excursion, including tax.

Moorea Fishing Charters, *Tel. 77.02.19; halfon@mail.pf; www.halfon-vip-tours.com.* Jean Pierre Halfon has a 29-ft. Riviera fishing boat with a flybridge, 200 HP diesel Volvo engine and luxury accommodations for 6 guests. There are two game fishing chairs, two outriggers and all the fishing equipment is provided. His **V.I.P. Tours** offer deep sea fishing, lagoon tours, a full-day excursion with fish and ray feeding and a BBQ on a private motu.

Tahiti Fishing Center, *Tel. 31.01.11; brunodamo@mail.pf; www.tahiti-fishing-center.com.* This is the sport fishing center of Moorea. They have a 19-ft. boat and a 30-ft. boat used for deep sea fishing expeditions and they can organize fishing in all the island groups of French Polynesia.

Dolphin & Whale Watching Eco-Tours

The following service providers are licensed by the government to operate dolphin and whale watching excursions:

Dolphin & Whale Watching Expeditions is owned by Doctor Michael Poole, *Tel/Fax 56.23.22; cell 77.50.07; dwwe@mail.pf; www.drmichaelpoole.com,* whose fiberglass boat will seat up to 40 people. On Sun. and Thurs. mornings a 3-4 hr.

DOLPHIN & WHALE WATCHING EXPEDITIONS

Dr. Michael Poole, *Tel/Fax 56.23.22; cell 77.50.07; dwwe@mail.pf; www.drmichaelpoole.com,* is an American marine biologist who lives in Moorea and has devoted his life's work to the study of dolphins and whales. He is a very good teacher who loves sharing his knowledge with other people. The enthusiasm he feels for the mammals he studies in their natural environment is very contagious. Michael and his staff lead 3-4 hour **Dolphin & Whale Watching Expeditions** on Thurs. and Sun. mornings and special tours for passengers on ships. A maximum of 40 people are picked up at their respective hotel docks between 8 and 9am, and Michael or one of his staff boards the boat at the Moorea Pearl Resort pier. The search begins, as you head through the lagoon or through a pass into the open ocean. The wild spinner dolphins (*Stenella longirostris*) are the easiest to find and the most fun to watch because of their acrobatic aerial leaps. Michael and his staff will tell you that 150 of these mammals live around Moorea all the time.

When the sea is calm and the mammals seem approachable, you can sometimes swim with the rough-toothed dolphins, pilot whales and humpback whales. The giant humpback whales can be seen and heard singing off Moorea between July and early November, when they come up from Antarctica to mate and give birth. These are the most exciting mammals to watch as they frolic close to the shore and splash in the vicinity of the surprised surfers, who ride the waves beside the passes.

Dolphin & Whale Watching Expedition (see sidebar) is guided by Doctor Michael Poole or his staff, which takes you through the lagoon and outside the reef to search for, observe and learn about the dolphins and whales that inhabit local waters. Time permitting, a snorkeling stop is offered inside the lagoon. This tour costs 8.000 CFP for adults, half price for children 3-12, and free for children under 3. Supplementary excursions are sometimes made on Sat., and special group charters can be arranged.

Manu Eco Tours Catamaran, *Tel./Fax 56.28.04; cell 79.03.28. Manu* is a 10.8 meter (36-ft.) motorized catamaran owned by Bernard Calvet, which operates out of the Nautical Center at the Intercontinental Moorea. A 4-hr. eco-tour around the island takes you to look for dolphins and whales (between July and early November), and also includes snorkeling with the rays and fish, for a minimum of 4 passengers at a cost of 8.500 CFP per person. A 3-hour snorkeling and ray-feeding cruise for a minimum of four people costs 7.000 CFP each, departing daily at 9:30am and 1:30pm and also includes a visit to Cook's Bay and Opunohu Bay. A half-day private charter for 6 passengers is 55.000 CFP. You can also join a sunset cruise. See information under *Sunset Cruises* in this chapter.

Moorea Deep Blue, *Tel. 76.37.27; jeromedambrin@hotmail.com; www.mooreadeepblue.com.* Jerome Dambrin's dolphin and whale watch excursions (in season) take you outside the pass to visit the sharks in the deep blue ocean, then back inside the lagoon to pet the sting rays and search for the spinner dolphins. Morning and afternoon tours last for 4-5 hours and snorkeling tours are also available as well as private tours for eight people. Snorkeling gear provided.

Moorea Mahana Tours, *Tel. 55.19.19,* at the Intercontinental Moorea Resort & Spa, has a full-day Dolphin Watch (and Whales between July-Oct.) boat tour around the island with a picnic on the motu for 10.850 CFP, or 7.400 CFP without picnic.

These excursions also include dolphin and whale watching (in season):

Moorea Dolphin Expedition, *Tel. 56.38.75/78.42.42; info@dolphinlagoonarium.com; www.mooreadolphin-expedition.com.* This excursion is operated by Paul Courset and Harold Wright, who worked with Club Med on Moorea until it closed in 2001. Their fully covered catamaran *Rava IV* makes trips around the island to look for the spinner dolphins and they also sight humpback whales between July and late October. Harold makes a stop to let the passengers play with the stingrays—an activity that he created in 1996. Another highlight of this excursion is a visit to Motu Ahi, where the tourists can snorkel among the fish, sharks, rays and turtles in the enclosed lagoonarium. This tour lasts for 4-5 hrs. and costs 8.000 CFP per person. Special rates for children.

Moorea Boat Tours, *Tel. 56.28.44/78.68.86.* Heifara Dutertre has 2 boats for dolphin and whale watches and private tours.

Lagoon Excursions, Snorkeling, Ray Feeding & Picnics on the Motu
    Hiro's Tours/What To Do On Moorea, *Tel. 78.70.10/22.56.18;*

wtdmoorea@mail.pf; www.hirotour.com. Hiro Kelley's **Motu Picnic Tour** features photo stops, a visit to Cook's Bay and Opunohu Bay, a shark show and ray feeding, snorkeling, and a sumptuous barbecue picnic on a *motu* islet, with punch, beer and soft drinks included. This 6-hr. tour is 5.000 CFP (cash only) and includes free pick-up service.

Moana Lagoon Tour, *Tel. 55.21.10/55.21.11; www.albert-transport.net*. Albert Transport and Activities has earned a good reputation for their barbecue picnic on the *motu*, which takes place every Tues., Wed., Fri. and Sun. During the 6-hour excursion you will view Cook's Bay and Opunohu Bay from the water and stop to feed the stingrays, enjoy a shark show and go snorkeling. Mask and snorkel supplied. Pick-ups at hotels included.

Moorea Mahana Tours, *Tel. 55.19.19*. They have excursions from the Intercontinental Moorea that will take you in a covered outrigger speed canoe to snorkel and meet the lagoon sharks and feed the stingrays, including a picnic on the motu for 6.500 CFP. Without picnic it costs 4.500 CFP.

Day Sailing Excursions & Sunset Cruises

Tahiti Cruise & Moorea Sailing, *Tel. 72.23.45, www.tahiticruise.pf* (under construction). The *Margouillat* is a 43-ft. luxury catamaran that provides half-day sailing and lagoon snorkeling, sailing sunset cruises and private cruises.

Lagoon Games, *Tel. 55.12.12/71.11.35, félix.patrick@mail.pf; www.catamaran-polynesie.com* is located at the Sofitel Ia Ora Moorea Nautical Activities Center. They provide sailing cruises aboard the 42-ft. deluxe Leopard catamaran *Kokiri*. A half-day sail is 9.500 CFP and a 7-hr. excursion with on-board picnic is 14.500 CFP. Private sailing tours are 65.000 CFP for a half-day and 98.000 CFP for a full day. The skipper, barman and chef are included in rates. The *Kokiri* can also be rented by the day or week.

Polynesian Spirit, *Tel. 77.97.19/56.11.74; kaveka.free.fr*. The *Kaveka* is a traditional Polynesian outrigger sailing canoe that makes half-day sailing and snorkeling tours for a maximum of 5 passengers, for 7.500 CFP per person. A sunset sailing cruise is 5.900 CFP.

Manu Catamaran, *Tel./Fax 56.28.04; cell 79.03.28. Manu* is a 10.8 meter (36-ft.) motorized catamaran that operates out of the Nautical Center at the Intercontinental Moorea. The sunset cruise leaves the dock every afternoon at 4:30-5pm and returns 1 1/2 hrs. later for a minimum of 4 passengers. Drinks are included in the price of 4.500 CFP.

Tuatini Activities Moorea, *Tel. 74.32.50; glassbottomboatmoorea@hotmail.com*. A 2 1/2-3 hr. sunset cruise aboard a glass bottom boat on the lagoon in Haapiti costs 4.500 CFP per person. Boarding is on the beach at Hotel Hibiscus and Taina is the female captain.

Sailing – Charter Yachts

Kokiri, *Tel. 71.11.35, félix.patrick@mail.pf; www.catamaran-polynesie.com* is a 42-ft. deluxe Leopard catamaran built in 2003 that can be chartered for the day or by the week. There are four double cabins. A skipper is required for inexperienced sailors. Weekly rates start at 2.900 Euros during the low season.

Scuba Diving

A qualified English-speaking instructor heads each dive center in Moorea. All diving equipment is available, and dive packages with special lodging can be arranged. If you are not a certified diver bring a health certificate from your doctor with you. The protected lagoons, passes and outer coral reefs offer ideal conditions for scuba diving year-round in water temperatures that range from 77° to 86° F.

There are more than a dozen dive sites no deeper than 75-90 ft. that you can discover with the following diving professionals.

Ia Ora Diving, *Tel. 77.86.44 or 55.12.12; www.iaoradiving.com.* This PADI dive center is located at the Sofitel Moorea Ia Ora Beach Resort. Certified divers leave the hotel beach daily at 8am and 10am, and pay 7.200 CFP for one dive and 12.400 CFP for 2 dives the same morning. An introductory dive for beginners is 7.500 CFP, and a night dive is 9.800 CFP for a minimum of 4 divers. They also have sunrise dives. Packages are available for 5 and 10 dives and certifications can be given for PADI, FFESSM, CMAS, ANMP and CEDIP. Ray feeding is 5.500 CFP.

MOOREA'S BEST DIVE SITES

Moorea's dive sites outside the reef offer special treats of swimming with the large lemon sharks and a rendezvous with the friendly giant-sized Napoleon fish. Divers also see black and white-tip sharks, gray sharks and moray eels.

The water is clear with insignificant currents, assuring easy dives that attract scuba divers from all over the world. One of the most popular sites is "Le Tiki", where you'll be able to see wild sharks, including lemon sharks more than 2.4 m (8 ft.) long. The Toatai Pass through the barrier reef offers drift diving among nurse sharks, leopard rays and schools of jackfish. A site known as "Napoleon Plateau" offers Napoleon fish that weigh up to 80 lbs., as well as sharks. Inside the lagoon is a site called "The Wreck", which is an artificial haven for fish, with the ship's hull spread over 82 ft., complete with anchors, chains and a gangway. Other sites include the "Ray Corridor," "The Canyon," "The Blue Island," the "Shark Dining Room," the "Bali Hai Wall," "Temae," "Atiha," the "Avamotu Pass" and the "Taotaha Pass," all offering a concentration of eels, barracudas, coral fish, rays or sharks. A deep dive in the Garden of Roses lets you discover beautiful Coral Roses (Montipora). The depth for these dives is usually 60-70 ft., with an average visibility of 150 ft. and sometimes more than 250 ft. Many of the dive spots are less than 10 minutes by boat from the shore.

Moorea Blue Diving, *Tel. 55.17.04/74.59.99; www.mooreabluediving.com.* This small dive center is based at the Moorea Pearl Resort & Spa and is owned by Lino and Solange Facondini. Lino is a BEES 1/OWSI PADI/CMAS** instructor/ MF1 FFESSM, and a shark diving specialist. They leave the resort each morning at 7:30am for 2 dives, returning at noon. An exploration dive is 6.800 CFP, 2 dives are 13.850 CFP, an introductory dive is 7.500 CFP, and a night dive is 8.500 CFP. A package of 5 Fun dives is 32.500 CFP and 10 Fun dives costs 59.500 CFP. The rates include all the equipment, which is new. PADI certification is 45.000 CFP, not including the open water diving book. Other diving certificates possible.

Moorea Fun Dive, *Tel. 56.40.38; www.moorea-fundive.com.* This dive shop is located at PK. 27 in Haapiti, and is operated by Gregory and Catherine Kister. They are both PADI master instructors and Nitrox instructors. Their equipment includes a 24-ft. aluminum boat for 14 passengers, but they limit the diving to 10 people with one dive guide for a maximum of 5 divers. All the necessary equipment is provided. They charge 6.400 CFP for an exploration dive, 12.000 CFP for two dives and 32.700 CFP for a 6-dive package. Whale watching excursions during season (July-Oct.).

TOPDIVE-Bathys, *Tel. 56.31.44/56.38.10/74.51.91; www.topdive.com.* This PADI 5-star center is located at the Intercontinental Moorea Resort & Spa and at the Hilton Moorea Lagoon Resort & Spa. A free pick-up service is available to take you to either resort, depending on the dive location of the day. The six members of the staff run an efficient 5-star operation. The experienced PADI instructors speak English with a strong French accent and you will need to pay close attention to the dive briefing to understand. They take a maximum of 18 people on their high powered speed boats and the boat trips alone can be worth the dive. The dive gear is quite new (Aqualung) and Nitrox is available for the same price as air. A Fun dive or Introductory dive costs 7.900 CFP and 2-tank dives are 14.500 CFP. A 6-dive inter-island package for 1 diver is 41.000 CFP and a 10-dive inter-island Gold Pass for 1-2 divers is 67.000 CFP. A TOPDIVE-Bathys specialty is the Moorea Shark Experience during which you swim with lemon sharks. Certifications are available for PADI and ANMP. You can also sign up for a Dolphin Encounter for 9.000 CFP, which is available year-round. The whale-watching expeditions are 12.000 CFP and available only between Aug. 1 and Oct. 31. A snorkeling excursion is 2.500 CFP.

Scubapiti Moorea, *Tel. 56.20.38/78.03.52; www.scubapiti.com.* Daniel Cailleux runs this popular dive center, which is located on the property of Les Tipaniers in Haapiti. He is a French State supervisor BEES 1, 1st degree French federal monitor, CMAS instructor, and monitor for PADI and ANMP (Association National des Moniteurs de Plongée). Daniel and his partner Henri and their highly qualified instructors are available to take you for an exploration or first dive for 6.100 CFP. A 2-tank dive is 11.600 CFP and a 4-6 dive package is 5.490 CFP per dive. Lessons are available. Most dives are drift dives and they do no shark feeding. A cameraman records your dives, which you can then see on an instant replay system.

More Water Fun

Aqua Blue, *Tel. 56.53.53/73.24.40; aquablue_pf@hotmail.com* is a novel way to say hello to the fish in the lagoon in Moorea. This activity is based at the Intercontinental Moorea Resort and is available daily except Sunday. You do not have to be a certified diver nor even a swimmer to discover this new sensation. A qualified diving instructor will help you to put on a funny looking yellow diving helmet that weighs 40 kg (88 lbs.). But you don't feel the weight when you are under the water, and you can actually walk around on the bottom of the lagoon just as you would walk on any land, wearing special water shoes. An air hose connected to a compressor on board the boat allows you to descend to a depth of 3.7 m (12 ft.). Your Aqua-Walk lasts 30 min. and costs 7.500 CFP. Free transfers.

Aquascope, *Tel. 55.12.12/71.11.35.* You'll find this excursion at the Sofitel Ia Ora Moorea. Aquascope is a half submarine that puts you under the surface of the water, where you can view the coral gardens and colorful fish without getting wet. The cost is 6.600 CFP for 30 min. or 9.900 CFP for an hour for a maximum of three adults.

Moorea Dolphin Center, *Tel. 55.19.48; www.mooreadolphincenter.com.* This organization is based at the Intercontinental Moorea Resort & Spa. You can participate in encounter programs with trained dolphins that live inside a lagoon park. A 30-min. encounter combines elements of hands-on contact, education, fun and adventure, for 15.500 CFP for adults and 10.000 CFP for a child 8-11 years. A 30-min. Apnea is 26.000 CFP. A 1-hr. Special Romance for couples starts at 11am and costs 50.000 CFP, and a 30-min. Family program is 58.000 CFP.

Lagoonarium of Moorea, *Tel. 78.31.15; lagoonarium@mail.pf; www.lagoonarium.com.* This activity is operated by Matahi and Aiata on Motu Ahi, at PK 8 in Afareaitu. Stop at the Curios *fare* on the seaside beside the road and a shuttle boat will take you to the motu. The fee is 2.900 CFP for each adult and 2.300 CFP per child, which allows you to spend the day on the motu, snorkeling in a lagoonarium filled with tropical fish of all colors. You can swim with the stingrays, baby reef sharks, moray eels, and turtles in a protected marine zone inside the lagoon. Fins, facemasks, snorkels, plastic shoes, safety jackets and kayaks are provided. Some of the organized lagoon excursions come here for their barbecue picnic on the motu. There is a kitchen, grill and refrigerator, as well as toilets and showers. A few simple A-frame shelters provide shade for a nap. Open daily from 8am to 4pm, with last departure at 1pm and last return at 4pm.

Lakana Fly Kite Surfing, *Tel. 70.96.71; bdflyfr@yahoo.fr.* David Bourroux is a young Frenchman who gives lessons in kite surfing and he speaks good English. He is based adjacent to Moorea Locaboat next door to Les Tipaniers on the site of the former Moorea Beach Club (Moe Moea).

Polynesian Parasailing, *Tel. 55.19.19* is operated by Moorea Mahana Activities and is based at the Intercontinental Moorea Resort. You can float over Moorea's lagoon without getting your feet wet. You have a 10-12 min. ride aloft, up to 180 m (600 ft.) above the lagoon, where all you can hear is the wind. This activity is available for 7.550 CFP per person or 11.250 CFP tandem for one adult and one child. The other hotel activity desks also sell this excursion.

SHOPPING

When you take a guided circle island tour of Moorea the bus or 4-wheel drive vehicle will most likely stop at a boutique and a pearl shop, which are probably owned by the guide's family or friends. If you rent a car or scooter or bike around the island you'll have a better chance of finding out which shops you prefer.

My favorites are the shops that sell locally made products, rather than clothes, pareos and souvenir items imported from Bali. **Coco Blanc** is in Centre Tumai on the mountainside at PK 2.7 in Tiaia, between the airport and Maharepa. Jean-Luc, the talented owner, creates jewelry from Tahiti cultured pearls, nacre, bone, tou, tutu, purau and other local wood. He also sells Marquesan wood sculptures, pareo outfits, shirts and lamps made by Tahiti Art, and he carries Te Mana shirts from Tahiti for men and women. **Green Lagoon Art Gallery**, on the mountainside around PK 3.8 in Tiaia, presents oil canvases by Nataly Jolibois and sculptures of driftwood, wood and metal and wood and stone by Hans Jörg Stübler.

There are a few curio shops and boutiques in and close to the Maharepa Center, where you'll also find the post office and banks. **La Maison Blanche** is one of the most popular tourist stops, even though most of their curios are imported. **Van der Heyde Art Gallery**, on the mountain side at PK 7, is owned by Aad van der Heyde, a Dutch artist whose oil paintings are displayed all around his enclosed garden. Inside his shop you'll find authentic primitive art from throughout the South Pacific and sculptures of coral and wood from the French Polynesian Islands. He also sells Tahitian cultured pearls and unset *keshis*.

Art Marquisien is in the Cook's Bay Center across from Hotel Kaveka. In addition to carvings of wood, bone, stone and mother-of-pearl, they also have Marquesan tapa and *tifaifai* bed covers or wall hangings. **Rev'Deco** is also in the center, displaying Polynesian designs for bed and table linen, handmade *tifaifais* for baby beds and an interesting choice of home decorations.

Maeva Center, across the road from Club Bali Hai, is a small artisan's village. At **Robert Aka's** shop, you can find slit wooden toere drums, Tahitian ukuleles, carved umete bowls and coconut bras, as well as seashells from the Marquesan Island of Ua Pou. The **Gilles Fraysse Galerie** are paintings made with sand, and at **Natural Mystic** you will find wood sculptures, pyogravure, airbrushed pareos and fashion accessories. Some of the shops sell locally made clothes, *pareos* and grass dancing skirts, and there is also a deli and beauty shop/massage parlor here.

Honu Iti Boutique, PK 8.5 in Cook's Bay, has Tahitian clothing and souvenirs, as well as pareos and trinkets imported from Indonesia. They also have some pearl jewelry. **Boutique Ra**, on the mountainside at PK 12.8 in Pihaena, displays the bamboo artifacts made by American expatriate, Ruth Konvalinka, as well as paintings, stone and coral sculptures created by local artists and artisans. On the mountainside at PK 13.5 in Pihaena will see a sign for **Tahiti Stained Glass**.

This is the atelier of **Tom Newbrough**, an American who makes stained glass windows, lamps, candle covers and fish mobiles. **Kaimana Boutique** at the Hilton Moorea Lagoon Resort & Spa is well-stocked with gift items, silk painted pareos, tropical clothing, men's shirts and T-shirts. Look for the sign **Tifaifai Papetoai** on the lagoon side of the road near Snack Mahana in Papetoai. Miri makes pretty wall hangings or bed covers called *tifaifai* in Tahitian. **Atelier du Chat** is on the mountainside at PK 24 in Tiahura. Their exquisite Oceanian Art sculptures includes jewelry made of bone and black pearls. **Envies d'Alleurs** is a nice boutique next to the Vet's office at PK 25 in Tiahura. They carry some pretty European fashions as well as *pareos* and unusual souvenir items.

In the hotel area of Haapiti you'll find a number of boutiques that carry *pareos*, T-shirts, swimsuits and gift items. **Le Petit Village** is a small shopping center with an ABC store, pearl shops, boutiques and a magazine stand. Be sure to visit **Creativ'** on the upstairs level. The dresses, pareos, jewelry, sculptures, and other high quality arts and crafts are all made locally. You should also visit the **bazaars** at the boat docks in Cook's Bay and Papetoai village when a cruise ship is in port. Local artisans set up display stands under awnings to sell their *pareos*, tee-shirts, dresses and beachwear, costume jewelry made of shells and mother-of-pearl, woven hats and bags and numerous other souvenirs that are made in Moorea.

Tahitian Cultured Pearls

Eimeo Fine Jewelry, *Tel. 56.47.07*; *www.eimeofinejewelry.com* is located on the same road as the Moorea Fruit Juice Factory at PK 12 in Cook's Bay. Open Mon.-Fri. 10am-4pm. This cute little cottage is the workshop and showroom of Elizabeth (Beth) Eyler-Wong, a very talented American jewelry designer, jeweler and goldsmith.

In 2007 Beth won first prize for a pair of pearl earrings she created for the 5th national edition of the Tahitian Pearl Trophy design competition, and took second prize for an 18kt gold ring containing a big keshi pearl, two Tahitian cultured pearls and a rose tourmaline. Beth's distinctive designs tend to have an Etruscan look, combining cultured pearls with chalcedony, moonstone, tourmaline and other semi-precious stones. She took the jewelry design course at the Gemological Institute of America (GIA) in 1977, and worked in the best jewelry stores in Southern California before moving to Moorea in 1988. Now she has one of the best jewelry shops on this island, with designs for all tastes and prices for all budgets. Have a look at her website, and you will agree.

Eva Perles, *Tel. 56.10.10*; *www.evaperles.com*, is next to the Banque de Tahiti in Maharepa. Eva and Thierry Frachon are the very amiable hosts in this pleasant shop, and their selection of fine Tahitian cultured pearl jewelry will be sure to please you. Eva was trained as an art metalist in Wisconsin during her college years, and now uses this knowledge to design and fabricate a lot of the jewelry she sells. She has also completed the pearl course given at the Gemological Institute of America, as well as the Accredited Jewelry Professional training. Her first goal is to educate people so that they will be free to choose the best for themselves, no matter where they buy their pearls. She never pushes for a sale, choosing instead to share her passion with the visitor, opening them up to the uniqueness of this magical gem, to recognize the true beauty of each pearl, even though that beauty may not be perfect. Eva also displays some of her paintings in the gallery, as well as works by other resident artists.

Golden Nugget Perles, *Tel. 56.13.05,* is on Motu Temae close to the public beach and the Sofitel Moorea Beach Resort. You take the coral sand road opposite the post office at PK 0 in Temae and follow the signs pointing to Kerebel Jeweller. Kerebel is a goldsmith who creates most unusual jewelry, which often reflects his interest in the American Southwest. Some of his masculine rings are a golden or silver eagle set with a big Tahitian cultured pearl. His paintings are also on display in his gallery.

Island Fashion Black Pearls, *Tel. 56.11.06,* at PK 6.9 in Pao Pao, is open Mon.-Sat. from 9am-6pm. Owner Ron Hall is an American from California, who sailed to Tahiti with Peter Fonda aboard the yacht *Tatoosh* in the mid-1970s and settled in Moorea. Ron was one of the first successful Tahitian cultured pearl salesmen on the island, and some of his customers return time and again to add to their collection from his impressive selection of quality pearls and jewelry. He also carries bikinis, beach wear, *pareos* and Hawaiian style shirts. Transportation from your hotel is provided on request.

Pai Moana Pearls, *Tel. 56.25.25; www.paimoana-pearls.com* is located on the mountainside in Haapiti close to Le Petit Village. Canadian Peter Ringland arrived in Tahiti in June 1978 aboard his 70-ft. sailing yacht *Seer* and discovered the lagoons of the Tuamotu archipelago during the four years he ran diving charters. In 1987 Peter sold his yacht and invested in a pearl farm in Manihi, which he named Pai Moana, the Polynesian name he was given when he married Kiki, a Tahitian schoolteacher from Moorea. Pai was the ancient Tahitian hero, who, according to legend, threw a spear from the island of Tahiti, making a hole in the top of one of Moorea's tallest mountains. That hole is still there today. Moana is Tahitian for the word ocean. So Ringland became "Hero of the Ocean".

Today Peter Ringland is CEO of SARL Gem Pearls, DBA Pai Moana Pearls. "This is a French Polynesia company that is completely integrated vertically with its own pearl farm. There's no middleman; therefore, we can offer the best quality and prices on the island," Peter said. His 3 children have become the second generation of pearl experts at Pai Moana. Their specialty is strands of pearls of all lengths, sizes, shapes and colors. Free transfers provided.

SAB Boutique, *Tel. 56.44.55/70.51.04; sabmoorea@mail.pf; www.annsimonblackpearl.com.* This little pearl shop was formerly named Ann Simon Boutique (ASB). It is located in the shopping center across the street from the Banque de Tahiti in Maharepa. I wrote in previous editions of this book that each time I went inside this jewelry shop I was impressed by the friendliness of the very helpful sales staff who speaks good English. I also wrote that I like the beautiful colors and quality of the pearls, the originality of the settings, and their reasonable prices, adding that everyone I have sent here agrees with me and usually buys some of the fine pearls, which they happily set on request. Ann Simon went back to France in 2010 and the very friendly sales lady I wrote about is now the owner of the pearl shop. Her name is Sabine Quere (SAB) and she is from Brittany. She worked for Ann Simon for 7 years and bought the shop in 2010. Be sure to stop by and meet Sabine when you're in Moorea and let her show you her lovely pearls. Free shuttle service is also available.

Tahia Pearls, *Tel. 55.05.00; www.tahiapearls.com. US Customer Service Center toll free Tel. 888/328-8266. Open Mon.-Sat. 9am-5:30pm and on Sun. 10am-5pm. Courtesy shuttle transfers available.*

Look for the sail-like canopies on the red building across the road from the former Club Med in Haapiti. This business began as The Black Pearl Gem Company in 1993, and has now developed from one small sales room to a highly successful chain of 6 pearl shops with a team of 15 employees. In addition to the main showroom in Moorea, you will also find Tahia Pearls across from the boat dock in Papeete, at the Moorea Pearl Resort, the Intercontinental Resort and Thalasso Spa Bora Bora, in the center of Bora Bora's Vaitape village, and on board the *M/S Paul Gauguin* cruise ship.

Tahia Haring is a young Polynesian-Swiss woman from Moorea, who is President and CEO of her own company as well as an award-winning jewelry designer and a former Miss Moorea. Her exclusive Tahitian pearl jewelry features only rare pearls in the most exotic colors from the top 1% of each pearl harvest. These stunning top-of-the line colors are harvested in a pearl farm in Fakarava and include varying nuances of blues, greens and purple, as well as the rare peacock.

Everyone At Tahia Pearls speaks very good English, in addition to a few other languages, and the service is friendly and helpful, never pushy. The a/c showroom is designed to make shopping for your pearls an enjoyable and memorable experience. The Moorea boutique also has a private, luxuriously appointed VIP Lounge to accommodate those clients who, because of the high value of their selections, wish to complete their transaction in an atmosphere of privacy and seclusion.

Woody's Black Pearl Paradise, *Tel. 56.37.00/79.45.70*, is beside the lagoon at PK 23.9 in Papetoai, 400 m. from Intercontinental Moorea. Free shuttle service. Woody Howard is an American resident of Moorea who creates exquisite sculptures from the roots of trees and local wood. He also makes guitars. Woody has now added a Tahitian cultured pearl showroom to his gallery, selling pearls from his own farm in the Tuamotu atolls. His jewelry has won top prizes in the Tahitian Pearl Trophy design competitions.

MASSAGES & SPAS

Hélène'Spa, *Tel. 55.19.70; reservation@helenespa.com; www.helenespa.com.* This award-winning spa was created in 1999, and was the first Polynesian spa in

French Polynesia. It has been ranked for many years among the most beautiful Spas in the world. Hidden in the exuberant foliage of private tropical gardens on the grounds of the Intercontinental Moorea Resort & Spa, there are 9 treatment areas in an indoor/outdoor Polynesian jungle setting of thatched roofs, bamboo walls, basaltic rock walkways, river baths, waterfalls and rain showers.

Hélène Sillinger is a qualified professional, certified in naturopathy. Using holistic secrets transmitted from wise Polynesian healers, she has created a range of Tahitian cares inspired by unique recipes. Her Polynesian Escapes packages of Well-Being Rituals suggest 6 combinations that last from 35-145 min. and cost from 11.500-38.400 CFP. The Herenui Love Ritual For Two starts with a traditional river bath, followed by a soft body scrub with fresh coconut pulp, a smooth body wrap with fresh coconut milk, a mask and plant lotion for a beauty care, a relaxing rain shower and Polynesian massage, topped off by a bath filled with fresh exotic flowers. A traditional drink and tropical fruits is included in the cost of 22.000-89.000 CFP per couple, for 35-145 min. A la carte treatments include Tahitian massages for 9.400 CFP for 25 min. up to 30.200 CFP for 100 min. Or you can choose an aromatic spa with tropical essential oils, a fresh flower bath, traditional river bath, regenerating rain shower, scrubs and vegetal wraps. Hélène'Spa also provides facial care, manicures, pedicures, makeup and waxing. They are open daily from 10am-6pm. Book your appointment 24 hours in advance.

Harmony Esthétique, *Tel. 56.55.54/Tel. 72.49.75; betrancourtc@mail.pf; www.tahitihotspot.com.* This Beauty Shop and Spa is located in the Cook's Bay Center in Maharepa, across the road from the former Cook's Bay Hotel and the cruise ship dock in Cook's Bay. Open Tues.-Sat. 8:30am-5:30pm. Chantal has more than 15 years' experience in the beauty care business and she has a nice gentle touch with facials and waxings. The Spa has a Hammam and Jacuzzi, and her services include body scrubs, wrapping, waxing, hair removal, manicures and pedicures. She also does make-up for weddings and other special occasions, and permanent makeup for the lips, eyes and beauty marks. Her facials are 5.700-11.000 CFP and she uses Matis products made in France. A 40-min. Aroma-reflexology treatment is 4.500 CFP and a 45-min. relaxing massage is 6.300 CFP. Chantal also has another outlet at Tiki Village in Haapiti, which is called **Harmony Tiki**, *Tel. 55.02.50.*

Legends Beauty, *Tel. 55.15.15*, is the spa at Legends Resort Moorea. Zen Spa Treatments include a foot bath with purau flowers and noni leaves, reflexology and a 90-min. massage (Relaxation, Sports or Thai), for 22.000 CFP. Coconut treatments for 30.000 CFP start with a body or face scrub, a 90-min. massage, and then a traditional Polynesian hair care treatment with coconut milk. A rain shower can be added to any treatment for 3.000 CFP. Body Treatments give you a choice of a 60 or 90 min. massage, and a body or face scrub. After-sun care with tamanu oil is 10.000 CFP for 30 min.

LeSpa, *Tel. 55.12.12*, is on the beach at Sofitel Moorea Beach Resort, offering 7 tranquil treatment rooms and 2 Jacuzzis with panoramic views across the lagoon.

There is an outdoor unheated pool and a solarium. Their signature massages feature the Moroccan Caress, a relaxing massage with circular movements. Another favorite is the Ancestral Paradise, which starts with a flower bath and is followed by a traditional Tahitian massage. Facials, manicures and pedicures are also available.

Moorea Lagoon Spa, *Tel. 689/55.10.40; 55.10.77; spamanager@hilton-moorea.pf;* is located on the beach level at the Hilton Moorea Lagoon Resort & Spa. The staff of Polynesian technicians includes massage therapists who are well trained to pamper you, and a menu of indulgences that will tempt all your hedonistic tastes. Their signature massage, Moorea Forever, is a Taurumi deep massage that was performed by the ancient Polynesians with long flowing movements along the length of the body using primarily the forearms as well as the hands and fingers, in combination with the breath. The continuous flowing movements performed as a dance can be likened to the waves of the ocean, washing away all tension in the body. The Spa manager recommends warm Vanilla Tiare monoi oil with this treatment. A 60-min. massage is 12.500 CFP. A Moorea Volcanic massage is applied with heated oiled stones and starts at 14.500 CFP for 60 min. You may choose a Hawaiian Lomilomi massage, a Top and Toe head and foot reflexology, a 90-min. Dream Body Ritual for 24.000 CFP, or a 120-min. Body to Body Skin Ritual for 30.000 CFP. A Nirvanesque Black Pearl Facial begins with a purifying hammam therapy, followed by a Tahitian Black Pearl clay treatment for the face, and a 5-step facial with Nuxe products. A final touch is a 20-min. Indian Head and scalp massage. This 90-min. ritual is 24.000 CFP. Romance Rituals for couples are available in the Royal couple suite or the Sandalwood suite. The "Crème de la crème" begins with a vanilla lace skin scrub, and continues with a Polynesian symphony spa and 4-hands massage. The next step is a coconut mousse skin delight, and then a Facial Crème Merveilleuse by Nuxe. This 2-person treat lasts for 200 min. and costs 65.000 CFP. It also includes a Tiare Tahiti lei, 1/2 bottle of champagne and spa nibbles in the Jacuzzi.

Manea Spa, *Tel. 55.17.97*, is the spa at the Moorea Pearl Resort and Spa. There are 3 rooms for massages, facials, hair and body and care, and a room with a Vichy shower and 2 massage tables. Facilities include a Hammam, Jacuzzi and rain shower, but no sauna. A special outdoor Watsu pool is used for Rumavai massages performed in the water. Manea Spa carries its own line of 100% natural products made from local herbs, fruits, flowers and plants. These oils and cosmetic creams can be purchased at the Spa. The house special in Moorea is the Monoi Painapo, a complete massage of 30, 50, or 80 min. using monoi oil made from locally grown pineapple.

Treatments range from a 30-min. massage for 8.500 CFP to a 3 hour and 20 minute Tohora Manea combination for 36.000 CFP for one person and 63.000 CFP for two. A 50-min. Hohoa Ofai, hot & cool stone facial is 15.000 CFP. Manicures, pedicures, waxing, and scalp exfoliation are also available.

Philippe Girodeau, *Tel./Fax 689/56.40.42, cell 77.54.79*, is my preferred massage therapist. He will bring his massage table to your room and make you feel like a new person after he works on your body, mind and soul. He opens your chakra energy centers and heals your aches and pains with magnetism and a pair of very strong hands. He charges about 10.000 CFP, but the massage lasts more than an hour.

TATTOOS

Masters of the art can design tattoos for those of you who wish to wear a permanent souvenir of your trip to Moorea. All the tattooers are required to follow strict standards of hygiene. The cost of a Maohi tattoo depends on the design, and you'll pay around 10.000 CFP for a simple drawing.

Albert Tattoos, *Tel. 28.18.44; abouttatou@yahoo.fr*. Located beside Le Cocotier Restaurant at PK 5 in Maharepa. Open Mon.-Sat. 9am-12pm and 12:30-6pm. Albert charges 6.000 CFP for a small simple tattoo and 10.000 CFP per hour for larger designs.

Gilles Lovisa, *Tel. 77.58.23; www.lovisatattoo.com*. Gilles is a Frenchman who moved to French Polynesia in 1993 and learned to tattoo from the local tattoo masters. He works out of his house beside the lagoon at PK 5 in Maharepa, 150 m. (492 ft.) from Moorea Pearl Resort. Look for the blue *pareo* tied on a pole beside the road.

Moorea Tattoo, *Tel. 76.42.60/56.25.33; www.mooreatattoo.com*. James Samuela is a young Tahitian man who specializes in traditional tattoos, and also uses the tattoo machine on request. He studied at l'Ecole National des Beaux Arts in Paris and learned tattoo techniques from local tattoo masters who now come to admire James as he works. His tattoo shop is at his home on the mountainside of the road at PK 32 in the Varari section of Haapiti. James speaks English and is married to Laurel Samuela, an American woman who owns True Tahiti Vacation and Dive Tahiti Blue, as an online tour operator.

Purotu Tattoos, *Tel. 56.22.92/77.57.59; www.purotu.com* is located on the mountainside at PK 5.5 in Maharepa. He also works out of his house at PK 12.8 in Pihaena, next door to Boutique RA. Laurent Purotu is a world-famous tattoo master and is noted for his original designs. He is a talented artist and sculptor. His brother also tattoos in the Maharepa shop.

Tehuitua Tattoo, *Tel. 71.92.50*. Beside lagoon at PK 27 in Haapiti. Open Mon.-Sat. 8am-6pm. All style tattoos.

Taniera Tattoo, *Tel. 56.16.98, tanieratatoo@mail.pf*, is located on the mountainside at PK 27.3 in Haapiti, across road from Restaurant PK 0. He is noted for his personalized Tahitian tattoos.

You can also get tattooed at **Tiki Village**.

Note: Some of Moorea's most popular tattoo masters are no longer living on the island. Roonui Anania and Tautu Ellis have moved to Canada and Chimé has been in Europe since 2008.

PRACTICAL INFORMATION

Banks

All the banks are closed on Sunday and holidays. They charge a commission for each transaction, which varies from bank to bank. They all have an ATM ready cash window.

Banque de Tahiti, *Tel. 55.00.55,* is on the lagoon side near the Maharepa Post Office. Open Mon.-Fri. 8am-12pm and 1:30-4:30pm. They will exchange traveler's checks and currency, but charge a higher rate for their services. **Socredo Banque,** *Tel. 47.00.00,* is in the same shopping center as the Maharepa Post Office, Open Mon.-Fri. 8am-12pm and 1:30-4:30pm. They do no exchanges unless you have an account with them. Across the road in the Centre Noha is the **Banque de Polynésie,** *Tel. 55.05.80.* Open Mon.-Fri. 7:45am-12pm and 1:15-3:45pm, and on Sat. morning. They will not exchange traveler's checks, but will exchange currency. There is also a **Banque de Polynésie** branch located in Le Petit Village in Haapiti, *Tel. 55.04.30.* Open Mon.-Fri. 8am-12pm and 1:30-4:30pm.

Books, Newspapers & Magazines

•**Kina Maharepa,** *Tel. 56.22.44,* is in the same commercial center as the Post Office and Socredo Banque. They sell magazines, newspapers, books, tobacco, office supplies, phonecards, Tahitian calendars and Loto tickets.

•**La Pirogue,** *Tel. 55.05.30,* is in Le Petit Village in Haapiti. They sell newspapers, magazines, books, tobacco, stamps, phonecards, souvenirs, and Loto tickets, and they rent DVD's.

Churches

If your hotel is in the Cook's Bay area, the Protestant church at PK 5 in Maharepa is a good choice. The Protestant church Ebenezer at PK 22 in Papetoai Village is octagonal and was built on the site that was once the royal Marae Taputapuatea, where heathen gods were worshipped. The first church in the South Seas was built here in 1827 and rebuilt in 1889. It has since been restored a few times. Another Protestant church is located at PK 35 in Haapiti, and the beautiful Catholic Church, Eglise de la Saint Famille Haapiti, is at PK 24 on the mountainside.

Saint Joseph's Chapel at PK 10 beside Cook's Bay contains a large mural depicting a Polynesian Nativity scene, painted in 1946 by Swedish artist Peter Heyman. The members of this little church wrote a letter to the Pope, asking permission to have a religious painting made, with Mary, Joseph and the Christ child portrayed as Polynesians. The Pope agreed to their proposal, stipulating that the painting should be a mural so that it would always remain in the church and not be transported elsewhere. When the building began to deteriorate, a new church was built next door, where services are still held. A wealthy Moorea resident had the chapel restored in 1999, and it is now used for weddings, baptisms and other special occasions.

Dentist

Dr. Fréderic Avet and Dr. Nicole Lebreton, *Tel. 56.32.44*, share offices in the Centre Noha, opposite the post office in Maharepa, They have modern equipment and good dental knowledge and techniques. Dr. Nicolas Marchadier, *Tel. 56.47.51*, is at PK 27.2 on the mountainside in Haapiti.

Doctors – Medical Services

In the Maharepa area Dr. Marie-Paule Gévolde, *Tel. 56.18.18*, has an office on the mountainside at PK 4.4, and Dr. Augustin Lejeune, *Tel. 56.30.31*, is at PK 6. Dr. Fréderic Foucher and Dr. Mei-Ling Esposito, *Tel. 56.32.32*, have offices in the Centre Noha, opposite the post office in Maharepa. Dr. Franck Gaudard and Dr. Jean-Marc Jouve, *Tel. 56.44.63*, are general practice doctors whose offices are above the pharmacy in Maharepa. Dr. Brigitte Busseuil, *Tel. 56.29.19*, and Dr. Yann Perchoc, *Tel. 56.47.47*, are also in Maharepa. Dr. Dominique Barraille, *Tel. 56.27.07*, and Dr. Jean-Yves Lafitte, *Tel. 56.15.55*, are in the Haapiti area. Dr. Smagghue, *Tel. 56.24.91*, is an English-speaking cardiologist whose office is above the pharmacy in Maharepa.

Moorea also has two medical laboratories and a radiology lab, a pediatrician, psychoanalyst, an orthophonist, several physiotherapists, and osteopaths/chiropractors. I can recommend Pierrick Renaud, *Tel. 79.57.67*, because he has treated me. His wife, Agnés Valentin, *Tel. 26.65.60*, is Moorea's only chiropodist (foot doctor) and she also treats me on a regular basis.

Drugstores

Pharmacie Tran is at PK 6.5 in Maharepa, *Tel. 55.20.75*. The hours are 7:30am-12pm and 2-6pm Mon.-Fri., 8am-12pm and 2:30-4:30pm on Sat., and 8-10am on Sun. and holidays. The **Pharmacie of Haapiti** is located on the mountainside at PK 30.5, *Tel. 56.38.37/56.41.16*. They are open Mon.-Fri. from 8am-12pm, and 3-6:30pm; on Sat. from 9am-12pm and 4-6:30pm; and on Sun. and holidays from 9-11am.

Eye Doctor – Glasses

Dr. Véronique De Chasteigner, *Tel. 56.50.51*, is an ophthalmologist whose office is located in the Centre Raehau behind Optique Moorea. She speaks English and is very thorough and professional.

Optique Moorea, *Tel. 56.55.44*, is in the small shopping center across from the Banque de Tahiti. Optician Frederic Baron can make or repair glasses and he is very helpful.

Hospital

The small government **Hospital of Afareaitu** is at PK 9 in Afareaitu Village, *Tel. 56.24.24/56.23.23*. *Tel. 17* or *56.22.22* for ambulance service. Seriously ill or injured patients are evacuated by helicopter or airplane to Mamao Hospital in Tahiti.

Internet Service
You can go to the following places to check your email:
Photo Magic, *Tel. 56.59.59/71.69.51*, is adjacent to La Plantation Restaurant in Haapiti. Open daily 8am-6:30pm. You can bring your own laptop and connect to ADSL with WiFi and Skype for one hour at 450 CFP and two hours at 850 CFP. Unlimited package rates are also available.
    Iguane Rock Café, *Tel. 56.17.16*, is in Le Petit Village in Haapiti. They are open Mon.-Sat. from 8am-8pm, and have computers with WiFi in a back corner. They charge 650 CFP per hour.
    Manaspot, *Tel. 50.88.88; www.manaspot.pf* has WiFi machines at the Post Office in Maharepa and Papetoai, and at Te Fare Potée Snack at the Vaiare Ferry Quay. You can buy prepaid cards for 1-100 hours, from 660-19.800 CFP, and you can even order them online and pay by credit card.
    Hotspot Wi-Fi Zone card machines are located at several of Moorea's hotels and family lodgings, restaurants and snacks, and there are 300 outlets in French Polynesia, where their Surfer packages can be used. You can buy 10-100 hours for 4.000-20.000 CFP, including free hours. *Tel. 83.16.41; www.hotspot-wdg.com.*
    Internet WiFi service is also available at all the big hotels, and many of the family pensions, usually at extra cost.

Laundry
    La Laverie Beatrice, *Tel. 56.17.19/70.64.65*, at PK 5.5 in the Orovau Center in Maharepa, facing the Banque de Tahiti. This pick-up and delivery laundry service is open Mon.-Sat. They do washing, spin drying and ironing.

Marina
    The **Marina of Vaiare**, *Tel. 56.26.97; rporoi@mail.pf;* Rocky Poroi is in charge of this marina, which has 120 places for sailboats and deep-sea sportfishing boats up to 60 ft. on the pontoon and 60 places for boats on the embarkment. Showers, restrooms, telephone box and WiFi Internet access. An enlargement project is on the drawing board.

Police
    The French *gendarmerie* is at PK 7 in Maharepa, *Tel. 17* or *Tel. 55.25.05*. Open daily 7am to 12pm and 2 to 6pm. The municipal police (*mutoi*) have a station in Afareaitu, *Tel. 56.36.36*, and in Papetoai, *Tel. 56.14.10*. Dial *18* to reach the *Pompier* (Fire) Station.

Post Office & Telecommunications Office
    The **Maharepa Post Office**, *Tel. 56.10.12*, is located in the shopping center at PK 5.5. Hours are 7:30am-12pm and 1:30-4pm Mon.-Thurs., and on Fri. it closes at 3pm. It's also open on Sat. 7:30-9:30am. All telecommunications and postal services are available here. **Papetoai Post Office**, *Tel. 56.13.15*, is on the

lagoon side in the center of Papetoai village. Open Mon.-Thurs. from 8am-12pm, and from 1:30-4pm and until 3pm on Fri. Open on Sat. from 8 to 10am.

Tourist Information

Moorea Visitors Bureau is also called the **Comité de Tourisme de Moorea**, *Tel. 56.29.09/75.01.01/27.76.07; ctm@mail.pf; www.gomoorea.com.* Their office is at the Vaiare Ferry Dock and the English-speaking hostess meets the boats when they arrive from Papeete each morning. She distributes brochures and flyers on Moorea's activities, restaurants, shopping and where to stay on the island. Open Mon.-Sat. from 8am-1pm. Closed on Sun. and holidays. Hiro Damide is president.

Wedding Ceremonies

Tahitian Weddings are performed at the **Tiki Theatre Village** for lovers who get married back home and want to splurge for a fun-filled colorful wedding ceremony in the authentic tradition of old Polynesia. It's not just newlyweds who are getting married in the Tahitian style, but also loving couples who are celebrating their anniversaries or who want to renew their vows. Some couples are now choosing to get married legally at the town hall (mairie) and then to celebrate their wedding with the traditional Polynesian ceremony. This ritual takes place on a *marae* stone altar with a Tahitian priest officiating. **Olivier Briac** and his Tiki Village artisans will transform you into a Tahitian prince and princess for your wedding ceremony for a marriage made in Paradise. There is even a floating *fare* in the lagoon where you can spend your honeymoon. Contact Olivier Briac at B.P. 1016, Haapiti, Moorea, *Tel. 689/55.02.50; Fax 689/56.10.86; tikivillage@mail.pf; www.tikivillage.pf.*

13. Huahine

Huahine (WHO-ah-HEE-nay) is a magical island. I discovered the special qualities of Huahine in 1977, when I was shipwrecked on the reef in Parea, on the south end of Huahine Iti, during a dark and stormy night, while sailing with American friends aboard their luxury yacht. The story has a happy ending, because the yacht was saved and we were adopted into a Tahitian family in Parea. I stayed there for six weeks just because the people were so nice.

On that first morning in Parea, from the cockpit of the yacht that was embedded on the coral reef, I watched the early dawn turning the whole world pink from the mountains to the village to the sea. There is a certain light and color of the air on this island that I haven't found anywhere else. The senses are heightened so that the colors of nature seem more vivid, the air more calm, yet at the same time charged with a feeling of anticipation. I realized that I was listening more intently for—perhaps the primeval call of the jungle.

I still have the same feeling for Huahine. The people are happy and relaxed and they have maintained their traditional lifestyle of fishing and farming. Family and friends are more important than television and Internet. The mountains of Huahine form the shape of a beautiful Tahitian woman when seen from the sea in the moonlight. And there's a definite aura of sexual energy in the air.

Huahine is 175 km. (110 mi.) northwest of Tahiti, the nearest of the Leeward Society Islands to the capital of Papeete. The two islands that comprise **Huahine-Nui** and **Huahine-Iti** (big and little Huahine) are connected by a bridge and have a combined surface area of 73 sq. km. (28 sq. mi.). Legend claims that the two islands were once united and the isthmus was formed when Hiro, a great warrior and god of thieves in Polynesian mythology, sliced his canoe through the island, dividing it and producing two beautiful bays on each side of the isthmus. Folklore tells us that Hiro used the Leeward Islands as his favorite hangout, and on Huahine you can see Hiro's paddle and parts of his anatomy in the stone formations of the cliffs overlooking the channel.

A common barrier reef surrounds the two islands, with several passes providing openings from the sea to the deep harbors. Offshore *motu* lie inside the reef, where watermelons and cantaloupe are grown in the white coral sand. These islets are surrounded by white sand beaches, ideal for a picnic outing with snorkeling in the living coral gardens.

A paved road winds 32 km. (20 mi.) around the two islands, passing through the little villages of Fare, Maeva, Faie and Fitii on Huahine Nui, and Haapu, Parea, Mahuti, Tefarerii and Maroe on Huahine Iti. The modest homes of the 6,070 inhabitants are built beside the lagoon in the small villages. Another paved road, called *la route transversale*, crosses part of the island of Huahine Nui, and is best explored by Land Rover or Jeep or any 4WD vehicle, which are called 4x4 (*quatre-quatre* in French and pronounced like cat-cat). This road is close-hemmed by giant ferns and vines that look as though Tarzan might be seen swinging around these parts. Skirting the shoreline and climbing a little higher into the fern-covered mountains, you will see spectacular views of natural bays and seascapes, with the white foam of the indigo ocean leaping into spray on the coral reef, giving birth to sapphire and emerald lagoons. One multihued bay near the village of Haapu is pointed out on tours as "Gauguin's palette." All around both islands are plantations of vanilla, coffee and taro, and groves of breadfruit, mango, banana and papaya. Trees of *purau* and kapok grow among tangled masses of untamed wilderness. Swiftly flowing streams make their way from their mountain origins, winding through the *mape* forests to form delightful pools for fresh water shrimp.

Mou'a Tapu is the sacred mountain overlooking the prehistoric village of Maeva, which is built beside Lake Fauna Nui. The mountain forms a pyramid, and the people of Maeva say there is a power spot on its summit, which is 429 m. (1,407 ft.) high. A tiki of white coral and a Tiare Taina (gardenia) bush are found here. You can reach this spot by going up the road where the television antenna is located on the southern side of the mountain.

According to ethnohistory, Maeva was the ancient capital of Huahine, and all its ruling families lived there and worshipped in their individual *marae* temples of stone. The great Marae Manunu on the coral islet on the opposite side of Maeva Village was the community temple for Huahine Nui, and Marae Anini at Point Tiva in Parea was the community *marae* for Huahine Iti.

European Discovery

Lieutenant James Cook (who was later promoted to Captain) was the first European to discover Huahine, when he anchored the *Endeavour* in the harbor of Farenui-Atea on July 15, 1769. You can see the islands of Raiatea, Taha'a and Bora Bora from Huahine, which Cook named a Society of Islands, 'because they lay contiguous to one another'.

Cook returned to Huahine in 1773 aboard the *Resolution*, along with the *Adventure*, under the command of Captain Tobias Furneaux. When the two ships set sail, a young man from Raiatea who lived in Huahine went with them. His name was Mai but the Englishmen call him Omai. He became the first Tahitian to discover England, where he was presented to King George III on July 17, 1774. Cook brought Omai back to Huahine in 1777 during his third and final voyage to the South Seas.

After Cook's departure there were few Europeans who visited Huahine, until 1808-09, when a party of Protestant missionaries from the London Missionary Society made it their headquarters for nearly a year. When Christianity was adopted in Tahiti in 1818 the missionaries returned to Huahine and opened a station. The Reverend William Ellis in *Polynesian Researches* tells a first-hand account of this story.

HUAHINE'S ARCHAEOLOGICAL SITES

The royal village of **Maeva** was the traditional headquarters of Huahine, the capital of a complex and highly centralized system of government. This was the only place in the entire Polynesian triangle where the royal families lived side by side. The people of Maeva say that the sacred mountain of Mou'a Tapu protected them. Each of the eight district chiefs of Huahine held court at Maeva and ruled in his province through envoys. Each royal household had a marae stone temple in Maeva as well as in his provincial seat. When the children of each household approached maturity, they, too, each had a temple erected. Consequently, there are some 200 marae in Maeva.

Doctor Yosihiko H. Sinoto, Senior Anthropologist of the Bernice P. Bishop Museum in Honolulu, restored several of the marae temples in Maeva Village and on nearby Matairea Hill in 1967 and 1968. He also restored the stone fish weirs in Lake Fauna Nui, which were used by the ancient fishermen of Maeva. Doctor Sinoto has restored some 200 sites, including 35 marae temples, plus council platforms and housing sites on Matairea Hill in Maeva Village. Inside the Fare Pote'e, an oval-shaped traditional meeting house that is built over Lake Fauna Nui is a museum where you can pick up a map of Matairea Hill. Follow the cultural and scenic hiking trail to visit the restored sites and learn the story of the royal village.

Huahine's warrior-queen Teha'apapa defended her island against the aggressions made by the men of Bora Bora, and she won a great naval battle against the forces of Tahiti's Queen Pomare, who tried to gain control of Huahine. In 1846 Teha'apapa won a land battle against French troops at Maeva, and 24 Frenchmen are buried in Maeva Village, surrounded by seven broken cannon. Huahine defended its independence until 1888, when the regent Marama accepted the French protectorate. In 1898 Huahine became a French colony, but it was not until 1946 that the people of Huahine became French citizens, 58 years after the residents of Tahiti.

ARRIVALS & DEPARTURES

Arriving By Air

Air Tahiti has 3-6 flights daily between Tahiti and Huahine. The 40-minute non-stop flight is 12.530 CFP one-way for adults, and 23.260 CFP round-trip, tax included. There is also a direct flight from Moorea on Mon., Tues., Thurs., Fri. and Sat., which costs 14.830 CFP one-way. You can fly from Raiatea to Huahine every day except Sun. for 7.030 CFP, and there are 1-2 flights daily from Bora Bora, for 9.330 CFP. **Air Tahiti reservations:** Tahiti, *Tel. 86.42.42;* Moorea, *Tel. 55.06.02;* Huahine, *Tel. 68.77.02/60.62.60.*

If you have hotel reservations then you will be met at the airport and driven to your hotel. Several of the family pensions also provide airport pickups. There is an **Avis** counter where you can rent a car. A couple of small boutiques and a snack bar are located in the airport terminal.

You can also get to Huahine by chartering an airplane in Tahiti from **Air Tahiti**, *Tel. 86.42.42*; or **Pol'Air**, *Tel. 74.23.11*.

Arriving By Boat

All the inter-island transport boats dock at the quay in Fare village, the main town of Huahine, and it would be advisable to arrange with your hotel or pension to have someone meet you when you arrive in the middle of the night. The car rental agencies will also meet you at the Fare quay. A travel agency and visitors information center is across the street from the quay.

Hawaiki Nui, *Tel. 54.99.54/Fax 45.24.44, contact@stim.pf.* This 12-passenger ship leaves the Motu Uta dock in Papeete each Tues. at 4pm and arrives at Fare quay in Huahine on Wed. at 2am. The Thurs. trip leaves Papeete at 4pm, and arrives in Huahine on Fri. at 4:30pm, after visiting Raiatea, Bora Bora, Taha'a and Raiatea again. The cost of sleeping on deck is 2.000 CFP per adult and a berth in one of the 4 double cabins costs 5.400 CFP from Papeete to all the Leeward Islands. Children pay half-fare. Meals are available on board. Cars are 11.600-16.900 CFP round-trip.

Departing By Air

You can fly from Huahine to Raiatea (1-3 flights daily) or Bora Bora (1-3 flights daily except Wed.), or return to Moorea (1 flight daily) or Tahiti (4-6 daily flights) by **Air Tahiti**, *Tel. 68.77.02/60.62.60* in Huahine. Tickets can be purchased at the airport or at the Air Tahiti office in Fare village. If you already have reservations and a ticket and need to reconfirm your flight, most hotels will take care of this for you or you can do it yourself one day in advance. Check-in time at the airport is one hour before scheduled departure.

Departing By Boat

You can continue on to Raiatea, Taha'a and Bora Bora by boat from Huahine, or you can return to Papeete.

Hawaiki Nui, *Tel. 68.78.03* (Huahine); *Tel. 54.99.54* (Tahiti), leaves Huahine for Raiatea, Bora Bora, Taha'a and back to Raiatea each Wed. at 3am. On Fri. it leaves Huahine for Tahiti at 7pm, arriving in Papeete on Sat. at 5am.

ORIENTATION

To get from the airport in Huahine to the hotels you will turn right to reach the road that circles the island of Huahine-Nui. When you come to this road you will turn right to go to the main village of **Fare** (pronounced Fah-rey) and the land base for Te Tiare Beach Resort. Turn left if you want to go to **Maeva Village**. You can drive in either direction to reach Huahine-Iti, where Hotel Relais Mahana and a few pensions are located. If you arrive by boat you will disembark on the dock at Fare, right in the center of Huahine's "downtown" area. Fare looks like a sleepy little village, shaded by acacia and South Seas almond trees, but it certainly wakes up on boat days when the passenger or supply ships arrive. Then you have traffic jams in the center of the village. On the waterfront street opposite the quay are the Banque de Tahiti, a couple of snack bars and small restaurants, two pensions, car, scooter and bicycle rentals, service station, scuba diving center, a supermarket, general merchandise and clothing stores, boutiques, a photo shop and jewelry shop. The post office, *gendarmerie*, private doctors, pharmacy and a 15-bed dispensary are within easy walking distance.

GETTING AROUND HUAHINE
Car, Scooter & Bicycle Rentals
Armelle Location, *Tel. 77.79.99; armelle@mail.pf* has a counter inside the Boutique Te Nahe Toetoe in Fare village and at Te Nahe Toetoe Pension in Parea. She charges 6.600 CFP for 24-hrs. for a 5-place a/c Chevrolet Aveo or a 5-place Hyundai Getz with a/c. These rates include taxes, unlimited mileage and insurance. Gas is extra.

Avis Huahine, *Tel. 68.73.34; Fax 68.73.35; avis.tahiti@mail.pf.* They have a sales counter at the airport and at the Mobil service station behind the Super Farenui store in Fare village. A 5-place a/c Ford Fiesta is 9.680 CFP for 8 hrs., and a 5-place Hyundai Getz is 12.600 CFP for 24 hrs. Rates include taxes, unlimited mileage and insurance. Gas is extra.

Europcar *Tel. 68.82.59; huahine@europcar.pf* has a sales office facing the post office in Fare and a sales desk at the Relais Mahana, *Tel. 68.71.62.* A 4-place Hyundai Io with a/c rents for 8.000 CFP for 8 hrs. A 5-place a/c Fiat Panda or Hyundai Getz rents for 9.300 CFP for 8 hrs. and an a/c 5-place Renault Sandero is 11.500 CFP for 8 hrs. Scooter rates are 4.800 CFP for 4 hrs., 5.800 CFP for 8 hrs. and 6.200 CFP for 24 hrs. These rates include unlimited mileage and third party insurance. Gas is extra.

Fare Maeva Location, *Tel. 68.75.53/29.82.98; faremaeva@mail.pf; www.faremaeva.com.* The sales counter is on the waterfront street in Fare village, in the same building as Snack Maeva. You can rent a 4-place a/c Fiat Panda for 7.500 CFP for 4 hrs., 8.000 CFP for 8 hrs., and 9.200 CFP for 24 hrs. A 5-place Fiat Punto is 8.500-9.000-9.800 CFP. A scooter rents for 5.000 CFP a day, and a bike is 1.000 CFP-1.500 CFP.

Huahine Location, *Tel. 68.86.49; huahinelocation@mail.pf.* The sales office is located at Pension Mauarii in Parea on Huahine Iti. An a/c 5-door Hyundai Getz rents for 4.900 CFP for 4 hrs. and 6.000 CFP for 24 hrs., including unlimited mileage and insurance. Gas is extra.

Bicycles/Boats/Kayaks
   Europcar, *Tel. 68.82.59*, rents bikes for 1.200 CFP for 4 hrs. and 1.600 CFP for 8 hrs. Longer rentals possible.
   Huahine Lagoon, *Tel. 68.70.00*, on the quay of Fare adjacent to Pension Chez Guynette. You can rent beach bikes, kayaks, and small boats.

Taxis
   Taxi service is provided by **Enite Excursions**, *Tel. 68.82.37/73.05.07.*

Le Truck
   The local transportation service, *le truck*, operates between the boat dock in Fare and the outlying villages around Huahine Nui and Huahine Iti, coordinating their runs with the arrivals and departures of the inter-island ferries and school hours. The name of the destination is painted on the wooden sides of each *le truck*. Although the fares are affordable for all budgets, hopping aboard a *le truck* is not recommended if you don't know your way around Huahine, and especially if you don't speak any French or Tahitian. But if you are adventurous, this is a fun way to discover the island and its inhabitants.

WHERE TO STAY
Huahine Nui – Deluxe
   TE TIARE BEACH RESORT, *B.P. 36, Fare, Huahine 98731. Tel. 689/ 60.60.50; Fax 689/60.60.51; res@spmhotels.pf; www.tetiarebeachresort.com; www.spmhotels.com. Located on the coast of Fitii, 20 min. by boat from the main village of Fare. 41 bungalows. AE, MC, V.*
   This 4-star hotel is owned by American businessman Rudy Markmiller, and is managed by Tahiti-based South Pacific Management as a Pearl Resort. It opened in March 1999 and closed in Feb. 2007 for a big sprucing up program that included new roofs and varnish for the woodwork. A soft-goods renovation of the property was completed in 2010 and a Manea Spa was also added.
   Te Tiare Beach Resort was included in Condé Nast Traveler's 2011 Gold List winners for the world's finest hotels, resorts and cruise lines. In 2010 Te Tiare Beach Resort listed among the best in the world in Condé Nast Traveler's 23rd Annual Reader's Choice Awards.
   The accommodations consist of 19 garden bungalows, 6 beach bungalows, 5 lagoon bungalows and 11 deep overwater bungalows, beside and over the lagoon in the district called Fitii. The hotel property can be reached only by boat, about a 12-min. ride from Fare village to the resort. All of the bungalows face west, so guests may enjoy the island's spectacular tropical sunsets as well as admire the nearby islands of Raiatea and Taha'a. Your first impression when you arrive here will be a sense of spaciousness and total tranquility. The reception, lobby, lounge, main bar, restaurant and boutique are built over the lagoon, suspended over the water on sturdy concrete pilings. The motif of this complex is tastefully Polynesian,

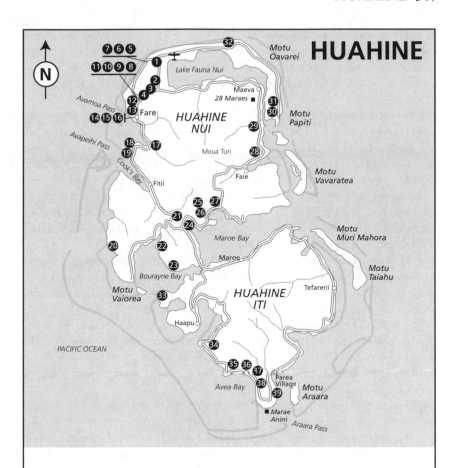

1. Huahine Airport
2. Motel Vanille
3. Chez Ella
4. La Petite Ferme
5. Fare Maeva
6. Pension Vaihonu
7. Pension Mama Roro
8. Chalet Tipanier
9. Rande's Shack
10. Fare le Fare
11. Pension Ariitere
12. Maitai Lapita Village
13. Pension Meherio

14. Pension Enite
15. Chez Guynette
16. Huahine Lodge
17. Pension Poetaina
18. Fare Ara L'ile Sauvage
19. Chez Henriette
20. Te Tiare Beach Resort
21. Hotel Bellevue
22. Pension Tupuna
23. Fare Iita
24. Villas Bougainville
25. Huahine Vacances
26. Villas Standing

27. Residence Loisirs Maroe
28. Pension Te Nahe Toe Toe
29. Au Motu Mahare
30. Pension Tifaifai & Café
31. Vanaa Camping (Delord)
32. Pension Fetia
33. Pension Hine Iti
34. Pension Te Nahe Toe Toe II
35. Pension Mauarii
36. Hotel Relais Mahana
37. Chez Tara
38. Fare le Parea
39. Huahine Camping (Ariiura)

with a huge thatched roof, ceiling fans, shell chandeliers, rattan tables and chairs, bamboo and woven pandanus decorations, and a Tahitian trio playing island tunes in the evening, while lovely *vahines* dressed in Polynesian colors and flowers take your order and serve you an excellent meal that combines French and local style cuisine.

On land the hotel site covers 28.17 acres (11.4 ha.) of tropical plants and flowers and flat ground. The deluxe bungalows are among the largest rooms you will find in Tahiti and Her Islands. You may not even want to leave your room because they are so comfortable. You don't even have to go out to eat if you want to order from room service, which is available from 7:30am to 9:30pm.

Each bungalow features a king-size bed comprised of 2 mattresses that can be transformed into 2 twin beds. There is a living room with sofa, chairs and tables, a/c and ceiling fan, a wet bar, refrigerator, coffee and tea facilities, cable TV, video, IDD telephones, and a separate dressing room in which you will find a personal safe. The overwater bungalows have a large Jacuzzi bathtub and a separate shower with powerful water pressure. (The water at Te Tiare Resort comes from a fresh underground spring, which is filtered, offering you a very high quality of drinking water.) All the bathrooms have separate toilets and hair dryers. There is twice-daily maid service to bring you more towels, bath gels and lotions. All the doors and windows are screened and you even have blackout curtains for more privacy. The terraces for these units are L-shaped and partially covered, with deck chairs for sunbathing or reading and snoozing in the shade. A ladder leads down a few steps into the shallow lagoon.

Next to the lagoon are a free form swimming pool and beach restaurant and bar, as well as the water sports facilities. Complimentary activities include scheduled boat transfers to and from the main town of Fare, snorkeling equipment, Polynesian outrigger paddle canoes, kayaks, beach volleyball, ping-pong and board games. Optional activities include land tours by 4WD, horseback riding, sunset catamaran cruises, lagoon tours by outrigger speed canoe, picnic on a motu, jet-skiing, scuba diving and sailboat excursions. Car, scooter and bicycle rentals, as well as Jeep safaris and other land excursions, are operated from the Te Tiare land base in Fare village. You can also enjoy a relaxing massage in the Manea Spa or in the privacy of your bungalow or practice your asanas with a yoga teacher. See more information under *Massages & Spas* in this chapter.

There are two computers in the overwater lounge and you can buy tickets at the reception. You can also connect your laptop to WiFi in the reception, lobby, bar and beach bar. A boutique of Tahiti's cultured pearls is located in the overwater restaurant/bar/reception complex. Special evenings at the Ari'i Restaurant at Te Tiare Resort are accompanied by a Polynesian dance group. See more information under *Where to Eat* in this chapter.

Various cultural demonstrations are given each evening at the Hawaiki Nui Bar at 6pm, while Tahitian musicians play romantic island songs to complete your dream come true. Honeymooners and couples celebrating anniversaries or other special events can contact the hotel directly for a list of the Romantic Rendez-Vous programs that are designed especially for lovers. These even include a non-binding Polynesian wedding ceremony on the white sand beach, with the bride and groom arriving by outrigger paddle canoe. Children under 15 are given free accommodation when sharing a room with their parents. Meals are also free for children and reduced rates are allowed for transfers.

Superior

MAITAI LAPITA VILLAGE HUAHINE, *B.P. 403, Fare, Huahine 98731. Tel. 689/68.80.80; Fax 689/68.80.68; booking@huahine.hotelmaitai.com; www.hotelmaitai.com. Beside lagoon 2 mi. from airport and 0.5 mi. from center of Fare (10-min. walk). AE, MC, V.*

The Maitai Lapita Village opened on Aug. 1, 2011, with 32 spacious bungalows situated on 7.5 acres (3 hectares) of land, on the former site of the Hotel Bali Hai Huahine. There are 15 Premium Lake bungalows built at the edge of a palm-shaded natural lake dotted with water lilies, and 5 Premium Garden and 12 Garden bungalows spread across the property, surrounded by tropical plants and flowers. The construction of the bungalows and public areas combine the natural products of the island with a blend of modern materials. The restaurant, bar and pool open onto the soft white sand beach and a lagoon that offers excellent swimming in the clearest shades of turquoise and blue.

Creating this hotel is a dream come true for owner/designer Peter Owen, an American expatriate who is often referred to as "Pita-the-Potter" because of the beautiful pottery he and his family produce in Huahine. They also own Huahine's only pearl farm. Peter and his partners in the Lapita Village project wisely chose Hotel Management & Services (HMS) to operate their hotel in the 3-star category of Le Maitai Hotels, under the umbrella of the Pacific Beachcomber S.C. Richard Bailey, who is also an American expat., is President and CEO of this company, which owns 4 Intercontinental Resorts & Spas in the Society Islands, plus the *Paul Gauguin* cruse ship, Hotel Le Maitai Polynesia in Bora Bora and Maitai Rangiroa Lagoon Resort.

Maitai Lapita Village was built with great respect to the environment. The hotel is largely supplied by photovoltaic renewable energy and the area's eco-system is preserved through the use of non-polluting waste treatments and cleaning products. Native trees and traditional medicinal plants were planted around the hotel, recreating an authentic atmosphere.

The bungalows at Maitai Lapita Village Huahine are patterned after the former canoe house or *fare va'a* of the ancient Polynesians. The decks fronting the rooms are decorated with stylized canoe prows, and the furniture on the terrace of the Premium lake bungalows is in the shape of a canoe. Traditional paddles or *hoe* decorate the walls of the bungalows, and the wooden chairs and benches were designed in the form of *turua*, the seats used by the ancient chiefs. The style of the reception and restaurant-bar is inspired by the architecture and carved ornamentation of the houses of ancient Polynesian chiefs. The motifs on the bungalow gables & posts, walkways, light posts and kitchen walls recall the ruddy terracotta color and designs of the Lapita pottery, and the décor of the bungalows reflects the archaeological artifacts of the ancient Polynesians who lived and worked on this site. In memory of the late artist, Bobby Holcomb, who lived on Huahine from 1976-1991, copies of his paintings decorate the walls of the rooms. These designs were based on the legends and tales of Huahine. In the hotel's reception is a large triptych of Bobby's tribute to Lapita pottery.

The 12 Garden Bungalows are 39 sq.m (420 sq. ft) and there are 6 blocks of 2 connecting units under the same roof with a dbl. bed and a sofa bed in each unit. These rooms can be booked separately for 20.150/26.850 CFP sgl/dbl during the low season and 22.165/29.535 CFP sgl/dbl during the high season. The 5 Premium Garden bungalows are 42 sq.m (452 sq. ft.), including a large terrace. They have a king-size bed and 2 single beds, and sell for 22.400/29.850 CFP sgl/dbl in low season and 24.640/32.835 CFP sgl/dbl in high season. The 15 Premium Lake Bungalows have 42 sq.m (452 sq. ft.) including a terrace of 38 sq.m (409 sq. ft.). They have a king size bed and 2 single beds and are priced at 24.640/32.835 CFP sgl/dbl during the low season, and 27.100/36.120 CFP sgl/dbl during the high season. These rack rates will decrease starting April 1, 2012. All bungalow rates include taxes, as well as an American breakfast. There is no accommodation surcharge for children under 16 years who share the room with their parents. They also have a reduction in meal rates. The costs of meal plans had not been definitely decided before my deadline in Aug. 2011. See more information under *Where to Eat* in this chapter.

The bungalows are equipped with a/c, satellite/cable TV, IDD telephone, paid WiFi access, minibar, in-room safe, coffee/tea making facilities, iron and board, private bathroom with a separate shower, hair dryer, and a terrace or patio. In addition to the restaurant, bar and swimming pool, there is a boutique with a museum area. Services include transit rooms, laundry services, ice machines, and guests have free use of the snorkeling equipment, table tennis and kayaks on request. The fitness room and game room are also open to guests. Bikes, cars and quads can be rented, and other paid activities include jet ski excursions, fishing, sailing, scuba diving and surfing in the pass.

One of my favorite activities at this hotel site is to awaken with the dawn so that I can photograph the lake and its bridges during a very brief magical moment, when the luminescence of the sky is reflected in the still water, shaded by the palm trees and lakeside bungalows. And just before sunset time I love to swim in the warm lagoon in front of the hotel. On the horizon lie the neighboring Society Islands of Raiatea, Taha'a and Bora Bora.

Down the beach toward Fare village, which is just a 10-min. walk from the hotel, cruising yachts anchor near the shore and come to the hotel bar to relax with a cold beer, Bloody Mary or Maitai. It is easy to feel the magic of Huahine here in this setting of peaceful beauty.

THE "LAPITA VILLAGE" MUSEUM
TELLS THE STORY OF THE POLYNESIAN PEOPLE

The term Lapita refers to the ancestral culture from which the Polynesians emerged. It refers to the people who navigated some 4,000 years ago from South East Asia through Melanesia to Polynesia, voyaging in great double-hulled sailing canoes. Traces of the passing of the "Lapita people" were revealed in archaeological excavations from which a very particular pottery-making tradition was identified for the first time in the 1950's. Lapita sites with their typical "incised" and "dentate stamped" pottery are to be found all the way from the Bismarck Archipelago in Melanesia to the islands of Tonga and Samoa in Western Polynesia. The latter date to c.1200 BC. It was in the 3 archipelagoes of Fiji, Tonga and Samoa that a true Polynesian culture emerged from the "Lapita cultural complex" over a period of 2,000 years. From c.750 AD the Polynesians settled East Polynesia. Among the earliest sites attesting to the presence of Polynesians in the East are the VAITO'OTIA and FA'AHIA sites on Huahine, located on the grounds of the Maitai Lapita Village Huahine.

The naming of "Lapita Village" is in remembrance of the ancient village that existed for centuries on the site around which the hotel is built. Numerous artifacts dating from c.850 to 1450 AD were uncovered here in 1974. These included stone adzes, hammer stones, grinding & polishing stones for stone tool manufacture and pearl shell fishhooks, bonito lures and pendants fashioned from both pearl-shell and whale bone. Wooden objects were also retrieved from water logged conditions that had preserved them. These included wooden food bowls (*umete*) and parts of a voyaging canoe, canoe bailer and coconut fiber cordage (*nape*). The canoe elements are the best preserved and most ancient discovered to date in Polynesia. The most spectacular find were fragments in both wood and whalebone of ancient war clubs known as *patu*. Up until this time these war clubs were only known from New Zealand and were presumed to be a uniquely New Zealand Maori weapon. The discovery points to the origin of these clubs being in tropical Polynesia and taken with the first settlers to New Zealand. The *patu* disappeared in the Society Islands after the first millennia AD. Some of these objects are displayed in the museum at Maitai Lapita Village. During hotel construction an on-site archaeologist supervised the ongoing work guaranteeing the protection of the archaeological deposits and structures still on the site. The latter are visible today and serve as a living museum.

One of these is the *marae* (open air stone temple) of the village called marae Tahuea, which was restored in the 1980's. Captain James Cook mentioned this marae during his visit to Huahine in 1769.

The rich history of the site of the Maitai Lapita Village is told in the form of a chronological exhibition in the hotel museum. From the early settlement period throughout ancient times to the arrival of Europeans and up until the 19th century historic period. The resources include relevant artifacts, illustrations, explanatory texts and diverse artworks. You can also visit marae Tahuea and the excavated areas where the archaeological finds were discovered.

– *Excerpt from Maitai Lapita Village presentation written by Mark Eddowes, an archaeologist-anthropologist living in Huahine.*

Family Pensions, Guest Houses, B&B, Backpackers' Lodgings, & Campgrounds
Moderate
CHALET TIPANIER, *Tel. 689/68.78.91/78.05.69; chalet.tipanier@mail.pf;*
www.pension-huahine.com. No credit cards.
2 modern chalets each with 2 upstairs rooms in Fare, 5 min. from airport, 7 min. from Fare center and 328 ft. (100 m.) from the lagoon. Equipped kitchen, bathroom with hot water, mosquito net TV, fan, WiFi Internet. Free transfers, bicycles, and swimming pool. They have a 1-Tiare rating.
MOTEL VANILLE, *B.P. 381, Fare, Huahine 98731. Tel./Fax 689/68.71.77; www.motelvanille.com. Located beside the road 1 km. (0.62 mi.) from the airport, 1 km. from the beach, and 1 km. from Fare village. Free transfers and breakfast. MC, V.*
This small family hotel has a 1-Tiare rating from Tahiti Tourisme. It is the first lodging you come to when leaving the airport, as it is built on the corner between the airport road and the circle island road. There are 5 bungalows with a choice of sleeping accommodations for 2-4 people, private bathroom with hot water, and a terrace. All the Tahitian style *fare* units are built of local woods, bamboo and thatched roofs, and the windows are screened. There are fans, in-room safes and mosquito repellent. They are set in a tropical garden around a swimming pool, and you cannot see the ocean from here. Bicycles are free for guests and a restaurant-snack is located on the premises.
PENSION POETAINA, *B.P. 522, Fare, Huahine 98731. Tel. 60.60.06/ 78.86.39/28.92.13; pensionpoetaina@mail.pf; www.poetaina.com. Located on the mountainside of the road in Fare village, 3 km. (1.8 mi.) from the airport and 1 km. (.62 mi.) from the ferry dock. Free transfers. MC, V.*
Jean-Pierre Amo and his wife Damiana have built a big 3-story white concrete house in the South Seas neo-colonial style, with a huge sun deck on the top floor. There are 4 rooms with a double and single bed, sharing 2 communal bathrooms and hot water; 3 family rooms with a/c, a double bed, single bed and private bathroom; and a family room with a king size bed, single bed, private bathroom and kitchenette. Downstairs is a living room with TV and activity area, a kitchen and dining room, which are all shared, as well as the big terrace and swimming pool. Breakfast is included. Jean-Pierre also operates Poetaina Cruises, providing a choice of lagoon excursions and picnics on the motu. Bicycles, horseback riding, scuba diving and all other activities can be arranged through the pension. See *Lagoon Excursions* in this chapter.
HOTEL BELLEVUE, *B.P. 21, Fare, Huahine 98731. Tel. 689/68.82.76; Fax 689/68.85.35; hotelbellevue@mail.pf. Located on the mountainside overlooking Maroe Bay, 6 km. (4 mi.) from the airport and 5 km. (3 mi.) from the ferry dock in Fare village. MC, V.*
Most visitors to Huahine see the Hotel Bellevue when they are riding around the island in a tour bus. It is perched on the top of a knoll overlooking the panoramic scenery of Maroe Bay and the hills beyond. This is one of those places

that is discovered by travelers who have the time to get to know an island, its people and its delightful secrets.

Each of the 10 colonial style bungalows contains a double bed with mosquito net, a private bathroom with hot water provided by solar heating, fans, and individual terraces overlooking the fresh water swimming pool and the view of Maroe Bay. 5 of these units are equipped with their own kitchen, and guests staying in the other bungalows without kitchens share the communal kitchen.

This small hotel opened in 1980 and was enlarged to 15 bungalows and a pool in 1985. Some of the units have now been closed. It is owned by Eliane and François Lefoc, a Chinese couple from Huahine who are noted for the delicious seafood they served in their public restaurant before they turned the kitchen over to their guests. Meals are still served to in-house guests on request. The Lefocs do not speak much English, but they say a lot with their eyes and gestures. Eliane will drive you to Fare village for supplies or you can also walk down to the road and catch *le truck*. She will also show you their impressive garden of fruit trees. Table tennis, mini-billiards, baby foot and bocci ball are free activities.

PENSION VAIHONU, *B.P. 302, Fare, Huahine 98731. Tel. 689/68.87.33/ 79.20.65/71.96.03; Fax 689/68.77.57; vaihonu@mail.pf; www.vaihonu.com. Located beside the sea at PK 1 in Fare, between the airport and the village. Free transfers. MC, V.*

If you are coming from Fare village look for the dirt road just past La Petite Ferme; turn left there and head toward the sea; turn left again at the last road before you get to the end at Fare Maeva; continue a short distance until you see the Vaihonu sign.

Available for guests are 2 concrete 2-level duplexes, 5 small wooden beach huts facing the sea, and a 7-bed dormitory. The duplex cottages are equipped with 2 double beds and a ceiling fan upstairs, and on the ground level there is a bright, cheerful kitchen with a dining area, plus a private bathroom. The windows are screened and the floors are tiled. Each beach hut has a double bed and screened windows and guests share the kitchen and bathroom (cold-water showers) with anyone staying in the dorm. Sheets are furnished and regularly changed for all guests, but you must bring your own towels when staying in beach huts or dorm. Laundry service and wireless Internet access are available and guests can use bikes free of charge.

Owner Etienne Faaeva also owns Huahine Explorer and he or his brother Daniel can organize your safari excursions and other activities. They both speak English. This is a family of excellent musicians, and if you are in residence during one of their frequent barbecue parties, you'll truly enjoy the beautiful island songs they sing while playing the guitar and ukulele. The restaurant serves Chinese and local style dishes on request. See *Where to Eat* in this chapter.

FARE MAEVA, *B.P. 675, Fare, Huahine 98731. Tel. 689/68.75.53/29.82.98/ 72.27.85; Fax 689/68.70.68; faremaeva@mail.pf; www.fare-maeva.com. Located* *beside the sea on the outskirts of Fare, 3 km. (1.8 mi.) from the ferry dock and 1 km. (.62 mi.) from the airport. Free transfers. MC, V.*

Ten yellow concrete bungalows with sheet metal roofs are built in a garden setting 20 m. (66 ft.) from the sea. Each small unit is a/c and furnished with cheerful colors and contains a double bed, a salon with 2 single beds, dining area and equipped kitchen, a private bathroom with cold water, and a terrace. 4 bungalows have easy access for handicapped guests. There are also 5 a/c rooms with a double bed and a private bathroom. Restaurant Tehina is part of the pension, where you can eat all your meals if you don't want to cook. See information under *Where to Eat* in this chapter. Guests have free use of the swimming pool. You can also rent a car, scooter or bicycle here and the reception people will help you organize your tours and excursions. Tahiti Tourisme gave this pension a 1-Tiare rating.

FARE ARA L'ILE SAUVAGE, *B.P. 891, Fare, Huahine 98731. Tel./Fax 689/ 68.75.08; cell 74.96.09; fare-ara@mail.pf; www.fare-ara.blog.fr. On the mountainside, 5 min. from the center of Fare. Free transfers. No credit cards.*

Tinau Ropati has 2 comfortable bungalows for rent in Hamene, each with 2 bedrooms, living room, equipped kitchen, bathroom with hot water, washing machine, TV, fan, house linens and mosquito net. Free activities include WiFi Internet, bikes, canoes, snorkeling gear, barbecue grill and visits to a vanilla farm. Packages also include the bungalow with a car and boat.

PENSION ARIITERE, *Tel. 689/74.40.30; Fax 689/68.82.26; pensionariitere@mail.pf; www.pensionariitere.com. V.*

There are 4 clean and tidy bungalows with fans and 2 a/c rooms in this 1-Tiare rated pension in Fare, a 10 min. walk from the village and 5 min. walk from the beach. There are cooking facilities in the bungalows and a communal kitchen beside the swimming pool, and meals can be served on request. WiFi Internet access, free bikes and kayaks. Scooter and boat rentals possible. Owners Juanito & Iva Lee provide friendly, helpful service. A bungalow for 2 people with a/c and breakfast is 7.500 CFP and a room for 2 is 6.300 CFP, including a/c and breakfast.

They also have a small house on a white sand beach for rent for 13.500 CFP a day for 4 people. This includes a 5-seat car.

Economy

CHEZ GUYNETTE CLUB-BED, *B. P. 87, Fare, Huahine 98731. Tel./Fax 689/68.83.75; chezguynette@mail.pf. In the center of Fare village, opposite the ferry dock and 3 km. (1.9 mi.) from the airport. All major credit cards.*

This is my favorite place to stay in Huahine when I want to meet all kinds of interesting people while sitting on the terrace facing the road and beach in the middle of Fare village. If you arrive in Huahine by inter-island ferryboat you can walk across the road from the boat dock and you'll be at Chez Guynette. The hostel has 7 large rooms, each with a double bed and 1-2 bunk beds, and a private bathroom with hot water. There is also an 8-bed dormitory, sharing 2 communal bathrooms with hot water, and a big, clean and homey kitchen where you can cook your own food. A washing machine is also available for guests. The windows are all screened and each room has a ceiling fan. Olivier and Laurence LeBrun, a young French couple, are the new owners, and they have improved the bathrooms with new tiles and made new bed covers. Information on the activities available on Huahine is posted in the reception area. See information under *Where to Eat* in this chapter.

You'll be right in the center of village life on a small tropical island here, with the benefit of walking across the road to a white sand beach for a wonderful swim in the warm lagoon, or watching the inter-island freighters and luxury passenger ships coming and going.

PENSION ENITE, *B.P. 37, Fare, Huahine 98731. Tel./Fax 689/68.82.37; cell 73.05.07. Located at the end of the waterfront street in Fare. No credit cards.*

This is one of the oldest pensions on the island, with 8 rooms located next to the lagoon. Guests share a living room with TV and a bathroom with hot water. Owner Enite Temaiana has earned a worthy reputation for the cuisine she serves her guests in the open-air restaurant. EP or MAP. She also operates a taxi service and will take you on excursions around the island.

PENSION FETIA, *B.P. 73, Fare, Huahine 98731. Tel./Fax 689/68.81.62; cell 72.09.50; pension-fetia@gmx.fr; www.ifrance.com/polynesie_pension-fetia. On the beach at Motu Maeva, 2.5 km. from the airport and 5 km. from boat dock in Fare village. No credit cards.*

Réjane and Pierre Ah-Min have 5 bungalows in a coconut grove beside the ocean shore on Motu Maeva. Made of wood, bamboo and stone, they can sleep a couple or up to 8 guests. Each bungalow has mosquito nets over the beds, fan, private bathroom with hot water, and a kitchen with micro-wave. Réjane's generous meals are served family style in a restaurant overlooking the ocean.

RANDE'S SHACK, *B.P. 112, Fare, Huahine 98731. Tel./Fax 689/68.86.27; cell 22.10.13; randesshack@mail.pf. On the beach between the airport and boat dock, a short walk from Fare village. Min. of 3 nights required. No credit cards.*

American expatriate Rande Vetterli and his Moorean wife Emere Roometua have 2 fully equipped houses that are set in a garden full of fruit trees. The houses are very clean and completely screened, with full kitchens, private bathrooms, hot water, linens, fans, TV, washing machines and bicycles. You will need to provide your own toiletries and car transportation and there is no maid service available. A 15-min. walk along the white sand beach or on the road will bring you to Fare village, where you can find restaurants and supermarkets. You can also spend hours snorkeling in the marvelous lagoon in front of the property. Rande's Shack is highly recommended by discerning Canadian friends who visit Huahine frequently. They think this is the best buy in French Polynesia and stay here each year for 2-3 months.

PENSION MEHERIO i HUAHINE, *Tel. 689/60.61.35; Fax 689/60.61.36; cell 30.53.32; meherio.huahine@mail.pf; www.huahine-meherio.com. Located 10 min. by car from the airport and 2 min. from Fare village. MC. V.*

This 3-Tiare rated lodging is in the midst of a lovely flower garden of Tiare Tahiti, gardenias and hibiscus, 200 m. (656 ft.) from the public beach of Fare. There are 3 buildings covered with woven bamboo, with the reception in the middle building and the 7 rooms divided in 2 side buildings. Each room is decorated in a colorful Polynesian style with woven bamboo wall coverings, pareo curtains and bedding, and paintings by local artists. There is a double bed, mosquito net, electric fan and a private bathroom and covered terrace. Two rooms are equipped for people with reduced mobility. The rooms are cleaned every 2 days.

Breakfast and dinner are served in the restaurant, which is closed at noon. The meals feature local products, and the Sunday morning breakfast also contains coconut bread and *firi firi*, the famous Tahitian doughnut. There is a TV and DVD player in the lounge, as well as a small library and board games. WiFi access is extra. A safety deposit box is available at the reception and laundry service is optional. Guests have free use of the kayaks, snorkeling equipment and bicycles, as well as the lounge chairs and parasols. All the island's activities and excursions can be arranged on request.

FARE IITA, *B.P. 629, Fare, Huahine 98731. Tel./Fax 689/68.70.21; cell 26.26.80; farepapaya@fare-iita.net; www.fare-iita.net. On mountainside in Bourayne Bay. No credit cards.*

The Papaya House (Fare Iita) is in Bourayne Bay, between Huahine Nui and Huahine Iti, and has been given a 1-Tiare rating by Tahiti Tourisme. You can cook your own meals or let Christine Delaplagne, your French landlady and neighbor, do it for you. This 4-bedroom wooden house is from Chile, and includes a bathroom with bathtub, a bathroom with shower, plus an outdoor shower. There is an American style kitchen and a big covered terrace, plus solar hot water, fans, mosquito nets, TV and paid Internet access. This is a good choice for families as there are 2 kids next door. Daniel, the landlord, will transfer you to the beach for a fee, and you can paddle a kayak, or rent a boat without license.

AU MOTU MAHARE, *B.P. 772, Fare, Huahine 98731. Tel. 689/77.76.97; motumahare@yahoo.com; www.aumotumahare.blogspot.com. On a motu on Huahine's northeast side of the island facing the sunrise. No credit cards.*

Kim Fabre operates this Robinson Crusoe type lodging in a coconut plantation on the edge of the lagoon facing Maeva. The 2 local style *fares* have a private bathroom and share the kitchen and thatched roof dining shelter. Hammocks, sun loungers and ocean kayaks are provided, as well as transfers.

Huahine Iti – Moderate

RELAIS MAHANA, *B.P. 30, Fare, Huahine 98731. Tel. 689/60.60.40; Fax 689/68.85.08; relaismahana@mail.pf; www.relaismahana.com. Located at Avea Bay on Huahine's best white sand beach, (25 km.) 15.5 mi. from the airport, on the southwest side of Huahine Iti, just outside Parea Village. Round-trip transfers 4.098 CFP. All major credit cards.*

This 3-star hotel opened in 1985 with 12 bungalows, and added more units over the years. Then the hotel closed in Nov. 2006 for rebuilding, adding new bungalows and remodeling some of the old ones. It reopened in March 2007 with 32 units, including deluxe and superior bungalows in the garden and on the white sand beach, plus 10 garden rooms with connecting doors. The superior bungalows, on the right side of the reception area, were only redecorated as they were still fairly new. These are the larger units usually occupied by families. The new rooms and deluxe bungalows on the left side of reception are built of balau wood from Bali. They have thatched roofs, tiled floors, woven wall mats, and a covered terrace with wicker table and chairs. The deluxe bungalows have a king size bed and a twin bed and the superior units have a king and 2 twin beds. The bedding is all white with accent cushions. All the rooms have ceiling fans, a long vanity desk with telephone, flat screen TV with satellite cable; coffee/tea making machines, and mini-bar. The bathrooms in the deluxe units have a separate toilet, a shower with rainshower and wand nozzles, a hair dryer and an iron in the closet. In all 12 of the deluxe bungalows you can step down from the shower into a walled garden with a locked gate that opens with your room key. Glass doors between the bathroom and bedroom may give a feeling of space, but they allow no privacy in either room, and there is no fresh air circulation in the bedroom when the sliding glass doors to the terrace are closed. There is maid service twice a day. Owner Franck Guillot has now added free WiFi Internet service in the rooms. He has also transformed one of the beach bungalows to the right of reception, which is now a spa with a Jacuzzi and sun deck. See information under *Massage* in this chapter.

There is a restaurant and bar in the main building, where breakfast and dinner are served. Lunch is normally served on the terrace, where there is a barbecue grill. See more information under *Where to Eat* in this chapter.

The white sand beach in front of the hotel curves along the aqua and deep turquoise waters of Avea Bay, which offers some of the island's best coral gardens for snorkeling. This bay is also a haven for cruising yachts and the swimming here is especially delightful. During the renovations of 2006-2007, the hotel's long pier was also rebuilt. The hotel grounds at the edge of the beach are partially shaded by enormous trees. These include tamanu, almond, miro (rosewood), tahinu, tiare kahaia and purau (wild hibiscus) trees. A bench has been built into the convoluted root system of an ancient almond tree that has grown together with a tamanu tree, a coconut palm and some bushes. This is a wonderful place to relax and watch the sunset.

Free activities include beach towels, snorkeling gear and kayaks. The hotel works with the local suppliers for rental cars, scooters, bikes, beach buggies, Quads, horseback riding, and 4WD tours. Relais Mahana has its own 12-place outrigger speed canoe that is used to take the in-house guests on a lagoon excursion and picnic on Motu Ara Ara facing Parea village. Following a morning discovery of the lagoon, the pearl farm, snorkeling in the coral gardens and feeding the sacred eels of Faie, you arrive on the white sand beach of Motu Ara Ara for a picnic of grilled fish and meats, fresh fruits and drinks (punch, beer, fruit juice, mineral water or coffee). The picnic tables are placed in the shallow lagoon water to keep you cool while you dine. A traditional *fare potée* with a roof of coconut fronds provides shade, and lounge chairs allow you to relax. There are 2 toilets and a changing cabin on the motu. After lunch you will board the outrigger canoe again and visit the friendly rays that live in the lagoon.

PENSION MAUARII, *B.P. 473, Fare, Huahine 98731. Tel. 689/68.86.49/ 73.90.26; Fax 689/60.60.96; vetea@mail.pf; www.mauarii.com. Beside a white sand beach in Parea, 17 km. (10.6 mi.) from the ferry dock and 19 km. (11.8 mi.) from the airport. All major credit cards.*

This Polynesian style pension has a 3-Tiare rating and is close to Parea village on Huahine Iti, beside the island's most beautiful lagoon and white sand beach. Accommodations include 4 bungalows in the garden, 1 bungalow on the beach, and 3 rooms on the beach. Each unit has a private bathroom with hot water. There are also 2 standard rooms in the Fare Mauarii that share a bathroom. All the units are clean and attractively decorated, with ceiling fans and mosquito nets over the beds, but there are no screens on the windows. Only the 5-person Monett garden bungalow has a kitchenette and refrigerator.

Guests have free use of kayaks, snorkeling gear and lounge chairs. Manager Vetea Breysse also owns Huahine Locations, and you can rent an a/c car or bicycle at the reception desk. You can also book island tours by 4WD vehicle and lagoon excursions. The Heremiti Dive Center is on the premises. Chez Mauarii Restaurant has a very good reputation for its food, and the menu includes fish and seafood specialties, as well as tasty Chinese dishes. See more information under *Where to Eat* in this chapter.

Note: On July 22, 2011 Tahiti Nui Travel (the largest travel agency in Tahiti) posted a notice on their website that they were permanently ending their partnership with Pension Mauarii following serious complaints about the quality of service and accommodation. Some folks love it here and others obviously don't.

FARE IE PAREA, *B.P. 746, Fare, Huahine 98731. Tel./Fax 689/60.63.77; cell 78.61.74; www.tahitisafari.com. Located on a white sand beach in Parea 20 km. (12.4 mi.) from the airport, 30 min. by car from Fare. No credit cards.*

These cottages are actually 4 canvas tents like you would stay in on an African safari. They are built on a wooden platform with a deck and the beach units contain a private bathroom, while the garden cottages share a communal exterior bathroom. The beach bungalows also have a private kitchen in a *fare potée* shelter adjacent to the tents, and guests staying in the garden tents share a communal kitchen. Each tent contains 1-2 big beds for a maximum of 4 people, and they have teak furniture, lamps, and electric floor fans. All the windows and doors are screened, but several guests have complained that the mosquitoes find their way inside.

The bikes and kayaks are free for guest use, and you can rent a scooter or car at the reception. The managers will also help you arrange your excursions or order take-out meals from the nearby snacks, which can be delivered to your cottage.

They will also show you Marae Ta'iharuru on the white sand beach in front of the Fare Ie property, and the very powerful Marae Anini at the end of Point Tiva. WiFi Internet access available.

Fare Ie Fare, *Tel./Fax 60.63.77; Cell 78.32.95; fareiehuahine@mail.pf; www.tahitisafari.com* has 2 tent cottages beside the lagoon just 2 km. (1.2 mi.) from the airport and a 15-20 min. walk to Fare village. These beach cottages are 60 sq. m. (646 sq. ft.) and can sleep up to 4 people. Each unit has a private bathroom, but the kitchen is communal. Nora & Sabrina, your hostesses, deliver fresh bread and pastries to you each morning for your complimentary breakfast. Bicycles, snorkeling, and fishing gear are available, as well as kayaks and beach chairs. WiFi Internet access.

Villa Rentals With Cars & Boats

In the Maroe Bay area there are furnished villas to rent, and a car and boat are usually included. All villas have access to the water, and there are 2 tennis courts, a swimming pool and a marina in this complex of rental villas.

HUAHINE VACANCES, *B.P. 10, Fare, Huahine 98731. Tel./Fax 689/ 68.73.63; cell 689/77.47.08; www.huahinevacance.pf. At PK 10 on the north shore of Maroe Bay. Free transfers. MC, V.*

Michel & Jacqueline Sorin have 3 modern white plantation-type villas for rent beside Maroe Bay, each with 3 bedrooms and 1-2 bathrooms. They include a fully equipped kitchen, hot water, screened windows, mosquito nets, baby bed, washing machine, TV, barbecue grill, house linens, and a covered porch facing the bay. There is direct access to the water. Baby-sitting is available, but no housekeeping. A car and boat are included in the package. This villa has a 1-Tiare rating.

VILLAS BOUGAINVILLE, *B.P. 258, Fare Huahine 98731. Tel. 689/ 60.60.30/79.70.59; Fax 689/60.60.31; www.villas-bougainville.com. At PK 10, Maroe on the north shore of the bay. Free transfers. MC, V.*

Raphael Matapo has 4 modern houses built on 2 acres (1 ha.) of land near the water in Maroe Bay. Each villa is at least 1,000 sq. ft. (90 sq. m.) and contains a living room with ceiling fan and satellite TV, DVD player, bedrooms with a ceiling fan or optional a/c. There is a fully equipped kitchen, dining area, private bathrooms with hot water, covered terrace, washing machine, household linens, outdoor barbecue and fishing rods. A long dock has a palapa type shelter at the end, with a table and chairs. The house is cleaned once a week and a groundskeeper rakes leaves daily. Baby sitting services and cribs are available. Included with each villa is a new 5-door car with a/c, and a motorboat with 9.9 HP or 15 HP motor. Reports on this place are very positive.

Other villas in the Maroe Bay complex include: **Residence Loisirs Maroe**, *Tel. 689/42.96.09/68.88.64,* with a 4-bedroom villa; **Villas Standing**, *Tel. 689/82.49.65/ 78.09.36; Fax 689/85.47.69; villas-standing@iaroana-huahine.com* with 4 villas and a bungalow. Rental prices on request.

Other Family Pensions, Guest Houses, Bed & Breakfast, Backpackers' Lodgings & Campgrounds on Huahine Nui and Huahine Iti
Chez Ella, *Tel. 689/68.73.07/28.35.91; chezellahuahine@yahoo.fr; www.iaorana-huahine.com.* There are 2 houses and a cottage, all with kitchens, next door to Motel Vanille near the airport. MC, V. **Chez Henriette,** *Tel. 689/68.83.71,* has 6 bungalows with kitchenettes in Haamene Bay. **Huahine Lodge,** *Tel./Fax 689/68.70.64; cell 30.39.66; huahinelodge@mail.pf.* 3-story concrete guest on mountainside in Fare with 12 rooms, fans, bathrooms with hot water, laundry, TV, WiFi, restaurant & bar. No credit cards. **La Petite Ferme,** *Tel./Fax 689/68.82.98; lapetiteferme@mail.pf.* Beside the road between the airport and Fare, with a 5-bed dormitory. **Pension Hine Iti,** *Tel./Fax 689/68.74.58,* has a 3-story house for 6 people in Haapu. **Pension Mama Roro,** *Tel./Fax 689/68.84.82; www.pensionteroro@yahoo.fr.* This 2-Tiare guest house has two bungalows with kitchens close to the sea and airport, across the road from Pension Vaihonu. **Pension Te Nahe Toetoe,** *Tel./Fax 689/68.71.43/77.79.99; www.pension-tenahetoetoe.net* is in Faie and has simple rooms as well as a dormitory, plus meals, free bicycles and paddle canoes. MC, V. They also own **Pension Te Nahe Toetoe** in Parea on Huahine Iti which has 4 bungalows, 1 fare and camping space on a very nice white sand beach. Bring your own tent. AE, MC, V. **Pension Tifaifai & Café,** *Tel. 77.07.74; uberi05@yahoo.fr.* This B&B is on a large property in Maeva. Flora Nordman has 2 rooms, each with private bathroom and hot water and fridge. 5.500 CFP sgl; 7.400 CFP dbl. Breakfast included. **Pension Tupuna,** *Tel./Fax 689/68.70.36; cell 79.07.94; lorettafranck@mail.pf; www.pensiontupuna.com* is in a coconut plantation near Bourayne Bay, with 3 very small local style bungalows that have a 1-Tiare rating. **Chez Tara,** *Tel. 689/68.78.45/72.98.76,* has 2 garden bungalows and 1 tree house beside the lagoon at Avea Bay in Parea on Huahine Iti. A local style restaurant on the premises serves good meals, with *ma'a Tahiti* on Sunday.

Backpackers and campers will find inexpensive accommodations at **Vanaa Camping and Snack (Pension Delord)** *Tel. 689/68.89.51,* on Motu Maeva, which has 13 small *fares* and a campground. **Huahine Camping** (also called **Ariiura Camping**), *Tel./Fax 689/68.85.20,* has cabins, tents and a campground on a white sand beach in Parea village on Huahine Iti. Guided ecology walks. Owner Hubert Bremond also has a garden of traditional medicinal plants. Room 2.000 CFP single; camping 1.000 CFP per person.

WHERE TO EAT
Deluxe
TE TIARE BEACH RESORT, *Tel. 60.60.50. Open daily for B, L, D. AE, MC, V.*
Arii Restaurant, the main restaurant, is built over the water, where you can see numerous fish swimming in the clear water. During dinner guests frequently see manta rays performing their ballet just below the restaurant terrace.

A Continental breakfast is 2.000 CFP and an American breakfast is 3.000 CFP. At lunch you have a choice of casse-croute sandwiches or paninis, burgers, salads and cold appetizers, or a hot dish of shrimp, grilled salmon, calamari, lamb chop, or steak. There are also several vegetarian dishes and a Junior menu. The a la carte dinner choices include fresh lagoon fish, red tuna, shrimp, lobster and crab (in season), poultry and New Zealand meats, priced from 1.200-3.100 CFP. You can order wine by the glass or a bottle of wine from France, Italy, Spain, Chile, California, New Zealand and Australia. Special evenings at the Ari'i Restaurant sometimes include a Polynesian buffet or a Seafood buffet and are accompanied by a Polynesian dance group.

Hawaiki Nui Bar is built over the water adjacent to the reception. They serve all your favorite libations plus some exotic cocktails of their own.

Beach Restaurant and Bar is built between the swimming pool and the white sand beach. This covered shelter can seat 40 people and is used for wedding receptions and other private parties. Drinks and snacks are served during the day, and the luncheon menu is the same as in the Arii Restaurant. No dinner is served here.

Superior

MAITAI LAPITA VILLAGE HUAHINE, *Tel. 68.80.80. Open daily for B., L., D. Coffee shop open 6am-10pm. Live entertainment on Fri. & Sat. nights. AE, MC, V.*

An American breakfast is 2.835 CFP. Lunch is approximately 3.150 CFP per adult, and dinner is 4.725 CFP per adult. The approximate MAP rate for breakfast and dinner is 7.560 CFP, and AP for all meals is 10.710 CFP per person per day.

RELAIS MAHANA, *Tel. 60.60.40. Te Nahe Restaurant is open daily for B, L D. All major credit cards.*

Breakfast and dinner are served in the 2 seaside dining rooms and you eat lunch outside on the terrace. Some of the tables are partially covered by the roof of the restaurant, while others are open to the elements, or covered by a big umbrella. Containers of carnelian and purple bougainvillea border the dining terrace. An American breakfast buffet is 2.568 CFP. Lunch choices include burgers and fries for 1.500 CFP, pizzas for 1.350-1.600 CFP, *poisson cru* for 1.900 CFP, raw vegetable plates 1.250 CFP, fish and seafood for 1.500 CFP, or grilled meats for 2.100 CFP. An a la carte dinner has main course choices for 1.900 CFP and a set menu is 5.350 CFP. Wine is sold by the carafe or bottle, and you can also order a cold pression of Hinano beer. A Buffet dinner with a Polynesian dance show is held on occasion, and costs 5.800 CFP.

CHEZ MAUARII, *Tel. 68.86.49, beside lagoon at PK 17 in Parea. Open daily 7:30am-9pm for B.,L.,D. AE, MC, V.*

This beachside restaurant is noted for its fresh seafood specials and local dishes. For breakfast you can order fruit, eggs and bacon or pancakes for 1.700 CFP. For lunch and dinner lagoon and ocean fish are served with a variety of sauces, priced from 1.800-3.200 CFP. Meats are 2.350 CFP. Shellfish choices are 2.700 CFP. You'll pay 6.500 CFP for crab and lobster in season, and 5.000 CFP for *varo*, a sea centipede that is a rare and tasty delicacy from the lagoon. You can buy wine by the glass, carafe or bottle. Their temperature-controlled wine cellar contains 60 bottles of red Bordeaux Grand Crus, as well as French champagne and Chilean wines. Tahitian food is available any day of the week, including the staple diet of the Polynesians—*punu puatoro* (canned corned beef) and *mitihue* (fermented coconut milk), for 1.500 CFP, or a Polynesian plate for 2.650 CFP.

Moderate

RESTAURANT BAR NEW TEMARARA, *Tel. 68.70.81, is at the edge of the lagoon at the beginning of Fare Village when you come from the airport. Open Mon.-Sat. Food served 11am-2pm and 6-9pm. MC, V.*

Marc Garnier, who also owns Huahine Nautique, is the energetic owner of this popular restaurant/bar. Burgers and fries are 1.000 CFP. The menu features fresh fish such as mahi mahi and tuna for 1.950 CFP, poisson cru and other appetizers for 1.600-1.800 CFP, lobster (at dinner only when in season) for 3.200 CFP, and you can also get a filet mignon steak for 2.250 CFP.

RESTAURANT TEHINA, *Tel. 68.75.53/29.82.98/72.27.85; beside the sea at the Fare Maeva pension at PK 3, near Huahine airport. Open daily for B, L, D. except Sun. noon. MC, V.*

The dining tables of this restaurant are placed on a covered terrace beside the small swimming pool, overlooking the ocean. There is a *fare potée* (gazebo shelter) where groups can eat. They specialize in barbecue and fresh local fish dishes and the main courses often include tuna with mustard sauce, shrimp curry or steak with pepper sauce.

LE MAHI MAHI, *Tel. 68.70.55*, is on the waterfront street of Fare.

LES DAUPHINS, *Tel. 68.89.01*, is on the mountainside of the circle island road, adjacent to the post office in Fare. Frenchman Robert Cazenave serves international cuisine and local specialties, such as stuffed crab. Prices average 2.000 CFP for the main course. Open daily except Mon. for L.,D.

CHEZ TARA, *Tel. 68.78.45; restaurantcheztara@gmail.com*, is close to the Relais Mahana in Parea, where you can eat right next to a beach of powdery white sand while sitting at a table under the shade of a tonina tree. There is also a big covered dining area. Tino, the Chinese-Tahitian chef from Parea village, serves delicious local style meals as well as French dishes, and a ma'a Tahiti feast of traditional Tahitian food is presented on Sundays. Open daily at 5pm.

Economy

CHEZ GUYNETTE, *Tel. 68.83.75, facing the waterfront of Fare village. Open 7am-3pm daily except Wed. MC, V.*

This is a great place to eat breakfast or just to stop in for a coffee, smoothie or beer and meet people while you watch what's happening on the waterfront. They serve breakfasts, light lunches, hamburgers and fish dishes. You can order a shish-kabob of tuna, mahi mahi or steak for 1.000 CFP, including an accompaniment. The snack is busy most of the day, and especially in the mornings.

RESTAURANT VAIHONU, *Tel. 68.87.33, is beside the sea, between the airport and Fare village. Open daily for B, L, D. MC, V.*

Even if you are not staying at Pension Vaihonu, you are welcome to join Etienne Faaeva and his group for a good meal in a relaxed setting beside the sea. You may order your meals 2 hrs. in advance from a menu of Chinese and local style dishes.

HAAMENE PIZZA, *Tel. 68.71.70, is on the mountainside of the road in Fare village on the way to Fitii, between the French gendarmerie and Pension Poetaina. Open Tues.-Sat. from 12-2pm and every night from 6:30-9pm. Closed Sun. noon and Mon. noon. No credit cards.*

American residents of Huahine, as well as visitors, say that the pizzas made by this Polynesian family are the best they have tasted in Tahiti and Her Islands. You can order from a menu of 14 medium or large pizzas.

ROULOTTES

You'll also find a few *roulottes* (mobile diners) and small snack bars on the quay of Fare, which are open during the day and evening, and some of them are still there when the inter-island boats arrive from Papeete or Bora Bora during the wee hours of the morning. Didier's Roulotte serves pizza.

SEEING THE SIGHTS

Fare Pote'e is a museum and handcrafts center built over the water at Lake Fauna Nui in Maeva Village. It is a replica of a traditional meetinghouse of classic Polynesian oval shape, with a high curved roof of pandanus thatch, bamboo walls, and a bamboo covered floor. The exhibits include a variety of useful tools that were used by the Polynesians before the arrival of the Europeans. Kites, canoes, tops and other traditional games are also displayed, as well as musical instruments and a copy of the wooden headrest used by Omai, the first Tahitian to discover England. Arts and crafts made by the residents of Huahine are for sale, and you can get a map of the hiking trails on nearby Matairea Hill, where you can see the restored *marae* temples of stone, the house and council platforms and other work in progress.

Huahine Nui Pearl Farm & Pottery, *Tel. 78.30.20; www.huahinepearlfarm.com* is owned by American expat Peter Owen and his Tahitian wife, Ghislaine. This is Huahine's only black pearl farm. They are open daily from 10am-4pm, and offer a free tour by boat to visit the pearl farm, leaving the Marina of Faie every 15 min. You can see some of their pearl jewelry in their overwater boutique. Also on display are samples of their creative pottery. You are welcome to snorkel in the mini-farm and see how the oysters are suspended under water. This area is not as deep as the pearl farm but it has lots of tropical fish to goggle back at you.

Land Tours
    Island Eco-Tours, *Tel./Fax 68.79.67; pauljatallah@mail.pf; www.islandecotours.net.* Paul Atallah is an American archaeologist who offers half-day tours by 4WD Ford Ranger that will give you an in-depth briefing on Huahine's unique charm, history, culture and tropical flora as you discover the authentic island, mountains, valleys, rivers, beaches, islets and people. This is also an interesting botanical experience for lovers of nature and green open spaces. But the main advantage that sets Paul's tours apart is his extensive knowledge of the ancient *marae* temples and other archaeological sites. He worked with Professor Yoshiko H. Sinoto to help restore the stone *marae* in Huahine and in other islands and the knowledge he gained through his scientific research helps to make his tours even more interesting. Paul charges 5.000 CFP per person for his tour if you book directly through him. He also leads group tours by *le truck* and does private archaeological walk-about tours on Matairea Hill in Maeva Village.
    Huahine Explorer, *Tel. 68.87.33; Fax 68.77.57; cell 79.20.65 h-explorer@mail.pf; www.vaihonu.com.* Etienne Faaeva has three 8-passenger Land Rovers to take you to discover the magical wonders of the two islands. Etienne and his brother Daniel are very good tour guides. They speak excellent English and know all about the legends and history of their native island. The Explorer Tour is 4.500 CFP per person and takes you around Huahine Nui and Huahine Iti. You will see the watermelon, cantaloupe and noni plantations, visit the *maraes*, fresh water eels, and enjoy the panoramic views. A Combined Tour is 12.000 CFP, which lets you discover Huahine by land and lagoon. After you have visited the island by 4x4, you will board a comfortable canoe to visit a black pearl farm, snorkel and swim, and have lunch and a coconut show on a *motu* islet. The tours operate daily and water and fruit juices are served on board during each excursion.
    Huahine Land, *Tel. 68.89.21/78.58.31, Fax 68.86.84.* This excursion is operated by Joel House, an American who has lived in French Polynesia for more than 3 decades. He has 3 8-seater Mitsubishi 4x4 vehicles and English-speaking guides who lead the half-day excursions. The tour begins at 8am or 1pm and takes you off the track into the hidden valleys and sites of the two islands.
    Enite Tours, *Tel. 68.82.37,* has big buses and mini-vans that are used for Circle Island Tours and Archaeological Tours.
    Gérard Temaiana, *Tel. 68.83.19/73.45.88,* of Parea on Huahine Iti operates a *le truck* service for large groups.

SPORTS & RECREATION
Hiking
    Huahine Camping, at PK 18 in Parea, *Tel. 68.85.20,* leads hiking expeditions into the flatlands, valleys, plateaus and mountains of Huahine. These Camping Ecology outings leave from the Huahine campground at 9am, and return at 1pm. Your qualified guides will teach you all about the traditional medicinal plants that you will see growing along the pathways.

Horseback Riding

La Petite Ferme, *Tel./Fax 68.82.98; lapetiteferme@mail.pf.* The little farm is located on the ocean side of the road between Fare Village and the airport. Anne-Celine Moriquand and Eric Ciceron will take you riding on trained Marquesan horses along the beach and on the shores of Lake Maeva for 7.500 CFP for 2 hrs. An all-day outing with a gourmet picnic is 18.000 CFP per person. An island tour by horseback can be organized for 3-5 days, and 1-hr. buggy rides are 3.000 CFP per person.

Boat Rental

Huahine Lagoon, *Tel. 68.70.00.* Jean-Luc Eychenne rents 13-ft. aluminum boats with a 15-h.p. motor that you need a license to pilot. All safety equipment is included for a maximum of 4 people. Masks, fins and snorkel are included, as well as icebox and map of the lagoon. Gas is extra. Rental kayaks and bicycles are also available.

Lagoon Excursions, Picnics on the Motu, Jet-Ski & Shark Feeding Excursions

Huahine Nautique, *Tel. 689/68.83.15; Fax 689/60.67.75; reservation@huahine-nautique.com; www.huahine-nautique.com.* Marc Garnier has a 12-passenger 36-ft. long glass bottom boat, 2 speed boats, 4 covered outrigger speed canoes and 12 Wave Runner Jetskis, as well as an 8-passenger mini-bus that he uses to transfer his clients from their hotel, pension or cruise ship to the marina or boat dock. A new addition to his fleet is a houseboat with sleeping accommodations for 4 people. Marc's tours are highly praised by former customers, and some of the participants on Internet forums say that he offers the best excursions in the Leeward Islands. His tours are well described on his website, along with special Internet discounts.

On the **Island Picnic** tour you will take a boat ride around part of Huahine Nui and all of Huahine Iti by outrigger speed canoe, with stops to visit the stingrays and eagle rays, snorkeling in a big coral garden, and a picnic on a small motu islet. On the way back to Fare you will stop and watch your guide feeding the black tip lagoon sharks. This full-day excursion is 9.500 CFP per person.

A **Private Picnic** Luxury Lagoon cruise can be made by Jetski or on board Marc's comfortable catamaran, which is complete with a toilet and shower on board, as well as a sunbathing deck and awning for shade. After visiting the cultured pearl farm in Faie Bay and snorkeling in the coral gardens of Tefarerii, Marc's guide will take you to a motu islet where he will set up a table and chairs in the shallow lagoon and shade them with a gazebo type tent. You will be served a Royal lunch that includes grilled lobster and champagne. Then you continue on around Huahine Iti and return to the dock around 3pm. This unforgettable treat is priced at 95.000 CFP per couple.

Shark Feeding excursions take on another dimension with Huahine Nautique, due to the unique submerged platform that lets you descend from the boat into the lagoon without the risk of getting coral cuts. You can also observe the sharks being fed while standing on a structure especially built for this purpose, 4 m. (13 ft.) above the water's surface. This excursion costs 4.500 CFP per passenger.

A guided 2.5-hr. **Safari Jet** excursion aboard a Wave Runner Jetski costs 25.000 CFP per Jetski, and includes a stop on a *motu*, snorkeling in a coral garden, meeting the gray stingrays and spotted eagle rays, and a cocktail in a hotel.

You can rent Mark's **Houseboat** for a party of 12 or 4 people can sleep on board in king size beds. Amenities include an American kitchen with bar, sink and stove-top cooking, a shower and separate water-closet, two decks with chairs, an audio system and Internet access. Imagine gazing at the stars in Huahine's night sky and being lulled to sleep by the gentle motion of the lagoon.

Poetaina Cruises, *Tel. 60.60.06/78.86.39/28.92.13; pensionpoetaina@mail.pf; www.poetaina.com.* This company is headed by Jean Pierre Amo, who also owns the Poetaina Pension. He has a 43-ft. outrigger speed canoe for 6-38 passengers and a 43-ft. double-decker catamaran named *Te Aito* that can accommodate up to 70 passengers. The excursion begins at the Fare quay daily at 9:30am and returns at 4pm, taking you around Huahine Nui and Huahine Iti inside the lagoon, with a stop at Vaiorea motu for snorkeling and a visit to a pearl farm. Lunch is served in the clear shallow water of the lagoon and you sit with your feet in the water as you dine. This all-day picnic excursion is 9.800 CFP per adult.

Sailing Yachts

Sailing Huahine Voile, *B.P. 661-98731 Fare, Huahine, Tel./Fax 689/68.72.49; cell 689/23.23.79; eden@sailing-huahine.com; www.sailing-huahine.com.*

Claude and Martine Bordier's 50-ft. sailboat *Eden Martin* is based in Huahine, offering half- and full-day sailing cruises, sunset cruises and private charters. The half-day cruise departs daily at 9am from the quay in Fare and sails down the lagoon to Motu Vaiorea, where passengers snorkel in the coral garden and swim beside the white sand beach of Hana Iti, arriving back at the Fare quay at 1pm. The cost is 7.200 CFP per person. The full-day cruise is 12.500 CFP and lasts from 9am-5pm, following the same course as the half-day cruise during the morning. From Hana Iti the cruise continues on to Avea Bay, where lunch is served on board. You can then relax or visit the reef by dinghy before sailing back. Snorkeling gear is available on board. A sunset cruise for a minimum of 4 leaves the Fare quay at 4:30pm and returns at dusk. The cost of 6.600 CFP per person includes cocktails, and champagne can be ordered at extra cost.

The *Eden Martin* can also be chartered for 2-5 passengers to cruise the Society Islands or the Tuamotu Archipelago. A 7-day/6-night cruise in the Leeward Islands is 69.000 CFP per day or 483.000 CFP for 7 days, and includes boat rental, skipper and fuel for the main engine. A good cruise for scuba divers is the 7-day/6-night cruise in the northern Tuamotu Islands, which begins in Rangiroa and ends in Tikehau, or the 12-day/11-night cruise to the central Tuamotu Islands, sailing from Makemo to Tahanea, then to Fakarava. Preferential conditions for Internet reservations.

You can also rent a sailboat from one of the yacht charter companies based in Tahiti, Moorea or Raiatea and sail to Huahine, or you can arrange for a yacht to be delivered to Huahine in time for your arrival. See chapter on *Planning Your Trip*.

Scuba Diving

Mahana Dive, *Tel. 73.07.17; Fax 68.76.63; www.mahanadive.com*. This dive center is based next to the *gendarmerie* in Fare village and is managed by Annie Brunet. She and another qualified instructor lead exploratory dives and baptism dives. 4-dive packages are also available.

Pacific Blue Adventure, *Tel. 68.87.21/71.96.55; Fax 68.80.71; www.divehuahine.com*. This dive shop is located on the quay in the main village of Fare. Patrice Quinet and Michel Goyet are international PADI and CMAS diving instructors who lead lagoon and ocean dives for beginners and certified divers. Their dives begin at 9am, 11am and 2pm daily, taking a maximum of 10 divers to the best sites inside the lagoon or in the open ocean, adapting to the diving level of the participants. The cost is 6.200 CFP for one dive and 23.600 CFP for 4 dives, including equipment, transfers and taxes.

Heremiti Dive, *Tel. 68.86.49/27.90.57; Fax. 60.60.96; morgancalabuig@hotmail.fr*. This dive center is based at Pension Mauarii in Huahine Iti, providing underwater discoveries for beginners or certified divers.

Surfing

American surfers discovered the passes of Huahine in the early 1970s, and a couple of them are still here, now sharing their favorite surf spots with their children. The local surfers jealously guard the passes with the best breaks, and a few foreign surfers have been given black eyes when they intrude. The big attraction in Huahine is the consistency and perfect shape of the waves rather than their size. Three of the best breaks are in the Fare area, and another good site is at the Ara Ara pass in Parea on the southern tip of Huahine Iti. Try to find a local surfer to accompany you to the passes, which may eliminate any problems from the other surfers.

SHOPPING

In addition to the boutiques and pearl shops in the resort hotels, you can also find original creations and some imported items in the boutiques in Fare and around the island.

The **Rima'i Te Nui Taue** has the most original clothing and souvenir items, including pottery made by Peter Owen, an American resident of Huahine, who owns **Huahine Pearl and Pottery** at his pearl farm in Faie. See information under *Seeing the Sights* in this chapter.

Pearl Treehouse, *Tel. 72.09.96; pearltreehouse@mail.pf; www.pearltreehouse.com. Open daily 10am-4pm. MC, V*. Ray Marks is an American expat who has built a unique pearl shop in the branches of an almond tree beside the beach in Fare. If you're coming by land, then take the access road across from the post office, next to Europcar. You'll find the Pearl Treehouse to the right of the newly built Lapita Village (site of the former Hotel Bali Hai). Ray is the partner of Peter Owen in the pearl farm in Faie, the only pearl farm in Huahine. He is quite proud of their selection of quality Tahitian pearls and his sales assistants will help you select your own special souvenir from Huahine.

Vana Creations, *Tel. 68.72.49/23.23.79; martine@tahiti-arts.com; www.artisanat-tahiti.com.* Martine Bordier (sailboat *Eden Martin*) makes and sells original handmade necklaces from the green or purple pencil sea urchins found on the coral reefs. You can shop online.

Galerie 'Umatatea, *Tel. 68.70.79/27.27.17; melanie@polynesiapaintings.com; www.polynesiapaintings.com.* The studio and showroom of Melanie Dupré includes her paintings of Huahine in oils and watercolors. Located on Motu Maeva across the road from Vanaa Camping.

Fare Rima'i Na Miri, *Tel. 72.01.66/73.58.73.* This boutique of dresses, pareos and mother-of-pearl jewelry is located at Pension Mauarii in Parea. Open daily.

Julien and Bernard Nicolas are a father and son team of artists who paint tableaux of Polynesian scenes using 80 different colors of soil found in the ground in Huahine. Their atelier is located in Haarimea Bay.

MASSAGE & SPAS

Patricia Matthews Nanua, *Tel. 68.72.32/77.94.65,* is an Australian expatriate and long-time resident of Huahine who does intuitive healing massages, working with the body's energy. She also gives private yoga lessons. Her base is Te Tiare Resort, and she will also come to your house, room or yacht to work her wonderful magic on your body.

Relais Mahana Spa, *Tel. 60.60.40.* You can relax in a Jacuzzi on the sundeck of a beach bungalow while gazing at the opalescent lagoon of Avea Bay. Then enjoy a hot stone massage or let your senses come alive with a massage of crushed pearls. All the products are natural and are made at the cosmetology lab in Tahiti.

PRACTICAL INFORMATION
Banks
Huahine has two banks located in the main village of Fare. Both have ATM windows: **Banque de Tahiti**, *Tel. 68.82.46;* and **Banque de Polynesie**, *Tel. 60.63.51.* **Banque Socredo**, *Tel.60.63.60,* is located on the mountainside of the circle island road in Fare village.

Doctor
There are four private doctors in Fare who speak English, and the 15-bed government medical center is on the mountainside in Fare, *Tel. 68.82.48.* There is also a dentist, *Tel. 68.88.00,* as well as two physiotherapists.

Drugstore

The **Pharmacy of Huahine**, *Tel./60.61.41/60.62.41,* is on the circle island road of Fare, on the way to the post office, one block inland from the waterfront. Open Mon.-Fri. 7:30am-12pm and 2:30-5pm; on Sat. 8am-12pm; and on Sun. & holidays 10-11am. The pharmacist speaks English.

Internet

AO API–New World, *68.70.99; aoapi2000@yahoo.com* is a cyber center located upstairs above the pharmacy on the waterfront in Fare Village; They also have Xerox facilities and can print out digital photos and color photocopying.

HIME PC, *Tel. 68.75.81,* is in Fare.

Video Shop Huahine, *Tel. 60.67.40; videoshop@mail.pf.*

Te Tiare Beach Resort, *Tel. 60.60.50,* has a computer corner with WiFi connections in their overwater lobby, and you can hook up your laptop to the data port on the telephone in your bungalow.

Police

The French gendarmerie, *Tel. 60.62.05,* is beside the lagoon in Fare.

Post Office and Telecommunications Office

The **Post Office,** *Tel. 68.86.35,* is in Fare on the circle island road. All telecommunications and postal services are available here. Hours are 7am-3pm, Mon.-Thurs., and 7am-2pm. on Fri.

Tourist Bureau

Huahine Tourism Committee, *Tel. 68.70.31/73.40.42* is a tourist information office located on the waterfront street in Fare. Open Mon.-Sat. 7:30am-3pm. The Tahitian hostess will give you brochures on all the lodgings and activities and answer your questions with a smile.

14. Raiatea

A panorama of green carpeted mountains, azure shoals and indigo bays greets your eyes as your Air Tahiti flight descends at **Raiatea** (Rye-ah-TEY-ah). The Temehani plateau rises to heights of 792 m (2,598 ft.) in the north, and Mount Tefatoaiati touches the clouds at 1,017 m (3,336 ft.) in the south. Small coral islets seem to float at the edge of the bays, rising from the submarine foundation that surrounds Raiatea and the smaller island of Taha'a. Eight passes provide entry into the vast lagoon.

Raiatea does not have the glamour of its neighboring island of Bora Bora. There are no white sand beaches except around the *motu* islets, and the tourist facilities do not include world-famous luxury resorts. Neither does it have the dramatic skyline of Moorea or the majesty of the mountains of Tahiti. Raiatea's big attractions include the ideal conditions the island and its surrounding lagoon and ocean offer for year-round sailing, scuba diving and fishing. There are 4 major yacht charter bases on the island, 2 scuba diving centers and several game-fishing boats.

Raiatea is 220 km. (136 mi.) to the west-north-west of Tahiti. It is the largest of the Leeward Society Islands, which also include the high islands of Taha'a, Huahine, Bora Bora and Maupiti, plus the coral atolls of Tupai, Mopelia, Scilly and Bellinghausen. It has a surface area of 170 sq. km (105 sq. mi.) and is shaped rather like a triangle. When I look at a map of Taha'a and Raiatea together and see the barrier reef that protects the two islands, I think that it looks like a *penu*, the phallic-shaped stone pestle used by the Polynesians to prepare their traditional medicines of plants and herbs. Taha'a is the head of the *penu* and Raiatea is the base.

Havai'i, The Sacred Island

Raiatea means "clear sky" and is still referred to as the **Sacred Island of Havai'i**, the ancestral home of the **Maohi** people. The Polynesian Creation Chant tells how Havai'i was created by the god Ta'aroa, as the birthplace of land, the birthplace of gods, the birthplace of kings and the birthplace of man. And it was to Havai'i, deep within the sacred Temehani mountain, that the souls of the dead must return. According to Polynesian mythology, fragments of the sacred island broke off to create other lands, swimming like a fish to become the Windward Islands of Tahiti, Moorea, Maiao, Mehetia and Tetiaroa. Havai'i was also the cradle of royalty and religion in Eastern Polynesia, as well as the center of the Maohi culture, history and heraldry.

Ta'aroa, the creator god, was considered too aloof for the dynamic religion that soon developed among the ancient Polynesians. He was eventually retired to the background, along with the god **Tane**, while **Oro**, the son of Ta'aroa, came to be revered as the god of war, harvest, music and the founder of the famous Arioi society of troubadours and comedians. Long before Oro was born at Opoa the national *marae* of Havai'i or Havaiki was called Tinirauhinimatatepapa o Feoro, which means "Fruitful myriads who engraved the rocks of Feoro."

When Oro became very powerful and was acknowledged as the supreme every day god of the earth and sky, the name Feoro was changed to Vaiotaha, meaning "Water of the man o' war bird," because this bird was Oro's shadow and the water meant human blood. To his *marae* were taken most of the heads of decapitated warriors, which were cleaned and stacked in shining white rows on the black stones of the temple. The name was later changed to **Taputapuatea**, which means, "Sacrifices from abroad," and it became an international *marae*, where chiefs were brought for investiture. All other *marae* temples were founded by bringing a sacred stone from Taputapuatea or one of its descendant *maraes*.

The sacred pass of **Te Ava Moa** at Opoa in Raiatea offered frequent scenes of grandeur as great double canoes from many islands sailed into the lagoon, streaming long pennants from Hawaii, Tonga and New Zealand. The deep-toned sound of drums and the conch shell trumpets announced the arrival of delegations from island kingdoms throughout the Polynesian triangle, who were members of a friendly alliance.

At Opoa, the **Tamatoa** dynasty was reputed to go back 30 generations to **Hiro**, who was Raiatea's first king. Tradition says that Hiro and his associates built a great canoe and sailed away to Rarotonga and New Zealand, leaving two of his sons behind. One succeeded him as King of Raiatea and the other was the King of Bora Bora. During the meetings of the friendly alliance at Opoa, King Tamatoa was entitled to wear a red feather belt or *maro*, a sign of the highest honor, as he welcomed the visiting delegations. Each group of pilgrims brought human sacrifices to offer to the bloodthirsty Oro, and awesome ceremonies were held in the open-air temple of Marae Taputapuatea for the festivity of the gods, to render respect and sacrifices to Oro on his home soil.

These pagan rites ended with the arrival of the missionaries. Oro and the lesser gods were banished and Marae Taputapuatea is now silent, except for an occasional reenactment ceremony, which does not involve human sacrifices!

European Discovery

Captain James Cook was the first European to discover Raiatea, when he anchored the *Endeavour* in the lagoon at Opoa in July 1769. On board the ship was a man named **Tupia**, a native of Uliatea, as the island was then called. Tupia was the rejected lover of **Queen Purea** in Tahiti, and he and his servant boy Tayeto sailed with Cook when the *Endeavour* left Uliatea 11 days later. Both of the Polynesians died in Batavia in October 1770, of scurvy or malaria or both.

Cook returned to Raiatea in September 1773, and took a young man from Raiatea to England with him. This was a 22-year old fellow named Mai (**Omai**) who was then living in Huahine. Cook brought Omai back to Huahine in 1777 and once again visited Raiatea on a prolonged visit before sailing to Hawaii, where he was killed.

A number of other explorers touched at Raiatea following Cook's visits, but very few of them wrote about their experiences. After them came the traders and whalers, whose primary objective was to recover from scurvy, get provisions and find a woman.

John Williams from the London Missionary Society arrived in Raiatea in 1818, when he was just 21 years old. A few years later he founded the town of Uturoa. The island remained under the influence of the English Protestant missionaries long after Tahiti had come under French control. The people of Raiatea are still predominantly Evangelical. Following a *coup de force* in Tahiti by French **Admiral Du Petit-Thouars** in 1842, there followed a long period of instability. The French did not attempt a real takeover until 1888. In 1897, more than 50 years after the conquest of Tahiti, two war ships filled with French marines mounted a full-scale attack, with massive fire-power, driving the Raiateans back, until the surrogate chief Teraupoo was captured and exiled to New Caledonia. The French flag first flew over Raiatea in 1898.

Raiatea Today

The Raiatea airport is at the northern tip of the island and the town of Uturoa is southeast of the airport. A mostly paved road encircles the island for about 150 km (93 mi.), following the contours of the deeply indented coastline, with occasional forays into the exuberant vegetation of the valleys. You can drive for several miles without seeing any houses or people. Raiatea's 12,545 inhabitants live beside the road in Uturoa and in the villages and hamlets of Avera, Faaroa, Opoa, Puohine, Fetuna, Vaiaau, Tevaitoa and Apooiti.

Driving in a southeasterly direction from Uturoa you will see the **Hotel Hawaiki Nui** on your left, and you will pass impressive new homes and lovely flower gardens on both sides of the road. By the time you reach Avera you are in the country and at PK 6 you will round a curve to the right that takes you down the deeply indented road that winds quietly around the edge of the **Faaroa Bay**. Your senses are heightened as you breathe in the perfumes of fresh mountain ferns, wild mangoes, kava, kapok and ripening breadfruit.

This bay merges with the **Apoomau River**, which is navigable by small ships and boats for a distance of 4 km (2.5 mi.) into the interior. At the mouth of the river is a spring containing effervescent water. A woman from Raiatea told me that people come from Hawaii and New Zealand to drink this water, which is guarded by the spirit of the spring. She said that photos taken here always show an extra person, or part of a face, which is supposedly that of the spirit. But this image fades in time.

A road from Faaroa Bay takes you into the interior of the island for 8 km (5 mi.), connecting with Fetuna at the southern tip of the island. Winding through the fertile valleys and wide flatland, you will pass plantations of pineapple, tapioca, papaya and vanilla, and farms with horses, cows, pigs and chickens. Far below the lacy fronds of acacia trees bordering the road you can see the wild, untamed southern coast of Raiatea. If you continue along the coastal route instead of cutting across the valley, you will come to **Marae Taputapuatea** at PK 32, 19.2 miles from Uturoa center, just beyond the village of Opoa. This is Raiatea's most famous landmark. The huge slabs of coral flagstone and basaltic rock slumber under the shade of coconut palms, a shrine to Polynesia's rich and varied Maohi culture.

Between Puohine and Fetuna a road has been built along an embankment, with small *motu* islets, some with just one coconut tree, within wading distance from the shore. The pre-fabricated box-like houses on stilts that you will see are supposedly built to withstand cyclones like those that destroyed the former homes on these sites. The Tahitian government sells these houses to qualified property owners at very low cost.

Along the west coast you will see mountain streams meandering to the sea and gaily-colored cocks following their harem of clucking hens. Some of the fishermen still use stones to enclose their fishponds instead of wire netting. You can see them mending their fish nets on the beach, while their children play in the shallows of the lagoon. There are no stores in these remote settlements, except for the mobile *magasins* operated by the Chinese vendors, who make their daily rounds with fresh *baguettes*, frozen chickens and Piggy Snax.

The lagoon narrows between Vaihuti and Vaiaau Bays, with palm-shaded *motu* islets on the reef edge of the lagoon. Sharp peaks delineate the central mountain chain and in Vaiaau valley are remnants of fortifications that were built by the warriors of Faterehau, the great chiefess of Raiatea, who opposed the takeover by the French in 1897.

TIARE APETAHI-RAIATEA'S ENDANGERED FLOWER

In the heights of the sacred Temehani Mountain grows the **Tiare Apetahi**, refreshed by the cool, dense clouds and mountain showers. When touched by the first rays of the rising sun, this rare white flower bursts open with a slight exploding sound.

The five-petal Tiare Apetahi is the symbol of Raiatea, and it is believed that this particular variety of the Campanaulacées family grows nowhere else in the world. Legend says that the delicate petals represent the five fingers of a lovely Tahitian girl who fell in love with the son of a king and died of a broken heart because she could not hope to marry him.

In order to protect the rapidly disappearing Tiare Apetahi, which the flower vendors in Raiatea were selling at the airport, the local government has declared it an endangered species. Offenders may be fined up to one million French Pacific francs if caught. Repeat offenders can be given a stiff fine and imprisoned.

Behind Tevaitoa village the magnificent **Temehani Plateau** rises in formidable walls of basalt. The historic peaks shimmer in shades of blue and gray, and countless waterfalls cascade in misty plumes to splash far below into crisp pools fringed with tropical fern trees and shrubbery. **Marae Tainuu** is on the shoreline in the middle of the village. The Protestant church here is the oldest on the island, and partially covers the flagstones of the *marae*. Petroglyphs engraved in the basaltic stones include a Polynesian sundial and 10 turtles, depicting a sort of Polynesian treasure hunt that the Maohi warriors had to perform to achieve valor and esteem.

Copra drying in the sun, pigs grunting in the mud and pearl farms in the lagoon just beside the road are left behind as you arrive at Apooiti Bay and see the sleek charter yachts moored at **Apooiti Marina**. Soon you round the north end of the island, pass in front of the airport and end your tour back in Uturoa.

Although there is an increase in the flow of traffic in the town center, the lifestyle here is still unhurried and the calm, friendly feeling of a small island lingers still. It is this wonderful magic of Polynesia that tempts you to return again to Raiatea.

ARRIVALS & DEPARTURES
Arriving By Air

Air Tahiti has 6-9 flights daily between Tahiti and Raiatea, including several direct flights for the 40-min. connection. The fare is 14.130 CFP one-way for adults, and 26.260 CFP round-trip, tax included. You can also fly direct to Raiatea from Moorea each Mon., Tues., Wed., Fri. and Sun., with a stop in Huahine on Mon. and Fri. You can fly direct from Bora Bora to Raiatea daily except Tues. and there are direct flights from Maupiti to Raiatea each Tues., Fri. and Sun. The one-way Moorea-Raiatea fare for adults is 14.830 CFP, between Huahine-Raiatea it is 7.030 CFP, Bora Bora-Raiatea is 7.730 CFP, and from Maupiti to Raiatea the one-way fare is 8.330 CFP. **Air Tahiti reservations:** Tahiti, *Tel. 86.42.42*; Moorea, *Tel. 55.06.02*; Huahine, *Tel. 68.77.02*; Raiatea, *Tel. 60.04.44*; Bora Bora, *Tel. 60.53.53*; Maupiti, *Tel. 60.15.05*.

If you have reservations with a hotel, pension or yacht charter company, then you will be met at the airport and driven to your hotel. Avis and Hertz have sales counters at the airport and there are also taxis that meet the arrival of each flight.

You can also get to Raiatea by chartering an airplane in Tahiti from **Air Tahiti**, *Tel. 86.42.42*; or **Pol'Air**, *Tel. 74.23.11*.

Arriving By Boat

All the inter-island transport boats dock at the quay in Uturoa, the main town of Raiatea, and it would be advisable to arrange with your hotel or pension to have someone meet you when you arrive in the middle of the night. The car rental agencies will also meet you at the Uturoa quay. The boat schedules are subject to change, so check with the Raiatea Tourism office, which is adjacent to the quay.

Hawaiki Nui, *Tel. 54.99.54; Fax 45.24.44; contact@stim.pf*. This 12-passenger cargo ship has 4 double cabins and deck space. It leaves the Motu Uta dock in

Papeete each Tues. at 4pm and arrives at the Uturoa quay in Raiatea on Wed. at 5:30am, after stopping in Huahine. The Thurs. trip leaves Papeete at 4pm, and arrives in Raiatea on Fri. at 3:30am. The ship continues on to Bora Bora and Taha'a and returns to Raiatea on Fri. at 4:30pm on its way back to Huahine and Tahiti. The cost of sleeping on deck is 2.000 CFP per adult and 1.000 CFP per child, and a berth in one of the cabins costs 5.400 CFP per adult and 2.700 CFP per child from Papeete to all the Leeward Islands. Meals are available on board the ship. A car is 11.600-16.900 CFP round trip from Tahiti to all the Leeward Islands.

Maupiti Express II, *Tel. 66.37.81/78.27.22/72.30.48; www.maupitiexpress.com.* This 140-passenger boat transports passengers between Raiatea and Bora Bora and from Bora Bora to Maupiti. In Raiatea it docks at the Uturoa quay where all the Taha'a boats tie up. It arrives in Uturoa direct from Bora Bora and Taha'a at 8:35am each Wed. and Fri., and at 5:35pm each Fri. and Sun. The one-way fare from Bora Bora to Raiatea is 4.000 CFP and round-trip is 5.000 CFP. The fares from Maupiti to Raiatea are 5.000 CFP and 7.000 CFP. Passengers under 12 years pay half-fare.

Enota Transport Maritime, *Tel./Fax 65.61.33.* Enota Tetuanui has 3 covered launches that can transport passengers each between Taha'a and Raiatea. *Te Haere Maru V* leaves from the east coast of Taha'a twice a day, starting from Faaaha, stopping in Haamene (at 6:30am and 12pm) and Vaitoare for the trip to Uturoa. *Te Haere Maru IV* leaves from the west coast of Taha'a twice a day, with stops at Tapuamu (5:30am on Mon. and 5:45am Tues.-Sat. and again at 11:45am), Tiva, Poutoru and Marina Iti, and then makes the 15-minute crossing to Uturoa. *Te Haere Maru VI* goes around the island of Taha'a as needed.

Tamarii Taha'a I, *Tel. 76.37.20,* can transport a maximum of 66 passengers in a 46-ft. aluminum boat that operates a shuttle service between Taha'a and Raiatea. The boat leaves the Patio boat dock at 5:30am and 11am Mon.-Fri., and at 5:30am on Sat. Stops are made at Murifenua, Tapuamu, Tiva, Hatupa, Patii, and Poutoru, then continue on to Uturoa.

Tamarii Taha'a II, *Tel. 76.37.20.* This sturdy 47.5-ft. boat was formerly the *Maupiti Express I.* It leaves Ra'ai dock in Taha'a at 5:20am Mon.-Sat., arriving in Uturoa at 6:40am. A second service starts in Haamene at 11am, arriving in Uturoa at 11:40am. The fare starts at 600 CFP for the closest docks.

Departing By Air
You can fly from Raiatea to Bora Bora, Maupiti and Huahine, or return to Tahiti by **Air Tahiti**, *Tel. 60.44.44/60.04.40* in Raiatea. There is no direct return flight service between Raiatea and Moorea. Tickets can be purchased at the airport. Check-in time at the airport is one hour before scheduled departure.

Departing By Boat
You can continue on to Taha'a, Bora Bora and Maupiti by boat from Raiatea, or you can return to Papeete with a stop in Huahine.

Hawaiki Nui, *Tel. 54.99.54* (Papeete), *Tel. 66.42.10* (Raiatea); *Fax 45.24.44,* leaves Raiatea for Bora Bora and Taha'a each Wed. at 7:30am, returning to Raiatea at 4:30pm, and then departs for Tahiti at 5:15pm, arriving in Papeete on Thurs. at 5am. It leaves Raiatea each Fri. at 5:30am for Bora Bora and Taha'a and returns to Raiatea at 4:30pm, then leaves at 5:30pm on Fri. for Huahine and Tahiti, arriving in Papeete at 5am Sat. morning.

Maupiti Express II, *Tel. 66.37.81/78.27.22/72.30.48/www.maupitiexpress.com.* The boat departs from the Uturoa quay each Wed. at 4pm for Taha'a and Bora Bora, arriving in Vaitape at 5:35pm. On Sun. it leaves Raiatea at 2pm and 6pm, arriving in Bora Bora 1h:35min. later. During the school period the *Maupiti Express II* leaves Raiatea at 2pm and 6pm each Wed. and Fri. During school vacations there is a 4pm departure each Fri. for Bora Bora. The one-way fare to Bora Bora is 4.000 CFP. Passengers under 12 years pay half fare. The captain is not allowed to transport passengers from Raiatea to Taha'a only.

Enota Transport Maritime, *Tel. 65.61.33. Te Haere Maru V* leaves from the boat dock in Uturoa at 10:30am and 4:30pm for the east coast of Taha'a, stopping in Vaitoare, Haamene and Faaaha. *Te Haere Maru IV* leaves from the boat dock in Uturoa at 10:30am and 4:30pm for the west coast of Taha'a, stopping at Poutoru, Tiva and Tapuamu. The crossing takes 20 to 45 minutes, depending on your destination, and the one-way fare is 650 CFP. *Te Haere Maru VI* is used as needed.

Tamarii Taha'a I, Tel. 76.37.20. This 46-ft. aluminum catamaran leaves the Uturoa boat dock Mon.-Fri. at 10am and 4pm, and on Sat. at 10am. Stops are made in Poutoru, Patii, Hatupa, Tiva, Tapuamu, and Murifenua, arriving in Patio at 11:15am and 5:15pm Mon.-Fri., and on Sat. at 11:15am.

Tamarii Taha'a II, Tel. 76.37.20. This sturdy 47.5-ft. boat was formerly the *Maupiti Express I*. It leaves Uturoa dock Mon., Tues. and Thurs. at 10.20am, 3:30pm and 4:20pm. On Wed. and Fri. it leaves Uturoa at 10am and 4pm. Stops are made at Vaitoare, Amaru Quay, Haamene and Ra'ai.

ORIENTATION

The town center of **Uturoa** (oo-too-RO-ah), which means, "long jaw," is 2 km (1.2 mi.) south of the airport. This is the second largest town in French Polynesia. Here you will find the administrative seat for the Leeward Islands. Buildings reminiscent of former colonial days stand adjacent to modern government buildings, post office, banks, boutiques, general stores, supermarkets and small restaurants. There is a hospital, *gendarmerie,* courthouse, a Catholic school, a lycée, technical schools and boarding facilities for students from throughout the Leeward Islands. A community nautical center and marina are on the edge of town, and the public market, port facilities and shipping warehouses in the center of Uturoa provide the focal point of a relaxed pace of business life.

Mount Tapioi rises 294 m (964 ft.) behind Uturoa, with a TV relay at the summit. You can hike or drive 3.5 km (2.2 mi.) to the top in a 4WD, where you'll enjoy the panoramic view of Taha'a and Huahine, Bora Bora and Maupiti.

Big government projects have modernized Uturoa's public facilities. A wharf provides 430 m (1,410 ft.) of docking space for visiting cruise liners as well as the inter-island cargo/passenger ships from Tahiti. On or adjacent to the quay are the port captain's office, warehouses, cold storage for fish, public restrooms, arts and crafts center and public gardens. A Gare Maritime shopping mall also embellishes the waterfront, with fancy 2-story buildings painted pink. Granite from Portugal was imported to pave rue Tiare Apetahi in front of the mall. In addition to the restaurants, pearl shops, boutiques, gift shops and florist shop downstairs, the Tahiti Tourism Bureau occupies an enormous space on the ground level, and the post office has a branch upstairs.

Uturoa's downtown area has been improved with a new public market and a by-pass road on the hill behind the main street, to ease the flow of traffic on the main street. There are also traffic round-abouts at each end of town.

The modernization program has meant the loss of the Fare Vanira, a little wooden shack on the main street that was built in 1938. This was the domain of "Madame Vanilla," Jeanne Chane, a lively Chinese woman who sells dried vanilla beans, powdered vanilla and extract. She is the third generation of vanilla experts in her family and has won many diplomas and silver cups as a vanilla professional. Just follow the fragrance of vanilla and you will find her now operating out of a container on the site of her former store—still counting her vanilla beans.

The improvement program, the economic downturn and lack of tourists have resulted in the closing of some of the restaurants in Uturoa. The Seahorse and L'Espadon in the Gare Maritime are no longer in business, and my favorite, Moemoea, had to close in June 2011 because its building was sold. The Club Zenith Discotheque in the Léogite Building, which was Raiatea's only nightclub, has also closed.

GETTING AROUND RAIATEA
Car, Scooter & Bicycle Rentals

Avis Raiatea, *Tel. 66.34.06/; Fax 66.16.06*; has taken over the defunct Europcar business. Sales offices are located at the airport, at the main office between the airport and Uturoa, and at the Hawaiki Nui Hotel, *Tel. 66.05.00.* A 5-door Fiat Panda rents for 6.700 CFP for 4 hrs., 8.250 CFP for 8 hrs., and 9.700 CFP for 24 hrs. A 5-door Fiat Panda with a/c costs 7.700 CFP for 4 hrs., 9.200 CFP for 8 hrs., and 10.700 CFP for 24 hrs. A 5-place a/c Renault Clio or Hyundai Getz rents for 8.700 CFP for 4 hrs., 10.200 CFP for 8 hrs., and 11.700 CFP for 24 hrs.

Scooter rates are 5.000 CFP for 4 hrs, 6.000 CFP for 8 hrs., and 6.500 CFP for 24 hrs. These rates include unlimited mileage and third-party insurance. Gas is extra.

Hertz Raiatea, *Tel. 66.35.35/78.23.32; Fax 66.13.66; hertz.raiatea@mail.pf.* Hertz has taken over the agency that used to be Avis. There is a counter at the airport and the main office is just before the airport. An a/c Citroen C-1 is 7.500 CFP for 4 hrs., 9.300 CFP for 8 hrs. and 11.500 CFP for 24 hrs. A 5-place a/c

Hundai Getz or a 5-place a/c Citroen C-3 is 8.550 CFP for 4 hrs., 10.300 CFP for 8 hrs., and 12.500 CFP for 24 hrs. Taxes, unlimited mileage and insurance are included.
Moana Rent A Car, *Tel./Fax 66.29.11; cell 75.08.30, moanarentacar@gmail.com,* is located at Garage Motu Tapu close to the airport.

Bicycles
Avis, *Tel. 66.34.06,* rents bicycles for 1.800 CFP for 4 hrs., 2.400 CFP for 8 hrs., and 3.500 CFP for 24 hrs. Longer rentals possible. The hotels and many of the pensions also rent bikes.

Taxis
There are at least 10 taxis in Uturoa and you can usually find one at the Uturoa airport for each flight arrival. A taxi stand is located at the boat and ferry dock in the center of Uturoa. The Raiatea taxi drivers pride themselves on their good reputation, although there is a variance in the fares they charge. Taxi fare from the airport to Uturoa center is 1.000 CFP and from the airport to the Hawaiki Nui hotel is 1.500 CFP, plus 100 CFP for baggage. The rate from the port in Uturoa to Hawaiki Nui is 800 CFP. The fare from the airport to Raiatea Lodge is 2.000 CFP and from the port or town of Uturoa to Raiatea Lodge the cost is 2.500 CFP. The hourly rate is 4.000 CFP, and 1.800 CFP for waiting time. A circle island tour by private taxi is 20.000 CFP. Germain Guilloux taxi: *Tel. 72.30.54;* Dalida Brodien, *Tel. 74.22.71;* Marc Tiatia, *Tel. 73.70.16.*

Le Truck
A *le truck* service operates between the public market in Uturoa and each village, coordinating their schedules with the arrivals of the ferries and school hours. They charge a minimal fee to transport passengers to their destination in Raiatea.

Taxi Boats
Taxiboat, *Tel./Fax 66.49.06; cell 79.62.01/79.62.02; VHF 16.* Dominique Lucas, who also owns Hotel Hinano Api, has a 10-passenger boat and will pick you up at the airport, the quay in Uturoa or from any boat dock specified. He will also take you on lagoon excursions. Daily service provided.
Limousine Boat, *Tel. 65.64.00/79.63.81; tahaa-marine@mail.pf.* Christophe Citeau also has a taxi boat for private transfers or excursions. See more information in chapter on Taha'a.

WHERE TO STAY
Deluxe
OPOA BEACH HOTEL, *B.P. 919, Uturoa, Raiatea 98735. Tel. 689/ 60.05.10; Fax 689/66.19.87; resa@opoabeach.com; www.opoabeach.com. Beside the*

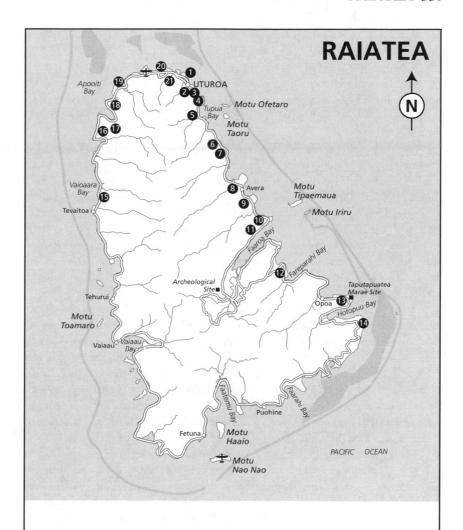

1. Uturoa Boat Dock
2. Residence Le Dauphin
3. Hotel Hinano Api
4. Hawaiki Nui Hotel
5. Pension Tepua
6. Pension Manava
7. Les 3 Cascades

8. Pension Yolande
9. Pension Opeha
10. Vini Beach Lodge
11. La Croix du Sud
12. Pension Te Maeva
13. Hotel Atiapiti
14. Opoa Beach Hotel

15. Villa Temehani
16. Raiatea Lodge Hotel
17. Laura Lodge
18. Sunset Beach Motel
19. Marina Apooiti
20. Pension Tiare Nui
21. B&B Raiatea Bellevue

lagoon at PK 37 on the south coast of the island, 35 min. from the airport and 10 min. from Marae Taputapuatea. Round-trip minibus airport transfers 4.500 CFP. MC, V.
Although this hotel and restaurant are not close to the town of Uturoa, this is the place I would recommend for anyone who wants to spend a few days in a small boutique hotel built in a picture postcard setting. A true bonus is the friendly attention you will receive from the owners, Eric and Nicole Barbace, and their well-trained staff.

I met Eric and Nicole while they were managing the Vahine Island Resort from 2001-2005, and I will never forget his genuine helpfulness and her delicious 5-star cuisine. Now they have designed and built their own charming hotel, which opened in May 2009, between a dense forest and a small beach of finely crushed shells overlooking Opoa Beach, the bird motu and the island of Huahine on the horizon.

There are 9 attractive wooden bungalows painted white with a blue roof, situated in the garden, around the swimming pool or on the beach. Each spacious suite (538 sq. ft. -50 sq. m) has a very comfortable 4-poster king-size bed with embroidered linens, a mosquito net, ceiling fan and a safety box in the bedroom. There is a daybed/sofa in the living room, along with a desk and stool, wireless Internet access, flat screen TV and DVD player, radio-CD player, telephone, mini-bar, and coffee making facilities. The large bathroom contains an Italian shower, separate water closet and hair dryer. Lounge chairs and a hammock provide easy relaxing on the covered terrace, reached through the sliding glass doors. Eric and Nicole carefully chose local materials for the decoration of their tropical hotel, whose basic color is varying shades of white. They have added the Polynesian touch with fibers from the coconut tree, roots from the miki miki bushes, seashells, and accent colors of yellow and orange. Disabled facilities are also available.

The hotel's amenities include a gastronomic restaurant (see information on *Where to Eat* in this chapter), bar, activities desk, car rental, boutique, Internet access, laundry service and baby-sitting on request. The swimming pool, kayaks, snorkeling equipment, outrigger paddle canoe, bocce ball, line fishing, games and books are free for guest use, as well as twice-daily boat transfers to the Bird Motu (islet) in the lagoon facing the hotel. You can also visit a fishing village or go into town for shopping in Uturoa.

The staff of Opoa Beach Hotel have earned a good reputation with former guests for their professionalism and knowledge of the local sites and the island's history. Paid activities they lead include snorkeling excursions, a picnic on the motu, lagoon fishing, guided walks, a day-tour by boat to Taha'a, mini-bus transfers to the Vaiorie mini-golf practice range nearby, a visit to Marae Taputapuatea and to explore the Faaroa River.

Opoa Beach Hotel is the ideal choice for honeymooners who are seeking a small romantic paradise "far from the madding crowd". Families with small children will also appreciate the lagoon, which is shallow water for the first 50 yards from the beach.

Although this gem of a hotel has a 3-star rating, many guests think it offers 4-star accommodations with a simple elegance and an authentic welcome.

Superior

RAIATEA HAWAIKI NUI HOTEL, *B.P. 43, Uturoa, Raiatea 98735. Tel. 689/60.05.00; Fax 689/66.20.20; reservation@hawaikinui.pf; www.hawaikinui.com. Beside the lagoon, 2 km (1.2 mi.) south of town. All major credit cards.*

Situated on the fringe of the lagoon in Tepua Bay, this 3-star hotel has 28 rooms and bungalows built in the Polynesian style with thatched roofs and bamboo furniture. The hotel opened as the Hotel Bali Hai Raiatea in 1968, presenting the world's first bungalows built over the water. These old units require frequent renovation and the roofs were replaced following damage caused by Cyclone Oli in February 2010.

Patricia Russmann Maurin, the new manager, headed Tahiti Manava Visitors Bureau for several years and has managed other hotel properties in the Society Islands. She has taken charge of renovating the bathrooms in all the bungalows, as well as making other needed improvements. All the units are screened and equipped with a king-size bed or 2 twin beds, plus a single bed, ceiling fan, mini refrigerator, radio, telephone, coffee and tea facilities, in-room safe and hairdryer. An iron and board are available on request. The garden bungalows have an interior lounge area and the overwater units provide a spacious terrace with direct access to the lagoon. A glass floor in the overwater bungalows lets you watch the fish at night as they feed in the coral gardens below. The garden rooms and bungalows all have a/c.

Adjacent to the Nordby Restaurant is an indoor-outdoor bar and a fresh water swimming pool that overlooks the lagoon. There is no beach here, but there is a pier for sunbathing. Snorkeling equipment is provided free of charge as well as kayaks. Hemisphere Sub Diving Center will take qualified divers to visit the *Nordby* wreck at the bottom of the giant aquarium close to the hotel pontoon. Pronounced "Nordbou", this 3-masted barque was built of iron in 1873 in Dundee, Scotland, under the name *Glencarn* for a British ship owner. It was sold in 1893 to the Winther Shipbuilders in Denmark. It sank in August 1900 in front of Teavarua pass in 25 m. (82 ft.) of water.

WiFi connections are available in all the bungalows and in the reception-restaurant-bar area. Cost is 500 CFP for 1 hr. Guest services also include room service, laundry service, and a snack service in the afternoon. Happy Hour is held at the bar on Wed. and Fri. from 6-7pm, with live Polynesian music. You can rent cars, scooters and bicycles, and there is a boutique adjacent to the lobby. There is an on-site dive center and an excursion desk. You can participate in the fish feeding at the end of the pontoon each morning, and you can also join others for a snorkeling excursion in the shallow water beside Motu Ofetaro, opposite the hotel. Or you can be dropped off at the *motu* and they will pick you up later. See *Where to Eat* in this chapter for information on the restaurant and bar.

RAIATEA LODGE HOTEL, *B.P. 680, Uturoa, Raiatea 98735. Tel. 689/ 60.01.00/66.20.00; Fax 689/66.20.02; raiateahotel@mail.pf; www.raiateahotel.com. On the mountainside at PK 9.8 in Tumaraa, 5 min. by car from the airport and 10 min. from Uturoa center. The charter yacht bases at Apooiti Marina are 4 km (2.5 mi.) from the hotel. MC, V.*

This 2-story colonial style hotel opened as the Hotel Tenape in 1999, then was known as the Hotel Miri Miri before being renamed the Raiatea Lodge Hotel. In 2008 the hotel was bought by Olivier and Karine Le Maux, a very outgoing young French couple who speak good English and are supported by a friendly staff. In their first three years the occupancy rose from 10% to 60%. In 2009 the Raiatea Lodge Hotel was the recipient of TripAdvisor's "best hidden gems of the South Pacific" nomination, and in 2010 it was acclaimed by TripAdvisor for "Best Service" and "Best Bargain".

This international 3-star hotel is situated on 4.9 acres (2 ha) of land on the northwest coast of Raiatea, with 120 m. (394 ft.) of lagoon frontage across the road. The 15 rooms have been redecorated with colorful modern bedding. They contain a king-size bed or twin beds, a/c, ceiling fan, refrigerator, TV with CNN and Internet WiFi access in some rooms, telephone, individual safe, and a separate bathroom with a hot water shower. Each room has a large balcony with a view over the lagoon and there are adjoining rooms for families.

Public facilities include a restaurant and bar, swimming pool and pool bar, lounge, activities desk and small gift shop. A long wooden jetty has been added, allowing for easy access into the lagoon where the snorkeling is interesting. Boats for scuba diving and lagoon excursions make pick-ups at the pier. Guests have free use of snorkeling equipment, fishing gear, 2-person kayaks and bicycles. There is no charge for canoe transfers to nearby Motu Miri Miri and other boat trips are arranged on certain days. Massages can be arranged by appointment.

See *Where to Eat* in this chapter for more information on the hotel's very popular gourmet restaurant.

Moderate
SUNSET BEACH MOTEL, *B.P. 397, Uturoa, Raiatea 98735. Tel. 689/ 66.33.47; Fax 689/66.33.08; sunsetbeach@mail.pf; www.sunset-raiatea.pf; Beside the lagoon in Apooiti, 5 km (3 mi.) from the ferry dock and 2 km (1.2 mi.) from the airport. Free round-trip transfers. MC, V.*

This small family hotel offers one of the best values and most pleasant experiences in the islands, and boasts a 3-Tiare rating. The 20 American style wooden cottage type houses or bungalows are placed far apart on a 24.7-acre (10 ha) property that is still a working coconut plantation. The bungalows are all on the waterfront with a fabulous view of Taha'a and Bora Bora. Each bungalow has screened windows and sliding glass doors, and contains a bedroom with a double bed, a living room with 3 single beds and television, ceiling fan, picnic table, kitchen, bathroom with solar hot water, covered terrace and carport. A narrow strip of white sand beach fronts the property, and you can sunbathe on the long private pier or feed the fish at the end of the dock. Snorkeling equipment, outrigger paddle canoes and volleyball are provided. You can rent a bicycle, scooter, car, or a motorboat. Free car transfers are provided for shopping expeditions in town.

Separated from the bungalows by a large garden is a campground for up to 25 tents, with a large kitchen and big covered dining terrace. Campers share the communal cold-water bath facilities, with access to a pay phone, luggage room and library on the premises.

Sunset Beach is owned and managed by Moana Boubee, whose enthusiasm and friendliness are welcome assets, and he speaks good English. There is no restaurant, but a breakfast including fresh fruit grown on Moana's farm will be delivered to your bungalow on request. You can also order bread or croissants the night before and pick them up at the reception in the morning.

HOTEL ATIAPITI, *B.P. 884, Uturoa, Raiatea 98735. Tel./Fax 689/66.16.65; atiapiti@mail.pf; www.atiapiti.com. Beside the lagoon at PK 31 in Opoa, near Marae Taputapuatea, 30 km (18.6 mi.) from the ferry dock and 32 km (19.8 mi.) from the airport. MC, V.*

This 3-Tiare rated accommodation is the closest to the famous Marae Taputapuatea. Round-trip transfers from the airport are 3.900 CFP. 7 concrete bungalows with wood shake roofs are well spaced in 2.5 acres (1 ha) of land beside a narrow strip of white sand beach. The grounds are planted with fruit trees, rainbow shower trees and lots of flowers. Each of the 4 beach bungalows has a bedroom with a king-size bed, living room with tamanu wood furniture, a kitchenette, mini-bar, bathroom with hot water, and a terrace overlooking the sea and the distant island of Huahine. The 2 garden bungalow suites contain a lounge with a double bed and 2 single beds, a small room with a single bed, a kitchen, terrace, and a bathroom with hot water. All the bungalows can accommodate up to 5 people. A lagoon villa for 1-6 people has 2 bedrooms and 2 bathrooms, a kitchen and a big covered terrace with a dining table and chairs, a lounge and hammock and an open space for sunbathing. All the units are colorfully decorated and have a ceiling fan, TV and free WiFi.

Marie-Claude Rajaud, the energetic French woman who owns this small family hotel, speaks English and Spanish, and opens the restaurant to outside guests at lunch only. See more information under *Where to Eat* in this chapter. Free activities include snorkeling from the long pier or pontoon, line fishing, ping-pong, society games and a lending library. Rental bicycles are available, as well as kayaks and outrigger paddle canoes. Optional activities include a guided visit to the Marae of Taputapuatea, and walking tours take you into the valleys on the wild southern end of Raiatea. You can join a 4WD excursion around the island, go horseback riding, scuba diving and deep-sea fishing, and take a boat trip to a nearby *motu* or to Taha'a.

VINI BEACH LODGE, *B.P. 1384, Uturoa, Raiatea 98735. Tel. 689/ 60.22.45/78.48.34; Fax 689/60.22.46; vinibeach@mail.pf; www.raiatea.com/*

vinibeach. On the seaside in Faaroa Bay at PK 12 in Avera, 7.4 mi. southeast of Uturoa center and 15 km from the airport. No credit cards.

This comfortable guest house is owned by a Polynesian family and has been awarded a 2-Tiare rating by Tahiti Tourism. It contains 5 hillside bungalows and 2 units beside the water overlooking the Faaroa River. The first of these attractively decorated bungalows was built in 2003 and each unit can sleep 4 people. The windows and doors are screened, and there is a ceiling fan, kitchen, bathroom with hot water shower and a terrace and balcony. TV available in some rooms. Guests can use the swimming pool, bicycles and kayaks. Excursions and rental cars arranged. Round-trip transfers are 1.220 CFP per adult and lunch or dinner is 2.500-3.300 CFP. Paid Internet access.

LAURA LODGE, *B.P. 1700, Uturoa, Raiatea 98735. Tel. 66.15.57/25.43.23; Fax 689/66.20.44; laura-lodge@hotmail.pf; www.lauralodgeraiatea.com. On mountain side on west coast of Raiatea, facing Miri Miri Pass, Taha'a and Bora Bora, 5 min. from airport. No credit cards.*

Marie-Laure and Serge Angermann have been praised by their former guests as the ideal hosts for their bungalow, which has a 2-Tiare rating from Tahiti Tourism. There is a double bed and a sofa bed in the 377 sq. ft. (35 sq. m) guest house, plus a well-equipped kitchen, washing machine, iron and ironing board, bathroom, hair dryer, ceiling fan, mosquito net and covered private terrace. TV and Internet connections are provided, and guests have access to the barbecue grill, swimming pool, bicycles, kayak, snorkeling equipment, fishing rod, and books. The bungalow is in a spacious private garden setting behind the Raiatea Lodge Hotel, whose restaurant serves fine cuisine. Laura Lodge guests can also use the long private pier over the lagoon.

PENSION MANAVA, *B.P. 559, Uturoa, Raiatea 98735. Tel. 689/66.28.26; Fax 689/66.16.66; manava@free.fr; www.manavapension.com. On mountainside in Avera, 6 km (3.7 mi.) southeast of town. Free round-trip transfers. MC, V.*

This family pension has earned a 2-Tiare rating from Tahiti Tourism. Roselyn and Andrew Brotherson have 4 clean and attractive bungalows and a large house, located in a pretty setting of trees, grass and flowers, across the road from the lagoon. Two bungalows have individual kitchens and toilets with solar hot water; 2 have individual toilets with hot water and share a kitchen. In the large house are 2 bedrooms with shared kitchen and a communal bathroom with hot water. Each bungalow has screened windows and a covered terrace. All the rooms have an electric fan and bed linens are furnished. If you want to eat dinner in a local restaurant someone from the pension will drive you to the good dining places, and the restaurant will drive you back after dinner or the Brothersons will come get you. Car, bicycle and scooter rentals can also be arranged.

Manava Excursions is across the road, where Andrew Brotherson will take you on an outrigger canoe ride to Taha'a for the day, complete with a picnic on a *motu*. Or you can join a half-day boat tour to visit the Faaroa River and Marae

Taputapuatea. You can also be dropped off on a *motu* and picked up later. There are no excursions on Sat.

PENSION TE MAEVA, *B.P. 701, Uturoa, Raiatea 98735. Tel./Fax 689/ 66.37.28; cell 73.01.22; temaeva@mail.pf; www.temaeva.com. On the mountainside at PK 23 in Opoa, 25 km (15.5 mi.) from the airport and 23 km (14.3 mi.) from the boat dock. No credit cards.*

You'll have a panoramic view of the *motu* islets of Avera from this mountainside retreat, which is 7 km (4.3 mi.) north of Marae Taputapuatea. It's far from the sea, far from the main village and tourist attractions, far from noise, far from everything. The two modern style bungalows have a double bed and single bed, fan, refrigerator, terrace and private bathroom with hot water. Amenities include a laundry room, international phone and Internet access. Guests can use the swimming pool and bicycles. Owner Claudine Leclerc-Hunter has been awarded a 2-Tiare rating by the Tahiti Tourist office for the quality of her pension. Camping is available for 1.500 CFP per person. MAP and AP meals available.

PENSION YOLANDE, *B.P. 298, Uturoa, Raiatea 98735. Tel/Fax 689/ 66.35.28. Beside the lagoon and white sand beach at PK 10 in Avera. No credit cards.*

Yolande Roopinia has operated this friendly Polynesian style pension for many years and was recently awarded a 2-Tiare rating from Tahiti Tourism. She has 4 comfortable and attractively decorated studios with a double bed and single bed, fan and mosquito net, a bathroom with hot water, and a kitchenette with fridge. All meals available. Free use of outrigger canoes and kayaks.

VILLA TEMEHANI, *B.P. 972, Uturoa, Raiatea 98735. Tel./Fax 689/66.12.88; cell 77.54.87; www.vacances-tahiti.com. Beside the lagoon of Tevaitoa, 10-min. from airport. No credit cards.*

Marie-Claude Rosnarho and Roland Marti have a big wooden house with 3 bedrooms on Raiatea's west coast in the middle of a tree-shaded garden beside the lagoon. There is a view of the Temehani valley and plateau on one side and the sunset, a motu, Taha'a and Bora Bora on the other side.

Tahiti Tourism rates this as a 2-Tiare guest house. Each room has a double bed with mosquito net, ceiling fan, refrigerator and hair dryer. Some rooms include a private bathroom with hot water. Guests share the living room with TV, telephone and free Internet access. Hammocks and deck chairs provide relaxing comfort on private terraces. MAP meals available. Bikes, kayaks, snorkeling equipment and a library are provided free of charge.

LA CROIX DU SUD, *B.P. 769, Uturoa, Raiatea 98735. Tel./Fax 689/ 66.27.55. On the mountainside at PK 12, overlooking Faaroa Bay. No credit cards.*

This pension with a 1-Tiare rating has a lovely panoramic view from a large covered terrace and is surrounded by a flower garden, with a swimming pool in the front yard. Hostess Annette Germa is Marquesan and worked in the charter boat business for many years with her late husband, Eric Germa. The three bedrooms are clean and attractively furnished, each with a double bed, mosquito net, ceiling fan and private bathroom with hot water. TV is available in the living room and MAP or AP meals are served on request.

LES 3 CASCADES, *B.P. 123, Uturoa, Raiatea 98735. Tel. 689/66.10.90/ 78.33.28; tbt@mail.pf; www.tahaa.net. On mountainside in Avera, 6 km (3.7 mi.) southeast of town. MC, V.*

This was formerly called the Kaoha Nui Ranch and since it was taken over by Bruno Fabre in Nov. 2010 it is also called l'**Excursion Bleue**. Lodging is in a fully equipped bungalow for 3, or in a 4-bedroom house with 2 single beds and a fan in each room, plus shared bathroom facilities with hot water. Be aware that the walls do not go all the way up to the ceiling in these rooms. House linens and anti-mosquito products are furnished. Guests have use of the kitchen and share the dining room. They can also have drinks or meals in the Club House and Restaurant, where there is a TV and free WiFi Internet access.

The property includes a stable of horses you can ride for 3.000 CFP an hour. You can join a guided hike to the waterfalls (Les 3 Cascades) in the valley, rent bicycles, or take an outrigger excursion to visit the Faaroa River, Marae Taputapuatea, or Taha'a. See information for l'Excursion Bleue under *Lagoon & Motu Excursions* in this chapter.

PENSION OPEHA, *B.P. 726, Uturoa, Raiatea 98735. Tel./Fax 689/66.19.48; cell 79.88.92; pension.opeha@mail.pf; www.pension opeha.pf. Beside lagoon at PK 10.5 Avera. No credit cards.*

Emma Tautoo will greet you at her clean family pension, which has 5 bungalows designed to accommodate 3 adults or a family of 4. Three bungalows have a king size bed and a convertible couch and the other 2 units have 2 single beds and a couch. Each bungalow has a/c, private bathroom with hot water, a kitchen equipped with a fridge, gas stove with oven, micro-wave oven, and a washing machine. There is also a TV and free access to the Internet, plus free use of kayaks and outrigger canoes. A 28-ft. aluminum boat is available to take you to Motu Nao Nao, to visit Faaroa River and Marae Taputapuatea, or to go to Taha'a for the day for 5.500 CFP per person.

PENSION TEPUA, *B.P. 1298, Uturoa, Raiatea 98735. Tel. 689/66.33.00; Fax 689/66.32.00: pension-tepua@mail.pf; www.pension-tepua.com. Beside the lagoon in Tepua Bay, 2.5 km (1.5 mi.) south of Uturoa center. AE, MC, V.*

Guylaine Ungaro-Alves runs this lodging, which is used by backpackers, scuba divers and other visitors on a tight budget. The compact space contains a seaside bungalow, a bungalow facing the pool, and a garden bungalow; all with a queen size bed and two single beds, ceiling fan, kitchenette and private bathroom. There are also 3 rooms with a double bed, 1 room with a single bed, and a 12-bunk dormitory. The rooms and dorm have ceiling fans and guests share the bathroom facilities and kitchen. All the bathrooms have hot water showers. There are refrigerators in all the bungalows.

The restaurant serves breakfast and dinner to the in-house guests and there is also a bar, swimming pool and a pier over the lagoon. There's a lot squeezed into one small space here, and all land and sea activities that are available in Raiatea can be arranged at the pension. Guests also have paid access to the Internet and telephone.

HOTEL HINANO API, *B.P. 1689, Uturoa, Raiatea 98735. Tel. 689/ 66.13.13/70.82.40; Fax 689/66.14.14; bajoga-hinano@mail.pf; www.hotel-hinano-tahiti.com. On the main street in the center of Uturoa, a 2-min. walk from the ferry dock. MC, V.*

This old budget family hotel has added the name "api" (new) as well as changed owners. Farhida and Dominique Lucas now manage this lodging, which is upstairs in the Uturoa town center. The 10 motel-type rooms have a/c or ceiling fans and can sleep 3 people. They have private bathrooms with hot water shower, a fridge, cable TV and WiFi access to Internet. A microwave oven, iron and hair-dryer are available at the office and breakfast is served on request. Several good restaurants and snack bars are just a few steps away.

Economy

Other budget lodgings include: **Bed & Breakfast Raiatea Bellevue,** *Tel./Fax 689/ 66.15.15; www.raiateabellevue-tahiti.com.* 3 rooms and 2 studios with kitchenettes and small pool on top of a steep hill north of Uturoa center. **Pension Tiare Nui,** *Tel. 689/66.34.06/78.33.53; Fax 689/66.16.06; tiarenui@mail.pf; www.raiatea.com/ tiarenui.* This 1-Tiare pension is adjacent to Europcar Agency near the airport, who has special packages for bungalow and car or bungalow, car and boat rental. The 4 bungalows can sleep 1-3 people and have a private bathroom, fan, TV, WiFi and kitchenette. **Residence Le Dauphin,** *Tel. 689/66.39.39/77.23.14; residenceledauphin @mail.pf.* 8 new furnished a/c studios with private bathroom for rent by day or month in Uturoa center above Anuanua Gallery and Optique Te Mata Oa.

WHERE TO EAT

Deluxe

OPOA BEACH HOTEL, *Tel. 60.05.10. Beside the lagoon at PK 37 on the south coast of the island, 35 min. from the airport and 10 min. from Marae Taputapuatea. Open daily for B.,L.,D. MC, V.*

Nicole Barbace, part-owner and chef, has a well-earned reputation for her amazingly inventive cuisine, starting with the delicious breakfasts she serves in her romantic and lovingly decorated restaurant. Continental breakfast is 1.900 CFP and an American breakfast is 2.300 CFP. An a la carte lunch is 3.000 CFP and dinner is 5.700 CFP. MAP and AP meal plans available for in-house guests. Nicole is from Paris and she used to own a gastronomic restaurant in Grasse, France. She picked up a few more culinary ideas when she and her husband, Eric, lived in Kenya and Guadeloupe before moving to Taha'a to manage Vahine Island, and then to Raiatea to open their own hotel and restaurant. Nicole's 5-star cuisine features fresh fish and seafood, mainly organic vegetables, and fabulous desserts, including the best coconut cake I have ever eaten. I highly recommend this restaurant.

RAIATEA LODGE HOTEL, *Tel. 60.01.00, Open daily for BLD. MC, V.*
This high end, fine-dining restaurant is set in a big open-sided and attractively decorated space overlooking the gardens, swimming pool and the lagoon across the road. The classy cuisine of excellently prepared French, Italian and Tahitian dishes is complemented by Raiatea's largest wine selection. Main courses are priced between 2.200 and 2.600 CFP. This restaurant has one of the best chefs in the Leeward Islands and the wait staff is well trained, friendly and attentive.

Superior to Moderate
RAIATEA HAWAIKI NUI HOTEL, *Tel. 60.05.00. Open daily for BLD. All major credit cards.*
The Marquesan chef de cuisine of the Nordby Restaurant takes pleasure in pleasuring guests, and his culinary skills guarantee the accomplishment of his goal. Try his melted chocolate fondant and you'll understand. The Continental breakfast buffet is 1.800 CFP and you'll pay 800 CFP more for eggs. Lunch is simple with a choice of salads, steaks and burgers. Dinner is much more elaborate with an interesting menu of French, international and Polynesian cuisine. The menu changes every six months featuring appetizers from 1.500-2.000 CFP and main courses from 2.000-3.000 CFP. The bar serves a variety of exotic cocktails, and snacks are available at the bar from 2-6pm. Special evenings with a Polynesian dance show are organized when the hotel is full. A Sunday brunch is presented once a month.

ATIAPITI RESTAURANT, *Tel. 66.16.65, is located at Hotel Atiapiti, PK 31, beside the lagoon in Opoa, near Marae Taputapuatea. Open daily for B and daily except Sat. for L. Closed for D. Guests not staying in the hotel-pension are welcome at lunch only. MC, V.*
Owner Marie-Claude Rajaud likes to serve fresh fish, crab and lobster from the lagoon, which she says is still not polluted. The river shrimp she prepares can be served with saffron or curry. She also cooks chicken with Coca-Cola, grilled New Zealand beef, and she makes a sumptuous coconut cake. Fresh fruits from the garden are also served. Meals are à la carte and there is a well-stocked bar and a good wine list. Breakfast is 1.500 CFP and the lunch menu is 2.500-3.200 CFP.

TE HOA YACHT CLUB, *Tel. 66.40.00, open daily 8am-11pm, with meal service ending at 9pm.*
This snack, restaurant and bar is located at the Apooiti Marina and used to be Le Club House Restaurant. Pierre (Pierrot) Dinard, who formerly managed the Raiatea Hawaiki Nui Hotel, and his associate Jean-Philippe have big plans for Te Hoa Yacht Club, which include adding a center of well-being (massage, sauna, Jacuzzi). They also plan to have a karaoke night, a Tahitian dance group on Friday nights and a Sunday morning brunch, then a Sunday buffet for 2.500 CFP per person.

JADE GARDEN, *Tel. 66.34.40, is on the mountainside of Uturoa's main street in the downtown shopping area. Open Wed.-Sat. from 11am-1pm and 6-9:30pm. Closed Sun., Mon. and Tues. AE, MC and V.*

There are 60 choices of Cantonese cuisine and local style food on the menu, plus the specials, such as Tapen Lou, the Chinese seafood fondue that requires a day's advance notice to prepare. I have always enjoyed my rather expensive meals here, which have included the steamed chicken with black mushrooms and ginger, the shrimp stuffed with taro, and taro steamed fried duckling. The a/c dining room is upstairs and has an elaborate ceiling decorated with gold dragons. The tables are covered with red or pink cloths and a vase of plastic flowers. You pay the owner, Soufa Chung, at the bottom of the stairway when you've finished eating.

LE NAPOLI, *Tel. 66.10.77; www.pizzerialenapoli.com is on the lagoon side of the road between Uturoa village and the airport. Open Tues.-Fri. for lunch and dinner, and on Sat. and Sun. evenings. Closed Sat. noon, Sun. noon and all day Mon. MC, V.*

This little restaurant is right beside the road near the airport, with shoji screens and bamboo walls. They serve really good pizzas and steaks cooked in a wood oven, as well as composed salads, Mahi Mahi and veal dishes. Pizza prices start at 1.490 CFP. Best to reserve.

CHEZ MICHELE, *Tel. 66.14.66, occupies the ground floor of the Hotel Hinano Api, facing the boat dock. Open for B.,L.,D. Closed Sat. night and Sun. No credit cards.*

You can get Polynesian food at all times in this small in-door, out-door restaurant that has been in business for many years. In addition to poisson cru, you can order *fafa* (Tahitian spinach), *uru* (breadfruit), taro, bananas and other Tahitian specials on request. The quality of the food is usually good, and includes Chinese and European dishes such as steak, chicken and fish, prepared in the local style. There are three choices of daily specials, which cost less than 2.000 CFP each.

BRASSERIE MARAAMU, *Tel. 66.46.64, is in the Gare Maritime building. Open for B.,L.,D, Mon., Tues, Fri; open for B.,L. Wed., Thurs, Sat. Closed at night on Wed., Thurs, Sat. and all day Sun. AE, MC, V.*

This Chinese restaurant is popular with local residents, who sometimes reserve the entire restaurant for private parties. You can have a breakfast of coffee, bread and butter for 350 CFP, poisson cru for 800-1.150 CFP, eggs or an omelet for 800 CFP, or fried fish for 800 CFP. The lunch and dinner choices are *ma'a tinito* (Chinese stew with pork, red beans, vegetables and macaroni) for 1.150 CFP, and other Chinese dishes of beef, chicken, fish or shrimp are 950-1.850 CFP.

Economy

There are small snack stands all around the island where you can buy casse-croûte sandwiches on baguette bread, *poisson cru, maa tinito* and other local dishes while driving around Raiatea. Several rolling food trucks called **Roulottes** park on the Uturoa waterfront at night, serving steak and fries, chicken legs and *salade russe* (red potato salad), *poisson cru*, brochettes of beef hearts, and grilled fish, along with soft drinks and juices in cartons. The prices are usually about 1.200 CFP per food order. You can also get casse-croûtes and other prepared foods in the well-stocked supermarkets in Uturoa.

SEEING THE SIGHTS

Hinerani Tours, *Tel. 66.25.75/72.49.66,* is owned by Lysis and Heiariki Terooatea, who have an 8-passenger Land Rover. They will take you on a 4-hr. tour into the interior of the island in the Faaroa valley, stopping at a botanical garden, splashing through rivers, and visiting Marae Taputapuatea. A combination all-day excursion takes you on a 4WD tour, then by boat to the Faaroa River, for a swim and picnic at Motu Iriru. Tourists enjoy this smiling and charming Tahitian couple and appreciate the small number of people on their tours rather than having to go with a crowd.

Jeep Safari Raiatea, *Tel. 66.15.73/78.23.73,* is operated by Mirella and Petero Mou Kam Tse, who have four 4WD vehicles and a motorized outrigger canoe for 32 passengers that they use for combined land and lagoon tours. They have daily departures in the morning and afternoon for 4-hour tours through the mountain valleys, with stops at vanilla plantations, Marae Taputapuatea and a pearl farm. You will learn about the botanical treasures of the hidden valleys and tropical plantations and all about the cultivation of the pearl oyster. A half-day tour is 5.000 CFP per person. Boat tours for 4-32 passengers will take you to the *motu* for a picnic.

Raiatea 4x4 Discovery, *Tel. 66.24.16/78.33.26; raidiscovery@mail.pf* is operated daily at 8:30am and 1pm by Maria Cowan and Gérard Duvos. Their 4x4 safari tours by open air Land Rover or an a/c Isuzu Trooper include a lot of personal attention and good explanations of the plants, flowers, sites and history of Raiatea.

Raiatea Tourism, *Tel. 66.20.86/78.33.13; raiateatourisme@mail.pf.* Christophe Bardou has a 45-seat a/c bus that is used to transfer groups between the airport and hotel or pensions or for tours around the island. He also provides 4WD excursions.

Trucky Tour, *Tel. 78.23.36* (Christian), *Tel. 75.66.02* (Nella); *Fax 66.10.47; millecam@mail.pf.* This very popular company has two 8-seater minibuses used for transfers to the airport, town, marina or to your hotel. They are very knowledgeable tour guides who do a lot of work with American tourists. An all-day tour is 5.000 CFP, which includes a sandwich and fruit.

Special Places to Visit

Marae Taputapuatea, at PK 32 in Opoa, faces Te-Ava-Moa pass on the east coast of the island. This is Raiatea's most famous landmark and the most significant archaeological site in the whole South Pacific area. This international *marae* has been in existence since 1600 A.D. and was the most important *marae* in eastern Polynesia during the pre-Christian era. Raiatea was then known as Havai'i, the Sacred Island. This marae was not always international and did not always carry the name of Taputapuatea. At a very remote time before the birth of the god Oro it was only the national marae of Havai'i (Raiatea) and its full name was Tini-rau-hui-mata-te-papa-o-Feoro (Fruitful myriads who engraved the rocks of Feoro), and its abbreviated name was Feoro. It contained 8 memorial stones representing the 8 kings who had reigned over the land. These stones later became 8 symbols of the royal insignia of the kings and queens in long succession afterwards. They were named: Te'iva, Feufeu, Nuna'a-e-hau, Te-ata-o-tu, Manava-taia, Huia-i-te-ra'I, Paie-o-te-fau-rua and Te-ra'i-pua-tata. On the seashore is **Marae Hauviri** with an investiture stone that served as a royal throne and as a measuring stone for warriors who served as representatives to the outside world. See introduction to *Raiatea chapter* for more information.

Marae **Tainuu** is located beside the sea at PK 15 in the little fishing village of Tevaitoa on the northwest coast of Raiatea. This marae has one of the most imposing *ahu* altars in the Leeward Islands. Petroglyphs engraved in the basaltic stones include a Polynesian sundial and 10 turtles, depicting a sort of Polynesian treasure hunt that the Maohi warriors had to perform to achieve valor and esteem. The chief's platform, called Taumatini, is at the edge of the road. Upstream from these ruins, on the hill there are several structures. First of all is the Marae Tetuira, which belonged to the chief and was considered to be very sacred. Above that a succession of small terraces takes you to the platform of the war chiefs, the *paepae* Taputuari'i.

La Vanillère is located at PK 33.5 Opoa in Hotopuu Bay, *Tel. 66.15.61/ 76.33.34; info@tahiti-vanille.com; www.tahiti-vanille.com.* If you are driving around the island with an organized tour be sure to stop at this vanilla farm with 18,000 vanilla plants and learn how the vanilla orchids are "married" by hand to cross-pollinate the flower that produces the vanilla bean. You can also buy dried vanilla beans, powder, extract and vanilla soap in their farm shop, or you order from their website. Hidden in the bushes nearby is a pretty waterfall where you can splash around in the basin, which is called "The Queen's Bathtub."

Pearl Farms you can visit include: **Anapa Pearl Farm**, *Tel. 70.76.07; www.anapapearls.com* is owned by Philippe Blanc, who says that "the best little pearl farm in the South Pacific", is located in Tevaitoa, in front of the Protestant church and Marae Tainuu. He invites the public to call for a free visit. Don't forget your snorkeling gear and they accept all major credit cards. **Tahi Perles**, *Tel. 60.20.20, tahiperles@mail.pf* at PK 4 in Avera, is owned by Roma and Moana Constant. Reserve for a tour of the pearl farm. **Vairua Perles**, *Tel. 66.12.12/ 66.38.39; vairuaperles@mail.pf* is located at PK 8.7 in Avera. The owner is Hundrew Brodien.

SPORTS & RECREATION
Horseback Riding
Pension 3 Cascades/L'Excursion Bleue is on the mountainside at PK 6 in Avera, *Tel. 66.10.90/78.33.28.* They have saddled Marquesan horses of Chilean stock. A 1 1/2 hr. ride is 3.000 CFP per horse.

Hiking
Raiatea Randonée, *Tel. 66.20.32/77.91.23; raiatearando@mail.pf.* Thierry is a licensed guide who belongs to an association of hiking guides. He leads hikes to the Faaroa Valley, the 3 cascades or waterfalls and Marae Taputapuatea.

Other hiking guides are: Paul of Hava'i Rando, *Tel. 66.13.77*; and Sandrine, *Tel. 76.38.00*.

Boat Rentals, Kayaks and Day Sailing

Avis, *Tel. 66.34.06*, rents boats with a 6-HP engine that requires no permit or a 15-HP engine that does require a license. The cost of either boat is 7.700 CFP for 4 hrs., 10.200 CFP for 8 hrs. and 11.450 CFP for 24 hrs.

Deep Sea Fishing

Game fishing is especially rewarding in the Leeward Society Islands, where prize catches of marlin, yellow fin tuna, mahi mahi and wahoo are frequent events. The Raiatea Haura Club holds local competitions several times a year, and the private charters report good fishing year-round.

Moanavaihi II Charter, *Tel./Fax 66.20.20; cell 72.10.57/72.03.38; jpconstant@mail.pf.* This Viking 40-ft. fishing boat is owned by Jean Pierre Constant, who is one of the top captains in the Leeward Islands. The boat is equipped with Shimano heavy tackle. Full-day fishing for a maximum of 6 people is 120.000 CFP with soft drinks and snacks.

N'Bopo Fishing, is operated by Jérome, *Tel. 28.33.71*, who speaks English. He can take up to 3 people for a 2-hr. or all-day fishing tour.

Lagoon & Motu Excursions

Faaroa River is a cool, green haven bordered by wild hibiscus *purau* trees and modern homes. One of the most popular excursions is to explore this historic river by outrigger speed canoe. Around the year 1350 hundreds of brave Maohi families left Raiatea from this river, navigating their voyaging sailing canoes by the wind, stars and ocean currents to settle in Hawaii, the Cook Islands, the Samoas and finally in New Zealand. Their Polynesian descendants are called Maori in New Zealand and Tahitians in French Polynesia.

A Day Tour to Taha'a Island takes you on a 30-min. boat ride across the protected lagoon that is shared by Raiatea and Taha'a. On the main island you will visit a picturesque little village and a vanilla farm. Then you will explore the lagoon by boat, visiting a pearl farm and stop on a *motu* islet to swim and snorkel in the clear lagoon waters. Most full-day excursions to Taha'a also include a picnic on the *motu*.

Trips to the Motu provide an ideal destination by canoe or speedboat, where you will find white sand beaches, privacy, and time for daydreaming and swimming in the lagoon. Taxi boats are available to drop you off and pick you up later, or you can arrange transfers with your hotel or pension. Should you wish to make a day of it, your hotel will pack a picnic lunch for you or you can buy food already prepared in the supermarkets in Uturoa or order a take-out dish from any of the restaurants and snack stands. Several of the *motu* islets around Raiatea and Taha'a are off limits to the public, as they are privately owned. Others are partially private while the rest of the *motu* is open to visitors seeking sun, sand and sea. On these sometimes fiercely protected properties you will see Tabu signs warning you to keep out. Some of the people who operate the boat excursions have access to private *motu* islets where they take their passengers.

Motu Iriru, located at the entrance to the Iriru pass on the east coast of Raiatea, is open to the public. The government has built a *fare pote'e* shelter here, along with a small changing room, shower, water faucets, toilets with handicap access, picnic tables and barbecue grills. You have to take your garbage away with you. To camp on Motu Iriru you need a permit from the commune of Taputapuatea. There are no mosquitoes, no nonos and no grouchy owners here. **Motu Oatara**, on the southeast side of Raiatea in front of Hotel Atiapiti, is also known as Bird Island. There is good snorkeling here. **Motu Nao Nao**, on the south end of Raiatea, is used by some of the boat service providers who take visitors to enjoy the pretty white sand beach. A 3,000-foot landing strip was built on this 65-acre flat islet by the US Navy Seabees during World War II. **Motu Ceran** (Motu Mahaea on a map of Taha'a) has fences to close off some of the private properties, but you can visit one part of the islet for a nominal fee and use the beach. **Motu Atger** (also known as Motu Toahotu) is also privately owned. Boat excursions take their passengers to visit a lagoonarium and marine park beside this *motu*, which is called "Titi ere ere" (black breasts). There are toilets on the islet, as well as a few small bungalows to rent (see information on *Where to Stay* in Taha'a chapter.)

Here is just a partial list of the people who provide boat tours in Raiatea and Taha'a. You may also want to look at the lagoon excursions listed in the Taha'a chapter, as many of those excursions begin in Raiatea.

Faaroa Tours, *Tel. 66.32.70*, is owned by Noma Wong, who managed the Hotel Bali Hai in Raiatea for several years. (This hotel is now the Raiatea Hawaiki Nui). Noma has 3 outrigger speed canoes to take 6-36 passengers to visit the Faaroa valley and Apoomau River, with a stop at Marae Taputapuatea, and a swim at a *motu* islet with a white sand beach. This 4-hr. excursion starts at 8:30am or 1:15pm. She also offers half-day boat tours to Taha'a, or a full-day tour with a barbecue picnic on a *motu*.

Hinerani Tours, *Tel. 66.25.75; lysis@mail.pf.* Lysis and Heiariki Terooatea can take 6-12 passengers on lagoon excursions in their 27-ft. long covered boat. A combination land and lagoon excursion takes you on a 4WD tour, then by boat to the Faaroa River and for a swim and picnic at *Motu* Iriru. This all-day excursion is 8.500 CFP per person for a minimum of 8 people.

Jeep Safari Raiatea, *Tel. 66.15.73/79.62.21*, is operated by Mirella and Petero Mou Kam Tse, whose 32-place outrigger speed canoe *Hinatea* provides excursions inside the lagoon and picnics on the *motu*. A half-day tour is 5.000 CFP.

L'Excursion Bleue (formerly Taha'a Pearl Tour), *Tel. 66.10.90/78.33.28; tpt@mail.pf; www.tahaa.net*, is owned by Bruno Fabre, who has outrigger speed canoes with awnings that he uses to transport 4 to 12 passengers for half- or full-day excursions. On the all-day tour, from 9am to 5pm, your guide will take you to a vanilla plantation and a pearl farm on the main island of Taha'a. He will present the eco system and history in a pleasant ambiance. You will be served a local type meal on a *motu* islet with a lagoonarium, and then you can drift snorkel in the best spots. Bring plastic shoes, a towel and snorkeling gear. This excursion including beverage is 8.500-12.000 CFP depending on where he picks you up. An underwater photographer will capture the memories for you on digital camera. Private tours are available for 47.000 CFP for 2 and 69.000 CFP for 4 people. MC, V and Paypal.

Lagon Aventures, *Tel./Fax 66.34.45; cell 79.26.27; h.clot@mail.pf; www.lagonaventures.com.* Hubert Clot operates this activity at Marina Apooiti and provides free transfers from the hotels and pensions. He leads kayak trips that can also include camping in tents on a motu for 1-3 days and fishing for your own dinner. Half-day trips will take you to explore Faaroa River or you can kayak around the island of Taha'a in a day trip.

Manava Excursions, *Tel. 66.28.26, manava@free.fr; www.manavapension.com.* This company is owned by Andrew Brotherson of Pension Manava. He provides excursions by a 27-ft. boat with a sun awning, offering half-day trips to the Faaroa Bay, Apoomau River and Marae Taputapuatea for 4.900 CFP. An all-day trip to Taha'a to visit a pearl farm, fish park, vanilla plantation and stop for a swim and picnic of grilled fish and fresh fruits at a *motu* costs 7.800 CFP. He will also take you to a nearby *motu* and return at your convenience, for 1.500 CFP per person. No excursions on Sat.

West Coast Charters, *Tel. 66.45.39/79.28.78.* Tony and Marie Tucker are a very friendly couple who speak good English. He's from South Africa and she is French. They offer a program of scenic lagoon excursions around Raiatea and Taha'a aboard their two boats with sun awnings. A full-day circle island tour of Raiatea includes a visit to Marae Taputapuatea and a snorkeling stop at a *motu*. A half-day Raiatea River Tour takes you along Faaroa River and to Motu Iriru for a swim or to snorkel at Motu Oatara. Or you can visit Marae Taputapuatea. A full-day boat trip to Taha'a takes you to visit a pearl farm and vanilla plantation, to feed the turtles, rays, tropical fish and sharks at a marine park, and snorkeling on a spectacular coral drop and in coral gardens.

Sailing Charter Yachts

Archipels Croisières (Dream Yacht Charter), *Tel. 689/66.18.80; Fax. 689/ 66.18.76; polynesie@dreamyachtcharter.com; www.dreamyachtcharter.com. Jérome Touze, base manager, cell 30.55.02; François Guais, customer service, cell 28.42.64.*

Archipels Cruises operated a nautical base in Moorea for several years, and have now transferred their base to the Apooiti Marina in Raiatea since they were purchased by Dream Yacht Charter in 2009. The Archipels fleet consists of 3 Harmony monohulls 47-52 ft. long and 5 Marquises and Eleuthera catamarans 56-60 ft. in length, which can be chartered only with a skipper. Dream Yacht Charter also has 8 Catana catamarans from 41-50 ft. long that can be chartered to sail yourself (if qualified). All of these yachts are based permanently in Raiatea, except during the high season, when 1-2 yachts are kept in Rangiroa.

You can also simply book a cabin for one of the regular sailing programs that operate throughout the year with 4-11 day cruises in the Leeward Islands and in the Tuamotu atolls. These include the Bora Bora Pearl Dream, Huahine Dream and Rangiroa Dream, which are all mini-cruises of 4 days/3 nights; the Tikehau Dream of 5 days/4 nights, the Atoll Dream or Bora Bora Dream, with 8 days/7 nights; and the unique Polynesia Dream of 11 days/10 nights, which takes you from Tahiti to Moorea, Huahine, Raiatea, Bora Bora, and Taha'a, ending in Raiatea.

The Moorings, *B.P. 165, Uturoa, Raiatea 98735. Tel. 689/66.35.93/78.35.93; Fax 689/66.20.94; moorings@moorings.pf; www.moorings.com.* The nautical base is located at Apooiti Marina, 1 km (0.6 mi.) from the Raiatea airport and 4 km (2.5 mi.) from the boat dock in Uturoa.

The Moorings has been operating in Raiatea since 1985. In 2007 both The Moorings and Sunsail operations were taken over by First Choice Holidays, headed by Patricia Hubbard in Raiatea. The Moorings has an average fleet of 20 yachts, including 14 Beneteau Dufour monohulls 36-52 ft. long monohulls and 6 Leopard de Robertson & Caine catamarans 42-47 ft. long. You have a choice of 3, 4 or 5 cabins in a frequently renewed fleet. Yachts can be chartered bareboat, ready to sail away or with skipper and hostess/cook. Provisioning is available on request.

Sunsail, *B.P. 331 Uturoa, Raiatea, 98735 Tel. 689/60.04.85; Fax 689/ 66.23.19; sunsail.tahiti@mail.pf; www.sunsail.com.*

This nautical base was formerly operated by Stardust Yacht Charters with a nautical base in Faaroa Bay. The Sunsail company, as well as The Moorings, was taken oven by First Choice Holidays and in September 2007 the Sunsail base was moved to Apooiti Marina, but it still maintains a separate office. Sunsail's fleet of 14 boats includes 6 monohulls 34-50 ft. and 8 catamarans 38-46 ft. Bareboat charters for a minimum of 3-days are available for sailing in the Leeward Islands. The yachts can also be chartered ready to sail away, complete with fuel, water, dinghy and outboard engine, bed linens and towels, barbecue grill and charcoal, snorkeling equipment and with complete provisions on request. Optional services include skippers, hostess-cooks and kayaks.

Tahiti Yacht Charter, *Tahiti office: Monette Aline, B.P. 364, Papeete, Tahiti 98713; Tel. 689/45.04.00; Fax 689/42.76.00; tyc@mail.pf; www.tahitiyachtcharter.com. Raiatea base: Tel. 689/66.28.86; Fax 689/66.28.85.*

Tahiti Yacht Charter is a 100% locally owned company. They have a fleet of 28 catamarans, most of them less than 2 years old, all based at the Apooiti Marina in Raiatea, with Papeete as a possible departure point. The catamarans are from 38-46 ft., including the Lagoon 380, Lavezzi 40, Lagoon 440, Nautitech 441, Orana 44, Bahia 46, and Lagoon 500.

Their sailing range is mainly the Leeward Islands, including Maupiti when weather conditions allow it. You can also sail to the Tuamotu and Marquesas

Islands with a Tahiti Yacht Charter skipper on board. Charter rates vary according to seasons. The 4 day/3 night cruises to Bora Bora or Huahine or cruising inside the lagoon of Raiatea and Taha'a start at 1400 euros (167.064 CFP) per person. A 7 day/6 night "Tahiti Twosome" private cruise, ideal for honeymooners and other romantic couples, starts at 2,750 euros (328.162 CFP) per person. For the same price 2 or more people in the same party of friends/family can sail from Fakarava to Toau and back to Fakarava on a 7 day/6 night Tuamotu Atoll cruise.

This company is very service oriented and keeps creating new and original programs and cruises targeted to couples as well as families or groups of friends. The staff and crew speak English. All the skippers have their own fishing rod. The "Tropiques" boat models have generator, water maker, a/c and 2 kayaks, and 2 floating hammocks on board. Boats are equipped with WiFi (for email retrieval from your own laptop) and VOIP telephones (call your country at your local telephone rates).

Atara Royal, *Tel. 66.17.74/79.22.40; Fax 66.17.67; myc@mail.pf; www.motoryachtchartertahiti.com.* This 46-ft. Grand Banks Europa motor yacht can be chartered for cruises in the Leeward Islands of French Polynesia. It was built in 1999 and has two Caterpillar 375 HP engines. Accommodations include 1 double cabin with ensuite bathroom, 1 twin cabin, crew quarters, a/c, water maker, TV, video and DVD players, 2 stereos, dinghy with 40 HP engine, plus equipment for fishing. With the boat cruise is linked a day on the private Atara Motu in the lagoon of Taha'a. Leeward Islands Discovery Cruises include sailing programs of 4 to 15 days, honeymoon specials, day charters and private diving cruises with a CMAS-PADI Instructor.

Catamaran Tane, *Tel./Fax 66.16.67; cell 73.96.90; charter.tane@mail.pf; www.chartertane.free.fr.* This 46-foot catamaran was specially designed for sailing in the tropics and has been based in Raiatea for many years. Owners Christian and Martine are the captain and hostess, providing personalized cruises for 2-6 passengers. Custom charters in the Leeward Islands include 5-days/4-nights and 7 days-6 nights, and longer cruises will take you to the Tuamotu and Austral Islands on request. Private cruises, day cruises and sunset cruises are also available. E-mail them for rates.

Scuba Diving

A short boat ride takes you to the **natural aquarium** at Teavapiti, and 50 different exciting dive spots are found in the four most beautiful passes of the Raiatea-Taha'a lagoon. These include exploring a sunken three-masted yacht, the hull of a Catalina seaplane, feeding gray sharks, barracuda, moray eels and the Napoleon fish that inhabit an underwater wall. The Octopus Grotto is a cave 120 m (394 ft.) long at a depth of 50 m (55 ft.); a dive for experienced divers only. There are rainbow-hued Jack trevally fish, caves of orange corals, black coral forests and dancing coral gardens of blues, violets and yellow.

Hémisphere Sub Plongée, *Tel. 66.12.49/72.19.52; Fax 66.28.63; hemissubdiving@mail.pf; www.hemispheresub.com* is based at the Marina Apooiti. A team of qualified instructors (considered the best) led by dive masters Sedira Farid and Durie Julien offers French CMAS-certification courses and PADI lessons. Daily diving excursions leave the marina at 8am, 10am, 2pm and 7pm to discover the lagoon, passes, caves, wreck and open ocean depths around Raiatea and Taha'a. Daily introductory dives; night dives on the wreck are available on request. A day tour with a picnic lunch on a *motu* and diving cruises can also be arranged. They also have a dive center at Hawaiki Nui Hotel. Rates are 6.000 CFP per dive, 7.000 CFP for an introductory dive, 7.500 CFP for a night dive and 54.300 CFP for a 10-dive package.

Te Mara Nui Plongée, *Tel./Fax 66.11.88; cell 72.60.19, temaranui@mail.pf; www.temaranui.pf.* This dive center is located at the Marina in Uturoa and is open daily. Floriane Voisin, the manager, is an international CMAS ** instructor and BEES 1 State instructor. An introductory dive or exploration dive is 5.600 CFP, an initial dive is 5.900 CFP; a night dive is 6.900 CFP and a 10-dive package is 50.000 CFP. A 2-dive outing with a picnic on the motu is 11.500 CFP.

Niyati Plongée, *Tel. 79.10.54; niyati.plongee@yahoo.fr; www.niyatiplongee.com.* Sail and dive aboard a Bavaria 49 monohull cruiser based at Apooiti Marina. Jeep and Valou Stoessel are experienced dive instructors who provide Scubapro equipment, a dive boat for 6, and comfortable accommodation on board their yacht. Private diving lessons available.

Water Skiing, Wakeboard and Windsurfing

Soul Rider, *Tel. 20.70.65; all-or-nothing@hotmail.fr; http://tahitisoul.rider.free.fr.* This water ski and wakeboard school in Uturoa is open to the public daily from 7am-6pm. The sessions can start from your hotel. A 15-min. baptism is 2.000 CFP and a 10-min. perfectioning is 2.500 CFP and 10 min. on the buoy is 1.500 CFP. Lessons are available.

Raiatea Windsurfing, *Tel. 20.76.69; raiateawindsurfing@hotmail.fr* is located at the Marina of Uturoa. Lessons in windsurfing and stand-up paddle surfing are available for adults and children.

SHOPPING

La Palme d'Or, *Tel. 60.07.85,* on Uturoa's main street, sells pearl jewelry. Tico Pearls, *Tel. 60.06.88,* has an impressive showroom in the Maritime building. They also sell wood and coral sculptures by the late Mara, Tahiti's most renown coral sculptor. Rai-Teva, *Tel. 60.04.20,* in the Maritime building, is a jewelry shop that carries a good selection of small pearl earrings. This size black pearl is not easy to find in most shops. They also carry a fashion collection of jeans, tops and other clothes. Vairua Perles, *Tel. 66.38.39,* is on the Uturoa waterfront. In addition to 18-karat gold jewelry, they carry engraved mother-of-pearl shells and pottery.

Sephora Boutique, *Tel. 66.21.21,* is in the pink Gare Maritime building on the Uturoa wharf. They carry woven hats, tapa covered photo albums, paintings and other gift items, as well as pearls. Te Fare Boutique, *Tel. 66.17.17,* is behind the Gare Maritime across the street from the Arts and Crafts Village. They offer a colorful selection of Polynesian art deco linens, pottery, basketwork and jewelry. Arii Creation, *Tel. 66.35.54,* on Uturoa's main street, sells locally made fabrics, pareos and tee shirts. Wasa Nui Shop in downtown Uturoa, *Tel. 66.18.00,* sells pareos, T-shirts and Indonesian clothes. My Flower, *Tel. 66.19.19,* is a florist and gift shop in the Maritime building. Havai'i Sport, Tel. 60.25.20, is upstairs at the Gare Maritime building. This is the only sporting goods store in the Leeward Islands.

Be sure to visit the Arts and Crafts Village or "Fare Mama" adjacent to the ship dock in Uturoa. There are 10 thatched roof *fares* decorated with *tifaifai* wall hangings, where the artisan mamas display their hand painted dresses and pareos, woven hats and bags, woodcarvings and shell jewelry. You can also find locally made souvenir items. The Hawaiki Nui Association, *Tel. 66.12.37,* at the airport, sells *pareos* and tee-shirts, wood sculptures, and traditional woven hats and bags, plus seashell jewelry.

Anuanua Art, *Tel. 66.12.66,* is on the mountainside of the main street in Uturoa center. A unique selection of paintings, sculptures, etchings, pottery, tapa, sandalwood and seashell jewelry is on display. Some of the local painters, sculptors and other artists represented are: Erhard Lux, Jean-François Favre, Christian Deloffre, André Marere, Joannis, Martiale, Philippe Dubois, Maryse Noguier, Roland Marti's sculpture and Peter Owen's pottery. Open Mon. to Fri. 8am-12pm and 1:30-5:30pm, and on Sat. from 8am-12pm. Arts Expo Gallery, *Tel. 66.11.83,* is at Apooiti Marina, with paintings, lithographies, hand painted fabrics, shirts, jewelry, pearls and gifts.

Vanilla grown in Raiatea and Taha'a can be purchased at Tahiti Vanille upstairs at the public market in Uturoa center. Although the old Magasin Vanira on the mountainside in Uturoa center has now been torn down, you can still buy plump, fragrant vanilla beans from Madame Jeanne Chane, who now operates out of a container located on the site of her former store.

SPECIAL SERVICES, MASSAGE, NATURAL THERAPY, RELAXATION

Lylou Beauté, *Tel. 66.15.16,* is upstairs in the Socredo building across the road from the Arts and Crafts Village and the Uturoa wharf. Their services include manicures, pedicures, facial care, waxing, makeup and relaxing massages. Beauty shops in Uturoa include Style et Tendance Coiffure, *Tel. 66.21.77,* and Tehina Coiffure, *Tel. 66.10.20.*

TATTOO ARTISTS

Isidore Haiti, *Tel. 66.15.97/72.86.63,* specializes in Marquesan tattoos and has a very good reputation for his work. Ahi Tattoo, *Tel. 72.13.22/66.48.76;*

ahitahiti@yahoo.com, is at PK 3 in Apooiti. He does Polynesian and Oriental tattoos.

PRACTICAL INFORMATION

Banks
Raiatea has 3 banks, which are all located in the center of Uturoa. All of them have ATM windows. **Banque de Polynésie,** *Tel.60.04.50,* is open Mon.-Thurs. from 7:45am-3:45pm, and on Fri. 7:45am-2:45pm. **Banque Socredo,** *Tel. 47.00.00,* is open Mon.-Fri. from 7:30-11:30am and from 1-3:30pm; **Banque de Tahiti,** *Tel. 60.02.80,* is open Mon.-Fri. from 7:45am-12pm, and from 1-3:45pm.

Bookstores
Librarie d'Uturoa, *Tel. 66.30.80,* is in the center of town, on the mountainside of the main street. They have calendars and books (mostly in French) about Tahiti and Her Islands.

Drugstore
The **Pharmacie de Raiatea** is on the mountainside of the main street in Uturoa center, across the street from the Catholic Church, *Tel. 66.15.56* (emergency), *Tel. 66.34.44.* It is open Mon.-Fri. from 7:30am-5:30pm; on Sat. from 7:30am-12pm and on Sun. and holidays from 9-10:30am.

Hospital
There is a government hospital close to the boat dock in Uturoa, *Tel. 60.08.00* (all services) and *Tel. 60.08.01* (emergency), which serves all the Leeward Society Islands. Several private doctors and dentists have practices in Raiatea as well as physical therapists (kinésithérapeutes) and there is also an optician, **Te Mata Ora,** *Tel. 66.16.19.*

Internet
ITS Multimedia *Tel. 60.25.25.* Informatique Technologie Services is in the Gare Maritime building facing the Tahiti Tourist office. They have 6 computers with flat screens and ergonomically designed keyboards. Open Mon.-Fri. 7:30am-12pm and 1-5pm; on Sat. from 7:30am-12pm.
The Post Office, *Tel. 60.04.95,* in the Gare Maritime also has computer service, and several of the hotels and pensions have cyber point computers and Mana Hotspot WiFi connections for your laptop.

Laundry
Laverie Jacqueline, *Tel. 66.28.36,* is in Apooiti and will also pick up and deliver your laundry. She's closed Sat. afternoon and all day Sun.

Police
The French *gendarmerie* is close to the post office in Uturoa center, *Tel. 60.03.05* or *17*. The number for the Municipal Police is *Tel. 60.05.69*.

Post Office & Telecommunications Office
The **Post Office** has a branch at the Gare Maritime building on the boat dock in Uturoa, which is open Mon.-Thurs. from 7:45am-12pm and 1-3:30pm, on Fri. from 7:45am-12pm and 1-2:30pm, and on Sat. from 8-10am. The main post office, *Tel. 66.35.11*, is in a modern building north of Uturoa on the main road, facing the hospital. It is open Mon.-Thurs. 7:10am-3pm, on Fri. from 7am-2pm and on Sat. from 8-10am. There is an ATM window here. All telecommunications and postal services can be handled at either office.

Travel Agency
Tahiti Cruise & Vacation, *Tel./Fax 66.40.50; www.tahiti-and-vacation.com* is located in the Gare Maritime building, providing qualified travel services for individuals and groups.

Tourist Bureau
Tahiti Tourism, *Tel. 60.07.77, Fax 60.07.76, raiateainfo@tahiti-tourisme.pf.* This information center is located in the Gare Maritime Building on the quay in Uturoa, and is open Mon.-Fri. from 8am-4pm. Marianne Amaru is the very helpful hostess and she also speaks good English.
Te Tupuna Association, *Tel. 66.16.65, www.raiatea-vacances.com*, is headed by Marie-Claude Rajaud of Hotel Atiapiti. They publish an informative guide that features the family pensions and bed-and-breakfast lodgings, as well restaurants, activities and boutiques.

Yacht Services, Marinas & Nautical Bases
Apooiti Marina is at PK 3 in Apooiti, west of Uturoa center, *Tel. 66.12.20; Fax 66.42.20; VHF 68 or 12; noc_fr@yahoo.fr*. This is the home base of The Moorings, Sunsail and Tahiti Yacht Charter. There are 70 berths for boats up to 50 ft. with a maximum draft of 8 ft. Visiting yachts pay 160 CFP per linear meter plus tax for overnight stays. Water and electricity supplied. Contact the marina manager for extended stays. Sailboat rentals, sailing school, sail loft, scuba diving club, 2 restaurants and bars, laundry service.
Uturoa Harbor Master's Office, *Tel./Fax 66.31.52; Cell 78.36.94 (Port Captain); VHF Channel 16 or 12*. This is a public marina in the harbor of Uturoa that has a quay for liners up to 210 m. (688.8 ft.) Large vessels are welcome. There is also a nautical base with 100 berths for boats from 26-55 ft. and a maximum draft of 3 m. (9.8 ft.). A diving club is on the premises and fuel service is available in the Uturoa port complex adjoining the wharf. Overnight stays for up to 10 sailboats are free for one night only at the loading dock.

Uturaerae Marina is at PK 4.5 in Apooiti. This large marina is on the northwest side of Raiatea and is used by all vessels needing repairs or services, as well as by people on extended stays. It is privately owned by the **Chantier Naval des Iles** (Naval Shipyard of the Islands), *VHF Channel 72 or Tel. 66.10.10, Fax 66.28.41; raiatea.marine@mail.pf; www.raiateamarine.com.* This is the base of 4 companies that service the marine industry, providing construction and repair facilities for 30 vessels from 10-60 ft., including barges. Maximum draft 2.30 m. (7.5 ft.). Dry-docking, ships chandlery, take-away food, point phone.

Raiatea Carenage Services, *Tel. 60.05.45, Fax 60.05.46, VHF Channel 68; raiateacarenage@mail.pf; www.raiatea.com/carenage.* This full service boatyard has everything you need to repair your boat and sails and also provides long-term moorage during your absence. It is located at Uturaerae Marina and is managed by Dominique Goché, who speaks English.

15. Taha'a

This small circular island that is known today as **Taha'a** (or Tahaa) was settled by Maohi pioneers several hundred years ago, estimated between 850 and 1200 AD. They called the island Uporu, a name that is also found in Samoa (Upolu). Polynesian folklore declares that this island was the natal home of Hiro, the famous god of thieves in Polynesian mythology, whose favorite hangout was in the area we now call the Leeward Society Islands. Huge black volcanic boulders on Taha'a's east coast are considered parts of Hiro's body or objects that belonged to him.

During the 17th century the kings of Raiatea and Taha'a fought for possession of Taha'a. Bora Bora's feared warriors were more powerful, and both Taha'a and Raiatea were subjugated to the rule of Bora Bora's King Tapoa, descendant of Puni the Conqueror. Although the Leeward Islands became a possession of France in 1888, the French flag was raised in Taha'a only in 1897, following years of rebellion.

For many years you didn't hear much about the quiet little island of Taha'a, which formerly lived in the shadow of its big sister island of Raiatea and within sight of the glamorous island of Bora Bora. Then, without making much hoopla about it, Taha'a began stretching in many directions. Its reputation as Polynesia's **"Vanilla Island"** has now expanded to include 3 dozen pearl farms in the clear lagoon waters near the white sand beaches of the *motu* islets.

Word began to spread among cognizant travelers when the 9-bungalow Hotel Vahine Island was built on a private *motu* in the mid-1990s. In July 2002 the 5-star Taha'a Pearl Beach Resort & Spa opened 60 bungalow suites on Motu Tautau, a lovely little islet just a 5-min. boat ride from the main island of Taha'a. One of its best selling points is a clear view of Bora Bora across the sea. This hotel was designed to be the most luxurious resort in the entire South Pacific region. In Jan. 2004 Le Taha'a Private Island & Spa, as it was then called, was accepted as a member of the elite Relais et Châteaux. This chain and The Leading Hotels of the World, Ltd., have created the Luxury Alliance group, representing the most prestigious hotels in the world. Although the official name of the hotel today is Le Taha'a Island Resort & Spa, to most people it is simply "Le Taha'a."

The Taha'a Golf Resort that local developers planned to build on a 247-acre (100-ha.) motu located off the north coast of Taha'a has been put on a long hold due to the depressed economic situation. The project included a 199-room Raffles Hotel with 60 overwater bungalows, 10 beach villas and 43 hotel villas, each with 3 bedrooms and kitchenette for long stays.

The former Marina Iti hotel and yacht club on Taha'a was bought by a group of investors in 2005 and renamed the Taravana Yacht Club. According to investor/manager Richard Postma, an expatriate American who formerly owned Taravana

Island Sport Charters Bora Bora, the Marina Iti bungalows were planned to be replaced by three 3-bedroom villas plus 10 small bungalows. In May 2011 Richard told me that his investor backed down and the Taravana Yacht Club and Restaurant was shutting down.

Several Frenchmen with yachts have chosen the peaceful island of Taha'a as retirement retreats. There are good marina facilities and all yachts are welcomed.

Taha'a's inhabitants lead quiet, industrious lives, earning their living in agriculture, fishing and breeding livestock. Plantations of sumptuous fruits and vegetables add their lushness to the palette of vibrant colors you'll see all around the island. The produce from Taha'a is sold at the public market in Raiatea and the watermelons are shipped to the market in Papeete.

Taha'a is known as the Vanilla Island because of the numerous plantations of this aromatic "brown gold" that flourish in the fertile valleys. After the vanilla beans are harvested and laid out to dry, the whole village is filled with the rich perfume of vanilla. You can visit a vanilla plantation and some of the pearl farms that are built in the warm, clear lagoon near the *motu* islets.

Taha'a has no airport, but there are good port facilities, with service by inter-island ferry and cargo ships several times a week, and water-taxi or shuttle boat service from Uturoa. Taha'a has a *gendarmerie*, infirmary and dispensary, two post offices, banks and small general stores. Accommodations are available on a small but steadily growing scale, either in traditional Polynesian style hotels, elegant beach and overwater bungalows on a *motu*, a berth aboard a sailboat or a room in a village home. Wherever there is a room there is usually a good meal available. You can paddle a kayak or hire a boat and guide to visit the *motu*, where you can picnic on the white sand beaches. The protected lagoon is also ideal for sailing, windsurfing, kite surfing, jet-skiing, snorkeling and fishing. You can hike into the valleys or rent a car or bike to explore the island.

Taha'a still remains virtually undiscovered by the general tourist market, although it has awakened to the world of tourism. Peace, tranquility and natural beauty combine with the island's friendly, unhurried pace, offering you a relaxed and happy vacation with a taste of Polynesia of yesteryear. Wherever you go on this island you will find that the people smile and wave to you, nod their heads or raise their eyebrows in a traditional Polynesian greeting.

ARRIVALS & DEPARTURES
Arriving By Air

There is no airport on Taha'a. You can fly to Raiatea and take a boat to Taha'a. If you have made reservations at a hotel or pension on Taha'a, your host may send a boat to meet you at the airport. The dock is to the right of the terminal building as you face the street. There is no sign indicating this is where you should wait. You can sit at the snack bar and watch for the arrival of your boat. You can also go to the quay in Uturoa and get a regular shuttle boat to Taha'a or take a private taxi boat. **Tahiti Helicopter Service**, *Tel. 67.54.90*, opened an office in Bora Bora in

July 2011, and will provide helicopter transfers on request to the hotels with helipads.

Arriving By Boat

Hawaiki Nui, *Tel. 54.99.54 (Tahiti); Tel. 65.61.59 (Taha'a); Fax 45.24.44, contact@stim.pf.* This 12-passenger cargo ship has 4 double cabins and deck space. It leaves the Motu Uta dock in Papeete each Tues. at 4pm and arrives at the Tapuamu quay in Taha'a on Wed. at 2:30pm, after stopping in Huahine, Raiatea and Bora Bora. The Thurs. trip leaves Papeete at 4pm, and arrives in Taha'a on Fri. at 2:30pm, after going to Bora Bora and before returning to Raiatea and Huahine on its return trip to Tahiti. The cost of sleeping on deck is 2.000 CFP per adult and a berth in one of the cabins costs 5.400 CFP from Papeete to all the Leeward Islands. Children pay half-price. Meals are available on board the ship.

Maupiti Express II, *Tel. 66.37.81/78.27.22/72.30.48; www.maupitiexpress.com.* The *Maupiti Express II* leaves Bora Bora at 7am. on Wed., and Fri., arriving in Taha'a at 8:20am. The boat leaves Bora Bora at 3pm on Sun. and arrives in Taha'a at 4:20pm. The one-way fare from Bora Bora to Taha'a is 4.000 CFP and round-trip is 5.000 CFP. The fares from Maupiti to Taha'a are 5.000 CFP and 7.000 CFP. Passengers under 12 years pay half-fare.

Enota Transport Maritime, *Tel./Fax 65.61.33.* Enota Tetuanui has 3 covered speedboats that transport passengers between Raiatea and Taha'a. *Te Haere Maru V* leaves from the boat dock in Uturoa at 10:30am and 4:30pm for the east coast of Taha'a, stopping in Vaitoare, Haamene and Faaaha. *Te Haere Maru IV* leaves from the boat dock in Uturoa at 10:30am and 4:30pm for the west coast of Taha'a, stopping at Poutoru, Tiva and Tapuamu. On Sat. there is a 10:30am departure from Uturoa, but nothing on Sun. and holidays. The crossing takes 20 to 45 min., depending on your destination. *Te Haere Maru VI* makes stops all around the island.

Tamarii Taha'a I, *Tel. 65.65.29/76.37.20.* This 46-ft. aluminum catamaran leaves the Uturoa boat dock Mon.-Fri. at 10am and 4pm, and on Sat. at 10am. Stops are made in Poutoru, Patii, Hatupa, Tiva, Tapuamu, Murifenua and Patio. One-way fares are 1.000 CFP.

Tamarii Taha'a II, *Tel. 25.80.58.* This sturdy 47.5-ft. boat was formerly the *Maupiti Express I.* It leaves Uturoa at 10am and 4pm weekdays and at 10am on Sat. Stops are made at Vaitoare, Amaru Quay, Haamene and Ra'ai.

Taxi Boats

Limousine Boat, *Tel. 65.64.00/79.63.81; tahaa-marine@mail.pf.* Christophe Citeau has a 28-ft. teak and mahogany boat that can take up to 6 passengers on private excursions or transfers. Shower, towels, refrigerator, 2 salons, and snorkeling equipment. Hostess, champagne, picnic or snack basket available on request. He also takes care of the 5 boats used by Le Taha'a and has a glass bottom boat based at the Tapuamu boat dock.

Monique Taxi Boat, *Tel. 65.62.48*. Round-trip transfers btween Vaitoare and Uturoa are 12.000 CFP per person and other transfers are possible. Packages for a taxi boat and car start at 19.000 CFP for 1 person and cost 27.000 CFP for a maximum of 5 passengers.

Taxiboat, *Tel./Fax 66.49.06; cell 79.62.01/79.62.02; VHF 16*. Dominique Lucas has a 10-passenger boat in Raiatea that he uses for transfers and excursions.

Departing By Air

You can take a boat from Taha'a directly to the airport on Raiatea or go to Uturoa town by taxi boat and take a land taxi to the airport. Air Tahiti's number in Raiatea is *Tel. 60.04.44/60.04.40*.

Departing By Boat

Hawaiki Nui, *Tel. 54.99.54 (Papeete)*, *Tel. 65.61.59 (Taha'a)*; *Fax 45.24.44*, leaves Taha'a each Wed. at 3:30pm for Raiatea and Tahiti, arriving in Papeete on Thurs. at 5am. It leaves Taha'a each Fri. at 3:30pm for Raiatea, Huahine and Tahiti, arriving in Papeete at 5am on Sat. morning. The one-way deck fare is 2.000 CFP and a berth is 5.400 CFP for adults and half-fare for children.

Maupiti Express II, *Tel. 66.37.81/78.27.22/72.30.48*. The boat stops in Taha'a each Wed., Fri. and Sun. between Raiatea and Bora Bora. See schedule in the Raiatea chapter.

Enota Transport Maritime, *Tel. 65.61.33*. *Te Haere Maru V* leaves from the east coast of Taha'a twice a day, starting from Faaaha, stopping in Haamene (at 6:30am and 12pm) and Vaitoare for the trip to Uturoa. *Te Haere Maru IV* leaves from the west coast of Taha'a twice a day, with stops at Tapuamu, Tiva and Poutoru, and then makes the 15-min. crossing to Uturoa. The boat begins its journey at 5:15am Mon.-Fri. during school days, and at 5:45am during vacation time. They also make another trip starting at 11:45am. *Te Haere Maru VI* also provides service from Taha'a to Raiatea. One-way fare is 1.000 CFP.

Tamarii Taha'a I, *Tel. 65.65.29/76.37.20*, leaves the Patio boat dock at 5:15am and 11:25am Mon.-Fri., and at 5:15am on Sat. Stops are made at Murifenua, Tapuamu, Tiva, Hatupa, Patii and Poutoru, then the boat continues on to Uturoa, arriving at 6:30am and 12:30pm Mon.-Fri., and at 6:40am. on Sat. The fare is 1.000 CFP from Patio.

Tamarii Taha'a II, *Tel. 25.80.58*, leaves from the Ra'ai dock in Taha'a at 5:15am Mon.-Fri. It stops at Haamene, Amaru dock and Vaitoare, arriving in Uturoa at 6:40am. The 11am shuttle leaves Haamene and stops at Amaru and Vaitoare, arriving in Uturoa at 11:40am. On Sat. the boat leaves Ra'ai at 5:20am and arrives in Uturoa at 6:40am, with stops in Haamene, Amaru and Vaitoare.

Note: the boat schedules are subject to change without notice.

ORIENTATION

Taha'a lies 3 km (2 mi.) northwest of Uturoa, sharing the same coral foundation and reef-protected lagoon that surrounds the island of Raiatea. The shape of the island, with its scalloped shoreline, resembles a hibiscus flower. A narrow isthmus separates the deeply indented bays of Apu, Haamene and Hurepiti on the south of the island. Some 60 *motu* islets lie inside the coral reef in the north and this protective barrier is unbroken except by the two navigable passes of Toahotu on the southeast side and Tiamahana on the southwest coast. Yachts and even ships can completely circumnavigate the island inside the lagoon, often accompanied by porpoises.

Taha'a has a land surface of 88 sq. km (34 sq. mi.), and **Mount Ohiri**, at 598 m (1,961 ft.), is the highest peak of the volcanic mountain range. The mountains are not high enough to attract enough rain to meet the needs of the 5,094 residents, who live in the small villages of Patio, Pahure, Hipu, Faaaha, Haamene, Motutiairi, Vaitoare, Poutoru, Patii, Tiva, Tapuamu and Murifenua. **Tiva** is considered the prettiest village, **Tapuamu** has the main port facilities, **Patio** is the administrative center, and **Haamene Bay** is 6 km (3.7 mi.) long, providing good anchorage and a haven for sailors.

A road winds 67 km (42 mi.) through the coastal villages and up mountain roads, where you have panoramic views of the bays, offshore islets and the ever-changing colors of the sea beyond the white foam on the barrier reef.

GETTING AROUND TAHA'A
Car Rentals
Buggy Dive, *Tel./Fax 65.69.33; cell 33.67.02; www.buggydive.com*. Based in Apu Bay near the former Taravana Yacht Club. Rentals for buggy only start at 6.000 CFP for 2 hrs. See *Scuba Diving* in this chapter for Buggy + Dive programs.

Hibiscus Location, *Tel. 65.61.06/79.28.81*, is located at Hotel Hibiscus in Haamene. They rent cars and mountain bikes.

Monique Location, *Tel. 65.62.48*, is located in Vaitoare. She rents 5-place a/c Ford Fiesta and Citroen cars for 18.000 CFP for 24 hrs., gas not included. She also has packages that include taxi boat service and car rental for a maximum of 5 passengers, for 27.000 CFP.

Poerani Location, *Tel. 65.64.20/78.80.25*, is operated by Teva Ebbs in Haamene. He rents 3 Bugsters with open roof for 2 passengers.

Taha'a Rent-A-Car (Taha'a Location Voiture), *Tel./Fax 65.66.75; cell 72.07.71 www.hotel-tahaa.com*. Pension Le Passage in Faaaha rents 5-place a/c Logan cars starting at 6.500 CFP.

WHERE TO STAY
Prestige
LE TAHA'A ISLAND RESORT & SPA, *B.P. 67, Patio, Taha'a 98733. Tel. 689/60.84.00; Fax 689/60.84.01; reservations 689/50.76.01; resa@letahaa.com; letahaa@relaischateaux.com; www.relaischateaux.com/letahaa. Located on Motu*

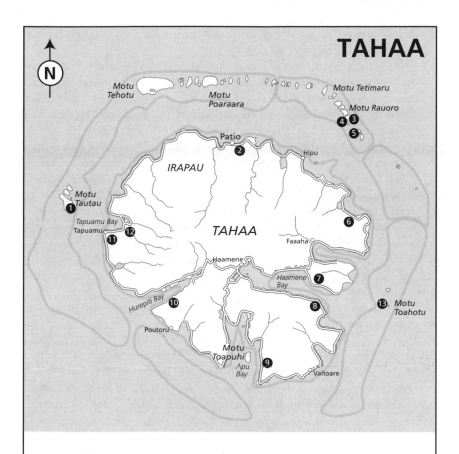

1. Le Taha'a Island Resort & Spa
2. Fare Pea Iti
3. Hotel La Pirogue
4. Motu Porou
5. Hotel Vahine Island
6. Le Passage
7. Pension Hibiscus
8. Tiare Breeze
9. Pension Api
10. Pension Vaihi
11. Pension Au Phil Du Temps
12. Chez Pascal
13. Pension Atger

Tautau, 35 min. by boat from the airport in Raiatea and 5 min. by boat from the main island of Taha'a. All major credit cards.

This 5-star 60-unit resort opened in July 2002 as the Taha'a Pearl Beach Resort & Spa, and the name was changed to Le Taha'a Private Island & Spa when it became associated with Relais et Châteaux in Jan. 2004. Another rebranding took place in 2007, in an effort to more accurately reflect its secluded location, thus changing the name to Le Taha'a Island Resort & Spa. As of Jan. 1, 2011 the property is managed by FHP (Financière Hôtelière Polynêsienne), a Tahiti-based company that is the major stockholder. Christine Chevalaz is the general manager.

This resort sanctuary has garnered its share of industry honors and has appeared on many lists of the world's best places to stay. Reached by boat from the airport on the neighboring island of Raiatea, 45 min. away, Le Taha'a is located on Motu Tautau, an offshore islet facing the island of Taha'a. Designed in pure, authentic Polynesian style, Le Taha'a sits in a stunningly beautiful natural setting of 40 acres (16 ha.). Long white sand beaches and an unimaginably translucent lagoon offer horizon vistas of Bora Bora's mystical silhouette and the lusciously green mountains of Taha'a.

The best local craftsmen have combined their know how and talent to produce an architectural gem. The 48 overwater units are 90 sq. m (969 sq. ft.) large, and they are classified according to the views they offer. The 20 Taha'a Overwater Suites face Taha'a's main island; the 10 Raiatea Overwater Suites reveal Mount Ohiri across the lagoon; the 7 Sunset Overwater Suites have a view of the lagoon and romantic sunsets; and the 8 Bora Bora Overwater Suites look out over the ocean and the island of Bora Bora. There are also 3 End of Pontoon Overwater Suites with a view of the lagoon and ocean. Each overwater unit has a wraparound deck outfitted with cushioned lounge chairs, thatched-roof dining areas and steps leading down to another solarium platform with a ladder that provides access to the lagoon. At the foot of the majestic bed in the center of the room, there is a see-through "lagoonarium" feature complete with nighttime lighting so that you can watch the tropical fish. Three of the overwater suites are equipped for disabled guests in a wheelchair and do not have direct access to the lagoon.

Each of the 10 Beach Villas faces the lagoon and has a terrace overlooking the beach. These spectacular villas have 180 sq. m (1,937 sq. ft.) of living space, including a private enclosed garden with a small private pool, shaded sitting area and an open sundeck. All of the above villas and overwater suites have a/c and ceiling fans, a full shower and separate bathtub, a king size bed or 2 twin beds, plus a sofa bed. They have IDD phones and Hotspot WiFi Internet access (500 CFP per hour), flat screen TV's with satellite cable, mini-bar, coffee/tea making facilities, individual in-room safe, ironing board and iron, hair dryer and magnifying mirror. The bathrooms contain a generous supply of Manea Spa products. Housekeeping service is provided twice daily and room service is available from 7am to 9:30pm.

Two Royal Beach Villas offer 250 sq. m. (2,690 sq. ft.) of living space, including 2 bedrooms, and 2 bathrooms with a full shower plus a bathtub in a tropical garden. They also have a spacious lounge with desk, 3 flat-screen TV's with DVD player, and a private enclosed garden and terrace with a private pool. These villas have all the same amenities as the 1-bedroom units, plus a few extras such as a Nespresso coffee machine and IPod dock, which are also available to guests staying in the Sunset, Bora Bora and End of Pontoon Overwater Suites. A VIP welcome, linen bathrobes and sea shoes are also provided in the End of Pontoon Overwater Suites and Royal Beach Villas, and snorkeling equipment is included for guests in the Sunset Overwater and Beach Villa units.

Le Taha'a offers 3 dining venues, including a casual beach restaurant, an open-air dining room artfully conceived in a cathedral-like structure built into the trees, and an intimate gourmet restaurant. Two bars offer a variety of spirits, wines and tantalizing tropical cocktails. There is also a boutique and pearl shop, and 4 transit-day rooms. The fresh water infinity swimming pool has swim-up bar stools at the Manuia Bar. Besides the pool, other free activities include a lighted tennis court, bocce ball, snorkel gear, kayaks, outrigger paddle canoes and a fitness center.

You can take a free shuttle boat from Motu Tautau to the main island of Taha'a and go exploring on your own or join an organized tour. At the activities desk in the hotel lobby you can book a Taha'a Discovery half-day safari tour by 4WD for 7.727 CFP, rent a jet ski with guide starting at 10.909 CFP for 30 min., water-ski or wake-board for 5.000 CFP for 20 min., take a catamaran day cruise for 46.818 CFP, a champagne sunset cruise for 24.090 CFP, or a private sunset cruise for two for 78.000 CFP. A picnic on a motu for a minimum of 4 is 12.045 CFP each. You can go sport fishing for 172.727 CFP for an all day outing. You can go scuba diving with the Taha'a Blue Nui Diving Center or get a relaxing massage at the Manea Spa, which are both located at Le Taha'a Island Resort & Spa.

There are many other ways to spend your day, including snorkeling in the magnificent coral gardens adjacent to the hotel, or lying in a *chaise longue* on Motu Paari, an islet just a few steps from the beach, while you gaze at the mountains of Bora Bora in the distance. You can even take a speedboat ride to Bora Bora for 100.000-300.000 CFP for 2 people. A regular boat transfer to the airport in Raiatea is 5.000 CFP and a private transfer for 2 is 15.000 CFP. There is a helipad on the hotel property and helicopter service between Bora Bora and Le Taha'a resumed in July 2011.

If ever a hotel was created with honeymooners in mind, it is here at Le Taha'a Island Resort & Spa. Contact them directly for a brochure on their Special Romantic Rendez-Vous services. These include Romantic Welcomes, Romantic Interludes, Romantic Escapades and Polynesian Wedding Ceremonies. They can also recommend several private tours for two. Families are also welcome, and special activities, beach toys and menus are provided for the children. See further information under *Where to Eat, Massages & Spas, Seeing the Sights* and *Scuba Diving* in this chapter.

Deluxe

HOTEL VAHINE ISLAND, *B.P. 510, Uturoa, Raiatea 98735. Tel. 689/ 65.67.38; Fax 689/65.67.70; vahine.island@mail.pf; www.vahine-island.com. Located on Motu Tuvahine (Island of the Woman), 15 km. (9.3 mi.) from the Raiatea airport and 12 km (7.4 mi.) from the ferry dock in Raiatea. 9 bungalows. All major credit cards.*

This private hotel is a member of the Small Hotels of the World chain and was named one of the "50 Dream Destinations" by *Islands Magazine* in Dec. 2010. It was also awarded 5th place in the 2011 TripAdvisor Travelers' Choice for the 10 Top Luxurious Hotels in the South Pacific.

Hotel Vahine Island is located on a 23-acre *motu* facing the village of Hipu on the northeast side of Taha'a, with a beautiful view of Bora Bora. Clients are greeted at the Raiatea airport and taken to Vahine Island by speedboat over the lagoon in 35 min. On this motu you will find white sand beaches, snorkeling in the coral gardens of the lagoon, and a calm setting for relaxing. The reception-lounge and dining room are on the beach facing the 3 overwater bungalows, and you walk through a coconut grove to get to the 6 units beside the beach. All the accommodations were refurbished in 2006, transforming 3 of the small beach bungalows into 3 deluxe beach suites. These new accommodations have a total floor size of 115 sq. m. (1,238 sq. ft.); the overwater bungalows have 70 sq. m. (753 sq. ft.), and the standard beach bungalows have 50 sq. m. (538 sq. ft.). The deluxe suites have a king size bed and the other categories have either king size or twin beds. All units include a bathroom with 2 sinks, potable water, a shower with hot water, separate toilets, hair dryer, IDD telephone, ceiling fan, minibar and coffee/tea facilities, CD and DVD player with LCD screen. The beach bungalows and suites have a deck with a hammock and a beach shower, and the 3 deluxe beach suites also have a sitting area with a sofa and two armchairs. The overwater bungalows have a sitting area with a sofa and aquarium table for fish-watching, and a covered terrace and hammock.

General Manager Sylvie Guerry and her friendly staff are constantly working to improve the property and they pay close attention to every detail to ensure guest satisfaction. Free Internet WiFi has been added in the bar, restaurant and beach area and a laptop is available at your disposal. In Feb. 2011 Sylvie announced the addition of air-conditioning in all the bungalows—without increasing the rates.

Activities free of charge include Polynesian outrigger canoes, windsurf board, lagoon kayaks, snorkeling equipment, fishing equipment for the reef, beach games, board games, fish feeding, and a large selection of DVD's and books in the library. A beach boy is on hand to take you snorkeling, to visit the reef, and to learn all about the coconut. Optional activities organized by the hotel include boat transfers to Raiatea and the main island of Taha'a, snorkeling excursions by outrigger speed canoe, visit to a pearl farm, sailing on a 14-ft. Hobie Cat, and small motor boats for 2-4 passengers. The management will help you to book any of the other excursions listed in this chapter. There is also a helipad on the premises. The restaurant and bar are open to the public, but reservations must be made for meals if you are not staying in the hotel. See more information in *Where to Eat* in this chapter.

The shallow water in the lagoon around Vahine Island is sometimes filled with spiny sea urchins and *bêche de mer*, the elongated black sea cucumber that lives on the white sand bottom. You have to step carefully through these obstacles to get to the deeper water where you can swim and snorkel.

Superior

HOTEL LA PIROGUE, *B.P 668, Uturoa, Raiatea 98735. Tel. 689/60.81.45; Fax 689/60.81.46; hotellapirogue@mail.pf; www.hotel-la-pirogue.com. Located on Motu Porou on the northern barrier reef facing Bora Bora, a 30-min. boat ride from the port of Uturoa and 35 min. by boat from the airport in Raiatea. Boat transfer 8.000 CFP. AE, MC, V.*

This 3-star hotel opened in June 2004 on Motu Porou, a private islet on the northern side of Taha'a, offering a superb view of the lagoon of Taha'a as well as the romantic sunsets over Bora Bora. Giuliano Tognetti and his wife Séverine and their two daughters welcome guests to their cozy little resort, which offers 1 beach suite, 4 beach bungalows and 4 garden bungalows. These are built in the local style of wooden walls and floors and thatched roofs of coconut fronds that were woven by the people of Hipu village. Each bungalow has a double bed, mosquito net, ceiling fan, television, teak and kohu furniture, DDD telephone and Internet connection for your laptop, a private bathroom with hot water shower, and a terrace with lounge chairs. Fresh water is piped in from the main island under the lagoon and electricity is provided by solar energy and an electric generator. The restaurant proposes a local menu, with seafood specialties and Polynesian nights organized. Room service is available from 8am to 9pm. Canoes, snorkeling equipment and fishing gear are free to in-house guests. Optional activities include boat excursions to visit pearl farms, a 4WD trip around the island or a picnic outing on a motu. A private shuttle boat transfers hotel guests from the port of Uturoa or the airport in Raiatea to La Pirogue on Motu Porou. See more information under *Where to Eat* in this chapter.

FARE PEA ITI, *B.P. 128, Patio, Taha'a 98733. Tel./Fax 689/60.81.11; cell 76.98.55; farepeaiti@mail.pf; www.farepeaiti.pf; Beside the lagoon 1.2 km. (0.7 mi.) from Patio village and 30 min. by boat from Raiatea airport. Round-trip boat transfers 15.000 CFP sgl; 9.400 CFP each for 2 or more; Continental breakfast 2.000 CFP, Dinner 5.500 CFP per person. AE, MC, V.*

The name of this charming place means "A little luck" in Tahitian, and you will indeed feel lucky to stay here, as this 3-star boutique hotel is part of the prestigious Chateau & Hôtels de France selection. It has also been given a 3-Tiare rating by the Tahiti Tourist office. In a dream landscape facing a garland of motu islets, owner Brigitte Guerre has built 3 attractive deluxe beach bungalows and 1 standard garden unit in the Polynesian style and has decorated them with refinement and a high quality of comfort. The beach bungalow facilities include a king size bed with very nice bedding and a mosquito net, ceiling fan, cable flatscreen TV and DVD player, a private bathroom with hot water shower, hair dryer, makeup mirror, linens, bathrobe, slippers, and Chateaux & Hôtels de France toiletries. The covered terrace includes a recessed kitchen area with hotplate, microwave, barbecue, fine china and silverware, and a stocked mini bar. There is daily housekeeping service and laundry service is optional.

A Continental breakfast of gourmet food is served on your dining terrace and dinner can be a private affair on your terrace or you can join other guests at the main table for this deliciously prepared table d'hôte meal. Lunch is prepared on request. There is a magasin food store, a restaurant, snack and roulotte in nearby Patio village for lunch or dinner. Beside the white sand beach at Fare Pea Iti there is a salt-water swimming pool with deck chairs, and a fitness area with exercise bike and running mat. Guests have free use of the snorkeling gear, outrigger paddle canoe, kayaks, bicycles, French bowls, badminton and ping-pong. In the main house there is a library with a relaxing area, board games and DVD films. WiFi Internet access is available in the bungalows.

Activities can include a tour of the island by car, a boat excursion with snorkeling for 8.000 CFP, a lagoon excursion with a picnic on the motu for 12.000 CFP each, and a sunset cruise with cocktail. A boat transfer to the motu is 3.000 CFP. A 3 1/2-hr. guided Jet-ski ride for two is 20.000 CFP. You can also have a massage, Tahitian dance lesson, a Polynesian tattoo or an arts and crafts demonstration, which are all extra.

TIARE BREEZE, *B.P. 178, Haamene, Tahaa 98734. Tel. 689/65.62.26/ 73.83.97; castagnoli@mail.pf; www.tiarebreeze.com. On hillside in Haamene, a 20-min. boat ride from airport in Uturoa. V.*

This Polynesian style thatched roof luxury bungalow has earned a 3 Tiare rating from the Tahiti Tourist office. It contains a king size bed and a single bed, a full bath with hot water shower and a half bath, a fully equipped kitchen bungalow including big refrigerator and ice-maker, barbecue grill, bar-dining area, entertainment center with CD player and stereo system, ceiling fan, and expansive decks overlooking the bay. Paid Internet access, fax and point phone. Bicycles, kayaks, snorkeling equipment and fishing A private pontoon has covered bar and dining area, with deck chairs for sunbathing. All activities can be arranged. Fresh island fruits and French pastries are delivered to your doorstep each morning.

Moderate

LE PASSAGE, *B.P. 150, Haamene, Taha'a 98734. Tel./Fax 689/65.66.75; cell 72.07.71; residencelepassage@mail.pf; www.hotel-tahaa.com. On the mountainside in Faaaha, a 30-min. boat ride from the airport in Raiatea. Round-trip transfers 8.000 CFP per person. No credit cards.*

Bruno and Marie-Thérèse Meunier-Coeroli have built 3 bungalows on the side of a hill in Faaaha on the wild east coast of Taha'a, facing the rising sun and overlooking Motu Atara, Vahine Island and Motu Mute, as well as the boat passage near the village of Patio. It has been given a 2-star rating by the Tahiti Tourist office. The furnishings and decorations are all done in good taste, offering two smaller units with a double bed and a private bathroom, and a 2-bedroom family bungalow with double beds and 2 bathrooms. Mosquito nets and electric mosquito repellents are provided. Each a/c unit has a covered terrace overlooking the marvelous lagoon. These units are marketed as formulas with a choice of lodging only, or deluxe villa formulas with access to the swimming pool, private pontoon and marina, BBQ *fare*, washing machine, library, kitchen, big-screen satellite TV, and an a/c car included throughout your stay. WiFi connections are free in all the rooms.

The biggest attraction at Le Passage is the gastronomic restaurant, where Marie-Thérèse practices her culinary arts. She specializes in fish and seafood, using local products and organically grown fruits and vegetables from her own garden. Free activities include kayaks, bicycles, ping-pong, snorkeling equipment, swimming pool, whirlpool bath, private marina and 4WD Landrover excursions. Optional choices include renting a 5-place Logan car with a/c starting at 6.500 CFP. A boat tour around the island of Taha'a with a picnic on a motu is 8.000 CFP each for a minimum of 2 people. Your hosts can also arrange deep-sea fishing and scuba diving excursions, as well as a relaxing massage with a cocktail included.

PENSION HIBISCUS, *B.P. 184, Haamene, Taha'a 98734. Tel. 689/65.61.06/ 79.28.81; Fax 689/65.65.65; hibiscus@tahaa-tahiti.com; www.hibiscustahaa.com/ www.tahaa-tahiti.com. At the end of Haamene Bay, 20 min. by boat from the Raiatea ferry dock. Round-trip boat transfers between Raiatea and pension 3.000 CFP per person. AE, MC, V.*

This is classified as a 2-Tiare small family hotel with 7 small bungalows built in a tight space. It is also a nautical base. The smallest bungalow contains 2 double beds and a single bed, a private bedroom with hot water and a small terrace. The largest bungalow can sleep up to 10 people, with beds downstairs and on the mezzanine, plus a bathroom with hot water. All the bungalows have screened windows, refrigerator and fan. Some of the smaller bungalows share the toilet and shower facilities.

Across the road is the 200-seat restaurant and bar, which also serves as a yacht club. The ambiance at Leo and Lolita Morou's bar can become quite lively when a group of yachties tie up at the 7 moorings provided at the big pier and adjourn to the "watering hole." If you're looking for a rollicking good time, with lots of sea tales, this is your place. If you seek a tranquil, private environment, maybe the bungalows in back will give you enough distance from the noise to get a good night's sleep. You'll have to go further, however, to escape the sound of the *toere* drums when there is a dance group, so you may as well join them and learn to dance the hip-shaking *tamure*. Be prepared to chip in to pay for the entertainment when Leo passes the hat. He has a reputation for adding a lot of extra charges to the bill.

Terainui Tours is operated by Eric Morou, who handles all the land and lagoon tours at his family's pension. These include all the regular 4WD and boat excursions, picnics on the motu and transfers to a nearby motu. He will also take you on a sunset cruise, or rent you a car for your own discoveries of Taha'a. See more information under *Where to Eat* and *Yacht Services* in this chapter, as well as the sidebar on the *Hibiscus Foundation*.

PENSION AU PHIL DU TEMPS, *B.P. 50, Murifenua Patio, Taha'a 98733. Tel. 689/65.64/19/27.18.58; Fax 689/65.64.18; florenecombeau@gmail.com; www.pension-au-phil-du-temps.com. At PK 8 in Murifenua on mountainside of Taha'a's west coast, near the Tapuamu ferry dock. Take boat shuttle or taxi boat from Raiatea to Tapuamu dock. Free land transfers from Tapuamu dock to pension. V.*

Two small thatched roof bungalows are built on stilts beside the main house inside a fenced yard across the road from the lagoon and boat dock. Each unit has 2 single beds and a double bed in the mezzanine, mosquito screens, ceiling fan, TV, free WiFi connections, mini-bar, terrace and private bathroom with hot water. 2 rooms are also available in main house. European and Tahitian meals are served in the communal dining room on your private terrace. Flo is noted for her delicious desserts.

This small family pension has a 2-Tiare rating by the Tahiti Tourist office. It is managed by René and Flo, a young French couple who have packages that include free excursions if you choose the MAP or AP meal plan. Guests have free use of the bicycles, canoes and snorkel gear. Paid activities include kite surfing and scuba diving, lagoon tours around the island, picnics on the motu, boat transfers to Motu Tautau, and land tours by 4WD. You can also walk 1 km. (0.62 mi.) from the guest house to a botanical garden with 2 rivers. This is managed by the Mairie (town hall) and there is no charge.

PENSION ATGER, *B.P 308, Hamene, Taha'a 98734. Tel. 689/66.11.24/ 65.77.32/28.26.81; atgertheodore@mail.pf; www.pensionatger.com. Motu Atger is a private islet 1.8 mi. (3 km.) from Taha'a and 3.7 mi.(6 km.) from Raiatea. No credit cards.*

The *Tavaeura 2* shuttle boat can be rented for 8.000 CFP to take up to 5 passengers from Uturoa to Motu Atger. There are 4 modern bungalows with beds for 1 couple and 1-2 children and 1 double bungalow for a couple and 2 children or 2 couples in a bedroom and living room. Each unit has a beach-view terrace, private bathroom, solar for hot water, fan, hair-dryer and TV. Mosquito nets and repellant. WiFi service for a charge. MAP and AP meal plans with Continental or Tahitian breakfasts. Traditional Tahitian food served on Sundays. Free activities include kayaks and a visit to the lagoonarium. They will also take you around the island by boat, with stops to visit a fish park and snorkeling in the coral gardens at Motu Tautau.

Other Family Pensions

Pension Api, *Tel./Fax 689/65.69.88; cell 21.62.24.* 3 rooms in a thatched roof building beside the lagoon in Vaitoare, with kayaks, bicycles and snorkeling equipment. MAP and AP available. No credit cards.

Pension Vaihi, *Tel. 689/65.62.02/74.44.49. 3 fares* beside Hurepiti Bay, reached by a long rutted road. No English spoken. MAP and AP meals. No credit cards.

Chez Pascal, *Tel./Fax 689/65.60.42.* 4 simply furnished bungalows and 2 rooms on mountainside near Tapuamu ferry dock, with private bathrooms and hot or cold water. Communal dining room and kitchen. EP room 3.500 CFP per person and 6.000 CFP MAP for first night and 5.000 CFP afterward. No credit cards. Rental bikes.

Private Villa

MOTU POROU, *www.tahiti-villa.com is adjacent to Pension La Pirogue, 2 motus east of Vahine Island on Motu Porou, 5 min. by boat from Hipu village and 30 min. by boat from Raiatea. View of Taha'a, Raiatea, Bora Bora and Huahine.*

A wooden colonial style 3-bedroom, 3 bathroom house built in 2004 in 4 acres (1.5 ha.) of planted grounds can accommodate 8 adults and 1 baby. American style kitchen, potable water, solar energy, washing machine, TV, DVD, sound-blaster, library, covered terraces with banquettes and hammock. Gardener 3 times a week, optional maid, cook and hostess. Minimum stay of 3 nights at 420 euros (50.119 CFP) per night and 2,900 euros (346.062 CFP) per week.

WHERE TO EAT

Prestige

LE TAHA'A ISLAND RESORT & SPA, *Tel. 60.84.00. There are three restaurants and two bars. All major credit cards. Reserve.*

Restaurant Vanille is the main restaurant, situated in the heart of the resort on the upper level among the trees. A breakfast buffet is served from 7-10am and costs 3.600 CFP. Dinner is served nightly except Tues., from 7-9:30pm, featuring an international menu with an emphasis on fresh seafood and fish with French and Polynesian flavors. A 3-course set dinner menu is 7.500 CFP. A Manea Spa menu offers selections of light, healthy choices, and there is also a Vegetarian Menu. A seafood buffet and dance show for 8.800 CFP is served on Sat. evenings in July and August.

Restaurant Ohiri is an elegant room with a/c and seating for 18 that is open for dinner only on Wed.-Sun evenings. You must reserve to savor a gourmet Chef's Menu dreamed up by the Executive Chef. This culinary voyage of trendy delights presents a delicate fusion of French and Polynesian cuisine. This may be foie gras and pineapple tatin in a port wine sauce; lobster from the Marquesas Islands served in a buttery sauce; vanilla and pumpkin purée; and a slice of Brie cheese stuffed with truffle and pistachio. This restaurant is closed from January-April.

La Plage is the poolside restaurant that gifts you with a magnificent view of the lagoon and Taha'a island while you are enjoying your lunch, served daily from 12-3pm. You can order burgers and light dishes and serve yourself from the salad bar. A set luncheon menu of 2 courses is 4.700 CFP. La Plage is also the setting for

Polynesian Evening each Tues., when a Polynesian barbecue buffet is served, accompanied by a dance group and a fire dance performance. This theme dinner is 8.250 CFP per person.

Tehutu Bar is the hotel's main bar on the upper level, which is open daily from 3-11pm. except on Tues, when the Polynesian buffet and show are held at La Plage. You can cool off in the swimming pool and swim up for a tropical cocktail at the Manuia Bar, which is open daily from 10am-6pm. The bartender makes great cocktails, including a super Mojito.

For guests staying in the overwater suites a Canoe breakfast can be served on their covered terrace. The cost is 12.500 CFP for 2 people. Meal plans include MAP for 10.500 CFP and AP for 13.000 CFP per person. There is an obligatory supplementary charge for MAP and AP plans for dinner in the Restaurant Vanille on Dec. 24 and Dec. 31.

Deluxe

HOTEL VAHINE ISLAND, *Tel. 689/65.67.38. In-house guests are required to pay the MAP rate for breakfast and dinner for a 2-day minimum. All major credit cards. Reservations are required for guests not staying in the hotel.*

Bruno, the French master chef, worked in the best restaurants in Paris, including Maxim's and Le Doyen. His exquisite cuisine is very impressive, starting with the Continental breakfast, which includes fresh fruit salad, fruit juice, fresh croissants and bread, fresh homemade cakes, mango marmalade and other home-made jams, vanilla yogurt, a selection of cereals, tea and coffee. The American breakfast includes all of the above plus omelets or any style eggs cooked to please your taste. Lunch is served on the terrace overlooking the lagoon, with a choice of fresh salads, marinated fish or fish tartar, grilled fish, and sandwiches of smoked fish, crab salad or meats. In the evening the restaurant provides a romantic setting where the gastronomic dinners are served by candlelight. Chef Bruno's menu of local and French specialties proffers a selection of 2 starters, 2 main courses and 2 desserts. His notable dishes include tuna sashimi with local berries, pickled cabbage and fresh coriander, crispy shrimp with tender baby vegetables in coconut milk, Salmon of the Gods, tagliatelle of vegetables wrapped in banana leaf, farm-raised chicken stuffed with pota (a green leafy vegetable) and creamy curry and coconut sauce, almond cake with roasted mangoes and cinnamon honey, and chocolate chip pralines in blanc mange coco. A vegetarian menu can be prepared when requested in advance. A traditional Polynesian buffet is prepared on Sunday for a minimum of 10 people, and Polynesian music and a dance show can be performed on Wednesday evenings for a minimum of 14 clients.

The bar at Vahine Island is open all day, serving a fine selection of original cocktails and delightful flavors mixed from local fresh fruit juices and Polynesian spirits.

Superior
CHEZ LOUISE, *Tel. 65.68.88/71.23.06, beside the lagoon in Tiva village. Open daily with non-stop service from 8am-10pm. MC, V. Free transfers.*
Louise has earned a very good reputation for her crab and lobster and river shrimp specialties and other local style cuisine that is often flavored with vanilla. She serves a Marina Menu, which is a bamboo canoe filled with poisson cru, rock lobster (in season), grilled lagoon fish, shrimp, rice and bread for 4.900 CFP. A rare treat that you will find on her menu is *cigale de mer*, a very tasty slipper lobster that is priced at 3.350 CFP. Even more delicious and almost impossible to find on anyone's menu is *varo*, which Louise also serves for 5.650 CFP when it is in season. Special hooks and skills are required to capture these sea centipedes that live in pairs in a hole in the white sand bottom of the lagoon. Louise is considered "the" specialist in preparing *maa Tahiti* for groups. Prompted by some of the hotels and passenger ships to put the price up so that they can get a commission, she now charges 5.500 CFP per person, which includes a bottle of wine for 4 people. Otherwise, her prices have not changed in many years. Yachting people can tie their dinghy to the boat dock in front of the restaurant.
LA PIROGUE, *Tel. 60.81.45, on Motu Porou. B.,L.,D. AE, MC, V. Reservations are required for guests not staying in the hotel.*
A Continental breakfast is 2.000 CFP and an American breakfast is 2.250 CFP. In-house guests pay 8.000 CFP for a MAP and 11.500 CFP for AP meals. Their excellent meals feature fresh fish and seafood, local favorites and international cuisine. A la carte lunch usually consists of poisson cru, sashimi or tuna carpaccio, and a 3-course dinner costs around 5.000 CFP per person. They have added a new Japanese restaurant and serve 5-course "Teppanyaki" dishes for 7.800 CFP per person.

Moderate
RESTAURANT HIBISCUS, *Tel. 65.61.06. BLD, are served. AE, MC and V. Reservations are required for guests not staying in the hotel.*
The emphasis is on local specialties such as lobster, crab and varo, along with the fish catch of the day. The average 3-course meal costs around 3.500 CFP per person. The Hibiscus hosts a Tahitian *tamaara'a* feast for 4.250 CFP each Saturday night. Guests are expected to chip in 1.500 CFP to pay the musicians and dancers who entertain.
RESTAURANT TAHA'A MAITAI, *Tel. 65.70.85. On the waterfront in Haamene village. 3 moorings for boats. Open 10am-2:30pm and 6:45-8pm Tues.–Fri. Closed Sat. noon and open at night. Open Sun. noon and closed at night. Closed all day Mon. MC, V.*
Frenchman Bruno François caters to the local clientele, as well as French residents and visitors from many countries. He serves good, simple meals to suit all tastes: salads, poisson cru, fish, seafood dishes, burgers and fries, plus several choices of ice cream. You can also buy a beer or bottled wine.

Economy
SNACK MAC CHINA 99, *Tel. 65.67.81*. In Haamene village across road from post office. Breakfast, pastry shop and Chinese food to go.

SEEING THE SIGHTS
Land Tours
Guided excursions by 4WD vehicles take you on safari tours into the mountains and across the island, passing through Taha'a's luxuriant vegetation from bay to bay. Stops are made at lookout points to let you admire the panoramic views of the bays and lagoons. You will visit a tropical fruit garden and vanilla plantation, where you will learn about this fragrant "brown gold" and how it is "married" by hand. Most of the tours also include a visit to a cultured pearl farm, and some tours even include the turtle park. Most half-day tours cost 3.500-5.000 CFP per person.

Land tours are provided by: **Dave's Tours** (Dave Atiniu), *Tel. 65.62.42/ 77.18.91*; **Hibiscus Activities** (Terainui), *Tel. 65.61.06/79.28.81*; *hibiscus@tahaa-tahiti.com*; **Poe-Rani Tours**, (Teva Ebbs), *Tel. 65.64.20/78.80.25; rani-poe@mail.pf;* **Remuna Tours**, Remuna Teriipaia, *Tel. 65.63.28/72.93.28;* **Taha'a Discovery**, (Matahiarii Laughlin), *Tel. 65.66.67/79.28.92; tahaadiscovery@mail.pf;* **Taha'a Tours Excursion** (Edwin and Jacqueline Mama), *Tel. 65.62.18/79.27.56;* **Trucky Tours** (Christian), *Tel. 78.23.36;* (Nella), *Tel. 75.66.02; millecam@mail.pf;* and **Vaipoe Tours**, (Patricia Amaru), *Tel. 65.60.83/79.26.01; vaipoe.excursions@mail.pf.*

Vanilla Tours, (Alain and Christina Plantier), *Tel. 65.62.46; vanilla.tours@mail.pf; VHF 9*. Alain leads very informative 4-hr. ethno-botanical excursions by 4WD that begin on their property bordering the lagoon of Hurepiti Bay. 2 buoys available for yachts.

Hiking
Terapu Rando, *Tel. 65.69.55/76.70.01; terapurando@hotmail; www.raromatairando.over-blog.com*. Hiking guide Reynald Vaiho leads day hikes for 6-12 people.

Glass Bottom Boat, Lagoon Excursions & Cultured Pearl Farms
Glass Bottom Boat Tours inside the bubble of the 3-passenger "Jules Verne" begin at the Tapuamu pier and last for 45 min. for 4.000 CFP per person. Contact Christophe Citeau at *Tel. 65.64.00/79.63.81*.

Dave's Tours, *Tel. 65.62.42/77.18.91* is operated by Dave Atiniu in Haamene. He has a 28-ft. locally built Fiberglas boat with a sun awning that he uses for excursions that begin in Uturoa or Taha'a. Full-day excursions include snorkeling in the coral gardens and a picnic on a motu. These tours can also be combined with 4WD land excursions.

Mata Tours, *Tel. 66.17.33/74.11.43; matatours@tahaa.org*. Stéphane Toimata offers a half-day tour that takes you by one of his two outrigger canoes to feed the sting rays and fish, snorkel in a natural aquarium and enjoy fruit tasting while visiting a vanilla plantation, then to stop at a pearl farm. You can also opt for a half-day tour that includes shark feeding instead of the rays, as well as snorkeling, the vanilla plantation and fruit tasting. He also has private tours for 2-4 passengers, and the all-day tour includes a BBQ on the motu. Stéphane's English is not perfect, but the tourists enjoy his tours and his ukulele music.

Motu Pearl Village, *Tel. 65.66.67.79/28.93/72.33.01; VHF 8; motupearlvillage@mail.pf; www.motupearlvillage.com. AE, V.*

Sabrina Laughlin and her big Polynesian family of talented singers and musicians offer free bi-lingual guided tours of their pearl farm in Faaaha Bay. The pearl boutique is open daily 9:30am-5pm, except Sun. and the tours of the pearl farm are scheduled at 10am, 11:30am, 2pm and 3:30pm. The village is accessible by sea with a mooring and dock, and they have a 30-passenger motor launch and a 60-passenger covered catamaran that can accommodate large groups. They specialize in organizing barbecue picnics and Tahitian buffets for groups up to 200 people, which are served in their large covered hall, complete with a bar. They can provide VIP tours on request. Rentals and extras include bicycles, kayaks, mask and snorkel, diving equipment, boat transfers to the motu and fish parks, pick-ups at the hotels, "Iaoranet" cards for Internet access, and water fill-up for yachts. Optional visits can also be made by 4WD vehicles to visit a vanilla plantation and to see the panoramic sights of Taha'a. Water taxi service is available to go around the island and a new service is the Taha'a VIP Tour, with a half- or full-day of diving at the motu. Contact: *araia@mail.pf.*

Poe-Rani Tours and Pearl Farm, *Tel. 65.64.20/78.80.25 (Teva),77.17.95 (Linda); rani-poe@mail.pf; www.poeranisafari.com.* Teva and Rooverta Ebbs have a pearl farm in Haamene Bay that you can visit during a 4WD Safari Tour, a guided Jet-ski excursion or while driving a Bugster style vehicle. The Ebbs have all kinds of rentals. Guided excursions always include a visit to their Poe-Rani Pearl Farm, where you will learn about how the oysters are grafted and the beautiful cultured pearls are produced. You can also buy Tahitian products here.

Taha'a Tours Excursion, *Tel. 65.62.18/79.27.56.* Edwin and Jacqueline Mama provide lagoon excursions on board their motorized outrigger canoes, which include a visit to a pearl farm and a picnic and swim at a motu. These tours usually originate in Raiatea and can be combined with a 4WD land excursion in Taha'a.

Vaipoe Excursions, *Tel. 65.60.83/79.26.01; vaipoe.excursions@mail.pf.* Patricia and Daniel Amaru have 2 boats for 6-24 passengers, providing an all day boat and safari excursion from Raiatea to Taha'a, or departures from Taha'a. This outing includes snorkeling in the coral gardens, a picnic and swim at a motu and a visit to their **Vaipoe Pearl Farm** for 6.500 CFP per person. You can also combine this excursion with a 4WD Safari tour of Taha'a for 8.000 CFP per person. Patricia and Daniel, who are both Polynesian, have a long-standing reputation for their popular tours.

The Raiatea chapter also lists several tour operators under *Lagoon and Motu Excursions* who provide boat excursions to Taha'a and its motu islets. Some of these guides are: **l'Excursion Bleue**, *Tel. 66.10.90*; **Noma Tours**, *Tel. 66.32.70*; and **West Coast Charters**, *Tel. 66.45.39*.

SPORTS & RECREATION
Charter Yachts
Information on the yacht charter companies is given in *Raiatea* chapter.

Day Sailing
Bisou Futé Charter, *Tel. 65.64.97/79.11.42; Fax 65.69.08; jeanyvon@mail.pf; www.bisoufute.com.* This 51-ft. Beneteau monohull is owned by Jean-Yvon Nechachby and is based in Apu Bay, Taha'a. This yacht is available for full-day sailing cruises inside the Raiatea-Taha'a lagoon. Lunch is served on board or on a motu islet. Private cruises can be organized on request to other Society Islands.

Aapu Croisière Charter, *Tel. 65.75.08/25.12.38; aapu@mail.pf; www.aapu-croisiere.net.* This 50-ft. Beneteau monohull named *Wanda* is based in Apu Bay in Taha'a. A maximum of 10 passengers can sail around the island with a picnic on request. Sunset cruises possible. Long distance cruises in French Polynesia are available for 8 passengers.

See information on **Atara Royal** and **Catamaran Tane** under *Charter Yachts* in the Raiatea chapter. They also offer day sailing and sunset cruises.

Lagoon and Deep Sea Fishing
John's Fishing Tours, *Tel./Fax 66.33.44/79.71.74*. John is a retired police-man with a little red boat with a red cover and a huge motor. He can take 2-4 passengers snorkeling in the coral gardens at Motu Tautau, around the island of Taha'a or fishing for bonito, snappers and jackfish in the lagoon or between Taha'a and Raiatea or outside the reef. He also has a Jet-ski.

See the section on Deep Sea Fishing charters in the *Raiatea* chapter.

Scuba Diving
There are more than 25 recorded dive spots, including 8 passes, around Taha'a and Raiatea, all reachable by boat within 10-25 min. from Taha'a. You can see reef sharks and humphead wrasses year-round in water temperatures of 60-80° Fahrenheit. Of special interest to divers are underwater caves and a wrecked ship.

Taha'a Blue Nui Diving Center, Tel. 65.67.78/79.66.44; *tahaabluenui@mail.pf; www.bluenui.com* is located at Le Taha'a Island Resort & Spa on Motu Tautau. The dive instructor, Stéphane Hamon, can take certified divers for a Fun dive for 7.727 CFP, a night dive for 8.636 CFP, and a 2-tank dive for 13.818 CFP. An introductory dive or lesson is 7.727 CFP and a private dive is 22.727 CFP (two people minimum). Training and certification available for PADI, CMAS and FFESSM. Rates include basic equipment (instructor, boat

HIBISCUS FOUNDATION SAVES THE SEA TURTLES

Leo and Lolita Morou, who own the Hotel-Restaurant Hibiscus in Taha'a, started the **Hibiscus Foundation** in 1992. Their goals are to fight against underwater spearfishing and turtle poachers, and to rescue the turtles that have been injured or accidentally trapped in fish parks inside the lagoon near the passes. When they find these turtles Leo and his volunteer helpers shelter them in a special enclosure for a few days, then tag them for future identification before releasing the turtles into the open ocean. By March 2011 the Hibiscus Foundation had saved 1,460 turtles, mostly the Chelonia Midas, the green sea turtle, which is the most common and the tastiest. Several hawksbill turtles, Eretmochelys imbricata, the large-headed turtle, have also been rescued by Leo and Lolita, and their network of yachting friends.

In the olden days when the arii, the Polynesian chiefs, ruled the people, the honu (turtles) were considered sacred and their meat was reserved only for the kings, priests and keepers of the marae, where the Maohi people worshipped their god Oro. The marae that were dedicated to Oro were distinguished by stones that were shaped in the form of turtle heads, and turtle petroglyphs were carved in the basaltic rocks. The turtles are just as tapu (taboo, sacred or forbidden) today as they were then, because they have been declared an endangered species by the local government.

transfer to dive site, tank, regulator, weight belt, fins, mask, diving suit and underwater flashlight for night dives). Packages of 6 or 10 dives can be used in all the Blue Nui diving centers but cannot be shared between 2 people. Free transfers for divers staying in all the hotels and family pensions on Taha'a and also on cruise ships.

Taha'a Diving, *Tel. 65.78.37/24.80.69; contact@tahaa-diving.com; www.tahaa-diving.com.* Located in Tapuamu village, providing fast access to the reef on the western side of Taha'a. Instructor Michel Cordero and his assistant Marielle can take up to 6-8 divers to the most beautiful sites in Taha'a and Raiatea for scuba diving, snorkeling or a combined outing that includes diving and a picnic on the motu. Scubapro equipment includes tank, regulator, stab/BCD, mask, fins, diving suit, weight belt and boat transfer to the dive sites. Courses in PADI, CMAS and FFESSM provided on request. 10-dive packages can be shared between 2 people. Free transfer from your hotel by boat or car.

Buggy Dive, *Tel. 65.69.33/33.67.02; info@buggydive.com; www.buggydive.com.* Pascal and Sandrine Avila run this new PADI dive center and Aqualung partner, which is located in Apu Bay, close to the Taravana Yacht Club (now closed). You can combine a half-day of exploring Taha'a by Buggy in the morning and diving in the afternoon, or you can choose either the land or lagoon. A 26-ft. aluminum boat with a sun roof can take 10-12 divers to the best spots. Pascal is a BEES 1, MF 1 and PADI Dive Master and Nitrox monitor. He can take you for a first dive or exploration dive for 6.000 CFP, a 2-tank dive for 10.800 CFP, a night dive for 7.200 CFP, or a private dive for 36.000 CFP. A 5-dive package is 27.000 CFP and a 10-dive package is 54.000 CFP. Snorkeling excursions are 4.000 CFP.

SHOPPING
Pearl Farms and Boutiques
Champon Pearl Farm, *Tel. 65.66.26/78.33.58; champonb@mail.pf; www.tahiti-perle-online.com.* Owners Bernard and Monique Champon will organize boat transfers from Raiatea and explain all the operations of their pearl farm, which is located next door to the Taravana Yacht Club (now closed) at Point Toamaro in Apu Bay. Direct pearl sales are made in the boutique here or you can order them online. AE, M. and V accepted.

Love Here Pearl Farm, *Tel. 65.62.62/74.31.36; aiho.vaite@mail.pf; www.loveherepearlfarm.com* is located in Patio. Free visits Mon.-Fri. 8am-2pm.

Motu Pearl Village, *Tel. 65.66.67/79.28.93; www.motupearlvillage.com* in Faaaha sells pearls, keishis, mabes and pearl jewelry featuring Raka design creations. They also sell locally made clothing, *pareos*, curios, and traditional arts and crafts combining mother-of-pearl with local woods and woven coconut fibers. Free guided tours of their pearl farm 4 times daily except Sunday.

Poerani Farm, *Tel. 65.64.20/78.80.25*, and **Vaipoe Farm**, *Tel. 65.60.83/ 78.80.25*, both in Haamene Bay, sell pearls from their own farms, as well as locally made jewelry and arts and crafts. See more information under *Seeing the Sights* in this chapter. **Sophie Artisanant Boutique** in Hurepiti Bay, *Tel. 65.62.56*, sells hand painted *pareos*.

MASSAGES & SPAS
Manea Spa, *Tel. 60.84.16, maneaspa@letahaa.com; www.maneaspa.com.* This attractive spa is built of natural materials in Polynesian style at the edge of a saltwater lake on Motu Tautau, providing body and facial care for men and women, most of whom are guests at Le Taha'a Island Resort & Spa.

The Manea Spa features twin massage rooms beside the lake, a double massage room with Jacuzzi viewing the lake, as well as a double open-air Vichy-shower. Hotel guests are also free to relax in the Spa's beach Jacuzzi beside the Manea Spa. Treatments include traditional Polynesian massage, reflexology, exfoliation, body masks and wraps, facial care and hydration. A 30-min. massage starts at 8.182 CFP, a 50-min. massage starts at 13.636 CFP and an 80-min. Taurumi welcome massage is 17.273 CFP. You can get treated with a jet-lag massage, a warm stone massage, a ritual foot massage, a 4-hands massage and a massage over the lagoon. Facial care for ladies includes the 50-min. Hoho'a Vanira (vanilla facial) for 12.727 CFP and the Rouru Vanira is a 50-min. luxurious scalp massage using vanilla monoi on your hair, for 12.727 CFP, which also includes a foot massage. The ultimate choice of Manea Spa's signature treatments is the Here Nui, a unique and unforgettable body treatment for two that lasts for 3 hrs. 20 min. and costs 86.364 CFP per couple.

TATTOOS
Tavita Manea is a well-known tattoo artist who lives in Patio. He worked for many years at Tiki Village in Moorea. He does tattoos on request at Le Taha'a Island Resort & Spa and at most of the other hotels and pensions. Ask at the hotel's activity desk.

PRACTICAL INFORMATION
Banks
Banque Socredo, *Tel. 47.00.00,* is located in Patio, and **Banque de Tahiti,** *Tel. 65.63.14,* is in the Teva Uri building in Haamene.

Doctors
There is a government operated medical and dental center in Patio, *Tel. 65.63.31,* and a dispensary in Haamene, *Tel. 65.67.51.* Doctor Régis Rouveyrol has a private practice in Haamene, *Tel. 65.60.60,* and Doctor Raphael Dana, *Tel. 65.65.67,* has a private practice in Patio. Kati Anais, *Tel. 65.60.00,* and Jérôme Gence, *Tel. 65.61.11,* are physical therapists in Patio.

Drugstore
Pharmacie Taha'a, *Tel. 60.86.08,* is in the Commercial building in Haamene.

Police
A brigade of the French *gendarmerie* is posted in Patio and Haamene, *Tel. 60.81.05.*

Post Office and Telecommunications Office
There is a **Post Office** in Haamene, *Tel. 65.60.11,* and another in Patio, *Tel. 65.64.70.* All telecommunications and postal services are available.

Tourist Bureau
Comité du Tourisme de Taha'a, *Tel. 60.81.66/77.18.91; raiatea@tahiti-tourisme.pf* is located in the Maritime building (Gare Maritime) on the quay in Uturoa. Open Mon.-Fri. from 8am-4pm and on weekends when a cruise ship arrives. The hostess is well informed and very helpful.

Yacht Services
Hibiscus Yacht Club, *B.P. 184, Haamene, Taha'a 98733; Tel. 689/65.61.06/ 79.28.81; Fax 689/65.65.65; VHF 68-Hibiscus; hibiscus@tahaa-tahiti.com; www.tahaa-tahiti.com.*

The Hotel-Restaurant Hibiscus is at the entrance to Haamene Bay. There are 7 free yacht moorings and services include fresh water, showers, garbage disposal, message service and, on request, fresh bread can be delivered to your yacht daily except Sun. You can rent a car, join a 4x4 tour, or sign up for a variety of activities.

16. Bora Bora

When you tell your friends: "I'm going to **Bora Bora**," you can be sure that this simple phrase will bring envy and longing to their romantic hearts and stir a feeling of wanderlust in their vagabonding souls.

Bora Bora has become the center of tourism in Tahiti and Her Islands. Some of the world's famous stars of stage, cinema and television vacation here, flying their private jets to the international airport in Tahiti and on to Bora Bora, without a thought of seeing the other islands of French Polynesia. European royalty, sheiks, emirs, maharajas and international jet-setters find the serenity and privacy they seek on this magnificent little island. Cinematographers discover the ideal tropical setting for movies, often starring the islanders themselves.

Bora Bora, perhaps more than any other island in the South Seas, teases the imagination of travel writers, who search for adequate phrases of 'purple prose' to describe the spectacular beauty of its craggy, sculpted mountains, the palm-crowned islets that seem to float just inside the coral reef, surrounded by a confection of white sandy beaches that dip down into a lagoon of opalescent blues and greens.

Bora Bora lies 260 km. (161 mi.) northwest of Tahiti in the Leeward Society Islands. Your first glimpse of Bora Bora may be from the window of an Air Tahiti plane, at the end of a direct flight from Tahiti or Moorea. Bora Bora from aloft appears as a precious emerald in a setting of turquoise, encircled by a protective necklace of sparkling pearls. You will have a great view of Bora Bora as the ATR-72 banks for landing on Motu Mute. On most flights you will usually have the best

---

PAUL-EMILE VICTOR - THE COLORS OF BORA BORA
Paul-Emile Victor, a French polar explorer, artist and writer, retired to Bora Bora with his wife Colette, and lived on Motu Tane in Bora Bora until his death in 1995. His impression of seeing Bora Bora from the cockpit of an airplane in 1958, after a 25-year absence from the island, was published in the 1970s in *Distance*, the in-flight magazine of the former UTA-French airline: "...Never before had I seen waters the colour of the rainbow or like fireworks, springing right out of some maddened imagination, or from Gauguin's own palette. Waters the colour of bronze, of copper, gold, silver, mother-of-pearl, pearl, jade, emeralds, moonlight or the aurora borealis. The stars themselves seemed to have fallen into the sea, scintillating brilliantly on the lagoon's surface, in bright sunlight...Who could find the words, what poet the images, what painter even the colours, to describe this scene? I give up."

views of Bora Bora if you are sitting on the left side of the plane, but this all depends on the landing pattern used for that particular flight.

If you arrive in Bora Bora by cruise ship, inter-island ferryboat or by sailboat, you will also be impressed by the kaleidoscope of shimmering iridescence that greets your eye at every turn. Aquamarine. Lapis lazuli. Turquoise. Cobalt. Periwinkle. Sapphire. Emerald. Jade. Ultramarine. Indigo. You'll love counting the shades of color in the sparkling waters of Bora Bora's world-famous lagoon.

Mythology

Polynesian mythology claims that Ofai Honu, a volcanic boulder carved with petroglyphs of turtles, was possessed with godly power and mated with the Pahia Mountain, then called Hohorai. From their union a son was born, whose name was Firiamata O Vavau. This first great chief gave his name to the island and for many years this fabled paradise was known as **Vavau**, which means first-born. Legend says that Vavau was the first island that sprang up after the mythical creation of the sacred island of Havai'i (Raiatea). The beautiful little islet beside the pass of Vavau was named Motu Tapu, the sacred islet.

LEGEND OF HIRO

One of the most famous characters in Polynesian oral history was **Hiro**, god of thieves. Hiro hid out on **Toopua Island**, across Povai Bay from the main island. Using the dragonfly to distract attention, Hiro and his band of thieves robbed their victims at night, between sunset and the first cockcrow. Hiro's constant companion was a white cock, the moa uo. This rooster became excited when Hiro was trying to steal Toopua Island and began to crow, breaking the magic power and so enraging Hiro that he hurled the bird against the face of Pahia mountain, where the imprint still remains. Although Hiro abandoned his plan to steal the island, he detached a large chunk of it that is called Toopua-Iti, the islet that is separated by only a few feet from Toopua.

The view of Bora Bora's famous mountains of **Otemanu** (sea of birds) and the twin peaks of **Pahia** and **Hue** are best photographed through this opening, where just underneath the clear surface of the lagoon lie rocks known as **Hiro's Canoe**. Ashore on Toopua Island are giant stones said to have been left by Hiro and his son Marama, tossed about in a game played by the 2 giants. Deep inside the coconut forest is a gigantic rock, **Hiro's Bell** that used to reverberate when struck. This basaltic boulder was damaged during the construction of a hotel on Toopua Island, however, and now sits as a silent witness to Polynesia's past.

Geology

Bora Bora was formed by volcanic eruptions some three to four million years ago. It is one of the oldest in the chain of the Leeward Islands. Through eons and centuries it has been eroding and sinking. 1-2 miles inside the fringing reef rise the sharp cliffs of basaltic rock that form the central mountain chain running through the principal island of Bora Bora. Mount Otemanu, at 727 m. (2,384 ft.), Mount Pahia, at 661 m. (2,168 ft.), and Mount Hue at 619 m. (2,030 ft.), are the most spectacular chimney peaks of the crater that once spewed molten lava. The center of this sunken volcano lies far beneath the electric blue of Povai Bay, and the smaller islands of Toopua and Toopua-Iti are the opposite walls of the crater, formed when the earth erupted beneath the ocean. The Teavanui Pass is the only navigable break in the coral wall that has formed on top of the caldeira of the sunken volcano.

If you want to see what an atoll is like without heading out to the Tuamotu archipelago, then you should visit a *motu* in Bora Bora. These islets have the same flora and fauna of the atolls, with the advantage of having a high island just a 5-min. boat-ride away. Walk along the ocean side of a motu and you will find *miki miki* bushes, sea grape, pandanus, the South Seas rosewood tree called *miro*, the huge *tou* trees with their orange flowers and precious wood so desired by sculptors, *tamanu* trees whose fruit gives us a healing oil for the treatment of deep burns and cuts, the Australian pine, which is called *aito* in these islands, and the *tiare kahaia*, whose decorative branches are used in the construction of the typical Polynesian bunga- lows built by most hotel owners. Go for a walk along the seashore early in the morning and you will see the herons fishing, and during a picnic on the *motu* perhaps you will catch a glimpse of the lovely white fairy tern with its black button eyes.

ARRIVALS & DEPARTURES

Arriving By Air

Air Tahiti has 7-10 direct flights daily for the 50-min. hop between Tahiti and Bora Bora, as well as flights that stop in Huahine and/or Raiatea. More flights are added during high seasons. The fare is 16.530 CFP one-way for adults, and 30.760 CFP round-trip, taxes and airport shuttle boat in Bora Bora included. There are 2-3 flights daily from Moorea, either direct or stopping in Huahine or Raiatea. The one-way fare from Moorea to Bora Bora is 20.430 CFP, from Huahine to Bora Bora it is 9.330 CFP, and from Raiatea to Bora Bora the fare is 7.730 CFP. On Sun. there is a Maupiti-Bora Bora flight for 7.930 CFP.

Air Tahiti reservations: Tahiti, *Tel. 86.42.42;* Moorea, *Tel. 55.06.02;* Huahine, *Tel. 68.77.02/60.62.60;* Raiatea *Tel. 60.04.44/60.04.40;* Bora Bora, *Tel. 60.53.53/ 60.53.00;* Maupiti *Tel. 60.15.05/67.81.24.*

The **Bora Bora airport** is located *on Motu Mute*, a 15-min. boat ride to the main village of Vaitape or 10-15 min. by luxury launch direct to your deluxe hotel, depending on its distance from the airport. If your hotel doesn't have a private launch to the airport, then you will be met at the boat dock in Vaitape village and

BORA BORA TODAY

When the 5th edition of *Tahiti & French Polynesia Guide* was written in 2008 Bora Bora boasted 16 international class hotels and a dozen or so family pensions on the main island and the motu islets. When updating for the 6th edition in mid-2011, I had to cross out the Hotel Bora Bora, which closed for renovation in Oct. 2008, stating that it would reopen for its 50th anniversary in 2011. No news has been announced since then, but we all hope that Aman Resorts will succeed in having the road rerouted so that they can build their luxurious villas on the hillside and eventually rebuild on Point Raititi, the most beautiful hotel site on Bora Bora's main island.

Other hotel losses include Club Med, which closed temporarily in 2008, then announced in 2009 that they were not reopening. The Bora Bora Lagoon Resort, an exclusive Orient-Express property on Motu Toopua, suffered heavy damage due to Cyclone Oli in Feb. 2010, and has never reopened. That was also the end of the fabulous Marú Spa built in the branches of two banyan trees. The former Novotel Bora Bora Beach Resort was taken over by Antipodes, then closed on Dec. 31, 2010.

Pension Anau-Chez Teipo has closed, and two family pensions on small motus near the airport closed following Cyclone Oli. These are Mai Moana Island and Le Paradis. Due to a fire in 2010 Chez Nono on Matira Beach lost 2 small bungalows and the main house with a dorm and communal kitchen, but they are still in business with two beach bungalows. The Bora Bora Yacht Club lost 3 bungalows and their pier during Cyclone Oli. They have moved to the former TOPdive Hotel and Restaurant and are now the Mai Kai Marina & Yacht Club and the Mai Kai Lounge Bar.

Other businesses that have closed for various reasons include Matira Beach Restaurant, Sunset Boulevard Restaurant, Bora Bora Tours, Richard Postma's sportfishing/sailing catamaran *Taravana*, and Polynesia Hélicopteres (replaced by Tahiti Helicopter Service). Some of the snacks, rental car agencies, pearl shops, boutiques and art galleries have closed or changed owners, but there are more lagoon excursions now than ever before.

Although Bora Bora still has some challenging environmental problems to solve on shore, the island's world-famous lagoon continues to be a prize-winner. Each year since 2000 the island of Bora Bora has been awarded the Blue Flag (the European Pavillon Bleu) for their successful efforts in environmental management. These awards are for the quality of the water in the lagoon and the frequency of samples the health department takes from the water at hotels and public beaches.

In 2007 the mayor of Bora Bora, Gaston Tong Sang, also received the Marianne d'Or award, an environmental recognition for the island's 3 water treatment systems and desalinization plants. Bora Bora began its environmental improvement program in 1989 by providing its inhabitants and visitors with potable water. However, the water you get from your faucet in Bora Bora tastes and smells like chlorine. Therefore, the hotels recommend bottled water to their guests.

driven to your hotel. Land transportation from the Vaitape quay to the small hotels, pensions and campgrounds is also provided by *le truck* or mini-vans. The Air Tahiti office is located on the quay of Vaitape, and there are public phone booths just outside.

You can also get to Bora Bora by chartering an airplane in Tahiti from **Air Tahiti**, *Tel. 86.42.42*, or **Pol'Air**, *Tel. 74.23.11.*

Arriving By Boat

All the inter-island transport boats dock at the Fare Piti quay in Faanui, 3 km (1.9 mi.) from Vaitape village. It would be advisable to arrange with your hotel or pension to have someone meet you when you arrive. A *le truck* also provides service from the boat dock to the hotels in Matira.

Hawaiki Nui, *Tel. 54.99.54, Fax 45.24.44, contact@stim.pf* leaves the Motu Uta dock in Papeete each Tues. and Thurs. at 4pm. On the first voyage it arrives at the Fare Piti quay in Bora Bora at 10am on Wed., after stopping in Huahine and Raiatea. For the Thurs. departure the ship arrives in Bora Bora on Fri. at 9am after stopping in Raiatea. Passengers are limited to 12, who sleep on the deck for 2.000 CFP or in one of four cabins containing 2 berths and a toilet. A berth costs 5.400 CFP from Papeete to all the Leeward Islands. Meals are available on board the ship. Round-trip fares to transport a car are 11.600-16.900 CFP.

Maupiti Express II, *Tel./Fax 689/66.37.81* (Raiatea), *Tel. 67.66.69, Fax 60.37.16* (Bora Bora); *Cell 78.27.22/72.30.48; www.maupitiexpress.com.* The 140-passenger *Maupiti Express II* leaves Raiatea at 4pm each Wed. and arrives at the Vaitape quay in Bora Bora at 5:45pm. On Fri. it leaves Raiatea at 2pm and arrives in Bora Bora at 3:45pm, and on Fri. and Sun. it leaves Raiatea at 6pm, arriving in Bora Bora at 7:45pm. On Thurs. and Sat. the Maupiti-Bora Bora shuttle leaves Maupiti at 4pm and arrives in Vaitape at 5:45pm. The one-way fare is 4.000 CFP and round-trip is 5.000 CFP. Passengers under 12 years pay half price.

Departing By Air

The main office of **Air Tahiti**, *Tel. 60.53.53/60.53.00*, is at the boat dock in Vaitape village. Most of the hotels take care of reconfirming your departure flight, or you can do it yourself by telephone. The Bora Bora Navette, Air Tahiti's shuttle boat, leaves the Vaitape village dock 1:15 hrs. before each scheduled departure and check-in time at the Air Tahiti office on Motu Mute is 1 hr. before your flight departs. Air Tahiti has 6-10 flights from Bora Bora to Tahiti a day. Most of the flights are direct and the other flights stop in Huahine or Raiatea. There is a daily flight from Bora Bora to Moorea with a stop in Huahine, daily non-stop flights from Bora Bora to Huahine and 1-2 daily direct flights from Bora Bora to Raiatea except Tues. You can fly direct from Bora Bora to Maupiti on Sun. and via Raiatea on Fri. There are direct flights from Bora Bora to Rangiroa on Tues., Wed., Sat. and Sun., and a stop in Tikehau on Thurs. From Bora Bora you can fly to Fakarava each Tues. and Wed. with a stop in Rangiroa, and the flights from Bora Bora to

Manihi are on Tues., Wed. and Sun. with a stop in Rangiroa. There is a direct flight from Bora Bora to Tikehau on Thurs., and the Wed. and Sun. flights stop in Rangiroa.

Departing By Boat

Hawaiki Nui, *Tel. 67.72.39* (Bora Bora), leaves the Fare Piti dock in Bora Bora at 1pm each Wed. for Taha'a and Raiatea, then heads directly back to Papeete, arriving at 5am Thurs. On Fri. the ship leaves Bora Bora at 12pm, stopping in Taha'a, Raiatea and Huahine, and arrives in Papeete at 5am on Sat.

Maupiti Express II, *Tel. 67.66.69, cell 78.27.22/72.30.48*, leaves Bora Bora for Taha'a and Raiatea at 7am each Wed. and Fri., at 3pm on Wed., Fri. and Sun. It leaves for Maupiti at 8:30am each Thurs. and Sat. The trip to Maupiti is 1 hour and 45 minutes and gives you plenty of time to enjoy a day tour on one of the lovely motu islets. See chapter on *Maupiti* for further information. The one-way fare from Bora Bora to Taha'a and Raiatea is 4.000 CFP and round-trip is 5.000 CFP. The same rates apply for the Bora Bora-Maupiti voyage. Passengers under 12 years pay half-fare.

ORIENTATION

In the vicinity of the boat dock in **Vaitape village** you will find the *mairie* (town hall), *gendarmerie*, post office, banks, schools, churches, dispensary, pharmacy, Air Tahiti office, tourist information, arts and crafts center, food stores, small restaurants and snack stands, shops, boutiques and rental agencies for helicopters, cars, scooters and bicycles, plus service stations and public telephones.

Bora Bora's main island is only 10 km (5.2 mi.) long and 4 km (2.5 mi.) wide. A partially paved road circles the coastline, winding 29 km (18 mi.) through the villages of Vaitape, Faanui and Anau. You'll see little settlements of modest *fares*, the homes of Bora Bora's 8,992 inhabitants, which are often surrounded by flower gardens.

GETTING AROUND BORA BORA

Car & Bicycle Rentals

Avis Bora Bora has a sales office in Vaitape facing the quay, and another counter in Matira adjacent to the former Novotel (hotel is closed), *Tel. 67.70.15/ 67.70.03; avis.bora@mail.pf*, A 2-seat Bugway rents for 12.000 CFP for 2 hrs. and 14.000 CFP for 4 hrs. An a/c 3-door Fiat Panda is 9.000 CFP for 2 hrs., 10.850 CFP for 4 hrs., 12.300 CFP for 8 hrs., and 13.500 CFP for 24 hrs. A 5-place a/c automatic drive Hyundai Getz rents for 9.500 CFP for 2 hrs. and up to 15.200 CFP for 24 hrs. Rates for all rental cars include unlimited mileage and third-party insurance. Gas and flat tires are extra. Their bicycles are 1.400 CFP for 2 hrs. and 2.000 CFP for 24 hrs.

Taxis
    There are taxis in Bora Bora, but it is usually necessary to call them by phone. Most of them wait for customers at the boat dock in Vaitape. Each hotel and pension uses a bus, *le truck* or mini-van service to provide transfers between the hotel and the boat dock in Vaitape or Faanui, coordinating their runs with the arrivals and departures of Air Tahiti and the inter-island ferries. There is no official public transportation service on Bora Bora. See information under *Circle Island Tours* in this chapter.

WHERE TO STAY
On the Main Island
Deluxe
INTERCONTINENTAL BORA BORA LE MOANA RESORT, *B.P. 156, Bora Bora 98730. Tel. 689/60.49.00; Fax 689/60.49.99; Reservation Tel. 689/ 86.51.78; reservationspf@interconti.com; www.lemoana.intercontinental.com. Beside the lagoon on Point Matira. All major credit cards.*

    This hotel offers 62 junior suite bungalows with a choice of 50 units built over the water or 12 bungalows on the white sand beach. The modern Polynesian style bungalows have pointed pandanus thatch roofs and are beautifully furnished with contemporary wood and wicker furniture, live plants, natural fabrics, and paintings by resident artists. All the units have a/c and ceiling fans, a bathroom with separate shower and bath, and a private sun terrace with exterior shower. A king-size bed can be converted into twin beds, and in the living room is a sofa that can sleep a third person. There is a writing desk, fully stocked mini-bar, coffee and tea facilities, complimentary toiletries, hair dryer, iron and board, personal safety box, 2 flat screen TV's and stereo sound system, 2 international direct dial telephones with voice mail and data ports for Internet. 2 beach bungalows are wheelchair accessible.

    The overwater bungalows are the perfect haven for lovers. Room service is available from 7am to 9pm and you can even treat yourself to an American breakfast delivered by outrigger canoe to your private terrace. Lounge chairs on the terrace are ideal for hand-in-hand stargazing. Step down from your sun deck into the warm embrace of the clear lagoon for the feel of paradise. Or look through your glass table in the living room and watch the fish swimming around in the crystalline lagoon.

    Meals are served in the Noa Noa Restaurant and Terrace overlooking the white sandy beach. See more information under *Where to Eat* in this chapter. The Vini Vini Bar is beside the 2-level swimming pool, which is enhanced with a waterfall and tropical foliage. Four fully equipped transit bungalow units are available for day visitors or guests arriving before the 2pm check-in or departing after the 11am check-out. Public facilities and services include a reception desk that is open 24/24, a concierge and guest relations/activities center with a car rental desk, business center and computers for guest use with wireless data connection. There is also a Polynesian Natural Pearl Shop and a gift shop and newsstand.

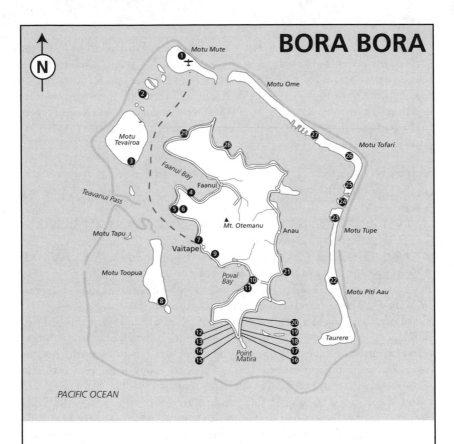

1. Bora Bora Airport
2. Blue Heaven Island
3. Bora Bora Pearl Beach Resort & Spa
4. Farepiti Wharf
5. Bora Bora Pension Noni
6. Sunset Hill Lodge
7. Vaitape Boat Dock
8. Hilton Bora Bora Nui Resort & Spa
9. Pension Moon
10. Rohotu Fare Lodge
11. Pension Rosina Ellacott
12. Temanuata Iti
13. Hotel Matira
14. Pension Chez Nono
15. Pension Robert et Tina
16. ICH Bora Bora Le Moana Resort
17. Chez Maeva Mason
18. Temanuata Beach
19. Le Maitai Polynesia
20. Sofitel Marara Bora Bora Beach and Private Island
21. Pension Bora Lagoonarium
22. Bora Bora Eden Beach Hotel
23. ICH Bora Bora Resort & Thalasso Spa
24. Le Meridien Bora Bora
25. Lagoonarium
26. St. Regis Resort & Spa
27. Four Seasons Resort Bora Bora
28. Bora Vaite Lodge
29. Bora Bora Condos

The Beach Boys at the Fare Plage will give you pointers on how to use the complimentary snorkeling gear, outrigger paddle canoes and kayaks. The Activities manager will explain the full range of land and water sports available and help you book your optional excursions.

Le Moana Resort has long been a favorite destination for honeymooners. When the overwater bungalows were refurbished in 2010 four of the most secluded suites in the furthest part of the lagoon were adorned in pristine white décor to offer the ultimate in honeymoon luxury. These White Villa Suites are ideal for newlyweds. Contact the hotel directly for information on romantic dinners and Polynesian wedding ceremonies that are performed on the beach or in the wedding chapel at the Intercontinental Bora Bora Resort & Thalasso Spa located on Motu Tiarepuomu, just a 15-min. boat ride away. A shuttle boat service between the two hotels operates 11 lagoon crossings a day, with the first shuttle leaving the dock at Le Moana at 7:45am and the last departure at 10pm. A shuttle bus from Le Moana to Vaitape leaves the hotel at 9:45am and 2:45pm, and departs from Vaitape at 11:15am and 5pm. One-way airport transfers by boat are 3.965 CFP per adult and 1.982 CFP for child 3-11 years.

When booking your room, ask for a bungalow that faces Mt. Otemanu and try to get as far away as possible from the noisy end of the resort closest to Point Matira, where there are several houses, children, dogs and roosters.

Superior
SOFITEL BORA BORA MARARA BEACH AND PRIVATE ISLAND,
B.P. 6, Vaitape, Bora Bora 98730. Tel. 689/60.55.00; Fax 689/67.74.03; H0564@sofitel.com; www.sofitel-frenchpolynesia.com. Beside the lagoon at the end of Taahana Bay, north of Point Matira on the east side. 95 units. All major credit cards.

The hotel Marara, (flying fish in Tahitian) was built by Dino de Laurentiis in 1977 to house the crew of his film, "Hurricane". When the Accor Group bought the hotel a few years later, it became the Sofitel Marara. The name was changed to Sofitel Bora Bora Beach Resort in mid-2006 following a major renovation project that upgraded it to a 5-star resort and spa. In 2010 the Sofitel Marara, located beside a white sand beach, and the Sofitel Motu on Motu Piti Uu'uta, merged into one resort that is now called Sofitel Bora Bora Marara Beach and Private Island.

This combination offers 95 luxury bungalows, distributed on the main island (called Beach) and on an authentic motu (called Private Island). Transportation between the two properties is provided on request by a 2-min. shuttle boat service. Accommodation choices include lagoon front, garden, beach, overwater, island lagoon view and island overwater. All the individual bungalows are crafted from wood and pandanus and have a private deck or terrace. The bungalows offer guests the patented Sofitel MyBed with canopy, as well as a plush sofa bed. Amenities include a/c, ceiling fan, plasma screen TV with cable/satellite, radio, IDD telephone with voicemail, Wi-Fi Internet access, work desk, in-room safety deposit box, iron, minibar, coffee/tea facilities and bathrobes. The mosaic tiled bathrooms have a rainshower, separate toilet with telephone, hair dryer and magnified mirror.

The overwater bungalows have spacious decks with bamboo screening for privacy and in-floor glass platforms that are illuminated at night for prime viewing of the natural marine life in the rich coral gardens below. Stairs from the covered terrace lead you directly into the inviting water, and snorkeling gear and beach towels are provided in each room. There is an outdoor shower on the lower sundeck.

The public areas of the resort also have a new look and new additions. On the Beach side the Latitude 16° is the main restaurant, serving French and international dishes, and La Suite is the gastronomic restaurant open only for dinner. Exotic cocktails are available in the Hurricane Bar, at Le Snack or on the deck beside the infinity swimming pool. Because the Private Island is a natural reserve of the reef heron, *egretta sacra*, or Manu Tuki in the Paumotu language of the Tuamotu atolls, this graceful bird is used as the logo for the Manu Tuki restaurant. You will enjoy spectacular views of the multihued lagoon as well as the highly praised cuisine served here. For more information see *Where to Eat* in this chapter. Room service is available in all bungalows during meal hours.

The Private Island features 3 beaches, one of which has sun all day long for sunbathing and snorkeling in the coral gardens surrounding the motu. People who have stayed here claim that the best snorkeling in Bora Bora is in the natural aquarium right beside this islet. For an unforgettable view of the sunset over the distant island of Maupiti be sure to climb the hill behind the hotel on Motu Piti Uu'uta.

The ambiance at the Sofitel Bora Bora Marara Beach and Private Island is lively, with a list of daily activities that are posted in the reception area. Guests have free use of snorkeling equipment, kayaks, outrigger paddle canoes and board games. The activities desk can book any land tour or lagoon excursion you want, plus rent you a car or bicycle. Round-trip shuttle bus service will take you to Vaitape village during the week or to church on Sunday. A dive center is located on the premises, and Le Spa at Sofitel provides body care, massages and flower perfumed Jacuzzi baths. There is something going on every evening, with nightly entertainment at the bar, including Polynesian dance shows. Non-binding Polynesian wedding ceremonies or legal conventional weddings are performed in the wedding *fare* beside the beach or on the hillside of the Sofitel Private Island motu. Contact the hotel directly for details and rates.

The Sofitel Bora Bora Marara Beach and Private Island made the Condé Nast Travelworld Gold List 2011 for the best rooms in the Australia/Pacific area. They were given 100 points for area location, design and activities, and 50 points for food service. This resort is also affiliated with the International Gay & Lesbian Travel Association and welcomes lesbian, gay, bisexual and transgender guests.

Moderate to Superior
LE MAITAI POLYNESIA, *B.P. 505, Bora Bora 98730. Tel. 689/60.30.00; Fax 689/67.66.03; booking@bora.hotelmaitai.com; www.hotelmaitai.com. At Taahana Beach in the Matira area, 15 km (9 mi.) from the ferry dock and 12 km (6 mi.) from Vaitape. All major credit cards.*

This 3-star medium priced hotel opened in June 1998 and added more rooms in 2000, offering 74 units, all with a/c. The 28 garden view rooms are located in 2-level concrete buildings behind the reception, Haere Mai Restaurant and Manuia Bar. The 20 ocean view rooms are located in adjacent buildings across the road from the lagoon. The mountainside rooms have 312 sq. ft. (29 sq. m) of living space and provide either twin or king size beds. Some of the ocean view rooms also have a day bed that can sleep a third person. The mountainside rooms are not recommended for anyone who has difficulty walking, as there are stone steps leading up to these units. The beach bungalows and overwater bungalows are all 323 sq. ft. (30 sq. m) in size and are built in the traditional Polynesian style, with thatched roofs and woven pandanus walls. These units all have king-size beds plus a daybed, and they also have a ceiling fan in addition to the a/c. All the hotel's rooms and bungalows are furnished with a writing desk, blackout curtains, TV Internet hook-up, direct dial telephone, personal safe, mini-bar fridge, coffee/tea making facilities, shower with massage nozzle, hair dryer, bath and beauty amenities, extension mirror and full length mirror in bathroom, and a sliding glass door onto a private terrace or balcony. The overwater bungalows have a glass-viewing table that enables you to see the abundance of fish swimming in the clear water below. Steps provide direct access into the lagoon and there is a shower on the landing below the terrace.

Maitai means 'all is well,' and you'll certainly have a good feeling about this place from the moment you enter the reception area and are welcomed by a smiling Tahitian host or hostess, who offers you a refreshing fruit punch. The reception desk, Haere Mai Restaurant and Manuia Bar are all under one huge woven pandanus roof. Also under this room are a jewelry shop, boutique and lounge, library and computer corner with Wi-Fi access in some public areas. Vivid shades of bougainvillea, hibiscus, colored leaves, tree ferns and hanging baskets of exotic ferns fill the gardens of the hotel and the South Seas setting is completed with a decor of tapa, bamboo and huge chandeliers of seashells.

Breakfast and dinner are served in the Haere Mai Restaurant, and the weekly buffets during high occupancy are popular events, accompanied by a Polynesian dance show. The Manuia Bar is a gathering place during Happy Hour, when the musicians play island tunes and demonstrations are given on how to make *poisson cru* or tie the *pareo*. The Tama'a Maitai Restaurant is located on the beach side of the property, a short walk from the reception area. This is a big open-sided restaurant with a thatched roof, situated between the road and beach. You can walk inside the stone wall that protects the beach bungalows from the noise of traffic. When the Haere Mai Restaurant is closed during certain seasons, the Tama'a Matai is open non-stop daily from 6 a.m. to 9 p.m. The burger bar atmosphere here is very casual, with indoor/outdoor seating at Formica tables. In addition to burgers and pizzas, they serve good salads, fish, seafood, grilled steak or chicken, as well as daily specials. You can also order fresh fruit juices, a glass of beer or house wine, or a bottle of wine. See information under *Where to Eat* in this chapter.

The reception desk remains open 24 hours a day and provides foreign currency exchange and fax service. There is also laundry service, a luggage storage room, changing room with shower for early arrival or late departure, and baby-sitting on request. Guests of Le Maitai Polynesia have free use of snorkeling equipment, kayaks and outrigger paddle canoes, which they can check out at the Sports Fare on the hotel's white sand beach. At the guest activities desk in the main lobby you can rent a car or bicycle and book a variety of land tours and lagoon excursions.

Le Maitai Polynesia was the first hotel in French Polynesia to have been awarded the Earthcheck Silver certification, and has now won this distinction for the second year. Like all the hotels in the Pacific Beachcomber Group, Le Maitai also participates in the international Reef Check program and has a "Green Team" of hotel staff members, including the in-house biologist/veterinarian, brainstorming ideas to conserve and protect the environment.

Moderate

HOTEL MATIRA, *B. P. 31, Bora Bora 98730. Tel. 689/67.70.51/79.15.95; Fax 689/67.77.02; hotel.matira@mail.pf; www.hotel-matira.com. On Matira Beach at the turnoff to Point Matira. AE, MC, V.*

This small hotel is on the beach side of the road right at the turn onto Point Matira. 14 modern Polynesian style bungalows are built in the garden and facing the white sands of Matira Beach. There are 2 beach bungalows, 4 with a lagoon view, 5 with a garden view and 3 standard units near the parking lot. Each of the bungalows has 2 double beds in the bedroom, a sofa bed in the living room, ceiling fan, small refrigerator, coffee and tea facilities, bathroom with hot water shower, and a terrace. There is no a/c and no TV or telephone. An iron and hair dryer are available at reception.

The hotel has no restaurant, but they work with Fare Manuia, just a few steps away. Several restaurants provide pick-up service for dinner. There is also the Tiare Market within easy walking distance and an excellent roulotte sets up shop practically across the street every evening. All activities and excursions, such as lagoon trips and mountain safaris are available. Arrival and departure transfers 1.500 CFP per adult and 1.000 CFP for child 4-11 years.

Small Family Hotels, Family Pensions, Guest Houses, Guest Rooms, Dormitories, Camping on the Main Island

ROHOTU FARE LODGE, *B.P. 400, Bora Bora 98730. Tel. 689/70.77.99; info@rohotufarelodge.com; www.rohotufarelodge.com. On mountainside overlooking Povai Bay, 4 km. (2.5 mi) north of Vaitape village. Free round-trip transfers. MC, V.*

For many years Israeli expatriate Nir Shalev was the friendly manager of the popular backpacker's hangout, Village Pauline. In 2005 he moved 50 m. (150 ft.) up the mountain slope and built 3 exotic wooden bungalows on stilts in the midst of a botanical garden. This unique lodging has been awarded a 3-Tiare rating by the Tahiti Tourist office—the only pension in Bora Bora in this category. There are two lagoon view bungalows for two people in each unit and a double-size mountain view bungalow for families, which has a separate bar-salon and an extra bed. Each bungalow has its own design, with teak floors and thatched roofs, a four-poster queen size bed with mosquito net, ceiling fan, safe, a bathroom with a marble floor, outdoor shower in a private garden, kitchenette with refrigerator, microwave oven, and coffee maker, plus a wide veranda. The bungalows and gardens are decorated with original works of art, including some erotic paintings and statues. Even the showers are suggestive!

You can relax in a rope hammock in a special hut facing the lagoon, browse through the library's collection of books, watch TV, log-on through the WiFi connection, ride a free bike to the main village, or take advantage of the free transfers Nir offers his guests to the beach, stores, shopping or wherever they want to go. He has all the information you need to book your activities to discover Bora Bora by land or lagoon. He also rents sturdy USA made sea kayaks, complete with snorkeling and fishing gear.

VILLAGE TEMANUATA, *B.P. 544, Bora Bora 98730. Tel. 689/67.75.61; Fax 689/67.62.48; village.temanuata@mail.pf; www.temanuata.com.* MC, V.

Temanuata Beach: *On the beach side at Matira, just past the turnoff to Point Matira. Breakfast basket delivered on request.*

This is a good location on Matira Beach, very close to restaurants, snacks, a food store, patisserie and activities. The 12 Polynesian style thatched roof bungalows sit in a spacious grassy area between the white sand beach and the road, adjacent to Restaurant Fare Manuia. They all have a terrace, private bathroom with hot water, double or single beds, a closet, refrigerator, electric kettle, ceiling fan and mosquito net. They are attractively decorated with pareo curtains and bedspreads and are cleaned daily. You can rent a bicycle at reception and Martine, the manager, will happily help you arrange your tours and excursions.

Temanuata Iti: *On the mountain side between Hotel Bora Bora and Point Matira, 10 min. from Temanuata Beach.*

Four large thatched roof bungalows are located in a private garden setting across the road from Matira Beach and the lagoon. These well furnished family units are equipped with a king size bed, ceiling fan, coffee and tea making facilities, TV, private bathroom with hot water, kitchen and a terrace. Bungalows are cleaned daily. Two complimentary bicycles are provided for each bungalow.

PENSION ROBERT ET TINA, *Vaitape, Bora Bora 98730. Tel. 689/67.63.55/ 79.22.73/73.53.89; Fax 689/67.72.92; pensionrobertettina@mail.pf; www.pensionrobertettina.com. Beside the lagoon at Point Matira.* MC, V.

This Polynesian family has 3 individual houses with a total of 15 rooms at the tip end of Point Matira. They all have kitchens, electric fans and bathrooms with cold water showers. You can rent a room and share the bathroom and kitchen or rent the entire house. A full-day circle island boat tour with Rohivai Tour includes shark feeding, visit to stingrays and manta rays, snorkeling in coral garden and picnic on a motu. This costs 9.000 CFP. A half-day excursion without picnic is 7.000 CFP.

CHEZ NONO, *B.P. 282, Bora Bora, 98730. Tel. 689/67.71.38; Fax 689/ 67.74.27; nono.leverd@mail.pf; www.cheznonobora.com. On the white sand beach of Point Matira, facing the Hotel Bora Bora and the distant island of Maupiti, 13 km (8 mi.) from the ferry dock and 6.8 km (4.2 mi.) from Vaitape village. MC, V.*

This guest house has always been considered as one of the best choices for a budget accommodation on Bora Bora, because of its excellent location right on the white sand beach of Matira, facing Maupiti and the sunset sea. In late 2010 a fire destroyed the big house, 2 twin bungalows, and the communal kitchen. The 2 round family bungalows were spared. These are Polynesian style fares with a big thatched roof and half-walls of woven bamboo, overlooking the incredibly beautiful lagoon. They can sleep a maximum of 4 adults and each has a bathroom with solar hot water, a fridge and a fan. A grocery store, patisserie and several restaurants and snack bars are within a 10-min. walk. The biggest drawback here is lack of privacy, as Matira Beach is Bora Bora's only public beach. Nono operates Teremoana Tours and has a motorized outrigger canoe that he uses to take his guests around the island with a picnic on a motu. His very popular excursions depart from the beach in front of his pension at 9:30am and return at 4:30pm. A lunch of *poisson cru*, grilled fish, coconut bread, cake, fresh fruit and *po'e* is served on the *motu*. The cost is 9.200 CFP per person.

CHEZ ROSINE MASSON (PENSION MAEVA), *B.P. 33, Bora Bora 98730. Tel./Fax 689/67.72.04; cell 72.76.66; pensionrosinemasson@mail.pf; www.tahitiguide.com. Beside the beach at Point Matira, 13 km (8 mi.) from the ferry dock and 6.8 km (4.2 mi.) from Vaitape village. MC, V.*

This is a very good location on Matira Beach with several restaurants, snacks, the Tiare Market food store, patisserie and various activities within easy walking distance. Tahiti Tourisme has rated this a 2-Tiare guest house. It was the former home of Polynesian artist Rosine Temauri-Masson and her late husband, the French painter Jean Masson, and it still has the decor and warmth of a home. The 2-story wooden house has 2 bedrooms on the ground floor, each containing a double bed, and the 3 rooms upstairs have a double bed in 2 rooms and a 3-bed dormitory in the other room. The rooms have a ceiling fan and mosquito net. The bathroom with hot water shower and the kitchen are communal. WiFi Internet, point phone, washing machine and iron are extra. Transfers are available from the airport boat dock in Vaitape village. Several of my friends have enjoyed staying here and getting to know Rosine, who still lives in the house.

BORA VAITE LODGE, *B.P. 197, Vaitape, Bora Bora 98730. Tel./Fax 689/ 67.55.69, cell 73.57.71; boravaite@mail.pf; www.boravaite.com. Overlooking the* *lagoon on the mountainside in Hitiaa Bay (6.2 mi.) 10 km. north of Vaitape center. No credit cards.*

Vaite and Alain Wernert formerly worked at the Hotel Bora Bora—she ran the boutique and he was chef de cuisine. They both speak English. In 2005 they opened their big 2-story concrete house to welcome guests, with meals and activities included. The guest accommodations consist of 3 rooms, 2 apartments and a studio with a 5-bed dormitory. The rooms can sleep 4 and have a ceiling fan, minibar, satellite TV and water fountain. The bathroom is shared. The apartments have a double bed and 2 single beds and a kitchen with dishes, oven, refrigerator, coffee maker, microwave and iron. All rooms are clean, attractively decorated and budget priced compared to most lodgings in Bora Bora. Rates start at 6.000 CFP sgl. and 8.400 CFP dble., and a bed in the dorm is 3.000 CFP. A Continental breakfast is 500 CFP and lunch or dinner is 2.800 CFP each. Internet is 500 CFP a day. Transfers are free for arrival and departure and 500 CFP if you want to go to Vaitape or to Matira Beach.

BORA BORA PENSION NONI, *Tel./Fax 689/67.71.48; cell 73.73.61; contact@nonipension.pf; www.nonipension.com. On mountainside facing Total Station in Vaitape, a 10-min. walk from the town center. No credit cards.*

This 3-room house in Vaitape village is owned by Denis and Gloria Tetuanui. Each room can sleep 3 people and has a private bathroom with hot water shower, a ceiling fan, safe, TV and refrigerator, plus a microwave on request. WiFi Internet is extra. The rate of 7.500 CFP for 1-2 people includes breakfast. You can also have lunch and dinner in their restaurant-snack, starting at 1.000-1.500 CFP, or walk to several nearby restaurants, snacks or roulottes. This friendly Polynesian family can also take you to a motu with a private white sand beach with cooking and bathroom facilities.

SUNSET HILL LODGE, *B.P. 58, Vaitape, Bora Bora 98730. Tel. 689/79.26.48; Fax 00 33 972129352; dreamland.bora@mail.pf; www.sunset-hill-borabora.biz. On mountainside facing Total Station in Vaitape, a 10-min. walk from the town center. No credit cards.*

Continue up the road that leads to Bora Bora Pension Noni and you will come to Sunset Hill Lodge, which is 16-32 ft. (5-10 m.) above the main road, with a good view of the lagoon and removed from the road noises. There are 5 lodgings here, but only 2 garden bungalows are available for short-term rental for 5.000 CFP per day. These units are nestled in a Zen garden with a little waterfall and fishpond to add to the tranquility. They contain a double bed, fan, TV, a small kitchen with gas oven, microwave, refrigerator, cutlery, crockery, coffee, tea, sugar, salt, pepper, oil and vinegar. The private bathroom has a hot water shower and there is a covered terrace. Free WiFi Internet is available in the office. The owner is Gerard Beon, a Frenchman who is highly praised by his guests for his helpfulness, which includes driving his clients to Matira Beach. He has kayaks for rent and will advise you where you can rent a bike. The TOPDIVE-Bathys dive center is just 328 ft. (100 m.) away, and there are several dining choices in the Vaitape area.

Other Accommodations on Bora Bora's Main Island
Bora Bora Condominiums, *Tel./Fax 689/67.61.21; marcolundi@mail.pf; www.marcolundi.com.* The rental condos include 10 on the mountainside and 4 overwater bungalows facing Bora Bora's airport, and are rented by the week, month or year. **Chez Rosina Ellacott**, *Tel./Fax 689/67.70.91/79.26.51; pensionchezrosina@mail at PK 4.5, on mountain side in Paparoa section of Pofai Bay,* has 7 rooms. No credit cards. **Pension Bora Lagoonarium**, *Tel. 689/67.71.34/ 79.73.67; www.boraboraisland.com.* Beside lagoon in Anau village. 3 garden bungalows with private bathroom; 4 rooms and 20-bed dormitory share bathroom and communal kitchen; camping space. Owners also have Lagoonarium water park on motu. **Pension Moon**, *Tel. 689/67.74.36; pensionmoon@mail.pf.* Muna Teriitehau has 4 bungalows with private bathrooms and kitchens, adjacent to Galerie Alain and Linda beside the lagoon in Pofai Bay. No credit cards.

Hotels & Pensions on the Motu
Prestige
FOUR SEASONS RESORT BORA BORA, *B.P. 547, Vaitape, Bora Bora 98730. Tel. 689/60.31.30; www.fourseasons.com/borabora. Reservations: USA and Canada 1 800/819-5053. On Motu Tehotu across the lagoon from Bora Bora's main island. 121 rooms. All credit cards.*

Former guests speak in superlatives and write with exclamation points when referring to this resort, making generous use of the phrases "awesome!, amazing!, great! and wow!!" This is definitely the choice dream resort of young honeymooners. The Four Seasons began accepting reservations in Sept., 2008, after all the other 5-star resorts were open on the motu islets facing Anau village and Mt. Otemanu on Bora Bora's main island. The owner and architect had the advantage of seeing how others had built their hotels, then refining the details, adding the cachet of the Four Seasons reputation for striking physical surroundings, opulence, and truly superior, attentive pampering service for affluent guests. They are still working on the service part in Bora Bora and are mostly successful.

The Four Seasons Resort Bora Bora is located on 54 acres (22 ha.), providing 121 spacious rooms in 100 bungalows built over the lagoon and in 7 magnificent villas on the beach. The overwater bungalows range in size from 1,080 sq. ft. (100 sq. m.) to 1,576 sq. ft. (146 sq. m.), offering views of the beach or lagoon and some with unobstructed views of Mount Otemanu. They all have a king-size- or 2 queen-size beds, and 8 units have a plunge pool built over the water. The 2-bedroom beachfront villas and the 4 premium beachfront villas with 2 bedrooms have a private pool and 3,228 sq. ft. (300 sq. m.) of living space, with 1 king- and 2-queen-size beds. The 3-bedroom luxury beachfront villa has a private pool and 5,380 sq. ft. (500 sq. m.) of space. There are 2 king-size and 2 queen-size beds in this enormous villa. The one-of-a-kind Otemanu luxury beachfront villa with private pool has 2 king and 2 queen beds, 3 full marble bathrooms, plus powder room, and can sleep 6 adults. The outdoor area of this presidential villa encompasses 2,152 sq. ft. (200 sq. m.) of expansive decks, a swimming pool, whirlpool, and shaded lanais, with spectacular views of the lagoon and Mount Otemanu.

Inspired by local architecture, the guest quarters offer an airy restful ambience, complete with teak wood furnishings, Polynesian artwork, high ceilings, and thatched roofs made from pandanus leaves. The overwater bungalows have sliding doors beside the deep bathtubs for panoramic, fresh air views of the lagoon and some of the units have private plunge pools. Snorkeling gear with masks and life vests are available on the large private terrace, which has chaise lounges, lagoon access and an outdoor shower. The bungalows also have separate showers and a double vanity in the marble bathrooms. There are four large glass panels, including one in the floor looking down into the lagoon. Services and amenities in the a/c rooms include satellite TV with plasma screens, CD player, DVD player, clock radio with MP3 adapter, wired or wireless Internet access, multi-line telephones with voicemail, built in safe, refrigerated private bar, coffee/tea maker, thick terry bathrobes, hair dryer, L'Occitane bath amenities, hypo-allergenic pillows on request, iron and ironing board, and twice-daily housekeeping service along with bottled water. Self-service laundry facilities are located close to all overwater bungalows.

The resort's facilities include the Tere Nui, an open-air all-day restaurant, the Arii Moana gourmet specialty restaurant, the Fare Hoa Beach Bar and the Sunset Restaurant and Bar, plus 24/24 hr. In-Room dining service. (See information under *Where to Eat* in this chapter). The Kahaia Spa offers 7 a/c treatment rooms, steam rooms, a mineral whirlpool, and an overwater cabana for treatments under the sun or stars. (See *Massages and Spas* in this chapter). There is a small open-air fitness center with overwater sunrise yoga platform. The main infinity pool is 131-ft. (40 m.) long and shaped like a wave, with 5 cabanas and poolside food and beverage service. There is also a splash pad for the little guests in the supervised Kids Club area, and a Young Adult center and private beach for teens on Chill Island, complete with indoor and outdoor games and sports. (See *Taking the Kids* in Chapter 7). Guests can play beach volleyball, badminton and bocce ball. There are 2 tennis courts with night lights, all-weather surface, rackets and balls. A library with a good selection of books, CD's, DVD films and board games is also provided. Complimentary activities also include equipment for non-motorized water sports—kayaks, windsurfing equipment, paddle boards, stand-up paddle boards, snorkeling gear, kayaks and outrigger canoes. Scuba diving and kite-surfing lessons are also available at a surcharge, and many other lagoon excursions can be reserved through the activities desk or the concierge.

The Ruahatu (Polynesian God of the Ocean) Lagoon Sanctuary is a research facility at the Resort's inner lagoon and a haven for more than 100 colorful species of fish, eagle rays, octopus, sea anemones, shrimp and other marine life. On-site marine biologist Oliver Martin is available for complimentary snorkeling tours with guests, who can participate in feeding sessions and learn about Polynesian ecology and coral grafting.

The Four Seasons Resort Bora Bora has a heliport, and they also welcome guests at the Bora Bora airport upon their arrival and transport them to the hotel pier aboard a 40-passenger catamaran. The cost of this transfer is added to your hotel bill. Lagoon excursions can be organized aboard this shallow-draft catamaran, including stargazing cruises, wedding receptions or adventurous group activity. A complimentary round-trip shuttle between the Resort and Vaitape village is made each morning, and the dinner shuttle costs 3.000 CFP per person round-trip.

Other facilities at Four Seasons Resort Bora Bora include a business center and impressive pavilions for meetings or events. Should you wish to get married during your stay, their wedding specialist can assist in every detail. You can have the ceremony on the beach, on a private motu or in the wedding chapel. Wedding packages include the romantic Poe Here – Pearl of Love ceremony for 410.000 CFP. Contact the hotel for full information.

ST. REGIS RESORT & SPA, *B.P. 506, Bora Bora, 98730. Tel. 689/ 60.78.88; Fax 689/60.78.60; www.stregis.com/borabora; www.starwoodhotels.com/ stregis. On Motu Ome'e, facing Anau village. Mandatory round-trip airport transfers by private launch 7.500 CFP per person. All major credit cards.*

Just a few days after the St. Regis Resort opened on June 20, 2006, actress Nicole Kidman and her new husband, Keith Urban, were honeymooning in the resort's Royal Estate. This ultra luxurious 3-bedroom retreat has 13,000-sq. ft. (1,207 sq. m). At the same time, "Desperate Housewives" star Eva Longoria and her boyfriend (now ex-husband), NBS star Tony Parker, also checked into the St. Regis Resort for their own romantic holiday. These power celebrity couples thus launched the St. Regis Resort, putting it on the world map as the latest "in" spot for high profile guests and anyone else in search of a spare-no-expense high-end luxury experience. By Jan. 2007 the St. Regis was being named the "Best Resort in the World" by travel magazines. The American comedy "Couples Retreat" was filmed here in 2009, which increased the resort's popularity even more.

Following the devastating visit of Cyclone Oli in Feb. 2010, the St. Regis closed the hotel for 4 months, reopening in June with newly resigned landscaping, re-sanded beaches, new fish species and coral growth in the Private Lagoonarium, retiled pools, and many other updates to maintain the St. Regis legacy of unsurpassed luxury.

The St. Regis Resort features 91 lavish overwater and beach villas, built on a 44-acre (17.8-hectare) property on a long motu islet across the lagoon from the village of Anau. The lush landscaping is edged by the largest expanse of beach access in French Polynesia. Le Méridien Resort and Intercontinental Bora Bora Resort and Thalasso Spa are to the left of St. Regis and the Four Seasons Resort is on its right. All four resorts face Bora Bora's famous Otemanu Mountain and have the Pacific Ocean beyond the barrier reef at their back door.

St. Regis Resort Bora Bora boasts a number of firsts for French Polynesia, including 5 Royal Overwater 2-Bedroom Pool Villas with 3,455 sq. ft. and private swimming pools suspended over the lagoon. The 2 Royal Oceanfront Beach Villas each provide 2,852 sq. ft. and 2 bedrooms, plus an infinity pool. They also have access to a private helicopter pad. The Royal Estate is located on a secluded cove with 3 separate pavilions, with magnificent tropical gardens bordering its own private white sand beach. In addition to the 3 bedrooms, the Royal Estate also boasts 2 luxurious living rooms, a chef's kitchen, and a dining room with sunset terrace. It has a private pool and a private spa area with treatment room, sauna, steam bath and Jacuzzi.

The 8 Overwater Villas, 24 Superior Overwater and 32 Deluxe Overwater Villas each offers 1,550 sq. ft. The 8 Premier Overwater Villas have 1,905 sq. ft., a Jacuzzi and a covered gazebo complete with daybed. The 4 Pool Beach One Bedroom Villas have 1,636 sq. ft., separate living rooms, a private outdoor garden with exclusive shower and a plunge pool. The 7 Premier Oceanfront One Bedroom Pool Villas have 2,702 sq. ft. and an outdoor garden with plunge pool and direct access to the beach. Some of the villas face Bora Bora's main island and the Otemanu mountain, while others have a view of the inner lagoon. The units built over the water all have a glass floor under the coffee table for fish watching. All the accommodation designs are contemporary and showcase exotic woods and re-gional art. Each villa is a/c and has ceiling fans, light dimmers, mini bar, in-room safe, coffee and tea maker, iron/ironing board, snorkel gear, hair dryer and magnified makeup mirror. The bathrooms also contain a deep bathtub and a separate shower with an oversize rain nozzle and a hand-held nozzle. Guests are truly pampered with big containers of Acqua di Parma bath products and Pratesi linens for the heavenly king size beds. (Watch out for the protruding black base under the mattress to avoid shin bruises). There are 3 telephones with voicemail, and wireless high-speed Internet for your laptop hook-up, which costs 3.000 CFP a day. Internet access is also available in the library/lounge in the main building. Each villa also has two 42-in. plasma TV's, Bose DVD/CD players, and MP3 docking stations. The resort has a library of CD's and DVD films.

In addition to the twice-daily maid service, room service, guest relations and 24-hr. concierge staff, the St. Regis also offers the "legendary St. Regis Butler service". Your butler is supposed to ensure that everything is available at the touch of a button, from arranging a day of yachting and diving to dinner on a private island and even packing your suitcases on request.

Guests have a choice of 3 restaurants, including Lagoon, the resort's signature overwater restaurant, as well as Sushi Take and Te Pahu, the Mediterranean Grill that offers all day dining. The Aparima Pool Bar & Grill serves snacks and drinks throughout the day, and the Lagoon Bar is a favorite destination for sunset cocktails. Room service is available 24 hours a day. See information in *Where to Eat* in this chapter.

The resort's main pool has a swim-up bar and the romantic Oasis pool has 6 private day-bed cabanas, each with its own private plunge pool that you must reserve. You can have lunch and drinks here too. Other water activities include snorkeling in the resort's man made lagoon, reef fishing, deep-sea fishing and the island's only catch and release fly-fishing at the resort's private lagoonarium.

The Miri Miri Spa is a 13,000 sq. ft. world-class spa located on a private island within the resort's lagoon. It features Tahitian and Pacific Rim treatments in 7 treatment rooms. See information under *Massages & Spas*. There is also a state-of-the art fitness center adjacent to the Spa, with Technogym equipment, open 24/24. Tennis players will enjoy the floodlit tennis court. Other activities (some may have a surcharge) include bicycles to ride around Motu Ome'e, outrigger paddle canoes, kayaks, Hobie Cats, windsurfing, and snorkeling gear. Optional excursions can be arranged to discover Bora Bora by land, lagoon or air, and a shuttle boat service take guests from the resort to the main village of Vaitape, returning 1-2 hrs. later.

St. Regis Resort in Bora Bora offers couples an array of wedding options— whether an intimate barefoot event on a private motu, a traditional Tahitian ceremony, or a reception in the resort's secluded beachfront 1,600 sq. ft. event villa. The resort offers an onsite St. Regis Travel Specialist who is available to assist with all individual and group travel planning needs. Families can take advantage of St. Regis' Creativity Club, which provides supervised activities for children. See information in chapter on *Taking the Kids*.

BORA BORA NUI RESORT & SPA, *B.P. 502, Vaitape, Bora Bora 98730. Tel. 689/60.33.00; Fax 689/60.33.01. info@hilton-borabora.pf; www.hilton.com/ frenchpolynesia. On Motu Toopua, southeast of the main island of Bora Bora, 6 mi. from Motu Mute domestic airport. Round-trip airport transfers by private launch 7.500 CFP per person. All major credit cards.*

Since Jan. 2009 the Bora Bora Nui Resort & Spa has been operated by South Pacific Management under the Hilton franchise, replacing the former Starwood Hotels Luxury Collection. This 5-star hotel has 122 luxury villas and suites located on 16 acres of lush, terraced hillside and on the water of a private, protected cove. The white sand beach is 600 m (1,968 ft.) long, one of the longest hotel beaches on the island of Bora Bora. The spacious accommodations offer a choice of beach, hillside and overwater units with views of Motu Toopua, Mt. Otemanu on the main island of Bora Bora, or the infinity of sky and sea on the horizon. There are 16 Lagoon View Suites (1,076 sq. ft.), 11 Hillside Villas (969 sq. ft.), 9 Garden Villas (969 sq. ft.), 38 Overwater Villas (1,022 sq. ft.), 44 Overwater Deluxe Villas (1,022 sq. ft.), 2 Royal Overwater Villas (1,453 sq. ft.), with a Jacuzzi on the deck, and 2 Presidential Overwater Villas (3,229 sq. ft.) that are built on two levels with 3 bedrooms, a living room, well-being center, a swimming pool and Jacuzzi adjoining the sundeck. Accommodations include non-smoking rooms, 4 rooms for handicapped guests and 16 connecting rooms. These are some of the finest overwater suites in French Polynesia and the Bora Bora Nui is one of the most beautiful resorts in the world. It was selected among the Top 10 Hotels in the South Pacific for Romance and also for Relaxation & Spa in the TripAdvisor Travelers" Choice 2011. CNN.com ranked the Hilton Bora Bora Nui in 1st place for the Five Most Spectacular Overwater Hut Resorts in the world.

The meticulously planned decor in all units features a stylish Polynesian motif with rich, exotic woods (Indonesian yellow balau walls, mahogany furniture, merbau decks, and teak outdoor furniture), plus Polynesian and Asian shell chandeliers. Paintings by resident painters adorn the walls in the living room and bedroom, and woodcraft objects were created by local artists. Tapa covered sconces are fixed in the corners of the living room, tapa covered sliding doors lead to the bathroom and there is a tapa covered lamp on the desk in the bedroom. There is a king-size or 2 twin beds in the bedroom and a daybed-sofa in the living room, complete with very comfortable mattresses. In-room amenities include individual a/c, ceiling fan, CD player with tuner, DVD players, 2 plasma screen color TV's with satellite channels including CNN, 3 direct dial telephones with data ports, voice mail and Internet access, electronic safe, and a mini-bar that is set up to bill your room the instant you remove an item from its place. Inside a wall of closets and shelves are two sets of snorkeling gear, a basket table for breakfast in bed, two plastic raincoats, shoe polish, electronic safe, iron and board. The pink marble bathroom is huge and very well lit. The floor and walls are tiled and there are dressing counters and lavabos on two opposite walls. On one side there is a magnified lighted makeup mirror, hair-dryer and a generous supply of personal toiletries. On the other counter are two pots for making coffee and tea, along with the supplies. Underneath the counter is a bathroom scale. There is an oversize bathtub and a separate shower with an overhead showerhead with a soft spray and a hand held shower nozzle with a jet spray. The toilet and bidet are in a separate room.

In the overwater villas and suites fish and coral viewing panels are provided in the living room, bathroom and on the deck, which is partially covered with a thatched roof. All the outdoor furniture is teak and includes two padded lounge chairs, a teacart and table and two dining chairs. A ladder leads to a lower platform, where there is a shower. From there you can dive into the deep water or descend slowly on another ladder to snorkel among the fish and coral gardens in the lagoon.

Should you decide to spend your entire day in your villa, be assured there is 24-hour room service. You can order a Continental, American, Fitness or Japanese breakfast to be served in your room, and the romantic Canoe Breakfast can be delivered by outrigger canoe to the overwater villas. For special theme dinners see *Where to Eat* in this chapter.

The resort's public facilities are just as impressive as the bungalows. The overwater reception area is set in a natural aquarium. Among 600 coconut trees and hundreds of other palms, pandanus trees and tropical plants in the immense gardens and along the white sand beach there are 2 restaurants, 2 bars, a meeting room, library and computer room with free Internet access, a gift boutique, art gallery, Robert Wan Pearls boutique, a Hina Spa built on the hillside, and a beauty salon for facials, manicures and pedicures. On top of the hill is a lovely little wedding chapel with a fabulous panoramic view. Secretarial and other business services are available, as well a tour and travel desk, same day laundry service, 2-day dry-cleaning, daily maid service and nightly turndown service, baby-sitting, private boat transfers between the airport and resort, electric shuttle carts and a heliport. Complimentary shuttle boat service between the resort and Vaitape village operates almost hourly.

One of the special touches offered is the food and beverage service that is brought to guests anywhere they may be in the pool and beach area. This includes complimentary sliced fruit, homemade cookies and sorbet that can even be delivered to you while you are enjoying the 10,000 sq. ft. infinity-edge swimming pool. Other complimentary activities include snorkeling equipment, canoes, kayaks and Hobie cats, as well as billiards and backgammon in the lounge, use of the fully equipped fitness center, sauna and steam bath. The activities desk staff can help you arrange your optional excursions, which include a "Day in Paradise" barbecue picnic on Motu Tapu for 15.000 CFP per person, complete with lobster, wine and champagne. This exquisite little islet is the private domain of Bora Bora Nui Resort. Romantic dinners and ideas, wedding ceremonies and special honeymoon suggestions are available on request.

Prestige
INTERCONTINENTAL BORA BORA RESORT & THALASSO SPA, *B.P. 156, Bora Bora 98730. Tel. 689/60.76.00; Fax 689/60.76.99; res. 689/ 86.51.78; boraboraspa@intercontinental.pf; www.boraboraspa.intercontinental.com. 83 units. One-way airport transfers by private launch is 4.362 CFP per person. All major credit cards.*

This 5-star resort opened on May 1, 2006, between "the two hearts" of Motu Piti A'au, a coral islet on Bora Bora's barrier reef, across the lagoon from the village of Anau on the main island. Some say that the 2 rows of overwater bungalows resemble the claws of a crab. This eco-friendly resort is the first hotel in the world to use an air-conditioning system operating with deep sea water, which is 90% more energy efficient than electricity, and eliminates the use of potentially hazardous compounds that deplete the ozone layer and provoke climatic change. The Sea Water Air-Conditioning (SWAC) system pumps cold water (41°F, 5°C) from an ocean depth of 3,000 ft. (915 m.) to cool down the villas by thermic exchange. This is also the first luxury establishment to propose a deep sea water Thalasso center and Spa in the South Pacific.

Each of the 80 overwater villas contains 65 sq. m. (700 sq. ft.) of space indoors and 100 sq. m. (1,076 sq. ft.) counting the terrace. All units are the same except for their view. The 19 Emerald Overwater Villas have a view of the beach and motu, the 22 Sapphire Overwater Villas have a view of the lagoon, the 25 Diamond Overwater Villas have an extraordinary view of the main island of Bora Bora, the 6 Diamond Otemanu overwater villas have a perfect view of Mt. Otemanu and the lagoon, and the 8 End of Pontoon Villas have the best view of all. Each of the overwater units contains a living room with a glass-bottom coffee table for viewing the sea life in the lagoon, a separate bedroom with a walk-in dressing room, a large and bright bathroom with black slate floors and big tubs overlooking the lagoon. There is a large shaded terrace with sun lounges and table, plus a spacious bathing deck with exterior fresh water shower. The bedrooms are furnished with a king size bed convertible into twin beds if required and in the living room is a sofa with a pull-out trundle bed. In addition to the seawater a/c, there are also 2 ceiling fans, 2 flat screened TV's with cable/satellite TV, pay-per-view in-room movies, high end video equipment, CD and DVD players, stereo sound system, 2 IDD telephones with voice mail, high speed Internet and WiFi connection, work desk with lamp, electronic safety box, a fully stocked mini bar, complimentary tea and coffee facilities. The bathroom has a separate shower and bathtub and double sink, plus separate toilets. There is a hair dryer and a complimentary range of guest toiletries. Room service is available 24/24 and there is next day valet and laundry service. Butler service is also available on request. All the villas are decorated in a contemporary architecture with Polynesian accents that include traditional dance costumes on the walls. Three rooms have accessibility standards.

Since the hotel opened, 3 Motu Family Suites have been added that can sleep 5 people. The "Heremoana" is a beach or overwater Junior Suite with beds in the bungalows and lounge. "Poe Vai" is an Overwater Suite comprised of 2 Junior Suites linked by a lounge with 2 single beds.

The hotel also offers 1,000 feet of private white sand beach, a freshwater infinity pool, 2 restaurants and bars, 12 transit bungalows, conference facilities, business center, concierge, guest relations/activities desk, car rental desk, boutique, a Tahia pearl shop, a fitness and aerobic room, tennis court, and helicopter pad. There is even an on-site guest self-laundry with washing machine and dryer. Although the hotel's decor can be described as trendy—especially the all-white Bubbles Bar with Lucite ceiling fans that was inspired by Philippe Starck—their overwater wedding chapel can only be called romantic. The view from the picture window frames a perfect view of Bora Bora's famous Otemanu mountain, and a large glass floor lets you admire the tropical fish swimming below you.

Romantic ceremonies may be an intimate blessing on a white sandy beach, a renewal of vows in the Blue Lagoon Chapel or on the hotel beach, or a wedding ceremony on the beach or in the hotel's glass-bottom Chapel. These can be followed by wedding ccake, champagne and a bed of flowers in your villa. Contact the hotel directly for a list of all their Romantic and Amenities Ideas, Romantic Dinners, and Romantic Ceremonies.

A free boat shuttle service operates between the Intercontinental Bora Bora Resort & Thalasso Spa and the Intercontinental Moana Resort Bora Bora. This 15-min. shuttle begins at 7:45am and continues at regular intervals until 10:30pm. Other free activities include kayaks, outrigger paddle canoes, tennis, volley ball, snorkeling gear, pareo tying lessons and palm frond weaving. For a fee you can even take gourmet cooking classes from the hotel's French chef. Special evenings at the IC Thalasso include a French buffet dinner with a Polynesian dance show each Mon. evening, a Japanese buffet one night, and an Island World Tour Dinner with show on Fri. night. Also see information under *Where to Eat* and *Massages & Spas* in this chapter.

HOTEL LE MERIDIEN BORA BORA, *B.P. 190, Bora Bora 98730. Tel. 689/60.51.51; Fax 689/60.51.52. Reservations 689/47.07.29; Fax 689/47.07.28; rez@lemeridien-tahiti.pf; www.lemeridien.com/borabora. 99 units. All major credit cards.*

With more than 1 km (.6 mi.) of white sand beach, accessible only by a 20-min. boat ride from the airport or 5 min. by boat from the main island of Bora Bora, Le Méridien covers more than 23.5 acres (9.5 ha) on Motu Tape, an islet across the lagoon from the village of Anau. This hotel opened in June 1998 and was the first international class hotel to be built on this chain of offshore islets. Today, the Intercontinental Bora Bora Resort & Thalasso Spa is on its left, and neighbors on the right are the St. Regis Resort & Spa and the Four Seasons Resort. In late 2005 the Le Méridien group was acquired by Starwood Hotels & Resorts and a big renovation project improved the bungalows and public buildings on the property. In 2009 the resort created a new class of accommodations, with 4 pool beach villas featuring 8x16 ft. pools connecting two existing beach bungalows. With breath-taking views of the interior lagoon and Otemanu Mountain, the new villas are ideal for families, and they have direct access to the interior lagoon for snorkeling and swimming in the Turtle Sanctuary. These renovations also included the remodeling of the premium overwater bungalows, giving them unobstructed views of Otemanu Mountain. A glass-bottomed overwater wedding chapel, a new infinity swimming pool on the main beach, and a new fitness center were also added. After closing 4 months for a major upgrade in 2010, the hotel reopened in Jan. 2011, with all beach and overwater bungalows featuring sleek, modern interiors. The bungalows, as well as the restaurants, bars and other public spaces now have a new pandanus thatched roof. The enhancements also include new teak wood docks leading to the overwater bungalows. The restaurants and bars were restyled with new fabrics, and the front desk and other public areas also received new contemporary lighting, fabrics and furniture.

Le Méridien Bora Bora has 59 bungalows and 22 premium bungalows built over the lagoon. These overwater units consist of a large bedroom with a sitting area, a walk-in closet and a spacious bathroom. There is also a partially covered outside deck and steps leading into the lagoon. Instead of the standard glass table that allows you to watch the fish in the lagoon underneath the overwater bungalows, Le Méridien has gone a step further and built a large glassed surface into the polished wood floor. The 6 beach bungalows, 4 beach suites and 4 beach villas with pools are adjacent to a shallow interior lagoon. The pool beach villas have 2 bedrooms and a living room overlooking a private terrace, plus a Jacuzzi and swimming pool. The 3 lagoon bungalows are located over the channel of the interior lagoon and they have no glass bottom floor. There are 4 handicap accessible bungalows and 1 lagoon bungalow is being used as the "Espace Bien-Etre" Spa. An a/c transit room has 4 private shower rooms.

All the resort's bungalows are built with natural materials of pandanus-thatched roofs and precious kohu wood, which is dark and heavy, similar to teak. Each bungalow has a/c and a ceiling fan, and they are furnished with a king-size bed or two twin beds. There is also a sofa bed, a big desk with a recessed make-up mirror, blackout curtains, cable/satellite flat-screen television, video on request, CD player, a mini-bar fridge, international direct dial telephone with Internet access, personal safe, and coffee and tea facilities. The bathroom contains two lavabos, a bathtub and separate shower, private toilet, a full-length mirror, magnified makeup mirror, and hair dryer. The premium overwater bungalows are located at the end of the deck with a direct view of Bora Bora's famous mountains. They also have a large balcony where you can have lunch or sunbathe while admiring the view in between your swims in the translucent lagoon, which is 13-20 ft. deep here. These units also have a DVD player.

The boat-shaped central building houses the reception area, activities desk, the Miki Miki Bar, boutique, lending library and a game room with billiards table. In the a/c lounge are modern computers for guests to use at no charge. Free WiFi is also available in the lobby and public areas, but you pay for this service in your bungalow.

Breakfast and dinner are served in the restaurant Le Tipanie that offers a close-up view of the private lagoon, complete with hungry fish looking for a handout. Le Tiare also overlooks the interior lagoon and features a refined cuisine. The chef caters to the taste preferences of the hotel guests, who are primarily French, Italian, American and Japanese, providing international and local cuisine. Lunch is served at Le Te Ava, a beachside restaurant where the atmosphere is informal and friendly. The Miki Miki bar serves cocktails and Fare Tupa beach snack serve light meals and liquid refreshments. See information under *Where to Eat* in this chapter. Room service is available 24 hrs. a day, with a limited menu between 10pm and 6am, and you can even order picnic baskets to take with you while exploring the delights of the beautiful white sand beach and aquamarine waters of Bora Bora's incredible lagoon.

The choices of activities and excursions available at Le Méridien include the fresh water swimming pool, free snorkeling equipment, beach volley, badminton, ping-pong, pedal boats, windsurf boards, kayaks and Polynesian outrigger canoes. You can join the Kainalu Canoe Club and go sailing in a traditional dugout canoe built in Hawaii. Or you can rent a 14-ft. Hobie Cat.

As part of their ever-expanding family friendly program, the hotel management has added a fully equipped children's playground. They provide small snorkeling gear for kids from 2 years old, small cha-cha sailboats and a small windsurf board that an 8-year old can handle. An exclusive treat for guests of all ages at Le Méridien is to visit the Turtle Observatory at the inner lagoon on the hotel property, where you can watch dozens of baby sea turtles being fed at 10:30 each morning. You can even swim with the turtles inside the clear waters of a *hoa* channel that flows from the ocean into the lagoon. A new Ecological Center has been built near the Turtle Sanctuary, and a French biologist explains that the hawksbill and green sea turtle eggs are hatched on the hotel's beach and the turtles are released from the nursery into the ocean a year later, then tracked by satellite as part of an environmental program. The ecological center is a joint effort with Le Méridien and the island's Ministry and Delegation of the Environment meant to assure a vibrant future for sea turtles and to provide educational programs for guests and local residents.

Honeymoon couples from Japan and other countries have their formal wedding ceremony in Bora Bora filmed in the romantic little chapel built over the lagoon. Some of these couples have already been legally married in their country. Others choose to make their wedding vows at the Bora Bora Mairie (town hall). Non-binding Polynesian Wedding Ceremonies are performed on the beach at Le Méridien on request. For further details you should contact the hotel directly.

BORA BORA PEARL BEACH RESORT, *B.P. 169, Bora Bora 98730. Tel. 689/60.52.00; Fax 689/60.52.22; reception@boraborapearlbeach.pf; www.spmhotels.com; www.spmhotels.pf; Reservations: Tel. 689/50.84.45; Fax 689/43.17.86; res@spmhotels.pf. 80 bungalows. All major credit cards.*

This 5-star resort is a member of The Leading Small Hotels of the World and has earned a well-deserved reputation as a honeymoon and family resort since it opened in June 1998. Among its many awards is the 2011 TripAdvisor Certificate of Excellence. This well-maintained property is located on 47 acres (19 ha) of land between the ocean and lagoon on Motu Tevairoa, facing Faanui Bay and the famous Otemanu mountain of Bora Bora. It is a 10-min. boat ride from the airport and a 15-min. boat ride to the main village of Vaitape. The entire hotel is built in the traditional Polynesian style, with pandanus thatched roofs, local woods, woven pandanus wall coverings and a decor that includes tapa wall hangings and paintings and sculptures by Polynesian artists.

There are 20 overwater bungalows, 30 premium overwater bungalows, 10 beach suites with Jacuzzi, and 20 garden pool suites. All units have a/c as well as ceiling fans, a well-stocked refrigerated mini-bar, coffee and tea making facilities, hair dryer, safety box, iron and table, magnifying mirror, 20" LCD satellite television with DVD player, CD player, and IDD telephones in the bedroom and separate toilets. There are twin beds or a king size bed and a day bed in each unit, as well as writing desks and reading lights. Amenities include a wide range of Manea toiletries.

Honeymooners prefer the overwater bungalows that are classified as premium because they offer the best views of the mountain and lagoon. These attractively decorated units have 658 sq. ft. (61 sq. m) of living space, with a glass bottom table and glass windows in the bathroom to observe more than 70 species of fish that have settled and developed in the To'a Nui coral nursery beside these bungalows. This park also has a colony of 4,000 corals that are regenerating in perfect ecological conditions. (See information on To'a Nui Coral Nursery in *Other Ways to Discover Bora Bora's Marine World* in this chapter). All the overwater units have a bathtub and a separate shower, as well as Internet outlets. Guests staying in the overwater bungalows may also have the pleasure of their breakfast being delivered by outrigger canoe for 12.000 CFP per couple.

The very popular beach suites provide 786 sq. ft. (73 sq. m) of living space and have an indoor-outdoor bathroom with a full shower in a tropical garden, and a private enclosed sundeck with a Jacuzzi. The a/c bedroom can be completely closed off, and anyone sitting or sleeping in the living room, which has a day bed, will have the benefit of a ceiling fan but no a/c. The premium and garden pool suites provide 872 sq. ft. (81 sq. m) of living space, which is great for families. There is a gazebo type shelter with a table and benches, a sundeck with 2 lounge chairs, a private plunge pool and a small tropical garden. A privacy fence surrounds this area and another wall protects the covered shower in the garden adjoining the bathroom. The bedroom can be closed off from the bathroom to take full advantage of the a/c.

Three overwater bungalows are well equipped for wheelchairs and the hotel has wide cement paths and easily accessible public areas. There is an elevator in the main building, from the reception area to the restaurant and bar upstairs, a disabled access toilet in the main building and a changing room for disabled guests at the Manea Spa.

The hotel has 3 restaurants, 2 bars, a boutique and pearl shop, movie theater/conference center/computer room with paid Internet access, lending library, a fresh water swimming pool and Jacuzzi, a/c fitness center, day-use bungalows, heliport, floodlit tennis court, mini golf, table tennis, volley ball court and bocce ball court, billiards, and a wide variety of optional activities and excursions. Hotel guests have free use of the snorkeling equipment, outrigger paddle canoes, kayaks, windsurf boards, competition canoe, Ping Pong, bocci ball, badminton and society games. On-site are the Blue Nui Dive Center and Manea Spa, both of which are top-rated in French Polynesia. See further information under *Where to Eat, Scuba Diving* and *Massages & Spas* in this chapter. A complimentary shuttle boat service is operated daily, with 19 departures from the hotel to the land base at the Pahia commercial center on the main island and 18 return crossings. A free bus service will take you between the land base and the Vaitape town center four times a day Mon.-Sat. The boat transfers between the airport and the hotel are 3.000 CFP per person one-way.

The Bora Bora Pearl Beach Resort & Spa is a favorite destination for honeymooners and other lovers who appreciate the romantic setting of this hotel. To make those moments together even more magical, you can have a non-binding wedding ceremony performed in the little wedding chapel or Polynesian style on the beach. Contact the hotel directly for a list of Romantic Welcomes, Romantic Interludes and Romantic Escapades.

This is also a family resort that allows free accommodations for children under 15 years old who are sharing a room with their parents and according to the existing bedding configuration. Transfers are free, as well as their meals ordered from the kids' menu. Children facilities include candies upon arrival, bathroom or beach toys, according to age group, and snorkeling equipment and life jackets are available for children.

Moderate

BLUE HEAVEN ISLAND, *B.P. 751, Bora Bora 98730. Tel. 689/72.42.11; eliealain@gmail.com; www.blueheavenisland.com. Free airport transfers. No credit cards.*

This private motu near the airport in Bora Bora is owned and operated by Monique LaVoie and Alain Elie, and it is a regular destination for scuba divers, yoga groups, corporate treats and family gatherings. The 5 comfortable Polynesian style bungalows are scattered throughout a tropical garden and are built of indigenous bamboo, thatched roof and shoji screens. Each unit contains a king or queen-size bed or 2 twin beds, with a mosquito net overhead. They have large closets, ceiling fans, bamboo furniture and colorful island accents. Solar energy provides lighting and hot water. There is a common living room outdoors and waterside lounging areas, a pontoon and kayaks for guest use. Meals and other activities are extra.

Other Lodgings on the Motu Islets

Bora Bora Eden Beach Hotel, *Tel. 689/60.57.60; Fax 689/67.69.76; borabora@mail.pf; www.boraborahotel.com.* A 12-bungalow eco-tourist hotel on Motu Piti A'au, a 15-minute boat ride across the lagoon from Anau village. This hotel has a fabulous view of Otemanu mountain and is favored by tourists who want to be on a motu without paying the cost of a 5-star hotel. Bring mosquito repellent and understand that you'll be taking care of yourself as there is no staff. The owner cooks the meals, which are reputedly very good.

WHERE TO EAT

Hotel Restaurants on the Main Island

INTERCONTINENTAL BORA BORA LE MOANA RESORT, *Tel. 60.49.00. All major credit cards.*

Noa Noa Restaurant and Terrace. *Open daily for breakfast, lunch and dinner.* A Continental breakfast is 2.743 CFP and a full American breakfast is 3.363 CFP. A Canoe breakfast delivered to your overwater bungalow is 7.416 CFP per person. A 2-course set luncheon is 3.800 CFP. Light snacks are served on the Vini Vini Bar Terrace for lunch and the *a la carte* dinner menu in the Noa Noa Restaurant lists hot and cold appetizers for 1.950 CFP, delectable choices from the Chinese Corner for 2.280 CFP, fresh lagoon and deep ocean fish and seafood dishes for 2.900 CFP, meat and poultry selections for 3.290 CFP, spiny lobster for 5.720 CFP, surf and turf (lobster and beef filet) for 4.980 CFP, and vegetarian dishes for 2.100 CFP. A 3-course set dinner is 7.120 CFP. A lavish seafood buffet under the stars is served each Sat. evening, during the *Soirée Merveilleuse* (marvelous evening), followed by a Polynesian dance show on the beach. The cost is 8.785 CFP. Special theme evenings also include a Tues. night Barbecue Buffet and Polynesian night on Thurs., with traditional foods and local entertainment.

The **Vini Vini Bar** has special cocktails and live music in the bar at sunset and during dinner in the Noa Noa Restaurant.

LE MAITAI POLYNESIA, *Tel. 60.30.00. All major credit cards.*

Haere Mai Restaurant, *in main building of Le Maitai Polynesia. Open daily for breakfast and dinner during high tourist season. May be closed at certain times of the year.*

An American breakfast buffet is served each morning for 2.576 CFP. Depending on the time of year a Seafood & Polynesian Specialties Buffet with a Tahitian dance show is presented once a week. The dinner menu on other nights features international cuisine with a French touch, such as dry ham or lobster stew, mahi mahi with vanilla sauce, and duck filet with orange caramel sauce. Starter courses are 1.360-1.995 CFP, fish is 2.240-2.630 CFP, meats are 2.190-2.890 CFP, and desserts are 1.010-1.210 CFP.

Tama'a Maitai Restaurant, on beach at Hotel Le Maitai Polynesia. Open daily with non-stop service from 11:30am-9pm. When the Haere Mai Restaurant is closed during certain seasons, the Tama'a Matai is open non-stop daily from 6am-9pm.

This is a big open sided restaurant with a thatch roof, situated between the road and beach in the Matira area. The burger bar atmosphere is very casual, with indoor/outdoor seating. Burgers are served on sesame buns and are good, priced 1.460-1.670 CFP, including fries. Burritos are 1.670 CFP, pizzas are 1.170-1.470 CFP, sashimi is 1.840 CFP, and a salad bar is served during lunch and dinner hours for 2.200 CFP, a T-bone steak is 2.885 CFP and grilled lobster is 3.990 CFP. There are daily specials for around 1.990 CFP. You can also order fresh fruit juices, a glass of beer or house wine, or a bottle of wine.

The **Manuia Bar** in the hotel lobby is open daily 5:30-10:30pm, and the **Beach Bar** is open daily from 9:30am-5:30pm.

SOFITEL BORA BORA MARARA BEACH & PRIVATE ISLAND, *Tel. 60.55.00. All major credit cards.*

On the Beach Side:

Latitude 16° is the hotel's main restaurant, serving B., L., D. in a pleasant decor that was inspired by tribal tattoos, with ironworks representing the local fishermen's nets. You can also dine on the terrace overlooking the lagoon. The only so-so meals feature international and local cuisine, with numerous theme evenings organized throughout the week and on weekends. Tapas are served on Sat.

La Suite, *Tel. 67.60.60, is open from 6-10pm on Mon., Tues., Thurs. and Sun.* This is the hotel's gastronomic restaurant in a chic, modern setting. French chef Nicolas Falcoz creates la nouvelle cuisine for gourmands and others who remember his refined dishes at the former La Matira Restaurant, where he worked for 5 years.

Le Snack offers a menu of healthy salads, burgers or fresh sandwiches for a casual meal served to you beside the pool.

Hurricane Bar was named for the famous Dino De Laurentiis movie filmed in Bora Bora in the mid-1970s. The bar is inlaid with red and silver mosaic tiles and sparkling mirrored lights to complement the red-cushioned chairs. Open daily from 10am-11pm, and live entertainment includes Polynesian shows several nights a week. They carry an extensive selection of cigars.

On the Private Island:

Manu Tiki Restaurant. *Open daily for B., D.* This restaurant is built on stilts on the hilltop of a motu, granting spectacular views of Bora Bora and its famous lagoon and mountains. The cuisine is French with a Polynesian accent and has earned a good reputation for quality. This cave has one of the most extensive wine lists in the region and cigars are also available.

Mako Bar *is open from 10am-11pm.* This lounge-bar overlooks the lagoon on the sunset side. Happy Hour daily. Enjoy after dinner drinks on the outdoor terrace or head to the cozy cigar cave. Picnic boxes, snacks and ice cream are also available.

Room service is available during meal hours for guests staying at either the Beach or the Private Island.

Hotel Restaurants on the Motu

FOUR SEASONS RESORT, *Tel. 60.31.30. All major credit cards.*

Tere Nui, *open daily for B.,L.,D.* This open-air thatched-roof all-day restaurant is adjacent to the beach facing Mt. Otemanu, with plantation-style ceiling fans adding to the airy comfort of the sea breezes. Breakfast is served from *6:30-11am*, presenting an opulent buffet of fresh fruit, fresh baked goods, an omelet station and other favorites, such as pineapple caramelized pancakes served with mango and papaya purée. Lunch is served from *11am-5pm* and dinner is from *6:30-9:30pm*, offering tempting choices of salads, burgers, wraps, tempura, shrimp curry, roast tuna and grilled lobster. Weekly themed dinners include Mediterranean night, which features a made-to-order pasta bar, and BBQ night.

Arii Moana, *open 6:30-9:30pm daily for dinner.* Offering romantic views of Bora Bora's lagoon and Mt. Otemanu beyond, this is the Resort's specialty restaurant, where you can dine indoors or outdoors on the terrace beside the water. The menu creations highlight the combination of Polynesian and French cuisine, accompanied by a good bottle of wine. Appetizers start you off with pan-fried foie gras served with kumquat chutney, passion fruit, and coconut shooter. Or you may prefer snow crab seasoned with lime and olive oil, herbs Tabbouleh, mango and coffee vinaigrette. Follow up with New Caledonian shrimp with vanilla oil, celery and sweet potato, with zucchini pesto. There is also spiced Australian rack of lamb, oriental style vegetables, and date purée with lime, and Black Angus beef fillet, plus Love to Share desserts.

Faré Hoa Beach Bar is adjacent to the main pool and is *open daily 10am-5pm.* You can enjoy a lunch of fresh salads, sandwiches, desserts or light snacks while relaxing in your pool cabana.

Sunset Restaurant Bar is *open daily from 4-11pm*, and is the place to be during that magical time of day when the tropical sun dips behind the horizon. The menu features freshly prepared sushi and other Asian-inspired dishes, plus cocktails with a unique twist.

In-Bungalow Dining is available 24 hours a day, and you can choose your meals from an extensive menu. Dining Experiences feature Taurua Romantic Dinners for two served in your bungalow or on the beach.

ST REGIS RESORT & SPA, *Tel. 60.78.88. All major credit cards.*

Te Pahu is the Mediterranean Grill beside the beach with all-day dining for B., L., D. Closed Thurs. night. The young French wait staff provide very attentive service. You can choose a Continental breakfast, a Healthy breakfast or an American breakfast. Or you can order à la carte. Luncheon choices include B.L.T. for 2.300 CFP, burgers with salad, fries, seasonal vegetables or fresh potato purée for 2.700 CFP, poisson cru for 2.900 CFP, a pizza for 3.300 CFP, or a grilled Wagyu flank steak for 4.800 CFP. Desserts are 1.700 CFP. The dinner specialties are the citrus shrimp ceviche, grilled tuna with herbs, swordfish confit in olive oil, roasted lamb with crusted black olives and Kobe sirloin. Healthy and vegetarian suggestions are also available. Theme dinners include Mediterranean dishes on Sun., a Polynesian dinner with dance show on Wed., and a lobster dinner on Fri.

Lagoon is the signature restaurant of the internationally acclaimed Chef Jean-Georges Vongerichten. This overwater restaurant features a limited but frequently changing menu of French and Asian influenced cuisine, using the freshest fish and ingredients indigenous to the islands. Try the bacon-wrapped shrimp with passion fruit mustard or the spiced chicken with coconut-caramel sauce and citrus salad. Appetizers and salads are 3.100-3.600 CFP and the main courses are 4.000-5.500 CFP, with desserts at 2.000 CFP. The wine cellar contains an awarded selection of fine wines spanning the old and new world. Open for dinner only.

Sushi Take is the sushi and sake restaurant at St. Regis. Salads are 900-2.600 CFP, sashimi is 4.000-4.500 CFP and sushi is 3.500-4.000. A Sushi Take combo of seaweed salad, sashimi and sushi is 9.600 CFP.

Aparima Pool Bar & Grill serves snacks and drinks throughout the day, and some guests take all their meals here. The **Lagoon Bar**, built over the water adjacent to Lagoon Restaurant, is a favorite destination for sunset cocktails. Try the Ginger Margarita or Pomelo-Mint Mojito and you'll surely want another one.

BORA BORA NUI RESORT & SPA, *Tel. 60.33.00. All major credit cards.*

Tamure Grill is open daily for B.L.D. This big open sided restaurant with a thatched roof and a floor of white sand is located next to the swimming pool and white sand beach. A Continental or American breakfast buffet starts the day. The luncheon menu includes burgers for 2.000 CFP, salads, poisson cru and tartars for 1.400-2.400 CFP, and pizza from 1.900 CFP. Tamure Snacks are also available at the Ta'ie'ie Beach Bar, which is at one end of the Tamure Grill. The Tamure grill is also open nightly for dinner from 6:30-9:30pm. The main courses are 2.100-2.500 CFP, and the chef's specialties include a Thai style chicken style skewer for

2.100 CFP. A Polynesian Island buffet is held on Tues. night for 8.500 CFP and includes entertainment by a Tahitian dance group at 8:30pm.

Iriatai is open for dinner nightly from 6-9:30pm. This panoramic restaurant is on the upper level of the central building. The Iriatai features a fusion menu with Polynesian, Pacific-Rim and Mediterranean influences. Starter courses are 1.800-2.700 CFP, fish and seafood dishes are 3.400-3.800 CFP, and meats are 3.200-4.500 CFP. Desserts are 1.600-1.750 CFP, and a composition of 5 desserts is 1.950 CFP. You can order wines from Napa Valley, California, New Zealand, Australia, South Africa, Chile, Italy, Rangiroa in the Tuamotu Islands, and all the wine producing regions of France. In addition to an impressive list of Grands Crus from Bordeaux, there is also a good selection of French champagnes available.

A pianist plays popular tunes in the **Upa Upa Bar** adjacent to the Iriatai to enhance the romantic atmosphere while you sip your after dinner *digestif.*

Room Service is available 24/24.

INTERCONTINENTAL BORA BORA RESORT & THALASSO SPA, *Tel. 60.76.00. All major credit cards.*

Le Reef Restaurant & Terrace. Open daily for breakfast and dinner. You can dine in a/c comfort or sit outside on the patio that overlooks the white sand beach and lagoon. A Continental breakfast is 2.743 CFP and an American breakfast is 3.363 CFP. A Romantic Canoe Breakfast with a half-bottle of champagne is 9.211 CFP, and a Romantic Breakfast served on the beach is 8.667 CFP, including a half-bottle of champagne. A 2-course set lunch is 3.800 CFP and a 3-course set dinner menu is 7.120 CFP. The MAP rate is 10.483 CFP and AP is 14.283 CFP. A Japanese buffet is 7.120 CFP. The French buffet on Mon. night and the Island World Tour Dinner each Friday cost 7.120 CFP, and include a Polynesian show. The à la carte menu for Le Reef includes a few vegetarian dishes, such as cucumber gazpacho married with "fromage blanc" ice cream, raspberry and tomato bruschetta. Among the appetizers you'll find seared foie gras served with dried fruit crumble and hibiscus flower sauce, for 2.950 CFP. A spoon of Aquitaine "Perlita" French caviar can be added at an extra charge of 2.390 CFP. The meat selections include "Wagyu" beef filet tournedos with apple fritter and meat stock, for 4.520 CFP.

Sand's Bar & Restaurant is built beside the resort's private 1,000 ft. of white sand beach, providing the perfect rendezvous for light meals between 11am-9:30pm, as well as snacks and exotic cocktails. A pizza or a steak sandwich with fries is 2.220 CFP, fish dishes are 3.200 CFP, a whole lobster is 6.910 CFP, and mean dishes start at 3.420 CFP. Desserts are 1.400 CFP.

Bubble's Bar & Terrace is the ultra trendy bar designed all in white for the resort's Japanese tourists. There's music every night but very few people. Drinks, exotic cocktails and light snacks are served from 10am-11pm.

HOTEL LE MERIDIEN BORA BORA, *Tel. 60.51.51. All major credit cards.*

Le Tipanie Restaurant, *open daily 7-10:30am for breakfast and 6:30-9:30pm for dinner.*

You can feed the fish in the interior lagoon while dining in this "Lagoon" side restaurant, where you can choose your favorite dishes from the buffet tables. The themes change each evening and may present a French buffet, Pacific buffet, Barbecue buffet, Asian buffet, Fisherman's buffet, Latino buffet, or a Mediterranean buffet. Polynesian shows are presented frequently.

Tiare Restaurant, *open daily 7-9:30pm for dinner. Must reserve.*

This is the "Laguna" side of the restaurant where diners choose their gourmet meals from a frequently changing menu that always includes some imaginative vegetarian dishes. To accompany these epicurean dinners you can order from an interesting list of wines from France, Chile, Australia and California.

Te Ava Restaurant, *open daily 10:30am-9:30pm for B.,L,D.*

Le Méridien's beachside restaurant Te Ava is adjacent to the fresh water swimming pool. In this relaxing atmosphere you can sit in a rocking chair and dig your toes into the white sand floor while enjoying your lunch. You can have a late Continental breakfast here. Lunch and dinner choices consist of salads, sandwiches, burgers, pasta, and pizzas, supplemented by grilled meats and seafood. Draft beer and wine by the glass or bottle are available.

Fare Tupa, *open daily 10am-5pm.*

This beach bar and snack serves Continental breakfast from 10-11:30am, and sandwiches, fresh drinks and ice cream from 10:30am-5pm.

Miki Miki Bar, *open from 3-11pm.*

This friendly bar is shaped like the prow of a ship, pointing toward Mt. Otemanu, providing a good setting for sunset and cocktails.

BORA BORA PEARL BEACH RESORT, *Tel. 60.52.00. All major credit cards.*

Tevairoa Restaurant is the hotel's main dining room, which sits 20 ft. (6 m) above sea level and overlooks the myriad hues of the blues and greens of the Bora Bora lagoon. It is open for breakfast and dinner, serving a refined international menu. An American breakfast buffet is 3.300 CFP. International dining with a French flair is featured for dinner, with à la carte selections or a 3-course set dinner menu for 6.500 CFP. A Polynesian buffet and dance show is presented each Mon. evening for 7.300 CFP, and a seafood buffet and dance show is held on Fri. for 7.900 CFP.

Miki Miki Restaurant and Bar is located beside the swimming pool, and is open daily for lunch. This is a great place to hang out during a hot tropical day, sipping cold Hinano pression beer and munching on cheeseburgers, club sandwiches, poisson cru, fish and chips, or grilled sirloin steak. Most of the guests sitting at the friendly bar or at the tables on the terrace are American honeymooners or young French families with children. The atmosphere here is very casual. A 2-course set luncheon menu is 4.000 CFP.

Fare Ambrosia, behind the Miki Miki Restaurant, features Italian specialties and is open nightly except Mon. & Fri. Open 6-9pm for dinner only and reservations are required.

Taurearea Bar upstairs is open daily 3:30-11pm, providing the perfect setting to admire the sunset as you gaze at the peaks of Otemanu and Pahia mountains. Happy Hour is held from 5:30-6:30pm, featuring Polynesian cocktails at half-price. Live music in the evenings.
Room Service is available 24/24.

Private Restaurants on the Main Island – Deluxe

LA VILLA MAHANA, *Tel./Fax 67.50.63; damien@villamahana.com; www.villamahana.com. On the mountainside between Vaitape village and the Hotel Bora Bora. Open Mon.-Sat. for dinner only. Free pick-up service. Reserve by email 2-3 months in advance. AE, MC, V.*

A young Corsican chef de cuisine named Damien Rinaldi Dovio opened this gastronomic restaurant in April 2004 and it became an immediate success. Residents and tourists alike must reserve months in advance during the high seasons, and when they leave the restaurant in a dreamy state of contentment, their comments in the guest book and by word of mouth are full of praise. This is indeed a unique experience that you do not want to miss when you visit Bora Bora, because people say that Damien, who studied at the prestigious Institut Paul Bocuse in Lyon, France, served them the best meal they have ever eaten. I highly recommend this restaurant as my favorite dining place in French Polynesia.

There are six small tables on the courtyard patio or inside the restaurant during rainy weather. The walls and gardens of this area are decorated with the bright, colorful paintings of Bora Bora artist Gigi and the Polynesian sculptures of JC. Another table for private dining is upstairs over the restaurant in the Tahitian room, which also has a couch. There is a small reflecting pool on the terrace. Damien will close the restaurant for private parties of up to 12 people.

Damien comes out of his kitchen to greet his guests, with a special smile for young honeymooners who dined here just a few nights ago. The gourmet menu features light cuisine influenced by Damien's origins, combined with Polynesian products and associated with the use of spices to magnify the flavors. He suggests several tempting à la carte menus, but his piece de resistance gives you a choice of a Polynesian or European menu. The Epicurean Experience begins with a light salad of shellfish and caviar on toast, followed by seared duck foie gras with sweet spices. The next course is king rock lobster risotto, followed by roasted beef tenderloin cooked in red wine and vanilla sauce, served with creamy gnocchi. Dessert for this feast is molten lava cake with a creamy chocolate sauce and Tahitian vanilla ice cream. The Exotic Menu includes seared ahi tuna with vanilla oil, Mahi Mahi curry and other marvelous taste treats that will tempt you to come back for more.

Damien also proposes a wine tasting menu to accompany his special menus. His impressive wine list includes Cristal rosé and Dom Perignon champagnes. Starting your evening with a glass of champagne seems a most fitting touch in this ambience of intimate hospitality. Should you go high end with the special menus, expect to pay up to $400 per couple, depending on your choice of wines. Damien's gourmet cuisine and the romantic atmosphere of Villa Mahana are worth it.

Superior
SAINT JAMES RESTAURANT, *Tel. 67.64.62. On waterfront in Helen's Bay Center. Open for lunch and dinner Mon.-Sat. Closed Sun. AE, MC, V. Free pick-up for dinner. Reserve.*
    This restaurant opened in Sept. 2007 in the building that was formerly La Pirate, and quickly became one of the most popular dining spots on the island. The French owners have remodeled and redecorated, placing tables and chairs beside the bay where guests can watch the magnificent Bora Bora sunsets as well as the manta rays that come to play in the evenings. Light lunches are served and the dinner menu features homemade foie gras as an appetizer. Main courses consist of fresh local products prepared French style with an emphasis on fish and seafood dishes, as well as excellent duck and beef selections. They also have a good wine list. There are 2 moorings for boats in front of the restaurant.
    BLOODY MARY'S, *Tel. 67.72.86; www.bloodymarys.com. On the mountainside in Pofai Bay, 5 km (3 mi.) from Vaitape. Open for lunch and dinner Mon.-Sat. and on boat days. Bar open 9:30am-11pm. Closed Sun. AE, MC and V. Free dinner transportation is provided from select locations.*
    Most American visitors feel they haven't seen Bora Bora unless they have been to this world famous restaurant and bar. A long list of celebrities who have dined at Bloody Mary's is posted beside the road, adding to the legend that began when the restaurant opened in June 1980. This is the kind of funky and fun place where people get to know one another very easily. You can't be too reserved while you are sitting on a tree stump at the bar under a huge thatched roof or wiggling your toes in the white sand floor while eating your dinner. Be sure to check out the surprise in the men's room that keeps most of the young clients in giggles throughout the evening.
    Appetizers start at 1.500 CFP, and include grilled shrimp, garlic crab, charred peppered sashimi, teriyaki fish kabob, and the house specialty, a very tender calamari steak that is breaded and sautéed in capers and white wine. Dinner time is show time, with an impressive selection of seafood, chicken and meats displayed on a bed of ice for your viewing and choosing pleasure. Fresh lagoon or deep ocean fish are priced around 3.000 CFP. Fresh local lobster is 8.000 CFP and a surf and turf combo is 7.500 CFP. New Zealand beef may be rib eye steak, New York strip steak or babyback ribs, for 3.000 CFP. You can also order a vegetarian plate. The main courses are accompanied by green salad, white rice, hot vegetables and fresh fruit. The dessert menu includes sumptuous coconut pie.
    Lunch is served between 11am and 3pm, which includes great burgers, including the Jimmy Buffet Cheeseburger in Paradise for 1.100 CFP. They also have salads, chicken quesadillas, a Reuben sandwich, fish and chips, and deep fried shrimp. Appetizers are served at the Tupa Bar between 3-9pm, which definitely

should be accompanied by the house's special drink, a Bloody Mary, which is only 650 CFP. They also serve cold draft Hinano, a good choice of wines, and an excellent frozen Margarita or Bloody Mary's Maitai.

Be sure to visit Bloody Mary's website to learn all about this fabulous restaurant and the people who work there. On this site you can read my stories that were written for the *Tahiti Beach Press*, recounting the celebrations for Bloody Mary's 30th anniversary, and the Jimmy Buffet concerts that really "rocked the rafters" of this famous funplace.

Bloody Mary's also welcomes cruise ship passengers and crew members, who are delivered by the ship's tenders to their sturdy 98-ft. long, well-lighted dock across the road from the restaurant and bar. Sailing yachts can anchor for short periods of time in the deep waters of Povai Bay, using one of 8 moorings provided by the "Bloody Mary's Yacht Club". From the dock you will enjoy an excellent view of Bora Bora's Mount Otemanu. Tie your dinghy to the dock and amble on over to the barefoot bar/restaurant for a cold drink and great food.

MAI KAI MARINA & YACHT CLUB, *Tel. 60.38.00; info@maikaimarina.com; www.maikaimarina.com. Marina information Tel 22.10.33; VHF: They monitor channel 16 and converse on channel 69. Situated facing the entrance of the Teavanui pass in Bora Bora. AE, MC, V. Free transfers with dinner reservations.*

Teiva & Jessica Tapare are a very personable Polynesian/American couple who ran the Bora Bora Yacht Club until Feb. 3, 2010, when Cyclone Oli destroyed most of the structures, including their home. They have now joined forces with Kito Sylvain, a realtor from a well-known family in Tahiti, and have moved to a site closer to Vaitape village that was formerly operated by TOPdive as a hotel, restaurant and dive center.

The Mai Kai Marina & Yacht Club and the Mai Kai Lounge Bar serve as a cozy Polynesian type hangout for local residents, tourists and visiting yachties. This is the ideal spot to sit next to the water and to experience one of Bora Bora's finest meals in a fun, relaxed atmosphere. Teiva and Jessica have a very good reputation as hospitable hosts who attract such personalities as Jimmy Buffet. The famous singer dined in their Bora Bora Yacht Club restaurant every night during his last visit to Bora Bora in Jan. 2010, when he performed 2 concerts at Bloody Mary's.

Teiva is a Tahitian-Paumotu born in Hawaii, who grew up in Tahiti and studied French cuisine in Paris for 7 years. Some of his recipes come from his grandmother's kitchen, like his renowned mashed potatoes. Teiva uses only the freshest ingredients, which highlight steak and seafood. Vegetarian dishes are available and many items can be prepared to cater to those with special dietary needs, making the dining experience feel as though you are being served by a private chef.

KAINA HUT, *Tel. 67.54.06, is on the mountainside in Pofai Bay. Open for dinner nightly except Fridays. Closed for lunch. All credit cards.*

A big thatch roof covers this open-sided Polynesian style restaurant that has a sandy floor, coconut wood furniture, pretty shell chandeliers and lots of plants and flowers. The menu changes frequently and presents a fusion of French cuisine with Polynesian and Asian ingredients. Appetizers feature seared tuna salad and mussels with garlic, and other choices may be seabass, steamed lagoon fish, or veal filet The signature dish here is crispy breadfruit gnocchis for 2.100 CFP, and a seafood platter is 5.800 CFP, which includes grilled lobster.

LE PANDA D'OR, *Tel. 67.62.70.* On mountainside in Vaitape village. Open for lunch and dinner. Closed Sun. MC, V.

The Golden Panda serves Polynesian Cantonese food in its 200-seat a/c restaurant and also does a good take-out business. Their extensive menu includes breaded fried shrimp, cuttlefish, Coquille St. Jacques, and seasonal delicacies such as sweet and sour crab, and shrimp and lobster sautéed with broccoli.

Moderate to Superior
RESTAURANT FARE MANUIA, *Tel. 67.68.08/72.52.84. On the lagoon side, just past the turnoff at Point Matira. Open daily 11:30am-10pm. MC, V. Free pick-up for dinner.*

This attractive little restaurant decorated in a Polynesian style offers non-stop service that includes 28 choices of pizza cooked over a wood fire, priced from 1.200-1.900 CFP. During the day they serve 15 choices of burgers from 1.400-2.000 CFP with fries, and 15 choices of paninis with fries for 700-1.000 CFP. The dinner menu of gastronomic French cuisine and fresh island specialties lists fish dishes starting at 1.800 CFP. Meat choices include lamb curry, or a grilled prime cut of beef with shallots for 3.900 CFP. A 3-course menu is 3.900 CFP. Try their yummy Mouelleux, a warm chocolate cup cake. They have a good wine list and they also feature a daily cocktail for 1.200 CFP.

LA BOUNTY, *Tel. 67.70.43, on mountainside in Matira, close to Hotel Maitai Polynesia. Open for lunch and dinner. Closed Mon. MC and V.*

This restaurant may need to spruce up its decor, but it has a good location and reputation and it so much more than just a pizza joint. Their specialty is beef fondue and their extensive menu includes such tempting choices as salmon with pepper sauce and a very good steak with a choice of sauces. Their wine selection is also good. This is where the locals eat because the food is good, the staff is friendly and attentive and the prices are decent.

Economy
BEN'S, *On mountainside in Matira, between Hotel Bora Bora and Point Matira. Open daily 8am-5pm. No credit cards.*

Ben Teraitepo, from Bora Bora, and his American wife, Robin, gave up their busy life in Southern California to settle in Bora Bora in 1987. They cook and serve home-style meals on their terrace across the road from the white sandy beach. Their menu includes Tex-Mex food, hot dogs, cheeseburgers, submarine sandwiches, American pizzas, lasagna, spaghetti with different types of sauces, and fresh fish. Prices are 700-1.600 CFP.

SNACK MATIRA, *Tel. 67.77.32, is beside the lagoon at Matira Beach, across the road from Ben's. Open 10am to 4pm. Closed Mon. No credit cards.* This simple 100-place beach snack serves sandwiches, burgers, *poisson cru* and pizza. Beer and wine are served with food only.

ALOE CAFÉ, *Tel. 67.78.88. In Pahia Center in Vaitape village. Open 6:30am-5pm Mon.-Sat. Closed Sun. No credit cards.*

This pastry shop and snack-restaurant was formerly l'Appetisserie. They serve crêpes, paninis, burgers, salads, kabobs, pork ribs, fresh fish and good pizza at very reasonable prices. They also provide Internet service. (See information under Cybercafé-Internet Service).

GARDEN CAFÉ, *Tel. 67.60.00. In Centre Mautera on mountainside in Tiipoto, just outside Vaitape village toward Matira. Open Mon.-Fri. 6am-3:30pm and 6-10pm, and on Sat. 6-10pm.*

You can order food to go or sit outdoors to eat your breakfast, lunch or dinner. Daily specials are 1.000-3.000 CFP and may be grilled lagoon fish with breadfruit chips and eggplant, braised beef with rice, shrimp in coconut milk cooked with pineapple and vegetables, roast lamb, or a mixed grill of sausage, chicken and beef, with fries. They also have free WiFi.

SNACKS AND ROULOTTES. Crêpes, burgers, pizzas, roast chicken and take-out Tahitian-Chinese dishes are available at small stands in Vaitape and the Matira Beach area. At least four *roulottes* (mobile diners) set up shop in Vaitape village at night, where you can enjoy a full meal for around 1.200 CFP. They all serve steak and fries, *brochettes* (kebabs), barbecued chicken legs, *poisson cru* and grilled fish. Roulotte Matira, across the road from the entrance to Point Matira, is noted for its good food.

SEEING THE SIGHTS

To explore Bora Bora by car or bicycle, start at the Vaitape boat dock, if you head south around the island. All along the water's edge of Pofai (or Povai) Bay you will see spectacular views of the **Otemanu Mountain**. Beside the lagoon at the edge of the town center of Vaitape you will see La Perla boutique, adjacent to the 2-story white building that houses the Robert Wan Tahiti Perles boutique. Along the edge of Pofai Bay you will see Moon B&B just before coming to Alain and Linda's Art Gallery on the right. There are usually gaily-painted *pareos* hanging on a line in front of the boutique. Across the road from the big sports complex and playground is a path that leads over the island to the village of Anau. The interior roads can only be traversed by mountain bike or on foot.

If you stay on the **circle island road** you'll see the Kaina Hut Restaurant, Villa Mahana, Bloody Mary's Restaurant and The Farm of Bora Pearl Company. Look to the right across the bay toward the point of Motu Toopua Iti and you will see some of the overwater bungalows at the Bora Bora Nui Resort & Spa. Continuing south on the main road, at Raititi Point, you will pass the entrance to the highly acclaimed Hotel Bora Bora (now closed).

On the mountainside past the Bora Diving Center and Bora Bora Gallery there is a trail leading to a battery of coastal defense guns on the hillside, relics of World War II when the American Armed Forces were stationed on Bora Bora. You can reach them in just a 10-min. hike up a walking trail east of the Matira Restaurant, which is now closed. Back on the circle-island road, Ben's Place serves American food on the mountainside and Snack Matira serves local style dishes beside the lagoon. A sign indicates the turnoff at Point Matira, where you can visit the Intercontinental Bora Bora Le Moana Resort and the Hotel Matira and have a swim at Matira Beach. Chez Nono has a pension right on the white sand beach and Chez Robert & Tina have 3 rental houses right at the tip of Point Matira. Once again on the main road, you'll see Fareani Curios on the left and Chez Maeva Masson and the Fare Manuia Restaurant on the right, next to Village Temanuata. Matira Pearls is across the road from them.

Heading along the east coast of Matira, Le Maitai Polynesia hotel is on both sides of the road, with beach, mountain and overwater bungalows. La Bounty Restaurant, Tiare Market, Nemo World dive shop, Sofitel Bora Bora Marara Beach and Private Island Beach Resort can also be seen along the way.

A steep hill leads you behind the Club Med Coral Garden Village (now closed) at **Faaopore Bay**, just before Paoaoa Point. You can visit a lookout point on a ridge above the bay by taking the tunnel under the road or by walking up the steps just beyond a boutique. A trail to the right of the hill will take you down to Marae Aehautai, where you will have a good view of Otemanu Mountain and the islands of Taha'a and Raiatea beyond the reef. Other *marae* are also located in this vicinity, as well as coastal guns from World War II. Shortly after the bay you will come to Pension Bora Lagoonarium on the lagoon side.

The road continues on to **Anau village**, which has some very modest homes sitting on rather marshy land with lots of land crab holes. Beside the lagoon are the land bases for the deluxe hotel resorts built on the motu islets facing the village. These are the Intercontinental Bora Bora Resort & Thalasso Spa, Le Méridien and the St. Regis Resort & Spa. The Lagoonarium is built on a motu between Le Méridien and St. Regis, and just past the St. Regis is the Four Seasons Resort. After passing a few houses on the road beyond Fitiiu Point, you'll come to Taimoo Bay. For the next few miles the only thing you will see are scattered houses, coconut plantations and *tupa* land crabs, until you come to the *Musée de la Mer*, the Marine Museum, which has replicas of famous ships that have visited Tahiti and Bora Bora.

Just before Point Taihi you'll see a steep track that leads up to a World War II radar station on top of Popoti Ridge. Across the lagoon you can see the Bora Bora airport on Motu Mute. Continuing on the circle island road you'll pass the Bora Bora Condos, which consist of 4 overwater bungalows and 11 mountainside apartments on stilts. Marlon Brando's estate owns 2 overwater bungalows and 1 on the mountainside. These condos are rented to visitors who wish to spend a week or more on the island.

At Tereia Point in **Faanui Bay** you'll see an old shipping wharf and a seaplane ramp that were built by the American Seabees during the war. Another US coastal gun is located on the hill above the concrete water tank, and right after the former submarine base is the Marae Fare-Opu, between the road and the bay. The stones of the temple are engraved with turtle petroglyphs. A road beside the Protestant church at the head of the bay runs inland, narrowing into an unmarked track that you can follow with a guide over the saddle of the ridge top to Bora Bora's east coast of Vairau Bay, south of Fitiiu Point.

On the western end of Faanui Bay is the main shipping wharf, where inter-island ferries and cargo vessels from Tahiti dock. This wharf was also built during the war. Just 100 m. west of the quay is the Marae Marotetini, a coastal *marae* that was restored by Dr. Yosihiko Sinoto in 1968. This was a royal temple and members of Bora Bora's chiefly families are buried nearby.

Around the bend from the Faanui boat dock is the Bora Bora Yacht Club, and on the hillside facing the island's only pass are 2 defense guns left over from the war. The Safari Tour excursions will take you to visit these guns. On 2 *motu* islets across the lagoon you will see the Bora Bora Pearl Beach Resort and the Bora Bora Lagoon Resort (now closed), as well as Motu Tapu, which is now the private domain of the Hilton Bora Bora Nui Resort & Spa. This little *motu* is famous for its white sand beach and is located just beside the Teavanui Pass, the only navigable entrance through the protective necklace of coral reef surrounding the island.

On the seaside just before you reach Vaitape village you will see the TOPDIVE-Bathys dive center. You will also find a good little *patisserie* in the Centre Commercial Le Pahia, or you can shop at Magasin Chin Lee, which is truly an establishment of village life in Bora Bora. In addition to cold juices and drinks you can choose a *casse-croûte,* sandwich, Tahitian and Chinese pastries or a take-away container of good hot food—usually rice and fish, chicken or meat. Royal Helen's Bay is another small shopping center beside the lagoon in Vaitape.

To end your do-it-yourself tour around the island, spend a little time in Vaitape village and you will be able to observe the daily drama of life on a small island. You'll discover that Bora Bora is not just a tourist island, but the residents have their own private interests, as well as looking after visitors from all over the world. You may see the children bursting from the confines of their schoolrooms into the Bora Bora sunshine. Their parents or big brother or sister, auntie or grandmother may be waiting for the little ones in the car or on a scooter parked in the shade of a flamboyant tree.

Have a look at the fruits and vegetables the vendors have carefully placed on small tables beside the road. Take a picture of the brightly colored lagoon fish strung on a line that the fisherman and his family are selling. Watch the adolescent boys and enjoy the flirting that goes on between them and the young *vahines*. Walk down to the *mairie* (town hall) and you'll see the stately Polynesians coming and going, taking care of business that involves division of their land, or the marriages, births and deaths of family members. At the post office you'll see local residents standing in line to pay their telephone bills or mail a letter. Even if they're in a hurry to check their mailboxes, they always have time to greet a friend with kisses on both cheeks, and to share a bit of gossip, a joke and a laugh.

Then go to the arts and crafts center beside the wharf, which is adjacent to the Bora Bora Tourist Information Center (Comité de Tourisme). While you're looking at the hand painted *pareos* and dresses, the shell necklaces and woven hats, be sure to exchange smiles with the "mama" who spends all day here, waiting to make a sale. Just lifting your eyebrows is a form of greeting and you'll be happy with the response when you see her eyes light up with friendly warmth. This is Bora Bora at its best.

Circle Island Tours

To fully appreciate the history and beauty of Bora Bora, climb aboard an excursion bus or a "le truck" and settle back to listen, learn and enjoy as the English-speaking guide tells all about this little island and its colorful past, exciting present and plans for tomorrow. While passing through the little villages on the 29-km. (18-mi.) circuit, you will see humble homes or modern concrete villas surrounded by pretty flower gardens, small snack stands and little boutiques selling *pareos* and shells. The *marae* temples, where Polynesians used to worship in pre-Christian days, are pointed out, along with the Quonset huts, naval base and heavy artillery guns, left behind by the 5,000 American soldiers, sailors and Seabees who made a "friendly invasion" of Bora Bora during World War II, who also left many blue-eyed children. If you book through your hotel activity desk you will pay 3.000-6.000 CFP for a circle island tour by a/c van and more for private tours.

Circle island tours, as well as taxi and transfer service is provided by the following companies:

Simplet Taxi, *Tel. 79.19.31/73.85.72; kayhaut@yahoo.fr,* is operated by Matahi "Simplet" Tefana, who worked as guest relations manager for Sofitel Marara for years until he retired. You will enjoy his comical comments and anecdotes as he drives you around the island. He has buses and air-conditioned vans.

Otemanu Tours, *Tel. 67.70.49; otemanu.tours@mail.pf;* provides a circle island tour daily, using a/c vans or *le truck* to show you the island. If you are on a ship or yacht they will pick you up on the dock in front of your tender. They charge 2.500 CFP per person for a 2 1/2-hr. tour and 10.000 CFP per hour for a private minibus tour for 6 maximum passengers. A transfer is 600 CFP and a private transfer is 3.000 CFP per person.

Dino's Tours & Excursions, *Tel. 79.29.65; dinostours@yahoo.fr.* Dino Dexter provides tours around the island in his a/c van. He also operates a land and water taxi service and has outrigger canoe tours around the island for groups or private parties, with a picnic on request. Be sure to visit his tattoo shop in Vaitape across from the boat dock.

Charley Taxi, *Tel. 67.64.37/78.27.71.* Charley works mostly at night when he transfers tourists between their hotels and the restaurants.

Mountain Safari 4x4 Excursions

Viewing Bora Bora's majestic beauty takes on new dimensions when you bounce up and down the rutted mountain trails in a Land Rover or Jeep on a photographic safari excursion. Your guide will tell you the story of the American military base that was established in Bora Bora during World War II and you'll visit the gun emplacements and radar station on Popoti Ridge. At the end of the trail you walk uphill through the bush, where you are rewarded with a 360° panoramic vista of an ancient volcano crater, the lagoon and coral reefs around Bora Bora and the neighboring islands. These include Taha'a, Raiatea, Huahine, Maupiti and the atoll of Tupai, which are all clearly visible from this height. These tours also circle the island, where your guide points out the *marae* stone temples used by the ancient Polynesians, and the war relics used by the Americans. These are very interesting and scenic tours, but are not for the faint-hearted, pregnant or lazily inclined tourist. When you book through the hotel activity desks you will be charged 7.600-8.500 CFP for this tour.

Tupuna Mountain Expeditions, *Tel. 67.75.06; tupuna.bora@mail.pf; www.safaribora.com.* Owner Dany Leverd has several 4-wheel drive (4x4) vehicles and good guides. This half-day morning or afternoon tour costs 7.600 CFP and includes a visit to Bora Bora's only cultured pearl farm, owned by Dany and his wife, Tea Suchard.

Vavau 4x4 Adventures, *Tel. 72.01.21; temana689@me.com; www.borabora4x4.com.* is operated by Heirama Fearon, whose American father, Steve, Fearon, owns Matira Pearls. Heirama and his English-speaking guides will take you on a historical and cultural tour by a/c Landrovers. Their off-road adventures include a visit to a fish farm, where you will learn about the effect these tropical fish have on Bora Bora's fragile ecosystem. Heirama's website includes photos and descriptions of the sights they visit. Call direct for rates.

Patrick's Activities/Maohi Nui Private Excursions, *Tel. 67.69.94/79.19.11; patrick@maohinui.net; www.maohinui.net.* Patrick Tairua or his guide will take you on a private 4WD safari excursion by Land Rover Defender to let you discover the "back-country" of Bora Bora. Security belts are installed in the back for every passenger and a white cover protects you from the sun and rain. Raincoats are available if needed. Patrick speaks very good English and will give you details on the geological formation of Bora Bora, the history of the religious sites and information on the American presence on the island during World War II. He leads an easy 20-min. walk into the forest to reach a site where you can see an old turtle petroglyph carved in a basaltic boulder. Along the way you can learn about the tropical plants growing here. Mineral water is provided during the tour. The hotels sell the Maohi Nui half-day safari tour for 52.500 CFP for 2-4 people. You can also combine a 4WD safari tour with a tour of the lagoon by outrigger canoe, or experience both tours and a Polynesian lunch on a beautiful motu. See information under *Private Lagoon Excursions and Picnics on the Motu* and *Wedding Ceremonies.*

ATV - Quad Tours

You can rent a quad all-terrain vehicle at Matira Jet Tours on Matira Beach, *Tel. 77.63.63*, and go for a ride on the motu. Combination jet-ski & quad tours are also available.

Helicopter Tours

Tahiti Helicopter Service, *Tel. 67.54.90; www.tahiti-helicopters.com* opened an office on Vaitape quay in July 2011. Their program of flight-seeing excursions includes a 15-min. tour of Bora Bora, the lagoon and motu islets, 30-min. and 40-min. tours of Bora Bora and the atoll of Tupai 20 km. northwest of Bora Bora, and special sunset tours over Tupai. You can even get married on Tupai. The wedding party of 5 maximum people boards the helicopter at the helipad located at Pago Pago on Bora Bora's main island, and the pilot flies you to Tupai for the ceremony, then returns to pick you up at the pre-arranged time.

Special Activities & Sightseeing Stops

Alain Gerbault's grave opposite the *gendarmerie* on Vaitape quay may be pointed out to you during your guided land tour. Gerbault was a Frenchman who had sailed the seven seas aboard his yacht *Firecrest* before dropping anchor in Bora Bora. He was most attracted to the young boys of Bora Bora, to whom he introduced the game of soccer. Due to the politics of war Gerbault left Bora Bora in 1941, and died on the island of Timor. His remains were brought back to his beloved Bora Bora in 1947, and a small tomb in the form of a *marae* was built in his honor.

Ancient temples of coral stone called *marae* are scattered around the island and on a few of the surrounding *motu* islets. The most easily accessible of these pre-historic sites of worship and human sacrifice are: **Marae Marotetini**, on a point by the lagoon between the Bora Bora Yacht Club and the Faanui boat dock; **Marae Taianapa**, on private property well off the mountain side of the road in Faanui, close to the Electra power plant; and **Marae Aehautai**, located on the beach at Fitiiu Point overlooking Anau Bay. **Fare Opu**, "House of the Stomach" is located between the lagoon and the road, close to the old navy docks in Faanui, immediately before the Faanui village. Petroglyphs of turtles are incised into 2 of the coral slabs. Turtles were sacred to the Maohi ancestors of today's Polynesians.

Matira Beach begins at the Hotel Bora Bora (now closed) and continues past the Hotel Matira and Chez Nono at Point Matira, and on around the point past the Bora Bora Intercontinental Le Moana Resort. It joins Taahana Beach at Le Maitai Polynesia and the Sofitel Marara Resort, but most people still refer to the entire area as Matira Beach. This is where you will find a concentration of hotels, pensions, boutiques, black pearl shops and all kinds of nautical activities. The west side of Matira Beach, facing the Hotel Bora Bora, is Bora Bora's most popular beach. The soft, white powdery sand slopes gently into the aquamarine lagoon, where the water is very shallow until you see the deepening shades of blue. Point

---

TUPAPAU

"Many vestiges of ancient times still linger on Bora Bora. The belief in **tupapau** (TWO-pow-pow), ghosts of the dead, is prevalent among the islanders. Walk alone on a dark Bora Bora night and you'll see why. It is still a common practice to keep a lamp lit at night to ward off these evil spirits. In 1973 my son Tom and I discovered a human arm and a portion of jawbone in front of the altar of Marae Marotetini. They had been pushed to the surface by land crabs digging their burrows. Despite warnings from the locals, we took the bones as souvenirs. Shortly after the discovery, my right arm became swollen to twice its normal size, followed by a swelling of the right side of my jaw. Upon taking the bones back to Los Angeles, Tom's leg was broken in several places during a freak motorcycle accident. This was followed by a period of family sickness and bad luck that didn't cease until we returned the bones to Marae Marotetini in 1976. In 1981, several giant human footprints were discovered at the water's edge near Marae Taianapa. The discovery was important enough to bring government officials and newsmen from Papeete to examine the huge prints and wonder at their origin. The elders of Bora Bora didn't wonder. They knew. The prints were an omen from the distant past." – from cinematographer Milas Hinshaw's booklet *Bora Bora E.*

Matira was named in memory of a British ship named *Mathilda* that was wrecked on Moruroa Atoll in the Tuamotus in 1792. Three of the survivors remained in Tahiti, forming the first European colony. One of the crew, James O'Connor, married King Pomare's cousin, and their granddaughter was named Mathilda. She married a chief of the Leeward Islands and they settled in Bora Bora, where part of their property included the beautiful point and sand beach now called Matira, the Tahitian pronunciation of Mathilda.

Musée de la Marine is on the back side of the island, between the villages of Faanui and Anau, *Tel. 67.75.24.* French architect Bertrand Darasse displays his collection of ship models, which includes the *Mayflower*, dated 1615, the *H.M.S.Endeavour* that brought James Cook to Tahiti in 1769, the *Boudeuse* and *Etoile*, commanded by **Louis Antoine de Bougainville**, **Captain Bligh's** famous *Bounty*, and **Alain Gerbault's** *Firecrest*, which he sailed to Bora Bora. There are also models of outrigger sailing canoes, *bonitiers* and *poti marara* boats that are still used in these islands. Admission to the maritime museum is free.

NIGHTLIFE & ENTERTAINMENT

Le Récif, *Tel. 67.73.87, north of Vaitape towards Faanui.*

This is Bora Bora's only public disco and it is open on Fri. and Sat. nights. The ambiance in this dark and crowded room is very Tahitian. If you are curious as to how the locals whoop it up, this is the place to experience it first hand. The drinking and dancing continue until the wee hours of the morning. Entry fee.

Heiva in Bora Bora – Where the Fête Goes On & On
During the month of July, the island of Bora Bora pulsates to the rhythm of the **Heiva**, which means festival in Tahitian. Some people still call this event the Fête or Tiurai, the Tahitian word for July. Whatever name you choose to call it, this is the most colorful time to visit Bora Bora.

Most of the islands have their own Heiva celebrations, but the Fête in Bora Bora is the best, because the villagers put so much enthusiasm and effort into building their *baraques* (barracks). These are carnival type stalls or booths that are made of thatched roofs and walls woven of palm fronds. They are decorated with multicolored *tifaifai* wall hangings, ferns, bright blossoms and *ti* leaves. These *baraques* are transformed into restaurants, pool halls, shooting galleries and carnival booths with a roulette-type wheel called *taviri*. If you place a bet you may win a bar of soap, sack of rice or sugar, bolt of *pareo* cloth, or even a live suckling pig.

Each village presents a singing group and a troupe of dancers in the Heiva competitions. Some of these performers are just as talented as the professional entertainers in Tahiti, as Bora Bora has long been recognized for producing excellent dancers, choreography and costumes. The competitions are a big social event, when old friends get together to catch up on the latest happenings and to swap a choice bit of gossip. The fruit-carriers' race, javelin-throwing contest, soccer matches and outrigger sailing canoe races are just warm-up events for the outrigger paddle canoe races.

July 14 is a good combination of old style Polynesian celebrations and the French version of honoring Bastille Day in the tropics. This is the time to drink champagne at the mayor's office, aboard a visiting French ship and at the glamorous resort hotels. A huge fireworks display ends the day's festivities, and an all-night ball gets underway a little later. Although there are only 2-3 weeks of planned events during the Heiva in Bora Bora, the Fête still goes on and on, well into the month of August. After all, building the *baraques* did require a lot of work. What's more, they provide a great meeting place.

SPORTS & RECREATION
Hiking & Trekking
Polynesia Island Tours, *Tel. 29.66.60/67.56.02; polynesiaislandtours@mail.pf; www.polynesiaislandtours.com.* Azdine is a Frenchman who leads cultural walks, hiking and trekking tours into the heart of Bora Bora. You will be introduced to the botany, archaeology, geology and legends of Polynesia. The Valley of the Kings is an easy 3-hr. walk that sells for 6.500 CFP; the Ancestors' Road or the Track of the Past is an easy full-day tour for 9.500 CFP; the Sacred Cave of Anau is a 6-hr. trek for advanced walkers and costs 12.000 CFP; and the 6-hr. climb up Mt. Pahia

(2,168 ft./661 m) is for experts only and costs 14.000 CFP. For this hike, you must be fit, in good health, and not prone to vertigo.

Taxi Boat & Boat Rental

La Plage, *Tel. 67.68.75/28.48.66; laplage.bora@hotmil.com*. Isabelle and Franck provide taxi boat service to visit a motu or with a Tahitian guide for private excursions and sunset cruises. They also rent boats that you can pilot yourself without a license or guide.

Manu Taxi Boat, *Tel. 67.61.93/79.11.62; fanfantaxiboat@mail.pf*. Jean-François Ferrand has 3 motorboats and can accommodate up to 20 passengers for hourly, daily and half-day excursions, transfers and rental. Picnic on a private motu on request.

Taxi Motu, *Tel. 67.60.61/77.33.23; taximotu@hotmail.com*. Ronan and Chloé Delestre have a 15-ft. boat for transfers to the motu and a 28-ft. covered boat for a maximum of 12 passengers.

Matira Jet Tours, *Tel. 67.62.73/77.63.63*, has a 27-ft. covered boat for half- or full-day rentals to visit the hotels, circle the island or snorkel. Airport transfers on request.

Moana Adventure Tours, *Tel. 67.61.41*, provides boat transfers upon request from the airport and resort hotels or private lodgings. A 17-ft. Boston Whaler with sun top or a Bowrider can be rented with a pilot, who will take you to places in the lagoon that visitors normally never get to see.

Deep Sea, Lagoon & Coastal Fishing

Sports fishing around Bora Bora is a very popular activity and the local fishing clubs hold tournaments throughout the year. There is even a Vahine Sport Fishing Club for the ladies, and any visiting female angler is welcome to join the competitions and fun. The fishing grounds are only a 20 min. boat ride outside the barrier reef, and the waters around Bora Bora are filled with marlin, yellowfin tuna, sailfish, wahoo, mahi mahi and bonito. The marlin are tagged and released at the anglers' request. Inter-island cruises are provided on request. The sea captains listed below all speak very good English.

Luna Sea, *Tel. 72.95.85, www.boraborasportfishing.com* is a Black Watch 34 that is a No Nonsense Big Game Fishing Boat built specifically for serious charter fishing in French Polynesian waters off the Leeward Society Islands. "Luna Sea" is based in Bora Bora but can easily fish the neighboring islands of Taha'a, Raiatea, Huahine, Tupai and Maupiti. The boat is dry, smooth, stable and very quick, and is equipped with Melton International Tackle custom-built rods from 8 lb. to 130 lb. test with Shimano Tiagra 2-speed reels and Shimano spinning reels. She has Top Shot gaffs and a Relax Marine fighting chair and outriggers. Captain Tepoe Pere has more than 30 years of local and international experience and his goal is to give you the very best service possible. A 4-hr. charter for fishing in the lagoon is 85.000 CFP, a 4-hr. deep-sea charter is 100.000 CFP, and a full day (8 hrs.) deep-sea fishing or transfer to Tahaa is 140.000 CFP.

Moana Adventure Tours, *Tel. 78.27.37; www.moanatours.com* uses a 17-ft. Boston Whaler for fishing close to the outside reef, where currents and high seas attract bonito, tuna, mahi mahi, jacks, barracudas and wahoo. A half-day lagoon fishing trip for max. 4 people is 43.000 CFP and a half-day coastal fishing excursion is 43.000 CFP for a max of 2 people. A 6-hr. trip to Tupai, an atoll 10 miles north of Bora Bora, includes 3 hrs. of fishing for giant trevally and huge barracudas.

Jourdain of Romantic Tours, *Tel. 71.91.07.* In addition to providing private Romantic Tours on board his 22-ft. boat **Betty,** Jourdain works with some of the hotels to take their guests on half-day fishing trips. The hotels charge 55.000 CFP for 4 hrs. of lagoon fishing and 75.000 CFP for 4 hrs. of offshore fishing. You can contact him directly and save 22% of the cost.

Lagoon Excursions by Outrigger Canoe or Speedboat

Bora Bora's lovely lagoon offers many surprises, pleasures and photographic treasures. **A Boat Trip Around the Island** normally includes time for snorkeling, exploring a small motu islet, searching for the graceful manta rays, sharing a kiss with the sting rays, diving for the giant mussels buried in the white sand lagoon bottom (the mussels are not removed from their habitat) and donning mask and snorkel to view the fish and coral in the natural aquarium. **Feeding the Sharks and Stingrays** is included in most **Circle Island Tours,** and is Bora Bora's most popular and thrilling excursion. A **Picnic on a Motu** combined with your boat tour can mean you eat freshly grilled fish and fruit and drink coconut water, or you may be served a gourmet lunch, complete with cold drinks and wine. All lagoon activities depend on the whim of the weather and sea.

The hotel resorts and cruise ships have an agreement with their own qualified guides and charge from 9.500-12.500 CFP for a 3-hr. boat tour around the island. A combined lagoon safari and motu picnic is 14.000 CFP. You may get a better rate if you contact the guides directly. Here are a few of the best known guides and excursions.

Shark Boy of Bora Bora, *Tel./Fax 67.60.93, cell 78.27.42; sharkboy@mail.pf.* Owner Evan Temarii has been operating Evan Activities for 26 years. He has 4 speedboats for 4-12 passengers and a catamaran for 60 passengers. On all his lagoon excursions you will be able to swim with the rays and watch the sharks being fed. Evan has starred in 2 movies filmed in Bora Bora: starting when he was 11 years old with *Heart,* made for the Wonderful World of Disney, followed by *Call It Courage* when he was 18. He traps the sharks with his bare hands and holds them over his head out of the water for the photographers. He said that he was the first one to tame the stingrays, and even taught them how to kiss.

Raanui Tours, *Tel. 67.61.79/79.43.14; www.boraborasafarilagoon.com* is operated by Arieta Onee Tepeva and her Tahitian family. They have 4 motorized outrigger canoes that include shark and ray feeding and snorkeling. They charge 6.300 CFP for a half-day excursion and 9.300 CFP for a full-day with a picnic on Motu Tapu. They also do private tours.

Teremoana Tours (Nono Tours), *Tel. 67.71.38; nono.leverd@mail.pf; www.cheznonobora.com.* Noel "Nono" Leverd also owns Chez Nono pension on Matira Beach. His very popular excursions aboard two 36-ft. outrigger speed canoes depart from the beach in front of his pension at 9:30am and return at 3:30pm. A lunch of poisson cru, grilled fish, coconut bread, cake, fresh fruit and *po'e* is served on the motu. Nono charges 9.130 CFP for the excursion and picnic, and half-price for children under 12 years old.

Bora Bora Lagoonarium, *Tel. 67.71.34; www.boraboraisland.lagoonarium.* A half-day excursion operated by Teura and Claudine Teheiura takes you to their Lagoonarium on the northern point of Motu Piti A'au. Fenced-in sections of the lagoon contain fish, sea turtles, rays, and a huge moray eel. The hotels charge 7.100-8.500 CFP for a half-day tour and 13.000 CFP for a full day with picnic.

BORA BORA'S SHARK FEEDING SHOW

Feeding the sharks is one of the most popular excursions on Bora Bora. Each morning the tourists board outrigger canoes to speed across the lagoon toward the barrier reef. When you make your own shark feeding tour, you will put on a mask and snorkel, and step into the clear waters of the warm lagoon, just inside the fringing reef. With just a few steps in water about 1.2 m (4 ft.) deep you will reach a rope that has been tied around 2 huge coral heads. You hold onto the rope for stability and watch through your mask as your guide performs the daily shark feeding show.

Thousands of tropical fish of all colors rush over to have a nibble at the huge head of tuna or mahi mahi that the guide holds out to them. You will see rainbow colored butterfly fish, black and white striped manini, the blue and yellow empress angel fish, the variegated and very territorial Picasso fish, plus many other families of more than 300 species of fish that inhabit the Bora Bora submarine gardens.

Gasps and squeals from the audience announce the arrival of the sharks as they appear for their breakfast. Sometimes you can see as many as a dozen sharks, about 1.5 m (5 ft.) long. These are the Carcharhinus Melanopterus, commonly known as the **blackfin** or **blacktip reef shark**.

The shark feeding show is so fascinating that you may forget your fear. As you are up current of the sharks and the Tahitian guides keep their attention diverted with the proffered fish breakfast, the sharks normally pay little attention to their observers. If you are bold enough, you can even help to feed these hungry sharks. And if your nerve fails you, then the outrigger canoe is just a few steps away.

Note: Some of the lagoon tours are now sold as Shark Observing or Shark and Ray Meeting instead of Shark Feeding.

Reef Discovery, *Tel. 76.43.43; www.reefdiscovery.pf.* This is one of the most popular activities in Bora Bora, mainly because Christophe Poch, a French Navy veteran who speaks perfect English, has an extensive knowledge of the marine life as well as the history of the island, and also because of the extra care and attention he gives to those who are not confident swimmers. Christophe takes you on a 3 1/2-hr. tour in his luxurious red speed boat with a sunshade and comfy leather seats. During the 4 snorkeling stops you will see manta rays, eagle rays, a kaleidoscope of lagoon fish, moray eels, reef sharks, tridacna clams and beautiful coral gardens. This tour is sold in the hotels for 10.900 CFP. Reserve in advance.

Private Lagoon Excursions & Picnics on the Motu

Private tours and excursions are very popular with Honeymooners in Bora Bora, and now there are several service providers who specialize in private boat tours around the island. They stop to let you swim in the coral gardens, feed the stingrays, observe the sharks and enjoy a romantic picnic on the motu.

Etienne Private Picnic, *Tel./Fax 67.63.14; cell 79.22.62.* Etienne was the first tour operator to provide a picnic in the water, and his private lagoon excursions and barbecues on the motu are highly praised. While you are swimming and snorkeling and enjoying the peace and quiet on the white sand beach of the motu, Etienne is preparing your lunch. He places a small table and 2 chairs in the shallow lagoon water, shades them with a big umbrella, dresses the table with a linen cloth and place settings, sets up his barbecue grill in the water and ices down the champagne in a bucket standing in the lagoon next to the table. The stylish lunch starts with mixed salad and poisson cru with coconut milk, and is followed by grilled lobster, mahi mahi and steak, accompanied by potatoes, and followed by a dessert of fresh fruit. There is beer, pineapple juice, Sprite and Coke in the cooler, and you can have wine if you prefer that to champagne. This 6 1/2-hr. excursion costs 40.000 CFP per person when booking through a hotel.

Etienne told me that most of the so-called private picnic tours, except for Patrick's Activities, take place on a motu near the Lagoonarium, and you can see other couples or small groups while swimming and dining.

Patrick's Activities/Maohi Nui Private Excursions, *Tel. 689/67.69.94/ 79.19.11; patrick.@maohinui.net; www.maohinui.net.* Patrick Tairua is well known and appreciated in Bora Bora for his private lagoon excursions, his ma'a Tahiti feasts on a private motu, private safari excursions by 4x4 Landrover, Polynesian wedding ceremonies, and his spectacular fire-dancing when he performs with his Maohi Nui dancers at the hotels several nights a week. Patrick is indeed a busy man because he is really good at what he does and he's dependable; therefore, he is in demand by the hotels and individual clients. He also has some well-trained assistants who have a long rich experience as boat captains, guides and musicians.

Patrick speaks good English and he will tell you about the Polynesian culture and legends of Bora Bora as he takes you around the lagoon in his famous flower-decorated yellow outrigger speed canoe made of wood that has a roof of coconut palm fronds. During a 3-hr. private tour around the island you will stop to snorkel in a coral garden, then to visit the friendly sting rays, which Patrick says are part of the family. The last stop is on the ocean side, where you can observe the black tip reef sharks. Patrick or his guides will assure you that they are perfectly safe and you are not their food. Snorkeling equipment is provided, as well as drinks: mineral water, fruit juice, soft drinks, and beer. Bring a beach towel, shoes or sandals, sunscreen and your cameras.

Patrick also has a æ-day tour and a full-day tour. Both of these tours include a traditional Polynesian lunch on a private motu islet. You can watch the opening of the underground earth oven, and your lunch will be served on an umbrella-shaded table set in the shallow lagoon water. The meal includes pork, chicken, tropical vegetables and local fruits and the food is cooked in banana leaves. Wine or champagne accompanies your lunch, according to your preference.

If you are going to be in Bora Bora only a short time, perhaps you would like to combine your Lagoon Tour and Polynesian lunch with a 4x4 Safari. Contact Patrick for his rates. The hotels sell the 1/2 day Maohi Nui Lagoon Tour for 2-4 people for 54.500 CFP and the Polynesian Island full-day tour for 130.000 CFP for 2-4 people. The exclusive tour of Bora Bora's lagoon with lobsters and champagne is priced at 118.500 CFP by the hotels. See information under *Mountain Safaris and 4x4 Excursions* and *Wedding Ceremonies*.

Keishi Tours (Pierrot Picnic), *Tel. 67.67.31/79.26.56; keishitour@mail.pf.* Pierrot Taati has 2 motorized outrigger canoes. He works with some of the hotels, taking their guests on boat excursions around the island with a private picnic on a motu, and the tourists are very happy with Pierrot's excursions.

Other private picnic tours are organized by **Ben Heriteau** of **Diveasy**, *Tel. 79.22.55;* **Bora Bora Photo Lagoon**, *Tel. 77.10.96;* **Keawai Excursions**, *Tel. 60.40.95/78.27.97;* **Moana Adventure Tours**, *Tel. 67.61.41/78.27.37;* **Romantic Tours**, *Tel. 71.91.07;* **Tanoa Private Tours**, *Tel. 76.17.98;* and **Teiva Tours**, *Tel. 67.64.26/73.75.74.*

Sailing Charter Yachts

There is no big yacht charter company based in Bora Bora. You can rent a sailboat from one of the charter companies based in Tahiti, Moorea or Raiatea and sail to Bora Bora, or you can arrange for a yacht to be delivered to Bora Bora in time for your arrival. See Chapter 6, *Planning Your Trip*, section on Cruises.

Day Sailing Excursions & Sunset Cruises

Bora Bora Voile, *Tel./Fax 67.64.30; cell 75.84.07; boraboraexcursion.com.* Taaroa III is a Formula 40 Fleury Michon racing catamaran that accommodates 2-10 people for the morning excursions around the island and 2-16 passengers for a sunset sailing cruise. A sail around the island, from 8:45am-12:30pm, costs 8.000 CFP and includes a swim in the lagoon. Sunset cruises vary according to the season and cost 6.000 CFP per person. Captain Laurent Navarro also does private charters.

Cap-Lagoon, *Tel. 72.47.12; www.cap-lagoon.com.* **Tapatai** catamaran can accommodate up to 18 passengers for a half- or full-day sailing excursion, a sunset cruise, romantic cruise or full moon cruise.

Hobie Cat 21, *Tel. 67.63.63/78.26.36; hobbiebora@mail.pf.* Olivier Ringeard provides a totally ecological way to sail across the lagoon of Bora Bora on a 21-ft. Hobie Cat. A 90-min. Toopua tour with snorkeling is 16.000 CFP per person and 21.000 CFP for a couple. A private island tour with sushi and champagne is 45.000 CFP for 1 person and 60.000 CFP for 2.

Motor Yacht Charters

ROA Yachting Company, *B.P. 511, Bora Bora 98730; Tel. 689/70.96.20; manager@roa-yachting.com; www.roa-yachting.com.* Motor Yacht Roa is a Falcon 77-ft. Fiberglass French-owned a/c luxury yacht that is based in Bora Bora since Aug. 2007, providing 4-7 day charters in the Leeward Islands, day trips for 4-12 passengers inside the lagoon of Bora Bora or to Taha'a, and sunset cruises There are 4 cabins, crew quarters for 3, private bathrooms, a fully-equipped kitchen, living room, cockpit, fly bridge, aft deck, sunbathing deck and swimming deck. You can also rent the boat and its crew for an "a la carte" cruise. Rates quoted on request.

Scuba Diving

Bora Bora's scuba diving clubs have qualified instructors who will introduce you to a large variety of diving spots inside the lagoon and beyond the barrier reef. Visibility is usually 20 to 30 m, with an abundance of marine life, including manta rays, sharks, barracuda, dolphins and turtles. The lagoon of Bora Bora is the only one in the world where a family of manta rays lives year-round. Initiation dives, fun dives and night dives are available, with up to 4 outings a day.

Bora Bora Blue Nui, *Tel. 67.79.07/60.52.00; Fax 67.79.07; boraborablue nui@mail.pf; www.bluenui.com.* This dive center is based at the Bora Bora Pearl Beach Resort, and is headed by Gilles Petre, who also supervises the Blue Nui Dive Centers in Taha'a, Manihi and Tikehau. He is an international CMAS ** monitor, State instructor BEES 1, PADI instructor and OWSI, and can give exams for CMAS, PADI and FFESM certificates. Rates are 8.500 CFP for a fun dive, 8.500 CFP for an initiation dive, and 9.500 CFP for a night dive, including all the equipment. Blue Nui offers packages of 6 or 10 dives that can be used in any or all of the 4 Blue Nui Dive Centers, but cannot be shared between 2 people. They also offer a DVD video service on request.

Bora Diving Center, *Tel. 67.71.84; boradiving@mail.pf; www.boradiving.com* adjacent to the Hotel Bora Bora (closed) on Matira Beach. The friendly staff includes PADI instructors as well as BEES1 and BEES2 French State instructors who speak English. You can dive in the morning for 1 fun dive (8.500 CFP) or a 2-tank dive in the afternoon (14.500 CFP). Introductory dives and certification courses are held in the afternoon. Free pick-up by boat or car. Private boat or rebreather on request.

Diveasy, *Tel. 79.22.55; Fax 67.69.36; diveasy@mail.pf; www.boraboraisland.com/ diveasy/index.html*. Ben Heriteau offers private dives for 1-4 people, and this is reportedly a good dive center for beginners. He is a State Instructor BEES 1, Class II B. Examinations are given for ANMP and CMAS certification. He is equipped with an underwater communications system to allow comments during the dive and underwater camera rental is available. Several hotels use his services for private dives with personalized guidance. They charge 50.000 CFP for 2 people for 1 dive, 80.000 CFP per couple for 2 dives, and 20.000 CFP per person to dive with the humpback whales during the season (July-Oct.). An eco-snorkeling excursion is 10.000 CFP per person for 4-6 people.

Nemo World Bora Bora, *Tel. 67.77.85; mail@nemoworld.pf; www. www.boradiving.com*. This dive center is located on the beachfront adjacent to the Sofitel Marara Resort and is now part of the Bora Bora Diving Center. The multilingual staff includes certified PADI and BEES1 dive instructors who lead 2-tank dives in the mornings for 14.500 CFP and introductory dives in the afternoon for 8.500 CFP. Video films can also be made of your dive.

TOPDIVE-Bathys Bora Bora, *Tel. 60.50.50; Fax 60.50.51; borabora@topdive.com; www.topdive.com*. This is the biggest dive center in Bora Bora, with a location in Vaitape and another at the Intercontinental Bora Bora Resort & Thalasso Spa. The Dive Master is supported by a team of 7, including 3 instructors who are qualified to give PADI and ANMP certification. The equipment used is Aqualung, with 110 steel tanks for Air and Nitrox and 4 completely equipped dive boats can take 11-21 passengers plus crew to the special dive sites inside the lagoon or outside the coral reef. Specialties include Nitrox, private dives and manta diving. Public rates for scuba diving start at 8.500 CFP for an introductory dive or fun dive, and a Blue Honeymoon for 2 includes introductory dives, shell necklaces, fruit juice and a DVD, for 26.000 CFP. A 10-dive Gold inter-island pass (TOPDIVE-Bathys & Blue Nui) is 70.000 CFP for 1 or 2 divers.

Other Ways to Discover Bora Bora's Marine World

Aqua Bike Adventure, *Tel. 76.60.61; www.boraboraunderwaterscooter.com*. Anyone from 7-77 years old can drive the 2-seater mini-submarine that is shaped like an upside down bowl. This 1/2-day experience includes a swimming stop at a white sand beach motu and costs 12.250 CFP per person.

Aqua Safari Helmet Dive, *Tel.28.87.77; Fax 67/61/98; aquasafari@mail.pf; www.aquasafaribora.com*. Experience an unusual way in which to discover what's under Bora Bora's world-famous lagoon. You put a funny looking square yellow helmet over your head and you can walk on the lagoon bottom at a 3-m. (10-ft.) depth, without getting your head wet. And you don't even have to know how to swim or dive to discover this new sensation. The helmet is attached to air bottles just like the divers wear; only the bottles remain on the boat while you wander around under the water, breathing as you normally do. A bilingual guide accompanies 4-5 people while a dive master stays aboard the boat to check on the air supply. This 30-min. Undersea Walk takes you to a natural coral formation near Toopua Island, where nobody else goes. Here you can see a large variety of fish and maybe even some rays in the blue depths. The hotels charge 8.600 CFP for this Helmet Dive.

Bora Bora Submarine, *Tel. 67.55.55/74.99.99; www.spiritofpacific.com.* The *Spirit of Pacific* is a yellow submarine that will take 4-6 passengers down to 25 m. (82 ft.) below the water's surface to observe the world of corals and their animal life. The cabin is a/c with a 360° viewing port. You are transferred by boat to the submarine, which remains inside the protected lagoon between Bora Bora's main island and Motu Toopua. There are 5 outings per day and the hotels charge 24.000 CFP for 35 min. dive, including transfers. Children under 12 years old pay half price.

To'a Coral Nursery and Coral Fare, *www.spmhotels.com.* The coral nursery at Bora Bora Pearl Beach Resort & Spa was started in 2001, and has welcomed more than 70 types of fish that have made a home among the 4,000 coral colonies that have been collected and preserved in the resort's lagoon. In an effort to further develop the rescue program, the "Coral Fare" offers a variety of activities that guests can choose from to help maintain and expand the nursery.

The Coral Colony Sponsorship allows guests to choose a young coral colony to place within the nursery with assistance from an expert, which will be documented with a photo and certificate of sponsorship. The Biorock Sponsorship expands the resort's biorock implantation program by providing guests the opportunity to preserve a biorock with their family name, which will be permanently bound to the rock through a natural calcifying process. In addition, guests can participate in a Saving Coral Colonies tour that takes participants to the donor reef to collect specimens to bring back to the resort to place within the nursery. This tour provides a more in-depth introduction into the overall rescue program. Finally, the expert staff can join guests on a snorkeling excursion through the coral nursery, as well as offer an FM snorkel to provide an underwater soundtrack for the up close marine exploration. The rate of 3.000 CFP includes a 1-hr. Coral Colony Sponsorship, a 1-hr. introduction to snorkeling at To'a Nui, a 1-hr. rental of an FM Snorkel, and the Sponsorship of a Biorock in the hotel.

Glass Bottom Boat Excursions

Moana Adventure Tours, *Tel. 67.61.41* or *78.27.37,* has a covered glass bottom boat that operates tours from all the hotels. The cost at the high-end hotels is 4.100-4.300 CFP, and half-price for children under 12.

Jet-Ski or Wave-Runner Excursions

You can rent a jet ski for 1-2 hrs., with guides to take you around the island inside the lagoon. You'll stop on the *motu* islets, snorkel in beautiful coral gardens, feed the fish, visit the aquarium and even dive with the sharks and stingrays. The rental costs are 20.000 CFP for 1 hr. and 27.000-28.000 for 2 hrs. when you book through the hotels.

Matira Jet Tours, *Tel. 67.62.73/77.63.63*, is operated by Rainui Besineau on Point Matira. **Miki-Miki Jet Tours,** *Tel. 67.76.44/72.10.76,* is owned by Karl Chang, also on the beach at Point Matira. Jet skis or Wave-Runners can also be rented from **Maitai Tours,** *Tel. 67.72.73/79.08.66*; **Moana Adventure Tours,** *Tel. 67.61.41/78.27.37*; **Moana Jet Boat,** *Tel. 67.68.10/75.62.02.*

Sea Kayaks

Bora Bora Kayak, *Tel. 70.77.99; www.rohotufarelodge.com.* Nir Shalev at Rohotu Fare Lodge rents single or double American made sea kayaks that include storage space, paddles, snorkeling gear, life vests. backrests, dry bags, fishing poles, and cooler.

Water-Skiing & Wakeboard

Bora Bora Lagoona Ski, *Tel. 73.53.77, bobwaterski@mail.pf.* Patrick works with several hotels providing all levels of waterskiing: bi-ski, mono-ski, wakeboard, barefoot and buoy skiing. A 15-min. tour is 9.000 CFP, a 30-min. session is 13.000 CFP. Private water-skiing and snorkeling boat rides around the island available.

Parasailing

Bora Bora Parasail, *Tel. 70.56.62/78.27.10; parasail@mail.pf.* Their base is located adjacent to the former Novotel Bora Bora Beach Resort in the south of the island. You can soar solo or duo from 330-990 ft. high above the Bora Bora lagoon for a fabulous view. The take-off and landing is gentle and you won't even get wet. No experience required. A 15-min. flight up to 100 m. (330 ft.) costs 18.000 CFP for 1 person and 25.000 CFP for 2. A 30-min. flight up to 300 m. (990 ft.) is 23.000 CFP solo and 32.000-CFP duo. There is no age limit to this thrilling flight, which was tested and approved by Walt Disney World. Half price for children under 12 years old. Free transportation.

Kite Surfing

A Kite Surf School is based at Matira Beach, *Tel. 29.14.15; adsurfsystem@gmail.com.* Kite rentals and lessons available.

SHOPPING
Art Galleries

Galerie D'Art Alain and Linda, *Tel./Fax 67.70.32, alainlinda@mail.pf; www.borabora-art.com.* This interesting art gallery is on the beach side of Pofai Bay, between Vaitape village and the Matira area. Linda is a German painter and her French husband, Alain, paints the *pareos* and tee shirts that they sell. Their gallery has a collection of paintings, sculptures, pottery, etchings and lithographs by the finest artists from the Polynesian islands. They also carry art books and tapa bark paintings. Both of these friendly folks enjoy meeting people and Linda has a lot of stories to tell you about the legends and life of the island, where they have lived for more than 3 decades.

Galerie d'Art Pakalola, *Tel. 70.75.60*, is upstairs next to the post office in Vaitape. Isabelle Kerrien's fine art gallery presents paintings and other lovely objects created by Polynesian artists.

Garrick Yrondi, *Tel. 60.57.15; yrondi.art@mail.pf; www.yrondi.pf/ www.yrondi.org.* This multi-talented artist displays his paintings, collages, sculptures and bronzes in his Villa Rea Hana mountainside gallery located behind Boutique Gauguin in Amanahune. Yrondi created the pink marble statue of *vahine ei'a*, the fish woman, which you should look for at the edge of the Motu Mute lagoon by the airport. This is the protector of Bora Bora.

Paarara Mountain Artist, *Tel. 67.65.31*, is located above Faanui Bay, overlooking the lagoon and the Bora Bora Pearl Beach Resort. **Emmanuel Masson** learned to paint from his father, Jean Masson, who was a very well known French artist who first discovered Tahiti in 1938. Years later he met Rosine Temauri from Bora Bora, who became his favorite model and student, and together they had four children. Emmanuel exhibits his paintings of Polynesian people and Bora Bora scenery in his art gallery, and all the Safari tours stop here. If you want to rent a car and drive there, you should turn off the main road beside the church in Faanui and follow the winding road up the mountain until you see his sign. You can even picnic in his garden and gaze at the lovely view.

Other galleries include: **Bora Bora Art Naea Studio**, on mountainside in Faanui, *Tel. 67.71.17*; and **Atelier Patine**, *Tel. 67.74.09*, in Nunue.

Tahitian Cultured Pearls

Some of the pearl companies from Tahiti and Moorea also have outlets in Bora Bora. These include **Robert Wan's Tahiti Perles,** *Tel. 67.50.24* and **Tahiti Pearl Market,** *Tel. 60.38.60*. **Tahia Pearls,** *Tel. 60.37.00*, has a shop in Vaitape village and at the Intercontinental Bora Bora Resort & Thalasso Spa, *Tel. 67.56.00*. They also have shops in Tahiti, Moorea and aboard the *Paul Gauguin* cruise ship.

Matira Pearls & Fashions, *Tel. 67.79.14, www.matirapearls.com* is a well-established shop on the mountainside just east of Point Matira. Owner Steve Fearon is an expat American who opened the first pearl shop on the island that was outside of the hotels. Steve's family used to be part-owners of the Hotel Bora Bora and the Hotel Tahara'a in Tahiti. The shop is open daily, presenting lovely quality pearls at attractive prices.

Bora Pearl Company, *Tel. 60.37.77/70.06.75, www.borapearl.com* is at Raititi Point near the Hotel Bora Bora property. Owners Dany Leverd and Tea Suchard of Bora Bora get their lovely pearls from a pearl farm in Taha'a and other sources, but they have also built a small pearl farm inside the lagoon, which is called **The Farm**. This is Bora Bora's only pearl farm, and visitors can learn all about how a cultured pearl is produced as they watch the process being demonstrated by trained technicians. A good sales gimmick here is to take a honeymoon couple in a boat to visit the grafted oysters suspended in wire baskets inside the lagoon and let the husband dive and choose an oyster. When the pearl is extracted, he then presents it to his bride. She can take it home unset or have the pearl drilled and set while they watch and drink champagne. This is an automatic stop for the Tupuna Mountain Safari Tours, which is also owned by Dany Leverd.

Arc en Ciel, Tel. 67.59.98/71.98.89, *iliana@mail.pf; www.arcencielborabora.com.* Owner Wendy Hebert is a very personable Polynesian who has more than 10 years' experience in the cultured pearl business and a certificate from the Gemological Institute of America (GIA). You'll enjoy meeting her and seeing her collection of Rainbow (Arc en Ciel) pearls. Wendy, as well as most of the pearl shops, will provide complimentary shuttle service to visit their showrooms.

La Pearla Joaillerie, *Tel. 67.63.91, designer@pearls-corp-borabora.com.* This is one of the newest additions to the pearl shops in Vaitape and you will enjoy visiting their sophisticated showroom beside the lagoon near the post office. Open daily 9am-6pm.

Clothing & Souvenirs

The Arts and Crafts Center at the Vaitape quay has grass skirts and coconut bras, shell jewelry and woven hats and bags that are handmade by the people who sell them, even though most of the seashells were imported.

Boutique Bora Bora, *Tel. 67.79.72,* is on the mountainside in the center of Vaitape village, displaying a collection of Polynesian arts & crafts, jewelry, home interior accents, fashion accessories and Polynesian epicurean delights.

Boutique Gauguin, *Tel. 67.76.67,* in Nunue, is a large shop that sells Paul Gauguin prints, black pearls, clothing and handcrafts.

Mom's Boutique, *Tel. 67.69.29,* in Vaitape next to Fashion Bora Bora is a good place to shop for traditional Polynesian clothes, pareos, handcrafts, curios and Kaenon sunglasses.

Bora Bora Shop, *Tel. 67.77.10,* is in the Royal Helen's Bay Center, selling T-shirts and surfwear for all the family. Pahia Center is a small shopping center beside the lagoon in Vaitape village with pearl shops, a few clothing boutiques and miscellaneous gift shops. Be sure to check out the hotel boutiques on the motu islets as well as the main island. All around the island you will find little boutiques and thatched roof stands that sell hand-printed *pareos*, tee-shirts, swimwear and all kinds of creative souvenir items that were actually made on Bora Bora. Don't be fooled into buying an authentic made-in-Bali carving that has the name Bora Bora stamped on it.

Bora Home is in the center of Vaitape village, featuring a collection of Polynesian arts and crafts, jewelry, home interior accents and fashion accessories.

Photos and Photographers

Bora Bora Photo Lagoon, *Tel. 77.10.96; damien@boraboraphotolagoon.com; www.boraboraphotolagoon.com.* Damien Dunand is a multi-lingual professional photographer who leads special photo safaris aboard a Bayliner B217 deckboat (party boat) with a sunroof, shower, bar, kitchen and stereo. His special 2-3 hr. cruises are designed for honeymooners and other vacationers who want souvenir photos of their trip to Bora Bora. He will take 200-300 photos in 2 hrs. and burn them to a CD and make them into postcards for you. See his website for details. **Cathy Camera Shop**, *Tel. 72.01.23,* works with several of the top hotels, to photograph or film any occasion such as weddings, anniversaries, gatherings, reunions or whatever you want for your souvenir album. **Loisirs Photo Video**, Tel. 60.58.35; Fax 60.58.36; lpv@mail.pf in Vaitape provides computer services for photo, video, hi-fi and sound, as well as printing. **Moe Productions**, *Tel. 67.52.89,* moeprod@mail.pf, provides professional photographic services.

MASSAGES & SPAS

Espace Bien-Etre, *Tel. 60.51.51,* is a massage and body care center located in one of the lagoon bungalows at Le Méridien. This place of well-being consists of two massage tables where you can indulge your hedonistic nature with a rubdown with coconut fiber, crushed coffee beans or sand perfumed with oils, followed by an aromatic bath or floral bath, a seaweed wrap, facial and a choice of massages.

Hina Spa, *Tel. 60.33.00,* is built on the hillside at the Hilton Bora Bora Nui Resort & Spa. There are 3 private and luxurious treatment bungalows hidden within the lush vegetation. You have an unsurpassed view of the azure waters of Bora Bora's world famous lagoon and Otemanu mountain from one terrace and a panoramic sweeping view of the lagoon and Pacific Ocean from the other side of the spa. Each Spa bungalow is equipped with its own Jacuzzi. Body massages, foot massages, body scrubs, body wraps and facials start at 8.500 CFP for 30-min. The Signature Therapies and Massages include a Ta'u Here-Time for Two Special that begins with a 30 min. skin-and-muscle softening hydrotherapy bath, followed by a relaxing body massage for 50 min. or 80 min. A Nehe Nehe 4-hr. treatment is 42.500 CFP for one person and 75.500 CFP for two, and begins with a floral foot bath, followed by a body scrub, body wrap, a Jacuzzi bath, champagne and sweets, then a relaxing body massage and a soothing facial.

Kahaia Spa at Four Seasons, *Tel. 60.31.30, www.fourseasons.com/borabora.* Open daily 8am-8pm. Spa treatments from 9am-7pm. You are encouraged to arrive 60 min. prior to your scheduled appointment in order to enjoy the Spa facilities, which include a steam room, outdoor vitality pool, sensory experience shower, drench shower, changing room with lockers, and separate relaxation lounges for female and male guests. The Kahaia Spa Suite has two treatment beds placed over glass windows open to views of the water below and from here you can see the Jacuzzi on the covered deck and the private lagoon bordered by coconut palms. The Kahaia Spa Suite package includes 2 hours of chosen treatments and 1 hour of relaxation, for 90.000 CFP per couple. There's a charge of 15.000 CFP for any extra treatment and a 10.000 CFP surcharge for a 1-hour coconut bath. The natural resources of French Polynesia are used in the treatments and rituals, such as monoi, tamanu, kahaia and vanilla. The Spa also features Osea's signature holistic treatments using 100% certified organic seaweed. Osea is the world's leading brand of marine-based natural skincare products. Kahaia Spa also offers a special massage, body scrub, facial and manicure just for teens.

Le Spa at Sofitel, *Tel. 60.55.00*, is located in 2 bungalows at the edge of the lagoon at the Sofitel Bora Bora Marara Beach, with 5 therapy rooms and outdoor Jacuzzis. Le Spa offers an array of massages and beauty treatments for individuals and couples. Tahiti's local plants and traditional Tahitian techniques are blended with Thalasso therapies to give you a feeling of relaxation and well being for body and soul. Also on offer are world-renowned beauty treatments from an exclusive partnership with Lancôme.

Manea Spa, *Tel. 60.53.85, maneaspa@borapearlbeach.pf; www.maneaspa.com.* This spa at the Bora Bora Pearl Beach Resort has earned an excellent reputation and won many awards. Spa manager Kamala Nayeli is from Arizona and has managed spas all over the world, and the massage therapists are well trained Polynesians. There are 8 treatment rooms spread over a 600 sq. m. (6,460 sq. ft.) area next to a lake in the heart of a tropical garden. You can choose a 30-min. monoi massage for 7.727 CFP, up to the Manea Manea, the ultimate body bliss, which lasts for 3 hr. 20 min. and costs 40.909 CFP for one and 68.182 CFP for two. The spa menu offers full body massage, body shaping, body wraps, hot stone healing, four hands massage, scalp massage and reflexology, after sun care, men's and women's facials, manicures and pedicures and waxing. There are also 2 saunas, 2 steam baths, a relaxation room, and the Manea line of 100% natural local products for complete body care. The Royale Pomare Suite, the Manea Spa's centerpiece, is a distinctive treatment room for honeymooners and couples, who can enjoy a private session that includes an exfoliating body polish, a coconut bath by candlelight, a relaxing couple's massage and a bottle of champagne. You can even get a tattoo in this spa. You may purchase a day pass for 1.818 CFP to enjoy full use of the spa even if you are not receiving treatment. This includes use of the gym, lockers, steam room, sauna, shower and relaxation lounge.

Miri Miri Spa, *Tel. 60.78.88*, is the world-class signature spa at the St. Regis Resort, Bora Bora. Occupying 13,000 sq. ft. of space on its own private island, the spa is accessible by a footbridge across its private lagoon. Tahitian and Pacific Rim treatments are available in 7 luxurious spa suites. These include Balinese, Table-Taï, Neuomuscular and Ayurvedic Abhyanga Massage.

Exclusive to Miri Miri Spa, Robert Wan, the world's largest cultivator and exporter of Tahiti pearls, has created signature spa treatments utilizing his luxurious cosmetic product line Pearl Spirit. These treatments integrate warmed black pearls, mother-of-pearl salve, mother-of-pearl powder, and mother-of-pearl body milk. Miri Miri Spa also uses Comfortone from Italy.

The founding principles of the Miri Miri Spa are based on the Seven Pillars of Well-Being. A 2-day package was designed using the principles of harmony, beauty, vitality, aqua, life balance, nature and nutrition. This 140-min. Miri Miri rejuvenation for two is 60.000 CFP. A 2-day Intimate Relaxation package is 73.000 CFP per couple for a treatment of 170 min.

Thalasso Deep Ocean Spa, *Tel. 60.77.00; www.boraboraspa.intercontinental.com.* This is the first thalasso spa in the world to harness the virtues of sea water from the ocean's depths. Built on a private motu at the Intercontinental Bora Bora Resort, the Deep Ocean Spa houses a complex of 13,200 sq. ft. (1,226 sq. m.), offering 14 treatment booths that are air-conditioned with water siphoned through a pipeline outside the coral that is 3,000 ft. (915 m. deep). This unique balneotherapy and thalassotherapy center was conceived by Dr. Tregger, who designed Monaco's thermal baths. It is managed by the Algotherm company, whose reputation and expertise extend all over the world.

From the Deep Ocean Spa's glass-floored overwater treatment suites, individual guests or couples can admire maritime flora and fauna during sessions designed to help you relax and replenish your body's minerals and restore equilibrium. The facilities also include multisensorial outdoor spas, a phlebological course, a fitness room with cardio training area, steam baths and showers to awaken the senses, a traditional *fare* to relax while facing the ocean, a meditation garden, tea lounge and iced bath. There are changing rooms for men and women and an elevator for guests in wheel chairs.

At the entrance to the Deep Ocean Spa are 3 fountains where you can sample the desalinated, extraordinarily purified deep sea water. This cold water (41°F, 5°C), contains an excellent complement of nutritional mineral salts. It is bottled under the label "Vai Moana" (the ocean source) right at the Spa, and is sold in the **Boutique by Algotherm** that is located at the entrance to the Deep Ocean Spa. Algotherm and Hei Poa products, clothing, jewelry and wellness books are also sold here.

A 20-min. marine deep sea hydro-massage bath with essential oils for 6.000 CFP is one of many à la carte choices for water treatments. An Algospa marine scrub and wrap lasts for 75 min. and costs 17.900 CFP. Facials include an eyelash tint for 5.300 CFP and an Algo performance facial for 21.500 CFP. The "Massages of the World" menu suggests a special 60-min. jet lag massage for 17.000 CFP or a 90-min. deep blue massage for 28.400 CFP. Discovery treatment packages offer a 2-hr. Detox for 34.800 CFP, a 2 1/2-hr. Honeymoon treatment for 2 in an overwater Spa Suite for 90.200 CFP, and a 5-hr. "Chill Out in Bora Bora" for 2 people for 143.200 CFP. Treatment packages for 3 or 5 days are also available, under the themes of Vitality, Deep Serenity, Natural Beauty, Pure Slimming, Honeymoon (for 2), and The Ultimate by Algotherm. Waxings, hot stone foot massage, hand bliss and foot bliss are also available for men and women, as well as delightful add-ons, such as a hot stone foot massage, collagen eyes or lips re-pulp care.

TATTOO ARTISTS

Bora Bora Ink, *Tel. 79.29.65, dinostours@yahoo.fr; www.boraboraink.com.* Polynesian Tattoo shop is across the road from the boat dock in Vaitape. Open Mon.-Sat. 9am-5pm. Owner Dino Dexter has always liked to draw and now he is realizing another of his lifelong dreams. He has been an actor, model, tour guide in California, Mister Bora Bora 1995, Mister Tahiti 2001 and 2nd runner-up for Mister France 2002. Then he returned to Bora Bora and skippered a 65-ft. sailing catamaran and started Dino's Tours & Excursions and Dino's Land & Water Taxi. In 2009 he opened a tattoo shop, along with Angelo, who has a diploma from the Arts and Crafts training center in Tahiti. You can see their tattoo designs on the website and make plans to get your own "tat" during your stay in Bora Bora.

Marama Traditional Tattoo, *Tel. 67.66.73/72.03.75,* is located on the lagoon side in Matira between Point Matira and Le Maitai Polynesia. Teriimarama Olson is a half-American half-Polynesian native of Bora Bora who designs the tattoo to suit the individual.

PRACTICAL INFORMATION

Banks

Bora Bora has three banks, which are all located in Vaitape village. **Banque de Tahiti,** *Tel. 60.59.99,* **Banque Socredo,** *Tel. 60.50.10,* and **Banque de Polynésie,** *Tel. 60.57.57.* All the banks have ATM windows.

Books, Magazines, Newspapers, Cigars

Maison de la Presse, *Tel. 60.57.75,* is located on the mountainside in Vaitape village, adjacent to the Gendarmerie. They sell coffee table books, travel guides, local and international newspapers and magazines.

Cybercafé/Internet Service

You can check your E-mail while enjoying your morning coffee and croissant at Aloe Café in the Centre Commercial Le Pahia in Vaitape village, *Tel 67.78.88; Fax 60.56.80; aloecafe@mail.pf.* They are open 6:30am-5pm Mon.-Sat. and have 4 speedy computers with WiFi, Skype, English or French keyboards, printers, scanners and webcams. Rates start at 400 CFP for 10 minutes.

Garden Café, *Tel. 67.60.00. In Centre Mautera on mountainside in Tiipoto, just outside Vaitape village toward Matira.* This Snack/Cyber Café has free WiFi and is open Mon.-Fri. 6am-3:30pm and 6-10pm, and on Sat. 6-10pm.

The Post Office has ManaSpot WiFi. Most hotels also have computers and WiFi Internet service available for their clients, sometimes without extra charge. You can also plug in your laptop to the Internet connection in your hotel room, which costs much more, of course.

Doctors

There are private doctors and a dentist at the Medical Cabinet in Nunue, *Tel.* *67.70.62*, and a government-operated dispensary is located in Vaitape, *Tel.* *67.70.77.* Dentists are located in the Pahia Center, *Tel. 67.70.61* and in Vaitape, *Tel. 67.69.42.* There are also 2 physiotherapists in Vaitape.

Drugstore

Pharmacie Bora Bora, *Tel. 67.70.30,* is located on the mountainside of the road in Vaitape village. It is open Mon.-Sat. 8am-6pm and on Sun. and holidays from 9-11am.

Police

The French *gendarmerie* is on the mountainside opposite the quay in Vaitape, *Tel. 60.59.05. The emergency number for police is 17.*

Post Office & Telecommunications Office

The Post Office is in Vaitape village on the circle island road near the quay, *Tel. 67.70.74.* Hours are 8am-3pm on Mon., 7:15am-3:15pm Tues.-Thurs., 7:15am-2:15pm on Fri., and 8-10am on Sat. All telecommunications and postal services are available here and there is an ATM window outside.

Tourist Information

Comité du Tourisme de Bora Bora (Bora Bora Tourism Committee) is located in Fare Manihini on the quay in Vaitape, *Tel. 67.76.36; info-borabora@mail.pf; www.borabora-tourisme.com.* Hours are 9am-12pm and 1-4pm Mon.-Fri., and on Sat. from 9am-12pm. They are closed on Sun. and holidays unless there is a ship in port.

Bora Bora Activites, *Tel. 73.54.22; gieboraboraactivites@mail.pf; www.borabora-tourisme.com* is associated with the Comité du Tourisme and is located in the 3 Tiki boutique in Vaitape.

Wedding Ceremonies

Patrick's Activities/Maohi Nui Private Excursions. *Tel. 67.69.94,79.19.11; patrick@maohinui.net; www.maohinui.net.* I watched Patrick Tairua perform a Polynesian wedding ceremony on the beach at one of the resort hotels in Bora Bora, and I thought it was the most touching, romantic sensation a couple in love could experience. The bride and groom were dressed in white pareos and wore a crown of flowers on their heads. Patrick, the *tahua* priest, was dressed in a yellow costume with a necklace of mother-of-pearl and feathers. He conducted the ceremony in Tahitian and translated the words into English, with a gentle look at the couple he was marrying (unofficially). It was a magical moment for everyone who watched this performance. The Polynesians use the word *mana* to describe a sacred power, and Patrick is definitely filled with this presence, this *mana*.

Patrick has created his own Maohi Nui programs of ceremonies that are very popular with couples who want to be married in the traditional Polynesian style or anniversary twosomes who wish to renew their vows. These unofficial weddings include choices of a 12-minute **Intimate** ceremony, a 15-minute **Simple** ceremony, or a **Traditional** ceremony that lasts for 30 minutes. All three rituals can be held on Matira Beach in a setting made of coconut leaves and hibiscus flowers, usually beginning in late afternoon.

For the Traditional and Simple ceremonies on Matira Beach, the couple wears the white pareos that are provided. The priest leads the ceremony and declares the husband "tane" and the wife "vahine" under the Polynesian tradition, before giving them a Tahitian name. The couple exchanges flower leis and crowns, which symbolizes harmony, before receiving the wedding certificate from the priest. The certificate is made on a fine peace of tree bark called "tapa". Songs, music and dances punctuate the entire ceremony. During the Intimate wedding on Matira Beach only the priest is present with the couple, and the vows and prayers stay the same as in the traditional ceremony. They also receive one wedding certificate made of tapa.

A Traditional Polynesian wedding can also take place on a motu islet, usually from 3:30-5:30pm, including the ride in a flower-decorated outrigger canoe to and from the motu. The wedding couple dress in their white pareos and flowers once they are on the motu, and two Polynesian "warriors" take them in their arms to meet the priest for the ceremony. The Maohi Nui group sings and dances during the 30-min. ceremony. A bottle of Moët et Chandon champagne is opened and the happy couple sip their bubbly as they watch the sunset and listen to the tunes played on a ukulele during their outrigger canoe ride across the lagoon back to their hotel. A Simple ceremony of 15 minutes is the same as the Traditional wedding except there are no warriors to carry them ashore as they are alone with the priest and one musician. The pareos, flowers, tapa wedding certificate and champagne are all included.

Maohi Nui's **Honeymoon Day** program is especially made for the couples who wish to celebrate their love with a 30-minute Polynesian wedding on a motu, as well as discovering Bora Bora's natural wonders with a lagoon excursion and Polynesian lunch or BBQ, if they prefer. The lunch comes with a good bottle of Moët and Chandon champagne, or red/white wine depending on the guests' preference. Contact Patrick Tairua for more information and rates.

Wedding Chapels

Bora Bora Pearl Beach Resort, Bora Bora Nui Resort & Spa, Four Seasons Resort, Intercontinental Bora Bora Resort & Spa and Le Méridien have wedding chapels for more classic type ceremonies.

You can also get married on a catamaran or underwater in Bora Bora. And now you can even get married legally at the town hall (Marie) on the island of your choice without having to establish residency in French Polynesia a month in advance. See information under *Getting Married* in Chapter 7 of this guide.

Yacht Clubs & Services

MAI KAI MARINA & YACHT CLUB, *B.P. 162, Vaitape, Bora Bora 98730. Tel. 22.10.33 (marina); Tel. 60.38.00 (restaurant); info@maikaimarina.com; www.maikaimarina.com. Situated at Lat. 16°29'S, Lon. 151°45'W. facing Teavanui Pass in Bora Bora. They monitor VHF channel 16 and converse on channel 69.*

This new boutique marina and yacht club opened in mid-2011 on the site of the former TOPdive hotel, restaurant and dive center near Vaitape village. It is managed by Teiva & Jessica Tapare, a Polynesian/American couple who ran the Bora Bora Yacht Club until Feb. 3, 2010, when Cyclone Oli destroyed their pier and dock, sushi bar and 3 overwater bungalows.

In addition to spectacular sunsets, the Mai Kai Marina & Yacht Club offers an array of services including an excellent waterside restaurant and bar. The marina has 25 moorings for vessels up to 60 ft., a 150 ft. mooring ball, a 98-ft. floating dock and a 48 ft. stationary dock with berths for mega yachts. This new yacht club provides all the facilities for yachts, including a water filling station, hot showers, laundry facilities, Wi-Fi internet services, trash disposal, re-provisioning, book exchange, and most of all fun. They will hold your mail or packages for your arrival.

BLOODY MARY'S YACHT CLUB, *Tel. 67.72.86; www.bloodymarys.com. On the mountainside in Pofai Bay, 5 km (3 mi.) from Vaitape. Open for lunch and dinner Mon.-Sat. and on boat days. Bar open 9:30am-11pm. Closed Sun. AE, MC and V.*

Sailing yachts can anchor for short periods of time in the deep waters of Povai Bay, using one of 8 moorings provided by the "Bloody Mary's Yacht Club". Tie your dinghy to the 98-ft. long dock and amble across the road to the barefoot bar/ restaurant for a cold drink and great food.

17. Maupiti

If you appreciate the beauty of Bora Bora but not the mass tourism and exorbitant prices, **Maupiti** offers similar scenery, peace and tranquility, as well as an authentic Polynesian experience, with genuinely friendly people who are not burned out by seeing too many tourists. If you want to find out what Bora Bora was like 40 years ago, then go to Maupiti. It offers so much more than sunshine, white sand beaches and a turquoise lagoon. The rhythm of life is slow and easy. There's gentleness to the place and the people that will answer a longing inside you to know the "real Polynesia." The villagers still smile and say "Ia Ora Na" when you meet. The longer you stay in Maupiti, the longer you will want to stay.

Lying just 40 km. (25 miles) west of bustling Bora Bora, Maupiti is considered the hidden jewel in the necklace of emerald islands and atolls that make up the Society Islands. Some people say it's one of the prettiest islands in the South Seas.

Like Bora Bora, Maupiti has a central island with a high mountain range of volcanic origins, and is surrounded by a shallow, sparkling lagoon with 5 long offshore *motu* islets bordered by beautiful white sand beaches. **Onoiau** is the name of a narrow pass leading into the lagoon. This formerly dangerous pass is more easily navigable since channel markers were added, but it can still be hazardous during high seas. The clear turquoise lagoon has pretty coral gardens, a plentiful supply of edible fish, lobsters, tridacna clams, *vana*, an edible sea urchin, and even *varo*, a sea centipede that is sought by gourmets. The *motus* provide coral gardens for watermelon and cantaloupe plantations, as well as secluded white sand beaches for sunbathing and excellent snorkeling grounds a few feet into the lagoon.

Mount Teurafaatiu rises 380 m. (1,246 ft.) above the central island, and is relatively easy to scale for panoramic views. **Point Tereia** on the main island is a lovely white sand beach in a natural environment, a favorite swimming site for the young people from the villages. Some of the older folks compare this beach to what Point Matira in Bora Bora was like many decades ago. From Point Tereia you can walk across the lagoon to the *motu*, in waist-deep water. Although you may encounter a few curious sharks, just hit the water hard with the palm of your hand and yell at them, and they will swim away. It works for the locals, and no tourists have been injured to date by the "friendly" sharks that grew up inside the lagoon.

Geologists say that Maupiti is the oldest of the high islands in the Society archipelago, and was formed some four million years ago.

Dr. Yoshihiko H. Sinoto and Dr. Kenneth P. Emory of the Bernice P. Bishop Museum in Honolulu excavated a burial site in Maupiti in 1962 and 1963, unearthing 13 skeletons from the ninth century. Inside the tombs on Motu Pa'eao were adzes, fishhooks, lures and sperm whale tooth pendants that date back to circa

850 AD. This is one of the oldest archaeological sites in the Society Islands, and one of the most important. Doctor Sinoto said that the whale tooth pendants were the first material cultural link between the Society Islands and the New Zealand Maoris. Other archaeological sites include 2 more *marae* on the *motus* and 2 *marae* on the high island. In the valley of Heranae are petroglyphs representing turtles, a sacred animal for the ancient Maohi people.

At one time there were 9 districts and 9 royal Maohi chiefs on Maurua Ite Ra, as Maupiti was then called. Chiefs came from other islands to meet at the royal Marae Vaiahu for gatherings that included investiture ceremonies. A huge boulder at the stone temple has been engraved with the names of these chiefs, who came from Rimatara, Raivavae, Rapa, Atiu in the Cook Islands, and Hawaii. One of these kings was said to have come from Malaysia.

The Dutch explorer Roggeveen discovered Maupiti in 1722; 45 years before Samuel Wallis discovered Tahiti. It was united with Bora Bora during the reign of the last royal family. The 9 villages of ancient times have dwindled to the 3 contiguous villages of Vai'ea, Farauru and Pauma, where most of the 1,248 inhabitants live.

ARRIVALS & DEPARTURES
Arriving By Air
Air Tahiti, *Tel. 86.42.42* in Tahiti; *Tel. 60.15.05* in Maupiti, has a flight from Tahiti to Maupiti each Tues., 2 flights on Fri. and a Sun. flight, all with stops in Raiatea. During the high seasons there are non-stop flights from Tahiti to Maupiti on Mon. and Wed., and an additional flight on Fri. with a stop in Raiatea. There are direct flights from Raiatea to Maupiti on Tues., 2 on Fri. and 1 on Sun. There is a direct flight from Bora Bora on Sunday and a Fri. flight from Bora Bora that changes planes in Raiatea. The Maupiti airstrip is located on a *motu* islet across the lagoon from the main village. If you have reservations for a place to stay then you will be met at the airport and taken by boat to the pension. Otherwise, you can catch a ride with one of the taxi boats that goes to the airport for each flight arrival. The one-way airfare between Tahiti and Maupiti is 16.930 CFP and the round-trip fare is 31.360 CFP. The one-way fare between Raiatea and Maupiti is 8.330 CFP, and 7.930 CFP from Bora Bora.

You can also get to Maupiti by chartering an airplane in Tahiti from **Air Tahiti**, *Tel. 86.42.42*, or **Pol'Air**, *Tel. 74.23.11*. **Tahiti Helicopter Service**, *Tel. 67.54.90*, *www.tahiti-helicopters.com* can also fly you from Bora Bora to Maupiti as a transfer or for a day tour. They can wait or come back for you at the end of the day.

Arriving By Boat
Maupiti Express II, *Tel. 689/67.66.69 (Bora Bora); cell phone 78.27.22/ 72.30.48; www.maupitiexpress.com*. This 140-passenger ship provides service between Raiatea, Taha'a, Bora Bora and Maupiti. The *Maupiti Express II* leaves Bora Bora on Thurs. and Sat. at 8:30am, arriving in Maupiti at 10:15am. The one-

way fare from Bora Bora is 4.000 CFP and round-trip is 5.000 CFP. Passengers under 12 years pay half-fare. If you want to take a day-trip from Bora Bora to Maupiti, you should contact Gérald Sachet at the above cell phone numbers. He is the owner/captain of *Maupiti Express II* and his wife runs the Pension Poe Iti, which serves as a land base for day-trippers. They have a small boat that is used for exploring the lagoon and motu islets. See information under *Where to Stay* and *Land and Lagoon Tours* in this chapter.

Departing By Air
Air Tahiti, *Tel. 60.15.05*; Tahiti Reservations *Tel. 86.42.42*. Air Tahiti has 4 flights from Maupiti to Papeete each week, stopping at Raiatea on Tues., twice on Fri. and once on Sun. During the high seasons there are direct flights to Tahiti each Mon. and Wed. There is a direct flight to Bora Bora on Sun.

Departing By Boat
Maupiti Express II, *Tel. 67.66.69/78.27.22/*72.30.48, leaves Maupiti at 4pm for Bora Bora each Thurs. and Sat. The trip takes 1:45 hrs. and the one-way fare is 4.000 CFP. Passengers under 12 years pay half price.

ORIENTATION
The main village is **Vai'ea**, where the town hall, Air Tahiti office, post office, church, school, airport boat dock, family pensions, snacks and a few small stores are located. This village suffered severe destruction in Nov. 1997 when Cyclone Osea destroyed 95 percent of the houses and buildings on the island. Most of the houses are now of the MTR variety, which is a box-like 'anti-cyclone' design, built on stilts. Each family has added their own touch of flowers and colored leaves planted around the houses to make them more attractive.

GETTING AROUND MAUPITI
By Bicycle
Maupiti Bike, *Tel. 67.80.11/71.29.97*, **Puanere Locations**, Tel. *67.81.68*, **Loana Manuarii**, *Tel. 67.81.46/*78.94.38, **Arieta Firuu**, *Tel. 67.80.63*, and others rent bikes for 1.000 CFP per day at the public boat dock in Vai'ea village. Bikes are also provided at some of the family pensions.

By Mini-Van
Visit Maupiti *Tel./Fax 67.80.95. cell 21.88.21*. Ui Teriihaunui provides excursions around the island in his 9-seat a/c Mercedes-Benz minibus. Day-trippers arriving on the *Maupiti Express* can spend the day with him and learn about life in Maupiti, as well as the history, geology and legends. Ui speaks French, but not much English.

By Boat
Maupiti Poe Iti Tours and Visit Maupiti provide boat excursions around the island and picnics on the motu. See information under *Lagoon Tours* in this chapter.

WHERE TO STAY & EAT
On the Motus – Moderate
LE KURIRI, *B.P. 23, Vai'ea, Maupiti 98732. Tel./Fax 689/67.82.23; Cell 689/74.54.54; kuriri@mail.pf; www.maupiti-kuriri.com. Beside the ocean on Motu Tiapa'a, an islet 15 min. by boat from the airport. MC, V.*

Since 2003 this lodging has been owned by Anne Marie Badolle and her husband, Camille Marjorel, a French couple who sailed their boat around the world before settling down in Maupiti. There are 4 bungalows built of natural materials that face the beach or the garden. 2 of the *fares* contain a double bed or 2 twin beds, plus a private bathroom with hot water. The 2 family *fares* have a double bed, mattresses on the mezzanine, a living room and a private bathroom with hot water. All the beds are covered by a mosquito net. Lighting is by solar power, and guests have access to telephone, fax and WiFi Internet service in the reception area. 2011/2012 rates are 12.600 CFP per person, which include lodging and half board (Continental breakfast and dinner), and airport transfers. Half-rate for children 2-12. A 1-course light lunch is 1.870 CFP and a full 3-course lunch is 2.860 CFP.

Rather than facing the inner lagoon, the view you'll have here is of the open ocean and Bora Bora in the distance, and if you get up early in the morning you can watch the sunrise behind Bora Bora. There is even a panoramic lookout deck built above the seaside dining area, for gazing at the sea and sky. The beach on the ocean side is always cooled by the trade winds and you can take a nice siesta under the thatched roof of the cushioned contemplation deck overlooking the sea. You can swing in a hammock or lie on a chaise longue. However, if you are visiting between Jul.-Oct. you may want to remain vigilant and be on the lookout for humpback whales. Snorkeling equipment and sea kayaks are free for guest use, as well as lagoon fishing and reef discovery walks. Paid activities and excursions are 3.000-4.500 CFP per person and include a boat tour around the island and a snorkeling excursion in the north of the island. Tahiti Tourism gives this pension a 3-Tiare rating. Anne Marie and Camille both speak English.

FARE PA'EAO, *B.P. 33, Vai'ea, Maupiti 98732. Tel./Fax 689/67.81.01; cell 72.81.25; fare.pae.ao@mail.pf; www.maupitilodge.com. On Motu Pa'eao, 10 min. by boat from the airport. MC, V.*

This pension has 6 bungalows of the FEI type that have become the standard Polynesian bungalow partially financed by the local government. Tahiti Tourism has awarded them a 3-Tiare rating. These are wooden bungalows with a wood shake roof, and the rooms have a double bed and a single bed, a ceiling fan, an electric anti-mosquito device, a mosquito net over the beds, a terrace and a private

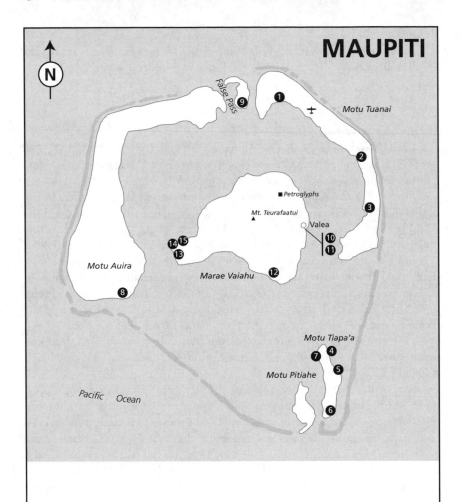

MAUPITI

Motu Tuanai

Petroglyphs

Mt. Teurafaatui

Valea

Motu Auira

Marae Vaiahu

Motu Tiapa'a

Motu Pitiahe

Pacific Ocean

False Pass

1. Pension Terama
2. Pension Poe Iti
3. Pension Marau
4. Pension Rose Des Iles
5. Pension Maupiti Village
6. Le Kuriri
7. Pension Papahani
8. Pension Auira
9. Pension Pa'eao

10. Pension Eri
11. Pension Taputea
12. Pension Tautiare
13. Pension Teheimana
14. Maupiti Residence
15. Tereia Beach

bathroom with cold water shower. MAP bungalow and transfer is 17.852 CFP sgl; 23.120 CFP dbl; taxes included. Breakfast and dinner are served in the communal dining room. Free kayaks are provided for guests, and an island tour by boat is 5.000 CFP per person. Lagoon and deep sea fishing available. The snorkeling is very good here and the sunsets are sometimes incredible. This pension is also known as Chez Janine, who has now retired. Her son Nelson Tavearii and his wife Lahaina are now in charge and they speak English.

PENSION AUIRA, *B.P. 2, Vai'ea, Maupiti 98732. Tel./Fax 689/67.80.26. Cell 72.24.24. On Motu Auira, 20 min. by boat from the airport. No credit cards.*

The beach here is very beautiful when it is clean, with soft white powdery sand and clear shallow water in the lagoon that is deep enough for swimming if you walk out into the blue water several feet distant. All of the former *fares* were destroyed by Cyclone Osea in 1997. Since then Edna Terai and her husband Gilbert, who are both Polynesian, have built 6 bungalows on the beach and in the garden, but they are now in need of repair and refreshing. Each of the rustic *fares* has a double bed, mosquito screens, a fan and a private bathroom with cold water. Family style meals are served in the main house. Campers can pitch their tent in the shaded garden or on the beach and they also have bathroom facilities with a cold water shower and can cook their meals in the kitchen, which has a refrigerator.

Edna can arrange for your boat excursions with a picnic or to watch the manta rays and feed the stingrays inside the lagoon. Her husband will take you by boat to the village on request, where you can bike around the island or hike in the mountains.

PENSION MARAU, *B.P. 11, Vai'ea, Maupiti 98732. Tel. 689/67.81.19/ 70.56.09/72.48.86; Fax 689/67.82.46; contact@pension-marau.com; www.pension-marau.com. On Motu Tuanai, 5 min, by 4WD from the airport and the village. No credit cards.*

This pension with 7 modern bungalows is on the same motu as the airport. Each bungalow has a double bed, a ceiling fan, a private bathroom with cold water, and a covered terrace. Mosquito repellents and house linens are provided, and the rooms are cleaned every 2 days. Polynesian type meals of lagoon fish, breadfruit, taro, sweet potatoes and plantains are served in a *fare pote'e* shelter. Paid activities include a 4WD tour around the main island, a boat tour inside the lagoon, deep sea fishing and a picnic on a motu. Kite surfing is also available. English is spoken.

PENSION POE ITI, *B.P. 39, Vai'ea, Maupiti 98732. Tel./Fax 689/67.83.14; cell 74.58.76; maupitiexpress@mail.pf; www.maupitipoeiti.com. On Motu Tuanai, 5 min. by boat or car from the airport and 5 min. by boat from the village. No credit cards.*

This pension opened in October 2004, with 4 bungalows built in a garden setting on the same motu where the airport is located. Tahiti Tourism has awarded them the top rating of 3 Tiares. The wooden bungalows are the government approved and subsidized units that are modern and attractive. Electricity is provided by wind generators. Each bungalow has a king size bed and a single bed,

A/C, TV and DVD player, a private bathroom with hot water shower and a private covered terrace facing the white sand beach and lagoon. The kitchen and restaurant/bar are located in separate buildings, and the spacious dining area can accommodate day visitors who come over from Bora Bora on board the *Maupiti Express II*, whose captain, Gérald Sachet, is also owner of Pension Poe Iti and Maupiti Poe Iti Tours. His wife, Joséphine Ah-Yun, manages the pension and takes care of guests. Bungalows are 9.000 CFP dbl, breakfast is 1.000 CFP, and other meals are 2.500 CFP per person. The snorkeling equipment is complimentary, as well as the kayaks and society games. Rental bicycles are also available. José provides free boat transfers to the village and airport. Maupiti Poe Iti Tours will drop you at Motu Tiapa'a and return later to pick you up, or you can join a boat tour of the lagoon and have a picnic on an uninhabited motu for charges.

PENSION PAPAHANI, *B.P. 1, Vai'ea, Maupiti 98732. Tel. 689/60.15.35/ 71.97.97; Fax 689/60.15.36; pensionpapahani@hotmail.fr. On Motu Tiapa'a, 15 min. by boat from the airport. No credit cards.*

This pension is located on the lagoon side of Motu Tiapa'a facing the pass and the village, and it has a beautiful beach of fine white sand. The 5 bungalows are very close together and are simply furnished with a double bed in the smaller units and a double bed in the family bungalows. Another bed can be added to the larger units on request. All the larger bungalows have ceiling fans, and the smaller units have electric fans. All units have mosquito nets, a bathroom with a hot water shower, and house linens. Vilna Tuheiava serves family style meals in the *fare pote'e* dining shelter beside the beach. Activities include a boat tour of the lagoon with a picnic on a motu. Snorkeling gear and kayaks are free for guests. Tahiti Tourism has awarded this family pension with a 2-Tiare rating. You'll get a taste of the authentic Polynesian life when you stay here.

PENSION MAUPITI VILLAGE, *Vai'ea, Maupiti 98732. Tel./Fax 689/ 67.80.08; Cell 689/70.13.69/76.03.69; maupitivillage@mail.pf. On Motu Tiapa'a, 5 min. by boat from the airport and 3 min. by boat from the village. No credit cards.*

There are 3 simple plywood bungalows beside a pretty beach on the ocean side of Motu Tiapa'a, with each unit containing 2 double beds with mosquito nets, and a bathroom with hot water. There is also a 3-bedroom house with a double bed and a single bed in each bedroom, plus a lounge with beds, and a communal bathroom with hot water. Another house has 2 bedrooms, a lounge-kitchen, refrigerator and 2 terraces. There is plenty of fresh water and solar electricity day and night. Audine Colomes, the owner/manager, speaks a little bit of English and serves fresh seafood, with Tahitian food served on Sat. Rates are 6.000-12.000 CFP per person including all meals. Free activities include kayaks and outrigger paddle canoes, table tennis, fishing gear, motu tour, a visit to the marae, and walking on the reef. Paid activities include a bicycle tour of the main island, a boat tour of the lagoon and deep sea fishing.

PENSION TERAMA, *Vai'ea, Maupiti 98732. Tel./Fax 689/67.81.96; cell 71.03.33; maupiti.terama@mail.pf; www.maupiti.terama.over-blog.com. On Motu*

Tuanai, 5 min. by boat from the airport and the village. Free round-trip airport transfers. No credit cards.

Melissa Firuu and her French husband, Marc Pinson, have built a 3-bedroom concrete house in the middle of a Tiare Tahiti plantation on the airport motu, but there are no neighbors and no noise in this remote area. There is a double bed in 2 of the guest rooms and 3 single beds in the other room. Both the interior and exterior bathrooms with cold water showers are shared. The kitchen is separate and a *fare pote'e* gazebo shelter serves as the dining room. Guests have use of the kayaks and can hop a ride to the village when Marc goes there to shop. Both Melissa and Marc speak some English and are very open and friendly. A room with breakfast and dinner is 7.000 CFP and half-price for children under 12 years.

On the Main Island

MAUPITI RESIDENCE, *B.P. 51, Vai'ea, Maupiti 98732. Tel./Fax 689/ 67.82.61; maupiti.residence@mail.pf. On Terei'a beach on main island, 20+ min. by boat from airport. MC, V.*

Two large, modern all-white *fares* are built on stilts right on the white sand of beautiful Tereia, the main island's only beach, which is also called "Lover's Beach". Each bungalow has 775 sq. ft. (72 sq.m.) of living space consisting of 2 rooms, a living room with TV and DVD player, an equipped kitchen, a bathroom with hot water, plus an outdoor shower, and Internet access. Beds are available for 4-5 people and a 1-2 night stay is 12.000 CFP for 1-2 guests, and 4.750 CFP per person for each additional night. A/C is available in one of the units at a surcharge. There is no restaurant on the premises. You can buy lunch at Snack Chez Mimi next door to the pension and Laï, the pension manager, will bring your dinner on request (for the cost of the restaurant meal plus a delivery charge), which you can eat on the terrace overlooking the beach and lagoon. She also brings a Continental breakfast "kit" to your bungalow each evening, which you can put together the following morning. Her husband Sammy will organize your lagoon excursions on request and transfer you to the village (1.000 CFP round-trip). Maupiti Nautique is also located on this property, providing interesting scuba diving and snorkeling excursions. Maupiti Residence also offers free activities that include sailing a 16-ft. catamaran, windsurfing, kayaks, bicycles, mountain bike, snorkeling gear, fishing tackle, beach volley ball, petanque (bocce ball), lounge chairs, hiking in the mountain, and you can also walk across the lagoon to another motu. Be warned that Tereia Beach is a popular gathering place for young people on weekends, who bring their boom blasters and party until late at night.

PENSION TAUTIARE VILLAGE, *B.P. 16, Vai'ea, Maupiti 98732. Tel./Fax 689/60.15.90; cell 32.42.67; pension-tautiare@mail.pf. On seaside in Hurumanu, 2 km. (1.2 miles) from the village. No credit cards.*

Dawn Domingo has a 4-bedroom guesthouse on the main island, located between the white sand beach of Tereia and the Vaiahu Marae. There is a hot water shower in the bathroom, plus a private terrace for each room. She charges 7.500-

11.000 CFP for a room; 500 CFP for breakfast and 2.500 CFP for lunch or dinner. Round-trip boat transfers are 1.650 CFP per person. Snorkeling equipment and kayaks are available for guest use, and bikes can be rented for 1.000 CFP per day. Boat tours around the island are 3.500 CFP per person for a half-day and 6.000 CFP for all day with a picnic on the motu. A fishing excursion in the lagoon is 2.500 CFP and deep sea fishing is 6.000 CFP per person (min. 2). Tahiti Tourism has awarded a 2-Tiare rating to this pension. Dawn speaks English.

Economy
PENSION ERI, *Vai'ea, Maupiti 98732. Tel. 689/67.81.29/77.32.33; Fax 689/67.80.32. Beside the lagoon in Vai'ea village, 700 m (763 yds.) from the ferry dock and 3 km from the airport. No credit cards.*

This is a popular pension with young French people and other travelers who want to stay on the main island, but it is very noisy here in the heart of the village. The 4-bedroom house is basic but very clean, with a double bed and a fan in each room. Guests share the kitchen, living room and bathroom with cold water and pay 3.000 CFP for a room, 5.500 CFP for a room and MAP, and 7.000 CFP for a room and all meals. Eri's daughter, Maeva Mohi, manages the pension, serving fresh fruits and vegetables from their farm, along with fresh fish. Snack Tarona is also close by. You can rent a bicycle or kayak, go by boat to the motu, fishing in the lagoon or on picnics to a white sand beach.

Other Bed & Breakfast Lodgings
PENSION TAPUTEA, *Tel./Fax 689/67.82.78; pension.taputea@yahoo.fr.* A 3-room house in the main village, 7.000 CFP MAP. **PENSION ROSE DES ILES**, *689/67.82.78/70.50.70; www.pension-rose-des-iles.com* has 3 rustic bungalows on the beach of Motu Tiapa'a and camping space for 4 tents. Juliette is from Brittany and is noted for her delicious meals. **PENSION TEHEIMANA**, *Tel. 67.80.11*, has 3 rooms located near Tereia Beach, and is owned by Ah-Yun Tehei. This was formerly Le Lagon d'Emeraude (Emerald Lagoon) that closed several years ago.

RESTAURANTS AND SNACKS
Pension Poe Iti, *Tel. 67.83.14/74.58.76.* Visitors who come over from Bora Bora for the day on board the *Maupiti Express II* usually eat their lunch at this restaurant/bar, which is located on Motu Tuanai near the airport. Gérald Sachet owns the pension, the boat and Maupiti Poe Iti Tours, and his wife José is reputed for her food. Lunch is 2.500 CFP.

Restaurant Tarona, *Tel. 67.82.46/71.99.45*, is located in Vai'ea village, serving local style cuisine. Owner Nicole Spitz works for the Commune of Maupiti and is also head of Maupiti's Tourism Committee.

Snack Chez Mimi is located at Tereia Beach, serving local style food.

SEEING THE SIGHTS

You can walk around the main island of Maupiti in about 2-3 hours, depending on your pace, and how many times you stop to take pictures, shake down a ripe mango from a roadside tree or stop for a swim in the inviting lagoon. A road circles the island for 9.6 km (5.9 miles). You can also bike around the island and visit the petroglyphs of turtles, the family and royal *marae* stone temples and other archaeological sites. The *maraes* are located on some of the *motu* islets, as well as the central island.

The hosts at each pension normally organize the activities for their guests, which include snorkeling and shelling, outrigger paddle canoes, fishing in the lagoon and pass for lobster and fish, and picnics on the *motu*.

Lagoon Tours, Picnics on the Motu and Fishing Excursions

Maupiti Poe Iti Tours, *Tel.74.58.76*, is owned by Gérald Sachet, who owns *Maupiti Express* and Pension Poe Iti. He has a 20-ft. long flat bottom aluminum boat that is used for lagoon tours and transfers to Motu Tiapa'a. A circle island tour by boat includes fruit tasting and coconut water for 2.500 CFP, and you can also have a picnic on request for 3.500 CFP. The boat will drop you off on Motu Tiapa'a and pick you up later for 1.000 CFP per person. See information on *Where to Stay* in this chapter.

Visit Maupiti, *Tel. 67.80.95/21.88.21,* is operated by Ui Teriihaunui. He will take up to 4 passengers all the way around the island in his 18-ft. launch for 3.500 CFP, and will include a picnic on the motu on request. Ui also has 2 kayaks and a 15-ft. polyester skiff boat for rent.

Taputu Fanny works with several of the family pensions to provide boat excursions. The rates charged the tourists are usually 3.500 CFP per person for a half-day lagoon tour and 6.000 CFP for all day with a picnic on the motu. A fishing excursion in the lagoon is 2.500 CFP and deep sea fishing is 6.000 CFP per person.

Scuba Diving and Snorkeling Excursions

Maupiti Nautique, *Tel. 67.83.80; www.maupiti-nautique.com.* Lionel Clin is a BEES1 scuba diving instructor who leads a maximum of 5 divers to explore 7 varied sites both inside the lagoon and outside the coral reef. You can watch the ballet of manta rays between late March and July, observe humpback whales from Aug. to early Nov. and swim with dolphins, grey sharks, and many species of fish throughout the year. No feeding is involved. An exploration dive or refresher dive is 6.500 CFP and a 5-dive package is 30.000 CFP.

Snorkeling Tours include a special outing with manta rays for 3.500 CFP, and the **Marine Trail Discovery** is an eco-tourist snorkeling activity for 3.500 CFP. A qualified guide leads you on this 90-min. excursion that takes you to 5 different sites to see the richness of the underwater flora and fauna.

PRACTICAL INFORMATION

Bank

A representative from Banque Socredo calls at Maupiti once a month, which is also an occasion for arts and crafts vendors to set up shop in the Salle Polyvalente at the *mairie* (town hall).

Doctor

Medical assistance is available at Maupiti's government operated Infirmary, *Tel. 67.80.18.*

Internet Service

Visitors can check their email messages on the computer at the *mairie* (town hall) in Vai'ea village, which will be connected in the wedding hall (*Salle des Mariages*) on request. You can buy a Mana Spot card at the post office to access WiFi Internet service.

Post Office

The telecommunications service is located in the *mairie* (town hall) and is open Mon.-Thurs. 7:30am-3pm, and on Fri. 7:30am-2pm. *Tel. 67.80.19.*

Tourist Information

Maupiti Tourism Committee, *Tel. 689/67.82.46/60.15.55/71.99.45; nicole.spitz@commune-maupiti.pf.* Nicole Spitz is the president. She also owns Tarona Snack.

18. Tuamotu Islands

The 77 atolls and one upraised island that form the **Tuamotu Archipelago** are mere specks of land out in the heart of the trade wind, lost in the vastness of the blue Pacific. Sprinkled across ten latitudes and covering a length of 1,500 km (930 mi.) and a width of 500 km (310 mi.), these are some of the most remote islands in the world.

This vast collection of coral islets conjures up castaway dreams on a tropical isle, the ultimate get-away for rejuvenation of the body and soul. Tiny green oases floating in the desert of the sea, with names as exotic as the trade winds and coconut trees. Here you will find wild windswept beaches, the sea and sunshine, and only the sound of the surf and the cries of the sea birds for company. Fragrant *miki miki* bushes blend their perfume with aromas of salt spray and blossoms from the *tiare kahaia*, *geo geo* and *gapata* trees. The lagoons shimmer with a brilliance of light and color unsurpassed, and a submerged landscape of untouched magic and awesome beauty awaits beneath the sun-gilded waters tinged in turquoise.

Polynesian explorers, sailing from their homeland in the West, settled on the lonely shores of these atolls centuries ago. Pakamotu, they called their new home—a cloud of islands. Outcast chiefs from Tahiti and the Marquesas Islands named them Paumotu, the Submissive or Conquered Islands, the isles of Exiles. European ships from many nations rode the treacherous reef in this maritime maze, thus adding the names Low or Dangerous Archipelago and the Labyrinth. The **Paumotu people** now call their home the Tuamotu—many islands.

More than 400 varieties of fantastic, rainbow-hued fish glint like ornaments of gold in the iridescent waters of the sheltered lagoons, providing hours of enchantment for snorkelers and scuba divers. On many of the atolls you can visit pearl farms and fish parks inside the lagoons, take boat tours to visit the various *motu* islets and picnic under the black-eyed gaze of the white fairy tern.

You can go on fishing expeditions, hunt for tiny shells to string into pretty necklaces, learn to weave hats, mats and baskets from palm fronds, and eat delicious seafood direct from its shell while you stand at the edge of a Technicolor reef. In the evening you can sit under a starlit sky, watching the Southern Cross as you listen to musicians playing island tunes on guitars and ukuleles. Their songs tell of old gods and heroes, the spirits of sharks and fish, destructive hurricanes, people lost at sea, shipwrecks on the treacherous reef, *vahines* and *l'amour*.

More than two dozen of these atolls have airstrips and regular air service from Tahiti, and inter-island trading schooners transport supplies and passengers. The lack of potable water remains a problem on many of these remote islands, while solar energy provides electricity and hot water for villages and remote pearl farms.

"MANY LAGOONS" BY RALPH VARADY

You have to see an atoll to get its feeling. It leaves a vastly different impression than a high island does. There is something about the atolls that is magnetic. They are lost and, for the greater part, deserted, full of flies and copra bugs. They are remote, a death trap in a hurricane, a danger to navigation and often inaccessible except by small boat. They offer the minimum of human comfort, their maximum asset being their copra; and yet there is something wonderful about them, and truly they belong to the list of nature's wonders.

Many of the islands are uninhabited and seldom visited. Nevertheless, the traveler who wanders into this maritime maze will be rewarded by what he sees. These Dangerous Islands are not sizable or comfortable, but they are rich in the realm of color. The debauch of color found in the Tuamotu lagoons is incomparable to that of any other island group.

Personally, I hope that these islands never have "facilities" so that they will be kept as they are now: unspoiled, beautiful and natural. It is good to know that some of these islands will remain out of reach of a fast-moving civilization."

This archipelago is rapidly being developed, with modern telecommunications services now reaching even the most distant of the settled islands.

The atolls of Rangiroa, Manihi, Tikehau and Fakarava, which are described in this chapter, offer international class hotels, small hotels, pensions or guest houses with simple accommodations. These are the destinations most frequently visited by travelers, but the number of visitors in the Tuamotus is so minute that these islands still offer a natural environment and miles of empty beaches.

You will also find accommodations in family homes and pensions on the atolls of Ahe, Anaa, Apataki, Arutua, Kaukura, Mataiva, Takapoto and Takaroa. Unfortunately, we are not able to give the details of each atoll in this book, but you can obtain a list of lodging facilities from Tahiti Tourisme or the Haere Mai Association. The contact numbers are listed in the *Basic Information* chapter under *Where to Find More Information About Tahiti & French Polynesia*.

RANGIROA

Rangiroa, also called **Rairoa**, means 'long sky' in the Paumotu dialect, the language of the Polynesian inhabitants. The coral ring encircling the pear-shaped atoll of Rangiroa contains more than 240 *motu* islets, separated by at least 100 very shallow *hoa* channels and three passes. The Tiputa Pass and Avatoru Pass on the north of the atoll are deep and wide enough for ships to enter the lagoon, and the Tivaru Pass on the west is narrow and shallow. A vast inland sea measures approximately 75 km (47 mi.) long by 25 km (16 mi.) wide, covering a distance of 1,020 sq. km (393 sq. mi.). This is the largest atoll in the Southern Hemisphere and one of the biggest atolls in the world.

The Dutch explorer Le Maire discovered Rangiroa in 1616, but the first European settlers did not arrive until 1851. The missionaries insisted that the population be grouped in Avatoru and Tiputa rather than dispersing in small villages around the atoll, where they could more likely continue their heathenistic practices. A cyclone in 1906 destroyed the village of Tivaru, and today the population of 3,384 inhabitants reside in the villages of Avatoru and Tiputa.

Rangiroa is the administrative center of the northern Tuamotu atolls. Children from the small atolls are sent to junior high school and technical schools in Rangiroa, where they are lodged throughout the school year, some of the students returning to their homes only during the two-month vacation in July and August.

Rangiroa's lagoon is world famous for unsurpassed scuba diving in the warmest and clearest water you can dream of. Favorite excursions include "shooting the pass," where hundreds of fish, moray eels and sharks swim beside and below you, swept along by the strong currents. You can view this exciting spectacle aboard a glass-bottom boat, or jump into the water with mask, snorkel, fins or even scuba diving bottles. Vacation memories are also made while paddling a kayak or outrigger canoe, sailing inside the lagoon, line or drag fishing, on boat excursions to the pink sand beach of Vahituri, while admiring the fossilized coral formations on Reef Island, and during a full day picnic trip to the Blue Lagoon or Green Lagoon.

Among this wealth of scenery is an attractive selection of international resort hotels, small hotels with thatched roof bungalows and simple family owned pensions with fresh lagoon fish on the menu. Across the lagoon from the villages are very basic sleeping facilities in camp-like settings that can be reached only by boat, where you can walk on beaches as remote as Robinson Crusoe's. On these beautiful little islets you can live a *sauvage* simplified life with freshly caught food from the reef and lagoon.

ARRIVALS & DEPARTURES
Arriving By Air
Air Tahiti has 1-3 direct ATR flights daily between Tahiti and Rangiroa. The 55-60 min. non-stop flight is 18.330 CFP one-way for adults, and 33.960 CFP round-trip, tax included. You can also fly from Bora Bora to Rangiroa with 75-min. direct flights on Mon., Wed., Fri. and Sun., and with a stop in Tikehau on Thurs., for 25.530 CFP one-way. Direct flight service is also provided to Rangiroa from Manihi each Tues., Wed., and Sun., for 12.130 CFP. There are direct flights from Tikehau to Rangiroa daily except Fri. and Sun. for 7.230 CFP.

If you have reservations with a hotel, pension, cruise line or yacht charter company, then you will be met at the airport and driven to your accommodation. **Air Tahiti reservations**: Tahiti, *Tel. 86.42.42, www.airtahiti.pf.*

You can also get to Rangiroa by chartering an airplane in Tahiti from **Air Tahiti**, *Tel. 86.42.42*, or **Pol'Air**, *Tel. 74.23.11*.

Arriving By Boat

Mareva Nui, *Tel. 42.25.53, Fax 42.25.57*, is a 181-ft. steel ship that transports cargo between Tahiti and the Tuamotu atolls. It leaves Tahiti every 15 days, arriving in Rangiroa three days later. There are 12 berths for the maximum number of passengers allowed, but no cabins on board. The one-way fare to Rangiroa is 10.100 CFP including all meals.

St. Xavier Maris Stella III, *Tel. 42.23.58*, can transport 12 passengers, sleeping in an a/c cabin or on the deck. The deck fare from Tahiti to Rangiroa is 7.070 CFP and a berth is 10.000 CFP per person, including meals. Bring your own sleeping mat, pillow and bed linen. Sometimes Rangiroa is the first stop after a 20-hr. crossing from Tahiti, and on other voyages it may be the 3rd island visited. The ship leaves Papeete every 15 days.

Departing By Air

Air Tahiti has 1-5 flights daily from Rangiroa to Tahiti, including up to 3 direct flights per day. You can fly direct from Rangiroa to Manihi daily except Thurs. and Fri., direct from Rangiroa to Tikehau on Wed., Fri. and Sun., and direct from Rangiroa to Fakarava on Tues., Wed., and Fri., and with a stop in Manihi on Sat. Tickets can be purchased at the Air Tahiti office in Avatoru. If you already have reservations and a ticket, reconfirmations should be made one day in advance, and most hotels will take care of this for you. Check-in time at the airport is one hour before scheduled departure.

Departing By Boat

The *Mareva Nui, Tel. 42.25.53, Fax 42.25.57*, calls at 11-12 other atolls after leaving Rangiroa each 15 days. *St. Xavier Maris Stella III, Tel. 42.23.58*, leaves Rangiroa every 15 days for Ahe, Manihi, and all the western Tuamotu atolls, before returning to Papeete. Fares are determined by length of voyage to Tahiti.

ORIENTATION

The villages of **Avatoru** and **Tiputa** are located on the northern coast of Rangiroa atoll, where most of the population lives beside the two deep passes, a 45-minute boat ride apart. A flat paved road 10 km (6.2 mi.) long extends from the Avatoru Pass to the Tiputa Pass, with the ocean on one side and the lagoon on the other side. Most of the hotels and pensions are on the lagoon side of this road and the airport is about halfway between the two passes. You will find churches, schools, post offices and small food stores in both villages and it is easy to walk around once you are there, but you will probably find that the people in Tiputa village are friendlier to visitors.

You can explore Avatoru village to the Tiputa Pass by car, scooter or bicycle. The road was repaved in mid-2011 to get rid of the dangerous holes. You have to take a boat across the Tiputa Pass to get to Tiputa village, which can be easily discovered in a short walk. Overlooking the Tiputa Pass is **Ohotu Point**, a favorite destination in late afternoon when dolphins can often be seen playing in the swift current that flows through the pass between the open ocean and the interior lagoon.

GETTING AROUND RANGIROA
The hosts at the hotels and pensions meet their guests at the airport and provide transportation to the lodgings. Taxi service is provided on the Avatoru side of the pass by **Taximen Rangiroa**, *Tel. 26.67.26*, who has a 5-passenger car; **Temeehu Taxi**, *Tel. 96.72.65/22.91.62*, has a 7-seat minibus; **Ignace Taxi**, *Tel. 77.28.02*, has a 9-seat minibus.

Maurice Taxi Boat, *Tel. 96.76.09/78.13.25*, is operated by Maurice Snow, who provides taxi boat service between Tiputa and Avatoru, as well as other lagoon transfers.

Car, Scooter & Bicycle Rentals
Rangi Rent-A-Car, *Tel./Fax 96.03.28, Cell 21.35.08*, was formerly Europcar. They have an office near Avatoru village and desks at the Hotel Kia Ora with rentals for cars, buggies, scooters and bicycles.

Location Arenahio is also known as **Location Pomare**, *Tel. 96.82.45/73.92.84; carpom@mail.pf*. Pomare Temaehu at Carole Boutique in Avatoru rents cars, scooters and bicycles.

J-J Loc, *Tel 96.03.13/27.57.82*. Jean-Jacques Gandy rents scooters and bicycles in Avatoru village.

WHERE TO STAY
Deluxe
HOTEL KIA ORA RESORT & SPA, *B.P. 198, Avatoru, Rangiroa 98775. Tel. 689/93.11.11; Fax 689/96.04.93; Reservations: Tel. 689/93.11.17; Fax 689/96.02.20; resa@hotelkiaora.pf; www.hotelkiaora.com. Beside the lagoon at Ohotu Bay, 2 km (1.2 mi.) east of the airport. Round-trip airport transfers provided. All major credit cards.*

The Hotel Kia Ora opened in 1973 as the Kia Ora Village, and for many years this was the only international class hotel on Rangiroa. The hotel closed in 2009 to rebuild and upgrade its facilities, with plans to reopen on Sept. 1, 2011. The hotel's capacity of 60 units includes 7 types of lodgings spread throughout 40 acres of gardens and coconut trees, and beside a white sand beach almost a mile long. New additions include garden villas with pools. The garden junior suites and a 2-bedroom garden suite also have private pools. The 19 beach bungalows have a bedroom with a king size bed and a living room with a single bed or day bed, with sliding doors to separate the two rooms. The 3 beach suites have a bedroom

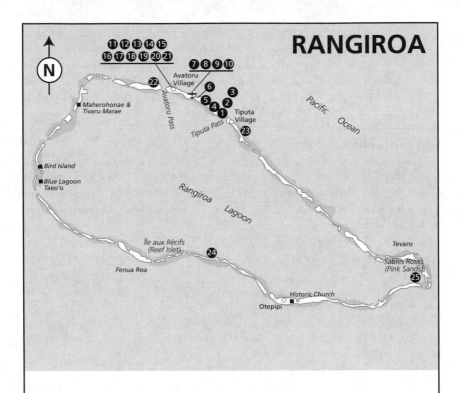

RANGIROA

1. Pension Glorine
2. Les Relais De Josephine
3. Chez Teina & Marie
4. Pension Bounty
5. Hotel Kia Ora Rangiroa
6. Maitai Rangiroa Lagoon Resort
7. Pension Cecile
8. Pension Tapuheitini

9. Raira Lagon
10. Pension Tuanake
11. Ariitini Village
12. Turiroa Village
13. Pension Martine
14. Pension Hinanui
15. Rangiroa Lodge
16. Camping Chez Nanua
17. Pension Henri

18. Pension Loyna
19. Pension Tevahine Dream
20. Pension Henriette
21. Le Merou Bleu
22. Lagon Vert
23. Chez Lucien
24. Hotel Kia Ora Sauvage
25. Motu Tetaraire

downstairs and another bedroom with two twin beds in the loft, plus a separate lounge, providing accommodations for four people. All these beach units have a Jacuzzi on the sundeck, facing a very white coral sand beach. Some of the deluxe beach bungalows offer an outdoor bathtub as well as a jet stream infinity pool instead of a Jacuzzi.

The 10 overwater bungalows are so beautiful, comfortable and romantic you'll never want to leave. They stand on a wooden pontoon over the jade and blue water and are made of thatched roofs, local woods and woven bamboo walls. They are spacious junior suites with a separate lounge and a glass bottom coffee table for fish watching. The decor is a subtle Polynesian design in cool colors to complement the blues and greens of the lagoon. Each overwater unit has a shiny, modern bathroom, with a new bathtub, as well as a big terrace. Steps lead from a private solarium into the inviting lagoon, a huge liquid playground of a thousand delights.

All the bungalows are built in a traditional Polynesian style that blends noble and precious materials with international class comfort. All units include a/c and ceiling fans and they are equipped with telephones, WiFi Internet connections, safety boxes, refrigerator/mini bar, and tea and coffee making facilities. In the beach and overwater bungalows a door separates the bedroom from the large bathroom. All the bathrooms have a big tiled hot water shower and some now have bathtubs. There is a hairdryer and the range of toiletries is replenished daily. Room service is provided on request.

In addition to an infinity swimming pool and adjacent Jacuzzi, the hotel provides free snorkeling equipment for its guests, outrigger paddle canoes, tennis, volleyball, basketball, *petanque* (French bowls), arts and crafts exhibits and frequent shows of Tahitian songs and dances. The Kahaia Lounge is equipped with a pool table, wide screen television with DVD and VCR players and films, computer with paid Internet access, library, and board games such as chess, backgammon, scrabble and dice. Another free service provided is round-trip transportation to attend services held each Sunday at the Catholic Church in Avatoru.

The activities desk in the hotel reception area can book your bicycle, scooter and car rentals, as well as excursions. These include glass bottom boat rides to snorkel and feed the sharks, lagoon tours to visit the dolphins and drift through the passes, picnic excursions to *motu* islets on the other side of the lagoon, deep-sea fishing, scuba diving, visits to a black pearl farm, boat rentals and excursions to visit the Kia Ora Sauvage. After a full day's activities, you can relax while enjoying a Thai or Oriental body massage or beauty treatment in the new overwater spa.

While sipping your exotic cocktail in the redesigned overwater bar and lounge you can look through the big glass floor windows to watch the tropical fish in the coral gardens below. The menu selections in the Kia Ora Resort's open-air dining room were chosen to please discerning clientele from all parts of the world. The luncheon menu features burgers with fries, pizza, pasta, chow mien, lagoon fish and a fresh fruit plate. The dinner menu offers several different choices each evening, which usually include fresh fish from the lagoon or deep ocean, as well as meat and poultry selections and an appealing dessert buffet. The wine cellar contains just the right vintage to enhance your meal, and the service provided by the friendly staff is also commendable.

HOTEL KIA ORA SAUVAGE RANGIROA, *(same contacts as for Hotel Kia Ora Resort & Spa). This hotel has also been closed for renovation and will reopen in 2012. 5 bungalows built on a private motu islet, one hour by boat across the lagoon to Motu Avae Rahi, 30 km (20 mi.) from the main village. AP meal plan is compulsory. All major credit cards.*

Motu Avae Rahi means "isle of the big moon". Here is your ultimate Robinson Crusoe Island—lost from the big world and all its problems. There are only 5 little thatched-roof bungalows on this 4-hectare (9.88-acre) islet. What you don't have here is of primary importance for your tranquility and totally relaxed getaway. No electricity, no telephones, no jet-skis, no excursion boats or helicopters buzzing around and overhead the lagoon, no cars, motorcycles and other traffic noises, and no roosters to crow all night. Your host and hostess and a staff of two assistants will take care of your meals, which are served family style in the restaurant-bar or on the beach. Your bungalow is an attractive *fare* built of local woods, and contains a king-size bed and a single bed with mosquito nets, a private bathroom with hot water shower and a terrace overlooking the white sand beach. Two kerosene lamps are placed on your front steps each evening.

Activities include boat trips to nearby *motu* islets, fishing for dinner in the lagoon and trips to the reef for appetizers. You can also paddle an outrigger canoe, windsurf or feed the sharks. In this little haven of peace, you can breathe pure sweet air, listen to the thunder of the surf on the reef, and gaze at the Southern Cross while lying on the secluded beach. This little hotel is a favorite retreat for honeymooners and other travelers in the know.

Superior

MAITAI RANGIROA LAGOON RESORT, *B.P. 17, Avatoru, Rangiroa 98775. Tel. 689/93.13.50, Fax 689/93.13.51; Reservations: Tel. 689/86.66.66, booking@rangiroa.hotelmaitai.com. Beside the lagoon, 150 m (492 ft.) from the airport. All major credit cards.*

This hotel opened in April 2004 as a Polynesian Resort Hotel, and the French group Accor took over management in August 2004. It was operated as a Novotel property until 2010 when it was acquired by the locally-owned Pacific Beachcomber group to become a member of the Maitai family of 3-star hotels. The 38 units consist of 22 Tapa garden view rooms with terrace, 10 Vini garden bungalows and 6 Lagoon view bungalows with terrace. There are 4 adjoining rooms for a family or they can be used as a suite, and there are also 2 rooms for reduced mobility guests. The twin beds can also be transformed into one king size bed, and the sofa beds in the lagoon and garden bungalows can sleep a third person. All units include individual a/c and a fan, teak furniture, satellite/cable TV, IDD telephone, safe deposit boxes, mini refrigerator and coffee and tea making facilities. The bathrooms are tiled, have a separate toilet, hot water shower and lavabo, and a hair dryer.

Public facilities include a reception area, where you will also find the activities desk and car rental center, as well as a small boutique. At the indoor-outdoor Lagon Bleu you can dine in the thatched-roof restaurant or under an umbrella on the terrace beside the beach. The breakfast buffet includes fresh tropical fruits, and at lunch you can choose poisson cru, salads, burgers, pizzas, pasta or the main course. The dinner menu features international and Polynesian cuisine. The beachfront bar is open daily from 10am to 11pm, serving Polynesian cocktails as well as standard drinks and fresh fruit juice. Local musicians and Tahitian dance shows are featured on special evenings.

There is a narrow strip of white sand in front of the restaurant and a long pier is built over the lagoon, where the snorkeling is superb. Complimentary activities include use of snorkeling equipment, kayaks, outrigger canoes, lagoon fishing, *petanque* (French bowls), and beach volleyball. Optional activities include bicycle, scooter and car rentals, glass bottom boat rides, day cruising on the lagoon with a skipper, picnics to the distant motu islets and scuba diving. WiFi is also additional.

MOTU TETA, *Motu Tetaraire, Tiputa, Rangiroa. Tel. 689/96.03.48; info@yourdreamisland.com; www.yourdreamisland.com. In US Tel. 559/447-2525. On a private motu on the southeastern side of Rangiroa, an hour's boat ride from airport. Minimum stay 3 days.*

Here is your own private hideaway with all the upscale comforts of an elegant Polynesian paradise. You will have this 9-acre (3.8 ha) Dream Island all to yourself during your stay. The main house is 2,250 sq. ft. (250 sq. m), built in the typical breezy Tahitian style with open beams and no windows. It has 3 bedrooms, 2 bathrooms, dining and living area, ceiling fans, and a kitchen complete with a private chef. A flat screen TV/DVD system with surround sound is complemented by a collection of music and DVD's. The guest bungalow, built in Bali, is 765 sq. ft. (85 sq. m) and has a bedroom and a wet bar, walk-in shower and ample storage. Each house has a large veranda overlooking the lagoon.

All meals are prepared to order and drinks include champagne, a diverse wine list and a well-stocked bar. Guests have unlimited use of all sports equipment and watercraft, which includes snorkeling gear, wind surfers, outrigger canoes, kayaks, a 14-passenger motor boat, 2 aluminum dinghies, kiting equipment, water-skis, and a 2-person float to be pulled by a motor boat. Your own personal guide is on hand to help you explore the most interesting islets and sites, with lots of time for picnics on uninhabited motu, snorkeling in the lagoon and fishing or hunting for lobsters on the ocean side of the reef.

Ralph Fäisi, the Swiss owner of Motu Teta, is the CEO of VisionOne, a high-tech multinational software company. He has chosen Ugo Angely of Oviri Tours as personal guide for the guests' lagoon activities, and Ugo's wife, Celine, is the property manager and chef de cuisine. Ugo grew up at the Hotel Kia Ora, where his father was one of the original owners. He and Celine spent many years taking care of guests staying at Kia Ora Sauvage and at the main hotel. They excel in their respective roles and they both speak English.

Moderate

LES RELAIS DE JOSEPHINE, *B.P. 140, Avatoru, Rangiroa 98775. Tel./Fax 689/96.02.00; relaisjosephine@mail.pf; http://relaisjosephine.free.fr. Beside the Tiputa pass close to the Ohotu boat dock, 5 km (3.1 mi.) from the airport. Free round-trip transfers. All major credit cards.*

This upscale family pension has earned a 3-Tiare rating from Tahiti Tourisme, although reports have been varied regarding guest satisfaction. Six attractive bungalows with thatched roofs are built in the garden and facing the pass. Each unit is furnished in a colonial style with a canopied double bed and single bed, a private bathroom with hot water and separate toilet, a dressing room with individual safe, a ceiling fan, desk, fridge, TV/DVD player, hair dryer, coffee and tea facilities and private terrace. Free WiFi Internet service. The bar terrace overlooks Tiputa Pass, where dolphins can often be seen dancing in the waves. There is no beach here and a wire fence is built between the pension and the rocky shore below. Madame Denise Thirouard Carrogio is noted for the gourmet cuisine and wines served in her restaurant, Le Dauphin Gourmand. Her clients are mostly French and Japanese. Activities can be arranged and there is a scuba diving center nearby. MAP or half-board is compulsory and the restaurant and bar are open to the public with advance reservations.

PENSION TEVAHINE DREAM, *B.P. 369, Avatoru, Rangiroa 98775. Tel./ Fax. 689/93.12.75; Cell 20.90.15; tevahinedream@mail.pf; www.tevahinedream.com. Beside the lagoon 5 km. (3.1 mi.) west of the airport and before Avatoru village. Free round-trip transfers. No credit cards.*

This new lodging is also called "Chez Norbert" and has already earned a reputation as the most charming pension on Rangiroa. Owners Norbert Lau and Thildy Gfeller and their 4 sons welcome their guests in a very friendly, authentic Polynesian manner that helps the visitors to feel at home, especially when sharing the delicious meals family style. Norbert speaks French and English and will help you arrange all your activities. They designed and built 3 beach bungalows and 1 garden bungalow that have thatched roofs in an A-frame, an open-air yet private shower with hot water, a crushed coral floor and a mini-garden. The 3 dreamy "Pearl Honeymoon" *fares* will sleep 2-3 people, and the big *fare* has accommodations for 6-8 guests, as well as its own kitchen. One bungalow has a small soaking pool. All units have a ceiling fan, mosquito nets, safe, free WiFi, refrigerator, private terrace and deckchairs. Breakfasts include 8 jams, breads, pastries, cheeses and fruit. Dinners are served in an outdoor setting and may be fresh fish, Chinese fondue or other specialties prepared by Norbert. The half-board (MAP) rate for a small bungalow is 12.500 CFP per person, which also includes the use of snorkel gear, bicycles, kayaks, a tour of the village in Norbert's a/c vehicle, a visit to the coral gardens and to watch the dolphins. The big bungalow with a kitchen is 25.000 CFP for 1-4 people and 30.000 CFP for larger groups. Meals can be added if desired. **RAIRA LAGON FAMILY HOTEL,** *B.P. 87, Avatoru, Rangiroa 98775. Tel. 689/93.12.30; Fax 689/96.02.92; rairalag.@mail.pf; www.raira-lagon.pf. At PK 1.5, beside the lagoon in Avatoru commune, 6.5 km (4 mi.) from the Ohotu boat dock and 800 m. (2,624 ft.) west of the airport. Free round-trip transfers. AE, MC, V.*

There are 10 small *fares* for couples or families, with single or double beds and a/c, ceiling fans, a small refrigerator and electric anti-mosquito gadgets. Each bungalow has a private bathroom with hot water shower, and there is a sliding glass door leading onto a small terrace. Rooms are cleaned daily. The restaurant is on the beach, serving a Continental breakfast, salads and sandwiches for lunch, fresh local fish and gastronomic French cuisine for dinner. There is also a small bar in the restaurant. The bungalows with a beach view are 12.000 CFP with breakfast only and 14.500-16.000 CFP MAP. Bungalows with a garden view are 11.000 CFP with breakfast and 13.000-14.500 CFP with breakfast and dinner. Beach chairs for guests are placed under the shade trees or on the fine sand beach and snorkeling equipment is provided. The managers, Sandrine and Jean-Frédérique, will help you to plan your lagoon excursions and scuba diving. They have their own excursion organization service provided, with a fast comfortable boat. They also have rentals for cars, buggies, and bicycles. The only drawback here is the sometimes noisy neighborhood.

LE MEROU BLEU, *B.P. 163, Avatoru, Rangiroa 98775. Tel./Fax 689/ 96.84.62, cell 79.16.82; lemeroubleu@mail.pf; www.merou-bleu.com. Beside the Avatoru pass, 5 minutes from the village. Free round-trip transfers from airport and Ohotu boat dock. No credit cards.*

The name of this pension means "Blue Spotted-Grouper" in English or "Roi" in Tahitian. Owner Sonya Friedrich is from Alsace and speaks very little English, but she has an American friend close by who helps with translations. The 3 small traditional style thatched roof bungalows are beside Avatoru pass, which is "the" surfing spot on Rangiroa. All the beds are protected by mosquito nets and electricity is provided by solar lighting and electric generator. The bungalows are small but nicely decorated with local woods, bamboo, sea urchin shells, and mother-of-pearl and dolphin mobiles. In a *fare potée* gazebo type shelter Sonya serves her specialties of couscous, West Indian dishes and local foods. A room and MAP meals are 15.084 CFP sgl, 28.156 CFP dbl. Bicycles are free for guests.

PENSION TUANAKE, *B. P. 21, Avatoru, Rangiroa 98775. Tel. 689/ 96.03.52/79.20.13; Fax 689/93.11.80; tuanake@mail.pf; www.pensiontuanake.pf. Beside the lagoon in Avatoru, 2.5 km (1.6 mi.) from the airport and 7.5 km (4.7 mi.) from the boat dock at Ohotu. Free round-trip transfers between airport and pension. MC, V.*

This popular family pension has been awarded a 1-Tiare rating by Tahiti Tourisme. There are 5 *fares* or bungalows on the white coral sand beach, with beds for 2, 5 or 6. Each *fare* is very clean and has a fan, safe, mosquito nets, terrace and private bathroom with hot water and a separate cold water shower outside. All guests share the big open-air living space and MAP meals are served here. There is a TV, pay phone and WiFi Internet service for guests.

This pension has a good reputation for the friendly, comfortable atmosphere that reigns here, with beach chairs to read in the shade or sunbathe on the coral sand beach. A hoa channel runs from the ocean to the lagoon on one side of the property and Gauguin's Pearl farm is on the other side. Owner Roger Terorotua passed away in 2011 and the pension is for sale.

PENSION BOUNTY, *B.P. 296, Avatoru, Rangiroa 98775. Tel./Fax 689/ 96.05.22; contact@pension-bounty.com; www.pension-bounty.com. Between the road and lagoon just past Hotel Kia Ora and 1/2 mi. from Tiputa Pass. Free round-trip transfers. AE, MC, V.*

This 4-bungalow family pension has been awarded a 2-Tiare rating by Tahiti Tourism. Built in 2004 of Kohu wood and red cedar, each of the double studios has a double or single bed, an equipped kitchenette, bathroom with hot water, mosquito screens on doors and windows, ceiling fan, personal safe, and a large deck. Free WiFi Internet provided. A studio with a bountiful breakfast is 7.500 CFP per person, and a studio with MAP meals is 11.000 CFP per person. Add 4.000 CFP for a single occupancy

A private paved road with night lights leads from the main road to the pension and directly to the nearby beach on Ohotu Bay. Owners Muriel and Alain Ruiz de Galaretta offer free use of bicycles to their guests and help them to organize their nautical activities. They speak English, French, Spanish and Italian. Alain is a level three diver and will direct you to the nearby dive centers. Special rates for divers. To preserve a quiet and tranquil atmosphere, children under 12 years are not allowed.

PENSION MARTINE, *B.P. 68, Avatoru, Rangiroa 98775. Tel. 689/93.12.25; Fax 689/96.02.51; cell 79.71.52; pension.martine@mail.pf. On the lagoon side near the airport and 5 km (3.1 mi.) from the village of Avatoru. Free round-trip transfers. MC, V.*

Martine Tetua's pension has a good reputation in Rangiroa and with former guests. There are 3 attractive and clean little bungalows, including a unit for singles, built beside the beach and lagoon. Each bungalow has a mosquito net over the beds, a ceiling fan, safe, private bathroom with hot water shower, and terrace. All guests share the living room and eat their meals in the dining room. A bungalow with half-board (MAP) meals is 9.000 CFP per person or 7.500 CFP each for 2-3 people. Your hosts will take you to visit their family pearl farm if you wish.

PENSION CECILE, *B. P. 98, Avatoru, Rangiroa 98775. Tel. 689/93.12.65; Fax 689/93.12.66; cell 77.55.72; pensioncecile@mail.pf. In Avatoru, 7.5 km (4.7 mi.) from the Ohotu boat dock and 2.5 km (1.6 mi.) from the airport. Free round-trip transfers. MC, V.*

There are 7 simply furnished bungalows beside the beach and in the garden, including 4 units of the standard government approved model. The 4 family bungalows will accommodate 2 adults and 3 children or 4 adults, and the 3 standard bungalows will sleep 2 people. Each unit has mosquito nets over the beds, a fan, and a private bathroom with cold water. The bungalows are 8.000-8.500 CFP, including excellent MAP meals served in an open-air dining room. Guests have free use of the kayaks. Cecile or her son Alban can help you arrange activities that include a visit to a pearl farm, fishing in the lagoon and lagoon excursions.

PENSION GLORINE, *Tel. 96.04.05; Fax 96.03.58; pensionglorine@mail.pf; 6 bungalows adjacent to the boat dock beside the lagoon and Tiputa Pass. No credit cards.*

Back in the early 1970s Glorine Toi was already reputed for her excellent fish dinners served in her low-budget family pension. Her son and daughter-in-law now run the pension, but Glorine still prepares her specialties for guests. 3 of the 6 bungalows are equipped with a kitchenette and the other guests can share a kitchen or enjoy the MAP meals for 8.000 CFP a day. A bungalow only is 4.000 CFP. The private bathrooms have cold water showers. Snorkeling equipment and bikes are provided for guest use.

TURIROA VILLAGE, *B.P. 26, Avatoru, Rangiroa 98775. Tel. 689/96.04.27/ 70.59.21; Fax 689/96.02.46; pension.turiroa@mail.pf. Beside the lagoon in Avatoru, 6 km (3.7 mi.) from the airport and 5 km (3.1 mi.) from Avatoru village. Free round-trip transfers. No credit cards.*

There are 2 garden and 2 beach bungalows, each containing a double bed and a mezzanine with single beds. These units have a kitchenette, private bathroom with hot water, a fan and a terrace. There is also a small *fare* with a private bathroom and hot water shower outside. A bungalow is 8.000 CFP for 1-4 people and breakfast is 500 CFP each. Your hostess, Mrs. Olga Niva, will take you to visit her family pearl farm and she also offers free transfers daily to the village. Kayaks are also free for guest use.

ARIITINI VILLAGE, *B.P. 18, Avatoru, Rangiroa 98775. Tel. 689/96.04.41, Fax 689/96.04.40. Located beside the lagoon at PK 4 in Avatoru, 5.6 km (3.5 mi.) from the Ohotu boat dock and 500 m (1,640 ft.) from the airport. Free round-trip transfers. No credit cards.*

Felix and Judith Tetua have 6 bungalows in a garden setting beside the coral sand beach and lagoon. 5 units contain 1 bedroom with a double bed and a single bed, a fan, private bathroom with hot water shower and a small terrace. There is also a 2-bedroom unit. A bungalow is 8.000 CFP per person including breakfast and dinner, which are served in the restaurant/snack, and there is a communal living room with TV.

PENSION LOYNA, *B.P. 82, Avatoru, Rangiroa 98775. Tel./Fax 689/ 96.82.09; cell 29.90.30; pensionloyna@mail.pf; www.pensionloyna.fr.st. 4 km (2.5 mi.) from airport and 2 km (0.8 mi.) from Avatoru village. Free transfers. MC, V.*

Loyna Fareea can sleep up to 30 people in a 3-bedroom house, a 2-bedroom *fare* and 3 big bungalows located 100 m. (328 ft.) from the lagoon, across the road. Group rates provided starting with 6 people. Ceiling fan, safe, and private bathrooms with hot water showers. Living room and dining room facilities are shared. A room with MAP meals is 7.500 CFP per person. The beach here is poor but the snorkeling is good, and the food served is very tasty. Loyna, who speaks some English, welcomes you in the warm Polynesian tradition.

Economy

RANGIROA LODGE, *Avatoru, Rangiroa 98775. Tel. 689/96.82.13; www.rangiroalodge.com. Beside the lagoon in Avatoru village, 8 km (5 mi.) from the Ohotu boat dock and 6 km (3.7 mi.) from the airport. No credit cards.*

Because of its location and facilities, this pension is appealing to low-budget travelers who want to stay in Avatoru and be able to cook their own meals. One-way airport transfers are 350 CFP. There are six simple rooms and two 3-bed dormitories in 2 rather run-down, rustic buildings built between the lagoon and the road—very close to the road. Single rates are 2.625-6.921 CFP and 12.888 CFP for the 2-bedroom villa (orange *fare*) with a kitchen. The limited camping space is 1.313 CFP per person per day. There is a communal equipped kitchen and a dining room on the coral beach. Snorkeling is good here and the mask, snorkel and flippers are available free for guests. The Raie Manta Club dive center is next door and has a Bed and Dive package for scuba divers. There is a pizzeria next door.

CHEZ LUCIEN, *B.P. 69, Tiputa, Rangiroa 98776. Tel./Fax 689/96.73.55; http://pensionlucien.free.fr. Near the pass in Tiputa village, 10 minutes by boat from the airport. Round-trip boat transfers 1.000 CFP per person. No credit cards.*

This well maintained pension is facing the lagoon at the edge of the Tiputa Pass. Lucien Pea has built 2 small bungalows and a 2-bedroom family bungalow, all with covered porches that overlook the pass. Each of the smaller bungalows has 2 double beds, a mezzanine with a double bed, a fan, refrigerator and a bathroom with hot water. The family bungalow has a double bed in each bedroom, 3 double beds on the mezzanine, a living room, fan, refrigerator and a communal bathroom with hot water. House linens are furnished. The meals are generous and pleasant, served in a covered dining room beside the lagoon. A room with breakfast is 4.725 CFP and a room with MAP meals is 6.825 CFP per person. Bikes, lagoon fishing and a visit of the village are free.

LAGON VERT, *B.P. 54, Avatoru, Rangiroa 98775. Tel. 689/79.24.66/ 77.28.85. On a motu at Lagon Vert (Green Lagoon), a 10-minute boat ride from Avatoru village. No credit cards.*

Punua and Moana Tamaehu have built 5 very simple Paumotu style *fares* of coconut fronds and kahaia wood on a motu islet called Lagon Vert (Green Lagoon). There is also camping space here. Each unit has a private bathroom with cold water shower. Electricity is provided by generator. Family style meals are served on a long picnic table under a *fare potée* shelter beside the lagoon. Free ground transfers are provided from the airport to the boat dock and you pay 1.000 CFP per person for the round-trip boat transfers to the motu. The *fare* and MAP meals of lagoon fish are 5.500 CFP per person. Campers pay 1.050 CFP EP or 4.500 CFP MAP per person, including taxes. Punua made history in 2010 when he was captain aboard the Tahitian sailing canoe *O Tahiti Nui Freedom* that went to China during a 4-month one-way voyage (see www.*otahitinui.com/vaa/en*). Punua is the man with the white beard.

Other Pensions

The pensions listed above are the most popular of the family lodgings that were available in Rangiroa at publication time. The other pensions near Avatoru village are: **PENSION HENRI**, *Tel./Fax 96.82.67; pensionhenri@mail.pf;* 2 bungalows on ocean side; **PENSION HENRIETTE**, *Tel. 96.84.68;* 1 bungalow in Avatoru village; **CAMPING NANUA**, *Tel./Fax 96.83.88; pensionnanua@hotmail.com.* 4 small *fares* & camping site beside lagoon in Avatoru; **CHEZ TEINA & MARIE**, *Tel. 96.03.94/30.20.39; Fax 96.84.44; pensionteina@mail.pf;* 7 bungalows and 3 rooms at Tiputa Pass. **PENSION TAPUHEITINI**, *Tel./Fax 689/96/04/07; cell 73.76.30; tapuheitini@mail.pf.* 3 bungalows beside lagoon 1 km. from Avatoru Village.

WHERE TO EAT – RESTAURANTS OUTSIDE HOTELS AND PENSIONS
Superior-Moderate

RANGIROA LAGOON GRILL, *Tel. 96.04.10, is beside the lagoon between the airport and Hotel Kia Ora. Open for L. D. daily except Tues. Free pick-up service. All credit cards.*

Owner Stéphane Croutelle was the assistant food & beverage manager at the Hotel Kia Ora before it closed for rebuilding. Now Stéphane has his own restaurant next door to the hotel, where he serves meals outdoors under the shade of trees. The menu includes good sandwiches for 950 CFP, fresh fish and lobster, plus French specialties such as Coquilles St. Jacques, Confit de Canard and Kobe Beef for 3.500 CFP. He also provides free Internet WiFi service.

VAIMARIO, *Tel. 96.05.96, is located on the ocean side of the road between the Hotel Kia Ora and the airport. Open for L, D, except on Wed. when they are closed all day and at noon on Sat. AE, MC, V. Free pick-up service at 7pm.*

For many years Pierre Meyrand was the restaurant manager for the Hotel Kia Ora before taking over the Vaimario. He and his Polynesian wife Estelle serve French cuisine that includes shrimp curry for 2.300 CFP and tournedos Rossini for 2.950 CFP, as well as crêpes and pizzas for 1.000-1.400 CFP.

LE KAI KAI, *Tel. 96.03.39, on lagoon side next door to Pension Martine and across road from L'Atelier Corinne. Open for lunch and dinner daily except Thurs. Round-trip transfers provided. MC, V.*

This restaurant is managed by Catherine Coconnier, who serves her guests French home cooking on an outdoor terrace with a thatch roof and coral floor. The starter courses are priced from 800-1.500 CFP. Main course dishes are 2.300-2.400 CFP, with choices of grilled mahi mahi, shrimp curry or shrimp with ginger sauce. A dish of Paumotu style roast pork is excellent for 1.500 CFP and beef filet with Roquefort sauce is 2.000 CFP. An extensive dessert menu has tempting choices, including crêpes, from 450 to 600 CFP. Free WiFi.

Economy
CHEZ AUGUSTE & ANTOINETTE (Chez Puhipuhi*), Tel. 96.85.01, is on your right opposite the marina at the entrance to Avatoru village when coming from the airport. Open Mon.-Sat. from 9am to 9pm. No credit cards.*

This is where the locals with big appetites go for very generous portions of mouth-watering dishes prepared local style. The menu includes fresh fish and Chinese dishes such as chow mien, lemon chicken and tamarind duck. Prices range from 1.000 to 1.250 CFP a plate.

PIZZERIA FILIPO, *Tel. 73.76.20,* is located beside the lagoon at the entrance to Avatoru. Salads and pizzas. Closed Wed.

SNACK CHEZ OBELIX is on the roadside adjacent to the Hotel Maitai, serving generous portions of local style meals.

SNACK DE LA MARINA, *Tel. 96.85.64, is at the Avatoru marina. Open daily for L. & D. except Mon .and Sun. noon. No credit cards.*

Henriette serves chow mien, poisson cru, sashimi, shish kabob, grilled fish or meats for 900-1.200 CFP a plate.

SNACK MOETUA (also called Snack Ohotu or Chez Marie-Jo), *Tel. 78.30.38,* is on the Ohotu quay, across the road from Pension Glorine, overlooking the Tiputa Pass. Open Mon.-Sat. 8am-5pm. Food served 11am-2pm only. Closed Sun. No credit cards.

Fruit juices, beer, *casse-croûtes* (400-650 CFP) omelets, grilled chicken, steak, shish kebabs, fish and hamburgers (400-800 CFP) are served on the overwater terrace.

SPORTS & RECREATION
Glass Bottom Boat Excursions
Matahi Excursions, *Tel. 96.84.48/79.24.54,* based at Ohotu Point on the Avatoru side of the Tiputa pass, is operated by Matahi Tepa and his daughter, Suzanne. They have two glass bottom boats that provide 2-hr. excursions, with departures made according to the incoming current in the pass. You'll view the amazing wealth of sea life from the dry comfort of the boat as you drift through the pass and stop at the fishermen's *motu* islet inside the pass.

Seascope Rangiroa, *Tel. 96.02.84/30.84.41, stephbonhart@yahoo.fr.* This is a 1-hr. excursion aboard an a/c semi-submersible that departs from the Ohotu dock beside Tiputa Pass. The viewing windows are 1m (3 ft.) below the water's surface. A 30-min. snorkeling stop is made at the natural aquarium of Nohi Nohi.

Snorkeling & Dolphin Watch Excursions
Rangiroa Activities, *Tel. 96.73.59/77.65.86,* has a 1 1/2-hr. snorkeling

excursion to the natural aquarium of Motu Nohi Nohi for 3.500 CFP; a 2-hr. boat excursion to watch for dolphins and to drift snorkel through Tiputa Pass for 5.000 CFP; and a 2-hr. Dolphin-watch Ecotour for 4.750 CFP. You may see the big dolphins (*Tursiops truncatus*), a family of spinner dolphins (*Stenella longirostris*), or more rarely, the black and white dolphins (*Peponocephala electra*) that live around the coast of Rangiroa.

Rangiroa Paradive, *Tel. 96.05.55*, leads snorkeling excursions to the natural aquarium for 3.500 CFP, drift snorkeling in Tiputa Pass and a 1 1/2-hr. Dolphin-watch Eco Tour, each for 4.200 CFP.

Lagoon Excursions, Picnics on the Motu, Fishing, Motor Boat Rental

The most popular destination of the lagoon excursions is the **Blue Lagoon**, which is an hour's boat ride from the hotels and pensions in Rangiroa, on the western edge of the atoll. This lagoon within a lagoon is formed by a natural pool of aquamarine water on the edge of the reef, known locally as Taeo'o. Several *motu* islets are separated by very shallow *hoa* channels, and you can walk from one white sand beach to another. Be sure to take along your T-shirt, hat, sunscreen, mosquito repellent, protective shoes and snorkeling gear. Don't forget your camera.

Each hotel or pension has its own private *motu* used for barbecue picnics, and the cost varies from 7.500-10.500 CFP for an all-day picnic excursion to the Blue Lagoon.

Reef Islet, also called **île aux Récifs** and **Motu Ai Ai**, is on the south end of Rangiroa, an hour's boat ride across the lagoon. Here you can walk through razor sharp raised coral outcrops called *feo* that resemble miniature fairy castles formed during four million years of erosion. This excursion is sold for 7.500-10.500 CFP, which includes a picnic on the beach. The pink sand beaches of **Vahituri**, or **Les Sables Roses**, are 1.5-2 hours by boat from Avatoru to the southeastern edge of the lagoon. The pink reflections in the sand are caused by Foraminifera deposits and coral residues. You'll enjoy swimming and snorkeling in the lagoon in this lovely area. The cost of this excursion ranges from 10.500-12.500 CFP, including a picnic.

Here are some of the excursion operators who will take you to discover the wonders of the Rangiroa lagoon.

Atoll Excursions/Watergames, *Tel. 96.04.49/26.73.27*. Hiria Arnoux has two motorboats used for snorkeling, lagoon excursions, picnics and fishing in the lagoon or deep sea. He also operates Watergames jet-ski excursions. Hiria's father, Serge Arnaux, was one of the original owners of the Kia Ora.

Oviri Excursions, *Tel./Fax 96.05.87/26.07.05*. Ugo Angely speaks good English. His father, Robin Angely, was one of the original owners of the Kia Ora and Ugo grew up at the hotel, then worked there for several years, managing the Kia Ora Sauvage. Ugo has two powerful motorboats available for excursions.

Pa'ati Excursions, *Tel. 96.02.57/79.24.63; revaultleon@mail.pf* is operated by Léon Revault. His full-day excursions for 4-9 people include a picnic on Motu Pa'ati and a stop at Pink Sand Beach or Reef Island.

Tane Excursions, *Tel. 96.84.68/72.31.51*, is operated by Marcel Tane Tamaehu, whose wife owns Pension Henriette, close to the Avatoru Marina. He has two locally built boats that he uses for lagoon fishing, deep-sea fishing, shooting the pass or for picnic excursions.

Tereva Tane E Vahine, *Tel. 96.82.51/70.71.38*. Jean-Pierre Tavita has two 24-ft. boats for 4-7 people. He specializes in picnic excursions to Reef Island.

Pearl Farms

Gauguin's Pearl Farm and Boutique, *Tel. 93.11.30/78.79.78, Fax 96.04.09; phcab@mail.pf.* This working pearl farm is operated by Philippe Cabrall. Free transfers from your lodging to the farm, which is built over the lagoon close to the airport. Free guided visits are given Mon.-Fri. at 8:30am, 10:30am and 2pm. You can watch the black-lipped oysters being grafted, cultivated and harvested during the season. The pearl boutique is open Mon.-Sat. 9am-5:30pm, and on Sun. from 10am-12pm and 2:30-5pm. Their reasonably-priced pearls have a very good luster and lovely colors, and they also have a pearl shop at the Hotel Kia Ora.

Visit a Vineyard & Wine Storehouse

Cave de Rangiroa, *Tel. 96.04.70/79.07.45; www.vindetahiti.pf.* You can visit the Dominique Auroy Estate Winery, a unique wine orchard on Motu Lagon Vert, where grapes are actually grown in the coral soil to produce red, rosé and white wine. A half-day excursion leaves Avatoru at 1pm and costs 8.000 CFP. When you return to the village you can taste the Rangiroa wines in the a/c cave near Avatoru. Or you can simply do some wine tasting without the boat trip.

Scuba Diving

The lagoon of Rangiroa is essentially a huge inland sea, with a maximum depth of about 27 m (90 ft.), which offers the finest and most abundant of nature's aquaculture. The two passes of **Tiputa** and **Avatoru** are submarine freeways for the passage of fish between the open ocean and the lagoon. The ocean normally has a moderate swell running and near the passes a five-knot current enters or exits rhythmically with the rise and fall of the tide. Static dives in or near the passes can only be done twice a day when the water is still and clear, which is normally at 12-hour intervals. Drift dives are possible on nearly any day, and these "shooting the pass" dives are exhilarating, as you are surrounded by hordes of fish, jacks, tuna, barracuda, manta rays, eagle rays, turtles, dolphins and sharks.

Between December and March huge hammerhead sharks gather to mate outside Tiputa Pass, and the graceful manta rays are most plentiful during their mating season between July and October. There are 15 popular dive sites inside the lagoon, in the passes and on the outer coral reef of Rangiroa. The following diving clubs have qualified instructors who speak English and schedule their dives between 8am and 2pm, depending on the tides, currents, swell and wind conditions. The cost of an exploration dive varies between 6.000-7.900 CFP, an introductory dive is 6.500-7.900 CFP, and a night dive is 8.500 CFP. They all accept credit cards and dive packages are available. Equipment is included, but you may feel more secure if you bring your own buoyancy compensator, regulator and depth gauge. You'll also need to bring your certification papers and a medical certificate if you are not certified. Transportation is usually provided from your hotel or pension to the dive center.

Blue Dolphins Diving Center, *Tel./Fax 96.03.01, bluedolphins@mail.pf; www.bluedolphinsdiving.com.* This busy dive shop is located at the Hotel Kia Ora. They offer Nitrox dives and the equipment is 100 percent Scubapro that is renewed every two years. **Raie Manta Club**, *Tel. 96.84.80/72.31.45; info@raiemantaclub.com; www.raiemantaclub.com.* The main office is beside the lagoon near Avatoru village, adjacent to Rangiroa Lodge, with whom they have a "Bed & Dive" program. They also have a dive center beside the Tiputa Pass. This is Rangiroa's oldest dive center, opened since 1985. Owner Yves Lefevre also has dive centers in Tikehau and Rurutu, all using Scubapro equipment. **Rangiroa Paradive**, *Tel. 96.05.55; rangiroa.paradive@mail.pf; www.rangiroaparadive.com.* This is a small family club of passionate divers located beside the Tiputa Pass between Chez Teina & Marie and Pension Glorine. Olivier Archambaud is co-head of the center and a Nitrox and rebreather instructor, and Cyril Abada is the Dive Master and the island's resident artist. 95% of their dives take place around Tiputa Pass and they also have special atmosphere dives.

The Six Passengers, *Tel/Fax 96.02.60/30.32.59; the6passengers@mail.pf; www.the6passengers.com.* This dive center moved in 2010 and is located beside a "hoa" channel between the Hotel Kia Ora and the Tiputa Pass. Owner Tanguy Bonduel said that they have a limit of 6 passengers for dives and diving picnics, and they also offer night dives. **TOPDIVE-Bathys**, *Tel. 96.05.60/72.39.55; rangiroa@topdive.com; www.topdive.pf.* This dive shop is located beside the lagoon just a minute's walk to the right of Hotel Kia Ora. It is a PADI center with modern equipment including NITROX. A 10-dive package can be used in any of the TOPDIVE centers on Tahiti, Moorea, Bora Bora and Fakarava. **Rangiroa Plongée**, *Tel. 27.57.82/96.03.13; rangiroaplongee@mail.pf; www.rangiroaplongee.pf,* is located at the Tiputa Pass, catering to a very limited number of divers.

Cruising, Sailing & Fishing Charters

Archipels Croisières (Dream Yacht Charter), *Tel. 689/66.18.80; Fax. 689/66.18.76; polynesie@dreamyachtcharter.com; www.dreamyachtcharter.com. Jérome Touze, base manager, cell 30.55.02; François Guais, customer service, cell 28.42.64.*

This Raiatea-based company also has a Marquises 57' or Eleuthera 60' catamaran based in Rangiroa during the high seasons. These luxurious sail catamarans are designed to accommodate up to 8 passengers. A 4-day/3 night Rangiroa Dream Cruise from Sat. noon to Tues. at 8am takes you to the Pink Sands area, to the wild side of the atoll and to the old village of Otepipi, all inside the vast lagoon. The cost per person starts at $1,357 in a double cabin and $1,812 in a single cabin.

SHOPPING

There is a well-stocked boutique at **Hotel Kia Ora** and an outlet of **Gauguin's Pearls**, which has another sales room at the **Gauguin's Pearl Farm**. **Boutique Ikimasho**, *Tel. 96.03.91*, is close to Magasin Kelly, selling black pearl jewelry. Free pick-up service. **Atelier Corinne**, *Tel. 96.03.13*, is close to the airport, selling black pearls and jewelry. **La Boutique Rangistyle** in Avatoru village sells gift items plus clothes for all the family made to order on request. **Coconut Boutique**, *Tel. 96.85.12*, in Avatoru village, carries gift items, cosmetics, French magazines, shirts and pareos. **Raie Manta Club Boutique** is adjacent to the scuba diving center in Avatoru. Here you will find a good selection of wildlife postcards, underwater video films, T-shirts and posters. **Pareos by Coucou** are on sale at Snack Obelix and **Valerie**'s pareos and T-shirts can be purchased at Rangiroa Plongée. Locally made arts and crafts are on display at the **Fare Artisanat** in Avatoru. **Vai Boutique** in Avatoru village sells clothing, pareos, gifts and souvenirs. **Boutique Vai Piti**, just outside Avatoru village, sells gifts, pareos, and magazines. **Miel de Rangiroa** is locally produced honey that is sold in the magasin stores in Avatoru.

PRACTICAL INFORMATION

Banks

Banque de Tahiti has a branch in Avatoru village close to the Catholic Church and the *mairie* (town hall), *Tel. 96.85.52*. It is open Mon., Tues., Thurs. and Fri., 8-11am and 1-4pm.

Banque Socredo is located beside the *mairie* of Avatoru, *Tel. 96.85.63*, and is open on Wed. and Fri. 8am-12pm, and on Mon. and Thurs. 1:30-4:30pm. They have an ATM. Banque Socredo, *Tel. 93.12.50*, also has an office at the *mairie* in Tiputa, which is open Mon. and Thurs., 8am-12pm.

Hospitals

A government operated medical center is located in Avatoru village, *Tel. 96.03.75*, and has an ambulance. There is an infirmary in Tiputa village, *Tel. 96.73.96*, and there are also private doctors and dentists in Rangiroa.

Internet

The hotels and several of the family pensions provide Internet service for their guests. The Post Offices in Avatoru and Tiputa have a computer with Mana HotSpot Wi-Fi service.

Magasins (Food Stores)

Magasin Daniel in Avatoru village sells wine, beer and a few fresh vegetables. You can also buy some supplies at **Magasin Kelly, Chez Henriette, Libre Service Teina Piti**, and **Libre Service Simone**. **Poissonnerie Teura** is a combination fish shop and **laundry service**, in Avatoru open from 7:30am-6pm. Clothes washed, dried and ironed, drop-off in the morning and pick-up in the afternoon.

Pharmacy

The **Pharmacie de Rangiroa**, *Tel. 93.12.35*, is in Avatoru village across the road from the Catholic Church. It is open Mon.-Fri. 8am-12:30pm and 3-6:30pm; on Sat. 8am-12:30pm and 4:30-6:30 pm; and on Sun. 10-11:30am.

Police

The French *gendarmerie* is beside the lagoon between Hotel Kia Ora and the airport, *Tel. 93.11.55*. Municipal Police of Avatoru, *Tel. 96.84.74*. You can also dial *17* for police.

Post Office & Telecommunications Office

A Post Office is located in Avatoru village, *Tel. 96.83.81* and another is in Tiputa village, *Tel. 96.73.80*.

MANIHI

Manihi is 520 km (322 mi.) northeast of Tahiti and a world removed from time and care. A tiny green oasis floating in the desert of the sea, with a name as exotic as the trade winds and a lagoon as pretty as a mother-of-pearl shell. Seen from the air, Manihi presents a picturesque palette of glimmering greens and blues, with white and pink beaches in a framing of feathery green coconut palms. A close range view of this crystal clear lagoon is even better, as you can see the vividly painted tropical fish feeding in the coral gardens on the white sand bottom, several feet below the water's surface.

Some visitors find that Manihi is still one of the friendliest villages in the Tuamotu Islands, although life for the 1,575 inhabitants has changed with the development of the cultured pearl industry. The first privately owned black pearl farm was started in Manihi in 1966. When it became known that the black-lipped oysters in this lagoon produced a high quality rainbow-hued pearl, Manihi became synonymous with the *po'e rava*. This is the local name for the rare and beautiful Tahitian cultured pearl.

Several dozen pearl farms were eventually built on stilts on almost every coral head inside the lagoon, which is about 8 km (4.9 mi.) wide by 27 km (16.7 mi.) long. Most of the people who live in Manihi were involved in the pearl business, even though they may have had other jobs as well. All but 10 or so of these pearl farms are now abandoned since the market for pearls took a dive, and the local government began demanding high taxes. All around the lagoon you can now see the buoys that once floated on the surface, marking the presence of pearl oysters suspended below the water in wire baskets.

Turipaoa, which is also known as Paeua, is a sun-baked little village with colorful houses of limestone and clapboard lining the three main roads, one of which extends to the end of the motu. The houses are shaded by breadfruit trees and bordered with frangipani, hibiscus and bougainvillea. This village is home to most of Manihi's 800 residents. The favorite hangout in the village is to sit on the benches under the shade of a giant *tou* tree with orange flowers beside the Turipaoa pass. Here the inhabitants can talk politics and gossip as they watch the comings and goings of the supply ships from Tahiti and the boats from the pearl farms.

ARRIVALS & DEPARTURES
Arriving by Air
Air Tahiti flies from Tahiti to Manihi 7 days a week with a stop in Rangiroa and sometimes in Tikehau. There is a direct Rangiroa-Manihi flight daily except Thurs. You can fly from Bora Bora to Manihi every Mon., Wed. and Sun., changing planes in Rangiroa. There is a flight from Tikehau to Manihi each Mon. and Wed., with a stop in Rangiroa and a Sat. flight with a change of plane in Rangiroa. You can fly direct from Ahe to Manihi each Fri. and Sun for 7.230 CFP for the 10-min. flight. The one-way fare from Tahiti to Manihi is 22.030 CFP and 28.630 CFP from Bora Bora to Manihi. The one-way fare from Rangiroa or Tikehau to Manihi is 12.130 CFP, the same price you'll pay to fly from Fakarava to Manihi each Thurs. **Air Tahiti reservations**: Tahiti, *Tel. 86.42.42*; in Manihi *Tel. 93.30.70*.

The airport is on a *motu islet* at the southwest end of Manihi, and the airstrip will accommodate ATR-72 aircraft. Transfers from the airport to the Manihi Pearl Beach Resort are made by boat or golf carts, just a 5-minute ride either way. Air Tahiti does not provide any boat transportation from the airport to the village, a 15-min. boat ride from the airport.

You can also get to Manihi by chartering an airplane in Tahiti from **Air Tahiti**, *Tel. 86.42.42*, or **Pol'Air**, *Tel. 74.23.11*.

Arriving By Boat
Mareva Nui, *Tel. 42.25.53, Fax 42.25.57*, is a 181-ft. steel ship that transports cargo between Tahiti and the Tuamotu atolls. It leaves Tahiti every 15 days for the 8-day round-trip voyage, and calls at Manihi after stopping at several atolls, which may include Makatea, Mataiva, Tikehau, Rangiroa and Ahe. There are 12 berths but no cabins and the one-way fare from Tahiti to Manihi is 17.000 CFP, including all meals.

St. Xavier Maris Stella III, *Tel. 42.23.58, Fax 43.03.73*, can transport 12 passengers who sleep on the bridge for 8.484 CFP between Tahiti and Manihi, including three meals a day. A berth in an a/c cabin is 16.000 CFP, meals included. Bring your own bedding. The ship leaves Papeete every 15 days and the itinerary varies, taking from 7-10 days for the round-trip voyage.

All the ships stop at the Turipaoa quay beside the pass in Manihi. See more information in Chapter 6, *Planning Your Trip*.

Departing By Air
Air Tahiti has daily flights from Manihi to Papeete, either direct or with a stop in Rangiroa or Fakarava. There are daily flights on Tues., Wed. and Sun. from

Manihi to Rangiroa, from Manihi to Tikehau on Mon., and to Fakarava on Thurs. and Sat. **Air Tahiti** reservations in Manihi: *Tel. 93.30.70,* and the airport number is *Tel. 96.42.71.*

Departing By Boat

St. Xavier Maris Stella III, Tel. 42.23.58, leaves Manihi every 15 days, stopping at several of the western Tuamotu atolls before returning to Papeete. Meals are served on board. *Mareva Nui, Tel. 42.25.53, Fax 42.25.57,* calls at 9-10 other atolls after leaving Manihi each 15 days. See more information under *Inter-Island Cruise Ships, Passenger Boats and Freighters* in Chapter 6, *Planning Your Trip.*

ORIENTATION

Manihi's only village, **Turipaoa**, is on Motu Paeua, 2.8 km (1.7 mi.) across the lagoon from the airport. The village is built next to the Tairapa Pass, which is 60 m. (197 ft.) deep and provides the only navigable entry into the lagoon. A sheltered basin with lights has moorings for several boats. In the village you will find a couple of *magasin* stores, a bakery, a snack, and a post office. There is no bank in Manihi.

WHERE TO STAY & EAT

Deluxe

MANIHI PEARL BEACH RESORT, *B.P. 1, Manihi Tuamotu 98771. Tel. 689/96.42.73; Fax 689/96.42.72; www.pearlresorts.com. Reservations: Tel. 689/ 50.84.45; Fax 689/43.17.86; res@spmhotels.pf. 39 bungalows. All major credit cards.*

All 6 editions of this guide book have featured the same photo of Manihi Pearl Beach Resort on the front cover. Look at the clear lagoon in this picture and you will understand why I recommend that you stay in an overwater bungalow. These coral heads are home to a vast array of tropical fish, Tridacna reef clams with colorful mantles, and even live Trochus shells. The glass top coffee table that allows you to view the fish below your bungalow has become almost *de rigeur* in overwater bungalows, but this hotel gives you additional fish watching possibilities with windows on 2 sides of a writing desk. Glass panels in the bathroom keep you in touch with what's happening in the lagoon at all times. A light can be turned on at night to attract the fish and you can even watch a family of blue, green, turquoise and red parrotfish nibbling their dinner while you're brushing your teeth after your own meal! Of course, you'll have a better view from your balcony or by getting into the water with all that fascinating fauna. A fish identification card is placed in the desk drawer of the overwater bungalows to help you recognize the various species of fish you're seeing.

This 4-star hotel with 39 units is a member of Select Hotels and offers a choice of 4 standard beach bungalows or 15 premium beach bungalows, 1 beach suite, 14 overwater bungalows and 5 premium overwater bungalows. They are built in traditional Polynesian style, with a roof of thatched pandanus fronds and wooden walls. Each unit has a king size bed or 2 twin beds, plus a day bed, all with off-white covers and accent cushions the color of the turquoise and emerald lagoon. They are equipped with a ceiling fan, mini-bar refrigerator, coffee/tea facilities, hair dryer, iron and board, international direct dial telephone with Internet connection, satellite TV, individual safe and sundeck. All units have a hot water shower and the superior beach bungalows have 2 entrances and an indoor garden with a coral floor. All bungalows have electric mosquito repellent plugs and laundry service is available.

The premium overwater bungalows are the same size as the overwater bungalows (51 sq. m. or 549 sq. ft.) but they are further apart, providing just a little more privacy. They also have a/c, CD player and bathrobes. There are 2 overwater bungalows designed for physically challenged guests in wheelchairs, and the hotel's public areas and pool are wheelchair accessible. The hotel staff will assist handicapped guests when being transferred by boat between the hotel and village or other boat excursions.

The Poe Rava restaurant serves deliciously prepared fish and French cuisine. An American breakfast buffet is 3.200 CFP, a 2-course set luncheon menu is 3.650 CFP, and a 3-course set dinner menu is 6.200 CFP. In addition to burgers, sandwiches, pizza and pasta, the luncheon menu may suggest a Cobb salad or a salad topped with fresh fried parrotfish that is breaded in coconut. The à la carte dinner menu offers fish and seafood dishes that include grilled lobster in season.

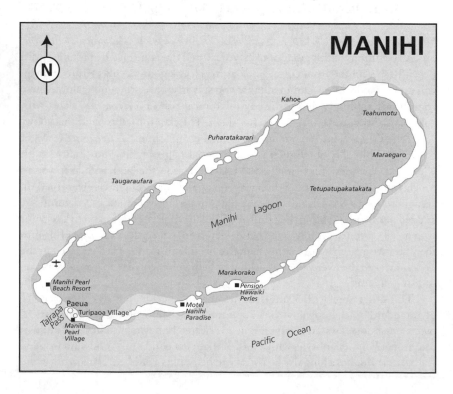

Chicken, lamb, veal and beef choices are also included on the limited menu. A local band plays island style music in the restaurant during dinner on some evenings and the hotel employees present a Tahitian dance show during the Polynesian buffet that is held on Fri. or Sat. night. Room service is available during meal hours and snacks can be ordered at the bar from 3-5pm.

The reception, bar, boutique, pearl shop, library-lounge and Manea Spa are all located in separate buildings. Beside the coral beach and the lagoon is a large fresh water infinity swimming pool, and the Manihi Blue Nui scuba diving center is adjacent to the pier. Another place to feed and admire the fish is at the snorkeling pier, which has a shower and steps leading into the lagoon. You can also walk across a shallow part of the lagoon to a small islet, where you can relax in a lounge chair or hammock and read your favorite beach book.

Free activities for hotel guests include use of bicycles, outrigger paddle canoes, kayaks, snorkeling gear, volleyball, badminton, petanque (bocce ball), mini-golf, and game room with billiards. There are 2 computers in the recreation room and WiFi connections are available in your room as well as in all parts of the hotel property. You can hook up your laptop to the Internet for 500 CFP for 1 hr. and 2.000 CFP for 5 hrs. There is free WiFi in the bar. A coconut show, pareo tying demonstration, traditional weaving lessons and tamure dance lessons are scheduled regularly at the Miki Miki bar. An interesting and free activity takes place at 7pm each Wednesday evening when guests accompany Celine, the Marquesan bartender, out to the airstrip to gaze at the huge bowl of stars and planets. There are no lights anywhere nearby, and you can clearly see the Milky Way, Southern Cross, Orion's Belt and all the other constellations visible in the Southern Hemisphere.

Paid excursions and activities include a visit to a pearl farm for 2.550 CFP, a picnic on an uninhabited motu islet for 9.200 CFP, hand line fishing for 2.050 CFP, drift snorkeling in the ocean for 1.950 CFP, and a sunset cruise for 2.035 CFP. A deep-sea fishing excursion for a 2-hr. minimum is 15.325 CFP.

Manihi Pearl Beach Resort is one of French Polynesia's most popular destinations for honeymooners and other loving couples. The hotel offers a number of suggestions for Romantic Rendez-Vous, such as the canoe breakfast that is delivered by outrigger paddle canoe and served on your terrace, just as you see in the cover photo. Contact them for details and prices and be sure to have a look at their website as they have installed a web cam to entice you.

As in all the Pearl Resorts, children under 16 years of age are allowed free accommodation when sharing a room with their parents and according to existing bedding configuration. Extra charge will apply when extra bedding is added. Free meals for children are included (except beverages, gourmet restaurant, room service, and mini bar) when ordering from special kids menu only. Transfers are also free of charge for children. Beach toys, games, bicycles with baby seats, life jackets, snorkel gear, drawing kit, candies and DVD are also provided for children.

Because the Manihi Pearl Beach Resort is a small hotel, it is easy to get to know the employees and other guests. The feeling here is that of a small village, yet you still have all the privacy you desire. One of the reasons I like to keep going back again and again is because nothing changes very much and I can see the same smiling faces each time I visit.

Moderate
MOTEL NANIHI PARADISE, *Turipaoa, Manihi 98771. Tel. 689/93.30.40/ 29.53.36; Fax 689/93.30.41; www.nanihiparadise.com. On Motu Kamoka, a private islet on the southeast side of the atoll, 10 km. (6.2 mi.) from airport. MC, V.*

Vaiana Dantin owns this holiday family pension, which has been given a 1-Tiare rating awarded by Tahiti Tourisme. This is a 3-acre property with 3 small bungalows containing 1-2 bedrooms, mosquito nets over beds, kitchenette with refrigerator, bathroom and a terrace facing west for enjoying sunset cocktails. Round-trip boat transfers 2.500 CFP per person. EP Rates: 10.979 CFP sgl./ 13.484 CFP dbl; MAP and AP meals available. Activities include boat transfers to the village, boat tours around the lagoon, snorkeling, shelling, fishing in lagoon, visits to pearl farms, picnics on an uninhabited motu, and transfers to the Manihi Blue Nui Dive center at Manihi Pearl Beach Resort. WiFi extra. Vaiana is one of the pioneers of *mabe* pearl (blister pearl) grafting in Manihi and she accepts credit cards in her on-site Mabe Factory of jewelry.

Economy
PENSION HAWAIKI PEARLS, *B.P. 51, Turipaoa, Manihi 98771. Tel. 689/ 96.42.89; Fax 689/96.43.30; contact Loana Buniet at pensionhawaikipearls@hotmail.fr; www.pensionhawaikipearls.com. On Motu Marakorako, 12 km (7.5 mi.) from the airport and main village. No credit cards.*

This pension was formerly called Pension Vainui Perles. It is located on a large motu owned by Frenchman Edmond Buniet in a remote location 30 min. by boat from the airport. Round-trip boat transfers are 1.000 CFP per person. There are 7 rooms available in 4 bungalows facing the lagoon. There are mosquito nets over the beds and a safe in each room. Solar power provides electricity, supposedly 24/ 24. Bring a flashlight just in case it is shut down during the evening. All guests share the bathroom facilities and potable water is available. A central refrigerator is available for guests. Meals are served on a shaded terrace next to the beach of white and pink sand. Two Polynesians take care of guests and the food is European and local style. Free activities include a library, kayaks, petanque (bocce ball), badminton, fishing in the lagoon, picnics on a motu and a visit to a private pearl farm. AP Rates: 12.000 CFP per person. Telephone, fax and Internet service are extra.

MANIHI PEARL VILLAGE, *B.P. 80, Turipaoa, Manihi 98771. Tel./Fax 689/96.43.38; Cell 70.45.00; pensionmpv@mail.pf. On lagoon side in Turipaoa village. No credit cards.*

John and Moea Drollet have 4 bungalows in Manihi's main village with sleeping accommodations for up to 3 people each. Each room has mosquito nets over the beds, a ceiling fan, safe, and a private bathroom with cold water shower.

Free TV and airport transfers. Sunset fishing is also available. A room for 1-2 people with MAP meals is 10.000 CFP.

SPORTS & RECREATION
Scuba Diving
Manihi Blue Nui Dive Center is located at the Manihi Pearl Beach Resort, *Tel./Fax 96.42.17; manihi.blue.nui@mail.pf; www.bluenui.com.* This well equipped dive shop has showers, lockers, hangers for wet suits and a covered aluminum boat for 16 divers. All diving gear and equipment is provided. Founder Gilles Petre, who is based in Bora Bora, supervises all the Blue Nui Dive Centers. His staff in Manihi are highly qualified instructors for PADI, BEES and CMAS. The rates are 7.727 CFP for 1 dive, initiation dives are 8.636 CFP, and night dives are 9.091 CFP. The Blue Nui Dive Centers in Manihi, Tikehau, Taha'a and Bora Bora all offer dive packages that can be used in any or all of the centers. These packages sell for 40.909 CFP for 6 dives and 65.455 CFP for 10 dives. Diving lessons available.

Dive Sites
Manihi offers excellent diving conditions in shallow, warm, clear water, with mild currents in the pass. The dive sites are only five minutes away from the dive center, reached by a comfortable speedboat that is custom designed for diving. The pass is south to north with the main wind from the east, and for beginners, a site outside the reef is used that is protected from the main wind by the village of Turipaoa.

Tairapa Pass is one of the most popular dive sites, offering drift dives with the incoming or outgoing currents. You'll feel as though you are soaring through space with the tuna, sharks, schools of barracuda, jack fish, rays and turtles. **The Drop Off** is a wall dive on the ocean side of Manihi, which descends from 3 to 1,350 m (10 to 4,500 ft.) deep. This site abounds with gray sharks, Napoleon fish, giant jack fish, schools of snapper and sea pike barracuda, plus the deep-sea fish like tuna and marlin. Each July thousands of groupers gather here to breed, offering one of the most fascinating underwater events in the world.

The Circus is the name given to a location between the pass and the lagoon, which is a favorite hangout for eagle and manta rays. Underwater photographers can get close to the graceful manta rays as they glide up and down in an average underwater depth of 9 m (30 ft.). These curious and friendly creatures sometimes have a wingspan up to four m (13 ft.) wide, and remain here all year long.

A scenic dive on the **West Point** of the ocean side reveals fire coral, antler coral and flower petal coral, among others, which are visible for up to 60 m (200 ft.) in the incredibly clear water. Shark feeding is best at **The Break**, a large cut in the outer reef, where a coral amphitheater provides the scenery for a multitude of reef sharks, including black tip, white tip, gray sharks and an occasional hammer head, who show up for the free handouts of tuna heads.

SHOPPING

The Manihi Pearl Beach Resort has the **Vahine Purotu Boutique** and **Pearls by Corrion** sells pearls and pearl jewelry on the premises. Just a 5-minute walk or an even quicker bike ride from the hotel is **La Boutique Mareva**, *Tel./Fax 689/ 96.41.38/93.30.25; marevacoquille@hotmail.com*. This is the home of Mareva and Guy Coquille, who formerly owned and managed the Kaina Village before it became Manihi Pearl Beach Resort. Mareva has a nice selection of Tahitian cultured pearl jewelry.

Poetai Perles, *Tel. 96.42.36/75.12.97*, is across the road from the airport, adjacent to **Rebeta Snack & Boutique**. There is a very limited choice of pearls, but you can buy a sandwich and juice or soft drink.

You can also buy pearls in Turipaoa village, where you may encounter some of the pearl farmers who have set jewelry as well as loose pearls. It is best to learn something about pearls first, so that you will be able to determine if the pearl is not a reject or a pearl that has been harvested early for control purposes. The best quality pearls stay inside the oyster for 18 months, and have a lovely orient or luster. See more information under Shopping in the *Basic Information* chapter.

Visits to a Pearl Farm

Pearls by Corrion, also known as **CJC Perles Manihi,** is the only pearl farm in Manihi that allows regular visits, conducted each Mon., Wed. and Fri. morning. The boat leaves the Manihi Pearl Beach Resort at 8am, with a minimum of two people, and the excursion lasts about 2 hours. During this time you will learn practically all there is to know about the *Pinctada Margaritifera* black lipped oyster that gives us this precious gift from the rainbow-hued lagoon of Manihi. The guide is well informed, as she also works in the Pearls by Corrion boutique located at the hotel, where you can buy pearls from the farm. Please do not expect to fly into Manihi at noon and be taken to a pearl farm that afternoon. It just doesn't work that way because the farm is on the other side of the lagoon and the boat and pilot may be otherwise occupied. The guided boat tour to the pearl farm costs 2.550 CFP per person.

MASSAGES & SPA TREATMENTS

Manea Spa, *Tel. 96.42.73; maneaspa@manihipearlbeach.pf;* www.maneaspa.com. A selection of massages is available for men, women and couples. Prices start at 8.000 CFP for a 30-min. Monoi Maitai massage for one or 12.909 CFP for two. You can also get a 50- or 80-min. massage, as well as body scrubs, hair, skin and body care, special care treatments for men, and hot stone healing. The specialty here is the Monoi Poe, named for the cultured pearls that come from Manihi's famous lagoon. This exotic stimulating massage is applied with a rope of black pearls that arouses all your senses as the masseuse slithers the pearls over your body. You've got to try it! This 50-min. treat is 13.455 CFP for one and 21.545 CFP for a couple. If you think you can stand an 80-min. session of this sensual experience, then you'll pay 18.636 CFP for one and 29.818 for two.

PRACTICAL INFORMATION
Banks
There are no banks in Manihi.

Hospital
A government-operated infirmary is located in Turipaoa village, *Tel. 96.43.67.* The nurse is on duty from 7-11am and from 4-6pm.

Post Office
A **Post Office and Telecommunications Office** is located in Turipaoa village facing the marina, *Tel. 96.42.22.* You'll find telephone booths in this building, as well as a couple more in the village and at the airport, and a public phone is located at the Manihi Pearl Beach Resort. They all accept phone cards.

TIKEHAU
Tikehau is a South Sea island dream come true, an escapist's haven of seclusion that is less than an hour's flight from Tahiti and just 20 minutes by plane from Rangiroa. Tikehau is one of the most popular atolls in the Tuamotu Archipelago, because of its natural beauty and the friendliness of the 400 inhabitants.

In the Paumotu language Tikehau means "peaceful landing" and when the Russian navigator Kotzbue discovered the atoll in 1815, he named it Krusenstern Island. The old village was destroyed by a cyclone in 1906 and the residents moved to higher ground and built their homes in Tuherahera on the southwest side of the atoll. Here you'll find the *mairie* (town hall), post office and telecommunications center, school, infirmary, three *magasin* stores, bakery, Protestant temple, Catholic church, Seventh-Day Adventist church, Sanito temple, a snack, and most of the pensions and guest houses. There is no bank in Tikehau. Three coral sand roads connect Tuherahera with the airport and the road follows the coast line around the *motu*, where you will see new settlements of the anti-cyclone type houses, as well as new concrete houses, which are built by the new generation who have moved back to the old village.

Most of the guesthouses or pensions are located between the airport and a pretty white sand beach. Tall, stately ironwood trees, *Casuarina equisetifolia*, also known as Australian pine or *aito*, border the beaches, and you can hear the wind whistling through the branches while you watch the white fairy terns soaring overhead.

The barrier reef surrounding Tikehau is almost continuous and the 150 m. (492-ft.) wide Tuheiava Pass, on the west coast, is the only entrance into the lagoon. Immediately to the left of the pass is Motu Teonai, which contains a small village of fishing families. Copra is produced in the old village of Maiai, on the northeast side of the atoll, and this is where you will find a religious community called Eden, where cruise boats are usually welcomed. The yachting families are happy to buy the organic vegetables and fruits grown in the gardens of Eden. Many members of this sect are Chinese from Tahiti who gather here during holidays and long weekends.

When Jacques Cousteau's research group made a study of the Polynesian atolls in 1987, they declared the lagoon of Tikehau to contain the most fish of any of the lagoons in French Polynesia. There has been no evidence of ciguatera fish poisoning in Tikehau, and all the lagoon fish are considered edible. The choice fish include parrotfish, grouper, long-nose emperorfish, soldierfish and jackfish. A few attempts were made to harvest the *Pinctada Margaritifera* oyster that produces pearls, but due to a lack of plankton in the lagoon, most of these pearl farms are now closed. Surfers seek the swells of the sea as it crashes on the reef beside Tuheiava Pass.

ARRIVALS & DEPARTURES

Arriving by Air

Air Tahiti flies direct from Tahiti to Tikehau daily with 55-min. flights and a flight on Fri. and Sun. that stops in Rangiroa. There is a direct flight from Rangiroa to Tikehau on Wed., Fri., and 2 on Sun. There is also a Mon. flight from Rangiroa that stops in Manihi. You can fly direct from Bora Bora to Tikehau each Thurs., and with a stop in Rangiroa on Wed. and Sun. A Sun. flight from Raiatea stops in Bora Bora and Rangiroa. **Air Tahiti reservations:** Tahiti, *Tel. 86.42.42*, in Tikehau *Tel. 96.22.66*.

The one-way airfare from Tahiti to Tikehau is 18.330 CFP; the one-way fare from Rangiroa to Tikehau is 7.230 CFP; and the one-way fare from Raiatea or Bora Bora to Tikehau is 25.530 CFP.

You can also get to Tikehau by chartering an airplane in Tahiti from **Air Tahiti**, *Tel. 86.42.42*, or **Pol'Air**, *Tel. 74.23.11*.

Arriving by Boat

Mareva Nui, *Tel. 42.25.53, Fax 42.25.57*, is a 181-ft. steel ship that transports cargo between Tahiti and the Tuamotu atolls. It leaves Tahiti every 15 days, stopping in Makatea and Mataiva before arriving in Tikehau. There are 12 berths on board but no cabin. The one-way fare from Tahiti to Tikehau is 7.350 CFP, including three meals a day.

St. Xavier Maris Stella III, *Tel. 42.23.58*, can transport 12 passengers, sleeping in an a/c cabin or on the deck. Bring your own bedding. The fare from Tahiti to Tikehau is 7.070 CFP on deck and 10.000 CFP for a berth in an a/c cabin, including 3 meals a day. The ship leaves Papeete every 15 days for 7-10 day voyages.

See more information in Chapter 6, *Planning Your Trip*.

Departing by Air

Air Tahiti has 1-2 daily flights from Tikehau to Tahiti, either direct or with a stop in Rangiroa plus a Mon. stop in Manihi. Direct flights from Tikehau to Rangiroa are daily except Fri. and Sun. There are flights to Manihi via Rangiroa on Mon., Wed. and Sat. **Air Tahiti reservations** in Tikehau, *Tel. 96.22.66*.

Departing by Boat

Mareva Nui, Tel. 42.25.53, calls at 12 other atolls after leaving Tikehau each 15 days, and the trip back to Tahiti takes 7 days. *St. Xavier Maris Stella III, Tel. 42.23.58*, leaves Tikehau every 15 days for Manihi, Fakarava and several other western Tuamotu atolls before returning to Papeete. Fares are determined by length of voyage to Tahiti. See more information under *Inter-Island Cruise Ships, Passenger Boats and Freighters* in Chapter 6, *Planning Your Trip*.

ORIENTATION

Most of the residents of Tikehau live in **Tuherahera village** on the southern end of the atoll, where small boats can enter the lagoon through a pass in the coral reef. The almost circular interior lagoon is 26 km (16 mi.) wide, bordered by white and pink sand beaches. A 10-km. (6.2-mi.) dirt road circles the *motu* of Tuherahera, which you can explore on a bicycle.

WHERE TO STAY

Deluxe

TIKEHAU PEARL BEACH RESORT, *B.P. 20, Tuherahera, Tikehau 98778. Tel. 689/96.23.00; Fax 689/96.23.01; welcome@tikehaupearlbeach.pf; www.spmhotels.com. Reservations: Tel. 689/50.84.54; Fax 689/43.17.86; res@spmhotels.pf. 37 units. All major credit cards.*

This 4-star hotel is located on Motu Tianoa, 3 km (1.9 mi.) east of Tuherahera village in a group of islets called Ohotu. The hotel opened in 2001 with 13 beach bungalows, 9 overwater bungalows and 7 premium overwater bungalows. A 2004 project added 8 premium overwater suites with a/c, which are so comfortable that you will want to move in for a long term.

All the bungalows have thatched roofs, walls of woven palm fronds, woven pandanus matting on the ceiling and split bamboo on the inside walls. The furniture is made of rich-toned local woods and consists of a king-size bed or 2 twin beds, a single daybed, writing desk, small table and chairs. There is a ceiling fan, telephone, satellite/cable TV, mini-bar, coffee-tea making facilities, safe, iron and board, umbrella and snorkeling gear in each room. The deluxe beach bungalows have a/c. The bathrooms in all the beach units open onto a garden and a high coral wall, and there are doors between the bedroom and bathroom. Each bathroom has a hair dryer and Manea amenities that are replenished daily when the rooms are cleaned. One of the nicest features of the beach bungalows is the partially covered terrace overlooking a beautiful white sand beach. You can recline in the lounge chairs on the sundeck and watch the sunrise or sunset, depending on which unit you have, and rarely do you see another person on the beach, nor even a passing boat. The very inviting lagoon is just a few steps away. This is the gentle side of the motu, so typical of the South Seas scenery that makes you dream of trade winds singing through the coconut palms, white sandy beaches that turn pink with the setting sun and a crystalline lagoon the color of green silk, turquoise and jade.

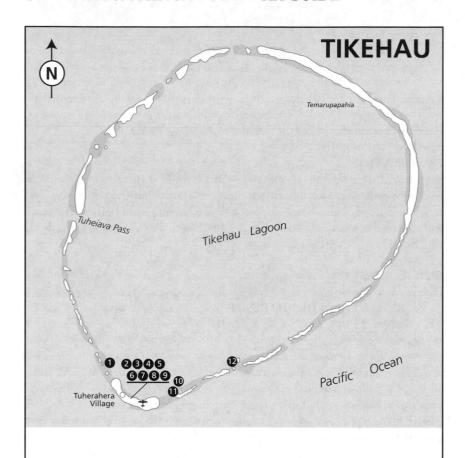

1. Ninamu Resort
2. Fare Hanariki
3. Tevahi Village
4. Aito Motel Colette
5. Tikehau Village

6. Pension Tematie
7. Panau Lagon
8. Chez Justine
9. Pension Hotu
10. Relais Royal Tikehau

11. Kahaia Beach
12. Tikehau Pearl Beach Resort

The original overwater bungalows are 55 sq. m. (595 sq. ft.), and are built over a *hoa* channel where the current flows from the ocean into the lagoon. Because the water can be as deep as 2 m (6.6 ft.) underneath some of the bungalows, the hotel management advises guests against swimming here when the current is very strong. You can stand on your balcony and see the waves crashing onto the coral reef and watch a family of reef herons fishing on a sandbar. The overwater bungalows have a glass window in the floor for fish watching. These units have all the same amenities as the beach units, with the addition of CD players in the premium overwater bungalows. One of the overwater units is equipped for guests in wheelchairs.

The fabulous premium overwater suites are 93 sq. m. (1001 sq. ft.) and are built over the lagoon just beyond the beach bungalows. These a/c units are furnished like all the other bungalows, but they also have bathrobes and bathtubs, as well as a big terrace partially covered with a thatched roof. There is a table next to a sofa and chairs under this *fare pote'e*, and there are 2 lounge chairs on the open sundeck. You have direct access into the lagoon by ladder from the swimming platform, plus a shower for rinsing off when you come back up. The fish are plentiful and greedy for free handouts of bread and croissants. There is also a glass table in the bedroom-sitting area designed for fish-watching.

In addition to the Poreho Restaurant and Tianoa Bar, the hotel has an activities desk at the reception area, plus an all-purpose room that can be used for meetings or a game room with a wide screen TV and DVD. There is also a sundries gift shop and boutique. Tikehau Blue Nui Dive Center is located on the hotel grounds, as well as Fare Manea Spa. Room service is offered during regular meal hours, and there is a 48-hr. laundry service and a secretarial service. The hotel grounds are fumigated daily to keep the mosquito and bug population to a minimum, and each room is furnished with an electrical repellent device, as well as bug spray.

The hotel's complimentary activities include an infinity swimming pool, kayaks, outrigger paddle canoes, snorkeling gear, volleyball, bocce ball, badminton, ping-pong, billiards and library. For optional excursions and activities you can take a boat trip to visit Bird Island on Motu Puarua and snorkel in the lagoon, for 5.909 CFP, or join a barbecue picnic on a pink-sand motu for 7.727 CFP. A local fisherman will also take 1-4 people for line fishing in the lagoon for 14.091 CFP, or trawling in the open ocean for 27.273 CFP for 2 passengers. A sunset cruise is 3.182 CFP. You can be dropped off on an uninhabited motu for 3.182 CFP, with a walkie-talkie and picnic and drinks if you so desire. A jetski excursion costs 16.364 CFP for 1 hr. and 45 min. or 11.818 CFP for a 1-hr. sunset ride. You can also sign up for a 2-hr. cooking lesson with the chef de cuisine for 5.455 CFP.

The hotel operates a daily boat service between the village and the hotel, providing 5 round-trip shuttles. You can take this free shuttle to the village and pick up a rental bike at the boat dock for 909 CFP for half a day. A bike ride around the village motu takes about 45 min. and it is a lovely trip. The people of Tikehau are very friendly to one another and to visitors.

The Tikehau Pearl Beach Resort is a member of Select Hotels & Resorts and a favorite destination for honeymooners. Contact the hotel for details on their Romantic Rendez-Vous Package, which includes a Canoe Breakfast for 2 for 11.600 CFP, a Blue Lagoon breakfast, a picnic for 2 on a secluded motu, or a gourmet picnic on the motu that includes champagne served at an elegantly dressed table.

As in all the Pearl Resorts, children under 15 years of age are allowed free accommodation when sharing a room with their parents and according to existing bedding configuration. Extra charge will apply when extra bedding is added. Free meals for children are included (except beverages, gourmet restaurant, room service, and mini bar) when ordering from special kids menu only. Transfers are also free of charge for children. Beach toys, games, life jackets and snorkel gear are also provided for children.

Superior

NINAMU RESORT, *Tuherahera, Tikehau 98778. Tel. 689/73.78.10/ 96.23.98; chris@motuninamu.com; www.ninamuresort.com. US reservations: Carissa Sanchez-Booking Manager, Tel. 1-949/842-5589; Fax 949/481-2424. carissa@motuninamu.com; Skype: Motuninamu. On Motu Ninamu 2.5 mi. north-west of Tikehau airport, a 10-min. boat ride from the pier in Tuherahera village.*

Ninamu means "blue" in the Tahitian language, and you'll be surrounded by all shades of blue when you visit this 18-acre private islet. Australian Chris O'Callaghan, part owner and resident manager, is the organizer of the Billabong Surfing competitions in Tahiti, and his partner founded Billabong. Chris has built 6 unusual bungalows on a private motu, and this little hidden gem resort opened in 2010. It has quickly become a choice destination for surfers, divers, fishermen and many others who seek a secluded haven "far from the madding crowds" and beaten paths of tourism. The bungalows can accommodate 16-18 people, and the unique architecture of local wood, coral rock and other locally found materials features spiral staircases leading to raised bedrooms with high end furniture, including canopy beds with king-size mattresses. The rooms also have fans and mosquito nets. The open air showers have privacy walls of tiled coral rock. This eco-friendly resort uses solar power for electricity and a reverse osmosis water processing system. The recreation building has a restaurant/bar, boutique, sitting area, library and TV-movie area. WiFi is free in the restaurant and living area. Chris and his wife Greta have a full-time chef and they serve good meals that include fresh fish and seafood as well as the organic fruits and vegetables they buy from the Garden of Eden located on another private motu in Tikehau.

Ninamu Resort has all the toys for exploring the atoll, and most of the activities are included in the daily rate of bungalow, AP meals and boat transfers, which is $350 or $400 depending on the season. They have snorkel gear, kayaks, kiteboards, surfboards, and lessons are available if desired. Deep sea fishing and scuba diving are extra.

Moderate
RELAIS ROYAL TIKEHAU, *B.P. 15 Tuherahera, Tikehau 98778. Tel./Fax 689/96.23.37, cell 72.17.18/72.17.19; info@royaltikehau.com; www.royaltikehau.pf. On Motu Varney, a private islet across channel from the end of the airport runway and 5 min. by boat from Tuherahera quay. MC, V.*

This high-end lodging opened in mid-2007 and now has 11 units consisting of 4 rooms upstairs in a concrete building and 7 locally constructed wooden bungalows on stilts, built over a *hoa* channel and beside the beach on a private motu. Each room can sleep 2 people. They have mosquito nets and a private bathroom with cold-water shower. The bungalows can also sleep 2 people and each has a fan, mosquito net and a private bathroom with hot water shower. Radios are provided in the *hoa* bungalows and in the rooms, and TV is available in the superior and beach bungalows. A family bungalow can sleep up to 4 people. All the accommodations have comfortable beds and attractive decorations. There is solar electricity plus an electric generator as back-up. A safety box is available at reception, and there is also a curio shop. Meals featuring Tahitian food with a seafood base are served in the overwater restaurant, and there is a lounge with a pool table, baby foot and rainy day games. Petanque (bocce ball) and volley ball are played on the beautiful white sand beach. Snorkeling equipment and kayaks are provided and lagoon excursions can be arranged for guests. Owners Jean-Claude and Monique Varney are well-known residents of Tahiti who both speak English. Their pension has become a success due to the fine quality of cuisine served here, their outgoing personalities, and a friendly staff. MAP rates range from 15.000 CFP sgl./26.000 CFP dbl. for a room to 23.000 CFP sgl./ 37.000 CFP dbl. for a superior beach bungalow. The family bungalow is 36.000 CFP sgl. and 60.000 CFP for 4 people. Reduced rates for children. Boat transfers between the airport and pension are 1.160 CFP one-way.

Economy
PENSION TEMATIE, *Tuherahera, Tikehau 98778. Tel./Fax 689/96.22.65. Beside the beach in Tematie village, 400 m (436 yds.) from the airport and 2 km (1.2 mi.) from the main village of Tuherahera. Free transfers. No credit cards.*

This original style pension is between Tikehau Village and Panau Lagoon, right on the pretty white sand beach that is shaded by *aito* trees (Australian pines) that whisper in the refreshing sea breezes. Owner Nora Hoiore is originally from Tikehau and her French husband, Yves-Marie Dubois, is an engineering consultant for airport landing strips. After living in Africa, St. Kitts, Indonesia and other countries for several years, they returned to Tikehau and built 3 bungalows for guests. Two of these units are octagon shaped and the walls are made of broken coral they collected from the reef. The smaller bungalows have a double bed and a single bed, and the family bungalow also has a mezzanine that will sleep two people. All the bathrooms are tiled and private, with cold water showers. The windows are screened and there is a portable fan. The bungalows are attractively decorated with Polynesian bed covers and woodcarvings.

Meals are served in the communal dining room. They both speak some English and can arrange activities for guests. They charge 9.000 CFP per person for a bungalow and MAP meals, and 11.000 CFP if you want 3 meals a day. You can also rent the bungalow without meals.

TIKEHAU VILLAGE, *Tuherahera, Tikehau 98778. Tel. 689/96.22.86/ 74.86.46; Fax 689/96.23.84; tikehauvillage@mail.pf. Beside the beach in Tematie village, 600 m (654 yds.) from the main village of Tuherahera and 400 m (436 yds.) from the airport. Free transfers. MC, V.*

This small family hotel is also called Chez Pae'a and Caroline, and is located between Aito Motel Colette and Chez Tematie on a pretty white sand beach next to the airport. There are 8 recently renovated thatched roof bungalows facing the beach. All rooms have tiled floors, ceiling fans and private bathrooms with hot-water showers, and terraces. You have a choice of double or twin beds and mosquito nets are available on request. A bungalow with MAP half-board plan is 13.000 sgl., 20.140 CFP dbl.

The beach side restaurant and bar are open to the public, but it is better to reserve in advance for meals. When business is good they have buffet dinners twice a week and a Tahitian feast is also prepared once a month or so, complete with Paumotu music.

Guests enjoy feeding the sharks and rays that come to the edge of the lagoon beside the white sand beach in search of handouts. Boat trips can be arranged with Naga Excursion to take you to visit other motu islets inside the lagoon, complete with a picnic. The Raie Manta Club diving center is located on the hotel premises. It is advisable to time your visit when the owners are on the premises.

TEVAIHI VILLAGE, *B.P. 42, Tuherahera, Tikehau 98778. Tel./Fax 689/ 96.23.04, Cell 74.85.29. Beside lagoon in Tuherahera village, 5 minutes from the airport and 400 m (1,312 ft.) from the quay. Free transfers. No credit cards.*

Noella Poetai operates this family pension that is located on the left of the community pier. There are four wooden bungalows of the government-approved model, built on stilts facing a pretty beach of white sand. Each unit has a double bed and a single bed, mosquito nets, a fan and TV, plus a private bathroom with cold water shower. You can sit on the covered terrace and watch flocks of sea birds as they fish in the lagoon and you can also watch the sunrise from here.

Meals are served in a restaurant on the beach that is also open to the public. The lagoon is shallow here, but you can swim if you walk further from shore. Noella rents a bungalow for 5.300 CFP per day; a bungalow with MAP meals is 7.450 CFP and with all meals it is 8.500 CFP. She also has rental bikes and will arrange your boat excursions on request.

AITO MOTEL COLETTE, *Tuherahera, Tikehau 98778. Tel./Fax 689/ 96.23.07; Cell 74.85.77/74.85.88. Beside lagoon between Tuherahera village and the airport. Free transfers. No credit cards.*

Colette has 5 thatched-roof A-frame bungalows built on stilts on the beach within easy walking distance from the village. Tall Australian pine trees (called Aito in Tahitian) line the beach, providing shade and the melody of their whispering sounds as their feathery fronds sway in the ocean breeze. Two bungalows contain 2 double beds, 2 bungalows have a double bed, and 1 bungalow has a double bed and a sofa. Each unit has a private bathroom with a cold water shower. There is a restaurant and bar on the beach where you can enjoy Colette's home cooking. A bungalow with MAP is 17.500 CFP dbl and with AP full-board she charges 22.800 CFP dbl. Colette doesn't speak much English, although she works at the airport for each Air Tahiti flight arrival and departure, so she can manage to communicate with non-French speaking guests.

Other Pensions
The pensions listed above are the ones I consider the best choices on Tikehau. You can also find accommodations and meals in the following lodgings, which are all located on a white sand beach. Their rates are 7.000-7.950 CFP per person for a bungalow, breakfast and dinner. Camping space is 3.000 CFP. **FARE HANARIKI**, *Tel. 689/96.23.58/21.69.33; farehanariki@mail.pf. 5 rooms.* **PANAU LAGON**, *Tel./Fax 96.22.99. 6 fares*; **CHEZ JUSTINE**, *Tel./Fax 96.22.87; cell 72.02.44. 5 fares* and campground; **PENSION HOTU**, *Tel. 96.22.89. 3 fares*; **KAHAIA BEACH**, *Tel. 96.22.77; Fax 96.23.75*, *5 fares* on a motu near airport.

WHERE TO EAT
Restaurant Poreho at Tikehau Pearl Beach Resort, *Tel. 96.23.00. Open daily for BLD. All major credit cards.*
An American breakfast buffet is 3.200 CFP, a 2-course set luncheon menu is 3.800 CFP, and a 3-course set dinner menu is 6.250 CFP. MAP meals are 9.200 CFP and AP meals are 12.500 CFP. You can get snacks at the Tianoa Bar from 2:30-4 pm.
Tevaihi Village, *Tel. 96.23.04.* The restaurant at this family pension is open to the public. No credit cards.
Tikehau Village, *Tel. 96.22.86.* A beachside restaurant/bar at this family pension welcomes the public. Regular buffet dinners and occasional Tahitian feasts served. MC, V.
Cathy's Snack in Tuherahera is also a good place to stop for lunch while you are biking around the village.

SEEING THE SIGHTS
You can view the beauty of the fish and submarine gardens through a snorkeling mask or while scuba diving with qualified instructors. Take a boat to **Motu Ohihi**, which is surrounded by shallow *hoa* channels and has a pink sand beach. Go to **Motu Puarua** and **Oe Oe**, the Bird Island where snowy white fairy terns and noddy birds nest. Snorkeling is especially good in Tikehau's crystal clear lagoon.
Boat excursions will take you to visit the fish parks and past one or more of the former pearl farms, and you have a choice of *motu* islets for a memorable picnic.

You can fish by line or spear, and Tuheiava Pass is a good surfing spot in December and January. From the quay you can see the manta rays performing their graceful ballet in the evenings during July and August.

On the main island bike through the coconut groves to the rose-colored reef, and take a guided land tour to the old village and surrounding area. Hina's Bell is a big rock beside the beach that resounds like a chime when struck. This is a lovely place to watch the sunset. Under the light of the tropical stars it becomes a romantic spot for lovers to meet.

SPORTS & RECREATION
Nautical Activities
Naga Excursions, *Tel. 689/74.84.85.* Roland Teriiatetoofa will take you in his boat with a sunroof to visit Bird Island, where hundreds of sea birds come to lay their eggs in the sand or on the bare limb of a tree. You can fish, snorkel and swim in the warm lagoon and then enjoy a Paumotu style picnic of grilled lagoon fish on an uninhabited motu. This all-day excursion also includes visiting a fish park and stopping on Eden Island, where there is a religious community. The cost is 7.500 CFP per person.

Scuba Diving
The dive sites are concentrated around the Tuheiava Pass at the southern or southwestern end of the atoll. The clarity of the water, moderate currents in the pass and impressive seascapes provide an exciting experience, especially when you are surrounded by white tip reef sharks, leopard rays, eagle rays, tunas, barracudas, jackfish, black surgeon fish, big groupers, napoleons and other brilliantly colored schools of tropical fish. You may even see the graceful manta rays gliding by.

Raie Manta Club Tikehau is located at Tikehau Village, *Tel./Fax 96.22.53; Cell 79.17.17; raiemantaclub@mail.pf; http://raiemantaclub.free.fr.* This dive center is owned by Yves Lefevre, who is also based in Rangiroa and Rurutu. The qualified English-speaking diving instructor takes a maximum of 5 divers for each outing, just a 20-min. boat ride from the village.

Tikehau Blue Nui, *Tel. 96.22.40/28.27.07; Fax 96.23.01; tikehaubluenui@mail.pf; www.bluenui.com* has their dive center at the Tikehau Pearl Beach Resort. The rates are 7.727 CFP for a fun dive, 8.636 CFP for a first dive and 9.091 CFP for a night dive. Dive packages can be used at any of the Blue Nui centers in Tikehau, Manihi, Bora Bora and Taha'a. A 6-dive package is 40.909 CFP and a 10-dive package is 65.455 CFP. A half-day private dive for two is 68.182 CFP. ANMP or PADI Open Water certification available.

MASSAGES & SPA TREATMENTS
Manea Spa, *Tel. 96.23.00; maneaspa@tikehaupearlbeach.pf,* is located in a beach bungalow at the quieter end of the hotel property. You can choose from a range of massages for 1-2 people that last for 30, 50, or 80 min., and start at 7.727

CFP for a 30-min. Monoi One. The specialty here is the Monoi Pape Miti, an unforgettable massage that is performed on a massage table placed in the lagoon. The cost for this 50-min. treat is 13.636 CFP for one and 23.636 CFP for two. The Monoi Ofai hot stone healing is 15.000 CFP for a 50 min. massage.

PRACTICAL INFORMATION
There are no banks and no *gendarmes* in Tikehau. The *mairie* (town hall) is located in Tuherahera village, adjacent to the post office and school. A new marina has been constructed.

Food Stores
There are 2 stores in Tuherahera village that provide frozen products, canned foods, a few fresh vegetables, wine and beer. You can buy fresh baguettes of French bread each morning. Yachts can find a limited quantity of fuel in the stores. A municipal cistern at the foot of the wharf can supply yachts with water.

Medical Services
There is an infirmary in Tikehau, *Tel. 96.23.49*, with a nurse but no doctor.

Post Office
The **Post Office and Telecommunications Office** is in Tuherahera village, *Tel. 96.22.22.* There is an automatic telephone cabin here.

Tourist Information
Comité de Tourisme de Tikehau – Teniu Hiti, is in Tuherahera village, *Tel. 96.22.42.*

FAKARAVA
Fakarava is the second largest atoll in the Tuamotu Archipelago, after Rangiroa, and its rectangular-shaped lagoon is 60 km. (37 mi.) long by 25 km. (15 mi.) wide. The atoll is 488 km. (303 mi.) east-northeast of Tahiti and southeast of Rangiroa in the central Tuamotus.

A direct flight from Tahiti to Fakarava is just 70 min., which is helping to turn this atoll into a popular destination for those who seek vacation experiences off-the-beaten path. The lagoon of Fakarava is a magnificent marine realm of sharks, graceful manta rays, giant sized fish and a whole parade of beautiful tropical fish.

The Commune of Fakarava includes 7 atolls that received an official seal of approval as a Biosphere Reserve in Dec. 2007. Aratika, Fakarava, Kauehi, Niau, Raraka, Taioro and Toau are now protected as part of the UNESCO Man and the Biosphere (MAB) global network.

Fakarava's special features are columns of water in the lagoon and ocean and the importance and diversity of its fauna and flora, including the kingfisher, the

Tuamotu palm tree and the lagoon crustaceans, such as *varo* (squill or sea centipede) and *tiane'e* (slipper lobster).

The **Garuae Pass** on the northwest coast is one km (.62 mi.) wide. It is the largest pass in French Polynesia and gives access to anchorages for yachts and even the big passenger liners that anchor in front of the village of **Rotoava** on the northeast coast facing the pass. The *Aranui III* calls here on the second day of its 14-day round-trip voyages between Tahiti and the Marquesas Islands. Rotoava village is home to most of the atoll's 1,674 population. This is where you will find a 3-star hotel, several family pensions, a couple of *magasin* stores, the post office, grade school, churches and town hall. Three scuba dive centers offer experienced divers a selection of dives among some of the most abundant fish life in all of French Polynesia.

On the southeast side of the atoll is **Tumakohua Pass**, which is 200 m. (656 ft.) wide and 12 to 15 m. (39 to 49 ft.) deep. The distance from pass to pass is 58 km. or 35 nautical miles and takes 1 1/2-2 hours by speedboat. In addition to scuba diving, a favorite activity here is to drift snorkel through the pass. Several decades ago Fakarava was the social, religious and cultural capital of the Tuamotu Archipelago, and was known to the *Paumotu* people in ancient times as Havaiki Nui. **Tetamanu** village was formerly the principal settlement on Fakarava. It is located on a very small *motu* beside the Tumakohua Pass, and only a couple of families live there today. There are 3 family pensions plus some simple accommodations for local folks who also seek the solitude of this remote side of Fakarava. There are no shops, no boutiques, nowhere to go on land except to visit the vestiges of the old village. There is the coral shell of an old Catholic Church that was built in 1862, the remains of a building that was a prison and the walls of the former Residence of the French Administrator of the Tuamotu Archipelago. Another church is dated 1874 and is more intact, but no mass is celebrated here anymore. A cemetery behind the church contains a few tombstones.

Inside the reef surrounding the atoll are 94 motu islets, mostly uninhabited except for sea birds. At the southern extremity is a very special motu called Irifa, where the lagoon provides a magical luminescence, a mirror reflection of hundreds of coconut palms that grow beside the beach that stretches on and on for several miles. Bring your mosquito repellent. Koka Koka motu is a favorite picnic destination for those in the know. Like many of the motu islets in Fakarava it is surrounded by pink sands, and in the crystalline lagoon you'll find a wealth of succulent fish that can be grilled for lunch. The forests are filled with trees that provide precious wood for building and carving: *kahaia, puatea, miro, tou, gnao gnao* and *autera'a*. Chances are you will also see a white fairy tern with black button eyes perched on the branch of a *tou* tree, along with her newly hatched chick. She provides no nest, but lays a solitary egg in the crook of a tree limb. Drinking coconuts are within easy reach without shinnying up the trunk. This is the domain of the *kaveu*, the giant coconut crab, which makes a very tasty dinner.

Whatever you do and wherever you stay in Fakarava, do not miss seeing the southern end of the atoll. Bring your camera and lots of film and a charged battery.

You may also want to bring your own booze and munchie snacks if you are staying on this side of the atoll.

ARRIVALS & DEPARTURES
Arriving by Air
Air Tahiti flies direct from Tahiti to Fakarava each Mon., Tues., Thurs., Sat. and Sun., with 70-min. flights. Each Tues., Wed. and Fri. the ATR flight from Tahiti to Fakarava stops in Rangiroa, with a change of aircraft on Tues. You can fly from Bora Bora to Fakarava on Tues. and Wed. with a stop in Rangiroa and a change of aircraft on Wed. **Air Tahiti reservations:** Tahiti, *Tel. 86.42.42* in Fakarava, *Tel. 93.40.25/93.40.20.*

The one-way airfare from Tahiti to Fakarava is 19.930 CFP, the one-way fare from Rangiroa to Fakarava is 7.230 CFP, and the one-way fare from Bora Bora is 28.630 CFP. The airport is 4 km. (2.5 mi.) from Rotoava village, connected by a paved road.

You can also get to Fakarava by chartering an airplane in Tahiti from **Air Tahiti**, *Tel. 86.42.42*, or **Pol'Air**, *Tel. 74.23.11.*

Arriving by Boat
Aranui III, *Tel. 42.62.40.* Fakarava is the first stop on the 14-day/13-night round-trip itinerary of the *Aranui III* between Tahiti and the Marquesas Islands. The ship leaves Tahiti on Sat. and arrives in Fakarava the following morning. The one-way fare is 15.444 CFP with lodging and 3 meals included. AE, MC, V.

Mareva Nui, *Tel. 42.25.53, Fax 42.25.57*, is a 181-ft. steel ship that transports cargo between Tahiti and the Tuamotu atolls. It leaves Tahiti every 15 days, arriving in Fakarava after stopping at 8 atolls in the Western Tuamotu Archipelago. There are 12 berths on board but no cabin. The one-way fare from Tahiti to Fakarava is 19.800 CFP including three meals a day per person.

St. Xavier Maris Stella III, *Tel. 42.23.58*, can transport 12 passengers who sleep on deck or in the a/c cabin. Bring your own bedding. The deck fare from Tahiti to Fakarava is 11.830 CFP per person, including 3 meals a day, and 30.000 CFP in a berth, meals included. The ship leaves Papeete every 15 days for 7-10 day voyages.

Cobia III, *Tel. 43.36.43*, leaves Tahiti at 3pm each Mon., arriving in Fakarava Wed. night or Thurs morning. There are accommodations for 12 passengers in 3 cabins. The one-way fare is 6.300 CFP, and no meals are available on board.

See more information in Chapter 6, *Planning Your Trip.*

Departing by Air
Air Tahiti flies direct from Fakarava to Tahiti each Tues., Wed., Thurs., Fri., Sat. and Sun. The Mon. flight and a Sat. flight from Fakarava stop in Rangiroa enroute to Tahiti. **Air Tahiti reservations** in Fakarava, *Tel. 93.40.25/93.40.20.*

Departing by Boat
Mareva Nui, Tel. 42.25.53, calls at five or more atolls after leaving Fakarava each 15 days, and the trip back to Tahiti takes 4 days or more. The cost is determined by the number of days required. *St. Xavier Maris Stella III, Tel. 42.23.58*, leaves Fakarava every 15 days for Papeete following an itinerary determined by freight to deliver or pick up. The *Cobia III, Tel. 43.36.43*, leaves Fakarava on Thurs. and arrives in Papeete on Fri. afternoon. See more information under *Inter-Island Cruise Ships, Passenger Boats and Freighters* in Chapter 6, *Planning Your Trip*.

GETTING AROUND
Fakalocation, *Tel. 78.03.37*, rents scooters and bicycles.
Joachim Dariel, *Tel. 93.40.15/74.16.16*, of Havaiki Pearl Guest House, has a 17-passenger truck used to transport visitors.

WHERE TO STAY
Superior
WHITE SAND BEACH RESORT FAKARAVA, *B.P. 19, Rotoava, Fakarava 98763. Tel. 689/93.41.50; Fax 689/93.41.51; res@whitesandfakarava.com; www.whitesandfakarava.com. Beside lagoon 10.5 km (6.5 mi.) from airport. 30 bungalows. All major credit cards.*

Fakarava's first and only hotel opened in September 2002, offering international class lodging and services just a 15-minute ride on the paved road from the airport and a 15-minute boat ride from the Garuae Pass, which offers nirvana for scuba divers in the kilometer-wide opening through the coral reef. Originally known as the Hotel Maitai Dream Fakarava, this 3-star boutique hotel was renamed White Sand Beach Resort Fakarava in 2009 when it was taken over by Fakarava Dream, whose President & CEO is Rudolf Jager.

The sturdily built bungalows sit on raised islands in groups of three above the quarter-mile white sand beach that stretches the length of the property. There are 9 a/c bungalows facing the magnificent lagoon, 6 beach bungalows in the second row and behind them are 15 bungalows, set in a garden of Tiare Tahiti bushes. All the bungalows have 45 sq. m (484 sq. ft.) of living space, plus a covered terrace. The walls and roofs are constructed with rich teakwood from Bali. Each unit is furnished with a king size bed that converts into twin beds. There is also a sofa bed, office desk and chair, ceiling fan, international direct dial telephone, satellite TV, refrigerator with mini-bar on request, coffee and tea making facilities, and individual safe. The furniture is made of coconut wood from Bali and Polynesian artwork adorns the walls. The indoor/outdoor bathroom is decorated with coral and has a powerful hot water shower and hair dryer. Bring your own makeup mirror if you are near sighted. There are also facilities for physically challenged guests. Children under 15 years can share the room with their parents at no extra cost, and baby cribs are available.

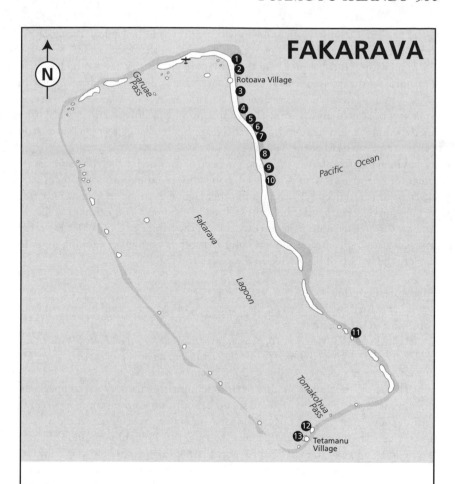

1. Relais Marama
2. Vahitu Dream
3. Havaiki Fakarava Pearl Guest House
4. Pension Rava
5. Vekeveke Village
6. Pension Paparara
7. White Sand Beach Resort Fakarava
8. Tokerau Village
9. Pension Kiria
10. Vaiama Village
11. Raimiti
12. Motu Aito Paradise
13. Tetamanu Village & Tetamanu Sauvage

The Kura Ora restaurant and Kiri Kiri bar overlook the lagoon. Buffet or à la carte meals are served in the 48-seat dining room, on the open terrace, or on the adjacent white sand beach where the tables are shaded by big umbrellas. The Paumotu waitresses are sometimes barefoot and shy, but always friendly if you smile at them. There is no room service. The bar is open from 10am-10pm, serving your favorite cocktails. Musical entertainment adds a Polynesian touch during special evenings. Internet service is available in the hotel's big reception area. You can buy a phone card at the front desk.

A long pier is built over the lagoon in front of the hotel, which is the departure point for boat trips to visit pearl farms, fish parks, remote motu islets, picnics on deserted beaches, deep-sea fishing and other lagoon excursions. Guests have free use of snorkel gear, kayaks and outrigger paddle canoes. You can rent a bike or arrange for a village tour or lagoon excursion at the front desk. TOPDIVE-Bathys is a scuba diving center on the premises that offers a range of exciting dives to explore the wealth of big sea life in the passes and lagoon.

Moderate/Economy

I have listed the Pensions on the North side of Fakarava atoll in order of their proximity to the airport.

RELAIS MARAMA, *B.P. 16, Rotoava, Fakarava 98763. Tel./Fax 689/98.42.51, cell 72.09.42/70.81.98; contact@relais-marama.com; www.relais-marama.com. On seaside in Rotoava village, 3.5 km (2.2 mi.) from airport. No credit cards.*

This is a popular bed and breakfast lodging with backpackers, campers and other budget travelers who prefer to spend a minimum amount on their sleeping facilities and save their money for scuba diving in one of the world's most spectacular lagoons. Owners Jacques Sauvage, a Frenchman, and Marama Teanuanua, a Paumotu man from Fakarava, speak English, French and Tahitian. They have built 8 bungalows and a 3-bedroom house, with two twin beds in each room. Rates are 5.000 CFP sgl. and 9.000 CFP dbl. for a garden bungalow, including breakfast. Camping space for 12 tents is available in a clearing overlooking the ocean for 2.000 CFP per person and tents are available at no extra cost. There are 4 communal bathrooms and 2 showers with cold water and guests can also use the washing machine. A *fare pote'e* shelter contains a kitchen/dining area that has two gas burners and two refrigerators, plus a sink and tables. There is also a barbecue grill. Guests can cook their own food here as the bungalows are rented without meals included, but you can order dinner from a choice of 7 dishes for 1.400 CFP if you reserve 24 hours in advance. Rainwater is used for drinking. There is a public telephone at the post office nearby, and there are 3 snacks, a roulotte and two small stores in the village. You can rent a bicycle and sign up for lagoon excursions and scuba diving.

HAVAIKI FAKARAVA PEARL GUEST HOUSE, *Rotoava, Fakarava 98763. Tel. 689/93.40.15/74.16.16; Fax 689/93.40.16; havaiki@mail.pf; www.havaiki.com.*

Beside lagoon 5 km (3.1 mi.) from airport and 600 m (1,968 ft.) past Rotoava village. Minimum stay 3 nights. AE, MC, V.

This is the most popular family pension on the north side of Fakarava. Owners Clotilde (Havaiki) and Joachim Dariel have built 5 plywood bungalows facing a pretty white sand beach, overlooking one of the most beautiful views of the lagoon and sky that Nature has created in these islands. There are 2 duplex garden view rooms on the second level of the main building across the road. Each of these bungalows and rooms contains a double bed and a single bed, mosquito nets, private safe, a private bathroom with cold-water shower, and a ceiling fan. There is also a communal hot water shower. In addition, there is a Robinson Crusoe type bungalow for one person, with a toilet and an open roof shower made of coral stones. Clotilde has a passion for flowers and she has placed big planters of hot pink bougainvillea, yellow and purple alamanda and other colorful flowers on both sides of the road to mark the limits of her land. Baskets of bright blossoms also hang under the eaves of each beach bungalow, and some of the shell mirrors in the rooms also contain fresh flowers. The 2011-2012 rates for a panoramic garden room are 12.950 CFP sgl, 19.900 CFP dbl; a beach bungalow is 16.950 CFP sgl., 23.900 CFP dbl. Round-trip airport transfers are 2.000 CFP. Meals are served at individual tables in the 100-seat dining room across the road from the beach, which is also open to the public in the evening. Breakfast is European style and dinner includes local and imported products prepared for European tastes. They also sell wine and beer. Lunch is served daily except Sun. (*Where to Eat* in this chapter). They also provide room service.

There is also a small pearl boutique in the dining/lounge/reception room. Here you can admire and buy the creations of Nicolas Dariel, Joachim's father, who is a goldsmith. Their family began Fakarava's first pearl farm in 1989, and you can see the grafting *fare* that is built overwater at the end of a very long pier in front of the pension. You can visit the pearl farm on request and even fish for your own mother-of-pearl oyster for 3.000 CFP. If there is no pearl inside, then you just keep fishing until you find one.

Free activities include kayaks, bicycles with baby seats, ping pong, table football, games and a children's park. Excursions are organized on request, which include snorkeling and fishing in the lagoon, visits to pearl farms, and picnics on uninhabited motu islets. Excursion rates range from 6.000-12.000 CFP. A half-day deep sea fishing trip is 52.000 CFP. Scuba diving centers can take you to explore the two passes of Fakarava. You can check your email on the Mana Spot WiFi service provided for 600 CFP for one hour. You can sit under a *fare potée* shelter that Joachim has built in the shallow lagoon beside the beach, or you can simply swing in a hammock and watch the setting sun slip behind the horizon at Garuae pass.

PENSION PAPARARA, *B.P. 88, Rotoava, Fakarava 98763. Tel./Fax 689/ 98.42.66; cell 74.69.10; pensionpaparara@mail.pf; www.fakarava-divelodge.com. Beside lagoon past Rotoava village, 10 km (6.2 mi.) from the airport. MC, V.*

This Polynesian owned pension opened in 1992 and is one of the oldest guest houses on Fakarava. It is located beside the lagoon just before the White Sand Beach Resort Fakarava. There are 2 beach bungalows with ceiling fans, private tiled bathrooms and cold-water showers, and 2 traditional style bungalows, each with a private bathroom and cold-water shower. One of the bungalows has a coral floor and a terrace hanging over the lagoon, where you can watch the parrotfish nibbling on the coral heads in the shallow water. All units have mosquito nets over the beds. They charge 9.000-11.500 CFP sgl, 16.000-19.000 CFP dbl. including breakfast and dinner, with digressive rates for longer stays.

Corina Lenoir and her husband Ato Lissant serve European and local style meals in a spacious dining room/bar in the garden or at a picnic table beside the lagoon. Bicycles are 1.000 CFP for a half-day and kayaks are 1.500 CFP a day. There is also a point telephone and WiFi service, both extra. Ato, who speaks English, operates Fakarava Explorer, providing boat excursions for snorkeling, dolphin watching, to visit various motu islets, for picnics and deep-sea fishing. Fakarava Diving Center is also located on the premises, offering scuba diving packages. (See *Nautical Activities* and *Scuba Diving* in this chapter).

VAIAMA VILLAGE, *Tel. 98.41.13/70.56.41; vaiama.village@mail.pf; www.fakaravavaiama.com. Beside lagoon 11 km. (6.8 mi.) from airport. MC, V.*

This pension is the next to last one on the north side of Fakarava atoll. There are 4 very simple *fares* beside the lagoon whose walls and roofs are made of palm fronds. Two of these *fares* are on stilts and one is 2-story, providing basic Tuamotu accommodations for 2-4 people, and the beds are covered with mosquito nets. All the *fares* have a ceiling fan, a terrace, and private bathrooms with cold water showers; some of the bathrooms are outside and have coral floors. There is also a communal TV room and free Internet access. A *fare* with breakfast and dinner is 12.500 CFP sgl. and 19.500 CFP dbl. Round-trip airport transfers are 1.500 CFP.

Breakfast is served at a picnic table on the beach and the dining room and kitchen are located inside a big *fare potée* shelter. Former guests from France and Tahiti have praised Dahlia's cooking as well as the warm family reception they received here. It was voted on TripAdvisor as the #1 place to stay in Fakarava. One of the best assets here is the open *fare* on the end of a long wooden pier. This was formerly the grafting house for the family's pearl farm and serves today as a place to relax, sunbathe and gaze at the sunset and starry sky. Steps lead into the natural aquarium just below. Bicycles and kayaks are provided free of charge for guests and you can fish from the pier or by boat in the lagoon. Ato of Pension Paparara is part of the family and he takes care of the lagoon excursions, including a picnic on a motu, which is additional to the meal plans.

TOKERAU VILLAGE, *B.P. 53, Rotoava, Fakarava 98763. Tel./Fax 689/ 98.41.09/88.06.82, cell 70.82.19/71.30.46; tokerauvillage@mail.pf; Beside lagoon 11 km (6.8 mi.) from airport. AE, MC, V.*

This attractive pension opened in February 2003 and has been awarded a 2-Tiare rating by Tahiti Tourism. It is located beside the lagoon just after the White

Sand Beach Resort Fakarava, and is owned by Flora and Patrick Bordes, who are assisted by their daughter, Gahina, who speaks English. The 4 bungalows built on stilts are the government backed models that consist of shingle shake roofs and wooden walls, a modern Polynesian style with *pueu* mats covering the walls, and room for a double bed and a single bed, desk and clothes closet in the bedroom/ sitting room. The rooms are colorfully decorated with *tifaifai* bed covers and photographs of old Tahiti hang on the walls. The beds have mosquito nets and there is a TV in each room, plus a fan on request. The private bathrooms have a cold-water shower. A covered terrace overlooks the French style garden with sculpted bushes and there are flowers everywhere. A bungalow with breakfast and dinner is 12.000 CFP sgl. and 22.000 CFP dbl., with a minimum of 2 nights required.

Polynesian style meals featuring fresh fish are served in a dining room near the beach, which is also open to the public. Bicycles and kayaks are provided free of charge for guests and car and boat excursions can be arranged on request. The scuba dive centers will come here to pick up clients who wish to dive.

PENSION KIRIA, *B.P. 89, Rotoava, Fakarava 98763. Tel./Fax. 689/98.41.83; cell 73.41.12; pensionkiria@mail.pf; www.pensionkiriafakarava.com. Beside lagoon 8 km. (5 mi.) past the village. No credit cards.*

After meeting the owners, Kareen Langomazino and Kahui (Jean) Lissant, I decided to stay at Pension Kiria the next time I go to Fakarava. Kareen is from Tikehau (and speaks English) and Kahui was born in Fakarava, lived in Tahiti for many years, then returned to his atoll. After operating a magasin and snack in Rotoava village, then trying his hand in pearl farming, he decided to open a family pension, where he can use his cooking skills while making his guests happy. The pension is named for their daughter Kiria. The 4 Paumotu style bungalows with thatched roofs and colorful Polynesian furnishings are named for neighboring atolls: Niau, Toau, Tepoto and Kauehi. Accommodations are available for up to 5 people. Each bungalow faces the lagoon and has a private bathroom with cold water shower, A bungalow with breakfast and dinner is 11.000 CFP sgl. and 19.000 CFP dbl., and 4.750 CFP for a child 5-12 years. Round-trip airport transfers are 2.000 CFP for adults.

Facilities include a kitchen and local style dining *fare*, a place to relax while reading or playing society games, and a coral sand beach with hammocks inviting you for a siesta under the shade of trees. Guests can use the kayaks free of charge and you can rent a bike for 4 hrs. for 1.000 CFP. Pension Kiria charges 4.000 CFP per adult for an excursion by car to visit the village, the old lighthouse beside the Garuae Pass, with a picnic near the *marae*, or to explore the uninhabited wild side of the atoll, with a picnic. A boat excursion with a picnic on a motu is 9.000 CFP, and a Robinson Crusoe adventure is 11.000 CFP. This includes a campfire bbq on the beach of a motu and sleeping under the stars. Children pay half-fare for all activities. Fishing expeditions and speed boat outings to visit nearby atolls can also be arranged. One of Kahui's many brothers is Ato Lissant from Pension Paparara and Fakarava Explorer, who organizes boat excursions. See information under *Nautical Activities* in this chapter).

Pensions on the South side of Fakarava atoll, close to Tumakohua Pass
MOTU AITO PARADISE, *B.P. 12, Rotoava, Fakarava 98763. Tel./Fax 689/ 41.29.00; cell 74.26.13; motu-aito@mail.pf; www.fakarava.org. On Motu Aito near the Tumakohua Pass and Tetamanu village, 55 km (34 mi.) by boat from the airport and Rotoava village. Minimum stay 3 nights. No credit cards.*

When Manihi and Tila Salmon and their 3 children settled on Motu Aito more than 20 years ago, the islet was only sand and coral. Today it is an oasis bordered by *aito* trees (also known as Casuarina, ironwood or Australian pine. There are also *tamanu* and *tou* trees for shade, flowering Tiare Tahiti bushes, frangipani and lovely green bird's nest ferns. The main abode is a big concrete house with an enormous family lounge filled with sofas or beds to accommodate the Salmon children and grandchildren when they come to visit, or to provide extra sleeping space for friends and an overflow of guests.

Manihi has built 6 Polynesian style bungalows for clients, which are very well constructed and thoughtfully decorated with driftwood, coral, seashells and fresh flowers. Each *fare* contains a double bed and a single bed and a mattress can be added if needed. Each unit is different and very originally designed, with walls and ceiling of woven palm frond and terraces trimmed with the very useful *kahaia* wood found in the atolls. Manihi also built the furniture, using local woods. There is an individual bathroom for each bungalow, with a private outdoor shower in a little garden of ferns and other green plants. Two enormous concrete tanks catch the rain and provide a plentiful supply of water for showers. Solar panels generate the electricity.

Manihi has expanded the size of the bungalows and Tila makes new curtains and bedspreads each year. Improvements include a fast boat that can get you from the main village to their motu in 90 minutes. The boat dock has been extended and a new bridge built to join the next motu. He has added lights for better fishing here at night, and has rebuilt his fish trap.

Activities include walking around the islets, swimming, boat trips to visit the pink sand beaches and bird island, the old village of Tetamanu with its Catholic church that was built in 1874, and snorkeling in the Tumakohua Pass (bring your own snorkeling gear). You can accompany Manihi on a tuna fishing expedition in the open ocean, or you can help him choose dinner from the abundant selection of fish in his fish trap. Everyone eats together at a big table on the dining terrace and fresh fish is the base of their meals. They do not sell any wine or beer, so bring your own and they will chill it for you.

It is also easy to get away on your own. You can walk across a shallow *hoa* channel to visit adjacent motu islets. Yours will be the only footsteps in the sand, as these are truly desert isles. Should you desire, Tila will pack you a picnic lunch and Manihi will drop you off on a pink sand beach and pick you up whenever you wish. They charge 14.740 CFP per person per day, which includes the bungalow, all meals, activities and taxes. The round-trip boat transfer from the airport is 3.000 CFP. The South Pass base for TOPDIVE-Bathy's dive center is located near Motu Aito Paradise, and their scuba diving charges are not included in the pension's rate. Tila and Manihi are both Polynesians and they warmly welcome their guests. They lived in New Zealand for 10 years and speak very good English. Their three children are now grown and the two boys are professional tattoo artists in Tahiti. Tikahiri is the name of their award winning musical group. See information on Aroma Tattoo Art and Manu Tattoo Art under *Tattoos* in the *Tahiti* chapter.

RAIMITI, *B.P. 144, Rotoava, Fakarava 98763; Tel. 689/71.07.63; raimiti@mail.pf; www.raimiti.com. On a big motu in the Tetamanu district, 60 km (37.2 mi.) from the main village of Rotoava and 15 km (9.3 mi.) from the nearest neighbor. AE, MC, V.*

Guests who have stayed at Raimiti since it opened in Sept. 2005 have a tendency to wax poetic in their verbose praises of the charms of this remote paradise when they sign the guest book or make their trip reports on Tahiti forums online. Raimiti means "between the sky and sea," and the beauty of this very special place really does make you want to describe it in superlatives.

Raimiti's 3 owners jokingly say that the pension is located at the 5028th coconut tree from the church in Rotoava, the main village on Fakarava. Eric Lussiez and Florian Pilloud, who formerly owned Pension Linareva and Le Bateau Restaurant in Moorea, joined forces with Raimaru (Junior), a Polynesian who worked for them. They all decided to make a dream come true in Fakarava and they have succeeded very well. They leased 14.8 acres (6 ha.) of land on a very large motu that is bordered on the east by the Pacific Ocean, on the west by the lagoon, on the north by an immense coconut forest and untouched natural environment and on the south by Irifa, one of the most beautiful beaches in Fakarava. The only way to get to this isolated area is by boat, which takes about 1 1/2 to 2 hours, depending on the weather and currents. You'll know you're there when you hear the sound of a *pu* shell (triton) heralding your arrival at the small boat dock, where 2 excited dogs, Rutu and Castor, and Eric's pet pig, Siki, wait to welcome you ashore.

There are now 9 sleeping units, which give you a choice of accommodations in identical "Fare Robinson" bungalows beside the lagoon or in the larger "Fare Crusoe" bungalows located on the reef side of the motu, with a panoramic view of the ocean. The lagoon-side units are built on stilts of coconut logs and the walls, roofs and windows are made of woven palm leaves, kahaia and other tropical woods. There are no doors and no keys—simply a curtain of pareo cloth over the entrance. A mosquito net hangs over the queen size bed and the private bathroom with hot-water shower is detached. The larger bungalows facing the ocean are made of gnao gnao and kahaia wood, as well as Brazilian mahogany. Each of these units has a king size bed and a single bed, plus an indoor bathroom with a hot water shower. Solar energy and oil lamps provide lights in the bungalows, and a powerful flashlight helps you to find your way to the "fare iti" (bathroom) in the middle of the night.

Raimiti's now extended dining room/bar/lounge/reception *fare* has a thatched palm roof, low walls of coconut stumps, a coral floor and stools made of coconut logs. It is imaginatively decorated with shells, coral, woven hats, wood carvings, pottery from Huahine and Moorea, and candles in sand-filled coconut shells.

Meals are announced by the sound of the pu shell. And what gourmet feasts they are! Your natural reaction will be to take a picture of the generous portions of creatively arranged food on your plate before you eat. A Continental breakfast is served buffet style. Lunch may include various kinds of salads and raw vegetables, as well as smoked salmon or whole boiled shrimp, followed by fruit and cheeses. Dinner is another true work of art and a delight for gourmands, with temptingly prepared vegetables to accompany the main courses of fish, seafood, poultry or meat. French style desserts may include crème caramel and Poire Belle Helêne. There is a limited supply of wines, beer and soft drinks, as well as sparkling water, or you can drink rain water.

The minimum stay is 2 nights and costs 54.000 CFP sgl./99.000 CFP dbl. when sleeping in a lagoon-side "Fare Robinson". The "Fare Crusoe" on the ocean side is 61.000 sgl/112.000 CFP. dbl for 1 night. The cost of your stay includes your lodging and all meals, boat transfers between the airport and Raimiti, and free use of snorkeling gear, kayaks and board games. It also includes your "Discovery" activities (try to avoid thinking in terms of structured, programmed "Excursions" here). These outings may be visits to the old village of Tetamanu, drift snorkeling in the Tumakohua Pass, visits to the pink sand beach of Irifa and to the fish parks inside the lagoon, picnics on a neighboring motu, or being dropped off at a secluded beach with a sandwich and water to make your own private discoveries. Scuba diving can be organized for an additional cost.

When you visit Raimiti you will be well taken care of by Eric, Junior, and their team of friendly Paumotu workers, as well as all the Raimiti pets. These include the dogs, pigs, rabbits, red-footed booby birds and herons that gather in the staff's kitchen at breakfast time. Florian, their Swiss partner, prefers his mountain home in the Swiss Alps, where he takes care of the reservations and other business for Raimiti that can be handled by modern communications. Raimiti accepts vegetarians and others who don't care for fish and seafood. They do request, however, that you advise them in advance so they can make you happy and get you well-fed during your stay at Raimiti. I suggest that you read their website before booking, so that you will better understand what to expect. The only shopping you can do at Raimiti is to buy some of the lovely pearl jewelry Eric stocks in the boutique. It's all made in Fakarava by knowledgeable pearl farmers and jewelers. If you read French you will enjoy reading Eric's daily journal, which recounts many of the details of life on a remote atoll. It reminds me Herman Wouk's 1965 novel written about running a hotel in the Caribbean, "Don't Stop the Carnival".

Other Pensions
The pensions listed above are just a few of the family lodgings that were available in Fakarava at publication time. The other pensions are: VAHITU DREAM, *Tel. 98.42.63*, 6-room house in Rotoava village. VEKEVEKE VILLAGE, *Tel. 98.42.80/79.13.77; www.pension-fakarava.com.* 4 bungalows beside lagoon 9 km (6 mi.) from airport. AE, MC, V. PENSION RAVA, *Tel. 75.03.76.* 1 room on beach adjacent to Havaiki Pearl Guest House. TETAMANU VILLAGE and TETAMANU SAUVAGE, *Tel. 77.10.06/78.03.67; Fax 42.77.70, tetamanuvillage@mail.pf; www.tetamanuvillage.pf.* Beside the pass in Tetamanu village on south end of atoll. 6 + 6 simple bungalows. The Tetamanu Dive Center is here.

WHERE TO EAT
Restaurant Kura Ora at **White Sand Beach Resort**, *Tel. 93.41.50, serves B, L, D. All major credit cards.* There is a buffet breakfast, an à la carte lunch of sandwiches and burgers, salads and other light selections served on the terrace or in the dining room. A set dinner menu is designed by the owner, who was trained as a Swiss chef. Bar Kiri Kiri is open 10am-10pm. A traditional show is performed on Fri. or Sat. evening, according to the season.

Havaiki Pearl Guest House Restaurant, *Tel. 93.40.15/74.16.16. AE, MC, V.* This 100-seat restaurant/bar is open daily for B.,L.,D. to in-house guests, except on Sun., when they close for lunch. You can order a sandwich for 500 CFP or a plate for 3.000 CFP. The public is invited in the evening. The à la carte dinner menu is displayed in the restaurant each morning, featuring a traditional and varied cuisine with specialties like fresh tuna sashimi, mahi mahi with honey, heart of oysters with coconut milk curry, and also French and Chinese dishes. Local musicians provide frequent entertainment and traditional dance shows are performed on special occasions. Call for pick-up service.

Restaurant Teanuanua, *Tel. 93.40.65; cecile.enoha@mail.pf.* Open for L, D. Free pickups. V. This lagoon-side restaurant-boutique is just a 5-min. walk from Havaiki Guest House. Menu selections include hamburgers, poisson cru, fried filet of parrotfish and steak, priced 1.300-3.000 CFP. Cecile, the French owner, also makes hand-painted pareos, caftans and tee shirts.

Tereka, *Tel. 98.42.13*, is a snack open only on weekends at the port. No credit cards.

There is a new **roulotte** in front of the dive center in Rotoava.

You can also arrange in advance to eat at some of the family pensions, such as Havaiki Pearl Guest House and Pension Paparara.

NAUTICAL ACTIVITIES
Fakarava Excursions & Fishing, *Tel. 689/98.42.83; menton@live.fr; www.fakaravaexcursionsandfishing.com.* Martine Adams offers half-day snorkeling tours for 6.000 CFP, a full-day snorkeling excursion with a picnic on a motu for

9.000 CFP, a full-day at Tetamanu and the south pass, and a picnic on Sables Roses, the pink sand beach, for a cost of 12.000 CFP, including the 3-hr. round-trip transfers. All the excursions are made on board a 26-ft. boat with a 260 hp inboard engine. Min. of 5 passengers required.

Sportfishing includes jigging, poppers, and bottom fishing for "paru" fishing, as well as lagoon fishing. Half-day boat rental for 2-4 fishermen is 40.000 CFP, and a full-day rental is 70.000 CFP. Underwater hunting is 15.000 CFP.

Fakarava Explorer, *Tel. 689/98.42.66/73.93.89; fakaravaexplorer@hotmail.com; www.fakarava-divelodge.com.* Ato Lissant of Pension Paparara has a 32-ft. offshore boat, *Taianui*, with a 250 hp outboard motor and sunshade that is used for excursions to discover the immense lagoon and passes of Fakarava. One of the best sites is the Lagoon of Teahatea, a refuge of numerous sea turtles, manta rays and sharks. This outing includes walking on the reef, learning how to fish in the lagoon, a picnic on the beach and time for a swim and relaxing on the motu. You can also visit Bird Island, drift snorkel in the passes, have a picnic on a pink sand beach, learn how to fish in the open ocean, or visit a pearl farm. A full-day outing to Tetamanu is 13.000 CFP for a min. of 5 passengers.

Havaiki Pearl Guest House, *Tel. 93.40.15.* Mateata is the captain of Joachim Dariel's boat trips and fishing expeditions. He will take you to the green lagoon of Teahatea on a half-day excursion for 6.000 CFP. Travel time is 80 min. with a stop on the way back to visit the north pass to look for dolphins. Other excursions include a half-day outing to Bird Island for 9.000 CFP, and a full-day visit to the south pass, Tetamanu village and a barbecue on the pink sand beach. Cost is 12.000 CFP and travel time is 3 hrs. Deep-sea fishing can be done inside the northern pass or offshore, where you may find tuna, mahi mahi, wahoo and maybe even swordfish. A half-day package for 2-4 fishermen is 52.000 CFP.

Tamatoa 2, *Tel. 98.41.14/70.81.99*, is a 24-ft. boat based at Pension Vaiama Village. Excursions for up to 12 passengers will take you for a half-day of snorkeling in the Garuae Pass for 6.000 CFP, to Bird Island with a picnic on a motu for 9.000 CFP, to the old village of Tetamanu for a picnic on the motu for 12.000 CFP, and fishing in the lagoon when the boat is available.

Cruise & Dive Charters

Aqua Tiki II. *Contact Aqua Polynésie, Tel. 00 33 1 64 90 50 10; Cell in Fakarava 73.47.31; aquatiki@aquapolynesie.com; www.aquapolynesie.com.* This 60-ft. (18 m) Fountain Pajot Eleuthera type catamaran takes 9 passengers (8 divers) maximum in 5 cabins: 3 standard cabins (2 with a double bed and 1 with twin beds), 1 VIP cabin and 1 forepeak perfect for low budget single passenger. Each cabin has its own bathroom. The brand new sailing yacht has all the comforts and mod-coms including a/c 3 hrs. a day, HiFi, TV and Blue Ray DVD player in the lounge. There is also full Scubapro equipment, and besides the skipper and hostess/cook, the crew includes a scuba diving instructor. You can rent a cabin or charter the whole boat for cruises that begin in Fakarava, take you to the neighboring atolls of Kauehi, Toau, Tahanea, Aratika and to the north and south passes of Fakarava, depending on the cruise program chosen. The 7-day/6-night cruise for divers during the low season starts at 2,100 per person in double occupancy, including taxes. There are also 9-17 day cruises in the Tuamotu Islands, as well the Leeward Islands. Departures are guaranteed with a minimum of 2 passengers. In addition to scuba diving, activities include snorkeling, water-skiing, wake-boarding, kayaking and big-game fishing. Please see information under the chapter on *Planning Your Trip*.

Tahiti Yacht Charter, *Tel. 689/66.28.80; www.tahitiyachtcharter.com; in USA 1- (800) 404-1010; 949-675-3519; marimktg@ix.netcom.com*. This locally owned company has a fleet of 28 catamarans that are from 38-46 ft., including the Lagoon 380, Lavezzi 40, Lagoon 440, Nautitech 441, Orana 44, Bahia 46, and Lagoon 500. A 7 day/6 night Tuamotu Atoll Cruise for 2-8 passengers in the same party starts at 3,000 euros (357.995 CFP) per person. Charter rates vary according to seasons. There will be a skipper/guide, hostess/cook on board and all meals will be served on the boat except for 2 dinners that you will eat ashore at your own expense. You board the yacht in Fakarava's Rotoava Village and the next day you will visit Tetamanu Village and the south pass. On the 3rd day you go to the pink sand beach of Sables Roses, and the next 3 days are spent visiting the neighboring atoll of Toau, then on the 7th day you will return to Rotoava village and have a light lunch on board before flying back to Tahiti, according to your Air Tahiti flight schedule. Activities during this voyage can include snorkeling, kayaking, line fishing, visiting uninhabited motu islets, and scuba diving (arranged with local dive center).

Scuba Diving

TOPDIVE-Bathys Fakarava, *Tel./Fax 98.43.76; cell 29.22.32; fakarava@topdive.com; www.topdive.com*. The main base is located at the White Sand Beach Resort Fakarava, and as of Jan. 2011 TOPDIVE-Bathys also took over the former Te Ava Nui dive center in Rotoava village. They have opened a second base near Motu Aito Paradise pension for those divers who want to be close to Tumakohua, the south pass at Tetamanu. The staff of 7 includes a dive master, 3 diving instructors, 2 boat pilots and a sales assistant.

At 8am and 10am the main base provides exploration (2-tank), introductory and certification dives and at 2pm they lead exploration dives for world class diving in the north pass of Garuae. Public rates for scuba diving start at 8.500 CFP for an introductory shore dive or fun dive. An introductory boat dive is 10.000 CFP. A 2-tank dive is 15.500 CFP. Open water certification courses are available and a 10-dive Gold package inter-island pass is 70.000 CFP. The diving rates include taxes and all equipment. This package can be used at 13 TOPDIVE-Bathy centers in Bora Bora, Moorea, Rangiroa, Fakarava and Tahiti. A special day trip from Fakarava north to Tetamanu on the south side to dive the Tumakohua Pass is 25.000 CFP per person, including 2 dives and a picnic on the pink sand beach. There is also a 1.500 CFP supplement per dive at Fakarava South.

Fakarava Diving Center, *Tel./Fax 93.40.75, cell 73.38.22; fdc@mail.pf; www.fakarava-diving-center.com* is located on the premises of Pension Paparara. Serge Howald is a BEES 1 diving instructor and his wife, Carine, pilots the spacious and comfortable dive boat, which is used for 5-6 divers only. Dives for all levels are made, either inside the lagoon, in the two passes of Fakarava, on the outer reef, deep sea and on the neighboring atoll of Toau, a 45-min. boat ride across the open ocean. All necessary diving gear is provided, including Aqualung wetsuits. A first dive is 6.500 CFP, an exploratory dive is 6.500 CFP, and a day-trip of 4-5 passengers to dive in the pass at Tetamanu is 18.000 CFP, which includes 2 dives and a picnic on a motu. 10-dive packages are 60.000 CFP and discounts are given for guests staying at Pension Paparara. MC/V.

SHOPPING
Buying Pearls & Visiting Pearl Farms

In Fakarava you need only mention the word "pearls" and you will be escorted to someone's house to look at the pearls that came from their family's former pearl farm. A few years ago there were 28 pearl farms in the lagoon of Fakarava, and today there are only half a dozen remaining, including some of the big names such as Robert Wan and Tahiti Pearls. Very often the pearls you will see at the arts and crafts exhibits on the boat dock or in private homes are pearls of poor quality. You can learn the difference by reading about Tahitian Cultured Pearls in the *Basic Information* chapter in this book. You should also be aware that jeweler's glue is not always used to set the pearls in these remote atolls, and you risk losing your pearl just hours after you buy it. If you cannot resist a piece of jewelry, then have a jeweler re-glue it once you get home. A few of the unset pearls selling at bargain prices may even be magnificent, but most of the really good pearls are shipped to Tahiti and sold at auctions. Here are some of the places you can trust for good quality, although some of the prices may set you reeling.

Pearls of Havaiki, *Tel. 93.40.15/74.16.16; havaiki@mail.pf; www.havaiki.com* is the pearl farm and boutique at Havaiki Pearl Guest House. Joachim Dariel, who owns the pension, also started Fakarava's first pearl farm in 1989 with his father, Nicolas Dariel, who is a goldsmith, painter and sculptor. The grafting *fare* is open for visits on request and you pay 3.000 CFP to fish for a pearl inside a mother-of-pearl oyster. A collection of Nicolas Dariel pearl jewelry creations is on display in the boutique at Havaiki, as well as the work of his Polynesian son and grandson. Here you will find some of the rarest pearls, from the largest to the most colorful gems as well as those of unusual shapes. The settings and quality of the pearls are good here, but expect to pay more. AE, MC, V.

Hinano Pearls, *Tel. 98.41.51/71.68.41; hinanohellberg@mail.pf* is a pearl farm 10 km. from Rotoava village. Free transfers are provided and there is no charge to visit the pearl farm, which is open on request, so be sure to reserve. Hinano also has a pearl boutique in Rotoava village next to the Catholic church, open Mon.-

Sat. 10am-4pm. AE, MC, V accepted. She has a very good reputation for the quality and prices of her pearls and jewelry.

Poeata Creations, *Tel. 77.25.65*; poeata-creations@mail.pf. Original jewelry at reduced prices.

PRACTICAL INFORMATION

There are no banks and no *gendarmes* in Fakarava. The municipal police station at the *mairie* (town hall) is located in the center of Rotoava village, *Tel. 93.40.40.*

Food Stores

There are 2 stores in Rotoava village that provide frozen products, canned foods, a few fresh vegetables, wine and beer. You can buy fresh baguettes of French bread each morning. One of the magasins sells fuel (diesel by the 200-liter drum only). They will deliver it to the quay for visiting yachts. They take credit cards. Open 7am-12pm and 3-6:30pm.

Hospital

A health care center with a nurse is located in Rotoava village, *Tel. 98.42.24.*

Internet

The Post Office has Internet access and some of the lodgings have WiFi access.

Post Office

The **Post Office and Telecommunications Office** is in Rotoava village, *Tel. 98.42.22.* Open 7-11:30am. There are telephone cabins here that take phonecards.

Tourist Information

Fare Manihini (Visitors Bureau) is located on the pier in Rotoava village. *Tel. 98.42.46.* Open Mon.-Fri. 10am-4pm. Hinano Hellberg, who owns Hinano Pearl Farm and Boutique, is in charge of the Comité de Tourisme. She asked me to request the female tourists to refrain from walking around the village half-nude in a tiny bikini. This is not a custom in the Polynesian Islands and the inhabitants want to avoid any provocations that may lead to rape or other aggressive behavior by the local men.

19. Marquesas Islands

The South Seas Island images of tranquil lagoons protected by coral reefs are not part of the scenery in the **Marquesas Islands**. Rising like a mirage from the swells of the cobalt blue Pacific, the rugged volcanic cliffs soar like rock fortresses thousands of feet above the thundering sea. The wild ocean beats endlessly against the craggy, sculpted coasts, unbroken by any barriers for almost 6,400 km. (4,000 mi.).

Beyond the tumbling breakers lie the fjord-like bays, the narrow shores and curving beaches of golden black sand. Sheltered coves reveal a turquoise tide with pink and white sand beaches. Behind the seaside cliffs the electric green grasslands wander gently upward. Brooding and black with frequent rains, the jagged peaks and spires become a fairy castle in the clouds of the setting sun.

Lying north-northwest by south-southeast along a 350-km. (217-mi.) submarine chain, the Marquesas Islands are all of volcanic origin. Scientists believe that these islands rose from the oceanic depths and their foundations are submerged 4,000 m. (13,120 ft.) below sea level. The island of Fatu Hiva is the youngest of the chain, with an age of only 1.35 million years, while the most ancient island in the Marquesas group is the uninhabited island of Ei'ao, which was formed 5.2 to 7.5 million years ago. This is the youngest group of islands in French Polynesia and the farthest removed from any continent.

The Marquesas Islands are 7.50 to 10.35 degrees south of the Equator, and 138.25 to 140.50 degrees west longitude. They form two geographical groups about 111 km. (69 mi.) apart, with a combined land area of 1,279 sq. km. (492 sq. mi.) for the 20 or so islands.

The southern group consists of the 3 inhabited islands of **Hiva Oa, Tahuata** and **Fatu Hiva**, plus a few smaller islets. The northern group comprises the 3 principal islands of **Ua Pou, Nuku Hiva** and **Ua Huka**, and several uninhabited islands, including **Eiao** and **Hatutu**, which lie about 80 km. (50 mi.) northwest of the other islands in the northern group.

Nuku Hiva, the administrative center of the northern Marquesas, is about 1,500 km. (932 mi.) northeast of Tahiti. Hiva Oa, the main island in the southern group, lies approximately 1,400 km. (868 mi.) northeast of Tahiti, a 3 1/2-hr. flight by Air Tahiti's 48-passenger ATR 42 airplanes. Marquesan time is 1/2 hr. ahead of the rest of the islands in French Polynesia. When it is 6am in Tahiti, it is 6:30am in the Marquesas.

The average temperature of the Marquesas is about 27 degrees Celsius (80 degrees Fahrenheit), with the hottest weather in March and the coolest temperatures in August. Although there is usually more than 80% humidity, the climate is healthy and fairly pleasant. The trade winds prevail between April and October,

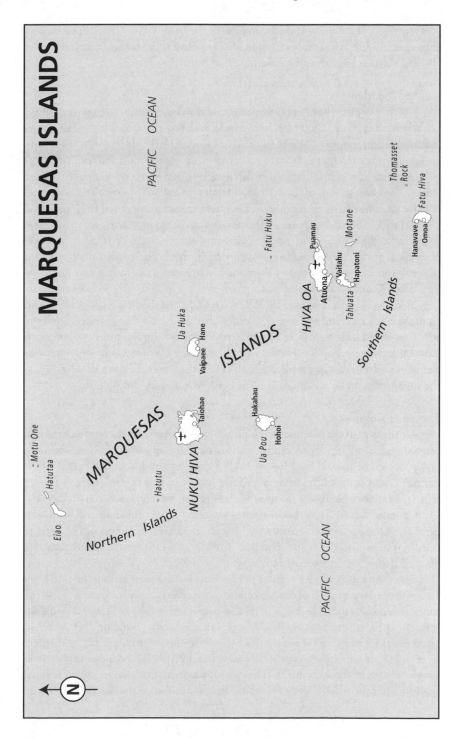

but at other times of the year there can be some hot, calm days. The annual rainfall varies greatly and is unevenly distributed. Fatu Hiva is the most verdant island of all because it receives the greatest amount of rain.

Land of the Men

Maohi people, whom the Europeans called Polynesians, settled in the valleys of these islands some 2,000 to 2,500 years ago, sailing their double-hulled canoes from Samoa or Tonga. Their legends tell of the god **Tiki**, ancestor of man, who conjured up a dozen islands from the ocean depths. These proud and fierce warriors were divided into clans, living in isolated valleys, separated by steep, knife-edge ridges. They had seasons of abundant food, but also seasons of draught, famine and tribal wars. They tattooed their bodies in intricate patterns learned from their god Tiki. As they evolved they made exquisite carvings in wood, stone, ivory and bone. They built their homes on *paepae* platforms, worshipped their gods in *me'ae* temples of stone, and were feared cannibals. In the northern islands they called their adopted home *Te Henua Te Enata*, and in the southern group it was *Te Henua Te Enana*, "Land of the Men."

In later years the descendants of The Men learned the origins of their islands from their legends, and had a story for the way their islands were named. Folklore tells that the islands were born of a marriage between the sea and sky. Their god Atua built a house: Nuku Hiva was its pointed roof; Ua Pou was its support posts or pillars; Ua Huka was the binding; Hiva Oa was the ridge pole; Fatu Hiva was the thatched roof; and Tahuata was the celebration of its completion.

European Conquerors

The history of the Marquesas with the arrival of the Europeans was varied and often tragic. In 1595 Spanish explorer Alvaro de Mendaña discovered the southern group, which he named Las Marquesas de Mendoza—in honor of the wife of his patron, Don Garcia Hurtado de Mendoza, Marquis de Canete, Viceroy of Peru. When Mendaña sailed away, some 200 islanders lay dead on the beach of Tahuata.

Captain James Cook claimed the southern group for England in 1774, estimating the population at 100,000. Joseph Ingraham of Boston discovered the northern group in 1791, and explorers from France, Germany and Russia also planted their flags on these distant shores.

These islands became a regular port-of-call for the men sailing the Pacific—crews hungry for a touch of land, women and recreation. Australians seeking the valuable sandalwood that grew in abundance in the valleys of the Marquesas brought their sailors to these shores. Later the American whaling ships arrived, often leaving behind those deserters who had jumped ship. Over the years there were all kinds of blackbirders, profiteers, beachcombers and adventurers who sought refuge in the Marquesas. They brought guns, alcohol, opium, smallpox, syphilis and other deadly diseases, which almost decimated the entire population.

In 1842 the whole archipelago was annexed to France under the name *Iles Marquises*. Catholic missionaries were installed and a new rule began. Yet the decline of the population continued. When the French took control in 1842 there were 20,000 people living in the Marquesas Islands, and 30 years later that number dropped to 6,200. The all-time low of 2,225 people was recorded in 1926, and 131 of this number were non-natives. The latest census of Sept. 2007 was 9,281, who are mostly Catholic.

Modern Marquesas

The Marquesas Islands today are quite modern, with electricity, international communications services, a radio and television station and efficient boat docks in the larger villages for the supply ships that provide regular service from Tahiti. The islands of Nuku Hiva, Hiva Oa, Ua Pou and Ua Huka have airports, and projects to build airports on Tahuata and Fatu Hiva still remain in the planning stage.

Farming and fishing are carried out on a family scale. The villagers live mostly from the land and sea, earning money for purchased supplies by copra production. For a few years the economy was boosted by the wild pickings of the *noni*, the *Morinda Citrifolia,* a potato-like fruit that grows on a tall bush. The juice from this fruit is sold worldwide by an American company as a tonic to cure anything from sore throats to syphilis, or as a panacea to heal a wide range of ailments from colds to cancers. The pulp is used in skin and hair care products, as well as a diet food supplement. While encouraging the exploitation of this business, the local government tried to discourage the islanders from abandoning their subsidized copra plantations in favor of planting *noni*. Their concerns proved accurate when the biggest noni company began buying the fruit for their Tahitian Noni Juice from Fiji and other countries at 20 CFP per kilo instead of paying 60 CFP per kilo to the Marquesans. Most of the Marquesans are now chopping copra again.

The *Aranui* cruises to the Marquesas Islands 17 times a year during its 14-day/ 13-night round-trip voyages from Tahiti. The ship calls at every principal valley and many smaller ones on each inhabited island. This is the most practical and enjoyable way to make a brief visit to the Marquesas, as the costs of land and sea transportation are very expensive for individual travelers. See information on the *Aranui* under *Inter-Island Cruises, Passenger Boats and Freighters* in the chapter on *Planning Your Trip.*

Accommodations are available in family pensions on each island and in one international class hotel on Nuku Hiva and another on Hiva Oa.

Activities in the Marquesas Islands include 4WD excursions, horseback riding, hiking over mountain trails and to inland cascades, picnics on the beach or in the mountains. You can go deep-sea fishing, on motorboat rides, scuba diving, visit the restored archaeological sites and stone tikis, and go to the workshops of crafts people to buy woodcarvings and tapa hangings.

A fragrant bouquet of flowers and herbs is worn in the hair or around the necks of the Marquesan women. This is called *kumu hei* in the northern group and *umu hei* in the southern islands. Their *monoi* is a delightful blend of coconut oil, sandalwood, spearmint, jasmine, gingerroot, pineapple, sweet basil, gardenia, pandanus fruit, ylang-ylang and other mysterious herbs. This is used as perfume, for massages, to seduce a boyfriend or to ward off mosquitoes.

On the subject of flora, since 1988 botanical exploration in the rugged Marquesas Islands has yielded 62 new species of ferns and flowering plants, bringing the total native species to 360, of which 18 are new discoveries. 11 of the 18 new species are ferns. Most of these new species are extremely rare and localized endemics, often confined to a single island. Many are known only from one or two localities harboring intact native vegetation that have so far escaped pressures from invasive plant species and feral animals. One of these rare ferns somehow managed to survive the voracious wild goats that roam the mountains of Ua Huka.

For further information on the hotels, pensions, restaurants, rental cars, boats, horses, and boat or land excursions; *tourisme@marquises.pf; www.marquises.pf.* You can also find information on the family pensions and guesthouses at: *haere-mai@mail.pf, www.haere-mai.pf.* Nuku Hiva will host the 8th edition of the Marquesas Festival of Arts from Dec. 15-18, 2011.

NUKU HIVA

In Marquesan mythology, **Nuku Hiva** was the first island to be raised from the ocean depths by the god Tiki, who created a wife from a pile of sand. Even today this beautiful emerald isle, located about 1,500 km. (932 mi.) northeast of Tahiti, is the leader of the Marquesas archipelago.

Captain Joseph Ingraham from Boston discovered Nuku Hiva in 1791, followed the same year by Etienne Marchand of France. When Russian Admiral Krusenstern landed in Taiohae Bay in 1804 they found an Englishman and a Frenchman who had deserted their ships to settle in Nuku Hiva. Cabry, the Frenchman, was tattooed from head to foot, just like his hosts in Taiohae.

With a surface area of 330 sq. km. (127 sq. mi.), Nuku Hiva is the largest island of the Marquesas group. The beauty of Nuku Hiva is truly breathtaking, whether viewed from the sea or the mountain heights. On the crenellated north coast is Taiohae Bay, a spectacular giant amphitheater dominated by emerald peaks and waterfalls. This is a welcome haven for cruising yachts from all over the world that drop anchor here after a month or more at sea. Taiohae is a pleasant village bordering the sea and serves as the administrative, economic, educational and health center of the Marquesas Islands. Here are the French and Territorial administrators, government buildings, *gendarmerie*, post office, general hospital, town hall, Air Tahiti office, banks and schools.

The 2,798 inhabitants live in the villages of Taiohae, Taipivai, Hatiheu, Aakapa, Pua, Ho'oumi, Anaho and Hakaui, which are separated by serrated mountain ranges, and connected by roads that are often best suited for 4WD vehicles and horses. These residents work for the government, the community, Catholic church or school system, or for themselves—chopping copra high in the mountains, fishing, raising cattle and other livestock, or sculpting bowls, platters, Marquesan ceremonial clubs, tikis and ukuleles.

The Notre-Dame Cathedral of the Marquesas Islands contains magnificently carved sculptures by craftsmen from each of the Marquesas Islands. You can visit the sculptors' workshops and arts and crafts centers in the villages of Taiohae, Hatiheu and Taipivai. You can rent a horse, a 4WD or pickup truck with chauffeur or a speedboat with pilot. A scuba diving center is located in Taiohae and the waters surrounding the island are rich with big fish, manta rays and an exciting variety of sharks. When Tahiti Helicopters opens its base in Taiohae in 2012, you will be able to take a helicopter flight to Hakaui Valley, with its steep gorges and Ahuii waterfall, one of the world's highest cascades, at an altitude of 350 m. (1,148 ft.). Near Hatiheu and Taipivai are ceremonial platforms, stone tikis and petroglyphs hidden deep in the valleys.

Taiohae has a few restaurants and snack bars, as well as general stores stocked with canned and frozen food, clothing and household items. Fresh vegetables are available some of the time. In Hatiheu you will find one of the best restaurants in the Marquesas Islands, as well as one of the most important ceremonial sites.

ARRIVALS & DEPARTURES
Arriving By Air
Air Tahiti, *Tel. 86.42.42*, in Nuku Hiva *Tel. 91.02.25*, flies ATR turbo jet planes from Tahiti to Nuku Hiva daily in 3 1/2 hrs. There are direct flights on Mon., Wed., Fri. Sat., one Sun. flight. The Tues. and Thurs., flights, as well as one Sun. flight, stop in Hiva Oa. Reminder: Marquesas Islands time is 30 min. ahead of Tahiti. The one-way airfare from Tahiti to Nuku Hiva is 32.230 CFP, and the round-trip fare is 59.460 CFP.

You can fly from Atuona to Nuku Hiva by ATR or Twin Otter plane daily for a one-way fare of 12.230 CFP. You can also fly direct to Nuku Hiva from Ua Pou aboard a Twin Otter 1-2 times a day except Mon., when it first stops in Ua Huka. There is a direct Twin Otter flight from Ua Huka to Nuku Hiva each Mon., Wed., Fri. and Sun., and the Tues. flight stops in Ua Pou. The one-way fare for the 25-30 min. flights from Ua Pou or Ua Huka to Nuku Hiva is 8.130 CFP.

A partially paved road from the Nuku Ataha airport to Taiohae village winds 48 km. (30 mi.) through the Toovii plateau, 800 m. (2,624 ft.) above the valleys of ferns, giant mango trees and coconut palms. The trip takes about 1 1/2 hrs. by 4WD vehicle and the still unfinished sections of the road are often very muddy and uncomfortable. **Tahiti Helicopters** will start an airport shuttle service in 2012.

You can also get to Nuku Hiva by chartering an airplane in Tahiti from **Air Tahiti**, *Tel. 86.42.42*, or **Pol'Air**, *Tel. 74.23.11*.

Arriving By Boat
The *Aranui* stops at the main port of Taiohae during its 14-day/13-night round-trip cruise program from Tahiti to Fakarava and on to the Marquesas. See

details in section on *Inter-Island Cruise Ships and Cargo/Passenger Boats* in Chapter 6, *Planning Your Trip.*

Departing By Air

There is a direct ATR flight between Nuku Hiva and Tahiti on Tues., Wed., Thurs., Sat. and Sun. On Mon., Fri., and Sun., a stop is made in Hiva Oa. There are also direct or 1-2 stop flights by ATR or Twin Otter from Nuku Hiva to Atuona daily. **Air Tahiti reservations** in Taiohae, *Tel.* 91.02.25; Nuku Ataha airport, *Tel. 92.01.45.*

Departing By Boat

The *Aranui* arrives in Taiohae Bay on the 5th day of its 14-day voyage from Tahiti to the Marquesas Islands. An alternative to taking the entire trip is to fly to Nuku Hiva and join the ship there, which will give you the opportunity of visiting all the inhabited islands in the Marquesas, with a stop in Rangiroa on the return trip to Tahiti. Or you can make the round of the Marquesas on board the ship and fly back to Tahiti. If you're just looking for a one-way passage from the Marquesas to Tahiti, the *Aranui* calls again at Nuku Hiva on the 11th day of its schedule, and from there goes to Ua Pou, Rangiroa and Tahiti, which will give you only 3 nights aboard the ship. See details in section on *Inter-Island Cruise Ships and Cargo/ Passenger Boats* in Chapter 6, *Planning Your Trip.*

ORIENTATION

The main village of **Taiohae** follows the semicircular curve of **Taiohae Bay** for about 3.5 km. (2 mi.), from the ship dock on the east to the **Nuku Hiva Keikahanui Pearl Lodge** on the west. During the summer months of Dec.-Mar. flowering flamboyant trees shade the road that passes through the village.

GETTING AROUND NUKU HIVA

Helicopter Flights

Tahiti Helicopters plans to open an office in Nuku Hiva in 2012.

Taxi & Transport Service

The one-way taxi fare between the Terre Deserte Airport to Taiohae village starts at 4.000 CFP per person. Your hotel or pension can arrange for your transfers when you reserve your accommodation.

Marie Jeanne Bruneau, *Tel. 92.01.84/70.05.89*, **Rose-Marie Transports**, *Tel. 92.05.96/74.36.76;* and **Joseph Tamarii**, *Tel. 92.00.84/77.09.84,* provide taxi service. See more information under *Land Tours* in this chapter.

Rental Cars

You can rent a self-drive 5-passenger 4WD vehicle from **Nuku Rent-A-Car**, *Tel./Fax 92.08.87/73.51.67; atachristian@mail.pf.* The office is located at the public boat dock. Rentals are also available at **Nuku Islands Excursions Marquises**, *Tel. 92.04.89/72.86.70/72.86.70*; **Kohuhunui Locations**, *Tel. 92.00.16/74.47.60*; and **Moana Nui Location**, *Tel. 92.03.30/72.86.65*, at the Moana Nui Pension/ Restaurant. They rent a 4x4 Suzuki for 11.000 CFP for 24 hrs. and a Toyota is 16.500 CFP. **Rose Corser** at **He'e Tai Inn**, *Tel. 92.03.82/73.53.12* also rents cars. A list of all the rentals can be obtained at the Nuku Hiva Tourism Committee in Taiohae village.

WHERE TO STAY
Superior
NUKU HIVA KEIKAHANUI PEARL LODGE, *B.P. 53, Taiohae, Nuku Hiva 98742, Marquesas Islands. Tel. 689/92.07.10; Fax 689/92.07.11; keikahanui@mail.pf. 20 bungalows overlooking Taiohae Bay, 2 km. (1.2 mi.) from the Taiohae pier and 48 km. (30 mi.) from the airport. All major credit cards.*

This 3-star hotel opened in 1999 with 20 local style bungalows built on stilts on the steep hillside overlooking Taiohae Bay. The grounds cover 15 acres (6 ha.) of tropical gardens of fruit trees and flowers. Each bungalow is 39 sq. m. (420 sq. ft.), and has a king size bed or 2 twin beds and an extra bed, plus a separate bathroom with hot water shower, and a terrace facing the bay. The bamboo walls and shingle roof of the bungalows are complemented by an interior of pandanus and tapa, which are beautifully blended to create a very pleasant decor. The rack rates are 26.000 CFP for a Garden Bungalow, 28.000 CFP for a Bayview Bungalow, and 31.500 CFP for a Premium Bayview Bungalow. Add 7.800 CFP per person for breakfast and dinner (MAP) and 10.000 CFP for all meals (AP). Each unit has a/c, a ceiling fan, a mini-bar refrigerator, satellite TV, tea and coffee facilities, IDD telephone, a safety box and hair dryer. Two rooms are well equipped for disabled guests using a wheelchair. Room service, laundry service and baby-sitting services are available.

The public facilities include Le Pua Enana gourmet restaurant and Le Tiki bar, the reception, boutique and tour desk, plus the fresh water swimming pool, from where you can gaze out at the lovely scenery of Taiohae Bay. The hotel's tour desk can help you arrange excursions and outings to visit the island by land, sea or air. One-way 4x4 airport transfers are 4.800 CFP per person and 20.000 CFP for a private transfer. See information in the sections on *Where to Eat, Land Tours, Horseback Riding, Motor Boat Rental,* and *Scuba Diving* in this chapter. **Note:** Financière Hôtelière Polynésienne (FHP), the major shareholder of this hotel, has taken over the management, replacing South Pacific Management (SPM).

Moderate
ROSE CORSER'S HE'E TAI INN, *B.P. 21, Taiohae, Nuku Hiva 98742, Marquesas Islands. Tel. 689/92.03.82/73.53.12; marquesasrose@gmail.com. On the western side of Taiohae Bay, 2 km. (1.2 mi.) from the Taiohae pier and 48 km. (30 mi.) from the airport. MC/V.*

This hotel complex opened in Dec. 2010 with 8 rooms in a 2-story building that was imported as a kit from the USA. The 6 single rooms have 2-3 twin beds that can be used as a king-size bed and a single. The suite of 2 rooms was designed for families, with a double and a twin bed in the bedroom and 2 twin beds in the living room, which also has a big TV and a mini kitchen with refrigerator and microwave oven. All the rooms are spacious and have a/c, a ceiling fan, a private bathroom with hot water, and a view of Taiohae Bay. They are all totally screened. A room with breakfast is 9.000 CFP sgl./10.500 CFP dbl; the MAP rate with room, breakfast and dinner is 12.000 CFP sgl./16.500 CFP dbl. The suite is 15.000 CFP dbl./20.000 CFP tpl., plus 3.000 CFP per adult for breakfast and dinner, and 1.500 CFP per child. Full-board (AP) with all meals is also available.

There is a restaurant and full service bar on the beach, where visitors from the yachts and cruise ships gather to enjoy Rose Corser's hospitality and the happy ambience generated by people who are having a good time. Rose caters to the boating community and this is an informal yacht club. She and her late husband, Frank Corser sailed their yacht to Tahiti in the early 1970s and settled in Taiohae in 1979, where they bought most of the west side of Taiohae Bay and immediately built a 6 bungalow hotel they called Keikahanui Inn. This is now the 20-bungalow Nuku Hiva Keikahanui Pearl Lodge.

Rose built a museum and boutique in the beautiful gardens of endemic trees and flowers just below her former hotel. Be sure to visit the Musée Enana Boutique and see Rose's collection of really good unique pieces of cultural art and creations. She also has sculptors working with her to carve exact replicas of the museum pieces.

The tourist services at He'e Tai (from the sea) include a rental car agency and excursion bureau. You can choose to drive yourself or go with a guide who knows the roads of Nuku Hiva, which can be dangerous on the mountain curves.

On frequent occasions, and always when a cruise ship is in port, Rose organizes cultural activities for her guests. These include a Marquesan feast cooked in the underground oven, music, a dance group, carving, tapa making and tattoo demonstrations. Rose will have a website before you visit. See more information under *Where to Eat, Shopping, Yacht Services & Internet Connections* in this chapter.

MAVE MAI, *B.P. 378, Taiohae, Nuku Hiva 98742, Marquesas Islands. Tel./ Fax 689/92.08.10; Cell 689/74.40.91; pension-mavemai@mail.pf; www.haere-mail.pf. On mountainside overlooking Taiohae Bay, 100 m. (328 ft.) from the boat dock and 48 km. (30 mi.) from the airport. D, JCB, MC, V.*

This is a 2-story white house on a hill located close to the shops and restaurants in Taiohae village. There are 8 clean and cheerfully decorated bedrooms on the ground floor or the second level, with a terrace or balcony overlooking the bay. All the rooms have a/c, a ceiling fan, a private bathroom with hot water shower, and a double and single bed. 2 rooms have a small kitchenette. A communal living room has a TV with DVD player, and paid Internet access. Guests can use the washing machine and swimming pool. MAP rates are 10.000 CFP sgl./18.000 CFP dbl.

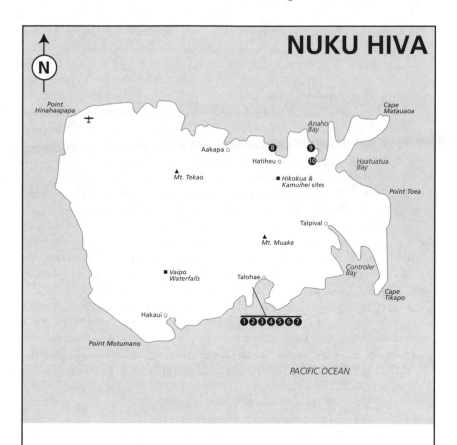

1. Nuku Hiva Keikahanui Pearl Lodge
2. Rose Corser's He'e Tai Inn
3. Pension Mave Mai
4. Pension Moana Nui
5. Paahatea Nui (Chez Justine & Julienne)
6. Chez Fetu
7. Pension Pua
8. Chez Yvonne (Hinako Nui)
9. Te Pua Hinako (Chez Juliette)
10. Pension Kao Tia'e

Owners Jean-Claude and Régina Tata have received a 1-Tiare rating from Tahiti Tourisme for their pension. They also operate the Kovivi restaurant, and guests are driven there for meals. An early breakfast is served at the pension on request. Round-trip airport transfers are 11.000 CFP. They will arrange day excursions for you or you can rent a self-drive 4WD vehicle from them for 12.000 CFP a day. Please see details under *Land Tours* in this chapter.

PENSION MOANA NUI, *B.P. 33, Taiohae, Nuku Hiva 98742, Marquesas Islands. Tel. 689/92.03.30/72.86.65; Fax 689/92.00.02; pensionmoananui@mail.pf; www.ifrance.com/pensionmoananui. On mountain side 600 m. (654 yds.) from the boat dock and 48 km. (30 mi.) from the airport. D, MC, V.*

This 2-story renovated building has 7 rooms upstairs, with single or double beds and private bathrooms with hot water showers. Each room has a/c and a ceiling fan. I stayed here in 1985 and the setting and tropical ambiance made me feel like I was in a Somerset Maugham movie. There's nothing fancy about this pension, but it's conveniently located if you want to be in Taiohae village, and Tahiti Tourisme has given it a 1-Tiare rating. A room with breakfast is 6.360 CFP sgl./8.890 dbl., and the MAP rate is 9.310 CFP sgl./14.790 CFP dbl. The restaurant downstairs serves good food for reasonable prices and the bar is popular with the locals. The manager, Charles Mombaerts, also has a one-bedroom a/c bungalow for rent, with a double bed and a single bed, private bathroom with hot water shower, a living room and dining room. He rents self-drive 4WD vehicles.

PAAHATEA NUI (CHEZ JUSTIN & JULIENNE), *B.P. 201, Taiohae, Nuku Hiva 98742, Marquesas Islands. Tel./Fax 689/92.00.97; paahateanui@mail.pf. Overlooking the bay at the west end of Taiohae village, 3 km. (1.9 mi.) from the quay and 45 km. (28 mi.) from the airport. No credit cards.*

This bed and breakfast pension has an excellent reputation and has a 1-Tiare rating. Julienne and Justin have 3 rooms and 6 bungalows in a garden setting across the road from the black sand beach. One of the bedrooms and all bungalows are equipped with a private hot water shower and toilet, and the other 2 rooms share the bathroom facilities. One of the family bungalows has a kitchen and other guests share a big kitchen. The bungalows also have a terrace, ceiling fan, TV and mosquito nets. All units are cleaned daily and guests can use the washing machine. A room for two is 7.900 CFP and a bungalow for two is 8.800 CFP, with breakfast and airport transfers included. No lunch or dinner served.

Budget lodgings in Taiohae

Chez Fetu, *Tel. 689/92.03.66*, has a bungalow for 3 with kitchen and cold-water shower in Taiohae, for 2.000 CFP per person per day. **Pension Pua**, *Tel. 689/92.06.87/21.47.53; Fax 689/92.01.35; claudepua@mail.pf* has 8 bungalows in the Nuku Hiva Village complex (now closed). Some units have kitchens. Bungalow rates are 4.000 CFP sgl./5.500 CFP dbl.; bungalow with kitchen 5.500 CFP sgl./7.500 CFP dbl.

Lodging Outside Main Village

CHEZ YVONNE (HINAKO NUI,) *B.P. 199, Taiohae, Nuku Hiva 98742, Marquesas Islands. Tel. 689/92.02.97; Fax 689/92.01.28; hinakonui@mail.pf. On mountain side in Hatiheu village, 500 m. (545 yards) from the Hatiheu boat landing, 75 km. (47 mi.) from the airport and 28 km. (17 mi.), 2 hours by car from Taiohae Bay. No credit cards.*

The 5 simple bungalows facing the sea and the restaurant next door are owned by Yvonne Katupa, who is also the mayor of Hatiheu. For many years she has been reputed for serving the best food in all the Marquesas Islands, and I definitely agree. The 4 standard bungalows have a double bed and the family bungalow can sleep three people. Each bungalow has a private bathroom with a cold-water shower. A room with half-board (MAP) meals is 8.000 CFP sgl./12.000 CFP dbl, and with all meals it is 11.000/18.000 CFP. A one-way airport transfer by 4x4 is 4.000 CFP per person. You can walk to the church, archaeological sites and to the artisan center. Be sure to visit Yvonne's new museum in Hatiheu village. A black sand beach is across the dirt road in front of the bungalows. Don't forget to protect yourself against the nonos, which can be vicious in Hatiheu. Guided excursions to Anaho village can be made by boat or 4WD.

KAO TIA'E, *B.P. 290, Taiohae, Nuku Hiva 98742, Marquesas Islands. Tel. 689/92.00.08. Beside the beach in Anaho Bay, 2 km. (1.2 mi.) from Hatiheu village, 30 km. (19 mi.) from Taiohae Bay and 77 km. (48 mi.) from the airport. No credit cards.*

It is worth staying here just to swim in beautiful Anaho Bay, bordered by a beach of soft pink sand. Raymond Vaianui owns a 5-bungalow pension with a double bed in each room, a private bathroom with hot water, and a terrace. For a bungalow and half-board (MAP) he charges 5.000 CFP per person, and 6.500 CFP for a bungalow and all meals. A one-way transfer by taxi from the airport to Hatiheu is 4.000 CFP, and from Hatiheu to Anaho by speedboat costs 7.000 CFP one-way.

Free activities include line fishing, swimming and shelling. You can hike the trail along the beach to Atuatua Bay and to the peaks overlooking the bay. You can also find a horse to ride along the beach if you just ask Raymond. Kao tia'e is Marquesan for the Tiare Tahiti bud and this family pension has a 1-Tiare rating from Tahiti Tourisme.

TE PUA HINAKO (CHEZ JULIETTE), *B.P. 202, Taiohae, Nuku Hiva 98742, Marquesas Islands. Tel. 689/92.04.14. Beside the beach in Anaho Bay, 2 km. (1.2 mi.) from Hatiheu village, 30 km. (19 mi.) from Taiohae Bay and 77 km. (48 mi.) from the airport. No credit cards.*

Juliette Vaianui is the mother of Raymond and she has a 2-bedroom house with a communal bathroom and cold water shower, next door to Pension Kao Tia'e. Her rates are a little less than his, and both pensions combine their meals and activities.

WHERE TO EAT

NUKU HIVA KEIKAHANUI PEARL LODGE, *Tel. 92.07.10. On hillside in Taiohae. All major credit cards.*

Le Pua Enana Restaurant is a 40-seat restaurant overlooking Taiohae Bay. Open daily for BLD, serving local, French and Continental cuisine. **Le Tiki Bar** has a bartender who is trained to make your favorite cocktail.

HE'E TAI INN, *Tel. 92.03.82/73.53.12. Beside the beach on western side of Taiohae Bay. Open daily for BLD. MC, V.*

Due to the 30-plus years that American expatriate Rose Corser has lived in Taiohae and worked with the cruising yachtsmen, her new restaurant has become known as an informal yacht club. She has a full bar license and her Friday night Happy Hour features a house special 'rum punch' and local music.

MOANA NUI, *Tel. 92.03.30. On the waterfront street of Taiohae village. Open daily for BLD except Sun. D, MC, V.*

This is the most popular gathering place in the village, serving French and local cuisine. Pizzas available at night only.

LE KOVIVI, *Tel. 92.03.85. On the waterfront street of Taiohae village. Open daily for BLD. D, MC, V.*

This restaurant is operated by the owners of Pension Mave Mai. The menu includes Chinese and local cuisine, and you can get take-away meals.

CHEZ YVONNE (HINAKO NUI), *Tel. 92.02.97 in Hatiheu village. BLD. Reserve. No credit cards.*

Although this popular restaurant is now called Hinako Nui, most people still refer to it as Chez Yvonne Katupa, because that's the name that earned it the reputation of serving the best food in the Marquesas Islands. I first ate here a few times in 1981, and many times since, and the food has always been excellent. The specialty here is the fresh water shrimp that are caught in the river nearby, which are battered and fried. Rock lobster is available during certain seasons. They also serve very tasty barbecued chicken legs, tuna fritters, roast pig and goat. The main course costs 1.500-3.000 CFP. This is where the *Aranui* passengers eat when they come to Hatiheu.

Nadia Crêperie on the quay in Taiohae is open Mon.-Fri., and is a meeting place for people from the yachts.

A small fruit market is open daily in Taiohae and the Sat. market is the best time to buy your fruits, vegetables and fish. It opens at 4:30am and closes early.

SEEING THE SIGHTS

The **Notre-Dame Cathedral of the Marquesas Islands** is located in the Catholic mission on the west side of Taiohae village. The cathedral was built in 1977, using stones from all the inhabited islands in the archipelago. The magnificent carvings were made by several of the local sculptors.

The **Herman Melville memorial** is a wooden sculpture made by Kahee Taupotini in 1992, which is on the bayside between the cemetery and the nautical club at the west end of the village. Melville wrote two books, *Typee* and *Omoo*, based on his short visit to Nuku Hiva in 1842, when he jumped ship from an American whaler and lived among the Taipi cannibals in Taipivai Valley for three weeks. The **Koueva** and **Temehea** sites in Taiohae were used for ceremonies during the 5th Marquesas Festival of Arts in December 1999. The *tohua* Koueva was the ancient site for public festivities in ancient times, and during the 1800s the Temehea was the residence of one of the great chiefs of Taiohae Bay. You can see the carved stones at each site, as well as the millennium tree that was planted at Temehea.

Behind Taiohae village you can have a panoramic view of Taiohae Bay and the island of Ua Pou from the summit of **Muake Mountain,** which rises 864 m. (2,834 ft.). You can get there on foot, by horse or by 4WD.

Hakaui Valley is on the southern coast, about a 20-min. boat ride from Taiohae. You'll have to hike inland over stones for about 2 hrs. to reach the **Ahuii waterfall.** This is one of the world's highest cascades, with a single jet of water tumbling from the basaltic rock at an altitude of 350 m. (1,148 ft.). You can also reach Hakaui from Taiohae on horseback, riding 12 km. (8 mi.) along a bridleway that ranges from 400-500 m. (1,312 to 1,640 ft.) in altitude. You'll appreciate the refreshing pool of water when you get to the waterfall. It's best to go with a guide, and take mosquito repellent, plastic shoes and your swimsuit with you. This valley was featured in the "Survivor" television series that was filmed in Nuku Hiva in 2001 and telecast in 2002.

Hatiheu, on the northern coast, is 28 km. (17 mi.) from Taiohae and 12 km. (7.5 mi.) from Taipivai. The road between the two villages has been improved and now offers a smoother and easier trip by 4x4. Hatiheu was the favorite village of the Scottish writer, **Robert Louis Stevenson,** when he visited the Marquesas Islands in 1888 aboard his yacht *Casco.* This is also my first choice on Nuku Hiva, for the beauty and layout of the village, for the food at Chez Yvonne Katupa's restaurant (also called Restaurant Hinako Nui) and for the **Hikokua** *tohua* in the valley, beside the road to Taipivai. This archaeological site is about 1 km. (.62 mi.) from Chez Yvonne, and it was restored for the Marquesas Festival of Arts that was held in Nuku Hiva in 1999. It is a large flat surface 120 m. (394 ft.) long, used for dances and other public ceremonies. The *me'ae* are decorated with ancient stone tikis and modern sculptures also decorate the *paepaes.*

At the entrance to the site is a phallic-shaped fertility tiki. It is said that infertile women who touch the tiki will soon become pregnant. A 20-min. walk further up the road from Hikokua brings you to **Kamuihei,** a sacred place shaded by numerous trees, including an impressive old banyan tree that is 14 m. (46 ft.) wide and said to be more than 600 years old. **Dr. Robert Suggs** found skulls in the branches of this tree when he was doing archaeological research in Nuku Hiva in the 1950s. The **Te i'ipoka** *me'ae* of boulders and stone platforms is located near the banyan tree in a mysterious dark jungle setting of *purau,* mango, breadfruit and *mape* chestnut trees, with giant ferns and *ape* leaves. There are also big pits that were used for storing "ma", a paste made from fermented breadfruit. In a riverbed behind the banyan tree are boulders carved with petroglyphs of fish, turtles and humans. After crossing a log bridge on the main path below the banyan tree you will come to Kamueihei *me'ae*, where you can hear the *upe'e* pigeons hooting in the banyan forest and smell the fragrance of the slim yellow flowers of the ylang ylang trees bordering 2 *tohua* complexes.

In 2011 Hatiheu's **Mayor Yvonne Katupa** opened a small archaeological **museum** inside the former school. Here you can see a collection of traditional artifacts found in the valley, as well as moulds that were made of the petroglyphs at Kamuihei. The masterpiece is a moulded boulder 5m (16.4 ft.) long that was carried by 20 men from the valley to the museum. French archaeologists **Pierre** and **Marie-Noëlle Ottino** worked with Mayor Katupa to preserve Kamuihei, which is the most popular tourist site on the island. **Gilbert** and **Cathy Banneville** came from a university in France to reproduce the petroglyphs for the museum.

In 1872 a French priest brought a white statue of the Virgin Mary to Hatiheu in 3 pieces and it was placed on one of the cathedral-shaped peaks overlooking the village, some 300 m. (984 ft.) above the sea. Once a year people from Hatiheu climb the peaks to clean the Virgin Mary statue. The Catholic Church in this village was rebuilt in 2003 and is ideally situated, facing the sea with a backdrop of rolling hills carpeted in shades of green.

Anaho is just a 10-min. easy boat ride from Hatiheu, and you can also get there by 4WD, horse or hiking the difficult 2-km. (1.2-mile) trail, which takes about 90 min. round trip. Anaho Bay is one of the loveliest spots in the Marquesas Islands, with good swimming in tranquil turquoise water and a crescent-shaped beach with golden-pink sand. Only a few families live in this valley, and the simple little chapel here is perhaps the smallest church in French Polynesia. The manta rays and leopard rays live in the depths of this bay, and the dreaded *nono* hangs out in the beach area. Bring your repellent.

Ha'atuatua Valley can be reached by hiking from Anaho beach, and the best way to visit it is with Dr. Robert Suggs, who is one of the guest lecturers aboard the *Aranui 3*. Dr. Suggs will lead you to the archaeological site he excavated on the Ha'atuatua beach in 1956 and 1957-58. In addition to the human bones, basalt adzes, fishhooks, mother of pearl ornaments and basalt flake tools he uncovered, he also found potsherds of a type of pottery that is known as "Polynesian Plain Ware." This undecorated household ware belongs to the Lapita pottery category of ceramics that was used by the Lapita peoples in Eastern Indonesia and Western Melanesia as far back as 2000-1900 BC. The pieces of potsherds that Dr. Suggs found at the Ha'atuatua site were believed to be brought by the first Polynesian settlers, which radiocarbon dating of the pottery indicates was around 125 BC. For more information on this subject you should read Dr. Suggs' books, which are listed in the chapter on *Basic Information*.

A road connects the Nuku Ataha airport in the **Terre Déserte** with **Aakapa** village. The wind-battered bushes, dried grasses and red earth in this desert land make you think you've been transported to an African savanna, and the only living beings you normally see are herds of wild goats. The panoramic scenery is incredible, with vistas of Motu Ehe and its bay edged with a beach of fine white sand. You pass through the sacred valley of Pua, where the last queen is buried, and the road leads up to a hill where you can look out over the bays of Akahea and Hapapani with a pink sand beach and turquoise waters. Then you see the sentinel peaks of Aakapa and follow the road into the little village.

The **Paeke archaeological site** in Taipivai has 2 *me'ae* temples and 11 tikis of reddish colored stone. The trailhead, about 4 km. (2.5 mi.) from where the valley begins, is not marked, so it is best to go with a guide. In 1957 American archaeologist Dr. Robert Suggs excavated **Te Ivi o Hou**, a *tohua* ceremonial site that is 274 m. (300 yds. long). You'll need a guide to reach this hidden site, way back in the valley. **Pukiki**, a guide who lives in Taipivai, is familiar with both sites. Protect yourself against *nonos* in the valleys as well as on the beaches.

Taipivai Valley is 16 km. (10 mi.) northeast of Taiohae, which you can reach in 30 min. by boat from Taiohae, or by 4WD over a now improved road that crosses the **Toovii Plateau**, which has an average altitude of 800 m. (2,624 ft.). A navigable river connects Contrôleur Bay with the village boat dock and follows the road through the village into the valley. American writer Herman Melville made this village famous with his published account of the Taipi tribe who welcomed him into their village in 1842. A '**Cite Melville**' sign marks the place where Melville was supposed to have stayed during his 3-week visit. It is on the left side of the Hatiheu road about 4.5 km. (2.8 mi.) from the bridge in Taipivai village.

Land Tours

Nuku Hiva Keikahanui Pearl Lodge. *Tel. 689/92.07.10.* The hotel's activity desk can arrange half-day excursions by 4WD vehicle for you to visit Taiohae village with an English-speaking guide, or you can take a half-day tour of the village plus the archaeological site of Koueva. A full-day 4WD excursion to Taipivai valley and lunch at Chez Yvonne in Hatiheu is about 9.000 CFP per person. A half-day excursion without lunch will take you to Taipivai valley.

Rose Corser's He'e Tai Inn. *Tel. 92.03.82/73.53.12.* Rose Corser has rental cars as well as an excursion agency and she uses the best English speaking guides on the island.

Temarama Tours, *Tel. 28.08.36/24.66.43, temarama.tour@hotmail.pf,* is owned by Richard Deane, who leads 4WD excursions. He speaks good English.

Jocelyne Henua Enana Tours, *Tel. 92.00.52/74.42.23; Fax 92.08.32; jocelyne@mail.pf; www.marquisesvoyages.com.pf.* Jocelyne Mamatui provides full-day safari excursions by 4WD vehicle to Taipivai, Hatiheu and the Aakapa lookout. She also has half-day tours from Taipivai to Ho'oumi, or to Muake Mountain and the Toovii Plateau. You can visit Taiohae village, the artisans and the Koueva site. Jocelyne also has all-inclusive package programs available to visit the other islands in the Marquesas group. Contact her directly for details.

Mave Mai Tours, *Tel. 92.08.10/92.00.01/73.76.01; Fax 92.08.10; pension-mavemai@mail.pf. D, MC, JCB, V.* Jean-Claude and Régina Tata, who own the Pension Mave Mai, also provide excursions by 4WD, which are sometimes combined with boat trips and hiking. You can take an archaeological tour by 4WD to visit the sites of Taipivai and Hatiheu and stop at the Aakapa Col for a panoramic view. At noon you will be taken by boat from Hatiheu to Anaho Bay where you will have a picnic of casse-croûte sandwiches and drinks, as well as time for swimming and enjoying the lovely white sand beach.

Nuku Hiva Excursions, *Tel. 92.06.80/77.32.81, Fax 92.06.44*, is owned by Marcel Huveke in Taiohae. He also provides 4WD tours to visit the archaeological sites and panoramic lookouts.

SPORTS & RECREATION
Hiking
Marquises Rando, *Tel. 92.07.13/21.08.74/29.53.31; frederic.benne@mail.pf; www.marquisesrando.com.* Frédéric Benne and William Teikitohe are both professional hiking guides who lead treks and walks in the mountains and hills. They can take you hiking on the ridges and Caldeira of Taiohae and the viewpoints of Nuku Hiva's South coast. This 5-1/2 hr. hike costs 6.600 CFP per person. A hike to the cliff edges of Aakapa and Hatiheu on the Northeast side of the island and to the observation sites of endemic birds from the Marquesas Islands takes 6 hrs. and costs 8.400 CFP. A 6-hr. hike to the Big Z Ridge and to Temokomoko Point offers views of Toovi, the Terre Deserte, Hakaui and the Hidden Valley, and costs 12.000 CFP per person. Included in all the hikes are transfers, sandwiches, cookies, hot and cold beverages, and the guide's services. Other hikes available on request.

Kimikamehameha Teikiteetini of Taiohae is another professional guide. He specializes in high mountain hiking. Get contact information from Nuku Hiva Visitors Bureau, *Tel. 92.03.73.*

Pua Excursions, *Tel. 92.02.94; Fax 92.08.14; claudepua@mail.pf.* Claude Gerard organizes full-day hikes requiring moderate skills. He also has trekking for several days, and 4x4 excursions.

Horseback Riding
Sabine and **Louis Teikiteetini** in Taiohae village, *Tel. 92.01.56/25.35.13*, have Marquesan horses for rent. They will organize excursions for you to explore the valleys by horseback.

Alphonse Teikiteetini, *Tel. 92.02.37*, also has horses for rent by the hour, half-or full day.

The Ranch is operated by Patrice Tamarii, *Tel. 92.06.35; danigo@mail.pf*, who has horses for rent. He can arrange 2-day excursions to Hakahui Cascade and to Hakatea, where you spend the night on the white sand beach. His 3-day outings will take you to the Terre Déserte.

Motor Boat Rental, Fishing & Excursions

The activities desk at the **Nuku Hiva Keikahanui Pearl Lodge** can arrange 2-hr. boat excursions around Taiohae Bay, a half-day dolphin trip with snorkeling, or a full-day boat excursion to Anaho Bay. Mixed land and sea excursions include a half-day boat excursion to Hakapaa bay, which includes a 1-hr. walk to 2 beautiful waterfalls. You can also take a full-day boat trip to Hakaui valley with a picnic. This excursion includes a 4-hr. walk to visit the waterfall.

Jocelyne Henua Enana Tours, *Tel. 92.08.32/74.42.23; Fax 92.00.52; jocelyne@mail.pf; www.marquisesvoyages.com.pf.* Jocelyne Mamatui organizes 7-hr. motorboat excursions to the Hakatea Valley and the Cascade of Hakaui. Bring your own sandwich and drinks. A 2 1/2 to 3-hr. outing will take you to the neighboring bays (Hakapaa, Taipivai, Hooumi, Hakahui, Hakatea, Colette), where you can snorkel and have a chance to see dolphins or manta rays. Contact her for the rates.

Marquises Plaisance, *Tel./Fax 92.08.75/73.23.48; e.bastard@mail.pf; www.marquises.pf.* Eric Bastard operates half- or full-day excursions in his 25-ft. boat, *Hitiaa*. He can take up to 5 people to visit Anaho Bay for a swim and picnic on the beach (picnic not included). He also combines a boat tour with hiking when he takes you to the Ahuii waterfall in Hakaui Valley. On the return boat trip you'll stop for a swim in Hakatea Bay. A half-day outing to the Southwest coast of Nuku Hiva also includes a swim at Hakatea Bay, and a half-day excursion to the Southeast coast of the island will take you from Taiohae to the site of the dolphins.

Scuba Diving

Centre de Plongée Marquises (CPM) is based at the Taiohae Quay, *Tel./Fax 92.00.88; marquisesdives@mail.pf; www.marquises.pf.* Xavier Curvat is a French Federal Instructor who has lived in the Marquesas Islands for 20-plus years. He is a PADI OWSI, BEES 1 and CMAS two-star instructor, and he can give exams for diving certificates. His dive boat is the 33-ft. *Makuita*, with complete equipment for 15 divers, plus a compressor and additional bottles. He can take you to more than 20 dive sites in the immediate proximity of Taiohae, or on day trips to Ua Pou, Ua Huka and the other islands in the northern Marquesas group. The water temperature in the Marquesas Islands is 28° C (82° F) all year.

You can see an abundance of marine life near the rocky points, where the water is oxygenated continuously by the surf. Among the profusion of color, species and movement, you may see red snappers, groupers, perch and other rock fish seeking shelter in the hollows of rock slides and caves sculpted in volcanic stones, hiding from their predators—tuna, surgeon fish, lionfish and four kinds of jacks or trevally. Curious manta rays, with their graceful ballet movements, will approach you for a closer look. And everywhere you will see sting, eagle and marble rays, lobsters, sponges and rare seashells. A little deeper you can observe barracudas and sharks. These may include reef sharks, silvertip sharks, Galapagos and silky sharks, hammerhead sharks and melon-head whales. You may even see one or more orcas, as they have been regular visitors in this area for the past several years.

Xavier Curvat specializes in helping film makers to shoot their movies in all the Marquesas Islands.

SHOPPING

Musée Enana Boutique, *Tel. 92.03.82/73.53.*12, is operated by Rose Corser in the garden adjacent to her hotel, the He'e Tai Inn. Rose is an American who has lived in Nuku Hiva since the 1970s and she buys carvings from the best sculptors in the Marquesas Islands. The boutique features a large variety of art objects as well as tapa and original paintings by local artists. She also has a small library and museum of Marquesan artifacts and handcrafts, and she loves to share her wealth of information about life in the Marquesas Islands. Rose and her late husband, Frank Corser, built the original Keikahanui Inn, which had 6 bungalows.

Beside the beach in Taiohae village is the (**Centre Artisanal du Nuku Hiva**), the arts and crafts workshop where you can buy all kinds of Marquesan jewelry, stone, bone and wood carvings, scented monoi oils, Marquesan pareos and T-shirts, and anything else made in the Marquesas.

You can visit the sculptors' workshops to buy carved bowls, platters, saddles, tikis, ceremonial clubs and intricately carved tables. You can also visit the arts and crafts centers to buy woodcarvings. **Damien Haturau**, *Tel. 92.05.56,* is the best known of the Marquesan sculptors. His works include the statues in the cathedral in Taiohae and the Virgin with Child at the Vaitahu church in Tahuata. Other noted wood carvers and stone sculptors include: **Edgard Tamarii**, *Tel. 92.01.67*; **Tahiahui Haiti, DamasTaupotini**, *Tel. 92.02.42*; **Pierrot Keuvahana**, *Tel. 92.05.58*; and **Philippe Utia**, *Tel. 92.00.51*. **Raphael Ah-Scha**, *Tel. 92.00.33,* is a wood carver and tattoo artist. If you're a serious collector, you can get a list of sculptors and arts and crafts centers from the Nuku Hiva Tourism Bureau.

PRACTICAL INFORMATION

Banks

Banque Socredo, *Tel. 92.03.63,* has a branch office in Taiohae. You can exchange currency and make credit card withdrawals here. The ATM machines are outside the bank.

Hospitals

There is a government-operated hospital in Taiohae, *Tel. 92.02.00*, and a dental center. The villages of Hatiheu and Taipivai each have an infirmary.

Pharmacy

Pharmacie Nuku Hiva, *Tel. 91.00.90,* is on the western side of Taiohae village. Open Mon.-Fri. 8:30am-12pm and 3-5pm; Sat. 9-11am.

Police

The French gendarmerie has an office in Taiohae, *Tel. 92.03.61/91.03.05; or 17.*

Post Office & Telecommunications Office

All telecommunications and postal services are available at the post office, which is close to the boat dock in Taiohae, *Tel. 92.03.50.* It is open Mon.-Thurs. from 7:30-11:30am 12-3:30pm, and on Fri. to 4:30pm. Outside ATM available.

Tourist Bureau

Nuku Hiva Visitors Bureau (Comité du Tourisme du Nuku Hiva) *Tel. 92.08.25/29.21.35; tourisme@marquises.pf; www.marquises.pf.* is located in the municipal market on the waterfront in Taiohae, opposite the *mairie* (town hall). Open Mon.-Fri. 7:30am-3:30pm, Sat. 7:30am-12:30pm. The hostess speaks English.

Yacht Services & Internet Connections

Rose Corser Yacht Club, *B.P. 21 Taiohae, Nuku Hiva, (ZIP 98742), Marquesas Islands; Tel. 689/92.03.82/73.53.12; rose.corser@mail.pf.*

Rose Corser is an American woman who sailed to Tahiti in 1972 with her husband Frank aboard their yacht *Corser*. After a couple more trips, they finally settled in Nuku Hiva in 1979, where they bought land and built a 6-bungalow hotel called the Keikahanui Inn. Rose and Frank ran the hotel together for the first 15 years, and Rose continued to run the hotel after her husband's death. She formed a partnership to build the 20-bungalow Nuku Hiva Keikahanui Pearl Lodge, which opened in Taiohae in September 1999. Once she was free of all connections with that hotel, Rose built another small first-class hotel all her own, which has 8 a/c guest rooms, a restaurant and bar located on her beachside property below the Keikahanui Pearl Lodge. **Rose Corser's He'e Tai Inn and Restaurant** also features yacht club activities. In addition to providing a service for mail and packages, she has facilities and equipment for faxes, e-mail and WiFi Internet connections for cruising yachts. Be sure to visit Rose's Musée Enana Boutique adjacent to her new hotel complex.

Nuku Hiva Yacht Services, *B.P. 461 Taiohae, Nuku Hiva 98742, Marquesas Islands. Tel./Fax 689/92.07.50; yachtservicesnukuhiva@yahoo.com.*

This service is operated by Anne Ragu and Moetai at the quay in Taiohae, who welcome the people who arrive aboard cruising yachts. They can help visiting yachts with entry formalities, visa extensions, provide general information on the weather, the Marquesas Islands and French Polynesia. They do laundry, mechanical repairs for boats, repair sails, and advise on where to buy duty free fuel, shop for provisions, rent a car, boat, horse or helicopter. They can organize hikes, guided excursions, visits to the wood sculptors' workshops and other arts and crafts vendors, and can even send you to a good tattoo artist. In addition to faxing facilities, they also have computers and provide WiFi Internet connections even from your yacht.

UA POU

When the Polynesians first settled on the island of **Ua Pou** they named it for the pillars of rock that resemble great cathedral spires. The mountain called Oave Needle, the tallest of the fantastic monoliths, thrusts 1,232 m. (4,040 ft.) into the clouds, and Ua Pou's dramatic silhouette is visible from Nuku Hiva, 35 km. (22 mi.) across the sea, and even from Ua Huka, some 56 km. (35 mi.) distant.

From the time of the old Polynesian chiefs Ua Pou has always been different from the rest of the Marquesas Islands. Although they formed tribes in the isolated valleys they recognized the authority of a single chief. The people seemed to be more peaceful, more unified and friendly, and the girls of Ua Pou are still considered the prettiest in all of Polynesia.

Ua Pou is the third largest island in the Marquesas archipelago, with 114 sq. km. (44 sq. mi.) of surface area. The 2,246 inhabitants live in the villages of Hakahau, Hakahetau, Haakuti, Hakamaii, Hakamoui, Hakatao, Hohoi and Anahoa.

The first stone church built in the Marquesas was constructed in Hakahau in 1859, and in Haakuti and Hakahetau villages there are small Catholic churches built on top of old *paepae* platforms. The main village of **Hakahau** has a dispensary, *gendarmerie*, bank, post office, food stores, boutiques, Air Tahiti office, port facilities, schools, small family pensions, plus a few simple restaurants and bars.

Ua Pou has experienced a cultural revival within the past several years. **Paepae Teavatuu** is a restored meeting platform in Hakahau, where traditional reenactments are held. The Marquesas Festival of Arts was held in Ua Pou in Dec. 2007. **Rataro** is a talented young singer from Ua Pou, who has become very popular throughout the Polynesian triangle and beyond. Videotapes and musical cassettes featuring his all-male performers are fast selling items throughout the islands. The **Kanahau Trio** is another popular singing group from Ua Pou.

The sculptors sell their wood or stone carvings from their homes and in the handcraft centers in the villages. Horseback or 4x4 vehicle excursions can be arranged to visit the **Valley of the Kings** at Hakamoui, archaeological sites in the interior valleys, to picnic on the white sand beach of Anahoa or to discover the flower stones (*phonolitis*) of Hoho'i, with their multi-colored drawings. Boats with pilot can be chartered for offshore fishing or to visit **Motu Ua**, a bird sanctuary on the south coast.

ARRIVALS & DEPARTURES

Arriving By Air

Air Tahiti, *Tel. 86.42.42* in Tahiti and *Tel. 91.52.25* in Ua Pou, has daily ATR flights from Tahiti to the Marquesas Islands of Nuku Hiva and Hiva Oa. A 19-passenger Twin Otter provides direct air connections from Nuku Hiva to Ua Pou daily except Mon., when the flight stops in Ua Huka. There are flights from Hiva Oa to Ua Pou Mon., Tues., Thurs. and Fri. From Ua Huka to Ua Pou there are direct flights on Mon. and Tues., and 1-stop flights on Wed, Fri. and Sun. One-way airfare from Tahiti to Ua Pou is 35.530 CFP; the one-way fare from Hiva Oa to Ua Pou is 9.730 CFP; the one-way fare from Nuku Hiva to Ua Pou is 8.130 CFP; and from Ua Huka to Ua Pou the cost is also 8.130 CFP.

If you have reservations with a pension then you will be met at Ua Pou's Aneou airport and driven to your lodging. Otherwise, you can get a taxi or hitch a ride. It's a 45-minute trip between the airport and Hakahau.

Tahiti Helicopters will open an office in Nuku Hiva in 2012.

Arriving By Boat

The *Aranui* includes stops at Hakahetau and Hakahau during its 14-day round-trip cruise program from Tahiti to the Marquesas. See details in section on *Inter-Island Cruise Ships and Cargo/Passenger Boats* in Chapter 6, *Planning Your Trip*.

Youri Bidal, *Tel. 92.50.29/78.70.05*, has a boat that makes transfers between Nuku Hiva and Ua Pou. **Antoine Tata**, *Tel. 92.54.41*, can also transport passengers in his boat.

Other motorboats can be rented in Nuku Hiva for trips to Ua Pou. See details in *Nuku Hiva* section.

Departing By Air

The **Air Tahiti** office in Ua Pou is next door to the post office in Hakahau, *Tel. 91.52.25/92.51.08*. There are 1-2 daily direct or 1-stop flights by Twin Otter from Ua Pou to Nuku Hiva to connect with the departure schedule of the ATR flights to Tahiti. Every day except Wed. and Sun. you can fly the Twin Otter from Ua Pou to Atuona, Hiva Oa, which may have 1 stop before reaching Atuona. There are direct flights from Ua Pou to Ua Huka on Mon. and Tues.; on Wed., Fri. and Sun. a stop is made in Nuku Hiva on the way to Ua Huka.

Departing By Boat

See information on the *Aranui* and in Chapter 6, *Planning Your Trip* (section on Inter-Island Cruise Ships and Passenger Boats). It is also possible to make arrangements with the numerous speedboats and *bonitiers* that frequently make the crossing from Ua Pou to Nuku Hiva.

ORIENTATION

The **Aneou airport** is located between Hakahetau and Hakahau, 30 min. from the main village. **Hakahau** is spread along the Bay of Hakahau and continues inland for several blocks. Sailboats drop anchor in the bay, adjacent to a concrete dock for inter-island ships. The "pillars" rise above the seaside cliffs, and are often covered by clouds. A paved road leads from the boat dock throughout the village, and it is also an easy walk from the dock to the village center, where you will find *magasins*, a few snack bars, a museum and the Catholic Church in the south end of the village.

A 22-km. (14-mi.) road from Hakahau to the airport and **Hakahetau** continues on to the tiny valley of **Haakuti** on the southwest side of the island, with a track from there to the village of **Hakamaii**, which is more accessible by boat. The road from Hakahau to the south leads to the villages of **Hakamoui**, **Haakau** and **Hoho'i**. A track leads from this road to **Pa'aumea**, but all the villages along this southeast coast are better reached by boat. The white sand beach of **Anahoa** is a 25-min. walk east of Hakahau. This is also a nice ride on horseback, where you have panoramic views of the volcanic mountains and Hakahau Bay. Look for the Restaurant Pukue'e sign, which also gives directions to Anahoa Beach.

GETTING AROUND UA POU
Taxi & Transport Service
    Gilbert Kautai, *Tel. 92.51.80*, and **Jules Hituputoka**, *Tel. 92.53.33*, provide taxi service in Hakahau village, and **Bertrand Ah-Lo**, *Tel. 92.51.97*, has a taxi in Hakahetau. **Noel Tata**, Tel. 92.52.29/31.88.13, also has a taxi.

WHERE TO STAY
Hakahau – Moderate
    PENSION PUKUE'E, *B.P. 31, Hakahau, Ua Pou 98745, Marquesas Islands. Tel./Fax. 689/92.50.83; cell 72.90.08; pukuee@mail.pf; http://chez.mana.pf/-pukuee. Overlooking Hakahau Bay, 12 km. (7.5 mi.) from the airport and 300 m. (984 ft.) from the boat dock. No credit cards.*

    For many years this pension was known as Chez Hélène et Doudou for owner Hélène Kautai and her French husband. Now their daughter Elisa Kautai and her French husband Jérôme Burns are in charge.

    The big 4-bedroom room house sits on a hill overlooking the boat harbor, with a good view of the sugar-loaf mountains of Ua Pou. Rooms have 1-2 single beds or a double bed. Guests share the 2 bathrooms with hot water. A very spacious terrace is also used as a dining area for the restaurant. Meals feature French cuisine and local products with a French flavor. Guests have often included government officials from Tahiti who are visiting the Marquesas as part of their duties as *fonctionnaires*. Round-trip transfers between airport and pension 4.000 CFP per person. Room and MAP are 6.200 CFP per person and AP with all meals is 8.700 CFP. WiFi is free and laundry is 1.000 CFP. Guests can also enjoy the spring water swimming pool or sign up for a guided excursion by 4WD for 10.000 CFP per car. Your hosts will introduce you to the best artisans and their products.

    CHEZ DORA, *Hakahau, Ua Pou 98745, Marquesas Islands. Tel. 689/ 92.53.69/72.90.57; Fax 689/92.53.99. 500 m. (1,640 ft.) from the quay of Hakahau and 10 km. (6.2 mi.) from the airport. No credit cards.*

    This is the home of Dora Teikiehupoko, who has a 2-story white house in the heights of Hakahau at the end of the village. One of the 3 rooms she rents to guests is large and comfortable and has a private bathroom with a hot water shower. The other two rooms are also rather large and the bath facilities are shared. A big covered terrace overlooks the bay. There are also 2 bungalows on the premises, each with a private bathroom and cold water shower. Dora has a reputation for preparing some of the best local style meals in town, which are served in the communal dining room. A room or bungalow with half-board (MAP) meals is 7.420 CFP and 9.540 CFP for a room and all meals. Airport transfers are extra and excursions by 4WD are 15.000 CFP per car.

PENSION VEHINE HOU, *B.P. 54, Hakahau, Ua Pou 98745, Marquesas Islands. Tel. 689/92.50.63/70.84.32; Fax 689/92.53.21; heato@mail.pf. Overlooking Hakahau Bay, 800 m. (2,624 ft.) from the quay of Hakahau and 13 km. (8 mi.) from the airport. MC, V.*

Tahiti Tourisme has awarded Pension Vehine Hou a 2-Tiare rating. This pension in the center of Hakahau village is also called Chez Claire, and is owned by Marie-Claire and Georges "Toti" Teikiehuupoko, who are both involved in the cultural activities in Ua Pou. She rents out 2 rooms in a big 2-story house and in 2 separate bungalows. The rooms contain a double bed and a single bed and guests share the living room, dining room, terrace and bathroom with hot water. The bungalows are equipped with a double bed and a private bathroom with hot water. Meals are served on the big covered terrace upstairs or you can eat in Snack Vehine on the ground floor, which Claire also manages. A magasin food store is across the street. A room or bungalow with MAP (2 meals a day) is 7.150 CFP per person, and for all meals it is 8.800 CFP per person. The round-trip airport transfers are 2.000 CFP per adult and 1.000 CFP per child. Excursions by 4WD can be organized for 15.000 CFP per car.

PENSION LEYDJ KENATA, *B.P. 105, Hakahau, Ua Pou 98745, Marquesas Islands. Tel. 689/92.53.19. On the hillside in Hakahetau village, overlooking the Bay of Hakahetau, 7 km. (4.3 mi.) from the airport. No credit cards.*

There are 2 big rooms, each with a double bed. Guests share a bathroom with hot water, plus the kitchen, dining room, living room and terrace. Tony Tereino, the owner, serves family style meals on the covered terrace of his big white house. A room with all meals is 7.420 CFP and round-trip airport transfers are 4.240 CFP for 1-4 people. He also organizes hikes, 4x4 excursions and horseback riding. Tony, who is a sculptor, has a contemporary museum on the premises, displaying paintings and sculptures as well as ancient objects.

HAKAMOUI PLAGE, *Hakahau, Ua Pou 98745, Marquesas Islands. Tel./Fax 689/92.53.28/70.67.94/30.30.71. Beside the sea in Hakamoui. No credit cards.*

Daniel Hapipi opened 4 new bungalows in July 2011 just a few steps from the beach in Hakamoui. Each unit has twin or double beds, mosquito nets, fans, a private bathroom with hot water, and a terrace. His restaurant is open every day for all meals and you can choose a half-board or full-board meal plan. The King's Valley is located just 5 km. (2.5 miles) from the main village, which you can visit on foot or by 4x4 vehicle. Daniel provides free transfers to Hakahau.

WHERE TO EAT

SNACK VAITIARE, *Tel. 92.50.95.* No credit cards. This snack serves good food.

SNACK VEHINE, *Tel. 92.53.21.* This is part of Pension Vehine Hou and is in the center of Hakahau village. The cuisine is Marquesan, Chinese and French. M, V.

CHEZ TI'PIE.RO, *Tel. 92.55.82/20.17.59.* Open Wed.-Sun. at noon. Lunch and dinner served on reservation. No credit cards.

Rose and Pierrot operate this family style restaurant in Hakahetau Valley, serving international cuisine with a Marquesan spirit.

SEEING THE SIGHTS

Saint Etienne Catholic Church in Hakahau village is on the site where the first church in the Marquesas Islands was built in 1859. The carvings inside this stone and wood church include a pulpit of *tou* wood that represents the prow of a boat with a fishnet filled with fish. Adam and Eve and the serpent in the Garden of Eden and other Biblical designs are also presented. The statue of Christ rests his feet on the head of a tiki and the Virgin Mary and Christ child have Polynesian faces. Alfred Hatuuku, who lives in Hakahau, created these exquisite carvings.

Excursions by horseback or 4WD vehicle will take you to visit the white sand beach of **Anahoa** and the flower stones of **Hohoi**. These amber colored stones are pieces of volcanic *phonolite* that make a pinging noise when struck. They were formerly used to make carving tools and as weapons. Recent studies show that these *phonolites* are 2.9 million years old and the light colored basalt, which is very rich in black minerals, is different from that found in other places. In the vicinity of Hakahetau and Hakamaii a very unusual basaltic stone was dated as 4 million years old. Archaeological sites in the **Valley of the Kings** in Hakamoui and Hakaohoka valley include *paepae* platforms, *tohua* ceremonial plazas, *me'ae* temples and tikis.

Above the village of **Haakuti** a small Catholic Church is built on a high *paepae* stone terrace. **Hakahetau** also has an interesting Catholic Church with a red tower. Hakanai Bay, 11 km. (7 mi.) from Hakahau, below the track leading to Hakahetau, is a good picnic spot. This cove is also called Shark Beach.

Te Menaha Taka'oa is the site of what was once a holy temple, dedicated to Te Atua Heato, one of the Polynesian gods worshipped by the ancient Marquesans. The German ethnologist Karl von den Steinen visited this sacred site in the 1800s, when it was still *tapu* (forbidden). Georges Toti Teikiehuupoko, *Tel. 92.53.21*, can guide you there.

SPORTS & RECREATION

Horseback Riding

Tony Tereino in Hakahetau, *Tel. 92.53.19,* can arrange horseback rides on request. A half-day ride costs 6.000 CFP and an all-day ride is 10.000 CFP, with a picnic on request.

Cultural, Hiking & Eco Tours

Georges "Toti" Teikiehuupoko, *Tel. 92.50.63/92.53.21,* speaks good English and enjoys sharing his knowledge of Marquesan culture and history. He is a schoolteacher and president of Motu Haka, the Society for the Preservation of Marquesan Culture, and he is also director of l'Académie Marquisienne. Toti is an excellent contact for information on local sites, history and archaeology. His wife, Claire, who runs Pension Vehine and Snack Vehine, is also leader of a Marquesan dance group in Hakahau.

Oatea is an Eco-Tourism agency created by Pascal Erhel Hatuuku in 2001 that specializes in cultural hikes and "green" excursions with a team of Marquesan guides whom Pascal helped train, complete with English lessons. The Marquesan guides will lead you on walking trails from Hakahau to the Vaiea waterfall, or from Hakahetau to Hakahau, over the mountains and through the woods, along the seashore and beach of Hakanai, following a cleared path that takes you to the Pokoio pass and through the Keaoa valley, where you will be tempted to climb the Poumaka peak for a breathtaking panoramic view of the island and sea. This 4-hr. walk is relatively easy for most people, but you can also go by 4WD if you prefer. Check with the Comité de Tourisme in Hakahau, *Tel. 92.53.86,* for more information on who is now leading these hikes.

Ua Pou Evasion, *Tel. 92.53.19,* is operated by Tony Tereino, who will guide you on half- or full-day walks to discover the flora and fauna, archaeology and history of the island. A half-day walk is 2.000 CFP per person and a full-day's outing is 3.000 CFP. Tony doesn't speak much English.

Ua Pou Rando, *Tel./Fax 92.50.83/72.90.08; pukuee@mail.pf.* Frenchman Jérôme Burns of Pension Pukue'e speaks English and leads discovery expeditions by 4x4 or on foot. The Hakahau-Hakahetau trail takes you across the mountains in a 2 hr. 15 min. walk. The Poumaka trek is a loop in the valley of Hakahetau up to the Poumaka peak and then a walk to the waterfall. Other treks can be organized on request, including bivouacs, or 4x4 car excursions with a picnic or lunch prepared by Marquesan families in the remote villages.

Motor Boat Rental & Fishing Excursions

The following locally built speedboats are available for inter-island transfers between Ua Pou and Taiohae or the Nuku Ataha airport on Nuku Hiva, for excursions around the island, and for fishing trips.

Oceane is a 24-ft. Fiberglas boat owned by Antoine Tata, *Tel. 92.54.87* that he uses for fishing expeditions and other charters.

Kukupa is a 24-ft. 8-passenger Fiberglas boat owned by Rudla Klima, *Tel. 92.53.86; Fax 92.53.37,* that is available for deep-sea fishing and boating excursions or transfers.

Tahia O Te Tai is a 24-ft. 8-passenger Fiberglas boat owned by François Keuvahana, *Tel./Fax 92.53.31* that can be chartered for fishing and guided excursions.

SHOPPING

Tehina Boutique in Hakahau sells curios, local clothing and perfumes. There is an arts and crafts center near the boat dock in Hakahau. Some 2 dozen wood or stone sculptors live on the island of Ua Pou, and you can visit their workshops beside their homes. One of the finest sculptors is Alfred Hatuuku, *Tel. 92.52.39,* who carved the pulpit in the Catholic Church. He lives between the seafront and Snack Vehine.

In Hakahau village **William Aka,** *Tel. 92.53.90,* makes and sells jewelry, small tikis, lizards and miniature saddles of semi-precious woods. Artisans in Hakahetau village include **Marcel Kautai,** *Tel. 92.52.37,* **Beo Makario,** *Tel. 92.52.54;* **Tony Tereino,** *Tel. 92.53.19;* Jacques **Kaiha,** *Tel. 92.50.31;* in Hakamaii village **Eloi Hikutini,** *Tel. 92.52.53,* carves wood sculptures and **Kina Vaiauri,** *Tel. 92.50.32,* does tattoos.

PRACTICAL INFORMATION
Bank
Banque Socredo, *Tel. 92.53.63,* is located in the same building as the Hakahau Mairie. The bank is open Mon.-Thurs. from 7am-3pm, and on Fri. from 7am-2pm. There is an ATM window outside the bank.

Hospital
A government operated dispensary with a medical team and dentist is located in Hakahau, *Tel. 92.53.75,* and every village has an infirmary.

Information Centers
The **Ua Pou Tourism Committee** is presided by Tina Klima, *Tel. 92.53.86;* She is also in charge of Air Tahiti in Ua Pou; *Tel. 91.52.25/70.63.13; escale.uap@mail.pf.*

Police
There is a French *gendarmerie* in Hakahau, *Tel. 91.53.05.*

Post Office & Telecommunications Office
The post office is in Hakahau. All telecommunications and postal services are available here. Phonecard telephone booths are located beside the post office, on the quay and opposite the Air Tahiti office. There is a ManaSpot WiFi service here.

UA HUKA
Welcome to **Ua Huka,** Marquesan cowboy country by the sea. On the southern coast untamed horses gallop freely in the wind on the tablelands. Herds of cows and goats graze in the ferns, wild cotton and scrub brush that grow in the desert-like topography on a vast plateau. Above this incredible and beautiful scene rises Mount Hitikau, the highest mountain at 855 m. (2,804 ft.). Breathtaking

panoramas of the rugged coast and the sparkling sea greet the eye at every turn on the narrow winding mountain road that connects Vaipae'e, Hane and Hokatu, the 3 valleys where the 592 inhabitants live. Ua Huka lies 35 km. (22 mi.) east of Nuku Hiva, and 56 km. (35 mi.) northeast of Ua Pou. It is the smallest of the inhabited islands in the northern Marquesas group, with just 81 sq. km. (31 sq. mi.) of land. This crescent-shaped island is 8 km. (5 mi.) long and 14 km. (8.7 mi.) wide.

Ua Huka is one of the most interesting of all the Polynesian islands. The fern-covered valleys conceal *tohua* ceremonial plazas, *me'ae* stone temples and *tokai* burial platforms for women who died while pregnant or giving birth. Among the ruins from the 7 tribes who formerly inhabited the island are petroglyphs that can be seen at the archeological site of Vaikiki valley. From Auberge Hitikau (Chez Fournier) in Hane you can hike uphill for 30 min. or so to **Me'ae Meiaiaute**, a restored temple terrace where you will see 3 *tiki* that are sculpted from slabs of red tuff. A 4th *tiki* is a smaller version of the Maki'i Tau'a Pepe statue found in Puamau Valley on Hiva Oa, only this one in Ua Huka has been beheaded. (Read *Manuiota'a*, a book that was written by **Dr. Robert C. Suggs** and **Burgle Lichtenstein**, for more information on this subject).

In 1964 and 1965, **Dr. Yosihiko H. Sinoto**, Senior Anthropologist at the Bishop Museum in Honolulu, excavated a coastal village in Hane that was buried under sand dunes 2 m. (6.6 ft.) high. Among his findings were 2 fragments of pottery, dating from around 380 AD, which Dr. Sinoto said is the oldest site yet discovered by anyone in Eastern Polynesia, and an important link between Western and Eastern Polynesia. Other renowned archaeologists believe that the Marquesas were settled between 500-200 BC. When Dr. Suggs excavated the Ha'atuatua site in Nuku Hiva between 1956-58, he discovered the first pieces of pottery ever found in Eastern Polynesia. The radiocarbon technique dated these shards at 125 BC.

An archaeological site named Manihina is located on a sandy beach not far from the arboretum in Ua Huka. Dr. Sinoto first noticed this site in 1964 when he was excavating the sand dune in Hane. In 1991 the mayor of Ua Huka wanted to take sand from the beach to use in construction. Before doing so he notified the department of archaeology at the Centre Polynésien des Sciences Humaines (CPSH) in Tahiti. Their research in 3 stages uncovered a burial site at Manihina that contained 39 human skeletons of both sexes, along with skeletons of 2 dogs and 11 pigs. Studies date this site between 1000 and 1400 AD. Although these were robust people in general, some of the human skeletons revealed that the old folks suffered from rheumatism and one of them had leprosy.

Captain Joseph Ingraham, of the American trading ship *Hope*, sailed by Ua Huka in 1791. The northern Marquesas islands were then visited in quick succession by Captain Marchand of the French ship *La Solide*; Lieutenant Hergest aboard the *Doedalus*, who surveyed the islands, and by Captain Josiah Roberts of the American ship *Jefferson* in 1793. Ua Huka was spared most of the carnage wreaked on the other Marquesas Islands by European discoverers, whalers and sandalwood seekers. During this period of discovery Ua Huka was named Ile Solide, Washington Island, Massachusetts, Ouahouka, Riou, Roahouga and Rooahooga.

Accommodations for tourists are available in the villages of Vaipae'e, Hane and Hokatu. These lodgings are located in separate houses and small bungalows, or in family homes or pensions.

ARRIVALS & DEPARTURES
Arriving By Air
Air Tahiti, *Tel. 86.42.42*, has daily ATR 42 flights from Tahiti to the Marquesas Islands of Nuku Hiva and Atuona. From Nuku Hiva you can connect directly to Ua Huka each Mon., Wed., Fri. and Sun., and a Tues. flight stops in Atuona. From Hiva Oa there are flights to Ua Huka on Mon., Tues. Wed., and Sun., either direct or with 1 stop. There are direct flights between Ua Pou and Ua Huka on Mon. and Tues., and 1-stop flights on Wed., Fri. and Sun. One-way airfare from Tahiti to Ua Huka is 35.530 CFP; the one-way fare from Nuku Hiva to Ua Huka is 8.130 CFP; the one-way fare from Atuona to Ua Huka is 9.730 CFP, and from Ua Pou to Ua Huka the cost is 8.130 CFP. If you have reservations with a pension then you will be met at the Ua Huka airport and driven to your lodging.

Arriving By Boat
The **Aranui 3** includes stops at Vaipae'e and Hane in its 14-day round-trip cruise program from Tahiti to the Marquesas. See details in the section on Inter-Island Cruise Ships and Cargo/Passenger Boats in Chapter 6, *Planning Your Trip.* Motorboats can be rented in Nuku Hiva for trips to Ua Huka. See details in Nuku Hiva section.

Departing By Air
Air Tahiti reservations in Ua Huka is *Tel. 92.60.44.* The Twin Otter flight leaves Ua Huka daily except Thurs. and Sat., connecting in Nuku Hiva for a direct flight to Tahiti on board the ATR plane. There are direct flights from Ua Huka to Atuona each Tues., Wed. and Sun., and flights with 1 stop on Mon. and Fri. Direct flights from Ua Huka to Ua Pou operate on Mon. and Tues., and the Wed., Fri., and Sun. flights to Ua Pou all go to Nuku Hiva first.

Departing By Boat
See information on the **Aranui 3** in Chapter 6, *Planning Your Trip,* section on Inter-Island Cruise Ships and Passenger Boats. Motorboats can be rented in Ua Huka to visit Nuku Hiva. Please see information in this chapter under Motor Boat Rentals.

ORIENTATION

Ua Huka's 3 villages of **Vaipae'e**, **Hane** and **Hokatu** are connected by a concrete road that winds along the edge of the cliffs for 14 km. (8.7 mi.). 4WD vehicles and horses are the means of transportation. The surf crashes against the steeply rising rocks of the coastline, creating a continuous spray that splashes high into the sky, reflecting the sun in multiple shades of blue. After a rain the hills and plains glimmer in varying shades of green, but the plateaus become brown and desolate during the arid seasons.

If you arrive by ship you will probably disembark in **Vaipae'e Bay**, also called Invisible Bay, because a wall of basaltic rock protects the bay from the open sea. Landings are made by small boat onto a concrete pier. Vaipae'e is the largest village on Ua Huka, with the *Mairie*, post office and the Vaipae'e Archaeological Museum of Marquesan artifacts all in the same complex. The Catholic Church in Vaipae'e is worth a stop to see the artwork in the windows. The 6 panels of stained glass include illustrations of the Immaculate Conception that feature a Marquesan Mary against a background of the Invisible Bay. She is complete with tattoos and a ukulele, while the panels are bordered by figures from the petroglyphs found in the valleys.

The Nukumoo airport is located between Vaipae'e and Hane villages and the arboretum is close to the small airstrip. **Hane Bay** is distinguished by Motu Hane that sits just offshore facing the pretty little village. This is a dark violet and red rock 152 m. (508 ft.) high, shaped like a sugar loaf. A structure of stones on top of this huge rock looks like a giant tiki has been carved there. In Hane there is a post office, an infirmary, schools and churches. Small *magasins* offer limited food supplies in Vaipae'e, Hane and Hokatu. Handcrafts centers and wood carvers' shops are found in each village.

The coast off Haavei is rich in sea life, filled with sharks, dolphins, manta ray, big turtles, lobster and a variety of fish. Boats with captains can be rented for deep-sea fishing and excursions to Anaa Atua grotto and the islets of Teuaua and Tiotio. On these bird islands thousands of white and sooty terns (*kaveka*), red-footed booby birds, blue noddy birds, frigates, tropic birds, petrels and shearwaters lay their eggs. They screech and squawk as they feed on the abundance of fish in this area, while their fluffy white fledglings sit on the hard ground of the upraised *motu* islets, waiting for dinner to be served.

WHERE TO STAY
Moderate
MANA TUPUNA VILLAGE, *Vaipae'e, Ua Huka 98744, Marquesas Islands. Tel. 689/92.60.08, Tel./Fax 689/92.61.01; manatupuna@mail.pf. In Vaipae'e valley, 5.5 km. (3.4 mi.) from the airport and 2 km. (1.2 mi.) from the Vaipae'e boat landing. No credit cards.*

Karen Taiaapu-Fournier is your hostess at Mana Tupuna Village, and she speaks good English and Spanish. 3 small wooden A-frame bungalows on stilts overlook Vaipae'e valley, where you can see goats and horses roaming freely and feeding on wild grass. Each of these *ha'e* contains a double bed and a single bed, a private bathroom with hot water, and a covered terrace. The furniture is made of bamboo and the posts on the terrace are sculpted coconut trunks from Ua Huka. Local style meals are served. A bungalow with MAP is 9.000 CFP sgl./17.000 CFP dbl. AP rates available. Round-trip transfers are 3.000 CFP.

LE REVE MARQUISIEN, *Vaipae'e, Ua Huka 98744, Marquesas Islands. Tel./Fax 689/92.61.84; Cell 689/79.10.52/71.52.95; revemarquisien@mail.pf. In Pahataua valley, 800 m. (2,624 ft.) from Vaipae'e village, 5 km. (3.1 mi.) from the airport and 1.5 km. (0.93 mi.) from the boat dock. Free transfers. No credit cards.*

Marie-France and Charles Aunoa have won a 2-Tiare rating for their 4 bungalows in the middle of a bird sanctuary. Each unit has a double bed, electric fan, mosquito net, terrace, and private bathroom with hot water. A sofa bed can be added for a third person and house linens are furnished. Guests can watch television or DVD films in a communal room and enjoy their gourmet meals of Marquesan, Tahitian, Chinese and French cuisine served in the restaurant. The room rates are 9.500 CFP sgl./11.500 CFP dbl. per day. Add 1.000 CFP per person for breakfast and 3.000 CFP each for lunch or dinner. They rent a 4x4 car with driver for 6.825 CFP per day, and they will organize sports activities, deep-sea fishing and walking excursions.

AUBERGE HITIKAU, *Hane, Ua Huka 98744, Marquesas Islands. Tel./Fax 689/92.61.74. In Hane village, 7 km. (4.3 mi.) from the airport and 11 km. (7 mi.) from the Vaipae'e boat landing. No credit cards.*

Céline Fournier and her family operate the Hitikau restaurant and bar, which is in the same big concrete house where the 3 simple bedrooms are located. The *Aranui* passengers have a luncheon buffet here whenever the ship is in port at Vaipae'e. Other groups also enjoy the feasts prepared by the Fourniers, and the in-house guests share the 6 toilets, 1 lavabo and a cold water shower with all restaurant guests. There is a big terrace in front that serves as the dining room for everyone who comes to eat the local style cuisine. A room with breakfast and lunch is 3.286 CFP per person and 5.936 CFP with all meals. Round-trip transfers are 2.000 CFP.

Economy

CHEZ ALEXIS, *Vaipae'e, Ua Huka 98744, Marquesas Islands. Tel./Fax 689/ 92.60.19; 76.56.84/79.09.48; scallamera.florentine@mail.pf. In Vaipae'e valley, 5.5 km. (3.4 mi.) from the airport and 2 km. (1.2 mi.) from the Vaipae'e boat landing. No credit cards.*

This is a concrete house with 3 rooms and a bungalow for rent beside the main road in Vaipae'e village. Look for the sign on the right. Each room contains a double bed and a single bed. One room has a/c. The living room with TV, the large kitchen, terrace and 2 bathrooms with hot water are shared. A standard room is 2.000 CFP per person and the a/c bungalow is 4.000 CFP. Breakfast is 1.200 CFP, lunch or dinner is 2.700 CFP. Round-trip transfers 2.000 CFP per person. You can rent a 4x4 vehicle with a driver for 8.000 CFP per day. Add VAT to all rates. Your host Alexis Scallamera will organize hikes for you on request.

CHEZ MAURICE & DELPHINE, *Hokatu, Ua Huka 98744, Marquesas Islands. Tel./Fax. 689/92.60.55. In Hokatu valley, 7 km. (4.4 mi.) from the airport, 13 km. (8 mi.) from the boat landing of Vaipae'e and 2 km. (1.2 mi.) from Hane village. No credit cards.*

At the entry to Hokatu village the Rootuehine home is the first house on the left. They have 3 hillside bungalows for rent overlooking the sea and Mount Hane. They are furnished with beds for 2-4 people, plus a fan, mosquito nets, safe, refrigerator, private bathroom with hot water, and a terrace. They also have facilities for disabled guests. A bungalow with MAP (half-board) is 5.700 CFP per person. Meals are served in the Rootuehine home in the village.

Round-trip transfers between airport and pension are 2.000 CFP per person. A 4WD vehicle is available for rent with driver and a small self-drive car rents for 10.000 CFP a day if you are not staying in this pension. Delphine speaks English and Maurice handles the land excursions and boat trips, which include a picnic.

CHEZ CHRISTELLE, *Vaipae'e, Ua Huka 98744, Marquesas Islands. Tel. 689/92.60.04/70.88.80; Fax 689/91.60.17. In Vaipae'e valley, 7 km. (4.4 mi.) from the airport and 2 km. (1.2 mi.) from the boat landing. It's the 7th house on the left from the bridge, 5 m. (16 ft.) after Chez Alexis. No credit cards.*

Christelle Fournier has a 4-bedroom concrete house with a double bed in each room. Guests share the living room, equipped kitchen, dining room, 2 bathrooms with cold-water shower, and terrace. There is also a large garden here. Round-trip transfers 2.000 CFP per person. A room is 2.000 CFP sgl./4.000 CFP dbl. and 1.000 CFP for a child under 12 years. Breakfast is 700 CFP, lunch or dinner is 2.000 CFP each. House can also be rented by the month. Add taxes. You can rent a 4WD vehicle with or without driver for 10.000 CFP per day, and take a boat trip to visit Bird Island for 3.000 CFP per person.

WHERE TO EAT

Whenever a ship arrives in Vaipae'e, the vendors sell fried fish, chicken legs, meats, banana fritters and sandwiches at the boat landing. Anne-Marie's snack at the Arboretum sells short-order food and soft drinks, and prepared food is also available from the *roulottes*, which may be a pick-up truck.

AUBERGE HITIKAU, *Hane village, Tel. 92.61.74. Advance reservations are needed for all meals. No credit cards.*

Breakfast is 700 CFP, and lunch and dinner are each 2.500 CFP. Feasts are prepared for groups, such as the *Aranui* passengers. These buffets may include kaveka (sooty tern) omelets, hard boiled kaveka eggs, goat cooked in coconut milk, *poisson cru*, sashimi, roast pig, goat and fish cooked in an underground oven, plus rice, *fei*, *uru*, banana *po'e*, cake and fresh fruit.

All the family pensions serve meals to their guests as well as to anyone else who reserves in advance.

SEEING THE SIGHTS

Papuakeikaha Arboretum, between Vaipae'e and Hane, *Tel./Fax 92.61.51*, is a botanical and plant nursery with more than 400 species of flora, including 144 varieties of citrus plants. Leon Lichtle, the former mayor of Ua Huka, started this nursery in the early 1970s. The gardens comprise 57 acres (23 ha.) and contain every kind of plant and flower you can think of that grows in this climate. There are huge trees of *miro* (rosewood), *tou*, bamboo, banyan, *uru*, teak, *puatea*, *pakai*, *cerrettes*, *tutui*, allspice, acacia, mangoes, mountain apples, custard apples, star apples, carambola and guava. You'll find several species of bananas and plantains, pomegranates, coffee, cacao, vanilla, hot peppers, hibiscus, auti and jasmine. Plus there are many bushes of Tiare Tahiti and Tiare Moorea. This is a refreshing stop in the shade of the lovely trees, as well as a very interesting and informative botanical lesson. The arboretum is open to the public from 8am-3pm Mon.-Fri. There is no admission charge.

Vaipae'e Archaeological Museum is adjacent to the Mairie or town hall of Vaipae'e on the left of the main road from the boat landing, *Tel. 91.60.25*. At the entryway is a small sandalwood tree, one of only a few that you will see in the Marquesas Islands. The small museum is filled with old photographs and ancient Marquesan artifacts, including replicas of a chief's burial grotto and a Marquesan stove. A collection of reproductions of ancient sailing canoes and outrigger canoes represents all the Polynesian archipelagoes. A contest is held each year at the end of June, when the sculptors carve reproductions of old Marquesan artifacts. The winner of this competition has the pleasure of seeing his creation sent off to Tahiti to be displayed in the Museum of Tahiti and Her Islands. Master sculptor Joseph Vaatete takes care of the museum in Vaipae'e, which is open Mon.-Fri. from 8am-3pm.

Hane Maritime Museum, *Tel. 91.60.25*, is managed by Joseph Vaatete, and is located beside the sea in Hane village. This small museum contains an old anchor, fishnets, ancient fishhooks, reproductions of outrigger canoes, and drawings of the Polynesian triangle, retracing the route of the first Polynesian sailors who settled the South Pacific islands. An arts and crafts center shares the building with the Musée de la Mer.

Hokatu Geological Museum, *Tel./Fax 92.60.55*, is managed by Maurice Rootuehine, and is open Mon.-Fri., 8am-3pm.

Museum of Wood "Jardin", *Tel. 91.60.25*, is another project realized by Léon Lichtle, the former mayor of Ua Huka, who planted the first seeds in the botanical nursery in the 1970s. This museum is in the magnificent setting of the Arboretum and pays homage to trees. Contact Joseph Vaatete if you want to visit, as it is open on request.

Hokatu Stone Museum, *Tel. 92.60.55*, is also managed by Joseph Vaatete and open on request. Here you will see a display of petroglyphs carved into basaltic stone.

Land Excursions

Land tours will take you to visit the 3 villages, the archaeological sites, arboretum, museums and the arts and crafts shops. To arrange for an excursion by 4x4 vehicle you can ask at the pension where you're staying, or you can hire the following people: **Alexis Scallamera**, *Tel. 92.60.19*, **Denis Fournier**, *Tel. 92.60.62*; **Marie-Louise Fournier**, *Tel. 92.61.08*; **Maurice Rootuehine**, *Tel. 92.60.55*; **Benoît Teatiu**, *Tel. 92. 61.22*; and **Firmin Teikiteepupuni**, *Tel. 92.61.07*. In Hokatu valley arrangements can be made at *magasin* Maurice, *Tel. 92.60.55*, for land tours, horseback riding and boat rentals. Some of the cars and 4-wheel drive vehicles can be rented without a driver. The rates are 6.000 to 12.000 CFP per day, depending on where you are staying when you rent the vehicle.

SPORTS & RECREATION

Horseback Riding

Seeing Ua Huka on horseback is the way to go. The small Marquesan horses you see wandering around the desert-like plains are descendants from Chilean stock imported in 1856. You can ride bareback or astride wooden saddles softened by piling on copra sacks. The cost of horseback riding in Ua Huka is 5.000 CFP per day, plus 2.000-3.000 CFP for a guide.

Alexis Fournier in Vaipae'e, *Tel. 92.60.05/92.60.72/92.60.19/76.56.84; scallamera.florentine@mail.pf*. He rents riding horses for half- and full-day excursions. There are others who have horses but not the permit to rent them.

Motor Boat Rental

Offshore excursions can be made by speedboat to visit Ua Huka's unusual sites. Half-day excursions and all-day outings with picnics are also possible. Boats with captains can be rented for deep-sea fishing and excursions to **Anaa Atua** grotto and the bird islands of **Teuaua** and **Tiotio**.

Bird Island or **Teuaua Motu** is a steep rock 6 m. (20 ft.) high, 150 m. (492 ft.) long and 100 m. (328 ft.) wide, lying offshore Haavei valley. Attracted by the numerous fish in this area, millions of sooty terns lay their eggs on the open ground on top of this small island. You have to climb to the top by rope, which is very tricky and dangerous. The small eggs are white with black spots and the yolk is very orange. People gather these eggs by the bucket to boil or use in omelets.

The imprint of human footsteps can be seen in the sand at low tide in the **Anaa Atua** grotto and they disappear during high tide. Petroglyphs can be visited at the pretty beach of **Hatuana**. The **Pahonu beach** near the airport is a good place to swim and can be reached by boat.

Alexis Fournier, in Vaipae'e, *Tel. 92.60.55/92.60.72*, has a locally built 20-ft. fishing boat for 6 passengers. Excursions around Ua Huka include half-day outings to Bird Island and Anaa Atua grotto, with a picnic for 7.350 CFP. Full-day excursions around the island of Ua Huka also include a picnic. In Vaipae'e you can rent a boat from **Joseph Teatiu**, *Tel. 92.61.28*, and **Jean Fournier**, *Tel. 92.61.74*.

Maurice Rootuehine, in Hokatu, *Tel. 92.60.55*, has a locally built 25-ft. fishing boat for 7 passengers, which is available for inter-island round-trips between Ua Huka and Nuku Hiva, and excursions around Ua Huka.

SHOPPING

Arts and crafts centers are located in the villages of **Vaipae'e, Hane** and **Hokatu**. The prices here are less expensive than in the other islands. You can also visit the sculptors' workshops at their homes. There are a dozen wood sculptors living in Hane Village, 14 wood sculptors living in Hokatu, and up to a dozen wood sculptors living in Vaipae'e village.

You will also find artisans who carve stone and bones. **Joseph Vaatete**, *Tel. 92.60.74*, is one of the most noted sculptors in wood and stone, who makes pieces for the museums in Ua Huka. He lives in Hane village, a couple of blocks from the sea, on the left side of the road that goes up the valley. You can recognize his house by the tree trunks and pieces of wood and stone in his yard. Two of Joseph's statues are located at the International Airport of Tahiti-Faaa, and another carving is located at the *Mairie* of Papeete. Joseph also takes care of the Vaipae'e Archaeological Museum adjacent to the *Mairie* of Vaipae'e, the Hane Maritime Museum, the Museum of Wood and the Hokatu Stone Museum. **Daniel Naudin**, *Tel. 92.61.03/ 92.61.35*, the best-known sculptor in Ua Huka who carves bones, lives in Vaipae'e. He creates designs combining wood and bone, and he is also a tattoo artist.

Magasin stores are located in each village and are also open on Sundays.

PRACTICAL INFORMATION
Infirmary
A government-operated infirmary is located in the village of Hane, *Tel. 92.60.58*.

Post Office & Telecommunications Office
A Post Office is located in the main village of Vaipae'e, *Tel. 92.60.26*, and in Hane village, *Tel. 92.60.46*. All telecommunications and postal services are available here.

Tourist Information
You can get information from the Ua Huka Tourism Committee–Tupehe Nui. *Tel./Fax 92.60.19; Cell 79.09.48; scallamera.florentine@mail.pf.* Alexis Scallamera is the president. He also owns the pension Chez Alexis.

HIVA OA

According to some Marquesan legends, **Hiva Oa** was the first island in this archipelago settled by the Polynesians before they reached Nuku Hiva. Archaeological findings support this theory, based on a charcoal sample taken from a fireplace in a rock shelter at Anapua. This site was excavated in 1981 by Pierre

Ottino of the ORSTOM research center in Tahiti, and the charcoal dates 150+-95 years BC. This is one of the oldest dates thus uncovered reflecting the presence of human occupancy in Eastern Polynesia.

Hiva Oa is located 1,400 km. (868 mi.) northeast of Tahiti. It is one of the youngest islands in the Marquesas chain, and has been described as a seahorse whose head faces the setting sun. The island measures 40 km. (25 mi.) long east to west and averages 10 km. (6.2 mi.) north to south. Atuona sits in the center of 3 adjoining craters, and Temetiu, whose peak reaches into the clouds 1,190 m. (3,900 ft.), crowns the ridge of mountains above the picturesque bays. The steep slopes of high altitude interior plateaus dominate this large fertile island of 330 sq. km. (127 sq. mi.). The 2,310 inhabitants live in the villages of Atuona, Puamau, Hanaiapa, Hanapaaoa, Nahoe, Tahauku and Taaoa, which are separated into isolated valleys by the dorsal spine and ridges.

The French painter **Paul Gauguin** came to Hiva Oa in 1901 in search of a primitive culture and savage wildness, and here he died in 1903. He is buried in Calvary Cemetery on a hill behind Atuona village. Fragrant petals from a gnarled old frangipani tree shower down on the simple grave, and a statue of Oviri, "the savage" stands at the head of the tombstone.

In the village of Atuona you can visit the **Paul Gauguin Center,** a complex of 3 large buildings on the original site where Gauguin lived. This center was inaugurated on May 8, 2003, during the commemorative services to honor the 100th anniversary of Gauguin's death in Atuona. The Gauguin Museum has some 100 reproductions of the French artist's paintings made in Tahiti and Hiva Oa, as well as sculptures, drawings, photographs, letters and other souvenirs of Gauguin. The entry charge is 600 CFP for adults and 300 CFP for 12-18 year olds. A replica of Gauguin's house, which he named **La Maison du Jouir** (House of Pleasure), is built beside the well into which Gauguin used to keep his liquor bottles, and there is a bamboo pole hanging out the window upstairs, which represents the pole Gauguin used to fetch his bottles of liquor from the well. This dried pit was uncovered during construction of the complex, and was filled with broken bottles, old paintbrushes, teeth and other cast off items. An open-sided shelter was erected near the sea for visiting artists, a replica of Gauguin's *Atelier des Tropiques,* where the ocean breezes fanned him as he painted. These Gauguin copyists are lodged in 4 bungalows on the premises. Across the street from the Gauguin Center is the Magasin Gauguin, where he used to buy his supplies.

A few graves distant from Gauguin's tombstone in Calvary Cemetery is the final resting place of the famous Belgian singer **Jacques Brel,** who lived in Atuona from 1975 until his death in 1978. Many of Brel's European fans make a pilgrimage to his grave, which is always decorated with flowers. When Brel was buried his mistress, Maddly Bamy, placed a plaque on his tombstone that contained an engraving of the two devoted lovers. The **Jacques Brel Memorial** is a black marble stele set in a stone overlooking the Hanakee Pearl Lodge and Atuona Bay east of Atuona. Brel wanted to build his house on this hillside, but was unable to do so because of his illness. There are 2 tracks leading to the site, and it is best to get clear directions before setting off on foot.

Jacques Brel's Beechcraft airplane, Jo Jo, has been restored and is on display in the **Jacques Brel Space** adjacent to the Gauguin Center. The **Traditional Arts Museum** (entrance is 500 CFP for adults and 250 CFP for 12-18 year olds) and an arts and crafts center are found in the area facing the **Pepeu** *tohua* meeting ground, where the ceremonies and dances were held during the Marquesas Festival of Arts in December 2003.

Atuona is the administrative center for the southern Marquesas. Framed in a theater of mountains with the Tahauku Bay providing safe anchorage, Atuona is a favorite port of call for yachts and copra/cargo ships. Atuona village has a *gendarmerie*, infirmary, new post office, bank, weather station, Air Tahiti office, restaurants and snack bars, stores and shops. There is a Catholic mission with a boarding school and a Protestant church.

You can rent a car with or without a driver or you can join an excursion by 4WD and visit the bays of Nahoe and Hanamenu, the black sand beach of Taaoa and the lovely white sand beach of Hanatekua. Near the little village of Hanaiapa is a cascade that splashes down a 249-m. (800-ft.) high cliff into the surging sea, wetting the black rocks so they sparkle like vaults of mica. Petroglyphs carved on stone have been found in the valleys of Eiaone and Punaei, and many other archaeological sites exist all over the island of Hiva Oa.

Gauguin's descendants still live in the Puamau valley, 48 km. (30 mi.) from Atuona. The restored archaeological site of I'ipona is also located in this valley. In this religious sanctuary is a *me'ae* on 2 large terraces, with 5 huge stone tikis. The most famous stone tiki represents the god Takai'i. Carved from porous red rock, this statue is 2.35 m. (7.7 ft.) tall, and is the largest stone tiki in French Polynesia.

You can also go deep-sea fishing, explore woodcarvers' shops, ride along a black sand beach on a Marquesan horse or charter a boat for a trip to visit nearby islands, including **Motane**, the sheep island. Accommodations on Hiva Oa are found in a 4-star hotel overlooking the cobalt blue Pacific and in small family pensions near the villages.

ARRIVALS & DEPARTURES
Arriving By Air

Air Tahiti, *Tel. 86.42.42* in Tahiti, *Tel. 91.70.90* in Atuona, flies ATR turbo jet planes from Tahiti direct to Hiva Oa each Tues., Thurs. and Sun. Flights from Tahiti stop in Nuku Hiva on Mon., Wed., Fri., Sat., and Sun., with a change of aircraft on Wed. and Sat., before continuing on to Atuona. The Wed. flight also stops in Ua Huka. The one-way fare from Tahiti to Atuona is 33.130 CFP and the round-trip fare is 60.760 CFP. The fare from Ua Pou to Atuona is 9.730 CFP, flying by Twin Otter direct or with 1-2 stops daily except Wed. and Sun. You can also fly direct from Ua Huka to Atuona on Tues., Wed., and Sun., and with a stop in Nuku Hiva on Mon. and a stop in Ua Pou with a change of planes on Fri. The one-way fare is 9.730 CFP.

You can also get to Nuku Hiva by chartering an airplane in Tahiti from **Air Tahiti**, *Tel. 86.42.42*, or **Pol'Air**, *Tel. 74.23.11*.

Arriving By Boat

The **Aranui 3** includes stops at Atuona, Puamau, and Hanaiapa in Hiva Oa during its 14-day round-trip cruise program from Tahiti to the Marquesas. See details in section on *Inter-Island Cruise Ships and Cargo/Passenger Boats* in Chapter 6, *Planning Your Trip*. The communal boat from Tahuata makes round-trips to Atuona once or twice a week. See further information in this chapter.

Departing By Air

Air Tahiti reservations in Atuona, *Tel. 91.70.90*. You can take an ATR plane from Atuona direct to Tahiti each Mon., Fri., and Sun. There are flights on each day of the week, with 1-2 stops and sometimes a change of aircraft before you reach Tahiti.

Departing By Boat

The **Aranui 3** leaves Tahuata on a Sunday and goes to Ua Huka, then to Nuku Hiva and back to Tahiti.

Tahuata Nui is a 48.6-ft. long aluminum hull boat that can transport 60 passengers between Atuona and Tahuata. The boat leaves the quay of Atuona at 12pm each Mon. for Vaitahu, and each Fri. the boat leaves Atuona at 4pm for Vaitahu and Hapatoni. The one-way fare is 1.000 CFP. Reserve at the Mairie of Tahuata, *Tel. 689/92.92.19; Fax 689/92.92.10*.

Te Hinaonaiki, *Tel. 92.76.97*, is the 8-passenger boat of Médéric Kaimuko of Atuona. He provides inter-island transfers to Tahuata for 30.000 CFP for 8 passengers and to Fatu Hiva for 65.000 CFP for a maximum of 8 passengers.

Vaipuna O Hanamenu, *Tel. 92.76.57/70.71.97/78.82.98*, is a bonito boat that can transport up to 8 passengers to Tahuata or Fatu Hiva.

See information under *Boat Excursions & Deep Sea Fishing* in this chapter and *Departing by Boat* in chapter on *Tahuata*.

ORIENTATION

A road 17 km. long (10.5 ft.) is built on the **Tepuna Plateau**, 440 m. (1,443 ft.) above the sea, connecting the airport with **Atuona village**. The town is at the north end of Taaoa Bay, 3 km. (1.9 mi.) from **Tahauku Bay**, also known as Traitors' Bay, which provides a safe harbor for yachts and the inter-island cargo vessels that dock at the concrete pier.

Three paved roads pass through Atuona and it is easy to walk around the town center, where most of the businesses and administrative offices are concentrated, as well as the medical facilities, churches and Catholic schools.

GETTING AROUND HIVA OA

When you make reservations with a hotel or pension your hosts will meet you at the airport or boat dock on your arrival. You can also organize your excursions at the place where you're staying. The cost of transfers and land tours varies according to the lodgings, which are listed under *Where to Stay*.

Taxi Service

Ida Clark Taxi - Vaite Transport, *Tel. 92.71.33/72.34.73*. She charges 1.500 CFP per person for one-way transfers between the airport and Atuona village, and 1.000 CFP per car for a transfer from the ship dock to the village. A visit around Atuona village is 4.000 CFP and Ida (who speaks very little English) can also drive you to visit the valleys and sites around the island. She charges 8.000 CFP to visit the Taaoa valley and 20.000 CFP for a trip to Puamau.

Car Rentals

With advance reservations a car can be delivered to the airport for your arrival. The gas station is located at the cargo ship dock at Tahauku Bay. Make sure there is a stockage of fuel on hand before signing your contract.

Atuona Rent-A-Car, *Tel. 92.76.07, cell 72.17.17*, operated by Abel Rauzy, has self-drive 4WD vehicles. A Suzuki Jimmy is 7.000 CFP for a half-day and 13.000 CFP for all day. A double cabin Toyota is 9.000 CFP for a half-day and 16.500 CFP for a full day.

David Locations, *Tel. 92.72.87; kmk@mail.pf,* is owned by David Kaimuko, facing Magasin Naiki in Atuona. He rents a 4WD self-drive vehicle for 12.000 CFP per day. Reserve 2 days in advance.

Hiva Oa Location, *Tel. 92.70.43/24.65.05.* Liliane Heitaa or Sandra Tamarii will rent you a Suzuki 4x4 for 6.500 CFP for a half-day and 13.000 CFP for all day.

WHERE TO STAY

Superior

HANAKEE HIVA OA PEARL LODGE, *B.P. 80, Atuona, Hiva Oa 98741, Marquesas Islands. Tel. 689/92.75.87, Fax 689/92.75.95; hiva.oa.pearl@mail.pf. On hillside overlooking Tahauku Bay, 7 km. (4.4 mi.) from airport and 2 km. (1.2 mi.) from boat dock. 14 bungalows. All major credit cards.*

This 3-star hotel is built on the hillside overlooking Tahauku Bay, above the port for the inter-island ships. The 14 bungalows include 6 Mountain View, 5 Ocean View and 3 Premium Ocean View categories, priced from 26.000-31.500 CFP per bungalow. Each unit is 39 sq. m. (420 sq. ft.) large, and has a king size bed or twin beds, plus an extra bed. They all have a/c, ceiling fan, TV, a mini-bar, tea and coffee facilities, IDD telephone, safe, shower with hot water, hair dryer and a sundeck. Laundry service is available and you can get a babysitter on request. Two of the ocean view bungalows are equipped for handicapped guests in wheelchairs.

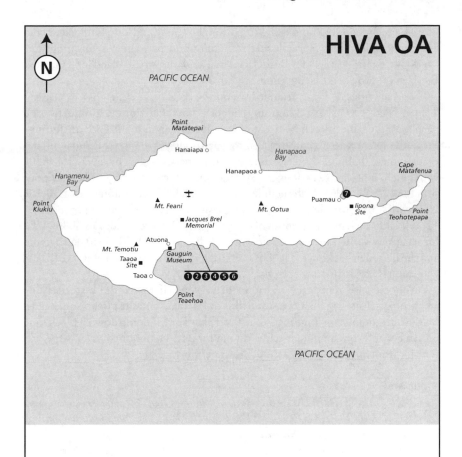

1. Hanakee Hiva Oa Pearl Lodge
2. Pension Kanahou
3. Temetiu Village
4. Relais Moehau
5. Pension Areke – Chez Kayser
6. Pension Ozanne
7. Pension Chez Marie-Antoinette

The main building houses the reception, boutique and a desk for excursions and car rentals. There is a gourmet restaurant and bar, and a swimming pool overlooks Traitors Bay, the Bordelais canal and the small island of Hanakee. Bicycles are provided free for guests.

The activities desk can arrange for your 4-wheel drive excursions to visit the Tehueto Petroglyphs for a 2-hr. tour that costs 4.500 CFP, or the smiling tiki and paepae for the same price. A 2 -hr. tour of Atuona village is 4.500 CFP, including the museum entry fee; a half-day tour to Taaoa valley is 4.500 CFP and a full day excursion is 10.500 CFP. You can also visit Hanaiapa valley by 4WD for 9.800 with lunch. Full-day excursions by 4x4 take you to Puamau valley and the Oipona sites for 12.500 CFP, which includes lunch at Chez Marie Antoinette or 10.700 CFP with a BBQ on the beach. You can visit the island of Tahuata by boat for 12.500 CFP each, for a minimum of 4 passengers. Horseback rides are 9.800 CFP for a half-day outing, and your choices include Punaei Creek, Tehueto petroglyphs and the Belvedere lookout of Jacques Brel's stele. A full-day ride is 16.500 CFP, and you can have a bivouac on horseback.

You can also rent a 4WD car to drive yourself to see the historical and archaeological sites, the famous stone tikis in Puamau, and the picturesque scenes of Marquesan horses swimming in the lovely bays or galloping down a black sand beach. See information under scuba diving for underwater discoveries. One-way transfer from airport by 4WD 2.200 CFP per person.

Moderate

PENSION KANAHAU, *B.P 101, Atuona, Hiva Oa 98741, Marquesas Islands. Tel. 689/91.71.31/70.16.26; Fax 689/91.71.32; pensionkanahau@mail.pf; www.pensionkanahau.com. No credit cards.*

Tahiti Tourisme has awarded this pension its highest rating of 3 Tiares. This 4-bungalow family pension owned by Tania Dubreuil opened in 2003 on the hillside of Atuona, overlooking Tahauku Bay, 9 km. (5.6 mi.) from the airport and 1 km. (0.62 mi.) from the boat dock. 2 of the wooden bungalows on stilts have a room with queen size bed with a mosquito net and the other 2 units have twin beds in the bedroom. Each unit also has a ceiling fan, a convertible sofa, a private bathroom with hot water, local TV, electric mosquito repellent, and a terrace overlooking the bay or the valley. A bungalow with breakfast is 10.727 CFP sgl./ 13.692 CFP dbl., for less than 4 nights. Add 3.416 CFP per person for dinner. Meals are served on a patio under a big shade tree with a marvelous view of the bay. The kitchen is also available for guests with children, and there is free laundry service. Round-trip transfers between the airport and pension are 3.416 CFP per person. Free transfers are provided to the village, including excursions to visit the points of interest in Atuona village, and the artisan workshops. Tania will also introduce you to the local cuisine, weaving, tapa making and Marquesas dancing. The Kanahau Restaurant is a popular hangout for people from the cruising yachts.

TEMETIU VILLAGE, *B.P. 52, Atuona, Hiva Oa 98741, Marquesas Islands. Tel. 689/91.70.60.70.72.07; Fax 689/91.70.61; heitaagabyfeli@mail.pf; www.temetiu.blogspot.com. On hillside in Atuona village overlooking Tahauku Bay. AE, MC, V.*

This welcoming family pension holds a 2-Tiare rating from Tahiti Tourisme. Six neat and clean bungalows have a beautiful view of Tahauku Bay. The 2 standard units contain a double bed or 2 single beds, and the 4 big bungalows have can sleep 3 people. All units have a private bathroom with hot water, a terrace, electric fan, TV, and electric anti-mosquito diffuser. The rooms are cleaned every 2 days and the towels are changed every day. There is a restaurant/bar and meals are served on the covered dining terrace overlooking the small swimming pool and the bay. There is also a communal living room with a TV, video and books, plus Internet access, and a small boutique of Marquesan arts and crafts. A standard bungalow is 6.880 CFP sgl./8.735 CFP dbl; and a big bungalow is 9.175 CFP for 1-2 people. Breakfast is 1.060 CFP and lunch or dinner costs 2.970 CFP per person for each meal. Round-trip airport transfers are 3.180 CFP per person. You can rent a self-drive 4WD vehicle for 13.000 CFP a day.

This is a favorite lodging because of its location, but mainly because of the owners, who are warm and very outgoing. "Gaby" is the former president of the Tourism Committee in Hiva Oa. His wife speaks English and will guide you on a complimentary tour of Atuona village and the other main points of interest. Gaby also has an Excursion business. See information under *Land Tours & Safari 4x4 Excursions* in this chapter.

RELAIS MOEHAU, *B.P. 50, Atuona, Hiva Oa 98741, Marquesas Islands. Tel. 689/92.72.69/70.16.34; Fax 689/92.77.62; www.relaismoehau.pf. On mountainside in Atuona, 9 km. (5.6 mi.) from the airport and 3 km. (1.9 mi.) from Atuona quay. MC, V.*

This pension has been given a 2-Tiare rating by Tahiti Tourisme. Gisèle and Georges Gramont have 7 spacious guest rooms in their 2-story white house, with a choice of a double bed or two single beds. Each room has a ceiling fan, TV, and bathroom with hot water shower. A big terrace spans the length of the house, offering a lovely view of Traitors Bay and Hanakee Rock. Free WiFi for guests with their own computers. Rooms are cleaned daily. Round-trip transfers between airport and pension 3.600 CFP per person. Room with breakfast 8.000 CFP sgl/ 12.110 CFP dbl. Meals are served in the restaurant on the premises, which is equipped with a wood-burning pizza oven. It is also open to the public. An *a la carte* menu features Marquesan, Polynesian and French cuisine. Excursions and guided tours can be organized on request to visit Hiva Oa and the sister island of Tahuata.

PENSION AREKE–CHEZ KAYSER, *B.P. 133, Atuona, Hiva Oa 98741, Marquesas Islands. Tel. 689/92.71.11/23.48.17; pension.hivaoa@yahoo.fr; www.pension-hivaoa.com. On the hillside overlooking Tahauku Bay, Point Taaroa and the island of Tahuata. No credit cards.*

Pierre-Alexandre Kayser is the French/German host at Chez Kayser's guest house, which is a 3-story house surrounded by luxuriant vegetation. There are 2 spacious rooms with a double bed and another big room with 1 double and 1 single bed. All 3 rooms have screened windows and a private bathroom with hot water shower. Rates for a room with breakfast and dinner are 10.500 CFP sgl./21.000 CFP dbl., for a min. of 2 days. Digressive rates for longer stays. Airport transfers are 3.000 CFP per person and excursions in close proximity to Atuona village are free.

All guests share the kitchen, living room with plasma screen TV, and the game room, library and covered decks. There is a bar, a professional billiards table, babyfoot game, potable water fountain, and a swimming pool. Guests also have telephone and WiFi service at a charge.

PENSION OZANNE, *B.P. 43, Atuona, Hiva Oa 98741, Marquesas Islands. Tel/Fax 689/92.73.43; Cell 20.07.32/23.07.40. No credit cards.*

This pension is on the hillside on the eastern edge of Atuona, providing accommodations in a 3-bedroom house and 2 bungalows. One of the rooms in the house has been renovated and now has a double bed, a kitchen and private bathroom. Guests share the living room and terrace. The bungalows each have a double bed and a single bed, a kitchen, and private bathroom with cold water. A room with half-board is 8.000 CFP for a couple., and a bungalow with MAP is 9.000 CFP dbl. Round-trip airport transfers 3.000 CFP per person. Add taxes.

The Marquesan style meals are eaten with the family under a *fare pote'e* shelter overlooking the black sand beach and ocean. Owner John Ozanne Rohi speaks English and is very friendly. His wife, Mary Jo, takes care of the pension and John and his sons take care of their boats. They can take you fishing or on excursions to visit other islands.

PENSION CHEZ MARIE-ANTOINETTE, *Puamau, Hiva Oa 98741, Marquesas Islands. Tel. 689/92.72.27/70.92.24; Fax 689/92.75.28; heitaa.etienne@mail.pf. No credit cards.*

This pension is in the valley of Puamau, on the northeast coast of Hiva Oa, 40 km. (25 mi.) from the airport and 3.5 km. (2.2 mi.) from the quay in Puamau. It is on the right hand side of the road that leads to the I'ipona or Oipona archaeological site with the 5 big tikis. There are 3 simply furnished rooms in the home of the former mayor, Bernard "Vohi" Heitaa, with a double and a single bed in each room. The bathroom with hot water is shared, as well as the living room with TV and the dining room. A room with breakfast and dinner is 5.830 CFP per person; and a room with all meals is 6.890 CFP per person per day; half price for child under 10 years. Add taxes.

Marie-Antoinette cooks the local style meals. She serves lunch for 2.200 CFP per person to those who stop here during day excursions to Puamau valley. Reserve in advance.

She also has a big yard with lots of noni trees and other kinds of fruit trees and flowers. There is also an arts and crafts display here. According to Marie-Antoinette, the tomb of Vehine Tetoiani, the last queen of Puamau valley, is also located on her property in the **Tohua Pehe Kua.** Although the queen was given a Christian burial when she died in 1926, two *ti'i* statues were placed beside her tomb. Those tikis are now beside the road.

Economy

Bungalows Fa'e Isa, *Tel./Fax 689/92.73.33,* owned by Aline Saucourt. She has 2 bungalows for rent by the day, week or month, which contain a double bed, equipped kitchen and bathroom with hot water, with a view of the mountain and Atuona village. Rates are 4.000 CFP sgl/, 5.000 CFP dbl. Weekly rates are 30.000 dbl. and monthly rates are 80.000 CFP for 1-2 people. No credit cards.

Communal Bungalows of Atuona, *Tel. 689/92.73.32; Fax 689/92.74.95; commune@commune-hivaoa.pf.* Claire and René Terme take care of the town hall's bungalows that are located in Atuona village, 200 m. from the beach. These units have beds, kitchenette and bathroom and are rented by the day for 3.000 CFP sgl, 2.500 CFP per person dbl., and 1.000 CFP for each additional person. Monthly rates are 50.000 CFP for 2 occupants and 70.000 CFP for 4 people, including electricity but no hotel services. No credit cards.

WHERE TO EAT

HANAKEE HIVA OA PEARL LODGE, *Tel. 92.75.87. Open daily for BLD. All major credit cards.*

An American breakfast is 2.800 CFP; the 3-course set tourist menu is 4.250 CFP. The MAP with breakfast and dinner is 7.800 CFP and AP with all meals is 10.000 CFP. Rates include taxes. The chef's specialties include fresh fish and locally caught seafood. You can sit on the terrace overlooking the bay and listen to Jacques Brel music during Happy Hour, which is held at the bar every Friday evening. There is a Marquesan dance show on special evenings.

HOA NUI, *in Atuona village, Tel. 92.73.63. No credit cards. Reserve.*

This is where the *Aranui* passengers eat when they visit Atuona. They get to enjoy Marquesan feasts of roast pork, curried goat, fresh river shrimp, smoked red chicken, *fafa poulet*, macaroni fritters, fried breadfruit, banana *po'e* and other delicious treats. Breakfast and lunch are served for walk-ins, but you'll need to reserve to enjoy the Chinese and Marquesan dishes they serve at dinner for 1.900-2.500 CFP.

RELAIS MOEHAU, *Tel. 689/92.72.69/70.16.34; Open daily L., D., Free transfers. MC, V.*

This is a family pension with a public restaurant. An *a la carte* menu features Marquesan, Polynesian and French cuisine, and pizzas are cooked in a wood-burning pizza oven. You can order take-away pizza.

TEMETIU VILLAGE, *Tel. 92.73.02. BLD. Reservations are necessary. AE, MC, V.*

Meals are served on their terrace overlooking Tahauku and Taaoa bays. Breakfast is 1.060 CFP and lunch or dinner costs 2.970 CFP. Lobster and shrimp specialties are featured, along with goat in coconut milk and other Marquesan foods.

SNACK MAKE MAKE, *Tel. 92.74.26, on the mountainside in the center of Atuona village near the Post Office. Open Mon.-Fri. 8:30am-1:30pm and 6-8pm, and Sat. until 1:30pm. Closed Sat. night and all day Sun. No credit cards.*
The Chinese owners still serve good hamburgers and cold beer, but they specialize in Chinese dishes priced from 1.200-2.000 CFP.

CHEZ MARIE ANTOINETTE, *Tel. 92.72.27/70.92.24, in Puamau,* is open daily, serving a lunch of Marquesan food to day-trippers who come to visit the stone tikis at Me'ae Iipona. Reserve.

SEEING THE SIGHTS

In the center of Atuona you can visit the Paul Gauguin Museum and Maison du Jouir in the Gauguin Center, Jacques Brel Cultural Center, Traditional Arts House, arts and crafts center and the sacred site of Tohua Pepeu, which was restored for the 1991 Marquesas Festival of Arts and used again as a stage during the 2003 Marquesas Festival of Arts. In Calvary Cemetery behind Atuona village you can visit the graves of French artist Paul Gauguin and Belgian singer Jacques Brel. The tourist office erected a stele or memorial to Brel in 1993 on a piece of open ground a few km. east of Atuona, overlooking the Hanakee Hiva Oa Pearl Lodge. This can be visited by 4WD, horseback, or on foot.

Sightseeing highlights away from Atuona include a visit to **Puamau Valley** to see the giant tikis at the **I'ipona** (or Oipona) archaeological site; the tiki and *paepae* platforms of **Taaoa Valley**; the petroglyphs on the **Tehueto** site in the **Faakua Valley**; the **Moe One tiki** in **Hanapaaoa Valley**; and the *paepae* and pretty little village of **Hanaiapa Valley**, where you can visit wood carvers' workshops and watch the surfers riding the waves in this popular surf spot.

Land Tours & 4x4 Safari Excursions

Gabriel Heitaa of Temetiu Village, *Tel. 91.70.60/70.01.71/70.72.07; heitaagabyfeli@mail.pf.* Gaby leads guided 4x4 excursions to Puamau. The 2 1/2-hour ride to Puamau is a one-way distance of 48 km. (30 mi.). You will be taken to visit the famous tikis, the queen's grave, and return by way of Jacques Brel's stele. This is an all-day trip and you can include lunch for 2.000 CFP per person. You'll pay an entry fee of 200 CFP at the archaeological site of Oipona. Another excursion takes you to the restored archaeological site of Taaoa. This is a distance of 7 km. (4.4 mi.) and a 15-20 min. ride from Atuona and costs 4.000 CFP. You can also visit the village of Hanaiapa, where you can buy tapa bark paintings and woodcarvings. This excursion costs 10.000 CFP, which includes the petroglyphs.

André Teissier, *Tel. 92.73.51,* is a well-informed English-speaking guide who leads excursions to the historical sites in Hiva Oa.

Marie Thérèse Tehaamoana Deligny, *Tel. 92.71.59/72.80.70,* can take up to 4 passengers in an a/c 4x4 vehicle to visit the archaeological sites.

Frida Peterano, *Tel. 92.79.66/70.72.02*, is an English-speaking guide who will show you the highlights of Hiva Oa by 4WD.

SPORTS & RECREATION
Hiking
Moana O Te Manu Excursions, *Tel./Fax 92.74.44 (Atuona), Tel. 92.75.68 (Hanaiapa), cell 24.64.58/23.68.90*. Henry Bonno is a professional Marquesan guide who can take you around the island by foot or 4WD to Taaoa, Puamau, and Hanaiapa. He also organizes camping trips on request.

Hiva Oa Trek, Alain Tricas (*Tel. 20.40.90*) and his son Teiva Tricas (*Tel. 20.38.00*) are professional guides who can suggest a choice of hiking trails, especially to explore the Taaoa valley, which is rich in archaeological sites. To hike Taaoa, Tehueto and the old cemetery, they charge 1.000 CFP per hr.

Horseback Riding
Hamau Ranch, *Tel./Fax 92.70.57, cell 28.68.21; hamauranch@mail.pf*. Lucien "Pako" Pautehea, leads "green tourism" expeditions by horseback to explore any of the dozen trails he knows, starting from Atuona. He is a nature lover and enjoys sharing his knowledge of the Marquesan fauna and flora with small groups of 3-4 riders. He uses 15 different trails for his rides, according to the riding level of his clients. You can ride by the hour, half day or all day, and hunting rides can also be organized. Free transfers provided from your hotel or pension.

Etienne Heitaa, *Tel. 92.75.28*, has Marquesan horses for rent in Puamau, with a guide if requested.

Boat Excursions & Deep Sea Fishing
Te Hinaonaiki is a 36-ft. bonito boat owned by Médéric Kaimuko, *Tel. 92.76.97*. Picnic excursions to Hapatoni or Vaitahu on Tahuata are 30.000 CFP for 8 passengers, and a trip to Fatu Hiva is 65.000 CFP for 8 passengers.

Vaipuna O Hanamenu, *Tel. 92.76.57/70.71.97/78.82.98*, is a 12 m. (39 ft.) bonito fishing boat owned by Leo Rohi of Atuona that can accommodate 8 passengers. He charges 20.000 CFP for a round-trip from Atuona to Vaitahu on Tahuata and return, and 25.000 CFP for an outing that also includes Hapatoni. A round-trip to Fatu Hiva is 50.000 CFP plus 10.000 CFP to spend the night. Deep-sea fishing and picnics on request.

Scuba Diving
SubAtuona Plongée, *Tel./Fax 92.70.88, cell 27.05.24; eric.lelyonnais@wanadoo.fr; www.subatuona.com*. Hiva Oa's scuba diving center is headed by Frenchman Eric Le Lyonnais, a BEES1 monitor. He charges 7.000 CFP for one dive and 13.000 CFP for a 2-tank dive. He can take 4-8 people on all-day outings in his 9.5 m. (31-ft.) bonito boat **Te Pua O Te Tai**, for a picnic on the white sand beaches of Tahuata, with

a dive included on request. The excursion and picnic are 11.000 CFP per person, and 15.000 CFP including a dive. The outing without meal or dive is 8.000 CFP.

SHOPPING

One of several arts and crafts centers in Atuona is adjacent to the Gauguin Museum and a very good handcraft shop and boutique is across the road. You can buy tee shirts with Marquesan designs, hand-painted pareos, *monoi* oil made with sandalwood and a thousand flowers, and *mille fleurs* honey. Artisan shops are also located in Puamau and Taaoa.

Marquesas Creation, *Tel. 92.70.77*, is operated by Stéphanie Citeau and Jean-Baptiste Gueldry and is adjacent to Tohua Pepeu in the center of the village. They sell Marquesan shirts, pareos, T-shirts, tapa, sculpted wood and stone, and Marquesan seed necklaces. The **Atuona Artisans Association** is headed by Aline Saucourt, *Tel. 92.73.33*, and is located on the western side of Tohua Pepeu. **Jean and Nadine Oberlin**, *Tel. 92.76.34*, have the small boutique at the airport and they also exhibit their oil paintings, tapas, engraved gourds and other arts and crafts in Atuona village whenever a passenger ship is in port. **Curios Vaiaka**, *Tel. 92.74.03/26.68.02*, is owned by Simone Teriivahine, who sells jewelry and specializes in hand painted sheets.

If you want to buy woodcarvings you can visit the sculptors at their home workshops. The Atuona artisans include: **Jean-Marie Otomimi**, *Tel. 92.76.55*, who carves wood sculptures; **Gilbert "Tuarai" Peterano**, *Tel. 92.70.64*, who carves on wood, stone and bone; **Fernand Tetuaveroa**, *Tel. 92.74.07*, who carves stone "penu" pestles; and **Maurice "Mori" Poevai**, who lives close to the *me'ae* Poevau in Puamau, and carves wood sculptures.

TATTOOS

Tuarae Peterano, *Tel. 92.70.64*; **Santos Nazario**, *Tel. 92.70.11*;

PRACTICAL INFORMATION
Banks

Banque Socredo, *Tel. 92.73.54*, has a branch on the main street in Atuona, next to the Air Tahiti office. There's an ATM window outside that is open during banking hours: Mon.-Fri. 7-11:30am, and 1-4pm.

Hospitals

There's a government-operated infirmary in Atuona, *Tel. 92.73.75*, a dental center, *Tel. 92.78.17*, an infirmary in Puamau, *Tel. 92.74.96*, and first aid stations in Nahoe and Hanapaaoa.

Internet, Laundry and Yacht Services

Sandra Wullaert in Atuona, wears a lot of hats. She is the Hiva Oa agent of Polynesia Yacht Services, and can help visiting yachts with entry formalities, visa extensions, and advice on where to shop for provisions, duty free fuel, rental cars, and have the boat repaired if necessary. She also operates Cyber Services and has WiFi Internet access. She charges 250 CFP per kilo to wash your clothes, and for 400 CFP a kilo she will wash, dry and fold your laundry. She also sells wooden guitars made locally by David Fabre. *Tel./Fax 92.79.85, cell 23.22.47, VHF 11; cyber-services@mail.pf.*

Pharmacy

You'll find Atuona's drugstore (Pharmacie) in the Mairie (town hall) complex, *Tel. 91.71.65/26.27.75.* Open Mon.-Fri. 8am-12pm and 2:30-5:30pm, and on Sat. 8:30-11:30am.

Police

The French *gendarmerie* has a brigade in the center of Atuona, *Tel. 91.71.05.* Dial *17* for emergency.

Post Office & Telecommunications Office

The post office is located adjacent to the town hall (*mairie*) in the center of Atuona village, *Tel. 92.73.50.* It is open Mon.-Thurs. from 7:30am-12pm and from 12:30-4:30pm, and on Fri. until 2pm. There is also a post office in Puamau, *Tel. 92.71.55.*

Visitor Information

Comité de Tourisme de Hiva Oa (Hiva Oa Tourism Committee), *Tel/Fax 92.78.93/70.45.18; comtourismhiva@mail.com; www.marquises-hivaoa.org.pf* is located in a small building in front of the Paul Gauguin Center in the village of Atuona. There is also an annex office at the boat dock when ships arrive.

Ernest Teapuaoteani works for the Mairie (town hall) of Atuona, *Tel. 92.73.32,* and he is a good source of information on Marquesan culture, dance and history. He speaks English.

TAHUATA

Tahuata has the only coral gardens in the Marquesas and the prettiest white sand beaches. There is no airport, although plans are underway to eventually construct a runway. Nor is there any helicopter service, but you can easily reach Tahuata by boat from Hiva Oa, which is just an hour's ride across the Bordelais Channel. This is a popular port-of-call for cruising yachts that drop anchor in coves with beautiful secluded beaches accessible only by boat. The *Aranui 3* passengers enjoy visiting the friendly little village of Hapatoni and playing on the beach at Hanemoenoe whenever the ship stops there.

Tahuata is the smallest populated island in the Marquesas archipelago, with only 50 sq. km. (19 sq. mi.) of land. A central mountain range crowns the crescent shaped island, reaching 1,040 m. (3,465 ft.) into the ocean sky.

It was in Tahuata's Vaitahu Bay that Alvaro de Mendaña's expedition of 4 caravels anchored in 1595. He named the island group *Las Marquesas de Garcia de Mendoza de Canete*, in honor of the wife of Peru's viceroy. The Spanish explorer came ashore at Vaitahu Bay, which he named *Madre de Dios*, Mother of God. It was here that the first crosses were raised and mass was held. When the Spanish-Peruvian ships set sail, 200 inhabitants lay massacred on the beach.

Following Captain James Cook's visit in 1774, Vaitahu's harbor was named Resolution Bay. When the first Protestant missionaries came in 1797, the generous local chief left his wife with missionary John Harris, with instructions that he should treat her as his own wife. Harris fled when the wife and 5 of her women friends visited his room.

The French took possession of the Marquesas in Vaitahu, establishing a garrison at Fort Halley in 1842. Monuments, ruins and graves of the French soldiers killed during the skirmishes can be seen in Vaitahu, but no indication is given for the Marquesans who lost their lives. The Catholic missionaries chose Tahuata as the site of their first Marquesan church. The Catholic Church that stands today in Vaitahu was built in 1988 with funds from the Vatican. It has a stained-glass window depicting a Marquesan Madonna, plus carvings from the wood sculptors.

Although Tahuata's past has been violent and grim, the 706 inhabitants live a quiet life today, working peacefully in their verdant valleys, raising livestock and making copra. The rich waters surrounding the island attract an amazing variety of fish, sharks and even whales.

Boat day in Tahuata's small villages is a main event when a ship arrives with food and supplies. Getting ashore in Hapatoni has always been dangerous, and this process is now easier with the addition of a jetty that was built to protect the enlarged concrete quay so that the communal boat can dock here. The 60 residents of Hapatoni are especially welcoming. The seafront road is made almost entirely of ancient paved stones and is shaded by the sacred *tamanu* trees.

ARRIVALS & DEPARTURES
Arriving By Boat
Aranui 3 includes stops at Vaitahu and occasionally at Hapatoni during its 14-day round-trip cruise program from Tahiti to the Marquesas. See details in section on *Inter-Island Cruise Ships and Cargo/Passenger Boats* in Chapter 6, *Planning Your Trip*.

Tahuata Nui is a 48.6-ft. long aluminum hull boat operated by the Commune of Tahuata that transports 60 passengers between Atuona and Tahuata. The boat leaves the quay of Atuona at 12pm each Mon. for Vaitahu, and each Fri. the boat leaves Atuona at 12pm for Vaitahu and Hapatoni. The one-way fare is 1.000 CFP. Reserve at the Mairie of Tahuata, *Tel. 689/92.92.19; Fax 689/92.92.10*.

Philippe Tetahiotupa, *Tel. 92.92.65*, has a 5-passenger boat *Tehaumate* that makes private transfers between Atuona and Vaitahu. The round-trip fare is

22.000 CFP for the boat. **Louis Timau**, *Tel. 92.93.19*, charges 15.000 CFP for a round-trip for up to 6 passengers for a round-trip between Atuona and Tahuata. **Hervé Barsinas**, *Tel. 20.35.43*, charges 15.000 CFP for 4-5 passengers for inter-island round-trip transfers. **Frédéric Timau**, *Tel. 92.92.28*, charges 18.000 CFP for the round-trips between Atuona and Tahuata.

Departing By Boat
　　Tahuata Nui, *Tel. 92.92.19*, is Tahuata's communal boat that leaves Vaitahu each Mon. and Fri. at 6:30am for Atuona. The boat stops at Hapatoni village each Fri. enroute to Hiva Oa. The one-way fare is 1.000 CFP and reservations are a must. See information above under *Arriving by Boat* for private boat transfers.

ORIENTATION
　　You can walk from the boat landing to the small village of **Vaitahu**. Hapatoni is just a 10-min. boat ride from Vaitahu, or you can take the road between the 2 villages. The **Valley of Hanatehau** is a 30-min. horse ride from Hapatoni. A track joins Vaitahu and **Motopu** in the northeast, a distance of about 17 km., which is ideal for riders. **Hanatetena** was formerly approachable only by boat and getting ashore through the turbulent surf is a dangerous maneuver. A road now connects this small valley with Hapatoni, Motopu and Vaitahu.

WHERE TO STAY & EAT
　　PENSION AMATEA, *Vaitahu, Tahuata 98743, Marquesas Islands. Tel./Fax 689/92.92.84, cell 76.24.90/29.37.49. Located in the center of Vaitahu village, with access to the sea. Free transfers from quay. No credit cards.*
　　There are 4 rooms in a big white concrete house owned by Marguerite Kokauani and her husband, François. Each room contains a double bed and guests share 2 bathrooms with cold water shower, as well as the living room, dining room and terrace. They charge 7.000 CFP per person for a room with breakfast and dinner, and 10.000 CFP for a room with all meals. The beach is close by and you can easily walk around the village from here. Land and sea activities are also available on request. They provide round-trip transfers between Vaitahu and Hapatoni for 12.000 CFP, and to visit Motopu for 15.000 CFP.
　　PENSION VAIKEHUNUI, *B.P. 83, Atuona, Hiva Oa 98741, Marquesas Islands. Tel. 689/92.92.48/92.93.56; www.haere-mai.pf. In Hanatetena Valley, 12 km (7.4 mi.) from Hapatoni and 22 km (13.6 mi.) from Vaitahu. No credit cards.*
　　This 5-room family pension is owned by Sabina and Pierre Nakeaetou. It opened in 2010 and is located on a hill near the village of Hanatetena, with a view of the Pacific Ocean. One of the bedrooms has a private bathroom with cold water shower and the other 4 rooms share 2 bathrooms with cold water. Sabina serves the meals and guests can also use the kitchen. The rate of 3.600 CFP per person per day includes the room and all meals. They pick up their guests from the quay in Hapatoni village. Activities include 4x4 excursions to visit the island.

SEEING THE SIGHTS

Vaitahu is the main village, and the small museum **Haina Kakiu** is located in the *mairie* (town hall), which contains exhibits, photos and illustrations of an archaeological site excavated in Hanamiai. **Monuments** in Vaitahu commemorate the 400th anniversary of the Spanish discovery of the Marquesas Islands; the 150th anniversary of **Iotete**, the first Marquesan chief; French Admiral Dupetit-Thouars; and the French-Marquesan battle of 1842. There are also the remains of a French fort and the graves of French sailors.

The big **Meipe Eia** in Hapatoni was renovated by the youths from the village. **Petroglyphs** can be found in the Hanatu'una valley, which can be reached by boat or horseback from Hapatoni. There are also stone **petroglyphs** in Hanatehau and **archaeological sites** in Vaitahu valley.

In front of the **Notre Dame de l'Enfant Jesus Catholic Church** in Vaitahu is a wooden statue of the *Virgin with Child* that is nearly 4 m. (13 ft.) tall. This beautiful work of art was carved by **Damien Haturau** of Nuku Hiva, whose Christ child is holding an *uru* (breadfruit) as an offering.

SHOPPING

A specialty of Tahuata is the fragrant *monoi* oil made from coconuts, herbs and flowers, sandalwood, pineapple and other aromatic plants. You will also enjoy the smoke flavored dried bananas wrapped in leaves. Wood carvers have their workshops in the valleys of Vaitahu, Hapatoni, Hanatetena and Motopu.

One of the best bone carvers in the Marquesas is Teiki Barsinas, *Tel. 92.93.24*, who lives in Vaitahu. Other noted sculptors in Vaitahu are: Edwin Fii, *Tel. 92.93.04*, and Felix Fii, *Tel. 92.92.14*. In Hapatoni contact Frédéric Timau, *Tel. 92.92.55*, Ernest Teikipupuni, *Tel. 92.92.51*, Paul Vaimaa, *Tel. 92.93.20*, Jules Timau, and Sébastien "Kehu" Barsinas, *Tel. 92.92.38*. Be sure to visit the handcrafts center in Hapatoni for woodcarvings.

Felix Barsinas in Vaitahu, *Tel. 92.93.23*, is one of the best tattoo artists in the Marquesas and passengers aboard the *Aranui 3* can arrange to get a tattoo during their time ashore, providing it doesn't take too long. Edwin and Felix Fii are also tattoo masters whose designs are very original.

FATU HIVA

The beautiful island of **Fatu Hiva** will show you the mysterious Marquesas you have dreamed of discovering. Deep within **Hanavave Bay** you may feel that you are inside a gigantic cathedral, a green mansion of moss and fern covered mountains, often encased in misty rain. White patches of goats and sheep look down from their green mansions above the quiet harbor. Nature's chiseled image of the Polynesian god Tiki is visible in the mountain formations, which may give inspiration to the talented sculptors of wood and stone. This is the famous Bay of Virgins, so named by Catholic missionaries, who said that the phallic shaped stone outcrops were formed as veiled virgins.

When the Spanish explorer Alvaro de Mendaña sighted the island of Fatu Hiva in 1595, he believed he had discovered Solomon's kingdom, complete with gold mines. He named the island La Magdalena and killed his first Polynesian on the shore of Omoa village.

The wild, spectacularly beautiful island of Fatu Hiva is the most remote, the furthest south and the wettest and greenest of the Marquesas Islands. Stretching 15 km. (9.3 mi.) long, a rugged mountain range is topped by Mt. Tauaouoho, at 960 m. (3,149 ft.), overlooking 80 sq. km. (31 sq. mi.) of land.

Fatu Hiva is about 70 km. (43 mi.) south of Hiva Oa, and can be reached by private bonito boats, speedboats, yachts or inter-island ships. Although government plans include building an airport here sometime in the future, the only approach is still by sea, and this view alone is worth a trip to the Marquesas Islands.

The jungle greenery begins at the edge of the sea, which is like blue glass after a rain. Narrow ravines, deep gorges and luxuriant valleys briefly open to view as your boat glides past, close to the sheer cliffs that plunge straight into the splashing surf.

Due to the abundant rain and rich, fertile soil, sweet and juicy citrus fruits fill the gardens. Large, tasty shrimp live in the rivers that rush through each valley and rock lobsters are plentiful in the submerged reefs offshore Omoa.

Fatu Hiva is a center of Marquesan crafts. In the villages you will see the women producing tapa cloth from the inner bark of mulberry, banyan or breadfruit trees. They hammer the bark on a log until the fibers adhere, and when it is dry they paint it with the old Marquesan designs like their ancestors wore as tattoos. Sculptors carve the semi-precious woods of rosewood, *tou* and sandalwood, as well as coconuts, basaltic stones and bones. They produce bowls, platters, small canoes, turtles, tiki statues and war clubs. You are welcome to visit their workshops at their homes.

You can rent a horse for a bareback ride into the valley, charter a motorized outrigger canoe to explore the coastline and line fish, swim in the rivers or open ocean, go shrimping or lobstering with the locals, and if you're really adventurous, you can join a Marquesan wild pig hunt.

Smoke flavored dried bananas are a specialty of the industrious people of **Omoa village**. Fatu Hiva's special bouquet is the *umu hei*—a delightful blend of sandalwood powder, spearmint, jasmine, ginger root, pineapple, vanilla, sweet basil, gardenia, pandanus fruit, ylang-ylang and other mysterious herbs. This seductive concoction is all tied together and worn around the neck or in the long hair of the women.

ARRIVALS & DEPARTURES
Arriving By Boat
Aranui 3 includes stops at Hanavave Bay and Omoa during its 14-day round-trip cruise program from Tahiti to the Marquesas. See details in Chapter 6, *Planning Your Trip*, section on Inter-Island Cruise Ships and Cargo/Passenger Boats.

Auona II, the 51-ft. catamaran owned by the Commune of Omoa, sank at its mooring in April 2011. It used to be a big joke in Fatu Hiva that their boat spent more time on land than it did in the sea, due to so many repairs it had to undergo. Now it is sitting at the bottom of the bay. You can charter a boat in Atuona to visit Fatu Hiva. See information in *Hiva Oa* chapter.

Departing By Boat

The best advice is to leave on the boat that brought you here, unless you're staying a long time and have made other arrangements that you can count on.

Private boats can be rented in Omoa for transfers to Atuona. **Joel Coulon,** *Tel. 92.81.17,* can transport 4 passengers and the one-way fare is 40.000 CFP for the boat. **Xavier Gilmore,** *Tel. 92.81.38,* also charges 40.000 CFP for a one-way trip and 80.000 CFP for a round-trip to Atuona.

ORIENTATION

The 629 inhabitants of Fatu Hiva live in the villages of **Omoa** and **Hanavave,** which are separated by 5 km. (3 mi.) of sea. Omoa, in the south of the island, is a wide-open valley with a black sand beach lined with several outrigger canoes. Just behind the beach are a soccer field and a paved road that leads through the village past the little Catholic Church, which has a red roof and a lovely background of mountain peaks and spires. Beautiful flower gardens, pamplemousse (grapefruit) trees, citrons and oranges, bananas and other tropical fruit trees surround almost every house. This village is clean and the people are open and friendly. A spring-fed river runs through the village, bordered by ferns and flowers, and villagers say it is safe to swim in this water, as there are no pigpens beside the river.

Getting ashore in Omoa can be an adventure in itself, as the small boat landing is slippery. When the ocean is wild, as it often is, the whaleboat bobs up and down beside the pier and you have to time your jump with the crest of the waves.

A protective seawall has been built on the left bank of Hanavave Bay, which greatly facilitates the problem of getting ashore. The ship's whaleboat or barge discharges passengers at a concrete quay, where they are welcomed by the artisan group. The tourists are led to the arts and crafts center, where tables are covered with tapa cloth paintings, sculptures, monoi oil, dried bananas, seashells and other wares for sale.

A serpentine path winds over the mountains between Omoa and Hanavave, offering a 17-km. (10.5-mile) challenging hike and panoramic views through the curtains of rock. Majestic waterfalls are visible from the path deep inside **Vaie'enui Valley.** In Hanavave valley you should avoid swimming in the basin at the bottom of the waterfall, as it is polluted and you risk catching leptospirosis. Facilities include food stores, a post office, a town hall and primary schools in each village.

GETTING AROUND FATU HIVA
Car Rentals
Lionel Cantois, *Tel. 92.81.84*, Henri Tuieinui, *Tel. 92.80.23*, Didier Gilmore, *Tel. 92.80.86*, Xavier Gilmore, *Tel. 92.82.08*, Roberto Maraetaata, *Tel. 92.81.02*, and Joseph Tetuanui, *Tel. 92.80.09*, all have a 4WD vehicle they will use to drive you to Hanavave. Cars have to be rented with a chauffeur, as the roads are very rugged.

WHERE TO STAY
Economy
PENSION CHEZ LIONEL, *B.P. 1, Omoa, Fatu Hiva 98740, Marquesas Islands. Tel./Fax 689/92.81.84; chezlionel@mail.pf. Free round-trip transfers from boat landing to pension. No credit cards.*

Tahiti Tourisme has given this pension a 1-Tiare rating. It is the last residence in the village, located beside a river 1.5 km. (.9 mile) from the quay. Lionel and Bernadette Cantois rent a room in the main house, which has a double bed and a single bed. As in many Polynesian homes, the walls do not go all the way to the ceiling. You share the bathroom with hot water and the living room with the family. A small bungalow next to the house has a double bed and a single bed, a fan, kitchenette and tiled bathroom with hot water. Two rooms can also be rented in their son's house on the premises, sharing the bathroom and kitchen. There is a double bed and a single bed in one room and 2 single beds in the other room. Meals are served on a big covered dining terrace in the main house, where guests can also watch TV. A room with breakfast is 4.500 CFP sgl./6.500 CFP dbl. Bungalow and breakfast costs 6.500 CFP sgl./8.500 CFP dbl. Lunch is 1.000 CFP; and a 3-course dinner is 1.500-2.250 CFP per person.

Lionel has a 4WD that he uses to take guests over the mountain road to Hanavave for 15.000 CFP. You can include a picnic lunch on this excursion. He will also take you to visit Omoa valley where there are waterfalls, ancient paepae and petroglyphs. He also has a small boat and can take guests fishing. He can take you hunting by horseback if you stay 8 days. You can also take a refreshing bath in the spring-fed river that gurgles behind his house.

CHEZ NORMA ROPATI, *Omoa, Fatu Hiva 98740, Marquesas Islands. Tel./Fax 689/92.80.13. No credit cards.*

Norma's guesthouse is in the middle of the village, and it is totally surrounded by beautiful flowers and colorful bushes and shrubs. The 4 bedrooms she rents are equipped with a double bed. The living room, dining room, terrace and communal bathroom with hot water are all shared. She charges 4.100 CFP per person for a room and 2 meals a day.

WHERE TO EAT
Chez Lionel is also a public restaurant. There are two *magasin* stores in Omoa village that sell food supplies and cold beer, and there is also a *boulangerie* that bakes long *baguette* loaves of French bread. There are no snacks or restaurants.

SEEING THE SIGHTS

The most beautiful sight in Fatu Hiva is the **Bay of Virgins** in Hanavave, which is best seen from the sea. In Omoa a giant **petroglyph** featuring a huge fish and stick figures is engraved in a boulder at the edge of the village, and there are stone *paepae* house terraces in the valleys. A private collection of ancient Marquesan woodcarvings that belonged to former chief **Willie Grelet** are on display in a house owned by his grandchildren in Omoa. The **Catholic Church** in Omoa, with its red roof, white walls and rock fence, is one of the most picturesque scenes in any Marquesan village.

A 17-km. (10.5-mile) **hiking trail** will lead you across the rugged mountains between Omoa and Hanavave village. Walking alone in the mountains of Fatu Hiva is not recommended, even if you are an experienced hiker.

SPORTS & RECREATION
Horseback Riding

In Omoa village you can rent a Marquesan horse with a wooden saddle for daily excursions to Hanavave Bay or to ride around Omoa Valley. Contact Roberto Maraetaata, *Tel. 92.81.02*, or Isidore Mose, *Tel. 92.80.89.*

Boat Rental

You can rent an outrigger canoe with an engine and guide to get from Omoa to Hanavave Bay or vice-versa. Skimming across the incredibly blue water close to the untamed shore and gazing up at the rock formations and the wild cattle and goats staring down at you are moments to remember forever.

Lionel Cantois at Pension Lionel, *Tel. 92.81.84*, has a small boat he uses to take his guests fishing. Other rental boats: in Omoa contact Xavier Gilmore, *Tel. 92.81.38*, or his brother Napoléon. They have an aluminum speedboat. Joel Coulon, *Tel. 92.81.17*, has a locally made *poti marara* fishing boat, and Roberto Maraetaata, *Tel. 92.81.02*, has a boat for hire. Jacques Tevenino, *Tel. 92.80.71*, Mathias Pavaouau, *Tel. 92.80.45*, also have boats. In Hanavave call Daniel Pavaouau, *Tel. 92.80.60.*

Deep Sea Fishing

The Marquesan men are experienced fishermen and you can arrange with your pension to accompany one of them. Most of the boats used for fishing are the outrigger speed canoes or *poti marara* wooden boats.

SHOPPING

Most of the women in Fatu Hiva make tapa bark paintings, which they sell in their arts and crafts center adjacent to the *mairie* (town hall). They also take or send their tapa creations to Papeete for arts and crafts exhibits. Appoline Tiaiho, *Tel. 92.80.66*, in Omoa village is one of the most noted tapa makers. When passengers from the *Aranui 3* or other ships visit the village, she demonstrates how the bark cloth is made. Marie-Noëlle Ehueinana, who also lives in Omoa, has won prizes for her tapa paintings.

Their *monoi* is a delightful blend of coconut oil, sandalwood, spearmint, jasmine, ginger root, pineapple, sweet basil, gardenia, pandanus fruit, ylang-ylang and other mysterious herbs. This is used as perfume, for massages, to seduce a boyfriend or to ward off mosquitoes. Some of the men even consider drinking it. The women wear an *umu hei* bouquet of flowers and herbs in their hair or around their necks, which has an enticing aroma. Dried bananas are also a specialty here.

In the village of Hanavave the artisans have started displaying their tapa, carvings and other handcrafts on tables near the dock whenever a ship comes to call.

Fatu Hiva has several sculptors in both villages. They carve wood, stone, shell and even coconuts, creating lovely designs taken from the ancient Marquesan tattoos. There are at least a dozen sculptors in Omoa village and two or three in Hanavave. Some of the noted sculptors are: Stéphane Tuohe, *Tel. 92.80.11*, David Pavaouau, *Tel. 92.80.45*, and Marc Barsinas, *Tel. 92.80.44*.

PRACTICAL INFORMATION
Doctors
A government-operated **infirmary** is located in Omoa village, *Tel. 92.80.36*, and a **First Aid Station** (*Poste de Secours*) is in Hanavave village, *Tel. 92.80.61*.

Post Office and Telecommunications Office
There is a **post office** in Omoa Village, *Tel. 92.83.74*, and in Hanavave, *Tel. 92.82.32*.

Tourist Information
Comité de Tourisme de Fatu Hiva, *Tel. 689/92.81.84*, is located at Pension Chez Lionel, and the president is Lionel Cantois.

20. Austral Islands

In the Polynesian language the **Austral Islands** of French Polynesia are collectively known as *Tuhaa Pae*, referring to the 5 parts or islands that make up the archipelago. Folklore tells of Maui, the South Seas Superman, who fished up this chain of islands from the sea, using a magical fishhook that now forms the tail of Scorpio in the sky. This same hero is said to have cut away the great octopus that held the earth and the sky together, and he pushed up the sky so that people could walk upright. The arms of this octopus fell to the earth to form the Austral Islands, with Tubuai as its head.

Tane was a powerful god who used his many colored seashells to help separate the earth and sky, decorated the Austral heavens with twinkling stars, a golden sun and silvery moon, cool winds and billowing clouds. Ro'o, God of Agriculture and the Harvest, can be seen as a gilded rainbow and heard as the voice of thunder. Ruahatu-Tinirau, a Polynesian Neptune known as God of the Ocean and Lord of the Abyss, is said to have a man's body joined to a swordfish tail. Everyone knows that this powerful god lives in the reefs of Raivavae. And Tuivao, a fishing hero from Rurutu, sailed on the back of a whale to an enchanted island ruled by the goddess Tareparepa. Fleeing her spell Tuivao rode his whale to the island of Raivavae, where the mammal landed so hard on the beach that its imprint is still seen there today.

Past and present blend in harmony in the Austral Islands today. Islands of quiet beauty, peace and pride; these are Polynesia's Temperate Isles.

The Austral Islands include the high islands of **Rurutu, Tubuai, Rimatara, Raivavae** and **Rapa**, plus the low, uninhabited islands of **Maria** (or Hull) and the **Marotiri** (or Bass) **Rocks**. These islands lie on both sides of the Tropic of Capricorn, extending in a northwest-southeasterly direction across 1,280 km. (794 mi.) of ocean. They are part of a vast mountain range, an extension of the same submerged chain that comprises the Cook Islands 960 km (595 mi.) further to the northwest.

The 141 sq. km. (54 sq. mi.) of land surface in the Austral Islands is home to some 6,669 Polynesians, who live peaceful lives in their attractive villages, where their houses and churches are usually built of coral limestone or concrete. Due to the rich soil and the cooler climate of the Australs, good quality vegetables can be produced, including taro, manioc, potatoes, sweet potatoes, leeks, cabbage and coffee, as well as apples, peaches, figs and strawberries.

Archaeological diggings in these isolated islands have uncovered habitation sites, council platforms and *marae* temples in the village of Vitaria on Rurutu, showing man's presence around the year 900 A.D. Tubuai, Rimatara and Raivavae also have ruins of open-air *marae* stone temples, and giant sized stone *tikis* have been found on Raivavae that resemble those in the Marquesas Islands and on Easter

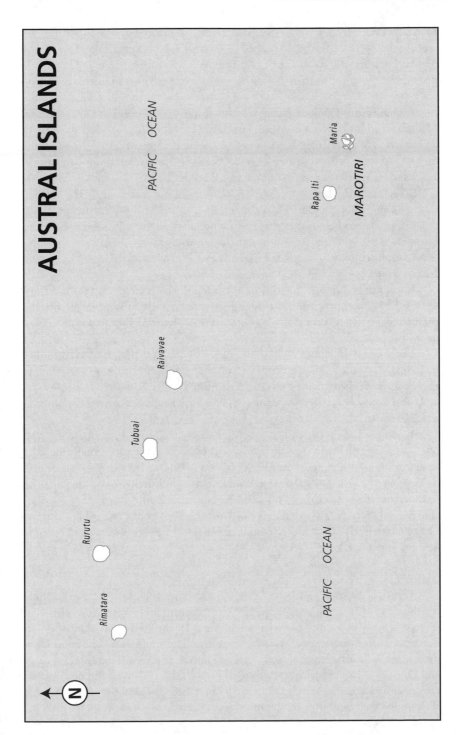

AUSTRAL ISLANDS

Island. On Rapa there are the remains of 7 famous *pa* fortresses on superimposed terraces that were found nowhere else in Polynesia except New Zealand where the Maori people settled. Exquisite woodcarvings, now in museums, tell of an artistic people highly evolved in their craft, who were also superb boat builders and daring seafarers.

Captain James Cook discovered Rurutu in 1769 and Tubuai in 1777. Fletcher Christian and his band of mutineers from the H. M. S. *Bounty* tried to settle in Tubuai in 1789, but were forced to flee the island because of skirmishes with the men of Tubuai. Spanish Captain Thomas Gayangos discovered lovely Raivavae in 1775 and remote Rapa was first sighted by English Captain George Vancouver in 1791. Rimatara, the lowest of the high islands, was not found until 1821, when Captain Samuel Pinder Henry of Tahiti arrived, returning the following year with 2 native teachers who converted the entire population to the Protestant religion. Evangelism still predominates, although there are now Mormon, Adventist, Sanito and Catholic churches, as well as Pentecost and Jehovah's Witnesses. The Austral Islands have all flown the French flag since 1901.

European and South American crews aboard whalers and sandalwood ships during the 19th century brought epidemic diseases to the islands, which practically decimated the strong, proud and highly cultured Polynesian race that once existed in the Australs.

The Austral Islanders today have many of the advantages of civilization, including electricity, potable water, telephone service, the Internet and satellite television. There is regular air service to Rurutu, Tubuai, Rimatara and Raivavae, and the *Tuhaa Pae II* cargo ship from Papeete brings supplies to all the islands on a regular basis.

Accommodations for visitors are provided in small pensions, where you will often eat, sleep and live in close proximity to the host family, which usually includes small children. Other guests may be people from Tahiti who are in the islands on business for the local government, school system or a church group. They may be technicians who have come to repair some broken machinery or bakery oven, or commercial representatives who take orders for school books and other supplies. Or it's just as likely you'll meet a couple of travelers from Norway who have come here to write a book.

RURUTU

Rurutu is the most northerly of the Austral Islands, lying at 22°27' Latitude South and 151°21' Longitude West, 572 km. (355 mi.) southwest of Tahiti. A very pretty island with a circumference of 30 km. (19 mi.), Rurutu is an upthrust limestone island with steep cliffs rising dramatically from the sea. The crannies in these bluffs were formerly used as shelters and burial chambers. There are also caves and grottoes decorated with stalactites and stalagmites. Rurutu's highest mountain, **Manureva**, reaches an elevation of 385 m. (1,263 ft.), and the coral reefs that surrounded the island eons ago are now raised *makatea* bluffs some 90 m. (300 ft.)

high above the sea. Rurutu does not have the wide lagoons found in the Society Islands or in Tubuai and Raivavae. Swimming and snorkeling are still possible in certain areas, however, and there are a few white sand beaches. The original name of this island was *Eteroa*, which means a long measuring string. The current name of *Rurutu tu noa* is an old Polynesian saying that means a mast standing straight. *Manureva* (soaring bird) was formerly the name of one of Rurutu's famous sailing boats that carried produce between the islands. The men are still noted sailors, and several of them work aboard the inter-island cargo ships that serve as a lifeline between Tahiti and the remote islands of French Polynesia.

The people of Rurutu were also highly skilled wood carvers. Most of the ancient tiki statues were destroyed by the missionaries, and one of them, the statue of the Rurutu ancestor god A'a, was taken to London by John Williams, one of the pioneering missionaries. This original tiki, which is 45 in. tall and weighs 282 lbs., is in the Museum of Mankind in London, but 5 plaster of Paris molds of the A'a statue were made by the British Museum. One of them was willed to the people of Rurutu by an American man who died a few years ago. This statue is now on display in the Mairie in Moerai village. Christi's has evaluated each of the A'a tiki statues to be worth $50,000. A Rurutu dance group made a wooden replica of the A'a tiki for a Heiva performance in Tahiti and this big statue now stands as guardian in front of Pension Le Manotel in Moerai.

In the old village of **Vitaria** is the **Marae Taaroa** or Arii, which dates from the year 900. This is the oldest known site of man's habitation in the Austral Islands. Nearby is a council platform and 70 house sites of a former village and warriors' house. In ancient times the warriors of Rurutu were feared for their strength. Today they are admired for their industriousness, seamanship, dancing skills and physical beauty.

The 2,210 handsome, intelligent and industrious Polynesians who live in the 3 villages of Moerai, Avera and Hauti, have houses of white concrete or coral limestone, bordered by flower gardens and low fences of white limestone.

In the main village of **Moerai** there is a *gendarmerie*, a post office and infirmary, a bank, primary and junior high schools, a few small *magasin* stores, bakeries, snack bars and roulottes (mobile diners). Each village is dominated by a Maohi Protestant Church, with smaller buildings for the Catholic, Mormon, Adventist, Pentecostal and Jehovah's Witness faiths.

The men harvest their taro, potatoes, tapioca, sweet potatoes, cabbages, leeks and carrots. The women form artisan groups to weave specially grown fibers of *paeore* pandanus into attractive hats, bags and mats, which are sold both locally and in Tahiti. The people of Rurutu enjoy a pleasant communal spirit, working together, singing *himenes* in their churches, and pitching in to prepare a big feast.

A New Year's custom on Rurutu is to visit each house in the village, where you are sprinkled with talcum powder and eau de cologne before entering. Once inside the house, you can enjoy the refreshments and admire the women's nicest woven products and *tifaifai* bed covers and wall hangings. Also during the month of

January the youth groups of the Protestant churches participate in a ritual called the *Tere*. A long caravan of flower-decorated pickup trucks, 4WD vehicles and motorcycles makes a tour of the island, stopping at each historical site, where one of the orators recites the legends of each significant stone or cave. One of the stops is on top of a mountain, where you have a lovely view of the village of Avera. Here is the Ofai Maramaiterai (intelligence that lightens the sky), which folklore claims is the center and origin of the island.

During the *Tere* circle island tour and also during the 2-week Heiva Festival in July the young men and women of each village prove themselves in a show of strength. Following a custom called *amoraa ofai*, unique to Rurutu, they attempt to lift huge volcanic stones to their shoulders. The village champions hoist one sacred stone that weighs 150 kg. (330 lbs.). This accomplishment is followed by exuberant feasting and dancing.

Another big event in Rurutu, as well as in all the Austral Islands, takes place during the month of May, when the Protestant parishioners gather in their temples for a religious fête called Me. The "mamas" dress for this occasion in their white gowns and elaborate hats and blend their voices with those of the men to sing their *himenes* and to donate money to support the church's projects for the coming year.

Activities on Rurutu include horseback riding and hiking to waterfalls, where refreshing showers cascade into fern bordered pools. The limestone grottoes form a natural stage for cultural reenactment ceremonies and cinematographers from all parts of the world come here to film these natural formations. Circle island tours by 4WD wind over concrete or dirt roads into cool valleys where fields of wild miri (sweet basil) scent the breeze. Picnic lunches can be packed for these trips or to play in the sun on deserted white sand beaches. Humpback whales can be seen offshore Rurutu during the austral winter months of July-Oct., and observation platforms have been built across the bluffs overlooking the ocean at each end of Moerai village.

The aroma of pineapple mingles pleasantly with *ylang ylang*, Tiare Tahiti, wild *miri* basil and *avaro*, some of the fragrant flowers, fruits and spices that are used to make the welcoming leis you will smell as soon as you arrive on this island of fragrant perfumes.

ARRIVALS & DEPARTURES
Arriving By Air

Air Tahiti has a 95-min. direct ATR flight from Tahiti to Rurutu each Mon., a Mon. flight that stops in Tubuai, a flight each Wed. with a stop in Rimatara, a Fri. flight with a stop in Rimatara, a Fri. flight that stops in Raivavae, and a Sun. flight with a stop in Tubuai. The one-way airfare from Tahiti to Rurutu is 22.030 CFP; from Tubuai to Rurutu the fare is 11.730 CFP; from Raivavae to Rurutu is 15.330 CFP, and from Rimatara it is 9.530 CFP. **Air Tahiti reservations:** Tahiti *Tel. 86.42.42; Rurutu Tel. 93.02.50;* Tubuai, *Tel. 93.22.75.*

You can also get to Rurutu by chartering an airplane in Tahiti from **Air Tahiti**, *Tel. 86.42.42*, or **Pol'Air**, *Tel. 74.23.11.*

Arriving By Boat

Tuhaa Pae II, *Tel. 41.36.06/41.36.16, Fax 42.06.09; snathp@mail.pf* makes 3 voyages a month from Tahiti to the Austral Islands, calling at Tubuai, Rimatara, Raivavae and Rurutu, then returning to Papeete. This itinerary changes according to the freight requirements of each voyage. The one-way fare to Rurutu is 3.817 CFP on the deck and 7.348 CFP for a berth in a cabin. Meals are extra. See further information in Chapter 6, *Planning Your Trip*.

Departing By Air

You can fly from Rurutu direct to Tahiti on Wed., Fri. and Sun. The Mon. flight stops in Rimatara and a Fri. flight stops in Tubuai. **Air Tahiti reservations** in Rurutu, *Tel. 93.02.50.*

Departing By Boat

The **Tuhaa Pae II** calls at Moerai village in Rurutu on its way back to Papeete or enroute to the other Austral Islands, according to the needs of the islanders. You can purchase your ticket on board the ship.

ORIENTATION

The oblong-shaped island of Rurutu is 10 km (6.2 mi.) long and 5.5 km (3.4 mi.) wide, or 36 sq. km (14 sq. mi.) in circumference. The main village of **Moerai** on the east coast is about 3 km (2.5 mi.) from the airport, connected by a paved road, which also extends to the village of **Hauti,** also on the east coast. Another concrete road links Moerai with **Avera**, a village 6 km (3.7 mi.) distant, located on the western coast. Avera has a small harbor for fishing boats, within the island's only real bay. The road around the island does not circle the coastline, but climbs up and down, from sea-level to almost 200 m (656 ft.), with panoramic views of white sand beaches and lagoons alternating with craggy cliffs and limestone caves and grottoes. The interior roads are bordered by fields of potatoes and taro and plantations of pandanus, bananas, coffee and noni. There are also several off-track dirt roads that can be explored by 4WD, horseback or on foot.

GETTING AROUND RURUTU

Car, Scooter & Bicycle Rentals

If you reserve a room at a family pension most, but not all of them will provide free round-trip transportation between the airport and their lodging. They charge for other transfers requested.

Rurutu Rent A Car, *Tel. 93.02.80, Fax 93.02.81, pensiontemarama@mail.pf,* is located at Pension Temarama in Unaa, between the airport and Moerai village. They also rent bicycles.

Total Station Tauamao, *Tel. 94.07.04/72.78.01*, in Moerai, has rental cars.

WHERE TO STAY

RURUTU LODGE, *B.P. 87, Moerai, Rururu 98753. Tel. 689/93.03.30/ 79.09.01; Fax 94.02.15; www.rurutulodge.com. Beside lagoon in Unaa Vitaria, close to airport.*

This small 2-star hotel is the only international class lodging in the Austral Islands. The 9 bungalows made of stone walls with thatched roofs are operated by Raie Manta Club, the scuba diving center headquartered in Rangiroa. They have rebuilt the old Hotel Rururu Village bungalows, providing 3 choices of accommodations: beach, garden and standard. A bungalow for 2 people is priced from 8.000 CFP. All units have a parquet floor, woven mats on the walls, a full-sized bathtub and separate toilets. The main building houses the reception, dining room and bar, library and dive shop. Reports are that the place is still rather run down. There used to be a swimming pool and tennis court, but they are no longer in service. There is a white sand beach in front of the property, but the waves are quite strong here most of the time. Scuba diving is the main theme, as well as snorkeling with the whales during the peak season of July-Oct., when the humpback whales come up from Antarctica to give birth and mate. Because there is no barrier reef, the whales come in close to shore, and it is easy to swim with them from a safe distance and have good visibility in the transparent water. Other activities include biking, hiking and horseback riding.

PENSION TE MARAMA, *B.P. 68, Moerai, Rururu 98753. Tel. 689/93.02.80/ 72.30.20; Fax 689/93.02.81; pensiontemarama@mail.pf. On mountainside in Unaa with access to the sea, 2 km (1.2 mi.) from the airport and 500 m (1,640 ft.) from the village of Moerai. Free round-trip transfers between airport and pension. AE, MC, V.*

This is a big two-story white house with 8 bedrooms located just outside the main village of Moerai. Each attractively decorated room has one or two double beds, a writing desk, ceiling fan, and a private bathroom with hot water shower, and some rooms have a TV. Daily maid service and clean towels. Each floor also has a living room with sofas, a television and bookshelves. A long, wide covered balcony outside the rooms overlooks the ocean, which is only about a block from the pension, and they have a swimming pool and hot water Jacuzzi in their front yard. A bar and restaurant are on the ground floor, where well-prepared meals are served family style. Dinner is accompanied by a pitcher of red wine. Owners Tania and Landry Chong also operate Rururu Rent A Car and they can arrange island tours, a special picnic, hiking excursions, horseback riding, fishing and diving expeditions. WiFi and pay telephone service available.

PENSION LE MANOTEL, *B.P. 11, Moerai, Rururu 98753. Tel./Fax 689/ 93.02.25, cell 689/74.35.42; manotel@mail.pf; www.lemanotel.com. On the mountainside, 6 km (3.7 mi.) from the airport and 2 km (1.2 mi.) from the boat dock in Moerai village. MC, V.*

Hélène and Yves Gentilhomme have 6 wooden bungalows in a lovely garden of flowers and ferns, located in Peva, across the road from a long white sand beach

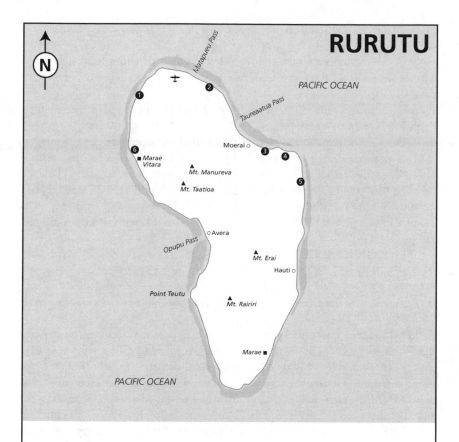

1. Rurutu Lodge
2. Pension Te Marama
3. Heiata Nui Guest House
4. Home Sweet Home
5. Pension Le Manotel
6. Pension Teautamatea

that is shaded by tamanu trees. Each colorfully decorated unit has a double bed, a single bed, a fan and television, a private bathroom with hot water shower and a covered terrace with two lounge chairs. Héléne cooks delicious local style meals that are served in the restaurant and Yves makes the confiture (jam). The water is potable.

Yves is past-president of the Rurutu Comité de Tourisme and he speaks a little English. He can provide land tours by 4WD and will take you to visit the grottoes, caves, beaches and blowhole, with or without lunch included. He can also put you in touch with a qualified hiking guide. Just across the road from Le Manotel you can easily see the humpback whales swimming close to shore during their visit each July-October. A bungalow with half-board (MAP) meals is 9.200-11.050 sgl., and 12.900-15.300 CFP dbl., according to season. The round-trip from airport is 1.000 CFP per person. This friendly pension has been given a 3-Tiare rating by Tahiti Tourisme.

PENSION TEAUTAMATEA, *B.P. 35, Moerai, Rurutu 98753. Tel. 689/ 93.02.93/70.34.65; Fax 689/93.02.92; www.teautamatea.blogspot.com. Across the road from the lagoon in Vitaria, 3 km (1.9 mi.) from the airport and 6 km (3.7 mi.) from Moerai quay. Free round-trip transfers between airport and pension. No credit cards.*

This modern house in Vitaria is situated in a magnificent coconut grove shading an archaeological site that includes the royal *Marae Tararoa*. There are 4 guest bedrooms with 1-2 double beds and wooden furniture built by the multi-talented owner, Viriamu Teuraurii. There is a ceiling fan in each room and disabled facilities are available. The 4 private bathrooms all have hot water showers, and a hairdryer is available on request. Guests can use the high-speed WiFi Internet without charge, and there is also a TV at their disposal. There is a pretty white sand beach across the road that faces the setting sun.

Viriamu's wife, Elin, is a Biologist from Wales and speaks English and French. She takes care of the pension and cooks the meals, which may include carpaccio of thazard (wahoo), spiced breadfruit soup, sweet potato gratin, and banana crêpes flambé served with homemade vanilla ice-cream. She serves coffee grown in Rurutu. Elin also makes jams from the local fruits, as well as monoi oils, soap and incense. Viriamu's mother is known for her hats, bags, mats and other crafts woven from the special *paeore* pandanus leaves grown in Rurutu. A room with MAP meals is 8.500 sgl., 13.200 CFP dbl, and 2.700 CFP for a child 4-12 years. They also offer the full-board (AP) plan. A traditional underground *ahima'a* oven is prepared every Saturday evening for lunch on Sunday. This feast requires 4 people min. and costs 3.500 CFP or 1.000 CFP extra for MAP guests.

Their bicycles are free for guest use. Viriamu and Elin can provide or arrange for various excursions. A half-day guided cave visit is 3.000 CFP and a full-day excursion by 4WD vehicle is 5.000 CFP, including a picnic. Viriamu also has rental horses. (See information under *Horseback Riding* in this chapter). For information and fun, read Elin's stories at *www.lifeinrurutu.blogspot.com*.

HEIATA NUI GUEST HOUSE (Chez Louis et Paulette), *B.P. 02, Moerai, Rurutu, 98753. Tel. 689/94.05.82/72.30.06; Fax 689/94.07.83; chambredhotesheiatanui@mail.pf. On mountainside in Moerai Village, 3 km. (1.8 mi.) from the airport and 200 m. (656 ft.) from the port. Free round-trip airport transfers. No credit cards.*

This 2-story white house in the center of Moerai faces the Protestant Church, where the parishioners gather almost every evening to sing their *himenes*. Tahiti Tourisme has awarded a 2-Tiare rating to the owners, Louis and Paulette Teinaore, who are active members of the community. Louis is the current president of Rurutu's Comité de Tourisme, which is based at their guest house. His wife operates the popular Snack Paulette, serving local style cuisine.

There are 4 rooms upstairs, each with a ceiling fan, and private bathroom with hot water. Two of the rooms have a double bed and a single bed and the other two rooms have 2 double beds and a single bed. Each room has a balcony overlooking the port or the mountains. The rooms are cleaned and linens changed every three days. Bed and breakfast rates start at 7.350 CFP sgl./9.450 dbl., and a room with MAP (half-board meals) is 9.450 CFP sgl./14.700 CFP dbl. The full-board (AP) plan is also available. Half-price for children 2-12 years.

Other Family Pensions:

HOME SWEET HOME, *Tel. 689/77.76.87*, is a 3-bedroom house in Moerai Village, built like the bow of a ship and overlooking the sea. Owners Jean-Claude and Virginia are a young Polynesian couple who have even included a honeymoon suite that has a king size bed, bathtub, terrace and private entrance. Guests can cook their own meals or let Virginia cook for them. This B&B also caters to traveling salesmen.

WHERE TO EAT

Visitors usually take their meals in the pension where they are staying. If you wish to dine in another pension then you must reserve in advance.

The **Omiri Ferme** (Farm), *Tel. 94.02.39*, in Moerai, makes various kinds of yogurts and confitures, and on Fri. nights you can get pizzas and fresh homemade pasta to go. There are also a few snack bars and roulottes that are located near the schools and at the port in Moerai. These include **Snack Paulette**, *Tel. 94.05.82*; **Snack Tetua**, *Tel. 94.07.82*; **Snack Piareare**, *Tel. 94.04.95*, **Snack Tiare Hinano**, *Tel. 94.05.00*; and **Roulotte Norma Poetai**. Most of the Chinese food stores sell prepared dishes to go, and it's best to shop before noon. There are also 3 bakeries turning out fresh baguettes daily.

SEEING THE SIGHTS

Some of the interesting sites you will want to visit in Rurutu are the grottoes and *marae* temples of Vitaria, the Tetuanui Plateau and dam, the beautiful view of Matotea between Vitaria and Avera, the Lookout Point at Taura'ma, where you can see the villages of Avera and Hauti, the Trou de Souffleur (spouting hole) and the beautiful white sand beaches of Naairoa, Narui and Peva, the Vairuauri Grotto at Paparai, and the Underwater Grotto of Te Ana Maro at Teava Nui.

You may also be interested in visiting the final resting-place of **Eric de Bisschop**, a French explorer who was noted for his ocean voyages in unseaworthy rafts. He died at Rakahanga in the Cook Islands in 1972, and is buried in the second cemetery of Moerai, off the main road, south of the village. All the pensions can provide a 4WD excursion to visit the highlights for about 5.000 CFP per person.

Hiking

Retii Mii, *Tel. 94.05.38*, is Rurutu's only trained hiking guide. He will take you on excursions that may include a visit to the Metuari'i domain on the north coast of the island. You can visit the Matonaa promontory overlooking Moerai village, and climb to the summits of Teape, Taatioe and Manureva mountains, which shouldn't present any major difficulty unless you are subject to vertigo. The Ana Aeo grotto in Vitaria resembles a baroque cathedral with its stalactites and stalagmites. President François Mitterand came here in 1990 when he was still president of France, and this grotto became a stage where the traditional songs and dances of Rurutu were performed. Following this visit the residents now calls this Mitterand Grotto. The Pito circuit covers the beautiful south end of the island, with its numerous beaches of white sand. You will climb plateaus and explore numerous grottoes, cross the cliffs and follow a road that takes you from Avera to Auti villages. The Peva circuit between the villages of Moerai and Auti is the shortest hike in distance, but the richest in various kinds of sites. This is where you will find the most beautiful grottoes on the island, complete with stalactites and stalagmites. The Varirepo grotto is comprised of two immense chambers with a ceiling that is 20 m high. One of the calcite formations is in the amazing shape of a giant sized *cocoro* (penis) that stands 2 m. high.

Horseback Riding

Viriamu Teuruarii at Pension Teautamatea in Vitaria, *Tel. 93.02.93/70.34.65*, leads horse treks into the mountains. A short trek across the island's agricultural plateau lasts about 2 hours and costs 5.000 CFP. A 3-hour trek for more experienced riders costs 7.500 CFP.

SPORTS & RECREATION

Safari And Quad Bike Tours

Le Manotel, Tel. 93.02.25/72.35.42. Yves Gentilhomme leads 4x4 Safari Tours.

Rurutu Baleines Excursions, *Tel. 94.07.91/70.30.53*, provides Safari Tours to discover the mountains and valleys of the island.

Rurutu Quad "Rimorimo", *Tel. 94.06.07/78.95.38*, takes you on mountain trails and off-track.

Boat Rentals, Sports Fishing and Whale-Watching Excursions
Rurutu Baleines Excursions, *Tel. 94.07.91/70.30.53; www.rurutu.pf. Princesse Inanui* is a 16-passenger Bertram fishing boat that is used for deep-sea fishing, excursions around the island, and for whale watching between the months of July and October. The captain and crew are all certified in first aid and life saving at sea.
Pierre Harua in Avera, *Tel. 94.06.36,* also has a boat for rent with a skipper.
Nahuma Tavita, *Tel. 94.06.51,* has a boat used for excursions. He charges 8.000 CFP for adults and 5.000 CFP for children.

Diving
Raie Manta Club Rurutu is based at the Rurutu Lodge, *Tel. 96.84.80/74.07.03; www.raiemantaclub.free.fr,* and is managed by Eric Leborgne. Their main tourist season is from July-Oct., when the humpback whales (*Megaptera novaeangliae*) come up from the cold Antarctic waters. The calm waters and low predation in the warmer waters of the tropics allow the females to calve in peace after their 11-12 month gestation period. Two observation platforms have been built on either side of Moerai village to watch the whales, which are easily sighted as the reef is close to the shore. The islanders say that when the orange flowers of the *Erythrina* (Indian coral) tree start to blossom this is a sure sign that the whales will arrive at any moment. The air temperature in Rurutu may drop to 15° C. (59° F.) in July-Aug., but the ocean temperature doesn't get any cooler than 21-22° C. (70 to 72° F). Although more whales are sighted each year in Tahiti and Moorea, visitors from several countries make their reservations months in advance so that they can dive with the humpback whales in Rurutu because the water is so clear. Sept. is usually the best month.

SHOPPING
The "mamas" of Rurutu are noted for their finely made hats, baskets, tote bags, mats and other woven products. You can visit the arts and crafts shops in each village and you will also see the women sitting together on the grass or on their front terraces, creating an outlandish hat for them to wear to church or a beautiful traditional hat for you to buy. The Artisans Association has stands at the airport. In the small *magasin* stores you can buy confitures made in Rurutu, as well as 500-gram (1 lb.) bags of Cafe Teautoa, which is 100% Arabica Cafe de Rurutu.

PRACTICAL INFORMATION
Banks
Banque Socredo, *Tel. 94.04.75,* has an agency in Moerai village, open Mon.-Fri. 7:30-11:30am and 1-4pm. There is also an ATM distributor in the Socredo building that accepts only Visa cards. Open 6am-10pm daily.

Doctors
There is a small medical center in Moerai, *Tel. 94.03.30,* and an infirmary in Avera village, *Tel. 94.03.21.*

Pharmacy

The pharmacy is located on the main road in Moerai, *Tel. 93.02.85.* Emile Leconte is the pharmacist.

Police and Fire

The French *gendarmerie* of Rurutu, *Tel. 93.02.05,* is located in Moerai. The municipal police (*mutoi*) *Tel. 94.03.38,* and Fire Station, *Tel. 73.17.55,* are also in Moerai.

Post Office

The Post Office and Telecommunications Center is in Moerai, *Tel. 94.03.50.* Open Mon.-Fri. 7am-12pm and 12:30-3pm. They have Internet service, a card telephone and an ATM.

Tourist Bureau

Rurutu Visitors Bureau. The **Comité de Tourisme (Tore Anuanua)** is located at the Heiata Nui Pension in Moerai, *Tel. 94.05.82/72.79.38; rurututourisme@mail.pf; www.rurutu.info.* Louis Teinaore is president.

TUBUAI

Tubuai is 568 km (352 mi.) due south of Tahiti, located just above the Tropic of Capricorn in the center of the Austral Island group, offering a pleasant combination of the tropics and temperate zone.

This is the largest of the Austral Islands, with a land area of 45 sq. km. (17 sq. mi.) and a population of 2,216 inhabitants. An immense turquoise lagoon is bordered by brilliant white sand beaches and dotted by 7 palm shaded *motu* islets, surrounded by superb snorkeling grounds. From the village of Mahu the reef is 5 km. (3 mi.) from the shore. These shallow lagoon waters provide an ideal nursery for colorful and delicious tropical fish, clams, sea urchins and lobsters. There are 3 main passes and several smaller passes through the coral reef into the lagoon, and cargo ships can offload supplies at a concrete pier near Mataura village. This sheltered harbor is located close to the former site where Fort George was established by Fletcher Christian and his mutineers from the *H.M.S. Bounty* when they tried to settle on Tubuai in 1789. This was one of the most important events in the history of Tubuai, when the mutineers tried twice to live on the island, but were fought off by the unfriendly warriors of the island.

Captain James Cook discovered Tubuai in 1777 during his 3rd voyage to Tahiti, but he did not go ashore. The London Missionary Society sent native teachers to the island to convert souls to Christianity in 1822 and the Protestant faith is still predominant in Tubuai. The first Mormon missionary to settle in these islands arrived in Tubuai in 1844, and this religion is today an important part of the lifestyle.

Tubuai is the administrative center for the archipelago, and the main village of **Mataura** has the administrative offices, town hall, gendarmerie, small hospital, post office, schools and some of the churches. Chinese families operate the island's 5 grocery stores and 2 bakeries. Electricity and hot water are provided in the small bed and breakfast pensions, where you can also share lunch and dinner with the host family in their big dining room, or cook your own meals in a well-equipped kitchen. Activities can be arranged at your pension to visit the island by car or bicycle or to explore the motu islets and lagoon by boat. Hiking is popular here and can easily be accomplished without a guide.

Tubuai is a pretty island with gentle slopes and contours. It does not have the dramatic coastlines of Rurutu, Raivavae and Rapa, and the people here seem to lack the zestful spirit, the *joie de vivre* that you'll find on Rurutu. This is one of the few remaining islands in French Polynesia where the untreated tap water is still totally safe for consumption, even for babies.

ARRIVALS & DEPARTURES
Arriving By Air
Air Tahiti has a 1:45 hr. direct flight from Tahiti to Tubuai each Sun. and Mon. A Mon. and Wed. flight also stops in Raivavae, and the Fri. flight stops in Rurutu. The one-way airfare from Tahiti to Tubuai is 24.330 CFP; the fare from Rurutu to Tubuai is 11.730 CFP; and from Raivavae to Tubuai the one-way fare is 11.530 CFP. **Air Tahiti reservations:** Tahiti *Tel. 86.42.42;* Tubuai *Tel. 93.22.75.*

You can also get to Tubuai by chartering an airplane in Tahiti from **Air Tahiti,** *Tel. 86.42.42,* or **Pol'Air,** *Tel. 74.23.11.*

Arriving By Boat
Tuhaa Pae II, *Tel. 41.36.06/50.96.09; Fax 42.06.09; snathp@mail.pf* makes 3 voyages a month from Tahiti to the Austral Islands, calling at Tubuai, Rimatara, Raivavae and Rurutu, then returning to Papeete. This itinerary changes according to the freight requirements of each voyage. The one-way fare to Tubuai is 4.046 CFP on the deck and 7.789 CFP for a berth in a cabin. Meals are extra. See further information in Chapter 6, *Planning Your Trip.*

Departing By Air
You can fly direct from Tubuai to Tahiti each Wed. and Fri. The Mon. departure from Tubuai makes a brief stop in Raivavae before returning to Tahiti and the Sun. flight stops in Rurutu on its way to Tahiti. More flights are added in July and August. **Air Tahiti reservations** in Tubuai, *Tel. 93.22.75.*

Departing By Boat
The **Tuhaa Pae II** calls at Tubuai enroute to the other Austral Islands or on its way back to Papeete. You can purchase your ticket on board the ship.

ORIENTATION

Tubuai is an oval shaped island with no indented bays. Two mountain ranges rise from the heart of the island, with **Mount Taitaa** the highest peak at 422 m (1,393 ft.) in altitude. A 24-km (15 mi.) paved road circles the island, connecting the quiet villages of **Mataura, Taahuaia** and **Mahu**. The airport is about 4 km (2.5 mi.) west of Mataura village and the ship wharf is on the east side of Mataura. Beside the pretty Protestant church in the center of Mataura village a transversal road heads inland and crosses the island from Mataura to Mahu, passing through fertile plains and marshlands, where taro, potatoes, sweet potatoes and peaches grow alongside coffee, corn and oranges. The island is bordered by soft sandy beaches that range in color from white to rose and yellow to ochre, an artist's palette of at least 8 varying shades. Most of the houses are built on the mountain side of the road because of the high seas and strong winds during the winter months of July and August. Australian pine trees and hedges of white lilies are planted on the beach side of the road to serve as wind breaks.

The residents of Tubuai are still recovering from the devastation caused by Cyclone Oli that bombarded their island on Feb. 4-5, 2010. More than 200 houses on the N and NE side of the island were destroyed by winds of up to 250 km. (155 mi.) per hour. The 9m. (30 ft.) high waves swept tons of sand, coral and rocks from the lagoon as far as 250m. (820 ft.) inland, pulverizing everything in its path. Some 20 km. (12.4 mi.) of the circle island road has been rebuilt, and the lost homes have been replaced by pre-built ready-made "anti-cyclone" MTR kit houses issued by the government. The vegetation along the shore has found new life, but the centuries old trees that were uprooted in the center of the island are gone forever.

GETTING AROUND TUBUAI

You will be met at the airport or boat dock by someone from the pension where you've reserved accommodations. Check with your host for car and bicycle rentals. There is no public transportation system.

Europcar Tubuai, *Tel./Fax 95.04.12; Cell 73.81.84.* Vii Maurinui rents a Nissan 4x4 with double cab for 15.000 CFP a day. A Fiat is 10.000 CFP and a Twingo is 9.000 CFP per day, and a Van is 10.000 CFP. Bikes are 1.500 CFP.

Tubuai Center*, Tel. 93.24.65/72.25.93; Fax 689/93.24.06; tubuaicenter@ mail.pf;* rents cars, kayaks and pedal boats.

WHERE TO STAY

PENSION TOENA, *B.P 146, Mataura, Tubuai, 98754; Tel./Fax. 689/ 95.04.12; Cell 73.81.84; toena@mail.pf; www.toena.pf. On mountainside in Taahuaia, 8 km. (5 mi.) from airport, 5 km. (3.1 mi.) from Mataura and 1 km. (.62 mi.) from the circle island road. Free airport transfers. No credit cards.*

This small family pension has been given a 2-Tiare rating by Tahiti Tourisme. The Maurinui Vii Tahuhuatama family has built 2 bungalows and a guest house on a hill overlooking the lagoon, the ocean and the tropical sunrise. The 1-bedroom

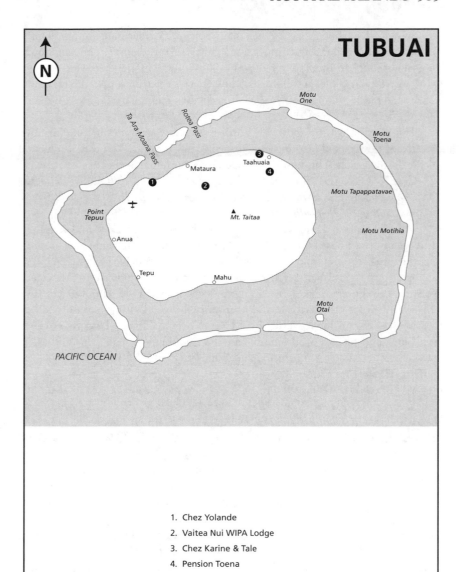

1. Chez Yolande
2. Vaitea Nui WIPA Lodge
3. Chez Karine & Tale
4. Pension Toena

bungalow with a living room, kitchen, bathroom and terrace rents for 6.500 CFP per person with breakfast and dinner, and 7.500 CFP for all meals. The 2-bedroom bungalow has 2 bathrooms and rents for 6.000-7.000 CFP per day per person for MAP or AP plan. The guest house is 5.500 CFP per person for MAP and 6.500 CFP for all meals. All the rooms are equipped with a ceiling fan and mosquito nets over the beds.

The pension is surrounded by a lush garden and activities include making wreaths of flowers and learning how to make tifaifai quilts. You can also have a picnic on the beach. This family also operates a car rental agency.

CHEZ YOLANDE, *B.P. 23, Mataura, Tubuai, 98754. Tel./Fax 689/95.05.52. On the mountainside in Mataura, 2 km (1.2 mi.) from the airport and 3 km (1.9 mi.) from the boat dock. No credit cards.*

This 1-Tiare rated family pension is located in a modern, clean and attractive 2-story concrete house. There are 5 guest rooms with comfortable beds, ceiling fans, private bathrooms and hot water showers. A/C is available in some rooms. A big open terrace and balcony overlook the beach and lagoon across the road. Yolande Tahuhuterani takes care of the students' meals in the school in Mataura village and she is also active in the Mormon Church. During her absence her pension guests are looked after by her employees. Circle island tours, boat excursions and picnics on the motu can also be arranged. This pension has an excellent reputation for its cuisine and both MAP and AP plans are available. Airport transfers are extra.

VAITEANUI WIPA LODGE, *B.P. 141, Mataura, Tubuai, 98754. Tel. 689/ 93.22.40/73.10.02; Fax 689/93.22.42; maletdoom@mail.pf; www.vaiteanui.com. Beside the cross-island transversal road in Mataura, 5 km (3 mi.) from the airport and a 10-min. walk inland from the circle island road in the heart of Mataura village. No credit cards.*

Wilson "Wipa" Doom, a local personality involved in lagoon activities, tourism and cultural events, now manages this family pension that was formerly operated by his relatives, the Bodin family. He speaks English and likes to talk about his culture. The motel-like concrete structure situated behind the kitchen contains 5 rooms that were completely renovated in 2010. The walls are thin, but the rooms are clean, with screened windows, and a double bed with a foam rubber mattress. There are also 3 bungalows for guests. All rooms have mosquito nets and a private bathroom with hot water shower. Room rates are 4.235 CFP sgl./6.960 CFP dbl. Add 4.115 CFP per person for breakfast and dinner, and 6.415 CFP for all meals. Reduced rates for children under 12 years. Round-trip airport transfers are 550 CFP for adults and 275 CFP for children.

Meals are served on a big covered terrace or in the family style dining room, where there is a lounge area with a small boutique, bookshelves, board games, TV, a point phone and free WiFi Internet access. The pension is conveniently located near the post office, food stores, banks, hospital, pharmacy, churches and town hall. Wilson can arrange all activities for you (see *Sports & Recreation* in this chapter).

CHEZ KARINE & TALE, *B.P. 34, Mataura, Tubuai, 98754. Tel. 689/ 93.23.40/75.68.56; Fax 689/93.22.76; charles@mail.pf. On mountainside in Taahuaia, 6 km (3.7 mi.) from the airport and 2 km (1.2 mi.) from Mataura quay. No credit cards.*

This cute little bungalow is across the road from a white sand beach, furnished with a double bed and 2 single beds, living room, kitchen, private bathroom with hot water shower, and a terrace facing the lagoon. The windows are screened and there is a ceiling fan, plus a TV and washing machine. It rents for 5.000 CFP sgl./ 8.000 CFP dbl. per day, plus taxes, including breakfast. No lunch or dinner served. Bicycles rent for 1.000 CFP per day.

Karine Tahuhuterani is an American woman from California who grew up in Tahiti and married her childhood sweetheart from Tubuai. She and Charlie (Tale) live next door to the bungalow, and she is the Air Tahiti agent in Tubuai.

WHERE TO EAT

Guests usually take their meals in the pension where they are staying unless they can prepare their own meals. Should you wish to dine at another pension, please reserve in advance. **Restaurant Mere**, *Tel. 95.04.17/76.25.68*, in Taahuaia, serves Chinese cuisine, and **Mara'ai**, *Tel. 95.08.32/73.62.20*, in Tamatoa, serves local dishes. Snack stands open and close according to what is happening on the island. **Libre Service Tien Hing** in Mataura village is the biggest food store, and each morning they sell casse-croûte baguettes and prepared dishes such as chow mein and other Chinese dishes to take away.

SEEING THE SIGHTS

Mount Taitaa is an attraction for hikers, who will enjoy the view from the summit, which is 422 m. (1,384 ft.) high. Your pension host will drop you off beside the track and it's an easy round-trip hike of 3 hrs. to get to the top. Other hiking trails are also interesting and easily reached. Your pension can arrange car tours around the island and you can also bike around.

SPORTS & RECREATION

Land and Lagoon Excursions

Tubuai Evasion, *Tel. 95.01.21/75.97.76; www.tubuai-evasion.com.* Gilles and Nathalie Kints organize half-day mountain hikes for 3.900-4.500 CFP, half-day 4x4 excursions for 4.500 CFP, visits to the marae, bike tours and cultural workshops. They also lead lagoon excursions, snorkeling tours and fishing in the lagoon and offshore.

Wind's Islands Program Australs (W.I.P.A) is operated by Wilson Doom, *Tel./Fax 95.07.12, Cell 73.10.02; maletdoom@mail.pf.* He guides historical excursions and 4x4 visits to the marae. He also provides island tours inside the lagoon aboard his 24-ft. motorboat, transfers to Motu One for a 2-3-hr. swim, and a 9am-4pm excursion that takes you around the island, with a local style picnic lunch on the motu. Wilson serves poisson cru, *pahua* (reef clams) and freshly grilled fish. This all-day outing is 7.000 CFP per person. He also has a kite surfing group and welcomes international kite surfers from many countries.

Scuba Diving
La Bonne Bouteille, *Tel/Fax 95.08.41, cell 74.90.97; labonnebouteille@mail.pf; www.labonnebouteilleplongee.com.* "The Good Bottle" is operated by Laurent Juan de Mendoza, originally from Nice, who is a BEES 1 sports educator instructor and Sea Guide. His boat is specially equipped for scuba divers and he has all the necessary diving equipment available in his center located at Mataura Quay. He teaches scuba diving and also has free-dive outings, as well as diving with the humpback whales between July and late October.

SHOPPING
An artisan center is located beside the old town hall in the main village of Mataura, selling woven hats, mats, bags, clothing, *pareos* and *tifaifai* bed covers. Handcrafts are also on display at the airport prior to Air Tahiti arrivals and departures.

PRACTICAL INFORMATION
Banks
Banque Socredo, *Tel. 95.04.86,* has an agency in Mataura village behind the Protestant church. **Banque de Tahiti**, *Tel. 95.03.63,* is in Mataura village.

Doctors
There is a medical center in Mataura, which serves all the Austral Islanders, *Tel. 93.22.50.*

Pharmacy
Mataura, *Tel. 95.03.28/93.25.00.*

Police
French *gendarmerie, Tel. 93.22.05.*

Post Office
There is a Post Office and Telecommunications Center in Mataura, *Tel. 95.03.50.*

Tourist Bureau
The **Tubuai Visitors Bureau** (Harii Taata Association), *Tel./Fax 95.07.12, Cell 73.10.02; maletdoom@mail.pf,* is in Mataura, presided by Wilson Doom, who speaks English.

RIMATARA

Located 538 km (334 mi.) southwest of Tahiti and 150 km (93 mi.) west-south-west of Rurutu, the circular island of Rimatara is the smallest and lowest of the inhabited Austral Islands. The land surface is only 8 sq. km. (3 sq. mi.) and Mount Vahu is the highest peak at 83 m. (274 ft.). A narrow fringing reef hugs the uneven shore of the island and there is no lagoon.

Far removed from the beaten path of tourists and even cruising yachts, Rimatara has no sheltered boat harbor or dock, and no hotel. For some of the island's 797 inhabitants (Sept. 2007 census), who live in blissful isolation from the world's problems and turmoil, Rimatara is a joyful and tranquil refuge. Several of the young people, however, are slowly leaving their island for Tahiti, where they can find jobs and a livelier lifestyle. Since the opening of an airport in 2006, the islanders now have more freedom of travel, and visitors can more easily get to Rimatara.

When the *Tuhaa Pae II* anchors offshore **Rimatara** every few weeks to bring supplies, the passengers come ashore by whaleboat, surfing over the reef in turbulent waves that beat against the island's limestone cliffs. Upon landing on the beautiful white sand beach of Amaru the visitors are required to follow an old custom of the island and walk through a cloud of smoke to purify them before being welcomed ashore.

ARRIVALS & DEPARTURES

Arriving By Air

The Mon. flight from Tahiti to Rimatara stops in Tubuai and Rurutu and the Wed. and Fri. flights are direct. Airfares from Tahiti are 24.930 CFP one-way and 45.960 CFP round-trip; and from Rurutu to Rimatara the one-way fare is 9.530 CFP, and from Tubuai to Rimatara the fare is 17.930 CFP. **Air Tahiti reservations** in Tahiti, *Tel. 86.42.42.*

You can also get to Rimatara by chartering an airplane in Tahiti from **Air Tahiti**, *Tel. 86.42.42*, or **Pol'Air**, *Tel. 74.23.11*.

Arriving By Boat

Tuhaa Pae II, *Tel.41.36.06, Fax 42.06.09; snathp@mail.pf* makes 3 voyages a month from Tahiti to the Austral Islands, calling at Tubuai, Rimatara, Raivavae and Rurutu, then returning to Papeete. This itinerary changes according to the freight requirements of each voyage. The one-way fare to Rimatara is 3.817 CFP on the deck, and 7.348 CFP for a berth in a cabin. Meals are extra. See further information in Chapter 6, *Planning Your Trip.*

Departing By Air

There is a direct flight from Rimatara to Tahiti on Mon.; the Wed. flight stops in Rurutu, and the Fri. flight stops in Rurutu and Tubuai.

Departing By Boat
The **Tuhaa Pae II** calls at Rimatara enroute to the other Austral Islands or on its way back to Papeete. You can purchase your ticket on board the ship.

ORIENTATION
Amaru is the principal village, with the town hall, *gendarmerie*, post office and infirmary, plus a school and a couple of stores. **Anapoto** and **Mutuaura** villages are reached by dirt roads. There is a severe water shortage during dry seasons.

WHERE TO STAY & EAT
PENSION UEUE, *Amaru, Rimatara, 98752; Tel./Fax 689/94.42.88; cell 74.66.13; ueue.rimatara@mail.pf; www.pensionueue.pf; 4 bungalows in Amaru village. Free airport transfers. No credit cards.*

Each of the 4 small white wooden bungalows has a covered terrace leading to a pretty garden of flowers. Each unit has a double bed and a single bed, a fan, mosquito repellent, and a private bathroom with hot water shower. Services include a restaurant/snack, covered dining terrace, living room with TV, safe, a point pay phone, and Internet access on request. Activities to visit the island can be arranged with the hosts, Georges and Claudine Hatitio.

RAIVAVAE
Raivavae is one of the most exquisite islands in the South Pacific, rivaling even Bora Bora with its natural beauty. Fern covered Mount Hiro reaches 437 m. (1,442 ft.) into the mist of clouds. Sea birds soar around some 2 dozen picturesque islets that seem to float on the emerald lagoon protected by a distant coral reef. Beaches of soft white powdery sand surround these motus, forming graceful swirling patterns of lagoons within lagoons.

Located 632 km (392 mi.) southeast of Tahiti, this island of 16 sq. km (6 sq. mi.) remained aloof from the world of tourism until 2002, when the small airport opened, providing Air Tahiti connections to Papeete 2-3 times a week, depending on the season. Although the airport represents a giant step forward into modern times, tranquility still reigns on Raivavae, even in the 4 pretty villages of **Rairua, Mahanatoa, Anatonu** and **Vaiuru**. These neat and clean villages, with their pastel colored limestone houses, are home to the island's 940 inhabitants. The women of Raivavae compete with one another to see who can make the most original hat to wear to the Evangelical church services. Some of the decorations consist of plastic fruit, golf balls and even blinking lights.

Raivavae has long held the attention of anthropologists, archaeologists and biologists, who come here to study the people and their customs, the remains of stone temples and tiki statures or to make an inventory of the birds, snails and aquatic insects. These included J. Frank Stimson in 1917, Thor Heyerdahl in 1956 and Donald Marshall in 1957. John Stokes of the Bishop Museum in Hawaii led an archaeological mission to Raivavae in 1921 to record the oral traditions and inventory the archaeological sites. The people agreed to loan 5 of their tikis to the Bishop Museum, which have never been returned. Thor Heyerdahl's expedition resulted in the loss of 7 more tikis that were carried away without permission of the local authorities and are now in the Museum of Oslo. 2 of the tikis from Raivavae were shipped to Tahiti in 1933 and are now standing on the grounds of the Paul Gauguin Museum in Tahiti. Chilean archaeologist Edmundo Edwards made an inventory of the sites in 1986 and 1991 on behalf of the Culture and Patrimony Service at the Museum of Tahiti and Her Islands and his findings are reported in his book published in September 2003: *Ra'ivavae: Archaeological Survey of Ra'ivavae, French Polynesia*. More than 600 archaeological structures have been found on Raivavae, including 80 marae still remaining. A short walk inland from the coastal road, just to the west of Mahanatoa village you can see Raivavae's only remaining tiki, which is 2 m. high. There are 20 tikis on Pomoavao marae, which is on the Matahariua land facing the airport, but these are incomplete fragments.

Raivavae's climate and fertile soil are ideal for growing crops of taro, potatoes, carrots, cabbages, coffee and citrus fruits. Sandalwood trees are also numerous on this island. There is a plentiful variety of seafood in the lagoon, including lobster, sea snails and tridacna clams. Due to a high level of ciguatera that affects the lagoon fish and clams, most of the family pensions serve only deep-sea fish at their tables.

ARRIVALS & DEPARTURES
Arriving By Air
Air Tahiti flies has a 1 hr. and 55-min. direct flight from Tahiti to Raivavae each Wed. and Fri. There is also a flight each Mon. that stops in Rurutu and Tubuai. The one-way airfare from Tahiti to Raivavae is 26.930 CFP; the fare from Rurutu to Raivavae is 15.330 CFP, and from Tubuai to Raivavae it is 11.530 CFP. There is no flight between Raivavae and Rimatara. Air Tahiti reservations: *Tahiti Tel. 86.42.42/86.41.84; Raivavae Tel. 95.44.33.*

You can also get to Raivavae by chartering an airplane in Tahiti from Air Tahiti, *Tel. 86.42.42*, or Pol'Air, *Tel. 74.23.11.*

Arriving By Boat
Tuhaa Pae II, *Tel.41.36.06, Fax 42.06.09; snathp@mail.pf* makes 3 voyages a month from Tahiti to the Austral Islands, calling at Tubuai, Rimatara, Raivavae and Rurutu, then returning to Papeete. This itinerary changes according to the freight requirements of each voyage. The one-way fare to Raivavae is 5.502 CFP on the deck and 10.591 CFP for a berth in a cabin. Meals are extra. See further information in Chapter 6, *Planning Your Trip.*

Departing By Air
You can fly from Raivavae direct to Tahiti on Mon., and the Wed. flight stops in Tubuai enroute to Tahiti. There is also a Fri. flight with stops in Tubuai and Rurutu. Air Tahiti reservations in Raivavae, *Tel. 95.44.33.*

Departing By Boat
The **Tuhaa Pae II** calls at Raivavae on its way back to Papeete or enroute to the other Austral Islands, according to the needs of the islanders. You can purchase your ticket on board the ship.

ORIENTATION
The island of Raivavae is 9 km. (5.6 mi.) long and 2 km. (1.2 mi.) wide. On the western shore of the island is Rairua village, where there is a port for cargo vessels, a *mairie* (town hall), small infirmary, post office, *gendarmerie*, primary school and a couple of old Chinese stores with a poor selection of supplies. A road, either concrete or dirt, connects the villages and a cross-island road provides a shortcut route over a mountain saddle from Rairua on the western side to Vaiuru on the southern coast. The airport is 6 km. (3.7 mi.) from the ship dock, built on a landfill between Rairua and Vaiuru.

Most of the houses are built on the mountain side of the coastal road and hedges of white spider lilies border the beach side to serve as a windbreak. Tall Australian pine trees also help to protect homes from the strong austral winds and big ocean swells that arrive during the winter months of July and August. Picturesque Protestant churches adorn each village, where the faithful parishioners gather several times a week to sing and pray.

GETTING AROUND RAIVAVAE
You will be met at the airport or boat dock by someone from the pension where you've reserved accommodations. There is no public transportation system on Raivavae and no taxi service outside the pensions.

Car & Bicycle Rentals
Ataha Location, *Tel. 95.43.69/28.92.35*, at Pension Ataha in Vaiuru charges 10.000 CFP per day for a rental car. He has 10 bicycles that he rents for 500 CFP for a half-day and 1.000 CFP for a full-day.

Pension Nuruata, *Tel./Fax 689/95.42.83; cell 78.63.50*, has a rental car for 7.000 CFP a day.

WHERE TO STAY & EAT
RAIVAVAE TAMA INN, *B.P. 17, Rairua, Raivavae 98750. Tel./Fax 689/ 95.42.52; raivavaetama@mail.pf; www. raivavaetama.com. Beside the sea in Anatonu village, 6 km (3.7 mi.) from the airport and 8 km (5 mi.) from the boat dock. Free airport transfers. No credit cards.*

Emmy Teupoo White and her American husband, Dennis, have built 3 wooden bungalows overlooking the beach in Anatonu village, Each well-furnished bungalow has a queen size bed and one or two twin beds, mosquito nets, ceiling fan, TV, and a bathroom with hot water shower. There is also a sundeck where you can sit and watch the lagoon, or you can walk a few steps past a row of *aito* trees

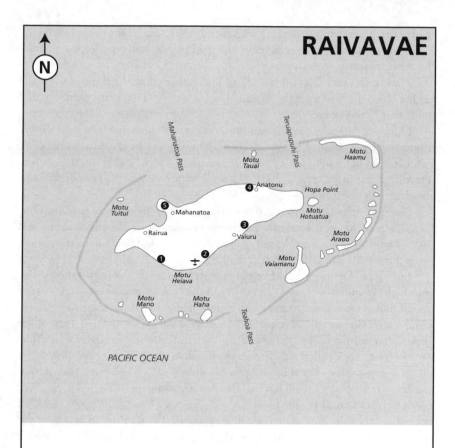

1. Pension Chez Linda
2. Pension Nuruata
3. Pension Ataha
4. Raivavae Tama Inn
5. Pension Moana

(Australian pines) and you are on a white sand beach. This is the only place on the island where you can stay beside the beach, and you are lulled to sleep at night by the gentle murmur of the waves.

There is also a small family house and 2 beautifully furnished bungalows in the garden across the road from the lagoon. The beds are covered with colorful tifaifai quilts that Emmy made.

Emmy's delicious and generous meals are served family style in their dining room or on the patio of the main house. She worked in the San Bernardino, California school system for 15 years, in nutrition, cafeteria and catering, before returning home to Raivavae in 2001. She was also president of the Friends of Tahiti association in California.

Fare Toa Angelique, a magasin store that is run by their daughter and son-in-law, is across the road from the beachside bungalows, and besides being well stocked with supplies, provides fax service. A phone booth is on the corner and a pretty Protestant church is just next door.

Emmy and Dennis will take you in one of their big 4WD's to visit the *maraes,* and their son-in-law will take you fishing in the lagoon or for a picnic on one of the 29 motus around the island.. You will be able to visit the exquisitely lovely Motu Vaiamanu, which the residents of Raivavae call "la piscine", as it resembles a vast swimming pool. The Whites will also take you camping on a motu where they have a house. They will make a fire on the beach at night and you can sing under the stars. On request they will drop you off all by yourself and bring your dinner at night. Otherwise, you will have all the privacy you wish.

Rates for a bungalow with breakfast and dinner are 8.500 CFP sgl./6.500 CFP per person dbl. The bungalow with all meals is 10.000 CFP sgl./8.000 CFP per person dbl. Activities are 2.500 CFP each. Bicycles and kayaks are 500 CFP for a half-day.

The Raivavae Tama Inn is an excellent place to stay if Emmy is in residence. Her meals are generous and varied and well prepared, and she is very warm and welcoming. The story is not at all the same whenever she has to leave the island, so be sure to confirm that she will be at home when you make your reservations.

PENSION CHEZ LINDA, *B.P. 45, Rairua, Raivavae 98750. Tel./Fax 689/ 95.44.25; cell 21.20.87; pensionchezlinda@hotmail.fr; www.pensionlindaraivavae.pf. Across road from lagoon and airport runway in Rairua village. Free airport transfers. No credit cards.*

There are 4 wooden bungalows in the garden, each with a double bed and a single bed, a ceiling fan, private bathroom with hot water shower, and a balustrade. Linda also rents 2 guest rooms with a communal bathroom inside her big white concrete house. Meals are served family style in the open sided dining room, which is covered by an immense roof and overlooks the beach across the road. She charges 10.000 CFP sgl./12.500 CFP dbl. for a bungalow and half-board (MAP) meals, and 7.000 CFP sgl./10.000 CFP. dbl. for a room and MAP.

A circle island tour is offered guests free of charge. Paid activities include a visit to the archaeological sites for 2.000 CFP, guided hiking excursions for 3.000 CFP and a picnic on the motu for 4.500 CFP. A bike rents for 1.000 CFP a day. Linda speaks English.

PENSION ATAHA, *B.P. 37, Rairua, Raivavae 98750. Tel./Fax 689/95.43.69; cell 28.92.35; pension.ataha@live.fr. Across the road from lagoon in Vaiuru village, 2.5 km (1.6 mi.) from the airport. Round-trip airport or boat dock transfers included. No credit cards.*

Terani Tamaititahio and his wife Odile have a one-story concrete house beside the road, with 2 bedrooms containing a double bed and fan, a shared bathroom with a very small bathtub and hot water, small living/dining area and an open terrace facing the lagoon. They also rent 3 studios with private bathrooms and hot water and an open terrace. These are equipped with a fan, TV and electric kettle. Rates including breakfast and dinner are 10.000 CFP sgl./14.000 CFP. dbl. Local style meals are served, featuring tuna and mahi mahi. Guests can use the washing machine for 1.000 CFP per load. Bicycles are 1.000 CFP a day, a cross-island tour by car is 3.000 CFP a picnic on the motu is 4.500 CFP and a boat tour of the lagoon with a picnic is 13.500 CFP. Terani has a car for rent for 10.000 CFP a day.

They have a small cabin on Motu Rani, which they call Ataha Sauvage, which has a kitchen and toilet, but no electricity. They will take you there by boat and you can buy a *casse croûte* sandwich and a bottle of water and spend the day by yourself on the motu. Or they will prepare a picnic for you.

Other Guest Lodgings

Pension Moana, *Tel. 689/95.42.66/76.81.17; moanapension@mail.pf.* This is a 3-bedroom concrete house with kitchen owned by Madame Haamoeura Teehu. Located on a private road near Mahanatoa village, between the airport and Rairua boat dock. Beach across road and food store nearby. You can rent a room only or a room and meals. No credit cards.

Pension Nuruata, *Tel./Fax 689/95.42.83; cell 78.63.50.* This is a 2-story concrete house on the mountainside in Rairua near the airport, with 4 guest rooms and 2 communal bathrooms with hot water. Free transfers and paid excursions to visit the island and lagoon. A rental car is 7.000 CFP a day. EP, MAP and AP plans available. No credit cards.

SEEING THE SIGHTS

No matter where you stay in Raivavae your hosts can arrange for a circle island tour by 4WD and they can usually find someone with a boat who will take you to visit the fabulous motu islets on the southern and eastern parts of the reef. Do not miss going to Motu Vaiamanu, which the islanders call motu piscine. This is the most beautiful motu I have ever seen in all my island hopping days in the South Seas. You arrive by boat from the main island and step onto a perfect white sand beach of white powdery sand. Then you walk a few feet through the shady grove of ironwood trees (Australian pines) to the other side of the motu, and a breathtaking vision opens up before you that will make you very happy you brought your camera. This lagoon within a lagoon is even better than Blue Lagoon in Rangiroa. Miles of soft white sand beach mingle with the shallow water of the tides, which reflect the patterns of white clouds. You can walk across this swimming pool to another motu that is closer to the reef or you can follow the curve of the beach to the spot where the tridacna clams are still found in abundant plenty in knee-deep water. Unfortunately, 2007 studies have found that they have high levels of toxic ciguatera. You can picnic here or continue on to explore some of the other motus, and you can also camp out on many of these uninhabited islets.

Archaeological sites on the main island include the one remaining big stone tiki, in a clearing just west of Mahanatoa village, Marae Maunauto on the south coast, where there is the grave of a princess, and Marae Pomoavao, facing the airport. You'll need a guide to take you to Marae Poupou at Vai Otorani stream in the valley, a short walk inland from the transversal road. Many of the big slabs of volcanic stone are still standing around this immense structure.

SHOPPING
Woven hats, bags and mats, as well as wood carvings are sold at the airport when Air Tahiti arrives. Handcrafts centers are located in Mahanatoa, Vaiuru, Rairua and Anatonu, but they are not usually open except for special occasions.

RAPA
Remote **Rapa** stands proudly alone 1,074 km. (666 mi.) southeast of Tahiti, below the tropical zone, where the temperature can drop to 5 degrees Celsius (41 degrees Fahrenheit) during the austral winter in July and August. Rapa-Iti, as the island is also called, has a strong cultural connection to Rapa-Nui, the Polynesian name for Easter Island. Archaeological ruins include strong *pa* fortresses built among volcanic pinnacles. **Mount Perehau**, the tallest of six peaks, reaches 650 m. (2,145 ft.) above the island, whose fjord-like coastline has 12 deeply indented bays. Several sugar loaf-shaped islets lie just offshore and there is no fringing reef in these cold waters. White puffs of sheep and wild goats perch on precipitous cliffs over the sea and bay, and herds of cattle roam the velvety green mountain ranges.

Rapa's 506 inhabitants live in **Haurei Village** and in the smaller village of Area, which is reached only by boat across Haurei Bay. There is a town hall, post office, infirmary, weather station and school. A cooperative store provides the villagers with basic supplies and many of the homes have television and telephone service. There is no airport in Rapa, and the *Tuhaa Pae II* supply ship docks in Haurei Bay every 6-8 weeks, the island's only regular connection to the outside world. This ship usually stays only a few hours at the dock before returning to Tahiti.

ARRIVALS & DEPARTURES
Tuhaa Pae II, *Tel.41.36.06, Fax 42.06.09; snathp@mail.pf* calls at Rapa once every 2 months during its visits to the Austral Islands. The one-way fare from Tahiti

to Rapa is 7.523 CFP on the deck, and 14.481 CFP for a berth in a cabin. Meals are extra. See further information in Chapter 6, *Planning Your Trip*.

WHERE TO STAY & EAT
   CHEZ JEAN TITAUA, *Ahurei, Rapa 98751. Tel. 689/95.72.59; Fax 689/ 95.72.60.* Near the quay in Haurei village. No credit cards. This is a 1-bedroom house with a living room, dining room, kitchen, terrace and private bathroom with hot water. House linens are furnished.

21. Glossary of Tahitian Terms

In addition to the Tahitian words, this glossary also contains a few French and English terms that are used in Tahiti and Her Islands. The **Tahitian alphabet** contains 13 letters. A is pronounced ah, as in father, E is pronounced e, as in fate, F is pronounced fa as in farm, H is pronounced he as in heaven, I is pronounced i as me, M is pronounced mo as in mote, N is pronounced nu as in noon, O is pronounced o as in go, P is pronounced p as in pat, R is pronounced ro as in rode, T is pronounced t as in time, U is pronounced u as in rule, V is pronounced v as in veer.

The Tahitian dialect abounds in vowels, such as Faaa, the name of Tahiti's largest commune, where the international airport is located. This is pronounced Fah-ah-ah, but most people lazily forget the last syllable. Tahitian words have no "s" for the plural. There are no hard consonants in the Tahitian alphabet, such as the letter "B;" however, the name Bora Bora is accepted as the legal name for the island that was formerly called Pora Pora.

a'ahi - tuna, *thon* on French menus
ahima'a - underground oven used for cooking traditional Polynesian food; also *hima'a*
ahu - the most sacred place on a marae, an altar that took many forms, including pyramid shaped
aita - Tahitian for "no"
aita e peapea - no problem; also used as "you're welcome"
aita maitai - no good
aito - ironwood tree, also a strong warrior
aparima - a Polynesian story-telling group dance
api - new, young
arii - Polynesian high chief, a sacred being or princely caste
arioi - a religious sect or fraternity in the Society Islands in pre-Christian days
atoll - a low coral island, usually no more than six feet above sea level
atua - Polynesian gods
baguette - long loaf of crusty French bread
barrier reef - coral reef between the shoreline and the ocean, separated from the land by a lagoon
belvédère - panoramic lookout
bonitier - bonito boat
BP - *bôite postale*, post office box
breadfruit - a football-size starchy green fruit that grows on a breadfruit tree, eaten as a staple with fish, pork or canned corned beef and coconut milk

bringue - a party or fête, usually with lots of music, singing, dancing and Hinano beer

cascade - French for waterfall

casse-croûte - sandwich made with *baguette* bread

CEP - *Centre d'expérimentation du Pacifique*; the French nuclear-testing program that was carried out in French Polynesia from 1966-1996

CFP - *cours de franc Pacifique*; the French Pacific franc is the local currency

chevrette - French for sea shrimp, as opposed to fresh water *crevettes*

CMAS - *Confédération Mondiale des Activités Subaquatiques*; the World Underwater Federation, France's scuba diving equivalent to PADI

copra - dried coconut meat used to make oil and monoi

coral - a white calcareous skeletal structure inhabited by Madreporaria, organisms that comprise the living polyps inside the skeletal pores, giving color to the coral

croque madame - also called *croque vahine*, is a toasted ham and cheese sandwich with a fried egg on top

croque monsieur - toasted ham and cheese sandwich

cyclone - tropical storm rotating around a low-pressure 'eye'; the equivalent to a typhoon in the western Pacific and a hurricane in the Caribbean

demi-pension - half board (bed, breakfast and dinner), see also *pension complète*

demis - half caste Tahitian-European

e - Tahitian for "yes"

espadon - French for sword fish

faa'amu -to feed; an informal child adoption system in Polynesia

faa'apu - farm

fafa - the green tops of the taro plant, similar to spinach

fafaru - stinky fish dish

fare - traditional Polynesian house, home, hut

fare iti - little house, outdoor toilet

fare manihini - visitor's bureau

fare moni - bank

fare ohipa - office

fare pape - bathroom

fare pote'e - chief's house or community meeting place, oval shaped

fare pure - church

fare purera'a rahi - cathedral

fare rata - post office

fare taoto -sleeping house

fare toa - store

fare tutu - kitchen

fei - plantain, Tahitian cooking banana

fête - festival, party, celebration

fiu - bored, fed up

fringing reef - a coral reef along the shoreline

FFESSM - *Fèderation Française des Activités Subaquatiques*, or French Underwater Federation of Scuba Divers

gendarmerie - French national police station

goëlette - French for schooner; inter-island cargo or freighter ships

haere mai - come here

haere maru - take it easy

haura - swordfish or marlin

heiva - festival, an assembly for dancing

heiva vaevae - big festival parade

here here - romance

high island - an island created by volcanic action or geological upheaval

himenes - Tahitian for songs or hymns

hinano - flower of the pandanus tree, girl's name, Tahiti's favorite beer

Hiro - Polynesian god of thieves; Raiatea's first king was named Hiro

hoa - shallow channel across the outer reef of an atoll that carries water into or out of the central lagoon at high tide or with big ocean swells

hoe - ceremonial canoe paddle

honu - turtle

ia ora na - hello, good morning, good afternoon, good evening, pronounced similar to "your honor" (yore-ronah)

ia'ota - marinated fish salad, *poisson cru*

ipo - a dumpling made with breadfruit and coconut water

iti - small, little

kaina - a slang term similar to hick or hillbilly, usually applied to out-islanders; country music

kava - mildly intoxicating drink made from the root of piper methysticum, the pepper plant; a fruit tree

kaveu - coconut crab

keshi - a pearl without a nucleus

lagoon - a body of normally calm water inside a coral reef

leeward - on the downwind side, sheltered from the prevailing winds

le truck - Tahiti's former public transportation system, now mostly replaced by modern buses.

LMS - London Missionary Society, the first Protestants to bring the Gospel to Tahiti in 1797

ohipa - work

opani - out of order, broken, closed

maa - food, also spelled **ma'a**

maa tahiti - traditional Tahitian food

maa tinito - Chinese food

maa tinito haricots rouge - a popular dish with red beans, macaroni, pork or chicken mabe - blister pearl that is grown inside the mother-of-pearl shell

maeva; manava - greetings, welcome

magasin - small food store

mahi mahi - dolphinfish, *dorade Coryphène*

mahu - Tahitian for transvestite or homosexual male

maitai - good; also a potent rum drink

maiore - another name for uru or breadfruit

mana - spiritual power

manahune - the common people or peasant class in pre-European Polynesia; servants, tillers of the soil, fishermen, prisoners of war and slaves

manuia - cheers, a toast to your health

mako, mao - shark

maniota - manioc root

manu - bird

maoa - sea snails

Maohi - Tahitian Polynesians; the ancestors of today's Tahitians, some of whom sailed to New Zealand and are called Maori

mape - Tahitian chestnut

maraamu - southeast trade winds that can often blow for days, bringing rain, rough seas and cooler weather

marae - traditional Polynesian temple of coral or basaltic stone, usually built with an ahu altar at one end

marara - flying fish

mauruuru - thank you

mauruuru roa - thank you very much

me'ae - Marquesan word for marae

mei'a - banana

meka - a melt-in-your-mouth swordfish from the ocean depths. French menus sometimes list it as *espadon de nuit*

miti ha'ari - fresh coconut milk poured over traditional Tahitian foods

miti hue - a fermented coconut milk used as a dipping sauce for breadfruit, taro, fei, bananas, fish, pork and canned corned beef

mona mona - sweet, candy

monoi - oil made from coconut oil, flavored with Tiare Tahiti, ylang ylang, pitate and other flowers, also with sandalwood powder or vanilla. It is used as an emollient, perfume, hair dressing, suntan oil and mosquito repellent

mo'o - lizard

mo'o rea - yellow lizard, name of the island of Moorea

more - Tahitian grass skirts made from the purau tree

mou'a - mountain

motu - a coral islet inside the lagoon, between the outer reef and a high island

mutoi - Tahitian municipal police

nacre - mother-of-pearl shell

naissain - larva of an oyster

nao nao -mosquito

navette - shuttle boat

nehenehe - pretty; handsome

neo neo - stinky smell

noa noa - fragrant, sweet smelling

nohu - stone fish

noni - Marquesan for *Morinda citrifolia*, a plant whose juice is used as a tonic

nono - sand flea; also Tahitian word for *Morinda citrifolia*

nucleus - a small sphere of calcium carbonate that is grafted into the gonads of the pearl oyster to produce a pearl. The fresh water mussel from the Mississippi River provides the best nucleus and helps to produce the finest black pearls

nui - big, new

oa oa - happy, joyful, merry

ono ono - barracuda

Oro - Polynesian god of war who demanded human sacrifices at the *marae* in pre-Christian days

otea - legendary group dance performed in grass skirts

PADI - Professional Association of Diving Instructors, the American system of scuba diving

pae pae - stone paved floor of pre-European houses or meeting platforms

pahua - clam; *bénitier* on French menus

painapo - pineapple, *anana*

pandanus - palm tree with aerial roots whose leaves are used for weaving roofs, hats, mats and bags

pape - water

pareo, pareu - a sarong-like garment that is hand-painted or tie-dyed

pass - channel through the outer reef of an atoll or the barrier reef around a high island that allows water to flow into and out of the lagoon

Paumotu - inhabitants of the Tuamotu atolls

peapea - problems, worries

pension - boarding house, hostel

pension complète - full-board (bed and all meals)

penu - pestle

pétanque - also known as *boules*, bocce-ball or bocci-ball; a French game of bowls, where metal balls are thrown to land as near as possible to a target ball. A very competitive sport in Tahiti

peue - mats woven of coconut or pandanus fronds

pia - beer

pirogue - French word for outrigger canoe

PK - *poste kilometre*, the number of kilometers from the *mairie* or post office

plat du jour - daily special, plate of the day

po'e - a sticky pudding made with papaya, bananas or pumpkin, corn starch and coconut milk

poe rava – a beautiful pearl that comes from the *Pinctada Margaritifera*, the black-lip oyster

poisson cru - fish marinated in lime juice and served cold with tomatoes, onions, carrots, cucumbers and coconut milk. In Tahitian it's *i'a ota*

popaa - foreigner, Europeans, westerners, white people

popoi - fermented breadfruit eaten as a bread substitute or sweetened with sugar and coconut cream as a dessert

poulet - French for chicken

poulet fafa - chicken cooked with taro leaves and coconut milk

pu - conch shell blown to announce the arrival of a delegation, visitors, dancers, or the fish truck

puaa - pig, the basic food for all Tahitian *tamaara'a* feasts

pua'a'toro - beef; canned corned beef, the staple of the South Seas

purau - wild hibiscus tree, whose inner bark is used to make grass skirts

rae rae - a slang term for *mahu*, usually implying homosexuality

raatira - the intermediary caste of the ancient Polynesian society, between the *arii* and the *manahune*

rori - sea slug, sea cucumber

roulotte - mobile dining van

sennit - woven fiber from coconut husks

siki - dark skinned people

Taaroa - Polynesian creator god

tahua - priests of ancient Polynesian religion

taioro - fermented grated coconut sauce that may contain *pahua* clams or *maoa* sea snails

tamaara'a - Tahitian feast

tama'a maitai - enjoy your meal, *bon appetit*

tamure - Tahiti's national hip swiveling, rubber-legging dance

tane - man, husband, boyfriend, Mr.

tapa - bark-cloth, traditional clothing of the pre-European Polynesians; wall hangings

tapu - tabu, taboo, sacred, forbidden

taramea - crown-of-thorns starfish that eats the coral animals and destroys the reefs

taro - root vegetable that is one of the staple foods in Polynesia

tarua - a tuber usually cooked in the *ahima'a* oven

tatau - Tahitian word for tattoo

tiane'e - slipper lobster; *cigalle de mer* on French menus

tiare - flower

Tiare Tahiti - fragrant white petalled *gardenia taitensis*, Tahiti's national flower

tifaifai - colorful bed and cushion covers or wall hangings sewn in patchwork or appliquéd designs

tii - Tahitian name for human-like wooden or stone statues that had a religious significance in pre-European Polynesia

tiki - a Marquesan word for the Tahitian *tii*; some of these statues are still found on the *me'ae* in the Marquesas Islands

Tinito - Tahitian name for Chinese

tiurai - Tahitian for July, the major festival of July

TPE - *traitement paiement electronique*, an automatic teller machine equivalent to the ATM. Nobody calls this a TPE, however, but a *distributeur*

toe toe - cold

toere - wooden slit drum played for Tahitian dance shows

tohua - a place for meetings or festivals in pre-European Polynesia

tupa - land crab

tupapau - spirit ghosts of the Polynesian religion, still feared by some people

ufi - a huge root vegetable similar to yams, cooked in underground *ahima'a* oven

umara - sweet potato

umete - wooden dish or bowl used for serving foods or holding fruits and flowers

upa upa - music

uru - breadfruit

vaa - Tahitian word for outrigger canoe

vahine - Tahitian word for woman, wife, Ms.

vehine- Marquesan word for woman, wife, Ms.

vana- black sea urchin whose meat is good to eat

vanira - vanilla

varo - sea centipede, a gourmet's delicacy

V.A.T. - value added tax; called T.V.A. in French Polynesia

vea vea - hot

vivo - nose flute

VTT or vélo or tout terrain - mountain bike

windward - facing the wind; the opposite of leeward

4x4 or 4WD - a 4-wheel drive vehicle, such as a Land Rover, Jeep or pick-up truck

GENERAL INDEX

AAD VAN DER HEYDE GALLERY 290

Adventure Eagle Tours 30, 195
Adventure Travel Company The 62
Afareaitu 139, 225, 226, 252, 298
Afareaitu waterfalls 227, 274
Ahe 17, 20, 31, 73, 79, 110, 460, 462, 480

Ahuii Waterfall 519, 527, 531
AIDS 99
Air Calédonie 68
Air Charters 75
Air France 68
Air Passes 73-74
Air Moorea 223
Air New Zealand 68, 69
Air Tahiti 18, 22, 24, 62, 64, 67, 69. 72, 73,
    75, 90, 130, 142, 225, 228, 303, 304,
    330, 334, 335, 365, 385, 387, 389, 390,
    449, 450, 461, 462, 480, 481, 488, 499,
    514, 518, 519, 520, 534, 535, 542, 550,
    551, 560, 574, 575, 583, 588, 589, 590,
    591, 596
Air Tahiti Nui 68, 69
Aman Resorts 388
Amaru 44, 47, 589, 590
Amaru Quay 336, 364, 365, 589, 590
American Consulate 59, 218
Anaa 17, 460
Anaa Atua Grotto 543, 547
Anaho 518, 525, 528, 531
Anahoa 534, 536, 538
Anapoto 590
Anatonu 590, 592, 596
Anau 390, 400, 401, 402, 406, 408, 422,
    423, 427, 428, 429
Apataki 17, 79, 460
Apooiti Marina 83, 206, 334, 342, 348,
    355, 357, 358, 360
Apoomau River 332, 353
Apu Bay 366, 380, 381, 382
Aqua Tiki II the 84, 510-511
Araara Pass 31

Arahoho Blowhole (see Blowhole of
    Arahoho) 190, 196
Aranui the 17, 24, 32, 77-79, 259, 498,
    499, 517, 519, 526, 528, 535, 542, 544,
    545, 551, 561, 562, 564, 565, 568
Aratika 84, 86, 497, 511
Archipels Croisières 24, 83, 354, 477
Area 596
Aremiti Ferry 76, 225
Aremiti V 76, 216, 217, 223-224, 225
Art Galleries 102, 145, 212, 388, 438
Arue 110, 131, 137, 139, 143, 152, 189,
    205, 214
Arutua 79, 460
Assembly of French Polynesia 51, 53, 93,
    113, 121, 145, 187
Assistance the 49
Astronomy 210
Atallah Paul 30, 324
Atara Royal the 380
Atimaono 43, 50, 128, 156, 181, 191, 201
ATMs (also see Money) 101, 218, 297,
    444, 445, 478, 532, 533, 560, 581, 582,
    604
Atoll 14, 16, 17, 23, 31, 33-34, 35, 37, 38,
    41, 44, 50, 55, 79, 86, 387, 460
Atua god 516, 598
Atuona 519, 520, 542, 549, 550, 551, 552,
    554, 557, 558, 559, 560, 562
Austral Islands 15, 18, 24, 32, 33, 43, 48,
    49, 56, 70, 74, 79, 81, 86, 87, 118, 120,
    122, 124, 192, 356, 570, 572, 574, 575,
    582, 583, 589
Avatoru 31, 86, 460, 461, 462, 463, 465
Avea Bay 316, 317, 320
Avera 332, 344, 345, 346, 351
Avis 88, 146, 227, 236, 304, 305, 334, 337,
    338, 352, 390

BACKPACKERS 20, 161, 162, 312, 320,
    346, 502
Baggage: allowances 66-67, 69, 74-75;
    storage 67, 142, 160

Bailey Dick 81, 89, 90
Balboa Vasco Nuñez de 47
Bali Hai Hotels 89, 103, 215
Bali Hai Mountain 103
Banking (see Money & Banking)
Barrier reef (see Coral reefs)
Bars 30, 92, 99, 116, 121, 135, 136, 137, 146, 155, 198
Bay of Virgins (see Hanavave)
Beachcomber (see InterContinental Resorts)
Bellinghausen (Motu One) 16, 330
Belvedere Lookout: Moorea 23, 215, 274, 275, 280; Tahiti 24, 176-177, 202; Atuona 554
Birds 11, 12, 37-39, 46, 140, 183, 246, 388, 459, 494, 495, 496, 498, 508, 530, 543, 590
Bishop Museum 107, 303, 448, 541, 590, 591
Bisou Futé the 84, 380
Bisschop Eric de 580
Bligh Captain William 48-49, 104, 140, 167, 189, 428
Bloody Mary's Yacht Club 447
Blowhole of Arahoho 196, 220
Blue Lagoon 461, 475, 596
Boenechea Don Domingo de 48
Books 57, 100, 104, 107-110
B.P. (bôite postale) 105
Bora Bora 50, 73, 74, 76, 82, 85-86, 385-386, 388; History 387; Where to Stay 391-412; Where to Eat 412-422; Seeing the Sights 76, 422-428; Nightlife 428-429; Sports 429-438; Shopping 438-441; Massages & Spas 441-443; Tattoos 444; Internet 444; Practical Information 444-445; Weddings 95, 445-446
Bora Bora Yacht Club (Mai Kai Marina & Yacht Club) 388, 420, 447
Bordelais Channel 561
Botanical gardens (see Gardens)
Boudeuse the 190, 428
Bougainville Admiral Louis-Antoine de 47, 140, 153, 187-188, 428
Bougainville Park 187, 219
Bougainville's anchorage 190
Bounty H.M.S. 48-49, 50, 103, 140, 167, 189, 428, 572, 582

Bounty Tunnel 185
Brando Marlon 12, 16, 98, 103-104, 109, 423
Breadfruit 35, 46, 48-49, 138, 189, 190, 269, 270, 272, 302, 332, 479, 527-528, 564, 565, 578, 598
Brel Jacques 549-550, 554, 557, 558
Brendan Vacations 61
Business hours 92
Buying Land in Tahiti 111
Byron Commodore John 47

CALENDAR OF FESTIVALS & EVENTS 123-129
Calvary Cemetery 549, 558
Camping 72, 203, 250, 252, 320, 324, 328, 345, 354, 400, 456, 472, 473, 502, 559, 594
Canoe Racing 54, 208
Car rentals 60, 64, 87, 146-147, 158, 227, 305, 337-338, 366, 390, 465, 552, 554, 567
Catamaran Tane the 84, 356
Cathédrale de l'Immaculate Conception 188
Census 42, 144, 226, 517, 589
Centre d'expérimentation du Pacifique (CEP) 50, 599
CFP 101, 102
Chamber of Commerce 66
Changing money (see Money & Banking)
Charter Boats (see Yachting)
Children travel with 130-134
Chinese 29, 36, 43, 124, 137, 149, 161, 171, 172, 174
Chinese Temple 123
Chirac Jacques 50-51
Christian Fletcher 104, 167
Churches Catholic 217, 255, 274, 297, 359, 465, 478, 487, 498, 506, 512, 518, 526, 528, 534, 535, 538, 540, 543, 551, 562, 564, 566, 572
Churches Protestant 124, 142, 186, 189, 192, 198, 217, 218, 273, 297, 302, 334, 351, 424, 487, 550, 562, 573, 574, 579, 584, 588, 592, 594
Ciguatera 18, 97, 488, 591, 596
Climate (see Weather)

Club Mediterranee (Club Med) 109, 225, 251, 276, 285, 293, 388, 423
Cockfighting 210
Coco Beach - Moorea 270, 276-277
Consulates in Tahiti 218
Cook Captain James 47, 109, 140, 153, 189, 302, 311, 331-332, 428, 516, 562, 572, 582
Cook Islands 18, 38, 43, 47, 67, 69, 73, 81, 118, 148, 352, 580
Cook's Bay – Moorea 215, 222, 225, 226, 233, 235, 236, 237, 262, 274
Coral reef 17, 33, 39, 40, 41, 84, 97, 207, 287, 301, 328, 366, 385, 424, 572, 574, 598, 600
Corser Rose Yacht Club 529, 533
Cost of Living & Travel 92-93
Cousteau Jacques 86, 488
Cousteau Jean-Michel 81
Crafts (see Arts & Crafts)
Credit cards 102-103
Crossroads Travel, Inc. 61, 132
Cruises & charters (see Boats & Yachting)
Cultural center 66, 123, 129, 145, 186, 189, 558
Currency Exchange (see Money & Banking)
Custom Tahiti Travel 61
Customs Allowances 71-72
Cyclones 97, 164, 243, 333, 341, 388, 402, 420, 447, 450, 453, 461, 487, 584, 599

DANCE LOCAL STYLE 201
Dangers Natural 41-42
Darwin Charles 33-34
Dave's VIP Tours 195
Day Tours 215-217
Deep Nature Spa by Algotherm 82
Deep Sea Fishing (see Fishing)
Demi the 44
Destination Management Companies 64
Diadème 14, 202
Diarrhea 35, 96, 98-99
Discos & Jazz 199-200
Dive Tahiti Blue 63, 64, 296
Diving 17, 31, 41, 54, 63, 67, 85, 86, 155, 207, 239, 287-288, 327, 356-357, 380-382, 435-436, 457, 461, 476-477, 485,

496, 511-512, 531, 559-560, 581, 588
Doctors 95, 96, 218, 298, 328, 359, 383, 445, 478, 569, 581
Doedalus the 541-542
Dolphin H.M.S. 47, 189
Dolphin Center (ex-Dolphin Quest) 133, 215, 244, 275, 289
Dolphins 12, 17, 40, 86, 256, 257, 284, 457, 463, 465, 469, 475, 476, 510, 531, 543,
Dolphin watch 23, 206, 209, 284-285
Dory III 80
Dream Yacht Charter 24, 83, 354-355, 477-478
Drugstores (see Pharmacies)
Duff the 49
Dupetit-Thouars Admiral Abel 37, 49, 564
Duty-free shopping 71-72, 82, 143, 155, 211, 212, 220, 533, 561

EASTER ISLAND 47, 62, 69, 115, 188, 596
Eden Martin 84, 326
Edwards Captain Edward 49
Edwards Edmundo 110, 591
Eels blue-eyed sacred 164, 318, 324
Eiao 17, 33, 514
Eiaone 550
Electricity 93, 142, 205, 360, 371, 406, 453, 454, 459, 469, 472, 484, 492, 493, 506, 572, 583
Ellis Reverend William 108, 302
Emory Dr. Kenneth P. 448
Endeavour H.M.S. 47, 153, 189, 302, 331-332, 428
Entrance requirements 57-59
Etablissements Français de l'Océanie (EFO) 49, 50
Etoile the 190, 428
Europcar 88, 146, 227, 305, 306, 328, 337, 347, 463, 585
Exchange rates (see Money & Banking)
Expatriates 44

FAAA (FAA'A) 22, 42, 50, 51, 59, 67, 68, 69, 72, 76, 82, 101, 106, 125, 126, 141, 146, 147, 154, 211, 220
Faaaha 335, 364, 365, 366, 372, 379, 382

Faakua valley 558
Faanui 389, 390, 410, 423-424, 427, 428, 439
Faaroa (Bay, River, Valley) 31, 202, 332, 340, 344, 345, 346, 350, 351, 352, 353, 354, 355
Faaopore Bay 423
Fa'arumai Waterfalls 190, 196
Faie 301, 319, 320, 323, 325, 327, 328
Fai Manu the 84
Fakarava 14, 16, 17, 20, 23, 24, 29, 31, 32, 73, 78, 79, 80, 84, 86, 104, 115, 326, 497-500; Where to Stay & Eat 500-509; Sports 509-512; Shopping 512-513; Practical Information 513
Fangataufa 50, 51, 185
Fare (Huahine) 301, 304, 305, 306, 308, 310, 312, 313, 314, 315, 316, 320, 322, 323, 325, 327
Fare Hape 196, 197
Fare Piti 389
Fatu Hiva 514, 516, 517, 551, 564-567; Where to Stay & Eat 567; Seeing the Sights 568; Sports 568; Shopping 568-569; Practical Information 569
Fatu Huku 17
Fauna 106, 387, 443, 457; Land-Based 36-39; Ocean Reef & Lagoon 34, 39-42, 86, 481, 497, 539, 559
Fautaua 14, 139, 202
FEI (Fond d'entraide aux îles) 165, 451
Festivals (see Calendar of Events)
Fetuna 101, 332, 333
Financière Hôtelière Polynesiénne (FHP) 90, 368, 521
Firecrest the 427, 428
Fire dancing 30, 159, 264, 272, 273, 278
Fire walking 125
First Choice Holidays 83, 355
Fishing 17, 18, 23, 78-79, 90, 157, 204, 205, 226, 282, 283, 284, 352, 356, 363, 369, 370, 371, 372, 373, 380, 404, 430, 431, 453, 454, 456, 457, 459, 461, 465, 467, 475, 477, 483, 491, 492, 503, 509-510, 511, 525, 531, 534, 539, 543, 547, 548, 556, 559, 568, 569, 581, 594
Fitii 301
Fitiiu Point 423-424, 427

Flora (see Flowers)
Flowers 15, 34, 35, 95, 107, 188, 189, 190, 193, 195, 445, 517; How to Wear Your Flowers 34; Tiare Apetahi 333
Food & Drink (general) 135-139
Food Plants - Traditional 35; Imported 35-36; Chinese 36
Fort George 582
Fort Halley 562
French Colonialism 49-50
French Embassies & Consulates 59-60
French High Commissioner 51
French Polynesia 50
French takeover 49
French the 44
Friends of Tahiti 66
Fun Sun Vacations 63
Furneaux Tobias 302

GAMBIER ISLANDS 15, 33, 40, 41, 42, 43, 75, 80, 111-112
Game fishing (see Fishing)
Gardens: Tahiti 129, 185, 190, 191, 193, 194; Moorea 276, 277; Ua Huka 541, 546
Garuae Pass 86, 498, 500, 503, 505
Gauguin Paul Museum 110, 190, 192, 220, 558, 591
Gauguin Paul 191, 192, 549-550
Gauguin Paul M/S 12, 24, 70, 81-82, 293, 309, 439
Gaulle General Charles de 50, 187
Gayangos Captain Thomas 572
Geography (see Land)
Geology 33-34, 387
Gendarmes 51, 51, 87, 143, 146, 261
Gerbault Alain 427, 428
Gibson Mel 104
Gneisenau the 188
Golf 128, 191, 201, 226, 230, 232, 259, 273, 279-280, 340, 411
Government 51-53, 145,
Green Lagoon 461, 472, 510
Grelet Willie Chief 568
Grey Zane 124, 204
Grottoes of Mara'a 191, 220

HAAKAU 536

Haakuti 534, 536, 538
Haamene Bay 320, 335, 364, 365, 366
Haapiti 31, 32, 216, 225, 226, 229, 243-252
Haapu 301, 302
Ha'atuatua Valley 528, 541
Haavei 543, 547
Haere Mai Federation 64
Hakahau 534, 535, 536
Hakahetau 534, 535, 537, 538, 539, 540
Hakamaii 534, 536, 538, 540,
Hakamoui 534, 536, 537, 538
Hakanai Bay 538, 539
Hakaohoka 538
Hakatao 534
Hakaui Valley 518, 519, 527, 530, 531
Hall James Norman 110, 152
Hall James Norman House and Library 110, 189, 192
Hall Ron 282
Hanaiapa 549, 550, 551, 554, 558, 559
Hanamenu 550, 551, 559
Hanamiai 564
Hanapaaoa 549, 558, 560
Hanatehau 563, 564,
Hanatekua 550
Hanatu'una Valley 564
Hanavave 564, 565, 566, 567
Handcrafts (see Arts & Crafts)
Hane 541, 542, 543, 545, 546, 548
Hanemoenoe 561
Hao 17, 80, 86
Hapatoni 551, 559, 561, 562
Harris John 562
Hatiheu 29, 518, 519, 525, 526, 527, 528, 529, 530, 532
Hatutu 17, 33, 514
Haumana 84
Haurei 596, 597
Hauti 573, 575, 580
Havai'i 140, 330, 331, 350, 358, 386
Havaiki 46, 47, 331, 503, 512
Havaiki Nui 498
Havaiki Fakarava Pearl Guest House 32, 500, 503, 509, 510, 512
Hawaiki Nui Hotel 332
Hawaiki Nui the 76, 304, 334, 335, 364, 389

Hawaiki Nui Va'a Outrigger Canoe Race 128, 210
Hawaiian Airlines 69
Health 85, 95
Heiva Festivals 54, 66, 104, 125, 126, 145, 191, 193, 210, 574
Heiva in Bora Bora 428
Helicopter Service & Tours (see Tahiti Helicopter Service)
Henry Captain Samuel Pinder 572
Henry Teuira 107, 141
Hertz Rent-A-Car 88, 146-147, 334, 337
Heyerdahl Thor 107, 108, 590, 591
Heywood Peter 49
Hibiscus Turtle Foundation 381
High Islands 14, 16, 17, 37, 40, 47
Hiking 167, 201-203, 209, 280-281, 324, 351, 378, 429-430, 528, 530, 539, 559, 568, 580, 583
Hikokua Tohua 527-528
Hinshaw Milas 428
Hipu 366, 370, 371, 375
Hiro 222, 301, 331, 362, 386, 600
Hiro's Bell (Rock) 386
Hitia'a 202-203
Hiva Oa 514, 516, 517, 548-552; Where to Stay 552-557; Where to Eat 557-558; Seeing the Sights 558-559; Sports 559-560; Shopping 560; Practical Information 560-561
Hohoi 534, 538
Hohorai (see Mount Pahia)
Hokatu 541, 543, 545, 546, 547, 548
Hokule'a Beach 146, 186
Holidays public 93, 138, 216
Honeymoon Resorts 26
Ho'oumi 518, 529
Horseback Riding 80, 203-204, 226, 281, 325, 351, 530, 547, 559, 580
Hospitals, infirmaries, dispensaries 95, 130, 145, 218, 298, 359, 478, 487, 513, 518, 532, 540, 560, 583, 586
Hot Spots 51, 232
Hotel Chains International; Locally Owned 89-90
Hotel Management & Services (HMS) 90, 309
Hotels general 18-20, 88-89

Huahine 301-306; Where to Stay 306-320; Where to Eat 320-323; Seeing the Sights 323-324; Sports 324-327; Shopping 327-328; Massages 328; Practical Information 328-329
Huahine Nui Pearl Farm & Pottery 324
Hurepiti 366, 375, 378, 382

I'IPONA (OIPONA) 550, 556, 558
Immigration and visa requirements 57-59, 71, 115, 142, 143, 212, 220-221
Immunizations (see Vaccinations)
Ingraham Captain Joseph 516, 518, 541-542
Inter-island ships to: Windward Society Islands 76; Leeward Society Islands 76-77; Marquesas Islands 77-70; Tuamotu Islands 79-80; Austral Islands 80-81
Internal Autonomy 51-52, 93, 125
Internet Service 99-100
Iotete Chief 564
Iles du Vent 15-16
Iles Sous le Vent 16
Island Adventures Air Tahiti 64
Island Eco-Tours 324
Island Escapes by Goway 63
Island Fashion Black Pearls 292
Island Stays 74
Islands in the Sun 61

JEFFERSON THE 541
Jardins de Paofai 145, 185-186
Jetabout Island Vacations 61
Jet-skis 283, 369, 437-438
JohnnyJet 60

KAHAIA SPA AT FOUR SEASONS 401, 441-442
Kamuihei site 527, 528
Kauehi 17, 79, 84, 497, 505, 511
Kaukura 17, 79, 460
Kayaks 283, 306, 352, 584
King George III 302
King Pomare (see Pomare family)
King Tamatoa 331
King Tapoa 362
Krusenstern Admiral Johann 487, 518

LAGOONARIUM Tahiti 193, Moorea 289, Taha'a 353, Bora Bora 432
Lagoon excursions 31, 285-286, 325-326, 352-353, 378-379, 431-434, 457, 475-476, 496, 509-510, 587
Lake Fauna Nui 302, 303, 323
Lake Maeva 325
Lake Vaihiria 196, 197
LAN Airlines 69
Land 33-34
La Solide 541
Laundry service 155, 157, 205, 219, 220, 299, 478, 552
Laval Father Honoré 15
Leeteg, William, Edgar 30, 195
Leeward Society Islands 23, 42, 47, 76, 301, 330, 352, 359, 362, 385, 430
Le Maire 47, 461
Les Sables Roses (see Vahituri)
Le truck and buses 123, 124, 141-142, 148, 157, 161, 176, 216, 229, 306, 338, 389, 600
Limousine service 147-148
Living in Tahiti 92, 111
London Missionary Society (LMS) (see Missionaries)
Loti The Marriage of 202
Luckner Count Felix von 188

MAEVA VILLAGE 302, 303
Maeva maraes 302, 303
Magazines 14, 21, 106-107, 297, 402, 444, 478
Magellan Ferdinand 47
Mahana Park 162, 193
Mahanatoa 590, 591, 595, 596
Maharepa 29, 105, 107, 226, 233-237, 273
Mahina 176, 189, 202
Mahu 199, 200, 582, 584, 601
Mahuti 301
Mai (see Omai)
Maiao 16, 42, 49, 330
Mail 105-106
Mairies (town halls) 93-94, 106, 188, 199, 217, 219, 226, 245, 300, 374, 390, 410, 424, 446, 450, 458, 478, 487, 497, 498, 513, 533, 546, 557, 561, 564, 566, 569, 583, 586, 590, 592, 596

Maison de la Culture 129, 186, 211
Maison de la Perle 145
Mai Kai Marina & Yacht Club (see Bora Bora Yacht Club) 388, 420, 447
Makatea 47, 79, 267, 480, 488, 572
Makemo 17, 86, 326
Manea Spa 27, 159, 214, 234, 295, 306, 308, 368, 369, 375, 382-383, 411, 442, 483, 486, 491, 496-497
Mangareva 15, 43, 47
Manihi 79, 86, 89, 112, 114, 133, 159, 292, 479-481; Where to Stay & Eat 481-485; Sports 485; Shopping 486; Massages & Spas 486; Practical Information 487
Maohi 42, 47, 94, 124, 125, 186, 196, 208, 218, 239, 296, 330, 333, 334, 352, 367, 381, 427, 516, 573, 601
Maohi Nui Private Excursions (See Tairua Patrick)
Maoris 47, 311, 352, 572, 601
Maps (where to buy) 100
Mara'a Grottos (see Grottos of Mara'a)
Maraes 14, 23, 30, 35, 141, 186, 598, 601; Fare Hape 196, 197; Marae Arahurahu 191; Marae Titiroa 274, 280; Marae Manunu 302; Marae Anini 302, 319; Marae Tainuu 334, 351; Marae Taputapuatea 351, 353; Marae Aehautai 423, 427; Marae Fare Opu 427; Marae Marotetini 424, 428; Marae Taianapa 427; Marae Vaiahu 449, 455; Marae Taaroa or Arii 573; Marae Pomoavao 591, 596
Marama (son of Hiro) 386
Marama Regent 303
Marama Tours Tahiti 63, 159, 195, 197, 201, 215
Marathons (see Tahiti Nui Marathon)
Marchand Captain Etienne 518, 541
Marché le 92, 139, 188, 210, 211, 213
Mareva Nui the 462, 480, 499, 500
Maria Island 18, 570
Marinas 83, 124, 131, 142-143, 178, 179, 201, 204, 205, 206, 208, 299, 323, 334, 336, 348, 354-357, 360-361, 362, 476, 487, 497

Maris Stella St Xavier III the 79, 462, 480, 488, 489, 499
Maroe 301, 312, 313, 319
Marotiri Rocks 570
Marquesas Festival of Arts 518, 527, 534, 550, 558
Marquesas Islands 15, 17-18, 24, 29, 32, 33, 37, 38, 44, 47, 49, 55, 70, 74, 76, 77-79, 86, 108-110, 192, 203, 514-518
Marquesans 43, 517, 538, 562
Marriage (see Weddings)
Marriage of Loti the 202
Maroto Valley 196
Massages & Spas 27, 213-214, 293-296, 382-383, 441-443, 465, 486, 496-497
Masson Emmanuel 439
Masson Jean 398
Masson Rosine Temauri 398
Mataiea 43, 161, 191, 193, 196
Matairea Hill 303, 323, 324
Mataiva 17, 20, 79, 460, 480
Mataura 583, 584, 586, 587
Matavai Bay 47, 48, 49, 127, 152, 154
Mathilda the 428
Matira Beach 32, 128, 428, 432, 439, 446
Matira Pearls 440, 423
Matira Point 393, 396, 397, 398, 440, 423, 448
Matotea 579
Maupiti 16, 19, 23, 32, 33, 47, 73, 83, 86, 355, 448-451; Where to Stay & Eat 451-456; Seeing the Sights 457; Sports 457; Practical Information 458
Maupiti Express II the 76-77, 335, 336, 366, 449, 450
Maupiti Nautique 457
Maurua Ite Ra (see Maupiti)
Me'ae 516, 527, 528, 529, 538, 541, 550, 558, 560, 601
Medical kit (see Health)
Mehetia 16, 33, 49, 330
Melville Herman 109, 526, 527, 529
Mendaña de Neira Alvaro de 47, 562, 565
Michener James 109
Miri Miri Spa 27, 404, 442-443
Missionaries Catholic 49, 517, 562, 564
Missionaries Protestant 49, 124, 302, 332, 562

Mitterand François 50, 188, 580
Moana Adventure Tours 430, 431, 434, 437
Moe One tiki 558
Moerai 573, 574, 575
Mohotani 17
Money and Banking 101-102
Monoi 129, 211, 442, 518, 560, 601
Monoi Road, The 194
Moorea 12, 16, 20, 22, 23, 24, 49, 222-229; Where to Stay 229-259; Where to Eat 259-273; Seeing the Sights 273-277; Nightlife 277-279; Sports 279-290; Shopping 290-293; Massages & Spas 293-296; Tattoos 296; Internet Service 299; Practical Information 297-300; Wedding Ceremonies 300
Moorea Boat Dock (Papeete) 223
Moorea Boat Dock (Vaiare) 223
Moorea Ferry 224, 225
Moorea Fruit Juice Factory & Distillery 136, 274, 275, 276
Moorea Green Pearl Golf Course 226, 259, 273, 279-280
Moorea Marathon 123-124
Moorea Tropical Garden 275, 276
Moorings The 355
Mopelia 16, 188, 330
Morinda Citrifolia (see Noni)
Moruroa 50, 51, 107, 185, 428
Mosquitoes 36, 77, 96, 108, 131, 193, 197, 246, 318, 353, 518
Motane 550
Mother-of-pearl 49, 111-112, 113, 114, 601
Motopu 563, 564
Motu Ahi 256, 287, 289
Motu Ai Ai 475
Motu Auira 453
Motu Avae Rahi 466
Motu Iti 17
Motu Maeva 315, 320, 328
Motu Mute 373, 385, 387, 389, 423, 439
Motu Nao Nao 346, 353
Motu Oe Oe 495
Motu Ohihi 495
Motu Pa'eao 448, 451
Motu Puarua 491, 495

Motu Taeo'o (see Blue Lagoon)
Motu Tapu 338, 386, 406, 424, 431
Motu Tevairoa 410
Motu Tiapa'a 451, 454, 456
Motu Toopua (see Toopua)
Motu Ua 534
Motutiairi 366
Motu Vaiamanu (motu piscine) 594, 595
Mou'a Puta 222, 236, 280, 281
Mou'a Roa 103, 222, 273
Mou'a Tapu 302, 303
Mount Aorai 202
Mount Hitikau 540
Mount Hue 387
Mount Manureva 572-573, 580
Mount Marau 196, 197, 201
Mount Muake 527, 529
Mount Ohiri 366, 368
Mount Orohena 190
Mount Otemanu 386, 387, 393, 400, 401, 402, 403, 404, 406, 407, 408, 410, 412
Mount Pahia 12, 386, 387, 411, 418, 429
Mount Perehau 596
Mount Rotui 222, 236, 240, 274, 280
Mount Taitaa 584, 587
Mount Tapioi 336
Mount Tefatoaiati 330
Mount Temehani 330, 333, 334, 345
Mount Temetiu 549
Mount Teurafaatiu 448
Mount Tohive'a 222, 273
Mount Vahu 589
Movies & DVD/Videos 103-104
Murifenua 364
Musée de la Marine 428
Museum Gauguin (see Paul Gauguin Museum)
Museum Pearls (see Tahiti Pearl Museum)
Museum of Tahiti & Her Islands 110, 156, 191, 193, 546, 591
Mutuaura 590
Mutiny on the Bounty 103, 104, 109, 167
Mutoi Police 51, 299, 601

NACRE (see Mother-of-Pearl)
Nahoe 549, 550, 560
Naudin Daniel 548
Nautical Centers & Clubs 204-205, 282-

283, 286, 509-510
New Cytherea 78, 190
Newspapers 21, 106-107, 217, 297, 444
Niau 79, 497, 505
Noni Nono (*Morinda Citrifolia*) 35, 78, 517, 602
Nono (sand flea) 35, 37, 77, 97, 273, 353, 525, 528, 529, 602
Nordhoff Charles (see Nordhoff & Hall)
Nordhoff & Hall 109
Nuclear testing 50-52
Nuku Hau the 80
Nuku Hiva 86, 95, 514, 516, 517, 518-521; Where to Stay 521-525; Where to Eat 526; Seeing the Sights 526-530; Sports 530-532; Shopping 532; Practical Information 532-533
Nuku Hiva Yacht Services 533

OAVE NEEDLE 534
O'Connor James 428
Ofai Honu 386
Ofai Maramaiterai 574
Oipona (see l'ipona)
Omai 110, 302, 323, 331
Omoa 565-566
One Tree Hill 189
Onoiau Pass 448
Opoa 331, 332, 333
Opunohu Agricultural School 103, 274, 275
Opunohu Bay 216, 240, 241, 242, 274, 276, 277, 281
Opunohu Valley 12, 23, 128, 215, 226, 274, 280, 281
Oro god 331, 350, 381, 602
ORSTOM 549
Ottino Pierre & Marie-Noëlle 528, 548-549
Owen Peter & Ghislaine 309, 323, 327, 328, 358

PA'AUMEA 536
Pacific Beachcomber SC (PBSC) 12, 81, 89, 90, 309, 396, 466
Pacific Experimentation Centre (see CEP) 50
Packing tips 56-57, 67, 99, 115

Pacific Battalion Monument 50, 187
Pacific Princess the 70
PADI Travel Network 63
Paea 108, 147, 178, 191
Paeke site 529
Paepaes 78, 185, 351, 516, 527, 534, 538, 554, 558, 567
Pahure 366
Pai Moana Pearls 292
Painapo Beach 29, 216, 269, 272-273
Pandora H.M.S. 48-49
Paoaoa Point 423
Pao Pao 29, 139, 226, 228, 274, 280, 292
Pao Pao Valley 236, 274
Papara 31, 43, 126, 128, 163, 182, 191, 201, 202, 208, 220
Papeari 110, 181, 182, 190, 192, 193, 194
Papeete 183-189, 194, 202, 210-213
Papeete By Night 198-201
Papeete Port (see Port of Papeete)
Papeete Yacht Quay 206-207
Papenoo Valley 196-197
Papetoai 226, 237-243
Paradise Tours 63
Parea 14, 31, 301, 302, 305, 316, 317, 319, 320, 322, 324, 328
Pareo (also Pareu) 14, 22, 56, 95, 111, 188, 210, 213, 215, 227, 316, 328, 358
Paroa cave 191
Parasailing 239, 282, 289, 438
Passports 57-58, 59, 71
Patii 335, 336, 364, 365
Patio 366, 371, 372, 373, 383
Patrick's Activities (see Tairua Patrick)
Pauma 449
Paumotu 43, 394, 420, 459, 460, 472, 474, 487, 494, 496, 498, 502, 505, 508, 602
Pearl farms 31, 86, 112, 114, 213, 278, 292, 293, 309, 317, 323, 351, 379, 382, 439-440, 476, 479, 486, 512-513
Pearl Museum 112, 186, 189, 192
Pearl Resorts 90, 133-134, 159-160, 483
Pearls (see Tahiti cultured pearls and black pearls)
People of Tahiti 44
Pepeu Tohua 550
Petit Village le 187, 216, 217, 227, 228, 229, 275, 291, 297

Petroglyphs 196, 334, 381, 386, 424, 427, 449, 457, 519, 528, 541, 546, 547, 550, 554, 558, 564
Pharmacies/Drugstores 95, 96, 98, 145, 219, 220, 298, 329, 359, 383, 445, 479, 532, 561, 582, 588
Pinctada Margaritifera (see Tahitian Cultured Pearls)
Pirae 126, 139, 145, 148, 152-154, 176, 177, 189, 194, 203, 218
Pitcairn Island 48, 109
PK (poste kilometre) 273, 602
Place Tarahoi 187, 188
Place To'ata 124, 125, 127, 145, 186, 189, 219, 220
Place Vaiete 137, 189, 200, 217, 220
Pleasant Holidays 62
Point Matira (see Matira Point)
Point Ohutu (also Ohotu)
Point Raititi 388
Point Taihi 423
Point Tiva 302, 319
Point Venus 31, 48, 49, 123, 177, 189, 190, 220
Pol'Air 75
Polynesians the 43, 56, 194, 311, 324, 330, 445, 534, 548
Polynesian migration 46, 47, 193
Pomare family 49, 125
Pomare I King 141
Pomare II King 35
Pomare IV Queen 49, 187, 191
Poole Dr. Michael 12, 31, 284
Popoti Ridge 423
Population 42, 43, 44, 144, 186
Porapora (see Bora Bora)
Port of Papeete 71, 142, 205
Port Royal 49
Postal service 105, 244, 299
Poutoru 335, 336
Pouvanaa A Oopa 145, 185, 186, 187, 190
Povai (Pofai) Bay 386, 387, 396, 420, 447
Pritchard George 49
Progress Pact 52
Protestants (see Missionaries Protestant)
Providence H.M.S. 49
Puamau 541, 550, 554, 556, 558, 560
Puka Puka 47

Punaauia 59, 124, 131, 137, 148, 154-159
Punaei 550, 554
Puni Chief 362
Puohine 332, 333
Purea High Chiefess 37, 331

QANTAS AIRWAYS 68, 69
Qantas Vacations 61
Queen Pomare IV (see Pomare family)
Queen Teha'apapa 213, 303
Queen Victoria 49
Quiros Pedro Fernández de 47

RADIO 110
Raiatea 14, 16, 20, 23, 28, 30, 32, 33, 44, 47, 73, 76, 330-338; Where to Stay 338-347; Where to Eat 347-349; Seeing the Sights 350-351; Sports 351-357; Shopping 357-358; Massage 358; Tattoos 358; Practical Information 359-360; Yacht Services 360-361
Rairua 590, 592, 595, 596
Raivavae 18, 49, 70, 74, 80, 192-193, 449, 570, 590-592; Where to Stay & Eat 592-595; Seeing the Sights 595-596; Shopping 596
Rangiroa 12, 14, 16, 20, 23, 25, 26, 28, 31, 73, 79, 83, 86, 114, 460-463; Where to Stay 463-473; Where to Eat 473-474; Sports 474-477; Shopping 478; Practical Information 478-479
Rapa 18, 33, 43, 80, 570, 572, 596-597; Where to Stay & Eat 597
Raraka 79, 497
Raroia 107
Real Estate 111
Reef (see Coral reefs)
Reef Island (Ile aux Récifs) 461, 476
Reine Blanche la 49
Relais et Chateaux Le 90, 246, 368
Resolution Bay (see Vaitahu)
Resolution the 302
Restaurants Bora Bora: Bloody Mary's 419; Bora Bora Yacht Club 420; Fare Manuia 421; Kaina Hut 420; La Bounty 421; Saint James 419; Villa Mahana 418-419
Restaurants Moorea: Aito 266-267; Blue

Pineapple 235-236; Honu Iti 260; Le Cocotier 261; Le Mahogany 261; Le Mayflower 268-269; Painapo Beach 269, 272-273; Rudy's 261-262

Restaurants Tahiti: Blue Banana 179; Casa Bianca 180; Chez Loula et Remy 182; Coco's 178 ; Restaurant Jimmy 173; Le Belvedere 24, 176-177; Le Lotus 167-168; Les Trois Brasseurs 173-174; Quai des Iles 179 ; Pink Coconut 178; Western Grill 180

Restrooms Public 137, 142, 186, 220

Retiring in Tahiti 111

Rikitea 80

Rimatara 18, 74, 80, 570, 572, 574, 589-590

Roberts Captain Josiah 541

Roggeveen Jacob 47, 449

Rotoava 498

Roulottes les 24, 29, 72, 135, 137, 161, 189, 216

Rurutu 15, 18, 24, 43, 54, 74, 80, 86-87, 570, 572-576; Where to Stay 576-579; Where to Eat 579; Seeing the Sights 579-580; Sports 580-581; Shopping 581; Practical Information 581-582

SAFETY (see Dangers)

Sailing (see Boats sailing cruising and fishing and Yachting)

Samuela Laurel & James 63, 64, 94, 252-253, 296

San Lesmes the 44, 47

Scharnhorst the 188

Schouten 47

Scilly 16, 330

School 145, 176, 180, 192, 226, 274, 275, 280

School holidays 54-55, 158

Scooters (see Car rentals)

Scuba diving (see Diving)

Sculptors (Wood Carvers) 189, 358, 387, 519, 522, 532-533, 540, 546, 548, 560, 564, 569

Sea of Moons 76, 144, 154, 157, 178, 189, 215, 222, 257

Seasons (see Weather)

Seeadler the 188

Sejours dans les Iles (see Island Stays)

Sexually transmitted diseases 99

Shark Feeding 23, 42, 131, 326-327, 356, 431, 432

Sharks 17, 39, 40, 41, 85, 86, 110, 207, 287, 448, 476, 519

Ships travel by passenger liner 69-70

Shopping 111 (also listed under each Island)

Sinoto Dr. Yosihiko H. 303, 324, 424, 448, 449, 531

Smith Harrison Willard 181, 190, 192-193

Snorkeling (see Lagoon Excursions)

Society Islands 15-16, 17, 23, 31, 33, 37, 39, 42, 43, 44, 54, 56, 73

Sofitel Hotels 89

South Pacific Management (SPM) 90

South Pacific Tours 64

Starwood Hotels & Resorts 89, 156, 404, 408

Stevenson Robert Louis 527

Stone lifting (amoraa ofai) 124, 125, 574

Suggs Dr. Robert C. 527, 528, 529, 541

Sunburn 98

Sunsail 83, 355

Sunspots International 62

Surfing 31, 54, 124, 127, 208, 255, 277, 327, 469, 492, 496

Surf School 162, 208, 209

Swain Tahiti Tours 62

TAAHANA BEACH 393, 427

Taahuaia 584, 587

Taaoa 549, 550, 551, 554, 557, 558, 559

Taapuna 31, 124, 143, 159, 208

Taaroa god 603

Taaroa III the 534

Tahaa 14, 16, 20, 23, 25, 26, 27, 28, 33, 47, 76, 81, 83, 84, 86, 87, 88, 89, 98, 112, 125, 362-366; Where to Stay 366-375; Where to Eat 375-378; Seeing the Sights 378-380; Sports 380-382; Shopping 382; Massages & Spas 382-383; Tattoos 383; Practical Information 383; Yacht Services 384

Tahara'a Lookout Point 189

Tahauku Bay 550

Tahia Pearls 82, 212, 293, 439

Tahiti 11, 14, 16, 22, 24, 31, 33, 34, 36, 42, 43, 44, 48, 50, 52, 54, 55, 58, 140-148; Where to Stay 149-167; Where to Eat 167-183; Seeing the Sights 183-198; Nightlife 198-201; Sports 201-210; Shopping 210-213; Massages & Spas 213-214; Tattoos 214-215; Practical Information 217-220; Internet Service 219; Yacht Services 220-221
Tahiti and Her Islands (see French Polynesia)
Tahiti cultured pearls 17, 52, 56, 72, 112, 113, 115, 127, 153, 212-213, 215, 239, 290, 291, 379, 439-440, 486, 512
Tahiti Discount Travel 62
Tahiti Faaa International Airport (see Airports)
Tahiti Helicopter Service 75-76, 198, 281, 363-364, 388, 427, 449
Tahiti Iti 144, 148, 163-164, 195, 207, 208, ; Where to Stay 164-167; Where to Eat 182-183; What to Do 209
Tahiti Legends 62
Tahiti Nui 33, 131, 140, 144, 190, 195, 196
Tahiti Nui Satellite (TNS) 120
Tahiti Nui Television (TNTV) 120
Tahiti Nui Travel 64
Tahiti Pearl Museum 213
Tahiti Pearl Regatta 125
Tahiti Perles 213, 239, 422, 439
Tahiti Safari Expedition 196-197
Tahiti Tourisme 55, 61, 65, 100, 104, 121, 123, 124, 128, 183, 219, 220
Tahiti Tours 64
Tahiti Travel 62
Tahiti Travel Planners 62
Tahiti Vacations 62
Tahiti Yacht Charter 24, 83-84, 205-206, 355-356, 360, 511
Tahitians 34, 35, 41, 43, 50, 108, 116, 130, 138, 141, 190, 198, 208, 215, 236, 278, 352
Tahitian Feasts 272-273
Tahua To'ata (see Place To'ata)
Tahua Vaiete (see Place Vaiete)
Tahuata 17, 514, 516, 517, 532, 554, 561, 562-564; Where to Stay & Eat 563; Seeing the Sights 564; Shopping 564

Taiarapu Peninsula (see Tahiti Iti)
Taimoo Bay 423
Taiohae 519, 520, 529
Taiohae Bay 518, 520
Taipivai 527, 529
Tairapa Pass 481, 485
Tairua Patrick, 95, 426, 433-434, 445-446
Takai'i tiki 550
Takapoto 17, 79, 460
Takaroa 17
Tamanu Canyon 196
Tamatoa King (see King Tamatoa)
Tapa 290, 405, 410, 446, 558, 565, 568, 569, 603
Tapuamu 335, 336, 364, 365, 366
Taravao 29, 131, 137, 144, 148, 164, 165, 166, 176, 182, 183, 191, 203, 209, 218, 220
Taro 15, 18, 35, 46, 136, 138, 170, 173, 269, 270, 272, 302, 570, 573, 575, 603
Tattoo 42, 53, 64, 214, 252, 277, 296, 358-359, 383, 425, 442, 444, 516, 522, 532, 533, 540, 543, 548, 560
Tattoonesia 128
Tautira 31, 48, 108, 123, 124, 148, 167, 182, 208
Taxes 20, 78, 117, 119, 227
Tax Refunds 117
Taxi Boats 338, 352, 364, 449, 463
Taxis 20, 24, 31, 66, 121, 142, 228, 306, 334, 338, 391, 425, 463, 520, 525, 535, 536, 552
Teahupoo 31, 32, 54, 110, 127, 148, 164, 165, 166, 182, 183, 202, 208, 209
Te Ana Maro Grotto 580
Te Ava Moa Pass 331
Teavanui Pass 387, 424
Tefarerii 301, 325
Te Hoa Yacht Club 348
Tehueto site 554, 558
Te Ivi o Hou site 529
Tekura Tahiti Travel 64
Telephone services 105, 116, 117-118, 119, 540, 552, 556, 572
Television 120
Temae 127, 216, 223, 226, 229, 232, 233
Temperature (see Weather)

Tennis 132, 134, 155, 157, 158, 204, 239, 244, 319, 369, 401, 404, 407, 411, 465
Te Pari 144, 164-165, 166, 201-202, 208, 209
Tepua Bay 341, 346
Teraupoo Chief 332
Tereia Point - Bora Bora 423=424
Tereia Point – Maupiti 448, 455, 456
Te Reva Nei Tours & Transport 164-165
Territorial Assembly (see Assembly of French Polynesia)
Tetamanu 498, 506, 507, 509, 510, 511, 512
Tetiaroa 12, 14, 16, 38, 89, 98, 109, 176, 185, 206, 207, 330
Tevaitoa 332, 334, 345, 351
Thalasso Deep Ocean Spa 27, 443
Three Cascades of Fa'arumai 190, 220
Tiamahana Pass 366
Tiare Moorea 547
Tiare Tahiti 34, 68, 91, 129, 194, 211, 222, 277, 455, 525, 546, 574, 601, 603
Tiarei 190, 196, 220
Tifaifai 111, 124, 129, 153, 155, 188, 211, 239, 290, 291
Tikehau 14, 16, 17, 25, 26, 31, 32, 86, 89, 90, 134, 159, 487-489; Where to Stay & Eat 489-495; Seeing the Sights 495-496; Sports 496; Massages & Spa 496-497; Practical Information 497
Tiki 302, 527, 538, 541, 543, 550, 554, 558, 564, 565, 573, 590, 604
Tiki god 516
Tiki Village, Tiki Village Theatre 27, 94, 215, 216, 271, 272, 275, 277-278, 294, 296, 300, 383
Time (of day) 120-121
Tipping 121
Tiputa 460, 461, 462, 463, 468, 472, 473, 474-475, 476, 477, 478
Tiva 302, 319, 335, 336, 364, 365, 366
Tivaru 460, 461
Toahotu 183, 353, 366
Toau 17, 31, 79, 84, 86
Tohua sites 527, 528, 529, 538, 541, 550, 557, 558, 560
Toilets Public (see Restrooms)

Toopua & Toopua Iti 386, 387, 388, 404, 422, 435, 437
Toovii Plateau 519, 529
Torea Nui Transport & Safari 223, 228, 275
TOPdive-Bathys 31, 207, 282, 288, 399, 424, 436, 477, 502, 511
Tour Operators in North America 61-63
Tour Operators in Tahiti 63-64
Tourist offices (see Tahiti Tourisme)
Traitor's Bay (see Tahauku Bay)
Transportation public (see Le Truck)
Travel Agents (see Tour Operators)
Traveling On Your Own 72, 148
Trees Sacred 36
Trekking 203, 429, 530
Trouble Staying out of 115-117
Truck the (see Le Truck & Buses)
True Tahiti Vacation 64, 296
Tu (see Pomare I King) 141
Tuamotu Islands the 16-17, 256, 267
Tubuai 570, 572, 573, 574, 582-584; Where to Stay 584-587; Where to Eat 587; Seeing the Sights 587; Sports 587-588; Shopping 588; Practical Information 588
Tuhaa Pae II the 80
Tuhaa Pae IV the 80-81
Tuherahera 487, 489, 492, 495, 497
Tumakohua Pass 498, 506, 508, 511
Tupa 37, 423
Tupai 16, 47, 426, 427, 430, 431
Tupapau 428, 604
Turipaoa 479, 480, 481, 484
Turtles 40, 133, 193, 289, 334, 381, 386, 409-410, 427, 432, 449, 457, 510, 543
Tuvahine Island (see Vahine Island)
T.V.A. (see Taxes) 20, 21

UA HUKA 17, 37, 38, 55, 74, 514, 516, 517, 518, 519, 531, 534, 540-543; Where to Stay 543-545; Where to Eat 545-546; Seeing the Sights 546-547; Sports 547-548; Shopping 548; Practical Information 548
Ua Pou 17, 74, 514, 516, 517, 519, 527, 531, 534-536; Where to Stay 536-537; Where to Eat 538; Seeing the Sights

538; Sports 538-539; Shopping 540; Practical Information 540
U.S. Consulate 59, 218
Uturoa 332, 333, 334, 335, 336-337, 338, 339, 357-359

VAATETE JOSEPH 546, 548
Vaccinations 99, 130
Vahine Island 26, 28, 89, 340, 348, 362, 370-371, 373, 375, 376
Vahituri (Les Sables Roses)
Vaiaau 332, 333
Vaiare Bay 280, 281, 299
Vaiare ferry terminal 216, 223, 224, 225, 227, 229, 273, 299, 300
Vai'ea 449, 450
Vaie'enui Valley 566
Vaikiki Valley 541
Vaima river 191
Vaipae'e 541, 542, 543
Vaipahi Gardens and Cascade 191, 193, 220
Vaipuu river 190
Vairau Bay 424
Vairuauri Grotto 580
Vaitahu 551, 559, 562
Vaitape 293, 336, 387, 389, 390, 391, 393, 394, 398
Vaitoare 335, 336, 364, 365, 366, 374
Vaiuru 590, 592, 596
Vancouver Captain George 572
Vanilla 106, 111, 136, 137, 167, 211, 214, 248, 260, 265, 274, 275, 276, 277, 295, 302, 314, 333, 337, 350, 351, 352, 354, 358, 362, 363, 375, 376, 378, 379, 382
Varady Ralph 460
V.A.T. (see Taxes)
Vavau (see Bora Bora)
Vegetarian & Vegan meals 82, 138, 139, 169, 171, 173, 174, 264, 269

Viaud Louis Marie Julien (see The Marriage of Loti) 202
Victor Paul-Emile 385
Visas (see Immigration)
Visitors Bureaus (see Tourist offices)
Vitaria 570, 573, 576, 578, 579, 580

WALLIS CAPTAIN SAMUEL 37, 47, 140, 153, 189
Wan Robert (Robert Wan Pearl Museum), 112, 186, 189, 192, 213, 239
Water drinking 97
Weather 55, 202
Website Forums & Bulletin Boards 64-65
Websites useful 65
Weddings (Getting Married) 93-95, 300
Weights & measures 121-122
Whales 24, 40, 41, 54, 86, 100, 206, 209, 256, 257, 283, 284, 285, 436, 451, 457, 531-532, 574, 576, 578, 581, 588
Williams John 332, 573
Windward Islands 15-16, 144, 330
Women travelers 116-117
Wood carvers (see Sculptors)
World of Diving & Adventure Vacations 63
World Wars I & II 187, 188

YACHT FACILITIES & SERVICES 220, 360, 384, 447, 533, 560-561
Yachting 23, 125, 377, 381, 487-488, 518; charter sailboats 84, 206, 286-287, 354-356, 380, 434-435, 477, 511; cruise and dive charters 84, 510-511; motor yacht charters 356, 435 ; formalities for pleasure boats 70-71, 533

ZÉLÉE 188

LODGING INDEX

WINDWARD ISLANDS
Tahiti
Ahitea Lodge 151
Bonjouir Lodge Paradise 165-166
Chez Flotahia 166-167
Chez Jeannine 167
Chez Lola 160
Chez Myrna 152
Fare Maithe 167
Fare Ratere 163
Fare Suisse 151
Heitiare Inn 163
Hiti Moana Villa 162-163
Hotel Le Meridien Tahiti 156-157
Hotel Royal Tahitien 153
Hotel Tahiti Nui 149
Hotel Tiare Tahiti 149-150
Intercontinental Tahiti Resort 154-156
La Vague Bleue 165
Manava Suite Resort 158-160
Meherio Iti 167
Papara Village 163
Pension Chayan 164
Pension Damyr 160-161
Pension De La Plage 161
Pension Otaha 161
Pension Puea 163
Pension Te Hihi O Te Ra 167
Pueu Village 167
Punatea Village 166
Radisson Plaza Resort Tahiti 152
Relais De La Maroto 198
Relais Fenua 162
Sofitel Maeva Beach Tahiti Resort 158
Taaroa Lodge 161-162
Tahiti Airport Motel 160
Tauhanihani Village Lodge 165
Te Miti 162
Te Pari Village 165
Vanira Lodge 164-165

Moorea
Atiha Lodge Moorea 258

Atuana Lodge 257
Camping Nelson 252
Club Bali Hai 235-236
Dream Island 247
Faimano 257
Fare Arana 254-255
Fare Aute 255
Fare D'Hôte Tehuarupe 254
Fare Edith 253
Fare Hamara 241
Fare Maeva 233
Fare Manuia 258
Fare Nani 257
Fare Pole 258
Fare Tapu Lodge 251
Fare Vaihere 242-243
Fare Vaimoana 257-258
Fenua Mata'i'oa 246-247
Green Lodge 230, 232
Haapiti Surf Lodge 256
Hilton Moorea Lagoon Resort & Spa 237-240
Hotel Hibiscus 249-250
Hotel Kaveka 234-235
Hotel Les Tipaniers 248-249
Intercontinental Moorea Resort & Spa 243-245
Les Tipaniers Iti 249
Legends Resort Moorea 245-246
Maheata 242
Mark's Place Moorea Bungalows 255
Moorea Beach Lodge 250
Moorea Fare Miti 251
Moorea Golf Lodge 232
Moorea Pearl Resort & Spa 233, 234
Motel Albert 237
Nature House Of Mou'a Roa 258
Pension Motu Iti 241-242
Pension Tifai 258
Residence Linareva 253-254
Robinson's Cove Villa 240-241
Sofitel Moorea Ia Ora Beach Resort 229-230

Taoahere Beach House 248
Tarariki Village 258
Te Fare Mihi 251-252
Te Nunoa Bungalow 252-253
Te Ora Hau 256-257
Vaihau Village 258
Villa Corallina 247-248
Village Temanoha 236

LEEWARD ISLANDS
Huahine
Ariiura Camping (see Huahine Camping)
   320
Au Motu Mahare 316
Chalet Tipanier 312
Chez Guynette Club-Bed 314-315
Chez Ella 320
Chez Henriette 320
Chez Tara 320
Fare Ara L'Ile Sauvage 314
Fare Ie Fare 319
Fare Ie Parea 318-319
Fare Iita 316
Fare Maeva 313-314
Hotel Bellevue 312-313
Huahine Camping 320
Huahine Lodge 320
Huahine Vacances 319
La Petite Ferme 320
Maitai Lapita Village Huahine 309-311
Motel Vanille 312
Pension Ariitere 314
Pension Enite 315
Pension Fetia 315
Pension Hine Iti 320
Pension Mama Roro 320
Pension Mauarii 318
Pension Meherio i Huahine 315-316
Pension Poetaina 312
Pension Te Nahe Parea 320
Pension Te Nahe Toetoe 320
Pension Tifaifai & Café 320
Pension Tupuna 320
Pension Vaihonu 313
Rande's Shack 315
Relais Mahana 316-318
Residence Loisirs Maroe 319

Te Tiare Beach Resort 306-309
Vanaa Camping and Snack 320
Villas Bougainville 319
Villas Standing 319

Raiatea
Bed & Breakfast Raiatea Bellevue 347
Hotel Atiapiti 343
Hotel Hinano Api 347
La Croix Du Sud 345-346
Laura Lodge 344
Les 3 Cascades 346
Opoa Beach Hotel 338-341
Pension Manava 344-345
Pension Opeha 346
Pension Te Maeva 345
Pension Tepua 346-347
Pension Tiare Nui 347
Pension Yolande 345
Raiatea Hawaiki Nui Hotel 341
Raiatea Lodge Hotel 342
Residence Le Dauphin 347
Sunset Beach Motel 342-343
Villa Temehani 345
Vini Beach Lodge 343-344

Tahaa
Chez Pascal 375
Fare Pea Iti 371-372
Hotel La Pirogue 371
Hotel Vahine Island 370-371
Le Passage 372-373
Le Taha'a Island Resort & Spa (Relais et
   Chateaux) 366-369
Motu Porou 375
Pension Api 374
Pension Atger 374
Pension Au Phil Du Temps 374
Pension Hibiscus 373-374
Pension Vaihi 375
Tiare Breeze 372

Bora Bora
Blue Heaven Island 412
Bora Bora Condominiums 400
Bora Bora Eden Beach Hotel 412
Bora Bora Pension Noni 399

Bora Nui Resort & Spa (Hilton) 404-406
Bora Bora Pearl Beach Resort 410-412
Bora Vaite Lodge 398-399
Chez Nono 398
Chez Rosina Ellacott 400
Chez Rosine Masson 398
Four Seasons Resort Bora Bora 400-402
Hilton Bora Nui Resort & Spa 404-406
Hotel Le Meridien Bora Bora 408-410
Hotel Matira 396
Intercontinental Bora Bora Le Moana Resort 391-393
Intercontinental Bora Bora Resort & Thalasso Spa 406-408
Le Maitai Polynesia 395-396
Pension Bora Lagoonarium 400
Pension Maeva Masson 398
Pension Moon 400
Pension Robert et Tina 397-398
Rohotu Fare Lodge 396-397
Sofitel Bora Bora Marara Beach Resort and Private Island 393-394
St. Regis Resort & Spa 402-404
Sunset Hill Lodge 399
Village Temanuata (Temanuata Beach Temanuata Iti) 397

Maupiti
Fare Pa'eao 451-453
Le Kuriri 451
Maupiti Residence 455
Pension Auira 453
Pension Eri 456
Pension Marau 453
Pension Maupiti Village 454
Pension Papahani 454
Pension Poe Iti 453-454
Pension Rose Des Iles 456
Pension Taputea 456
Pension Tautiare Village 455-456
Pension Teheimana 456
Pension Terama 454-455

TUAMOTU ISLANDS
Rangiroa
Ariitini Village 471
Camping Nanua 473

Chez Lucien 472
Chez Teina & Marie 473
Hotel Kia Ora Resort & Spa 463-466
Hotel Kia Ora Sauvage Rangiroa 466
Lagon Vert (Green Lagoon) 472-473
Le Merou Bleu 469
Les Relais De Josephine 468
Maitai Rangiroa Lagoon Resort 466-467
Motu Teta 467-468
Pension Bounty 470
Pension Cecile 470-471
Pension Glorine 471
Pension Henri 473
Pension Henriette 473
Pension Loyna 471-472
Pension Martine 470
Pension Tapuheitini 473
Pension Te Vahine Dream 468-469
Pension Tuanake 469-470
Raira Lagon Family Hotel 469
Rangiroa Lodge 472
Turiroa Village 471

Manihi
Manihi Pearl Beach Resort 481-484
Manihi Pearl Village 484-485
Motel Nanihi Paradise 484
Pension Hawaiki Pearls 484

Tikehau
Aito Motel Colette 494-495
Chez Justine 495
Fare Hanariki 495
Kahaia Beach 495
Ninamu Resort 492
Panau Lagon 495
Pension Hotu 495
Pension Tematie 493-494
Relais Royal Tikehau 493
Tevaihi Village 494
Tikehau Pearl Beach Resort 489-492
Tikehau Village 494

Fakarava
Havaiki Fakarava Pearl Guest House 502-503
Motu Aito Paradise 506-507

Pension Kiria 505-506
Pension Paparara 503-504
Pension Rava 509
Raimiti 507-508
Relais Marama 502
Tetamanu Sauvage 509
Tetamanu Village 509
Tokerau Village 504-505
Vahitu Dream 509
Vaiama Village 504
Vekeveke Village 509
White Sand Beach Resort Fakarava 500-502

MARQUESAS ISLANDS
Nuku Hiva
Chez Fetu 524
Chez Yvonne (Hinako Nui) 525
Kao Tia'e 525
Mave Mai 522-524
Nuku Hiva Keikahanui Pearl Lodge 521
Paahatea Nui (Chez Justin & Julienne) 524
Pension Moana Nui 524
Pension Pua 524
Rose Corser's He'e Tai Inn 521-522
Te Pua Hinako (Chez Juliette) 525

Ua Pou
Pension Pukue'e 536
Chez Dora 536-537
Hakamoui Plage 537
Pension Vehine Hou 537
Pension Leydj Kenata 537

Ua Huka
Auberge Hitikau 544
Chez Alexis 544-545
Chez Christelle 545
Chez Maurice & Delphine 545
Le Reve Marquisien 544
Mana Tupuna Village 543-544

Hiva Oa
Bungalows Fa'e Isa 557
Communal Bungalows of Atuona 557

Hanakee Hiva Oa Pearl Lodge 552-554
Pension Areke-Chez Kayser 555-556
Pension Chez Marie-Antoinette 556-557
Pension Kanahau 554
Pension Ozanne 556
Relais Moehau 555
Temetiu Village 555

Tahuata
Pension Amatea 563
Pension Vaikehunui 563

Fatu Hiva
Chez Norma Ropati 567
Pension Chez Lionel 567

AUSTRAL ISLANDS
Rurutu
Heiata Nui Guest House 579
Home Sweet Home 579
Pension Le Manotel 576-578
Pension Teautamatea 578
Pension Te Marama 576
Rurutu Lodge 576

Tubuai
Chez Karine & Tale 587
Chez Yolande 586
Pension Toena 584-586
Vaiteanui WIPA Lodge 586

Rimatara
Pension Ueue 590

Raivavae
Pension Ataha 595
Pension Chez Linda 594-595
Pension Moana 595
Pension Nuruata 595
Raivavae Tama Inn 592-594

Rapa
Chez Jean Titaua 597

About the Author

Jan Prince has lived in Tahiti and Moorea since 1971. She is a travel writer and journalist, and has also written about Tahiti for Fodor's travel guides, *The Los Angeles Times, Time Magazine, Tahiti Magazine, Pacific Islands Monthly*, and many other publications. She is currently the senior writer for the *Tahiti Beach Press,* a 20-page English-language magazine that is published once a month and distributed weekly in hotels and other tourist locations.

You may e-mail her at *janprincemoorea@mail.pf* only for questions and comments relating to this book – not to assist in travel or other arrangements. Please understand that she cannot help you with real estate, employment or immigration inquiries.

Jan's website is *www.janprince.net,* where she will post periodic updates for this book.

Open Road Publishing

Open Road's *Best Of* guides match the time you *really* have for your vacation with the right amount of information. No fluff, just the best things to do and see, the best places to stay and eat. Includes one-day, weekend, one-week and longer trip ideas – featuring beautiful color photos and maps! Now what could be more perfect than that?

Best Of Guides

Open Road's Best of Arizona, $12.95
Open Road's Best of The Florida Keys, $12.95
Open Road's Best of New York City, $14.95
Open Road's Best of Southern California, $14.95
Open Road's Best of Northern California, $14.95
Open Road's Best of Vermont, $14.95
Open Road's Best of Guatemala, $9.95
Open Road's Best of Belize, $14.95
Open Road's Best of Costa Rica, $12.95
Open Road's Best of Panama, $14.95
Open Road's Best of Italy, $14.95
Open Road's Best of Paris, $12.95
Open Road's Best of Provence & The French Riviera, $12.95
Open Road's Best of Walt Disney World & Orlando, $9.95

Family Travel Guides

Open Road's Italy with Kids, $14.95
Open Road's Paris with Kids, $16.95
Open Road's Caribbean with Kids, $14.95
Open Road's London with Kids, $12.95
Open Road's Best National Parks With Kids, $12.95
Open Road's Washington, DC with Kids, $14.95

Order now at www.openroadguides.com